THE OXFORD ENCYCLOPEDIA OF
THE BIBLE AND THEOLOGY

THE OXFORD ENCYCLOPEDIA OF
THE BIBLE AND THEOLOGY

Samuel E. Balentine

EDITOR IN CHIEF

VOLUME 2

KIN–WOR

OXFORD
UNIVERSITY PRESS

OXFORD
UNIVERSITY PRESS

Oxford University Press is a department of the
University of Oxford. It furthers the University's objective
of excellence in research, scholarship, and education
by publishing worldwide.

Oxford   New York
Auckland   Cape Town   Dar es Salaam   Hong Kong   Karachi
Kuala Lumpur   Madrid   Melbourne   Mexico City   Nairobi
New Delhi   Shanghai   Taipei   Toronto

With offices in

Argentina   Austria   Brazil   Chile   Czech Republic   France   Greece
Guatemala   Hungary   Italy   Japan   Poland   Portugal   Singapore
South Korea   Switzerland   Thailand   Turkey   Ukraine   Vietnam

Oxford is a registered trademark of Oxford University Press
in the UK and certain other countries.

Published in the United States of America by
Oxford University Press
198 Madison Avenue, New York, NY 10016
www.oup.com

Library of Congress Cataloging-in-Publication Data
The Oxford encyclopedia of the Bible and theology / Samuel E. Balentine, editor in chief.
volumes cm.—(The Oxford encyclopedias of the bible)
Includes bibliographical references and index.
ISBN 978-0-19-023994-7 (v. 1 : alk. paper)—ISBN 978-0-19-023995-4—(v. 2 : alk. paper)—
ISBN 978-0-19-985869-9 (set : alk. paper)   1. Bible—Dictionaries.   2. Theology—
Dictionaries.   I. Balentine, Samuel E. (Samuel Eugene), 1950–
BS440.O927   2015
220.3—dc23   2014038886

1 3 5 7 9 8 6 4 2

Printed in the United States of America on acid-free paper

ABBREVIATIONS USED IN THIS WORK

א	Codex Sinaiticus
// or ‖	parallel passages
§	section
A	Codex Alexandrinus
ʾAbot	*ʾAbot*
ʾAbot R. Nat.	*ʾAbot de Rabbi Nathan*
Acts	Acts of the Apostles
Acts Andr.	*Acts of Andrew*
Acts John	*Acts of John*
Acts Paul	*Acts of Paul*
Acts Pet.	*Acts of Peter*
Acts Thom.	*Acts of Thomas*
Add Dan	Additions to Daniel
Add Esth	Additions to Esther
Adol. poet. aud.	Plutarch, *Quomodo adolescens poetas audire debeat*
Ag. Ap.	Josephus, *Against Apion*
Agr.	Tacitus, *Agricola*
Alex.	Plutarch, *Alexander*
All.	Heraclitus, *Allegoriae (Quaestiones homericae)*
Amos	Amos
Ant.	Josephus, *Jewish Antiquities*
Ant. rom.	Dionysius of Halicarnassus, *Antiquitates romanae*
Apoc	Apocalypse of John (Revelation)
Apoc. Mos.	*Apocalypse of Moses*
Apol.	Plato, *Apologia*
1 Apol.	Justin, *Apologia 1*

As. Mos.	*Assumption of Moses*
B	Codex Vaticanus
b.	Babylonian Talmud
B. Bat.	*Baba Batra*
Bapt.	Tertullian, *De baptismo*
Bar	Baruch
2 Bar.	*2 Baruch*
Barn.	*Barnabas*
B.C.E.	Before the Common Era (= B.C.)
Bel	Bel and the Dragon
Ben.	Seneca, *De beneficiis*
Ber.	*Berakot*
Bib. Ant.	Pseudo-Philo, *Liber antiquitatum biblicarum*
ca.	*circa*
C. Ap.	Josephus, *Contra Apionem* (*Against Apion*)
CD	Cairo Genizah, *Damascus Document*
C.E.	Common Era (= A.D.)
Cels.	Origen, *Contra Celsum*
cf.	*confer*, compare
ch./chs.	chapter/chapters
1–2 Chr	1–2 Chronicles
Civ.	Augustine, *De civitate Dei*
1–2 Clem.	*1–2 Clement*
Col	Colossians
col./cols.	column/columns
Comm. Jo.	Origen, *Commentarii in evangelium Joannis*
Comm. Matt.	Origen, *Commentarium in evangelium Matthaei*
Comm. Rom.	Origen, *Commentarii in Romanos*
Contempl. Life	Philo, *On the Contemplative Life*
1–2 Cor	1–2 Corinthians
Cupid. divit.	Plutarch, *De cupiditate divitiarum*
d.	died
Dan	Daniel
Deus	Philo, *Quod Deus sit immutabilis*
Deut	Deuteronomy

Deut. Rab.	*Deuteronomy Rabbah*
DH	Deuteronomistic History
Dial.	Justin, *Dialogus cum Tryphone*
Did.	*Didache*
Dion.	Athanasius, *De sententia Dionysii*
Doctr. chr.	Augustine, *De doctrina christiana*
DSS	Dead Sea Scrolls
Dtr	Deuteronomist
E	Elohist source in the Pentateuch
Eccl	Ecclesiastes
ʿEd.	*ʿEduyyot*
ed.	editor (pl., eds.), edition
Embassy	Philo, *On the Embassy to Gaius*
1 En.	*1 Enoch*
Ep.	Seneca, *Epistulae morales*
Eph	Ephesians
Epict. diss.	Arrian, *Epicteti dissertationes*
Epist.	Jerome, *Epistulae*
Ep Jer	Letter of Jeremiah
1–2 Esd	1–2 Esdras
Esth	Esther
ESV	English Standard Version
Eth. eud.	Aristotle, *Ethica eudemia*
Exod	Exodus
Exod. Rab.	*Exodus Rabbah*
Ezek	Ezekiel
Ezra	Ezra
4 Ezra	*4 Ezra*
frag.	fragment
Fr. Matt.	Origen, *Fragmenta ex commentariis in evangelium Matthaei*
Gal	Galatians
Gen	Genesis
Gen. Rab.	*Genesis Rabbah*
Geogr.	Strabo, *Geographica*

Giṭ.	*Giṭṭin*
1 Glor.	Dio Chrysostom, *De gloria i (Or. 66)*
Gos. Mary	*Gospel of Mary*
Gos. Phil.	*Gospel of Philip*
Gos. Thom.	*Gospel of Thomas*
Hab	Habakkuk
Haer.	Irenaeus, *Adversus haereses*
Hag	Haggai
Ḥag.	*Ḥagigah*
HB	Hebrew Bible
Heb	Hebrews
Heb.	Hebrew (biblical citations and language)
Herm. *Mand.*	Shepherd of Hermas, *Mandate*
Herm. *Sim.*	Shepherd of Hermas, *Similitude*
Herm. *Vis.*	Shepherd of Hermas, *Vision*
Hist. an.	Aristotle, *Historia animalium*
Hist. eccl.	Eusebius, *Historia ecclesiastica*
Hom. Gen.	Origen, *Homiliae in Genesim*
Hom. Lev.	Origen, *Homiliae in Leviticum*
Hos	Hosea
Ḥul.	*Ḥullin*
Ign. *Magn.*	Ignatius, *To the Magnesians*
Ign. *Rom.*	Ignatius, *To the Romans*
Ign. *Smyrn.*	Ignatius, *To the Smyrnaeans*
Inst.	Quintilian, *Institutio oratoria*
Ios.	Philo, *De Iosepho*
Isa	Isaiah
Is. Os.	Plutarch, *De Iside et Osiride*
J	Yahwist source in the Pentateuch
Jas	James
Jdt	Judith
Jer	Jeremiah
Job	Job
Joel	Joel

John	John
1–2–3 John	1–2–3 John
Jonah	Jonah
Jos. Asen.	*Joseph and Aseneth*
Joseph	Philo, *On the Life of Joseph*
Josh	Joshua
Jub.	*Jubilees*
Jude	Jude
1–2 Kgdms	1–2 Kingdoms (Septuagint)
3–4 Kgdms	3–4 Kingdoms (Septuagint)
1–2 Kgs	1–2 Kings
Kil.	*Kil'ayim*
KJV	King James Version
KTU	*Die keilalphabetischen Texte aus Ugarit*
Lacr.	Demosthenes, *Contra Lacritum*
Lam	Lamentations
Laps.	Cyprian, *De lapsis*
Leg.	Philo, *Legum allegoriae*
Let. Aris.	*Letter of Aristeas*
Leuc. Clit.	Achilles Tatius, *Leucippe et Clitophon*
Lev	Leviticus
Lev. Rab.	*Leviticus Rabbah*
Lib. ed.	Pseudo-Plutarch, *De liberis educandis*
lit.	literally
Luke	Luke
LXX	Septuagint
m.	Mishnah
1–2 Macc	1–2 Maccabees
3–4 Macc	3–4 Maccabees
Mal	Malachi
Marc.	Tertullian, *Adversus Marcionem*
Mark	Mark
Matt	Matthew
Meg.	*Megillah*
Mem.	Xenophon, *Memorabilia*

Menaḥ.	*Menaḥot*
Metam.	Apuleius, *Metamorphoses*
Mic	Micah
Mid.	*Middot*
Midr.	*Midrash*
Moʾed Qaṭ.	*Moʾed Qaṭan*
Mor.	Plutarch, *Moralia*
Mos.	Philo, *De vita Mosis*
Moses	Philo, *On the Life of Moses*
ms/mss	manuscript/manuscripts
MT	Masoretic Text
Mut.	Philo, *De mutatione nominum*
NAB	New American Bible
Nah	Nahum
NASB	New American Standard Bible
Nat. d.	Cicero, *De natura deorum*
n.d.	no date
NEB	New English Bible
Neh	Nehemiah
NHC	Nag Hammadi Codex
Nid.	*Niddah*
NIV	New International Version
NJB	New Jerusalem Bible
NJPS	*Tanakh: The Holy Scriptures: The New JPS Translation according to the Traditional Hebrew Text*
NKJV	New King James Version
Noet.	Hippolytus, *Contra haeresin Noeti*
n.p.	no place
NRSV	New Revised Standard Version
NT	New Testament
Num	Numbers
Num. Rab.	*Numbers Rabbah*
Obad	Obadiah
Odes	*Odes of Solomon*
OG	Old Greek

OL	Old Latin
Opif.	Philo, *De opificio mundi*
Or.	Dio Chrysostom, *Oration*
OT	Old Testament
P	Priestly source in the Pentateuch
P.	Papyrus
p.	page (pl., pp.)
Paed.	Clement, *Paedagogus*
Pan.	Epiphanius, *Panarion (Adversus haereses)*
Pat.	Tertullian, *De patientia*
Pesaḥ.	*Pesaḥim*
Pesiq. Rab.	*Pesiqta Rabbati*
Pesiq. Rab Kah.	*Pesiqta de Rab Kahana*
1–2 Pet	1–2 Peter
Phil	Philippians
Phlm	Philemon
Piet.	Philodemus of Gadara, *De pietate*
Pirqe R. El.	*Pirqe Rabbi Eliezer*
Pol.	Aristotle, *Politica*
Pol. *Phil*	Polycarp, *To the Philippians*
Praescr.	Tertullian, *De praescriptione haereticorum*
Pr Azar	Prayer of Azariah
Princ.	Origen, *De principiis (Peri archōn)*
Pr Man	Prayer of Manasseh
Prot.	Plato, *Protagoras*
Prov	Proverbs
Prov.	Philo, *De providentia*
Ps(s)	Psalm(s)
Ps 151	Psalm 151
Pss. Sol.	*Psalms of Solomon*
Pud.	Tertullian, *De pudicitia*
Q	*Quelle*, a hypothetical source used by Matthew and Luke
QG	Philo, *Quaestiones et solutiones in Genesin (Questions and Answers on Genesis)*

1QH[a]	Qumran Cave 1, *Thanksgiving Hymns*[a]
1QIsa[a]	Qumran Cave 1, *Great Isaiah Scroll*
1QM	Qumran Cave 1, *War Scroll*
1QpHab	Qumran Cave 1, *Pesher Habakkuk*
1QS	Qumran Cave 1, *Rule of the Community*
3Q15	Qumran Cave 3, *Copper Scroll*
4Q169	Qumran Cave 4, *Nahum Pesher*
4QDeut[n]	Qumran Cave 4, *Deuteronomy Scroll*
4QMMT	Qumran Cave 4, *Halakic Letter*
11QPs[a]	Qumran Cave 11, *Psalms Scroll*[a]
11QT[a]	Qumran Cave 11, *Temple Scroll*[a]
Qidd.	*Qiddušin*
Qoh	Qoheleth
Rab.	*Rabbah*
Rab. Perd.	Cicero, *Pro Rabirio Perduellionis Reo*
REB	Revised English Bible
Resp.	Cicero, *De republica*
Rev	Revelation
rev.	revised
Rom	Romans
Roš Haš.	*Roš Haššanah*
RSV	Revised Standard Version
Ruth	Ruth
S	Codex Sinaiticus
Šabb.	*Šabbat*
Sacr.	Philo, *De sacrificiis Abelis et Caini*
1–2 Sam	1–2 Samuel
Sanh.	*Sanhedrin*
Sat.	Juvenal, *Satirae*
Serm. Dom.	Augustine, *De sermone Domini in monte*
Sg Three	Song of the Three Young Men
Sib. Or.	*Sibylline Oracles*
Sipra	*Sipra*
Sipre	*Sipre*
Sir	Sirach

Somn.	Philo, *De somniis*
Song	Song of Solomon
Soṭah	*Soṭah*
SP	Samaritan Pentateuch
Spec.	Philo, *De specialibus legibus*
Spec. Laws	Philo, *On the Special Laws*
Strom.	Clement of Alexandria, *Stromata*
Sukkah	*Sukkah*
supp.	supplement
Sus	Susanna
Syn.	Athanasius, *De synodis*
t.	Tosefta
T. Ash.	*Testament of Asher*
T. Benj.	*Testament of Benjamin*
T. Dan	*Testament of Dan*
T. Gad	*Testament of Gad*
T. Iss.	*Testament of Issachar*
T. Jos.	*Testament of Joseph*
T. Jud.	*Testament of Judah*
T. Levi	*Testament of Levi*
T. Naph.	*Testament of Naphtali*
T. Reu.	*Testament of Reuben*
T. Sim.	*Testament of Simeon*
T. 12 Patr.	*Testaments of the Twelve Patriarchs*
T. Zeb.	*Testament of Zebulun*
Taʿan.	*Taʿanit*
Tanḥ.	*Tanḥuma*
Theaet.	Plato, *Theaetetus*
1–2 Thess	1–2 Thessalonians
1–2 Tim	1–2 Timothy
Titus	Titus
Tob	Tobit
Trad. ap.	Hippolytus, *Traditio apostolica*
Trin.	Augustine, *De Trinitate*
v./vv.	verse/verses

Virt.	Philo, *De virtutibus*
Vit. Apoll.	Philostratus, *Vita Apollonii*
vol.	volume (pl., vols.)
Vulg.	Vulgate
War	Josephus, *Jewish War*
Wis	Wisdom of Solomon
y.	Jerusalem Talmud
Yad.	*Yadayim*
Yebam.	*Yebamot*
Yoma	*Yoma*
Zech	Zechariah
Zeph	Zephaniah

THE OXFORD ENCYCLOPEDIA OF
THE BIBLE AND THEOLOGY

K

KINGDOM OF GOD (HEAVEN)

The "Kingdom of God" (heaven) is of great importance in the preaching of Jesus and in early Christian literature. It is a concept that is rooted in Israel's scriptures, a concept that in the time of Jesus had developed in new ways largely in response to Israel's experience at the hands of foreign nations.

The Kingdom of God in the Old Testament. The concept of the Kingdom of God is founded on the conviction that Yahweh (the Lord), the God of Israel, is king. It is he who reigns over Israel, over the nations, and over the whole earth. The kingdom, kingship, or reign of God is expressed in a variety of ways, sometimes explicitly, sometimes only implied. While other vocabulary comes into play in describing God as king, the primary vocabulary is *malak* ("he rules"), *melek* ("king"), and *malkutah* ("kingdom"). The Greek equivalents, which appear in the Septuagint, the New Testament, and some of the intertestamental literature, are *basileiein* ("to rule"), *basileus* ("king"), and *basileia* ("kingdom").

God as judge and redeemer. God's role as king is implied in his actions as judge, redeemer, warrior, and savior, actions that were expected of kings in the ancient Near East. Many of these elements come together in Isaiah 33:22: "For the LORD is our judge, the LORD is our ruler, the LORD is our king; he will save us."

Traditions and testimonies of God's royal work are found throughout Israel's scriptures, beginning with the Exodus itself. God commands Moses to tell the people of Israel, "I am the LORD, and I will bring you out from under the burdens of the Egyptians, and I will deliver you from their bondage, and I will redeem you with an outstretched arm and with great acts of judgment" (Exod 6:6). God's judgments fall upon Egypt and upon other nations that oppose Israel in the wilderness. The second generation of the wilderness is reminded that "it is because the LORD loves you, and is keeping the oath which he swore to your fathers, that the LORD has brought you out with a mighty hand, and redeemed you from the house of bondage, from the hand of Pharaoh king of Egypt" (Deut 13:5; cf. Deut 23:14).

The prophets give expression to similar ideas. According to Jeremiah, the Lord will judge the nations and all the wicked (Jer 25:31; cf. Isa 66:16; Ezek 30:19). And, of course, even against Israel will God on occasion bring judgment (Isa 3:14; Ezek 20:36). But this judgment is ultimately redemptive, for the Lord will judge and purge Israel (Mal 3:5).

Because God is Israel's king, Isaiah exhorts the nation to have courage in the face of enemies (Isa 35:4). As king, God acts as a warrior, protecting his people and giving them victory (Zeph 3:17; Zech 9:16). In an eschatological setting the prophet anticipates that God will rescue the people and bring them salvation

(Isa 25:9). The Psalter affirms the same sentiments (Pss 7:8; 9:7; 106:47).

As king, God also visits, or inspects, his people. The Exodus was the result of God's visitation of his oppressed people (Exod 4:31). Visitation is often a good thing, as in Genesis 21:1 (whereby Sarah was enabled to conceive), 1 Samuel 2:21 (whereby Hannah was enabled to conceive), and Ruth 1:6 (in which God's visitation resulted in the end of famine). But God's visitation can bring judgment (Isa 29:6).

God's role as redeemer finds frequent expression in the Prophets and the book of Psalms. In 2 Isaiah Yahweh is many times called "redeemer" and "holy one" (41:14; 43:14; 48:17; 49:7; 54:5), sometimes in contexts of endearment and intimacy, envisioning God as mother (Isa 44:24), husband (54:5), or father (63:16). God has "comforted his people" and "redeemed Jerusalem" (52:9). God is the "LORD of hosts" (47:4), who is "the first and…the last," the only God (44:6), the "Mighty One of Jacob" (49:26). God "will come to Zion as Redeemer, to those in Jacob who turn from transgression" (59:20). The day will come when Israel will know that the Lord is her savior and redeemer (60:16). Echoing the Isaianic tradition, Jeremiah confesses, "Their Redeemer is strong; the LORD of hosts is his name" (Jer 50:34). The Psalmist addresses God as his rock and redeemer (Ps 19:14; cf. 78:35), a God who "redeems the life of his servants" (Ps 34:22).

God as king. Israel's scriptures explicitly affirm God as king in several places. In what is probably the earliest tradition, Yahweh consoles Samuel the prophet and priest when Israel demands a king, like other nations have (1 Sam 8:5–6): "they have not rejected you, but they have rejected me from being king over them" (1 Sam 8:7).

This breach is in part healed in the kingship of David, the man whose character is after God's heart (1 Sam 13:14). David is adopted as God's son (Ps 2:7; cf. 2 Sam 7:14; Ps 89:26). If Israel's kings are God's sons, it is implied, then God is himself Israel's great king. In a sense, David's kingdom is an adumbration of God's kingdom (which becomes clearer in Chronicles).

Isaiah and his tradition explicitly speak of God as king. In his theophany, Isaiah sees God as the enthroned king (6:5). In another context the prophet confesses God is the ruler and king who will save the people (33:22). In 2 Isaiah the Lord identifies himself as "the King of Jacob" (41:21) and "the King of Israel" (44:6).

Similarly, Jeremiah refers to God as "king" (Jer 10:10; 51:57), the "LORD of hosts" (48:15), the one who resides in Zion (8:19). He is Israel's everlasting king (10:10). Significantly, Israel's God is also the "King of the nations" (10:7). This language is echoed in Zephaniah, who calls God "the king of Israel" (3:15), and in Zechariah: "the king, the LORD of hosts" (14:16), and "King over all the earth" (14:9). In Malachi God, the "LORD of hosts," says of himself, "I am a great King" (Mal 1:14).

The Psalter frequently speaks of God as king. The Psalmist petitions God as king (Pss 5:2; 10:16; 29:10; 44:4; 47:6; 68:24; 72:12; 98:6; 145:1; 149:2); including as "king over all the earth" (47:2, 7). God is also the "great King above all Gods" (95:3), a "mighty King," who loves justice, establishes equity, and executes justice and righteousness in Israel (99:4).

The Kingdom of the Lord. To speak of God as king, either of Israel, of the nations, or of the whole earth, implies the idea of a Kingdom of God. The expression "Kingdom of Yahweh" occurs twice in Israel's scriptures, both in Chronicles and both in close association with David's royal house. Near death, David declares that God had "chosen Solomon my son to sit upon the throne of the Kingdom of the LORD over Israel" (1 Chr 28:5). After the death of Solomon, Jeroboam and the men of the northern tribes of Israel, who had abandoned Judah, are challenged: "And now you think to withstand the Kingdom of the LORD in the hand of the sons of David" (2 Chr 13:8).

The kingdom of Israel is understood as the "Kingdom of the LORD," over which David and his descendants have been placed. Accordingly, when his succession was confirmed, "Solomon sat on the throne of the LORD …as king" (1 Chr 29:23). The importance of this statement becomes apparent when it is compared to its older parallel: "Solomon sat upon the throne of David his father; and his kingdom was firmly established" (1 Kgs 2:12). For the Chronicler, the throne of David is, in a sense, the throne of the Lord. We encounter the same interpretive gloss in the story of the queen of Sheba who visits Solomon. The older parallel reads,

"Blessed be the LORD your God, who has delighted in you and set you on the throne of Israel!" (1 Kgs 10:9). In Chronicles it becomes, "Blessed be the LORD your God, who has delighted in you and set you on his throne as king for the LORD your God!" (2 Chr 9:8). The throne of Israel has become the Lord's throne.

What was implicit in Samuel and Kings has become explicit in Chronicles. The kingdom of Israel is in reality the Kingdom of Yahweh. David's throne is in reality Yahweh's throne. Indeed, "throne of the LORD" is sometimes just another way of speaking of the "Kingdom of the LORD." The Psalmist declares, "But the LORD sits enthroned forever, he has established his throne for judgment" (Ps 9:7). The Lord may be present in his temple, but his "throne is in heaven" (Ps 11:4). Indeed, "The LORD has established his throne in the heavens, and his kingdom rules over all" (Ps 103:19; see also Isa 66:1; Lam 5:19). The idea of God sitting on a throne is ancient, reaching back at least to the time of the prophet Micaiah: "I saw the LORD sitting on his throne, and all the host of heaven standing beside him on his right hand and on his left" (1 Kgs 22:19; 2 Chr 18:18), which recalls Isaiah's vision (Isa 6:1). When all of the relevant data are assembled, it becomes clear that the concept of Yahweh as king of Israel and king of the whole earth runs throughout Israel's scriptures, even if the precise phrase "Kingdom of the LORD" occurs only twice and the phrase "Kingdom of God" never occurs.

Kingdom of God Language and Expectation in Intertestamental Literature. Kingdom of God language and expectation become more explicit and variegated in intertestamental literature. Some of this developing tradition becomes foundational for Jesus and early Christian theology.

Daniel. Probably composed in the 160s B.C.E., Daniel is an important witness to kingdom ideas in the intertestamental period. The book envisions a succession of four human kingdoms or empires that will be smashed by the kingdom that "the God of heaven will set up." This will be the final kingdom, "which shall never be destroyed" (Dan 2:44; cf. 4:34; 6:26). The Babylonian king later confesses, "His kingdom is an everlasting kingdom, and his dominion is from generation to generation" (Dan 4:3; see also 4:37). Even before the final Kingdom of God makes its appearance, God in fact "rules the kingdom of men" (Dan 4:17, 25, 31; 5:21). In his night vision Daniel learns that "the kingdom and the dominion and the greatness of the kingdoms under the whole heaven shall be given to the people of the saints of the Most High; their kingdom shall be an everlasting kingdom, and all dominions shall serve and obey them" (Dan 7:27; cf. 7:14).

Daniel's concept of a kingdom of and for the "saints" represents yet another development in the Kingdom of God idea. In older tradition the kingdom was primarily identified with David and his descendants. In the postexilic period, as seen in Chronicles, the kingdom becomes much more closely linked to God himself. In Daniel the kingdom is linked with God's people and their representative, the "one like a son of man," who receives authority and kingdom from God.

Dead Sea Scrolls. Although the precise phrase "Kingdom of God" does not appear in the Scrolls, the concept nevertheless occurs many times. In the eschatological blessings of the second appendix to the *Rule of the Community*, the congregation is instructed to say of the priest, "May you serve in the temple of the kingdom" (1QSb 4:25–26). Given the context, it is almost certain the kingdom to which reference is made is the Kingdom of God. A later blessing speaks of the renewal of the covenant and the establishment of "the kingdom of his [God's] people forever" (5:21).

Most of the references to the Kingdom of God in the Dead Sea Scrolls occur in texts known as *Songs of the Sabbath Sacrifice*. Six fragmentary copies were recovered from cave 4 (4Q400–4Q405) and a seventh from Masada (MasSS). In these texts one finds some 20 references to God's kingdom (though almost always using the personal pronoun). Examples include "his kingdom" (4Q403, frag. 1, col. i, line 32), "his lofty kingdom" (4Q403, frag. 1, col. i, line 8; frag. 1, col. i, line 14; 4Q405, frag. 3, col. ii, line 4; MasSS, 2:20), "his glorious kingdom" (4Q403, frag. 1, col. i, line 25; 4Q405, frag. 23, col. i, line 3; col. ii, lines 11–12), "all His kingdom" (4Q403, frag. 1, col. i, lines 32–33), "your kingdom" (4Q400, frag. 1, col. ii, line 3; frag. 2, line 1; 4Q401, frag. 14, col. i, line 7), "your glorious kingdom" (4Q401, frag. 14, col. i, line 6), and "the glorious kingdom of the King of all the g[ods]" (4Q405, frag. 24, line 3).

Only a small portion of these songs has survived. If these scrolls had survived in full, we would have dozens more references to God's kingdom.

There is little doubt that the concept of God's rule was very important to the Qumran community. They anticipated the coming of this kingdom in its fullness, at which time the community's enemies would be vanquished and a righteous priesthood would be reestablished in Jerusalem. The *War Scroll* declares, "So the kingdom shall belong to the God of Israel, and by the holy ones of his people he shall act powerfully" (1QM 6:6//4Q491, frags. 14–15, line 7). God's kingdom will be established and the righteous of Israel will reign forever (1QM 12:15–16). The covenanters of Qumran praise God for the restoration of the kingdom (and temple) and for its glory (1QM 12:7; 4Q212, frag. 54, line 18). Other scrolls that praise God for his kingdom include 4Q286 (frag. 7, col. i, lines 5–7), 4Q287 (frag. 5, lines 10–11), 4Q302 (frag. 3, col. ii, lines 9–10), and 1QHa (3:27).

The arrival of this kingdom, of course, would be preceded by a great battle. Here too the Kingdom of God is presupposed. Lying behind the expectation of the great eschatological battle between the Sons of Light and the Sons of Darkness (1QM and copies) is the concept of two warring kingdoms—the Kingdom of God and the kingdom (usually "dominion") of Belial (or Satan). Belial and his evil spirits march in lockstep with their human allies (the Kittim). Opposing them will be God's angels and their allies, the righteous of Israel.

The concept of the kingdom in the Scrolls seems to reflect the multifaceted dimensions seen in the Old Testament. The Scrolls anticipate a Davidic Messiah who will defeat Israel's enemies, which is consistent with preexilic models, yet the Scrolls also associate the kingdom with God (as in Chronicles) and speak of it as given to his people (as in Dan 7).

Other literature. Several other writings from the intertestamental period speak of the Kingdom of God or of God as king. According to *Jubilees* 1:28, God is "king" who rules "upon Mount Zion forever and ever." In anticipation of Israel's restoration, the patriarch Dan prophesies that "the Holy One will rule [*basileuon*] over them" (*T. Dan* 5:13). The author of the *Testament of Moses* predicts the appearance of

God's kingdom after Israel endures a period of wrath (*T. Mos.* 10:1, 3). Because of Israel's sin "the Kingdom of the Lord" (*he basileia kuriou*) will be taken away (*T. Benj.* 9:1), but when Israel repents and is restored the nation will worship "the King of heaven" (10:7; the concluding relative clause, "who appeared upon earth in the form of a man in humility," is an obvious Christian gloss). According to the patriarch Joseph, God's "kingdom is an everlasting kingdom [*basileia aionos*], which will not pass away" (*T. Jos.* 19:12). In the *Testament of Abraham*, the patriarch asks about God's immortal kingdom (*T. Ab.* A 8:3). In the Greek version of the *Life of Adam and Eve*, we hear of the "throne of God," which was "fixed where the Tree of Life was" (*L.A.E.* 22:4; cf. 32:2).

The author of the *Psalms of Solomon* refers to "the Kingdom of our God [*he basileia tou theou hemon*]" that "is forever over the nations in judgment" (*Pss. Sol.* 17:3). Here we find the exact Greek phrase "Kingdom of God" (*he basileia tou theou*) that appears in the gospels.

In two of the major parts of the book of *Enoch*, the kingly rule of God is envisioned. In the Book of the Watchers (*1 En.* 1–36), God is described as an "eternal King (*1 En.* 9:4; 25:7)," "King of Kings (12:3)," and "King of the Universe" (25:3–5; 27:3). We also hear of God's "throne" (9:4; 18:8; 25:3). In the Book of Dream Visions (*1 En.* 83–90), God is addressed in exalted royal terms: "LORD King, great and powerful in your majesty, LORD of the whole creation of heaven, King of Kings and God of the whole creation" (84:2).

The concept of the Kingdom of God can be presented in metaphorical terms, often in service of wisdom themes: "When a righteous man fled from his brother's wrath, she [Wisdom] guided him on straight paths; she showed him the Kingdom of God [*basileian theou*], and gave him knowledge of angels" (Wis 10:10). Philo speaks similarly of God as king (*Cher.* 29; *Agr.* 51, 78; *Migr.* 146; and others). The word "kingdom" can sometimes be used in a metaphorical or philosophical sense, as in 4 Maccabees 2:23: "The one who adopts a way of life in accordance with it [the Law] will rule a kingdom [*basileusei basileian*]."

These intertestamental traditions range from the second century B.C.E. (Daniel, *Jubilees*, and *1 Enoch*

1–36) to the first century B.C.E. (*Testaments of the Patriarchs*, Wisdom of Solomon, *Psalms of Solomon*, Dead Sea Scrolls) and the early first century C.E. (*Testament of Moses*, Philo). These texts show that the concept of the Kingdom of God was well known among the Jewish people and could be envisioned and employed in a variety of ways. The most common conception, however, was eschatological.

Kingdom of God in the Proclamation and Actions of Jesus. As portrayed in the New Testament Gospels, the Kingdom of God stands at the very center of Jesus's proclamation. Indeed, the Kingdom of God is itself the gospel or good news, for which Israel has waited: "The time is fulfilled, and the Kingdom of God is at hand; repent, and believe in the gospel" (Mark 1:15).

Jesus's understanding of the good news of the Kingdom of God reflects the good news proclaimed in the book of Isaiah. The good news (or good tidings) is the appearance of God (Isa 40:9), the announcement of his reign (52:7), and his saving, redemptive work (61:1–2). Some of these texts are quoted or alluded to in Jesus's preaching (e.g., Isa 61:1–2 in Matt 11:5//Luke 7:22 and in Luke 4:18–19). Jesus's wording and interpretation reflect how Isaiah was paraphrased and interpreted in Aramaic.

Proclamation. The theme of the Kingdom of God is the subject of many of Jesus's parables. Response to the kingdom is likened to seed that is sown (Mark 4:3–20 [that it is the *kingdom* is made explicit in the parallel at Matt 13:19], 26–32). Petitioning God that his kingdom come is the basic theme of one's prayer (Matt 6:10). Seeking the kingdom is one's first priority (6:33); it is valuable above all else (13:44, 45–46, 47–48). Those who are blessed are those who will enter the Kingdom of God (Matt 5:3, 10), no matter what the cost (Mark 9:42–50).

Wealth, greed, hypocrisy, unwillingness to forgive, and indifference toward the poor and hungry may prevent people from entering the Kingdom of God (Matt 18:23–35; 23:13; Mark 10:17–31). Divided loyalties, folly, and lack of preparation may also shut a person out of the kingdom (Matt 25:1–13; Luke 9:61–62). The warnings to be prepared and to watch (as in Mark 13 and parallels in Matthew and Luke) have to do with entering the Kingdom of God, even when this is not explicitly stated.

The Kingdom of God is a central feature in the Words of Institution at the Last Supper: "Truly, I say to you, I shall not drink again of the fruit of the vine until that day when I drink it new in the Kingdom of God" (Mark 14:25). The coming kingdom involves struggle (Matt 11:12) but is certain (Mark 9:1). Still, the time of its coming is not known (Matt 24:14; 25:13; Mark 13:8, 32; Luke 17:20–21). The crucifixion of Jesus for claiming to be the "king of the Jews" (Matt 27:37; Mark 15:26; Luke 23:38; John 19:19) serves as a grim reference to the earlier proclamation of the Kingdom of God.

Healing and exorcism. A striking feature in Jesus's preaching is his linking of the Kingdom of God with healing and exorcism. Healing and exorcism are not incidental to Jesus's proclamation; they are illustrative and demonstrative.

Jesus appoints 12 apostles (lit. "ones sent") to "preach and have authority to cast out demons" (Mark 3:14–15; 6:7–13). In Luke the linkage between proclaiming the gospel of the Kingdom of God and healing and exorcism is made more explicit: "And he called the 12 together and gave them power and authority over all demons and to cure diseases, and he sent them out to preach the Kingdom of God and to heal" (Luke 9:1–2, 6).

The link between the Kingdom of God and exorcism is clarified when Jesus is accused of being in league with Beelzebul (or Satan). To this charge (see Matt 12:24; Mark 3:22; Luke 11:15) Jesus retorts, "And if I cast out demons by Beelzebul, by whom do your sons cast them out? Therefore they shall be your judges. But if it is by the finger of God that I cast out demons, then the Kingdom of God has come upon you" (Luke 11:19–20; cf. Matt 12:28). The expression "finger of God" brings to mind the confession of Pharaoh's magicians that the mighty works of Moses and Aaron are from the "finger of God," that is, from God himself (Exod 8:19). In Jewish interpretation Pharaoh's magicians were in fact in league with Satan. Accordingly, Jesus's allusion to the confession of the magicians is rhetorically effective. Jesus affirms that his exorcisms are not the result of magic or Satan's assistance; they are the result of God's kingly power.

Jesus sees in the exorcisms tangible and powerful evidence of the presence of the Kingdom of God. This explains the linkage of kingdom proclamation and healing and exorcism in the missionary charge to the 12 apostles. Healing and exorcism constitute supporting evidence that the Kingdom of God is in fact breaking into the world.

The reference to the divided kingdom in Mark's version of the dispute about exorcisms implies that Jesus thinks of Satan's sphere of power as a kingdom, a kingdom at war with the Kingdom of God (Mark 3:24–26). The last part of the quotation, "is coming to an end" (*telos echei*, lit. "has an end"), finds a significant parallel in the *Testament of Moses*, where, after a season of persecution and suffering, we are assured, "Then his [God's] kingdom will appear throughout his whole creation. Then the devil will have an end.… For the heavenly One will arise from his kingly throne" (*T. Mos.* 10:1, 3). The Latin "will have an end" (*finem habebit*), apart from the tense itself, is an exact parallel to Mark's "is coming to an end." The progress of the Kingdom of God requires the retreat and eventual destruction of the kingdom of Satan. Accordingly, the exorcisms are evidence of the dismantling of Satan's kingdom.

Another important component in Jesus's reply to the charge of being in league with Beelzebul is seen in his analogy of plundering the strong man's house (Mark 3:27). What is remarkable is that Jesus has implied that he has bound Satan. In saying this Jesus has claimed to be "stronger than" Satan (as in fact the tradition is worded in Luke 11:21–22). Such a claim assumes a very close association between Jesus, who acts on God's behalf, and God himself.

The New Testament Gospels. Mark and Luke regularly speak of the "Kingdom of God" (*basileia tou theou*). The expression occurs some 14 times in Mark and 32 times in Luke. Although "Kingdom of God" occurs in Matthew only four times, the Evangelist's preferred language, "Kingdom of heaven" (*basileia tou ouranou*), occurs some 32 times. The difference is purely formal and reflects Matthew's tendency, probably observed in the synagogue of his day, to avoid pronouncing the name of God. In addition, "kingdom" appears without further qualification many times in Matthew. These too refer to the Kingdom of God. In all, there are some 54 references to the kingdom (of God/heaven) in the Gospel of Matthew.

Matthew also uniquely speaks of the "sons of the kingdom" (8:12; 13:38). The second reference is positive: the good seed of the parable of the wheat and tares are the sons of the kingdom. However, the first passage, which is embedded in the story of the healing of the centurion's servant (Matt 8:5–13//Luke 7:1–10), warns that the sons of the kingdom "will be thrown into outer darkness." Here the sons of the kingdom are Israelites, who by heritage and patriarchal promises expect to enter the Kingdom of heaven and sit at table with Abraham, Isaac, and Jacob. But because of unbelief and refusal to repent, they will be excluded. Other less likely candidates, such as those who "come from east and west," will be included. These Matthean parables seem to serve as warnings to ethnic Israel: failure to repent and embrace Jesus's kingdom proclamation will result in being excluded from the kingdom.

The function of "Kingdom of God" in the Gospel of John is quite distinctive. The expression occurs only twice, both times in John 3 (at vv. 3 and 5), in the well-known conversation with Nicodemus. Jesus tells the teacher that he must be born from above (or anew) and must be "born of water and the Spirit," if he is to see or enter the Kingdom of God. In Johannine theology the Kingdom of God seems to have become part of the Evangelist's theology of salvation and mystical union with Christ (as seen esp. in John 14–16).

Kingdom of God Language and Expectation in the New Testament. Given the prominence of the Kingdom of God in the preaching of Jesus, it is surprising how little a role this language plays elsewhere in the New Testament. We do find, however, some interesting developments.

Preaching of the early church. The expressions "kingdom" and "Kingdom of God" occur eight times in the book of Acts. During the 40 days the risen Jesus was with his disciples, Luke says he was "speaking of the Kingdom of God" (1:3). This leads to the disciples' question, "Lord, will you at this time restore the kingdom to Israel?" (1:6). The question is not answered; the disciples are simply told that they are not "to know times or seasons," which are known only to God (1:7). They are to wait for the Holy Spirit and then bear witness to Jesus (1:8). This occurs on the Day of Pentecost (Acts 2). Then Philip preaches the "good news about the Kingdom of God and the name of Jesus Christ" (8:12). Acts also makes the kingdom an important element in Paul's initial preaching (14:22; 19:8) and continuing teaching (20:25; 28:23, 30–31).

What is interesting to observe in the book of Acts is not only the few occurrences of "kingdom" or "Kingdom of God" but how in a number of occurrences reference to the kingdom is expanded to include something about Jesus. The message is no longer simply the message of Jesus, viz., the in-breaking of the Kingdom of God; the message is just as much about Jesus himself, his suffering and death, and, more importantly, his exaltation.

The letters of Paul and other letters. In his early letters Paul speaks several times of the kingdom. He reminds the Thessalonians that God called them "into his own kingdom and glory" (1 Thess 2:12) and explains that their suffering makes them "worthy of the Kingdom of God" (2 Thess 1:5). "Kingdom of God" appears five times in 1 Corinthians. Some of these mentions refer to present existence (4:20) and some to the final eschatological kingdom (6:9, 10; 15:23–24). In Galatians Paul repeats his warning that the wicked "shall not inherit the Kingdom of God" (Gal 5:21).

There is no reference to the kingdom in Paul's theologically weighty letter to the Romans. Pauline theology, especially Christology and ecclesiology, are developed largely without reference to the Kingdom of God. To speak of "inheriting" the Kingdom of God (as in 1 Cor 6:9, 10; Gal 5:21) is another way of saying "saved." Paul's use of "Kingdom of God" really says very little about God's reign. As in the book of Acts, the concept of the kingdom has been redefined in the light of the death and resurrection of Jesus.

The Kingdom of God scarcely appears in the remainder of the New Testament letters, appearing only four times. James reminds his readers that God has chosen the poor to be "heirs of the kingdom" (Jas 2:5). The author of Hebrews quotes Psalm 45:6 and applies it to Jesus (Heb 1:8) and later exhorts his readers to be "grateful for receiving a kingdom that cannot be shaken" (Heb 12:28). The author of 2 Peter assures his readers that "an entrance into the eternal Kingdom of our Lord and Savior Jesus Christ" has been provided for them (2 Pet 1:11).

Revelation. The words "king," "kingdom," and "reign" occur several times in Revelation but only twice in reference to the Kingdom of God. In the first passage loud voices in heaven say, "The kingdom of the world has become the Kingdom of our Lord and of his Christ, and he shall reign for ever and ever" (11:15). Later a loud voice in heaven says, "Now the salvation and the power and the Kingdom of our God and the authority of his Christ have come" (12:10). The royal power of God and his Christ in the book of Revelation, however, goes well beyond these two passages. Throughout the book the reign of God (see 11:17) is depicted, either implicitly or explicitly. The message of the book is that the reign of God and his Christ will triumph over all kings and kingdoms.

Apostolic Fathers. In the Apostolic Fathers most references to the Kingdom of God are quotations of or allusions to specific New Testament passages. A few passages speak of the "Kingdom of Christ."

Kingdom of God. In *1 Clement* readers are reminded of how after the resurrection of Jesus the apostles "went forth…preaching the good news that the Kingdom of God was about to come" (42:3). Later in the letter God is addressed as "heavenly Master, King of the ages" (61:2). Then, *2 Clement* speaks of the "coming kingdom and eternal life" (5:5) and exhorts readers to "love one another, so that we all may enter into the Kingdom of God" (9:6), later promising, "if we do what is right in God's sight, we will enter his kingdom and receive the promises" (11:7) and exhorting, "Let us wait, therefore, hour by hour for the Kingdom of God" (12:1).

In two of his letters Ignatius reiterates Paul's warning that the wicked "will not inherit the Kingdom of God" (*Eph.* 16:1; *Phld.* 3:3, 5:3). The Shepherd of Hermas explains that "the saved may enter the Kingdom of God" (*Sim.* 12:3), adding that those who do not receive the name of God's Son "will not enter the Kingdom of God" (*Sim.* 12:8, 16:2–3).

The author of *Barnabas* states that those who learn and walk in the Lord's righteous requirements "will be glorified in the Kingdom of God" (*Barn.* 21:1). The author of *Diognetus* explains that it is by God's goodness and power that we are enabled "to enter the kingdom" (*Diogn.* 9:1).

Kingdom of Christ. The qualification seen in the book of Acts in which the Kingdom of God is linked to Jesus gives way in the Apostolic Fathers, not surprisingly, to references in the Apostolic Fathers to the "Kingdom of Christ." The author of *1 Clement* says that the righteous "will be revealed when the kingdom of Christ visits us" (50:3). In the *Martyrdom of Polycarp* readers are exhorted to follow the example of Polycarp so that they will "be found in the Kingdom of Jesus Christ" (22:1). The writer of the narrative, who identifies himself as one Pionius, hopes to be gathered together with Christ's "chosen ones into his heavenly kingdom" (22:3). The author of *Barnabas* speaks of the "Kingdom of the Lord" (4:13), by which he probably means Christ. This is supported by what he states later, when he says that "the Kingdom of Jesus is based on the wooden cross" (8:5).

Kingdom of God in the Targums and Early Rabbinic Literature. The concept of the Kingdom of God appears in early Jewish prayers, the Aramaic paraphrases of scripture known as Targums, and in early Rabbinic literature. Although the Targums and rabbinic writings are late, they do contain early traditions that in some cases shed light on some of the literature of the Second Temple period in which references are made to the Kingdom of God.

The Qaddish and synagogue prayers. The theme of the Kingdom of God appears in some ancient Jewish prayers. In its earliest form, the Qaddish, probably inspired by Ezekiel 38:23, was made up of two simple petitions: "May his great name be made holy; may his kingdom be established in your lifetime." The two petitions of the Qaddish appear at the beginning of the Lord's Prayer: "Father, holy be your name. Your kingdom come" (Luke 11:2; cf. Matt 6:10). The eleventh benediction of the Amidah ("standing") or Shemoneh Esra ("eighteen") prayer petitions God, "Alone be King over us, O LORD, in mercy and compassion, in grace and justice! Blessed are you, O LORD, a King who loves grace and righteousness."

Targums. Although the targumic and rabbinic materials postdate Jesus and New Testament literature, they do contain old traditions that in some cases can be traced to the time of Jesus and even earlier. In several passages references to God, his appearance, or his reign in the Hebrew scriptures are paraphrased, "the Kingdom of God is revealed" (*Tg. Isa.* 24:23, 31:4, 40:9, 52:7; *Tg. Ezek.* 7:7, 10; *Tg. Obad.* 21; *Tg. Mic.* 4:7, 8; *Tg. Zech.* 14:9). It has been plausibly argued that Jesus's proclamation of the arrival of the Kingdom of God reflects this Aramaic language, a language that emerged in the synagogue and later was preserved in the written Targums.

Rabbinic literature. A common exhortation in early Rabbinic literature is to "take the yoke of the Kingdom of Heaven upon" oneself. This meant embracing rabbinic "orthodoxy" in life and thought. It also implies, of course, preparing oneself for entering the Kingdom of God, or the "World to Come," beyond one's mortal life. Closer to the concept of a coming kingdom is a tradition credited to Eliezer ben Hyrcanus, a student of the first-century authority Yohanan ben Zakkai. When asked when the wicked will be blotted out, the great rabbi is remembered to have replied, "At the time when idolatry will be eradicated together with its worshipers, and God will be recognized throughout the world as the One, and his kingdom will be established for all eternity" (*Mek.* on Exod 17:14 [*Amalek* §2]).

[*See also* Apocalypticism; Authority and Order; Covenant; David; David, Son of; Ecclesiology; *and* Kings and Kingship.]

BIBLIOGRAPHY

Beasley-Murray, George R. *Jesus and the Kingdom of God.* Grand Rapids, Mich.: Eerdmans, 1986.
Chilton, Bruce. "Regnum Dei Deus Est." *Scottish Journal of Theology* 31 (1978): 261–270.
Chilton, Bruce. *God in Strength: Jesus' Announcement of the Kingdom.* Biblical Seminar 8. Sheffield, U.K.: JSOT Press, 1987.
Chilton, Bruce. "The Kingdom of God in Recent Discussion." In *Studying the Historical Jesus: Evaluations of the State of Current Research*, edited by Bruce Chilton and Craig A. Evans, pp. 255–280. New Testament Tools and Studies 19. Leiden, The Netherlands: Brill, 1994.

Chilton, Bruce, ed. *The Kingdom of God in the Teaching of Jesus.* Issues in Religion and Theology 5. London: SPCK; Philadelphia: Fortress, 1984.

Chilton, Bruce, and J. I. H. McDonald. *Jesus and the Ethics of the Kingdom.* London: SPCK; Grand Rapids, Mich.: Eerdmans, 1987.

Collins, John J. "The Kingdom of God in the Apocrypha and Pseudepigrapha." In *The Kingdom of God in 20th-Century Interpretation,* edited by Wendell Willis, pp. 81–95. Peabody, Mass.: Hendrickson, 1987.

Collins, John J. *Daniel.* Hermeneia: A Critical & Historical Commentary on the Bible. Minneapolis: Fortress, 1993.

Dodd, C. H. *The Parables of the Kingdom.* London: Nisbet, 1935.

Elbogen, Ismar. *Jewish Liturgy: A Comprehensive History.* Philadelphia: Jewish Publication Society; New York and Jerusalem: Jewish Theological Seminary of America, 1993.

Evans, Craig A. "Defeating Satan and Liberating Israel: Jesus and Daniel's Visions." *Journal for the Study of the Historical Jesus* 1 (2003): 161–170.

Evans, Craig A. "Jesus' Exorcisms and Proclamation of the Kingdom of God in the Light of the Testaments." In *The Changing Face of Judaism, Christianity, and Other Greco-Roman Religions in Antiquity,* edited by Ian H. Henderson and Gerbern S. Oegema. Studien zu den Jüdischen Schriften aus hellenistisch-römischer Zeit 2. Gütersloh, Germany: Gütersloher Verlagshaus, 2006.

Evans, Craig A. "Exorcisms and the Kingdom: Inaugurating the Kingdom of God and Defeating the Kingdom of Satan." In *Key Events in the Life of the Historical Jesus: A Collaborative Exploration of Context and Coherence,* edited by Darrell L. Bock and Robert L. Webb, pp. 151–179. Wissenschaftliche Untersuchungen zum Neuen Testament 247. Tübingen, Germany: Mohr Siebeck, 2009.

Haufe, Günter. "Reich Gottes bei Paulus und in der Jesus Tradition." *New Testament Studies* 31 (1985): 467–472.

Hengel, Martin, and Anna Maria Schwemer, eds. *Königsherrschaft Gottes und himmlischer Kult im Judentum, Urchristentum und in der hellenistischen Welt.* Wissenschaftliche Untersuchungen zum Neuen Testament 55. Tübingen, Germany: Mohr Siebeck, 1991.

Klein, Günter. "'Reich Gottes' als biblischer Zentralbegriff." *Evangelische Theologie* 30 (1970): 642–670.

Koch, Klaus. "Offenbaren wide sich das Reich Gottes." *New Testament Studies* 25 (1978): 158–165.

Ladd, George Eldon. "The Kingdom of God—Reign or Realm?" *Journal of Biblical Literature* 81 (1962): 230–238.

Ladd, George Eldon. *Jesus and the Kingdom: The Eschatology of Biblical Realism.* New York: Harper & Row, 1964.

Lattke, Michael. "On the Jewish Background of the Concept 'Kingdom of God.'" In *The Kingdom of God in the Teaching of Jesus,* edited by Bruce D. Chilton, pp. 72–91. Issues in Religion and Theology 5. London: SPCK; Philadelphia: Fortress, 1984.

Longman, Tremper, III, and Daniel G. Reid. *God Is a Warrior.* Studies in Old Testament Biblical Theology. Grand Rapids, Mich.: Zondervan, 1995.

Patrick, Dale. "The Kingdom of God in the Old Testament." In *The Kingdom of God in 20th-Century Interpretation,* edited by Wendell Willis, pp. 67–79. Peabody, Mass.: Hendrickson, 1987.

Perrin, Norman. *The Kingdom of God in the Teaching of Jesus.* New Testament Library. London: SCM, 1963.

Perrin, Norman. *Jesus and the Language of the Kingdom: Symbol and Metaphor in New Testament Interpretation.* London: SCM; Philadelphia: Fortress, 1976.

Schlosser, Jacques. *Le Règne de Dieu dans les Dits de Jésus.* 2 vols. Etudes bibliques. Paris: Gabalda, 1980.

Vanoni, Gottfried, and Bernard Heininger. *Das Reich Gottes: Perspektiven des Alten und Neuen Testaments.* Die Neue Echter Bible, Themen 4. Würzburg, Germany: Echter, 2002.

Viviano, Benedict T. "The Kingdom of God in the Qumran Literature." In *The Kingdom of God in 20th-Century Interpretation,* edited by Wendell Willis, pp. 97–107. Peabody, Mass.: Hendrickson, 1987.

Viviano, Benedict T. *The Kingdom of God in History.* Good News Studies 27. Wilmington, Del.: Glazier, 1988.

Weiss, Johannes. *Jesus' Proclamation of the Kingdom of God.* Chico, Calif.: Scholars Press, 1985. English translation of *Die Predigt Jesu vom Reiche Gottes,* first published in 1892.

C. A. Evans and J. J. Johnston

1 AND 2 KINGS

See Historical Narratives (Joshua—2 Kings).

KINGS AND KINGSHIP

Kingship in the ancient world was the social linchpin in the organization of a city state or empire. As a supreme deity ruled the heavens as king, according to the myths, so a human king ruled the earth. Kings unified societies in actual and symbolic ways. (1) They were military leaders, often leading troops in battle; and Egyptian texts portrayed the pharaoh as winning battles single-handedly. (2) They were responsible for enforcing laws, sometimes as a supreme court of appeal, and at times promulgating advisory law codes, especially in Mesopotamia (Ur-Nammu, 2000 B.C.E.; Lipit-Ishtar, 1850 B.C.E.; Hammurabi, 1750 B.C.E.; and others). (3) They often led public worship and offered sacrifice. (4) Significant trade connections were created under royal aegis, and empires, like the Akkadian Empire of Sargon in 2350 B.C.E., arose to protect trade routes. (5) Food distribution in lean years was facilitated by royal taxation of surplus crops in good years. (6) In Egypt and Mesopotamia upkeep of irrigation systems was a royal responsibility. (7) Kings undertook monumental building projects, especially temples (like Solomon's Temple), usually after military victories (unlike Solomon). (8) Kings symbolized the people, and the ruler's health supposedly assured good crops. Kings embodied the national fertility, often performing seasonal rituals. (9) Above all, kings represented the gods to the people; they were the "shepherds" of the people.

In Egypt the pharaoh was the incarnate god Horus in life and Osiris after death. In Mesopotamia a king was the "steward" of the gods, often said to be in the "image" or "likeness" of a god and therefore commissioned to "rule" (the language of Gen 1:26–27); and he was the "adopted son" of a deity. He maintained order on earth by strong rule, as the gods similarly maintained order in the cosmos. The Sumerian King List declared that kingship descended from the heavens at the beginning of time (Frankfort, 1948; Launderville, 2003).

Israelite Kingship. The biblical view of kingship (which may or may not be the view of historical Israel and Judah) shared much in common with the ancient world, although biblical authors sensed that kingship came later in their history and was not viewed in such elevated fashion. Biblical kings defeated national enemies by leading troops (Pss 2:9; 21:10–12; 45:5), and sometimes they died in battle (Ahab, 1 Kgs 22:29–38; perhaps Josiah, 2 Kgs 23:29). Credit was given to God, however, for truly winning the victories (Pss 18:48–50; 144:1, 10). Kings were portrayed as judges (David, 2 Sam 14:1–11; Solomon, 1 Kgs 3:16–28), and they pro-

claimed the Law (Jehoshaphat, 2 Chr 17:3–9; Josiah, 2 Kgs 23:2). Texts speak of how there was chaos in the land without kings (Judg 17:6; 18:1; 19:1; 21:25). Kings led worship, offered sacrifice (1 Sam 13:9–10; 2 Sam 6:13–18; 24:25; 1 Kgs 3:4, 15; 8:5, 62–64; 9:25; 12:32–33; 13:1; 2 Kgs 16:12–15), and sometimes reformed the cult (Asa, 1 Kgs 15:12–14; Hezekiah, 2 Kgs 18:4; Josiah, 2 Kgs 22:3—23:25). Although not revered as a deity (presumably), the biblical king was called the "adopted Son of God" (2 Sam 7:14; Pss 2:7; 89:26–27; Isa 9:6), in symbolic fashion. Kings assured prosperity, fertility (Ps 72:3, 6), and justice (Pss 45:4, 7; 72:1–4).

In the twentieth century several scholars suggested that kings of Jerusalem participated in a New Year's festival that entailed symbolic dying and rising god imagery in which the king reenacted the role of the deity. That theory has fallen into disrepute. But many still suggest that an annual New Year's coronation ceremony of the king or Yahweh (or both) was celebrated using royal psalms (Pss 2; 21; 72; 110; 132) and enthronement psalms (Pss 47; 93; 96–99).

Yahweh was often portrayed as the "king" of Israel or the entire world (Exod 15:18; Num 23:21; Judg 8:23; 1 Sam 8:7; 10:18–19; 12:12; Pss 47:2, 7; 95:5; 97:1; 99:1–2; 145:11–13; 146:10; Isa 6:5; 24:21–23; 33:22; 41:21; 46:4; 52:7; Jer 10:6–10; Mic 2:13; Zech 14:9, 16–17). God ruled by virtue of defeating the cosmic waters or the forces of chaos (Pss 74:12–15; 89:9–13), by defeating earthly opponents (Pss 48:4–8; 68:28–35; 96:10–13; Isa 43:15–17; Zeph 3:14–20), and by creation of the world (Ps 74:15–17).

In the Bible the Hebrew words for "king" (*melek*) and "kingship" (*mĕlukâ*) may come from an Arabic word meaning "to possess" or an Assyrian and Aramaic word meaning "to counsel" or "to advise." In Greek the words for "king" and "kingship are *basileus* and *basileia*. Since the king was "anointed" in Israel, the word *messiah* was also used.

Coronation rituals, which are difficult to reconstruct, probably were influenced by Egyptian models. Psalms 2, 21, 72, 110, and 132 may have been used in the ceremony. Symbols of royal authority may have included a scepter (Ps 45:6), an ivory throne (2 Sam 14:9; 1 Kgs 2:12, 19; 10:18–20; Ps 45:6), and a crown (2 Sam 1:10; 2 Kgs 11:12; Pss 89:39; 132:18), whose appearance is totally unknown to us. A person became king either by being the eldest son (primogeniture), by being selected by the previous king (1 Kgs 1:20), by being elected by landed gentry (2 Kgs 11:14), by being placed on the throne by a foreign conqueror (2 Kgs 24:17), or by being called by a prophet (1 Sam 9:1—10:16; 16:1–13; 1 Kgs 11:29–39; 2 Kgs 9:1–13).

With the disappearance of kings after the Babylonian Exile (586–539 B.C.E.), the Jews gradually transferred the language of kingship, especially those hopes for a future ideal king (Isa 9:6–7; 11:1–5; Jer 23:4–6; 33:14–16; Mic 5:2–4; Zech 9:9–10), into an eschatological future kingdom. The "anointed" king or Messiah was envisioned as a dramatic personage and eventually as a semidivine figure from the heavenly realm. Christians connected this image to Jesus and saw the anticipated eschatological kingdom as the Kingdom of God that Jesus proclaimed. Jesus refused the role and title of king (Mark 15:2; Matt 27:11; Luke 23:2; John 6:15), but he entered Jerusalem as a king (Matt 21:5). Later Christians spoke of Jesus as a king who established the everlasting Kingdom (Rom 14:11; 2 Pet 1:11; Rev 1:5) to be consummated someday in dramatic fashion (1 Cor 15:24–28; 1 Tim 6:15; Rev 14:14; 17:14; 19:15–16), and they described him as being born a king (Matt 2:2).

Biblical Criticism of Kings. Considering the great esteem given to kings in the ancient world, it is remarkable that biblical texts could challenge kings and kingship so often. As such, the Bible is a revolutionary intellectual document; and it has, in part, inspired the emergence of democratic thought in the modern age.

With their acerbic assault on economic injustice in Israel, the prophets often leveled judgment against their own kings, who generally were the chief culprits in the victimization of the poor (Amos 7:11; Hos 5:1–2; 7:5–7; 8:4; 10:3–4; 13:10–11; Jer 21:1—22:30; Ezek 12:10–14; 34:2–10).

The Deuteronomistic History (Joshua, Judges, Samuel, Kings; 622–560 B.C.E.) maintained that kings were in a covenant relationship with God and under the authority of the divine word as mediated through the Torah and the prophets. The historians assessed most of the kings of Israel and Judah as bad, save for Hezekiah (ca. 725–700/690 B.C.E.) and Josiah (636–609 B.C.E.). Biblical historiography contrasts with the excessive laudatory nature of ancient Near Eastern writings. For example, royal prowess in battle was praised in the ancient world, but in the Bible God won the battles, as exemplified by Joshua's defeat of Jericho (Josh 6:1–27). Most significantly, Deuteronomy 17:14–20 limited royal power by law, an action unique in the ancient world (until the English Magna Carta in 1215).

The Deuteronomistic History adduced accounts wherein prophets authorized kings to rule (Samuel and Saul, 1 Sam 9:1—10:16; Samuel and David, 1 Sam 16:1–13; Elisha and Jehu, 2 Kgs 9:1–13). Prophets condemned kings (Samuel and Saul, 1 Sam 13:7–15; 15:1–35; Nathan and David, 2 Sam 12:1–15; "man of God" and Jeroboam I, 1 Kgs 13:1–10; Ahijah of Shiloh and Jeroboam I, 1 Kgs 14:7–16; Jehu ben Hanani and Baasha, 1 Kgs 16:1–4; a nameless prophet and Ahab, 1 Kgs 20:35–43; Elijah and Ahab, 1 Kgs 21:17–29; Micaiah ben Imlah and Ahab, 1 Kgs 22:17–23).

Stories in the Deuteronomistic History ridiculed or condemned kings. Gideon (perhaps Israel's first true king, considering his son's name, Abimelech, means "my father, the king") was portrayed as foolish with the wet fleece (Judg 6:11–40) and totally dependent upon God for his victory over Midian (Judg 7:1–25). Abimelech, who tried to be king, died ignominiously (Judg 9:1–57), inspiring an antiroyal parable by Jotham (Judg 9:8–15). Samuel's sermon in 1 Samuel 8:11–18 condemned kings in general and probably foreshadowed Solomon's excesses. As 1 Samuel described the tragic decline of Saul, it provided sad commentary on kings. Lest we idealize David, we are told of his seduction of Bathsheba and murder of Uriah (2 Sam 11:1–26). Attention was paid to Absalom's revolt in 2 Samuel 15–19, a serious humiliation for David. Placing the great Davidic dynastic oracle (2 Sam 7:4–17) with these other narratives bespeaks the grace of God in contrast to the sinfulness of royalty. Unlike victorious Egyptian and Mesopotamian rulers who built temples after their triumphs, David was not permitted to do so (2 Sam 7:1–7). David's census of Israel, probably for military conscription, brought plague upon Israel (2 Sam 24:1–25). The humiliating portrayal of David as old and impotent (1 Kgs 1:1–4) implied potential crop failure for the nation by ancient understandings. In

1 Kings 1–11 one sees hints of Solomonic oppression: his reign began with a bloodbath (1 Kgs 2:13–46), tribal structures were replaced by administrative districts (1 Kgs 4:7–19), accumulated horses and chariots betokened military excess (1 Kgs 4:26; 10:26–29), people were forced to work on building projects (1 Kgs 5:13–18; 9:15; 12:4), Israelite land was sold to Tyre (1 Kgs 9:10–14), and foreign gods were introduced into Israel (1 Kgs 11:1–13). Rehoboam was portrayed as foolish in losing the northern kingdom (1 Kgs 12:1–20). Ahab was portrayed as tyrannical in seizing Naboth's vineyard (1 Kgs 21:1–16). Elijah and Elisha brought food, rain, and life (by resurrecting people) to the common folk, when this was the responsibility of kings (1 Kgs 17:1—2 Kgs 13:21). The sheer number of these narratives reflects a significant critique of kingship by the biblical text.

In the Pentateuch (550–400 B.C.E.) one likewise discovers a subtle and symbolic critique of kings. The man and the woman in Genesis 1–2 were characterized with royal images ("image," "likeness," and "have dominion"; Gen 1:26–27), but they were the simple ancestors of all humanity. Antediluvian ancestors in Genesis 4–5 were simple folk, not semidivine kings who lived thousands of years, as in the Sumerian King List. None of them even lived for one thousand years. The Tower of Babel account (Genesis 11) ridiculed the efforts of Assyrian and Babylonian kings in building ziggurats, often with prisoners of war, like the Jews. The lowly midwives defied mighty pharaoh (called "king of Egypt" in this text, Exod 1:15–21). Moses was an antiking. Although saved in a basket in the river, like Sargon of Akkad (2350 B.C.E.), he lived with the poor, confronted pharaoh, and defeated him and his gods with plagues until the divine pharaoh died in the sea; and he led slaves to freedom.

In the later novellas the royal critique is more explicit. Joseph and Daniel interpreted dreams (Gen 41:1–36; Dan 2:1–45; 4:4–27) when the king's men failed. The three friends and Daniel refused to recognize royal divinity and survived despite the royal attempt to kill them (Dan 3:1–30; 6:1–28). Vashti's refusal to show herself defied the Persian king and humorously threw the empire into confusion (Esth 1:10–22).

The New Testament also recounts criticism of royal power. John the Baptist challenged Herod Antipas for his marriage (Mark 6:14–29; Matt 14:1–12; Luke 3:19–20; 9:7–9). Wise men duped Herod and helped save Jesus (Matt 2:12). Jesus's saying "render unto Caesar" what is due to him (Mark 12:17; Matt 22:21; Luke 20:25) probably meant "render" him "nothing." Christians defiantly stole Caesar's royal titles ("Lord," "Savior," and "Benefactor"), as well as other idioms, and attributed them to Jesus and his kingdom (Gnuse, 2011, pp. 129–140).

Later Use of Royal Imagery. The Christian tradition has used royal imagery in its theology to speak of Jesus as king over all creation. Throughout Western history, European kings have appealed to biblical texts and the accounts of kings unfortunately to defend their absolute authority. More meaningful is the use of the biblical passages by thinkers who helped to develop and inspire democratic beliefs (Gnuse, 2011, pp. 1–13). For example, Deuteronomy 17:14–20 was read aloud as a challenge to the authority of kings when the English executed Charles I in 1649. During the American Revolution Thomas Paine quoted 1 Samuel 8:11–18 extensively in his pamphlet *Common Sense*.

[*See also* Justice, Justification, and Righteousness; Kingdom of God (Heaven); Politics and Systems of Governance; Prophets and Prophecy; *and* War (Holy War).]

BIBLIOGRAPHY

Ahlström, Gösta. *Royal Administration and National Religion in Ancient Palestine.* Studies in the History and Culture of the Ancient Near East 1. Leiden, The Netherlands: Brill, 1982.

Brettler, Marc Zvi. "King, Kingship." In *The New Interpreter's Dictionary of the Bible*, edited by Katherine Doob Sakenfeld, Vol. 3, pp. 505–512. Nashville, Tenn.: Abingdon, 2008.

Eaton, John. *Kingship and the Psalms.* 2d ed. Biblical Seminar 3. Sheffield, U.K.: Sheffield Academic Press, 1986.

Frankfort, Henri. *Kingship and the Gods.* Oriental Institute Publications. Chicago: University of Chicago Press, 1948.

Gnuse, Robert. *No Tolerance for Tyrants: The Biblical Assault on Kings and Kingship.* Collegeville, Minn.: Liturgical Press, 2011.

Lasine, Stuart. *Knowing Kings: Knowledge, Power, and Narcissism in the Hebrew Bible.* Atlanta: Society of Biblical Literature, 2001.

Launderville, Dale. *Piety and Politics: The Dynamics of Royal Authority in Homeric Greece, Biblical Israel, and Old Babylonian Mesopotamia.* Grand Rapids, Mich.: Eerdmans, 2003.

Whitelam, Keith. "King and Kingship." In *The Anchor Bible Dictionary,* edited by David Noel Freedman, Vol. 4, pp. 40–48. New York: Doubleday, 1992.

Robert Karl Gnuse

KNOWLEDGE

Knowledge (*daʿat*), very much like its associative term "wisdom," can be examined in two ways: as a concept broadly defined and as a social marker. This dual approach is buttressed by scholarship on the social history of ancient wisdom literature (Perdue, 2008). To know, to have knowledge, to be known, to lack knowledge are not just abstract terms about cognitive abilities or data collection and analyses but also markers of social stature and space, as well as methods of being in the world.

The reader of the Hebrew Bible first encounters knowledge in the creation narrative in Genesis. Represented by a tree, knowledge is at once part of the material world, accessible to humans, but also a prerogative of the divine. Materially, the tree functions as the subject–object of speech and touch and sight and desire and (forbidden) food (3:5–6). Socially, the tree symbolizes boundary making/crossing, with potential deadly effects (Gen 2:16–17; 3:3). Cumulatively, engagement with the tree of knowledge affects the body and the mind and impacts constructions of physical space; it produces a sense of material and spatial self-awareness and belonging. An "otherness" of knowledge, perceived as a divine prerogative, is felt: cognitively as fear (Gen 3:10) and materially as life lived in unfamiliar, extraterritorial landscapes (Gen 3:22–24; cf. Jos. 2:9). As a prerogative of the divine, the tree represents the prophetic concept of "knowledge of God" (Hos 4:1; 6:6), synonymous with "knowledge of God's to know my ways" (Isa 58:2), a

broad concept for divine actions and their impact on human identity. Knowledge, then, is "the reflective assessment of information acquired either through sensory perception or by revelation" (Crenshaw, 2008, p. 539) or "*any* cognition, from minimal awareness to elevated sagacity" (Fox, 2000, p. 31, italics original). But knowledge is also the navigation of one's cognitive, material, and social world.

To know is to know how. Verbal forms of *daʿat* may describe procuring tactical military information by inference (1 Sam 14:12) or the application of previous experiences of divine power and identity to new circumstances (Jer 16:21). Nominal forms refer to "opinion" (Job 32:6; 36:3, 10, 17), to exceptional talent or familiarity with something ("knower of knowledge," Dan 1:4; "knower of the sea," 1 Kgs 9:27; 2 Chr 8:18; "knower of mourning," Amos 5:16; "knower of sickness," Isa 53:3), and to skills in craft (Exod 31:3; 35:31; Isa 44:19; Jer 10:14).

Conversely, to act without knowledge is to act without premeditation, socially interpreted as unintentional, random action outside the framework of communal history and religion (Deut 4:42; 19:4; Lev 5:17–18). Here, the opposite of knowledge is forgetfulness or abandonment of previous traditions (Hos 2:8 [MT 2:10]; 4:6; 8:14; 13:4–6). This lack of knowledge manifests itself, if Sigmund Freud's psychohistorical theory was correct, as cognitive repression and latency rather than erasure. Once generated, knowledge cannot be destroyed, not even that which is forbidden (Gen 3:22) or hidden away in the hearts of fools (Ps 14:1, 4). However, lack of knowledge is not simply intellectual agnosticism (Job 34:35; 35:16; 38:2; 42:3) but social vulnerability: persons "without knowledge" are subjected to artistic ridicule (Isa 44:19; Jer 10:14); destruction and loss of life (Hos 4:6; Job 18:21; 36:12); danger from the mythical forces of death, Sheol (Isa 5:13-14); and, in the sexualized context of warfare, being violated (Num 31:18).

Framing Knowledge. According to Sirach 3:25, knowledge is a precondition for wisdom, just as eyes are a precondition for sight. Studies in cognitive linguistics lend themselves to the study of knowledge as a function of language but also of worldview. Metaphor and analogy are methodologically critical because they constitute a "cognitive paradigm in light of which the language user organizes his or her complex knowledge of what is described metaphorically" (Jinto, 2009, p. 226).

Gerhard von Rad examined the phenomenology of knowledge—theological and secular—as a product of spiritual and historical transitions; there was no sense of "absolute knowledge" devoid of secular and faith traditions and experiences immersed in the complexities of history and the possibilities of the unknown, which compelled Israel to perceive knowledge as a function of the human intellect and as a divine gift. Such complexity around the sociology of knowledge is evident in the literary forms that ancient sages used to describe the construction and transmission of knowledge, including proverbs, numerical sayings, didactic poems, autobiographical stylizations, parallelisms, and dialogues (von Rad, 1972, pp. 24–73).

The book of Proverbs combines individual experience and worldview. To engage the exploration and pursuit of knowledge (1:1–7), the sage presents a hypothetical scenario, a worldview populated by powerful characters, for Proverbs 1–9. Spatially, an outer layer has impersonators of Sheol (1:10–19) and personified Folly (9:13–18); an inner layer has personified Wisdom (1:20–33; 9:1–6). Knowledge is constructed, transmitted, and evaluated in relation to these powerful characters, whose social embodiments may reflect the economic and gendered politics of the Yehud community (Yoder, 2001, p. 101; Washington, 1994, pp. 217–242). To know is to construct specific forms of social identity.

Similarly, the poem in Job 28 combines wisdom/knowledge-related terminology, worldview, and social function: there are human and divine searches (28:3, 27); the human search is incomprehensive because of limited worldview (inability to "see," 28:7, 21), in contrast to the deity who sees everything (28:24, 27); and the testimony from a personified underworld, Deep, Sea, Abaddon, and Death (28:14, 22), is partial at best. Nevertheless, the cumulative effect of the quest for wisdom, summarized in 28:27 as "seeing, discussing, establishing, and exploring" comprises a sociology of knowledge that partly reflects two royal

forms of wisdom acquisition—"wisdom by exploration and wisdom by revelation" (Crenshaw, 2008, p. 539). When human, divine, and netherworld experiences and worldviews intersect, divine ordering—based on the deity's comprehensive worldview—produces knowledge that is connected to creation's revelatory and structuring power (Jones, 2013, pp. 488, 493–496). Qoheleth, too, explores knowledge, wisdom, and folly in the context of the significant sociopolitical and economic changes of the Persian period, changes that obliged Qoheleth to combine knowledge gained from individual "observations" with reflections on the macrostructure: "a new world of rapid political, social, and economic innovations, many of which were initiated and determined in seats of power that the ordinary citizens of the vast empire could hardly comprehend" (Seow, 2008, pp. 189–217; Fox, 1987, pp. 150–154).

On the one hand, then, knowledge is a social phenomenon, rooted in experience and social consciousness (Job 9:28; 10:2, 7). On the other, knowledge is rooted in the multifaceted nature of wisdom (Job 11:6), the ultimate basis of God's discriminating judgments (Job 11:11). Misalignment between individual experiences, cultural worldviews, and social histories is viewed as evidence of a lack of knowledge, a claim explained as a function of the ephemeral nature of individual/generational life (so Bildad in Job 8:9) or, fueled by his quest for justice, as a function of what Job sees as social (Job 7:10) cosmic (9:2, 5), personal (9:21), and generational (14:21) repression. Although the knowledge-ability of Job's experience is self-evident to human consciousness and creation (12:3, 9; 13:2) and even comprehensible to Job and his immediate interlocutors (15:9), still knowledge is more than consciousness and more than rational analyses of empirical facts. Rather, *knowledge is also effect*—for Job, effect of painful inadequacy in the presence of divine knowledge (14:5–6; cf. 15:2).

Technologies of Knowledge. The production, transmission, and experience of knowledge occur through various cognitive and material technologies. These can be grouped as (1) personification and textualization and (2) food and sexuality.

Personification and textualization. The personification of qualities, attributes, and objects constituted part of the intellectual heritage of the ancient Orient, from as early as the third and second millennia B.C.E. Personified concepts included "Authoritative Utterance," "Understanding," "Sight," "Hearing," "Intelligence," "Destiny," "Justice," and "Law/Right" (Kitchen, 1960, p. 4). In biblical wisdom literature, personification includes Sheol, Abaddon, the Satan, Folly, and Wisdom. In biblical mythology (Ezek 28:1–19; Ps 82:6–7), the garden of Eden is a place of wisdom, knowledge, and destruction, with cherubs (Ezek 28:11; Gen 3:24) and trees and serpents. Embodied but also transcending local cartography, knowledge is familiar and unfamiliar, local and extraterritorial, revealed and secretive. It is perhaps this worldview that underlies Paul's description of secret and revealed wisdom/knowledge brought together in the conflation of the person of Jesus Christ and the crucifixion tree (1 Cor 2:6–16).

Secret knowledge in ancient Mesopotamian and biblical literature constitutes the basis for the analogy between divine councils and royal councils and governance (see Prov 25:2). Because knowledge of and from the divine was generally deemed secret, divination/revelation became the point of contact between the human and the divine realms. Through textualization, the ad hoc process of divination "became the model for a scholarly mythmaking strategy to extend divine knowledge permanently into human history as written texts." Because the ancient Mesopotamian "scholars" (*ummânū*) "constructed a scribal myth of succession" that reached back to the antediluvian sages, these scholars could claim that their texts originated from the divine realm but were received "in history" through a scribal process, which in turn made these scholars "exclusive bearers of the textualized secret of the gods" (Lenzi, 2008, pp. 27, 36–37, 67, italics original). The tradition continues with the identification of Wisdom with the Torah in Sirach (24:23). Personification and textualization thus create a symbiotic relation: cosmologically, between divinity and humankind; politically, between the governor and the governed; and pedagogically, between the instructor and the instructed.

A key inflection point in the cosmology, the politics, and the pedagogy of knowledge is the trope of the "child" in biblical wisdom literature. In Job, children at once are beneficiaries of Job's knowledge and wealth but also represent the domain of knowledge beyond Job's grasp or control, the domain of secret knowledge and its ethical demands on Job (Job 1:4–5; 42:10–17). In Proverbs, children are often the addressees and the subject of multiple reflections. Yet, the book is rhetorically introduced as the Proverbs of a son (1:1; cf. Eccl 1:1). The trope of the child as learner-teacher is pedagogically useful, as evident when an instructor-parent speaks to his son in the third person, "When I was a son with my father, tender, and my mother's favorite, he taught me and said …" (Prov 4:3–4). This double self-styling of son as learner and teacher creates the rhetorical and social space where the transformation of the child-apprentice into an expert is critical to the articulation and the embodiment of knowledge (Prov 1:2, 4, 7). Similarly, the ancient Egyptian treatise on knowledge, the *Book of Thot*, construes the successful student as one who acquires knowledge of the sacred geography of Egypt and becomes an active participant in the functioning of the universe (Schneider, 2008, p. 41).

The learner's response to instruction (spoken/written) and Wisdom (embodied) is critical to the very construction of knowledge itself. Personified Wisdom is an itinerant character looking to infuse her audience with her teachings or her breath (Prov 1:23; cf. Wisdom as the breath of God's power in Wis 7:24–25). Similarly, the authors of Sirach (24:1–22) and Enoch (*1 En.* 42:2) portray Wisdom as an itinerant character searching the cosmos for a dwelling place among humans (cf. Prov 1:24, 28–29).

This reciprocal, relational character of textual and embodied knowledge is implied in the divine–human relationship around the tree of knowledge. Michael Rosenak proposes that "perhaps the knowledge in question is about human obedience to God, so that it was not they, but He, who was for a time 'ignorant.' God did not yet know, as it were, whether humans would choose good or evil" (Rosenak, 2001, p. 14). In this sense, it is the liminality and unpredictability, rather than the incomprehensibility of human activity, that define knowledge or the lack thereof as a relational concept. It is this liminality and unpredictability that generate "new" knowledge, both for humans with respect to the divine ("surely Yahweh is in this place and I did not know," Gen 28:16) and for the divine with respect to humans ("now I know that you fear God," Gen 22:12). This unpredictability of knowledge informs Qoheleth's search for meaning (Eccl 10:14–15; 11:2, 6).

Knowledge, food, and sexuality. Cultural studies emphasize the relationship between food and speech, food and sexuality, and food and memory (Feeley-Harnik, 1995, pp. 565–567). Indeed, as Mary Douglas argued, "those we know at meals we also know at drinks. The meal expresses close friendship" (1972, p. 66). Similarly, for Chinua Achebe, eating and the verbal art of proverbial speech are closely linked: proverbs are "the palm oil with which words are eaten" (1994, p. 7).

From the very opening chapters of the Hebrew Bible, food, sexuality, and knowledge are connected. We are introduced to a world of food and food production—plants, fruits, trees, the ground, etc.—but also a world of human sexuality and communication. God's words and actions—prohibiting eating from the tree of knowledge and preventing a predictable, knowledge- based human attempt to access the tree of life—are premised on a basic relation between food, speech, sexuality, and knowledge (Gen 3:5–6). Knowledge is a form of nourishment, soul food (Prov 24:13–14); and a lack of knowledge can indicate a breakdown in the sociomythology of food production, consumption, and life (Gen 4:9; Prov 24:12). The phrase "knowledge of good and evil" is often associated with food and the enhancing or diminishing of life span (Gen 2:17; 3:5, 22; Isa 7:14 [7:15, MT]; 2 Sam 19:35 [19:36, MT]). An itinerant group reconstituting its genealogical and political identity in the wilderness gathers around food and drink and laughter, while making claims about knowledge (Exod 18:11–12, 16, 20) or the lack thereof (Exod 16:12, 15; 32:1–6).

The metaphorical association of food with knowledge infuses teachings about knowledge (Prov 1:4, 7), introduced by a hypothetical simile of sinners impersonating Sheol (a place devoid of knowledge, Eccl 9:10), the insatiable monster of Canaanite mythology that threatens to swallow up everything (Prov 1:12–13; cf. Job 2:3). Personified Wisdom and Folly have "houses" to which they invite guests (9:1, 14) and passersby to feasting (9:2, 5, 17). Qoheleth's search for wisdom and knowledge takes place in gardens of feasts (Eccl 1:16—2:6). And the narrative plot of Job's story is framed around his children eating (ʾkl) and drinking (Job 1:5, 13), divine fire consuming (ʾkl) Job's property (1:16), and the gathering of Job's former acquaintances ("those who knew him") to eat and drink (42:11).

Concurrently, personified Wisdom states that she is the tree of life (Prov 3:18), a claim that alludes to the barred tree of life in Genesis. What is barred from humans in the Genesis text as a result of human acquisition of knowledge becomes available—in the person of Woman Wisdom, through knowledge. Access to wisdom is described in emotional, erotic language: as if seeking a bride, the young man undergoing instruction is urged to find wisdom (Prov 3:13) and hold fast to her (3:18); Wisdom, described as a "sister"—a term that conveys romantic endearment (Song 4:9, 10)—promises to reciprocate love (8:17). Holding knowledge in one's lips is synonymous with the infatuation of romantic and erotic embrace, reserved for one's lover (Prov 5). Wisdom and knowledge are the objects of human affections, not unlike lovers (Yoder, 2005, pp. 73–88). In the garden of Eden story, sexuality is linked with the acquisition of knowledge not just in the procreation story (Gen 4:1) but also in the morphology of "cunning" and "nakedness" (ʿrm) that frames human acquisition of knowledge (Gen 3:1–11). Thus, although the divine–human interaction around the tree of knowledge may refer to the pursuit of "the widest possible knowledge," the role of sexuality is undeniable (Bailey, 1970, pp. 147–150).

Elsewhere, the Egyptian *Book of Thot* personifies knowledge as a nurse from whose breast the disciple drinks milk. The acquisition of knowledge itself is expressed in highly sexual language: "the vulva is impatient for the teaching, may I enter its threshold" (cited in Schneider, 2008, p. 42). Additionally, Qumran texts (1QSa) and gnostic writings develop the relation between knowledge and sexuality. The gnostic book of Baruch, for example, contains three principles, two male ("Good" and "Elohim") and one female ("Edem"). The tale is one of lovers, the heavenly "elohim" and the earthly "edem," both characters drawn from the biblical creation story and depicting the emergence of (secret) knowledge and wisdom in sexualized terms (Barnstone and Meyer, 2006, pp. 119–134). Similarly 1 Corinthians 2:6–16 may not only have gnostic resonances and polemical undertones but also suggest that knowledge is a function of divine self-disclosure that fits into a larger divine plan of governance (Healy, 2007, pp. 138–156).

The Politics of Knowledge. The books of Proverbs (10:1; 25:1; cf. 31:1) and Ecclesiastes (1:1; 4:13–15; 8:1–5) discuss the production and use of wisdom and knowledge in relation to royal institutions and functions of kings. Although the book of Job does not ascribe royalty to him or his friends, the *Testament of Job* lends them that title (*T. Job* 7:1–8). The association of knowledge and wisdom with royalty and royal figures plays into two tropes: (1) the secrecy and mystique that surrounds royal figures, royal councils, and governance. It is this trope that nourishes the legend of Solomon's (re)quest for wisdom and knowledge (1 Kgs 3:4–28; 4:29–34; 10:1–13). Elsewhere, the Ziusudra traditions of ancient Sumeria emphasize the link between wisdom, kingship, and antediluvian knowledge so that "wisdom was very much linked from earliest times to the mystique of the monarchy, an institution that came down from heaven twice according to the Sumerian King List" (Beaulieu, 2007, p. 6). (2) The genealogical note identifying the author as "son of David" (Prov 1:1; Eccl 1:1; cf. Prov 30:1) symbolically depicts the transmission of knowledge in the face of political transition to be as powerful as biological, primordial identity formation.

To be politically unaware is dangerous; it depicts an inability to manage space, even the most intimate spaces of one's bedchamber (2 Sam 4:7, 11; 2 Kgs 6:12; Eccl 10:20). There is a direct relation between the monarch's ability to know and the maintenance of power structure (Lasine, 2001, pp. 77–78). Lack of knowledge creates a crisis of identity and affinity and obfuscates the power dynamics that

govern the divine–human cosmos (Job 38:2; 42:3; cf. Job 28:13, 23). Cultural amnesia (Exod 1:8) and the lack of religious awareness (Exod 5:2) are politically unforgiving and must be rectified through knowledge, even if violently transmitted (Exod 14:4, 18). As the primary narrative custodian of itinerant knowledge and its competing political claims, Rahab's statements about her lack of knowledge ("I do not know," Josh 2:5) and her knowledge ("I know that the LORD has given you," Josh 2:9) move the concept of knowledge beyond objective, apolitical "facts" or "memory" to knowledge as strategy of survival. In the political cosmos, analogous to the divine cosmos, "the tree of knowledge" functions to arrange "avenues of encounter between people and God, between the man and the woman, and between people and their natural environment" (Rosenak, 2001, p. 15). As a tool and function of governance and survival, knowledge construction and dissemination is part of the mechanism by which humankind and divinity attempt to hold together and navigate an immensely diverse cosmos, in the process shrinking time and space through travel and memory, reinterpreting the past, forging new experiences and alliances, and producing new consciousnesses and structures.

Knowledge, Epistemology, and Pedagogy. Biblical wisdom literature has pedagogical scenarios where knowledge is not only theorized but also socially performed. On the one hand, knowledge is the product and function of human endeavor: it can be acquired through empirical search (Eccl 1:16, 18; 7:25) or broadly reflected on (Eccl 7:12); knowledge can be taught (Prov 1:4, 23) but can also be resisted, a function of what personified Wisdom calls "hatred of knowledge" (1:22, 29). On the other hand, knowledge is a (divine) gift (Prov 2:6, 10), not because knowledge is alien to the world but because as a gift, knowledge/wisdom becomes a metaphor for establishing social structure, analogous to the way royal grants established the social stature of the recipients as well as enhanced their economic fortunes (Seow, 2008, pp. 199–202).

The epistemological architecture from which knowledge emerges is complex. Biblical wisdom presents a "sophisticated picture" of how people can be drawn into a community of "meaning and memory" (Alexander, 1999, p. 155). The acquisition and enjoyment of knowledge are a function of human endeavor and of "arbitrariness." God may give wealth to a man but then authorize a stranger (*nokrî*) to enjoy (consume, *ʾkl*) it (Eccl 6:2). In Proverbs, Folly (sometimes referred to as a strange woman, *nokriyyāh*//*ʾiššāh zārāh*, Prov 2:16) and the impersonators of Sheol populate the world of knowledge, alongside Wisdom; in Job, the Satan and Yahweh function as mirror opposites. This worldview is itself based on a prior epistemological view that Michael Fox calls the "coherence theory of truth" (Fox, 2007, p. 675), according to which the world functions in patterns of norms and anomalies. In order to nourish this epistemological and cognitive scale of reference, credible instructors are pedagogically able to see (and therefore know) and link the "end" to the "beginning" (Prov 1:15–19; Eccl 7:8; Job 8:7; 42:10; Isa 42; Rev 1). This strategy of hindsight–foresight attempts to abbreviate and structure the production and transmission of knowledge.

Pedagogically, the portrayal of knowledge as a fruit of human endeavor and as a gift accomplishes two things. First, it creates a cognitive, emotive, and evaluative analogy between experiential knowledge and hypothetical or imaginative knowledge. Many sayings in Proverbs 10–29 imply verifiability through experience, which gives sanction to the teachings (Brueggemann, 1972, p. 18). Similarly, for Qoheleth, knowledge is acquired through a process of discovery, rational inquiry, and argumentation (2:14; 9:11), a process of "introspective reporting" that construes knowledge not just as a product of prior experience but also as something new: "knowledge is subsequent to and dependent on observation" (Fox, 1987, p. 148). Second, it gives knowledge its complex human and social character, played out in "public" spaces. "To publicly articulate knowledge," writes Achille Mbembe, consists, to a large extent, "in making everything speak—that is, in constantly transforming reality into a *sign*, and, on the other hand, filling with reality things empty and hollow in appearance." Within this world of contrasted and contrasting signs and meanings, "the great epistemological—and therefore social—break" is "not between what is seen and what is read, but between what is seen (*the visible*) and what is not seen

(*the occult*), between what is heard, spoken and memorized and what is concealed (*the secret*)" (Mbembe, 2001, p. 144, italics original). The pedagogy is public, not just in the sense that knowledge is theoretically available and accessible to anyone and everyone but in the sense that accessibility is played out in public. The depictions of Folly are not just that she is a shadowy character in the streets (Prov 7:9–12) but also that, devoid of knowledge, she ultimately makes self-incriminating statements in the public about stolen water and bread eaten in secret (Prov 9:13–17).

Conclusion. Knowledge is the cognitive and emotive ability and process by which humankind, divinity, and creation forge a cosmology and a methodology of coexistence. Knowledge is forged and nursed in an epistemological ecosystem that draws on metaphors from food and sexuality, rationality, and cosmology. The intimacy involved in the search, the acquisition, and even the lack of knowledge plays itself out in the mapping and definition of human, social, and political bodies and spaces. Human senses and desires are summoned, their passions and seductions examined, liminal spaces navigated, empirical and hypothetical scenarios invoked, debates and memories forged and repressed, and identities constructed to grapple with a complex world where the voices that speak range from those of the parent/instructor to alluring, charismatic and itinerant figures, to the rumors of the netherworld. Knowledge is, in this sense, bold, dogmatic, and engaging, often demanding unequivocal responses from her audience but at the same time acting more like a catalyst that spurs the apprentice into (sometimes) different, unpredictable actions than like anesthesia that numbs the audience into a single position or mindset (cf. Prov 26:4). To know is to know how; it is to form character and identity.

[*See also* Education; Family; Genesis; Hospitality; Wisdom; *and* Wisdom Literature.]

BIBLIOGRAPHY

Achebe, Chinua. *Things Fall Apart.* New York: Anchor, 1994.

Alexander, Hanan. "A Jewish View of Human Learning." *International Journal of Children's Spirituality* 4, no. 2 (1999): 155–164.

Bailey, John A. "Initiation and the Primal Woman in Gilgamesh and Genesis 2–3." *Journal of Biblical Literature* 89, no. 2 (1970): 137–150.

Barnstone, Willis, and Marvin Meyer, eds. *The Gnostic Bible*. Boston and London: New Seeds, 2006.

Beaulieu, Paul-Alain. "The Social and Intellectual Setting on Babylonian Wisdom Literature." In *Wisdom Literature in Mesopotamia and Israel*, edited by Richard J. Clifford, pp. 3–19. Boston: Brill, 2007.

Brueggemann, Walter. *In Man We Trust: The Neglected Side of Biblical Faith*. Richmond, Va.: John Knox, 1972.

Crenshaw, James L. "Knowledge." In *The New Interpreter's Dictionary of the Bible*, edited by Katharine Doob Sakenfeld, Vol. 3, pp. 539–546. Nashville, Tenn.: Abingdon, 2008.

Douglas, Mary. "Deciphering a Meal." *Daedalus* 101, no. 1 (1972): 61–81.

Feeley-Harnik, Gillian. "Religion and Food: An Anthropological Perspective." *Journal of the American Academy of Religion* 63, no. 3 (1995): 565–582.

Fox, Michael V. "Qohelet's Epistemology." *Hebrew Union College Annual* 58 (1987): 137–155.

Fox, Michael V. *Proverbs 1–9: A New Translation with Introduction and Commentary*. Anchor Bible 18A. New York: Doubleday, 2000.

Fox, Michael V. "The Epistemology of the Book of Proverbs." *Journal of Biblical Literature* 126, no. 4 (2007): 669–684.

Healy, Mary. "Knowledge of the Mystery: A Study of Pauline Epistemology." In *The Bible and Epistemology: Biblical Soundings on the Knowledge of God*, edited by Mary Healy and Robin Parry, pp. 134–158. Colorado Springs, Colo.: Paternoster, 2007.

Jinto, Job Y. "Toward a Poetics of the Biblical Mind: Language, Culture, and Cognition." *Vetus Testamentum* 59 (2009): 222–243.

Jones, Scott C. "Job 28 and Modern Theories of Knowledge." *Theology Today* 69, no. 4 (2013): 486–496.

Kitchen, Kenneth A. "Some Egyptian Background to the Old Testament." *Tyndale House Bulletin* 5–6 (1960): 4–18.

Lasine, Stuart. *Knowing Kings: Knowledge, Power, and Narcissism in the Hebrew Bible*. Atlanta: Society of Biblical Literature, 2001.

Lenzi, Alan. *Secrecy and the Gods: Secret Knowledge in Ancient Mesopotamia and Biblical Israel*. State Archives of Assyria Studies 19. Helsinki: Neo-Assyrian Text Corpus Project, 2008.

Mbembe, Achille. *On the Postcolony*. Berkeley: University of California Press, 2001.

Perdue, Leo G., ed. *Scribes, Sages, and Seers: The Sage in the Eastern Mediterranean World*. Göttingen, Germany: Vandenhoeck & Ruprecht, 2008.

Rad, Gerhard von. *Wisdom in Israel*. Translated by James D. Martin. London: SCM, 1972.

Rosenak, Michael. *Tree of Life, Tree of Knowledge: Conversations with the Torah*. Boulder, Colo.: Westview, 2001.

Schneider, Thomas. "Knowledge and Knowledgeable Men in Ancient Egypt: Queries and Arguments about an Unsettled Issue." In *Scribes, Sages, and Seers: The Sage in the Eastern Mediterranean World*, edited by Leo G. Perdue, pp. 35–46. Göttingen, Germany: Vandenhoeck & Ruprecht, 2008.

Seow, Choon-Leong. "The Social World of Ecclesiastes." In *Scribes, Sages, and Seers: The Sage in the Eastern Mediterranean World*, edited by Leo G. Perdue, pp. 189–217. Göttingen, Germany: Vandenhoeck & Ruprecht, 2008.

Washington, Harold C. "The Strange Woman of Proverbs 1–9 and Post-exilic Judean Society." In *Second Temple Studies 2: Temple Community in the Persian Period*, edited by Tamara C. Eskenazi and Kent H. Richards, pp. 217–242. Sheffield, U.K.: JSOT Press, 1994.

Yoder, Christine Roy. *Wisdom as a Woman of Substance: A Socio-economic Reading of Proverbs 1–9 and 31:10–31*. Berlin and New York: De Gruyter, 2001.

Yoder, Christine Roy. "The Objects of Our Affections: Emotions and the Moral Life in Proverbs 1–9." In *Shaking Heaven and Earth: Essays in Honor of Walter Brueggemann and Charles B. Cousar*, edited by Christine Roy Yoder, Kathleen M. O'Connor, E. Elizabeth Johnson, et al., pp. 73–88. Louisville, Ky.: Westminster John Knox, 2005.

Kenneth Ngwa

L

LABOR

The Bible offers no theological treatment of labor. It is simply recognized as the normal human condition. The works of God receive the most attention in the sacred texts (e.g., Acts 2:11). Similarly, the problem of leisure is unknown in the Bible. Humans work from dawn to dusk (Ps 104:22–23). However, the command to rest on the sabbath (Exod 20:8–11) reveals that labor is not the main purpose of human life (Qoh 2:23). Humans are to continue the creative work of God and then enter into God's own rest. The true purpose of labor is the glory and service of God (Isa 58:13–14). The Pauline school was the first to provide a Christian interpretation of labor, repeating the notion of the Hebrew Bible that it should be service primarily. In the fourth century, monasticism turned labor into a problem to which the Middle Ages gave a negative evaluation. After the Reformation, however, labor lost its negative value and took on a liturgical dimension. The Industrial Revolution effected a sea change in the understanding of human labor, and the consequences of rapid technological developments in the contemporary world challenge theologians to shed light on emerging problems hitherto unknown.

Labor in the Bible. The historical time frame recorded in the Bible (beginning with Abraham in 2000 B.C.E. and extending to 2 Pet about 150 C.E.) lies within the archaeological Bronze (3200–1200 B.C.E.) and Iron (1200–600 B.C.E.) Ages and extends into the Hellenistic era (300 B.C.E.–300 C.E.). Despite significant human evolutionary progress in this period, geographically the terrain remained challenging to till. Water supply was unpredictable. Conquest and foreign occupation co-opted labor for the benefit of the conquerors, leaving precious little for the workers. It is thus understandable that the challenge of human subsistence in these periods allowed little time for reflection on the deeper meaning of human labor. The biblical witness demonstrates that the later writings of the New Testament first sketched elements of a theological reflection upon human labor. According to the biblical tradition, labor was not a curse but rather a divine commission (Gen 1:28; 2:15; Exod 20:9; Deut 5:13). Created in the image of God (Gen 2:26), humanity was made in the image of its Creator. God's chief works celebrated in the Bible are creation (giving life) and redemption (restoring meaning to life), also known as salvation (rescue from hopeless situations). In John's Gospel, Jesus promised that "the one who believes in me will also do the *works* [*erga*] that I do, in fact, will do greater *works* than these…" (John 14:12). The models are presented in Jesus's *erga* and *semeia* (signs), which echo God's *erga*: giving life (John 4:46–54; 6:1–14; 11:1–44) and restoring meaning to life (John 2:1–11; 5:1–9; 6:16–21; 9). The Pauline school noted that labor or work is service rendered not so much to human beings as to God (Col 3:22–41; Eph 5:4–9). The letter of James presented a positive view of labor when it noted that faith entails practical activity, work (Jas 2:18–26), and serves to guard against materialistic greed (Jas 4:13—5:6).

Postbiblical Period. Believers were expected to labor diligently and avoid idleness (2 Thess 3:6–12). The community intervened on behalf of unemployed fellow believers. They supported learning a new craft, provided capital to a worker starting a trade, or supplemented insufficient income. This welfare system was the special duty of ministers (deacons), who were supervised by the overseers (bishops).

In the fourth century, the monastic system raised a special problem. Some literally interpreted Jesus's instructions (Matt 6:22–34) not to be anxious, not to toil, and devoted themselves solely to prayer, leaving everything else to God. Others lived by Paul's warning: "Anyone unwilling to work should not eat" (2 Thess 3:10). In his treatise *On the Work of Monks* (*De Opere Monachorum*), Augustine denied that these verses contradicted each other. He urged monks to fulfill their physical labors but also to save time for prayer. Caesar of Arles (fifth century C.E.) cautioned priests not to spend more than three hours a day cultivating their gardens lest they neglect the souls committed to their care. The fifth-century document "Sayings of the Desert Fathers (and Mothers)" (*Apophthegmata Patrum*) echoes these sentiments, which were ultimately given clear expression by St. Benedict in his *Rule*: *ora et labora* (pray and labor). This pair of words does not describe two spheres of life but rather one unified activity: to pray while laboring. Thus, in the medieval monastic period, labor took on a theological meaning: the labor of a sinful person was a work of penance, and the monk was a penitent par excellence.

Slowly, however, contemplation began to separate itself from work, and the active (working) life, labor, was given a negative interpretation. Thomas Aquinas said that action is less perfect than contemplation (*Summa Theologica* 2–2ae, qq. 179–182). In the Middle Ages, labor was viewed as a necessary tool for fighting against laziness or a means for mastering the body but nothing more. This was the argument of the mendicants (see Bonaventure, *De Paupertate Christi: Contra*

Magistrum Guilelmum in *Opera Omnia* 14 [Paris: Vives, 1868], p. 406).

However, the end of feudalism, the emergence of towns, and the growth of guilds of skilled craftsworkers in the cities initiated a change in outlook. Members of the guilds looked after one another and gradually developed into beneficent societies and religious associations. They even celebrated feasts and seasons of the year so that liturgy and life as well as prayer and work began to be connected.

Reformation. In the Reformation, labor lost the negative value it acquired in the Middle Ages. Martin Luther denied the medieval insistence on tension between action and contemplation. He believed that one can serve God and neighbor in the midst of the world. But this means practicing an occupation (German *Beruf*), which in the German language led to interpreting the occupation as a vocation (*Berufung*). Luther said, "The first and highest of all noble and good works is faith in Christ" (*Weimarer Ausgabe* 6:204). Thus, labor took on an explicitly liturgical dimension. Whatever labor a person might do, the believer works before God. The believer's work participates therefore in the logic of worship that does not recognize a distinction between the active life and the contemplative life.

Industrial Revolution. The rise of the merchant class turned most laborers into wage earners. This was exacerbated by the Industrial Revolution, which produced industrial, machine-based, and capitalist work. On the one hand, labor was the concrete place in which a worker developed his or her humanity. The worker could create an identity. On the other hand, in the capitalist scheme, the worker became quantifiable and marketable, and labor entailed mindless repetition ruled by machines and clocks (see Pickering, 2004, for an indigenous reaction to this oppression). In other words, the locus of humanization became the locus of alienation. The worker became someone other than himself or herself.

The Contemporary Era. Studies in the contemporary era have identified two kinds of labor: instrumental and expressive. The vast majority of workers were involved in instrumental labor. This is a job that provides sufficient financial support and security so that the laborer can afford to engage in his or her passion outside of the job during leisure time. Many musicians and artists find themselves in this situation. They wait tables or sell real estate during the day in order to practice their passion in the evening. Expressive labor is that which a person would do even if no one paid for it. Musicians, artists, and teachers who are fortunate to have acquired a paid position, a significant minority of the working population, are in this category. If they should lose their gainful employment, they will nonetheless continue their passion by resorting to instrumental labor.

However, the present problem in labor is unemployment and underemployment. It would seem that the labor market was unprepared for the rapid changes caused in the marketplace by technological advances. Unemployment results not only from the globalization of the economy that makes it feasible and cost-effective to transfer jobs to countries where labor costs are less but also from serious lack of technological skills among laborers in search of employment. Underemployment or taking a job for which one is "overqualified" may put food on the table, but in the present economy it might not even qualify as instrumental labor. The laborer may be too dispirited or exhausted to be able to use precious leisure time to pursue her or his passion.

Theology of Labor. No theology of labor is possible unless it is also a theory of social justice. The theologian must discern and describe the conditions of a nonalienating relationship of the laborer to the work performed. As noted, the first attempt at a(n implicit) theology of labor worked out in the monastic tradition succinctly expressed by St. Benedict did not last very long. The Roman Catholic Church renewed the attempt beginning in 1891 with an encyclical by Pope Leo XIII, *Rerum Novarum* (Rights and Duties of Capital and Labor), which called for a partnership between management and labor. A succession of encyclicals followed that further dwelt on this theme, the most recent being *Laborem Exercens* (On Human Work), by Pope John Paul II (1981). At its conclusion, the pope sketched elements of a spirituality of work. In large measure, he echoed the sentiments of modern theologians who have reflected on this theme.

Yet already in 1955, the French theologian Marie-Dominique Chenu drew on the biblical tradition and argued that the worker can and should become a creator. To begin with, the worker can create (develop) himself or herself. In actual tasks, the worker can become a collaborator (with God) of creation. Pope John Paul II echoes these thoughts. He writes that if the human person was created in the image of a Creator God, then the human person "shares by his work in the activity of the Creator and… within the limits of his own human capabilities, man in a sense continues to develop that activity, and perfects it as he advances further and further in the discovery of the resources and values contained in the whole of creation" (*Laborem Exercens* n. 25).

In addition to Chenu (1966), the theologians listed in the bibliography have contributed valuable fresh insights to the construction of a theology of work. Agrell's (1976) focus on the diverse views of work in the New Testament indicates that they reflect the ambiguity of work in Genesis 2–3. His model is helpful for appreciating the diversity of traditions in the early church even if it skirts the question of the relational character of work. Apart from human work's continuation of God's creative activity, what is the relationship of an individual's work to fellow human beings? Volf (2001) tackles this question and broadens the discussion. While retaining a focus on creation, he also draws on pneumatology and eschatology. The end is not the destruction of the world but rather its transformation. Thus, work in the Spirit is work in the new creation. The nature of work is transformed from alienation to humanization. Humans must enjoy work because they cooperate with God in bringing about a new creation.

However, it is Cosden (2006) who takes up these threads and integrates them in a more complete theology of work. Building on Volf and Pope John Paul II, among others, Cosden recognizes the threefold nature of work as instrumental, relational, and ontological. The purpose of work coincides with God's purpose for all creation: to honor God and to give humans enjoyment. Moreover, since work is relational and ontological, it will not cease in the new creation, which will be consummated but not negated. The Holy Spirit enables human beings to imagine a new creation and to labor to begin the process of building it here and now.

Further Research. The dramatically changed situation of labor in the contemporary world compared to the ancient world of the Bible and subsequent centuries poses a new challenge to theologians. Even using the best methodology for cross-cultural interpretation, there may be precious few and only very general insights in the Bible to serve modern concerns and interests. For example, retirement and the problems accompanying leaving aside one's lifelong labor was simply not an issue in the ancient world, where life expectancy might not have extended beyond the age of 40. Moreover, in the concluding section of *Laborem Exercens* Pope John Paul II links toil with suffering, relying on a debatable distinction between labor and toil posited by some biblical scholars: "The Christian finds in human work a small part of the Cross of Christ and accepts it in the same spirit of redemption in which Christ accepted his Cross for us" (n. 27). Perhaps few but fellow ethnics would find these words helpful when dealing with instrumental work, underemployment, or unemployment. This advice reflects specific cultural values that are not universal (Pilch and Malina, 2009).

One promising avenue of research that might shed light on contemporary issues would be a fresh critical review of Emile Durkheim's *The Division of Labor* such as that conducted by Wallwork (1984). One of Durkheim's lifelong preoccupations was the relationship of religion to social structure and solidarity. It could be rewarding to reexamine his theory of structural functional differentiation and the role of religion within it, particularly since he examined ancient Israel, Greece, and Rome among the primitive societies characterized by mechanical solidarity. The six-stage theory of sociocultural change upon which Durkheim based his ideal types of mechanical and organic solidarity enhanced by alternative evolutionary proposals, including sociobiology, would be a rewarding research project.

[*See also* Creation; Discipleship; Holy Spirit; Joy; Nature and Natural Resources; Paul; *and* Prayer.]

BIBLIOGRAPHY

Agrell, Göran. *Work, Toil, and Sustenance: An Examination of the View of Work in the New Testament, Taking into Consideration Views Found in the Old Testament, Intertestamental, and Early Rabbinic Writings.* Translated by Stephen Westerholm. Lund, Sweden: Verbum H. Ohlsson, 1976.

Chenu, Marie-Dominique. *The Theology of Work: An Exploration.* Translated by Lilian Soiron. Chicago: Henry Regnery, 1966. English translation of *Pour une théologie du travail* (Paris: Seuil, 1955).

Cosden, Darrell. *A Theology of Work: Work and the New Creation.* Eugene, Ore.: Wipf & Stock, 2006.

Luborsky, Mark R. "The Retirement Process: Making the Person and Cultural Meanings Malleable." *Medical Anthropology Quarterly* 8, no. 4 (1994): 411–429.

Pickering, Kathleen. "Decolonizing Time Regimes: Lakota Conceptions of Work, Economy, Society." *American Anthropologist* 106 (2004): 85–97.

Pilch, John J. "Work, Labor." In *The Westminster Theological Word Book of the Bible*, edited by Donald E. Gowan, pp. 540–542. Louisville, Ky., and London: Westminster John Knox, 2003.

Pilch, John J., and Bruce J. Malina. *Handbook of Biblical Social Values.* Grand Rapids, Mich.: Baker House, 2009.

Volf, Miroslav. *Work in the Spirit: Towards a Theology of Work.* Eugene, Ore.: Wipf & Stock, 2001.

Wallwork, Ernest. "Religion and Social Structure in *The Division of Labor*." *American Anthropologist* 84 (1984): 43–64.

John J. Pilch

LAMB OF GOD

A lamb is a young sheep, usually one year old or less. To sheepherders and farmers in the ancient Near East, lambs were valuable commodities. In the Hebrew Bible lambs are especially prominent in the vocabulary of sacrifice. To offer a lamb in sacrifice to God was to give to God a valuable possession. In John's Gospel Jesus is twice identified as the "Lamb of God"; in Revelation the image is frequently applied to the risen Jesus, who reigns with his Father in heaven.

Torah. The most prominent Hebrew words for "lamb" are *śeh* and *kebeś*. A precise distinction between these terms is not clear. In Genesis 22:7–8, as Abraham prepares to offer Isaac as a sacrifice to God, Isaac asks, "Where is the lamb [*śeh*] for a burnt offering?" Abraham assures him that God will provide the lamb [*śeh*]. In Exodus, Leviticus, and Numbers, *kebeś* is the more common term. The legislation regarding daily offerings (Exod 29:38–46; Num 28:1–8) stipulates that two-year-old lambs (*kebaśîm*) are to be offered: one in the morning, the other in the evening. In the rules about sacrifices throughout Leviticus, a lamb is almost always present as part of the prescribed offering (Lev 3:7; 4:32, 35; 5:6–7; 9:3; 12:6, 8). When in Numbers 7 Moses finishes the Tabernacle's arrangement and consecrates the altar, the leaders of Israel's 12 tribes bring various offerings, which include lambs to be sacrificed. In the lists of sacrifices prescribed for the various feasts on the Jewish calendar in Numbers 28–29, lambs are mentioned at every point: daily offerings, sabbath offerings, monthly offerings, and the offerings for Passover, Weeks, Trumpets (or New Year), the Day of Atonement, and Booths. According to Torah, the lambs were to be sacrificed in Israel's worship first at the Tabernacle, later in the Jerusalem temple. Describing the ideal temple worship renewed in the New Jerusalem, the prophet Ezekiel (ch. 46) looked forward to a restoration of the sacrificial system, with appropriate offerings that regularly include lambs (*kebaśîm*).

In the instructions for preparing the Passover meal in Exodus 12:3–10, the other Hebrew word for "lamb" (*śeh*) appears several times. In Exodus, the Passover meal commemorates the divine protection given to the Israelites, enslaved in Egypt, from the plague of the death of the firstborn. The smearing of the lamb's blood on the family's doorpost symbolized that protection. While the original character of Passover remains mysterious, other biblical texts (e.g., Num 28:16–25) prescribe the sacrifice of lambs on Passover at the tabernacle or temple (or both). It is not clear whether the Passover meal described in Exodus 12 is a "sacrifice" as such; it appears to be a memorial meal at which the Israelites recall God's saving action on behalf of their ancestors (and, by extension, of themselves). No mention is made of forgiveness of sins through the lamb's slaughter. In most of the Jewish tradition, Passover has been observed mainly as a festive meal held in private homes.

The Servant of the Lord. From the perspective of Christian theology the most important mention of a lamb arises in the fourth Servant Song of Isaiah 52:13—53:12. There the Servant is said to have been "like a lamb [*śeh*] that is led to the slaughter." (The phrase also occurs in Jeremiah 11:19, though there the word is *kebeś*.) The image conveys physical weakness and execution; the Servant's sufferings are given atoning or expiatory value in the fourth Servant Song: "He was wounded for our transgressions … and by his bruises we are healed" (53:5; see also 53:6, 11–12). This usage clearly assumes the sacrificial contexts of other biblical references to lambs, applying the term metaphorically to an individual (the prophet or the leader of the exilic community) or to the community itself (the prophet's circle, exiles, perhaps all Israel) in the sixth century B.C.E. that had suffered greatly. Israel's exile in the early sixth century was primarily interpreted as LORD's just punishment for his people's failure to worship him properly and to observe his commandments. The return from exile is based on the conviction that Israel had received from the LORD's hand "double for all her sins" (Isa 40:2). In Second Isaiah, it was the expiatory or atoning sufferings of the Servant, whoever or whatever he was, that allowed LORD to wipe away Israel's guilt and to make possible its return home.

Gospels and Acts. In the New Testament there are three Greek words for "lamb": *arnen*, *amnos*, and *arnion*. Again, these terms are not precisely differentiated. The first appears only in Luke 10:3, when Jesus sends out his disciples "like lambs [*arnas*] into the midst of wolves": the disciples are warned to expect opposition and to remember that from a worldly perspective they appear as powerless as lambs before predators like wolves. In John 21:15–17 followers of the risen Jesus are referred to as "lambs" (*arnia*) and "sheep" (*probata*).

Probably the most famous "Lamb of God" texts appear in John 1:29, 36. In John 1:29, John the Baptist declares Jesus to be "the Lamb [*amnos*] of God who takes away the sin of the world." The image clearly associates Jesus with the offering of lambs in sacrifices that atone for sins. The expression as a whole points toward the "hour" of Jesus (his passion, death, resurrection, and exaltation) in which his expiatory suffering will bring about a new and better relationship with God. The figure of the Deutero-Isaianic Servant (identified as *amnos* in the Greek version of Isaiah 53) may also be evoked. In John 1:35, John the Baptist again identifies Jesus as "the Lamb [*amnos*] of God." The Johannine passion-week chronology (13:1; 18:28; 19:31, 42) suggests that Jesus dies on the cross at precisely the time when the Passover lambs were being sacrificed in the Jerusalem temple. Similarly, in 1 Corinthians 5:7 Paul proclaims, "Our paschal lamb [*pascha*], Christ, has been sacrificed."

According to Acts 8:26–40, the biblical passage that so puzzled the Ethiopian eunuch was Isaiah 53:7–8, especially the part in which the Servant is compared to a sheep (*probaton*) led to the slaughter and to a lamb (*amnos*) silent before its shearer. Philip's task was to show the Ethiopian eunuch that the text was really talking about Jesus. Likewise, 1 Peter 1:19 reminds Gentile Christians that they have been "ransomed" from their futile ways through "the precious blood of Christ, like that of a lamb [*amnos*] without defect or blemish." Here the themes of Christ as the Lamb/Servant of God and the expiatory value of his sacrificial death come together.

Revelation. The risen Christ is described nearly 30 times in Revelation as the "Lamb of God" (e.g., 5:6, 8, 13; 6:1, 16; 7:9, 10, 14, 17; 8:1). The Greek word is *arnion*, which can refer to a sheep of any age. Although *1 Enoch* 89:41–50 apparently alludes to Israel's earliest kings as warrior rams, the connection of this text with Revelation is dubious. In John's vision of the heavenly court (Rev 5), a search commences for someone worthy to open the scroll sealed with seven seals. That someone turns out to be "a Lamb standing as if it had been slaughtered" (5:6). Here and elsewhere the image brings together the motifs of lambs offered in sacrifices and the Suffering Servant led to slaughter. Ironically, in Revelation, the "slain Lamb" has conquered death and now merits the worship accorded to God in the heavenly court

(5:8, 12, 13). The Lamb opens the seals, thus revealing what is to come (6:1; 8:1). In the interlude of Revelation 7, the great multitude proclaims that salvation belongs to the Lamb (7:9) and that "the blood of the Lamb" has effected their salvation. Revelation affirms a triple paradox: their robes have been "made white" in the Lamb's blood (7:14), the Lamb shares the divine throne (7:15, 17), and the Lamb will now become the shepherd (7:17).

The second half of Revelation celebrates the victories of the risen Jesus as the Lamb (*arnion*) of God, not only in the paschal mystery but also in the future as John sees it. In 12:11, the Great Red Dragon (a satanic figure) has been conquered "by the blood of the Lamb." In 13:8, those who follow the Beast from the Sea (i.e., the Roman emperor) do not have their names written in "the book of life of the Lamb that was slaughtered" (see also 21:27). By contrast, in the vision of the 144,000 (Rev 14:1–5), the Lamb stands triumphant on Mount Zion; the redeemed, called "the first fruits for God and the Lamb," are said to "follow the Lamb wherever he goes." In a prelude to the vision of the seven bowls of God's wrath, the angels "sing the song of Moses, the servant of God, and of the Lamb" (15:3–4), celebrating the justice and glory of God. Under the power of the imperial Beast, the kings of the earth "make war on the Lamb"; nonetheless, "the Lamb will conquer them, for he is Lord of lords and King of kings" (17:14).

Near its conclusion, Revelation describes a festive celebration of the marriage supper of the Lamb (19:7, 9); the bride clothed in linen (the church?) stands in contrast to the lurid Beast and the Prostitute (the goddess Roma) in chapter 17. The vision of the New Jerusalem begins with the angel's promise to show John "the bride, the wife of the Lamb" (21:9). The city needs no temple and no source of light, since "its temple is the Lord God the Almighty and the Lamb" and "the glory of God is its light, and its lamp is the Lamb" (21:22–23). In the vision of the river of life, the Lamb again shares the divine throne with God (22:1, 3): a final confirmation of Revelation's high Christology.

Theological Legacy. The biblical "Lamb of God" echoes many things: ancient Israel's sacrificial system, the Passover lamb, the Servant of the Lord in Second

Isaiah, John the Baptist's description of Jesus the Lamb of God who takes away the world's sin, and Revelation's depiction of the risen Christ as the slain Lamb.

The liturgical prominence of the *Agnus Dei* (Lat "Lamb of God") in the Mass has evoked many musical compositions based on its words by such composers as Bach, Haydn, Mozart, Schubert, and Beethoven. Through the centuries many artists have painted and sculpted images of Christ as the Lamb and as the shepherd. In Christian theology, the image of Christ as the Lamb of God has set some of the terms for debates about the role of sacrifice in Christology.

In the Roman Catholic Mass today, the prayer of praise known as the *Gloria* celebrates Jesus as the "Lamb of God" and addresses him as "you who take away the sins of the world." In the Communion ritual, the priest breaks the bread, and all say or sing, "Lamb of God, you take away the sins of the world, have mercy on us." Both of these liturgical uses highlight the sacrificial and expiatory character of Jesus's death. The Invitation to Communion begins with the words, "Behold the Lamb of God," thus inviting believers to participate in "the supper of the Lamb," which in turn evokes the language of the latter parts of Revelation.

[*See also* Christology; Festivals and Holy Days; *and* John and the Johannine Epistles.]

BIBLIOGRAPHY

Johns, Loren L. *The Lamb Christology of the Apocalypse of John: An Investigation into Its Origin and Rhetorical Force.* Tübingen, Germany: Mohr Siebeck, 2003.

Laws, Sophie. *In the Light of the Lamb: Imagery, Parody, and Theology in the Apocalypse.* Wilmington, Del.: Michael Glazier, 1988.

Mekkattukunnel, Andrews George, ed. *Lamb of God: Essays in Johannine Theology.* Kottayam, India: Oriental Institute of Religious Studies, 2010.

Nielsen, Jesper Tang. "The Lamb of God: The Cognitive Structure of a Johannine Metaphor." In *Imagery in the Gospel of John,* edited by Jörg Frey et al., pp. 217–58. Tübingen, Germany: Mohr Siebeck, 2006.

Schneiders, Sandra M. "The Lamb of God and the Forgiveness of Sins in the Fourth Gospel." *Catholic Biblical Quarterly* 73, no. 1 (2011): 1–29.

Tuohy, Séamus. "Communion in the Supper of the Lamb." In *The Word Is Flesh and Blood: The Eucharist and Sacred Scripture,* edited by Vivian Boland and Thomas McCarthy, pp. 164–174. Dublin, Ireland: Dominican Publications, 2012.

Daniel J. Harrington

LAMENTATIONS

See Megillot.

LAND

Land was the primary material resource in the biblical world, essential, together with sun and rain, for producing food. Land meant different things to the majority who produced food and a dominant minority who did not but who benefited from food production. Producers found meaning mainly in local use rights, weather, soil, and terrain. Nonproducers strove to aggrandize lands, through conquest, coercion, manipulation (especially of debt), and marriage, and to exercise the authority to rent, tax, and otherwise control lands.

History. In Palestine, the main users of land were food-producing households residing in rural settlements dependent on rain agriculture made precarious by uncertain rainfall and encumbrances imposed by elites. Land was held by the patriarchal household in three ways according to the form of allocation. *Communal* allocation of land-use rights to arable land was through periodic repartition by lot. This facilitated the fencing of rotating fallow grounds for grazing and contributed to local solidarity. *Proprietary* allocation, comparable to freehold, was made by sale or grant and typically applied to vineyards, orchards, and private gardens, that is, property requiring long-term investment. Grants by sovereigns could be nominally permanent, but grantors did not scruple to rescind them through opportunism and caprice. Although evidence is sparse, temple lands may at times have been allocated by prebendal grants, as elsewhere in the ancient Near East, which however tended to become heritable. *Common* allocation applied to the use of outback for pasturage.

Each form of allocation had a broader territorial analog, of concern mainly to nonproducers; the territorial grant, by God as grantor and based ultimately on conquest, was perhaps the most important for the Bible.

Homeland was the "land of birth" (Heb. *môledet*) or "land of our fathers" (cf. Gk *patria*), particularly of fathers' graves. Landholding was regularly sanctioned by cultic or religious practice, centered at a local level on household or clan burial sites, at a regional level on saints' tombs, and at a monarchic territorial level on a temple and dynastic burial sites.

Local land use was tied to a wider political economy that influenced the extent, intensity, and nature of food production. The periodic extension and contraction of settlement characteristic of the ancient Near East was shaped less by climate or terrain than by political strategy and circumstance. The balance between plant cultivation and animal husbandry was decided mainly in response to political and economic pressures and opportunities created by nonproducers. The greatest pressure was the creditor's use of debt to encumber the holdings of producers, leaving them vulnerable to appropriation through foreclosure. This process, perennial in agrarian societies, led to land consolidation and agricultural intensification (*latifundialization*). Mixed subsistence agriculture benefiting producer households tended to give way to commodity production benefiting nonproducers, who traded produce in return for luxury or military goods of little use to producers. On the principle of comparative advantage, lowlands were dedicated to grains, highlands to grapes and olives, and dry lands to sheep and goats. For producers, serfdom or loss of land was a calamity whose effects are recurrently described in the Bible (e.g., 2 Kgs 4:38–41; Mic 3:1–2). A land-consolidating regime could produce an abundance of food, which however was available to producers only through handouts or in markets at a dire disadvantage. In the extreme, land consolidation pushed producers into hinterland husbandry where possible. Despite productive success, latifundialization fostered a stasis in productivity affecting the entire preindustrial era since producers lacked the incentive to increase production and nonpro-

ducers, whose vocation was war, lacked the know-how.

Tribal Israel. Archaeological evidence for the Early Iron Age, roughly the twelfth and eleventh centuries B.C.E., shows a spreading tide of self-sustaining highland villages engaged in a plentiful mixed agriculture, in the absence, unusually, of dominating or centralizing forces. The implication is that the pressures of agricultural consolidation and intensification were held at bay by the tribal politics of early Israel that provided the social stability essential for viable agriculture. The tribal alliance known as Israel formed prior to this spread of settlement, as is clear from the single nonbiblical reference to premonarchic Israel in a stela of the pharaoh Merneptah from the late thirteenth century B.C.E. What counted for Israelite lands at that time is not known. The sons of Israel comprised a typical tribal formation: a variable network of nested and interlocked kinship relationships, both real and putative, formed both against urban powers, as expressed in a deep-seated antimonarchic ethos, and in partnership with them. The extent of the Israelite sphere of influence is unknown; it was probably wide and certainly variable. The territory and social order overseen by the tribal collective must be seen as a dominion, without which the early Israelite spread of settlement would not have been possible. This dominion was sanctioned by a cult of Yahweh, the god of Israel, an avatar of the Canaanite deity El, located probably in Bethel or Shiloh. It was with reference to this dominion that every subsequent claim to sovereignty over the land of Israel was made.

Tribal monarchies. Tribal Israelite resistance to intensification lasted only so long. Tribal monarchies were not unusual, and in time an Israelite monarchy formed, with Saul or before, and with it the usual nonproducers' distortions of land access and use. The monarchy claimed sovereignty over the Israelite dominion for taxing produce and labor (*corvée*) and promised protection in return. The monarchic guarantee of justice was always open to tribal skepticism, which in Israel lasted for the entire period of the Bible's formation. This wariness was embodied in prophetic constraints, direct and indirect, including the corpus of written Prophets produced by the monarchic courts themselves. The monarchic claim over Israel was proprietary, asserted by the royal household, and as such heritable, or dynastic.

Israelite monarchic sovereignty was held or claimed over a territory acquired by conquest or coercion, held by force or threat (often with outsider help), and defended against opposing claimants. Tribal elder approval may at times have contributed to monarchic legitimacy. Sovereignty was warranted by the appropriated cult of Yahweh, in urban settings given the trappings of the temple god Ba'al. The divine sanction was actualized by prophetic appointment, a remarkable concession to tribal interference, part of the cost of winning the tribal dominion. Written records of prophetic sanction of territorial sovereignty, however, were held in the courts and temples of successive monarchic capitals. The longest-lasting and now best known was the Temple in Jerusalem, Davidic property in the Davidic city. The Temple, founded by David or his son Solomon, was an institution whose exaltation forms the main theme of the Prophets and that endured in name for 1,000 years, until the colossal structure begun by Herod the Great in about 20 B.C.E. was destroyed in 70 C.E.

Partly because of the strength of tribal tradition and partly because of location amid competing great powers, Israelite monarchic sovereignty was tenuous and rickety. Israelite dynasties were short lived—one or two generations—except for three generations of the house of Omri and five of the house of Jehu. Two dynastic circumstances played the leading role in shaping the biblical account of monarchic sovereignty over territorial Israel. The first was the survival of the house of David in Jerusalem and Babylon for over four centuries after their overthrow as kings of Israel; the second was the fall of Samaria in 722 B.C.E. to the Assyrians and therewith the end of Israelite dynastic sovereignty over the erstwhile dominion of Israel until the second century B.C.E.

The fall of Samaria together with the continuance of the house of David occasioned the house of David's irredentist assertion of sovereignty over the dominion of Israel. It is not unusual for territorial sovereignty to develop irredentist or revanchist claims because regimes cannot keep intact the extent of their sovereignty indefinitely. The house of David had a long run, but its sovereignty over political Israel, and thus the dominion under Israelite rule, lasted only two generations, those of David and Solomon. A revanchist claim to Israel was declared at least under Hezekiah in the late eighth century B.C.E. and Josiah in the late seventh century B.C.E., in both cases as vital to programs of Temple refurbishment and radical cultic and sociopolitical centralization. The programs included, as often in the ancient Near East, a debt remission that amounted to a return of lost lands to food producers and the weakening of extended households of opposing land-consolidators. Hezekiah's revanchism, part of wider political ambitions, met Assyrian resistance. Josiah, too, failed in his claim, though the exact circumstances are debated. Jerusalem fell to Nebuchadnezzar in 598 B.C.E., and the court of King Jehoiachin was transported to Babylonia. After the second fall of Jerusalem in 587 B.C.E. and the death of his ruling uncle, Jehoiachin inherited the Davidic claim, represented in texts coming from heirs of the Davidic court, which lasted intact into the fifth century B.C.E. and then, under Persian domination, vanished.

Persian, Greek, and Roman periods. Under Persian and Greek rule, nominal Israelite territory was reduced to Jerusalem and a small Judahite hinterland for the next 300 years. The Israelite dominion lay in abeyance until its gradual recovery under the Hasmoneans, sparked by a Temple restoration still celebrated as Hanukkah, during the late second century and early first century B.C.E. Their territory, probably the largest ever under an Israelite's rule, fell under Roman control in 67 B.C.E. and into the hands of the Herods as Roman clients from 39 B.C.E. to 70 C.E. An armed rebellion against Roman rule wracked the land in the first Jewish war, which resulted in the fall of Jerusalem and the Temple, making an Israelite sovereignty again problematic. Following a second Jewish defeat in 135 C.E., rabbinic leaders exercised a short-lived sovereignty under Roman auspices over portions of the territory described as Israelite in scripture, in the face of a Samaritan cult that had taken root two centuries before in the Israelite heartland.

Out of rabbinic rule came the Mishnah, which elaborated on laws governing Jewish life in the land, with however an ideal rather than real Temple center. In the wake of the Jewish wars, the emergent Christian churches, which knew the geographical location of Jesus's burial but not of his body, gradually followed a different approach to land as God's territory, in theory dispensing with it altogether, in fact eventually falling in with or under the headship of emperors and kings ready to aggrandize territory in any location in the name of Christ.

Bible. Since the Bible reflects mainly nonproducer politics, whether royal, priestly, or colonial, it represents land mainly as territory. A territory's extent was perennially variable, depending on changes in rulers' overt and covert power. This is one reason that biblical descriptions of Israelite dominion (e.g., Gen 15:18; Num 34:1–15) or parts thereof vary significantly. Another is that as urban pronouncements such descriptions are promotional or imaginary: no specification of territory in the Bible accurately depicts the land ever ruled by an Israelite federation or monarch. The one ingredient that detailed specifications, all from the Davidic monarchy, have in common is the assumption, theoretical but traced to early Israel, that the dominion of Israel comprises the sum of tribal territories (e.g., Josh 13–19; Ezek 47:13—48:29). This is so, whatever the social reality of Israelite tribalism at the time.

The most common form of landholding in the Bible is the land grant, particularly by regional sovereigns or God—not surprisingly since the Hebrew scriptures consist mostly of court or temple documents. The Hebrew word for grant (*naḥlâ*) and its cognate verb developed the nuance of "inheritance, inherit" and are often so translated because grants were typically heritable. Rural repartition by lottery is alluded to in a number of passages (e.g., Mic 2:5; Pss 16:5–6; 125:3). Decrees of debt remission, both periodic and one-time, furthered retention by producers of lands at risk of seizure for debts and form a significant motif in both Torah and Prophets (e.g., Exod 21:1–11; Lev 25:8–55; Deut 15:1–18; Isa 5:8–10).

Yahwist strand. The earliest representation of Israelite territory is found in the Yahwist (J) narrative strand in Genesis, Exodus, and Numbers, a work from the house of David thought by many to have been the narrative foundation of the Torah. The land is Canaan—perhaps the one-time Egyptian New Kingdom sector of that name—mythically conceived of as a land exuding milk and honey, which is to say nearly devoid of grain cultivation (see Isa 7:14–25) because inhabited only by urban Canaanites and pastoralist Israelites. Yahweh confers this territory on Israel's grandfather Abram and later on Israel by a monarchic grant sealed by oath (Gen 12:7; 13:14–17; 28:13–15). The territory, inhabited by several peoples, is only vaguely defined as the land visible from the heights of Bethel. A contemporaneous formula for the territory, "from Dan to Beer-sheba" (e.g., Judg 20:1; 1 Sam 3:20; 2 Sam 3:10), probably names border cults marking bounds of an Israelite dominion. Once in Palestine, Abram confirms the grant by establishing a cult of Yahweh at Shechem, then at Bethel (Gen 12:7–8). Another tradition places Abram's burial in Hebron, a seat of Davidic ascendancy (Gen 23:17–20; 25:9–10). The grant includes more than pasturage and thus is anticipatory, looking forward to the Israelites taking possession sometime after a trek as fugitive slaves through the desert from Egypt. How the narrator thought this possession would occur is unclear because the story ends with the blessing of the fugitive horde on the brink of arrival (Num 22:41—24:19). The only hints of a conquest are those introduced later in light of the Deuteronomistic story of conquest (Josh 1:1—12:24).

Following the overthrow of the house of David in Israel, J was supplemented by additions giving it a non-Davidic slant (so-called JE). The number of cults sanctioning territorial control was expanded. The extent of territorial Israel was not revised since the kings of Israel were usually reluctant to concede the rule of Judah.

Deuteronomistic History. What is anticipated in the Torah, the full possession of Canaan by outsiders (e.g., Gen 12:1–7), is fulfilled in the first book of the Prophets, Joshua, through conquest and colonization. Although it includes more ancient ingredients, the story of Joshua originated in the bid by the house of David, by the same token reluctant to concede the rule of Israel, to recover the sovereignty of Israel. Following Deuteronomy, which laid down laws obligatory for holding the land (e.g., 4:1–2, 25–27; 5:29–30; 6:10–19; 11:8–9; 13–17), Joshua forms the beginning of the Deuteronomistic History (DH), consisting of Deuteronomy through 2 Kings (without Ruth). The DH is, in essence, the house of David's account of its sovereignty over the dominion of Israel.

The revival of the Davidic claim to Israel after the fall of Samaria was the likely reason for the plot of the DH that gave shape to the sources incorporated: law and covenant laid down by Moses, which, unlike JE, make the political nation's possession of Canaan contingent on popular obedience to Yahweh (Deuteronomy); the conquest of Canaan; the futility of decentralization in the era of intermittent champions described in Judges; the resolution of political threat and turmoil through a centralizing cult and rule in Jerusalem (i.e., the remainder of the DH that includes Saul's selection as king, David's usurpation, Solomon's succession and building of the Temple, the deplorable secession of Israel under Jeroboam, the hostilities and alliances between the house of David and the kings of Israel, the fall of the house of Omri as declared by Elijah and Elisha, the fall of Samaria, and, in some form, the reign of Hezekiah.) The basic theme is that tribal Israel is to conquer and hold its land contingent on obedience to the commands of Yahweh, who ordered the Israelites to keep his cult in a single location (Deut 12:1–14), an order, it turned out, that only a king in Jerusalem could carry out. David conquers the location, and Solomon establishes the cult.

Though the house of David's loss of sovereignty over most of the dominion of Israel is provisionally warranted, it does not justify violating the law of Yahweh's exclusive cult by the kings of Israel, who with little regard for dynastic turnover are uniformly condemned for "the sin of Jeroboam" (e.g., 1 Kgs 15:30; 16:2, 19, 26), that is, the flouting of the sacred prerogatives of Jerusalem in compliance with God's law of centralization. Only the house of David's recovery of the dominion of Israel, as foreshadowed by Joshua's conquest and colonization, can keep the dominion of Israel in Israelite hands.

The Davidic irredentist project was thus retrojected into the Israelite past as the military fulfillment of the land grant to Abram and Israel in a conquest and colonization of Canaan—nominally tribal but plainly monarchic—under Moses's appointed successor, Joshua. The historical occasion for the story was not the Early Iron Age origin of Israel in Palestine but the Assyrian-period aspiration of the house of David, the marginal and tenacious rump Israelite monarchs. The DH adopts J's concept of the land as occupied by Canaanites—now the perennial warring and trading class infringing royal prerogative—and other peoples inhabiting the cities of a land primed for agricultural productivity. The boundary the DH locates at the Jordan River is determinative but not absolute (e.g., Deut 1:1; Josh 1:1–2, 10–15; 3:1—5:12; 13:1–13; 22:1–34); it is a reflex of Assyrian administrative policy, the Jordan rarely if ever having functioned as a border among the region's inhabitants.

This history of Davidic sovereignty from the court of Hezekiah was revised at least twice, first in the court of Josiah, whose revision bears the most explicit marks of composition (1 Kgs 13:1–3; 2 Kgs 22:1—23:25), and then in the court of Jehoiachin or a successor in exile (2 Kgs 25:27–30). As in J, the fulfillment of the revanchist vision is absent in the version from Hezekiah, at least as far as appears in the Bible, and etiolated in the version from Josiah, who campaigns against the cults of Israel but does not end up holding the dominion of Israel. Whether Josiah allied with Assyria or opposed it, the Assyrian and Egyptian presence made fulfillment problematic.

Latter Prophets. The ensuing Babylonian conquest made fulfillment impossible, for the time being, and under Jehoiachin the vision took a different form, in ancillary documents that now make up the Latter Prophets, highlighting instead the glorification of Jerusalem. The concept of land in the book of Jeremiah as governed by its Deuteronomic composition conveys the prophet's charge that until the ruling class in exile recognizes the violation of the Mosaic covenant as the reason for their loss of land, they will not recover the land; the deportees' role now is to make life in Babylon a proof of this realization (e.g., Jer 24; 29; 32).

Ezekiel's priestly vision depicts a recovery of the Israelite dominion by a combined Judah and Israel under a Davidic head (Ezek 34:23–24; 37:15–28). The dominion is highly idealistic: the land from the Jordan to the Mediterranean is segmented by east–west boundaries into 13 slices, one each for the 12 tribes and one for a new temple and adjacent capital city (Ezek 47:13–21; 48:1–35). This city is taken by most interpreters to be Jerusalem, but its location in the center of its segment and its separation from the temple indicates otherwise. Ezekiel's concept is indebted to the Deuteronomic notion of the Jordan River as a boundary and to a theoretical egalitarianism. Ezekiel's idealism is akin to that of the priestly strand in Torah, in which arable land keeps the sabbath by being fallowed every seventh year (Lev 25:1–7), hopeless as a field system in Palestine, the shortfall being regularly made up by a double production in the sixth year, a climatic impossibility. Similarly, the priestly strand stretches the periodic debt remission from seven years to forty-nine, putting the recovery of mortgaged lands out of reach for virtually the lifetime of most producers (Lev 25:8–55).

Other books of the Latter Prophets, foremost Isaiah, also look forward to a restoration but primarily in terms of Jerusalem (Isa 2:2–4; 12:1–6; 35:1–10; 40:1—55:13; 59:20; 60:1—61:7; 62:1–12; 65:17–25; 66:5–13; Joel; Mic 4:1–4; Zeph 3:14–20; Hag; Zech). In the face of the changeableness of territorial sovereignty, the cult center from which it will spring provides a sacred and secure focal point and one that imperial powers might grasp (Isa 41:2–4; 44:24—45:7).

Torah and Prophets. The Torah concept of territory is categorical, proleptic, and vague; the prophetic concept is contingent, fulfilled, and idealistic. Jerusalem goes unmentioned in the one and serves as the dazzling focal point of the other. These two dominant concepts of land, of the Torah and Prophets, created the great conceptual divide with respect to the land: the Torah constituting Israel off the land and the Prophets admonishing Israel in the land. In the end God's grant is both absolute and contingent. In the Torah it is definite but in the future; in the Prophets it is conditional but undergirded by the grant to David and especially Zion. The ultimate significance of this bifurcation is the preservation of the Torah itself, which constitutes a people without specifying a ruling regime, which is left to the Prophets. This distinction made the Torah perpetually adaptable under a continuing succession of regimes.

The New Testament sees the overthrow of the center of Zion, the Temple, and with it the territorial claims of the Davidic king—until he returns to claim a universal dominion. New Israel is based not on land but on covenant—the off-the-land concept of the Torah. This is a reflex of the dominance of Paul (Rom 4:1—5:2; Gal 2:15—5:1) in the canon and what became the prevalent Christian understanding during the first three centuries, in which territorial holdings, whatever their role in the earliest church, came to play little or no role. In the view that prevailed, the paradigm for trust in God is Abram's trust in Yahweh with respect to not the grant of land but the grant of an heir ("seed"; Gal 3:15–18). The church as Israel is thus "off" the land, hence portrayed, for example, in the earliest Gospel, Mark, as on the way through the desert (e.g., Mark 6:31, 32, 35; 9:2–8; 10:32, 52); and as for those "on," or holding, the land, from the church's perspective the prophetic sanctions fall on Zion as territorial center, annulling its sacred sovereignty over the land (Mark 11:20–25; 13:1–31).

Postbiblical and Contemporary Developments. Judaism developed its own version of existence absent a Jewish land, making the laws of Torah and their juridical elaboration, the Mishnah, primary in self-governing communities within imperial contexts still possessing, in theory, temple and land, the hope for which did not die. The church in the Roman sphere was adopted by the imperial head, and in this aspect territorial interests returned to the church. A great basilica was constructed over Jesus's gravesite, the transept and apse of which later became the Church of the Holy Sepulcher. This merger of church and state led to a long history of ecclesiastical landholdings, in both alliance with and opposition to ruling powers, and church-sanctioned takeovers in the name of biblical religion. The example of the United States is ambiguous only because of the disestablishment of religion.

In the late nineteenth and twentieth centuries, a nationalist movement with territorial interests blossomed in a segment of Judaism. It gained in importance through its gradual settlement of Palestine under Ottoman and British rule, burgeoned in the wake of the Holocaust, and in mid-century formed a state, whose territory, while in ancient Israelite lands or close by them, corresponded to no ancient Israelite bounds. Nevertheless, these interests were expressed in terms of "the land of Israel," a nationalist concept that located a Jewish right to Palestine in a revival of the venerable, if variable, dominion of Israel, held, in democratic guise, through purchase, conquest, colonization, and outsider help.

[*See also* Exile and Dislocation; Historical Narratives (Joshua—2 Kings); Inheritance (Heir); Jerusalem (Zion); Labor; *and* Nature and Natural Resources.]

BIBLIOGRAPHY

Benvenisti, Meron. *Sacred Landscape: The Buried History of the Holy Land since 1948.* Berkeley: University of California Press, 2000.

Borowski, Oded. *Agriculture in Iron Age Israel.* Winona Lake, Ind.: Eisenbrauns, 1987.

Davies, W. D. *The Gospel and the Land: Early Christianity and Jewish Territorial Doctrine.* Berkeley: University of California Press, 1974.

Davies, W. D. *The Territorial Dimension of Judaism.* Berkeley: University of California Press, 1982.

Hoffman, Lawrence A., ed. *The Land of Israel: Jewish Perspectives.* Notre Dame, Ind.: University of Notre Dame Press, 1986.

Hopkins, David. *The Highlands of Canaan: Agricultural Life in the Early Iron Age.* Sheffield, U.K.: Almond, 1985.

Janzen, Waldemar. "Land." In *Anchor Bible Dictionary,* edited by David Noel Freedman, Vol. 4, pp. 143–154. New Haven, Conn.: Yale University Press, 1992.

Sand, Shlomo. *The Invention of the Land of Israel: From Holy Land to Homeland.* London: Verso, 2012.

Stavrakopoulou, Francesca. *Land of Our Fathers: The Roles of Ancestor Veneration in Biblical Land Claims.* New York: T&T Clark, 2010.

Wright, Christopher J. H. *God's People in God's Land: Family, Land, and Property in the Old Testament.* Grand Rapids, Mich.: Eerdmans, 1990.

Robert B. Coote

LEVITICUS AND NUMBERS

Since the beginning of historical-critical research on the Pentateuch, the books of Leviticus and Numbers have played only a marginal place in scholarship. Leviticus was considered a pedantic priestly and ritualistic book, and the same held true for Numbers, a book that looks quite confusing and contains strange rituals and laws. In almost all theologies of the Old Testament that have been written in the past 100 years, very little space has been allotted to these books, with one exception: the discussion of the commandment to love one's neighbor in Leviticus 19:18–34.

According to Jewish tradition, however, the study of the Torah should begin with the "book of the priests," that is Leviticus, as the center of the Pentateuch. This idea is also found in the organization of the Pentateuch, which can indeed be understood as placing Leviticus at its very heart (Zenger, 1999), while the books of Genesis and Deuteronomy function as the outer frame of the Torah. In Genesis 6 Yahweh limits human life to 120 years, and in Deuteronomy 34 Moses dies at the age of 120. The first promise of the land that Abraham receives in Genesis 12 is also quoted in the last chapter of Deuteronomy. In addition, Jacob's blessing of his 12 sons in Genesis 49 has a parallel in Moses's last words about the 12 tribes of Israel in Deuteronomy 33. The books of Exodus and Numbers constitute the inner frame. In the book of Exodus the people arrive at the mountain of Sinai (Exod 19) and stay there until Numbers 10, when they depart toward the plains of Moab. The murmuring stories in Exodus 15–17 have parallels in the revolt stories in Numbers 11–20. The book of Leviticus, located at Sinai, finds its center in chapter 16, framed by the rituals about sacrifices and purity in chapters 1–15 and by texts about the holiness of the community and offerings in chapters 17–27. Leviticus 16 deals with a complex ritual about the purification of the sanctuary and the community. This ritual of Yom Kippur (the Day of Atonement), performed each year, provides the possibility of divine forgiveness and offers a new start. This central message of Leviticus shows that the book is concerned about the possibilities of reconciliation between humans and between Israel and its God.

Research has emphasized the importance of the books of Leviticus and Numbers, for a number of reasons. There is growing interest in the so-called Priestly texts (P) of the Pentateuch, whose theology is much more subtle than commonly alleged. In the current discussion about the extent and the end of the original P document, several scholars have argued that its conclusion can be found in Leviticus 16 (Köckert, 1999; Nihan, 2007). Then, P would have told a story starting with the creation of the world (Gen 11:1—2:3) and ending with the establishment of a sanctuary and the rituals through which Israel is able to encounter its God (Lev 1–16). If P ended in Leviticus 16, the second part of the book of Leviticus and the so-called P texts in Numbers are of later origin. In current European research, at least, these are often considered to be the most recent texts in the Pentateuch. They were written down in the last decades before the Torah was promulgated in the middle of the Persian era, around 400–350 B.C.E. Many of those texts can be understood as forerunners of the hermeneutics of interpretation and actualization of the divine law.

The Book of Leviticus: Rules for the Encounter with God. It has often been noted that Leviticus 17–26, although reminiscent of the P style, displays some important stylistic and, especially, theological differences. First of all, we find the refrain "You shall be holy, for I, the LORD your God, am holy." In contrast to Leviticus 1–16 where "holiness" is restricted to the priesthood, Leviticus 17–26 exhorts the whole community to become "holy." For this reason, Leviticus 17–26 is called the "Holiness Code" (Klostermann, 1877) and has often been understood as an independent law code added later to the book of Leviticus. However, Leviticus 17 does not really offer an introduction to an independent document (Joosten, 1996), and all chapters presuppose the fiction of a divine revelation during the sojourn at Mt. Sinai. Therefore, the best solution is to consider Leviticus 17–26 (Lev 27 is a later appendix) as a supplement to the P legislation, written from the very beginning to follow Leviticus 1–16. One may even speak of a "Holiness

school" (Knohl, 1995) that not only composed Leviticus 17–26 but also inserted several other texts into Exodus and Leviticus (Exod 12:14–20, 43–49; 31:12–17; Lev 11:43–45; 16:29–34a).

The theology of the conclusion of the Priestly code (Lev 1–16). For priestly theology, sacrifices play a major role. They regulate the relation between the human and the divine spheres. The origin and function of sacrifices are still under discussion. Does the sacrifice arise out of the "*do ut des*" principle ("I present you an offering so that I will get back divine favor" [Tylor, 2009])? Or is it a means to calm the divine anger or to regulate human violence (Burkert, 1984)? One can find these elements in the P texts, yet their first aim is to create a community between God and Israel through the idea of a common meal (Marx, 2003). In the lists of Leviticus 1–3 (Lev 4–7 might be a later addition [Nihan, 2007]), the P writers distinguish different types of sacrifices with different functions. The holocaust sacrifice (ʿolâ, burnt offering) is the most important since the entire animal is burnt so that it belongs exclusively to God via the smoke that rises to heaven. The other sacrifices imply that the sacrificial animal is shared among the priests, the person, or the family bringing the sacrifice and the deity (who receives mostly the noncomestible parts of the animal). This is especially the case for the šĕlamîm-offering ("sacrifice of well-being," Lev 3), a festive meal that manifests or restores a state of well-being with God. The redactors of Leviticus 4–5 have added other sacrifices that are particularly concerned with the idea of atonement ("sin offerings" for deliberate and nondeliberate transgressions). There are also cereal offerings (Lev 2) for several occasions. The origin of the grain offering (minḥâ) is perhaps to be found in a rural context and in the offering of first fruits (v. 14). It is a ritual of thanksgiving to the deity for granting a good harvest.

The exclusion of leaven and honey from the list of possible offerings can be explained by their propensity to fermentation so that their prohibition reflects another major priestly concern: the distinction and separation between pure and impure, between sacred and profane (Douglas, 1999, pp. 163–166). For the priestly worldview this is a fundamental distinction;

hence, it is important that persons with bodily impurities be excluded from the divine sphere. At the same time, the "pure" people must be protected in order to avoid contamination (Lev 12–15). In the context of priestly theology, the importance of the purity of the community may also be related to the anthropological statement of Genesis 1:26 about humankind as created in the image of God.

The distinction between clean (edible) and unclean (not edible) animals has often been explained through hygienic or religious reasons (importance of certain animals in nonyahwistic cults [Kornfeld, 1965]) or because unclean animals are not equipped with the right kind of locomotion for the environment (land, water, air) in which they live (Douglas, 2010, pp. 69–71). Without rejecting these explanations, one should first look for the theological rationale of this distinction. According to the ideal creation in Genesis 1, humans (and animals) are supposed to be vegetarians, and it is only after the Flood that God allows humans to eat animals (Gen 9:3–4). Against this backdrop, the more specific regulations in Leviticus can be understood as an attempt to also provide a more nuanced account of the created order. It also sets Israel apart from other nations as a "priestly" people (Houston, 2003; Nihan, 2007). In this sense, Leviticus 11 (paralleled in Deut 14) prepares the ground for the later *kashrut* regulations and has a function similar to Passover and circumcision, which are marks of belonging to the Israelite community.

Yom Kippur in Leviticus 16 combines two different rituals: a purification ritual and an elimination ritual. The ritual for purifying the temple has parallels in the Babylonian New Year festival that the deported priests may have known from their time of exile in Babylon. In Leviticus 16, the high priest has taken over the role of the Babylonian king. The elimination rite in which a goat, symbolically carrying the sins of the community, is sent to the desert is the origin of the word "scapegoat" that one finds in many languages. The goat is sent to Azazel, apparently a demon or a satyr. The goat is not a sacrifice. Rather, the power of the sins that the goat carries is broken by moving them to a place where they cannot do harm anymore

(Milgrom, 2004). The fact that this ritual is repeated every year reflects the need for forgiveness and God's willingness to offer a fresh start.

The call for holiness and the integration of the alien. Leviticus 17–26 was added to the P torah in Leviticus 1–16 in order to clarify or modify certain priestly concepts. The P writings insist on the blood taboo for the consumption of animals (Gen 9:1–7) and, at the same time, underline the importance of blood for purification purposes. However, they do not provide an explanation for the specific status of blood. The opening of the Holiness Code offers the only text where the cultic importance of blood is explained:

> For the life of the flesh is in the blood [cf. Gen 9:4]; and I have given it to you for making atonement for your lives on the altar; for, as life, it is the blood that makes atonement. Therefore I have said to the people of Israel: No person among you shall eat blood, nor shall any alien who resides among you eat blood. (Lev 17:11–12)

These verses also show how the Holiness Code includes the alien (*gēr*) in the cultic system of Israel. In many cases, the Holiness Code places the *gēr* on the same level as the Israelite (Lev 24:22). The *gēr* appears as a wealthy person who can even buy Israelites as slaves for a limited time (Lev 25:47–54). The alien is integrated in the temple cult and allowed to offer sacrifices (Lev 22:18–19). Also, the commandment to love one's neighbor as oneself (Lev 19:18) also applies to the alien: "you shall love the alien as yourself, for you were aliens in the land of Egypt" (19:34). The major difference between the *gēr* and the Israelite is the possession of land, from which the alien is excluded. But even this difference is somewhat qualified through the affirmation that Yahweh is the "real" owner of the land: "The land shall not be sold in perpetuity, for the land is mine; with me you are but aliens and tenants" (25:23).

Leviticus 19 and 25 clearly show a concern for social justice, as well as for the protection of the poor and the weak, which connects the Holiness Code to the Deuteronomic code (Deut 12–26). The call to become "holy" in Leviticus 17–26 may therefore be linked to the assertion that Israel is Yahweh's holy people in the book of Deuteronomy (7:6; 14:2; 26:19).

Sexuality and procreation. According to P theology, sexuality is, above all, a means for procreation, as stated in the creation account: "Be fruitful and multiply, and fill the earth and subdue it" (Gen 1:28). The Holiness Code affirms and further explicates this restrictive view. In Leviticus 15:24, it is not strictly forbidden for a man to have intercourse with a woman during her menstruation, although he is declared "impure" for seven days if he comes in contact with menstrual blood. In Leviticus 18:19, it is forbidden to have sexual relations during a woman's menstrual period, and Leviticus 20:18 even states that the man and the woman "shall be cut off from their people," an expression that refers to the death penalty. Leviticus 18 contains a long list of illicit sexual relations, mostly related to incest but not exclusively, repeated in Leviticus 20 and put under the death penalty. The interdiction of sexual intercourse between two men in Leviticus 18:22 and 20:13 ("If a man lies with a male as with a woman, both of them have committed an abomination; they shall be put to death") has received much attention and was used— and unfortunately still is—to discriminate against gay men. It is anachronistic to use these and other verses from Leviticus 18 and 20 uncritically for a contemporary sexual ethics. In order to understand these texts, one must bear in mind that ancient societies practiced a clear distinction of genders with regard to sexual roles: the man was active, the woman passive. A homosexual relation could not be tolerated, mainly because it represented a confusion of these assigned roles (Römer and Bonjour, 2005). A theological understanding and critique of chapters 18 and 20 must take into account the historical and sociological contexts in which these texts were written.

The Book of Numbers: Death and Life, Rebellion and Reconciliation. The book of Numbers does not have a clear organization. One can understand it as marking the passage from the first wilderness generation to the second, which corresponds with the two censuses in Numbers 1 and 26. The first part, especially chapters 11–21, contains rebellion stories of the first generation of the Exodus, which is doomed to die in the wilderness, whereas the second part of the book (chs. 26–36) deals with the second generation, which has the chance to enter the Promised Land as long as they do not imitate the faults of the first generation. Olson (1985) summarized the theology of the book of Numbers as follows: "The death of the old and the birth of the new." Every reader of the book has to decide whether she or he wants to belong to the first or second generation. This idea can also be found in Deuteronomy 30:15–20: "See, I have set before you today life and prosperity, death and adversity.... Choose life so that you and your descendants may live."

A cycle of rebellions. The most prominent theme of the book of Numbers is found in the rebellion stories in Numbers 11–21, which highlight the people's ongoing revolt against Moses, Aaron, and Yahweh. These rebellion stories have a concentric structure:

A (11:1–3) introduction: Yahweh's anger and Moses's intercession
B (11:4–23) the people's complaint about food and Moses's rebellion against Yahweh
C (12) Miriam's and Aaron's rebellion against Moses
  D (13–14) the people's complaint about the Exodus and the conquest
C′ (16–17) the Levites' and other groups' rebellion against Aaron
B′ (20:1–13) lack of water; Moses's and Aaron's rebellion against Yahweh
A′ (21:4–9) the people's rebellion against God: Yahweh's anger and Moses's intercession

This structure highlights the necessity of Moses's intercession, which is why Yahweh decides not to annihilate the people entirely. This negative assessment of the time of the wilderness, which contrasts with the older tradition in the prophets (Jer 2:2–3; Hos 2:16–17), results from the reflection on the catastrophe of the destruction of Jerusalem and the Babylonian Exile. In the Deuteronomistic History, this cataclysm is the result of the people's and the kings' disobedience, which already begins after the conquest of the land (see Judg 2). When in the first half of the Persian period the books of Joshua to Kings were separated from

Deuteronomy, which then became the end of the Torah, the question of when Israel started to disobey God is projected back into the time of the wilderness. This provides the Pentateuch with a reflection about the people's inability to conform to the divine Law.

Even Moses, who in the book of Numbers appears as the exemplary intercessor, is depicted negatively in some chapters. In Numbers 11, he complains about Yahweh's cruelty and wishes to die. According to the original form of verse 15, which was altered by the Masoretes, Moses says, "If this is the way you are going to treat me, put me to death at once—if I have found favor in your sight, do not let me see your wickedness" (the original text had *rāʿātekâ* ["your wickedness"] which the Masoretes changed into *rāʿtî* ["my misery"]). According to Numbers 20, Moses and Aaron have to die before entering the land because they did not keep Yahweh's commandments exactly (e.g., Yahweh asked Moses to take his staff and to speak to the rock to obtain water, whereas Moses speaks to the people and strikes the rock with his staff). In contrast to Deuteronomy 1:37, where Moses's death outside the land is explained by the fact that as the leader of the community he has to share the fate of the first wilderness generation, Numbers 20 insists on his own individual responsibility. The debate about collective and individual responsibility appears in several texts of the Hebrew Bible (Ezek 18:2–4) and continues in our own time.

The Ongoing Necessity for Interpretation and Actualization of the Torah. The book of Numbers and some late insertions in the book of Leviticus can be understood as forerunners of midrashic literature. Numbers 27 explicitly states that, after the revelation of the Law at Mt. Sinai, there remain "open cases," not anticipated by the Law. In this chapter, the daughters of Zelophehad claim they should inherit their father's land since he died and had no sons. So Moses brings the case before Yahweh, who accepts the daughters' claim and tells Moses to add a new law (27:8–11). However, the case is not ultimately settled. In the last chapter of the book (Num 36) people from Zelophehad's clan complain that this new law endangers the prosperity of the tribe since, in the case of women marrying someone from another tribe, their land would be lost. Thus, the Law is modified, without consultation of Yahweh again: "Every daughter who possesses an inheritance in any tribe of the Israelites shall marry one from the clan of her father's tribe, so that all Israelites may continue to possess their ancestral inheritance" (v. 8). Therefore, the book of Numbers ends with its actualization.

The same phenomenon occurs in Leviticus 10, which belongs to the latest additions of the book (Nihan, 2007). The chapter opens with the story of an illicit sacrifice presented by two sons of Aaron, who are then put to death. Moses then accuses Aaron of not having eaten his part of a sin offering and, thus, of having transgressed the Law (Lev 6:17–23). In Leviticus 10:16, it is said that Moses inquires about the sin offering, which in Hebrew corresponds to the repetition of the root *dāraš* ("to seek"). Aaron then explains that he cannot eat meat because he is mourning his dead sons, and Moses accepts this as an interpretation of the Law. According to the Masoretes, the double *dāraš* constitutes the middle of the Torah, which means that the center of the Torah is the quest for its understanding and application.

[*See also* Atonement; Blessings and Curses; Exodus; Foreigner; Historical Narratives (Joshua—2 Kings); Sacrifice and Offerings; *and* Torah.]

BIBLIOGRAPHY
Burkert, Walter. *Anthropologie des religiösen Opfers: Die Sakralisierung der Gewalt.* Munich: Carl Friedrich von Siemens Stiftung, 1984.

Douglas, Mary. *Leviticus as Literature.* Oxford: Oxford University Press, 1999.

Douglas, Mary. *Purity and Danger: An Analysis of Concepts of Pollution and Taboo.* Routledge Classics. London and New York: Routledge, 2010. First published 1966.

Houston, Walter J. "Towards an Integrated Reading of the Dietary Laws of Leviticus." In *The Book of Leviticus: Composition and Reception*, edited by Rolf Rendtorff and Robert A. Kugler, pp. 142–161. Leiden, The Netherlands, and Boston: Brill, 2003.

Joosten, Jan. *People and Land in the Holiness Code: An Exegetical Study of the Ideational Framework of the Law in Leviticus 17–26.* Vetus Testamentum Supplements 67. Leiden, The Netherlands: Brill, 1996.

Klostermann, August. "Ezechiel und das Heiligkeitsge-setz." *Zeitschrift für die lutherische Theologie und Kirche* 38 (1877): 401–445.

Knohl, Israel. *The Sanctuary of Silence: The Priestly Torah and the Holiness School.* Minneapolis: Fortress, 1995.

Köckert, Matthias. "Leben in Gottes Gegenwart: Zum Verständnis des Gesetzes in der priesterschriftlichen Literatur." *Jahrbuch für Biblische Theologie* 4 (1999): 29–61.

Kornfeld, Walter. "Reine und unreine Tiere im Alten Testament." *Kairos* 7 (1965): 134–147.

Marx, Alfred. "The Theology of the Sacrifice According to Leviticus 1–7." In *The Book of Leviticus: Composition and Reception*, edited by Rolf Rendtorff and Robert A. Kugler, pp. 103–120. Leiden, The Netherlands, and Boston: Brill, 2003.

Mathys, Hans-Peter. *Liebe deinen Nächsten wie dich selbst: Untersuchungen zum alttestamentlichen Gebot der Nächstenliebe (Lev 19,18).* Orbis Biblicus et Orientalis 71. Fribourg, Switzerland: Universitätsverlag; Göttingen, Germany: Vandenhoeck & Ruprecht, 1986.

Milgrom, Jacob. *Leviticus: A Book of Ritual and Ethics: Continental Commentaries.* Minneapolis: Fortress, 2004.

Nihan, Christophe. *From Priestly Torah to Pentateuch: A Study in the Composition of the Book of Leviticus.* Forschungen zum Alten Testament 2/25. Tübingen, Germany: Mohr Siebeck, 2007.

Olson, Dennis T. *The Death of the Old and the Birth of the New: The Framework of the Book of Numbers and the Pentateuch.* Brown Judaic Studies 71. Chico, Calif.: Scholars Press, 1985.

Römer, Thomas, ed. *The Books of Leviticus and Numbers.* Bibliotheca ephemeridium theologicarum Lovaniensum 215. Leuven, Belgium: Peeters, 2008.

Römer, Thomas, and Loyse Bonjour. *L'homosexualité dans le Proche-Orient ancien et la Bible.* Essais bibliques 37. Geneva, Switzerland: Labor et Fides, 2005.

Schwartz, Baruch J. "'Profane' Slaughter and the Integrity of the Priestly Code." *Hebrew Union College Annual* 67 (1996): 15–42.

Tylor, Edward Burnett. *Primitive Culture: Researches into the Development of Mythology, Philosophy, Religion Language, Art, and Custom.* 4th ed. Whitefish, Mont.: Kessinger, 2009. First published 1903.

Zenger, Erich. "Das Buch Levitikus als Teiltext der Tora/des Pentateuch: Eine synchrone Lektüre mit kanonischer Perspektive." In *Levitikus als Buch*, edited by Heinz-Josef Fabry and Hans-Winfried Jüngling, pp. 47–83. Berlin: Philo, 1999.

Thomas Römer

LIFE AND LIFE FORCE

In some of the latest texts in the Old Testament, there are at least two different views of what happens when a human life ends. One is found in Ecclesiastes, where the sage Qoheleth considers if there is any difference between animals and humans with regard to dying and death. As usual in this book, the answer is not exactly straightforward but cast in the form of a rhetorical question: "Who knows whether the human spirit goes upward and the spirit of animals goes downward to the earth?" (3:21). While there cannot be certainty, Qoheleth suggests there is no empirical reason to believe that the "spirit" of animals behaves any differently from the "spirit" of humans. Either one goes "down" and not "up," meaning that the *rûaḥ* disappears in the underworld, whereas the body returns to the ground from which it was made. The book of Daniel, on the other hand, develops a very different idea of what happens when people die or, more precisely, when righteous people die. While their bodies fall by the wayside, as it were, there is in fact something that goes up and continues the life of an individual person beyond physical death: "Those who are wise shall shine like the brightness of the sky, and those who lead many to righteousness, like the stars forever and ever" (12:3). Despite their differences, Qoheleth and Daniel share the assumption that humans are compound beings, which, in Daniel, means that there is a component of a human person that can continue even in a nonembodied form.

Anthropological Foundations. Given this basic anthropological consensus between two vastly different biblical traditions, it is somewhat surprising that much of the discussion in Old Testament anthropology seems to have taken for granted that the Old Testament presents an essentially holistic or unified view of a human person. This assumption finds its most pointed expression in Hans Walter Wolff's seminal monograph *Anthropology of the Old Testament* (1974). In the first part of this book, Wolff offers "an anthropological language primer." This is to say that the Old Testament combines a variety of different perspectives on the human person, without ever giving in to the multicentric anthropology that one finds, for example, in classical Greek philosophy with the distinction between *physis* and *psyche*.

Wolff defines a number of aspects that characterize human life, usually in relation to particular bodily functions or organs: the heart (*lēb*) stands for human reason, the kidneys for conscience, the throat (*nepeš*) for human neediness, the flesh for finitude, and, finally, the spirit (*rûaḥ*) expresses human empowerment. Wolff insists that these categories are analytical rather than ontological and that, according to the "Hebraic" view, a human person is an organic unit, although there is no terminology in the Old Testament that captures precisely this unity. It may be worth noting that the reason for Wolff's insisting on this particular aspect is not merely exegetical; as he mentions in passing in the introduction to his anthropology, any account of the Old Testament's view of the human person cannot ignore the fact that some of the most gruesome violence in the history of humankind occurred in the name of racial or ethnic superiority. Obviously, Wolff has the Third Reich in mind, when people were refused the right to exist based on what the Nazis considered ethnic or genetic defects. Wolff argues that the Bible does not support any such discriminatory judgment of the human person but rather starts from the assumption that every single human being, in all its facets, is an image of God.

Wolff's methodology has been largely influential well beyond the scope of Old Testament studies. Emma Brunner-Traut, Jan Assmann, and Ulrike Steinert have published a number of important contributions to the field of ancient Egyptian and Mesopotamian anthropology, employing semantic approaches to the subject that are quite similar to Wolff's. As one can expect, these, too, lead to the question of whether the different layers of a human person all point to some sort of hub or center.

Assmann (2009) argues that in the case of ancient Egypt the heart was considered as a midpoint and that, when the texts mention the heart, they envision human wholeness. Brunner-Traut and Steinert, on the other hand, conclude that most ancient Near Eastern texts depict humans as multicentric entities. Brunner-Traut (1988) uses the image of a lay figure (*Gliederpuppe*) to illustrate the Egyptian perception of a human being as intentionally compartmentalized into different "spheres of existence," both in the here and now and in the afterlife. Some of these spheres of existence, like the *Ka*, "soul," are not fully activated until the physical body dies. An individual's experience of oneness or, at the opposite end, of being fractured depends on how these different spheres (or centers) interact with each other. For Mesopotamia, Steinert (2012) offers a typology that comprises anthropological notions such as the head (*qaqqadu*, *rēšu*), the hand (*qātu*), the throat (*napištu*), the dream-soul (*zaqīqu*), and the intellect (*tēmu*). She concludes that Mesopotamian anthropologies go well beyond any simple dichotomy between "body" and "soul" and that they also resist construing a human person around any one particular capacity, such as self-consciousness or reason. This is to say that ancient Near Eastern anthropologies start from complex and experientially saturated descriptions of human life, without immediately trying to reduce this complexity to a transcendental core.

To give a specific example, Psalm 84:2 (MT 84:3) uses a series of anthropological key terms: "My soul [*nepeš*] longs, indeed it faints for the courts of the LORD; my heart [*lēb*] and my flesh [*bāśār*] sing for joy to the living God." On a Wolffian reading, the terms "soul," "heart," and "flesh" are essentially interchangeable and the accumulation of these terms expresses the Hebraic sense of "self." In a different perspective, however, these anthropological categories delineate distinct spheres of existence that overlap or interact in the concrete instances of human life.

Vitality and Life. Moving from these general observations about some current developments in Old Testament/ancient Near Eastern anthropology to a particular topic, it is the notion of life itself that poses interpretative challenges. If one asks what distinguishes living beings from dead matter, the answer is not altogether clear and varies between different traditions. The creation account in Genesis 1, for example, defines two different types of life and, thus, two different life forces. First, there is a basic potency for life already in the primordial ground, from which plants and vegetation emerge. Interestingly, God does not create plants but simply commands that the earth bring forth "vegetation: plants yielding seed, and fruit trees of every kind on earth that bear fruit with the seed in it" (Gen 1:11). This also establishes how life, at this level, continues: plants yield seed, and seed puts forth plants. Second, there is what Genesis 1:20–21, 24–25 calls "living beings" (nepeš ḥayyâ): the sea monsters, the fishes, the birds, and the field animals. The meaning of this phrase does not become clear until Genesis 9:4, which provides a definition of nepeš ḥayyâ: "Only, you shall not eat flesh with its life [nepeš], that is, its blood." In addition to being "earth creatures," animals and humans have this particular life force called nepeš. One can debate whether the blood itself is the nepeš or if it is the medium that carries the nepeš.

Be this as it may, the distinction between body and nepeš becomes ritually significant in the dietary laws of the Holiness Code (Lev 17:11–16), where separating flesh and blood is a prerequisite for the consumption of any kind of meat. The notion is that, while it is permissible to eat meat as something that comes from the ground and normally returns to it, the nepeš belongs to God as its Creator. It is never said that the nepeš returns to God and, in this sense, would be something like an immortal "soul." However, there is a clear understanding that the kind of life that distinguishes humans and animals from plants and "dead" matter is something that God gives to (or creates in) a living being and that he reclaims when life ends. Because animals and humans have a life force that exceeds the level of primordial vitality, they can live in accordance with the particular tasks that they are given: to be fruitful and multiply and fill the earth. One can argue that there is even a third tier in the ontological system of Genesis 1, which, however, is reserved for humankind alone, namely, being created in the image of God. It is in this context that the priestly text talks about gender difference (Gen 1:26, 28), the relationship between the generations (Gen 5:1–4), and in most general terms about the respect for the life of any other human being (Gen 9:4–6). Humans are prohibited to kill one another not because of the nepeš that they have but because of the image of God that they are.

Nepeš as Life Force. Even from this brief delineation it becomes clear that Genesis 1 establishes a subtle taxonomy of life, depicting humans as complex beings that participate in several different forms of life. However, the concept of nepeš draws the line between what one could call primitive vitality and life as something that has a particular place and purpose in the world that God creates. The idea of a life force as something distinct from the physical body that establishes a particular connection between the creator and the created world is attested well beyond the Genesis texts. Especially in the Psalms, the nepeš is the particular part of a human being that flourishes when it experiences the presence of God and suffers when this connection is broken. One of the key images in this regard is the "longing" for the enlivening presence of God (Ps 84:1–4). While the physical body with its senses and modes of perception locates the human being in the natural and social world, the nepeš belongs to the divine sphere, which means more specifically the temple and the cult. The nepeš desires to behold the face of God, and it enjoys the beauty of God's temple, where it belongs and where it truly prospers. This offers important insights for any Old Testament anthropology because the temple is not only God's dwelling place on earth but, via the nepeš, also a constitutive part of a human person. Without the cult, humans are not fully complete. While they may function in certain ways, there is a clear sense of deficiency and emptiness when the nepeš has no vital connection to its creator.

This raises the question of whether the connection between the nepeš and God continues even beyond death. In other words, does the nepeš concept segue into an Old Testament doctrine of immortality? Bernd Janowski (2013) and Johannes Schnocks (2009) argue that especially the Psalms move in this direction, although the two authors differ on how far the notion of immortality is developed.

A key text in this regard is Psalm 49 (cf. Pss 16; 73; 88) because it ties the experience of both death and resurrection to the nepeš. The first half of this psalm echoes the position that one also finds, for example, in Qoheleth: everyone dies and everyone's life force goes down to Sheol, which is not "hell" in the medieval sense but a place far from the presence of God with no life in it: "Truly, no ransom avails for one's life, there is no price one can give to God for it. For the ransom of life [*nepeš*] is costly, and can never suffice, that one should live on forever and never see the grave" (Ps 49:7–9 [MT 8–10]). While death is everyone's fate, the psalmist nevertheless expresses confidence that God will reclaim the faithful from the bonds of Sheol; and here, again, the *nepeš* plays a crucial role: "But God will ransom my soul [*nepeš*] from the power of Sheol, for he will receive me" (Ps 49:15 [MT 16]; cf. Pss 16:10; 88:3). Particularly remarkable about Psalm 49 is that it assigns the *nepeš* the role of personhood in a way that goes beyond its function of a life force. The hope that the psalmist expresses here is that the *nepeš* holds the individual pattern of a human being. However, this idea is not developed further in the Psalms or elsewhere in the Hebrew Bible. The closest parallel is Psalm 73:26, where the locus of an immortal self is not the *nepeš* but the "heart" (*lēb*): "My flesh and my heart may fail, but God is the strength of my heart and my portion forever."

This cultic concept of a life force was vulnerable to the crisis of the sixth century B.C.E., when the Temple was destroyed and parts of the Judean population were deported to Babylon. Psalm 42 seems to reflect precisely on the dilemma that occurred when the world around the belief system of ancient Israel started to change dramatically. Psalm 42 records the lament of one of the exiles, apparently a member of the Korahite temple singers, who is no longer able to feel and perceive the nearness of God: "As a deer longs for flowing streams, so my soul [*nepeš*] longs for you, O God.... My tears have been my food day and night, while people say to me continually, 'Where is your God?' These things I remember, as I pour out my soul [*nepeš*]: how I went with the throng, and led them in procession to the house of God, with glad shouts and songs of thanksgiving, a multitude keeping festival" (42:1, 3–4 [MT 2, 4–5]). The *nepeš* despairs and in fact wastes away because it has lost the connection to its life-giving center.

The response to this crisis seems to have been twofold. With the old cultic worldview having fallen victim to the rapidly changing political landscape, some of the theologies of the exilic and postexilic periods abandoned the idea that the *nepeš* was the life force in a human being that also established a unique and intimate divine–human connection (cf. Gen 2:4–7; 6:3; Eccl 3:21; Job 32:8; 34:14–15; Ps 104:27–30). Rather, these theologies now redefine the life force as the *rûaḥ* ("spirit") that God gives or, literally, breathes into every human being. This takes us back to the Primeval History, where this *rûaḥ*-based understanding of the life force occurs in the second account of creation in Genesis 2. On the other hand, there are theologies that keep the *nepeš* but reenvision the place where it connects with the divine sphere. According to Psalm 119, for example, the *nepeš* does not desire to behold the face of God in the Temple but to hear the voice of God in the words of scripture.

***Rûaḥ* as the Life Force.** Genesis 2 builds its account of the creation of Adam and Eve around the same phrase that was already introduced in Genesis 1, namely, the "living being" (*nepeš ḥayyâ*). However, the text goes into much greater detail about the creation of humankind. There are basically two ways of translating Genesis 2:7. The first is the rendering in most major English translations: "Then the LORD God formed man from the dust of the ground, and breathed into his nostrils the breath of life; and the man became a living being" (e.g., KJV, NIB, NRSV). It emphasizes that Adam as a "living being" emerges from the mixing of two components, a physical body and the *nišmat ḥayyim* ("breath of life"). The second translation is less common, although it may be linguistically preferable: "Then the LORD God formed Adam from the dust of the ground. Then he breathed into his nostrils the breath of life, *and thus* Adam became a living being" (e.g., TNK; italics added). The emphasis in this version is on the breath of life as the distinctive characteristic of humankind. While plants and animals have bodies, the divine breath is reserved for humankind alone. Even more important, however, is that Genesis 2:7 introduces a different understanding of the life force that separates humans from animals. While the term *nepeš* is the generic expression for "living being," the actual life force is now the "breath of life," which comes directly from

God and enlivens the physical body beyond the vitality that comes from the primordial ground. This spirit-concept of the life force is not tied to the cultic world of Psalm 49 or even Genesis 1; it is intrinsically universalistic since it does not require any specific point of orientation (such as the Temple).

As many of the exilic and early postexilic theologies show (Schuele, 2012a), the idea of God's presence in the form of God's Spirit was a productive paradigm in a time when the world had lost any definite center and when dislocation and Diaspora had become permanent realities for many nations and ethnic groups throughout ancient antiquity. Thus, it is no surprise that there are several different variations of the *rûaḥ* as life force.

In contrast to Genesis 2, Psalm 104 views the divine *rûaḥ* as that which enlivens humans and animals alike and on which they depend: "These all look to you to give them their food in due season; when you give to them, they gather it up; when you open your hand, they are filled with good things. When you hide your face, they are dismayed; when you take away their breath, they die and return to their dust. When you send forth your spirit, they are created; and you renew the face of the ground" (Ps 104:27–30). The last sentence emphasizes that created matter and the divine spirit form the dual matrix of all life. The spirit or breath of God sets the rhythm of the created order, which eliminates the need for any mediating instances. One finds the same sentiment of the omnipresence of God's spirit in Psalm 139, which is a long meditation on God's presence in the world. When the psalmist asks where one can hide from God's *rûaḥ* (v. 7), the answer is already implied: there is no corner between heaven and earth that the *rûaḥ* cannot permeate. However, it is also worth noting that even in Psalms 104 and 139, arguably some of the youngest texts of the Psalter, the older cultic theology left its imprint since there are still references to God's hiddenness (104:29; 139:12, 15), which is reminiscent of the same motif in some of the cultic psalms (cf. Pss 13:1; 27:9; 44:24; 51:11; 69:17; 88:14; 102:2; 143:7).

Scripture as Temple. While one can argue that in a number of biblical traditions the *rûaḥ* apparently replaced the *nepeš* as the life force, this is not the only development that took place, as one can see in the so-called Torah psalms (1; 19; 119). The question of God's presence in the world and how this presence can be experienced directs the reader's attention to the Word of God and, more specifically, to God's Torah. While it is not clear whether the term "torah" points specifically to the Sinai legislation (perhaps even the five books of Moses) or means "law/instruction" in a broader sense, the form of God's presence here is the word as either written down or conveyed orally. It is certainly no coincidence that in these psalms the word of God is what the *nepeš* desires. The terminology is strikingly similar to the cultic psalms, suggesting that the new point of orientation for the *nepeš* is not the temple or any other physical space but the word of God as something that speaks to the *nepeš* from beyond space and time; compare Psalm 84:2, "My *nepeš* longs, indeed it faints for the courts of the LORD" (author's translation), with Psalm 119:81, "My *nepeš* longs for your salvation; I wait for your word" (author's translation).

In this view, the word and the Torah of God have become a spiritualized temple to which the *nepeš* is drawn as to its fountain of life (Ps 119:25). Psalm 19:8 (19:7 NRSV) says that the Torah, literally translated, "returns" the *nepeš*, which probably means that it restores it to life (cf. Ps 119:28). This symbiosis between human *nepeš* and divine Word can hardly be overestimated with regard to some of the core convictions in both Judaism and Christianity. The idea that the Word of God and its forms of embodiment, such as the Torah, the prophets, and the gospels, are of existential significance and that they offer a living connection between God and humankind has its roots in the transformation of the ancient Israelite temple theology into a theology of word and scripture. What made this theological transformation possible was the anthropological assumption that there is something in a human being that both depends on and indulges in the nearness of God.

[*See also* Anthropology; Creation; Exile and Dislocation; Genesis; Image of God; Psalms; Sacrifice and Offerings; Tabernacles, Temples, and Synagogues; Torah; *and* Word (Logos).]

BIBLIOGRAPHY

Assmann, Jan. "Konstellative Anthropologie: Zum Bild des Menschen im alten Ägypten." In *Der Mensch im Alten Israel: Neue Forschungen zur alttestamentlichen Anthropologie*, edited by Bernd Janowski and Kathrin Liess, pp. 95–120. Freiburg, Germany: Herder, 2009.

Brunner-Traut, Emma. "Der menschliche Körper—eine Gliederpuppe." *Zeitschrift für Ägyptische Sprache und Altertumskunde* 115 (1988): 8–14.

Di Vito, Robert A. "Old Testament Anthropology and the Construction of Personal Identity." *Catholic Biblical Quarterly* 61 (1999): 217–238.

Janowski, Bernd. *Arguing with God: A Theological Anthropology of the Psalms*. Louisville, Ky.: Westminster John Knox, 2013.

Schnocks, Johannes. *Rettung und Neuschöpfung: Studien zur alttestamentlichen Grundlegung einer gesamtbiblischen Theologie der Auferstehung*. Göttingen, Germany: Vandenhoeck & Ruprecht, 2009.

Schroer, Silvia, and Thomas Staubli. *Body Symbolism in the Bible*. Collegeville, Minn.: Liturgical Press, 2001.

Schuele, Andreas. "Made in the 'Image of God': The Concepts of Divine Images in Gen 1–3." *Zeitschrift für die Alttestamentliche Wissenschaft* 117 (2005): 1–20.

Schuele, Andreas. "The Notion of Life in the Anthropological Discourse of the Primeval History." *Hebrew Bible and Ancient Israel* 4 (2012a): 483–501.

Schuele, Andreas. "The Spirit of YHWH and the Aura of Divine Presence." *Interpretation* 66 (2012b): 16–28.

Sommer, Benjamin. *The Bodies of God and the World of Ancient Israel*. New York: Cambridge University Press, 2009.

Steinert, Ulrike. *Aspekte des Menschseins in Mesopotamien: Eine Studie zu Person und Identität im 2. und 1. Jt. v. Chr.* Leiden, The Netherlands: Brill, 2012.

Wolff, Hans Walter. *Anthropology of the Old Testament*. Minneapolis: Augsburg Fortress, 1974.

Andreas Schuele

LIGHT AND DARKNESS

From ancient times "light and darkness" formed a merism (contrasting pair). In the ancient Near East (including Israel) light was seen as the ultimate condition for life on earth, and in creation stories light is often mentioned as one of the first aspects created to make life on earth possible. Light and darkness have become common metaphors for "the good" and "the bad." The merism has led to the idea of dualism, well known in Persia (Zarathustra) but also attested in ancient Egypt in the binary opposition of the gods Horus and Seth.

The Ancient Near East: Ancient Egypt. In ancient Egypt it was a common idea that light was created in the primordial beginning of the world. Time before creation was designated as "united darknesses," meaning the ultimate form of darkness. The world of the dead was seen as a land of darkness, in which no light could penetrate unless it was protected. Every night the dead had to be freed from the chains of darkness. Only the damned remained in eternal darkness. The god Osiris was the master of the primordial darkness. Darkness was seen as the realm of the forces of the enemy, the Apophis serpent who formed a constant death threat to the created world and the living. With the help of Seth, this monster had to be defeated every night. The daily kindling of light in the temple cult symbolized the victory of light over darkness. It therefore expelled not only darkness but also enemies. The beams of the sun god Re also sustained creation and expelled darkness. The acme of the Egyptian belief in the ultimate need of light was reached in the sun anthems for the god Aton during the Eighteenth Dynasty at Amarna. Also, the conflict between the good god Horus and the evil Seth was often expressed in contrasting terms like light and darkness. Sun and moon were the eyes of Horus, god of heaven. According to the myths, the eye of Horus was wounded time and again by Seth but was always healed; therefore, the so-called Udjat-eye (the healed eye of Horus) has been developed into a symbol for everything that secured life and light on earth. Artists shaped it into marvelous amulets, protecting those who wore it.

The Ancient Near East: Ugarit. In the texts of Ugarit (thirteenth century B.C.E.) the contrast between the power of light and the power of darkness occurs frequently. In a mythological text (*KTU* 1.100) a tree, probably the tree of life, has been poisoned by Ḥorrān, a rebelling god who is known as the Prince (*šr*, in later Islam a name of the Devil) and the Destroyer (*'bd*; cf. Abbadon/Abaddon in 1 QHᵃ 11:16 from Qumran and Rev 9:11). The evil god placed a venomous serpent in the tree that has become a tree of death. As a result the whole world withered and a poisonous fog enveloped everything in deep darkness. A divine being called Adam was sent to the earth to detoxify the tree but failed and was bitten by the serpent. Only the sun goddess Šapšu seemed able to save the world by summoning all the great gods to charm the snake. In the end the evil god Ḥorrān himself appeared to be the one who expelled the poison by uprooting the tree of death.

The sun goddess often plays a crucial role in expelling the forces of darkness: she expels not only Ḥorrān but also Yam, the sea god who dwells in the deep dark of the sea (*KTU* 1.2:3.11), and Mot, the god of death and the underworld. In an incantation (*KTU* 1.82:5–7) she is invoked to bring to life to a girl who has made a covenant with death, and together with the god Baʿal she seizes the serpents that attack the girl. Serpents, scorpions, and demons were all related to the gods of the netherworld, Mot and Ḥorrān. Because Šapšu visited the netherworld every night (at the end of the day she was supposed to descend into the earth), she was able to expel the powers of evil in the underworld by her light. The helpers of Mot were "sons of darkness" (*bn.ġlmt*; cf. the Qumranic "sons of darkness") who obscure the day (cf. Amos 5:18–20; Zeph 1:15). They also color the wings of fate brownish (*KTU* 1.4:7.54–58). Šapšu gets dusty, and the heavens are soiled by Mot (death, *KTU* 1.6:2.24–25).

In the Ugaritic myths, the seasonal pattern of the year seems to form the background of these concepts. In nature the sandy sirocco winds obscure the sun in spring and autumn. However, these phenomena were taken as symbols for all evil powers. Yearly the combat with the evil ones returned and the god Baʿal defeated them time and again, albeit with the help of Šapšu and Baʿal's spouse Anat. There are no texts that mention offspring of Šapšu, who could be called children of light. The combat always concerns Mot and his children of darkness, on the one side, and Šapšu and the other good gods, on the other side. As in Hittite texts, the benevolent expression of a good Ugaritic king is expressed by calling him the "sun" whose face "shines" upon his subjects.

The Ancient Near East: Mesopotamia. In a Sumerian text dated ca. 2000 B.C.E. the god An lightens heaven and darkens the earth before starting his work of creation. The Babylonian Šamaš Hymn (originating from the second millennium B.C.E. but transmitted in many later copies) identifies the sun god Šamaš as the illuminator of the whole heaven, who makes light in the darkness above and below. His radiance spreads like a net over the earth and brightens the gloom of the distant mountains (lines 1–6, 176–177), and he gives wisdom to humankind (line 149). Šamaš enlightens the darkness in the underworld and cares for the spirits of the dead (line 31). Indeed, he is the light of everything (line 34), and his glare reaches down to the abyss so that the monsters of the deep behold his light (line 38). He is the supreme one in the pantheon (line 46) and scans the plans of all the lands (lines 49–50).

The Old Testament. According to Genesis 1, God's first creative activity concerned the light and the separating of light and darkness (Gen 1:2–3). Beforehand the entire world had been enveloped in darkness. This was complemented by the creation of the lamps in heaven (in the biblical account sun and moon are not deities) on day four (Gen 1:14–18; cf. Jer 31:35). Isaiah 45:7 seems to refer to God's creative separation of light and darkness, while also using them as metaphors for peace and evil (cf. Isa 45:19). According to Job 26:10, the horizon forms the dividing line between light and darkness. From the creation forward, darkness forms the opposite of light, and this opposition is often used as a merism referring to good and bad. "Light and darkness" (*phōs kai skotos*) is used as a parallel of "nights and days" in the Old Greek text of Daniel, and the two pairs are summoned to praise God.

One of the seven plagues in Egypt is darkness, while at the same time the people of Israel had light (Exod 10:21–23). Amos 5:8 refers back to primordial times when God turned deep darkness (*salmawet*) into morning and darkens the day into night, but the prophet warns those who long for the day of the Lord (Amos 5:18, 20; also 8:9), for this time it will not be a day of light (*ʾôr*) but a day of darkness (*ḥôšek*). The prophet Isaiah warns people who exchange light and darkness, good and bad (Isa 5:20; cf. Job 17:12). Light turned into darkness is a common image for God's punishment (Isa 5:30; Jer 13:16; Ezek 32:8; Zech 14:6; Job 22:25; Lam 3:2), whereas God's power to create light in the darkness was presented as promising imagery (2 Sam 22:29; Isa 9:2; 42:16; Mic 7:8–9; Zech 14:7; 112:4; Job 29:3). The presence of God often is accompanied by light (Exod 13:21; 14:20; Ps 104:2), and God is designated as light replacing sun and moon (Isa 60:19–20) or when describing a situation of righteousness and salvation (Isa 60:18, 21; cf. Isa 30:26). God may shine on his people as it is prayed for in the priestly blessing (Num 6:24–26; cf. Ps 4:7[6]; 31:17[16]; 67:2[1]; 76:5[4]). This resembles Egyptian representations of the beams of the sun god ending in tender, bslessing hands that still glimmer through this imagery.

God also gives insight and knowledge by his light (Isa 2:5; Prov 29:13). Psalm 56:13 and Job 33:30 explicitly mention the "light of life" that God may shine upon humankind. Second Isaiah often uses the imagery of light and darkness. He contrasts Babylon the enemy that has to go into darkness (Isa 47:5) with the exiled Israelites who are called from darkness into the light (Isa 49:9), even becoming a light to the nations, radiating God's light (Isa 42:6; 49:6; 60:1–3; see also Isa 58:8). Several biblical and extra-biblical personal names also declare God a light of humankind, e.g., Uriel (God is my light) and Uriah (the Lord is my light). Similarly, Psalm 27:1 says, "The LORD is my light and my salvation." Psalm 119:105 takes God's word as a lamp for the feet and a light to one's path. A lamp in those days was merely a wick in an oil lamp, so one should not expect that stumbling becomes impossible.

Qumran. The *War Scroll* (1QM, dated in the second half of the first century B.C.E.) describes the combat between the sons of light (*bny ʿwr*) and the sons of darkness (*bny ḥwšk*). The "sons of light" was a favorite designation of the Qumranic Essenes for their own community (e.g., 1QS 1:9–10; 2:16; 3:13, 24–25; 1QM 1:1, 3, 7). This title relates them to the Prince of Lights (*šr ʿwrm*, also *šr mʾwr* in 1QM 13:10), who has the dominion over the sons of justice, who walk on paths of light (1QS 3:20). The sons of darkness are the

Kittim and all other traditional enemies of Israel as well as the "violators of the covenant" from among Israel (1QM 1:2) and the "cursed ones" (1QS 2:17). They are related to the angel of darkness (*mʾlk ḥwšk*, also called Belial). He has the dominion over "the sons of deceit, who walk on paths of darkness" (1QS 3:20–21) and had to be defeated by the sons of light. After the war, the sons of light will shine to all the edges of the earth (1QM 1:8). The dualism between light and darkness has an ethical meaning, referring to righteousness and evil, respectively. According to the Essenes' *Rule of the Community* (first quarter of the first century B.C.E.), God created two spirits among humankind, the spirit of truth and the spirit of deceit (1QS 3:13—4:16, esp. 3:18–19). On the day of visitation God will judge both armies, and the sons of darkness will go to the abyss until their final destruction (1QS 3:13).

New Testament. The imagery of light and darkness is taken over in the New Testament where the promised light in the darkness (Isa 9:2) is interpreted as the coming of Jesus (Matt 4:16; cf. John 3:19). The emphasis is put on the contrast between good and evil (Matt 6:23; Luke 11:35; John 3:19). Light and darkness are even explicitly related to the power of God and Satan, respectively (Acts 26:18; cf. Rom 13:12), undeniably showing some form of dualism. Satan is said to disguise himself as an angel of light (*aggelos phōtos*) as his servants disguise themselves as servants of righteousness (2 Cor 11:14–15). Light in general stands for righteousness (Eph 5:9), whereas darkness is related to evil, hatred (1 John 2:9), and death (Luke 1:79; Eph 5:14).

In Gethsemane, Jesus hands himself over to the high priests and declares that now is their hour, the reign of darkness (Luke 22:53); and when Jesus dies, the land is in darkness for three hours and the sun stops shining (Luke 23:44–45). After Jesus's resurrection, the women see two men in shining garments (Luke 24:4); and it is said that his appearances come at dawn, the time when the change from darkness to light occurs (Matt 28:1; cf. Luke 23:54). Often this contrasting use of light and darkness has been traced back to Persian religion (Zarathustra) with its two spirits, Spenta Mainyu, who is good and who works through the highest god Ahura Mazda, and Angra Mainyu, who is evil. However, the idea of a world of darkness, death, demons, and enemies (see also Matt 8:12; 22:13; 25:30) opposite to a world of light with the good god/gods and righteous people appears already in religious texts of ancient Egypt (especially from the Amarna period on) and Ugarit, as well as in the Old Testament.

The imagery of Second Isaiah that the blind people will be led into the light and their eyes opened recurs in the New Testament (e.g., Rom 2:19). Moreover, the followers of Jesus must become lights to others (Matt 5:14–16; Acts 13:47, quoting Isaiah texts; 26:23) and must shine forth as lights in the world (Phil 2:15); they are "children of light" (John 12:36; Luke 16:8; Eph 5:8; 1 Thess 5:5). In Luke 16:8 the "sons of light" are opposed to the "sons of this world." In 1 Peter 2:9 they are described as those called out of the darkness into God's light, whereas 2 Corinthians 6:14 harshly concludes that light and darkness have nothing to do with each other. The images again refer to righteousness as the opposite of lawlessness. In John, Jesus is often described as the light for the world (John 8:12; 9:5; 11:9; 12:35–36; see also 1 John 1:5). People believing in him will come out of the darkness (John 12:46). The Bible ends with the image of light, making God the great light that replaces sun and moon (Rev 22:5; cf. Isa 60:19–20).

Theological Significance of the Imagery of Light and Darkness. Some of the people of Judah saw the Exile as an experience of darkness (Lam 3:2). But Second Isaiah (Isa 40–55) opposes a completely pessimistic view. He emphasizes that it is indeed God who has created this darkness (not any other god) but that he also will reverse this situation. In the end God will create light (Isa 45:7). This is a typically monotheistic statement about God. At the end of exile, darkness will be the fate of the enemy, not of God's people (Isa 47:5). In the New Testament, the imagery of light and darkness is taken up again, especially in the Gospel of John: Jesus is the light of the world (John 8:12; 9:5). Nevertheless, Matthew also knows Second Isaiah's double meaning of light: not only the servant will become a light but so will the entire nation. In Matthew 5:14 Jesus takes up this wider

meaning: those who will follow him must show themselves to be the light of the world.

[*See also* Apocalypticism; Creation; Devils and Demons; *and* Underworld and Hell.]

BIBLIOGRAPHY

Aalen, Sverre. *Die Begriffe "Licht" und "Finsternis" im Alten Testament, im Spätjudentum und im Rabbinismus.* Skrifter: Utgitt av Norske Videnskaps-Akademi i Oslo, II. Historisk-Filosofisk Klasse. Oslo: J. Dybwad, 1951.

Aalen, Sverre. "'ôr." In *Theologisches Wörterbuch zum Alten Testament*, edited by G. Johannes Botterweck, Vol. 1, pp. 160–182. Stuttgart: Kohlhammer, 1973.

Berlejung, Angelika. "Licht/Finsternis." In *Handbuch theologischer Grundbegriffe zum Alten und Neuen Testament*, 2d ed., edited by Angelika Berlejung and Christian Frevel, pp. 303–304. Darmstadt, Germany: Wissenschaftliche Buchgesellschaft, 2009.

Böcher, Otto. "Licht und Feuer" (esp. "Licht und Feuer II: Altes Testament und antikes Judentum"). In *Theologische Realenzyklopädie*, edited by Gerhard Müller, Vol. 21, pp. 83–121, esp. 90–97. Berlin: De Gruyter, 2000.

Colpe, Carsten. "Lichtsymbolik im alten Iran und antiken Judentum." *Studium Generale: Zeitschrift für die Einheit der wissenschaften im Zusammenhang ihrer Begriffsbildungen und Forschungsmethoden* 18, no. 2 (1965): 116–133.

Grieshammer, Reinhard. "Licht." In *Lexikon der Ägyptologie*, edited by Wolfgang Helck and Wolfhart Westendorf, Vol. 3, pp. 1033–1034. Wiesbaden, Germany: Harrassowitz, 1980.

Hempel, Johannes. "Die Lichtsymbolik im Alten Testament." *Studium Generale: Zeitschrift für die Einheit der wissenschaften im Zusammenhang ihrer Begriffsbildungen und Forschungsmethoden* 13, no. 6 (1960): 352–368.

Hornung, Erik. "Licht und Fisternis in der Vorstellungswelt Altägyptens." *Studium Generale: Zeitschrift für die Einheit der wissenschaften im Zusammenhang ihrer Begriffsbildungen und Forschungsmethoden* 18, no. 2 (1965): 6–83.

Hornung, Erik. "Dunkelheit." In *Lexikon der Ägyptologie*, edited by Wolfgang Helck and Wolfhart Westendorf, Vol. 3, pp. 1153–1154. Wiesbaden, Germany: Harrassowitz, 1975.

Müller-Winkler, Claudia. "Adjatauge." In *Lexikon der Ägyptologie*, edited by Wolfgang Helck and Wolfhart Westendorf, Vol. 3, pp. 824–826. Wiesbaden, Germany: Harrassowitz, 1986.

Schwankl, Otto. *Licht und Finsternis: Ein metaphorisches Paradigma in den johanneischen Schriften.* Freiburg, Germany: Herder, 1995. See esp. pp. 52–73.

Westendorf, Wolfhart. "Horusauge." In *Lexikon der Ägyptologie*, edited by Wolfgang Helck and Wolfhart Westendorf, Vol. 3, pp. 48–51. Wiesbaden, Germany: Harrassowitz, 1980.

Marjo C. A. Korpel

LOGOS

See Word (Logos).

LORD

In the English Bible tradition the word "lord" is used to designate a person having authority, power, or influence. Its capitalized forms, "Lord" and "Lᴏʀᴅ," are employed in reference to God, Jesus, and occasionally the Holy Spirit.

Old Testament/Hebrew Bible. In the Old Testament several Hebrew words are translated "lord" or "Lᴏʀᴅ." Isaac blessed his son Jacob (Gen 27:29, 37): "Be lord (*gĕbîr*) over your brothers, and may your mother's sons bow down to you." The Hebrew word translated "lord" connotes the head of a family. Isaac's blessing grants his second born authority over his brothers, extended family, and, by extension, surrounding peoples.

The Hebrew word *adonai* occurs more frequently for persons in authority. Some of the earliest in the canon refer to the patriarchs (Gen 23:6; 32:4) as heads of family and Joseph as vicegerent over Egypt (Gen 42:10; 45:9). Given his significance in the tradition, it is no surprise that Moses is also called "lord" (e.g., Num 36:2). The title is applicable not only to those inside the covenant community; it can also refer to foreign kings and generals: for example, Sisera (Judg 4:18); Hanun, king of Ammon (2 Sam 10:3); and Ben-hadad, king of Aram (1 Kgs 20:14). Far more frequently, however, Israel's kings are called "lord": Saul (1 Sam 26:15), David (1 Sam 25:25; 29:10; 2 Chr 2:14), Solomon (1 Kgs 3:17; 2 Chr 13:6). It makes no difference whether a king is viewed positively or negatively; the term "lord" is deemed appropriate for Israel's rulers (e.g., Ahab in 1 Kgs 18:11). The phrase "my lord the king" becomes commonplace in referring to David and Davidic kings. Other notable leaders (e.g., Ezra 10:3) are addressed as "lord" because they are considered religious authorities. Similarly, prophets of Israel may be called "lord" since they speak and act on heaven's behalf (1 Kgs 18:7 [Elijah]; 2 Kgs 4:16 [Elisha]).

The Hebrew word *adonai* is employed even more frequently to refer to God (e.g., Gen 18:27; Exod 4:10; Deut 9:26) and heavenly messengers. When used in reference to God, *adonai* is translated with an initial capital: "Lord." Though rare in the Pentateuch, the title becomes more common in the Second Temple period. It may be used by itself or in combination with other titles. Angels, because they are messengers of God, carry heavenly authority and so may properly be addressed as "lord" (lowercase in English translation). The prophet Zechariah, for example, speaks to his angelic guide as "my lord" when being directed through a series of visions (Zech 1:9; 4:4).

Perhaps the most significant use of "Lord" in the Old Testament is its translation of the divine name (Heb., *YHWH*). While there are many titles given to the God of Israel in the Hebrew Bible, there is only one name by which God is to be known: the name revealed to Moses in the wilderness (Exod 3:13–15; 6:2–3; 20:2). The name (referred to as the *tetragrammaton*, "four letters") occurs about 6,800 times in the Old Testament (e.g., Gen 2:4; Exod 17:15; Judg 6:22; 1 Sam 25:26; Ps 8:1; 23:1; Isa 40:3). Its sacredness is reflected in the prohibition of its use in any empty or idle way (Exod 20:7). The *Shema* (Deut 6:4) emphasizes the oneness of God as well as the unique covenantal relationship between Israel and her God (cf. Isa 45:5, 6, 11).

The majority of modern English translations render the tetragrammaton "Lᴏʀᴅ." The capitalization of each letter distinguishes this use from "Lord," a word used to translate other Hebrew words for God or persons in authority, and signals to the reader that God's unique covenant name lays beneath the translation. The *Oxford English Dictionary* reports the use of "Lᴏʀᴅ" for the divine name as early as the eleventh century C.E.

The most influential English translation (KJV, 1611) renders most occurrences of the divine name as

"LORD." Nevertheless, in seven places it represents the name "Jehovah," a combination of the consonants of *YHWH* (Latinized to *JHVH*) with the vowels of *adonai* (Exod 6:3; Ps 83:18; Isa 12:2; 26:4). Three of these usages refer to place-names important in the narrative (e.g., Jehovah-jireh; Gen 22:14). For centuries Jehovah becomes effectively "God's name" in English.

Later translations expanded the ways in which the divine name is rendered. The Jerusalem Bible (1966), for example, uses "Yahweh" to translate the tetragrammaton. Others use "Yahweh" in select places (e.g., Exod 6:3) but generally render the divine name "LORD" (NLT, 1996/2004; HCSB, 1999/2002). A few translations represent the divine name "Jehovah" throughout (YLT, 1898; ASB, 1901; NWT, 1961). The Complete Jewish Bible (1998) substitutes "Adonai" (Heb., "Lord") for the tetragrammaton. James Moffatt's translation (1935) and The Voice Bible (2012) translate the divine name as "the Eternal." Still, the majority of modern translations continue the practice of rendering the divine name "LORD" (ESV, 2011; NRSV, 1989; NAS, 1977).

While most occurrences of the divine name are translated "LORD," the name may be translated "God" when used in combination with *Adonai*. So the Hebrew address *Adonai YHWH* is generally rendered "LORD God" (e.g., Deut 9:26; 1 Kgs 2:26; Ps 69:6; Isa 61:1). Although the expression occurs throughout the Old Testament, it is most frequent in Isaiah, Jeremiah, Ezekiel, and Amos.

There are a number of phrases utilizing the word "Lord" in the Hebrew Bible. "The angel of the LORD," for example, refers to an angel in whom the name of God dwells (Exod 23:20–21). In some cases it is difficult to distinguish between the angel of the Lord and the Lord himself (Gen 16:7–14; 22:11–18). "The day of the LORD" is a common reference to a coming day of judgment (first mentioned in Amos 5:18–20). Israel's preexilic prophets regard it as a day to be feared because God's people are not likely to escape God's wrath (Isa 2:12–22; Ezek 7:7–12). Postexilic prophets, however, associate the phrase with a promise of blessing and security to Israel while threatening

judgment against her enemies (Zech 12–14; Joel 3–7; Mal 3:2). The title "LORD of hosts" occurs about 240 times in the Hebrew Bible, to underscore God's sovereignty over celestial or angelic powers (e.g., 1 Sam 1:3; Ps 24:10; most frequently in Isa, Jer, Hag, Zech, and Mal). In the Psalter the community of the faithful is commanded to "Praise the LORD" (e.g., Ps 111:1; 147:1; 150:6). This directive is so common that the Hebrew expression *hallelujah*, "praise-Yah" (a shortened form of Yahweh), becomes typical in liturgical usage.

In Daniel 2:47 and 5:23 the English word "Lord" is used to translate the Aramaic *mārēʾ* in reference to God as the "Lord of kings" and "Lord of heaven."

New Testament. In the New Testament the English word "lord" or "Lord" translates two Greek words. The Greek word *despotēs* is rendered in some versions "lord"—in others, "master"—when referring to slaveowners (e.g., 1 Tim 6:1–2; 1 Pet 2:18). It is also used in referring to God in prayerful address (e.g., Luke 2:29; Acts 4:24) and Jesus as sovereign (Jude 1:4).

The most significant Greek word translated "lord" or "Lord" in the New Testament is *kyrios*. Like the Hebrew word *adonai*, *kyrios* is employed with regard to divine and human referents. In Greco-Roman antiquity the word was used in various ways: (1) in the vocative form as polite address (Arrian, *Epict. diss.* 4.1.57; P. Giess. 61.17, 85.16); (2) in regard to masters or owners of property including slaves, houses, businesses, or land (Aristotle, *Pol.* 2.9; Arrian, *Epict. diss.* 4.1.59, 116, 145); (3) in expressing the divinity of rulers (P. Oxy. 1.37.5; 2.246.30, 33, 36); (4) in reference to the gods and goddesses of various religions (e.g., P. Oxy. 1.110 [Sarapis]; *Corpus inscriptionum graecarum* 5070 [Hermes]; Plut *Is. Os.* 40 [Isis]). The same patterns of usage are reflected in the New Testament (e.g., Matt 27:63; Mark 12:9; Gal 4:1; 1 Pet 3:6; 1 Cor 8:6–8; Eph 4:6) with one exception: pious Jews apparently refuse to call the emperor *kyrios* because of the word's close association with the name of God (cf. Josephus, *War* 7.10.1.418–419).

In Greek versions like the Septuagint, *kyrios* designates people who possessed authority: heads of families, husbands of wives, owners of livestock, masters of slaves, and kings (e.g., Gen 27:29, 37; Exod 21:4; 28; 1 Sam 1:15; 2 Sam 16:4; Isa 1:3). *Kyrios* also translates several Hebrew words for God including *adonai* (e.g., Josh 3:11; Ps 97:5 [LXX 96:5]; Mic 4:13; Zech 4:14) and *ʾelohim* (e.g., Gen 21:2; Exod 3:4; Judg 6:20; Isa 61:10; Dan 1:2, 9). *Kyrios* is the word of choice for translating the tetragrammaton (more than 6,000 times). Exactly how early this translational practice emerged is difficult to say because the manuscript tradition is not uniform. Still, there are good reasons to conclude that Greek-speaking Jews vocalized *kyrios* instead of the divine name when reading scripture in synagogue services during the late Second Temple period. This communal practice is reflected in the manuscript tradition.

Under the influence of the Septuagint, New Testament writers employ *kyrios* to refer to God in various contexts. The Synoptic Gospels and Acts frequently refer to God as *kyrios* (e.g., Mark 5:19; 13:20; Matt 11:25; Acts 17:24). Likewise, the apostle Paul employs the title *kyrios* for God the Father, particularly in quotations from the Old Testament containing the divine name (e.g., Rom 4:7–8; 9:27–29; 1 Cor 3:20; 2 Cor 6:18). Without exception these are translated "Lord."

The New Testament's use of *kyrios* in reference to Jesus requires more explanation. It is not uncommon for Jesus to be addressed in the gospels as *kyrie* in polite address (Mark 11:3; 14:14; John 6:68; 13:13–16). Such usage requires no thought of his divinity, only respect for him as a revered rabbi or teacher. Interestingly, Jesus's opponents never call him "Lord," only "Teacher" or "Rabbi." Yet even in the gospels the word appears to take on transcendent significance (e.g., Mark 1:2; Matt 12:8; John 20:18; 20:28; 21:7). In particular, Jesus's quotation of Psalm 110:1 proves instructive (Mark 12:36–37): "The Lord said to my Lord, 'Sit at my right hand, until I put your enemies under your feet' (ESV)." The question posed and the explanation offered by Jesus imply an indirect messianic claim. The frequent Christological use of Psalm 110 by New Testament writers demonstrates that they interpret this psalm as describing something of Jesus's messianic and transcendent significance (e.g., Acts 2:34; 1 Cor 15:25; Heb 1:3).

Within his letters—the earliest New Testament documents—Paul employs *kyrios* most frequently as an honorific for Jesus. The confession "Jesus is Lord" and belief in the resurrection stand at the center of his gospel (Rom 10:9–13). For Paul the church is constituted of those who "call upon the name of our Lord," by whom he means the risen Jesus (e.g., 1 Cor 1:2 ESV). In fact, the apostle deems the *kyrios* title an appropriate honorific for Christ precisely because of the resurrection (Rom 1:3–4). Remarkably, Paul expresses this conviction by associating Jesus with the divine name in Old Testament quotations. For example, in contrast to the many gods and lords worshiped by pagans, Paul reworks the central creed of Israel (Deut 6:4–6) to include "one God, the Father" and "one Lord, Jesus Christ" (1 Cor 8:6). Though distinct and ultimately subordinate to the Father, this revised *Shema* links Christ with God's oneness and his name ("Lord"/*kyrios*/Yahweh) and credits Jesus as an agent of creation and redemption.

While scholars debate its significance, the majority considers the Philippian hymn (Phil 2:6–11) an extraordinary example of the apostle's high Christology. In the hymn's last half, God exalts and bestows on the humbled, crucified Jesus the name above all names (likely, "Lord"/*kyrios*/Yahweh). Universal acclamation of Jesus is expressed in language taken directly from Isaiah 45, the most stridently monotheistic passage in the Hebrew Bible. The acclamation "Jesus Christ is Lord" associates Jesus with the divine name (*kyrios*/Yahweh) and accords completely with the will of God (Phil 2:9–11).

Scholars debate the origin and significance of the title "Lord" as it was applied to Jesus. In the twentieth century Bousset (1913) argued that it was not until Christianity moved into a Hellenistic environment that the title "Lord" would have been applied to Jesus. Jewish monotheism, Bousset believed, would have precluded such a confession among Palestinian Jewish Christians. Accordingly, pagan usage of the term clarifies what Christians meant when they called Jesus "Lord." Hurtado (1988, 2005) argued that it is possible to account for the Christological use of *kyrios* and religious devotion to Christ by appeal to Jewish notions of divine agency and powerful religious experiences that convinced Jesus's earliest Jewish followers that he had conquered death and was now clothed with divine glory. The *maranatha* invocation ("O Lord, come!": 1 Cor 16:22 [NKJV]; cf. Rev 22:20; *Did.* 10:6) provides evidence that Aramaic-speaking Christians called Jesus "Lord" either as an invocation of his presence in worship or as a prayer for his return. The fact that Paul does not translate this Aramaic phrase in a letter addressed to Greek-speaking Christians in Corinth indicates it was already an accepted part of Christian liturgy and practice.

The connection between "Lord" and Spirit is less pronounced in the New Testament than its patrological and Christological associations. Still, Paul brings the "Spirit" into close association with "Lord": "the Lord is the Spirit, and where the Spirit of the Lord is, there is freedom" (2 Cor 3:17). The context of this passage involves the spiritual transformation that takes place when people behold "the glory of God in the face of Christ" (3:16—4:6 NASB). Given Paul's use of the term "Lord" elsewhere, it is likely to have Christological import here as well.

The word "Lord" is employed in the New Testament in several key phrases. John is in the Spirit on "the Lord's Day" (Rev 1:10), a likely reference to the first day of the week, or Sunday (1 Cor 16:2). Apparently Christ-believers began gathering on this day in honor of Jesus's resurrection. Paul addresses certain abuses associated with "the Lord's supper" (1 Cor 11:20) in Corinth. During this meal the community rehearsed the words Jesus spoke over the cup and the bread on the night of his betrayal (cf. "the cup/table of the Lord" in 1 Cor 10:21). Paul's corrective is the earliest historical reference to what in later church history is known as "the Eucharist" or "holy communion." When offering comfort to the Thessalonians, Paul claims to have "the word of the Lord" on the future of those who have fallen asleep in Jesus (1 Thess 4:13–18). Whether this refers to a known saying of Jesus from the gospels or an *agraphon* is unclear. In each of these cases "the Lord" refers to Jesus.

Postbiblical Usage. Later generations of Christian writers and theologians tended to use *kyrios* for God and/or Christ according to patterns laid down by New Testament writers. Psalm 110 continued to be cited as a way of declaring the unique role and dignity of both the Lord God and the Lord Messiah (*Barn.* 12:10; Justin, *Dial.* 32, 126). The *maranatha* invocation, first evidenced in 1 Corinthians 16:22, is picked up and used in its untranslated, Aramaic form (cf. Rev 22:20) among the first Greek-speaking readers of *Didache* (10:6).

At the same time individual writers among the Apostolic Fathers exhibited their own unique interests. In *1 Clement*, for example, there is increased usage of *despotēs* ("Lord") to refer to God, particularly in creational, covenantal, and legal contexts (e.g., *1 Clem.* 8.2; 20.11; 33.2; 40.1). Polycarp employed *kyrios* exclusively as a Christological title (e.g., Pol. *Phil.* 1.1–2; 12.2). As in the New Testament, there is some ambivalence to the use of "Lord"; the question of whether a particular *kyrios* refers to God or Christ must be determined by context. When *kyrios* introduces a known saying of Jesus from the gospels, the referent is clearly Christ (e.g., *2 Clem.* 6.1; *Did.* 9.5). When employed in formulaic passages such as "the Lord Jesus Christ" in introductions and benedictions, Christ is also surely in view. Similarly, when a writer speaks of the suffering of the Lord, his taking on flesh or coming as Savior, Christ is to be understood as *kyrios* (Ign. *Phld.* 4.1; 9.2; *1 Clem.* 12.7). However, when *kyrios* introduces or is contained in Old Testament passages, the referent is typically God the Father (e.g., *1 Clem.* 22.1; Justin, *Apol.* 1.37; *Dial.* 27). Writers in this generation also exhibit an increasingly Christological interpretation of the Old Testament (Justin, *Dial.* 129).

[*See also* Christology; Day of the Lord; Ecclesiology; Family; God and Gods; Holy Spirit; Kings and Kingship; *and* Servant of God.]

BIBLIOGRAPHY

Bacchiocchi, Samuel. *From Sabbath to Sunday: A Historical Investigation to the Rise of Sunday Observance in Early Christianity.* Rome: Pontifical Gregorian University Press, 1997.

Bousset, Wilhelm. *Kyrios Christos: A History of the Belief in Christ from the Beginnings of Christianity to Irenaeus.* Translated by John E. Steely. Nashville, Tenn.: Abingdon, 1970. First German edition published in 1913.

Brueggemann, Walter. *Theology of the Old Testament: Testimony, Dispute, Advocacy.* Minneapolis: Fortress, 1997.

Capes, David B. *Old Testament Yahweh Texts in Paul's Christology.* Wissenschaftliche Untersuchungen zum Neuen Testament 2/47. Tübingen, Germany: J. C. B. Mohr, 1992.

Fitzmyer, Joseph A. "The Semitic Background of the New Testament *Kyrios*-Title." In *A Wandering Aramean: Collected Aramaic Essays*, pp. 115–142. Society of Biblical Literature Monograph Series 25. Missoula, Mont.: Scholars Press, 1979.

Foerster, Werner, and Gottfried Quell. "*Kyrios.*" In *Theological Dictionary of the New Testament*, edited by Gerhard Kittel and Gerhard Friedrich, Vol. 3, pp. 1039–1098. Grand Rapids, Mich.: Eerdmans, 1965.

Fossum, Jarl E. *The Name of God and the Angel of the Lord: Samaritan and Jewish Concepts of Intermediation and the Origin of Gnosticism.* Wissenschaftliche Untersuchungen zum Neuen Testament 1/36. Tübingen, Germany: J. C. B. Mohr, 1985.

Hay, David M. *Glory at the Right Hand: Psalm 110 in Early Christianity.* Nashville, Tenn.: Abingdon, 1973.

Hurtado, Larry. *One God, One Lord: Early Christian Devotion and Ancient Jewish Monotheism.* Philadelphia: Fortress, 1988.

Hurtado, Larry. *Lord Jesus Christ: Devotion to Jesus in Earliest Christianity.* Grand Rapids, Mich.: Eerdmans, 2005.

Jenni, Ernst. "Yahweh." In *Theological Lexicon of the Old Testament*, edited by Ernst Jenni and Claus Westermann, Vol. 2, pp. 522–526. Translated by Mark E. Biddle. Peabody, Mass.: Hendrickson, 1997.

Marshall, I. Howard. *Last Supper and Lord's Supper.* Grand Rapids, Mich.: Eerdmans, 1981.

Rad, Gerhard von. *Old Testament Theology: The Theology of Israel's Historical Traditions.* Translated by D. M. G. Stalker. New York: Harper & Brothers, 1962.

David B. Capes

LORD'S PRAYER

The Lord's Prayer (as Protestants refer to it) or *Pater Noster* (among Catholics) is likely the best-known and best-loved prayer in Christianity. It was recorded by two gospel writers as an important teaching from Jesus, included in a first-century manual of Christian practices (the *Didache*), interpreted by teachers in the church from its early years until the present, and incorporated into liturgies and is prayed often by believers.

The First-Century Context. Scholars have long debated whether Jesus's prayer has primarily a future orientation (for God's kingdom to come fully) or a present emphasis (concern for Jesus's followers now). In recent years a greater understanding of the New Testament in the first-century Mediterranean world has persuaded many interpreters that Jesus taught his disciples to resist Roman rule while practicing God's justice in their present lives. When they so live, they share in God's work to renew creation, as God had long promised (e.g., Isa 11:1–9). Appreciating the context of first-century Roman rule is crucial for understanding Jesus's prayer.

The Roman Empire was the dominant reality in the first-century Mediterranean world. Israel, where Jesus and his followers lived, was an occupied country, subject to Roman political arrangements (client-kings like the Herods and the collaboration of local ruling elites), economics (taxation), and violence. Apostles like Paul, Barnabas (Acts 13:2–4), Andronicus, and Junia (Rom 16:7) traveled to urban areas where refugees from imperial wars abounded, the imperial cult flourished, and local ruling elites sought the patronage and favor of the emperor or his surrogates. As it spread, Roman rule brought power and prosperity for a few and difficult lives for most. In a world where religion, politics, and economics were inextricably intertwined, Roman propaganda declared that their ordering of the world was according to the plan of the gods.

In addition, cultural anthropologists describe the culture of that time as patriarchal: dominated by concerns for honor, oriented toward groups rather than individuals, and concerned about the present rather than the future. Most Roman subjects could focus only on surviving today and tomorrow.

Three Early Versions of the Lord's Prayer

Matthew 6:9–13	Luke 11:1–4	Didache 8:2
Pray then in this way: Our Father in heaven, hallowed be your name. Your kingdom come. Your will be done, on earth as it is in heaven. Give us this day our daily bread. And forgive us our debts, as we also have forgiven our debtors. And do not bring us to the time of trial, but rescue us from the evil one.	He was praying in a certain place, and after he had finished, one of his disciples said to him, "Lord, teach us to pray, as John taught his disciples." He said to them, "When you pray, say: Father, hallowed be your name. Your kingdom come. Give us each day our daily bread. And forgive us our sins, for we ourselves forgive everyone indebted to us. And do not bring us to the time of trial."	And do not pray as the hypocrites, but as the Lord commanded in his Gospel, pray thus: "Our Father in Heaven, hallowed be thy Name, Your Kingdom come, Your will be done, as in Heaven so on earth; give us our daily bread today, and forgive us our debt as we forgive our debtors. And lead us not into temptation, but deliver us from the Evil One, for yours is the power and the glory for ever."

The Prayer in the New Testament. Jesus proclaimed the arrival of God's kingdom in such a world. As he did so, he called his followers to live in God's reality rather than Caesar's. According to the writers of Matthew and Luke, Jesus taught his disciples to pray the Lord's Prayer. As one may see from the table, the versions presented by these Evangelists are similar, though not precisely the same. Their narrative contexts, however, are quite different. The prayer in Matthew is near the midpoint of the Sermon on the Mount (6:9–15). In Luke some disciples notice Jesus praying and ask him to teach them to pray (11:1–4). Apparently, the prayer derives from the Q material, a collection of Jesus's sayings, which both Matthew and Luke used in composing their gospels. From the early days of Jesus's movement, then, this prayer was remembered and passed down to his followers.

The prayer begins boldly with its address to "[Our] Father [who is in heaven]." In our time the maleness of the term "father" has required attention. In the first-century patriarchal world fathers were the heads of households, which were the basic building blocks of society. Households made up villages and cities, which made up states, which made up the empire. Thus, Caesar was the *pater patrie* (father of the fatherland), the head of the "household" of the Roman Empire. His "children" owed him respect, loyalty, obedience, and gratitude since he provided for their well-being. But Jesus taught his followers to pray to "our father who is in heaven," not to "our father who is in Rome."

To pray to "our father" is also to pray as family members and heirs of the householder, not as slaves or hired help. Our best knowledge of Jesus's first followers indicates they would not have been considered members of high-ranking families in their world, but Jesus invited them into his family (Mark 3:34). In Jewish tradition the description of God as father first appears in the Exodus story: Israel was God's firstborn son (Exod 4:22–23). For Jews, then, God as father had long been associated with freedom and dignity. Jesus's prayer begins by calling on that association.

The prayer's first petition is for God's name to be "hallowed" or honored. Children in Jesus's world honored their father's name by respecting their father and, thus, living as he taught them. The next two petitions (not in Luke) are for God's kingdom—God's rule, reality, and actuality—to come and for God's will to be done "as in heaven, so also on earth" (Matt 6:10, lit.). According to the gospels, wherever Jesus went, there went God's kingdom. Jesus not only proclaimed the kingdom; he also demonstrated it as he lived God's will. Consequently, readers of the gospels know that God's will and kingdom call for God's children to practice compassion, generosity, inclusion, justice, forgiveness, healing, and service to the "least of these," as Jesus did (Matt 25:31–46). The contrast with Rome's exclusive, competitive, and oppressive rule is stark. When Jesus's followers commit themselves to God's purposes, the radical new reality of God's kingdom—not the Roman emperor's—orients their living, and so they honor God's name. Therefore, the prayer petitions God to enable Jesus's followers to join themselves to Jesus's practices and to promote them, thereby honoring God's name.

The final three petitions focus on concrete struggles to live in God's new reality. First is "Give us each day our daily bread" (Luke 11:3) or "Give us this day our daily bread" (Matt 6:11). The use of "our" is telling, for eating in the Bible so often is concerned with community: thus, the messianic banquet (Isa 25:6–10), Jesus's eating with "tax collectors and sinners" (Matt 9:9–13), and the Last Supper (John 13–17). The attention to bread that is "sufficient" or "daily" (in Greek *epiousion* suggests either translation) brings to mind the manna in the wilderness that God supplied daily for the Israelites during the Exodus (Exod 16). They were to gather enough manna for their families for that day, trusting God to provide again tomorrow. In addition to attending to physical needs, the manna story taught a significant theological lesson that is surely invoked in Jesus's prayer: followers can trust that God has provided enough. Thus, hoarding indicates lack of trust in God's care. Ironically, hoarding also creates the scarcity the hoarder fears: when some have too much, others will have too little. What happens then? Resentment, mistrust, competition, and eventually violence will ensue; the community is destroyed; and the Kingdom of God is confused with that of Caesar.

The next petition invokes God's forgiveness. In Matthew, those who pray ask God to "forgive us our *debts*" (6:12). Luke's version reads, "forgive us our sins" (11:4). Either term denotes unmet obligations toward God that create a breach in the community's relationship with God. Jewish tradition had long portrayed God as gracious and merciful, slow to anger, and abounding in steadfast love (e.g., Exod 34:6; Ps 86:15). Jesus's prayer invites followers to call on God's grace again. This time, however, there is a corollary: those praying ask God to forgive them *as they also* forgive their debtors. Matthew and Luke both use the language of "debts" in this part of the petition. In the context of first-century empire, the literal meaning of the term was surely intended. Roman economic practices had made many Roman subjects into debtors. The "least of these" were most vulnerable to debt, which inhibited their ability to obtain "daily bread" for their families. This two-part petition, therefore, asks God to forgive any breach in the relationship with God as petitioners live justly toward brothers and sisters in God's household, forgiving whatever debts may be incurred so that daily bread is possible for everyone. The petition means that Jesus's followers will not act like citizens of the empire and will not respond as the older brother in the parable of the prodigal (Luke 15:11–32) or Matthew's merciless servant (18:23–34).

Matthew adds a final petition, structured in poetic parallelism: "Do not bring us to the time of trial [*peirasmos*], but rescue us from the evil one" (6:13). The Evangelists recount Jesus's temptation (*peirazō*) in the wilderness by Satan to choose to meet immediate needs, to "test" God, and to gain power by worshiping Satan (Matt 4:1–11; Luke 4:1–13)—in short, to go a different way from the one leading to Gethsemane and Golgotha. They also record Jesus's telling his disciples in Gethsemane to pray so that they would not enter into temptation (*peirasmos*; Matt 26:41). Instead, the disciples slept. When the arresters came, the disciples produced a sword and chose violence, which Jesus promptly rejected (Matt 26:51–56). These two stories, which use the same root word as in the prayer (Gk *peira-*), suggest that the trial petitioners hope to avoid, the evil from which they need rescue, is doubt in the way of God. If they doubt that love and all that goes with it—grace, mercy, justice, forgiveness, and nonviolence—overcome evil, they will succumb to the temptation to use weapons of evil—force, violence, and conquest—to defeat evil. Whenever they do, the Kingdom of God again resembles the kingdom of Rome.

The last phrase of the prayer as it is commonly prayed ("for thine is the kingdom, the power, and the glory forever") is not part of the best New Testament manuscripts of the prayer. The *Didache* (late first century) includes it, indicating that it was added early. This doxology is a final statement of hope in God and allegiance to God's purposes for the world, not Caesar's.

Jesus's prayer, then, is a bold request to participate in God's re-creation of the world according to God's designs for love and justice rather than Rome's desire for power and wealth. It is a subversive prayer of allegiance to God's kingdom in the midst of imperial rule.

The Prayer in Christian History. Since it was gathered into early Q material, recorded by Matthew and Luke, and included in the *Didache*, we know the that Lord's Prayer was cherished since the first days of Jesus's followers. Apparently, its bold hope for life as God's children even under Roman oppression resonated powerfully for the first Christians.

The prayer continued to appeal. The earliest surviving commentary on the prayer is Tertullian's (*Or.*, ca. 198). Origen (*Or.*, ca. 233) and Cyprian (*Dom. or.*, ca. 251) were among third-century church leaders who interpreted the prayer. By the fourth century it was both a regular part of Eucharistic liturgies and among the last instructions new believers received before baptism. The Roman Catholic Church continues to recite the prayer during Eucharist, immediately before the sign of peace.

Early believers prayed the prayer during set hours of prayer, a practice that would continue in the creation of the divine office. Augustine counseled the faithful to pray it three times daily (*Serm. Dom.*, ca. 393). As Western monasticism developed, the prayer was included among the daily practices of the monks. When Latin became the language of the Western church, the prayer was translated into that language; hence, the Catholic name for the prayer is *Pater Noster* (Lat "our father"). After the Reformation many, though not all, Protestant groups continued to pray the prayer as part of their regular worship and Eucharistic liturgies. They did so, however, in their own languages rather than in Latin, hence the Protestant title "the Lord's Prayer."

Ancient or contemporary, Protestant or Catholic, nominal or devout in their faith, Christians have prayed and continue to pray this prayer. It holds a unique place in Christian history.

[*See also* Exodus; Forgiveness; Glory; God and Gods; Holiness; Hope; Kingdom of God (Heaven); Kings and Kingship; Luke–Acts; Matthew; Politics and Systems of Governance; *and* Prayer.]

BIBLIOGRAPHY

Carter, Warren. *The Roman Empire and the New Testament: An Essential Guide*. Nashville, Tenn.: Abingdon, 2006.

Crosby, Michael. *The Prayer That Jesus Taught Us*. Maryknoll, N.Y.: Orbis, 2002.

Crossan, John Dominic. *The Greatest Prayer: Rediscovering the Revolutionary Message of the Lord's Prayer*. San Francisco: HarperOne, 2010.

Hahn, Scott. *Understanding Our Father: Biblical Reflections on the Lord's Prayer*. Steubenville, Ohio: Emmaus Road, 2002.

Johnson, Elizabeth A. *She Who Is: The Mystery of God in Feminist Theological Discourse*. New York: Crossroad, 2002.

Mendonca, Jose Tolentino. *Our Father Who Art on Earth: The Lord's Prayer for Believers and Unbelievers*. Mahwah, N.J.: Paulist Press, 2013.

Mitzi L. Minor

LORD'S SUPPER

Early Christians referred to a communal meal that recalled Jesus's final meal with his disciples before his death as the "Lord's supper" (1 Cor 11:20, or "table of the Lord," 1 Cor 10:21) or the "Eucharist" (*Did.* 9.1, 5; Ign., *Smyrn.* 6.2; 8.1). The term "Eucharist" is derived from the verb *eucharistein* ("to give thanks") that introduces Jesus's words and actions in connection with bread and one of the cups of wine (Luke 22:17, 19; 1 Cor 11:24). The Synoptic Gospels present this meal as the Passover celebration (Mark 14:17–31; Matt 26:20–35; Luke 22:14–38), while John's Gospel places it on the evening before the day of preparation so that Jesus's death coincides with the slaughter of the Passover lambs (John 13:1—14:31). John's version of the final meal lacks the core element of the Christian ritual, Jesus's words associating bread and wine consumed with the body and blood shed on the cross, but the Evangelist incorporated that tradition as the conclusion to a long discourse on Jesus as the bread of life (John 6:51–58).

Focusing on the action of breaking and sharing bread among the participants (1 Cor 10:17; Luke 22:19) produced an alternate designation for the Christian celebration "breaking bread" that is employed in

Luke–Acts (Luke 24:30, 35; Acts 2:42; 20:7, 11; 27:35). While it is clear that the blessing and sharing of bread and wine initially occurred within the context of a full meal, at some point the consumption of blessed bread and wine was separated from that context. Christians began to use the word *agapē* ("love") for the larger communal meal ("love-feasts," Jude 12; Ign., *Smyrn.* 8.2). Scholars disagree over how early the bread and wine ritual was detached from the larger meal. Some suggest that the tensions between well-fed, even drunk, Christians and those who had nothing in Corinth (1 Cor 11:17–34) were facilitated by transferring the loaf and cup rite with associated hymns and scripture reading to the conclusion of the communal gathering.

Although the events being remembered at the Lord's Supper are associated with an annual religious festival, the Passover, early Christians did not treat the Lord's Supper as an annual feast or a substitute Passover. Instead, they gathered weekly on "the Lord's day" (Rev 1:10) or "the first day of the week" (Acts 20:7) to commemorate the resurrection. In that setting the eschatological time frame that situated the rite between Jesus's death on the cross and his second coming is partially shifted by the risen Lord's presence in the meal ("proclaim the death of the Lord until he comes" [1 Cor 11:26b], "I will never again drink…until that day when I drink it new with you in my Father's Kingdom" [Matt 26:29; cf. Mark 14:25; Luke 22:18], "I shall not eat it [this Passover] again until it is fulfilled in the Kingdom of God" [Luke 22:16]). Incorporating the resurrection permits the Christian meal ritual to express the full paschal mystery of the Lord's death and resurrection that calls together a new covenant people.

Meals and Religious Associations. The Christian ritual consumption of a small amount of bread and wine that had been blessed using a formula handed down from Jesus's last supper ceased to look anything like sacrificial banqueting as it was known in either the Jewish or the pagan religious world. Scholars disagree over whether or not the descriptions of a Passover meal from latter rabbinic sources can be employed to fill out the Evangelists' statements that Jesus was celebrating a Passover meal with his disciples. Minimally, the Mishnah (ca. 200) indicates that the blessing of cups of wine before and/or after the bread may be connected to that setting (*m. Pesaḥ* 10.4–5). Although Christians easily associated their ritual bread and wine with the manna and water provided for the Israelites in the desert (1 Cor 10:3–4; John 6:30–51) and equated Jesus's death with the Passover lamb (1 Cor 5:7; Rev 5:9–14), they did not consider their meal a Passover.

Discovery of rules for a communal meal ritual practiced by the new covenanters among the Dead Sea Scrolls generated considerable excitement among New Testament scholars when one of them described a communal assembly in which the new bread and wine would be blessed first by the messiah of Aaron (a priest) and then by the messiah of Israel (1QSa 2.11–22). That rite defined the boundaries of the community since participants had to be full members in a state of ritual purity. It also suggested an association between the coming of messianic figures and a blessing of bread and wine. However, the lack of any detailed links between this set of meal regulations and the gospel narratives of Jesus's meal with his followers makes it unlikely that this sectarian practice was the basis for the Christian Eucharist.

Religious banqueting, that is, the consumption of meat or other foodstuffs offered to a deity, was a ubiquitous form of communal celebration in the ancient world. Public, civic festivals were only part of the picture. A wide range of private associations gathered to dine in honor of a deity revered by the group or thought to provide special benefits to those connected with a particular trade. Some constructed their own dining spaces; some had agreements to share space in an area belonging to another group; some temple complexes appear to have provided dining areas for hire; or dining may have occurred outdoors, as in the case of large public sacrifices. Faced with accusations against Christians, the Roman governor of Bithynia, Pliny (ca. 110), investigated the group. He reported that they met in the early morning on a certain day to sing hymns to Christ as god and returned later in the day for a meal but dropped the latter when he forbade such meetings of private associations (Pliny the Younger, *Ep.* 10.96.7).

Civic banquets often limited food distributions to enrolled citizens, and private associations controlled membership lists, with assessed dues and fines for failure to attend or misbehavior at a banquet. However, individuals could participate in multiple groups. Paul's first references to the Lord's Supper address those Christians who saw nothing wrong with continuing to attend banquets associated with other deities. Believing in the divine honoree was not a requirement for participation. By comparing Christian baptism and Eucharist to the Israelites under Moses, Paul points out that God punishes idolatry even among his own people (1 Cor 10:1–13). Therefore, Christians should not be indifferent to joining in other religious banquets. It involves participating in the cup and table of demons (1 Cor 10:14–22; "set a table for the demon," Isa 65:11 LXX).

One might expect Paul to deal with the disorderly behavior at the Christian meal (1 Cor 11:17–34) as other religious associations did, by designating an individual in charge with the authority to fine or punish those who disrupt the banquet. He does not. In both examples, Paul appeals to the religious meaning of the Christian meal to distinguish it from religious practices that might seem comparable. The metaphorical translation of "body" from the physical body of Christ on the cross to the bread that has been blessed, broken, and distributed, to the community itself as "body of Christ" creates a seamless web of relationships. Similarly, Paul uses the *koinōnia* ("sharing,"; "fellowship, communion") in the blood and body of Christ as a relationship that excludes other forms of belonging. Although such religious exclusion was well established among Jews, it was not obvious to non-Jewish converts. Even the requirement that only baptized persons can participate in the Eucharist will have to be spelled out in second-century Christian rules (*Did.* 9.5; Justin Martyr, *1 Apol.* 65.1).

The Eucharistic Formula. Paul bolsters his case for regulating the Corinthian celebration of the Lord's Supper by appealing to the tradition of Jesus's words establishing the rite that he had received and handed on to them (1 Cor 11:23–25). These words of institution that are also represented in the gospels form the central core of the Christian Eucharist. The formal stability of the wording indicates that they

Jesus's Words over the Bread and Cup

1 Cor 11:23–25	Luke 22:19–20	Mark 14:22–24	Matt 26:26–28
"took a loaf of bread	"took a loaf of bread	"While they were eating he took a loaf of bread	"While they were eating, Jesus took a loaf of bread,
and when he had given thanks	and when he had given thanks,	and after blessing it,	and after blessing it,
he broke it and said,	he broke it and gave it to them, saying,	he broke it, gave it to them, and said,	he broke it, gave it to the disciples and said
'This is my body that is for you.	'This is my body, which is given for you.	'Take; this is my body.'	'Take, eat; this is my body.'
Do this in remembrance of me.'	Do this in remembrance of me.'		
In the same way he took the cup also, after supper, saying,	And he did the same with the cup after supper, saying	Then he took a cup, and after giving thanks he gave it to them and all of them drank from it. He said to them,	Then he took a cup, and after giving thanks he gave it to them, saying, 'Drink from it all of you;
'This cup is the new covenant in my blood.	'This cup that is poured out for you	'This is my blood of the covenant,	for this is my blood of the covenant
Do this, as often as you drink it, in remembrance of me.'"	is the new covenant in my blood.'"	which is poured out for many.'"	which is poured out for many, for the forgiveness of sins.'"

had been adopted as ritual formulae from a very early period. Two variants exist, one represented in Paul and Luke (1 Cor 11:23–25; Luke 22:17–20), the other in Mark and Matthew (Mark 14:22–24; Matt 26:26–28). These formulae incorporate an interpretation of Jesus's death into the rite.

Luke's Gospel has an additional cup blessing before the bread that introduces the eschatological saying about drinking in the kingdom, "after giving thanks he said: 'Take this and divide it among yourselves; for I tell you that from now on I will not drink of the fruit of the vine until the kingdom of God comes'" (Luke 22:17–18). The Evangelist's crucifixion account is consistent with that statement. It omits the offer of sour wine familiar in other versions (Mark 15:36; Matt 27:48; John 19:28–29, requested by Jesus to fulfill the scriptures). The first cup saying also incorporates a command to consume the contents that is comparable to the "take, eat" associated with the bread in the Mark/Matthew tradition. The second cup saying in Luke includes a phrase, "is poured out for you," which suggests a different ritual gesture from consuming the contents. In other ritual settings a wine libation might be poured on the ground during a banquet in honor of a deity or the blood of a sacrificial victim captured in a bowl to be poured on the altar next to which the animal was slaughtered or sprinkled on those assembled as in the covenant sacrifice offered by Moses. Since all versions of the words of institution interpret the cup as a sign that Jesus's death establishes a new covenant, the shift from blood poured out (Mark/Matt) to a cup poured out may have been influenced by that scene in which Moses sprinkles half the blood of the sacrificed oxen on the people after they have accepted the covenant just read to them. "Moses took the blood and dashed it on the people and said, 'See the blood of the covenant that the LORD has made with you in accordance with all these words'" (Exod 24:8).

The expressions "for you" or "for many" represent the death of Christ as the source of salvation for others who could not achieve a right relationship with God for themselves (1 Cor 15:3, 29; 2 Cor 5:14; Rom 5:6; 8:32). Forgiveness of sins (Matt 26:28) is part of the picture, but entry into a new covenant

implies both a new life freed from the power of sin and participation in the community of believers. The remembrance formula taken from the Passover tradition (Exod 12:14; Deut 16:3) did not intend for the faithful to become a group of historical reenactors. Nor is the Christian meal the kind of annual meal memorializing the dead, also well known to a Roman-period audience as some scholars have suggested. Liturgical remembering (*anamnesis*) requires making the past events of salvation an effective part of the present (Deut 5:2–3). Paul reminds the Corinthians that the meal involves a communal responsibility to "proclaim the Lord's death until he comes" (1 Cor 11:26). Inappropriate behavior to others who make up the ecclesial body of Christ is cause for the same sort of divine retribution that people associated with sacrilegious acts (vv. 27–29).

Eucharistic Presence. The liturgical words of institution do not resolve the question of how to interpret the "is" that connects body and blood with bread and wine/cup, respectively. The passion narrative setting emphasizes the distance between the last meal of Jesus with his disciples and the "coming again" of the Lord at the end of days. God's presence to the community that assembles for the meal is through the Spirit operating in and through the "body of Christ" that is the church. Stories of the risen Lord appearing to disciples gathered for a meal (Luke 24:36–43; John 20:19–23, 26–29) sometimes initially disguised as an unrecognized stranger (Luke 24:13–35, "how he had been made known to them in the breaking of the bread"; John 21:4–14) suggest an opening toward finding Christ present in the meal.

A number of liturgical and theological shifts in the patristic and early medieval periods led the Latin West to focus on the "elements" as Christ and to transfer the sacrificial action from the self-offering of Christ on the cross to the ritual actions of the priest at the altar. In that context the words of institution spoken over the bread and wine mark their transformation from ordinary bread and wine into the real body and blood of Christ, referred to as "transubstantiation" since the twelfth century C.E. Devotion to the sacred presence of Christ led to pious practices such as elevation of the host and chalice, Eucharistic devotions, as well as declining reception of communion among the laity. By contrast Greek patristic tradition treats the Eucharist as representing sacramentally the mystery of Jesus's historical work of redemption. At the end of the fourth century C.E. Ambrose expressed the idea that Christ's words "this is my body" and "this is my blood" transform the reality of the bread and wine (Ambrose, *Myst.* 9.52, 54; *Sacr.* 5.14).

The Eucharistic thanksgiving prayers in *Didache* 9.1–4 and 10.2–4 (late first century C.E.) over the cup and bread do not repeat the words of institution but thank God for Jesus as vine of David (cup), the life and knowledge made known through Jesus (bread), as well as the unity of the church gathered from the ends of the earth (broken bread gathered). Justin Martyr does not report the content of the prayers and thanksgiving offered by the president of the assembly. Apparently, the whole anaphora to which the people have responded with their "Amen" makes the elements sacred food for the assembled community, which the deacons convey to absent members (*1 Apol.* 66.5). Exchange of Eucharistic bread between the diverse house churches of the second century C.E. served to signal their unity, while refusal to do so indicated that a particular group was considered heretical or schismatic. Thus, the widespread agreement that baptism was a requirement for participation in the Eucharist (*Did.* 9.5; Justin Martyr, *1 Apol.* 65) was no longer sufficient if members of one church considered the beliefs or practice of another deviant. Christian churches remain divided over whether or not the invitation to communion should be extended to all the baptized whether or not they are members of the denomination in question. Those who consider the bread and wine to be transformed into the real Christ rather than being part of a symbolic reminder of Christ's death for us generally restrict communion.

Jesus, Meals, and Ministry. The various modes of banqueting associated with religious cults in antiquity mark boundaries between those eligible for its benefits and outsiders, whether the markers are Jewish in the case of Passover or the meal consumed in ritual purity of the Dead Sea covenanters, citizen-ship in the case of public sacrifices, or inclusion in the member roles of a private association. There would be nothing remarkable about Christians establishing criteria for who may eat of the Lord's Supper and who is to be excluded if the gospels did not include stories about Jesus at meals during his ministry challenging the very concept of protecting the holiness of God's people by excluding the sinner, the ritually impure, the marginalized. A notoriously sinful woman disrupts the good order of a formal meal in Simon the Pharisee's house and departs with her sins forgiven (Luke 7:36–50). Jesus is roundly criticized for dining with tax collectors and sinners (Luke 15:1–2; 19:6–9).

Jesus rejects the add-on customs of hand purification and washing transferred from requirements of priests serving in the Temple to the table fellowship of the pious (Mark 7:1–23). And he illustrates his teaching with stories in which banquets are thrown for the wrong sort of reason, return of a disgraced son (Luke 15:11–32) or the despised, poor, and homeless being treated as a rich man's guests (Luke 14:16–23). Banqueting in God's kingdom is open to all comers, Jesus suggests. John's Gospel has Jesus teach the disciples a lesson in humble service by washing their feet at his last meal (John 13:12–17). Therefore, some Christians believe that the "table of the Lord" should mirror Jesus's meals and be open to everyone present, even young children and nonbelievers.

[*See also* Covenant; Cult and Worship; *and* Ecclesiology.]

BIBLIOGRAPHY

Borgen, Peder. "'Yes', 'No', 'How Far?': The Participation of Jews and Christians in Pagan Cults." In *Early Christianity and Hellenistic Judaism*, edited by P. Borgen, pp. 15–43. Edinburgh: T&T Clark, 1996.

Bradshaw, Paul F. *Eucharistic Origins.* Oxford: Oxford University Press, 2004.

Byars, Ronald P. *The Sacraments in Biblical Perspective.* Louisville, Ky.: Westminster John Knox, 2011.

Pecklers, Keith F. *Liturgy: The Illustrated History.* Mahwah, N.J.: Paulist Press, 2012.

Smith, Dennis E. *From Symposium to Eucharist: The Banquet in the Early Christian World.* Minneapolis: Fortress, 2003.

Taussig, Hal. *In the Beginning Was the Meal: Social Experimentation and Early Christian Identity*. Minneapolis: Fortress, 2009.

Pheme Perkins

LOVE

Love relationships are described, recommended, and regulated in the literature of almost all human societies. The love theme is present in the Bible from the earliest documents of the Hebrew Bible (ca. 1000 B.C.E.) to the more recent documents of the New Testament (ca. 100 C.E.). It is used to describe and regulate human relationships and, on the basis of these experiences, to articulate a variety of theological understandings of the relationship between God and humankind (theology) and the role of Jesus Christ within that relationship (Christology).

Hebrew Bible. Relationships of love are described in the cultures and languages of Egypt and Mesopotamia, prior to and parallel with biblical literature. The Hebrew root for "love" (*'āhab*) is found across all forms of literature in the Hebrew Bible, other nonbiblical Hebrew texts, and works in other Semitic dialects. The etymology of the expression is debated, but it is widely agreed that "the emotional experience is the germ cell for the development of the concept of *'āhab*" (Haldar and Wallis, 1974–1977, p. 102). The overall use of the expression in the Hebrew Bible indicates a positive attraction to, and search for, the other (see Deut 11:22; 30:20; Prov 18:24; Isa 1:23; Ps 40:17; 43:3) as well as faithfulness to the loved one (Jer 31:3; Hos 11:4); and its opposite is hatred (see 2 Sam 13:15; Ps 109:4).

Love language addressing everyday secular relationships.

- *Sexual love*: Isaac and Rebekah (Gen 24:67), Jacob and Rachel (Gen 29:18, 20, 30), Samson and Delilah (Judges 14:16; 16:4, 15). Hebrew uses another verb for the act of sexual intercourse (*yāda'* = to know). Sexual love is celebrated by such passages as Proverbs 5:18 and 30:18–19 and the Song of Songs, which situates a poetic celebration of the joy of the fulfillment of sexual yearning within the Hebrew scriptures.

- *Love among parents and friends*: Abraham and Isaac (Gen 22:2) and Jacob's love for Joseph (Gen 37:3). Love is divided between Isaac's partiality for Esau and Rebekah's love for Jacob (Gen 25:27–28). Ruth loved her mother-in-law (Ruth 4:15). Jonathan's love for David is proverbial (1 Sam 18:3; 20:17). Saul's love for David (see 1 Sam 16:21) may have soured, but David's love for both Saul and Jonathan is expressed in his lament after their deaths (2 Sam 1:23–26). Love is also used to describe special relationships between masters and servants (Exod 21:5; Deut 15:16).

- *Love as part of community behavior*: The Wisdom Literature expresses concern for the need for love between parent and child (Prov 13:24; 16:13; 17:17) and in a family (Prov 15:17). This love is based upon one's ethical responsibilities (12:1; 29:3; see also the negative 15:12). The wise man loves wisdom itself, and this leads beyond ethical responsibilities to a true love that has its basis in God (Pss 33:5; 37:28; 99:4). On the other hand, the tyrant loves evil and lying (52:5–6).

- *Love for neighbors and enemies*: God's design of mutual love generates the golden rule (Lev 19:18, "You shall love your neighbor as yourself"). No one should be so obsessed with his or her own interests when this would harm his or her neighbor. Love for fellow human beings extended into love for the stranger (Lev 19:34; Deut 10:18–19), but in Israel this meant people dwelling in the land. There is no call to love enemies of the nation.

The theological use of love language. As a covenanted people Israelites love one another with "steadfast love" (*ḥesed*). A strong feeling of security because of the guidance and protection of God was widely expressed (see Pss 31:24–25; 103:11–13; 2 Sam 7:14). The sentiment that God surrounded the just with righteous love is late (see Ps 146:8; Prov 3:12; 8:17, 21; 15:9; Neh 13:26), while God's love for the Patriarchs (see Deut 4:7), Solomon (2 Sam 12:24), and even Cyrus, King of Persia (Isa 48:14), is associated with the influence of the thought of the Deuteronomist.

Hosea's presentation of God's relationship with God's people through the figure of marriage is new.

Hosea's use of the word *ʾāhab* steers clear of notions of physical desire or lust by insisting on loyal affection. Israel's path as the loved one of God who gave herself to foreigners as a harlot (Hos 8:9) leads to a husband's wrath, antipathy, and divorce, in keeping with Israel's concept of love and marriage. But God's love transcends these concepts, overcomes his wrath (14:4–8), and draws them to him with the bonds of love (11:4). Once established, this imagery is used by other prophets. Jeremiah speaks of Israel's "prostitution" (Jer 2:2, 20, 23–24, 25; 3:3–4, 13; 30:14; 44:17). Yet God draws Ephraim to himself again in love (31:3–4). Ezekiel uses the marriage figure to describe the tragedy of Israel's infidelity (Ezek 16:33, 36, 37; 23:5, 9–11), but there is no message of a loving restoration. Deutero-Isaiah also uses the image of marital and maternal love to describe the relationship between God and an unfaithful people (Isa 43:4; 49:14–16; 51:17–19), and here, as in Trito-Isaiah (62:4–5; 63:9), God works to restore a right relationship by means of his love and compassion. The figure of love appears occasionally in other places within the prophetic tradition (e.g., Zeph 3:17; Mal 1:2). Only sometimes is a link made with the marriage bond (see Mal 2:11).

The "Deuteronomist" is a term given to a tradition that most likely had its origins in the northern kingdom prior to its collapse in 931 B.C.E. (see 2 Kgs 22:3—23:3). It is a theological reflection upon Israel's call to blessedness, failure, and punishment and is found across many of the historical books of the Hebrew Bible (Joshua—2 Kings), in some prophetic traditions (especially Jeremiah), and most systematically in the book of Deuteronomy. The Deuteronomist regarded the relationship between Israel and God as a covenant that paralleled the treaties between unequal parties, established in the ancient Near East between lower figures and a royal suzerain. God generated Israel through a loving gift: the forefathers, the Exodus, the promise of the land, and the promise that they would become a great people (Deut 7:8, 13; 23:5–6; 30:16, 20). Because of all that God has done, there is only one possible path for Israel: love of God and fidelity and devotion to that love (Deut 6:1–5). As God had initiated the covenant, the only acceptable

response from Israel, the privileged partner in this treaty, was love and obedience. The Deuteronomist addressed the failure of Israel, repeatedly calling the nation to obey the "commandments" (5:10; 7:9), to serve God (10:12; 11:13), to obey God's voice (30:20), and to walk in God's ways and cleave to God (11:22; 19:9) as signs of love for God. Israel must make a choice between life and good or death and evil (30:15–16). God's love for Israel brings with it a required theological and social response, that Israel love God. Other nations are to see this way of life based on love and acknowledge it (see Judg 5:31).

Recognition of God's love and the attempt to return that love find expression in the Psalms, with a strong focus on the cult and ritual of the Temple in Jerusalem where the cult was eventually centralized. Israel rejoices in God's presence (Ps 27:4), loves God's sanctuary (Isa 66:10; Pss 26:8; 122:6–9), and calls upon God's name there (Pss 5:12; 69:36–37). Israel's love for God's sanctuary is matched by God's love for the gates of Jerusalem (Pss 51:20–21; 87:1–2). In the Temple and in the cult the social ramifications of love were sometimes in danger of being obscured.

Qumran. The Deuteronomist's understanding of the initiative of God's love is central to the Qumran community (CD B 2:20–21, A 8:15–18, B 1:28–30, A 3:2–4, A 8:17). God has a special love for the spirit of light found in the community and takes pleasure in its works (1QS 3:26). The community responds by loving God and one another (1QH 14:26, 15:10; 1QS 1:3, 9). In this way they preserve the holy community (1QS 2:24; 5:4, 25; 8:2). Only those who love God can be admitted to the community (1QS 2:26–3:3, 1QH 2:14). By contrast, they must detest the sons of darkness (1QS 1:10). While God's love remains strongly in place, absence of a command to love people outside the community indicates the sectarian nature of the community.

Greco-Roman Thought. Plato's reflection on the ideal transcendent Good, manifested in human love, and Aristotle's movement of matter to form by being loved suggest some perennial reflection upon love. The focus of the Greco-Romans was upon human experiences and is reflected in the vocabulary of *eros*, *phileō* (to love) and *epithymia* (desire). Ovid (43 B.C.E.–17 C.E.) sang the praises of sexual love, but the

Cynics and the Stoics of the first century (Epictetus [ca. 55–135 C.E.] and Seneca [ca. 4–65 C.E.]) were suspicious of it. They saw perfect love reflected in control over one's emotions, especially on the part of the philosopher. Musonius Rufus (ca. 30–101 C.E.), Plutarch (46–120 C.E.), and Lucian (ca. 120–ca. 180 C.E.) praised marriage but pointed to the possible corruption of true love. They suggested an inner search for the true meaning and expression of love.

New Testament. The phenomenon of the Christian scriptures depends upon the event of Jesus of Nazareth. The texts that narrate Jesus's story (the gospels) are not objective history, but one can trace the beginnings of Jesus's articulation of the centrality of love to its further theological and socioethical developments in the letters of Paul and the Gospels of Mark, Matthew, and Luke. It reaches its most spectacular articulation in the Gospel of John and the accompanying Johannine letters (1–3 John).

Jesus of Nazareth. Studies of Jesus's teaching on love focus upon *words* found in the Gospels that can be traced back to him. This approach is somewhat one-sided. He not only said things; he also did things in relationships. This can be difficult to trace in detail, but one should not ignore the evidence in the gospels that Jesus was a man of compassion, mercy, and forgiveness. The later insistence of the author of 1 John that the Christian should attempt to "ought to walk just as he walked" (1 John 2:6) and Paul's request that his Christians have in themselves the mind of Christ and to imitate him, as he was an imitator of Christ (Phil 2:5; 1 Cor 4:16–17; 11:1; 1 Thess 1:6–7; 2:14), suggest a lasting memory of Jesus's lifestyle.

Within the Synoptic tradition only two statements of Jesus insist upon the centrality of love. Mark 12:28–34 reports a request from a scribe that Jesus indicates the first commandment. Jesus responds by joining the command to love God above all things with all one's heart, soul, mind, and strength, found in Deuteronomy 6:4–5, and the command to love one's neighbor as oneself, from Leviticus 19:18. The other love command that can be traced back to Jesus is his striking statement: "Love your enemies" (Matt 5:44; Luke 6:27; omitted in Mark). These two traditions (Mark 12:28–34; Q 6:27) are widely accepted as going back to Jesus himself. Nowhere in the Old Testament, Jewish literature, Philo, Josephus, or Qumran can the combination of Deuteronomy 6:4–5 and Leviticus 19:18 be found. Apart from the Synoptic parallels (Matt 22:37–39; Luke 10:27), Jesus's teaching on the combination of love of God, the first of all commandments, and love of neighbor, the second, as greater than any commandment does not play a role in early Christian literature. The same can be said for his command to love one's enemies.

Jesus was part of a tendency of his time to locate simple and essential statements that articulated the heart of Israel's life and practice as he joined the passages from Deuteronomy and Leviticus. He broke new ground in commanding love of God and love of neighbor as greater than any other way of responding to God. He stretched the command to love beyond these limits by insisting upon love for one's enemies. From these "words" of Jesus one can solidly suspect that Jesus's loving lifestyle was driven by love for God, love for neighbor, and even love for his enemies. This was "just as he walked."

Paul. The love of God, the love of Jesus Christ, and the love that the Christian expresses in response to God's saving action in Jesus Christ are central to the Pauline message. The initiative in this process lies entirely with God, who showed love for us while we were yet sinners (Rom 5:8). Christ died for us, and we were thus reconciled with God by means of the death of God's Son. In Romans 8:31–39, Paul is lyrical in his description of the immensity of the saving love that God has made available through Jesus Christ, our Lord. Equally lyrical is his description of the never-ending quality of Christian love, the greatest of all gifts, in 1 Corinthians 12:31c—13:13.

This must be understood within the context of Paul's presentation of God's action in rendering the sinner (Rom 1:18—2:20) righteous through the death and resurrection of Jesus (Rom 1:16–17; 3:21–26). Indeed, it is not only that the sinner is rendered righteous but also that God's action in and through Jesus Christ takes place within an apocalyptic framework. God's righteousness is understood as the power and sovereignty of God for the salvation of the entire creation. This notion can be grasped in the light of Paul's presentation of Jesus's death and resurrection as a "new creation" (2 Cor 5:17; Gal 6:15). For Paul, the Jewish notion of a beginning of all time (*Urzeit*), where the glory of God was manifested, was lost by the disobedience of Adam and the entry of sin into the world (Rom 5:12). This situation can be held at bay by means of observance of the law, confident that at the end of all time (*Endzeit*) God will again assert his sovereignty and the glory of the origins will be restored. However, Paul reinterprets that situation. He draws the *Endzeit* into human history. For Paul, the situation of sin generated by one man's disobedience was overcome by another man's unconditional obedience. Jesus Christ's act of unconditional obedience to God, emptying himself of his likeness to God, taking on the condition of a slave, and humbling himself unto death, even death upon a cross (Phil 2:5–8), reversed the post-Adamic situation of hopeless sinfulness (Rom 5:19). "Where sin increased, grace abounded all the more" (Rom 5:20).

But the traditional expectation of a final end of all time was still in place. Paul uses older traditions (e.g., 1 Thess 5:13–18) and his own formulae (1 Cor 15:51–57; Phil 3:20–21) to refer to an event that is to come in the uncertain future. He gives instruction to his churches on how they are to live the "in-between time." There is a strong sense of living between God's gift of the new creation in and through the death and resurrection of Jesus (Rom 1:16–17; 3:21–26) and the final coming of God and Jesus Christ at the end of time. Believers wait in hope and love through the in-between time (Rom 8:24–25). The creation waits with eager longing, as do those who already enjoy the first fruits of the Spirit groaning inwardly (Rom 8:23).

Already caught up in the anticipated presence of the glory of the end time, given by God through the obedient death and resurrection of his Son, yet aware that the end time is yet to come, the Christian lives the law of love. The law does not save; that has been effected by the death and resurrection of Jesus. But the commandments of the law are still in place. They guide the believer in a response to God's love and grace. Paul never suggests that the law's commandments are invalid. This is made particularly clear in Romans 13:8, where Paul teaches that "the one who loves his neighbor has fulfilled the law" (author's translation). He spells this out with explicit references to the law in verses 9–11, concluding that all the commandments "are summed up in this word, 'Love your neighbor as yourself.' Love does no wrong to a neighbor; therefore, love is the fulfilling of the law" (vv. 10b–11). In Galatians 5:13–14, the call to freedom resulting from God's saving action sets the believer free "through love [to] become slaves to one another. For the whole law is summed up in a single commandment, 'You shall love your neighbor as yourself.'" Although the verb "to love" is not found, its practice within the community is indicated in Galatians 6:2: "Bear one another's burdens, and in this way you will fulfill the law of Christ."

Jesus Christ is the model of how the law must be lived, responding to the loving initiative of God. Christ has made the believer his own (Phil 3:12); God's own love has been bestowed. Living in the in-between time, believers must "be clothed with Christ" (Rom 12:14; Gal 3:27–28; 1 Cor 12:12–13; Col 3:10), live no longer for themselves but for Christ who lives in them, "and the life I now live in the flesh I live by faith in the Son of God, who loved me and gave himself for me" (Gal 2:20; see also 2 Cor 5:14–15). For Paul, repeating the obedient love of Jesus Christ is the way of a believer in the in-between time. The believer has been claimed by love. "As a new man in Christ, the believer *is* love; that is the total meaning of his life and the reason why his obedience is the yielding of his whole life to God" (Furnish, 2009, p. 200).

The Synoptic Gospels. Apart from Jesus's identification of love for God and neighbor as the most important commands in response to the scribe in Mark 12:30–31 and the indication that Jesus looked upon the rich man and loved him (10:21), the Gospel of Mark does not address God's love or the love of Jesus. Jesus's teaching on love of God and neighbor is also recorded in Matthew 22:37–39 and Luke 10:27. Matthew also singles out Jesus's command to love one's neighbor (Matt 5:43). To these words of Jesus, which they received from Mark, Matthew, and Luke, both add Jesus's teaching on the need to love one's enemy (Matt 5:44; Luke 6:27). But Matthew and Luke have their unique contributions to the biblical teaching on love.

The key to Matthew's contribution is 22:37–40. Telling the story of Jesus in a largely Jewish-Christian setting, the relationship between Jesus and the law and the prophets is a matter of crucial importance. For Matthew, all the law and the prophets depend upon the love of God and neighbor (v. 40). This basic supposition plays out in other places where Jesus instructs the people on the need to forgive (6:14–15; 18:21–22, 23–35) and in his regulations on how one should deal with one's enemies (10:17–25) and with one's errant brother (18:15–17). These instructions reflect an early Christian community coming to grips with both outside and inside pressures in the growing tensions between postwar Judaism and emerging Christianity. The high point in Matthew's exposition of the theme of love is found in the last of his five discourses (25:31–46). The situation of a struggling community is again found here, but Matthew's Jesus reaches beyond the community itself to a broader sense of God and neighbor. The word "love" never appears in the discourse, but final judgment will be meted out according to the believer's treatment of the needy neighbor. Service to that neighbor is service to Christ (vv. 40, 45). If the law and the prophets depend upon the command to love God and neighbor (22:37–40), then they are fulfilled in the love and service of others. Not to love in this way will lead to eternal punishment (v. 46).

Jesus's teaching on the need to love God continues in Luke (10:27). Luke's Jesus also asks for love of one's enemy (6:27, 35). The command to love one's neighbor is not explicit but radicalized Luke's insistence that the believer is to be merciful as the heavenly Father is merciful, doing good, lending, and expecting nothing in return, just as the Father is kind to the ungrateful and the selfish (6:35–36). The Lukan ideal of Christian love is most clearly found in the description of the early Christian community as living a genuine *koinōnia* ("fellowship"). Christians are to be devoted to the common good (Acts 2:42; 9:31), selling their possessions to share with all, according to need (2:44–45; 4:32, 34–37), and ready to respond to the needs of others (11:28–29). This ideal is not found in love commands in the gospel but in the numerous uniquely Lukan narratives of Jesus's care and forgiveness for the socially unacceptable

(7:1–9, the Roman centurian; 7:11–17, the widow of Nain; 8:1–3, women in his ministry; 17:11–19, the Samaritan leper; 23:34, forgiveness of his executioners; 23:39–43, the crucified criminal), in his parables that focus upon the marginal (14:15–44; 15:11–32; 16:1–8, 19–31, etc.), and in his instructions not to judge others (6:37–42). Within the narrative of Luke–Acts, love of God, neighbor, and enemy is reflected in the compassion, service, and care for all, even one's enemies, and in showing restraint, forgiving, and sharing with others. This was the way of the Lukan Jesus and the way of the believer in Acts.

The Gospel and letters of John. The theme of love dominates the Gospel and letters of John. It has been claimed that Johannine Christianity, in a way similar to the Qumran sectarians, reflects a move into a sectarian Christianity. John never mentions love of neighbor or enemy but insists that the believers "love one another" (John 13:34–35; 15:12, 17; see also 17:21, 23, 26). The Gospel and the letters must be taken separately as the narrative of the Gospel and the teaching of the letters reflect different literary worlds and slightly different times, with the Gospel predating the letters. The Gospel states clearly that Jesus does the will of the one who sent him, perfecting the task given to him (John 4:34). He must make God known (17:3) and, thus, bring eternal life to all who believe in him (17:2; 20:30–31). The God Jesus must make known is a God who so loved the world that he gave his only Son, not to judge the world but to make possible eternal life (3:16–17). First John 4:8 (cf. v. 16) takes this understanding of God one step further by baldly stating "God is love." The task of Jesus is to make known a God who loves. He does this by means of his unconditional loving response to his Father, when he is "lifted up" on the cross so that he might draw everyone to himself (3:14; 8:28; 12:32–33; 19:25–27). Within the narrative world of the Fourth Gospel it is not only what Jesus says that communicates the message of love but also, especially, what he does.

On the cross the love of God is made visible, and by means of the cross Jesus returns to the glory that was his before the world was made (11:4; 12:27–28; 13:1, 18–19, 31–32; 17:1; 19:28–30). All subsequent believers will look upon the pierced one (19:37). Jesus asks that his disciples be swept up into the love that unites the Father and the Son (17:24–26) and manifest in their lives Jesus's own unconditional and self-giving love (13:34–35; 15:12, 17). The ongoing mission of the Johannine church is entrusted to the ministry of Peter, who must swear his love and commit himself to martyrdom for the glory of God (21:15–19) and to the witness of the disciple whom Jesus loved (21:20–24).

First John repeats the Gospel's teaching on love (3:15–16, 17, 18, 22–24; 4:7–8, 9–10, 12, 15–16, 18–20; 5:1–3), but there are problems in this loving community. Some have left the community, and they are judged severely (2:19). In 2 John 10 the author instructs a Johannine community not to accept anyone who does not live by the "true doctrine" (doubtless that of 1 John). But in 3 John 9–10 a leader of another community, Diotrophes, is following this regulation and not allowing the author of the letters into his community. The Johannine communities are experiencing a severe breakdown in their relationships. What has happened to this early Christian community, founded on Jesus's command to love as he loved (see John 13:34–35; 15:12, 17)?

All Johannine Christians were asked to be beloved disciples (John 20:29), made holy by God so that they may be the holy sent ones of the Father, as Jesus was the holy sent one of the Father (17:18–20). It appears that Johannine Christianity did not succeed. The failure was not the result of the formation of an early Christian sect. Never in the Gospel of John (unlike Qumran) are hatred and rejection of others commanded. Both 2 and 3 John come close and indicate that Johannine Christianity failed because the command to make God known to the world by loving as Jesus had loved them was easier to talk about than to live. Whatever we make of its failure within the early Christian church, Johannine Christianity has left us its story of Jesus, which it must have told and retold, despite (or perhaps because of) their struggles. We would not have the Gospel of John as part of the Christian canon if this were not the case. This is not a sectarian tract, written for the private mutual exhortation of a secret enclave.

Assessment. There is no single biblical understanding of love. Jews and Christians have always seen love as essential to their way of life, their understanding of God, whose love called them, and Christians have always seen love as essential to the role of Jesus Christ, whose love saved them. Both Jews and Christians have been admired and despised across the centuries for features of relationships that depend upon love: admired for those whose self-gift in love is unquestionable, despised for a sectarian and self-centered love that is concerned only with preservation. There are many shades between these extremes. The Bible offers no complete or satisfactory presentation of the profound human phenomenon and experience of love. Nor does it articulate a complete theology and/or Christology based upon love. The biblical development and articulation of the love theme is a limited response to "all aspects of the Christian praxis of love…divine and human love… salvation, sexuality and forgiveness in the light of love" (Jeanrond, 2010, p. 23). The tendency to transform the complexities of love and care for others into a bloodless spirituality of love is to be avoided "to lift all human differences and forms of otherness to a higher spiritual level in the name of love" (cf. Jeanrond, 2010, p. 44). There are many elements in the history of love and the social locations of love that the biblical tradition does not face. It addresses only a small part of the imperative to love found at the heart of the Jewish and Christian scriptures. Nevertheless, it has played, and continues to play, an important role in the religious and secular understanding and regulation of human relationships, theology, and Christology. It deserves a place at the table when the complexity of the human condition and its relationships with God in religious traditions and with one another in a secular traditions are under consideration.

[*See also* Election; Ethics, Biblical; Grace; Hospitality; *and* Mercy and Compassion.]

BIBLIOGRAPHY

Burridge, Richard A. *Imitating Jesus: An Inclusive Approach to New Testament Ethics*. Grand Rapids, Mich.: Eerdmans, 2007.

Furnish, Victor P. *The Love Command in the New Testament*. London: SCM, 1973.

Furnish, Victor P. *Theology and Ethics in Paul.* 2d ed. New Testament Library. Louisville, Ky.: Westminster John Knox, 2009.

Haldar, Alfred O., and John T. Wallis. "*ʾāhabh*, etc." In *Theological Dictionary of the New Testament*, edited by Gerhard Kittel and Gerhard Friedrich, Vol. 1, pp. 99–118. Grand Rapids, Mich.: Eerdmans, 1964.

Jeanrond, Werner G. *A Theology of Love.* London and New York: T&T Clark, 2010.

Meier, John P. "Widening the Focus: The Love Commands of Jesus." In *A Marginal Jew: Rethinking the Historical Jesus*, Vol. 4: *Law and Love*, pp. 478–646. Anchor Yale Bible Reference Library. New Haven, Conn.: Yale University Press, 2009.

Moloney, Francis J. *Love in the Gospel of John: An Exegetical, Theological and Literary Study.* Grand Rapids, Mich.: Baker Academic, 2013.

Quell, Gottfried, and Ethelbert Stauffer. "*agapaō*, etc." In *Theological Dictionary of the New Testament*, edited by Gerhard Kittel and Gerhard Friedrich, Vol. 1, pp. 21–55. Grand Rapids, Mich.: Eerdmans, 1964.

Sakenfeld, Katherine Doob, and William Klassen. "Love." In *The Anchor Bible Dictionary*, edited by David Noel Freedman, Vol. 4, pp. 374–396. New York: Doubleday, 1992.

Sanders, Jack T. *Ethics in the New Testament: Change and Development.* Philadelphia: Fortress, 1985.

Stählin, Gustav. "*phileō*, etc." In *Theological Dictionary of the New Testament*, edited by Gerhard Kittel and Gerhard Friedrich, Vol. 1, pp. 113–171. Grand Rapids, Mich.: Eerdmans, 1974.

Francis J. Moloney

LUKE–ACTS

Analysis of the theology of the two-part narrative conventionally called "Luke–Acts" addresses the story's representation of *theos*, the character of God. God speaks and acts in the narrative through a variety of agents and means, notably Jesus, the Holy Spirit, and prophets and witnesses commissioned by Jesus and authorized by the Spirit. This divine stamp on the story concerns the status and future of a people (ecclesiology) and their engagements with the world (ethics). Other theological loci necessarily come into view, notably Christology (the identity, significance, and work of Jesus), pneumatology (the Spirit of God), soteriology (the meaning and modes of salvation), and eschatology (perspectives on the future and history's culmination). Moreover, Luke's writings betray intensive concern with issues of social status and wealth, of power and authority; the theological interpreter must therefore locate Jesus and the emergent movement for which he is *kyrios* (sovereign Lord) in the geopolitical reality of empire (i.e., Roman hegemony under an emperor). Such an ambitious scope and the inescapable ambiguity that attends interpretation of a narrative (whose reading may vary with the location, commitments, and interests of diverse readers) necessitate a sketch in this article that can only be partial, selective, and shaped by one reader's sense of what matters most for theological interpretation.

Historical Context. The formal preface of Luke 1:1–4 signals that the narrator aims to deliver secure, reliable (*asphaleia*) teaching to readers. Within the religious pluralism of the Roman Empire in the late first or early second century C.E. and in the midst of a sustained contest for a legitimate stake in the religious heritage of Judaism in which Jesus-followers participated during this era, Luke's two-volume literary project was an exercise in legitimation. Historical experience raised important questions for Luke's readers and those with whom they interacted. How may a movement that affirms its rootedness in Israel's scriptures and hopes rightly lay claim to the Jewish story when it is increasingly spurned by Jews and embraced by non-Jews? Sharp debate persists over the images of Judaism encountered in Luke's writings, a debate sustained in part because of the ambiguity and ambivalence in the presentations of Judaism and the Jewish people in Luke–Acts. Moreover, how does a movement whose founder (Jesus) and a key proponent (Paul) were executed through Roman judicial process have a legitimate place in the empire? (Beyond the narrative in Acts, later accounts report Paul's execution: *1 Clem.* 5.5–7; *Mart. Paul*; Eusebius *Hist. eccl.* 2.25.) Once prevalent readings of Luke–Acts as an apologetic text portraying benign relations between "the Way" and the empire have increasingly yielded to readings that discern in Luke–Acts a sharp critique of Roman imperial rule and culture.

God's Saving Initiative. Although debate about the genre(s) of Luke and Acts continues unabated (with proposals ranging from biography to epic, from historical monograph to novel), most scholars locate Luke's writings within Jewish and Greco-Roman historiographical traditions. Luke's central concern with the purposes of God, enacted within the ongoing history of God's people, weds historical interest and theological commitment, positioning Luke–Acts as a continuation of biblical (OT) histories. The narrative consistently foregrounds the announcement and fulfillment of the divine purpose (*boulē*) in a manner that repeatedly displays the capacity of God's will and word to overcome every obstacle, whether demonic or imperial, whether expressed in betrayal and desertion from within or in persecution from outside. Accordingly, the crucifixion of Jesus by order of Pontius Pilate, the Roman governor (26–36 C.E.), is answered by divine vindication in Jesus's resurrection and exaltation to a position of power (Luke 23–24; Acts 1–2). Violent opposition to the movement by Saul (Paul) gives way to a stunning role-reversal wherein the persecutor becomes a powerful and persecuted proclaimer of the message (Acts 9). Paul's career closes on a note of unhindered preaching of the message of *God's* empire in the heart of Rome (Acts 28:30–31), even as Paul the prisoner awaits eventual execution. God's effective purpose, whether embraced or opposed by human characters in the narrative, gives coherence to the Lukan writings.

God's purpose (*boulē*) is centered on salvation (*sōtēria* or *sōtērion*), understood less as military deliverance from enemy domination (see Luke 1:71) than as the restoration of God's people Israel. This restoration is concretized in acts of healing, liberation, hospitality and social acceptance, forgiveness, and status role-reversal: the equipping of God's people to fulfill their divinely given vocation to bring illumination and blessing to the nations, including Gentiles (e.g., Luke 2:30–32; Acts 3:25; 13:46–48; 15:14–18). This restoration and equipping are effected through the message and actions of Jesus, the Spirit-anointed prophet-Messiah through whom God's sovereign rule reconfigures humanly constructed social worlds, as well as through commissioned agents (apostles and other followers in concert with them). First in Galilee and ultimately in Rome and beyond, "to the ends of the earth" (Acts 1:8), their words and alternative social practices attest the sovereignty of a counter-

ruler: both Jesus and God bear the status of *kyrios* (Lord). God restores Israel "despite the negative way some receive this restoration" (Salmeier, 2011, p. 153). The narrative thus depicts continuity—fulfillment of ancient promise to Israel in the movement associated with Jesus the Messiah—but also discontinuity, glimpsed both in the mixed reception accorded the Messiah and in the inclusion of Gentiles among the covenant people of God. Yet there is more to this seeming discontinuity than meets the eye: the incorporation of Gentiles within Israel fulfills ancient promise, for Israel thus actualizes its divine vocation of conveying salvation to the nations (Luke 24:45–48).

Jesus, Prophetic-Messianic Agent of Divine Rule. As prophet and Messiah anointed by the Spirit (Luke 3:21–22; 4:18–19; Acts 10:38), Jesus undertakes a mission to Israel that centers on *aphesis*, a "release" that takes concrete form in acts of healing, exorcism, and forgiveness of both debt and (especially) sin. The prophet-Messiah invites any and all into the realm governed by God, enacting that reign in emblematic, celebratory meals (e.g., Luke 14:15–24; cf. 13:23–30). The divine realm is configured by both horizontal and vertical reversals, as Jesus extends God's hospitality to persons on and beyond the social margins (sinners, tax collectors, and poor, sick, or disabled persons) while those at the center who enjoy the advantage of high status turn a cold shoulder and find their place at the table in jeopardy (e.g., Luke 5:27–32; 7:36–50; 13:10–17; 15:1–32; 18:9–17; 19:1–10). Centering on compassionate embrace of sinners, the horizontal reversals and boundary-transgressing hospitality of Luke's Gospel extend in Acts to Gentiles, especially devout God-fearers as transitional recipients of the message (programmatically, in the person of the pious centurion Cornelius; Acts 10). The introduction of Jesus's mission already anticipates these later developments (Luke 2:29–32; 3:4–6; 4:18–19, 25–27).

Jesus sets out to restore Israel as a people aligned with divine aims and commitments, with the call of 12 apostles symbolizing that project of restoration (Luke 6:12–16; 9:1–6). The result, however, is not unanimous embrace of the prophetic message or of the Messiah's rule but, instead, a divided people (thus, Simeon's prophetic oracle in Luke 2:34–35). From the beginning of Luke to the end of Acts, the narrative presents a divided response to God's saving initiative (culminating in Acts 28:23–28). Nevertheless, because Luke narrates the triumph of God's word and divine sovereignty, divided human response is not the last word. The scriptural pattern of prophets repudiated by their people (Luke 4:24; 13:33–35; Acts 7:51–53), of a Messiah who exercises ironic rule by way of a Roman cross, continues to give shape to the story of Israel and of God's unceasing commitment to its deliverance in ways that defy expectation (Luke 24:21). Jesus is Lord, the authorized agent of God's reign, and all who call upon him will receive the salvation promised to God's people (Acts 2:21, 39); God must validate this authority through the resurrection of Jesus after his rejection and execution (Acts 2:36; cf. Luke 19:11–27).

As Jesus in the Gospel forms a community of followers shaped by the values and commitments of God's reign, so also the mission in Acts welcomes any who accept the message of God's salvation: Judeans in large numbers (Acts 2:41; 6:7), Samaritans (8:4–25), and then Gentiles (10:1–48). When the message moves beyond conventional social boundaries, drawing Samaritans and later non-Jews into the movement, the divine Spirit intervenes, authorizing their inclusion (8:14–17; 10:44). As the mission advances, despite hurdles and obstacles, the word and, thus, the community of God grow (19:20).

The Holy Spirit: Continuing Witness to God's Word and Work. The Spirit empowers Jesus's liberative mission of "release" (Luke 4:1, 14, 18–19; Acts 10:38). After Jesus's crucifixion, resurrection, and exaltation, the Spirit directs the course of a mission that begins in Jerusalem and extends to the farthest reaches of the earth, energizing and equipping Jesus's followers for that mission (Luke 2:49; Acts 2:1–13, N.B. 16–21, 33). In tandem with mighty acts of release, their proclamation of the word continues the pattern of Jesus's ministry in the Gospel.

Before placing the stamp of divine commissioning and empowerment upon Jesus's ministry, the Holy Spirit summons witness to the fulfillment of scriptural promise in the births of the baptizing prophet John and the Messiah Jesus. The Spirit's role in animating proclamation receives emphasis in Luke 1:67 (Zechariah) and 2:25–27 (Simeon): this becomes the primary mode of the Spirit's activity in the book of Acts as Jesus's followers face hostile opposition (Acts 4:29–31; 7:55) just as he assured them they would (Luke 12:11–12). The Spirit provides divine authorization and empowerment for Jesus's liberative mission, then guides and emboldens the proclamation and witness of Jesus's followers to the end of the narrative and beyond, "to the ends of the earth" (Acts 1:8). The Spirit is presented as speaking a divine message in the voice of an Old Testament character like David (Acts 4:25; cf. 2:30–35); thus, Luke's readers may surmise that it is Spirit-aided interpretation of scripture that forges the connection between human and divine speech (Acts 2:17).

Eschatology and Ethics in the Meantime. Luke's distinctive development of eschatological traditions claimed scholarly attention in the wake of Conzelmann's pioneering redaction-critical analysis (1960), which placed in the foreground the problem of the Parousia's delay and found in Luke a solution that deferred Jesus's return to the remote future. Luke's Gospel pictures the salvific activity of God's realm as present in significant measure in Jesus's public ministry (2:29–32; 11:20; 17:20–21; 19:9–10; cf. 23:43). Nevertheless, the reign of God remains a matter for fervent prayer and hope (11:2); that hope encompasses Jesus's decisive return as the human one anticipated by Daniel 7, by whom the faithful will be delivered (Luke 21:27–28) and in whom divine judgment is vested (cf. Acts 17:31). The completion of God's sovereign purpose for the world is imminent neither during the time of Jesus's ministry nor during the early mission narrated in Acts nor even in connection with the destruction of the Jerusalem Temple (Luke 21:5–9, 20–24); still, that fulfillment remains a vital hope in the time of Luke's readers (21:29–31). In the meantime, the community nourished by the teaching of Jesus and his followers is summoned to vigilance and persevering faith and faithfulness (12:35–53; 17:22—18:8; 21:34–36). They will give bold public witness to the reigning presence of God through the Lord Jesus ("Lord of all," as Peter puts it in Acts 10:36). They will also participate in a distinctive set of practices as members of the community that gathers around the Lord's chosen apostolic leaders.

Jesus's own enactment of God's reign shapes the community of disciples (apostles plus many others), which is marked by distinctive social practices that run counter to the culture over which the Roman emperor presides. Vertical status reversals subvert concern for the privilege of status and preoccupation with honor-seeking (Luke 1:51–53; 6:20–26; 14:7–11; 16:15; 18:14, 15–17). Commitment to radically generous sharing of wealth sets aside concern for reciprocal benefit (14:12–14; 18:18–30). Hospitality embraces outsiders and the socially and economically marginalized (5:27–32; 14:16–24; 15:1–32; 18:15–17; cf. 7:36–50; 19:1–10). Luke's second volume depicts a movement characterized by such practices: generous sharing of possessions sustains a community where none is in need, at least for a while (Acts 2:45; 4:32–37; cf. 11:27–30). And with significant prompting by God (through visions and interventions by the Spirit), Jesus's followers welcome Samaritans and Gentiles into their company (8:14–17, 25; 10:1—11:18). After the pattern of Jesus, his followers extend compassion to the sick and disabled (3:1–10; 5:12–16; 14:8–10; 19:11–12).

Theology and ethics are thus intertwined. If God is gracious and extends mercy beyond humanly constructed, culturally normed boundaries, then those who live in the domain ruled by God should enact inclusive hospitality and generous benefaction without expectation of reward (Luke 6:27–36). If God's reign is defined by vertical status reversals that privilege the poor and powerless, the sick and young, then those who exercise leadership among God's people should not seek advantage of power and position. Jesus himself serves as the model for emulation in this regard (22:24–27). Nevertheless, the recurring pattern of human resistance overmatched by divine redemptive initiative, evident even in the narrative's conclusion (Acts 28:17–31), indicates that the hope-engendering message borne by witness to the farthest reaches of the world and enacted in distinctive social practices will continue, beyond the narrative's ending, not because of human fidelity but rather because of God.

Continuing Challenges for Theological Interpretation. Judged at the bar of Paul's theology of the cross by some interpreters in the last half of the twentieth century, Luke was for some time found wanting. Subsequent scholarship shows fresh appreciation of Luke's distinctive theological vision, even though important concerns linger.

Multiculturalism and triumphalism. Luke's narrative offers a panoramic vision of one universal people of God, transcending ethnic, cultural, and religious boundaries and (implicitly) supplanting the general histories of Luke's era that pictured world history's culmination in Roman imperial rule (e.g., Dionysius of Halicarnassus, *Ant. rom.*; Diodorus of Sicily, *Library of History*). Charges of triumphalism against Luke exaggerate: Acts leaves readers expecting a still-future completion of God's mission of salvation, for which Rome has become a fresh point of departure (28:17–31). Still, Roman imperial rule remains largely untouched at the story's end, as the fact of Paul's imprisonment makes clear. Luke's depiction of a movement that embraces cultural difference is helpful for readers in the complex, culturally diverse global reality of the twenty-first century. Nevertheless, the bold claim this narrative advances—that there is one God worthy of worship and one Lord through whom salvation comes—is provocative in a religiously plural world, whether in the first or the twenty-first century (Acts 4:12; 14:11–18; 17:23–25). Evaluations of the Lukan narrative, however, should also attend to its counterimperial and countercultural impulses, radically framed as reversals of social status and honor that subvert any triumphalist claims.

Anti-Judaism? One of the most vigorous and heated ongoing debates regarding Luke's theological perspective centers on the narrative's ambivalent representations of the Jewish people, religion, and institutions. Luke–Acts has both spirited defenders, who perceive it as affirming Jewish religion and people, and sharp critics, who brand its story "anti-Jewish" or "anti-Semitic." Luke anchors the narrative in the history, hopes, and people of Israel, embedding Jesus's life and ministry in that story. Luke's two volumes portray both Jesus and his followers as serious readers of Jewish scripture and as Torah-observant, though their interpretation and practice of the Law and the Prophets is shaped by Jesus's own reading and practice (Luke 6:1–11; 10:25–37; 14:1–6; 16:16–31; 18:18–23; Acts 15:12–29). Yet the narrative presents an Israel divided in response, first to the ministry of Jesus and later to the mission of his successors—with increasingly negative portrayals of Jewish people as each narrative moves toward its close—while that mission also incorporates Gentiles (e.g., Luke 23:13–25; Acts 13:44–51; 18:5–6, 12; 19:8–10; 28:17–28). The plot of Luke–Acts intimates that the movement's future demographics will place Gentiles in the majority, with increasing Jewish resistance. Appeals to scripture for the legitimacy of this development root the movement in Judaism but at the same time give rise, for some readers, to the disconcerting sense that Luke's story is supersessionist: Have the groups for whom Luke writes, who have appropriated the promises for Israel, supplanted Israel? How one appraises this mix of continuity and discontinuity informs one's theo-ethical engagement with Luke's writings.

Women in Luke–Acts. The debate over representations of women in Luke–Acts has proved spirited and durable. Some see in Luke's story affirmation of women's standing within the company of disciples; others concede that women play a prominent role in the narrative but charge Luke with consigning women to restricted, conventional social roles. Is Mary, hospitality-conscious Martha's sister, a model of passive listening (compared with men who are authorized to speak) or of authentic discipleship (Luke 10:38–42)? Luke's bent for pairing women and men offers prophetic Anna alongside Simeon—but only Simeon's oracle is delivered as direct speech (Luke 2:25–38); similarly, Acts 21:8–11 gives Philip's four prophetic daughters no spoken lines, which are reserved for Agabus instead. To what degree does Jesus's liberating vision, with its reversals of social status and relativization of social advantage, affect the status of women in Luke's account?

The narrative's ambivalence regarding women reflects the cultural constraints of Luke's own social location. Nevertheless, their activity—including Spirit-inspired Elizabeth and Mary (Luke 1:39–56); Mary Magdalene, Joanna, and Mary on Easter morning (24:1–11); successful merchant and house church–hosting Lydia (Acts 16:14–15); Priscilla, who instructs Apollos (18:26)—also places them in the ranks of prophets and teachers empowered for service as "eyewitnesses and ministers of the word" (Luke 1:2).

Political theology: Luke–Acts and empire. "These people who have been turning the world upside down have come here also.… They are all acting contrary to the decrees of the emperor, saying that there is another king named Jesus" (Acts 17:6–7). So say at least some detractors of the movement, whose emergence within the Roman Empire Luke chronicles. In a similar vein, the Roman prefect Pontius Pilate hears accusations that Jesus is a subversive teacher guilty of sedition (Luke 23:2, 5, 14). The message and social practices of both Jesus and his followers suggest that critics have raised legitimate concerns. Yet, even as Pilate hands Jesus over to crucifixion after a cursory interrogation, he dismisses the charges against the prisoner as unfounded (23:3–4, 14–15, 22). Likewise, even as King Herod Agrippa II (r. ca. 50–ca. 93 C.E.) and Festus, the Roman governor of Judea (ca. 59– ca. 62 C.E.), prepare to dispatch Paul to Rome to present his judicial appeal to the emperor (Nero, though unnamed in the narrative), Agrippa emphasizes the prisoner's innocence (Acts 26:30–32). Such mixed signals regarding the disposition of "the Way" within the imperial order point to the complexity of the challenge facing Luke and the emergent Christian groups for which he is writing. The movement's aims, values, commitments, and practices are shaped by its allegiance to a sovereign other than the emperor. But Luke expresses no prospect of a real-world replacement of the Roman Empire by God's dominion (*basileia*), at least not until the eschatological consummation (Luke 21:24–33).

In the meantime, Luke's critique of imperial culture and its structures of economy and power must be subtly nuanced. The followers of the Messiah-Lord Jesus on their mission to the farthest limits of the earth will navigate the Roman world as a law-abiding people who are adherents of a legitimate, venerable, and ancient religion, that is, as claimants to the history of the Jewish people. The narrative thus depicts deep "cultural disruption" but not "sedition" (Rowe, 2009, p. 149). The governing image for this disruption is resurrection rather than insurrection. Thus, the reader finds within this artful story not a "platform for revolution" but an alternative way of life that is to be pursued within alternative communities (Rowe, 2009, p. 150). The political theology that informs Luke's two volumes features a world turned upside down—symbolically, ideologically, and, to at least some degree, practically—by Christians' allegiance to their Messiah-Lord as they carry out a world-encompassing mission authorized by the sovereign God whose rule Jesus has announced and enacted. Luke–Acts invites, indeed forcefully presses, a crucial question: What implications does such a theopolitical vision have for readers' critical engagement with the geopolitics of the twenty-first century?

[*See also* Christology; Conversion; Discipleship; Ecclesiology; Eschatology; Ethics, Biblical; Forgiveness; Gentiles; Gospel; Holy Spirit; Joy; Judaism; Kingdom of God (Heaven); Mercy and Compassion; Parable; Paul; Repentance; Salvation History; Soteriology; Wealth and Poverty; *and* Witness.]

BIBLIOGRAPHY

Balentine, Samuel E., ed. "The Book of Acts." *Interpretation* 66, no. 3 (2012).

Bartholomew, Craig G., Joel B. Green, and Anthony C. Thiselton, eds. *Reading Luke: Interpretation, Reflection, Formation*. Scripture and Hermeneutics 6. Grand Rapids, Mich.: Zondervan, 2005.

Bock, Darrell L. *A Theology of Luke and Acts*. Biblical Theology of the New Testament. Grand Rapids, Mich.: Zondervan, 2012.

Bovon, François. *Luke the Theologian: Fifty-Five Years of Research (1950–2005)*. 2d ed. Waco, Tex.: Baylor University Press, 2006.

Conzelmann, Hans. *The Theology of Luke*. Translated by Geoffrey Buswell. New York: Harper & Row, 1960. English translation of *Die Mitte der Zeit*, first published in 1954 (Tübingen, Germany: J.C.B. Mohr).

Darr, John A. *On Character Building: The Reader and the Rhetoric of Characterization in Luke–Acts*. Literary Currents in Biblical Interpretation. Louisville, Ky.: Westminster John Knox, 1992.

Green, Joel B. *The Theology of the Gospel of Luke*. New Testament Theology. Cambridge, U.K.: Cambridge University Press, 1995.

Jervell, Jacob. *The Theology of the Acts of the Apostles*. New Testament Theology. Cambridge, U.K.: Cambridge University Press, 1996.

Keener, Craig S. *Acts: An Exegetical Commentary*. Vol. 1: *Introduction and 1:1—2:47*. Grand Rapids, Mich.: Baker Academic, 2012.

Marshall, I. Howard. *Luke: Historian and Theologian*. Grand Rapids, Mich.: Zondervan, 1970.

Marshall, I. Howard, and David Peterson, eds. *Witness to the Gospel: The Theology of Acts*. Grand Rapids, Mich.: Eerdmans, 1998.

O'Toole, Robert F. *The Unity of Luke's Theology: An Analysis of Luke–Acts*. Good News Studies 9. Wilmington, Del.: Michael Glazier, 1984.

Rowe, C. Kavin. *World Upside Down: Reading Acts in the Graeco-Roman Age*. Oxford: Oxford University Press, 2009.

Salmeier, Michael A. *Restoring the Kingdom: The Role of God as the "Ordainer of Times and Seasons" in the Acts of the Apostles*. Princeton Theological Monograph Series 165. Eugene, Ore.: Pickwick, 2011.

Seim, Turid Karlsen. *The Double Message: Patterns of Gender in Luke–Acts*. Edinburgh: T&T Clark, 1994.

Squires, John T. *The Plan of God in Luke–Acts*. Society for New Testament Studies Monograph Series 76. Cambridge, U.K.: Cambridge University Press, 1993.

Tannehill, Robert C. *The Narrative Unity of Luke–Acts: A Literary Interpretation*. 2 vols. Philadelphia and Minneapolis: Fortress, 1986–1990.

Tyson, Joseph B. *Images of Judaism in Luke–Acts*. Columbia: University of South Carolina Press, 1992.

Verheyden, Joseph, ed. *The Unity of Luke–Acts*. Bibliotheca Ephemeridum Theologicarum Lovaniensium 142. Louvain, Belgium: Leuven University Press, 1999.

John T. Carroll

MALACHI

See Book of the Twelve (Minor Prophets).

MARK

No biblical writing systematizes its theology. While Romans and Hebrews offer sustained articulations of early Christian faith, Mark does not. For convenience one may abstract and coordinate aspects of Markan theology; in so doing one betrays the narrative form in which the Evangelist leads the reader on a jagged journey of faith. This essay offers something like analysis of movements and leitmotifs extracted from their symphonic context. Comprehension of Mark's theology depends on reading the gospel whole.

The Kingdom of God, Its Agent, and Power. Mark opens (1:1), "The beginning of the good news of Jesus Christ, the Son of God." This theme is recapitulated in Jesus's introductory announcement (1:15): "The time is fulfilled, and the kingdom of God has come near; repent, and believe in the good news." Within and between these framing assertions, much of this gospel's theology is compressed.

- "The good news" (*euangelion*; see also 1:14; 10:29; 13:10; 14:9) concerns the coming of God's "kingdom" or dynamic sovereignty (*basileia*) over mortal life and human monarchies. God's mysterious dominion is bursting into the theater of human life (4:11, 26, 30); old structures cannot contain it (2:18–28; 3:31–35; 7:1–23; 10:2–12, 35–45).

- Jesus, God's anointed (*christos*), heralds this good news, summoning others to trust it (1:15). Jesus mediates the kingdom by exercising divine authority to exorcise unclean spirits (1:21–28; 5:1–20; 7:24–20; 9:14–29) to heal infirmities (1:29–34; 3:1–6; 5:21–43; 7:31–37; 8:22–26; 10:46–52), to forgive sins (2:1–12), and to confront others (3:19b–35; 11:15—12:44)—in a moment of crisis even himself (14:36)—with God's will. Where Jesus is, there is God's kingdom.

- The kingdom's advent, activated by Jesus, is presaged in the scriptural prophecy of preparing "the way of the Lord" (1:2–3; cf. Exod 23:20; Mal 3:1; Isa 40:3), itself personified by John the Baptist in Elijah's guise (1:4–8; 6:14–29; 9:9–14; cf. 2 Kgs 1:8; 21:1–26; Zech 13:4). John's message of repentance (*metanoia*, "turning of the mind") and forgiveness (*aphesis hamartiōn*, "release from sins") anticipates Jesus's proclamation (Mark 1:15). Many of Jesus's astonishing deeds (4:35–41; 6:30–52; 8:1–10) recollect prophetic activity in Israel (2 Kgs 4:8–37, 42–44) and God's own mighty works (Exod 16:4–21; Ps 107:23–30).

- The Holy Spirit attends Jesus's baptism (1:8–11; cf. 3:29; 13:11; 14:38; Isa 42:1–5; Ezek 2:2; 3:12–15). Immediately afterward, the Spirit drives Jesus into the wilderness for 40 days of satanic temptation (1:12–13; cf. Deut 8:2; Neh 9:21). The gospel's remainder is suffused by Jesus's assault of diabolical powers (3:11, 23, 26; 4:15; 5:12; 6:7), temptations of him and of his disciples to abandon the kingdom's mandates (8:11–13, 31–33; 10:35–41; 14:1–2, 10–11, 29–42, 43–53, 66–72), and apocalyptic foreshadowing of distress and eventual redemption (4:13–20, 26–32; 8:34—9:1; 9:38–50; 10:42–45; 13:1–37; 14:22–28).

From this précis emerge distinguishing features of Markan theology.

1. Formally, it unfolds as a brisk narrative, with Jesus its principal protagonist (1:1). Compared with other gospels (Matt 5:1—7:28; Luke 12:1—18:14; John 13:12—17:26), Mark rarely pauses for Jesus to offer uninterrupted instruction (4:1–32; 13:5–37); by comparison with other Synoptics, the teaching in Mark is more opaque than clarifying (cf. Mark 8:15/Luke 12:1; Mark 9:13/Matt 17:12–13).

2. Substantively, Markan theology is coherent but not systematically coordinated. Past (Israel's history), present (first-century Judea and Galilee, 1:5, 14; cf. 6:14–29), and future (eschatological completion) are tightly telescoped. As God's beloved son (1:11), Jesus preaches God's gospel on God's behalf (1:14) at the Spirit's behest (1:10–12). While Mark assumes no doctrine of the Trinity, its three "persons" and their dynamic interaction are in play (cf. Matt 28:19; Eph 2:18).

3. Though not an apocalypse in genre, Mark's gospel is eschatologically saturated. The heaven's rending and the Spirit's descent (1:10), encounters with Satan, wild beasts, and angels (v. 13) are elements in Hellenistic Jewish apocalypticism (Isa 64:1, Ezek 1:1; *1 En.* 72.1; *As. Mos.* 10.1; *T. Naph.* 7:7). Though rare, "the kingdom of God" is also an apocalyptic metaphor (*1 En.* 10:1—11:12; *Pss. Sol.* 17.1), and some strands of Jewish messianism are eschatological (CD 6.7011; *Pss. Sol.* 17:1—18:13; *4 Ezra* 11–12; *2 Bar.* 40, 72).

4. Unresolved tension is distinctive of Mark. In its prologue (1:1–15) this trait is conspicuous. The very first word signals the gospel's *archē*, "be-

ginning" (v. 1), with no terminus indicated. The identity of the "messenger [sent] to prepare [the] way" (v. 2) is equivocal because it is unclear whether it refers to John or to Jesus. Jesus is addressed from heaven as God's son, overheard by the reader (v. 11), and intuited by unclean spirits (1:24; 3:11); no one else in Mark is privy to his identity at the start (cf. Matt 3:17; Luke 2:49; John 1:29–34). Unlike Matthew 4:11 (cf. Luke 4:13), Jesus's temptation does not end in obvious triumph (Mark 1:13; cf. 3:27). Jesus does not proclaim that God's dominion has fully arrived; rather, "the time [*kairos*] is fulfilled, and the kingdom has come near" (1:15; cf. 9:1; 13:32–27; 14:25). "Belief in the good news" lies in a gap between the kingdom's inauguration and consummation.

God. Mark's 48 occurrences of *theos* are unique in the New Testament because they predicate almost nothing about God (9:37; 11:25; 12:27 are exceptions). Attributes of God may be inferred from Mark's fourteen sayings about "the kingdom of God," which is not coterminous with Israel or any geopolitical entity, neither an inner spirituality nor a utopian dream. God's *basileia* is anticipated (9:1; 14:25; 15:43) yet secretly erupting in history (Mark 4:22; cf. Matt 13:18–23; Luke 17:20–21). A gift from God, not a human achievement (Mark 4:26–29; 10:23–27; cf. Luke 12:32, John 3:3), the kingdom upends conventional expectations (Mark 4:30–32; cf. Matt 20:1–16; Luke 9:59–60). Its acceptance demands radical sacrifice (Mark 9:42–50) and infant dependence (10:13–15). The kingdom's ineluctable mystery, simultaneously revelatory and concealing (4:11–12; cf. Rom 11:25–36; 1 Cor 1:18—2:13), is developed in Jesus's references to God's transcendence (Mark 11:12—12:34).

To God belongs compassionate but final judgment over Israel, all the nations, and their religious custodians (11:17–18; 12:1–12; cf. Ps 96:13; Isa 2:4; Ezek 7:27). Secular power is relativized by God's sovereignty, which encompasses all of life without reduction to sectarian theocracy (Mark 12:13–17; cf. Rom 13:1–13). Through scripture (Exod 3:2, 6, 15), God affirms his enduring life and power over death (Mark 12:18–27).

No commandment is greater than Israel's complete love of the one and only God (Deut 6:4–5) and love of neighbor as one's self (Lev 19:18; Mark 12:28–34; cf. Luke 10:27; Rom 13:9; Gal 5:14; Jas 2:8). Throughout Mark, Jesus's teaching is radically theistic: membership in Jesus's family is defined as doing "the will of God" (3:35); discipleship to Jesus turns satanic when Peter sets his mind "not on divine things but on human things" (8:33); repeatedly, the criterion of Jesus's fidelity is acceptance of all that "the Son of Man must [*dei*] undergo great suffering" because it is God's will (8:31; cf. 9:34; 10:33–34; 14:36). The Resurrection decisively verifies God's own fidelity to his beloved Son (1:11; 9:7; 14:28; 16:6–7).

Jesus. Because he perfectly represents the one who sent him (9:37; 12:6; cf. John 5:30; 13:20) and instantiates the kingdom's values, Jesus is uniquely positioned in Mark to convey God's good news. A key metaphor is "sonship": used absolutely ("Son" 12:6; 13:32) but more often with predicates of Jesus's likeness to God (1:1; 3:11; 5:7; 14:61; cf. Jer 31:20 [referring to Israel], Sir 4:10c [protectors of the poor], Philo, *Spec.* 1 58.318 [the virtuous]). Compared with some other New Testament Christologies, Mark's appears functional rather than ontological: Jesus is God's Son through obedience, not by origin (cf. Matt 1:21–23; Luke 1:35; John 5:19–24; Heb 1:2). Although acclamations of Jesus as God's Son occur at critical points in the narrative (1:11 [Jesus's baptism; cf. Gen 22:2; Ps 2:7; Isa 42:1]; 9:7 [his transfiguration]; 15:39 [his death]), to claim this title's primacy in Mark outruns the evidence. "Son of God" complements other aspects of the Evangelist's presentation of Jesus and counterbalances other modes of reference to him, none of which adequately encompasses everything Mark asserts.

Compared with other New Testament witnesses—especially Luke–Acts, Paul, and Hebrews—Mark rarely refers to Jesus as "Christ" (= "Messiah" 1:1; 8:29; 9:41; 14:61; 15:32) or "Lord" (1:3; 2:28; 11:3; 12:37). By contrast with Matthew (e.g., 1:1; 21:9, 15), Mark seems especially leery of "Son of David": only a blind man so addresses him (10:47–48), and 12:35–37 implies that title's inappropriateness for Jesus (cf. Rom 1:3; 2 Tim 2:8; Rev 22:16).

By far, Mark's most common appellation for Jesus is the most enigmatic: "Son of Man." This self-identification carries several connotations: an earthly, authoritative figure who can transgress conventional Jewish piety (2:10, 28; cf. Isa 56:2, which assumes Torah's strictures), an apocalyptic figure to come (8:38; 13:26–27; 14:62; cf. Dan 7:13–14; *1 En.* 69:27–29; *Sib. Or.* 5.414–33), or—by a ratio of three to one—a figure that must suffer and be vindicated by God (8:31; 9:9, 12, 31b; 10:33–34, 45; 14:21, 41; cf. Ezek 4:1—5:17; 12:1–28; 24:15–27; Wis 1–6). These three nuances are mutually interpretive, begging coordination with other designations (like "Son of God") within Mark's narrative framework, which presents Jesus as the teacher whose insight is uniquely authoritative (2:23–28; 7:6–15) and the healer whose power over hostile forces will be consummated (1:21–28; 13:26–27; 14:62) only after he has relinquished his life for others (10:45). What sets the Markan "Son of Man" apart from other Jewish apocalypticism is its emphasis on his death, with a redemptive consequence that extends beyond Israel. Significantly, the single point in Mark at which all major ascriptions of Jesus converge is his acceptance of the high priest's oblique affirmation of him as Christ and Son of God, which seals the Son of Man's death warrant (14:61–64).

The Holy Spirit. Compared with Luke–Acts (Luke 1–2; Acts 2:1–42; 10:1—11:18), John (14:15–26; 16:13–15); and the Pauline tradition (Rom 8:1–30; Gal 5:16—6:10; Eph 2:1–22), Markan pneumatology is underdeveloped. Nevertheless, the Spirit is the power that propels Jesus's ministry (Mark 1:8, 10, 12), particularly his assault against unclean spirits that plague human life (1:23, 26; 5:2, 8; 7:25; 9:17, 20, 25). To confuse Jesus's healing power with diabolism is an unforgiveable blasphemy against the Spirit (3:22–30), presumably because it drives the accuser away from the genuine agent of God's forgiveness (2:10; cf. 1 John 5:16–17). Beyond the Spirit's presence with Jesus, his persecuted followers may rely on the Spirit to provide them testimony in their hour of trial (Mark 13:11).

Responses to God's Sovereignty: Discipleship and Resistance. As Christology and pneumatology follow from the second Evangelist's view of God, so also is discipleship (incipient ecclesiology) a coefficient of

Christology. Discipleship in Mark is "following Jesus" at his command (1:16–20; 2:13–14; 3:13–19a), extending his authority over demonic forces while healing the sick and feeding the hungry (6:7–13, 30–44; 8:1–10). Disciples who abandon family and property for the sake of Jesus and the gospel are reintegrated into a new family around him that does God's will (3:31–35), assured they will receive a hundredfold of all they have lost and, in the age to come, eternal life (10:28–31). With such rewards come persecutions (10:30c): intrafamilial betrayals, beatings, and susceptibility to deceit (13:5–27), all of which must be endured to the end (13:13b, 32–37).

As the Son of Man's vindication depends on giving up his life for others (8:31–32a; 9:31–32; 10:33–34), so do self-denial and taking up one's cross constitute the essence of discipleship (8:34). Mark reiterates this hard dedication paradoxically: saving one's life by losing it (8:35); becoming first by being last and servant of all (9:35); receiving the kingdom as a powerless child (10:13–16); giving up everything for heavenly treasure (10:17–25); achieving greatness only by self-enslavement (10:43–45); preaching that provokes temporary futility, punishment, and universal hatred (13:10–13a; cf. 4:14–19). Such self-sacrifice is distinguished from masochistic despair by Jesus's insistence that all is done for the gospel's sake (1:15; 8:35; 10:29), united with Jesus's newly inaugurated covenant (14:22–25) and assured of redemption by his own sacrifice (10:45; 14:24) plus the promise of his post-Resurrection persistence (14:28).

Moral responsibility. Upon receiving Jesus's word, rootless disciples may jump for joy, but "when trouble or persecution arises on account of the word, immediately they fall away" (4:17). On the night of their master's arrest, the Twelve are equally glib and traitorous (14:29–31, 50–52, 66–72). Jesus's interpretation of the sower parable (4:3–8) identifies another temptation besetting discipleship: being "sown among the thorns," wherein "the cares of the world, and the lure of wealth, and the desire for other things come in and choke the word, and it yields nothing" (4:18–19). That is the experience of a devout man whose many possessions block his inheritance of eternal life (10:17–22). Though less developed than in Luke (12:15–21;

16:1–13, 19–31; 19:1–10), Mark is pointedly concerned about the danger of wealth, which perverts filial responsibility (7:6–13; cf. Exod 20:12; 21:17; Lev 20:9; Deut 5:16); eases divorce, whose economic burden fell primarily on the woman (Mark 10:2–9); and encourages fraud (Mark 10:19b, seemingly interpolated from Deut 24:14 into the Decalogue's second table [Exod 20:9–17; Deut 5:13–21]). By contrast, the child who owns nothing (Mark 10:13–17), the plutocrat who gives all to the poor (10:21; cf. Deut 15:6–15; 24:10–22), and the poor widow who relinquishes everything (Mark 12:41–44) are models of discipleship. For both Old Testament prophets (Isa 3:13–17; Mic 2:1–2) and Hellenistic moralists (Diodorus Siculus, *Bibliotheca historica*, 21; Plutarch, *Cupid. divit.*; cf. Eph 4:19; Col 3:5), avarice is peculiarly pernicious for its rupture of the social fabric. Likewise, Mark is sensitive to malicious conduct that violates communal responsibility (7:20–22; 12:38–40). Written when the Jerusalem Temple was on the verge of destruction or had already been destroyed (13:1–2; 15:38), the Second Gospel defines defilement as evil that comes from within (7:14–15, 23) and specifies mutual forgiveness, underwritten by God, as normative among disciples (11:24–25).

The Twelve. More so than any other Evangelist, Mark portrays the Twelve severely. Their understanding of Jesus's teaching and intentions deteriorates as the gospel unfolds (e.g., 4:13, 40–41; 5:31; 6:37, 51; 7:17–18; 8:4, 14–21; 9:18c–19, 32, 38–41; 10:13–14, 32). Many of these passages have Synoptic parallels, though Luke (8:45; 9:13, 45; 18:34) and especially Matthew (8:27; 9:20–22; 13:51–52; 14:28–33; 16:7–12; 17:19–20, 23b) soften Mark's presentation. Three times in Mark, Jesus explains the implications of his passion for discipleship (8:31—9:1; 9:31–37; 10:33–34, 42–45); three times the disciples miss or reject the point, bickering among themselves for exalted status (8:32–33; 9:33–34; 10:35–41). None of the Twelve appropriates power available only through prayer (9:28–29); one of them colludes with Jerusalem's chief priests to betray Jesus (14:10–11, 43–46); three sleep during his anguish in Gethsemane (14:32–42); another triply denies knowing him (14:66–72); all forsake him, fleeing at his arrest (14:50–52). Simon Peter, the Twelve's spokesman (1:36; 8:29; 9:5–6; 10:28; 11:21; 14:29–31) and *primus inter pares* (1:16–18, 29; 3:16–19a; 5:37; 9:2; 13:3; 14:33), is singled out most unflatteringly (8:32; 9:5–6; 14:29–31, 37, 66–72). Among all of Jesus's opponents in this gospel, only Peter is addressed as Satan (8:33); his last words about Jesus are devastating: "I do not know this man you are talking about" (14:71). The reason Mark gives for the Twelve's incomprehension and miserable failure raises as many questions as it answers: "their hearts were hardened" (6:52; cf. 7:17–18; 8:17). Despite their receipt of "the secret [*mysterion*] of the kingdom of God," they are as blinded and deafened by it as others (4:10–13; 8:18–21).

In the biblical tradition God hardens hearts (Exod 4:21; 7:3; 10:1, 20, 27; 14:8; 17; Deut 2:30; Isa 6:9–13; John 12:37–41; Acts 28:25–29; Rom 11:7–8, 25), usually for a season until repentance is ripe. Those traditions, however, also emphasize human culpability (Exod 8:15, 32; Pss 36:1; 58:2; Isa 29:13–14; Zech 7:8–14; Rom 1:24–25). The same paradox crystallizes in Mark (14:21): "For the Son of Man goes as it is written of him, but woe to that one by whom the Son of Man is betrayed! It would have been better for that one not to have been born."

The anonymous. Discipleship in Mark is often demonstrated by shadowy, mostly nameless figures that briefly take the stage before disappearing. These include Simon's mother-in-law, who after being healed by Jesus serves him (1:30–31); sufferers of various infirmities, within Israel and on its frontiers, who approach Jesus with justified confidence that he can cure them (1:33–34b, 40–45; 2:10b–12; 3:1–5, 7–10; 5:18–20; 7:31–38); surrogates for the sick, who demonstrate faith (1:32; 2:1–5; 5:21–24a, 35–36; 7:24–30; 9:14–29); a well-intentioned scribe, who discerns Torah's deepest intent (12:28–34; cf. Lev 19:18; Deut 6:4; 1 Sam 15:22; Hos 6:6; Mic 6:6–8); a desperately poor widow, who invests in a lost cause (the Temple) "everything she had, all she had to live on" (12:41–44); a woman whose lavish gift to Jesus is a beautiful, anticipatory anointing of his body before its burial, forever remembered in the gospel's universal proclamation (14:3–9); many other female ministers who observe Jesus's crucifixion, death, and burial long after the Twelve have abandoned him (15:40–41, 47;

16:1–2); and Joseph of Arimathea, "a respected member of the council, who was also himself waiting expectantly for the kingdom of God," who boldly asks Pilate for Jesus's body and properly buries it, in the Twelve's absence (15:42–46; cf. John's disciples in 6:29). Mark's central segment, exposing the Twelve's blindness to Jesus's teaching, is framed by tales of faltering yet eventual restoration of visual perception (8:22–26; 10:46–52).

The adversaries. Though Jewish opponents are criticized (3:6, 22–30; 7:1–13; 10:1–5; 12:9–40), the vitriol occasionally directed in other gospels toward Pharisees and Jesus's other coreligionists is absent from Mark (cf. Matt 23:1–39; John 8:12–59; Acts 28:17–28). Instead, Mark emphasizes the bottomless irony that Israel's most devout leaders fail to recognize their king and collude with Rome's imperial forces to destroy him (15:25–32). Representative antagonists repeatedly speak the truth of the gospel without intention or comprehension: "You are the Messiah, the Son of the Blessed One?" (14:61, the high priest's quizzical claim); "He saved others; he cannot save himself" (15:31, the chief priests and scribes' paraphrase of 10:45); "Truly this man was God's Son" (15:39, Jesus's Gentile executioner). In Mark, Jesus is misunderstood and betrayed by almost everyone: his family (3:19b–21, 31), countrymen (6:1–6a), Jerusalem's crowds (15:11, 13–14), and the Twelve (3:19a; 8:32–33; 10:35–41).

Faith and fear. Jesus's mighty works are not noteworthy for their happy endings; the miracles performed by Apollonius of Tyana (Philostratus, *Vit. Apoll.*) and Hanina ben Dosa (*b. Yebam.* 121b, *b. Ta'an* 24b) were also successful. Jesus's works are important for what they disclose about disciples' faith. To know Jesus in Mark is to see beneath the Galilean prophet, recognizing him as God's eschatological agent who is retaking the field of a damaged creation from the diabolical forces of its occupation and restoring the ecology of God's sovereignty on earth (3:7–12; 5:1–20). When Jesus is so regarded, his parabolic teaching becomes intelligible, important, and trustworthy. As in Paul (Rom 4:1–25; 2 Cor 4:13—5:10; Gal 3:1–29), faith is humanity's trust in God in the face of manifestly hopeless situations (Mark 4:35—6:1–6a). Unlike those described in John's Gospel (2:11;

4:46–54), Jesus's mighty works in Mark do not stimulate faith. The sequence flows in reverse: first comes faith, fostering conditions in which God's power to heal, executed by Jesus, can be realized (Mark 5:23, 34a). Neither a cluster of belief (1 Tim 3:9; 4:6; Jude 3) nor an arrow released irrevocably toward its target, faith oscillates: it swings from confidence to panic, caught for a time by weak mortals before slipping from their grasp (Mark 5:33–36; 9:23–24). Because faith is a matter more of volition than of cognition, its opposite is cowardice (4:40) or fear (5:15, 33, 36), which repudiates Jesus's authority to wield God's healing potency (6:3c–4; 11:27–33). Those thinking themselves close to Jesus, friends of the family (6:1–6a) and even the Twelve (4:40; 5:31), are at best imperceptive (5:31), at worst craven (4:40). The powerless tap reservoirs of persistent trust that elude those with commonplace authority (7:24–30). At Gethsemane (14:32–42) and Golgotha (15:21–33), Jesus himself exhibits the depth of trust that activates self-sacrificial service to God for the gospel's sake. At the empty tomb female disciples, who continued with Jesus longer than all others, flee in fear after learning of his resurrection (16:1–8; cf. the risen Jesus's reassuring appearances in Matt 28:8–20; Luke 24:13–52; John 20:11–21:25; 1 Cor 15:3–8). Mark leaves the reader to ponder the continuing mystery of disciples' fear when confronted by cryptic evidence of Jesus's own fidelity and that of the God who raised him from death.

Concluding Assessments. Owing to its association with Peter and the Roman church, the Second Gospel's normative status was firm and unchallenged from the mid-second century. Yet its canonicity did little to stimulate its use in liturgies, commentaries, and quotations: "present but absent" in the patristic and medieval periods, Mark's distinctive theological voice was submerged beneath those of Matthew and John and by a general tendency to harmonize the gospels (Schildgen, 1999). Mark's stature was elevated in the nineteenth century as scholars increasingly accorded it special importance as the earliest gospel. For decades thereafter, exegetes disparaged its shaping of inherited traditions; eventually redaction critics recognized Mark's theological achievement, which became generally acknowledged.

Concentrating on the secret of Jesus's identity, Wrede (1901) was the first modern scholar to give full weight to the early church's "dogmatic" transmission of Mark's sources. Wrede's seminal study proved a mixed blessing. While opening the way for due appreciation of Markan theology, he projected onto the Gospel a reading tailored to fit his own hypothetical reconstruction of primitive Christianity while setting generations of critics on the dubious task of differentiating the earliest gospel's redaction of practically irrecoverable traditions (save the LXX) and focusing twentieth-century scholarship almost exclusively on Christology. "The Messianic Secret" is an imprecise label for a more complex phenomenon in Mark: only at 8:29–30 is confession of Jesus's *messiahship* rebuked; elsewhere Jesus accepts it (14:61–62). The Evangelist lays an obscure trail of suppressing Jesus's identity and activities (1:34–35; 3:11–12; 5:43; 7:36; 8:26; 9:9, 30), which are impossible to hide (5:19–20; 6:14a, 53–56; 7:36–37; 9:14–15). Dramatizing an apocalyptic precept—"For there is nothing hidden, except to be disclosed; nor is anything secret, except to come to light" (4:22)—Mark's narrative situates its characters and readers in that stressfully ambiguous time between the kingdom's arrival and its fulfillment (1:15; 13:13b).

If, as Dibelius (1951, p. 125) suggested, "The historian…must endeavor to illuminate and somehow to present the meaning of events" and if Mark was the earliest of Jesus's ancient biographers, then Mark—not Luke—is long overdue for recognition as Christianity's earliest theological historian. Mark established the basic format for the story of Jesus, the Messiah of Israel and of the nations, as the church chose to remember it—the template to which Matthew, Luke, and John adhered. Moreover, Mark does not simply tell a story about Jesus; he creates conditions under which readers may *experience* the peculiarity of God's good news: hurried into successive exegetical potholes (e.g., 4:1–34; 7:24–20; 8:14–19; 11:11–19), suspended within interlaminated stories of almost unbearable tension (e.g., 3:19b–35; 5:21–43; 14:53–72), stuck with the women in the Gospel's final, unresolved chord (16:1–8). Systematic theology coordinates and explains; the Second Gospel hurls one into the kingdom's mystery. After two millennia Mark's genius may no longer be hidden but is at last coming to light.

[*See also* Apocalypticism; Christology; Discipleship; Eschatology; Ethics, Biblical; Faith; Family; Fear; Gentiles; God and Gods; Gospel; Holy Spirit; John the Baptist; John and the Johannine Epistles; Judaism; Kingdom of God (Heaven); Luke–Acts; Matthew; Miracles; Parable; Prophets and Prophecy; Redemption; Repentance; Resurrection; Sickness, Disease, and Healing; Son of God; Son of Man; *and* Soteriology.]

BIBLIOGRAPHY

Black, C. Clifton. "Christ Crucified in Paul and in Mark: Reflections on an Intracanonical Conversation." In *Theology and Ethics in Paul and His Interpreters: Essays in Honor of Victor Paul Furnish*, edited by Eugene H. Lovering Jr. and Jerry L. Sumney, pp. 184–206. Nashville, Tenn.: Abingdon, 1996.

Black, C. Clifton. *Mark: Images of an Apostolic Interpreter.* Studies on Personalities of the New Testament. Minneapolis: Fortress; Edinburgh: T&T Clark, 2001.

Black, C. Clifton. "Does Suffering Possess Educational Value in Mark"? In *Character Ethics and the New Testament: Moral Dimensions of Scripture*, edited by Robert L. Brawley, pp. 3–17. Louisville, Ky.: Westminster John Knox, 2005.

Black, C. Clifton. "The Face Is Familiar; I Just Can't Place It." In *The End of Mark and the Ends of God: Essays in Memory of Donald Harrisville Juel*, edited by Beverly R. Gaventa and Patrick D. Miller, pp. 33–49. Louisville, Ky.: Westminster John Knox, 2006.

Black, C. Clifton. "Mark as Historian of God's Kingdom." *Catholic Biblical Quarterly* 71 (2009): 64–83.

Black, C. Clifton. *Mark.* Abingdon New Testament Commentaries. Nashville, Tenn.: Abingdon, 2011.

Black, C. Clifton. *The Disciples According to Mark: Markan Redaction in Current Debate.* 2d ed. Grand Rapids, Mich.: Eerdmans, 2012.

Black, C. Clifton. "*Endzeit als Urzeit*: Mark and Creation Theology." In *Interpretation and the Claims of the Text: Resourcing New Testament Theology*, edited by Jason A. Whitlark, Bruce W. Longenecker, Lidija Novakovic, et al. pp. 89–102, Waco, Tex.: Baylor University Press, 2014.

Dibelius, Martin. *Studies in the Acts of the Apostles.* Edited by H. Greeven. Translated by M. Ling. New York: Scribner's, 1956. English translation of *Aufsätze zur Apostelgeschichte*, first published in 1951.

Donahue, John R. "A Neglected Factor in the Theology of Mark." *Journal of Biblical Literature* 101 (1982): 563–594.

Henderson, Suzanne Watts. *Christology and Discipleship in the Gospel of Mark.* Society of New Testament Studies Monograph Series 135. Cambridge, U.K.: Cambridge University Press, 2006.

Lightfoot, R. H. *History and Interpretation in the Gospels.* London: Hodder & Stoughton, 1935.

Marshall, Christopher D. *Faith as a Theme in Mark's Narrative.* Society of New Testament Studies Monograph Series 64. Cambridge, U.K., and New York: Cambridge University Press, 1989.

Marxsen, Willi. *Mark the Evangelist: Studies on the Redaction History of the Gospel.* Nashville, Tenn., and New York: Abingdon, 1969. English translation of *Der Evangelist Markus: Studien zur Redaktionsgeschichte des Evangeliums*, first published in 1956.

Schildgen, Brenda Deen. *Power and Prejudice: The Reception of the Gospel of Mark.* Detroit: Wayne State University Press, 1999.

Telford, William R. *The Theology of the Gospel of Mark.* New Testament Theology. Cambridge, U.K.: Cambridge University Press, 1999.

Via, Dan O., Jr. *The Ethics of Mark's Gospel: In the Middle of Time.* Philadelphia: Fortress, 1985.

Wrede, W. *The Messianic Secret.* London and Cambridge, U.K.: James Clark, 1971. English translation of *Messiasgeheimnis in den Evangelien: Zugleich ein Beitrag zum Verständnis des Markusevangeliums*, first published in 1901.

C. Clifton Black

MARRIAGE

The institution of marriage as seen in scripture was broadly the same as in surrounding cultures. Over time, there were variations in the assumed number of partners, in their relative status, in assumptions about suitable candidates for marriage, and in the admissibility of divorce.

Preexilic Israel. In preexilic Israel, even though the majority of marriages may well have been monogamous, the practice of elite households made polygyny the cultural norm. Thus, Jacob had two full wives and two others whose status was subordinate to theirs. A household might include one or more such subordinate wives or concubines. Similarly, the household of David included a large number of wives, each constituting a subhousehold with her children.

Marriage was patriarchal in several senses. Residence was patrilocal, with the wife being attached to the husband and the husband's family. The husband was the public face of the marriage and, in terms of the prevailing honor/shame morality, carried the honor of the household, while the wife was the bearer of its "shame," that is, having the responsibility of avoiding public disgrace.

Wives were not always merely subordinate, as in the example of Abigail (1 Sam 25) or the woman of Shunem (2 Kgs 4). And women could be heirs of their paternal houses, a situation provided for in Torah (Num 36). Divorce was available to the husband (Deut 24:1–3).

As elsewhere in the ancient Near East, multiple wives were as much a sign of a man's social prominence as were large holdings in land or cattle. The Decalogue reflects this perspective in the way it links the coveting of the neighbor's property and of the neighbor's wife (Exod 20:17). This is not to say that wives were merely a form of property. Even when a man married his own slave, Torah prohibits returning her to slave status if he is displeased with her (Deut 21:10–14).

Most marriages represented an alliance between the families of the people being married, with the wife (and subsequent children) forming the physical embodiment of that pact. This aspect of marriage also lay behind levirate marriage, which required that a wife widowed before she had borne children be married to her late husband's brother (Deut 25:5–10).

In particular, the king's need for multiple alliances tended to result in multiple marriages. These marriages and their offspring, in turn, created a context for complex dynastic struggles among the king's various subhouseholds.

Polygyny also provided the framework for the incest laws of Leviticus 18:6–18. Some of the content of these laws reflects the widespread human concern to rule out marriage with close relatives. But the code shows a particular focus on offenses younger males in the polygamous household might commit against the honor of older males: father, uncles, and older siblings and half-siblings. The concern (as with adultery, too) was that intercourse with a woman who belonged to another man's sphere constituted a kind of theft—less of property than of honor. Thus, adultery was always defined in terms of a man's having intercourse with a woman married to another man, not in the broader modern sense.

Postexilic Judaism. We have less information about marriage in the early postexilic period. There was, however, a reaction against marriage with outsiders and a turn toward endogamy. Ezra (10) and Nehemiah (13:23–30) are both regarded as purging existing interethnic marriages, while the author of Ruth, on the other side of the debate, emphasized the presence of Moabite ancestry in the royal family. With the later spread of Greek influence, polygamy largely gave way to monogamy. There was never any conclusive judgment in favor of monogamy either in the Bible or in Judaism, but Christianity took it as a norm.

Identification of a theology of marriage in the Hebrew scriptures is problematic. Genesis 2:18–25 is sometimes read as offering such a theology, but if the story were truly intended to address marriage, it is difficult to explain why it is phrased in a way that assumes matrilocal residence, an arrangement otherwise unknown in ancient Israel. It is simpler, on the whole, to read it as an etiological story about the importance of erotic desire in human life.

The Hebrew scriptures make little connection between marriage and romantic love. The love of Elkanah for the childless Hannah (1 Sam 1) is treated as something worthy of note. The Song of Songs celebrates passionate love but with no clear reference to marriage. Marriage is rather the principal context for fulfilling the command to multiply (Gen 1:28), and, together with the birth of children, it is seen as a particular blessing of human life (Eccl 9:7–10; Pss 127; 128).

Marriage was also used as a theological metaphor for the relationship of God and Israel. Israel, as wife, was to show unswerving devotion to its husband, who might be justifiably angry at any betrayal (Hosea; Isa 62). Worship of other gods was often referred to metaphorically as "harlotry."

New Testament. In the New Testament, Jesus gives limited attention to marriage and does not give family a high valuation. Indeed, he keeps his own family at arm's length and calls his disciples away from theirs. He promises future rewards for those who leave parents, wives, and children (Mark 3:31–35; 10:28–31; Luke 18:29–30).

Jesus does, however, reject divorce and remarriage (Mark 10:2–9). He validates this by reading Genesis 2:23–25 as establishing a permanent relationship, one more like immediate kinship than like existing conceptions of marriage. He further dismisses the allowance for divorce of a wife as merely a concession to male hardness of heart. He thus effectively refashions the wife's status into that of permanent member of the family. Paul achieved a comparable result when he declared that husband and wife "own" one another equally (1 Cor 7:1–5).

The rise of ethnically mixed Christian communities raised questions about suitable marriage partners. The postexilic Jewish practice of endogamy would have forbidden marriage between the Jews and Gentiles in the community. Paul accepted existing mixed marriages but may have retained a kind of endogamy, redefined in terms of the Christian community: Christian widows might remarry only "in the Lord" (1 Cor 7:39).

We also find in the New Testament era signs of a new regard for celibacy. In the Hebrew scriptures, virginity was valued in women before marriage, and men practiced temporary sexual abstinence for reasons of purity. At the beginning of the Common Era, however, we find some Jews making celibacy a life practice (e.g., the Therapeutae). Paul went so far as to encourage all unmarried Christians to refrain from marriage, if possible, because the demands of the endtimes outweighed the traditional concern for family continuity (1 Cor 7:25–38).

Jesus says that there is no marriage in heaven (Mark 12:18–27). Luke understood this as an accommodation to the abolition of death, which left no need for new generations of humanity (20:34–36). Despite this marginalization of marriage, however, some New Testament writers used it positively as an image for the relationship of Christ and the church (2 Cor 11:1–3; Rev 21:2), which could serve, in turn, as a model for marital behavior (Eph 5:22–33).

Postbiblical Times. A further elevation of virginity at the expense of marriage came about with the historic turn toward Late Antiquity. It is apparent in second-century texts such as the *Acts of Paul and Thecla*, which took the Encratite position that only those who reject sexual intercourse are fit for heaven. This esteem for virginity was not exclusively Christian. A growing negativity about the human body is apparent in the art and philosophy of Late Antiquity.

Rabbinic Judaism ultimately rejected this tendency, insisting on the value of the body and asserting that sexual pleasure, not simply procreation, was an integral element of marriage. Christians moved more in step with the culture at large.

Monasticism was in the forefront of this shift, first in the form of women who vowed themselves to virginity while still living at home, then in the troops of men (and some women) who struck out into the deserts of Syria and Egypt to live as anchorites. Other voices, such as Clement of Alexandria (ca. 150–ca. 215), maintained the value of marriage as a school of piety; but even they were suspicious of the erotic element in it. Some married couples vowed themselves to sexual abstinence, although this was eventually prohibited by church authorities. Efforts to maintain a value for marriage equal to that of celibacy largely failed, most conclusively in the conflict between Jovinian and Jerome. Both men were celibate, but Jovinian maintained that Christians could achieve true holiness within marriage, while Jerome insisted that only sexual abstinence made this possible.

Christians retained existing Greco-Roman practices for solemnizing marriage, though now in the terms of their own faith. Furthermore, early Christian practice, still followed by the Eastern Orthodox, regarded Jesus's words on divorce and remarriage as an ideal rather than a legal requirement. In the fourth century, however, the Western church chose a different course by defining indissolubility as of the essence of marriage. At the same time, concubinage was still widely tolerated, although understood as a form of fornication, not of marriage.

Around 1200, Western Christianity began to take a more positive view of marriage. While celibacy was still considered the superior form of Christian practice and was now demanded of all clergy, a new tendency to regard marriage as a sacred estate appeared. Its inclusion among the sacraments coincided with a new effort by spiritual leaders to describe how a Christian marriage might promote the salvation of its partners.

If the medieval Western church adopted a newly positive stance toward marriage, the Reformation actively reversed the polarity that had dominated since the fourth century and declared marriage to be the normative context for Christian practice. Monastic orders were disbanded, and parish clergy were expected to marry.

More Recent Times. The nuclear family, now regarded as traditional in North Atlantic cultures, took form in the early industrial era. Marriage came to be seen more in terms of the married couple themselves, alone or with their children, and this image was projected back into the past, even into scriptural texts written with quite different family types in mind.

These developments, along with the shift away from an honor/shame culture, laid the foundation for feminist critique of the ancient presuppositions of patriarchy. A sharp distinction between male and female roles seemed increasingly without foundation. Women sought and gained equal rights before the law and in government, and this could not leave the institution of marriage untouched. It was now the product not of an agreement between the families of origin but of the choices of two particular people, who must consciously maintain and renew the relationship, a shift acknowledged in the recent concern on the part of churches for premarital preparation. This also formed the background for the relaxing of Protestant opposition toward divorce and remarriage.

Understanding marriage as a commitment between two equal persons made it more difficult to say exactly how or why same-sex life partnerships differed from heterosexual ones. Some argue that a kind of complementarity between male and female is essential to marriage. This then raises the question of whether some version of patriarchy is therefore also theologically essential. Others emphasize rather the commitment to lifelong partnership. Some suggest that friendship in the scriptures provides a more helpful theological foundation for contemporary egalitarian marriage than the patriarchal and polygamous presuppositions encoded in much of the Bible's more direct discourse on the subject. On such a basis, marriage can be equally open to same-sex couples.

[*See also* Ethics, Biblical; Family; Freedom and Slavery; Friendship; Honor and Shame; *and* Love.]

BIBLIOGRAPHY

Boyarin, Daniel. *Carnal Israel: Reading Sex in Talmudic Culture.* Berkeley: University of California Press, 1993.

Brooke, Christopher N. L. *The Medieval Idea of Marriage.* Oxford: Oxford University Press, 1989.

Brown, Peter. *The Body and Society: Men, Women, and Sexual Renunciation in Early Christianity.* New York: Columbia University Press, 1988.

Countryman, L. William. *Dirt, Greed, and Sex: Sexual Ethics in the New Testament and Their Implications for Today.* Rev. ed. Minneapolis: Fortress, 2007.

Hays, Richard B. *The Moral Vision of the New Testament: A Contemporary Introduction to New Testament Ethics.* San Francisco: HarperSanFrancisco, 1996.

Hunter, David G., trans., ed. *Marriage in the Early Church.* Sources of Early Christian Thought. Minneapolis: Fortress, 1992.

Jordan, Mark D., ed. *Authorizing Marriage? Canon, Tradition, and Critique in the Blessing of Same-Sex Unions.* Princeton, N.J.: Princeton University Press, 2006.

Reynolds, Philip Lyndon. *Marriage in the Western Church: The Christianization of Marriage During the Patristic and Early Medieval Periods.* Supplements to Vigiliae Christianae 24. Leiden, The Netherlands: Brill, 1994.

L. William Countryman

MARY

The mother of Jesus is named Mary in the Synoptic Gospels and Acts. She is also referred to in John and Galatians and has been a focus of theological reflection since at least the second century C.E. The most extensive biblical treatment of her is found in Luke 1–2, early Christian chapters that are already theologically rich. For example, the Annunciation narrative (Luke 1:26–38) recalls the creation of the world (Gen 1:1–3), inviting the reader to see God's action in Christ as the radical re-creation of the cosmos;

Mary's visit to her cousin Elizabeth (Luke 1:39–45) recalls the journey of the Ark to Jerusalem (2 Sam 6:1–11), suggestive of Jesus's identity as the Word of God.

Mother of God. Marian theology (Mariology) is highly developed in the Orthodox and, especially, the Catholic Church. All theological reflection upon Mary stems ultimately from her status as mother of the Word of God incarnate (the divine motherhood). The Council of Ephesus (431 C.E.) confirmed that the title *Theotokos*—"God-bearer," or "Mother of God"—was a correct designation for her since it is the correlate of the fact that the son she bore was both divine and human.

The doctrine of the divine motherhood has its scriptural foundation in Luke 1:26–38 and Matthew 1:18–25, with Luke's Annunciation narrative being of primary importance for most Mariology. Since at least the second century, Mary was regarded as both a moral and a physical agent in the Incarnation. Thus, Ignatius of Antioch wrote "Jesus Christ our Lord" was "born and unborn, God become man…from Mary and from God" (Ign. *Eph.* 7). Justin Martyr (ca. 100–ca. 165) and Irenaeus (ca. 130–202) emphasize her willing acceptance of God's word in her assent to Gabriel's message. Irenaeus develops the motif of Mary as the "new Eve" (*Epid.* 30–33; *Haer.* 3.22) in parallel to Paul's designation of Christ as "the new Adam": whereas Eve gave ear to the word of the serpent and brought death to the world, Mary gave ear to the angel and brought life (*Haer.* 19.1).

The role of Mary as subordinate partner in the work of redemption was developed by Augustine, who contends that, just as both sexes were involved in bringing about the Fall, so also it was necessary for both sexes to be involved in the work of redemption; otherwise, the redemption would not have been complete (*Agon.* 22, 24). A gendered reading of Mary's significance for soteriology is found mainly in the West, where it has been elaborated in the work of von Balthasar (1975, 1978). The predominant tradition in both East and West understands Mary as representing humanity or creation as a whole: on behalf of the whole world, she receives the angel's message with joy and she gives the Word of God his human flesh (see Luke 1:43, 47).

The bodily incarnation of the Son of God is necessary for the passion and crucifixion, which means that any mainstream Christian teaching must acknowledge the unique, and uniquely important, position that is occupied by the woman who gave Christ his human body. This position is enhanced in those Christologies that maintain that the Incarnation is itself salvific. For example, Cyril of Alexandria (d. 444) writes that, in being conceived by Mary, Christ consecrated all human conception (*Third Letter to Nestorius*). This claim comports with Galatians 4:4–5: in uniting himself to humanity in Mary, God gave all humanity the possibility of being divinized.

Mediation. It was by means of Mary that God came to dwell bodily upon earth. Catholic theology has understood this mediatorial function to belong to Mary not just in history but perpetually, as she intercedes for the world's salvation. The wedding feast at Cana (John 2:1–11) is often cited in support of the importance of Mary's intercession since the mother of Jesus appeals to her son on behalf of the host whose wine has run out, whereupon Jesus turns water into wine. Queen Esther's interceding with King Ahasuerus (Esth 8:3–8) has customarily been seen as a type of Mary's intercession with Christ, but the underlying rationale for belief in Mary's constant and effective mediation is her childbearing, as narrated in Luke and Matthew. Catholic and Orthodox theology interpret the relevant gospel texts by use of analogy, or a kind of sacramental thinking: as Mary was the means of linking God to creation in the Incarnation, so she continues to be a bond between God and creation throughout time.

Her mediatorial role in the gospels reveals a pattern established by God that will be maintained in perpetuity, and explains why it is good to seek her intercession. Thus, early and medieval authors, such as Bernard of Clairvaux (ca. 1090–1153), write of Mary as the "bridge" between heaven and earth, or the "neck" between Christ, who is the head, and the church, which is his body (cf. Eph 5:23; Col 1:18). Some Catholic writers have extended this argument: since God chose to come into the world through Mary, it is through her that he continues to give all grace. This argument from analogy, or claim for continuity of the kind that occurs in the sacraments, was developed by Louis de Montfort (1673–1716), who contended that the coming of Christ at the end of time would be preceded by an "age of Mary."

Virginity. Although some modern biblical commentators (e.g., Schaberg, 1995) have argued that the gospel narratives do not attest to Mary's virginity when Jesus was conceived, the customary readings of both Luke and Matthew uphold the doctrine of the virginal conception. This is the most natural reading of Luke 1:26–38, wherein Mary inquires of the angel how she will conceive since she has not had sexual relations (v. 34). As early as the second century some texts hold that Mary not only conceived but also gave birth without change in her bodily condition: *in partu* virginity. The most important of these early witnesses is the *Protevangelium of James* (mid-second century), which narrates the midwife's examination of Mary after Christ's birth, finding that she still had a virgin's anatomy. The theological purpose of this story seems to be a demonstration of Christ's divinity: only God could be born in such a miraculous way. Indeed, for early Christian writers like Athanasius (*Inc.* 8), the significance of the virginal conception is its correlation with the doctrine of the Incarnation: the fact that Christ was born of a woman shows that he is truly human, while the fact that he was born of a virgin shows that he is divine. Although the doctrine of the *in partu* virginity was not universally accepted in the earliest centuries (e.g., Tertullian, *Carn. Chr.* 23.1–5), during the patristic period it became the accepted teaching in both East and West (*Tome of Pope Leo* [451]; Ambrose, *Ep.* 42.4–6; Ephrem, *Hymns on the Nativity* 12), together with the teaching that Mary remained a virgin throughout her life: before, during, and after childbirth (Augustine, *Serm.* 51.11, 18; Lateran Council [649 C.E.]).

Several Old Testament texts are believed to have provided types of Mary's virginity. Since Mary bears in her body the very presence of God, she is, as it were, a new Temple; thus, the Temple may be seen as a type of the Virgin. In Catholic and Orthodox tradition, both Ark and Temple are common images for the Mother of God. In reading Ezekiel, then, the Temple is understood in just this way: the door through which the Lord has entered but which remains forever closed (44:2), is read as a type of Mary's virginity (e.g., Jerome, *Jov.* 1.32). Other Old Testament types of the unbroken virginity include the burning bush (Exod 3:2), which foreshadows the mystery whereby Mary's virginity was not destroyed by her childbearing (e.g., Proclus, *Oratio* 1.1). The "sealed fountain" and the "enclosed garden" of the Song of Songs (4:12) were understood to be symbols of the life of virginity and of moral integrity in general (e.g., Ambrose, *Myst.* 9.55). These images were applied to Mary (Jerome, *Adv. Jov.* 1.31) and became commonly used in the visual arts to signify Mary's fruitful virginity. As with other Old Testament types of the Virgin, these symbols retain such meaning in present-day spiritual exegesis (Haffner, 2007, p. 15).

A further theological meaning of Mary's virginity is eschatological. At the expulsion from Eden, one of the curses laid upon Eve is that she will have pain in childbirth (Gen 3:16). Mary's *in partu* virginity is implicitly painless. This shows that, with the Savior's coming into the world, the consequences of the Fall are being reversed. Following the ancient principle that perfection consists of integrity without variety, division, or composition, Mary's unbroken body signifies a future world that will be brought to its final deification: a restoration to its original likeness with God. In the act of Incarnation, there is a movement of descent and ascent, whereby the Son of God descends to take corruptible human flesh from his earthly mother, and she, in turn, is blessed with a heavenly state of incorruptibility. Because of the Incarnation—God's becoming human so that humans could become like God—in Mary, through whom the Incarnation was realized, deification is already fully accomplished.

Mary at the Cross. In addition to the Lukan narrative of Jesus's birth, John 19:25–27 has been of considerable importance in Mariological thinking since the late Middle Ages. Origen (ca. 182–254 C.E.) taught that the beloved disciple stands for every Christian, who should therefore receive Mary as his or her mother; but this teaching was unusual in the early church. Augustine held that Jesus's commissioning of the beloved disciple to care for his mother was of purely personal significance; this understanding was not radically altered until the twelfth century, when Rupert of Deutz (ca. 1075–1129) took up the motif of Mary's becoming the mother of Christians at the crucifixion (although the more general idea that Mary was mother to Christians was already in circulation, e.g., in the medieval hymn "Ave maris stella"). The doctrine of Mary's "spiritual motherhood" has been widespread in Catholicism since that time; it underlies Pope Paul VI's proclamation of Mary as "mother of the church" (Vatican II, Session 3, 21 November 1964).

Of greater theological importance has been the motif of Mary's suffering at the cross. In a *kontakion* (hymn) by Romanos the Melodist (seventh century), Mary stands for the congregation in her attempts to understand why the innocent Christ must suffer and die; gradually Christ brings her to the revelation that his death is for humanity's salvation. In the West it became common to assert, "What Christ suffered in his body, Mary suffered in her soul" (e.g., Arnold of Bonneval [d. ca. 1156], *On the Praises of Holy Mary*, PL 189); this claim contributed to the notion that Mary played an active part in Christ's work of redemption. Authors from the seventeenth century onward argued that at the crucifixion Mary actively offered her son for the world's salvation: as Christ was born of the divine Father and a human mother, so, at the moment of his death, his mother again undertook a human act that corresponded to the Father's offering of his only Son. This belief, in turn, was one element that gave rise to the notion that Mary acted in the office of priest or deacon at the crucifixion (e.g., Chirino de Salazar [1575–1646] and authors of the French school, cited in Laurentin, 1952, and Scheeben, 1946).

Mirroring Christ. In many respects Mary's life has been presented from early times as a mirror to that of Christ. The *Protevangelium of James* (2–3) presents Mary as conceived by parents who thought they were barren (on the model of the conceptions of Isaac [Gen 18] and Samuel [1 Sam 2]); moreover, her mother's pregnancy was announced by the angel Gabriel. In the *Protevangelium of James* 7 Mary was presented by her parents to the Temple when she was three years old, a continuation of the echo of

Samuel and a parallel to the presentation of Christ (Luke 2:22–40). Early traditions of the end of her life tell of her dormition (falling asleep, or death) and Assumption (her bodily translation to paradise), in which her bodily ascent reflects Christ's own Ascension (Acts 1:6–11; see Shoemaker, 2002). These doctrines develop Mary's reflection of Christ in her office as the new Eve, her spiritual suffering, and her heavenly mediation. The theological significance of these claims is their demonstration that a human can be conformed to Christ's likeness, thus presenting an image of what it is to be saved. Fundamentally, however, Mary's mirroring of Christ seems based on the premise that God orders the work of salvation, not merely according to principles of mechanical necessity but also according to congruence, or fittingness, a notion important in Catholic theology. God orders the world according to principles of beauty and justice. Hence, Mary's status as Mother of God lends to the believer confidence that God will have bestowed upon her certain other dignities.

Immaculate Conception. The best-known application of the principle of fittingness is in the doctrine of Mary's Immaculate Conception: she was conceived without original sin. In defense of the Feast of Mary's Conception, this doctrine had become widely accepted in the Western church by the late Middle Ages. It was made a formal dogma of the Catholic faith in 1854, two centuries after the debate had effectively been settled. Medieval theologians argued that since God made Mary the God-bearer, the highest honor bestowable upon any creature, we can be certain that God will have bestowed upon her every other spiritual blessing that is possible (e.g., Eadmer of Canterbury [ca. 1060–ca. 1126], *Tractate on the Conception of Saint Mary*). A number of biblical texts were adduced in support of the doctrine. Proverbs 9:1, in which Wisdom builds her house, was interpreted by early writers as signifying the Incarnation: Christ, who is Wisdom, forms his human body, the house (Hippolytus, *Fr. Prov.* 9:1; Bede, *In Proverbia*). Since that body is the body of Mary and he dwells in her, Wisdom's house came to be identified with Mary; moreover, it was argued that the dwelling place prepared for the Son of God would be as excellent as possible. In the case of a human being, this would mean perfect freedom from every moral flaw. However, the figure of Wisdom soon came to be identified with Mary herself.

Proverbs 8:22–31 and Sirach 24:14–16, which refer to the presence of Wisdom with God from before the foundation of the world, were customarily used as the readings for Marian feasts, such as her Assumption and birthday. Likely, these readings were chosen because Wisdom is often identified with the Word incarnate (1 Cor 1:24); their use for Marian liturgies highlighted Mary's essential part in the Incarnation. This reading supported the opinion of Scotist theologians, who held that God had ordained the Incarnation "from before the sin of Adam was foreseen" (so that the Incarnation was ordained for the world's final glorification and not primarily as a remedy for sin). From this it followed that the woman from whom Christ took human flesh must, in the same act of predestination, have been ordained to be the God-bearer. Wisdom's claim that she was "born" from, or "conceived" by, God (Prov 8:24) could thus be applied not only to Christ but also to Mary: conceived in the mind of God from before the world's foundation. If Mary was ordained to be the Mother of God "from before the sin of Adam was foreseen," then this status as God-bearer must take priority over Adam's sinfulness—an argument against Mary's having contracted original sin. While *Ineffabilis Deus*, the document containing the papal definition of 1854, does not uphold the Scotist Christology, it states that God eternally foresaw both the Fall and the Incarnation as its remedy. Its theological implication is that Mary was ordained from eternity to be the Mother of God, and the wisdom texts remain applicable to her.

Another biblical text commonly used in support of the Immaculate Conception is Song of Songs 4:7: "You are all fair, my love, and there is no stain in you." The custom of interpreting the bride in the song as Mary was normal in twelfth-century Christian interpretation. The bride was first understood as a figure for the church, alternatively for the Christian soul (each having a spousal relationship to Christ, the bridegroom [Eph 5:25–27]); Mary is likewise a figure for both of these. The notion of both the church and the soul as the virgin mother of Christ is found in the early church fathers, and the figures became interchangeable (Clement, *Paed.* 1.6.21; Origen, *Fr. Matt.* 281).

Mary's association with the biblical figure of Wisdom is also found outside the Catholic Church. The Lutheran mystic Jakob Boehme (1575–1624) taught that Mary was the mirror of Sophia. In the Russian Orthodox Church, Sergei Bulgakov (1871–1944) presented Mary as the "created Wisdom of God," the counterpart to Christ who is "uncreated Wisdom."

Neither the Assumption nor the Immaculate Conception is a scriptural teaching, but modern Catholic theologians hold that these doctrines are part of the "fuller meaning" (*sensus plenior*), gradually disclosed, of the readings used for these feasts in the Catholic liturgy (Rahner, 2000, p. 105). The celestial woman of Revelation 12:1 is reckoned to be both the church and the Virgin assumed into glory; the immaculate Virgin is the first fruit of the Devil's defeat by Christ, the fulfillment of the prophecy that the serpent's head would be crushed (Gen 3:15).

New Theological Trends. In liberation theology a text of particular importance is Mary's prophetic Magnificat (Luke 1:46–55). Liberation theologians present Mary as the humble woman of Nazareth, who fearlessly proclaims the justice of God's Kingdom, thereby representing and encouraging other men and women in their struggle for freedom from oppression.

Feminist theologians are divided in their interpretations of Mary. Some emphasize that Mary is an ordinary woman in solidarity with other women in their struggles (see Johnson, 2006). Others tend to draw on historical-critical biblical studies. Still others, considering the inspiration of a female figure in glory to be important, favor the "high" Mariology taught in traditional Catholicism, wedding it to a new sense of women's dignity (see Gebara and Bingemer, 1999).

Future Marian theology will undoubtedly have to take account of feminist concerns, as well as ecological ones. The figure of Wisdom will probably be of key importance in this development, as will New Testament theologies of the new creation.

[*See also* Adam, Last; Allegory and Typology; Anthropology; Atonement; Christology; Creation; Ecclesi-

ology; Eden; Eschatology; Ethics, Biblical, *subentry*
New Testament; Hermeneutics, Biblical; Holy Spirit;
Luke–Acts; Megillot; Redemption; Wisdom; Wisdom
Literature; *and* Word (Logos).]

BIBLIOGRAPHY

Balthasar, Hans Urs von. "The Marian Principle." In *Eluci-dations*. Translated by John Riches. London: SPCK, 1975.

Balthasar, Hans Urs von. *Theodrama: Theological Dra-matic Theory.* Vol. 3: *The Dramatis Personae: Persons in Christ.* San Francisco: Ignatius, 1978.

Boss, Sarah Jane, ed. *Mary: The Complete Resource.* London: Continuum; New York: Oxford University Press, 2007.

Gebara, Ivone, and Maria Clara Bingemer. *Mary, Mother of God, Mother of the Poor.* Translated by Phillip Berry-man. London: Burns and Oates, 1999.

Haffner, Paul. *The Mystery of Mary.* Chicago: Hillendbrand, 2007.

Johnson, Elizabeth A. *Truly Our Sister: A Theology of Mary in the Communion of Saints.* London and New York: Continuum, 2006.

Laurentin, René. *Marie, l'église et le sacerdoce.* Vol. 1: *Étude historique.* Paris: Nouvelles éditions latines, 1952.

Maunder, Chris, ed. *Origins of the Cult of the Virgin Mary.* London: Continuum, 2008.

Rahner, Karl. "The Fundamental Principle of Marian Theology." Translated by Philip Endean and Sarah Jane Boss. *Maria: A Journal of Marian Studies* 1 (2000): 86–122.

Schaberg, Jane. *The Illegitimacy of Jesus.* Sheffield, U.K.: Sheffield Academic Press, 1995.

Scheeben, M. J. *Mariology.* 2 vols. Translated by T. L. M. J. Geukers. St. Louis, Mo., and London: Herder, 1946.

Shoemaker, Stephen. *Ancient Traditions of the Virgin Mary's Dormition and Assumption.* Oxford: Oxford University Press, 2002.

Sarah Jane Boss

MATTHEW

A gospel is a narrative. Narratives do not develop theologies; they tell stories with implicit theological convictions. This entry summarizes and highlights Matthew's story of Jesus, with a hint at some of its underlying convictions.

Presuppositions. The following interpretation of Matthew is based on some basic literary and historical assumptions concerning structure, sources, historical situation, and authorship.

Structure. Because Greek manuscripts have nei-ther sections, chapters, nor subtitles, New Testament scholars offer different proposals for the arrangement of Matthew's Gospel. Two main narrative sections in the Gospel may be identified: (1) Jesus's public ac-tivity in Galilee from the beginning until the turning point in Caesarea Philippi (4:17—16:20) and (2) Je-sus's journey to Jerusalem, ending with his passion and resurrection (16:21—28:20). An unusual narra-tive prologue precedes these two sections (1:2—4:16). The Evangelist marks five great discourses with a similar final clause ("Now when Jesus had finished saying these words"): the Sermon on the Mount (chs. 5–7), the missionary discourse (chs. 10), the parable discourse (ch. 13), the community discourse (ch. 18), and the eschatological discourse (ch. 24–25). Their number reminds one of the Pentateuch's five books. They do not advance the story but are addressed di-rectly to the readers in Matthew's churches. In this they differ from other discourses in the Gospel (e.g., 11:7–25; 21:28—22:14; 23:1–39).

Source critical presuppositions. On the generally accepted two-source hypothesis, the Evangelist used Mark's Gospel (in a slightly different version from ours) and a sayings source, Q, plus some special ma-terials from mostly oral traditions. Mark was his main source. After a very free use of Mark 1:2—2:22 and 4:1—5:43 in chapters 3–10, Matthew follows closely Mark's order in chapters 12:1—28:10. Matthew's Gospel is a new version of Mark; generically, it is neither a catechetical book nor a biography. Departing from his use of Mark, Matthew uses the sayings source as a mere collection of materials, excerpting it in ac-cordance with his own thematic viewpoints and thereby destroying Q's structure. The Evangelist also arranges the five great discourses; in most cases Markan materials are followed by a mixture of Q and special materials.

Historical situation. The conflict of Jesus's disci-ples with the majority of Israel, led by the Pharisees, is the traumatic experience developed in Matthew's new version of Mark's Gospel. Whether this is an internal Jewish conflict, with Matthew's congregations a deviant group within Judaism (Konradt, 2007; Overman, 1990; Sim, 1998), or whether the "parting of the ways" has already taken place, with the Matthean congregations no longer part of Judaism (Foster, 2004; Stanton, 1992) remains controversial. Probably, Matthew's congregations were minority groups gathering in assemblies with their own scribes and leaders, apart from synagogues in which Pharisees were the majority. Matthew's readers celebrate the Lord's Supper, not Passover; their initiation ritual is baptism, not circumcision. Whether they are considered "outside" of Judaism is impossible to determine because at that time no Jewish authority existed to define "normative" Judaism.

Author, time, and place. Antioch or another great city in Syria was probably the Gospel's place of origin. Matthew was likely written not long after Jerusalem's destruction, maybe between 80 and 90 C.E. Its author was an influential Jewish-Christian teacher, though not the apostle Matthew, in spite of the antiquity of that ascription.

Matthew's Story of Jesus. Matthew's narrative may be divided into three parts: a short prologue (Matt 1:1—4:16) and two main sections. They begin with almost the same words in 4:17 and 16:21.

The prologue. The book's title (lit., "Book of Genesis of Jesus the Messiah, the Son of David, the Son of Abraham," Matt 1:1) leads Matthew's Jewish-Christian readers to expect a new book of Genesis (i.e., a book with biblical authority) that tells of Jesus, the Davidic Messiah. "Son of Abraham" is open to different interpretations. Matthew then opens his narrative with a prelude (1:2—4:16) that introduces the Gospel's most important Christological and salvation-historical perspectives. Formula quotations ("All this took place to fulfill what was spoken"), especially numerous at the beginning of the Gospel (1:22–23; 2:5–6, 15b, 17–18, 23), are important for interpreting the prologue. Jesus, of Davidic descent (thus, the genealogy 1:2–16), will be called "Emmanuel," a biblical term signifying the presence of the God of Israel with his people (1:23). "Conceived from the Holy Spirit" (1:20), Jesus will be called "Son of God," as witnessed by the prophet (1:15) and proclaimed by the heavenly voice at his baptism (3:17). The temptation story (4:1–11) shows

that Jesus, the Son of God, is obedient to the will of God. Many geographical indications allude to the course of salvation history. The way of Jesus begins in the Davidic city of Bethlehem (2:6). Threatened by King Herod, who is supported by the priests and the scribes of "all Jerusalem" (2:3–4), the infant Jesus's family flees to Egypt, then settles in Nazareth (for which reason Christians will be called "Nazoreans," 2:23). Finally, the adult Jesus withdraws to "Galilee of the Gentiles" (4:15). This prologue anticipates the way of Jesus that Matthew will narrate in the whole Gospel.

Other signals indicate that Jesus's future will be among Gentiles: the four pagan women in the genealogy (1:3, 5a, 5b, 6b), the "wise men from the East" (2:1–12), and the children of Abraham that God is able to raise from stones (3:9). The reader begins to understand the meaning of "son of Abraham" in the book's title (1:1): Abraham is the father of the proselytes, not only the father of Israel (Gen 17:1–8).

The proclamation of the kingdom in Galilee. Matthew's first main section (4:17—16:20) is introduced, "From that time Jesus began to proclaim: 'Repent, for the kingdom of heaven has come near'" (4:17). In the following chapters the Evangelist narrates how Jesus is "teaching in their synagogues and proclaiming the gospel of the kingdom" and how he "cures every disease and every sickness among the people [of Israel]" (4:23). The programmatic Sermon on the Mount (chs. 5–7) exemplifies Jesus's teaching; the sequence of healing stories and other miracles in chapters 8–9 exemplifies his healing. When teaching on the Mount, Jesus acts like Moses, but his authority—unlike that of the Jewish scribes (7:29)—is even higher than that of Moses, through whom God had spoken to "those of ancient times" (5:21, 33). In content, the sermon consists of ethical commandments, principles, and exemplary rules. It will be the content of the disciples' missionary preaching to the world: go and teach the nations "everything that I have commanded you" (28:20).

When healing the lepers and the blind, casting out demons, and raising the dead among his people Israel (chs. 8–9), Jesus acts as "Son of David" (9:27). The Son of David is not a military or political leader who frees his people from Roman rulers; rather, he is a meek, peaceful redeemer who heals the sick and the outcasts of Israel. In this way the story of Jesus transforms traditional Jewish messianology.

At chapter 10 the Evangelist inserts the missionary discourse, brought forward from Mark 6:7–13 and expanded with materials from Q (= Luke 10) and other texts. Jesus conveys to his 12 disciples the same authority he has. Their task is to proclaim the gospel of the kingdom and to heal the sick, just as he does; they do these things in the same way Jesus did, absolutely poor and defenseless; and they will share Jesus's fate, persecuted and required to take up the cross. Like Jesus, whose activity is limited (almost) exclusively to Israel (4:25), the 12 disciples are sent only to "the lost sheep of the house of Israel" (10:5–6). The message of this discourse is this: "The disciple is to be like the teacher, and the slave like the master" (10:25). Discipleship means conformity with Jesus in every respect.

From the beginning of his public activity Jesus meets with resistance on the part of the Jewish leaders: according to 9:33–34 the ordinary people are positively amazed, but the Pharisees suspect Jesus as casting out demons in the name of the devil (similarly, again in 12:23–24). The Pharisees and the scribes—in Matthew's own time the leaders of the majority synagogues in Israel (see 23:2)—are Jesus's most prominent enemies. In Matthew 11–12 the split in Israel gets deeper: "this generation" (11:16), the cities of Galilee (11:20–24), "the wise and the intelligent" (11:25), and the Pharisees (12:2, 14, 24, 38) stand on one side. The "infants" (11:25), those who "are weary and are carrying heavy burdens" (11:28), the sick, the "crowds" (12:15), and the true family of Jesus that "does the will of my Father in heaven" (12:50) stand on the other. The Christological perspective is widened: 11:27 anticipates the Son's universal lordship, which will become visible in the Gospel's last episode (28:18). Matthew 12:38–40 anticipates the coming resurrection of the Son of Man, according to the model of Jonah. The formula quotation in 12:18–21 once more opens the horizon to the Gentiles.

From chapter 12 on, Matthew follows closely Mark's narrative. His distinctive accent is on the threefold "withdrawal" of Jesus from hostile Jewish leaders to the desert, to Phoenicia, or to the other side of the lake (12:15; 14:13; 15:21; cf. 16:4–5). In these places those with Jesus witness special events: feedings of the multitudes, which prefigure the Eucharist of the Church (14:13–21; 15:32–39); the stilling of the storm, prefiguring experiences of Jesus's disciples in "the storms of life"; the healing of the daughter of a Canaanite woman (15:21–28), yet another signal of hope for the Gentiles. Inserted into this section we find the third of the great discourses, the Parables (ch. 13). At the end of his last withdrawal, Jesus and his disciples are in the district of Caesarea Philippi, in the utmost north of the Holy Land, where Peter, as spokesperson of all the disciples, confesses Jesus as Son of God, the basic confession upon which the church will be built (16:16–19).

The way to Jerusalem, to the cross, and to resurrection. Matthew introduces his second main section (16:21—28:20), "From that time Jesus began to show that he must go to Jerusalem and undergo great sufferings" (16:21). The next subsection (16:21—20:34) details three predictions of suffering, each followed by the disciples' refusal to claim their own suffering. In this subsection Jesus teaches his disciples, the nucleus of the future church, about the requirements, experiences, and dimensions of discipleship. Suffering, reversal of worldly ranking, marriage, and poverty are among this section's chief topics. In its center the so-called community discourse (Matt 18) is inserted: discipleship entails respect of the "little ones," fellowship, forgiveness of sins, and love. The center of this discourse is the promise of Emmanuel: "Where two or three are gathered in my name, I am there among them" (18:20; cf. 1:23).

At 21:1–11 Jesus enters Jerusalem as the nonviolent Messiah, riding on a donkey. He is applauded by the city's enthusiastic crowds as "Son of David" and "the prophet Jesus from Nazareth." In the Temple he engages in three courses of dispute with his opponents. First, he tells them three parables (21:28—22:14), progressively disclosing the course of salvation history. God's judgment is announced to the leaders of Israel after the wicked tenants have murdered the Son (21:42–44). In the parable of the wedding banquet, after the destruction of Jerusalem (22:7) the king's servants will be sent to the people on the streets to invite them—surely an allusion to an incipient mission to the Gentiles (22:8–10). But an invitation to the royal banquet is no guarantee of security: the guest without a wedding robe will be thrown into the outer darkness (22:11–13)—a warning for the church, which is a mixed body of good and evil people (cf. 13:24–20). Second, a collection of controversies follows (22:15–46): Jesus refutes different groups of Jewish adversaries, Sadducees and Pharisees, who are all united in their hostility toward him. Third, the sevenfold woe discourse against the Pharisees and scribes describes them as negatively as possible (23:13–33). A twofold announcement of judgment terminates the woes: the blood of all the righteous murdered in Israel will come upon this generation (23:35–36); Jerusalem will be left desolate (23:38). Jerusalem's destruction is interpreted as God's punishment for the murder of the prophets, of Jesus, and of his disciples. Then Jesus and his disciples leave the Temple—forever (24:1–2). In the following eschatological discourse (chs. 24–25), the main emphasis lies on warnings to the church, which still must face the last judgment with the parousia of the Son of Man. To belong to the church does not insure security; one strives for works of love in fear yet at the same time with confidence in the judge of the world, who is revealed to the disciples as their Lord, the Emmanuel who has accompanied and protected their lives (25:31–46).

The Gospel ends with the story of the passion and the resurrection. Jesus is innocent; he is depicted as the just one, who is obedient to the will of the Father as proclaimed in the Sermon on the Mount (26:30, 42, 51–54, 63–64; 27:4, 12–14, 19, 24). In his obedience Jesus is truly the Son of God (27:42–43, 54). The conflict with Israel's leaders comes to its climax. They pursue their goal to have Jesus executed without much ado by lucrative means. The 30 pieces of silver leave their bloody trail throughout the rest of the story (27:3–10; 28:12–15). In a bizarre yet key episode, inserted by Matthew into the Markan narrative, "the whole people" (*pas ho laos*) responds to Pilate's handwashing with what one could call a "conditioned self-curse": "His blood be on us and our children" (27:25).

For Matthew the destruction of Jerusalem in 70 C.E. is the fulfillment of these words; he thinks neither of a condemnation of Israel in the last judgment nor of an everlasting curse on the Jewish people. Only after Jesus's death does God intervene with awe-inspiring signs (27:51–53). Jesus's resurrection leads to death ("the guards shook and became like dead men," 28:4) and to life for the women and all the disciples. The Gospel ends with a twofold outlook: first, on the incredulity that will prevail among "Jews" (note: not "all Jews") until today (28:11–15); second, and most important, on the full authority of Jesus over the universe, the ensuing mission of the disciples to "all the nations," and their protection by the Emmanuel, Jesus, who will always be "with them, to the end of the age" (28:18–20).

Matthew's Theology. How may we conceptually summarize Matthew's theology, narrated in his story of Jesus? The following attempt to "translate" Matthew's narrative into theological concepts might be helpful for theological comparisons, but it cannot retain the power of Matthew's narrative.

Narrated Christology. This Gospel has a very high Christology: Jesus is "Emmanuel," "God with us" (1:23; 28:20). "Emmanuel" means that humans can experience God in history, narrate his story, and follow him. In this biblical concept God is "close" to humanity. Matthew's high Christology is very different from later Christian forms of high Christology, expressed in ontological categories influenced by Platonic philosophy in the Greek church. Terms traditionally construed as "Christological titles" become part of Matthew's narrated Christology of the "Emmanuel." Thus, "Son of Man" is not a "title" whose meaning is defined by its background in Jewish apocalyptic texts. Rather, it is defined by the story of Jesus: "Son of Man" is a self-designation which embraces the whole of the way of Jesus, his humility and his human authority, his suffering and death, his resurrection and exaltation, and his parousia as judge of the world (Hare, 1990). "Son of God" is not a title defined by its traditional Jewish or Christian uses, such as the royal Messiah, the one born of a virgin, or a man with divine power. Rather, Matthew's *story* shows who the Son of God is: a humble, just man, obedient to

God until his death but at the same time the unique representative of God, revealed by God, and confessed by humans. "Son of David" is not the Davidic Messiah of traditional Jewish expectations. The story of Jesus demonstrates this concept's transformation. The Son of David is the healer of the sick among his people, the nonviolent, meek ruler of Israel.

An ethical gospel. Matthew's book is an ethical Gospel. He knows no distinction between "indicative" and "imperative." Rather, his theology follows the Jewish model of "covenantal nomism": the law, as fulfilled and newly proclaimed by Jesus in his Sermon on the Mount, is the greatest gift of the "Emmanuel" for his disciples and for the nations, just as Torah is the greatest gift of God for his chosen people Israel. The radical commandments of Jesus are embedded into the story of Jesus, just as the promulgation of Torah is embedded into the Old Testament's story of God with Israel. Jesus's commandments lead to the experience of the heavenly Father's presence. This is shown by the Sermon's central section (Matt 6:1–18), particularly by the Lord's Prayer at its center (6:9–14).

Salvation history. Most scholars regard Matthew 28:16–20 and the mission to all the nations as the culmination and goal of the whole Gospel (differently Sim, 1998). There is less agreement, however, whether the mission to all the Gentiles replaces the mission to Israel or whether this last command of the exalted Lord means that the once exclusive mission to Israel (10:5–6) is expanded to include the mission to all the nations. The latter seems more probable, as 10:23 suggests (Konradt, 2007; differing from Luz, 2001). However, Matthew does not leave much room for hope for a conversion of Israel (13:13–17; 23:37–39). In his day most Jews are listening to the Pharisees as their leaders, not to Jesus and his disciples. Matthew's Gospel reflects this traumatic experience. One might call his theology of Israel "proto-supersessionist." "The kingdom of God will be taken away from you"— that is, from the leaders, not from the people of Israel—"and given to a people"—not to new leaders, but to an *ethnos*—"that produces its fruits" (21:43). Matthew does not say that the kingdom will be given to the church or to the Gentiles. Rather, a chance is opened to the church, insofar as it brings forth good fruits.

Church as discipleship. Matthew's "ecclesiology" is one of discipleship. Its key aspects are found in Matthew 10: to follow Jesus; to take him as a model; to imitate him in his humility, poverty, nonviolence, sufferings, and even martyrdom. There is not yet a clear and standardized use of the word *ekklesia*, either for the universal church (16:17) or for the local congregation (18:17). There is no distinction between the visible and invisible church: disciples of Christ are always visible. Nor does Matthew distinguish the "true" church from other Christian communities: every church is church only insofar as it is obedient to Jesus. Matthew recognizes no hierarchical structures in a church: the "little ones" are its center, forgiveness of sins and mutual love its *notae*, presence of the Emmanuel its promise (18:20). Neither does Matthew draw a clear distinction between "the old people of God," Israel, and "the emerging Christian church," except for one criterion: that disciples' "righteousness [must] exceed that of the scribes and the Pharisees" (5:20). The church must prove itself by its "good works" (5:16). In these respects Matthew's emerging ecclesiology became a model for minority churches, monastic movements, the churches of the radical Reformation—not so much for the great mainline churches.

[*See also* Allegory and Typology; Christology; Discipleship; Ecclesiology; Eschatology; Ethics, Biblical; Forgiveness; Gentiles; Gospel; Judaism; Justice, Justification, and Righteousness; Kingdom of God (Heaven); Mercy and Compassion; Parable; Repentance; Salvation History; Scripture; *and* Soteriology.]

BIBLIOGRAPHY

Davies, William D., and Dale C. Allison. *A Critical and Exegetical Commentary on the Gospel According to Saint Matthew*. 3 vols. Edinburgh: T&T Clark, 1988–1997.

Fiedler, Peter. *Das Matthäusevangelium*. Theologischer Kommentar zum Neuen Testament 1. Stuttgart: Kohlhammer, 2006.

Foster, Paul. *Community, Law and Mission in Matthew's Gospel*. Wissenschaftliche Untersuchungen zum Neuen Testament 2, Reihe 177. Tübingen, Germany: Mohr-Siebeck 2004.

Hare, Douglas R. A. *The Son of Man Tradition*. Minneapolis: Fortress, 1990.

Keener, Craig S. *A Commentary on the Gospel of Matthew*. Grand Rapids, Mich., and Cambridge, U.K.: Eerdmans, 1999.

Konradt, Matthias. *Israel, Kirche und die Völker im Matthäusevangelium*. Wissenschaftliche Untersuchungen zum Neuen Testament 215. Tübingen, Germany: Mohr-Siebeck 2007.

Luz, Ulrich. *Matthew 8–20*. Translated by James E. Crouch. Hermeneia. Minneapolis: Fortress, 2001.

Luz, Ulrich. *Matthew 21–28*. Translated by James E. Crouch. Hermeneia. Minneapolis: Fortress, 2005 a.

Luz, Ulrich. *Studies in Matthew*. Translated by Rosemary Selle. Grand Rapids, Mich.: Eerdmans, 2005 b.

Luz, Ulrich. *Matthew 1–7*. Translated by James E. Crouch. Hermeneia. Minneapolis: Augsburg, 1989. Fortress, 2007.

Nolland, John. *The Gospel of Matthew*. New International Greek Testament Commentary. Grand Rapids, Mich.: Eerdmans; Bletchley, U.K.: Paternoster, 2005.

Overman, J. Andrew. *Matthew's Gospel and Formative Judaism: The Social World of the Matthean Community*. Minneapolis: Fortress, 1990.

Sim, David. *The Gospel of Matthew and Christian Judaism: The History and Social Setting of the Matthean Community*. Studies of the New Testament and Its World. Edinburgh: T&T Clark, 1998.

Stanton, Graham N. *A Gospel for a New People: Studies in Matthew*. Edinburgh: T&T Clark, 1992.

Ulrich Luz

MEGILLOT

The "Five Scrolls," or *Megillot* (Hebrew for "scrolls"), is the collective name for the books Ruth, Song of Songs, Ecclesiastes, Lamentations, and Esther. Originally, these books had nothing more in common with each other than they did with other Old Testament books. All were canonized in the third part of the Hebrew Bible, the Writings, though. After some initial variability, the order of the books in this part of the Hebrew canon became fixed so that the five books were arranged according to the alleged times of their composition (see the order in the *Biblia Hebraica Stuttgartensia*).

In the Greek Bible, the five books were not kept together (see the order in Christian Bibles). Ecclesiastes and Song of Songs appeared among the Poetical Books, whereas Ruth and Esther were placed among the Historical Books and Lamentations with the Prophetic Books, following Jeremiah. Although these changes are mainly due to misunderstandings (neither Ruth nor Esther is a historical book, and Lamentations was not composed by Jeremiah), they also reflect the diversity of the five books. None of them is at the center of the Old Testament tradition, yet each is a little "pearl." Together, they give unique insight into diverse aspects of the world of ancient Israel.

Only in medieval Judaism did the five books grow together into a distinct collection: the "Five Scrolls," read in the synagogue at Jewish festivals. By the Second Temple period, Esther was read liturgically at the festival of Purim. In the eighth century C.E., the post-Talmudic tractate *Soferim* (14:3, 18) mentions the liturgical use of Esther (Purim), Song of Songs (Passover), and Ruth (Shavuot, Feast of Weeks). Eventually, Ecclesiastes was connected with Sukkoth (Feast of Tabernacles). Some of the links between the books and the festivals are clear (Esther, Lamentations), while others are more random (especially Ecclesiastes). In this liturgical use, the proper order of the books is Song of Songs, Ruth, Lamentations, Ecclesiastes, Esther, following the cycle of the liturgical year (see the order in Jewish Bibles).

Ruth. In four chapters, the book of Ruth unfolds the story of the Moabite Ruth and her Judean mother-in-law Naomi. Ruth 1:1 dates the events to the time of the judges. The book is not a historical report, though, but a theological narrative. Its date of origin is difficult to determine. Thematic foci and connections with other books make an origin in postexilic times likely.

Ruth 1 starts with a famine, a trip from Bethlehem to Moab, two marriages with Moabite women, and the death of three men. Having lost her husband Elimelech and her two sons, Naomi decides to return to Bethlehem. Ruth, one of her daughters-in-law, insists on following her. The remaining chapters all deal with the problems of widows, who, lacking male support, have a difficult position in a patriarchal society. Ruth 2 depicts Ruth gleaning in the fields of Boaz. Whereas he has heard about her solidarity with

Naomi, she learns only later who he is: a relative of Elimelech and thus one of the family's "redeemers." Ruth 3 unfolds how Ruth, following Naomi's advice, throws herself at the uncovered "feet" (a term with sexual overtones) of Boaz one night and suggests that he be her "redeemer." Boaz is willing but informs her that he must first ask a closer relative. This conversation takes place in Ruth 4 and reveals that the "redeeming" consists of both marrying Ruth and buying the field of Elimelech, to "maintain the dead man's name on his inheritance" (Ruth 4:5, 10). This arrangement is not attractive to the other relative, leaving Boaz free to buy Elimelech's field and marry Ruth. Their marriage is blessed with a son, Obed, described as the grandfather of David.

Although at first glance Ruth might be mistaken for a harmless family story, it clearly is more. With its explanation of the role of the "redeemer" (see especially Ruth 4:5), it creatively combines two laws from the Torah: Leviticus 25:23–28 (on the return of sold land in the jubilee year or earlier through "redemption" by a close relative; see also Jer 32:7–9) and Deuteronomy 25:5–10 (on levirate marriage). Similarly, Ruth 2 reflects an interest in the social laws of the Torah as it reads like a narrative explanation of the laws on gleaning in Leviticus 19:9–10; 23:22 and Deuteronomy 24:19, also reflecting their references to the poor, foreigners, and widows.

Introducing Ruth as a Moabite and describing her faithfulness, the book of Ruth takes a clear stand against xenophobic tendencies found elsewhere in the Old Testament. Probably, it is arguing against a special hatred of both Moabites (see Deut 23:4–7 [NRSV, vv. 3–6]; Num 25:1–5; Ezra 9:1; Neh 13:1) and foreign women (see Ezra 9–10; Prov 2:16–19, etc.)

Narratively, the book of Ruth unfolds a theology of God's unspectacular presence. Although there are no miracles and revelations, God is present in the life of the two women and their families. Although Ruth and Naomi belong to the weak in society, their solidarity mirrors God's solidarity and their plans mirror God's plans. This is reflected most clearly at the end of the book in the birth of Obed, which shows that the marriage of Ruth and Boaz is not only blessed but also a sign of life for Naomi (see Ruth 4:17) and

connects the foreigner Ruth with David (and Jesus; see Matt 1:5).

Song of Songs. Song of Songs (Song of Solomon, or Canticles) is one of the most unusual books in the Bible. It deals with love and desire and, with one possible exception (Song 8:6), never mentions God. Early on, the book was interpreted allegorically, which secured its (controversial) canonical status. Read as a dialogue between Yahweh and Israel, Christ and the church, Christ and Mary, or Christ and the believer, Song of Songs is a very religious book. Thus, it became important both in Judaism and in Christianity. Pointing to Solomon (see 1 Kgs 5:12) as the author of "the song of songs," its superscription (Song 1:1) gives the book additional weight.

Critical scholarship has made clear that Song of Songs was not written by Solomon and originally was not meant to be read allegorically but, rather, has to do with the erotic love of humans. Beyond that, there is little consensus. Regarding date, many scholars argue that the final composition is late (third century B.C.E.), but at least for individual songs a much earlier origin (eighth–sixth centuries B.C.E. or even earlier) is conceivable as well. Regarding content and genre, the similarity to ancient Near Eastern and especially Egyptian love poetry is noteworthy. Some of these ancient Near Eastern texts involve a goddess and a king and might have had a cultic connection (sacred marriage rites). Most of them, however, are purely worldly. Scholars dispute whether Song of Songs is a more or less random collection of such worldly love songs or whether it is a consciously arranged composition.

What is clear is that Song of Songs consists of several love songs, both monologues and dialogues, spoken by one (or several) pair(s) of a female and male lover and some others. There is no continuing story line, but the tone remains the same throughout the book. The lovers are full of longing, describing the desirability of each other's bodies and the restrictions imposed on their desire by society and talking or dreaming about meetings in a garden, the fields, or the privacy of home. These descriptions are full of metaphors, insinuations, and double entendres. As little as Song of Songs is meant to be read allegorically, neither is it meant to be read literally.

Beyond issues of how to understand single verses and passages, the understanding of the book depends on the question of its purpose and setting in life. Connected to the question of whether it is a collection of independent love songs or a purposefully arranged composition, this question is as fundamental as it is hard to answer. Assuming that the canonization of Song of Songs was not a total misunderstanding, some connections with other Old Testament books might be important. By referring to Solomon, the superscription implies a connection between Song of Songs and wisdom (cf. 1 Kgs 5:9–14 [NRSV, 4:29–34]; Prov 1:1; Eccl 1:1). And indeed there are thematic overlaps with wisdom books, especially with Ecclesiastes (focus on joy; see, e.g., Eccl 9:9) and Proverbs (praise of woman wisdom; see, e.g., Prov 9; 31). With the motif of a closed garden with trees and water, Song of Songs is reminiscent of Genesis 2–3. It is further connected with the paradise story as it describes man and woman as equal partners (Gen 2:18, 23) and humans in harmony with nature (Gen 2:15, 19–20). Does it perhaps, despite its silence about God, also contain a religious dimension, implying that through such harmony and equality humans are also close to God?

Ecclesiastes. According to Ecclesiastes 1:1, the book of Ecclesiastes contains "the words of Qoheleth, the son of David, king in Jerusalem." Thereby, the book both claims to be written by Solomon—the real name of David's son who became king in Jerusalem—and reveals that this claim is fictitious—there never was a son of David by the name of Qoheleth. The language and the content of the book indicate that it belongs among the youngest books of the Old Testament. Most scholars date it to the third century B.C.E., when Judah was under Ptolemaic rule. The name *Qoheleth* is a feminine participle from a Hebrew verb that means "to come together, assemble." Both the feminine form and the use of the article in Ecclesiastes 12:8 (and probably Eccl 7:27) indicate that *Qoheleth* was originally not a name but a title. Latin *Ecclesiastes* and English *preacher* are attempts to imitate the Hebrew.

The alleged Solomonic authorship, which connects Ecclesiastes with Proverbs, Song of Songs, and Wisdom, is especially important in Ecclesiastes 1:12–2:26. Here, the "king" introduces himself and speaks about his royal endeavors. At the end, he comes to a very negative conclusion: despite all his wisdom, wealth, and achievements, there is no permanent gain (Eccl 2:11); like the fool, he must die (Eccl 2:14–16), leave all his goods to an heir (Eccl 2:21), and be forgotten by everyone (Eccl 2:16). The "king" realizes that his power is limited, that at the end it is not he but God who decides whether he will receive wisdom and joy (Eccl 2:26). For the "king," this is an unbearable thought. Ecclesiastes 3–12 contains similar reflections on death and other limitations, but here the conclusions are often more positive. Furthermore, there are no indications anymore that the narrative "I" is a king. According to one convincing theory, the author of the book plays with two different perspectives: the one of the "king," which he presents in Ecclesiastes 1:12—2:26, and his own, which he presents in Ecclesiastes 3:1ff. Whether this author's name indeed was Qoheleth or whether Qoheleth is the name he chose for his narrator remains an open question. The bulk of the book is framed with verses about Qoheleth in the third person. Ecclesiastes 12:9–14 is probably a later addition by someone who wanted to give the book a more pious ending. Ecclesiastes 1:1–2 and 12:8 might well go back to the author who wrote the rest of the book. He frames his reflections with a motto that summarizes Qoheleth's message with the Hebrew word *hebel*, which literally means "breath, vapor." This term is difficult to translate as Qoheleth uses it sometimes in a neutral sense of "transient, fleeting" without further qualifications but sometimes in a negative sense of "worthless, fruitless."

Qoheleth's reflections prove him a sage, although not a traditional one. Against the worldview of traditional wisdom, as found, for example, in Proverbs, he points out that neither wisdom nor righteousness is a guarantee of success. Reflecting further on humans' inability to understand God's doings (Eccl 3:11; 8:16–17) or to know their future (Eccl 3:21–22; 6:12), Qoheleth encourages his audience to accept life as it is and deal with its challenges as best as possible

(Eccl 7:14; 11:5–6). Instead of despairing over the incomprehensibility of God's doings, it is better to trust that God created the world good (Eccl 3:11; 7:29). Instead of getting angry about the injustices in the world, it is better to remember that nobody is perfectly just (Eccl 7:20; 9:3). Instead of being afraid of death, it is better to enjoy life (Eccl 8:15; 9:7–10). Instead of being depressed because there are no everlasting "gains" (Eccl 1:3; 5:15 [NRSV, v.16]), it is better to realize that one's "lot" consists of everyday joys, which are a gift from God (Eccl 3:12–13; 5:17–18 [NRSV, vv. 18–19]).

Lamentations. The book of Lamentations consists of five poems (corresponding to the book's five chapters) that lament the destruction of the city and Temple of Jerusalem (587 B.C.E.). Connecting this catastrophe with God's wrath and humans' sin and expressing hope for God's mercy, the poems are an attempt to "digest" it theologically. Similar city laments are known from ancient Mesopotamia; a famous example is the lamentation over the destruction of Ur.

According to the superscription in the Septuagint and later Jewish tradition, Lamentations was composed by Jeremiah (see also 2 Chr 35:25). As this connection is not made in the Hebrew Bible, it is most likely not historical. Although four of the five poems of Lamentations are acrostics, that is, their lines or stanzas start with consecutive letters of the alphabet, and the last one is reminiscent of the alphabet in that it consists of 22 verses, each has individual features. Hence, the poems were probably composed by different people. At least some of them likely date to the time shortly after the fall of Jerusalem. Whether they were used in the mourning rituals mentioned in Jeremiah 41:5 and Zechariah 7:3; 8:19 is disputed.

In trying to come to terms with the catastrophe of 587 B.C.E., all the poems of Lamentations speak about the tragic events and subsequent misery in Jerusalem. In addition to references to the plundering and destruction of the Temple and the destruction of the city, most of the poems contain graphic depictions of the inhumanity of the enemies, the atrocities of war, and the subsequent desolation. Lamentations 1 depicts Jerusalem as an abandoned and defenseless widow who has nobody to comfort her (Lam 1:2, 9, 17, 21).

Lamentations 2 in particular, although also the other poems, blame(s) God for the misery of Jerusalem and describes God as an enemy who wrathfully destroys everything and mercilessly attacks daughter Zion (Lam 1:12; 2:1–6, 21–22; 3:43; 4:11; 5:22). Similar statements appear in Lamentations 3. Here, however, the target of God's wrath is not Jerusalem but an individual (compare Job).

Going one step further, other passages explain the connection between Jerusalem's misery and God differently, namely, by pointing to Jerusalem's transgressions. Lamentations 1:5 states that God made Jerusalem suffer because of "the multitude of her transgressions" (see Lam 1:8, 18, 20; 3:42; 5:7, 16). In Hebrew thinking, sin and punishment are closely related. Hence, in Lamentations 4:6 it is unclear whether the comparison of Jerusalem to Sodom is about the cities' sin or their punishment. The words used in Hebrew can mean both. In a different way, the connection is made clear in Lamentations 5:7 as this verse talks about the sins of the ancestors that their children have to bear.

Finally, Lamentations addresses the possibility of God's mercy. In the form of a psalm of individual lament, Lamentations 3 especially expresses the hope that God's faithfulness is great and God's love and mercy will not come to an end (Lam 3:22–23). This hope is connected less to an awareness of wrongdoing (but see Lam 3:42) than it is to a wish that enemies be punished (Lam 3:46–66). Theologically more subtle is Lamentations 5:19–22, in which the hope for restoration is grounded in a confession of God's enduring presence.

Esther. The book of Esther narrates a conflict between the Persian Haman and the Jew Mordecai that endangered the entire Jewish people. The book is named after Esther, a Jewish woman who became the Persian queen and through her courage saved her people from annihilation. The story is set in the time of King Ahasuerus (Xerxes I, fifth century B.C.E.) and contains many details about the Persian court. Other details are also conspicuous, for example, a Jewish woman becoming the Persian queen, Mordecai coming from the family of Kish (Esth 2:5; cf. 1 Sam 9:1–2), and his enemy Haman being an Agagite (Esth 3:1), an allusion to the war between Saul and Agag (1 Sam 15) and Israel's enmity with the Amalekites (Exod 17:8–16; Deut 25:17–19). Hence, scholars agree that Esther is not a historical report but rather historical fiction, a narrative that addresses the problems of life in the Diaspora. It was probably written between the fifth and the third centuries B.C.E. Besides the Hebrew version (printed in Jewish and Protestant Bibles), the book is also handed down in a longer Greek version with many additions (printed in Catholic Bibles) and a shorter Greek version, which ends with Esther 8:17.

The story is both enthralling and horrible: Esther 1–2 introduces Esther and Mordecai and explains how Esther became the new queen. In Esther 3 Haman enters the picture, and from here on the story is about life and death. Angered by Mordecai's refusal to bow down to him, Haman develops a plan to destroy all the Jews. He convinces the king to enact an edict with a date for all the Jews in the Persian Empire to be annihilated. As Esther 4–5 unfolds, Esther, urged by Mordecai, risks her life to save her people. Without being asked, she approaches the king, which could lead to her execution. The king, however, greets her favorably and tells her that he will grant her every wish. Esther does not tell him her request at first but only invites him and Haman to a first and then a second banquet. Interwoven with these banquet scenes in Esther 5–8 is the motif of rise and fall: Haman has high aspirations and plans to have Mordecai hanged. Eventually, however, it is he who ends up at the gallows, whereas Mordecai is honored. With the personal aspect of the conflict between Haman and Mordecai resolved, Esther 8 returns to the political dimension. Though Haman is dead, the edict still threatens all the Jews with death. As no edict of a Persian king can be revoked (Esth 8:8), the only solution is to release a counteredict that allows the Jews to fight back. And so it happens in Esther 9: to prevent their annihilation, the Jews kill thousands of their enemies. The book ends with an explanation of how the Purim festival is connected to this story: its name derives from the *pur* (Persian for "lot") that

Haman threw to determine the day to kill the Jews (Esth 3:7; 9:24–26), and it is celebrated annually in remembrance of this day.

Theologically, the book of Esther is interesting as (in its Hebrew version) it never mentions God. Nevertheless, it clearly assumes that behind the scenes God is present (see especially Esth 4:14). At the same time, by focusing on Esther, a Jewish woman in a foreign king's court, the story makes the point that anyone may come into a situation where he or she is specially needed (Esth 4:14). The most challenging part of the story, theologically, is its bloody end. Knowing that the literary brutality is a reaction to actual brutality against Jews in the Diaspora helps to understand it. Nevertheless, the justification, if not the glorification, of the slaughtering of thousands of people remains problematic.

[*See also* Festivals and Holy Days; *and* Wisdom Literature.]

BIBLIOGRAPHY

Ruth

Fischer, Irmtraud. "The Book of Ruth: A 'Feminist' Commentary to the Torah?" In *Ruth and Esther: A Feminist Companion to the Bible*, edited by Athalya Brenner, pp. 24–49. Feminist Companion to the Bible, Second Series 3. Sheffield, U.K.: Sheffield Academic Press, 1999.

Nielsen, Kirsten. *Ruth: A Commentary*. Old Testament Library. Louisville, Ky.: Westminster John Knox, 1997.

Trible, Phyllis. "Ruth, Book of." In *The Anchor Bible Dictionary*, edited by David Noel Freedman, Vol. 5, pp. 842–847. New York: Doubleday, 1992.

Song of Songs

Exum, J. Cheryl. *Song of Songs: A Commentary*. Old Testament Library. Louisville, Ky.: Westminster John Knox, 2005.

Fox, Michael V. *The Song of Songs and the Ancient Egyptian Love Songs*. Madison: University of Wisconsin Press, 1985.

Ecclesiastes

Fox, Michael V. *A Time to Tear Down and a Time to Build Up: A Rereading of Ecclesiastes*. Grand Rapids, Mich.: Eerdmans, 1999.

Kruger, Thomas. *Qoheleth: A Commentary*. Hermeneia. Minneapolis: Fortress, 2004.

Seow, Choon-Leong. *Ecclesiastes: A New Translation with Introduction and Commentary.* Anchor Yale Bible 18C. New Haven, Conn.: Yale University Press, 1997.

Lamentations

Berlin, Adele. *Lamentations: A Commentary.* Old Testament Library. Louisville, Ky.: Westminster John Knox, 2002.
Dobbs-Allsopp, F. W. *Lamentations.* Interpretation. Louisville, Ky.: Westminster John Knox, 2002.

Esther

Berlin, Adele. *Esther: The Traditional Hebrew Text with the New JPS Translation.* JPS Bible Commentary. Philadelphia: Jewish Publication Society, 2001.
Fox, Michael V. *Character and Ideology in the Book of Esther.* Columbia: University of South Carolina Press, 1991.

Annette Schellenberg

MERCY AND COMPASSION

Mercy and compassion are multivalent themes throughout the Bible, which characterize aspects of both God's dealings with humanity and relationships among human beings. Their legacy pervades Jewish and Christian theology, worship, and practice.

Classical and Hellenistic Contexts. Whereas the terms "mercy" and "compassion" appear synonymous in modern usage, such was not always the case in the ancient world. In the classical era Aristotle taught that "mercy" (*eleos* or *oiktirmos* and cognates) is an emotion, not a virtue that human beings feel when they see another person suffer an undeserved misfortune to which they also might be subject (*Rhet.* 2.8, 1386a25–27). *Eleos* may be translated as "pity"; to feel it one must be at the proper distance from the sufferer, vulnerable to suffering but not in the midst of it. Suffering consumes one's attention to the detriment of attending to others, whereas invulnerability engenders indifference. By contrast, compassion (*sympatheia*, from *sympaschō*) denotes intimately shared suffering. Insofar as the gods are invulnerable to human suffering, they cannot be relied on to show either mercy or compassion, though they may on occasion do so.

In the Hellenistic era, however, mercy and compassion are correlated in some texts, such as Diodorus Siculus's description (first century B.C.E.) of a grief-stricken father who "induced pity [*eleos*] and intense sympathy [*sympatheia*] in everyone" (*Library of History* 12.24.5). Compassion may soften one's heart and render it merciful: thus, Achilles Tatius (first to second centuries C.E.), "A human being who listens to the sufferings of others is somehow disposed to mercy [*sympathēs de pōs eis eleon*] and mercy frequently is the patron of affection [*philia*]" (*Leuc. Clit.* 3.14.3). Notably, the translators of the Septuagint (third century B.C.E.) use *eleos* to translate *hesed*, variously denoting covenant loyalty and faithfulness, steadfast love, and mercy toward sinners; the cognate adjective *eleēmōn* is used to translate *ḥānûn*, "compassionate" or "gracious." The Hebrew adjective *raḥam*, also meaning "compassionate," becomes *oiktirmōn*, "merciful." *Raḥam* most frequently appears with *ḥānûn* (*eleos* LXX) to invoke God in public or private prayer (2 Chr 30:9; Neh 9:17, 31; Pss 86:15; 103:8; 111:4; 145:8; Joel 2:13; Jonah 4:2). Thus, the Septuagint translates compassion, covenant loyalty, faithfulness, and mercy in terms of mercy as a divine attribute.

Divine Mercy: The Hebrew Bible. Biblical texts display a fluid understanding of both mercy and compassion, locating the source of both in God. In the foundational self-revelation to Moses on Sinai (Exod 34:6), God is named "The LORD, the LORD, a God merciful [*raḥămîm/oiktirmōn*] and gracious [*ḥānûn/eleēmōn*], slow to anger and abounding in steadfast love [*ḥesed/polyeleos*] and faithfulness." This formulaic revelation of God on Sinai as "merciful" and "gracious" occurs throughout the Hebrew Bible and the New Testament (e.g., Jonah 4:2; Pss 86:15; 103:8; 145:8; Rom 9:15). It is the foundation of God's covenant relationship with Israel and of Israel's existence as a people called by God (Exod 34:6; Rom 9:15). God's mercy on disobedient Israel (Exod 34:6) leverages both Moses's intercession on behalf of Israel (Num 14:18) and Joel's call to repentance (Joel 2:13), based on the premise that God will be merciful. It is also the basis for Israel's national confession and restoration after the Exile (Neh 9:17).

Divine mercy thus connotes both covenant faithfulness for God's elect people and compassion for sinners, whether Israelites (Ps 103:8) or Gentiles (Jonah 4:2). Indeed, while divine mercy and compassion are particularly displayed through the covenant with Israel, they extend to all God's creation (Ps 145:8). This theme is picked up by Hellenistic Jewish texts: "For you are merciful [*eleeis*] to all…and you overlook people's sins, so that they may repent. For you love [*agapas*] all things that exist, and detest nothing that you have made" (Wis 11:23–24; also Sir 2:11; 16:11–12). Here, notably, God's mercy and love are based in creation, extend to all creatures, and potentially lead to repentance for all people. The same theme occurs in *Joseph and Aseneth* (first century B.C.E.–second century C.E.), where the revelation of the God of Israel as "a pitying [*eleēmōn*] God, and merciful [*oiktirmōn*]" (11:10) gives the Gentile Aseneth courage to repent of her idolatry.

Assurance of God's mercy and grace is ubiquitous in the Psalms and central in later benedictions and prayers (4Q381 47.1; Sir 48:20; 50:19; *Pss. Sol.* 5:1–2; 10:7–9; Wis 15:1; 2 Macc 8:29). The benediction of Aaron in Numbers 6:24–26, invoking God's mercy and peace, is echoed in later liturgical formulas (Sir 50:22–24; 1QS 2.3–4) and the rabbinic Eighteen Benedictions (*Shemoneh Esreh*). Invocations of God's mercy are central to the *Amidah*, or "standing prayer," in Jewish liturgy to this day.

In summary, in the Hebrew Bible and postbiblical literature divine mercy is the foundation of Israel's relationship with God. Mercy is elective and creates a people by calling them into this covenant relationship. In this sense, God's mercy and compassion define a particular people—Israel—by virtue of their reception of divine love, apart from any deserving (Deut 7:7–8). Israel owes its ongoing existence to God's freedom to be merciful. The divine attributes of mercy and compassion undergird prophetic calls to repentance and their promise of Israel's restoration. Intrinsic to the notion of mercy is that it is given to the undeserving and unfitting. This quality implies that God's mercy is not limited to one people but rather is implicit in creation and given to all people. It is the divine quality most frequently invoked in

prayers for forgiveness of sins and for deliverance from harm.

Divine Mercy: The New Testament. In the New Testament mercy and compassion characterize Jesus's ministry to the undeserving: those of low status, the poor, and the outsider. Jesus is the Son of David who responds to pleas for mercy by healing, exorcizing, and delivering people in need (Matt 9:27; 15:22; 17:15; 20:30–31; Mark 10:47–48; Luke 16:24; 17:13; 18:38–39). The Psalms' frequent invocation of God as merciful now appears in petitions invoking the mercy of Jesus, who responds with concrete acts of healing and deliverance. In this way Jesus enacts and embodies God's attributes as revealed in the covenant with Israel (Luke 1:50, 54, 58, 72, 78; 4:17–21), intentionally extending those attributes beyond the bounds of the covenant people (Luke 4:24–27) by healing outsiders such as the Gerasene demoniac (Mark 5:19) and the daughter of the Canaanite woman (Matt 15:22). Jesus also interprets divine mercy as the calling of sinners rather than the righteous, quoting Hosea 6:6 to rebuke those who criticize his fellowship with public sinners (Matt 9:13). The exercise of mercy and justice is at the heart of true worship (Matt 12:7) and is the central import of the Mosaic law (Matt 23:23).

Jesus's compassion has an emotional component as well, conveyed by the Greek word *splanchnois*: literally, "inward parts," metaphorically referring to "the heart," the seat of the emotions. The cognate verb *splanchnizomai* may be translated as "moved with compassion or pity" and frequently describes Jesus's response to human need (Matt 9:36; 14:14; 15:32; 20:34; Mark 6:34; 8:2; Luke 7:13). That response, in turn, embodies the compassionate mercy of God (*splanchna eleous theou*), prophesied by Zechariah, the father of John the Baptist (Luke 1:78; cf. *Odes Sol.* 9:78).

In Paul's letters mercy most frequently refers to God's dealings with Israel, building explicitly on Exodus 34:6 (Rom 9:15; see also 9:18, 23; 11:30–32; Gal 6:16). The bestowal of mercy on the Gentiles is an extension of this covenant faithfulness (Rom 15:9). Paul also describes his own calling and ministry in terms of divine mercy (1 Cor 7:25; 2 Cor 4:1), perhaps because he sees his vocation as parallel to, and bound up with, God's calling and purposes for Israel, even through his ministry is primarily to the Gentiles (Rom 11:13–14). Apart from these instances, however, Paul employs the term "grace" (*charis*) rather than mercy to denote God's redemptive action on behalf of humankind. The source of this terminology is debated, as is its relationship to divine mercy. Perhaps *charis* avoids the ambivalent connotations of *eleos* in Greco-Roman literature and evokes the patronage system of benefaction in Roman society, to depict redemption through Christ as a gift for the undeserving. Yet the theological conviction of God's mercy toward the undeserving, rooted in God's self-revelation to Israel, is central to Paul's preaching and teaching.

In his undisputed letters Paul does not use the blessing of "mercy and peace"; rather, he opens his letters with a salutation of "grace and peace" (Rom 1:7; 1 Cor 1:3; 2 Cor 1:2; Phil 1:2; 1 Thess 1:1; Phlm 3). The combination of "grace, mercy, and peace" occurs as a closing blessing in 1 Timothy 1:2 and 2 Timothy 1:2. Divine mercy remains central to blessings throughout Christian liturgies, as evidenced by the formula *kyrie eleēson, Christe eleēson, kyrie eleēson* ("Lord have mercy, Christ have mercy, Lord have mercy"), which apparently derives from the invocations of God's mercy in the Hebrew Bible and may be documented as early as the fourth century C.E. (*Const. ap.* 8.6.4).

Human Mercy/Compassion. In both the Hebrew Bible and the New Testament, the exercise of mercy and compassion toward fellow human beings is an extension of divine mercy. One is to be merciful toward one's neighbor because this is what God is like and what God commands (e.g., Exod 2:21–27; Ps 111:4; Hos 6:6; Amos 1:11; Zech 7:9). Put succinctly, "Be merciful, just as your father is merciful" (Luke 6:36). Mercy is more than an emotion or a disposition; it issues in concrete acts of mercy such as almsgiving (*eleēmosynē*), which appears particularly in the Hellenistic Jewish texts of Sirach and Tobit as well as in the New Testament (Matt 6:2–3; Luke 11:41; 12:33; Acts 9:36; 10:2, 4; Jas 2:13). Almsgiving, the enactment of mercy, is simply assumed as the practice of devout Jews, Gentile God-fearers, and all who belong to Christ.

In the New Testament a further motivation for acts of mercy is Christ's identification with humanity in its poverty and need. In Matthew 25:35–40 Jesus teaches that at the last judgment the blessed who inherit the kingdom of God will learn that when they helped "the least of these" they in fact were serving the Lord. Paul develops a similar theme when exhorting the Corinthian Christians to give funds for the poor Christians in Jerusalem; he appeals not only to the example of Christ but also to fellowship with Christ and Christ's solidarity with those in need: "For you know the generous act [*charis*] of our Lord Jesus Christ, that though he was rich, yet for your sakes he became poor, so that by his poverty you might become rich" (2 Cor 8:9). Acts of mercy thus express communion with God in Christ through participation in a circle of giving and receiving.

The church fathers develop this theme in sermons enjoining almsgiving. Gregory of Nyssa (fourth century C.E.) describes mercy as "loving self-identification" with those in need (*Homilies on the Beatitudes* 5, *Gregorii Nysseni Opera* 7.2:126); Maximus the Confessor (seventh century C.E.) describes it as "voluntary self-identification" with others (*Mystagogia* 24, PG 91:71:713A). Such self-identification is a response to Christ's self-identification with all humanity and a mode of participation in that divine–human act. As Maximus puts it:

> If the poor person is "God," it is because of God's condescension in becoming poor for our sake [cf. 2 Cor 8:9] and in taking upon himself by his own sufferings the sufferings of each one "until the end of time" [cf. Matt 28:20], always suffering mystically out of goodness in proportion to each one's suffering. So all the more will that person be "God" who, in imitation of God's philanthropy, personally heals by his or her own initiative, but in a deiform way, the afflictions of those who suffer, and who exhibits in his or her merciful disposition the very same power of God's sustaining providence that operates in proportion to need. (*Mystagogia* 24, PG 91:713B)

Significantly, the early Christians included the collection and distribution of alms in their worship, as Justin Martyr records (*1 Apol.* 67.5–6). Their care for the poor became so notable that when the apostate emperor Julian (late fourth century C.E.) tried to reinstate pagan worship and undercut the influence of

Christian churches, he instructed the officials of pagan temples to erect shelters for the poor.

[*See also* Comfort and Mourning; Grace; Hospitality; Love; Prayer; Reconciliation; *and* Wealth and Poverty.]

BIBLIOGRAPHY

Blowers, Paul. "Pity, Empathy, and the Tragic Spectacle of Human Suffering: Exploring the Emotional Culture of Compassion in Late Ancient Christianity." *Journal of Early Christian Studies* 18, no. 1 (2010): 1–27.

Breytenbach, Cilliers. "'Charis' and 'Eleos' in Paul's Letter to the Romans." In *Grace, Reconciliation, Concord: The Death of Christ in Graeco-Roman Metaphors*, edited by C. Breytenbach, pp. 207–238. Leiden, The Netherlands: Brill, 2010.

Davies, Oliver. *A Theology of Compassion: Metaphysics of Difference and the Renewal of Tradition.* London: SCM, 2001.

Konstan, David. *Pity Transformed.* London: Duckworth, 2001.

Meeks, Wayne A. *The Origins of Christian Morality: The First Two Centuries.* New Haven, Conn.: Yale University Press, 1993.

O'Brien, Peter T., ed. *God Who Is Rich in Mercy: Essays Presented to D. D. B. Knox.* Homebush West, Australia: Lancer; Grand Rapids, Mich.: Baker, 1986.

Susan Eastman

MESSIAH

See Christ.

MICAH

See Book of the Twelve (Minor Prophets).

MINISTER AND MINISTRY

The notion of "minister" as a role within the community of faith derives far more directly from the New Testament than from the Old.

Ministry in the Old Testament (Hebrew Bible). There are at least three "offices" or "functions" in the writings of the Hebrew Bible that influence the New Testament understandings of ministry and our own understanding in the twenty-first century.

Elders. In Numbers 11:14 the people complain to Moses, and Moses complains to the Lord: "I am not able to carry all this people alone, for they are too heavy for me." God's response is to instruct Moses to appoint 70 elders "and they shall bear the burden of the people along with you" (Num 11:17). We can suspect that something of the role of Israel's elders echoes in the qualification for elders (i.e., presbyters) in the Pastoral Epistles and almost certainly in the story of Paul's instructions to the elders of Ephesus in Acts 20. Implicitly the elders are now to bear the burden of the people after Paul's death.

Prophets. The narratives of the calls of the prophets in the Old Testament, especially in Jeremiah 1, are echoed in the story of Paul's call to be an apostle in Galatians 1:13–17. Paul's whole understanding of the apostolic office and the church's thereafter is shaped by the view of the prophet as one commissioned and instructed by God. Further, the role of prophet continues as a gift of the Spirit in the churches Paul founds, and he explicitly contrasts the gift of prophecy to the gift of speaking in tongues (1 Cor 12:10; 14:39). For Matthew's community, some of the church leaders are also designated as prophets (Matt 23:34).

Priests. In Exodus 28 Aaron and his sons are designated by the Lord as priests, and the role of the priesthood continues in Israel and specifically in Jerusalem up through the time of Jesus's ministry, until the destruction of the Temple in 70 C.E. While no leader in the churches of the New Testament is specifically designated as a priest, in the book of Hebrews Jesus is himself explicitly the new high priest and early in the life of the church the role of presbyter moved in at least some congregations to the role of priest. The two priestly roles, sacrifice and intercession, are both essential components of ministerial office in many Christian communions in the twenty-first century.

Ministry in the New Testament. Two claims will help to understand the place of ministry in the New Testament. First, there is no clear evidence that ministerial offices as we understand them, with ordained persons set apart for special leadership in the churches, had been established by the time the last books of the

New Testament were written. Second, while considerable attention is paid to the role of leadership in the New Testament, there is no one consistent pattern of leadership that obtains across the canon. Understandings of leadership vary from generation to generation and almost certainly from one location to another.

Jesus. All four canonical gospels were written to claim and sketch the significance of Jesus's life, death, and resurrection for the writers' own communities. It is notoriously hard to be certain what claims we can make about the practices of the Galilean in the time before his crucifixion. Still, the gospels are unanimous in claiming that Jesus chose a smaller group of disciples from the larger circle of his followers. All four gospels also indicate that there were 12 of these especially chosen disciples. It may be that as Matthew indicates the number 12 is related to the 12 tribes of Israel and that in choosing 12 Jesus indicated his mission to declare the kingdom throughout Israel and Judea. In any case, it is quite clear that Jesus follows the example of John the Baptist in choosing a circle of disciples (see Matt 11:2; Luke 11:1). Furthermore, we can guess that Jesus shapes his practice with the practice of the ancient prophets in mind—Elisha was Elijah's disciple, Baruch was Jeremiah's.

Paul. The earliest written records we have concerning early Christian ministry are the writings of Paul. There is a consensus among scholars that at least seven of the letters attributed to Paul in the New Testament were written by him: Romans, 1 and 2 Corinthians, Galatians, Philippians, 1 Thessalonians, and Philemon. Other epistles, like Ephesians, 1 and 2 Timothy, and Titus, certainly draw on Pauline thought but probably reflect somewhat later developments in their understanding of ministry.

The starting point for Paul's understanding of ministry is his claim about his own ministry, that (like Peter and others) he is an apostle. At the beginning of four of his undisputed letters Paul refers to himself as an apostle (Rom 1:1; 1 Cor 1:1; 2 Cor 1:1; and Gal 1:1). His apostleship is defined in part by the fact that he has seen the risen Lord. Though Paul did not know Jesus prior to his crucifixion, he insists that his experience of the risen Lord makes him an apos-

tle as much as those like Peter who followed the Galilean Jesus and then witnessed his resurrection (Gal 1:11–12; 1 Cor 9:1; 15:8–9). His apostleship is further defined by his relationship to the churches he has founded. When he describes his role in relation to those churches, it is clear that he sees apostleship as an almost parental responsibility (1 Thess 1:7–8, 11). Because the apostle is one who is "sent" (the Greek word *apostello*, "I send," provides the fundamental meaning of the title), Paul stresses his role as one who is sent as an ambassador for Christ and his primary responsibility as to serve as a messenger, to preach the gospel.

For Paul, church leaders are also designated with other terms. He, along with others, is a "minister" or "deacon" (see 2 Cor 3:6). John N. Collins has suggested that for Paul the term "deacon" refers primarily to the responsibility of the church leader to represent Christ as a kind of emissary (Collins, 1990, p. 198). It is also clear that Paul has a kind of entourage of Christian leaders who travel with him and can be his emissaries to the churches he has founded, like Sosthenes (1 Cor 1:1) and Timothy (Phil 1:1). In addition, Paul recognizes various kinds of leaders in the churches to which he writes, although he does not define their responsibilities. In Philippians 1:1, Paul refers to overseers or bishops and the deacons at Philippi but without giving any indication of their exact function. It seems clear from 1 Corinthians that Stephanas is a leader of the church that meets in his house (1 Cor 1:16; 16:15–18). In Romans 16:3–5, it is implied that Prisca and Aquila have some authority because of the church meeting in their house.

The list of leaders in Romans 16 includes Phoebe as a "deacon" or "minister" and Junia as famed "among the apostles." There are passages in the Pauline letters that seem to downgrade the role of women in the church assembly, but there seems no question that women had the same kind of titles and responsibilities as men in the early Pauline churches.

Far more instructive than the brief reference to titles are Paul's two lengthy descriptions of the church as the body of Christ. Here church order depends far less on offices and far more on interdependent gifts (1 Cor 12:12–26; Rom 12:3–8). Remembering that Paul believes that Christ will come in glory in the near future, it is not surprising that he is little concerned with providing a manual for church order. The Spirit provides the various gifts of ministry to various members of the body.

Matthew and Luke. Matthew and Luke both draw heavily on the outline and stories of Mark's Gospel but pay more attention than Mark to the question of ongoing church life and ministry. Matthew's Gospel makes a distinction between the disciples and the "little ones" in Jesus's community. The disciples serve as a kind of foreshadowing and example for the church leaders of Matthew's time, and the "little ones" serve as a foreshadowing of church members.

Matthew also uses two terms that seem to refer to leaders in his own churches. One is "scribe." In 13:52, Matthew writes of the scribe "trained for the kingdom of heaven is like the master of a household who brings out of his treasure what is new and what is old." Christian leaders are interpreters of the Torah, who read scripture in the light of Jesus's story and decide what is binding and what is not. The other term "prophets" is mentioned in Matthew 23:34 and 37. Perhaps some leaders of Matthew's community were simply itinerant preachers who went from community to community.

Matthew pictures church leaders as those who "hold the keys to the kingdom of heaven." In Matthew 18, the keys are given to the whole company of the disciples (of church leaders or members). Here the power to bind and to loose is clearly the power to forgive (or not forgive) sins. In Matthew 16, however, the keys are given to Simon Peter. Now the authority rests more on one man than on the community, and binding and loosing is more a matter of right and wrong interpretation of both Moses's law and Jesus's.

Luke's Gospel is the first part of the two-volume work Luke–Acts. The fact that the author moves beyond Jesus's story to the story of the first generation of the church indicates his concern with ongoing right teaching and right order in the long period of waiting for Christ's return.

The understanding of ministry in Luke follows a narrative of succession. First, the Spirit falls upon Jesus, who begins his ministry in Luke 4. At his Trans-figuration, Jesus foretells the passing on of the Spirit to the apostles, and that prophecy is fulfilled in the story of Pentecost in Acts 2. The primary examples of authority are Peter and Paul. As the age of the apostles draws to a close, Paul bestows the responsibilities of ministry to the elders from Ephesus (Acts 20). The responsibilities of ministry include preaching the gospel, guarding against false teaching, and living with integrity and compassion among the flock.

The Gospel of John. John's Gospel seems almost deliberately to contrast its vision of ministry with that of Matthew and perhaps Luke. In John 13, the major role of the disciples is to wash one another's feet—to live out humility and love. In John 21, Peter is not so much the prince of apostles as the kindest among shepherds. In John 15's image of Christ as the vine and Christians as the branches, each branch is directly tied to the vine without any mediation of any ecclesiastical teacher, intercessor, or judge. Insofar as we can reconstruct John's community, it is deliberately more egalitarian than the communities behind the other gospels.

The later Pauline letters. Either Paul underwent something of a shift in his understanding of ministry or later disciples writing in his name authorized a more ordered view of ministry. In Ephesians, the image of the church is still that of a great body, but the body is defined by the Christian offices and not only by Christian functions: "The gifts he gave were that some would be apostles, some prophets, some evangelists, some pastors and teachers" (Eph 4:11). In 1 and 2 Timothy and Titus, the church has been around awhile and will continue into the indefinite future. There are defined offices (elders, bishops, deacons) and explicit requirements for office—having to do not only with ministerial skills but also with uprightness of life. The leader of the church functions like the leader of a Christian household.

Significance for Today. The primary significance of the variety of biblical understandings of ministry is precisely their variety. The differences in the twenty-first century among congregations and Christians around the meaning of ministry are already foreshadowed in the Hebrew Bible and displayed in the New Testament. In particular, the split between Catholic and Protestant in the Western church reflects in part Luther's great attachment to Paul, especially Galatians and Romans, versus the Catholic church's attachment to Peter and his authority, as presented in the Gospel of Matthew. It is not that one view is biblical and the other not. Both have biblical grounds; both rely on considerable and imaginative interpretation.

In particular, the history of the church shows the ongoing dispute about the authority of Rome. Catholic Christians see in Matthew a foreshadowing of Peter's role as bishop of Rome and of the developing authority of the Holy See. Others tend to see the passage as pertinent to Peter as foremost among the disciples, who like him will carry out their mission as scribes of the kingdom of heaven.

One striking feature of ministry in the New Testament is that there is no necessary tie between any particular church office and the administration of the sacraments. The connection between ordination and presiding may be a reasonable development between the Bible and the early church, but it is a development all the same.

Any attempt simply to recover the ministry of the first century is bound to be frustrated by the limits of knowledge and the variety of options that the New Testament presents. This does not mean that the words of the New Testament books and the evidence of the communities for which they were written may not provide continuing challenge, corrective, and caution.

[See also Authority and Order; Call; Cult and Worship; Discipleship; Ecclesiology; Priests: Priests and Priesthood; and Prophets and Prophecy.]

BIBLIOGRAPHY

Agosto, Efrain. *Servant Leadership: Jesus & Paul.* St. Louis, Mo.: Chalice, 1995.

Bartlett, David. *Ministry in the New Testament.* Philadelphia: Fortress, 1993. Reprint, Eugene, Ore.: Wipf and Stock, 2001.

Collins, John N. *Diakonia: Re-interpreting the Ancient Sources.* New York and Oxford: Oxford University Press, 1990.

Forestell, J. T. *As Ministers of Christ: Christological Dimensions of Ministry in the New Testament.* Mahwah, N.J.: Paulist Press, 1991.

Malherbe, Abraham J. *Paul and the Thessalonians.* Philadelphia: Fortress, 1987.

Meeks, Wayne A. *The First Urban Christians.* New Haven, Conn.: Yale University Press, 1983.

Schillebeeckx, Edward. *The Church with a Human Face: A New and Expanded Theology of Ministry.* Translated by John Bowden. New York: Crossroad, 1985.

Wilson, Robert R. *Prophecy and Society in Ancient Israel.* Philadelphia: Fortress, 1980.

David L. Bartlett

MINOR PROPHETS

See Book of the Twelve (Minor Prophets).

MIRACLES

Definitions of "miracle" vary. Some modern thinkers define miracles as "supernatural" events, accepting David Hume's (1711–1776) definition of miracles as violations of nature. Because biblical authors viewed God as active in creation, however, and because some of the most dramatic biblical narratives depict God as working *through* elements of creation, defining miracles as contradictions of nature excludes from consideration many biblical miracle accounts. Accordingly, other thinkers view miracles as "special" divine action in the sense that they are divine acts sufficiently extraordinary to command special attention. Thus, they are roughly equivalent to the biblical designation "sign" (Heb. ʾōt, Gk sēmeion). That is the basic definition of miracles employed in this article.

Miracle Reports in the Old Testament. Though the Hebrew Bible reports events that fit many later definitions of miracle, such events are typically referred to as "signs" or "wonders." The term "sign" (ʾōt) refers to an attestation or omen signifying something else: a rainbow as God's sign of a covenant (Gen 9:17), circumcision as a human sign of a covenant (Gen 17:11), or the Sabbath (Exod 31:13, 17). Frequently, such signifiers involve God's conspicuous displays of power. A wonder (mōpet; occasionally, peleʾ) includes events such as the Jordan's parting (Josh 3:5), an angel's ascending in a flame (Judg 13:19–20), or an idolatrous altar's splitting after its denunciation by a prophet (1 Kgs 13:3, 5).

Signs in the Exodus. By far the most pervasive use of the language of "signs" and "wonders" (especially together) in the Hebrew Bible applies to God's distinctive displays of power in bringing about the Exodus (Exod 7:3; Num 14:22; Deut 11:3; 26:8; 34:11; Neh 9:10; Jer 32:20). These signs include Moses's leprous hand, his staff's transformation into a snake (Exod 4:3–4; 7:9), and especially the judgments against Pharaoh and his people (Exod 7:3; 10:1–2; 11:9; Deut 4:34; 6:22; 7:19; 11:3; 26:8; 34:11; Neh 9:10; Pss 78:12; 43–51; 105:27; 135:9).

Such signs reveal God's glory or honor (Num 14:22; Jer 32:20) and God's compassion toward his people (Deut 4:37; 6:22–23), though even judgment against Israel can function as a sign (Deut 28:46). Signs also display God's powerful "hand" (Ps 78:42–43; Jer 32:21), "might" (Ps 77:14), or "power" (Bar 2:11). Like creation (Jer 10:12; 27:5; 32:17; 51:15), the Exodus display God's power (Exod 9:16; 14:31; 15:6; 32:11; Deut 4:37; 9:29; 34:12; perhaps Ps 74:13). Divine power invites praise (Ps 78:4; 147:5) and prayers for deliverance (2 Chr 14:11; 20:6); prophets sometimes promise God's future acts of power (Isa 63:1; Zech 4:6).

Theologically, most signs during the Exodus challenge national polytheism. Although scholars debate whether particular Egyptian deities are always in view, the Old Testament narratives depict the plagues against Egypt as judgments against Egypt's deities (Exod 12:12; Num 33:4). Likewise, antiquity respected deities who conquered the sea (Exod 14:10–29), and serpents played a significant role in Egyptian religion and magic (Num 21:8–9).

Deuteronomy emphasizes the Exodus generation's eyewitness experience (4:34; 6:22; 7:19; 29:3), probably for the purpose of underlining the wisdom of trusting and obeying the Lord. Signs invite obedient faith (Num 14:11); failure to respond with such faith after witnessing multiple signs leads to judgment (Num 14:22; cf. Exod 11:9; Ps 78:41–43). God's awesome works invite praise (1 Chr 16:9, 12); these works include not only creation (Ps 136:4) but also dramatic signs attending the Exodus (Exod 15:10–11; Ps 77:11–20). In eras dominated by suffering, the reported signs of earlier generations could seem a distant memory (Judg 6:13; Ps 74:9),

though writers also suggested that God could renew signs as needed (Judg 6:17, 21).

Other aspects of signs. One way that God's power is displayed in various sources is his use of ordinary instruments (e.g., Exod 4:17; 2 Kgs 4:2, 41). In contrast to some later definitions of miracles, biblical writers unabashedly portray God's conspicuous acts as working through elements or forces that God had already created. Thus, many scholars suggest that the language of the plagues in Exodus evokes a reversal of the gift of creation (as in the flood narrative, Gen 6:5—8:22). Similarly, God parts the sea and sends quail by using wind (Exod 14:21; Num 11:31). Exodus suggests that one's intellectual framework shapes one's interpretation of the events: apparently, Pharaoh's beliefs about his gods, perhaps also about his own divinity, made him resistant to what Exodus invites its readers to view as divine action (Exod 7:11–13, 22).

Nevertheless, ancient Israel did not expect all divine activity to be conspicuous. For example, Exodus suggests that Moses's inconspicuous rescue through water (Exod 2:3–10) was divinely ordered; the Hebrew term for his "ark" (Exod 2:3, 5) may recall that of Noah (Gen 7–9, the term's only other occurrence in the HB). Likewise, his rescue among reeds (Exod 2:3, 5) may prefigure Israel's deliverance through the sea of "reeds" (15:4, rendering literally the same Hebrew term). God's "ordinary" acts in creation could appear as "signs" (Ps 65:9; cf. Gen 1:14). Extraordinary signs that drew special attention appeared only when needed; thus, the miraculous provision of manna ceased once Israel obtained a more conventional food supply (Josh 5:12). Moreover, even extraordinary signs might not come in the span of time that mortals might expect (Ps 88:10, 12). Only a generation after Pharaoh drowns Israel's babies in the Nile (Exod 1:22) does God avenge them by turning the Nile to blood (7:19–21), slaying Egypt's firstborn (12:12, 29), and drowning Pharaoh's army (15:27–28).

Although Deuteronomy views the Exodus signs as distinctive to Israel's experience (Deut 4:34), both it and other biblical writings acknowledge that signs or wonders could be performed in the name of other deities. A prediction in the name of other gods might prove accurate (Deut 13:1–2), even though the prophet merited death for leading Israel away from God's covenant (13:5). Pharaoh's magicians are able to simulate, on a smaller scale, the first three plagues but eventually concede the greater power of Israel's God (Exod 7:11, 22; 8:7, 18–19; 9:11).

In the Pentateuch (Exod 3:12; Deut 13:1–2) at times and especially in the prophets (Isa 7:11; 8:18; 20:3; 37:30; 38:7; Jer 44:29; Ezek 14:8; cf. 1 Sam 2:34; 10:7) "signs" generally designate prophetic actions or omens. Nevertheless, events corresponding to later definitions of miracles are described, such as Hezekiah's healing (2 Kgs 20:7) and especially the narratives in the Elijah–Elisha cycle: blinding, unlikely pregnancy, fire from heaven, and control of rain (1 Kgs 17:1; 18:37–39, 44–45; 2 Kgs 4:16–17; 6:18), as well as the kind of experiences common in later accounts about Jesus: the healing of a leper (2 Kgs 5:14), multiplication of food (1 Kgs 17:13–16; 2 Kgs 4:3–7, 42–44), raisings from the dead (1 Kgs 17:21–23; 2 Kgs 4:33–35), and restoration of sight (2 Kgs 6:20).

Stories such as those in the Elijah–Elisha cycle may have been transmitted in prophetic circles. In such circles the reports may have functioned as ideal models for prophetic power; although the later prophets speak more often of fulfilled predictions, narratives about Isaiah also depict dramatic signs, such as the reversal of sunlight on stairs (Isa 38:7–8) and the destruction of an army (Isa 37:36). Stories about later Jewish and Christian holy men are often modeled on Elijah. For the presumed audience of 1–2 Kings, however, the dramatic events reported about Elijah's circle particularly reinforce Israel's guilt in again straying so soon from the covenant.

Miracle Reports in the New Testament. Developing some models in the Hebrew Bible, New Testament accounts of miracles heavily shaped subsequent Christian views of the subject. The prominence of miracles in accounts of Jesus is conspicuous: roughly 30 percent of Mark's Gospel details miracle reports. The Greek term often translated "miracles," *dynameis*, refers to acts of power. Although the term does not convey this sense earlier in biblical sources, Jewish tradition sometimes links signs with God's power (Exod 9:16; Bar 2:11). In many cases these acts of power can also be viewed as "signs" (*sēmeia*) that draw attention to or explain some divine activity.

Ancient miracle reports. Although the earliest traditions about Jesus stem from Galilee, the Gospels circulated in a broader Mediterranean environment. In this environment traveling diviners and fortune-tellers were common (Juvenal *Sat.* 6.548–591). Many used secretive magic for love charms or cursing rivals. Healing shrines account for a majority of extant healing claims; suppliants often reported experiencing dreams and then cures at sanctuaries of Asclepius. Legends of wonder-workers who had lived many centuries earlier also circulated.

The closest non-Jewish parallel to the Gospels' accounts about a healing sage is Apollonius of Tyana (ca. 15–100 C.E.), most of whose activity is dated after Jesus's ministry. Yet our primary source for Apollonius, especially for his alleged parallels with Jesus, is Philostratus (ca. 170–245 C.E.), whose work appeared after the Gospels were in wide circulation. Earlier historians and biographers reported prodigies and apparently supernatural cures (Tacitus *Hist.* 4.81, Suetonius *Vesp.* 7) but did so infrequently because they were not concentrating on miracle-workers.

Some scholars (especially Vermes) have developed comparisons of Jesus with some Jewish charismatic sages, citing Honi the Circle-Drawer (first century B.C.E.) and Hanina ben Dosa (first century C.E.) as primary examples. With a few exceptions the reports about their miracles appear centuries after these figures lived (*m. Ta'an.* 3.8; *b. Ber.* 34b). Nevertheless, a primarily Jewish milieu for the earliest reports about Jesus's miracles makes sense. Probably relevant to contemporary healing figures would be exorcists, reported in this period especially in Jewish circles (Josephus *Ant.* 8.46–48; Matt 12:27//Luke 11:19; Acts 19:13; cf. 4Q242). Although extrabiblical support for miracle-working figures is limited, Luke calls Simon a public worker of "magic" in Acts 8:9–11.

The closest earlier analogies to Jesus's miracles appear in the biblical Elijah–Elisha cycle, which could have offered a model for Jesus or those who recounted stories about him. Elijah was associated with the end-time (Mal 4:5–6; Sir 48:10). Some other first-century Jewish prophetic figures reportedly promised, though failed to deliver, an eschatological sign (parting the Jordan or making walls collapse: Josephus *Ant.*

20.97, 167–170). Although they did not offer healing or deliverance from spirits, they probably sought to imitate Moses or Joshua, fitting the expectation of a new Moses (Deut 18:15–18).

Jesus's miracles. A strong majority of historical Jesus scholars recognize that his contemporaries regarded him as a miracle-worker, whatever explanations one might offer for those works. This feature of Jesus's ministry is attested in all the sources, including the earliest: Mark (e.g., 1:21–34) and Q (Matt 11:5//Luke 7:22; Matt 11:21//Luke 10:13; Matt 12:28//Luke 11:20). Josephus's few comments about Jesus seem to depict him as a miracle-working sage (the probable sense of the earliest version of *Ant.* 18.63). Early critics of the Gospel accounts, such as Celsus and some rabbis, acknowledged Jesus's performance of unusual feats but attributed them to sorcery (cf. Mark 3:22//Matt 12:24//Luke 11:15).

Unlike other reported miracles outside Christian sources, Jesus's signs were eschatological and intimately connected with the kingdom he proclaimed. In what is probably some of the earliest tradition (Matt 11:5//Luke 7:22), Jesus interprets his signs as fulfilling Isaiah 35:5–6 and 61:1 and their promise of the restoration of creation (Isa 35:1–2) and of Israel. Likewise, in Matthew 12:28//Luke 11:20, Jesus explains that his deliverance of people from demonic powers demonstrates that God's promised reign is present or impinging on the present. This interpretation may also develop the motif of cosmic warfare found in ancient Israelite narratives (e.g., Moses's contest with Pharaoh's magicians). Healings and deliverance thus offer a foretaste of God's reign, the divine ideal of the kingdom. As in the Hebrew Bible, signs also increase the accountability of those who witness them (see Matt 11:21//Luke 10:13).

Nevertheless, even if the kingdom is believed present in some sense, most New Testament writers portray its consummation in the future. For this reason, healings do not represent creation's full deliverance but merely a foretaste. Healings were not eternal; even those raised from death would eventually die again. The temporally limited benefits portended a better world; in the meantime, Jesus's crucifixion and resurrection implied that God was active in the face of suffering and injustice.

In the Gospels, Jesus's miracles are not simply exhibitions of power; most of his reported signs also suggest divine benefaction. In Luke's theology, for example, healings and deliverance work against the devil's malevolent purposes (Acts 10:38); the people of God are empowered to combat suffering. In the Gospels, Jesus's miracles display grace in several ways. First, the content of most reports involves healing and deliverance, clearly a benefit for those restored. Such acts thus do not solely solicit attention for Jesus; they reveal the *nature* of the kingdom. Benefactions for the needy cohere with the Gospels' depicted character of Jesus's ministry in other respects (e.g., Mark 10:13–14, 48–49). Second, Jesus sometimes touches the ritually impure to cure them, although his contemporaries would view him as thereby contracting temporary impurity (Mark 1:41; 5:41; cf. 5:25–34). This picture coheres with the Gospels' portrait of Jesus offering himself on behalf of others (Matt 8:16–17; Mark 10:45; 14:22–24).

Finally, the signs of Jesus's benefaction suggest political implications. Healings display concern for the broken or needy, who also figure in Jesus's teachings (e.g., Matt 5:3–12//Luke 6:20–23). Jesus tends to pursue the marginalized more than respectable members of society: sinners, the poor, children, and the sick, including the ritually impure. Jesus's focus on the infirm, rather than cultivating alliances with the politically powerful, coheres with other Jesus tradition about a new kingdom of radical dependence on the Father rather than on human power (Matt 6:25–33//Luke 12:22–31). This pattern also coheres with the sources' portrayal of Jesus's submission to execution by the powerful (Mark 8:31; 9:31; 14:41; cf. John 10:17–18), apparently depending on the Father to raise him (Mark 14:28; Matt 16:21; 17:23; 20:19). Jesus's performance of his signs may have effectively committed him to eventual martyrdom (cf. John 2:3–4, in view of "hour" elsewhere in John).

The language of "signs and wonders" evokes especially Moses's works in the Exodus narratives, as do the wilderness feedings (Mark 6:41–42; 8:6–8). This evocation becomes even clearer in the Fourth Gospel. Like Moses's first plague, Jesus's first sign transforms water (Exod 7:20; John 2:11). Signs also reveal God's glory in Exodus (16:7, 10; cf. Num 14:22) and in John (2:11; 11:40). People sometimes responded to Moses's signs with faith (Exod 4:30–31; 14:31); likewise, in the Fourth Gospel those who see signs may believe the Father and Jesus (John 14:1, 11). Whereas Moses offers manna or the Torah, Jesus is himself the true bread (6:31–35) and the Word (1:14–18).

Miracles and theological ambiguity. People in antiquity responded to miracle claims in varying ways. Those who disagreed with particular figures' claims could attribute their extraordinary works to sorcery. Luke attributes to sorcery the works of Simon (Acts 8:9–11), and already in Mark Jesus's critics apparently charge him with sorcery, which often invoked the help of spirits (Mark 3:22). The charge of sorcery applied most commonly to those whose works were practiced in secret rather than in public and to those who performed such works for selfish gain rather than public good; the Gospels have additional reason to stress the public and nonaffluent character of Jesus's ministry. Early Christians believed that false prophets could perform signs (Acts 8:9–11; cf. Exod 7:11). They apparently expected these particularly in the end times, which they probably believed was at hand (Mark 13:22; Matt 24:24; 2 Thess 2:9; Rev 13:13–15). For Matthew (7:22–23), God values obedience above miracle-working.

Even in the Gospels, miracles do not persuade all observers (e.g., John 10:25; 11:45–46; 12:37). Jesus performed few miracles where faith was lacking (in Mark 6:5–6, he could not do them; in Matthew 13:58, probably adjusted for christological reasons, he did not do them). In Mark, Jesus enjoins silence not only about his identity (1:25; 3:11–12; 8:29–30) but also about those of his miracles not already performed in public (1:44; 5:43; 7:36; 8:26). The silence may have been to avoid further increasing crowds (2:2; 3:7–10) but may also relate to his identity and the mystery of the kingdom (4:11–12; cf. Dan 2:30, 44, 47).

Against some scholars, it is unlikely that Mark polemicizes against miracles, given their dominant role in his narrative. Among other expressions of radical discipleship in Mark, Jesus expects disciples to exercise faith for miracles (11:22–24; probably 9:18–19, 28–29; perhaps 4:38–40). Nevertheless, Mark rejects tri-

umphalism based on miracles. For example, though Jesus sends the disciples to cast out demons (6:7, 13, 30), these verses frame a much longer account of the prophet John's execution (6:14–29), which prefigures that of Jesus (9:12–13). Miracles cure some people; they do not entirely transform this world and obliterate suffering. For Mark, the deepest revelation of God's purpose is the cross: God is acting even when human blindness and injustice temporarily prevail.

The limited purpose of signs becomes still more evident in the Fourth Gospel. John recounts signs so the hearer may believe (20:30–31). Jesus's signs invite faith (10:37–38; 11:15, 42; 13:19; 14:10–11, 29), and many become believers because of signs (1:50; 2:11, 22; 10:41–42; 11:45; 12:11; 16:30; 17:21; 20:8). Depending on the interpretation of 14:12–13, John may also anticipate the performance of signs among Jesus's followers. Nevertheless, the initial faith invited by signs proves inadequate if it does not proceed to full discipleship (2:23–24; 3:2–3; 4:48; 8:30–31; 9:18, 35–38). Moreover, demanding signs suggests inadequate faith (6:30; 7:4–5; 20:25), and Jesus refused to perform signs for skeptics (6:30–33; cf. Mark 8:11–12). The ideal is to believe based on the testimony of human witnesses and of the Spirit (John 20:25–31; cf. 15:26–27). Although John develops the inadequacy of "signs-faith," it already appears earlier in the Jesus tradition (Mark 8:11–12; 15:32; Matt 12:39//Luke 11:29; 1 Cor 1:22).

Miracles in the church. A distinctive emphasis on extraordinary signs persists in early Christianity. Miracles occupy roughly one-fifth of Acts, a book that depicts Jesus's first followers as continuing Jesus's mission of proclaiming and healing. The Spirit that empowered Jesus in Luke's first volume now empowers key disciples in the second, and signs become the most frequent means for drawing attention to the message about Jesus (e.g., Acts 3:10–12; 4:29–30; 8:6–7; 13:9–12; 14:3). Such signs are performed "in the name of Jesus" (3:6, 16; 16:18; cf. 19:13, 17; Luke 10:17), that is, authorized by the exalted Jesus. Jesus the healer in Luke's Gospel continues that work through his agents in Acts (9:34; 14:3); signs confirm the risen Jesus's exalted status as Lord at God's right hand (2:33).

Luke's account in Acts of the apostolic mission continues theological associations previously noted regarding Jesus, such as the association of miracles with compassion and power. Because Luke often associates "power" with miracles (Luke 4:36; 5:17; 6:19; 8:46; 9:1; Acts 3:12; 4:7; 6:8; 10:38), the promise of witnesses' power in Acts 1:8 may also imply signs.

Although Luke's focus is on key apostolic figures, especially Peter and Paul, miracles characterize not only apostles but also many other proclaimers (Luke 10:17; Acts 6:8; 8:7; 9:12–18). Because signs demonstrate that the eschatological era has arrived (see Acts 2:17), Luke presumably expects them to continue until Jesus's return.

This continuing emphasis on signs in early Christianity is not Luke's invention. It appears in "we" material, which many Lukan scholars attribute to an eyewitness (Acts 20:8–12; 28:8–10). Various early Christian sources report expectation of healings and other signs (Jas 5:14–16; cf. Rev 11:5–6, whose two witnesses, for some interpreters, represent the church).

Paul indicates that signs accompanied his evangelistic work in new areas (Rom 15:19) and appeals to his audience's witness of such signs (2 Cor 12:12). Possibly Paul's mention of the Spirit's power in evangelism (1 Cor 2:4; 1 Thess 1:5) also suggests miracles, though for Paul a deeper emphasis is God's power revealed in the cross (1 Cor 1:18–25) and in Paul's own weakness (2 Cor 4:7; 12:9; 13:4). Paul boasts in suffering rather than in visions or revelations (12:1–10).

Yet Paul also expects the Spirit to continue empowering the church in healings and miracles (1 Cor 12:9–10; Gal 3:5). In this context, these empowerments for ministry characterize some believers, while others receive different empowerments (1 Cor 12:5–7; though cf. 12:31 and 14:1, 39). Some scholars suggest that Paul's reference to (literally) "gifts of healings" in the plural (1 Cor 12:9) implies that some are gifted with faith for healing of particular kinds of infirmities.

Postbiblical Approaches to Miracles. Later rabbinic sources indicate that some contemporary Jewish followers of Jesus were known for healing, although some rabbis viewed this negatively (t. Ḥul. 2.22–23). Early church fathers often cited healings and exorcisms to support the truth of their faith; on a popular level, healings and exorcisms constituted the primary cause of Christian conversion in the fourth century. Christian

holy men competed with other figures of power in Egypt; one, a monk named Anthony (ca. 251–356 C.E.), was immortalized in an account by Athanasius (ca. 296–373 C.E.). Like some other leaders in the church, Augustine initially believed that miracles were no longer as active in their day as in the time of Jesus's first followers. Augustine's views changed, however; after just two years of keeping records, Augustine's diocese had collected 70 affidavits attesting miraculous cures, including raisings; and he knew of others not yet recorded (Civ. 22.8). The Eastern church, generally better educated than its Western counterpart, combined prayer for miracles with medicine and hospitals (a compatibility previously evidenced in the shrine of Asclepius at Cos).

During Augustine's time and throughout the Middle Ages, a primary point of contact for healing faith was relics. Though the authenticity of many or most of the relics may be questioned, apparently many people did experience cures. While subsequent hagiography surrounding particular figures sometimes makes historical details uncertain, miracles were widely attributed to missionaries evangelizing new regions.

Reacting against relics and other issues, the magisterial reformers rejected most contemporary miracle reports. Although they allowed for answered prayers and exceptional circumstances, their polemic against Catholic miracles led to a decline in miracle reporting among Protestants. Responding to Protestant polemic, Catholics began documenting miracles more carefully. Nevertheless, even some Protestants believed that some extraordinary experiences occurred; by the late nineteenth century they became increasingly open to the persistence of miracles. The shift occurred partly in response to the perceived epistemic inconsistency of accepting all biblical miracle claims while discounting all subsequent miracle testimony.

Much modern philosophic and theological discussion of miracles has engaged Hume's skepticism. Because much of Hume's argument rested on a perspective on natural law prevalent in his day, many modern discussions involve the relationship between putative miracles and nature. When applied to biblical texts, however, such discussions are etic; that is, they arise from external observers' categories. Biblical theology focuses instead on emic explanations, which arise from the biblical authors' worldviews. Biblical writers did not limit miracles to events without proximate natural causes (thus, Exod 14:21).

Beyond current philosophical discussion, various religious expectations regarding miracles continue to circulate. In the twenty-first century Protestants increasingly share with Catholic and Eastern Orthodox Christians belief in continuing miracles. Many emerging Christian movements in the majority world treat biblical miracle accounts as paradigmatic for ministry. Biblical examples provide a primary foundation for most such approaches.

[*See also* Creation; Deuteronomy; Devils and Demons; Exodus; God and Gods; Historical Narratives (Joshua—2 Kings); Holy Spirit; John and the Johannine Epistles; Kingdom of God (Heaven); Luke–Acts; Mark; Matthew; Pauline Letters; Prophets and Prophecy; Salvation History; *and* Sickness, Disease and Healing.]

BIBLIOGRAPHY

Burns, Robert M. *The Great Debate on Miracles: From Joseph Glanvill to David Hume*. Lewisburg, Pa.: Bucknell University Press, 1981.

Capps, Donald. *Jesus the Village Psychiatrist*. Louisville, Ky.: Westminster John Knox, 2008.

Cotter, Wendy. *Miracles in Greco-Roman Antiquity: A Sourcebook for the Study of New Testament Miracle Stories*. London: Routledge, 1999.

Cotter, Wendy J. *The Christ of the Miracle Stories: Portrait through Encounter*. Grand Rapids, Mich.: Baker Academic, 2010.

Duffin, Jacalyn. *Medical Miracles: Doctors, Saints, and Healing in the Modern World*. Oxford: Oxford University Press, 2009.

Earman, John. *Hume's Abject Failure: The Argument against Miracles*. Oxford: Oxford University Press, 2000.

Ellens, J. Harold, ed. *Religious and Spiritual Events*. Miracles: God, Science, and Psychology in the Paranormal 1. Westport, Conn., and London: Praeger, 2008.

Eve, Eric. *The Jewish Context of Jesus' Miracles*. Journal for the Study of the New Testament, Supplement Series 231. London: Sheffield Academic Press, 2002.

Houston, J. *Reported Miracles: A Critique of Hume*. Cambridge, U.K.: Cambridge University Press, 1994.

Kee, Howard Clark. *Miracle in the Early Christian World: A Study in Sociohistorical Method*. New Haven, Conn.: Yale University Press, 1983.

Keener, Craig S. *Miracles: The Credibility of the New Testament Accounts*. 2 vols. Grand Rapids, Mich.: Baker Academic, 2011.

MacMullen, Ramsay. *Christianizing the Roman Empire*. New Haven, Conn.: Yale University Press, 1984.

Mullin, Robert Bruce. *Miracles and the Modern Religious Imagination*. New Haven, Conn.: Yale University Press, 1996.

Pilch, John J. *Healing in the New Testament: Insights from Medical and Mediterranean Anthropology*. Minneapolis: Fortress, 2000.

Porterfield, Amanda. *Healing in the History of Christianity*. New York: Oxford University Press, 2005.

Theissen, Gerd. *The Miracle Stories of the Early Christian Tradition*. Edited by John Riches. Translated by Francis McDonagh. Philadelphia: Fortress, 1983.

Vermes, Geza. *Jesus and the World of Judaism*. Philadelphia: Fortress, 1984; London: SCM, 1983.

Craig S. Keener

MONSTERS

Biblical tradition is literally riddled with monsters—riddled in the sense that biblical monsters are legion, appearing throughout the canon, but also riddled in the sense that they often raise profound theological questions about the interplay of creation and chaos, familiarity and otherness, within the biblical God. Much like the monsters on ancient maps that indicated the world's *terra incognita* ("unknown territories"), biblical monsters draw our attention to the *terra incognita* of biblical theology.

Otherness Within. A monster is a personification of otherness within, the outside that has found its way inside, threatening our sense of meaning, order, and security. Monsters are, to borrow a biblical phrase, in the world but not of it, threatening figures of anomaly within the well-established and accepted order of things. As otherness personified, moreover, monsters are imbued with agency: they act, or threaten to act, upon us, imposing their otherness against our familiar understanding and experience of sameness and order.

One way to elucidate this paradoxical sense of the monster as a personification of otherness within sameness is Sigmund Freud's concept of the *unheimlich* ("unhomely" or "uncanny"). If the German word *heimlich* ("homely") refers to what belongs within the home, inspiring feelings of domestic safety and security, the *unheimlich* refers to that which threatens one's sense of "at-homeness," not from the outside but from within (Freud, 1955, pp. 222, 226; Beal, 2001, pp. 4–12). The *unheimlich* is what is in the house without belonging there, the outside that is inside—under the bed, in the basement, beneath the floorboards. The horror of the unhomely experience, then, involves the awareness that something that should be outside the house is inside it. It is an experience of otherness within sameness. Monsters, then, are inherently *unheimlich*.

For Freud, the *heimlich* represents one's conscious self and the *unheimlich* is what the one has repressed. Its reappearance, as return of the repressed, is experienced as an invasion of something alien and monstrous only because it has been so completely exorcised from consciousness.

For our interests, we may extend this notion of the monstrous as *unheimlich* to other dimensions of culture as well, from self to society to cosmos:

1. *Personally*, the monstrous is the *unheimlich* within the "house" of the body or self, threatening one's confidence in the meaning, integrity, and well-being of oneself as a subject.
2. *Sociologically*, the monstrous is the *unheimlich* within the "house" of society, threatening individual and collective confidence in the meaning, integrity, and well-being of society or culture.
3. *Cosmologically*, the monstrous is the *unheimlich* within the "house" of the world—in biblical–theological terms, the order of creation—which undermines confidence in the meaning, integrity, and well-being of the entire cosmos.

As *unheimlich* figure of otherness within, the monstrous is that which invades personal, social, and/or cosmic order and security, disturbing one's sense of at-homeness in oneself, one's society, and one's world. Monsters make us feel *not at home at home*. They are "there" in the house but cannot be comprehended by it or integrated into it. They are revelations of chaos and disorientation within order and orientation, re-vealing deep insecurities in our faith in ourselves, our society, and our world. In the context of Hebrew and Christian scriptures, these monstrous epiphanies are also and especially theological: monsters draw our attention to the *unheimlich* of biblical theology.

Hebrew Biblical Monsters. Hebrew biblical tradition is rife with what scholars often describe as "chaos monsters," monstrous personifications of chaos that potentially threaten the divinely ordained cosmic and/or sociopolitical order (see, e.g., Gunkel, 1895; Wakeman, 1973; Day, 1985; Levinson, 1987). Perhaps because most of these monsters find their way into biblical literature from other ancient Near Eastern mythological contexts (Gunkel, 1895; Wakeman, 1973; Emerton, 1982; Mobley, 2012, pp. 16–33), their identities can be slippery; they take on different forms and carry very different theological meanings in different texts. Thus, whereas the *tannin*, "sea monster" or "dragon" (cf. Ugaritic *Tunnan* in the Canaanite Baʿal–Anat cycle), is created by God in Genesis 1:21 and called upon to praise God in Psalm 148:7, it figures elsewhere as a threat to cosmic and/or social stability. In Jeremiah, for example, the city of Jerusalem, personified as a lamenting mother, describes King Nebuchadrezzar of Babylon as a voracious *tannin* that has eaten her alive:

> King Nebuchadrezzar of Babylon has devoured me,
>   he has crushed me;
> he has made me an empty vessel,
>   he has swallowed me like a monster [*tannin*];
> he has filled his belly with my delicacies,
>   he has spewed me out. (Jer 51:34)

Likewise in Ezekiel God describes the Pharaoh of Egypt as a monstrous *tannin* who must be slain for the sake of Israel:

> I am against you,
>   Pharaoh king of Egypt,
> the great dragon [*tannîn*] sprawling
>   in the midst of its channels,
> saying, "My Nile is my own;
>   I made it for myself."
> I will put hooks in your jaws…
> I will fling you into the wilderness,
>   you and all the fish of your channels;

you shall fall in the open field,

and not be gathered and buried. (Ezek 29:3–5)

Another monstrous name often associated with Egypt and closely related to the *tannin* is the boisterous sociopolitical enemy of God and Israel Rahab, whose name means "storm" or, figuratively, "arrogance" (e.g., Pss 87:4; 89:10; cf. Job 9:13).

Whereas the aforementioned biblical monsters are primarily sociopolitical, threatening the order and security of God's people Israel, other biblical monsters are primarily cosmological, threatening the order and security of creation. *Yam* (lit. "Sea" as a proper name; cf. Ugar *Yamm* in the Canaanite Baʿal–Anat cycle), for example, personifies the primordial deep, present before creation, and often appears on the edges of created order as a potential future threat. In the divine speech from the whirlwind in Job, God claims to have subdued Yam in order to establish the foundations of the world:

Who enclosed Yam behind doors

when he burst from the womb

when I made a cloud his diaper

and thick darkness his swaddling?

I imposed my limit on him

set a bar and doors, saying,

"This far you come and no farther

here your majestic waves stop." (Job 38:8–11, author's translation)

Although often seen as a biblical example of *Chaoskampf* ("chaos battle") against the forces of chaos, such a categorization risks overlooking the complexity of this remarkable text, which imagines God simultaneously controlling and nurturing the primordial chaos waters as a parent cares for a baby: enclosing, clothing, swaddling, setting limits, affirming power and majesty. Here Yam is both threat to the order of creation and part of the creative process (but cf. Job 3:8, in which Job imagines conjuring Yam as a means of undoing creation).

Most prominent among the biblical chaos monsters is Leviathan (cf. Ugar *Litan*; discussed at length in Emerton, 1982). Whereas Psalm 104 describes Leviathan as a playful part of the glorious order of creation

(v. 26), Psalm 74 identifies it with Yam as a many-headed figure of anticreation whom God violently destroyed in order to make the world. Crying out to God in a time of chaos and peril at the hands of the Babylonians, the psalmist prays for deliverance, recalling how God overcame the primordial sea and its monstrous denizens as the first act of creation:

You crushed Yam by your might,

broke the heads of the sea monsters upon the waters.

You smashed the heads of Leviathan,

gave him for food to the people of the desert.

You broke openings for springs and torrents.

You dried up ever-flowing rivers.

Your day, also your night.

You established light and sun.

You set up all the boundaries of the earth.

Summer and winter you made. (Ps 74:12–17, author's translation)

Thus, Psalm 74 envisions God destroying these chaos monsters in the beginning of creation. Isaiah 27, on the other hand, imagines that they are not dead yet or that they have come back to life and looks forward to a final judgment when God will slay them once and for all: "On that day the LORD will bring his fierce and mighty and powerful sword down upon Leviathan the fugitive serpent, upon Leviathan the twisting serpent, and he will slay the sea monster [*tannin*] in the sea" (Isa 27:1, author's translation).

The most theologically remarkable biblical appearance of Leviathan is in the final crescendo of the divine speech from the whirlwind in the book of Job (41:1–34; for a detailed analysis, see Beal, 2001, pp. 35–56; also Asma, 2009, pp. 63–73). Up to that point in the dialogue, Job's abysmal suffering has often led him to desire chaos against God's cosmos, even identifying with the chaos monsters Yam and Leviathan, whom he assumes to be God's anticosmic archenemies (e.g., 3:7; 7:12; 9:13–17; 26:12–13). Although he identifies with chaos monsters, even representing his voice of pain as a monstrous embodiment of chaos within God's world, he fully expects that God will smash him down just as God has smashed down other chaos monsters that threaten divine rule. Job identifies himself among the monsters and sees God as the ultimate monster killer. When God is finally roused to respond from the whirlwind (chs. 38–41), however, Job's expectations are horrifically demolished. His self-conception as a monstrous threat against the divinely ordained order of things is overwhelmed by a simultaneously wonderful and terrifying revelation of a God who does not slay or banish the chaos monster Leviathan but glories in it and identifies with it as an embodiment of cosmic horror. Job's identification with the monstrous over against God leads ultimately to God's identification with the monstrous over against Job. God outmonsters Job, pushing the theological horror one step beyond Job's wildest expectations.

The Dragon in Revelation. In the New Testament book of Revelation, or the Apocalypse of John, the seven-headed dragon "who is the Devil or Satan" (12:9; 20:2) is largely stitched together from Hebrew biblical images of chaos monsters. Although the author may have drawn some of the Devil's features from Greek and Roman mythologies (Collins, 1976, pp. 57–85), his primary resources were the biblical figures of Leviathan and the "sea monster" (*tannin*), both of which get translated into the Greek Septuagint as *drakon*, "dragon." The literary genealogy of John's dragon is complex, but three biblical visions of Leviathan and the sea monster appear to be especially influential (Beal, 2001, pp. 79–81):

In the Septuagint text of Ezekiel 29:3, the Hebrew "great sea monster" (*hattannîm haggādôl*) is translated into Greek as "the great dragon" (*ton drakonta ton megan*), whom God will ultimately "cast down" (*katabalo*, from the verb *ballo*, "cast"). Similarly, Revelation twice refers to this monster as "the great dragon" (*ho drakon ho megas* in 12:3, 9), and describes him being "cast out" (*eblethe*, also from *ballo*) of heaven by God (12:9).

In the Septuagint version of Psalm 74:12–14, both Leviathan and the *tannin* are translated into Greek as *drakon*, and this dragon, like the one in Revelation, has multiple heads (*tas kephalas ton drakonton*, "the dragon's heads," vs. 14; cf. Apoc 12:3, *tas kephalas outou*, "his heads").

Likewise, in the Septuagint text of Isaiah 27:1, both Leviathan and the *tannin* are translated as *drakon*. In that

text, moreover, the Hebrew epithet for Leviathan, *nāḥāš* ("serpent," as in "twisting serpent" and "fleeing serpent"), is translated into Greek as *ophis* ("serpent"), a term that Revelation uses as an epithet for the dragon (*ho ophis ho archaios*, "the archaic serpent"; Apoc 12:9; 20:2).

Revelation's dragon, then, is stitched together from old monster skins in order to make a new "ancient serpent" for a new cosmopolitical and theological crisis, that of Roman persecution of the early Jesus movement at the end of the first century. It is no accident that John's dragon is closest to the earlier biblical chaos monsters of Psalm 74, Isaiah 27, and Ezekiel 29 because they, too, represented threats not only to the cosmic order but also to the political order of Judah, understood theologically to be a microcosm of God's creation. In Psalm 74, God's victory over Leviathan was reason to hope for God's future victory over Babylon; in Isaiah 27, Leviathan is literally a personification of Babylon; and in Ezekiel 29, the sea monster personifies Egypt. In the latter two cases, the monster still lives, but the prophet anticipates that God will destroy it on a future judgment day. In the Apocalypse of John, these ancient monsters and the former enemies they symbolize emerge as personifications of a new battle-red monster of destruction and persecution, namely, late first-century Rome, its emperors, and its militia.

Yet the chaos monster's transfiguration in Revelation as "the Devil or Satan" is unprecedented. In Hebrew biblical tradition, neither Leviathan nor the sea monster (nor any other monster) is ever identified with the Devil or Satan, a figure who does not acquire the identity of ultimate anti-God until later, postbiblical Christian thought.

John's spectacular vision of the great red dragon in Revelation 12 helped launch a new diabolical career for the biblical chaos monster. Images of it as a figure of the Devil pervade the apocalyptic imagination of Christian visual culture throughout the Middle Ages and into our day. It also becomes a figure for European colonialist representations of the deities of other religions. Perhaps most significantly, it prefigures many monsters of horror culture, from the dragons who fight Saint George and Beowulf to Bram Stoker's Dracula (whose name comes from the Romanian *drakul*, which means both "dragon" and "devil") to William Blake's Great Red Dragon paintings, which in turn inspired the Hannibal Lecter of Thomas Harris's *The Silence of the Lambs* novels and the films made from them (Beal, 2001, chs. 6, 8, and 9).

Monsters and Biblical Theology. Monsters are inherently theological. In fact, their theological import is born in the word itself: "monster" derives from the Latin *monstrum*, which is related to the verbs *monstrare* ("show" or "reveal") and *monere* ("warn" or "portend") and sometimes refers to a divine portent. In this sense a *monstrum* is a message that breaks into this world from the realm of the divine. Even in the ancient and extremely cruel notion of "monstrous births" as revelations of divine judgment, the otherness of the monster is considered not only horrifically *unnatural* but also horrifically *supernatural*, bearing a message to those who behold it (Beal, 2001, pp. 6–7). So what might biblical monsters reveal, not only from God but also and especially about God? What biblical–theological reflections might biblical monsters invite?

One particularly suggestive focus for reflection is the ambivalent relationship between God and Leviathan. Different biblical texts represent Leviathan in mutually incompatible ways. On one extreme, Psalm 104 describes Leviathan as part of the order of creation, a sea beast that God "formed to play with" (cf. Ps 148). On the other extreme, Psalm 74 and Isaiah 27 envision Leviathan as radically outside the order of creation, a dreadful chaos monster that opposes the creator God and must be destroyed. This latter conception of Leviathan is shared by Job in his opening curse (3:7), in which he desires that Leviathan be stirred up against creation.

In the divine speech from the whirlwind, however, we encounter a disturbing combination of these two extremes: on the one hand, as in Psalm 74 and Isaiah 27, Leviathan is an embodiment of primordial chaos within creation; on the other hand, as in Psalm 104, God identifies with it. Here, then, is a vision of the world and of God in which chaos and order intertwine; and Leviathan emerges as a means of expressing that intertwining, thereby engendering a sense of uncertainty and cosmic horror that is deeply theological, going to the very core of the character of God.

Monsters like Leviathan help reveal tensions within biblical–theological understandings of the world and its creator God: on the one hand, confident in the stable, reasonable order of the cosmos, confident in our ability to articulate that order and live according to it, and confident in God as founder and guarantor of that order; on the other hand, haunted by monstrous forms of profound disjunction and disorder, shadowy revelations on the edge between creation and uncreation, cosmos and chaos. Haunted, too, by the lurking anxiety that God, like the world God created, is fraught with the same tensions. Biblical tradition is endlessly caught between cosmogonic visions of a stable moral universe, in which God has crushed the monsters and sits enthroned over chaos, and chaogonic visions of a world on the edge of collapse, in which the monsters are alive and well and it is not always clear whether God is with them or against them.

[*See also* Creation; Ezekiel; Isaiah; Jeremiah; Kingdom of God (Heaven); Lamb of God; Light and Darkness; Revelation; *and* Satan.]

BIBLIOGRAPHY
Asma, Stephen T. *On Monsters: An Unnatural History of Our Worst Fears*. New York and Oxford: Oxford University Press, 2009.
Beal, Timothy. "The System and the Speaking Subject in the Hebrew Bible: Reading for Divine Abjection." *Biblical Interpretation* 2 (1994): 171–189.
Beal, Timothy. *Religion and Its Monsters*. New York: Routledge, 2001.
Cohen, Jeffrey Jerome. "Monster Culture (Seven Theses)." In *Monster Theory: Reading Culture*, edited by Jeffrey Jerome Cohen. Minneapolis: University of Minnesota Press, 1996.
Collins, Adela Yarbro. *The Combat Myth in the Book of Revelation*. Missoula, Mont.: Scholars Press, 1976.
Day, John. *God's Conflict with the Dragon and the Sea: Echoes of a Canaanite Myth in the Old Testament*. Cambridge, U.K.: Cambridge University Press, 1985.
Emerton, J. A. "Leviathan and *ltn*: The Vocalization of the Ugaritic Word for the Dragon." *Vetus Testamentum* 32 (1982): 327–331.
Freud, Sigmund. "The Uncanny." In *The Standard Edition of the Complete Psychological Works of Sigmund Freud*, Vol. 17, translated by James Strachey. London: Hogarth, 1955.
Gunkel, Hermann. *Creation and Chaos in the Primeval Era and the Eschaton: A Religio-historical Study of Genesis 1*

and Revelation 12. Translated by K. William Whitney Jr. Grand Rapids, Mich.: Eerdmans, 2006. English translation of *Shöpfung und Chaos in Urzeit und Endzeit: Eine religionsgeschichtliche Untersuchung über Gen I und Ap Joh 12* (Göttingen, Germany: Vandenhoeck & Ruprecht, 1895).

Levinson, Jon D. *Creation and the Persistence of Evil: The Jewish Drama of Divine Omnipotence.* San Francisco: Harper & Row, 1987.

Mobley, Gregory. *The Return of the Chaos Monsters: And Other Backstories of the Bible.* Grand Rapids, Mich.: Eerdmans, 2012.

Wakeman, Mary K. *God's Battle with the Monster: A Study in Biblical Imagery.* Leiden, The Netherlands: Brill, 1973.

Timothy Beal

MOSES

Moses (Heb., Aram *Mōšeh*; Gk *Mōseis* or *Mousēs*; Lat *Moyses*) was the leader, Levitical priest, prophet, and teacher of Israel, whom the Deity commissioned to lead the nation out of Egyptian bondage through the Sinai wilderness and into the Promised Land. Moses presided over Israel during the revelation of the Deity's Torah ("Instruction") at Mount Sinai, which provides the foundations for Judaism's identities as nation and religion from antiquity through the present.

The Hebrew Bible. The primary narratives for Moses's life appear in Exodus, Leviticus, Numbers, and Deuteronomy.

Exodus, Leviticus, and Numbers. The narratives in Exodus, Leviticus, and Numbers present the fullest account of Moses's life and activities. Moses is born into the priestly tribe of Levi. His father is Amram; his mother, Jocheved. He has two older siblings: a sister, Miriam, and a brother, Aaron (Exod 2:1; 6:16–20; 7:7; Num 26:59; cf. 1 Chr 23:12–14). Moses's Levitical identity is crucial to the narrative. As a Levite he serves as intermediary between Israel and the Deity and as the teacher of the Deity's Torah to Israel (Lev 10:10–11). The biography of Moses appears in the form of a creation account for the nation Israel that combines multiple elements: the Deity's creation of the natural world, the Deity's intervention in the human world to defeat Pharaoh and to release Israel from Egyptian bondage, the Deity's revelation of Torah to Israel to provide the bases for a just and holy living society, and Moses's struggles with both Israel and the Deity to hold nation and God together. This narrative includes accounts of Moses's early life and commission by the Deity, his confrontation with Pharaoh and the crossing of the Red Sea, the wilderness narratives, and the Sinai–Revelation narratives.

Early life and commission by the Deity. The narratives concerning Moses's early life and commission by the Deity in Exodus 1–4 emphasize the impending conflict between the Deity and Pharaoh, Moses's formation as a leader for Israel, and the Deity's role as creator. As the people of Israel thrive in Egypt, a new pharaoh arises who fears the power of the growing nation. Many identify this pharaoh as Seti I (r. 1318–1304 B.C.E.), the father of Rameses II (r. 1304–1237 B.C.E.). Though the latter was one of the most powerful Egyptian pharaohs prior to Israel's emergence in the land of Canaan and seems to be the Deity's nemesis in the Exodus account, Pharaoh's historical identity plays no discernible role in the narrative. Considered as a god in Egyptian society, Pharaoh serves as a narrative foil for the Deity, who emerges as the true sovereign of creation and human events.

Pharaoh orders the Israelites enslaved and their newborn male children murdered. When Moses is born, his mother hides him in a basket and floats him down the Nile River under his sister's watchful eye. Ironically, Moses's basket is discovered by Pharaoh's daughter, who adopts him as her own and raises him as a prince in the Egyptian royal household. Such a motif is a common means to signal a future leader in the ancient world: Sargon I of Akkad (r. ca. 2334–2279 B.C.E.) was saved in a basket floated down the river; Cyrus the Great of Persia (r. ca. 558–529 B.C.E.) was abandoned as an infant to die in the mountains (Herodotus 1.107–130). Moses's Israelite identity and passion for justice emerge when he witnesses an Egyptian taskmaster beating a Hebrew slave. When Moses kills the taskmaster to protect the slave, he is compelled to flee to the Sinai, where he will encounter the Deity. Upon arriving in the wilderness, Moses rescues the seven daughters of Reuel (= Jethro, Exod 3:1), the priest of Midian, at a well.

Such a motif portends Moses's marriage to Zippo-rah, the daughter of Jethro (Exod 2:15b–22).

Moses's encounter with the Deity takes place on Mount Sinai in the burning bush episode (Exod 3), in which the Deity commissions Moses to go to Pharaoh to demand the release of the Israelite slaves. The burning bush apparently presupposes the *Rubus sanctus* or the *Cassia senna*, both native to the Sinai, which produce red flowers that appear to be aflame when viewed from a distance. A key motif in this story is the Deity's refusal to disclose the divine name. By stating that the name is "I am who I am" (Heb. ʾehyeh ʾăšer ʾehyeh), the narrative employs an *idem per idem* rhetorical device that defines a thing in relation to itself as a means to protect the sanctity of the divine name and to interpret its meaning. Egyptian religious practice presupposed that one who correctly pronounced a divine name in an incantation received the power of the deity in question. Israelite practice precludes such power; to protect its sanctity, the divine name is never pronounced in Judaism (with the exception of the high priest in the Jerusalem Temple on Yom Kippur). The use of the verbal phrase ʾehyeh, "I am," portrays the divine name, the Deity, as a form of the verb, *yihyeh*, "he is," to emphasize the reality and power of the Deity as sovereign of the universe. When Moses protests that he is a man of uncircumcised lips who cannot speak for the divine properly, the Deity orders that Moses's brother, Aaron, the future high priest (Num 17–18), go with him to act as his spokesperson. Such an arrangement anticipates the role of the high priest as representative and spokesperson for the Deity before the people. Moses appears to assume the role of oracle diviner who receives the divine word directly from the Deity.

Confrontation with Pharaoh. The narratives concerning the confrontation with Pharaoh in Exodus 5–15 likewise emphasize the conflict between the Deity and Pharaoh for mastery of creation as well as Israel's formation. The Deity instructs Aaron to cast his rod down before Pharaoh so that it will turn into a serpent; Pharaoh responds by commanding his magicians to perform the same feat. Snake charming is a well-known Egyptian practice, but the power behind such a feat is ascribed to the Deity. Aaron's serpent swallows those

of the Egyptians, but Pharaoh nevertheless hardens his heart and refuses to let the Israelites go.

The confrontation then turns to the plagues, the first nine of which serve as etiologies to explain the origins of natural features of creation in Egypt and Israel. Moses's rod, a symbol of his Levitical role, becomes the instrument by which the plagues are initiated, thereby pointing to the future recognition of the Levites as priests and agents of the Deity's power. The first nine plagues appear in three triads. The first triad includes the waters of the Nile turned to blood, frogs, and gnats, all of which are linked to the natural cycles of the Nile, which floods in the spring and covers the land with reddish-colored mud and frogs, which in turn allows gnats to breed. The second triad includes flies, cattle disease, and boils, all natural occurrences that result from the flooding and dead frogs and other creatures that appear when the waters recede. The third triad is hail and thunder, locusts, and darkness, all of which are natural occurrences. Darkness is a reference to the desert hot winds, *ḥamsin* (Arabic) or *sharav* (Hebrew), which occur at times of seasonal transition and block the sun with blowing dust and dirt.

The tenth plague, the death of the firstborn, is a key element in the narrative that celebrates the redemption and consecration of the firstborn in Israelite law (Exod 13:1–2; 34:19–20). As the example of Samuel, firstborn to his mother Hannah indicates, firstborn sons originally were consecrated to serve as priests in Israel (1 Sam 1–3). Numbers 3:5–13, 40–51; and 8:5–19 stipulate that the Levites will later replace the firstborn of Israel in this role. Thus, the tenth plague against Egypt constitutes an etiology for an early form of priestly service in Israel that later gives way to the consecration of the tribe of Levi as Israel's priesthood.

The culminating event of the confrontation is the crossing of the Red Sea. The designation of the Red Sea is drawn from the Greek Septuagint, *Thalassēs Eruthras* (Exod 15:22), whereas the Hebrew reads *yam suph*, "Sea of Reeds," in reference to the swamps around Lake Manzeleh (known as *Pa tjoufi*, "Land of Reeds," in Egyptian records). The account of the emergence of dry land in the midst of the sea functions as a creation narrative that sees to the deliverance of

Israel and the destruction of Pharaoh's armies before the Deity.

Revelation at Sinai. Exodus 19—Numbers 10 constitute the Sinai pericope in which the Deity employs Moses to reveal the Torah to Israel. The portrayal of Mount Sinai in the wilderness as the location for divine instruction constitutes a paradigm for the later Jerusalem Temple. The theophanic portrayal of divine presence as cloud and lightning is based on the imagery of incense smoke and the flaming lamps of the Temple. Moses instructs the people to purify themselves and to avoid treading on the mountain in anticipation of conduct expected at the Temple.

The revelation of divine Torah provides the basis for the covenant between the Deity and Israel. Interpreters have noted the role that ancient Near Eastern treaty texts, particularly the suzerain-vassal treaties of the Assyrian Empire, have played in defining the relationship between the Deity and Israel. Although the Assyrians would have used royal officials, such as the *rabshakeh* ("chief cupbearer" in 2 Kgs 18–19; Isa 36–37), to negotiate treaties on behalf of the Assyrian king, Moses appears here as a Levitical priest who represents both Yahweh before the people and the people before the Deity. The Deity is configured as a powerful suzerain monarch who enters into a treaty relationship with a weaker vassal. The Deity therefore self-identifies in Exodus 20:2–3, "I am the LORD, your God, who brought you out of the land of Egypt," in keeping with treaty forms in which the Assyrian king identifies himself and presents a brief history of relations between his kingdom and that of his proposed vassal. The stipulations of the relationship appear in the legal commands: "you shall have no other gods beside me" (Exod 20:3), "you shall not murder, you shall not commit adultery, you shall not steal, you shall not bear false witness against your neighbor" (Exod 20:13–16), much as Assyrian laws stipulate the obligations of the vassal to the suzerain.

Other laws appear as case laws, like those from the Mesopotamian law codes: for example, "when a man schemes against another and kills him, you shall take him from my altar to be put to death" (Exod 21:14). Blessings for observance of the stipulations and curses for failing to observe them motivate observance: thus, "if you follow my statutes and observe my commands and do them, I will grant your rains in their season so that the earth will yield its produce and the trees of the countryside their fruit" (Lev 26:3–4). Likewise, blessings and curses appear at the conclusion of Assyrian treaties.

The Sinai narrative presents a number of law codes and narratives that provide both the civil and sacred laws governing Israelite and Judean social life. Indeed, Exodus 18 presents Moses, acting on the advice of his father-in-law Jethro, as the founder of the Israelite court system. These laws function as the legal basis for constructing a just and holy living society. Although the laws do not govern every imaginable legal situation that might arise in a living society, the legal instructions found in the Torah serve as the basis for establishing legal precedents to be applied to different situations that might arise in the Israelite court system. The goring-ox laws, found both in Hammurabi's law code and in Exodus 21:28–36, provide the basis for determining liability in cases in which an ox might injure or kill another person. If it is a first-time event, the ox is killed and its carcass is shared by the owner and the injured party. If the ox is known to have injured in the past, the owner is held liable. These principles may then be applied to other situations involving injury, death, and personal liability. Likewise, the ritual counting of sabbatical and jubilee years in Leviticus 25 provides the basis for defining terms of debt service, assignment of land, and the redemption of property in the economy of ancient Israel and Judah.

The wilderness narratives. The wilderness narratives in Exodus 16–18 and Numbers 11–36 (see also Exod 32–34) focus especially on the conflicts between the Deity and Israel, Israel and Moses, and Moses and the Deity. The people complain that they lack food; the Deity provides them with manna and quail, thereby explaining the origins of manna and the migratory patterns of birds in the Sinai wilderness (Exod 16). The people demand an idolatrous golden calf for worship when Moses spends 40 days on Mount Sinai receiving the tablets of the covenant from the Deity, prompting the Deity to attempt to destroy the tablets (Exod 32–34). The people challenge Moses's leadership repeatedly (e.g., Num 11). The Deity vows to destroy

Israel when they express fear of the Canaanites after hearing the reports of the spies (Num 13–14). Moses intercedes and challenges the Deity when the Deity proposes to destroy Israel and make Moses into a new nation. Instead, the Deity destroys the wilderness generation but allows the next generation entry into the Promised Land of Israel (Exod 32:9–14; Num 14:11–38). In the end, even Moses is denied entry into the Promised Land when he commits sin at the rock of Meribah, most likely because he and Aaron did not purify themselves following the burial of their sister Miriam (Num 20).

Several major theological issues underlie these narratives. First is the need for a priesthood to mediate the relationship between the Deity and Israel. the Deity appears as the Holy God of Israel whom human beings cannot approach without first sanctifying themselves. Consequently, the wilderness narratives focus on the institution of the tribe of Levi as the priesthood of Israel who will represent Israel before the Deity and the Deity before Israel. The Levites demonstrate their zealousness for the Deity in the narrative of the golden calf by purging Israel of those who had sinned (Exod 32–34). Likewise, Numbers 17–18 recounts the choice of Aaron and the Levites to serve as priests in the place of firstborn sons. Indeed, Aaron's grandson, Phineas, received the eternal covenant of priesthood, which allowed his descendants to serve in the Jerusalem Temple for his actions in purging the people of sin (Num 25).

The second is the question of theodicy: Is the Deity a righteous, present, and powerful god? The narratives certainly establish the Deity's power, but the question of the Deity's righteousness is under scrutiny. In the incidents of the golden calf (Exod 32–34) and the spy narrative (Num 13–14), Moses must stand up to the Deity and remind the Deity that the Deity has obligations to fulfill toward Israel as well. The result is the well-known liturgical portrayal of the Deity's mercy and judgment in Exodus 34:6–7 (cf. Num 14:18): "The LORD, the LORD, a compassionate and gracious God, slow to anger, abounding in fidelity and truth, extending fidelity to the thousandth generation, forgiving iniquity, rebellion, and sin, but certainly not acquitting due punishment, visiting the iniquity of

the ancestors upon the children and the children of the children upon the third and fourth generation."

The question of Israel's sins is another important issue: to what extent does Israel merit punishment? The use of the golden calf episode is especially instructive insofar as the golden calves are a major motif in the condemnation of the northern kingdom of Israel in the books of Kings. Israel's first king, Jeroboam ben Nebat, erected golden calves at the sanctuaries at Beth El and Dan for Israel's worship (1 Kgs 12:25–33; 2 Kgs 17). Exodus 32–34 deliberately employs the paradigm of the golden calf to justify Yahweh's punishment of Israel, specifically northern Israel, and thereby to deflect charges that the Deity was unable to protect Israel in the face of the more powerful Assyrian Empire and its god, Assur. Such a motif defends the Deity on the part of faithful Israelites or Judeans who chose not to abandon their God but to take responsibility themselves for the disasters that befell them.

Deuteronomy. The book of Deuteronomy presents Moses's last speeches to Israel while encamped on the plains of Moab on the day before they take possession of the land of Israel. Although Moses's speeches are portrayed as a repetition of the revelation of the Deity's Torah at Mount Sinai (= Mount Horeb), the laws presented by Moses in Deuteronomy represent a complete revision of earlier laws from Exodus and Numbers. Even Moses himself appears differently. Whereas in Exodus—Numbers Moses is a Levite, in Deuteronomy he is a prophet—indeed, the prophet par excellence (Deut 18:9–22). These differences point to different origins for Deuteronomy. Whereas the Moses narratives in Exodus, Leviticus, and Numbers derive from E and J strata of ninth- to eighth-century northern Israel and eighth- to seventh-century Judah and the P stratum of fifth- to fourth-century Judah, Deuteronomy derives from the sixth-century program of religious reform and national restoration sponsored by King Josiah of Judah (r. ca. 640–609 B.C.E.).

According to the account of his reign in 2 Kings 22–23, Josiah's reform was based on the discovery of a Torah scroll during Temple renovations. Insofar as Josiah's reforms correspond to laws now found in Deuteronomy, interpreters have reasoned that the scroll must have been a version of Deuteronomy. The references to

Shechem in Deuteronomy 27 and the absence of references to Jerusalem, among other features, prompted earlier scholars to conclude that Deuteronomy must have originated in northern Israel; but the emphasis on the centralization of worship in Deuteronomy at the place where the Deity causes the divine name to dwell has convinced later scholars that Deuteronomy is a Judean work written to support Josiah's program.

Moses appears in Deuteronomy as both teacher and innovator of the traditions of Israel. Deuteronomy's revision of earlier laws is especially intended to support the Jerusalem Temple as the one place for worship of the Deity and teaching concerning the Deity's will. Whereas the Ten Commandments in Exodus 20 portray the Deity as the creator, the version in Deuteronomy 5 portrays the Deity as Israel's redeemer from Egypt, which threatened Judah in Josiah's time. Whereas Exodus 20:19–23 allows multiple altars in the land, in keeping with northern Israelite practice, Deuteronomy 12:1—13:1 allows only one, in keeping with Josiah's program of centralization based on the Jerusalem Temple.

Deuteronomy's legal revision gives greater rights to women and the poor, which indicates Josiah's interests in supporting the people of the land, who placed him on the throne following the assassination of his father Amon (2 Kgs 21:23–24). For example, the slave laws in Exodus 21 and Deuteronomy 15 differ markedly. Exodus 21:1–11 stipulates that when a man becomes a slave for reasons of debt, he will serve his master for six years. At the end of that time, he will go free; but his master is not obligated to provide him with any support, and the master will retain any wives assigned to him and children born to the wives. This is a powerful incentive to remain a slave. Women do not go free at all because they will be married into the master's house. Deuteronomy 15:1–18 gives greater rights to both men and women in debt slavery. The man will go free after six years of service, but the master must provide for him so that he has a greater chance to begin a new life. Women likewise go free after six years of service. Deuteronomy 34 recounts Moses's death and burial in a place known only to the Deity as leadership passes to Joshua ben Nun, who will guide Israel into the Promised Land.

The New Testament. Moses appears more frequently in the New Testament than any other figure from the Hebrew Bible. In most cases, he functions as a representative of Judaism, which has been fulfilled or superseded by the revelation of Jesus in Christianity.

Synoptic Gospels and Acts. Mark, Matthew, and Luke–Acts generally refer to Moses in relation to the Torah, or *nomos* ("law"), as it is designated in the New Testament. Moses appears with Elijah in the transfiguration scene in which both talk with Jesus (Matt 17:3–4 = Mark 9:4–5 = Luke 9:30, 33). At the end of the scene, a voice speaks from the midst of a cloud, "This is my son, my chosen, listen to him." Matthew (23:2) refers to "Moses's seat" and presents Jesus as seated like Moses while teaching from a mountainside, a deliberate attempt to portray Jesus as Moses's successor. Stephen's speech before the high priest in Acts 7 summarizes much of Moses's life in an attempt to portray Israel's rejection of Moses as an analogy and prelude to the rejection of Jesus.

John. John likewise presents Moses in parallel with Jesus in order to portray Jesus's superiority. The "law" given through Moses is fulfilled by the "grace and truth [which] came through Jesus Christ" (1:17). Whereas Moses lifts up a serpent in the wilderness, John 3:14 presents Jesus as the one who must be lifted up. John claims that God spoke to Moses (9:29) and that Moses gave the "law" (7:19), but the Fourth Gospel also claims that Moses wrote about Jesus (1:45; 5:46) in an attempt to assert that those who believe in Moses must also believe in Jesus. John 9:28 nevertheless contrasts those who continue to follow Moses with those who follow Jesus.

Pauline epistles. Paul refers to Moses only in Romans and 1–2 Corinthians. In Romans 5:14 he states that "death exercised dominion from Adam to Moses"; he refers to Moses as the one to whom God spoke the "law" (Rom 9:15) and as the one who wrote the law (Rom 10:5; 19:1; 1 Cor 9:9). Paul argues in 1 Corinthians 10:2 that all who passed through the sea in the Exodus were baptized into Moses in the cloud and the sea. In 2 Corinthians 3:7–18 he contrasts the dispensation of condemnation with the dispensation of righteousness. The dispensation of condemnation came with such splendor that Moses had to veil his face, whereas the dispensation of righteousness or the spirit comes with greater splendor and yet does not require a veil. When Moses is read, the veil lies over the minds of Jews, whereas Christians with unveiled face behold the glory of the Lord.

Other New Testament works. Revelation 15:3 refers to the song of Moses, sung by those who have conquered the beast (cf. Exod 15). Jude 9 portrays a dispute between the angel Michael and the devil concerning the body of Moses. Clement of Alexandria (ca. 150–ca. 215) and Origen (ca. 185–254) maintain that this refers to the burial of Moses as recounted in the *Assumption* (or *Testament*) *of Moses*, although the relevant section is not extant. Second Timothy 3:8 compares the men of Jannes and Jambres, who opposed Moses (cf. Exod 7:11, where the magicians of Pharaoh are unnamed), with heretics who oppose the truth.

Rabbinic Literature. Rabbinic literature views Moses as the greatest Jewish teacher or rabbi of all times, the man with whom God speaks face to face, the greatest prophet, and the recipient of divine Torah. At the same time, rabbinic literature is careful to assert that Moses is a mortal human being with his own human shortcomings and not a divine or semidivine figure. God—not Moses—is the source of the Torah revealed to the Jewish people at Mount Sinai.

Rav and Samuel state that 50 gates of understanding were created in the world and all but one were given to Moses: "You have made him [Moses] but a little lower than the angels" (*b. Ned.* 38a, interpreting Ps 8:6). All the prophets saw God as those who look through a dim glass, but Moses saw God as one looks through a clear glass (*b. Yebam.* 49b). According to one sage, Moses did not really die but still serves God as he did on Mount Sinai (*b. Soṭah* 13b). Moses and Aaron were righteous throughout their lives (*b. Meg.* 11a). Their humility was greater than that of Abraham: whereas Abraham spoke of himself as dust and ashes (Gen 18:27), Moses and Aaron declared that they were nothing at all (Exod 16:8). The whole world exists only on account of the merits of Moses and Aaron (*b. Ḥul.* 89a). God appeared to Moses in a burning bush to illustrate that the Jews were as indestructible as the bush (*Exod. Rab.* 2:5).

Moses is the rabbi par excellence in rabbinic literature because he was given both the written and the oral Torah at Mount Sinai as well as all interpretations of the Torah that would ever be developed. The rabbinic view of the development of new teachings concerning the Torah is expressed in the account of God's transport of Moses to the yeshivah (rabbinic academy) of Rabbi Akiva. Moses sat at the back of the room with the beginners and was perturbed that he could not understand what Akiva said, but he was relieved when Akiva declared that he had received his teachings from Moses at Mount Sinai (*b. Menaḥ.* 29b). Moses's preeminence is expressed by the statement that he lived for 120 years; but the great rabbinic teachers R. Hillel, R. Yohanan ben Zakkai, and R. Akiva also lived for 120 years, divided into three periods of 40 years (*Sipre Deut.* 327).

Moses died with the kiss of God (*Deut. Rab.* 11:10; *b. B. Bat.* 17a). He was buried by God in a grave that cannot be seen: to one standing in the valley it looks as though it is on a mountain peak and to one on a mountain peak it looks as though it is in the valley.

[*See also* Canaan and Canaanites; Covenant; Creation; Cult and Worship; Decalogue; Deuteronomy; Election; Exodus; Freedom and Slavery; Holiness; Idols and Idolatry; Israel and Israelites; Land; Leviticus and Numbers; Miracles; Priests and Priesthood; Prophets and Prophecy; Revelation; Theophany; *and* Torah.]

BIBLIOGRAPHY

Finkelstein, Jacob J. *The Ox That Gored.* Transactions of the American Philosophical Society 71, part 2. Philadelphia: American Philosophical Society, 1981.

Ginzberg, Louis. *The Legends of the Jews.* 6 vols. Philadelphia: Jewish Publication Society, 1968.

Herodotus. *I: Books I–II.* Translated by A. D. Godley. Loeb Classical Library. Cambridge, Mass., and London: Harvard University Press, 1996.

Knierim, Rolf P., and George W. Coats. *Numbers.* Grand Rapids, Mich., and Cambridge, U.K.: Eerdmans, 2005.

Lee, Won W. *Punishment and Forgiveness in Israel's Migratory Campaign.* Grand Rapids, Mich., and Cambridge, U.K.: Eerdmans, 2003.

Levenson, Jon D. *Sinai and Zion: An Entry into the Jewish Bible.* Minneapolis: Winston, 1985.

Levine, Baruch A. *Numbers.* 2 vols. Anchor Bible. New York: Doubleday, 1993–2000.

Levinson, Bernard M. *Deuteronomy and the Hermeneutics of Legal Innovation.* Oxford and New York: Oxford University Press, 1997.

McCarthy, Dennis J. *Treaty and Covenant: A Study in Form in the Ancient Oriental Documents and in the Old Testament.* Rome: Pontifical Biblical Institute, 1978.

Milgrom, Jacob. *Leviticus.* 3 vols. Anchor Bible. New York: Doubleday, 1993–2001.

Nicholson, Ernest W. *The Pentateuch in the Twentieth Century: The Legacy of Julius Wellhausen.* Oxford: Oxford University Press, 1998.

Pritchard, James B. *Ancient Near Eastern Texts Relating to the Old Testament.* Princeton, N.J.: Princeton University Press, 1969.

Propp, William H. C. *Exodus.* 2 vols. Anchor Bible. New York: Doubleday, 1999–2006.

Sarna, Nahum M. *Exploring Exodus: The Heritage of Biblical Israel.* New York: Schocken, 1986.

Sweeney, Marvin A. *King Josiah of Judah: The Lost Messiah of Israel.* New York and Oxford: Oxford University Press, 2001.

Sweeney, Marvin A. *Reading the Hebrew Bible after the Shoah: Engaging Holocaust Theology.* Minneapolis: Fortress, 2008.

Tigay, Jeffrey H. *Deuteronomy.* Philadelphia and Jerusalem: Jewish Publication Society, 1996.

Van Seters, John. *The Life of Moses: The Yahwist as Historian in Exodus–Numbers.* Louisville, Ky.: Westminster John Knox, 1994.

Marvin A. Sweeney

MYSTERY AND MYSTERY RELIGIONS

A "mystery" (*mystērion*) was a secret rite, something on which silence must be kept, or in general something hidden. It could be used of the "secrets of life," a secret medicine, or magical formulae. Plato used "mystery" metaphorically for philosophical teachings (*Theaet.* 156a; *Gorg.* 497c; cf. Matt 13:11 and parallels). Jewish apocalyptic literature employed the word for divine secrets, especially those related to eschatology. The Greek translation of Daniel 2:28–29 used it to render the Aramaic *raz*, "secret," with reference to God's future plans that only God can make known. This usage prepared for the New Testament usage, especially in Pauline letters for the previously unknown purposes of God now made known in Christ, with particular reference to the incorporation of Gentiles in the people of God. "Now to God who is able to strengthen you…according to the revelation of the mystery that was kept secret for long ages but is now disclosed" (Rom 16:25–26). "The mystery that has been hidden throughout the ages and generations but has now been revealed to his saints. To them God chose to make known how great among the Gentiles are the riches of the glory of this mystery, which is Christ in [among] you, the hope of glory" (Col 1:26–27; cf. Eph 3:3, 4, 9).

Greek Mysteries. By far the most common use of *mystērion*, usually in the plural (*mystēria*), was for the rites of initiation into certain religions; and this usage was the basis for applying the word to secular secrets. In the technical sense, a "mystery" was a secret ceremony by which individuals were brought into a relationship with a deity and assured of certain benefits. The ceremonies were effective in and of themselves. The *mystēs*, the "one initiated," was not to reveal what was involved in the initiation. Although a fair amount is known of the public ceremonies associated with the mystery religions, their secrets were well enough kept that we must speculate on details. The original Greek mysteries were rooted in the land and related to the cycle of nature. They were designed to assure fertility, safety, and well-being.

Most famous in classical Greece were the mysteries of Demeter celebrated at Eleusis, near Athens. There were three grades of initiation. The "lesser mysteries" were designed to purify initiates. There are references to fasting, sacrifices, being sprinkled or bathing in the Illisos River outside Athens, singing of hymns, and bearing a sacred vessel. The "greater mysteries" attracted more attention and covered 10 days. There was a preliminary washing in the sea, and a sow was sacrificed to Demeter and her daughter Persephone. Then a great public procession of the worshippers, the initiates, and their families led by priestesses made the 14-mile journey from Athens to Eleusis. The initiation included "things enacted," perhaps a pageant enacting the myth of Persephone, Hades, and Demeter; "things said," perhaps explaining the ceremonies; and "things shown," the most important part of the ceremony, performed by the *hierophant* ("the one who makes things appear"), accompanied by the kindling of a great fire. The highest grade of initiation, *epopteia*, involved an additional vision of sacred objects.

The Eleusinian Mysteries were a "local" mystery because one had to go to Athens and Eleusis to receive the initiation, but those eligible to receive initiation were gradually increased to include all citizens of the Roman Empire. Other notable ancient local Greek mysteries were at Andania in the Peloponnesus, at Panamara in southwest Asia Minor, and those of the "mother of the gods" and the Cabiri at the island of Samothrace.

Most influential of those mysteries not tied to a locality and which thus could be celebrated anyplace were the mysteries of Dionysus. The worship of Dionysus (god of wine, Lat *Bacchus*) had wider aspects—ecstatic dances, eating the raw flesh and drinking the blood of an animal, more conventional banquets, dramatic contests, processions. Initially, most participants in Dionysus worship were women, but later men were included.

Although the term "mysteries" was applied to other aspects of the cult of Dionysus, mystery initiations proper were added in the Hellenistic age. These could include children as well as adults. There seems not to have been as tight a control of secrecy as in the mysteries of Demeter, for scenes in art may depict elements of the initiation. This is especially true if the frescoes in the *Villa Item* ("House of the Mysteries") outside Pompeii represent Dionysiac ceremonies. Central to the initiation, which included flagellation (representing punishments in the afterlife?) followed by an ecstatic dance, was the uncovering of objects in a basket (*liknon*), apparently featuring especially a phallus. The original emphasis was likely on fertility, but the symbolism seems to have been extended to life-giving power. The Dionysiac mysteries came to be interpreted as promising a blessed afterlife; hence, Dionysiac scenes were commonly included on sarcophagi and funerary monuments.

Eastern Mystery Religions. As the worship of deities from the Near East spread into the Greek world, their Hellenization included the addition of secret initiations. The most successful of these eastern cults came from Egypt, especially under the influence of the Ptolemies, but the popularity of the Egyptian deities continued after the Ptolemaic dynasty was absorbed into the Roman Empire. Osiris and his sister/wife Isis were old and important Egyptian deities, but in the Hellenistic age a new god, Sarapis (Lat *Serapis*), a combination of Osiris and Apis the bull god, was paired with Isis. Their worship spread widely in the Mediterranean world, as witnessed by surviving sanctuaries and artworks. Public daily ceremonies at the temples and two annual festivals attracted attention.

There were three classes of adherents of the Egyptian deities: the ordinary faithful, who might attend the daily ceremonies and join a procession; the initiates, who could enter the temple, wore linen, and took part in the ceremonies; and the various levels of priests. Initiation was not for everyone but seems to have been required to become a priest.

The most circumstantial account of an initiation into a mystery religion to survive was written by Apuleius, *Metamorphoses* 11, in the mid-second century. Lucius (standing for the author) received three initiations—first into the cult of Isis at Corinth. There was a purificatory washing and fasting from meat and wine for 10 days. Clothed in a new linen robe, Lucius was brought into the interior of the temple in the dead of night. He was next led on a symbolic journey through the heavenly realms, and then in bright lights he saw the gods and worshipped them. Apuleius's allusions tell enough that initiates would know what he described but the uninitiated would be left with only the impression made on him. With a torch in his right hand and palm leaves on his head, Lucius was placed on a wooden platform in the presence of an image of Isis, and he was presented to the gaze of the crowd. Three days of banqueting celebrated his "birthday" as an initiate. When Lucius went to Rome, the goddess instructed him to receive an additional initiation into the mysteries of Osiris. Later, the goddess gave another vision instructing a third initiation, this time into the lower order of priests, the *pastophori*.

Initiation brought a person under the special protection of Isis and gave freedom from the control of fate and magic. There was no explicit promise of immortality, but there was one of a bliss after death.

Other eastern cults for which mysteries are attested include that of the Syrian goddess Atargatis of

Hierapolis, a goddess of nature, fertility, motherhood, and ruler of animals. The nature of her mysteries is unknown. What attracted the attention of Greek and Latin authors in the early empire were the itinerant priests (*galli*), who in a frenzy stripped off their clothes and castrated themselves, thereafter wearing women's clothes and belonging in a special way to the goddess.

More information is available about the cult of Cybele and Attis from Phrygia. The daily activities of a week-long festival in March are known from a fourth-century source, but how these relate to mysteries is not known. Much attention has been given to the taurobolium in the cult of Attis, mainly attested in the second century and later. The person receiving the rite stood in a deep pit that was covered with a wooden lattice platform. A bull was brought to the platform and killed with a spear; the initiate below raised his face and drank from the blood that flowed down. Most of the early inscriptions relate the rite to a sacrifice for the welfare of the individual or others. The later inscriptions indicate an act of personal consecration, perhaps in preparation for the afterlife. Some of the inscriptions describe the person as "reborn" for a period of about 20 years (with the presumable need to repeat the rite), but one from the late fourth century says "reborn for eternity."

A significant expansion of the worship of the Persian deity Mithra (*Mithras* in Greek and Latin) occurred in the second to fourth centuries. Literary references from the Roman period are rare, so what is known derives largely from the numerous Mithraic sanctuaries and their art that survive. The central scene in the sanctuaries, in either sculpture or painting, was Mithras slaying a bull, an event with cosmological significance, a creative act either releasing life and energy or demonstrating power over the stars and fate.

Through the twentieth century the prevailing interpretation of Mithraism traced its origin to Persian religion that entered the Roman world in the first century B.C.E. Since the latter part of the twentieth century an alternative explanation that connects Mithraism with astral religion and astronomical speculation has prevailed.

Only men were admitted to membership, and from the size of the sanctuaries for initiations and cult meals each community must have been relatively small. Mithraism appealed especially to soldiers and administrative officials on the frontiers of the empire from Britain to Syria, but there was a significant presence among merchants and city dwellers at Rome and its port Ostia.

A pebble floor mosaic from a mithraeum at Ostia depicts the seven grades of initiation and three symbols associated with each (the grade itself, the function of each grade, and the planetary god associated with it): raven (Mercury), bride (Venus), soldier (Mars), lion (Jupiter), Persian (Moon), Heliodromus (Sol), and Father (*pater*, Saturn). The initiate took an oath of secrecy before admission and, according to paintings, was led through the ceremonies naked. Some sources indicate physical ordeals endured in the initiation. All adherents received an initiation, at least to the first grade.

Mystery Religions and Christianity. To claim certain Christian practices and doctrines as derived from the mystery religions was at one time fashionable, but studies have shown the limitations of many of these claims. There are methodological problems in the comparison because of the chronological lateness and scarcity (the initiates for the most part kept their secrets) of the evidence. Those ideas seen as parallel turn out to have significant differences. The "dying and rising" gods of paganism are based on the cycle of nature and have little in common with the presentation of Jesus's one-time physical resurrection. The terminology of "regeneration" is rare in the mysteries and occurs as a metaphor for a new life and not specifically as a moral renewal. The salvation offered by the mysteries was a deliverance from fate and the terrors of the afterlife, not a deliverance from sins. The application of water in the mysteries was a preliminary purification, not the initiation itself as with Christian baptism. Sharing meals with religious connotations was a common activity in paganism, Judaism, and Christianity; but the weekly memorial of the death and resurrection of Jesus and the specific note of thanksgiving (eucharist) were distinctive of Christian practice. Pagan critics of Christianity contrasted Christianity's welcoming of the unworthy with the requirement in the mysteries of meeting accepted social standards. Whereas one could acquire as many mystery initiations as could be afforded, in Christianity "initiation" was for the whole community and brought one into an exclusive fellowship.

By the second and third centuries Christians began to appropriate mystery terminology to interpret Christian ceremonies and ideas to pagans, and in the fourth century Christian ceremonies (especially baptism and the eucharist) began to be presented in terms of these concepts so that *mystērion* became the term in Greek roughly equivalent to the Latin *sacramentum*.

[*See also* Conversion; Cult and Worship; *and* Idols and Idolatry.]

BIBLIOGRAPHY

Bornkam, G. "*mystērion*." In *Theogical Dictionary of the New Testament*, edited by Gerhard Kittel and Gerhard Friedrich, Vol. 4, pp. 802–828. Grand Rapids, Mich., Eerdmans, 1967.

Burkert, Walter. "Mysteries and Asceticism." In *Greek Religion*, translated by John Raffan, pp. 276–304. Cambridge, Mass.: Harvard University Press, 1985.

Ferguson, Everett. "Greek Mysteries and Eastern Religions." In *Backgrounds of Early Christianity*, 3d ed., pp. 251–300. Grand Rapids, Mich.: Eerdmans, 2003.

Finkenrath, G. "Secret, Mystery." In *The New International Dictionary of New Testament Theology*, edited by Colin Brown, Vol. 3, pp. 501–511. Grand Rapids, Mich.: Zondervan, 1978.

Klauck, Hans-Josef. "The Fascination of the Mysterious: The Mystery Cults." In *The Religious Context of Early Christianity: A Guide to Graeco-Roman Religions*, pp. 81–152. Studies of the New Testament and Its World. Edinburgh: T&T Clark, 2000.

Metzger, Bruce. "Considerations of Methodology in the Study of the Mystery Religions and Early Christianity." *Harvard Theological Review* 48 (1955): 1–20. Reprint, Brice Metzger, *Historical and Literary Studies* (New Testament Tools and Studies; Grand Rapids, Mich.: Eerdmans, 1968), pp. 1–24.

Meyer, Marvin. *The Ancient Mysteries: A Sourcebook: Sacred Texts of the Mystery Religions of the Ancient Mediterranean World*. San Francisco: Harper & Row, 1987.

Nock, A. D. "Hellenistic Mysteries and Christian Sacraments." *Mnemosyne* 5 (1952): 177–213. Reprint, *Essays on Religion and the Ancient World*, edited by Zeph Stewart (Oxford: Clarendon, 1972), pp. 791–820.

Everett Ferguson

N

NAHUM

See Book of the Twelve (Minor Prophets).

NATURE AND NATURAL RESOURCES

"Nature" and "natural resources" do not figure prominently as topics in biblical interpretation. Contributing to this is, first, that neither the Old Testament nor ancient Israel or other cultures in the surrounding ancient Near East or the Hellenistic-Roman world conceived of nature as a mechanical sphere unto itself open to scientific investigation in the same way that post-Enlightenment and post-Newtonian societies approach nature. Furthermore, biblical interpretation has tended to focus on God's acts within history in an attempt to differentiate biblical religion from religions of the surrounding cultures, which were closely related to nature.

In the ancient Near Eastern world, *nature* was first and foremost bound up in the concept of *creation*, linking the sphere of the *natural* closely with the sphere of the *supernatural*. Second, in the perspective of the ancients, nature connoted a notion not of something "pure" or "untouched by humans" but rather of something "dangerous" (although nature could be an object of philosophic reflection in Greco-Roman thought). This arose from the antagonistic and gen-erally uncontrolled view of the nonhuman world: it was not a tool to be used by humanity but a threat to be feared, avoided, and battled. Iconographic portrayals of Neo-Assyrian kings defeating lions as well as King David's claim to have defeated bear and lion while shepherding his father's flock bear witness to this motif (1 Sam 17:34–37). Third, as part of creation, nature and natural resources, generally speaking, were viewed as intrinsically good, even if not necessarily controllable in the world from which the Old Testament arose.

Consequently, the modern notion of "natural resources," as materials and components derived from the environment and available for human use, takes on a different light in the biblical views. Both those natural resources such as sunlight and rain, whose disbursement are uncontrolled by humans (ubiquitous resources), and those resources that only occur in small sporadic areas such as precious metals (localized resources) take on distinctive theological coloring in the biblical writings. Like modern notions, however, these resources are viewed positively and as desirable. This very desirability leads to their inherent danger, on the one hand, and their use as comparisons of value, on the other.

The physical geography and geology of the southern Levant influenced the approach to nature and natural resources in the Bible. First, Israel was mainly an inland-focused polity (unlike the Phoenicians and the Greeks) made up of different climatic and geographic zones. A coastal plain (usually controlled by the Philistines) gives way eastward to rolling hills, then rugged mountains, and the hot and arid decline to the Jordan River valley. Moving north to south, the region becomes progressively more arid, to the point where agriculture was no longer profitable in the Negev and the land could only be used as pasturage for flocks and herds. A particularly important feature was the lack of a central river system such as that of the Nile, Tigris, or Euphrates, found in the surrounding regions of Egypt and Mesopotamia. This factor meant dependence on well-timed rains for adequate grain production, rendering rain and the related agricultural yield as the most important natural resources. Finally, the region meant that precious metals were generally imported (except for the copper found in the Sinai and in the Negev, 30 kilometers from the Red Sea).

Old Testament. Within the Old Testament, conceptions of nature can be thought of along several lines. These include nature as a creation that is valued by God but can present dangers to humans, nature as comprising God-given resources to be used by humans, and nature as a subject existing beyond human society.

Nature, as God's creation, is good. The Bible begins with the creation and repeated affirmation of nature's "goodness" (Gen 1). This fundamental affirmation of the material world, unfolded throughout the Old and New Testaments, forms the basis for the appropriation of the goodness of nature—its resources—as blessings for the created beings, especially (but not solely) humanity. Job 9 does call this perspective into question however: because of Job's experience of injustice and his logical linking of God's role as judge with his role as Creator, he questions whether the creation is good. Nonetheless, the diversity of nature is generally viewed positively. In fact, nature, as nonhuman creation, is also granted a closeness to God: "Even the sparrow finds a home, and the swallow a nest for herself, where she may lay her young, at your altars, O LORD of hosts, my King and my God" (Ps 84:3). Such a perspective relativizes

the notion of nature and natural resources simply in terms of human use or value.

Following logically from the perspective in Genesis 1, numerous texts depict all natural resources of the world as belonging to God, as king and owner of the world (Ps 50:10: "For every wild animal of the forest is mine, the cattle on a thousand hills"). This perspective extends to the land itself (Lev 19; 25) and to precious metals and gems (e.g., Job 28:1–4).

God's presence in and reflected through nature and natural resources. Signs in nature were reflections of divine intent. For example, the rainbow of Genesis 9:13–16 marks God's self-reminder not to destroy the world by flood. A solar eclipse is documented for 763 B.C.E. in Assyria, and such events were viewed as divine portents.

Because all natural resources are ultimately God's possessions, they are distributed to creatures—both human and animal—in accordance with the divine will. Psalm 104, considered to be a reorientation of the Egyptian "Great Hymn to Aten [the divine sun]" from the Amarna reign of Akhenaten (r. 1379–1362 B.C.E.), displays Yahweh's broad concern for the creatures of the earth (v. 11) and for its resources (v. 14). Perhaps more surprising, provision of food for carnivorous animals is also included: "The young lions roar for prey, seeking their food from God" (v. 21; cf. Job 38:39–41; Ps 147:9). Unlike the Egyptian hymn's conflation of the sun and the deity, however, God is not to be identified with any specific created entity (Exod 20:4–6; Isa 44:6–20; 46:1–7). This provision for animals takes on a cosmic perspective, and several texts emphasize divine provision in locations distant from human presence: in Job 38:25–27, the rain also falls on desert, and in 39:1–18, God sustains animals beyond humans' reach and knowledge.

And, more than simply gifts, "nature"—understood as a region in opposition to "culture"—takes on a particular theological role as the location of special divine provision. In the Old Testament this is especially apparent in Yahweh's provision for the emerging people of Israel during the 40-year wandering in the desert. The desert, as a location remote from human domination, was understood as inhospitable to human flourishing. Therefore, Yahweh's ability to provide through the manna highlights the ultimately divine responsibility for all elements necessary for human flourishing (Exod 16; Ps 78:18–31).

Natural resources as blessings. Considerations of God as provider of the necessary resources for sustaining life often appear in connection with worship, thus designating Yahweh's provision as blessings coinciding with faith. In this context Psalm 144:12–14 focuses on the particular use of nature and its resources—both inanimate and animate—for human use as a response to choosing Yahweh as God (also for Eliphaz in Job 22:21). That this specific power resides with Yahweh is the subject of debate between Elijah and the priests of Baʿal in 1 Kings 18. Similar control of fertility is accorded to God's ability to make the earth yield crops (Ps 66:7; cf. 65:10–14). The distinctive link between natural provision and riches, on the one hand, and justice, on the other, converges in much of ancient Near Eastern thinking and in Psalm 72:15–16 in the concept of a just king being blessed with rich harvests and tribute of precious metals (cf. 1 Kgs 10).

Important in this regard is the ancient Near Eastern connection to the provision of natural resources as divine blessing. Deuteronomy 28:1–14 (cf. Lev 26:1–13) links political or religious obedience to natural fertility. Conversely, disobedience brings curses in the form of natural disasters (Deut 28; Lev 26; Amos 4:9; 7:1; Joel), a motif also present in the Aramaic Sefire Treaty Inscriptions (Stele I–II) from the mid-eighth century B.C.E. and in Neo-Assyrian treaties of the eighth and seventh centuries B.C.E. This line of thinking opened the logical possibility for interpreting all experiences of material goodness or poverty as a sign of divine approval or disapproval, which engendered philosophical problems when the "righteous" suffered or the "wicked" prospered (Eccl 3:16–17; Job).

Natural resources and the land of Israel/Palestine. The various genres of Deuteronomy 1–11, 26, 28, and 32 display a rich palate of the divine intent to shower the chosen people with gifts in the form of natural resources in the Promised Land. Perhaps most extravagant is the list in Deuteronomy 8:7–10. From the perspective of the ancient audience, this list includes the essentials of nature for a satisfied life: water, grain, and long-term ownership of land, which allows for the cultivation of grapevines as well as fruit and olive trees that require years of investment before their produce can be enjoyed. There is also metal necessary for tools, and perhaps even weapons. Recalling the Pentateuchal narrative, Deuteronomy 11 contrasts this vision with two others: the Nile-dominated life in Egypt, where people water crops (including those needing significant amounts of water, like vegetables) through irrigation, and the inhospitable desert, where only special divine provision kept the Israelites alive (cf. Num 11:5–10).

This vision hinges upon the people's adherence to the divine ordinances (8:6, 11–20), especially remembering that Yahweh, rather than the people themselves or another deity, is the origin of blessing. Deuteronomy 26:1–11 and 28:1–14 depict the results of obedience, which in large part consist of rich agricultural yields in areas where only God could act. Haggai 1:4–11 displays this logic, stating that the reason for the poverty among the residents of early Persian-period Judea (late sixth century B.C.E.) was their delay in building the Second Temple.

Resources such as precious metals typically appear in the Old Testament in connection with the king or the Temple (1 Kgs 6–7; Ezra 8:24–30). While these contexts are expected, they show Israel's participation in the general human tendency to use valuable material items to represent divine presence and sacred space.

One recurring image related to nature in the Old Testament, and in the archaeology and texts of the ancient Near East, is the paradisiacal garden. It is reflected in the legendary Hanging Gardens of Babylon, in the recent archaeological discovery of a lush garden at Ramat Rahel (approximately 5 kilometers from Jerusalem) in the Persian period of the sixth to fourth centuries, in Neo-Assyrian iconography, in the biblical creation in Genesis 2–3, and in images of eschatological restoration such as Ezekiel 47:1–12. The biblical and extrabiblical uses of this image combine numerous important features. Given the relative dryness of the region, water, especially flowing rather than stagnant water, was perennially in short supply. This made a lush garden the apex of wealth. Second, such gardens displayed mastery over the natural world, especially through the maintenance of diverse plants and animals, the latter often destined for royal hunts. For example, Persian rulers sought to grow plants in their gardens from species found throughout their empire for food (Xenophon, *Cyr.* 8.6.12–23; Diodorus Siculus, *Bibliotheca historica* 14.80.2; cf. Gen 2:8–9). Third, such installations were often bedecked with precious metals and gems (Gen 2:10–11; Ezek 28:13), which links them to temples, where gold and other precious materials adorned the earthly location of the divine (Exod 25–31).

Certain elements of nature took on special meanings for divine–human contact. In Old Testament texts this role generally fell to offerings, which were processed agricultural products—meat, grain products, wine, and oil—thus dependent on beneficial weather and other factors in the hands of God.

Nature as subject. Nature appears as a subject with at least three separate connotations—as threat, as worshiper, and as judge.

As the importance of the lions and other animals implies, nature often appears as a threat to humanity, and God uses nature as a means of punishment for humans. Lions and other wild animals exemplify the threats one might meet in the desert wilderness. Fiery serpents attack the Israelites in the wilderness (Num 21:5–9; cf. Job 30:1, where the wilderness is a place for bandits and jackals). Attacks by wild animals are found in the lists of curses (Lev 26:22), and Psalm 22:13–14, 17 picks up on this danger, comparing enemies to lions and bulls (cf. Amos 3:12). The sea is often personified as Leviathan, the sea monster. Playing off prebiblical portrayals in the Baʿal cycle (*KTU* 1.1–1.6) of the sea as a monster, Yahweh (like the Ugaritic deity Baʿal) conquers his enemy the sea (Pss 89:9–10; 74:12–14). Elsewhere Yahweh displays care for the natural world by providing food and boundaries for the sea monster (Job 38:8–11; 41; Ps 104:26). These depictions intend to lead the audience to worship of Yahweh (Pss 29; 97) and provide a provisional answer to the place of chaos in the world. According to Job 38:8–11, even chaos-inducing creatures like Leviathan have a divinely limited role to play in the world, even if their particular relation to God's providence remains hidden. The Jonah narrative illustrates several of these themes: the storm leads the non-Israelite sailors to worship the Israelite deity (1:16), God appoints a Leviathan-like fish to save Jonah by swallowing him (1:17), both human and animal residents of Nineveh perform acts of repentance (3:5–9), and God demonstrates concern for human and nonhuman life (4:6–11; cf. Gen 6–9).

Nature appears not only as a threat to humanity but also as a worshiper of God in its own right. Numerous texts describe the heavens (Job 38:7; Pss 19:1; 50:6; 96:11), day and night (Ps 19:2), earth and fields (Ps 96:12), hills (Pss 98:8; 148:9), animals (Ps 148:10; Isa 43:20; 66:23), desert (Isa 35:1–2), and seas (Isa 42:10) as praising, singing, shouting, and rejoicing before God.

A related role is granted nature in Job 31:38–40: Job calls the earth as judge between him and God, stating that if he has eaten the earth's produce without payment, "let thorns grow instead of wheat." The earth plays a similar role in Genesis 4:10–12, where it no longer will produce a yield for Cain after receiving the blood of his brother as a result of Cain's violence.

Finally, an important current with regard to natural resources that begins in the Old Testament but features more prominently in the New Testament is the relativization of the importance of natural resources. Two streams of thought converge on this opinion. The first, exemplified in Ecclesiastes 4:7–12 and 5:11–20, is that possession of material wealth, generally manifested by natural resources, does not actually bring about human joy and flourishing. Many texts from Proverbs place more value on acquiring wisdom, honor, and appropriate speech than gold and silver (3:13–18; 8:10, 19; 16:16; 20:15; 25:11; Job 31:24–25). The second line of thinking might be found in Isaiah 65:17–25, if interpreted as indicated that the present world will pass away, taking its goods with it.

Intertestamental and Greco-Roman Philosophical Background to the New Testament. Several important conceptual developments had taken place by the time of the emergence of the New Testament from its Greco-Roman and early Jewish environment. In Greek philosophy, Plato, especially in *Timaeus* 30a, took a decisive step, locating original perfection not in material reality but in the ideas behind them. According to this text, the creator (*demiurge*) then copied these into material creation. This theory allowed later followers to devalue the material world, including nature and its resources, in favor of immaterial or spiritual realities. On the other hand, Stoicism, which emerged in the third century B.C.E., tended to identify God as the organizing principle present within the material creation—nature—as a whole (pantheism). Both of these understandings exercise influence on New Testament and early Christian approaches to nature and its resources.

One inner-Jewish tradition, the rise of apocalypticism, emerged largely in an environment of crisis during the Hellenistic period (333–63 B.C.E.), where political stability was often lacking. A body of texts placed deliverance outside of normal human religious–political efforts and often placed the renewal of creation outside the reach of the current, humanly experienced world, which necessitated a radical in-breaking of divine presence and power that disrupted the established rhythms of the world. For example, while *1 Enoch* 101 and 102:1–3 emphasize God's control over nature and judgment coming through nature, *1 Enoch* 52 proclaims that those in control of precious metal resources are mountains that will undergo God's wrath, thus casting them as God's opponents. These trajectories served in Platonically influenced and postbiblical ascetic communities to redirect emphasis away from blessing understood as natural material resources to blessing immaterial.

Other responses to Hellenism appear in attempts to assimilate Jewish heritage with the new Greek world. Sirach 14, in similar strains to Ecclesiastes, promotes enjoyment of one's material wealth rather than hoarding for another to enjoy when one has died. Sirach also praises artisans such as the potter and blacksmith, whose skills are necessary for human flourishing (Sir 38), placing considerable value on material well-being, even if such skills do not provide the necessary wisdom to be a political leader.

Jubilees 13:6 names the wealth of trees Abraham encountered upon reaching Canaan, emphasizing the material blessing Abram receives for trusting God (cf. Deut 8:7–10). Nature also continues to function as threat (Tob 2:10; 6:3) and as intermediary of divine redemption, as seen in Tobit's use of fish gall to cast out a demon (8:3).

New Testament. The New Testament generally assumes the Old Testament in its approach to nature, viewing it as creation (κτίσις) (John 1:1–3; Col 1:15–16) by a beneficent deity, not as a separate Platonic demiurge. Like the Psalms and Prophets, several New Testament texts (Rom 8:22) depict nature as a subject; and just as in the Old Testament, nature can pose threats to humanity (Mark 4:25–41 and pars; Luke 10:19) and function as a sign of divine action (Matt 24:7–8, 17, 19). Furthermore, while the value of natural resources belongs to the foundational worldview, many New Testament texts react to the accumulation of such resources by those in power (Roman rulers, e.g.) by redirecting readers to goals beyond, or outside of, material gain (Mark 12:17; Luke 20:25).

Divine control of nature and its resources. Much like the Old Testament, New Testament texts affirm God's control of nature and its resources. Jesus calms the sea (Matt 8:23–27 and pars.), directs a miraculous catch of fish (Luke 5:1–11; cf. John 21:1–11), and multiplies the bread and fish (Matt 14:13–21 and pars.), demonstrating his connection with God, the ultimate controller of these goods, in correspondence to similar miracles in Exodus—Numbers.

Furthermore, like divine provision for all in the Old Testament, God and his agents provide sustenance for the whole world both by sending rain on the righteous and unrighteous (Matt 5:45) and by giving the necessities of life to nonhuman life (sparrows, Luke 12:6–7; ravens, Luke 12:24; and grass, Matt 6:25–34). This general provision offers an analogy with human life: God will also take care of humans, especially those who turn to him for assistance (Matt 6:11).

Nature as object and subject. Also in continuity with the Old Testament, nature emerges at various points as subject, especially in Romans 8:18–25, where creation is both passive in being subjected to futility at the will of another (cf. Gen 3:17) and active in its waiting and its groaning. Nature appears as worshiper in Revelation 5:13; but in 12:12 and 18:20 only the heavens rejoice, while earth and sea are lamented for their proximity to the dragon and the evil city. Nature also continues as threat, such as adversarial snakes and scorpions (Luke 10:18).

Colossians 1:15–20, however, proclaims the reconciliation of all creation through Christ. Overtures in Mark 1:12–13 continue the tradition of the reconciliation of nature with humanity in the emergence of the Kingdom of God. As in Isaiah 11:6–9 and 65:17–25, where God renews the cosmos through the establishment of divine rule, Jesus's appearance as the divine ruler brings about the reconciliation of humanity with the threatening creatures of the wild (Mark 1:12–13). Nature also appears as object when it is used to contribute to human flourishing or to make object lessons, as in Jesus's cursing of the fig tree because it did not yield fruit and his promise that one could move mountains by faith (Matt 21:18–22; Mark 11:12–14, 20–26).

God's presence in nature and natural resources as elements of divine–human ritual. The New Testament's ultimate affirmation of the material or natural comes in Jesus's humanity (John 1:1, 14; 1 John 1:1–3) and the reaffirmation of divine creation of everything (John 1; Col 1:15–16). Natural resources also continue to carry inherent value as a means of conveying or symbolizing closeness to the divine, much like offerings in the Old Testament, particularly through water baptism (John 1:26, 29–34; 3:22–23) and the ritual installation of the bread and wine at the last supper. The plain materiality of these rituals displays the continued presence of the divine in the basic resources—water and food—that appear in the Bible. Furthermore, though less emphatic than in the Old Testament, Romans 1:20 declares access to some divine qualities "Ever since the creation."

Relativization of the importance of natural resources. An important New Testament emphasis with regard to natural resources comes in the elaborations on Old Testament traditions that placed immaterial goals above the accumulation or enjoyment of material resources. Matthew 6:19–21 states this most clearly, exhorting the accumulation of treasure

in heaven. This logic appears more subtly in Jesus's elevation of the importance of living water and bread of life over the material goods themselves (John 4:7–14; 6:35–58). Nonetheless, the conception of the restored or new creation in Revelation 21–22 continues the use of the image of a "garden"—combined with a city—full of material good things, such as a fruit-bearing tree, flowing water, and overwhelming amounts of precious metals and stones.

Postbiblical Developments. Patristic thinking on nature primarily addressed questions raised by Neo-Platonism and Gnosticism, traditions that devalued materiality, even to the point of viewing it as evil. Gnostic writings generally viewed material creation as problematic, developing a Platonic preference for the immaterial. Marcion similarly rejected the Old Testament and much of the New Testament, in part because of God's role as Creator of the material world and its concomitant evil.

A number of early church writers, to combat these tendencies, affirmed the doctrine of *creatio ex nihilo* by God alone (e.g., Tatian, *Oratio ad Graecos* 5:1–3; Tertullian, *Herm.* 21:2–3). Irenaeus offers a sustained critique of any kind of demiurge or angel forming material creation on the basis of prior ideal blueprints, arguing for the perfect creation of the single God (*Haer.* 2).

Contributions to Current Discussions. While nature no longer poses a threat to humanity in the same way as in the ancient world and scientific investigation has changed the way nature is viewed, there are biblical resources worth considering when addressing the current global ecological crisis, which results from human action and gives rise to the question of humanity's place in the world and use of natural resources. Some biblical scholars have developed an approach called "ecological hermeneutics" (Davis, 2009; Habel, 2001, 2008; Rhoads, 2004), which places nonhuman entities as the subjects of interpretation. This perspective seeks to decenter humanity as the single, or central, object of concern for interpreters by highlighting biblical texts that lend support to the subjectivity of nature, rather than viewing nature and natural resources as simply background and instruments for a divine–human drama.

The collaboration between nature and humanity as co-worshipers (Ps 148) and co-groaners (Rom 8:18–27) is particularly worthy of reflection.

A second potentially fruitful contribution from biblical studies to current environmental issues arises from the long acknowledged and oft-abused designation of humanity as God's image—that is, royal representative—on earth. By recognizing the responsibility of caring for the weak explicitly as part of the ancient conception of kingship (cf. Ps 72:15–16), care for nature becomes part of the royal task. This notion of *imago Dei* would carry over to the very concern for the birds and lilies (Matt 6:26–28). These insights critique the notion that nature is simply an instrument for human use (White, 1967).

Finally, the Bible affirms nature and natural resources as good. Its focus on natural resources as most important for sustaining life—water and food—suggests a primary concern for providing the necessities for life, rather than the adornment of elites with riches.

[*See also* Blessings and Curses; Eden; Heaven and Earth; Image of God; Labor; *and* Land.]

BIBLIOGRAPHY
Brown, William P. *The Seven Pillars of Creation: The Bible, Science, and the Ecology of Wonder.* Oxford: Oxford University Press, 2010.
Claassens, L. Juliana M. *The God Who Provides: Biblical Images of Divine Nourishment.* Nashville, Tenn.: Abingdon, 2004.
Davis, Ellen F. *Scripture, Culture, and Agriculture: An Agrarian Reading of the Bible.* New York: Cambridge University Press, 2009.
Fretheim, Terence E. *God and World in the Old Testament: A Relational Theology of Creation.* Nashville, Tenn.: Abingdon, 2005.
Goldingay, John. "The World." In *Old Testament Theology* Vol. 2: *Israel's Faith*, pp. 648–732. Downers Grove, Ill.: InterVarsity, 2006.
Habel, Norman C. *The Earth Story in the Psalms and the Prophets.* The Earth Bible 4. Sheffield, U.K.: Sheffield Academic Press, 2001.
Habel, Norman C, ed. *Exploring Ecological Hermeneutics.* Society of Biblical Literature Symposium Series 46. Atlanta: Society of Biblical Literature, 2008.
Hendry, George Stuart. *Theology of Nature.* Philadelphia: Westminster, 1980.
Hiebert, Theodore. *The Yahwist's Landscape: Nature and Religion in Early Israel.* New York: Oxford University Press, 1996.
Rhoads, David M. "Who Will Speak for the Sparrow? Eco-justice Criticism of the New Testament." In *Literary Encounters with the Reign of God*, edited by Sharon H. Ringe and Robert C. Tannehill, pp. 64–86. New York: T&T Clark, 2004.
Rogerson, John W. "The Old Testament View of Nature." In *Instruction and Interpretation Studies in Hebrew Language, Palestinian Archaeology, and Biblical Exegesis Papers Read at the Joint British–Dutch Old Testament Conference Held at Louvain, 1976*, edited by Hendrik Antonie Brongers, pp. 67–84. Oudtestamentische studiën deel 20. Leiden, The Netherlands: Brill, 1977.
Schmid, Konrad. "Schöpfung im Alten Testament." In *Schöpfung*, edited by Konrad Schmid, pp. 71–120. Themen der Theologie 4; Uni-Taschenbücher 3514. Tübingen, Germany: Mohr Siebeck, 2012.
Vollenweider, Samuel. "Wahrnehmungen der Schöpfung im Neuen Testament." *Zeitschrift für Pädagogik und Theologie* 55 (2003): 246–253.
White, Lynn Townsend, Jr. "The Historical Roots of Our Ecologic Crisis." *Science* 155 (1967): 1203–1207.
Wischmeyer, Oda. "Physis und Ktisis bei Paulus: Die Paulinische Rede von Schöpfung und Natur." *Zeitschrift für Theologie und Kirche* 93 (1993): 352–375.
Zimmerli, Walther. *The Old Testament and the World.* Translated by John J. Scullion. London: SPCK, 1976.

Peter Altmann

NEHEMIAH

See Ezra, Nehemiah, and 1 and 2 Chronicles.

NUMBERS

See Leviticus and Numbers.

O

OATHS AND VOWS

The purpose of an oath in the biblical world was to assure the truth of a statement or the reliability of a promise. Persons who made an oath invited divine judgment on themselves if the statement proved false or the pledge unreliable (Thiselton, 2006, p. 309). Truthfulness was crucial to the stability of society, and those who would "swear deceitfully" represented a major moral problem (Ps 24:4). Thus, Hosea listed the misuse of oaths along with lying, murder, and adultery as examples of Israel's sins (Hos 10:4). Oaths also play an important role in the modern Western world, especially in court testimony. A false oath brings a charge of perjury and legal punishment. In the world that produced the Bible, however, people thought God enforced oaths, thus bringing the force of the curse inherent in the oath that was sworn.

Vows were also pledges of faithfulness that used the well-being of the vow maker as collateral. Vows may be distinguished from oaths, however, in that they were made exclusively by humans to God. Whereas oaths entailed swearing loyalty or faithfulness and thus could be made by God (Gen 22:16–18; Jer 22:5; Exod 32:13; Ps 132:11–12), vows were pledges of specific actions by humans to God, often made in return for God's help. Despite this distinction between oaths and vows, both terms could be used to describe a human pledge of faithful action. Thus, Psalm 132:2 includes both expressions in parallel to describe David's intention to make a home for the ark in Jerusalem: "he swore [*nišbaʿ*] to the LORD and vowed [*nādar*] to the Mighty One of Jacob."

Language and Logic of Oaths and Vows. The Old Testament most frequently connotes oaths and oath-making with the Hebrew root *šābaʿ*, meaning "to swear." Verbal forms of the root communicate the act of swearing (Gen 21:23–24), and noun forms connote what is sworn or pledged (*šĕbûʿâ*; 2 Sam 21:7). Another term used to connote oath-making, albeit less frequently, is *ʾālâ*, "to swear" (1 Kgs 8:1), and its nominal derivative that means "oath" (Lev 5:1; Neh 10:30). This term is significant in that it can also mean "to curse" (Judg 17:2). Noun forms likewise often refer to curses, either divine (Num 5:23; Deut 30:7; Isa 24:6) or human (Job 31:30; Ps 10:7). This negative meaning illustrates the close relationship between swearing an oath and uttering a curse. Those who swore truthfulness invited evil upon themselves if the oath was not honored.

It was common to enhance the statement of obligation by making reference to God as the guarantor of the oath (Keller, 1997, p. 1294). Hence, full expression of an oath in the so-called oath formula takes several distinctive forms through which ancient Israelites placed themselves under the Lord's potential punishment ("May the LORD do thus and so to me, and more as well if…"; Ruth 1:17; 2 Sam 3:35) or enhanced the force of the statement ("As the LORD lives…"; Judg 8:19; 1 Sam 14:39; 26:10, 16). When God pledged faithfulness God could only appeal to God's own authority to back the promise. Isaiah 45:23 is typical: "By myself I have sworn, from my mouth has gone forth in righteousness a word that shall not return: 'To me every knee shall bow, every tongue shall swear.'" The writer of Hebrews makes this a major point in explaining divine faithfulness: "because he had no one greater by whom to swear, he swore by himself" (Heb 6:13).

Since swearing an oath meant binding oneself to an irrevocable pledge, it is not surprising that oaths were sworn sometimes at sanctuaries or sacred places (Gen 26:28–31; Hos 4:15). The level of commitment in oaths is indicated by the accompaniment of symbolic acts such as raising the hands (Gen 14:22 [Heb.]; Rev 10:5–6). Hence, when Psalm 144:8 speaks of right hands that are false, it refers to those who swear oaths with no intention to abide by them. Abraham requires his servant to place his hand under his thigh when swearing an oath, thus linking it with procreation (Gen 24:2–9).

Some scholars speculate that swearing an oath is related in meaning to the number seven since the number appears to derive from the same Hebrew root (*šbʿ*). The implication is that one who swears an oath "sevens" herself or himself, that is, binds the self by means of a complete self-imprecation (Lehmann, 1969). The association of the number seven with oaths, however, is not clearly supported by any biblical text. Genesis 21:23–31 and 26:21–23 do explain the place-name Beersheba (lit. "place of seven" or possibly "place of the oath") with reference to the number seven and the making of an oath, but the connection is not explicitly stated and thus remains speculative (Keller, 1997, p. 1292).

The primary language of vow-making involves the Hebrew root *nādar*, "to vow." The verb means "to make a vow," and the noun refers to the "vow" itself (*neder*). The verb and noun appear frequently together in the expression "make a vow" (lit. "vow a vow;" Gen 28:20; Num 21:2; Deut 12:11, 17). This expression is used to pledge a gift or offering in the sanctuary (Deut 12:11, 17, 26) or, more generally, to devote oneself to service, as expressed in the Nazirite vow (Num 6:2, 5, 21).

Vows were sometimes part of an interaction with God in which the one making the vow did so in order to receive a favor from God. Two primary examples illustrate this use of the vow. In Numbers 21:1–3 the Israelites "made a vow" to the Lord as they prepared for war with the Canaanites: "If you will indeed give this people into our hands, then we will utterly destroy their towns" (v. 2). Israel vowed to put the Canaanites under the ban (thus, giving them as an offering to God instead of keeping them and their possessions as spoils) if God gave them victory. In a similar way and with the same pattern of speech, Hannah prayed for God to give her a son and vowed, in return, to give the child back to God for service at the sanctuary (1 Sam 1:11): "She made this vow [*wattiddōr neder*]: 'O LORD of hosts, if [*'im*] only you will look on the misery of your servant, and remember me, and not forget your servant, but will give to your servant a male child, then [*wĕ*] I will set him before you." Judges 11:29–40 uses the same terminology and the same sentence structure when it reports Jephthah's vow. He "made a vow" to the Lord saying, "If you will give the Ammonites into my hand then whoever [or whatever] comes out of the doors of my house" (vv. 30–31) will be the Lord's as a sacrifice. In each case the vow was for a specific situation in which the one(s) making the vow pledged to pay homage to God with sacrifice if God granted him or her success.

Inappropriate Oaths and Rash Vows. In the biblical world oaths and vows were like blessings and curses in that they were powerful speech that had almost magical power. Once spoken, they went out like an arrow toward its target that could not be taken back (e.g., the blessing of the firstborn in Gen 27:27–35 that could not be retracted). Hence, the Bible warns against inappropriate use of such speech. The irrevocable nature of vows is apparent in the story of Jephthah. When he realized his vow bound him to sacrifice his daughter, he "tore his clothes" and said, "I have opened my mouth to the LORD and I cannot take back my vow" (Judg 11:35). Numbers 30 nuances this understanding of the power of vows in the case of vows made by women who are married or who live in the house of their father. Since the patriarch was ultimately responsible for any pledge made by a member of his household, he could nullify a vow made thoughtlessly or irresponsibly.

The primary regulations on oaths relate to the connection between oaths and truthfulness. It was reprehensible to utter an oath with no commitment behind it (Jer 5:2; 7:9). Deuteronomy 5:13 reveals the essence of the problem by placing as parallels swearing in the name of the Lord and fearing and serving him (Keller, 1997, p. 1296). To swear by a deity was to declare allegiance. Hence, to swear falsely was to make a disingenuous declaration of piety. The Third Commandment may be understood in this context ("You shall not make wrongful use of the name of the LORD your God"; Exod 20:7; Deut 5:11). The second type of false oath is one that invokes the name of a foreign deity (Jer 5:7). Such an oath was problematic for reasons already stated, namely, that such an oath was an inherent declaration of faithfulness to the deity named in the utterance.

The Nazirite Vow. The Nazirite vow was a distinctive pledge of a person who dedicated himself or herself to holiness before God. Numbers 6:2 characterizes this as "a special vow" or perhaps better "an extraordinary vow" (*pālāʾ*; my translation; see Noth, 1968, p. 55). The term *nāzîr* means "one set apart." During the time of the vow the Nazirite was essentially divine property (Dozeman, 1994, p. 64). Thus, one who took the Nazirite vow pledged to separate himself or herself for a period of time by not drinking wine or strong drink or tasting anything made from grapes, by not cutting the hair, and by not touching a dead body (Num 6:3–8). The separation from all products of the vine may reflect a concern for the Israelites to separate from Canaanite culture, which was associated with wine and drunkenness (see Gray, 1903, pp. 61–63; Gen 9:18–29). Whether this association is correct or not, the Nazirite vowed to maintain holiness much like a priest (see Lev 21:10–15), but ordinary Israelites took the Nazirite vow and maintained priest-like holiness for a specific period of time. Samson and Samuel are unique in that their mothers gave them as Nazirites for life (Judg 13:7; 1 Sam 1:11).

Oaths in Wisdom Literature and the New Testament. The virtual absence of references to swearing oaths in the Wisdom material is striking. This is due most likely to wisdom's cautious view of the matter. Sirach 23:9 counsels, "Do not accustom your mouth to oaths, nor habitually utter the name of the Holy One" (cf. Eccl 9:2). James 5:12 is similar: "do not swear, either by heaven or by earth or by any other oath." It has a close parallel in Matthew 5:33–37, in which Jesus refutes the conventional idea of not swearing falsely by stating that one should not swear at all, either by heaven or by the earth or by Jerusalem. Matthew 23:26–23 does not so much renounce the practice of swearing oaths as it refutes the pharisaical ranking of oaths and making some lesser oaths more binding. This teaching highlights again the seriousness of the oath and the caution with which it should be used.

Despite the New Testament emphasis on not swearing, it remained an important part of the New Testament world, as it continues to be used in contemporary society. The story of Peter's denial of Jesus gives evidence of the ongoing role of oaths and the curses that accompany them. When Peter was identified as one of Jesus's followers, Peter first offered a simple negation (Matt 26:70). On the second such identification he made a more emphatic statement by swearing an oath (Matt 26:72). Finally, he swore an oath and uttered a curse (Matt 26:74). The oath and curse gave greater weight to Peter's denial and invited harm upon him if he was untruthful. Thus, the story of Peter illustrates the continuing role of swearing truthfulness or imposing a curse, but it also provides direct support for the sages' warning against swearing falsely.

[*See also* Authority and Order; Blessings and Curses; Covenant; Cult and Worship; Decalogue; Deuteronomy; Election; Ethics, Biblical; Festivals and Holy Days; Leviticus and Numbers; Priests and Priesthood; *and* Sacrifice and Offerings.]

BIBLIOGRAPHY

Davies, G. Henton. "Vows." In *The Interpreter's Dictionary of the Bible*, edited by George Arthur Buttrick, Vol. 4, pp. 792–793. Nashville, Tenn.: Abingdon, 1962.

Dozeman, Thomas. "The Book of Numbers." In *The New Interpreter's Bible*, edited by Leander Keck, Vol. 2, pp. 1–268. Nashville, Tenn.: Abingdon, 1994.

Floyd, Michael H. "Vow." In *The New Interpreter's Dictionary of the Bible*, edited by Katherine Doob Sakenfeld, Vol. 5, pp. 793–794. Nashville, Tenn.: Abingdon Press, 2006.

Gray, George Buchanan. *A Critical and Exegetical Commentary on Numbers*. International Critical Commentary 4. New York: Scribner, 1903.

Keller, C. A. "שבע šbʻni. to Swear." In *Theological Lexicon of the Old Testament*, edited by Ernst Jenni and Claus Westermann, Vol. 3, pp. 1292–1297. Translated by Mark E. Biddle. Peabody, Mass.: Hendrickson, 1997.

Lehmann, M. R. "Biblical Oaths." *Zeitschrift für Alttestamentlich Wissenschaft* 81 (1969): 74–92.

Noth, Martin. *Numbers: A Commentary*. Translated by James D. Martin. Philadelphia: Westminster, 1968.

Pope, M. H. "Oaths." In *The Interpreter's Dictionary of the Bible*, edited by George Arthur Buttrick, Vol. 3, pp. 575–577. Nashville, Tenn.: Abingdon, 1962.

Thiselton, Anthony C. "Oath." In *The New Interpreter's Dictionary of the Bible*, edited by Katherine Doob Sakenfeld, Vol. 4, pp. 309–312. Nashville, Tenn.: Abingdon, 2006.

Jerome F. D. Creach

OBADIAH

See Book of the Twelve (Minor Prophets).

OFFERINGS

See Sacrifice and Offerings.

P

PARABLE

Parables appear in both the Old and New Testaments, as well as in other ancient literatures, but are associated primarily with the teachings of Jesus in the gospels. It is generally thought that, if one wants to hear and understand the message of Jesus, one must read the parables. There are other texts that convey the teachings of Jesus, but the parables are an indispensable source.

Parables in General. The word "parable" is derived from the Greek word *parabolē*, a "comparison." As used in both biblical and nonbiblical texts, however, the meaning of the word is not limited to that etymology; it can designate a broad range of figures of speech. Within classical Greek literature a *parabolē* can indeed refer to a comparison (Plato, *Phileb.* 33b), but in other cases it can denote an illustration in narrative form (Plato, *Phaed.* 87b). According to Aristotle, parables are illustrations used to confirm a point being made within a larger discourse (*Rhet.* 2.20).

Within the Septuagint *parabolē* appears 46 times as a translation of the Hebrew word *māšāl*. The Hebrew term broadly refers to figures of speech (such as proverbs, oracles, fables, riddles, and maxims), and it is not used in places where one might expect it. If any story in the Old Testament may be classified as a parable, it would be that which the prophet Nathan tells David following the king's arranging the death of Uriah and taking Bathsheba as his wife (2 Sam 12:1–4). Yet it is not called a *māšāl*. The same is true of other stories that employ narration and resemble parables, as commonly understood, in content and function (e.g., 1 Kgs 20:39–40; Isa 5:1–7; 28:23–29).

Closer to the time of Jesus, parables appear in Rabbinic literature (e.g., *'Abot R. Nat.* 15.3, *Gen. Rab.* 1.15, *t. B. Qam.* 7.3), often introduced with the word *māšāl*. Whether the parables predate Jesus and may therefore have provided a model for him is uncertain. Of the more than 300 known parables in Rabbinic literature, most are from the second and third centuries C.E. Even if they predate Jesus, they differ in function from his. They serve almost exclusively as exegetical tools to explain biblical texts, while none of Jesus's parables do. (A possible exception is the good Samaritan in Luke 10:25–37, which is partially prompted by Lev 19:18.) The parables of Jesus serve as media for his own teaching; he teaches "as one having authority, and not as the scribes" (Mark 1:22).

The Parables of Jesus. The parables of Jesus are the most familiar units of his teaching. Moreover, they are characteristic of his manner of teaching. Containing rich imagery and frequent surprises, they have been treasured through the ages not only in the church but also in the larger culture.

Definition and number. Within the New Testament parables appear only in the Synoptic Gospels and are told only by Jesus. A passage in John (10:1–6) is called a "parable" in the King James Version, which the New Revised Standard Version translates a "figure of speech." The Greek word is *paroimia*, not *parabolē*; strictly speaking, John 10:1–6 is a Christological discourse, not a parable.

What material can be classified as a parable is debatable. One cannot always rely on explicit use of the term in the gospels. Some parables are introduced by a phrase like "he told this parable" (thus, the barren fig tree in Luke 13:6–9); in Matthew 13:36 the disciples ask Jesus to explain "the parable of the weeds of the field" (13:24–30, demonstrating that some parables had acquired names during the apostolic era). On the other hand, just because a unit is called a "parable" in the gospels does not mean that it must be classified as such. For example, is Jesus's saying about not placing a patch of new cloth on old clothes a parable? Luke so identifies it (5:36); Mark (2:21) and Matthew (9:16) do not. At Luke 4:23 Jesus says, "Doubtless you will quote to me this proverb [*parabolēn*], 'Doctor, cure yourself.'" Few would consider that aphorism a parable; consequently, the Greek word in this case is typically translated as "proverb."

What can be counted among the parables of Jesus depends on how one defines the term. Though no definition universally satisfies, at minimum a parable is a figure of speech in which the speaker draws a comparison between something mysterious (the subject under discussion) and something familiar, thereby instructing the hearer about an aspect of what is being taught. The unknown is illumined by the known. In the particular case of Jesus's teaching, a parable is a figure of speech in which a comparison is made between God's kingdom, character, or expectations and something in this world, real or imagined. By this definition, over three dozen units of gospel material may be considered parables.

The parables of Jesus: A listing. While others might be included, the following 37 units of Synoptic tradition appear in most lists of Jesus's parables. These are tabulated according to canonical sources, based on the standard two-source theory of gospel origins.

Parables appearing in Mark (five, most with parallels):
The sower (4:3–8//Matt 13:3–8//Luke 8:5–8)
The seed growing secretly (4:26–29)
The mustard seed (4:30–32//Matt 13:31–32//Luke 13:18–19)
The wicked tenants (12:1–12//Matt 21:33–46//Luke 20:9–19)
The waiting slaves (13:34–37//Luke 12:35–38)

Parables attributed to the Q source (a total of six):
The father's good gifts (Matt 7:9–11//Luke 11:11–13)
The wise and foolish builders (Matt 7:24–27//Luke 6:47–49)
The children in the marketplace (Matt 11:16–19//Luke 7:31–35)
The leaven (Matt 13:33//Luke 13:20–21)
The lost sheep (Matt 18:12–14//Luke 15:4–7)
The faithful and wise slave (Matt 24:45–51//Luke 12:42–46)

Parables distinctive of Matthew (10 in all):
The weeds in the wheat (13:24–30)
The treasure in the field (13:44)
The pearl of great price (13:45–46)
The dragnet (13:47–50)
The unforgiving slave (18:23–35)
The workers in the vineyard (20:1–16)
The two sons (21:28–32)
The wedding feast (22:1–14)
The ten maidens (25:1–13)
The talents (25:14–30)

Parables distinctive of Luke (numbering 16):
The two debtors (7:41–43)
The good Samaritan (10:25–37)
The friend at midnight (11:5–8)
The rich fool (12:16–21)
The barren fig tree (13:6–9)
The great banquet (14:16–24)
Building a tower (14:28–30)
The king going to war (14:31–33)
The lost coin (15:8–10)
The prodigal son (15:11–32)
The unjust manager (16:1–8)
The rich man and Lazarus (16:19–31)
The slave at duty (17:7–10)
The unjust judge (18:2–8)
The Pharisee and the tax collector (18:10–14)
The pounds (19:12–27)

In addition to the parables in the Synoptics, there are parables of Jesus in apocryphal writings, notably the *Gospel of Thomas* and the *Gospel of Truth*. Ten parables in *Thomas* have parallels in the Synoptics: the sower (Mark 4:3–8//*Gos. Thom.* 9), the mustard seed (Mark 4:30–32//*Gos. Thom.* 20), the weeds in the wheat (Matt 13:24–30//*Gos. Thom.* 57), the rich fool (Luke 12:16–21//*Gos. Thom.* 63), the great banquet (Luke 14:16–24//*Gos. Thom.* 64), the wicked tenants (Mark 12:1–12//*Gos. Thom.* 65), the pearl of great price (Matt 13:45–46//*Gos. Thom.* 76), the leaven (Matt 13:33//*Gos. Thom.* 96), the lost sheep (Matt 18:12–14//*Gos. Thom.* 107), and the treasure in the field (Matt 13:44//*Gos. Thom.* 109). *Thomas* contains four additional parables not found in the Synoptics: the wise fisherman (8), the disciples as little children (21), the woman with a jar (97), and the assassin (98). The *Gospel of Truth* (31–32) contains one parable also appearing in the Synoptics, the parable of the lost sheep (//Matt 18:12–14).

Types of parables. It is customary to classify Jesus's parables under three categories. Formally, there are two major types; if one considers content, a third emerges.

As oral compositions that make comparisons, parables share the linguistic field with similes and metaphors. Some, classified as "similitudes," can be considered extended similes. A simile is typically very brief, employing "like" as a connector ("stars *like* diamonds in the sky"); a similitude contains more explanatory detail. Among Jesus's parables, the parable of the leaven is considered a similitude: "The Kingdom of Heaven is *like* yeast that a woman took and mixed in with three measures of flour until all of it was leavened" (Matt 13:33//Luke 13:20–21). Four other parables can be classified as "similitudes": the parables of the seed growing secretly (Mark 4:26–29//*Gos. Thom.* 57), the mustard seed (Mark 4:30–32//Matt 13:31; Luke 13:18–19//*Gos. Thom.* 20), the treasure in the field (Matt 13:44//*Gos. Thom.* 109), and the pearl of great price (Matt 13:45–46//*Gos. Thom.* 76). In each of these, either "like" or "as if" (Gk *hōs* or *homoia*) is employed, and the verb is conjugated in the present tense (Eng "is"; Gk *esti*). Moreover, the comparisons are general, drawing upon illustrations from daily life.

Most of Jesus's parables can be classified as "narrative parables"; they contain a narrative in which a comparison is made, and the narrative is set in the past tense. These parables have a "once-upon-a-time" character, and they are imaginative, not based on commonplace observations of daily life. In fact, it is their atypical character that makes them so memorable. Among these are most of the parables of Jesus and certainly the most famous, including the parables of the prodigal son (Luke 15:11–32) and the workers in the vineyard (Matt 20:1–16).

Four parables are often placed in a third category. Although they can be considered a subset of the narrative parables, they may be called "parables of exemplary behavior." Providing models of conduct, these are more straightforward in meaning and invite application, whereas other narrative parables leave the hearer with enigmas to ponder. The four in this category, all appearing only in Luke, are the parables of the good Samaritan (10:25–37), the rich fool (12:16–21), the rich man and Lazarus (16:19–31), and the Pharisee and the tax collector (18:10–14).

Features and Themes of the Parables. Like other parables of antiquity, Jesus's parables use common metaphors drawn from everyday life. Yet the parables of Jesus contain distinctive elements and major themes.

Stylistic features. Jesus's parables are addressed directly to his hearers about matters important for their lives. This quality is most evident in cases where Jesus addresses his audience with such penetrating questions as "which one of you?" (Luke 14:28; 15:4), "suppose one of you" (Matt 12:11), "what woman?" (Luke 15:8), "Is there any among you?" (Matt 7:9//Luke 11:11), "what king?" (Luke 14:31), "who among you?" (Luke 17:7), "who then is the faithful and wise slave?" (Matt 24:45), "who then is the faithful and prudent manager?" (Luke 12:42); and "what do you think?" (Matt 18:12; 21:28). Alternatively, one finds the simple indicative "everyone then who hears" (Matt 5:24). Such opening phrases engage hearers immediately, putting them on the spot and eliciting a response.

A second distinctive feature is that, in spite of their use of common metaphors, Jesus's best-known parables do not portray human behavior in typical ways. The narrative leads the hearer from the familiar to a surprising twist at the end. For example, in the parable of the workers in the vineyard (Matt 20:1–16) the "eleventh-hour workers" receive pay equal to that of laborers who worked all day. Without knowing the prodigal's intent, the father runs to meet his returning son, who has squandered everything (Luke 15:11–32). In the parable of the marriage feast (Matt 22:1–10), the king orders that others, "both good and bad," be brought in as guests when the respectable, first invited, would not come. These surprises have a bearing on the message of the parables.

Major themes. The parables of Jesus refer primarily to three things: the nature of God, the Kingdom of God, and human conduct. All of these are intertwined but can be considered separately.

Regarding the nature of God, the parables do not describe God's attributes or discuss God's nature theoretically. Characteristic, instead, is the sense of God's intimacy and familiarity, conveyed through common metaphors: a father, king, shepherd, owner of a vineyard, or a woman who sweeps her house. Such concrete metaphors prevent abstractions.

The clearest affirmation about God is that God is good and gracious beyond human expectations. In the parable of the prodigal son, Jesus compares God to a father who *runs*—certainly not typical of a Middle-Eastern father in antiquity—to meet his wayward son who returns (Luke 15:20). Jesus portrays God as more loving and merciful than any human father one might know. Similarly, in the parable of the unforgiving servant (Matt 18:23–35), a king forgives his slave an indebtedness of 10,000 talents, an astounding amount, impossible to imagine. Moreover, God's love and goodness extend to persons not considered worthy of it by normal standards of judgment: God reaches out to the lost, as in the parables of the lost sheep (Matt 18:12–14//Luke 15:4–7) and the lost coin (Luke 15:8–10), and rewards those who work for only an hour in the parable of the workers in the vineyard (Matt 20:1–16). The actions of God as shepherd, woman, father, and wealthy landowner are not typical of ordinary persons in those roles. A masterly storyteller, Jesus portrays God through figures who act in extremely unusual, unconventional ways.

Although clearly loving and merciful, God is also a god of judgment. In the parable of the Pharisee and the tax collector (Luke 18:9–14) God has already made a judgment when, according to Jesus, the one man goes down to his house "justified" (Luke 18:14) but the other does not. God's judgment stands against those who, though lavishly forgiven, will not forgive others: the unforgiving slave is cast into prison (Matt 18:23–35). Similarly, the rich man is consigned to torment because of his arrogant, uncaring, and inattentive conduct toward Lazarus in this life (Luke 16:19–31). The parables of the weeds in the wheat and the dragnet (Matt 13:24–30, 47–50) use metaphors for a final judgment (reaping, gathering, and burning; sorting and casting away).

Frequently, the parables are about the Kingdom of God (or, in the language of Matthew's Gospel, the Kingdom of Heaven). Notable here are the similitudes. Often called "parables of the kingdom," they affirm the certainty of the growth of the Kingdom (or reign) of God (the parables of the seed growing secretly [Mark 4:26–29], the mustard seed [4:30–32], and the leaven [Matt 13:33]). Some parables affirm the joy of the kingdom's discovery (the parables of the treasure hidden in the field [Matt 13:44] and the pearl of great price [Matt 13:45–46]). In other cases a parable may begin by referring to the kingdom, even though the story that follows is actually about the ways of God in a more general sense (e.g., Matt 20:1–16; 25:1–13).

Finally, there are parables devoted to human conduct. Four of Jesus's parables teach exemplary behavior: true neighborliness (the good Samaritan), not trusting in an increase in material resources to make life more meaningful (the rich fool), caring for the needy (the rich man and Lazarus), and true piety before God (the Pharisee and tax collector). Other parables describe conduct expected of a disciple of Jesus as well, including the need to extend forgiveness (the unforgiving slave), the responsible use of one's gifts (the talents and the pounds), the need to leave judgment up to God (the weeds in the wheat), and faithful service until Christ comes again (the faithful and wise slave), even if his coming be far in the distant future (the ten maidens).

Jesus's Parables in Context: Ancient and Contemporary. The parables do not provide the totality of Jesus's teaching regarding God, God's Kingdom, and the conduct expected of a disciple. Nor do they convey balanced and nuanced teachings that can satisfy a fixed theological or ethical system. They express facets of Jesus's message; its entirety could not be neatly fitted into the parables. The parables are memorable for their vivid scenes, bold characterization, and hyperbole. They provoke the hearer—and the reader of the Gospels—to reconsider previously held views concerning God, God's Kingdom, and God's expectations and then to see new possibilities for thought and action.

During much of the twentieth century, it was usually assumed that, to hear the message of the parables, one must recover their original meaning in the setting of Jesus's ministry. Historical interest in the parables continues, including attempts to reconstruct the original form and wording uttered by Jesus. But other approaches have also flourished, including comparative research in Rabbinic literature, social–cultural studies, redaction–critical studies, and all that can be called literary–critical study, including rhetorical and semiotic analyses. According to many literary–critical approaches, the key to meaning is to be found within the limits of the text's form and structure, aside from its historical context, sources, and the elusive intentions of a given evangelist or Jesus himself. In addition, the investigation of parables within their respective Gospels has grown commensurately with literary–critical studies of those Gospels, recognized as literary works that employ parables within their plot and rhetorical structures. No single interpretive approach reigns supreme.

Because the parables are metaphorical, they generate multiple shades of meaning. They are open-ended, capable of various nuances because of what different hearers and readers bring to them. That does not mean that parables can be interpreted to say just anything. Restraints are imposed on interpretation by the particulars of the texts themselves and by the frames in which they are set (the ministry of Jesus, insofar as it may be known, and the literary contexts of the Gospels in which they appear). Although some have interpreted the parables as units that can be abstracted from their historical and literary contexts altogether, others maintain that those contexts are indispensable for interpretation because all forms of discourse are spoken in contexts. The power of the parables lies not simply in the extraordinary ideas they convey or in their didactic artistry, important as these things may be, but also in their ability to confront the interpreter, and the community of interpreters, then stirring the imagination to thought and action in light of the total biblical witness.

[*See also* Allegory and Typology; Christology; Justice, Justification, and Righteousness; Kingdom of God (Heaven); *and* Mercy and Compassion.]

BIBLIOGRAPHY
Bailey, Kenneth E. *Poet and Peasant: A Literary Cultural Approach to the Parables in Luke.* Grand Rapids, Mich.: Eerdmans, 1976.
Carlston, Charles E. *The Parables of the Triple Tradition.* Philadelphia: Fortress, 1975.
Crossan, John Dominic. *In Parables: The Challenge of the Historical Jesus.* 2d ed. Sonoma, Calif.: Polebridge, 1992.
Dodd, C. H. *The Parables of the Kingdom.* Rev. ed. New York: Charles Scribner's Sons, 1961.
Hultgren, Arland J. *The Parables of Jesus: A Commentary.* Grand Rapids, Mich.: Eerdmans, 2000.
Jeremias, Joachim. *The Parables of Jesus.* 2d ed. Translated by S. H. Hooke. Upper Saddle River, N.J.: Prentice Hall, 1972. English translation of *Die Gleichnisse Jesu.* (6th ed.; Göttingen, Germany: Vandenhoeck & Ruprecht, 1962).
Jülicher, Adolf. *Die Gleichnisreden Jesu.* 2d ed. 2 vols. Tübingen, Germany: J. C. B. Mohr (Paul Siebeck), 1899, Reprint, Darmstadt, Germany: Wissenschaftliche Buchgesellschaft, 1963.
Kissinger, Warren S. *The Parables of Jesus: A History of Interpretation and Bibliography.* American Theological Library Association Bibliography Series 4. Metuchen, N.J.: Scarecrow, 1979.
Longenecker, Richard N., ed. *The Challenge of Jesus' Parables.* Grand Rapids, Mich.: Eerdmans, 2000.
McArthur, Harvey K., and Robert M. Johnston. *They Also Taught in Parables: Rabbinic Parables from the First Centuries of the Christian Era.* Grand Rapids, Mich.: Zondervan, 1990.
Snodgrass, Klyne. *Stories with Intent: A Comprehensive Guide to the Parables of Jesus.* Grand Rapids, Mich.: Eerdmans, 2008.

Stern, David. *Parables in Midrash: Narrative and Exegesis in Rabbinic Literature.* Cambridge, Mass.: Harvard University Press, 1991.

Tolbert, Mary A. *Perspectives on the Parables: An Approach to Multiple Interpretations.* Philadelphia: Fortress, 1970.

Arland J. Hultgren

PAUL

Paul was the earliest Christian theologian—arguably the greatest—whose letters helped to shape Christian thought for all time. Paul himself insisted on the continuity between Judaism and belief in Jesus as the Messiah and maintained that his teaching was loyal to the Jewish scriptures. Nevertheless, his conviction that through the death and resurrection of Jesus Gentiles were now included in God's people was largely responsible for transforming belief in Christ from a Jewish sect into a worldwide religion.

Paul's influence is derived not only from the letters that can, with reasonable certainty, be attributed to the apostle himself but also from those written by others in his name and accepted by the early church into the canon. Unfortunately, there is no universal agreement about which letters fall into which category, but most scholars would include Romans, 1 and 2 Corinthians, Galatians, Philippians, 1 Thessalonians, and Philemon in the former group, while some would add Colossians and 2 Thessalonians. Galatians and 1 Thessalonians are thought to be his first letters, while Romans and Philippians are among his last. Those regarded as pseudonymous include the Pastoral Letters (1 and 2 Timothy and Titus), Ephesians (regarded by most scholars as post-Pauline), and possibly Colossians and 2 Thessalonians. Authors who wrote in Paul's name were interpreting his theology for the situations in which they found themselves, so continuing the Pauline tradition. Whether they understood him correctly or not, their work became part of the Pauline canon and was regarded for centuries as the teaching of Paul. Collections of Paul's letters appear to have been made at an early stage (see, e.g., 2 Pet 3:16), but—in a strange irony—it seems to have been Marcion who first drew up a "canon" of authoritative books (consisting of an abbreviated version of the Gospel of Luke and all the Pauline letters apart from the so-called Pastorals). He must have completely misunderstood them, however, since they are at total variance with his own belief, which saw the God of Judaism as a second god.

Paul's Life. Paul was born around the beginning of the Christian era, but knowledge of his life is sketchy since it was not his intention in his letters to impart autobiographical information. He included only details that are relevant to his arguments: from Philippians 3:4–6, for example, it is known that he was born into a Jewish family, could trace his ancestry to the tribe of Benjamin, and was a Pharisee, which meant that he was scrupulous in his observance of the Law; his zeal for Judaism had led him to persecute the Christian church—something he refers to again in 1 Corinthians 15:9 and Galatians 1:13, 23. Luke supplies a few more details, such as that Paul was born in Tarsus of Cilicia but studied in Jerusalem under the famous first-century rabbi Gamaliel (Acts 22:3). This is supported by Paul's exegesis of the scriptures, which betrays the marks of rabbinic training. His letters also demonstrate knowledge of Greek rhetoric, which suggests that he received the Greek education we would expect in a city such as Tarsus. Luke refers several times to the fact that Paul was a Roman citizen (Acts 16:37; 22:25–29; 25:11–12), and it was this that enabled him to appeal to Caesar. Paul never mentions this, but it may well have been true since many Diaspora Jews were Roman citizens. Paul worked at a trade (1 Thess 2:9; 1 Cor 9:3–18), and according to Luke, this was tentmaking (Acts 18:3). Luke also refers to a confrontation between Paul and Gallio, proconsul of Achaia (Acts 18:12); this can be dated, from an inscription, to 51–52 C.E.

Paul had initially persecuted the Christian community (Acts 9:1–14; 22:4–10). The traditional understanding of his story thereafter—his dramatic "conversion" on the road to Damascus and the "three missionary journeys" he undertook before his final voyage to Rome—is based on what Luke tells us in Acts. How much of this is historical is a matter of keen debate, especially as some of it appears to conflict with the references Paul himself makes to his travel plans. Much of Luke's account may be colored by his own agenda, and his accounts of Paul's preaching have to be treated with considerable caution. Paul was clearly Luke's great hero, and he was anxious to demonstrate, among other things, that Paul had offered the gospel to the Jewish people before turning to the Gentiles and that he was a loyal Roman citizen. Any problems he encountered were due to the Jews' rejection of the gospel and their consequent antagonism. Paul's own letters indicate that he visited Jerusalem a couple of times after becoming a Christian and that the other apostles recognized his call to evangelize the Gentiles (Gal 1:18–2:10). After spending some time in Antioch (in Syria), he extended his mission to include towns and cities in what is now Turkey, before moving into Greece, establishing small Christian communities wherever he went. He revisited some of these communities, and he planned to return to Jerusalem with a gift to Christians there from his churches, before setting off to Spain (1 Cor 16:1–9; Rom 15:22–29). Luke's account of this final visit to Jerusalem and his journey to Rome is recorded in Acts 21–28. According to tradition, Paul was beheaded in Rome in about 64 C.E.

Paul the Apostle. Paul believed himself to be an apostle, called by God for the specific task of taking the gospel to the Gentiles, though he was well aware that some Christians disputed his claim. This conviction not only led him to undertake arduous journeys, spreading the gospel throughout Asia Minor and Greece, but also shaped his theology. He makes three brief references to his call. In 1 Corinthians 9:1, his apostleship is linked with the fact that he saw the risen Lord—something he refers to again in 1 Corinthians 15:8, when he includes himself among the witnesses to Christ's resurrection. In Galatians 1:15, he explains the significance of his encounter with the risen Lord, claiming that God had set him apart before his birth and had by grace called him to proclaim his Son among the Gentiles.

The fact that Paul was changed from persecutor to apostle, described by Luke in vivid detail no less than three times (Acts 9:1–9; 22:3–16; 26:4–18), led to this event being known as his "conversion"; but Paul himself clearly thought of it more in terms of a call—an interpretation supported by Luke, who explains each time that Paul was being called to preach the gospel to Gentiles (Acts 9:15; 22:15, 21; 26:4–18). The label "conversion" was an unfortunate one, however, for though it was an appropriate term to describe the dramatic change in Paul, it appeared to suggest that Paul was converted from one religion to another and thus contributed to the hostility between Christianity and Judaism that developed in later centuries. At the time, however, there was no such thing as Christianity; to Paul the persecutor, believers represented a sect of misguided Jews who were guilty of blasphemy. Now he was persuaded that they were right. If the crucified Jesus had indeed been raised from the dead, then the God of Israel had vindicated him and revealed him to be his Son. Paul was in no way abandoning his Jewish faith but embracing what he believed to be its fulfillment.

Common to all three references by Paul to his call is the conviction that he had seen the risen Christ, a conviction that lies at the heart of Paul's theology. In Judaism, future resurrection was one of the marks of the eschatological age. The hope of this resurrection is expressed as early as Isaiah 26:19 and Daniel 12:1–3, and since it became characteristic of Pharisaic piety, it would have formed part of Paul's expectation: perhaps this is why he saw so clearly the implications of Christ's resurrection. The new age had dawned. It was no wonder that the Holy Spirit had been poured out, as Joel 2:28–29 had predicted (Acts 2:17). The prophets had also spoken of a day when the Gentiles would worship God (Isa 56:6–7), and that, too, was beginning to happen, for Gentiles were responding to the gospel and asking to be baptized as Christians: they were even receiving the gift of the Holy Spirit (Acts 10:1–48; Gal 3:1–5). We can understand why Paul began to speak of "a new creation" (2 Cor 5:17), for it seemed that the time of renewal and restoration promised by the prophets (Isa 65:17–25) had arrived.

Paul's Theology. It was Paul's conviction that the new age had broken in with the resurrection of Christ that led him to insist, so passionately, that Gentiles who were baptized "into Christ" were full members of God's holy people and had no need to become Jews first. Paradoxically, it was the Pharisee who had been so rigorous in his devotion to the Jewish Law and who had punished those Jewish believers in Jesus who had transgressed it, who recognized that the requirement of the Law—true holiness—had been fulfilled by Christ (Rom 8:3–4) and so was available for all who were "in him," both Jews and Gentiles. Christ was the *telos* (lit. "end") of the Law in the sense that he had achieved its goal, bringing righteousness to all who believed (Rom 10:4). Since the goal had been reached, the Law was no longer necessary and must not be imposed on those who had been set free from bondage and made children of God. In Galatians, where he was countering the arguments of certain Jewish Christians who had demanded that male Gentile converts be circumcised and take on all the obligations of the Law, Paul passionately argues that Gentile Christians are true "children of Abraham." He repeats his argument, in less strident terms, in Romans.

Like Galatians, all Paul's letters are pastoral in nature, written to deal with the particular problems that confronted his different congregations. This means that they do not set out to present a coherent statement of Christian belief but tend to deal with matters that have been misunderstood (e.g., the incidental reference to the institution of "the Lord's Supper" in 1 Cor 11:17–34) or to encourage Christians who are confronting opposition. The closest Paul came to writing a "systematic theology" is Romans, though even it concentrates on the particular issue of the fate of Israel and the role of the Gentiles within the people of God. So-called theologies of Paul attempt to do what Paul himself never did. Paul's understanding of the gospel was not something that came to him overnight; it developed throughout his ministry as he studied the scriptures anew in the light of Christ and thought through the implications of his faith.

Paul never abandoned the belief that God had called Israel to be his people and had revealed himself to them through the Law and the prophets. The gospel he preached had been "promised beforehand through his prophets in the holy scriptures" (Rom 1:2).

He repeatedly quotes from those scriptures to show how those promises have been fulfilled and insists that his gospel in no way undermines the Law (Rom 3:31). It is Paul's own understanding of those scriptures and of the role of the Law that has changed. Now he recognizes that the Law had been unable to deal with the problem of the power of sin, which had taken hold of humankind through the disobedience of Adam and brought death to everyone. Although it promised life, it had been unable to deliver it because of the frailty of the human condition (what Paul terms "flesh"). But by sending his Son to share our human condition, God has done what the Law could not do and has himself fulfilled in men and women what the Law required (Rom 8:3–4). So sin is replaced by righteousness and death, by life. Paul sees the Law no longer as the solution but as the *witness* to the solution (Rom 3:21).

This belief that Christ was fully human and had shared our human experience—a belief that he expresses in various ways in several of his letters (Rom 8:3; Gal 3:13; 4:4; 2 Cor 5:21; 8:9; Phil 2:7–8)—is fundamental to Paul's understanding of what God has achieved for humanity through Christ. Because the Son of God was born as a human being (Gal 4:4; Rom 8:3), men and women are enabled, through baptism "into Christ," to become "sons of God" (Gal 4:5–7; Rom 8:14–17). Paul's apparently sexist language here has been disguised in most modern translations, which therefore fail to convey Paul's point that Christians now share Christ's relationship to God—that of being "sons." In the ancient world, sons enjoyed privileges of status and inheritance denied to women. But now all who are "in Christ," both men and women, share his status, whether they are Jew or Gentile, slave or free (Gal 3:28). In Romans 8, Paul explains that those who share Christ's sonship share also in his glory (vv. 17, 18, 21, 29), an idea which reappears in Philippians 3:21; because Christ took the form of a slave, was born in human likeness, and shared the human lot, submitting even to death on a cross (Phil 2:6–8, REB), God has not only exalted him but enabled him to raise and glorify those who are "in him" (Phil 2:9–11; 3:21).

This Philippians passage demonstrates the close correlation between what would later be called "incarnation" and "atonement." It was essential that Christ was fully human in order to reverse what had been done by Adam, who by his sin had brought death into the world (Gen 3). Because Christ was human he was subject to death, and died, unjustly condemned as a malefactor (Gal 3:13; 2 Cor 5:21; Phil 2:8). At the same time, God himself was at work in Christ (2 Cor 5:19) since what the Son did, in dying for us, was done in obedience to the will of his father in order that we might be saved by his resurrection life (Rom 5:6–11). Romans 5:12–21 spells out the contrast between the disobedient Adam and the obedient Christ, through whom the grace of God was able to reverse the effects of Adam's sin and bring righteousness and life. These are effective through baptism into Christ Jesus, which means sharing his death to the life of sin and his resurrection to a life of righteousness—a life lived in right relationship with God, obedient to his will (Rom 6:1–19). Those who are baptized into Christ and who share his death and resurrection live no longer according to the "flesh" but according to the Spirit—the Holy Spirit of God, given to every believer (Rom 8:9), and the guarantee of life to come (Rom 8:23).

Christology. Paul commonly refers to Jesus as "Christ," and though this quickly came to be understood as a name, it is impossible that Paul himself would fail to remember that it was the Greek translation of the Hebrew "Messiah." Although he only once refers to Jesus's Davidic descent (Rom 1:3), he clearly believed that Jesus was the promised Messiah of Israel (Rom 9:5). As such, he was the representative of his people. Paul now sees Gentile Christians as members of that people, for he regularly addresses them as "saints" (i.e., those who were consecrated to God, members of his holy people) and applies to them passages once addressed to Israel (e.g., 2 Cor 6:16–18). God's people are now defined by their relationship to Christ, not the Law. To be a follower of Christ was to be a member of a community that is described both as a temple (1 Cor 3:16–17; 2 Cor 6:16) and as the body of Christ (1 Cor 12:12–31; Rom 12:4–5). This had come about not by circumcision and obedience to the Law but by baptism "into Christ," so sharing his status (Gal 3:15–18, 23–29). The

idea that Christians live "in Christ" lies at the heart of Paul's theology.

Paul frequently refers to "our Lord Jesus Christ." The title "Lord" would have been meaningful in the pagan world, where it was used of rulers and gods (1 Cor 8:5) and increasingly of the Roman emperors. For Paul, its significance lay in the fact that it was used in the Hebrew scriptures of God himself, and in 1 Corinthians 8:6 he deliberately transfers the divine title "to Christ." It is probably this name that is referred to in Philippians 2:11. Yet Christ's exaltation is said there to be to the glory of God himself, and Paul never addresses Christ as "God," preferring to speak of him as "Son of God," a term that conveys both unity of purpose and obedience to the Father's will. When the end of all things finally comes, the Son himself will be subject to God (1 Cor 15:28). The title "Son of God" occurs only occasionally—most significantly in passages where he is referring to or summarizing the gospel (Rom 1:3, 4, 9; 5:10; 8:3, 29, 32; 1 Cor 15:28; Gal 1:16; 2:20; 4:4, 6; 1 Thess 1:10). The title is one of great honor yet reminds the reader that Paul's theology remains theocentric; inevitably the gospel focuses on the figure of Christ, and thus appears christocentric, yet as Son Christ is obedient to the Father's will. The gospel is about what God does *through* his Son (Rom 1:1–4; 5:6–11; 8:3–4, 32; Gal 1:15; 4:4–7; cf. 2 Cor 5:16–21).

In 2 Corinthians 4:4 Paul describes Christ as the "image of God," an idea picked up and expounded in Colossians 1:15; both passages go on to refer to the creation narrative of Genesis 1. Unlike Adam, who failed to give glory to God, Christ is God's true image; and those who believe in him reflect his glory and are transformed into his image (2 Cor 3:18; cf. 1 Cor 15:42–49). In him, they become what he is. As both "Son of God" and "image of God," Christ is the pattern of what men and women were created to be and can, recreated in him (2 Cor 5:16), become again (Rom 8:29–30). Both titles describe what Christ is in relation to God, while at the same time depicting him as what men and women were created to be. Christ also takes over what Judaism had affirmed of the Law since he, like the Law, reflects God's glory and embodies the wisdom of God (1 Cor 1:30), by which

God had created the world (e.g., Prov 3:19). This idea developed into the wisdom Christology of Colossians 1:15–20 (cf. 1 Cor 8:6).

Life in Christ. Christ's death and resurrection are the focus of Paul's gospel. He employs many metaphors to describe what they achieve. The most common metaphor uses the verb *dikaioō*, which, though traditionally translated as "to justify," means literally "to right," that is, "to restore to a correct relationship." Other verbs used are *katallassō* ("to reconcile"; Rom 5:10–11; cf. 2 Cor 5:18–20) and *agorazō* ("to buy" and hence "redeem"; Gal 3:13; 4:5; cf. 1 Cor 1:30; Rom 3:24), implying release from slavery. In 1 Corinthians 5:7, Paul describes Christ as our *pascha*, "paschal lamb," while in Romans 3:25 he refers to him as an *hilastērion*, which, though often translated as "a sacrifice of atonement," probably means here "mercy-seat," as in the Old Testament (cf. Heb 9:5)—that is, the *place* of atonement. Sometimes he simply says that Christ died "for us" without further explanation, as in 1 Thessalonians 5:10: Christ "died *for us*, so that…we may live *with him*." But Christians must respond in faith, trusting in what God has done; if they are to share his risen life, they must also *die* with Christ to the old life of sin (Rom 6:1–11). They can also expect to share Christ's suffering and even his death (Rom 8:17; 2 Cor 4:7–12).

Final salvation lies in the future, when Christ will return and the final resurrection will take place (1 Thess 1:10; 1 Cor 15:23–24; Phil 3:20). Christians will have to give an account of their actions (1 Cor 3:10–13; 4:1–5). In the meantime, those who live "in Christ" must live "in newness of life" (Rom 6:4). Paul's ethical teaching is based on the assumption that those who are "in Christ" must become like him. As members of God's holy people they are subject not to the Law given on Sinai but to "the law of Christ" (Gal 6:2), which means "living by the Spirit" (Gal 5:16–18) and allowing the Spirit to bear fruit in their lives (Gal 5:22–26). The gifts of the Spirit are intended to benefit the whole community, which is why love (which should characterize everyone) is paramount (1 Cor 13). Gifts of ministry and leadership bestowed on individuals are intended to benefit all and should not be a source of pride (1 Cor 12). There is no sign of a structured ministry before the Pastorals, but the guidelines given there were highly influential on later patterns of ministry.

Paul's Influence on the Church. In spite of the opposition with which Paul had to deal—from fellow Christians (Gal 2:12; 2 Cor 10–13) as well as opponents outside the church (Phil 1:27–30; 1 Cor 15:32)—his influence was clearly widespread, as Acts testifies and as the composition of letters written in his name demonstrates. In the Pastorals, for example, Paul was regarded as the source of "sound" teaching and ethical guidance. The letters may contain fragments from Paul himself, but doctrinal statements are simply quoted, rather than being integrated into the argument, as was Paul's custom (contrast 1 Tim 3:16 with Phil 2:1–13). Rules are now laid down for "bishops" and "deacons" (1 Tim 3:1–13), and women are forbidden to teach (1 Tim 3:8–15); such restrictions suggest the need for discipline in charismatic societies. Paul, who had protested about living "according to Law," was now turned into the great lawgiver, laying down regulations that sometimes conflict with his teaching elsewhere.

Colossians includes warnings against the kind of philosophical teaching that may have developed into the gnostic beliefs popular in the second century C.E. In that century, too, Jewish Christians were in the minority. In mainstream Christianity, now almost entirely Gentile, the old debates about their admission were forgotten—indeed, Ephesians 2:11–22 suggests that they were already a thing of the past when that letter was written.

Because Paul's letters were addressed to particular situations, they were reinterpreted and even misunderstood when their original context was forgotten. When the debate about the status of Gentiles was over, increasing hostility between "Jews" and "Christians" meant that Galatians and Romans were understood as attacks on Judaism. This tragic misreading of the text contributed, in turn, to the conflict between Judaism and Christianity and encouraged anti-Semitism.

This process was encouraged by Marcion, whose misinterpretation of Paul fostered anti-Semitism and ensured that Christianity and Judaism were seen as separate religions. Meanwhile, early commentaries on Paul's letters were written by the Fathers, who plundered his writings to support their various Christological interpretations; but their comments often owed more to Greek culture than to Judaism. The interpretation of Paul's teaching in relation to every reader's own situation and outlook was inevitable—and became even more significant once his letters were regarded as canonical since their relevance to the life of the church was now seen as vitally important. Just as Paul himself had interpreted the Jewish scriptures in the light of his newfound faith in Christ, so his successors interpreted his writings in terms of their own beliefs and culture. Once Paul's writings were regarded as "scripture," his comments on particular topics were quoted as proof-texts.

One notable commentator on Paul was Irenaeus, who, in attacking the teaching of the Gnostics, insisted that the creator God of the Old Testament was also the Father of Jesus Christ. He developed the doctrine of "recapitulation" (a term taken from Eph 1:10, where the Greek verb is sometimes translated 'to gather up'), which was based on Paul's teaching about the way in which Christ reversed the consequences of Adam's actions. Irenaeus therefore stressed the importance of the incarnation. He summed up its significance in words that express well Paul's own teaching: "Christ became what we are, in order that we might become what he is" (*Haer. V. praef.*).

Once the debate about Gentiles was settled, the church was understood to be the "true Israel" and Paul's teaching about salvation was interpreted in wholly individualistic terms. Augustine, who was greatly influenced by Paul's work, saw the doctrine of grace as central to Pauline theology: through grace, men and women are justified by faith. Augustine developed the doctrine of original sin, based on Paul's teaching in Romans 1:18–23, 5:12–14, and 8:18–23. Since only divine grace can rescue human beings from the grip of evil, Augustine also emphasized the doctrine of predestination, in opposition to Pelagius, who insisted that divine grace does not destroy human freedom. The debate about free will and determinism has continued ever since. Noteworthy among medieval commentators is Peter

Abelard, whose understanding of the atonement was based on Romans. Although he insisted that Christ's crucifixion was essential, he rejected the view that God demanded Jesus's death as a sacrifice and stressed Jesus's supreme love in laying down his life for others—who should imitate his love and so gain salvation. In the Orthodox world, the emphasis was on the themes of incarnation and deification, rather than on judgment and justification.

Paul's Continuing Influence. Luther followed Augustine in seeing "justification by faith" as the heart of Paul's theology, and he made it his own distinctive teaching. Reacting against the teaching of the contemporaneous Catholic Church's widespread practice of granting indulgences, he interpreted the "works of the Law" attacked by Paul as "merit" and emphasized the contrast between "Law" and "gospel." Paul's theology was the core of the gospel for Luther, and at the center of this gospel lay the concept of "faith." His teaching has had a profound influence on Protestant exegesis to this in later centuries. Like Luther, Calvin wrote a commentary on Romans, and the influence of that book is clear in his theology. His logical approach led him to stress certain aspects of Paul's teaching, including the idea of predestination, which developed into the doctrine of double predestination stressed by his followers. Other Reformers, too, wrote commentaries on Romans, as did their Catholic opponents, all trying to prove the truth of their position from Pauline texts.

The invention of the printing press and the Reformers' insistence that the Bible should be available in the vernacular meant that its teaching was available to "ordinary" Christians, for whom it was now the great authority. Paul's letters were seen as his word to *them*, and the original context of his letters was forgotten: this provided spiritual comfort but also, in time, inevitably caused problems. Such problems arose because Paul's teaching was grounded in the social context of his day and included his instructions to women to have their heads covered when leading worship (1 Cor 11:1–10), his references to homosexual activity (e.g., Rom 1:26–27), and his instruction to the Romans to "be subject to the governing authorities" (Rom 13:1)—instructions that led many twentieth-century German Christians to submit to the National Socialist state.

With the Enlightenment came the attempts of F. C. Baur and the Tübingen school to see Paul in historical perspective, though the influence of Luther's interpretation remained. For them, there was a total opposition between Jewish Christianity and Paul's law-free gospel, and it was only in the second century that a synthesis was reached and early Catholicism emerged. Like Luther's interpretation, this reading was influenced by the contemporary zeitgeist, being indebted to Hegel. The nineteenth century was notable, also, for the emergence of the kenotic theory, which was based on Philippians 2:7. What did Paul mean by saying that Christ "emptied himself"? The answer, it was suggested, was that he abandoned the attributes of deity—omnipotence, omniscience, and cosmic Lordship. Those who advocated this theory were wrestling with the problems of reconciling the statements about Christ's divinity in the creeds with the belief in a truly human Jesus.

The influence of contemporary scholarship from fields outside the New Testament is demonstrated by the interpretation of Wilhelm Bousset, at the beginning of the twentieth century. He regarded Paul as a Hellenist, influenced by the mystery religions, and as the "founder" of Christianity. In contrast, scholars such as Albert Schweitzer emphasized his Jewish heritage, exploring apocryphal and pseudepigraphical writings and stressing the importance of Jewish eschatological hopes. Rudolf Bultmann attempted to demythologize Paul in order to make him comprehensible to his contemporaries. Karl Barth's influential *Commentary on Romans*, similarly, offered an interpretation of Paul for the twentieth century. Anti-Semitism influenced some interpretations, whether deliberately or unknowingly, detaching Paul—like Jesus—from his Jewish roots. In reaction, the Jewishness of Paul was reaffirmed, by G. F. Moore, whose insights were developed by W. D. Davies (who pointed to Paul's links with rabbinic teaching) and E. P. Sanders (who undermined the Lutheran interpretation of Paul by attacking the view that first-century Judaism relied on merit). Galatians and Romans were now seen by many commentators to be primarily concerned with the status of Gentiles within the people of God, rather than with an attack on "legalism." As a result, scholarly interest focused on Paul's Christology in relation to Judaism and the Roman world, the social context of his ethical teaching, and his use of rhetoric.

The way in which Paul is understood depends to a large extent on the presuppositions of his interpreters. A prime example of this is the modern debate on the meaning of the phrase *pistis Christou* (lit. "faith of Christ"). This has traditionally been understood to refer to the believer's faith *in* Christ, but many modern commentators maintain that it refers (primarily if not exclusively) to the faith of Christ himself, a faith that is shared by those who are "in him." Though often stated in grammatical terms, the real debate emerges from a renewed emphasis on the humanity of Jesus and a realization of the corporate nature of salvation, together with a new understanding of the relationship between Christology and soteriology in Paul. Once again, we see how contemporary theological understanding influences the way in which Paul is interpreted and how Pauline exegesis, in turn, influences contemporary theology.

Paul's enormous influence on Christian theology is a result of the fact that his letters (and those written in his name) were included in the canon. Yet it is their canonical status that has led to his words being quoted out of context and applied in ways that are far from Paul's original intention.

[*See also* Deutero-Pauline Letters; Gentiles; Grace; *and* Pauline Letters.]

BIBLIOGRAPHY

Babcock, William S., ed. *Paul and the Legacies of Paul.* Dallas: Southern Methodist University Press, 1990.

Baird, William. *History of New Testament Research.* Vol. 1: *From Deism to Tübingen*, Vol. 2: *From Jonathan Edwards to Rudolf Bultmann.* Minneapolis: Augsburg, 1992–2003.

Barth, Karl. *The Epistle to the Romans.* Translated by E. C. Hoskyns. London: Oxford University Press, 1933.

Baur, Ferdinand C. *Paul the Apostle of Jesus Christ: His Life and Works, His Epistles and Teachings.* 2d ed. 2 vols. Translated by Eduard Zeller. Peabody, Mass.: Hendrickson, 2003. First published 1873–1875.

Bousset, Wilhelm. *Kyrios Christos: Geschichte des Christusglaubens von den anfängen des christentums bis Irenaeus.* Forschungen zur Religion und Literatur des Alten und Neuen Testaments 4. Göttingen, Germany: Vandenhoeck & Ruprecht, 1913.

Bultmann, Rudolf. *Theology of the New Testament.* Vol. 1. Translated by K. Grobel. New York: Charles Scribner's Sons, 1954.

Davies, W. D. *Paul and Rabbinic Judaism: Some Rabbinic Elements in Pauline Theology.* 2d ed. London: SPCK, 1955.

Dunn, James D. G. *The Theology of Paul the Apostle.* Grand Rapids, Mich.: Eerdmans; Edinburgh: T&T Clark, 1998.

Furnish, Victor Paul. *Theology and Ethics in Paul.* Nashville, Tenn.: Abingdon, 1968.

Hays, Richard. *The Faith of Jesus Christ: An Investigation of the Narrative Substructure of Galatians 3:1–4:11.* 2d ed. SBL Dissertation Series 56. Grand Rapids, Mich.: Eerdmans, 2002.

Hooker, Morna D. *From Adam to Christ: Essays on Paul.* Cambridge, U.K.: Cambridge University Press, 1990.

Hooker, Morna D. *Paul: A Short Introduction.* Oxford: Oneworld, 2003.

Hooker, Morna D. *Paul: A Beginner's Guide.* Oxford: Oneworld, 2008.

Moore, George Foot. *Judaism in the First Centuries of the Christian Era: The Age of the Tannaim.* 3 vols. Cambridge, Mass.: Harvard University Press, 1927–1930.

Murphy-O'Connor, Jerome. *Paul: A Critical Life.* Oxford: Oxford University Press, 1996.

Neill, Stephen, and Tom Wright. *The Interpretation of the New Testament 1861–1986.* 2d ed. New York: Oxford University Press, 1988.

Sampley, J. Paul, ed. *Paul in the Greco-Roman World.* Harrisburg, Penn.: Trinity Press International, 2003.

Sanders, E. P. *Paul and Palestinian Judaism: A Comparison of Patterns of Religion.* London: SCM, 1977.

Schweitzer, Albert. *The Mysticism of Paul the Apostle.* 2d ed. English translation of *Die Mystik des Apostels Paulus* (London: A&C Black, 1953).

Stendahl, Krister. *Paul Among Jews and Gentiles.* London: SCM, 1977.

Westerholm, Stephen, ed. *The Blackwell Companion to Paul.* Oxford: Wiley-Blackwell, 2011.

Whiteley, D. E. H. *The Theology of St. Paul.* 2d ed. Oxford: Blackwell, 1974.

Wiles, Maurice F. *The Interpretation of St. Paul's Epistles in the Early Church.* Cambridge, U.K.: Cambridge University Press, 1967.

Wolter, Michael. *Paulus: Ein Grundriss seiner Theologie.* Neukirchen-Vluyn, Germany: Neukirchener Theologie, 2011.

Ziesler, John. *Pauline Christianity.* Rev. ed. Oxford and New York: Oxford University Press, 1990.

Morna D. Hooker

PAULINE LETTERS

Discussion of Paul's letters has often focused on identifying the central theme or doctrine of Paul's theology. The dominant view, especially among Protestants, has been that the center of Paul's theology is the doctrine of justification by faith. Some, however, have suggested other centers, such as a mystical relationship with Christ (Schweitzer) or the story of God's keeping covenant with God's people (Wright, 2013).

The dominance of Protestant acceptance of justification by faith as the central Pauline doctrine can be traced to the founders of the Protestant Reformation. Both Luther and Calvin identified it as the pivotal doctrine in Paul's theology. Support for identifying this doctrine as the center of Paul's theology came from the common understanding of Romans as Paul's *magnum opus*, the place in which he objectively set out his theology. Since justification is a prominent metaphor for how Christ facilitates the proper relationship with God in Romans, it was seen as the center of Paul's theology. This emphasis on finding a center of Paul's theology assumes, at times unintentionally, that Paul works as a systematic theologian and that his letters reflect the things most important in his theological system. But the content of Paul's letters is determined more by the situation they address than by a desire to set out a theological system. While some interpreters still use Romans as an outline of Paul's theology, others argue that Paul's theology can be understood more clearly if one approaches each letter individually, without assuming a particular center or allowing a single letter to dominate. This essay adopts the latter approach so that a full range of Paul's thought can emerge. I discuss the letters in chronological order, as best as can be determined, treating only those letters that are accepted by nearly all New Testament scholars as genuinely from Paul's hand.

First Thessalonians. Paul's earliest extant letter addresses two primary issues, both important for the earliest church: the meaning of persecution (1 Thess 3:1–5) and the fate of believers who die before the return of Christ (4:13–18). The experience of persecution called into question early church members' decision to worship only God, rejecting the worship of other gods who were thought to support the welfare of prevailing social and political systems. Hardships were commonly understood as signs that the gods were displeased. Persecution led some early church members to wonder if God was displeased with them or if they made a mistake in deciding to worship only God. Paul responds by reminding the Thessalonians that he and all of God's people are persecuted (1:6; 2:2, 14; 3:4). While this may assure them that they are God's people, it does not explain why God's people suffer.

Paul's response suggests that he understands persecution from within an apocalyptic worldview in which the powers of evil rule the economic, political, and social systems of the world. People who live for God reject the values embodied and imposed by those powers and systems. When those values are rejected, their proponents respond with coercion aimed at gaining conformity (2:18—3:3). That coercion is the persecution believers endure. Paul expects this to be the state of the world until the coming catastrophic intervention of God at Christ's Second Coming. Then God will regain control of the cosmos, vindicate the faithful, and punish those who inflict suffering on them (1:9–10). By these end-time acts God will be recognized as just and loving, as believers proclaim. Until then, the persecuted are encouraged that what they now endure will be more than worth it in the end (5:6–11).

The Thessalonians' second issue concerns eschatology directly. Some believed that the Parousia (Christ's Second Coming) would occur before anyone in their church had died (4:13). Paul's response sets out a chronology of the Second Coming's events that privileges the dead over the living. He asserts that the dead are raised before the living are transformed into the kind of existence given the resurrected. Thus, both the dead and the living will experience life in the presence of God.

Rather than speaking of its imminence, Paul emphasizes that this coming is unpredictable—it will come "like a thief in the night" (5:2). Such uncertainty occasions ethical exhortation: believers must live so that they are always ready for Christ's return. Paul regularly uses the Parousia and coming judgment to support his calls for proper living (1:9–10; 3:11–13; 4:3–6; 5:4–11, 23–24).

Eschatology plays a central role in this letter. It supports Paul's interpretation of persecution as he looks forward to vindication of the faithful at the judgment (1:9–10; 2:18–19). His description of the sequence of events at the Parousia assures the Thessalonians that death will not keep them from enjoying the blessings of life with God. This assurance demands proper ethical living because the Second Coming includes a judgment of all.

First Corinthians. The letter of 1 Corinthians addresses a raft of problems. Before attending to individual issues, Paul addresses the larger problem of the Corinthians' factiousness (1:11–17; 3:2–9, 21–23), arguing that it is an indication that they misunderstand spirituality. Some in the first century thought that contact with a god enhanced social power and financial success (Heliodorus, *Aeth.* 127; Ovid, *Epistulae ex Ponto* [Letters from the Black Sea], 1.1.45–58; Plutarch, Moralia, *On the Fortune of the Romans*, sec. 323F). Accepting this understanding of spirituality, the Corinthians evidently believed that Spirit-endowed church leaders should have impressive personalities and be able to take charge in ways demanding deference. Apparently, they selected leaders who had these abilities.

Paul responds by making "the message [or 'word' more literally] of the cross" (1:18) the epitome of spirituality. He argues that believers must evaluate all things through the lens of the cross. For Paul, the cross reveals who God is and how God wants God's people to live. It exemplifies the paradigm of putting the good of others ahead of one's own good. Jesus sets this example by his willingness to die for others. God vindicates this way of life by raising him from the dead. Paul defines true spirituality as a willingness to adopt the pattern of life epitomized in Christ's crucifixion. This manner of life diametrically opposed the Corinthians' expectations of benefits from contact with a god, but Paul contends it is what the Spirit enables believers to do.

Paul brings this construction of spirituality to bear not only on the question of leadership but also on how believers should conduct themselves in relation to one another. Believers must deny themselves the advantages of attending meals at temples because their presence could harm a fellow believer (chs. 8–9, esp. 8:7–13). Among the reasons they are all to eat the same food at the Lord's Supper is to affirm their oneness; no advantages should be claimed by emphasizing differences in social status (11:21–22). When exercising spiritual gifts in worship, the Corinthians should seek those gifts that build up the community rather than those that enhance the experience or prestige of the gifted (14:1–3). Citing what seems to be a Corinthian slogan, "All things are lawful for me" (6:12; 10:23), Paul qualifies its original meaning by adding "but not all things are beneficial" and "not all things build up." With these additions Paul orients decisions about conduct toward their effect on others.

Likewise, Paul affirms the way that believers should value one another. "The strong" must not attend feasts at temples because they might influence others to violate their faith by attending. Such harm overrides any exercisable "right" because fellow believers are those "for whom Christ died" (8:11). Believers must make moral decisions that are consistent with recognizing others as so important that Christ died for them.

Another prominent feature in 1 Corinthians is Paul's understanding of the church as a holy community. Replicating the ministry of Jesus, Paul sees the church as reaching out to sinners but also demanding genuine repentance that includes changing how they live. Believers must reflect the holiness of God. Paul instructs the church to expel a member whose sexual conduct is unacceptable because his presence threatens to contaminate the community (5:1–8). Business dealings among church members must be honest because swindlers have no place in a holy community (6:1–11). The importance of holiness is evident in the way Paul typically refers to believers in his letters: they are saints, a holy people, a people set apart

(Rom 1:7; 1 Cor 1:2; 3:16-17; 6:1-2; 14:33; 16:1; 15; 2 Cor 1:1; 9:12; 13:12; Phil 1:1; 4:21). Part of the reason for this emphasis on holiness is Paul's conviction that God's Holy Spirit lives in believers. In both personal and communal behavior, believers must manifest that presence of God (6:9–11, 18–20).

Paul's emphasis on spirituality in no way denigrates bodily existence; to the contrary, holy living invests bodily life with significance. Further, 1 Corinthians 15 is a discussion of the resurrection that affirms its bodily nature. Paul views the believer's resurrection existence as bodily; it conforms to the nature of Christ's resurrection. Resurrection bodies are composed of incorruptible material: not made up of "flesh and blood" yet a body, not a disembodied soul. Despite some seemingly ascetic tendencies (e.g., privileging celibacy; 7:8, 25–35, 40), Paul judges bodily existence as the proper way for humans to serve and to be in the presence of God.

While Paul's extensive discussion of spirituality and its manifestation in personal and communal ethics draws on Christ as the exemplar, the Christology of this letter includes other affirmations about Christ. Christ is the eschatological judge whom God has exalted as ruler of the cosmos (1 Cor 15:24–28). While God grants Christ this position, Christ remains subordinate to God. In addition, Christ's death serves as the means by which God forgives sin (1 Cor 15:3–5). Citing traditional authority for this claim, Paul offers no atonement theory; he simply accepts such a belief as foundational for the church's existence and for its soteriology.

Christology, then, is the basis on which Paul grounds the central arguments and exhortations of 1 Corinthians. Most often in this letter Christ is the exemplar for what God expects of God's people. The cross establishes the correct pattern for spirituality and ethics. Although remaining subordinate to God, Christ is the key figure in Paul's pneumatology, eschatology, and soteriology. The Spirit serves as the means of God's presence in believers' lives, granting gifts and demanding appropriate behavior. Paul assumes that the Corinthians believe in Christ's Parousia, which will include judgment of all, including believers. A life of holiness is an ethical expectation that grows out of both the Spirit's presence in one's life and the coming judgment.

Second Corinthians. While the historical occasion of 2 Corinthians is different from that of 1 Corinthians, the basic theological issues remain the same. Tracing the progress of Paul's debate is complicated by questions about this document's literary integrity. Despite the probable presence of multiple letters in the canonical 2 Corinthians, the practical issue overriding all involves the qualifications of genuine apostles. In this debate the theological question concerns the Spirit. Previous letters to the Corinthians failed to move them to reject the cultural expectation that contact with a god makes one impressive and powerful in word and deed. Now teachers who accept this perspective have arrived. Claiming the status of apostles, they call the church to reject Paul because of his weak demeanor and to accept and support them as their apostles because they manifest the Spirit's powerful presence.

No longer using the phrase "word of the cross," Paul continues to argue that the presence of God is seen in a willingness to put the good of others ahead of one's own good. He clarifies his view by using the death and resurrection of Christ as the dominant metaphor. This metaphor works in two ways. In some places Paul says that he and believers in general suffer now but will receive life and power after that suffering (13:4; cf. Rom 8:18–23). Elsewhere and predominantly, power and weakness appear simultaneously. Paul's sufferings and voluntary acceptance of disadvantage manifest weakness, but through this weakness the power and love of God are seen. His weakness demonstrates that any good that comes from his work is accomplished through God's power, the same power by which God raised the crucified Jesus. Adoption of this paradigm is required of those who look to the death and resurrection of Christ as the definitive revelation of God. In fact, God has given Paul a "thorn in the flesh" to make it obvious that it is God's power, not Paul's, that is visible in his apostolic labors (12:8–10).

Paul sets his apostleship within the framework of his eschatology. Early believers interpreted the resurrection of Christ as the inauguration of the end times, but they struggled to understand how to live in the "last days," which now extended over 20 years. All saw the gift of the Spirit as a blessing of the last days, even as they wondered what its presence meant for present life. Paul describes existence in the eschatological time as a "new creation" (5:16–17). Being that new creation demands a complete reorientation of values, determined by God's self-revelation in the death and resurrection of Christ. Thus, believers' participation in the eschatological time demands their recognition that God's power works through the weakness of putting the good of others first. Accepting this eschatological outlook, then, requires them to acknowledge that Paul is a genuine apostle.

The central theological affirmation of 2 Corinthians is that the lives of apostles and leaders—and by implication all believers—must conform to the death and resurrection of Christ. The revelation of God in that event is determinative for life in the eschatological new creation. Thus, the Spirit works through weakness and humility rather than through power and prestige. In 2 Corinthians the theological topics of pneumatology, eschatology, and ecclesial ethics are all intertwined and shaped decisively by the death and resurrection of Christ.

Galatians. Galatians addresses the place of Gentiles among the people of God. The specific question is whether Gentile church members should accept circumcision and observe the holy days and perhaps the food laws of Judaism. The early church's larger discussion of this issue revolved around questions about the identity markers for the people of God: Were Gentile believers in Christ fully members of the people of God without becoming proselytes to Judaism by being circumcised and taking up traditional Torah observance? It is unclear whether those whom Galatians opposes have such a theological agenda, but Paul's response is thoroughly theological.

Paul sets justification through Torah observance in opposition to justification through Christ (2:15–21). While this opposition has often been read as a contrast between justification by works and justification by faith, this skews Paul's argument. Paul contrasts two assertions; presumably, his readers agree with both. All agree that no one is justified (i.e., found not guilty before God) through observance of the Torah, and all agree that believers are justified through Christ. Jews of the first century saw the Law as the guide to fulfilling their part of the covenant relationship with God, not as a way to gain salvation. They knew their relationship with God was initiated by God's grace. Paul acknowledges that Jews know that justification does not come through Torah observance (2:15–16) yet caricatures the function of the Law: observing the "works of the Law" is the opposite of having faith (3:10–14).

Paul uses the phrase *pistis Iēsou Christou* to make a second assertion about justification. This phrase is usually translated "faith in Jesus Christ," but many interpreters think that a better rendering is "faithfulness of Jesus Christ." Thus, Paul would be asserting that justification comes to believers because of Christ's faithful obedience to the will of God. This interpretation does not remove the faith of the believer from the equation (2:16 notes that the readers believe), but it does shift the emphasis of the passage: the work of Christ rather than the act of the believer is central. Whichever is the more correct reading, Paul assumes that all his readers agree.

What his readers do not agree about is the contrast between these assertions and the conclusion Paul draws from it. He contends that acknowledgment of justification apart from "works of the Law" requires that Gentiles not accept circumcision for church membership. He argues that if Gentiles observe the Law as Jews do, their actions demonstrate that they believe in justification *by their own obedience* rather than by Christ's. While they may not have understood their actions in this way, Paul insists that it is the necessary implication. Gentile acceptance of circumcision and observance of Jewish holy days constitute a lack of trust in Christ's work of salvation. It thereby severs one's relationship with Christ to such a degree that one is no longer among the saved (5:4).

These radical oppositions are sometimes rhetorical exaggerations. Paul moderates and qualifies disparaging comments about the Law (e.g., 3:23–25) in the less polemical setting of Romans. His statements about the Law in Galatians do not reflect a carefully balanced theological position. He overdraws contrasts

to help his argument succeed because he believes so much is at stake.

The Spirit also figures prominently in the letter's argument. Paul asserts that possession of the Spirit alone is sufficient evidence to prove that Gentiles do not need to become Jewish proselytes (3:1–5). Because the Spirit's presence proves that God already has an intimate and saving relationship with them, the gift of the Spirit demonstrates that Gentiles do not need to begin Torah observance. Furthermore, the Spirit evokes the recognition that a person is a genuine heir of God's promises (4:6–7). Paul even asserts that the indwelling Spirit makes the Law unnecessary because the Spirit leads believers to do God's will (5:16–18).

Paul also draws on the meaning of baptism to oppose Gentiles' adoption of Torah observance. Quoting a baptismal liturgy (3:26–28), Paul reminds them that in baptism they take on the identity of Christ. This is crucial because Christ is the heir of the promise to Abraham. Believers' incorporation into Christ, then, makes them heirs as well. As heirs they receive God's blessings (3:29–4:7).

Finally, Paul argues that Gentiles do not need this kind of Torah observance because they live in the eschatological era. Markers such as circumcision convey no status because believers are a "new creation" (6:15). The era of the Law's functioning as the primary guide to serving God has passed. Because the coming of Christ opens new avenues of knowing the will of God for life, Gentile believers do not need it (3:23–4:7). Although Paul does not speak of functions the Law continues to have in Galatians, in Romans he speaks of it as "holy and righteous and good" (7:12). Christ-believing Jews continue to be Torah-observant as their way of being the people of God. And the Law continues to be the word of God, as seen in the many times Paul cites it as authoritative. He can even say that, while circumcision means nothing, "keeping the commandments of God is everything" (1 Cor 7:19). So the Law provides guidance, but observance of those aspects that distinguish Jews from Gentiles no longer determines who is counted among the people of God.

Galatians is well known for its soteriology, particularly for its assertion that faith is the means of attaining justification. But Paul also uses several other theological arguments to assert that Gentiles must not accept circumcision and Jewish food laws. The presence of the Spirit and the meaning of baptism provide important arguments for his view. Eschatology again plays an important role as Paul contends that the new age ends some kinds of usefulness for the Law.

Romans. Romans, the only letter Paul wrote to a church he did not found, has at least three distinct purposes: (1) to introduce Paul and his gospel so that he, as apostle to the Gentiles, can represent predominantly Gentile churches in Jerusalem (1:5–7; 15:14–19, 25–32), (2) to ask his readers for aid in expanding his mission to Spain (15:23–24, 28–29), and (3) to address a conflict between the Jewish and Gentile members of that church (chs. 14–15). To accomplish these purposes, Paul must lay out his gospel because this church knows him only by reputation. Paul shapes his presentation of himself and his teaching to accomplish these objectives.

As Paul introduces himself by describing the human need for the gospel and how the gospel addresses it, he has a constant eye on the question of the place of Israel in God's plan—a plan that involves the inclusion of Gentiles among the "people of God." This concern, as well as the need to encourage the Roman church to accept him as its apostle, substantively shapes his presentation of himself and the gospel.

Romans 1:16–17 sets out the central themes of the letter. As much as the gospel is about Jesus, Paul identifies it as the "power of *God*." It is a message about what God has done to provide salvation. Romans sets out a consistently theocentric presentation of the gospel. The apostle to the Gentiles asserts that the gospel is for all people, while affirming the continuing priority of Jews: the gospel is for "Jews first." Paul returns to this theme most explicitly in chapters 9–11, and many interpreters see it as a dominant undercurrent of the whole letter. Although exegetes disagree about the meaning of Israel's priority, all acknowledge that it is part of Paul's gospel. Paul also describes the gospel as a demonstration of the "righteousness of God," which in Romans 1 refers to a wide range of God's characteristics: most importantly God's holiness, justice, love, mercy, and faithfulness.

These attributes of God play major roles in the letter's arguments.

Paul's first tack in his explication of the gospel asserts that all people are guilty before God and thus deserve condemnation. Gentiles are guilty because they ignore what could be known about God in nature, choose to worship other things as gods, and indulge in grossly immoral behavior (1:19–32). Even Gentiles who reject the immoral behavior of their fellows engage in conduct they know is wrong and, thus, also deserve condemnation (2:1–16). Jews fall under a similar judgment because they know God's will through the Torah but fail to live in accord with it (2:17—3:8). Therefore, all deserve God's condemnation (3:9–20).

Having set out the human condition in such dark terms, Paul offers an eschatological and Christological solution. "From now on"—that is, in the eschatological time—all who trust in Christ's faithful obedience to God receive forgiveness (3:21–26). The work of Christ allows God to remain righteous while forgiving those who justly deserve condemnation. Christ's work allows God to restore humans to right relationship in a manner that is consistent with, even attested by, how God was already known in the Hebrew scriptures (3:21).

But Paul also recognizes a more systemic problem that separates God and humans. In his eschatological scheme, the forces of evil control the world and corrupt its social, economic, and political systems. These systems shape the world in such a way that humans are forced to participate in sin. Through sin, Paul argues, "death" (envisioned as an evil power) reigns in the world (5:12–21). It and other such powers have enslaved humans (6:5–23). Even as Christ frees believers from this enslavement, they must continue to live in this world, where they are still subject to evil's onslaughts.

Working within the apocalyptic eschatology that is also known in Second Temple Judaism (e.g., 2 Esd 3:22), Paul recognizes a yet deeper problem: there is something within humans that wants to sin (7:7–25). The only escape from this desperate situation is the eschatological gift of the Spirit that enables believers to live for God rather than capitulating to evil desires (8:1–17).

While Western theology has heightened attention to the theme of human guilt through acts of sin, Paul's discussion manifests a more complex understanding of the human dilemma. In this multifaceted analysis of the human condition, Paul offers a multidimensional eschatological solution that is grounded in the work of Christ that brings forgiveness, reconciliation, and the power to resist evil.

This complex analysis of the human condition and God's response to it faces a significant obstacle: by not recognizing the new act of God in Christ, Israel has rejected the gospel. This fact challenges the validity of Paul's gospel because it challenges the righteousness of God. God had called Israel as God's people. If the gospel suggests that God has abandoned them, then God is not trustworthy. If God has not been faithful to Israel, then believers in Christ must question whether God will be faithful to them. In a contorted and pained argument, Paul defends the faithfulness of God to Israel while also declaring that all salvation is in Christ (chs. 9–11). In the end, Paul is not sure how to reconcile those two foundational claims. Thus, this discussion ends with a doxology that expresses Paul's inability to know the mind of God and yet expresses his confidence that both claims are true (11:33–36). The gospel remains a demonstration of God's righteousness.

Romans' concluding chapters illustrate another important aspect of Paul's theology. For Paul, faith is not simply assent to a set of beliefs; it is an orientation of life. In Romans (chs. 12–15) and in nearly all his letters, he makes it clear that the claim to have faith is valid only if one's manner of life reflects the character of God seen in Christ.

The complex situation that Romans addresses led Paul to compose a different sort of letter from the others that we have from his hand. He gives a fuller analysis of the human situation and the gospel's response to it. Paul does not present a systematic theology; rather, he presents these ideas in coherent ways that help him accomplish the goals of the letter. He shapes this explication of his teaching to meet the letter's occasion.

Consistent with what is found in other letters, the primary actor in the gospel is God. Christ is God's agent of revelation and salvation. Christ both enables a right relationship with God and empowers believers to live for God as they are strengthened by the eschatological gift of the Spirit which comes to them through Christ. The apocalyptic interpretation of the present and the future, witnessed in other letters, shapes Paul's understanding of the human dilemma and God's response. An emphasis on justification distinguishes Romans and Galatians from other letters, which emphasize different metaphors to explain how Christ brings salvation and proper relationship with God. Paul's treatment of the need to privilege the good of others also echoes his more detailed responses to ecclesial conflicts in earlier letters. While it is present (12:10; 14:1–4; 15:1–3), there is also less use of the cross and resurrection as the paradigm for proper behavior within the church (15:1–3).

Philippians. While Philippians mentions joy and rejoicing repeatedly (e.g., 1:4, 18–19, 25; 2:17–18, 28–29; 4:2), its primary purpose is to address a conflict between two leaders (4:2–3). Even though this problem is mentioned explicitly only in chapter 4, Paul addresses it from the letter's outset.

The incarnation, death, and exaltation of Christ play a decisive role in Philippians but not as part of a discussion of soteriology or even of Christology. Paul quotes a liturgy that recounts those events. It is the primary support for the letter's central exhortation. Paul tells the Philippians they must adopt the "mind of Christ," seen in his descent from heaven and death. They do this by considering fellow believers better than themselves and by putting the interest of others ahead of their own (2:3–11). As in the Corinthian correspondence, the incarnation and death of Christ serve primarily as the paradigm for believers' attitudes and conduct. Philippians' central rhetorical strategy is to set out examples that the recipients (and especially the disputatious leaders) are to imitate. Christ is the fundamental exemplar, but Paul also presents his acceptance of persecutions and the lives of Timothy and Epaphroditus as examples for the Philippians to imitate. They serve this purpose because they follow Christ's example.

The liturgy about Christ continues past his death to emphasize that exaltation followed his willingness to privilege the good of others (2:8–11). Similarly, Paul looks forward to life with God after he endures difficulties (1:21–26) and reminds the Philippians of coming judgment and the future glorification of the faithful (1:28–30; 2:12–17; 3:17–21). The example of Christ demonstrates that God vindicates Christ's pattern of life. God's exaltation of Christ demonstrates that this countercultural and counterintuitive manner of life pleases God.

Eschatology plays a significant role in this letter. The coming judgment on persecutors and the wicked offers assurance to those who are suffering (1:28; 2:14–15; 3:18–19). Alongside these assurances are reminders that believers also face judgment and, thus, should conduct their lives with that reality in mind (2:12–16). Further, the hope of the resurrection demonstrates the superior value of life in Christ (3:7–11) and of the manner of life it demands (3:20–21). There is also an element of realized eschatology in Philippians. The steadfastness of believers is an eschatological sign of their salvation (1:27–30); Christ already reigns in heaven, the place where believers already have citizenship (3:20). By speaking of believers as citizens of a different realm, Paul reminds them of a new identity that they have through Christ.

The liturgy of 2:6–11 demonstrates that the church of the mid-50s already had a complex Christology. They proclaim Christ as a preexistent being and identify his condescension and death as the central elements of his saving activities. While proclaiming a preincarnation existence in "the form of God" (2:6), the liturgy also envisions Christ as subordinate to God; obedient to God (2:8), he is exalted and given his position as ruler of the cosmos by God (2:9–10).

Christ's death and resurrection in Philippians functions primarily as an exemplar for conduct within the church. Still, Paul believes in a Christ who was preexistent and brings believers salvation through the defeat of the powers of evil. Christ is also the initiator of the eschatological age: the one to whom all beings in the cosmos are ultimately answerable, including believers who are to remember that accountability as they live together as the church. Yet in all of this, God remains the primary actor. It is God who exalts Christ, and Christ remains subordinate in his

obedience, which has as its goal to bring honor to God. Philippians again shows Paul privileging the good of the community over the good of the individual. By supporting this ecclesial ethic with the liturgy of 2:6–11, Paul makes eschatology and Christology crucial elements of his argument.

Philemon. The short letter to Philemon concerns the return of a slave to his owner. Though Paul does little theological reasoning here, preferring other means of persuasion, some underlying theological tenets are evident.

The references to Philemon's love (vv. 4, 7) and Paul's basing of his appeal on love (v. 9) suggest that this is a recognized and foundational sanction for ethical decisions. It appears that love was recognized as a cardinal virtue in Paul's churches.

Another theological assumption involves the way fellow believers are to value one another. Paul says that Onesimus is no longer a slave but now a "beloved brother" (vv. 15–16). This assertion assumes that believers identify one another as family members who have the same status because all are brothers and sisters. While there is no development of this ecclesiology in Philemon, this reference to regarding slaves as brothers indicates that the church's valuing of members ran counter to cultural expectations when it valued slaves as peers of freeborn people.

Conclusions. This survey suggests that Paul draws on various elements of his theology to address the situation each church faces. In no letter does he simply teach about a theological topic for its own sake; each letter responds to debated issues or a church's conduct. Accordingly, these letters do not provide an easy outline of Paul's theology. He addresses topics based on what a church needs to consider, not because they are the most important elements in his theology. Still, from these letters one can discern some foundational components of Pauline thought.

In many places Christ serves as the exemplar for the conduct of believers. The orientation of privileging the good of others over one's own good, the way of living seen most clearly in the cross and resurrection, is fundamental in Paul's understanding of the faith. Thus, in imitation of Christ, Paul's ethics focuses on the community's good. The good of the individual is consistently superseded by the good of others, especially by the good of the whole church. Such regular attention to this manner of living indicates that ecclesial ethics is a crucial part of Paul's theological reflections with his churches.

At the same time, the work of Christ, particularly his death and resurrection, is the means of forgiveness and right relationship with God. No single metaphor, not even justification, dominates Paul's exposition of how this works. While justification is prominent in Romans and Galatians, it is absent from other letters, which speak of reconciliation or rescue from the powers. Paul sees what Christ has done as the means of right relationship with God, but there is no single way of describing it that captures all that he thinks it accomplishes and no single metaphor that dominates his description of it.

Throughout Paul's letters Christ is the inaugurator of the eschatological time. It is impossible to understand Paul's theology without recognizing that it is thoroughly eschatological. The church lives in the new age initiated by Christ. It enjoys the presence of the Spirit as an eschatological sign of God's presence. Paul constantly orients his churches to the future victory of God and its accompanying vindication of the faithful.

The presence of the Spirit as an eschatological gift is another constant in Paul's conversations with his churches. The Spirit's activity is evidence that the end-time has begun: it confirms believers' relationship with God and enables them to live for God. The Spirit also reveals the will of God and provides gifts that support the church's life and growth.

While Christ serves in such crucial ways, Paul's theology remains theocentric. Belief that the God of Israel is the only true God, the creator and rightful ruler of the whole cosmos, undergirds all of Paul's theological reflections. Christ is always the agent of God and remains subordinate to God. It is God who raises Christ from the dead and exalts him to the place of lord of the cosmos. Christ is the means through which God brings salvation and so reclaims the world for God's self.

While various letters emphasize different aspects, Paul's theology is remarkably consistent. Although one cannot discern a fully systematic theology of Paul, one can see many indispensable elements of his system of belief as he responds to the issues raised in his churches.

[*See also* Apocalypticism; Apostleship; Atonement; Baptism; Christology; Ecclesiology; Eschatology; Ethics, Biblical; Gospel; Holy Spirit; Justice, Justification, and Righteousness; Lord's Supper; Paul; Soteriology; *and* Torah.]

BIBLIOGRAPHY

Bassler, Jouette. *Thessalonians, Philippians, Galatians, Philemon. Pauline Theology.* Vol. 1. Minneapolis: Fortress, 1991.

Bassler, Jouette. *Navigating Paul: An Introduction to Key Theological Concepts.* Louisville, Ky.: Westminster John Knox, 2007.

Beker, J. Christiaan. *Paul the Apostle: The Triumph of God in Life and Thought.* Philadelphia: Fortress, 1980.

Campbell, Douglas A. *The Deliverance of God: An Apocalyptic Rereading of Justification in Paul.* Grand Rapids, Mich.: Eerdmans, 2009.

Dunn, James D. G. *The Theology of Paul the Apostle.* Grand Rapids, Mich.: Eerdmans, 1998.

Dunn, James D. G., ed. *The Cambridge Companion to St. Paul.* Cambridge, U.K.: Cambridge University Press, 2004.

Eisenbaum, Pamela. *Paul Was Not a Christian: The Original Message of a Misunderstood Apostle.* New York: HarperOne, 2009.

Furnish, Victor P. *Theology and Ethics in Paul.* New Testament Library. Louisville, Ky.: Westminster John Knox, 2009. First published 1968.

Gorman, Michael J. *Apostle of the Crucified Lord: A Theological Introduction to Paul & His Letters.* Grand Rapids, Mich.: Eerdmans, 2004.

Hay, David M., ed. *1 & 2 Corinthians.* Pauline Theology 2; Society of Biblical Literature Symposium Series. Atlanta: Society of Biblical Literature, 1993.

Hay, David M., and E. Elizabeth Johnson, eds. *Romans.* Pauline Theology 3; Society of Biblical Literature Symposium Series. Atlanta: Society of Biblical Literature, 1995.

Hays, Richard. *The Faith of Jesus Christ: An Investigation of the Narrative Substructure of Galatians 3:1–4:11.* 2d ed. Grand Rapids, Mich.: Eerdmans, 2002.

Johnson, E. Elizabeth, and David Hay, eds. *Looking Back, Pressing On.* Pauline Theology 4; Society of Biblical Literature Symposium Series. Atlanta: Scholars Press, 1997.

Martyn, J. Louis. *Theological Issues in the Letters of Paul.* Edinburgh: T&T Clark, 1997.

Matera, Frank J. *God's Saving Grace: A Pauline Theology.* Grand Rapids, Mich.: Eerdmans, 2012.

Ridderbos, Herman. *Paul: An Outline of His Theology.* Grand Rapids, Mich.: Eerdmans, 1975.

Schnelle, Udo. *Apostle Paul: His Life and Theology.* Translated by M. Eugene Boring. Grand Rapids, Mich.: Baker, 2005.

Schweitzer, Albert, *The Mysticism of Paul the Apostle.* 2d ed. London: A&C Black, 1953. English translation of *Die Mystik des Apostels Paulus*, first published in 1930.

Thompson, James W. *Moral Formation According to Paul: The Context and Coherence of Pauline Ethics.* Grand Rapids, Mich.: Baker Academic, 2011.

Watson, Francis. *Paul, Judaism, and the Gentiles: Beyond the New Perspective.* Grand Rapids, Mich.: Eerdmans, 2007.

Wolter, Michael, *Paulus: Ein Grundriss seiner Theologie.* Neukirchen-Vluyn, Germany: Neukirchener Theologie, 2011.

Wright, N. T. *Paul: In Fresh Perspective.* Minneapolis: Fortress, 2005.

Wright, N. T. *Paul and the Faithfulness of God.* Christian Origins and the Question of God 4. Minneapolis: Fortress, 2013.

Jerry L. Sumney

PAULINE LETTERS, DEUTERO

See Deutero-Pauline Letters.

PEACE

"Peace" translates as the Hebrew Bible's *šālôm* and the New Testament's Greek *eirēnē*. Each contributes significantly to the theological and ethical emphases of both testaments. In noun and verbal forms *šālôm* occurs approximately 250 times and *eirēnē* 100 times. *Eirēnē* occurs 199 times in the Septuagint, translating words other than *šālôm* and its cognates only 14 times. Iridescent in meaning, *šālôm* connotes wholeness and well-being (including health and material prosperity). The New Testament *eirēnē* lacks the notion of material prosperity and associates peace with self-sacrifice and servant discipleship, aspects of atonement theology.

Šālôm in the Hebrew Bible. "Shalom be to you" is a common greeting or form of blessing in Hebrew life (Judg 19:20; 1 Sam 25:6) or "within you (Ps 122:8). Similarly, "peace be upon Israel" occurs as blessing (Pss 125:5; 128:6). In addition to its primary meaning of "wholeness or well-being" and its less frequent meaning of (material) "prosperity" (Pss 37:11; 72:1–7; 128:5–6; 147:14; Isa 66:12; Zech 8:12), *šālôm* is an ethical imperative often theologically framed (Pss 34:14; 85:8–10; Zech 8:19). Israel's prophets regard *šālôm* as central to their eschatological vision with the messiah acclaimed as "Prince of Peace" bringing peace among the nations (Isa 9:2–7; Zech 9:9–11; cf. Isa 2:2–4; Mic 5:4–5a).

While scholars have understood the contextual focus of *šālôm* differently, their perceptions complement each other. Some hold that it emphasizes material well-being, others that it points more to relationship with God. Some see this relationship giving rise to a state or condition of wholeness and well-being. Whether condition or relationship, *šālôm* encompasses both personal and corporate dimensions of life, as is evident in Jeremiah's command to exiled Israel to "seek the welfare [*šālôm*] of the city" (29:7; LXX 36:7).

Šālôm is related to war but not exactly its antonym (in 2 Sam 11:7 David asks Uriah about the *šālôm* of the war). Yahweh is a warrior (Exod 15:3, though the LXX renders the phrase, "Yahweh crushes war"!). *Šālôm* is sometimes achieved through negotiated treaties (Deut 20:10–12; Josh 9:15; 10:1, 4; Judg 4:17; 1 Sam 7:14; 1 Kgs 5:12). Israel's royal ideology and imperial wars obstruct *šālôm*. Hence, Isaiah calls King Ahaz to courageous, quiet trust in God (7:7–9; 8:1–5; 30:15).

Theologically significant, Yahweh is self-designated as *šālôm* (Judg 6:24; cf. the "God of peace" appellation in Paul's letters and Hebrews). God ultimately is the source of peace (1 Kgs 2:23; Isa 52:7; 60:17; 66:12, 22) because peace flows from God's nature. The much-loved Moses/Aaronic benediction begins with "The LORD bless you and keep you" and ends with "the LORD...give you peace [*šālôm*]" (Num 6:24–26). Even sabbath rest celebrates God's creation-*šālôm* (Gen 2:1–4). Neville (2013, p. 190) proposes that John's prologue, echoing Genesis 1, "presupposes an

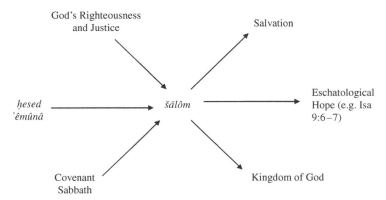

Fig. 1: Semantic field of shalom: corporate, relational, and eschatological

'ontology of peace.'" The canon begins and ends with a peaceontology (Gen 1–2; Rev 21–22; Neville, 2013, pp. 217–218), though Ollenburger (in Brenneman and Schantz, 2014) qualifies this: in some Psalms (e.g., 74:12–14) and Isaiah (51:9)—even Genesis 1:2—God's creating crushes chaos (violence?).

The theological significance of *šālôm*-peace is evident in its semantic field. On the left of Figure 1 are God's covenantal moral attributes (*ḥesed*/steadfast love and *ʾĕmûnâ*/faithfulness) that make *šālôm* possible (Exod 34:6; Pss 57:10; 108:4; 117:2). These together with justice (*mišpāṭ*) and righteousness (*ṣĕdāqâ*) describe God's character and initiative (Ps 89:14; cf. 99:4). These divine attributes are blended with salvation and *šālôm* in Psalm 85:7–13 (cf. Isa 9:6–7; 60:17–18). These and more Isaiah texts express eschatological hope (Isa 35; 55:12—56:1; 59–61). Isaiah affirms new visions of *šālôm* (52:7–10), including Israel as the Lord's suffering servant (53:5c; "whole" translates *šālôm*).

Rabbinic Reflection on Peace. Reflection on the meaning of *šālôm* continued in Judaism among the rabbis. Hillel defined the heart of Judaism as "love peace and pursue it" (*m. ʾAbot* 1.12). Aaron is the prototype of those who pursue peace and love for all creatures. Israel's prayers (Birkat ha Kohanin, the Qaddish, the "Amidah," the Birkat ha Mazon) end with a petition for peace, with hope that the peace that exists in the heavenly spheres shall also reign on earth (cf. the Lord's Prayer phrase "as in heaven, so upon earth" [author's translation]). In rabbinic texts as a whole,

Šālôm primarily signifies a value, an *ethical category*— the overcoming of strife, quarrel, and social tension,

the prevention of enmity and war. It is still, to be sure, depicted as a blessing, a manifestation of divine grace. The pursuit of peace is the obligation of the individual and the goal of various social regulations and structures. (Ravitsky, 1987, p. 685)

Rabbi Joshua ben Korha taught that "where there is strict justice there is no peace, and where there is peace there is no strict justice." Thus, he mediated the two by calling for a compromise, justice tempered with peace (*y. Sanh.* 1.5, *b. Sanh.* 6b). An opposing approach regarded truth, peace, and justice as inseparable: "By three things the world is preserved, by justice, by truth, and by peace, and these three are one: if justice has been accomplished, so has truth, and so has peace" (*y. Taʿan.* 4.2; Ravitsky, 1987, pp. 686–687).

Eirēnē. In the Greek apocryphal books *eirēnē* occurs frequently, especially in 1 Maccabees to describe political relations, which likely reflects secular Greek influence. Sirach's usage, however, is more reflective of the Hebrew *šālôm*: "The fear of the LORD is the crown of wisdom, making peace and perfect health to flourish" (1:18; cf. 28:9, 13, 16).

In Secular Greek. *Eirēnē* in secular Greek contrasts with war and often describes the prosperity that follows victory in war. But in addition to describing the social–political condition, *eirēnē* may denote virtue. Two paths to peace in Greek literature have been proposed, one whereby virtue is achieved heroically through war and a nonheroic means, work that produces peace and justice.

In classical Greek literature it is not always clear whether *eirēnē* refers to a sociopolitical condition or to the Greek goddess Eirēnē. Historians Herodotus (*Hist.* 1:87) and Thucydides (*History of the Peloponnesian War*, 2:61.1) speak of peace as a desirable sociopolitical condition, for humanitarian and political reasons. Euripides, recognizing that the spear-wielding Hellas would destroy herself, calls people to turn to the goddess Eirēnē. Eirēnē never emerged beyond minor goddess status in Greco-Roman culture.

To complement Eirēnē as a deity in the Greek-speaking East, Augustus introduced into Roman imperial politics the *Pax* cult in the Latin-speaking West. The earlier Roman *Concordia* cult was now nicely balanced with a *Pax* cult. The former was directed to internal policy; the latter, toward imperial policy. Pax Romana's *eirēnē* pacified foreign nations to enable concord and harmony at home. The Altar of Peace to Augustus on the field of Mars in Rome, erected in 9 B.C.E., discloses the means of Pax Romana: wars to subjugate the nations. Vespasian's Peace Temple, built 73–75 C.E., extols Rome's victory over the Jews, depicted on the Titus arch.

The Pax Romana was considered an ideal world of prosperity and order with a worldwide Greco-Roman language and culture. In contrast to the Pax Christi of the gospel of Messiah Jesus, Rome's "golden age" of Pax Romana was maintained by subjugation and oppression, which oppose and mock *šālôm*.

New Testament. We cannot know the precise degree of influence that the classical Greek use of *eirēnē* had upon New Testament writers. Since the Septuagint translated *šālôm* with *eirēnē, eirēnē* in the New Testament is rooted in the meaning of the Hebrew Bible's *šālôm* but not without new connotations that stem from the political context, such as anti-imperial motifs.

The semantic field of *eirēnē* highlights key theological concepts. Virtually every term in the *eirēnē* semantic field is both theological and ethical—as is *eirēnē* itself, thus indicating the inseparable nature of theology and ethics. It is essential to treat *eirēnē* in its broader semantic field associations, though word frequency alone indicates its scope and importance. On the left of Figure 2 are God's gifts through Jesus Christ, the fruit of the peace-gospel that restores relationship with God and fellow humans. On the right are the fruits of peace. The recurring double love and love of enemy commandments are foundational to peacemaking.

Jesus and the Gospels. Peace in the Gospels accrues meaning within the context of social and political conflict, as well as human alienation from God. The passion accounts narrate conflict between Jesus and the political powers. In all four Gospels Jesus responds nonviolently. Jesus's call to discipleship causes conflict within households: "Do not think I have come to bring peace to the earth; I have not come to bring peace but a sword" (Matt 10:34–38; Luke's parallel [12:49–53] in v. 51 reads "division" instead of "sword"). Jesus's peace is a radical call to discipleship that causes division and conflict within families and even churches.

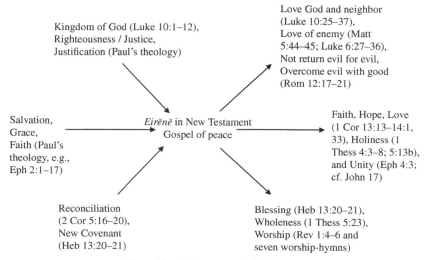

Fig. 2: The NT semantic field of *eirēnē*

Pervasive emphases on nonretaliation against evil and love of the enemy (Matt 5:38–48//Luke 6:27–36; Rom 12:17–21; 1 Thess 5:15; 1 Pet 2:21–23; 3:9–17) challenge disciples of Jesus to break the spiral of human violence through peacemaking. The parable of the Good Samaritan (Luke 10:27–36) and Jesus's encounter with the Samaritan woman (John 4) depict the peace-gospel. The "Golden Rule" captures the essence of peacemaking: "In everything do to others as you would have them do to you" (Matt 7:12). This assumes one desires peaceable treatment from others.

In the Synoptics, "Kingdom of God," "gospel," and *eirēnē* are interrelated. The Sermon on the Mount links the Kingdom of God to peace in the seventh beatitude, by identifying peacemakers (*eirēnopoioi*) as the "children of God" (Matt 5:9). The first (reconcile with brother or sister), fifth (do not resist evil with evil), and sixth (love your enemy) antitheses (supertheses) in Matthew 5:21–48 consist of peacemaking injunctions, with the sixth command to love the enemy as evidence of identity as "children of your Father in heaven" (5:45). God's perfect, complete (*teleios*) love (5:48) is thus manifest through these peacemaking actions.

In Mark's "way" (*hodos*) section (8:27—10:52) Jesus teaches costly discipleship as the way of peacemaking. Jesus's distinctive use of *eirēneuete* in Mark 9:50 admonishes his disciples to "be at peace with one another." This command contrasts to the disciples' vying for greatness in the coming kingdom and rivalry that foments strife.

Luke accentuates three related themes: announcing the gospel, Kingdom of God, and peace. While Mark uses "gospel" only as a noun, Luke uses the verb *euangelizesthai* "to announce the gospel," echoing the gospel-kingdom-peace proclamation of Isaiah 52:7. Luke uses *eirēnē* 14 times in the gospel and 7 in Acts. Texts that link "gospel" and "kingdom" are Luke 4:43, 8:1, and 16:16 as well as Acts 8:12. Those linking "gospel" and "peace" are Luke 2:10 and 14, heralding the keynote theme of the messianic age, "peace on earth." Zechariah's Benedictus assures that the baby born to Mary will "guide our feet into the way of peace" (Luke 1:79). Simeon thus praises God and says, "Master, now you are dismissing your servant in peace" (Luke

2:29). Acts 10:36 sums up Jesus's ministry as "preaching the good news of peace." Significantly, Luke 10:1–12 links "peace" and "kingdom." The message the 70 take to the people begins with a peace greeting: "Peace to this house" (v. 5). The one who receives the gospel is designated as "a son of peace" (v. 6; cf. with Matt 5:9, 45 RSV). The gospel-peace message is "the Kingdom of God" come to them (vv. 9, 11), whether or not they accept it. Jesus's statement in Luke 10:18, "I saw Satan fall like lightning from heaven" (RSV), declares God's peace-gospel victory, achieved through the nonviolent gospel announcement of God's reign. This contrasts with the empire's violent means of peacekeeping.

Peace (*eirēnē*) is one of Luke's narrative emphases in his distinctive journey section. The narrative begins with Jesus rebuking his disciples for desiring to destroy enemy Samaritans (9:51–55). Then the early and last narratives in the section (10:1; 19:28) are laced with Luke's peace accent. "Peace" occurs three times in 10:5–6, including the phrase, "son [child] of peace" (RSV), and twice again in 19:28–42. As Jesus enters Jerusalem the "whole multitude of disciples praise God joyfully" and loudly, saying "Peace in heaven, and glory in the highest heaven" (19:38). *Eirēnē* here antiphonally responds to the angelic choir's heralding Jesus's birth with "glory to God in the highest heaven" and "peace on earth" (2:14). The mood shifts, however, at the Pharisees' unbelief. Jesus weeps over Jerusalem for its coming judgment, saying, "If you, even you, had only recognized on this day the things that make for peace!" (19:42). Though rejected in Jerusalem, Jesus in resurrected power appears to and greets his disciples with "Peace be with you" (24:36).

In John's farewell address Jesus's abiding gift is peace (*eirēnē*) (14:27; 16:33), recurring three times in his postresurrection appearances ("Peace be with you" in 20:19, 21, 26). Jesus's peace contrasts with what the world gives; it frees from fear, "Do not let your hearts be troubled, and do not let them be afraid" (14:27). Jesus's promise of peace contrasts with the world's persecution. Within the larger conflictive ethos of John's Gospel, Jesus promises peace to those who abide in his love (13:34–35; 15:9–13; cf. 1 John 4:7–16). Jesus's post-resurrection greetings both reassure the despairing disciples of Jesus's abiding peace and empower them with the promised Holy Spirit for mission in the world (20:19–23).

Pauline writings. *Eirēnē* occurs 44 times in Pauline writings: 10 in Romans and 8 in Paul's theology of atonement link peace to conflict, battle, and victory (Col 2:12–15; 1 Cor 15:24–27; Rom 8:37–39; Eph 6:10–18), an essential aspect, even precondition, for God's peacemaking among humans, in relation to God's self and fellow humans. Atonement, peace, and justice are intrinsically interconnected in biblical theology.

A distinctive phrase, "God of peace," occurs seven times (Rom 15:33; 16:20; 1 Cor 14:33; 2 Cor 13:11; Phil 4:9; 1 Thess 5:23; 2 Thess 3:16). The appellation points to God's character as peacemaker. Further, Paul's salutations of "grace and peace" are not merely cultural but convey blessing emanating from the gospel, thus promoting a peace-formational ethos in early Christian communities. While Paul proclaims true peace through Christ, he believes his opponents promise false peace and foment dissensions (Rom 16:17–20; 1 Thess 5:3; cf. Phil 3:17–21; 1 Cor 6:12–20).

Romans 5:1–11 and Ephesians 2:14–17 are key texts in Pauline peace theology. Peace with God (Rom 5:1) is through justification by faith, declared in the context of God's wrath against sin (Rom 1:18–32), the primacy of faith (chs. 3–4), and human disobedience (5:12—6:23). In Ephesians Paul or a Pauline writer sums up Jesus's mission by joining two key Isaiah peace texts: "preaching peace" (*euangelizesthai eirēnē*), Isaiah's *mĕbaśśēr šālôm* (52:7), and the phrase "peace, peace to the far and the near," Isaiah's universal vision (57:19; cf. 42:6; 49:6; 52:10). For Paul this "far-and-near" peace depicts beautifully his role in contributing to God's expanding gospel of peace: Gentiles, those far, and Jews, those near, both made one through Christ's peace, which breaks down the dividing wall, kills the enmity, creates one new humanity, and thus makes peace.

Reconciliation is the outcome of God's peacemaking event through Jesus Christ, incarnating God's love for enemies (2 Cor 5:18–19). The cosmic goal of God's salvation in Jesus Christ is reconciling all things to God's self "by making peace through the blood of his cross" (Col 1:20). God's peacemaking is anchored fully in the cross of Jesus Christ, who disarms the powers (Col 2:15), forgives sins (Col 1:13–14; Eph 1:7), and unites formerly alienated parties, Jews and Gentiles, into one body in Christ with common access to God (Eph 2:15–22).

Peace with God bears the fruit of life in the Spirit (Gal 5:22–23; Rom 6:8; 8:9–11). "To set the mind on the Spirit is life and peace" contrasts with setting the mind on the flesh, which is death (Rom 8:6). Believers are called to peace (1 Cor 7:15) and make "every effort to maintain the unity of the Spirit in the bond of peace" (Eph 4:3–6; Col 3:15). Further, the peace of God is the power that "will guard your hearts and your minds in Christ Jesus" (Phil 4:7). Peace is thus both a gift and a virtue to strive toward, empowered by Jesus and the Spirit.

Hebrews, James, and Peter. Peace is significant in these writings as well. In Hebrews Jesus the priest resembling Melchizedek rules over the city of peace (Jeru-shalom): "His name, in the first place, means, 'king of righteousness.'" He is "king of Salem, that is, 'king of peace'" (Heb 7:2). The discipline Jesus's believers experience "yields the peaceful fruit of righteousness" (12:11). Believers are called to "Pursue peace with everyone" (12:14). A "God of peace" benediction (13:20–21) climaxes the epistle.

James contrasts "pure, peaceable" wisdom to earthly, devilish wisdom (3:17) and then (3:18) echoes and complements Isaiah 32:17, reversing the order between peace and justice: "a harvest of righteousness [justice] is sown in peace for those who make peace." Peacemaking is the way to peace and contrasts with conflicts, disputes, and war (4:1–4).

First Peter develops at length a nonretaliation ethic that appeals to Jesus as a model in enduring suffering, calling believers to "follow in his steps" (2:21). He quotes Psalm 34:12–15 to authorize turning from evil to doing good, seeking and pursuing peace (3:11). The epistle concludes characteristically, "Peace to all of you who are in Christ" (5:14).

Summary. In the New Testament, then, *eirēnē* has at least six denotations; a single use may encompass all or several of them: (1) relationship with God through salvation (Rom 5:1); (2) peace among humans, breaking down walls of enmity (Eph 2:11–22); (3) Christ's new creation peace, an alternative community to the Pax Romana (Luke especially); (4) peace with socio-political dimension (Luke–Acts) but also in lordship titles of Jesus Christ (Matt 2:3–4; John 20:28; 1 Tim 6:13–15); (5) peace with cosmic dimensions (Col 1:20; Eph 1:10; Rev 21:1); and (6) an inner peace that stills the human spirit and sustains safety (Phil 4:7, 9). All have theological import.

Peace in Reception History. Since *šālôm* and *eirēnē* have a range of meaning and the topics in their semantic fields have diverse interpretations, the reception history of the biblical teaching is difficult to assess.

Pacifism. The early church until the time of Constantine (r. 306–337) understood Jesus's peace teachings to be normative for faith and life. Hence, with some exceptions, they refused participation in war because serving in the military violated the commandment "Thou shalt not kill" and Jesus's teachings on peace, love of enemy, and nonretaliation. Numerous scholars, however, hold that the military's enforcement of emperor worship (idolatry) was the primary reason Christians refused military service. It seems, however, that both are foundational and necessarily entwined in the confrontation between obedience to scripture and loyalty to Roman religious, military culture.

The "just war" theory, developed first by Augustine but with emphasis on peace also, set forth conditions under which wars could be fought. This became the dominant view of the Christian church (cf. Aquinas's question 29 "Peace" in his *Summa*). In retrospective analysis few wars, if any, have met the just conditions.

Pacifism—or, better, refusal to retaliate—endured through the ages in minority groups: monastic communities, Waldensians, clerical orders of the Roman Catholic and Orthodox churches, most sixteenth-century Anabaptist groups and the Historic Peace Churches (Mennonites, Brethren, Hutterites, Amish) that own the Anabaptist legacy, as well as the Quakers. During the early 1900s liberal Protestants often espoused pacifism, for example, Walter Rauschenbusch and Reinhold Niebuhr. Faced with threatening World War II, Niebuhr shifted position: war is wrong but "necessary"—to stop the evil of Hitler's

holocaust. Karl Barth also espoused pacifism, except for *Grenze* cases, where God (existentially) may command otherwise.

In later decades "nonviolence" dominated Christian discussion but was not necessarily "principled pacifism." Since Tolstoy, nonresistance as true peace practice has continued mostly among conservative Peace Church groups. Rather, nonviolence (and sometimes nonretaliation) dominates antiwar sentiment. All three are "non" stances and shortchange the positive peacemaking emphasis of the New Testament gospel expressed in loving the enemy, killing enmity, being reconciled to opponents, and teaching holistic peaceable living, including creation care. Berry (2013) identifies three peacemaking types (Reinhold Niebuhr, Martin Luther King Jr., and Doris Janzen Longacre) that represent quite different responses to Jesus's and the New Testament's peacemaking calling. Liberation theologians espousing nonviolence exemplify another peacemaking model.

Peace Church conversations. Theological engagement between Historic Peace Church leaders and mainline church denominations occurred sporadically during the twentieth century. The multidenominational Fellowship of Reconciliation (U.S.) produced *A Declaration on Peace*, which affirms peace as "the will of God." Multidenominational discussions on peace theology, focused on biblical, ecclesial, and ecumenical dimensions of peace, include Lutheran, Orthodox, Reformed, Pentecostal, Churches of Christ, Baptist, Friends, Brethren, and Mennonite contributions. Many denominations, from Pentecostal to Catholic, Jewish, and Orthodox, have "peace fellowships" that testify to "pacifism" within their tradition. Though Catholic theology affirms just war, a strong witness to peace and justice is an essential part of the social teaching of its papal encyclicals.

Peacemaking. Peacemaking practices with most all Christian denominations developed in various forms throughout the last quarter of the twentieth century and the beginning of the twenty-first. These practices range from national and international relief and humanitarian agency efforts to street protests against political policies that obstruct peaceable relationships. The Quakers have for centuries excelled in diplomatic peacemaking (e.g., John Woolman's and William Wilberforce's witness). The 1960s civil rights antisegregation protests in the United States (in part the fruit of the Southern Christian Leadership Conference and Clarence Jordan's Koinonia Farm exemplifying integration at risk of life), the work of the Truth and Reconciliation Commission in South Africa, and church institutions divesting from investments in South Africa are notable "movements" inspired by the biblical peace and justice vision. Christian Peacemaker Teams, originating from Ron Sider's 1984 plea at the Mennonite World Conference in Strasbourg, France, have volunteers who monitor injustices in numerous countries, observing and seeking to obstruct violent engagements (e.g., Israeli demolition of Palestinian homes).

Other peacemaking developments attempt to end discrimination between Anglos and native populations dispersed by colonializing, in which native populations were severely devastated, for instance, the Truth and Reconciliation Commission of Canada seeking to heal the violence and pain inflicted by the settlers on the indigenous peoples. Restorative justice (both theory and practice) has emerged worldwide as an alternative to the retributive justice prevalent in legal courts. Creation care, inherent to scripture's peaceable vision (Gen 1; Rom 5–8; Eph 4:24), is also evolving in peacemaking praxis.

Peace in national and international politics. While the above discussion focuses mostly on ecclesial embodiment, witness, and action regarding peace, peace is usually the goal of politics as well, accomplished through various peacemaking or peacekeeping efforts (even missiles or submarines occasionally have peace-related names), to avert war and form peaceable relationships after war.

[*See also* Atonement; Eschatology; Kingdom of God (Heaven); Lord's Prayer; Mercy and Compassion; Politics and Systems of Governance; Reward and Retribution; Soteriology; Violence; *and* War (Holy War).]

BIBLIOGRAPHY

Berry, Elizabeth Malinda. "'The Mark of a Standing Human Figure Poised to Embrace': A Constructive Theology of Social Responsibility, Nonviolence & Nonconformity." Ph.D. diss., Union Theological Seminary, 2013.

Brenneman, Laura L., and Brad D. Schantz, eds. *Struggles for Shalom: Peace and Violence across the Testaments.* Studies in Peace and Scripture 12. Eugene, Ore.: Pickwick, 2014.

Brock, Peter. *Freedom from Violence: Sectarian Resistance from the Middle Ages to the Great War.* Toronto: University of Toronto Press, 1991.

Cochrane, Arthur C. *The Mystery of Peace.* Elgin, Ill.: Brethren Press, 1986.

Dear, John. *The God of Peace: Toward a Theology of Nonviolence.* Maryknoll, N.Y.: Orbis, 1994.

Durnbaugh, Donald F., ed. *On Earth Peace: Discussions on War/Peace Issues between Friends, Mennonites, Brethren and European Churches, 1935–75.* Elgin, Ill.: Brethren Press, 1978.

Eisenbeis, Walter. "A Study of the Root Shalom in the Old Testament." Ph.D. diss., University of Chicago, 1966. Published as *Die Würzel שלם im Alten Testament* (Berlin: Walter de Gruyter, 1969).

Enns, Fernando. *The Peace Church and the Ecumenical Community: Ecclesiology and the Ethics of Nonviolence.* Translated by Helmut Harder. Kitchener, Canada: Pandora; Geneva, Switzerland: World Council of Churches, 2007.

Gremillion, Joseph. *The Gospel of Peace and Justice: Catholic Social Teaching since Pope John.* Maryknoll, N.Y.: Orbis, 1976.

Gros, Jeffrey, and John D. Rempel, eds. *The Fragmentation of the Church and Its Unity in Peacemaking.* Grand Rapids, Mich.: Eerdmans, 2001.

Gwyn, Douglas, George Hunsinger, Eugene F. Roop, et al. *A Declaration on Peace: In God's People the World's Renewal Has Begun.* Scottdale, Penn.: Herald, 1991.

Long, Michael G., ed. *Christian Peace and Nonviolence: A Documentary History.* Maryknoll, N.Y.: Orbis, 2011.

Mauser, Ulrich. *The Gospel of Peace: A Scriptural Message for Today's World.* Studies in Peace and Scripture 1. Louisville, Ky.: Westminster John Knox, 1992.

Miller, Marlin E., and Barbara Nelson Gingerich, eds. *The Church's Peace Witness.* Grand Rapids, Mich.: Eerdmans, 1994.

Neville, David J. "Grace Elicits Correspondences: The Christian Theologian as Peacemaker." In *Embracing Grace—The Theologian's Task: Essays in Honour of Graeme Garrett,* edited by Heather Thomson, pp. 119–134. Canberra, Australia: Barton, 2009.

Neville, David J. *A Peaceable Hope: Contesting Violent Eschatology in New Testament Narratives.* Studies in Peace and Scripture 11. Grand Rapids, Mich.: Baker Academic, 2013.

Ravitsky, Aviezer. "Peace." In *Contemporary Jewish Religious Thought: Original Essays on Critical Concepts, Movements, and Beliefs*, edited by Arthur A. Cohen and Paul Mendes-Flohr, pp. 685–689. New York and London: Macmillan, 1987.

Snyder Belousek, Darrin W. *Atonement, Justice, and Peace: The Message of the Cross and the Mission of the Church.* Studies in Peace and Scripture 10. Grand Rapids, Mich.: Eerdmans, 2012.

Stassen, Glen H., and David P. Gushee. *Kingdom Ethics: Following Jesus in Contemporary Context.* Downers Grove, Ill.: InterVarsity, 2003.

Swartley, Willard M. *Covenant of Peace: The Missing Peace in New Testament Theology and Ethics.* Studies in Peace and Scripture 9. Grand Rapids, Mich.: Eerdmans, 2006.

Swartley, Willard M., ed. *The Love of Enemy and Nonretaliation in the New Testament.* Studies in Peace and Scripture 3. Louisville, Ky.: Westminster John Knox, 1992.

Wengst, Klaus. *Pax Romana and the Peace of Jesus Christ.* Translated by John Bowden. Philadelphia: Fortress, 1987.

Wink, Walter, ed. *Peace Is the Way: Writings on Nonviolence from the Fellowship of Reconciliation.* Maryknoll, N.Y.: Orbis, 2000.

Yoder, John Howard. *Christian Attitudes to War, Peace, and Revolution.* Edited by Theodore J. Koontz and Andy Alexis-Baker. Grand Rapids, Mich.: Brazos, 2009.

Yoder, Perry B., and Willard M. Swartley, eds. *The Meaning of Peace: Biblical Studies.* 2d ed. Studies in Peace and Scripture 2. Translated by Walter Sawatsky and Gerhard Reimer. Elkhart, Ind.: Institute of Mennonite Studies, 2001.

Willard M. Swartley

PENTATEUCH

See Deuteronomy; Exodus; Genesis; *and* Leviticus and Numbers.

PERSECUTION

Religious and ethnic persecution permeates the Bible as biblical writers frequently write on behalf of the persecuted community. They choose, however, not to describe Israel's acts of violence against others as persecution. Throughout Israel's history, many considered persecution a sign of God's punishment. God punishes Israel because of its disobedience; God punishes other nations because of their idolatry and mistreatment of Israel. Some Israelites understood God's punishment as a form of persecution (e.g., Jer 17:16–18), and others, like Job, challenged traditional theological thinking on the fine line between punishment and persecution (Job 19:21–22). Most ancient Israelites thought that Yahweh was intimately involved in the persecution and punishment of the nations of the world. If Yahweh did not *directly* initiate the persecution, God at least allowed it. Israel needed to appease Yahweh, in some cases, either by obedience or some other means in order to avoid persecution or punishment. The prophets share this theological perspective.

Later Jewish and Jewish Christian reflections distance God from their own persecution and associate it more closely with evil enemies or forces in the world. Among biblical writers, Paul is the only one who self-identifies as a (former) persecutor (Gal 1:13–14).

Ancient Israelite Attitudes toward Persecution. Even though the specific language of "persecution" (Heb. *rādap*) is rare in the Torah (Deut 30:7), scenes of persecution—for example, Israel's enslavement (in Egypt) and the so-called conquest of Canaan—are central to the overarching narrative. (The narratives, of course, offer Israel's perspective and rarely, if ever, provide insight into Canaanite reflections on these events.) According to the Deuteronomistic History, Yahweh will repay Israel's enemies for their persecution of Israel (Deut 30:7). And in their description of the conquest of Canaan, the destruction of the land and its people was placed under a "ban" (*ḥērem*; Deut 7; 20) and thereby set aside for complete destruction for Yahweh's sake.

During the United Monarchy, Saul's desire to annihilate the Gibeonites led to a three-year famine. Later, David appeased Yahweh's anger by turning over seven of Saul's sons (and grandsons) to the Gibeonites for public executions (2 Sam 21:1–14). Ancient Israelites believed firmly in God's sovereignty in the affairs of the world, including divine sanction for natural disasters in the land and physical persecutions. On one occasion David's prophet, Gad, approached the king with divine options for the people's punishment (2 Sam 24:11–25). David preferred Yahweh's direct judgment (or "mercy," as the text reads at 24:14) instead of external, human persecution, so Yahweh struck the land with pestilence.

The oracles of Isaiah are filled with themes of persecution. Assyrian persecution of the Syrians and the northern nation of Israel receives divine sanction—as a rod of Yahweh's anger (Isa 10:5–19). This punishing includes crushing infants, raping women, and looting homes (Isa 13). Isaiah's oracles also proclaim the persecution and destruction of the Moabites (Isa 16), Damascus (Isa 17), "rebellious" Israelites (Isa 30), and, eventually, the Assyrians (Isa 30:27–33). Despite the oracle, Israelites were called on to show mercy to their neighbors, becoming a "refuge" for the "outcasts" of Moab (Isa 16:4).

In Jeremiah's oracles, sabbath disobedience was emblematic of Israel's disregard for the covenant that led to Yahweh's terror, persecution, and eventual exile of the Judeans (Jer 17:14–27). Some Israelites disagreed with Jeremiah's rationale, so the Temple priests beat and imprisoned Jeremiah (Jer 20). Eventually, the Babylonians attacked and defeated Judah because Yahweh had turned against Judea (Jer 21:10). Yahweh's anger also ignited over Israel's unjust economic practices (Isa 5:8–24; 10:1–4; Jer 7; Amos 4–5; Micah 6; Ps 12:5).

Not only was the Babylonian Exile an act of Yahweh according to the prophets but Ezekiel's oracles stress Yahweh's forceful and decisive action against Israel's neighbors for their failure to come to Israel's defense, including Edom (25:12–14; 35:1–9) and the Philistines (25:15–17). Ezekiel's God is a God who annihilates (25:13 16; 35:3; 2 Sam 21) Israel's enemies, eliminating even their memory (Ps 34:16).

On other occasions, the language of persecution may be used in interpersonal conflicts or personal suffering. The psalmists cry out to Yahweh for protection from the enemy who wishes to do them (personal?) harm (Pss 3; 10; 12; 22; 55); on the other hand, the psalmists occasionally recognize the necessity of punishment for wrongdoing (Ps 7:1–5). Job also begs his friends not to imitate Yahweh, whose attention and persecution overwhelm him (19:22). From the author's perspective, Job's "persecution," though instigated by Yahweh, was carried out by one of the heavenly beings, the "Accuser" (Job 1:6–12). Here is an early attempt to distance Yahweh from Job's direct calamities. The absence of any divine name in the story of Esther may also indicate an attempt to distance Yahweh from the mass murders the Israelites committed against their enemies (Esth 9). The later Greek additions revise this omission and include, among other elements, Mordecai's acknowledgment that Israel's prayer to God brought deliverance.

Jewish Attitudes toward Persecution during the Hellenistic Period. The story of "Daniel" and the Maccabean literature are Hellenistic accounts of persecution memories in Jewish tradition. They preserve the memory of Israel's salvation from the enemy's attempt to destroy God's people.

The central motif of Maccabean literature was the persecution of the Jewish community by Antiochus Epiphanes (r. ca. 175–164 B.C.E.) (1 Macc 1; 2 Macc 5). A willingness to die for the sake of Torah lies behind the martyrdom stories integral to 2 Maccabees and represents a new moment in Israel's history. Also, Eliezar, an unnamed mother, and her seven sons represent a willingness to die on behalf of the entire nation in order to appease God's anger (2 Macc 7:38).

In the Maccabean literature, persecution was not only external. Jewish leaders violently retaliated against other Jews, who desired integration with their Hellenistic neighbors. Mattathias, along with the Hasideans, punished those Jews who had ignored the Law, forcibly circumcising boys and persecuting others (1 Macc 2:45–47). Judas Maccabeus was praised for continuing his father's policy (3:5).

In the Wisdom of Solomon, in the spirit of the older tradition, it is God who "pursues" the ancient enemies of God's people (19:2–4). Here even nature opposes those who oppress Wisdom's righteous followers: "for the universe defends the righteous" (16:17, CEB; cf. 16:15–19; 19:13–17).

Attitudes toward Persecution in the Early Christian Movement. Jesus repeatedly taught his disciples that persecution would be part of their expected future (Matt 5, 10, 23). Harassment would often come because of sectarian, religious differences (5:11; 10:18, 22).

The (Synoptic) Jesus teaches his disciples of the inevitability of both verbal (Matt 5:11) and physical (Matt 10:17) persecution (Matt 5:10–12). Persecution may come from local religious groups (10:17), family members (10:21), or Gentile leaders (10:18; cf. Luke 21:12–17). Jesus associates his followers with Israel's prophets, who likewise received persecution from fellow Israelites (5:12). In fact, he criticizes specific contemporary Pharisees for such persecution and places them in line with the ancestors who killed the ancient prophets (23:29–34; Luke 11:47–49). In Jesus's explanation of one parable, he emphasizes that "distress" (*thilpsis*) and "abuse" (*diōgmos*) scare his followers away (Matt 13:21//Mark 4:17), yet they should expect persecution (Mark 10:30) as a sign of the end of the age (Matt 24//Mark 13). Jesus challenges his disciples to receive harassment with joy. They should also pray for their persecutors (5:44; cf. Rom 12:14). But they should not relish the abuse nor seek it out. Jesus does not encourage martyrdom. When the opportunity arises, they should escape to the next village (10:23). Later, in Luke's report, Paul and Barnabas follow this strategy (Acts 13:50–51).

The Fourth Gospel distinctively uses the language of (verbal?) persecution to describe the treatment Jesus received from religious leaders on account of his sabbath activities (John 5:16). The Synoptic Jesus encountered debates over his sabbath practices but not immediate persecution (Matt 12:14). The Johannine Jesus informs his disciples that persecution will come from more than the religious community: "If the world hates you, be aware that it hated me before it hated you" (John 15:18).

The public execution of Jesus was evidence of Rome's power in the lives of religious sectarian groups in the eastern part of the empire. The beatings and insults he received and Jesus's final cries, in Mark, were signs of his agony, "My God, my God, why have you forsaken me?" (15:34) Luke and John present Jesus's death in a more noble manner, with a Jesus more in control of himself, portraying a death worthy of emulation: "Father, into your hands I commend my spirit" (Luke 23:46; cf. John 19:30). After all, Jesus is "the faithful witness" (*ho martys, ho pistos*; Rev 1:5).

Acts emphasizes the persecution of Jesus's followers. Stephen's speech reiterates Jesus's teaching on the past killing of the prophets (Acts 7:52; cf. Luke 11:47–49) and situates Jesus's crucifixion in the line of these prophets. Luke describes Stephen's death as a parallel to Jesus's own (Acts 7:59–60). Saul's presence at this scene is ominous (7:58; 8:1) as he becomes a leading persecutor of the Way (8:1–3; 9:1–5; Gal 1:13). His religious violence is a prominent and repeated memory in the Acts tradition (9:1–6; 22:1–8; 26:9–18). One common feature, in the repeated scenes, is the vision in which he heard, "Saul, Saul, why do you persecute me?" (9:4; 22:7; 26:14).

Paul's letters also highlight persecution. Paul alludes to his physical abuse of Jesus's followers and his attempt to shut down the sectarian group (Gal 1:13; 23; 1 Cor 15:9; Phil 3:6). On the other hand, Paul discusses the persecution he has suffered, patiently (1 Cor 4:12), after turning from persecutor to missionary preacher (Gal 1:23; 5:11; 2 Cor 6:3–10). He encourages fellow sufferers, as part of his Christian duty (2 Cor 1:3–11; Phil 4:13–14), with his (radical?) theological understanding: "always carrying in the body the death of Jesus, so that the life of Jesus may also be made visible in our bodies" (2 Cor 4:10; cf. Phil 3:10–11). Death of the body—suffering for a good cause—leads to life and peace for the community of faith (2 Cor 4:12). And for some early Christian thinkers, it builds character (Rom 5:3–4; Heb 10:33), though they do not claim that the persecution originates with God. The marks of persecution are the new religious identification markers on the body of God's followers, not the mark of circumcision (Gal 6:12–13). Like Jesus, Paul, too, recognizes future hardships for adherents to the new religious sect and advocates a policy of nonretaliation toward persecutors, blessing them instead (Rom 12:14; 1 Cor 4:12). In Paul's thinking, nothing—not even persecution—should separate God's elect from God's love (Rom 8:33–39); rather, Paul basks in the abuse, insults, and difficult situations because "whenever I am weak, then I am strong" (2 Cor 12:10).

Different types of persecution are raised in the later books of the New Testament, but there is less theological reflection on its meaning. One Pauline disciple extends Paul's teaching on the link between human suffering and Christ's death, implying that Paul's suffering completes Christ's sufferings (Col 1:24). That takes Paul's earlier rationale (2 Cor 4:10) to one possible conclusion. Claiming to speak in Paul's words, another Pauline disciple uses the abuse Paul received for his missionary activity to advocate for (and expand on) the idea that persecution is inevitable even for believers who simply choose "to live," not proclaim, "a godly life" (2 Tim 3:10–12). There is a fine line between this author's advice and the idea that one should seek out harassment in order to live a holy life. But no New Testament author discusses Paul's death directly. New Testament writers did not treat Paul's death as martyrdom.

The book of Revelation is filled with scenes of persecution as it exhibits language of apocalyptic war. It draws the themes of persecution and martyrdom together more closely than other New Testament documents. Antipas is the only explicitly named "witness" or "martyr" (*martys*) of the book (Rev 2:13) besides Jesus Christ (Rev 1:5). When the "dragon" was unable to attack successfully "the woman who had given birth to the male child," it "made war" (*poiēsai polemon*) on Jesus's followers (Rev 12:13–17). The language of warfare (*polemon*) between "good" and "evil" permeates the apocalypse (11:7–10; 13:7–10; 16:12–16), though believers will finally overcome in this apocalyptic drama (19:19–21; 20:7–10). More than other New Testament writers, the author of the apocalypse blames the devil for the persecution of believers (2:9–10): "I saw that the woman [i.e., Rome] was drunk with the blood of the saints and the blood of the witnesses to Jesus. (*tōn martyrōn Iēsou*; 17:6). More reflective of the older tradition, the author claims that God will avenge God's people with persecution of the enemy (Rev 2:18–23; 7:14–17; cf. 2 Thess 1:6). Yet, those who endure the external abuse will receive rewards at the end of the age (Rev 7:14–17; cf. 2 Thess 1:4; Heb 10:33). This final idea is the beginning point of theologies of martyrdom in early Christian traditions.

Challenges and Relevance in Contemporary Society. God's people, according to biblical literature, have a long history of suffering persecution. Frequently, later interpreters turn these stories into teachings of inevitable expectation of external persecution on behalf of the promulgation of the faith. Martyrdom has ancient roots but not ones widespread throughout biblical stories. With the exception of the Maccabean literature, possibly Jesus's death, and themes in the Apocalypse, few passages point in this direction. The development of stories encouraging martyrdom comes later in the early church. Some have called these stories themselves into question, arguing that the early church exaggerated Christian martyr stories in order to gain a rhetorical advantage in their ancient polemics. Some contemporary Christians have continued to utilize this "myth" in order to support unpopular cultural or political causes in the contemporary world, such as pacifism or the rights of the unborn.

On another level, womanist theologians rightly raise the concern about the value of redemptive suffering—that is, saying that dying for a good cause has a broader value for others—as a potentially dangerous message for those already on the margins of society. In Christian history, the message that "persecution" is a necessary experience for followers of Jesus has occasionally been utilized to encourage disenfranchised people to remain patient in their suffering. Religious and ethnic persecution permeates the Bible. Yet, it rarely presents persecution in a positive light.

[*See also* Atonement; Blessings and Curses; Covenant; Exile and Dislocation; Expiation; Good and Evil; *and* Violence.]

BIBLIOGRAPHY

Boyarin, Daniel. *Dying for God: Martyrdom and the Making of Christianity and Judaism.* Stanford, Calif.: Stanford University Press, 1999.

Castelli, Elizabeth. *Martyrdom and Memory: Early Christian Culture Making.* New York: Columbia University Press, 2004.

Frend, W. H. C. *Martyrdom and Persecution in the Early Church: A Study of a Conflict from the Maccabees to Donatus.* Grand Rapids, Mich.: Baker Book House, 1981. First published 1965.

Moss, Candida. *The Myth of Persecution: How Early Christians Invented a Story of Martyrdom.* New York: HarperCollins, 2013.

Pobee, John S. *Persecution and Martyrdom in the Theology of Paul.* Journal for the Study of the New Testament, Supplement Series 6. Sheffield, U.K.: JSOT Press, 1985.

Seibert, Eric. *The Violence of Scripture.* Minneapolis: Fortress, 2012.

Ste. Croix, Geoffrey de. *Christian Persecution, Martyrdom, and Orthodoxy.* Edited by Michael Whitby and Joseph Streeter. Oxford: Oxford University Press, 2006.

Emerson B. Powery

PETER

Peter, named Simon at his birth in Bethsaida (John 1:44; Gal 2:11, 14), was the son of John (John 1:42; 21:15–17) or Jonah (Matt 16:17). In Capernaum, Peter lived with his wife, mother-in-law, and brother Andrew, making a living by fishing (Mark 1:16–18, 29–34). The traditions of the Gospels have Jesus call these brothers as his first disciples. In the Synoptics they leave their family for a migrant lifestyle without possessions (Mark 1:16–18; 6:8–9; 10:28–29; Q Matt 10:37/Luke 14:26). Preparing Israel for the arrival of God's Kingdom, Jesus intended the 12 disciples to be a symbol of the restored tribes. He gave Simon the nickname "Kepha" (Aramaic for "rounded stone, precious stone, lump," in Greek transcribed as "Cephas," translated as "Petros"/"stone"; Mark 3:16; John 1:42), distinguishing him from another disciple (Mark 3:18). Neither "Kepha" nor "Petros" had been used as names before, except for one uncertain fifth-century B.C.E. "Kepha" attestation (Fitzmyer, 1979).

Before Jesus's crucifixion, the Gospels have Peter flee (Mark 14:50; John 16:32). His denial (Mark 14:66–72) is historical because after Easter there would have been no interest in inventing such an event. In Galilee, Peter was the first to have a vision of the deceased Jesus (1 Cor 15:5; Mark 16:7; cf. Luke 24:34). He convened other Jesus followers and experienced a second vision among the 12, a third one in a larger circle (1 Cor 15:5, 7).

Based on the conviction that Jesus had been resurrected, Peter and others founded a Jewish-Christian congregation in Jerusalem, which successfully missionized in Judea (Gal 1:22–24) and soon faced antagonism from Jewish authorities (Gal 1:13, 23; Phil 3:6; 1 Cor 15:9). Paul was one of the persecutors. After his conversion, however, he visited Peter for two weeks in Jerusalem around 34–35 (Gal 1:18).

In the Jerusalem congregation, Peter and others shared the leadership (Gal 1:18–19; Acts 1:13—6:7). At the apostles' convention in about 48, the "pillars" James, Peter, and John were the leaders (Gal 2:7–9); the pre-Easter circle of 12 had lost its importance. At the convention (2:1–10), Peter met Paul again. With Peter's consent and against some opposing Jewish-Christians, it was decided that Paul and Barnabas should continue the Torah-free Gentile mission, while the "pillars" missionized Jews with Torah observance. Although Peter, influenced by the Jesus tradition (e.g., Mark 2:15—3:6; 12:28–34), did not attribute any salvific relevance to Torah observance (Gal 2:12a), he recognized that Jewish believers in Jesus in the Jewish milieu of Judea should continue to observe the Torah. Finally, Paul agreed to raise money in his Gentile congregations for the poor among the Jerusalem Christians.

At the time of the convention, Paul considered Peter the leading missionary to the Jews (Gal 2:7–9). However, because Peter was traveling as a missionary, even to Syria (Gal 2:11; Acts 9:32—11:2), Jesus's brother James soon became the main leader among the Jerusalem Jewish Christians (Gal 2:12; Acts 12:17). Soon after the convention decision, Peter and Paul practiced table fellowship with Gentile Christians without observing the Torah in Antioch (Gal 2:11–21). However, when Torah-observant followers of James arrived from Jerusalem they would not join the fellowship. Peter therefore encouraged the Antiochian Christians to observe the Jewish dietary laws for the sake of joint table fellowship and congregational unity (Gal 2:13, 14d). Only Paul opposed Peter, accusing him of hypocrisy. But the Antiochians did not side with Paul, who consequently left the city. At the convention and in the Antiochian conflict, Peter was integrative and compromising, mediating between Jewish and Gentile Christians, which prevented a split between the two wings of the church. He later therefore was viewed as the foundational figure of the whole church.

Peter's subsequent life remains largely unknown. His wife accompanied him on his missionary trips; the congregations paid for their subsistence (1 Cor 9:5–6; more prominent than "the other apostles," Peter is especially mentioned here, as in Gal 2:7–9). Whether Peter visited Corinth, where Christians taught or baptized by him formed a Peter faction (1 Cor 1:12; 3:22), is unclear. When discussing the Corinthian apostle factions, Paul diplomatically spared Peter by using only himself and Apollos as examples when illustrating the absurdity of such factions (3:4—4:6). After the Antiochian confrontation, Paul in 1 Corinthians apparently tried to avoid another conflict with Peter. During Paul's last Jerusalem visit, Peter was not in town (Acts 21:18—23:11).

Sometime after Paul's Letter to the Romans, Peter probably reached Rome and was crucified in the Vatican gardens during the Neronian persecution in 64 (*1 Clem.* 5:1–4; 6:1–2; 1 Pet 5:1, 13; John 21:18–19; 3:36; Tacitus, *Ann.* 15.38–44; *Mart. Ascen. Isa.* 4.2f.; *Apoc. Pet.* Rainer frg.). That the author of Mark heard Peter preach (as Papias claimed according to Eusebius, *Hist. Eccl.* 3.39.15) cannot be proven but becomes plausible if both stayed in Rome in the early 60s. In the first half of the second century, Christians considered a simple grave at the Vatican to be Peter's tomb. Between 147 and 161, most likely around 160, they decorated it with a modest edicula, which is identical with the Peter "tropaion" mentioned by Gaius around 200 (in Eusebius, *Hist. Eccl.* 2.25.7). Constantine and/or Constantius II erected the original St. Peter's basilica above this tomb.

New Testament Peter Images. For Mark, Peter is the most important apostle. He is the first to see the resurrected Christ (16:7) and part of several inner circles of the disciples; he is the first one mentioned of the three (5:37; 9:2; 14:33; cf. 3:16–19) who witness Jesus conquering death (Jairus's daughter), being declared God's Son (the Transfiguration), and being distressed (at Gethsemane); he is the first mentioned of four in 1:16–20; 13:3, and of the 12 who preach and exorcise in 3:14–16. He is the first and last disciple mentioned by name (1:16; 16:7), being a witness of Jesus's work from the beginning to the end.

However, as speaker of the disciples (1:36–38; 8:29, 32–33; 9:5; 10:28; 11:21–24; 16:7), Peter also represents typical traits of discipleship, both positive and negative. Together with his brother, he is obedient to Jesus's call to fish for people (1:16–20), being promised eternal reward (10:28–31). After a long phase of incomprehension, Peter vicariously for all 12 disciples, confesses Jesus as Messiah (8:29). But as this insight is gained because of Jesus's miracles, it is deficient. From 8:31, the disciples, especially Peter (8:32–33), are challenged with new learning: only when Jesus's passion is experienced can his true identity as Messiah and God's Son be understood. The disciples' failure to accept both Jesus's and their own suffering (8:34–38) is exemplified especially in Peter (14:37). Representative of the disciples, he rejects the perspective of suffering (8:33) and is scolded (8:32–34). He also exemplifies the disciples' incomprehension (9:5–6). Although the denial story is peculiar to him (14:29–31, 54, 66–72), he is still representative of believers (see also 14:31c, 50) in the sense that persecuted readers can identify with his conflict. Without diminishing Peter's authority, Mark uses Peter's negative traits to show the ambiguous nature of discipleship, an existence that stands between faithfulness and failure.

Matthew takes over Mark's ambiguity (Peter is called first, confesses the Messiah, rejects the thought of suffering, and fails during Jesus's passion) but adds his own tendencies. "Peter," the most frequently used disciple name in Matthew, is emphasized from the beginning (4:18) in preparation for 16:18, whereas the absolute "Simon" appears only once (17:25).

Matthew's redaction emphasizes Peter's first place among the 12 (10:2). More than in other Gospels, Peter is the leading dialogue partner of Jesus (18:21; 15:15 vs. Mark 7:17; Matt 19:27b vs. Mark 10:28; Matt 17:24–27; Mark is followed in 16:22–23; 19:27; 26:33–35, except for 21:20). Some of his questions aim at Christian ethics. He thus is associated with teaching righteous conduct (also 16:19) and with confessing that Jesus is the Christ (16:16–17). Therefore, Jesus blesses him with the promise of 16:17–19 (only in Matthew).

The wordplay *petros* (stone)/*petra* (rock) in 16:18 is possible only in Greek; in Aramaic this playful use of two different but phonetically similar words is impossible. As a pre-Matthean logion, it most likely originated in a Greek-speaking congregation such as Antioch, where Peter had played an important role. That *petra* refers to Peter's confession is not likely, considering that not only 16:18a but also 16:19 focuses on the person of Peter; "this rock" clearly refers to 16:18a syntactically. As Peter was called first, saw the risen Christ first, and played a leading and integrative role after Easter, it seemed plausible to consider him the foundational rock of the universal church. The "keys" and "binding"/"loosing" (16:19; 18:18) concern Peter's proclamation: by teaching the Matthean Jesus's ethical commands (28:20), Peter opens the kingdom—instead of shutting it off from people as the Torah teaching by the Pharisees and scribes does according to Matthew (23:13). "Binding" and "loosing" designate authoritative decisions about ethical issues (cf. 23:23) and the power of disciplining (excommunication or forgiveness; 18:15–18; John 20:23). It does not apply so much, however, to binding assertions of salvation or condemnation (cf. Q Luke 10:5f, 10–16). In this way, Peter is the foundation of the church; he sustains its existence and opens heaven for people (7:14; 16:18–19).

Peter's preeminent role is counterbalanced by material that stands in tension with his elevation. Not only Peter but also all the disciples are empowered to bind and loose (18:18). In 23:8 and 4:18, 21, Matthew's redaction emphasizes that disciples are siblings. The other disciples join Peter's pledge to stand by Jesus even in the face of death (26:35; Mark 14:31). Their confession of Jesus's identity as God's son (14:33) precedes Peter's confession (16:16). In 28:7, Matthew eliminates Peter's name from his source, and he does not report that Peter was the first Easter visionary. Indeed, the last time Peter is mentioned by name is in the context of his denial (26:75). That Jesus forgives him is only implied when he commissions all 11 disciples to missionize (28:16–20). Matthew's redaction emphasizes Peter's failures as much as his preeminence: Peter's resistance to the thought of suffering is even more dramatic in 16:22b than in Mark 8:32. Jesus accordingly intensifies his reproach, directing it exclusively to Peter (Matt 16:23, unlike

Mark 8:33). Matthew also intensifies Peter's denial (Matt 26:72 vs. Mark 14:70 ff.).

In this ambiguous picture, Peter is not a guardian of church discipline and doctrine, superordinate to other disciples; instead, he is representative of the others, in both positive and negative respects. His sleepiness (26:40) and his little faith when walking on water (14:28–31, only in Matthew) are typical of the disciples (14:31; 6:30; 8:26; 16:8; 17:20; 28:17). Whereas his witnessing of Jesus's work from the beginning (first to be called; first vision, which laid the "rock" foundation for the church) was unique and cannot be reproduced, his commission to teach normatively (16:19) is the task of all disciples (18:18; 28:18–20).

For Luke–Acts, not the typicality but the historical uniqueness of the 12 is emphasized (Acts 1:21–26). More than Mark, Luke puts Peter in the center (e.g., Luke 5:1–11; 22:8, 31–34; 9:20; 24:34; 6:13–16; Acts 1:13, 15; 2:14, 37–42; 3:11–13; 4:8; 5:3, 8–13, 29; 8:45; 12:41) and alleviates his negative traits (Luke 9:22–23; 22:46, 57, 60; Matthew also omits Mark 14:31, 27, 50). Peter's denial is alleviated by the redactionally inserted pledge in Luke 22:33 (see also Peter living up to the pledge in Acts 5:18; 12:3–6). However, important decisions are made collegially (6:2–5; 8:14; 15:23–29), with Peter also working in a team (3:1–11; 4:1–7; 8:14–25; cf. Luke 10:1; 22:8).

The first half of Acts features Peter, who evangelizes Jews in Jerusalem, Judea, and Samaria, whereas the second half positions Paul in the center. Their speeches (e.g., 1:15–22; 2:14–36; 3:11–26; 10:34–43; 11:5–18; 17:22–31) direct the plot, with Peter, not Paul, initiating the mission to Gentiles (10:1–48, prepared for in 2:39; 3:25). Thereafter, Peter is only mentioned in 12:3–19 (when he is miraculously released from prison) and at the apostles' convention (15:7–11), where he supports the mission to Gentiles without the Torah, except for the stipulations in 15:29. Acts pictures both protagonists in more harmony (15:25) than they may have been historically, e.g., in the Antiochian conflict. Peter, as guarantor of ecclesiastical unity (Acts 8:14–25) and in consultation with the other apostles, legitimizes Paul's Gentile mission (10:1–11:18; 15:1–29), which helps Luke's agenda of composing an apologia of Paul.

In John, the relationship between the beloved disciple and Peter mirrors the relationship between John's congregations and the mainline church. Both figures symbolize groups, with Peter's importance being downplayed. The ambiguous material shared with the Synoptics (1:41–42; 6:68–71; 13:36–38; 18:15–18, 25–27) withholds the detail that Peter was the first to be called and the first to confess (1:40–42). Although he is the speaker for the 12 (6:67–71; 21:2 ff.), this function seems unimportant. Peter now is the problematic sword-bearer (18:10–11) with only limited understanding (13:1–11). Correspondingly, the beloved disciple is put in the limelight (20:2–10; 21:1–14 vs. Luke 24:9–12; 5:1–11). Showing himself superior to Peter, he alone remains at the foot of the cross (19:26; 16:32). Closer to Jesus than Peter (13:23–25; 21:20–23), he opens Peter's eyes (21:7) and wins the race to the tomb but generously lets Peter enter first (20:4–8). John's Christianity does not want to be a sect separated from the mainline church. Therefore, John's Gospel acknowledges that Peter is the universal shepherd and martyr (21:15–23; 13:36) who warrants the unity of the universal church (21:11; 17:20–23), but the Johannine Christians claim to have a deeper understanding of Christ.

In the fictive situation of 1 Peter, shortly before his martyrdom in Rome (5:1, 13), Peter strengthens congregations of Asia Minor (1:1, 6, 17) that are struggling with persecution (2:11–12; 3:14, 16; 4:4, 12–14, 16; 5:8–9), attempting to be a model for them (5:3). He instructs their presbyters as a "fellow presbyter" (5:1–11, literal translation from Greek text), calling himself "apostle" only in 1:1 (Greek text). The pseudonymous author usurps Peter's authority. But there is no evidence of a Petrine "school."

Second Peter, a fictitious farewell writing to the entire church (1:1, 13–15), stylizes Peter as a universal authority. The author attempts to secure the apostolic, including Pauline, heritage against false teachers, featuring Peter and Paul in harmony (3:2, 15–17). Peter's authority is used for a corrective rereading of Paul (3:16b; 1:20; 2:1, 19), especially with regard to Paul's eschatological perspective and Paul's concept of freedom (3:3–9; 2:2, 10, 13–15, 18–22). During Jesus's transfiguration Peter received his authority to interpret the doctrinal heritage (1:16–20), when he—as *epoptēs* (one who sees, e.g., the highest mysteries) as in the mystery religions or in philosophy—reached the highest level of initiation: as visionary (see also *Apoc. Pet.*), he witnessed an anticipation of Christ's Parousia in the transfiguration so that those denying the Parousia (3:4; 2:1) are refuted.

The historical Peter's leading, compromising, and integrating role and his unique and nonreproducible experiences of having been the allegedly first to be called by Jesus and the first to see the risen Lord made him a universal authority of the church in the eyes of later New Testament writers. At the same time, writers such as Mark and Matthew considered him representative of typical features of discipleship, both positive and negative.

Peter in Late Antiquity. In noncanonical documents, Peter's authority and martyrdom became dominant themes. Since the end of the first century in Rome, the memories of Peter and Paul as local martyrs were closely connected (*1 Clem.* 5:3–7; 6:1; Gaius in Eusebius, *Hist. Eccl.* 2.25.7; Ign. *Rom.* 4.3; Dionysius of Corinth, in Eusebius, *Hist. Eccl.* 2.25.8; Irenaeus, *Haer.* 3.1.1; Tertullian, *Praescr.* 36; Origen, in Eusebius, *Hist. Eccl.* 3.1.2–3; *Acts Pet. and Paul*).

Archaeological evidence. The veneration of Peter as a martyr, documented in archaeological evidence of Rome since the second century (at the Vatican) and jointly with Paul since the middle of the third century (graffiti under S. Sebastiano) paved the way for the cultic veneration of other martyrs in Rome after the persecutions of the third and early fourth centuries. The archaeological evidence in Rome shows that, as martyrs, Peter and Paul were invoked as intercessors before God—just as Christ was after his death. Christ's, Peter's, and Paul's martyrdoms were paralleled in early Christian art; for example, the two apostolic martyrs were frequently depicted as sacrificial lambs beside the Christ lamb. Christians believed that these martyrs' tombs made the universal importance of Christ's death tangible on the local level. Similarly, in popular pagan religiosity, the divine was perceivable on the local level in hero cults and local deities.

Despite the close Peter–Paul association, Peter is significantly more prominent in Roman catacomb paintings and sarcophagi reliefs. Some recurring motifs include (1) the story of Peter's denial that served as an illustration of God's grace and forgiveness (John 21), making Peter a person with whom many could identify; (2) a Moses–Peter typology, in which Peter reenacts Moses's miracle of bringing water from the rock by converting the soldiers who arrest him, thus giving them the water of life (later literary evidence is found in Pseudo-Linus's *Passio Petri* 5, fifth century; *Passion of the Saints Processus and Martinianus*, sixth century); (3) a second Moses–Peter typology, which makes Peter the teacher of the church (seen in his receiving of the scroll of Christ's law [*traditio legis*] or the keys [Matt 16:18–20; John 21:15–17]). As Christ's authoritative representative, Peter explains what Christ wants Christians to do (scroll) and possesses the power to forgive and to discipline (keys). By the middle of the third century, Roman bishops claimed the same authority for themselves. In Rome, subsequent depictions of Peter in art therefore alluded to the Roman bishop's authority. Accordingly, Peter appears significantly more often in sarcophagus reliefs commissioned by upper-class Christians than in catacomb frescos (ratio 1:8). Christians of worldly status and power liked to associate themselves with the authority of Peter and the Roman bishop, while less aristocratic Christians commissioning less expensive catacomb paintings avoided this association.

Literary sources. Around 180 Irenaeus anchored his fictive catalogue of Roman bishops (*Haer.* 3.3.3) not in Peter but in "the apostles." Likewise, around 200 Bishop Satornius of Antioch "received" Peter as well as the other apostles "as Christ" and acknowledged that they together represented Christ (Eusebius, *Hist. Eccl.* 6.12.3–6). Similarly, Origen understood Matthew 16:18 in light of 18:18 ("*we* become a Peter…a rock is *every* disciple of Christ"; *Comm. Matt.* 12.10, italics added). Bishop Stephen of Rome in the middle of the third century, however, applied Matthew 16:17–19 to himself alone. Nonetheless, Cyprian opposed him: Stephen "contends that he holds the succession from Peter, on whom the foundations of the Church were laid," which is "folly" (Cyprian, *Ep.* 74.17). Tertullian (*Pud.* 21) and Origen (*Comm. Matt.* 12:11) had contested similar claims earlier. Not until the end of the fourth century did the Western church accept the primacy of the Roman bishop (Bishop Siricius, r. 384–399; Rasmussen, 2001, p. 34). In the fifth century, Leo the Great finally suggested that Peter as primate of all bishops is to be honored in his successors (*Sermones ad Romanam Plebem*, 3–4).

In the second century, Papias anchored Mark's Gospel in Peter's "teachings" (Eusebius, *Hist. Eccl.* 3.39.15; cf. Irenaeus, *Haer.* 3.1.1), trying to secure its apostolic authenticity. Similarly, the Gnostic Basilides claimed Petrine heritage, with his teacher Glaucias allegedly having interpreted Peter (Clement, *Strom.* 7.17.106). Additionally, several pseudonymous writings besides 1 and 2 Peter appropriated Peter's authority. These include the *Gospel of Peter* (second half of the second century), the *Kerygma of Peter* (early second century), and the *Apocalypse of Peter* (second quarter of the second century).

In the influential *Acts of Peter* (originally from the end of the second century), Peter follows Simon Magus to Rome to stop his influence by preaching and performing miracles. He also propagates asceticism, which leads to his martyrdom. The *Pseudo-Clementines* describe the struggle between Peter and Simon Magus as well but not with the intention, as older research held, of creating a polarization between a Petrine mission to the Jews and a Pauline mission to the Gentiles.

Nag Hammadi writings have Peter proclaim a wide variety of messages. In the non-gnostic *Acts of Peter and the Twelve* (NHC 6.1; second to third centuries), Jesus commissions him and the other apostles to preach poverty and asceticism. Similarly, the *Actus Petri* (BG 4; second to fourth centuries) narrates non-gnostic stories about Peter the miracle worker, visionary, and preacher. On the other hand, the other *Apocalypse of Peter* (NHC 7.3; third century) contains polemics against mainline Christianity, while preaching dualism and docetic Christology and attributing a central role to Peter as receptor of gnostic revelations. The *Letter of Peter to Philip* (NHC 8.2; second to third centuries) deals with Christian suffering by propagating gnostic teachings given to Peter by the risen Jesus. Contrary to these images of Peter, in the gnostic *Gospel of Mary* (BG 1), Peter and Andrew become symbols of mainline Christianity by polemically questioning the legitimacy of gnostic teachings. A similarly critical attitude toward Peter as mainline church representative, and thus downplaying his authority, can be seen, e.g., in the *Gospel of Judas*, the apocryphal *Letter of James* (NHC 1.2), and the *Pistis Sophia*. The Gnostics thus used Peter as both a negative counterpart, representing the larger church that does not acknowledge the gnostic teachings, and a positive authority, supporting their doctrines. Either way, they recognize the unique authority that Peter enjoyed in late antiquity.

[*See also* Apostleship; Authority and Order; Ecclesiology; John and the Johannine Epistles; Luke–Acts; *and* Paul.]

BIBLIOGRAPHY

Bockmuehl, Markus. *The Remembered Peter: In Ancient Reception and Modern Debate.* Tübingen, Germany: Mohr Siebeck, 2010.

Böttrich, Christfried. *Petrus: Fischer, Fels und Funktionär.* Leipzig, Germany: Evangelische Verlagsanstalt, 2001.

Dschulnigg, Peter. *Petrus im Neuen Testament.* Stuttgart, Germany: Katholisches Bibelwerk, 1996.

Fitzmyer, Joseph A. "Aramaic *Kepha'* and Peter's Name in the New Testament." In *Text and Interpretation: Studies in the New Testament Presented to Matthew Black*, edited by Ernest Best and Robert McLachlan Wilson, pp. 121–132. Cambridge, U.K.: Cambridge University Press, 1979.

Gibson, Jack J. *Peter Between Jerusalem and Antioch: Peter, James, and the Gentiles.* Tübingen, Germany: Mohr Siebeck, 2013.

Gnilka, Joachim. *Petrus und Rom: Das Petrusbild in den ersten zwei Jahrhunderten.* Freiburg im Breisgau, Germany: Herder, 2002.

Gnilka, Joachim, Stefan Heid, and Rainer Riesner, eds. *Blutzeuge: Tod und Grab des Petrus in Rom.* Regensburg, Germany: Schnell & Steiner, 2010.

Grant, Michael. *Saint Peter: A Biography.* New York: Scribner, 1995.

Grappe, Christian. *Images de Pierre aux deux premiers siècles.* Paris: Presses Universitaires de France, 1995.

Grünstäudl, Wolfgang. *Petrus Alexandrinus: Studien zum historischen und theologischen Ort des zweiten Petrusbriefes.* Tübingen, Germany: Mohr Siebeck, 2013.

Heid, Stefan, ed. *Petrus und Paulus in Rom: Eine interdisziplinäre Debatte.* Freiburg im Breisgau, Germany: Herder, 2011.

Lampe, Peter. "Das Spiel mit dem Petrus-Namen—Matt. xvi. 18." *New Testament Studies* 25, no. 2 (1979): 227–245.

Lampe, Peter. "The Excavation Complex at the Vatican." In *From Paul to Valentinus: Christians at Rome in the First Two Centuries*, 3d ed., pp. 104–116. Minneapolis: Fortress; London: Continuum, 2006.

Lampe, Peter. "Archaeological and Iconographic Vestiges of Peter Veneration in Late Antiquity at Rome." In *Peter in Earliest Christianity*, edited by Helen Bond and Larry Hurtado. Grand Rapids, Mich.: Eerdmans, forthcoming.

Markley, John R. *Peter—Apocalyptic Seer: The Influence of the Apocalypse Genre on Matthew's Portrayal of Peter.* Tübingen, Germany: Mohr Siebeck, 2013.

Nau, Arlo J. *Peter in Matthew: Discipleship, Diplomacy, and Dispraise…with an Assessment of Power and Privilege in the Petrine Office.* Collegeville, Minn.: Liturgical Press, 1992.

Perkins, Pheme. *Peter: Apostle for the Whole Church.* Columbia: University of South Carolina Press, 1994.

Pesch, Rudolf. "Was an Petrus sichtbar war, ist in den Primat eingegangen: Die biblischen Grundlagen des Primats und seiner Weitergabe." In *Der Primat des Nachfolgers Petri im Geheimnis der Kirche: Studien der Kongregation für die Glaubenslehre*, edited by Gerhard Ludwig Müller, pp. 29–50. Würzburg, Germany: Echter, 2010.

Rasmussen, Mikael B. "Traditio Legis—Bedeutung und Kontext." In *Late Antiquity: Art in Context*, edited by Jens Fleischer, John Lund, and Marjatta Nielsen, pp. 21–52. Acta Hyperborea 8. Copenhagen: Museum Tusculanum, 2001.

Schultheiss, Tanja. *Das Petrusbild im Johannesevangelium.* Tübingen, Germany: Mohr Siebeck, 2013.

Wiarda, Timothy. *Peter in the Gospels: Pattern, Personality and Relationship.* Tübingen, Germany: Mohr Siebeck, 2000.

Zwierlein, Otto. *Petrus und Paulus in Jerusalem und Rom: Vom Neuen Testament zu den apokryphen Apostelakten.* Berlin: De Gruyter, 2013.

Peter Lampe

1 AND 2 PETER

See Catholic Epistles.

PHILEMON

See Pauline Letters.

PHILIPPIANS

See Pauline Letters.

POLITICS AND SYSTEMS OF GOVERNANCE

The phrase "systems of governance" designates the structures, institutions, and personnel that administer the sociopolitical order of a society. They involve such interrelated networks of power as the institutions of governance, the military, the economy, and ideological–religious sanctions.

Across the biblical canon, the words "government," "politics," and "democracy" do not appear in the New Revised Standard Version translation. This absence underscores profound differences between systems of governance in the ancient world and the contemporary Western world. In the latter, commonly held ideas about systems of governance frequently affirm that all people are equal, that all can have access to the governing process, and that governmental/political figures derive power from the people. The ancient world did not regard people as equal or participants in governing systems. And leaders and kings were often regarded as exceptional individuals chosen by the gods or God.

This article will survey systems of governance as they are presented in the Hebrew Bible narrative, then in the New Testament. With respect to the Hebrew Bible, the biblical narrative constructs diverse systems of governance. The narrative presentations often focus on religious and military dynamics but rarely offer details of daily governance or even consistently accurate historical depictions. Moreover, they offer mixed theological evaluations on the systems of governance.

Hebrew Bible. The rule of the Egyptian pharaoh constitutes the first major governing system in the Hebrew Bible narrative. It receives a mixed evaluation. Abram and Sarai, as vulnerable foreigners, employ deception to survive the power of Pharaoh's officials (Gen 12:10–20). God sends punitive plagues on Pharaoh's household for endangering them. By contrast, the Hebrew Joseph, betrayed by his brothers and taken to Egypt, flourishes under Egyptian rule (Gen 39–50). Surviving the seductive and power-abusive efforts of his master Potiphar's wife, he rises to a position second only to the king. God secures this advancement through Joseph's (God-given) ability to interpret Pharaoh's dreams.

But despite Joseph's successful self-benefiting accommodation, all is not well with the Egyptian monarchy. The Israelites' numerical growth in Egypt causes a new king to fear their alliance with an external enemy. He enslaves and "oppress[es] them with forced labor" (Exod 1:11). Using natural forces as weapons of war—polluted water, insect plagues, disease, thunder and hail, and the sea to drown Pharaoh's army—God thwarts Egyptian power to deliver the Israelites from slavery.

Theocracy and charismatic leadership. Theocracy under Moses as God's chosen agent now emerges. The Exodus narrative presents Moses's rule as originating with God (Exod 3) and maintained by God's use of Moses as spokesperson (the Decalogue, Exod 19–31). While the governance is charismatic, it does not remain uncontested by the people (Exod 32; Num 11). Heavy demands on Moses to exercise judgments (Exod 18) and the people's complaints about their limited diet (Num 11) result in the creation of subleadership structures, including the appointment of 70 elders. Also evident are prophets (Num 11:26–29; 12:6) who across the canon are presented in diverse relationships to the various systems of governance (Deut 13:1–5; 1 Sam 10:5–13; 1 Kgs 18–19; 22; Jer 27; Neh 9:26–32, etc.).

With Moses's death, theocracy continues as God appoints Joshua, "Moses' assistant" (Josh 1:1) as leader. As commander in chief, Joshua leads the Israelites in their successful, divinely directed campaign across the Jordan River in conquering Canaan. With control of the land secured, the territory is divided among the tribes who unite, prior to Joshua's death, in covenant loyalty to serve "the LORD our God" (Josh 24).

Tribal confederacy and judges. Details of tribal self-governance are thin in the narratives. Elders and priests perform governing functions; a female prophet, Deborah, administers justice (Judg 4:5). Especially important are spirit-empowered military rulers or "judges," who "as needed" unite tribes in successful wars against foreign powers (Judg 3:7–30; chs. 6–8; 11:29; 13:3–5). They do not instigate a hereditary line, impose taxes or levies, draft soldiers, or demand forced labor.

The accounts in Judges, though, offer few details about any wider governing functions for this tribal confederacy. Theological perspectives dominate. God empowers these leaders when the threatened people cry out to him. While the narrative shows the confederacy failing in the struggle against the Philistines' military threat and growing demands for continuity in strong leadership, it especially highlights the failure to acknowledge God's will. Gideon refuses demands that he and his successors rule over them by saying "the LORD will rule over you" (Judg 8:23). Dynastic human rule is rejected, at least at this point, as contrary to God's rule. When Gideon's son, Ahimelech, rules as king, his death by defeat in battle is presented as God's judgment (Judg 8:22–23, 56–57). After the troubling rules of Jephthah and Samson, chaos increases with the repeated refrains "in those days there was no king in Israel" (Judg 17:6; 18:1; 19:1; 21:25) and the condemnatory "all the people did what was right in their own eyes" (17:6; 21:25).

Deuteronomy, Joshua, Judges, 1 and 2 Samuel, and 1 and 2 Kings attest the theological perspectives of the Deuteronomistic History (DH). The Deuteronomistic theological agenda condemns the confederacy for not complying with the covenant or with God's will revealed in the Law of Moses. Punishment resulted; God delivered when the people turned to him (e.g., 1 Sam 12:6–15).

Monarchy. Monarchy emerges from this chaos with mixed theological evaluations (1 Sam 8). Negatively, it is said to imitate the nations, reject Israel's God as king, and lead to misrule by exploiting people, plundering produce, and slavery (1 Sam 8:4–22; 10:18–19). Positively, kingship is presented as sanctioned by God through Moses, as requiring obedience to the king, and as requiring the king's obedience to the law (Deut 17:14–20). Monarchy and loyalty to God are reconciled with the king as the agent of God's purposes. In the royal Psalms, like Psalm 2 or 72, the king is God's "son" or agent, representing God's rule and justice (also Prov 16:10, 13; 20:26, 28; 29:4, 14).

Saul, Israel's first king (1 Sam 10), has military success; but there are few other details about the system of governance during Saul's rule. He loses the kingship after violating a cultic practice before battle (1 Sam 10:8; 13) and failing to obey God's command to destroy the Amalekites completely (1 Sam 13:13–14; 15:10–35). Failure in faithful worship and obedience to God's will are recurring themes in assessing kings in 1 and 2 Kings. Saul's military style of rule gives way to centralized rule and administration in the united kingdom of David and Solomon.

The texts show David anointed initially as king of Judah and then of the united kingdom of Judah and Israel (1 Sam 16; 2 Sam 2:4; 5:1–15). He consolidates his power after struggles with Saul and the Philistines, claiming the throne after Saul's death (1 Sam 16—2 Sam 8). He establishes Jerusalem as the united kingdom's capital and center for worship. He secures the nation and his own position by defeating surrounding nations (2 Sam 8–10). He administers justice (8:15) and expands administration, appointing army commanders, bodyguards, a manager of forced labor, a "recorder" and chief scribe, and priests (8:16–18; 20:23–26). He does not appear to tax but does foster trade. His son Absalom claims the throne (2 Sam 15–18), and Sheba leads a revolt of alienated Israelites (19:41—20:22). The two revolts highlight ongoing problems for monarchic rule: power struggles involving members of the ruling family or its officials and resentment from regions who perceive themselves to lack royal favor.

The narrative emphasizes God establishing a dynasty for David's house to rule forever (2 Sam 7:13–14). The succession, though, after David's death is not smooth (1 Kgs 2:10–12). Solomon defeats Adonijah to become king and expands administrative activity. Like David, he appoints various officials including priests, recording secretaries, an army commander, a palace administrator, and one in charge of forced labor (1 Kgs 4:1–6). He subdivides Israel into 12 districts; a ruling official maintains order and levies supplies for the palace and personnel, including troops ("12,000 horsemen") and horses ("barley and straw"; 4:7–28). Solomon's extensive building program centers on the Temple and palace complex using Israelite and foreign conscript labor (1 Kgs 5:13; 9:21) and "550 officers"

(9:23). The narrative's theological perspective criticizes Solomon's building priorities: seven years for the Temple but 13 years for his own house (6:38; 7:1). Whereas the Lord's house is 60 by 20 by 30 cubits (6:2), Solomon's palace is 100 by 50 by 30 cubits (7:2–8). Solomon expands trade with greater international interactions (9:26–28) and faces Jeroboam's rebellion (11:26–40). Solomon falls to the Deuteronomic theological fault of worshipping foreign gods (11:4–13).

With Solomon's death the united kingdom dissolves into the 10-tribe northern kingdom under king Jeroboam (Israel) and the southern kingdom under king Rehoboam (Judah). Resentment of Solomon's heavy-handed demands of forced labor and taxation which Rehoboam plans to increase fuels the division (1 Kgs 12:18). Thereafter the narrative assesses the theological worthiness of each king in terms of loyalty to Yahweh ("good" kings) or involvement with idols and other gods ("bad" kings). There are few details about the system of governance. Attention falls on religious faithfulness and military contests.

The northern kingdom established worship of Yahweh as its official religion, but 1–2 Kings evaluates most of its 19 kings as unfaithful in observance. With external pressures from Aram/Syria and Assyria and internal instabilities from its numerous tribes and regional and cultural differences, regular conflict with coups and civil war marked the northern kingdom. Nine kings gained the throne by coups; seven were assassinated. By the mid-eighth century B.C.E., the prophets Amos and Hosea critically assess the elite-controlled governance. Amos attacks the elite's self-benefiting, oppressive political and economic treatment of peasants (Amos 4:1; 6:4–6). According to Amos, they sell the poor into slavery for debts, use bribes in court (2:6–8), levy grain (5:10–12), deprive peasants of justice (6:12), and defraud them in commerce (8:4–6) while building themselves splendid houses (3:15; 6:4). Hosea attacks Israel's foreign policy of alliance with Assyria as idolatrous and abandoning God and the covenant (Hos 8). He attacks king and priests who gain power and wealth through this alliance (Hos 5:1; 8:14) and laments social evils such as "swearing, lying…murder…

stealing…adultery…bloodshed" (Hos 4:2). The DH largely ignores these dimensions of governance; the worship of other gods explains Israel's defeat by and exile in Assyria in 722 B.C.E. (2 Kgs 17:7–23).

Israel's final demise resulted from King Hoshea's negotiation of Assyrian pressure as a vassal ruler. When he refused the annual tribute and seeks alliance with Egypt against Assyria (2 Kgs 17:1–4), Assyria invaded Samaria (722 B.C.E.). Some Israelites were deported to Assyria; others moved south into Jerusalem. Assyria settled foreigners in Israel, which was now the Assyrian province of Samaria. They were tasked with agricultural production, trade, and defense of Assyrian interests.

The southern kingdom, Judah, centered on Jerusalem and its Temple, lasted until 586 B.C.E. The DH commends only 4 of its 20 kings (Asa, Jehoshaphat, Hezekiah, and Josiah) as faithful to Yahweh. It praises Josiah, for example, for purifying religious observances but offers few details of his practices of governance. At an earlier time, the prophet Micah denounces economic sins that deprive people of property (2:1–11). He attacks rulers who destroy the people through injustice (3:1–12) and urges doing justice, loving kindness, and serving God (6:8; cf. Isa 1:16–17). The prophet Isaiah similarly denounces economic stratification and disadvantage for the poor (Isa 3:13–15). Foreign policy in the eighth and seventh centuries concerned negotiating Assyrian power as a compliant tribute-paying, vassal state (2 Kgs 18:13–16). The subsequent Babylonian threat provoked debate between those advocating submission and those advocating resistance by means of Egyptian alliance.

Nebuchadnezzar of Babylon takes King Jehoiachin prisoner in 597, captures Jerusalem, and installs Zedekiah as a puppet king. When Zedekiah withholds tribute, the Babylonians return in 586 to destroy the city and Temple, exile Jews to Babylon (2 Kgs 25:8–21), and imprison the rebellious Zedekiah. Judah became the Babylonian province of Yehud; a local figure, Gedaliah, of the pro-Babylonian family of Shaphan, became governor. This system of governance, though, was very conflicted; and subsequently Gedaliah was assassinated by Ishmael and his supporters (Jer 41:2–3). While 2 Chronicles 36:21 declares the land was depopulated, 2 Kings 25:12 indicates poor people remained as "vinedressers and tillers of the soil."

Colonial governance. By 539, Persia had defeated Babylon and established its empire centered on its king, Cyrus, whom at least one Judean prophet identified as the Lord's anointed or Messiah (Isa 44:28—45:1). Cyrus returned Jews to the province of Yehud (2 Chr 36:22–23), now part of the Persian administrative system of satrapies belonging to the province "Beyond the River" (Ezra 4:10). While details are scarce, the biblical texts present the postexilic system of governance as significantly different from the preexilic monarchy.

According to the biblical writings, Persian supervision permits Yehud to restore important markers of Judean identity. First, Yehud's system of governance comprised two appointed officials, a governor and a high priest. Providing some apparent "self-governance," Persia appointed Jews cooperative with Persian power to these positions: Sheshbazzar (Ezra 1:8–11; 5:14–16) and then governor Zerubbabel and Joshua the high priest, in office in 520 B.C.E. (Hag 1:1). Zerubbabel's descent from the exiled Davidic king Jehoiachin caused some to hope that his governorship would lead to restoring the Davidic monarchy, whether immediately or in the future (Hag 2:20–23). Another Jew, Nehemiah, became governor in 445 B.C.E. and ruled for 12 years. During severe economic hardship and shortage of food, poor farmers were forced to give up land and consign their children into slave labor when they could not repay loans. Nehemiah hears their complaints, brings "charges against the nobles and the officials," and effects restoration (Neh 5:1–13). Nehemiah abandons the burdensome custom of previous governors of receiving food provisions from the people for himself and his household of 150 or so members (Neh 5:14–18).

Second, the accounts present Persian rule as allowing the observance of native religion. They encouraged restoration of the Jerusalem Temple building and worship and of Jerusalem itself (Ezra 1:2). Ezra specifically mentions Cyrus returning Temple vessels taken in 586 (Ezra 1; 5:13) and narrates Darius after 520 B.C.E. confirming the rebuilding and reestablishment of sacrificial practices (6:3–15). Zerubbabel

completes the Temple's restoration (Zech 4:8–9), while the book of Nehemiah presents Nehemiah's chief task as rebuilding Jerusalem.

Third, the Persians permit observance of Torah. Nehemiah presents the idealized scenario of the priest-scribe Ezra reading the book of Moses with the people committing to observe it, maintain the Temple and priests, and observe festivals and sabbath (Neh 8–13). The issue of separation from the nations, especially involving mixed marriages, concerns both Ezra and Nehemiah; the latter also imposes sabbath observance that curtails agricultural and trade activities (Neh 13:15–22).

The biblical documents, whatever their historical value, say little about the system of governance beyond these measures. If they reflect historical realities, evident is not religious tolerance but a Persian policy that creates compliant and grateful subjects even while tribute and taxes are extracted. Ungratefulness or rebellion could be readily punished by military power and revoking self-governing privileges. Colonized Judeans, however, occupied a difficult in-between space, beholden to Persian favor yet with some autonomy and national/cultural markers. Co-opted as allies and representatives of Persian power and obligated to satisfy Persian commitments to order and economic benefit, elite Judeans also knew self-benefiting opportunities for power, wealth, and status. They also knew the ambivalent "third space" of hybridity, being colonized while also colonizing nonelites and their resources. So Nehemiah 5:1–13 attests rural crises from oppressive elite actions involving land control, famine, taxes, slavery, debt, and interest.

Theocracy and hierocracy. These accounts of Persian colonial rule end the biblical story of Israel and Judah in the Jewish and Protestant Hebrew Bible canons. Texts in the Apocrypha continue the story several centuries later, after the Macedonian Alexander the Great (356–323 B.C.E.) had defeated Persian power. The Ptolemies in Egypt and the Seleucids in Syria succeeded Alexander with control of parts of his empire and contesting the control of Judea, with the Ptolemies dominant in the third century B.C.E. and the Seleucids in the second. The books of 1–2

Maccabees narrate the military occupation of Jerusalem by the Seleucid Antiochus IV Epiphanes (r. 175–164 B.C.E.). They also recount his collection of tribute, ethnic cleansing, abolition of the worship of Israel's God and observance of Torah, appointment of governors (2 Macc 5:21–26), and installation of a statue of himself as Zeus Olympios in the Jerusalem Temple, which he designated the temple of Olympian Zeus (2 Macc 6:2). These actions provoked various responses from Jews including cooperation and alliance (1 Macc 1:11–16, 52), defiance and martyrdom (1 Macc 1:62–64; 2 Macc 7), military resistance (1 Macc 2–9), and reliance on God's intervention to save the faithful (Dan 1–6) and to end human empires and establish God's empire (Dan 7).

Judea reestablishes religious autonomy in rededicating the Temple in 164 B.C.E. The struggle to gain political independence centers on the Hasmonean line. After Judas's death, his brother Jonathan (160–143 B.C.E.) unites the roles of military leader and chief priest (2 Macc 10:20), along with diplomat in securing alliances with Rome and Sparta. His brother Simon follows (142 B.C.E.) as governor, military commander, and chief priest (1 Macc 13–16, esp. 14:41–43) and secures political independence from the Seleucids. The Hasmonean line continues after Simon's death (134 B.C.E.; 1 Macc 16:11–17) through his son John Hyrcanus, the military, political, and priestly leader until 104 B.C.E. Another son, Alexander Jannaeus, rules until 76 B.C.E., adding the title "king." His wife Salome Alexandra follows (76–67 B.C.E.), with her son as chief priest. Infighting and intrigue weaken the Hasmonean line, opening the way for Pompey Magnus to establish Roman rule in Judea in 63 B.C.E.

New Testament. The New Testament texts, written in the late first century and early second century C.E., emerge under Roman imperial power. Since Augustus's rule (d. 14 C.E.), central power resided in the hands of the emperor and senate in Rome. Administration of the empire's 40 or so provinces relied not on a large bureaucracy of civil servants but on imperial agents: governors, troops (in reality or by threat), and alliances with local elites and client kings.

Governors were appointed from the Roman elites. The Senate appointed proconsuls from its own members to administer senatorial provinces; the provinces of Asia and Africa were regarded as prestigious appointments. For the remaining 30 or so imperial provinces, the emperor appointed a senator or someone of equestrian status for smaller provinces (such as Judea) as governors. Primary responsibilities focused on maintaining societal order, suppressing opposition, and collecting tribute and taxes. Governors imposed authority through the reputation and reality of military force and alliances with local elites. Local elites used patronage and euergetism to administer local matters. Control of resources, both material (taxes) and human (slave labor), along with claims of divine sanction for Rome as chosen by the gods (Virgil, *Aen.* 1.278–279), also expressed and secured the imperial governing system.

The New Testament participates in and inscribes this imperial governing system. Emperors Augustus (Luke 2:1) and Tiberius (Luke 3:1) contextualize Jesus's birth and John the Baptist's ministry. Governors appear regularly: Pilate who crucified Jesus (Matt 27:2; Luke 20:20), Quirinius (Luke 2:2), and those Paul encounters in Acts: Sergius Paulus (13:7), Gallio (18:12), Felix (23:24), and Festus (26:30). Client kings, allies with and agents of Roman rule, include the Herodians (Matt 2; Mark 6; Acts 12; 25). Other kings benefit from trade (Rev 18:9–10). Soldiers (Luke 3:14; John 18:3; Phil 1:13) and tax collectors (Mark 2:13–14; Luke 3:12–13) are imperial officials. Elite beneficiaries often with landed wealth, power, and status appear (Matt 19:16–30; 20:1; Jas 5:1–6). So too do imperial victims, especially slaves (Mark 12:2–5) and the poor (Luke 14:21–24; Jas 2:1–7).

Jesus. Jesus's ministry occurs in Galilee, which was administered by the Rome-appointed client, Herod Antipas (ca. 21 B.C.E.–ca. 39 C.E.). Jesus avoids confrontation with Antipas and his cities of Sepphoris and Tiberias (honoring Herod's patron, the emperor Tiberius), though Herod wants to kill him (Luke 13:31) and supporters of Herod oppose Jesus (Mark 3:6). Antipas executes John the Baptist (Mark 6: 14–29) and may contribute to Jesus's death (Luke 23:6–12).

In Jerusalem, the Roman governor Pilate crucifies Jesus in alliance with the local Jerusalem elite and power group based in the Temple. Crucifixion was the death penalty for those understood to threaten Roman rule and order, such as insurrectionists and slaves. Jesus's death by crucifixion indicates that the ruling alliance understood him as a threat to Roman rule. This threat does not comprise a call to military revolt but comprises his proclamation of the "Kingdom" or "Empire" of God. It is not clear, though, whether Jesus saw himself as the "king" or "emperor" of this kingdom/empire or whether he was a prophet or sage announcing its coming or presence. Instructive, however, is that the crucifixion accounts identify Jesus as "king," suggesting he was understood to be a key and threatening agent in its establishment.

Gospels. The Gospels tell the story of Jesus some 40–70 years later, after Roman military power had destroyed Jerusalem and its Temple in 70 C.E. All the Gospels negotiate Roman rule with various and simultaneous strategies ranging from confrontation and resistance through imitation and accommodation.

Opposition is sounded in various ways. The Gospels ally the devil and Rome's empire when the devil offers Jesus control of "all the empires of the world" (Matt 4:1–11; Luke 4:1–13). Subsequently, the Synoptic Gospels name a demon "legion," the central unit of Rome's military, over which God has destructive power (Mark 5:1–20). One effect of this presentation is to secure the contrast and opposition between Rome's devilish empire and the Empire or Kingdom of God that Jesus proclaims and enacts.

The Gospels also announce Rome's world to be under judgment. Using Jewish "two-age" thinking, they anticipate Jesus returning to end the imperial world and establish God's rule in full (Mark 13; Matt 24–25; Luke 21). The imperial world is judged to be violent (Herod, Matt 2; Herod Antipas, Mark 6) but subject to God's power, even serving as God's agent in destroying Jerusalem in 70 C.E. (Matt 22:7). It is exploitative in that rich rulers fail to "shepherd" the people (Matt 9:36; Luke 6:24) and deprive the poor of resources (Mark 10:17–31). It is bad for people's health (Jesus's healings roll back imperial damage), unjust in administering "justice" for the benefit of elite alliances (Pilate and the Jerusalem leaders ally to crucify Jesus), and limited in power in not keeping Jesus dead (Mark 16; Matt 28; Luke 24).

But such emphases do not mean Jesus-believers are to abandon Rome's world or violently oppose it; they live a hybrid identity within it. Violence is prohibited to them (Matt 5:39, "Do not resist violently"; author trans.) since violence is an imperial strategy (John 18:36). They are to participate in imperial life (Luke 3:10–14) and, as is common with powerless groups under imperial power, occupy the third space of cooperation with and dissent from Roman rule. So they cooperate with the practice of *angaria*—supplying labor and material supplies—yet they dissent with exaggerated compliance that throws the ruling power off balance (Matt 5:38–42). They pay taxes as an apparently public act of compliance while reframing payment as an act that attests God's sovereignty and relativizes imperial claims (Mark 12:13–17; Matt 22:15–22; 17:23–27). They are also to form alternative communities that embody God's empire in the midst of Rome's. So Luke's Jesus evokes the sabbath tradition of Isaiah 61:1–2 to present a different societal vision in which acts of transformation repair the damage of Rome's world (Luke 4:16–17).

Disciples similarly repair imperial damage by healing the sick, casting out demons, feeding the hungry, welcoming the stranger, and lending to those in need (Matt 25:31–46; Mark 3:14–15; Luke 6:35). They pray for adequate bread and forgiven debts (Matt 6:9–13; Luke 11:2–4). Instead of "lording it over others" as the rulers of the Gentiles do, Jesus's followers renounce domination and tyranny, seek the good of others (Mark 10:42–45), and love one another (John 13:34–35). Ironically, the vision or fantasy of the final imposition of God's empire imitates and reinscribes imperial practices. The scenarios imagine God acting like imperial rulers, imposing God's rule and enacting violent punishment on those who do not welcome God's Empire.

Paul and other New Testament writers. Paul's letters reflect similar strategies. Paul presents the imperial world as passing away and God's reign about to be established (1 Cor 15:20–28). God's wisdom and purposes are hidden from and contrary to "the rulers of this age, who are doomed to perish" (1 Cor 2:6). In 1 Thessalonians 5, after citing the propaganda claim that the empire has brought "peace and security," he equates it with darkness and night under God's wrath. Yet Paul can also urge, in a much debated passage, submission to "the governing authorities…instituted by God" (Rom 13:1). Some have interpreted this passage as articulating a universal submissive stance toward governing authorities, but various factors, including the reference to paying taxes (13:6–7), suggest the matter is more complex. In chapter 12, Paul tells his readers not to conform to this world (12:1–2); to form communities marked by love, hospitality, and harmony (12:3–18; 13:8–10); to rely on God for vengeance (12:19–21); and to await God's eschatological intervention (13:11–14). These chapters offer various intermingling and simultaneous strategies for negotiating the Roman world including submission, nonconformity to the Roman world, the forming of alternative communities, and reliance on God for vengeance and establishing God's reign. Despite this mix of strategies, the post-Pauline tradition emphasizes an accommodationist stance, urging obedience to and prayer for the emperor along with "quiet and peaceable" living (1 Tim 2:1–2; Titus 3:1–2).

Beyond Paul, 1 Peter 2:17 commands honoring the emperor. Interpreters often claim this verse requires obedience but not participation in the prayers, sacrifices, games, and other festivities for the emperor that comprised the imperial cult. Several factors, though, require rethinking this claim of exception. First, participation in such prayers and sacrifices was standard "honoring" behavior. To refuse participation defeats 1 Peter's strategy of societal involvement to secure a good name. Second, the letter emphasizes honoring Christ in one's heart (3:15), suggesting that loyalty to Christ relativizes participation in public honoring. Third, other New Testament material indicates that abstinence from idols was by no means universally established among Jesus communities (1 Cor 8–10; Acts 15:29; Rev 2–3).

Finally, we should note Revelation's sustained and sharp critique of Rome's empire. It presents Jesus as "the ruler of the kings of the earth" (Rev 1:5). It rejects any imperial accommodation, including participation in imperial cult activities (Rev 2–3). The document reveals that, in its writer's perspective, true worship centers only on God and Jesus (Rev 4–5).

By contrast, the empire is under judgment (6:1—8:5; 15–18), it is in the devil's power (12–14), and God's triumph over it is at hand (19–22). These affirmations are declared in a context of dispute and division. Revelation 2–3 indicates that other believers in the seven churches in the province of Asia take a very different approach. Led by a teacher on whom Revelation's author bestows the hostile and pejorative nickname "Jezebel" (cf. 1 Kgs 16–21; 2 Kgs 9:30–37), some Jesus-believers actively participate in imperial society including the imperial cult.

Summary. Diverse systems of governance appear across the biblical writings. All are evaluated from a theological perspective. The narratives offer various evaluations, even of the same system. Repeatedly, systems of governance (monarchy, empire) are divinely ordained. While the biblical tradition generally expects obedience to governing systems, this is by no means a universal principle. Further, the tradition recognizes legitimate tensions between governing systems and loyalties to God and to Jesus that require active negotiation. Moreover, every system is relativized by the recognition that God rules over all rulers and by the expectation that the future establishment of God's rule will destroy all human rulers and systems.

[*See also* Apocalypticism; Authority and Order; David; Historical Narratives (Joshua—2 Kings); *and* Kingdom of God (Heaven).]

BIBLIOGRAPHY

Carter, Warren. *Matthew and Empire: Initial Explorations.* Harrisburg, Penn.: Trinity Press International, 2001.
Carter, Warren. *The Roman Empire and the New Testament: An Essential Guide.* Nashville, Tenn.: Abingdon, 2006.
Carter, Warren. *John and Empire: Initial Explorations.* London: T&T Clark, 2008.
Carter, Warren. *What Does Revelation Reveal? Unlocking the Mystery.* Nashville, Tenn.: Abingdon, 2011.
Friesen, Steven. *Imperial Cults and the Apocalypse of John: Reading Revelation in the Ruins.* Oxford: Oxford University Press, 2006.
Goodman, Martin. *Rome and Jerusalem: The Clash of Ancient Civilizations.* New York: Random House, 2007.
Gottwald, Norman. *The Politics of Ancient Israel.* Louisville, Ky.: Westminster John Knox, 2007.

Grabbe, Lester. *Ancient Israel: What Do We Know and How Do We Know It?* London: T&T Clark, 2007.

Horsley, Richard, ed. *Paul and Politics: Ekklesia, Israel, Imperium, Interpretation.* Harrisburg, Penn.: Trinity Press International, 2000.

Horsley, Richard, ed. *In the Shadow of Empire: Reclaiming the Bible as a History of Faithful Resistance.* Louisville, Ky.: Westminster John Knox, 2008.

Mann, Michael. "Revitalized Empires of Domination: Assyria and Persia" and "The Roman Territorial Empire." In *The Sources of Social Power.* Vol. 1: *A History of Power from the Beginning to A.D. 1760*, pp. 231–300. Cambridge, U.K.: Cambridge University Press, 1997.

Scott, James. *Domination and the Arts of Resistance.* New Haven, Conn.: Yale University Press, 1990.

Warren Carter

POVERTY

See Wealth and Poverty.

PRAYER

Prayer is an individual's or group's direct address to God that is generally initiated by humans (Werline, 2007a). While this definition seems straightforward, a few features of biblical narrative actually create some confusion in determining when to classify a text as a prayer. Within the Hebrew Bible, humans slip into conversations with God in which the dialogical language often contains formulations found in typical prayer texts. God may initiate these conversations. This has prompted some scholars to propose that nearly all conversations with God in the Hebrew Bible should be considered prayers (Miller, 1994). The Abraham and Moses narratives contain several instances (e.g., Gen 15:1–6; 18:16–33; Exod 5:22–23; 19:23–24; 32:31–34; Num 11:11–23). Frequent shifts between second-person and first-person addresses within psalms and prayers also generate some confusion about whether a text is a prayer to God or speech about God. Hannah's prayer in 1 Samuel 2:1–10 presents an interesting case. The passage begins with the phrase "Hannah prayed and said," while the

references to God in the prayer are in third person and align with what could be categorized as a hymn.

In the New Testament, conversations with Jesus, especially in the Synoptic Gospels when a person requests healing, include phrases that parallel prayers and the biblical psalms. Some modern interpreters suggest that some of these exchanges should be categorized as prayer. However, this position requires a higher Christology than that presented within the Synoptic Gospels and neglects to consider that any person asking assistance from a person holding a socially higher rank often employs rhetoric that resembles the language of petitionary prayer. Further, the Synoptic Gospels do not promote a practice of praying to Jesus; all prayers are directed to God.

In general, form criticism has dominated studies on prayer in the Hebrew Bible. Sigmund Mowinkel and Herman Gunkel set this agenda for generations of scholars with their magisterial work on the psalms. The establishment of a text's literary form and *Sitz im Leben*, the setting of a psalm within the worship of Israel, holds primary place in their method (Balentine, 1993). While not completely without value and merit, this approach faces some limitations. First, interpreters sometimes seem to imagine the existence of a "pure form," while biblical texts never quite match that form. Second, the reconstruction of a text's *Sitz im Leben* frequently rests on conjecture, especially in the psalms, which rarely offer a clear social setting for a psalm's performance within Israel. Scholars have turned to tradition criticism in order to highlight the way in which the elements of prayers are developed and adapted to new situations. As the psalms became the focus for the analysis of prayer, prayers embedded in biblical narratives suffered neglect until near the end of the twentieth century.

Studies on prayer in the New Testament followed a parallel course as form and redaction criticism became the primary approaches in the discipline. However, Jesus's use of "father" in the Lord's Prayer pushed Christology to the forefront of New Testament prayer studies. This especially gained momentum because of an incorrect interpretation of *'abba*, "father" in Aramaic, as equivalent to "daddy" (Jeremias, 1964). The Lord's Prayer, despite its complete Jewish character, now became a statement of Jesus's unique and intimate relationship to God, which his followers could also enjoy in some fashion as they prayed the prayer he taught them. Add to this the Christological hymns found in Pauline and Deutero-Pauline texts as types of prayers, and Christology established a firm grip on many studies.

Texts from Second Temple Judaism contain numerous prayers. The discovery and publication of the Dead Sea Scrolls added about 200 prayer, psalm, and hymn texts, as well as various liturgical materials imbedded in other documents, to the evidence (Chazon and Bernstein, 1997). Nevertheless, analysis of these prayers remains in its early stages. Overall, studies on biblical prayers have not fully integrated this material, except for citing parallels. By confining studies to canonical boundaries, conclusions about biblical prayers may be skewed or somewhat incomplete.

Characteristics of Biblical Prayer Language. Moshe Greenberg (1983) has shown that prayer language in the Hebrew Bible parallels conversations between humans, especially a person of a lower social level and a social superior. Whether praise or petition, the supplicant's language imagines the divine as being in a position to effect a change. Petitionary prayer in the Hebrew Bible especially draws on basic speech patterns of appeals made to a king for a favor or to correct an injustice. The speaker maintains a tone of politeness and deference by frequently using honorific titles such as "Lord" and referring to one's self as "servant" (Greenberg, 1983). For example, Solomon in his Temple dedication prayer refers to both David and himself with the term "servant" (1 Kgs 8:24, 25, 26, 28, 29, 30, 52, 53).

Further, a common word for the act of praying, "to cry out" (ṣʿq), occurs when a wronged person sues for justice (Greenberg, 1983; Miller, 1994). Miller explains that the word "prayer," *tĕfillāh*, and its cognate verb, *pālal*, have a basic meaning of presenting a case (1994). Psalm 109:7 provides a vivid example of this basic meaning: "When he is tried, let him be found guilty; let his prayer [*tĕfillāh*] be counted as sin." The many complaint and lament texts within the Hebrew Bible fit naturally with this concept of

pleading a case because the petitioner has been wronged (e.g., Pss 6; 7; 17; 18; 59). A delay in an answer, salvation, or vindication moves the prayer from a general petition to a complaint. Besides the pain of an illness or the dangers of enemies who are plotting against the petitioner, the individual suffers the possibility or reality of social "shame" (cf. Ps 22:7–8; and, e.g., Job 12:1–5). Also at risk are God's faithfulness and justice, as Jeremiah makes clear in one of his complaints, even though he seems to know, like Job, that God will win the argument if actually litigated:

> You will be in the right, O LORD,
>   when I lay charges against you;
>   but let me put my case to you.
> Why does the way of the guilty prosper?
>   Why do all who are treacherous thrive?
>   (Jer 12:1; cf. Job 13:18; 23:1–7)

In this particular passage, Jeremiah turns his cataloging of wrongs done to him to "lay charges" (*rîb*) and bring a "case" (*mišpaṭîm*) against God.

Other terms used to introduce prayer, e.g., "call" (*qārāʾ*), "seek" (*biqeš*), "entreat" (*ʿātar*), "supplicate" (*ḥānan*), also imagine a person making a request to a character of higher power who has the ability to offer some kind of favor or assistance (Miller, 1994, pp. 38–46). Prayers of praise and thanksgiving depict God as having answered a petition or as one who gives benefits to humans, whether personal deliverance, deliverance of God's people, the blessing of being God's people, or the blessing of creation (e.g., Pss 8; 22:22–26; 35:18; 42:5, 11; 104; Sir 51:1–12).

When humans offer penitential prayers, the issue of shame surfaces, this time because the wrong has been done against God, who in this constructed reality holds the highest place of honor. Ezra explicitly mentions that shame has come upon the people because of sin, and he accompanies this with postures demonstrating the anxiety of offending God:

> When I heard this, I tore my garment and my mantle, and pulled hair from my head and beard, and sat appalled....I sat appalled until the evening sacrifice. At the evening sacrifice I got up from my fasting, with my

garments and my mantle torn, and fell on my knees, spread out my hands to the LORD my God, and said, "O my God, I am too ashamed and embarrassed to lift my face to you, my God, for our iniquities have risen higher than our heads, and our guilt has mounted up to the heavens." (Ezra 9:3–6)

Similar language occurs in the prayer in Daniel 9:

Righteousness is on your side, O LORD, but open shame, as at this day, falls on us, the people of Judah, the inhabitants of Jerusalem, and all Israel…because of the treachery that they have committed against you. Open shame, O LORD, falls on us, our kings, our officials, and our ancestors, because we have sinned against you. (Dan 9:7–8; cf. Bar 1:15; 2:6)

These kinds of petitioners may seek forgiveness, reinstatement, or amnesty for what is sometimes expressed as "treachery" (*m'l*), an interesting term because it also carries priestly nuances.

The New Testament portrays a similar response to sin in the scene of the prayers of the Pharisee and the tax collector: "But the tax collector, standing far off, would not even look up to heaven, but was beating his breast and saying, 'God, be merciful to me, a sinner!'" (Luke 18:13).

Postures, Times, Places and Petitioners. Prayer in the Bible situates bodies in certain postures, at certain times, occasions, or circumstances, and sometimes in specific places. These all represent ways in which, among other possibilities, culture constructs experience and an individual self in relationship to the community. Culture determines these various elements related to prayer and in a sense inscribes them upon a person in the process of the practice. A person engaged in prayer does not simply think about prayer but bodily participates in the action. As an embodied cultural practice, prayer powerfully unites life circumstances, cultural expectations and ideals, and the understanding of the divine. Thus, prayer is a social action, even if performed alone, because it enacts what culture has taught the person. Prayer also establishes a culture's ethos and aesthetic through actions, words, performing characters, settings, and pageantry.

Postures. The Bible does not contain one uniform posture for praying. People pray standing (1 Kgs 8:22; Luke 18:10, 13), kneeling (Ezra 9:5; 3 Macc 2:1), and lying on the ground (Jdt 9:1; Matt 26:39). They also may lift their hands toward heaven (1 Kgs 8:22; Ezra 9:5; Pss 134:2; 141:2; 143:6; Lam 2:19; Tob 3:11; 3 Macc 2:1). Various other activities may accompany prayer, such as fasting, weeping, mourning, wearing sackcloth, and smearing ashes upon the body. People add these in times of great distress or when approaching God in recognition that they have sinned. These actions increase the intensity of the experience and provide a means to express deep emotions.

Times. The psalms mention prayers in the morning (e.g., Ps 5:3) and in the evening (e.g., Pss 92:2; 119:62) (Penner, 2012). Daniel prays three times each day (Dan 6:10). Several texts refer to prayer in relationship to the time of evening sacrifice (Ps 141:2; Ezra 9:5; Dan 9:21; cf. Exod 29:38–42), but there is no indication that this has become a fixed time for prayer. In Acts, Peter and John go up to the Temple with other Jews to pray at "three o'clock" (Acts 3:1), and an angel visits Cornelius at the same time of day while he is praying (Acts 10:3, 30). The Qumran scrolls refer to times for prayer and liturgies that align with the movement of heavenly bodies during the day and night, throughout the changing of the seasons, and festival times (e.g., 1QS IX–X; 1QH XX; 4Q408; 4Q409; 4Q503; 4Q504) (Penner, 2012). All evidence indicates that by the end of the Second Temple period neither Jews nor the early church followed a uniform time for prayer.

Types of petitioners. People from all social classes could pray; the action is not confined to religious officials. The Hebrew Bible includes prayers by prophets, priests, kings, and ordinary people. In the New Testament, all of Jesus's disciples may pray and are given directions about how to do this in the most proper manner.

When dealing with the sins of the people as a whole, several biblical texts depict Israel relying on a person who occupied a recognized religious office. The model for this kind of intercessor in the tradition was Moses (e.g., Num 11:2; 21:7). Texts in Jeremiah suggest that prophets may have participated in liturgical settings to intervene for the people in order to ward off an approaching danger or to seek forgiveness from God for the people's sins (Jer 7:16; 11:1–14; 14:1—15:9). However, Solomon's prayer in 1 Kings 8 establishes that the people may repair the relationship with God by confessing their sins in or toward the Temple. Still, this reference to the people praying would not preclude a ceremony in which a prophet, or perhaps a priest, would intercede for the people.

Various psalms, especially psalms of individual lament or complaint (e.g., Pss 10; 13; 22; 26; 42; 71), may have been spoken by anyone. Gerstenberger (2009) has proposed that some psalms may have originated and been offered within family and clan settings. Hannah's prayer gives evidence of prayer offered by women (1 Sam 1:10–12; 2:1–10). If one includes blessings within the category of prayer as a kind of indirect petition to God, Ruth shows men, women, and people from all social levels offering blessings as they meet and depart (e.g., Ruth 2:19–20; 3:10; 4:14). Hagar's anguished statement "Do not let me look on the death of the child" (Gen 21:16) also approaches the language of a prayer (Miller, 1994).

In the New Testament, prayer is not confined to Jesus as he gives the disciples instructions about how to pray. The disciples in Luke state that the followers of John the Baptist also engaged in prayer (Luke 11:1). Acts assigns a special practice of prayer and "serving the word" to the apostles (Acts 6:4). Otherwise, Acts includes a wide range of people praying, including Gentiles (Acts 10). The New Testament also refers to prayers of intercession, e.g., when Simon asks Peter and John to pray for him that he not suffer for attempting to buy the power of the Spirit (Acts 8:24) and when Jesus prays for all who follow him (John 17). James gives the elders the role of anointing the sick and praying over them when the ill call upon them: "Are any among you sick? They should call for the elders of the church and have them pray over them, anointing them with oil in the name of the Lord" (Jas 5:14). In Paul's churches, men and women prayed in church services (1 Cor 11:13), and the apostle prayed on behalf of his churches.

Prayer, priests, and temple. The connection between prayer and the Temple is complex. Petitioners pray or are instructed to pray in the Temple (1 Kgs 8:33), toward the Temple (1 Kgs 8:30, 35), toward the city (1 Kgs 8:44; Dan 6:10), or toward the land (1 Kgs 8:48). The Hebrew Bible records no prescribed prayers that priests offered within the Temple services. This led Yehezkel Kaufmann to make his famous pronouncement that in Israel "the priestly temple is the kingdom of silence" (1960, p. 303). The ʾašam offering refers to confession, but the regulations do not specify the content and the place of the confession. Most likely, as Milgrom (1991) argues, the confession took place before going to the sanctuary (Lev 5:5; Num 5:7). Nevertheless, confession functions to remove an inadvertent sin (mʿl) within a priestly ritual sequence that ultimately leads to the central sanctuary. For the Day of Atonement, Leviticus directs the high priest to "lay both his hands on the head of the live goat, and confess over it all the iniquities of the people of Israel, and all their transgressions, all their sins, putting them on the head of the goat" (Lev 16:21). However, the content of that confession remains unknown.

Joel depicts the priests participating in a communal lament over a plague of locusts. The priests deliver this prayer in the midst of a "solemn assembly" in which the people engage in fasting, weeping, mourning, and rending their clothes in repentance, counting on the tradition that God is slow to anger and abounding in steadfast love (vv. 12–13; see Exod 34:6–7). The prophetic voice gives the priests specific directions:

> Between the vestibule and the altar
>   let the priests, the ministers of the LORD, weep.
> Let them say, "Spare your people, O LORD,
>   and do not make your heritage a mockery,
>   a byword among the nations.
> Why should it be said among the peoples,
>   'Where is their God?' "
>
> (Joel 2:17)

The priests' prayer elicits the Lord's response as the culmination of a series of actions (2:18–29).

First Chronicles depicts David assigning roles to the Levites that surely involved prayer: "He appointed certain of the Levites as ministers before the ark of the LORD, to invoke, to thank, and to praise the LORD, the God of Israel" (1 Chr 16:4). The reference to Israel scattered among the nations in the prayer for salvation in 1 Chronicles 16:35–36 anachronistically fits the setting of the postexilic period and not the time of David. In many texts the Levites play musical instruments, offer thanksgiving and praise, and pray (cf. 1 Chr 16:5–36; 2 Chr 7:6; 8:14; 29:25–30; 30:21 [where priests join]).

Luke–Acts relates the Temple and prayer. The pious of Israel gather at the Temple to pray, whether they stand outside praying at the time of the offering of incense (Luke 1:10), praise God because the "consolation of Israel" has come (2:29–32), pray there as a prophetess (2:37), or attend the hour of prayer (Acts 3:1). A Lucan parable places a Pharisee and a sinner praying in the Temple (Luke 18:9–14).

Two factors lead to speculation about whether prayer replaces or stands in the stead of sacrifice: (1) the loss of access to the Temple through exile, by the distance created by living in the Diaspora, or as a result of its destruction, and (2) a group's abandonment of the Temple because of disagreement with the theology and practices of the priests. A previous generation of scholars quickly jumped to the idea that prayer functioned as a simple, easy replacement for sacrifice. Later studies encouraged seeing numerous complex positions as responses to these problems. For example, while the Qumran community did withdraw to the desert, its understanding of its relationship to temple worship developed over time. Further, some of the daily prayers (e.g., 4Q504) predate the founding of the community. Thus, it is impossible to know the function of these prayers before the community's founding and the reason the community first included the prayers in its liturgical collection (Falk, 2000). Further, while Daniel prays at the time of the evening sacrifice and the prayer contains a confession of sin, the precise relationship of the prayer to the temple cult remains difficult to determine (Dan 9).

Literary Functions. Authors and editors during the production of the biblical traditions crafted prayers to fit within the narratives, to conform to narrative goals, and to serve specific purposes (Balentine, 1993). As a result, the way in which people might have prayed in "real life" must be reconstructed and conjectured.

However, one can assume some verisimilitude between portrayals in texts and real practices. Authors employ prayer, in part, in order to develop characters, reveal something about them, establish them as heroes or antiheroes, and thus provide a moral model for their audience. Jacob's prayer before his encounter with Esau not only contributes to the tension of the encounter but also affords the patriarch a way to leverage God in the situation, which Jacob has already attempted with every human he encountered. Hannah's silent, anguished prayer at the "house of the Lord" at Shiloh conveys her deep sorrow about not having a child (1 Sam 1:9–13). Jonah's prayer (Jonah 2:1–10), which may have been inserted in the narrative at a later time, presents interesting character development problems. While the prayer does not contain a confession of sin, it moves the narrative along in its present form.

The Deuteronomistic histories and the texts influenced by them teach that prayer related to the people "turning" back to God triggers a change in their predicament. In this way, prayer sometimes functions as the turning point in a narrative with a cycle that generally has the following stages: the people sin; punishment comes upon them, usually in the form of pestilence or their enemies; the people repent and pray; and God delivers them. God's address in 2 Chronicles captures this turning point in the cycle and combines it with priestly rhetoric: "if my people who are called by my name humble themselves, pray, seek my face, and turn from their wicked ways, then I will hear from heaven, and will forgive their sin and heal their land" (2 Chr 7:14). To "humble" one's self in Chronicles becomes shorthand for repentance. This occurs in the case of Manasseh, who humbles himself and prays (2 Chr 33:10–13) and, because of this, God grants the king freedom from his imprisonment by a foreign invader. In addition, Chronicles is now able to explain the long reign of the person who was otherwise Judah's worst king.

Prayers can also drive or turn the plot within a narrative. The plot in Tobit begins its initial steps toward a resolution after the prayers of Tobit and Sarah (Tob 3:1–6, 10–15). While both pray that it would be better if their lives ended, the prayers display quite different formal features. Tobit's prayer adopts elements from the penitential prayer tradition as he situates his own predicament within the context of the suffering of the Jewish people—domination by a foreign power and exile. However, he strangely changes the prayer's tone in verse 6 by declaring that he unjustly suffers "insults." Sarah, on the other hand, protests her suffering based on her innocence. In response to these prayers, God sends Raphael to solve the issues in both characters' lives by weaving them together into a singular plot.

In the New Testament, Luke especially uses prayer to drive the narrative. The Gospel begins with the people outside the Temple praying at the time of the offering of incense while Zechariah is inside the Temple experiencing an angelophany that explains that God has heard the elderly priest's prayers for a child (Luke 1:13). Thus, prayers assume a prominent place in God acting within history in the coming births of John the Baptist and then Jesus (Holmås, 2005). According to Luke's depiction of Paul's speech before an angry crowd in the Jerusalem Temple, Paul began his mission to the Gentiles because of a vision of Christ that he received when he entered into a trance state while praying in the Temple (Acts 22:17–21). Luke clearly creates this story in order to set up a final series of pronouncements from Paul that the gospel now goes to the Gentiles, the culmination of Luke's theological project of the tragedy of Israel that the Evangelist sets in motion perhaps as early as the Magnificat (Luke 1:46–55) but certainly forms the heart of Jesus's inaugural sermon (Luke 4:16–30).

Prayer and the Moral Life of Community. Within narrative settings or letters like those of Paul, prayers possess significant rhetorical power to shape the audience's thoughts, dispositions, and actions. In part, prayers achieve this within a narrative because members of an audience understand the power of ritual action through their own past experiences. Although located within a story, prayers and other rituals can still trigger the people's culturally learned emotions and attitudes. Further, prayer relies on metaphors and traditions that may have deep roots within the religious person. The person may have heard the language since birth, or it may have been part of

the instruction needed to enter the community. Finally, prayers seem to be a meeting point, a nexus, between humans and the divine. Thus, the moral life evoked in the prayer achieves divine approval for adherents.

For example, the prayer in Ezra 9, in part, establishes boundaries for marriage and assigns social shame to those who cross them. Violation of the boundaries places the whole community in jeopardy of God's punishment and eventual destruction. The book of Ruth either models or reflects the daily practice of blessings that clearly negotiate the liminality of encounters and departures. Characters give special attention to their speech and postures in these moments because the ritual, in part, actualizes the relationships of social power. In the process of negotiating power relationships and boundaries, both Ezra and Ruth use ritual to connect individuals to the larger story of God's people. This happens through the careful choice of words and references to Israel's traditions that the characters integrate into the ritual.

In the Second Temple period, the Qumran scrolls provide a wealth of evidence for how a community could shape individuals. Liturgies and prayers held an important place in this ongoing process, and carefully crafted rhetoric, reinforced through instruction, accompanied ritual action (Newsom, 2007). The *Psalms of Solomon* also reveal a community that used the practice of prayer, and especially the declaration of God's righteousness, to shape the dispositions of the Jews within that group so that they accepted God's "discipline."

The Lord's Prayer and the instructions surrounding it in Matthew, Luke, and the *Didache* exhibit similar features. The Lord's Prayer is a Q tradition, appearing in Matthew 6:9–13 and Luke 11:2–4. Although Christians frequently recite the Lord's Prayer, it contains no distinctive Christian features. Only Matthew's and Luke's placement of the prayer within Jesus's teaching would lead later interpreters to think of the prayer as "Christian." Actually, the prayer's features resemble Jewish prayers from the time period and, to some degree, fall within a trajectory of Jewish prayers that include the Kaddish and the Eighteen Benedictions, the Amidah.

As mentioned, the address to God as "Father," *'abba*, does not equate to "daddy" in English. The title was apparently applied to revered Jewish teachers, as even Matthew 23:9 indicates: "And call no one your father on earth, for you have one Father—the one in heaven." The Hebrew Bible already used the metaphor "father" for God. For example, the penitential lament in Isaiah 63:7—64:12 appeals to God as "father":

> For you are our father,
>   though Abraham does not know us
>   and Israel does not acknowledge us;
> you, O LORD, are our father;
>   our Redeemer from of old is your name (Isa 63:16)
> Yet, O LORD, you are our Father (64:8a)

A prayer in Sirach twice addresses God as father (Sir 23:1, 4). This decision to address God with a family metaphor may rhetorically serve to unite a community as family, as all say the title together. This would fit nicely with traditions within the Gospels that speak of the community as a family or that reconfigure what constitutes family within life in the Kingdom of God (Werline, 2007a).

The opening petitions establish an eschatological tone for the prayer. "Hallowed" or "sanctify your name" evokes Hebrew Bible themes about the importance of protecting God's name from being profaned or dishonored. Ezekiel includes this theme as he speaks about the restoration of God's people from exile. By accomplishing this, God says, "I will sanctify my great name" (Ezek 36:23), for it had been profaned among the nations. A Jewish prayer, the Kaddish, includes a similar petition. The petition for the arrival of God's kingdom, God's end-of-time rule, stands in parallelism with the first petition and expands upon the way in which the sanctification should arrive. Several Second Temple Jewish texts speak of the arrival of God's Kingdom, and these texts imagine this as an overturning of the kingdoms of this world (Dan 7; *As. Mos.* 10). These first petitions, then, long for the day when earthly powers bow to God's power and a new era of justice commences.

The eschatological tone may carry forward into the petition for bread. The word often translated as "daily" (*epiousios*) is problematic. The word appears only in Matthew 6:11 and Luke 11:3 in the New Testament and nowhere else in Greek literature. Danker offers several possible interpretations: (1) bread necessary for existence, (2) bread for today, (3) bread for the following day, and (4) for the coming day, which refers to the arrival of the Kingdom (2000, p. 376). While certainty remains impossible, the final interpretation fits well with the first petitions in the prayer.

In Matthew's version of the prayer, Jesus says, "Forgive us our debts, as we also have forgiven our debtors" (Matt 6:12), while Luke's version states, "Forgive us our sins, for we ourselves forgive everyone indebted to us" (Luke 11:4). The term "debt" may function as a metaphor for "sin." In his explanation of the prayer in Matthew 6:14–15, Matthew's Jesus immediately switches from "debts" to "trespasses." This petition clearly brings the rest of the community into view as the person praying agrees to forgive those who have sinned against him or her, thus making community life possible. The prayer's eschatological tenor makes forgiveness all the more urgent and necessary.

Given the eschatological emphasis established in the prayer, the request "Lead us not into temptation" or, more properly, "Do not deliver us to the time of trial" requests that God deliver the petitioner from the great eschatological struggle. The final line in Matthew, "but deliver us from evil," or perhaps "the evil one," i.e., Satan, advances the thought of the previous petition. If this line does refer to Satan, then this would relate Matthew's prayer to the traditions of apotropaic prayers like those among the Qumran scrolls (Werline, 2007b).

Within the context of Matthew, the Lord's Prayer stands among a collection of directives about how to practice various pious acts (Matt 6:1–18). The text juxtaposes these actions over against the practices of rival groups labeled as "hypocrites." This approach to practice, including prayer, provides a way to draw clear boundaries between the group and "others"; in performing the ritual, people experience the difference. However, the group must also establish the attitude that members should have about those on the outside. Through practice, individuals become not simply culturally shaped but also morally shaped by the group. The *Didache* also places the prayer (*Did.*

8:2–3) in the midst of regulations about fasting (*Did.* 8:1). This text instructs the community to pray the prayer three times each day. However, the prayer also stands within a larger collection of liturgical and ritual practices, e.g., baptism and the Lord's supper, all of which give shape to the community (*Did.* 7:1—10:7).

Luke's placement of the Lord's Prayer also bears the markings of group formation but of a different kind (Luke 11:1). The disciples know that John the Baptist had taught his disciples to pray, and apparently this has given them one kind of distinguishing mark, which the disciples must have perceived as providing some benefit. The disciples wish for the same, and Jesus indicates that in addition God gives the Spirit to those who persistently ask (11:13; cf. Matt 7:7–11, which omits the reference to the Spirit).

Jesus's prayer on behalf of the disciples in John 17:1–26 also establishes boundaries and sets expectations for life within the community. This prayer concludes Jesus's farewell discourse (13:31—17:26). The literary form of this section most closely resembles the testament literature of Second Temple Judaism, in which a patriarch or prominent biblical figure addresses his children before he dies. These texts frequently offer moral exhortations to the children, which of course is especially aimed at the people alive at the time the text was actually written. This prayer specifically draws on the worldview and the metaphors of the Gospel's prologue (1:1–5, 9–14, 16–18). At the foundation of the prayer stands the Word, which has descended into the world to reveal and glorify the Father and establish a community of those who have believed in the Son (17:4–8). Jesus asks the Father to protect this group from the world, which is hostile to the Son and will also be hostile to those who accept him (vv. 11–12, 15). They have been "sanctified," "set apart" from the world through the truth of revelation they have received (vv. 17, 19). This language draws a bold boundary between those in the Johannine community and those on the outside. Jesus prays that those inside the community may be one as he and the Father are one (v. 11). This includes not only those who are already his followers in the Gospel narrative but also all those who will come to believe (vv. 20–21). Thus, Jesus

desires a community unified in love and purpose. The prayer is rhetorically powerful as it calls the community to live the life that Jesus desired for them in his final prayer. According to the prayer, this will be the work of God.

Paul tells his congregations that he prays for them and reveals the basic content of those prayers. Letter writers in the Greco-Roman world frequently and warmly informed their recipients that they entreated the gods on their behalf (Doty, 1973). In this, Paul proves no different. Paul claims that his prayers take the form of a thanksgiving (1 Cor 1:4; Phil 1:3–4; 1 Thess 1:2; Phil 4). Deutero-Pauline texts carry on this tradition (Eph 1:16; Col 1:3; 2 Thess 1:3; 2 Tim 1:3). The prayer reports in the genuine Pauline letters exhibit two basic themes: (1) Paul's continuing appeal that his congregations live a moral life because (2) the eschaton is near. Along with these two themes, Paul adds further causes for thanksgiving. In 1 Corinthians 1:4, the apostle seems to include a reference to the congregation's spiritual gifts with the phrase "grace of God." The prayer report in Philippians draws on themes from moral philosophy as Paul prays that members develop so that they have keen moral insight: "And this is my prayer, that your love may overflow more and more with knowledge and full insight to help you to determine what is best, so that in the day of Christ you may be pure and blameless, having produced the harvest of righteousness that comes through Jesus Christ for the glory and praise of God" (Phil 1:9–11). The concluding exhortations in Philippians combine prayer with the Stoic practice of reflecting on the virtues in order to bring moral advancement (Phil 4:4–9). Paul's blessing in the opening lines of 2 Corinthians extols God for supplying mercy and consolation, which should engender a community in which people console one another (2 Cor 1:3–4). These prayer reports and Paul's instructions about prayer in Philippians either demonstrate or regulate practice as a way to shape a moral community.

[*See also* Cult and Worship; Lord's Prayer; Sacrifice and Offerings; *and* Tabernacles, Temples, and Synagogues.]

BIBLIOGRAPHY

Balentine, Samuel E. *Prayer in the Hebrew Bible: The Drama of Divine–Human Dialogue*. Minneapolis: Fortress, 1993.

Barr, James. "'Abbā Isn't 'Daddy'." *Journal of Theological Studies* 39 (1988): 28–47.

Brown, Francis, S. R. Driver, and Charles A. Briggs. *A Hebrew and English Lexicon of the Old Testament*. Oxford: Clarendon, 1979.

Chazon, Esther G., and Moshe J. Bernstein. "An Introduction to Prayer at Qumran." In *Prayer from Alexander to Constantine: A Critical Anthology*, edited by Mark Kiley, pp. 9–22. London and New York: Routledge, 1997.

Danker, Frederick W., ed. *A Greek–English Lexicon of the New Testament and Other Early Christian Literature*. 3d ed. Chicago: University of Chicago Press, 2000.

Doty, William. *Letters in Primitive Christianity*. Philadelphia: Fortress, 1973.

Falk, Daniel K. "Qumran Prayer Texts and the Temple." In *Sapiential, Liturgical and Poetic Tests from Qumran: Proceedings of the Third Meeting of the International Organization for Qumran Studies, Oslo, 1998*, edited by Daniel K. Falk, Florentino Garcia Martínez, and Eileen M. Schuller, pp. 106–126. Studies on the Texts of the Desert of Judah 30. Leiden, The Netherlands: Brill, 2000.

Gerstenberger, Erhard S. *Der bittende Mensch: Bittritual und Klagelied des Einzelnen im Alten Testament*. Wissenschaftliche Monographien zum Alten und Neuen Testament 51. Eugene, Ore.: Wipf & Stock, 2009.

Greenberg, Moshe. *Biblical Prose Prayer: As a Window to the Popular Religion of Ancient Israel*. Berkeley: University of California Press, 1983.

Holmås, Geir Otto. "'My House Shall Be a House of Prayer': Regarding the Temple as a Place of Prayer in Acts within the Context of Luke's Apologetic Objective." *Journal for the Study of the New Testament* 27 (2005): 393–416.

Jeremias, Joachim. *The Lord's Prayer*. Translated by John Reumann. Philadelphia: Fortress, 1964.

Kaufmann, Yehezkel. *The Religion of Israel*. Chicago: University of Chicago Press, 1960.

Knohl, Israel. "Between Voice and Silence: The Relationship between Prayer and Temple Cult." *Journal of Biblical Literature* 115 (1996): 17–30.

Milgrom, Jacob. *Leviticus 1–16*. Anchor Bible 3. New York: Doubleday, 1991.

Miller, Patrick D. *They Cried to the Lord: The Form and Theology of Biblical Prayer*. Minneapolis: Fortress, 1994.

Newman, Judith H. *Praying by the Book: The Scripturalization of Prayer in Second Temple Judaism*. Society of Biblical Literature Early Judaism and Its Literature 14. Atlanta: Scholars Press, 1999.

Newsom, Carol A. *The Self as Symbolic Space: Constructing Identity and Community at Qumran*. Studies on the Texts of the Desert of Judah 52. Leiden, The Netherlands: Brill, 2004. Reprinted, Atlanta: Society of Biblical Literature, 2007.

Penner, Jeremy. *Patterns of Daily Prayer in Second Temple Period Judaism*. Studies on the Texts of the Desert of Judah 104. Leiden, The Netherlands: Brill, 2012.

Werline, Rodney A. *Pray Like This: Understanding Prayer in the Bible*. New York: T&T Clark, 2007a.

Werline, Rodney A. "Reflections on Penitential Prayer: Definition and Form." In *Seeking the Favor of God*. Vol. 2: *The Development of Penitential Prayer in Second Temple Judaism*, edited by Mark J. Boda, Daniel K. Falk, and Rodney A. Werline, pp. 209–225. Society of Biblical Literature Early Judaism and Its Literature 22. Atlanta: Society of Biblical Literature, 2007b.

RODNEY A. WERLINE

PREACHING AND PROPHECY

Proclamation in the New Testament is a multifaceted phenomenon. The first-century church was heir to both the Jewish prophetic and rabbinic traditions of teaching and preaching and the Greco-Roman rhetorical practices that were ever-present in the popular, philosophical, and religious life of the Mediterranean world. In some sense, the whole of the New Testament can be considered proclamation, but our interest is in formal expressions of proclamation that prefigure (although are not synonymous with) contemporary sermons. Among the numerous kinds of speech named in relation to such formal proclamation in the New Testament are announcing the good news (*euaggelizō/euaggelion*), preaching (*kērrusō/kērygma*), prophesying/prophet (*prophēteuō/prophētēs*), teaching (*didache*), witness (*martys*), comfort or exhortation (*paraklēsis*), and making disciples (*mathēteuō*). In addition, many times preaching is portrayed in the New Testament without the use of any technical vocabulary (e.g., Mark 2:2; Acts 13:46; 23:6; Rom 15:9; Eph 6:19). Instead of focusing on particular vocabulary, then, it is best to examine the various portraits of preaching that appear in the literature.

Gospels. The Gospels (especially the Synoptic Gospels) present Jesus as an itinerate, apocalyptic Jewish preacher and teacher. (The later ecclesiological distinction between preaching and teaching is not found in the New Testament.) The core of his message is the announcement of the advent of the reign of God (Mark 1:14//Matt 4:17). Juxtaposed to the current reign of Caesar, this message had both eschatological and political dimensions. Nevertheless, Jesus never defines the reign of God but only describes it, especially in his parables.

While much of Jesus's proclamation was likely passed down to the Gospel writers in the form of independent parables and *logia*, the Gospel narratives also present Jesus as preaching and teaching in the form of extended, somewhat thematically focused discourses (e.g., the parables and eschatological discourses in Mark 4 and 13, the Sermon on the Mount/Plain in Matt 5–7//Luke 6:17–49, and the Good Shepherd discourse in John 10:1–18).

The form of Jesus's preaching found in Luke 4:16–21 has been among the most influential on later homiletical practices. Jesus is in the synagogue, stands to read a text from Isaiah that describes the coming of God's Spirit upon the one anointed to proclaim God's good news (58:6; 61:1–2), and sits down to declare that the scripture has been fulfilled that day in their hearing. The church has found in this scene a paradigm for its preaching: the preacher is anointed by the Holy Spirit, the sermon is to be based on scripture, and the message should be applied to the contemporary situations of the hearers.

In the Synoptic Gospels, Jesus commissions his apostles also to proclaim the reign of God during his ministry (Mark 6:12; Matt 10:7; Luke 9:2; 10:9). But throughout the New Testament, apostolic preaching is primarily presented as a postresurrection phenomenon. Yet in spite of the patriarchy of the first century, the Gospels present women (and not members of the Twelve) as the first witnesses (in the sense of both the first to see and the first to testify) to the resurrection (Mark 16:1–8; Matt 28:1–10; Luke 24:1–12, 22, 24; John 20:1–18; contrast 1 Cor 15:5, in which Paul cites tradition that claims the risen Christ first appeared to Cephas and then the Twelve).

Acts. In Acts (Luke's second volume), however, the women do not remain at center stage, but rather one finds the apostles to whom the risen Jesus promises the Holy Spirit so that they might be his witnesses to the ends of the earth (1:8). In the fashion of ancient historiographers, Luke creates speeches for his main characters that are appropriate to the flow of the narrative. It is no surprise, then, to find that the sermons throughout Acts, though spoken by various characters, all sound quite similar and follow a consistent pattern.

This pattern is established with the first sermon in the narrative found in the story of Pentecost (ch. 2) and is similar to that found in Jesus's teaching in Luke 4: the Holy Spirit comes upon those gathered. Then Peter addresses the crowd by quoting scriptural texts and interpreting them for the situation of the hearers. But added to the pattern from Luke 4 are two new elements. First is a new narrative core to the proclamation appropriate for the postresurrection setting. Peter declares to those gathered in Jerusalem: *you* killed Jesus, *God* raised Jesus, and *we* are witnesses to the resurrection (2:23, 24, 32). The second added element is the response to the apostolic message. Those persuaded by the proclamation are baptized (2:37–41) and begin participating in the communal life of the church, which includes attending to continued apostolic teaching (2:42). Luke, however, never provides an example of an apostolic sermon preached to those in the church that includes the level of detail he uses in the evangelistic sermons.

As the proclamation of the resurrection is carried to Gentiles outside of Judea, Luke modifies the pattern slightly to fit the new audience. First, instead of quoting Jewish scriptures, which would have no authority for the Gentiles, other sources of authority are used (the most dramatic example is Paul's Areopagus sermon in Acts 17:22–31). Second, a pronoun shift is required in the narrative core of the message from *you* to *they* killed Jesus (e.g., Acts 10:39–41). Luke models Christian preaching that adapts rhetorically to new circumstances while maintaining a consistent message.

Paul. In Paul, the resurrection (or, better, the death and resurrection) of Christ remains the center of proclamation. He speaks most directly about the content of his preaching when dealing with conflict in 1 Corinthians. When dealing with divisions within the community, he emphasizes that his preaching focused on the cross (1 Cor 1:10—2:5). That this message included the resurrection is seen at the close of the letter where he reminds the Corinthians of the content of the tradition ("of first importance") that he proclaimed when he was with them as recounting the story of Jesus's "death for our sins in accordance with the scriptures" through a series of resurrection appearances including an appearance to him (15:1–8). Similar to the Gospels and Acts, then, Paul focuses his preaching on Christ's death and resurrection, draws on scripture in proclaiming that good news, and considers himself qualified to proclaim this message because he is a witness to the resurrection (v. 8).

Other than this, we know little about the content or form of Paul's oral proclamation and teaching. Paul does, however, provide some explication of his theology of preaching. He asserts that proclamation participates in God's salvific work in that faith comes by hearing the word of Christ proclaimed (Rom 10:14–17; cf. Paul's identification of his vocation as proclamation as opposed to baptism in 1 Cor 1:17). On the other hand, he dismisses rhetorical eloquence in his own preaching (1 Cor 1:17; 2:1–5; cf. what Paul reports others say about his manner of speech in 2 Cor 10:10). While this dismissal is clearly a rhetorical device by which Paul lifts up the effectiveness of his preaching, he makes an argument for the content of the Gospel being distinct from the abilities of the preacher (see also 2 Cor 4:5).

Paul also speaks about the importance of preaching within the community of faith when he is not present. He does so in the context of contrasting the gift of prophecy with that of speaking in tongues in 1 Corinthians 12–14. As he begins this section, Paul names a variety of manifestations of the Spirit (vv. 8–10; cf. Rom 12:6–8 and Eph 4:11 for similar lists). Of the nine gifts listed, five (and possibly six if discernment of spirits is included) refer to oral speech within the community. As Paul's argument advances, he uses a similar list in 12:28: "God has appointed in the church first apostles, second prophets, third teachers; then deeds of power, then gifts of healing, forms of

assistance, forms of leadership, various kinds of tongues." The first three items are persons or offices in the church, which he enumerates. They are followed by an unnumbered list of *charismata*. Here, it seems that even though Paul values the variety of spiritual gifts, he does prioritize them (see v. 31). The first three are highlighted in a way the others are not, and the three are all offices characterized by oral proclamation. Given that the role of apostle is reserved for a few, prophecy is highly important to Paul: it is second only to the work of apostles, the only item to appear in all of his lists of spiritual gifts, and the gift to which he calls all to aspire (1 Cor 14:1, 39).

In these lists, it is unclear whether words of wisdom and knowledge, prophecy, teaching, and revelation (see 14:30) are synonymous, related, or fairly distinctive. Likely they overlap in ways about which we cannot be precise from our distance (see 14:6). Prophecy is usually assumed to be inspired, perhaps even at times immediately revealed, speech that comes from God and is intelligible to the hearers. By contrast, Paul makes a strong distinction between prophecy and speaking in tongues. While he does not dismiss speaking in tongues as a gift of the Spirit, prophecy serves a purpose he values more. Whereas speaking in tongues is ecstatic, prophets can control what they say (14:32). Whereas speaking in tongues is a form of prayer (14:2), prophecy is proclamation to the community (14:22–25), building it up and offering encouragement and consolation (14:3). Whereas speaking in tongues requires interpretation for others to understand (14:2, 6–19, 23, 27–28), prophecy can be understood by and be edifying for all (14:3, 24).

An utterance claimed to be prophetic was not, however, to be accepted without questioning. Listeners must weigh what is said to determine if it is truly a word from God (1 Cor 14:29; 1 Thess 5:20). There could be false prophets or preachers who were simply mistaken.

Catholic Epistles. Even though Jesus's discourses as we have them are constructed by the Gospel writers instead of the historical Jesus, the sermons in Acts are constructed by Luke instead of the designated speakers, and Paul does not provide an example of Jesus's preaching, there may be some texts among the Catholic epistles that originated as actual sermonic material delivered to Christian communities. For instance, biblical scholars used to argue that 1 Peter was a baptismal homily because of the lack of clear recipients of the letter, use of baptismal imagery (1 Pet 3:21) and references to conversion, and the author's description of the letter's content as a word of encouragement and witness (5:12). In the twenty-first century, scholars more often argue 1 Peter is a real letter whose purpose is moral exhortation to some who are experiencing persecution.

Many scholars, on the other hand, assert that Hebrews and James have homiletical origins. Both are missing some of the standard elements found in ancient letters, and the ones present seem artificial. Hebrews is either an extended sermon or a collection of excerpts from oral "words of exhortation" (see Heb 5:11; 13:22). The writing draws extensively on scripture, interpreting texts in light of the Christ event and using those interpretations as the basis for calling the audience to lives of faithfulness. James is moral exhortation in line with the wisdom tradition and in the form of a diatribe (see Jas 1:22). In an approach strikingly different from Hebrews, James has very little Christological interest (see only 1:1 and 2:2). However, James does know something of Jesus's teachings (see 1:6; 2:8; 5:12) and uses them in the same way he draws on material from scripture.

This brief survey shows that preaching and prophecy in the New Testament is anything but monolithic in terms of theological content or homiletical form. This is, of course, true of preaching today as well. Nevertheless, almost all of the homiletical elements named above still find a home in different traditions defining the essence of Christian preaching: inspiration of the preacher, biblically based sermons, the centrality of the crucifixion and resurrection, distinction between evangelistic preaching and preaching to the community, and exhortation or consolation of the audience in relation to their circumstances.

[*See also* Authority and Order; Ecclesiology; Gospel; Holy Spirit; Revelation; *and* Story and Memory.]

BIBLIOGRAPHY

Edwards, O. C. "The Earliest Christian Preaching." In *A History of Preaching*, pp. 3–26. Nashville, Tenn.: Abingdon, 2004.

Old, Hughes Oliphant. *The Reading and Preaching of the Scriptures in the Worship of the Christian Church*. Vol. 1: *The Biblical Period*. Grand Rapids, Mich.: Eerdmans, 1998.

Osborn, Ronald E. *Folly of God: The Rise of Christian Preaching*. A History of Christian Preaching 1. St. Louis, Mo.: Chalice, 1999.

O. Wesley Allen Jr.

PRIESTS AND PRIESTHOOD

The priest in the Hebrew Bible is a religious specialist whose function is related particularly to cult places such as shrines and temples. He offers (or at least oversees) sacrifices for worshippers, looks after the shrine, makes enquiries of the Deity, gives rulings and blessings, and teaches the Law. Different parts of this profile are emphasized in different parts of the Hebrew Bible, depending upon what the authors' main concerns are. This entry will first consider historical questions relating to the development of the priesthood as it can be reconstructed from the Hebrew Bible. It will then examine priests' duties and consider the two main theologies of priesthood in the Hebrew Bible, before looking at a selection of postbiblical and New Testament understandings of priesthood.

History of the Priesthood. The historical-critical methodologies of the nineteenth and twentieth centuries as practiced in particular by the nineteenth-century German scholar Julius Wellhausen (1844–1918) viewed the history of priesthood as reflected in the Hebrew Bible in developmental terms. According to this schema, priesthood began as a relatively unregimented phenomenon at local shrines. Over time, however, a number of localized groups (including the Levites) developed their priestly competence to a high degree and gradually claimed the exclusive right to performing priestly duties so that those who were not members of the group no longer had the opportunity to carry out priests' duties.

A significant event in the history of priesthood was the passing of religious reforms by King Josiah in 622 B.C.E., which aimed to eliminate every shrine or temple in Israel except for the one in Jerusalem. Josiah's reforms meant that those who had served as priests in the outlying shrines lost their jobs, leading to competition among all the former priests as to who would serve as priests in the Jerusalem Temple. Ultimately, the Jerusalem-based priests claiming descent from Zadok, David's priest when Jerusalem was established as the capital of David's new monarchy (2 Sam 8:17) and the first priest in the temple subsequently built by Solomon (cf. 1 Kgs 4:4), claimed and retained the right to serve as full priests (Ezek 40:46), while other provincial priestly groups (the "Levites") were downgraded into assistant clergy (cf. Ezek 44:10–16).

Following the Babylonian Exile (586–538 B.C.E.), the restored community focused its identity around the Jerusalem Temple, which was the country's one remaining Yahwistic shrine; and in the absence of a restored monarchy, the role of the high priest developed to take over what had been the sacral aspects of the king's role, namely, representing the whole people before God at major religious festivals in Jerusalem and overseeing the Jerusalem Temple. Thus, from having all priests at effectively the same level and entitled to carry out all the same duties, the structure of the priesthood changed over time to become a priestly pyramid based on subgroups of descent within a larger group: all the tribe of Levi were entitled to be clerical assistants; but within that the sons of Aaron alone were entitled to be priests, and within that group eventually only the sons of Zadok were entitled to be high priests.

The Biblical Evidence. The outlined schema is arrived at by comparing the regulations about priests in Exodus, Leviticus, Numbers, and Deuteronomy with the narratives involving priests in Joshua—2 Kings. Joshua—2 Kings presents the story of Israel from its settlement in the land to its exile in Babylon, but its picture of priesthood is inconsistent with the detailed laws for high priests, priests, and Levites that appear in the books of Exodus, Leviticus, and Numbers, which precede the book of Joshua.

Exodus 28 describes Aaron and his sons being set aside for priesthood at God's command, with Aaron himself being the archetypal high priest; and Numbers 3 and 8 show the rest of the Levites being instituted as assistants to the priests. A genealogy in Exodus 6 makes both Moses and Aaron sons of Levi and shows the various levitical family lines that are used when allocating duties to different groups of Levites (Exod 6:16–25; cf. Num 3:17–39). Yet in Joshua—2 Kings there is no high priest as such (although there are chief priests of local shrines, including the Jerusalem Temple); there is no mention of priests having to be descended from Aaron; and indeed, some priests are not even descended from Levi (Judg 17:5; 2 Sam 8:18). Nor is there any evidence of Levites being assistant, nonsacrificing clergy as against the full priests who were the sons of Aaron.

The conclusion that Wellhausen drew from this is that the three-tier structure of high priest, priests, and Levites was not in fact known or instituted until after the Exile and that the materials in Exodus, Leviticus, and Numbers in which this structure is presented as originating from Moses's tryst with God at Sinai were a postexilic composition, retrojecting the laws for priesthood to the time of Israel's foundation in order to claim divine authority for what was actually an innovation. A counterargument might be that the books of Chronicles, which tell the story of much of the same period as Joshua—2 Kings, do show the three-tier priesthood in operation during that period. However, the books of Chronicles are widely acknowledged to be a later version of the history. They may well therefore be composed from a perspective that takes the three-tier priesthood for granted as present reality, whether or not it would have been so in the period that they describe.

More compatible with the picture of priesthood in Joshua—2 Kings are the laws about priests in Deuteronomy. These say very little about how the priesthood should be structured, merely assuming that all members of the tribe of Levi have the right to serve as priests and specifying the portions of the sacrifices to which they have exclusive right (Deut 18:1–8). Although styled as the last words of Moses, Deuteronomy in its present form is dated by many scholars to a time no later than the Babylonian Exile. Whether they are regarded as Mosaic or late monarchic, though, the laws in Deuteronomy are universally regarded as dating from the preexilic period and, thus, may be a truer reflection of priestly realities during that time.

Priests in the Prophetic Books. Aside from the narrative and legal material, evidence in the prophetic literature relating to priests and priesthood is limited and tantalizing. Nevertheless, it does seem to represent a similar range of views to those already outlined for the narrative and legal material.

Major Prophets. Of the three major prophetic books (Isaiah, Jeremiah, Ezekiel), the Exile-dated Ezekiel has the most explicit references to priests and their duties, stipulating in particular that the Zadokites should be priests in the restored Temple after the Exile and setting down some of the rules for their service (Ezek 44:9–31). Since Ezekiel himself is presented as a priest (Ezek 1:3), the book's concern with the priesthood is unsurprising. Isaiah has several passing references to priests that offer no independent information about the priesthood. Jeremiah has a slightly clearer narrative picture of ranks of priesthood at the Temple in Jerusalem during the late monarchy (Jer 19:1; 20:1; 29:25–26; 52:24) and apparently favors a levitical ideology of priesthood corresponding to that in Deuteronomy (Jer 33:17–22). Like Ezekiel, Jeremiah himself is pictured as a priest, in the sense that he is from a priestly family (Jer 1:1), although his kin are based outside Jerusalem in Anathoth, a location that links them implicitly with the disgraced priest Abiathar, who was Zadok's counterpart in the time of David but who forfeited the favor of Solomon by supporting Solomon's elder brother and rival claimant to the throne, Adonijah (1 Kgs 1:5–8; 2:26–27). Ezekiel and Jeremiah may therefore to some extent represent the perspectives of Jerusalem Temple priests and provincial priests, respectively.

Minor Prophets. In the Book of the Twelve (Hosea—Malachi) the references to priests are often in passing, although they associate the priests with teaching the Law and with offering sacrifices. Only one of the Twelve gives any hint about who was eligible to be a priest: in a critique of contemporary priestly practice, the fifth-century B.C.E. book of Malachi speaks

of the covenant with Levi that the priests are breaking by their misdemeanors (Mal 2:4–9). This implies that Malachi views the priests as descendants of Levi—as do Deuteronomy and Jeremiah—although it gives no evidence of the subgroups within the levitical corpus that are introduced in Exodus, Leviticus, and Numbers.

Duties of Priests. What, then, according to the various Hebrew Bible sources, were the details of priests' duties? In setting out what priests were thought to do, scholars often refer to a passage from the so-called Blessing of Moses in Deuteronomy 33. Here, Moses blesses the tribes of Israel individually before his death, and in referring to the tribe of Levi he says,

> Give to Levi your Thummim, and your Urim to your loyal one, whom you tested at Massah, with whom you contended at the waters of Meribah; who said of his father and mother, "I regard them not"; he ignored his kin, and did not acknowledge his children. For they observed your word, and kept your covenant. They teach Jacob your ordinances, and Israel your law; they place incense before you, and whole burnt offerings on your altar. Bless, O LORD, his substance, and accept the work of his hands; crush the loins of his adversaries, of those that hate him, so that they do not rise again. (Deut 33:8–11)

Although the passage is regarded by many as composite because the priestly persona changes from singular ("*he* ignored his kin") to plural ("*they* observed your word") and back again ("bless *his* substance"), it does describe the range of duties that priests can be seen as carrying out elsewhere in the Hebrew Bible. The first, perhaps surprising to modern sensibilities, is that of divination: the Urim and Thummim referred to in Deuteronomy 33:8 are shown in the Hebrew Bible narratives as sacred lots that were manipulated by priests in order to discern the Deity's will (1 Sam 14:41–42). The priests were the guardians of the technical skills associated with divination and enquired of the Lord using mechanical means, as opposed to prophets who claimed more direct verbal inspiration for their messages.

The reference in Deuteronomy 33:9 to Levi disregarding his family may be intended to evoke the tradition about Levites that is recounted in Exodus 32. Here, the Levites declare their loyalty to Yahweh by killing every Israelite, including members of their own families, who committed idolatry by worshipping the golden calf while Moses was on Mt. Sinai. As a result Moses tells the Levites that they have ordained themselves for service to God (Exod 32:25–29). The tradition establishes a strong link between Levites and zeal for God, thereby validating their claim to special duties in regard to the Deity and legitimizing a Levite priesthood.

The other two characteristics of Levites listed in Deuteronomy 33 are that they teach the Law to the people and offer incense and food sacrifices on the altar on behalf of the people. Both characteristics are associated with priests elsewhere in the Hebrew Bible. Hosea, for example, criticizes the priests for their failure to teach the Law to the people (Hos 4:6), as does Malachi (2:7–9); and in an intriguing narrative in 2 Kings 17:24–28, an exiled Israelite priest is sent back to Israel to teach Assyrian settlers there the "law of the god of the land." Priests officiating at sacrifices are also mentioned in the narrative and prophetic materials (1 Sam 2:12–17; 2 Kgs 16:15; Mal 1:6–8), although the most detailed picture of priests' sacrificial duties is in Leviticus, with the first seven chapters of the book describing the various kinds of sacrifice that are to be offered and the respective roles to be taken by priest and offerer in each case.

Priests' duties, then, are defined as mechanical divination of the Lord's will, officiating at sacrifices, and teaching the Law to the people. Given such a picture, it is understandable that priesthood is shown as hereditary: the skills required to function as a priest were such that they could be learned and transmitted from generation to generation and would probably be preserved and honed within professional guilds much like any other skill or craft. It also resonates with the Hebrew idiom for ordination of a priest, to "fill the hand" (*millēʾ yad*), which implies something physical and practical rather than sacral and spiritual and may evoke the priest manipulating the sacred portions of the sacrificial offerings during the ritual or receiving his allocated share of the offering as his payment.

Theology of priesthood: Deuteronomy. Although the sources broadly agree on the duties of priesthood, there are differing theological evaluations of the office. Two main theologies of priesthood can be seen in the Hebrew Bible. The first is the deuteronomic, epitomized in Deuteronomy itself, which although it contains the "priests' manifesto" of 33:8–11 just discussed, includes little detail in its legal stipulations about priests' duties. Priests are defined as "sons of Levi" (Deut 21:5), and their duties are defined by the umbrella phrase "[stand to] minister in the name of the LORD" (17:12; 18:5, 7), usually at the central sanctuary (17:8–9; 18:6–7).

The priests at the central sanctuary are given the responsibility of deciding legal cases that are too hard for local judges, presumably by using some form of divination or ordeal (17:8–9, 12); they are by implication the guardians of the Law, which has to be written out in their presence and given to the king (17:18); and they are entitled to certain portions of the sacrifices (18:1–4). They are to officiate with the judges in cases of false accusation (19:16–17), to reassure the troops before battle that the Lord is with them (20:2–4), to officiate in the ceremony to purge bloodguilt when a corpse is found (21:5), to bless the people in the name of the Lord (21:5), to teach the people what to do in a plague of leprosy (24:8), to receive the offerings of first fruits and tithes from the people (26:3–4), to curse those who disobey the Law (27:14–26), and to look after the copy of the Law written by Moses and read it out to the people every seven years (31:9–13). This is quite a nonsacral understanding of priesthood, in line with the outlook of Deuteronomy as a whole; it associates priests firmly with keeping the Law and finding out the will of God in order to instruct the people in it, rather than viewing priests as sacral mediators between heaven and earth. Assuming that there is no distinction between "Levites" and priests, the priests are also given the job of carrying the Ark of the Covenant (Deut 10:8–9), which contains the Law but which also functions in war—an interesting link, given that the priests have to bless the troops before they go out to war.

Theology of priesthood: Priestly materials. The second main theology of priesthood is embodied in the so-called Priestly materials in Exodus, Leviticus, and Numbers, which have a much more sacral outlook. They show a highly stratified society in which the priests are the guardians of cultic and ritual purity and have a primary role as sacrificial practitioners, to the extent that sacrifice requires the participation of a priest. Priests have to manipulate the blood of the sacrificial animal (Lev 1:5, 11, 15; 3:2, 8, 13; 4:5–7, 16–18, 25, 30, 34; 5:9), and in the types of sacrifice designated as sin or guilt offerings they have to consume the offering as the means of removing the impurity that the offerer's sin has generated (6:25—7:7). There are strict rules for how the priests conduct themselves and who they can marry (Lev 21:1–15), what they must wear when serving at the altar (Exod 28), and how they are to be ordained (Exod 29:1–36); there is also a strict boundary between sons of Levi in general and sons of Aaron in particular, the latter being the only ones among the sons of Levi who are allowed to serve as altar priests and eat the food from the sacrifices (Lev 7:29–36), while the former are what might be termed sanctuary support staff (Num 3:6–9).

Priestly service is understood in terms of "coming near to the Lord," and anyone who comes near without a specific commission to do so from the Lord himself will suffer the fate of being consumed by fire (Lev 10:1–3; Num 3:10; 16:1–11, 16–22, 35–40). Indeed, the ordination ritual and the special priestly clothing, especially that of the high priest, underline the link between the priests and sanctuary duties and define the prime locus of priestly activity as the sanctuary: the ritual itself (Lev 8—9) takes place within the sanctuary, requiring the ordinands to remain inside it for seven days as well as to be sprinkled with blood from a sacrifice and anointing oil, ending with Aaron being enabled to offer sacrifice; and certain elements of the high priest's clothing are made out of the same material as parts of the tent of meeting (Exod 28:4–8; cf. Exod 26:1, 31). Within this schema there is less direct emphasis on the priests as teachers of the Law, although of course it is implicit that they would need the knowledge of the Law to be able to carry out their duties correctly; and Aaron and his sons are commissioned to teach the people the difference between the clean and the unclean, between the holy and the common, and to teach them the Law (Lev 10:10–11).

There are various instances of what it means in practice to distinguish between clean/unclean and holy/common. Priests are to give rulings about what counts as a case of "leprosy" and to say when the leprosy has gone (Lev 13); they are to officiate at sacrifices designed to purify individuals from various types of impurity, including that generated by leprosy and genital discharges (Lev 14; 15:13–15, 28–30); they blow trumpets to mark festivals (Num 10:8, 10); and they may be required to value items or people that are dedicated to the Lord (Lev 27:8, 11–12, 14, 18, 21, 23). They also bless the people in the name of the Lord (Num 6:22–27). As for the Levites, they are described as being a substitute sacrifice for the first-born males of Israel (Num 3:12–13). As such, they are dedicated to the Lord in the service of the priests and the tabernacle (Num 8:19), a rationale that gives them sacral, if passive, dignity, quite different from the levitical etiology in Exodus 32, which shows them as warlike and zealous for the Lord.

Within this schema, too, the high priest has a particular role, in that he represents the whole people in his own person (Exod 28:12, 29–30; cf. Lev 4:3). In this capacity his tour de force is on the annual Day of Atonement, when he officiates both to purify the sanctuary from the defilement generated by the people's sins and to purify the people themselves from their sins (Lev 16). His elaborate ceremonial clothing bespeaks his representative function in that it includes a 12-stoned breast-piece, each stone engraved with the name of one of the tribes of Israel (Exod 28:15–21), and two shoulder stones for the breast-piece, on each of which is engraved the names of 6 of the 12 tribes of Israel (Exod 28:9–12). This allows him ritually speaking to bring the people of Israel into the sanctuary when he wears the clothing. Beyond this he has special duties of ritual maintenance in the sanctuary (Lev 24:1–9), and his death is the means whereby those who have committed accidental homicide are freed from bloodguilt, indicating that it has some sort of expiatory effect (Num 35:22–33). As a reflection of his exalted position in the ritual hierarchy, he is required to maintain an even stricter degree of ritual purity than the ordinary priests, being restricted in whom he can marry and in those for whom he is allowed to participate in mourning rites (Lev 21:10–15).

In this sacral view of priesthood the Urim and Thummim, the sacred lots used by priests for divination, are restricted to being a part of the high priest's ceremonial garb (Exod 28:30) and are never shown being used. Instead, the cultic system of sacrifices and the detailed instructions given by the Lord to Moses have become the resource via which priests make known the will of God to the people and vice versa.

Postbiblical Pictures of Priesthood. Broadly speaking, then, the materials in the Hebrew canon present two different theologies of priesthood: the sacral and the nonsacral. In both of these schemes the priests perform the same kind of duties (facilitating offerings at the sanctuary, teaching the Law, discerning the will of the Lord, ceremonies of ritual purification, blessing the people), but there is a difference in the internal organization and the sacral significance of both the priesthood and the community of which it is a part so that different aspects of the priestly role are emphasized in the different schemes. Turning to the literature of Second Temple Judaism that postdates the Hebrew canon, from ca. 200 B.C.E. to ca. 100 C.E., there are some distinctive developments in the picture of priesthood: the picture of the priests' duties is not significantly altered, but there is an increase in the sacrality of the priesthood, together with more detailed speculation about how the tribe of Levi comes to be granted the priesthood. For present purposes I shall consider four works in which priesthood appears: the Wisdom of Ben Sira (also known as Sirach or Ecclesiasticus) from the Apocrypha, the noncanonical books *Jubilees* and the *Testament of Levi*, and the Dead Sea Scrolls. All of these sources build on the picture of priesthood as presented in the documents of the Hebrew canon and adapt that picture to their own particular theological interests.

Wisdom of Ben Sira. In this work from an early second-century B.C.E. Jewish writer in Jerusalem, the priesthood, particularly the high priesthood,

receives sustained attention. As part of a list of great figures from Israel's past, Ben Sira extols Aaron and his grandson Phinehas as the ancestors of the priestly line and the high priestly line, respectively (45:6–22, 23–24), and a few chapters later gives an elaborate description of the high priest Simon II officiating at the Jerusalem Temple in Ben Sira's own day, aided by ranks of Aaronide priests (50:1–24). The details of the priestly rights and duties in these descriptions of priesthood (45:16–17, 20–22) correspond to those in the biblical record, but Ben Sira's evaluation of these (high) priests themselves is much more exalted. In chapter 45 Aaron is given 17 verses of description by comparison with the five that are given to Moses (45:1–5), and when wearing the high priestly vestments Aaron is pictured in quasi-supernatural terms of splendor, glory, perfection, and holiness (45:7–8, 10, 12–13). The priesthood's special relationship with the Deity is stressed by saying that God chose Aaron out of all the living to offer sacrifice (45:16), and twice Ben Sira asserts that God made an everlasting covenant with Aaron and his descendants for the priesthood (45:7, 15), language which goes beyond the biblical description (cf. Exod 28:1) and equates the granting of priesthood to Aaron with the granting of kingship to David. In chapter 50 the description of Simon officiating at the Temple for the daily sacrifice again emphasizes the glorious, unearthly nature of the scene and of the officiating high priest himself, implying that the ritual being carried out has cosmic significance and that the high priest embodies "a union of earthly and heavenly worlds" (Hayward, 1996, p. 72).

Book of Jubilees. Another second-century B.C.E. work with a distinctive view of priesthood is the book of *Jubilees*, which is a reworking of the biblical narrative from Genesis 1—Exodus 12. *Jubilees* shows how from the very beginning of history all the heroes of Israel followed the Jewish Law, and it includes a description of how Levi himself (rather than just his descendants) came to be granted the priesthood. In fact, *Jubilees* gives four versions of how Levi and his descendants are granted the priesthood.

In the first version, priesthood is a reward to Levi for his righteous zeal in killing the Hivites whose prince, Shechem, had slept with Jacob's daughter Dinah. The priesthood that is granted to Levi is said to reflect that of the angels in heaven who minister in the presence of the Lord (*Jub.* 30:18). In a second version, Jacob takes his sons Judah and Levi to visit his father Isaac, and Isaac is inspired by a spirit of prophecy to bless the two sons. In his blessing of Levi, Isaac grants him the priesthood (*Jub.* 31:12–17) and compares serving as priest in the earthly sanctuary with being a ministering angel in the presence of God (*Jub.* 31:14). Jacob then takes Judah and Levi with him to Bethel, where in a third version Levi dreams that he and his sons have been ordained priest of God Most High forever (*Jub.* 32:1). The fourth version of how Levi becomes priest is in *Jubilees* 32:2–3, where at Bethel Jacob offers to the Lord a tithe of everything he has, including his sons. In order to determine which son to dedicate to the Lord, Jacob counts from the youngest up, which makes Levi the tenth son, so Jacob ordains him priest. Levi subsequently serves as a priest in Jacob's presence at Bethel (*Jub.* 32:9). An additional aspect of the picture of Levi in *Jubilees* is that when Jacob dies he gives "all of his books and the books of his fathers to Levi, his son, so that he might preserve them and renew them for his sons until this day" (*Jub.* 45:15).

There seem to be several elements underlying this distinctive presentation in *Jubilees*. The first is the author's desire to show the Jewish Law as having been in effect from the very beginning of time, particularly in relation to cultic observances, which would require a priesthood and some sort of cultic instruction. The second is the author's desire to explain certain details of the biblical text that he deemed anomalous, especially again in relation to cultic observance. For example, in Genesis 28:22 Jacob promises one-tenth of all his possessions to the Lord, but the text never shows him actually paying the tithe; and in any case, without priests and functioning sanctuaries (which are absent from Genesis), how and where would he pay the tithes? The third element is the claim in Malachi 2:4–7 that God made a covenant with Levi, something that can only have happened in the patriarchal period but which is not shown in Genesis. A combination of explanatory exegesis and traditions related

to Levi, probably filtered through earlier works that elaborated on the idea of a covenant with Levi, enabled the author of *Jubilees* to smooth over some of the anomalies that he saw in the Genesis text using this extraordinary picture of Levi being instituted as primordial priest and the guardian of tradition (cf. Mal 2:7). This in turn enabled him to stress his own view of the importance of cultic observances and the dignity of the priesthood by showing earthly priesthood as a reflection of heavenly worship.

Testament of Levi. A second extracanonical work that shows Levi himself rather than simply his descendants being granted an eternal priesthood is the *Testament of Levi*, which is one of the *Testaments of the Twelve Patriarchs*. Like *Jubilees*, the *Testaments* can be dated to the second century B.C.E., and they present the last words of each of the sons of Jacob to their own sons.

In the *Testament of Levi*, Levi himself describes how he came to acquire the priesthood, in a narrative that has several points of contact with *Jubilees*. First, Levi dreams that he is being taken up into the heavens by an angel, where he is told by the angel and by God himself that he and his descendants will receive the priesthood (*T. Levi* 2:5–12; 4:2–4a; 5:2). He carries out the zealous act of taking vengeance on the Hivites and subsequently at Bethel receives a second vision in which seven angels invest him as priest by dressing him in the high priestly garments (*T. Levi* 8:1–10). Priestly privileges are promised too for Levi's descendants (*T. Levi* 8:11–17). Then, along with Jacob and Judah, he visits Isaac, who blesses him in accordance with the vision that Levi has received (*T. Levi* 9:2) and subsequently teaches him the law of the priesthood (*T. Levi* 9:6–14). Finally, Jacob sees a vision that Levi should be a priest and pays tithes to the Lord through Levi (*T. Levi* 9:3–5). Although some of the details are different, especially regarding Levi's initial dream, this fourfold heavenly justification for Levi's priesthood is reminiscent of that in *Jubilees*.

In addition to the various accounts of how Levi becomes a priest, the *Testament* speaks of the heavenly cult that is carried out in the presence of God by angels as they offer bloodless sacrifices for propitiation on behalf of the righteous (*T. Levi* 3:5–6). The implication is that Levi's priestly service on earth will be an imitation of the heavenly cult, as is stated in *Jubilees*. One element in the *Testament* that does not appear in *Jubilees*, however, is the vision of an eschatological priest whom God will raise up to implement judgment over the world and to initiate an era of glory and righteousness, including unbarring the way to Eden and binding the forces of evil (*T. Levi* 18). The figure is spoken of in terms that elsewhere are applied to a royal messianic figure, and a glory and significance are here attributed to the priesthood that far exceed what is granted it in the biblical materials. This exalted picture of the priesthood continues in the *Testament of Judah*, where Judah tells his sons to love Levi because God has subjected the kingship (granted to Judah and his line) to the priesthood (granted to Levi and his line) (*T. Jud.* 21:1–2).

The Dead Sea Scrolls. The Dead Sea Scrolls, found in caves near Khirbet Qumran on the northwest shore of the Dead Sea, are a collection of biblical, postbiblical, and sectarian manuscripts that were produced over the period 250 B.C.E. to 70 C.E. The community that produced and collected them had its origins in conflict surrounding the priesthood in Jerusalem, when in 167 B.C.E. a group of rebels of priestly descent was responsible for organizing armed resistance to the oppressive policies against Judaism put into effect by the Seleucid Greek emperor Antiochus IV Epiphanes. As related in 1 and 2 Maccabees, the Maccabean family, led by the brothers Judas, Simon, and Jonathan, succeeded in throwing off Greek imperial rule and establishing independent Jewish rule, and Jonathan, followed by his brother Simon, became ruling high priest even though they were not of the Zadokite lineage that had become the norm for those who claimed the right to the high priesthood. They and their descendants, often referred to as the Hasmoneans from the name of one of their ancestors (Josephus, *Ant.* 12.263), remained in power from when Jonathan claimed the high priesthood in 152 B.C.E. until the Roman general Pompey conquered Palestine in 63 B.C.E. However, not everyone welcomed their ascendancy, and scholars have long believed that the sectarian community at Qumran was founded and run by Zadokite priests who were opposed to the Hasmonean takeover of the Jerusalem Temple.

More recent scholarship has challenged the consensus that Zadokites founded the community, but the community's opposition to the contemporary Jerusalem priesthood has remained unquestioned. The *Commentary on Habakkuk* that was found among the Scrolls lambasts the "Wicked Priest" for ruling sinfully and defiling the Temple (1QpHab 8:4–14; 12:1–9), and the *Community Rule* scroll presents the community as a haven of holiness and its observances as an appropriate replacement for the presently corrupt Jerusalem cult (1QS 8:1–11; 9:3–5).

Priests appear frequently in the Scrolls and occupied a significant role in the community's ongoing life and thought. According to the *Community Rule*, the group was structured as a priestly hierarchy headed by priests and Levites (1QS 2:20–23; 6:4, 8–10), and speaking in anger against one of the community's priests would incur the penalty of a year's penance (1QS 7:2–3). The *Damascus Document*, which is an exhortation followed by a list of laws to be observed by members of the community, shows priests in similarly significant positions of leadership (CD 9:13–15; 10:4–6; 12:22—13:4; 14:3–8). Both documents also link the priesthood to eschatological and messianic expectations: the *Community Rule* refers to the Prophet and the Messiahs of Aaron and Israel (1QS 9:10–11), while the *Damascus Document* speaks of the Messiah of Aaron and Israel (CD 12:22—13:1; see also 1QSa 2:11–25).

Despite the fact that a number of the Scrolls, particularly the *Temple Scroll* (11QT), describe sacrificial rites involving priests, the general consensus is that there was no sacrificial worship at Qumran; instead, the community's own observances were regarded as the equivalent of sacrifices at the Temple. The Qumran priests would not therefore have serviced a sacrificial cultus. Nevertheless, in other respects the priesthood described in the Scrolls has clear affinities with the priesthood as described in the canonical literature. Indeed, as Florentino García Martínez (1999) argues, the Scrolls indicate that the priests at Qumran continued to carry out many of the traditional priestly duties that they had done for generations among the people of Israel: teaching, oracular divination, judicial decisions, and blessing the community.

However, two aspects of priesthood according to the Qumran documents go beyond the biblical picture. The first is the priests' involvement in war. While this is not a complete novelty—Deuteronomy 20 shows the priest encouraging the troops before battle, and Numbers 10:9 instructs that when the people go to war an alarm shall be blown with the priests' trumpets—at Qumran the priests are portrayed as commanders in an eschatological battle between the sons of light and darkness. In the battle, as described in the *War Scroll*, the priests wear special battle robes and control the progress of the battle by blowing trumpets to direct the action (1QM 7:10—9:10; 16:2–14; 17:10–15). They also encourage the troops before and during the battle (1QM 15:4—16:1; 16:14—17:9) and lead them in offering praise to God when it is over (1QM 13; 18:6—19:9). This is clearly a highly theologized picture, but it underlines the strongly liturgical conception of the community in which God's righteous guidance is mediated via the jurisdiction of priests in every aspect of its life. The second aspect of priesthood in the Qumran scrolls that goes beyond the biblical picture of priesthood is that of the heavenly priesthood: as in other documents from this period, there is a concept of the heavenly liturgy that is being enacted by angelic priests in a heavenly temple (4Q400; 4Q403 I ii 18–25). This implies that earthly priesthood is a copy or reflection of a heavenly office, a conception that gives the earthly priesthood supernatural gravitas. Both of these aspects of priesthood at Qumran serve to emphasize the enormous spiritual significance of the priests and to justify their claim to authority over the rest of the community.

Priesthood in the New Testament. Turning to the New Testament, the figure of the priest is much less theologically significant than in the Hebrew Bible and in documents from ancient Judaism. This is partly because at the time most of the New Testament documents were being written—that is, the mid-to-late first century C.E.—the emergent, eschatologically oriented Christian movement was not yet sufficiently separate or institutionalized to have developed a priesthood of its own; and in the New Testament

Jewish priests are often presented (doubtless to some extent polemically) as embodying institutional religious opposition to Jesus and his followers or as negative moral examples, such as the priest and Levite in the parable of the Good Samaritan (Luke 10:31–32). However, the concept of priesthood is theologically significant in the New Testament in two ways. First is in understanding the relationship between Jesus and Christian believers, as shown by the letter to the Hebrews. Here, the gravitas and sacrality of the high priest are transferred to Jesus, who is both priest and sacrificial offering in one. As such, he eliminates the need for a human priesthood to mediate between earth and heaven and for sacrifices as the medium of mediation. Second, in the New Testament documents, the concept of priesthood is democratized: the entire Christian community is seen as a priesthood (1 Pet 2:5, 9; Rev 1:6; 5:10; 20:6), an idea based on Exodus 19:6, where the people of Israel are referred to as a "holy priesthood." Such a democratization both defines the Christian community as one characterized by holiness and worship and presents its function as one of mediating between humankind and God and proclaiming the saving works of the Lord.

[*See also* Asceticism; Atonement; Cult and Worship; Ecclesiology; Expiation; Ezra, Nehemiah, and 1 and 2 Chronicles; Faith; Festivals and Holy Days; Idols and Idolatry; Jerusalem (Zion); Leviticus and Numbers; Minister and Ministry; Repentance; Tabernacles, Temples, and Synagogues; Torah; *and* Tradition.]

BIBLIOGRAPHY

Blenkinsopp, Joseph. *Sage, Priest, Prophet: Religious and Intellectual Leadership in Ancient Israel.* Louisville, Ky.: Westminster John Knox, 1995.

Blenkinsopp, Joseph. "The Mystery of the Missing 'Sons of Aaron.'" In *Exile and Restoration Revisited: Essays on the Babylonian and Persian Periods in Memory of Peter R. Ackroyd*, edited by Gary N. Knoppers and Lester L. Grabbe, with Deirdre Fulton, pp. 65–77. Library of Second Temple Studies 73. London: T&T Clark, 2009.

Fabry, Heinz-Josef. "Priests at Qumran: A Reassessment." In *The Dead Sea Scrolls: Texts and Context*, edited by Charlotte Hempel, pp. 243–262. Studies on the Texts of the Desert of Judah 90. Leiden, The Netherlands, and Boston: Brill, 2010.

Fletcher-Louis, Crispin H. T. "Some Reflections on Ange-lomorphic Humanity Texts among the Dead Sea Scrolls." *Dead Sea Discoveries* 7 (2000): 292–312.

García Martínez, Florentino. "Priestly Functions in a Community without Temple." In *Gemeinde Ohne Tempel—Community without Temple: Zur Substituier-ung und Transformation des Jerusalemer Tempels und seines Kults im Alten Testament, antiken Judentum und frühen Christentum*, edited by Beate Ego, Armin Lange, Kathrin Ehlers, et al., pp. 303–319. Wissenschaftliche Untersuchungen zum Neuen Testament 118. Tübingen, Germany: Mohr Siebeck, 1999.

Grabbe, Lester L. *Priests, Prophets, Diviners, Sages: A Socio-Historical Study of Religious Specialists in Ancient Israel.* Valley Forge, Penn.: Trinity Press International, 1995.

Grabbe, Lester L., and Alice Ogden Bellis, eds. *The Priests in the Prophets: The Portrayal of Priests, Prophets, and Other Religious Specialists in the Latter Prophets.* London: T&T Clark, 2004.

Grossman, Maxine. "Priesthood as Authority: Inter-pretive Competition in First-Century Judaism and Christianity." In *The Dead Sea Scrolls as Background to Postbiblical Judaism and Early Christianity: Papers from an International Conference at St Andrews in 2001*, edited by James R. Davila, pp. 117–131. Studies on the Texts of the Desert of Judah 46. Leiden, The Netherlands: Brill, 2003.

Haran, Menahem. *Temples and Temple Service: An Enquiry into the Character of Cult Phenomena and the Historical Setting of the Priestly School.* Oxford: Clarendon, 1978.

Hayward, C. T. R. *The Jewish Temple: A Non-Biblical Source-book.* London: Routledge, 1996.

Hempel, Charlotte. "The Sons of Aaron in the Dead Sea Scrolls." In *Flores Florentino: Dead Sea Scrolls and Other Early Jewish Studies in Honour of Florentino García Mar-tínez*, edited by Anthony Hilhorst, Emile Puech, and Eibert Tigchelaar, pp. 207–224. Journal for the Study of Judaism Supplement Series 122. Leiden, The Neth-erlands: Brill, 2007.

Hillel, Vered. "Demonstrable Instances of the Use of Sources in the Pseudepigrapha." In *The Dead Sea Scrolls: Texts and Context*, edited by Charlotte Hempel, pp. 325–337. Studies on the Texts of the Desert of Judah 90. Leiden, The Netherlands, and Boston: Brill, 2010.

Kugel, James. "Levi's Elevation to the Priesthood in Second Temple Writings." *Harvard Theological Review* 86 (1993): 1–63.

Kugel, James L. "How Old Is the Aramaic Levi Docu-ment?" In *A Walk Through Jubilees: Studies in the Book of Jubilees and the World of Its Creation*, pp. 343–364. Journal for the Study of Judaism Supplement Series 156. Leiden, The Netherlands, and Boston: Brill, 2012.

Kugler, Robert A. *From Patriarch to Priest: The Levi-Priestly Tradition from Aramaic Levi to the Testament of Levi.* Early Judaism and Its Literature 9. Atlanta: Scholars Press, 1996.

Kugler, Robert A. "Priesthood at Qumran." In *The Dead Sea Scrolls after Fifty Years: A Comprehensive Assessment*, edited by Peter W. Flint and James C. VanderKam, Vol. 2, pp. 93–116. Leiden, The Netherlands, and Boston: Brill, 1999.

Kugler, Robert A. *The Testaments of the Twelve Patriarchs.* Guides to the Apocrypha and Pseudepigrapha. Shef-field, U.K.: Sheffield Academic Press, 2001.

Leuchter, Mark, and Jeremy Hutton. *Levites and Priests in Biblical History and Tradition.* Ancient Israel and Its Literature 9. Atlanta: Scholars Press, 2012.

Mason, Eric F. *"You Are a Priest Forever": Second Temple Jewish Messianism and the Priestly Christology of the Epistle to the Hebrews.* Studies on the Texts of the Desert of Judah 74. Leiden, The Netherlands, and Boston: Brill, 2008.

Nelson, Richard D. *Raising Up a Faithful Priest: Community and Priesthood in Biblical Theology.* Louisville, Ky.: Westminster John Knox, 1993.

Newsom, Carol A. "'He Has Established for Himself Priests': Human and Angelic Priesthood in the Qumran Sab-bath *Shirot*." In *Archaeology and History in the Dead Sea Scrolls: The New York University Conference in Memory of Yigael Yadin*, edited by Lawrence H. Schiffman, pp. 101–120. Journal for the Study of Pseudepigrapha Supplement 8; Journal for the Study of the Old Testa-ment/American Schools of Oriental Research Mono-graphs 2. Sheffield, U.K.: JSOT Press, 1990.

Olyan, Saul M. *Rites and Rank: Hierarchy in Biblical Rep-resentations of Cult.* Princeton, N.J.: Princeton Univer-sity Press, 2000.

Rooke, Deborah W. *Zadok's Heirs: The Role and Develop-ment of the High Priesthood in Ancient Israel.* Oxford Theological Monographs. Oxford: Oxford University Press, 2000.

Schiffman, Lawrence H. "Temple, Sacrifice and Priest-hood in the Epistle to the Hebrews and the Dead Sea Scrolls." In *Echoes from the Caves: Qumran and the New Testament*, edited by Florentino García Martínez, pp. 165–176. Studies on the Texts of the Desert of Judah 85. Leiden, The Netherlands: Brill, 2009.

Seland, Torrey. "The 'Common Priesthood' of Philo and 1 Peter: A Philonic Reading of 1 Peter 2.5, 9." *Journal for the Study of the New Testament* 57 (1995): 87–119.

Teicher, J. L. "Priests and Sacrifices in the Dead Sea Scrolls: A Question of Method in Historical Research." *Journal of Jewish Studies* 5 (1954): 93–99.

VanderKam, James C. "Identity and History of the Com-munity." In *The Dead Sea Scrolls after Fifty Years: A*

Comprehensive Assessment, edited by Peter W. Flint and James C. VanderKam, Vol. 2, pp. 487–533. Leiden, The Netherlands, and Boston: Brill, 1999.

VanderKam, James C. "Jubilees and the Priestly Messiah of Qumran." *Revue de Qumran* 13 (1988): 353–365.

Deborah W. Rooke

PRIMEVAL HISTORY

See Adam (Primeval History).

PROCREATION

See Barrenness.

PROPHECY

See Preaching and Prophecy *and* Prophets and Prophecy.

PROPHETS AND PROPHECY

The prophetic voice thunders through the pages of scripture. Just as the wind blows where it wills, these God-pointing, God-revealing figures appear from all corners, from various occupations, lifestyles, and sectors of society. Like the divine word they claim to bear, they partake of the pure freedom of God and play a truly creative role in history. As channels of revelation and as covenantal mediators, they inject God's personal sovereignty into Israel's collective life. They make God a tangible factor in the course of Israel's history. The prophetic witness encounters readers in multiple divisions of the canon and in quite diverse ways: through poetry and prose; through song, legend, and story; through announcement and dramatic action.

Grasping the major role of prophets and prophecy in the Bible and theology involves elucidating their original social, historical, and ancient Near Eastern contexts. Of particular interest is the typical pattern of social interaction between heaven, the prophet, and the audience. A theological understanding of prophecy also entails appreciating the diversity of biblical prophetic theologies, how differing prophets defend at least three distinct divine covenants. So, too, competence in theological reading of prophetic scriptures includes appreciating the reception and shaping of prophetic texts by the faith community. The present scriptural shape of prophetic texts provides guidance for theological appropriation of their message. Finally, a discussion of prophets and theology is incomplete without treating the posthistory, reception, and consequences of prophecy.

The Prophets' Milieu: Ancient Near Eastern, Social, and Historical Contexts. Prophecy was known in Israel from the settlement era (see Judg 6:8), and its prominence increases markedly in texts about monarchic times (impressively, the Hebrew title *nābî'*, "prophet," occurs a little more than 300 times in the Bible as a whole). A great variety of prophetic literature appears in scripture, including multiple genres of prophetic communication. The historical books of Joshua through Kings, known in Judaism as the "Former Prophets," narrate significant prophetic activity in prose, emphasizing especially prophetic interaction with monarchic rulers. Attention to the power of the prophetic legend to shape readers' imaginations must figure significantly in interpreting this genre of writing as, of course, must attention to the course of the narrative plots about prophets' careers.

Beginning in the eighth century B.C.E., as urbanization and writing advanced in Israel, written anthologies of prophets' actual poetic speeches emerged. Some of these collections have now received scriptural status as the "Writing Prophets," that is, as the Bible's 3 Major and 12 Minor Prophets. Much of this prophecy is poetry, laden with expansive meaning and emotive power. It is also often messenger speech, akin to an Assyrian emperor's demands relayed via official representatives to a distant populace. Like an emperor's pronouncements, prophets' messenger speech aimed to convict and persuade and to place a people's fate in their own hands, not merely in the hands of their king (see 2 Kgs 18:28–35). Attention to such questions of form and genre must inform the interpretation of all the anthologized prophecies of scripture.

Prophets and prophecy played significant roles in the ancient Near East outside of Israel. Indeed, the phenomenon of prophecy occurs in many societies across cultures and history. Thomas Overholt (1989) has shown that prophecy, as it occurs cross-culturally, invariably works to link a human audience with a transcendent realm. He describes prophets as "channels" of the beyond. As channelers of the transcendent, prophets convey, or claim to convey, thinking or power from outside earthly, empirical reality.

Emar and Mari, ancient Syrian cities north of Canaan, have prophetic groups with names based on the same Semitic root "prophesy" found in the Hebrew of the Bible. The linguistic evidence about the Hebrew root from these cities shows that it conveys the idea of invoking gods. Such invocation, the original meaning of the Semitic root *n-b-ʾ*, appears intensively in 1 Kings 18:26, where both Elijah and his prophetic opponents invoke their respective deities for a display of power.

If the social-scientific model of "channel" is on target, then groups will concede the possibility of prophecy only if they believe in a transcendent reality. Significant for a theological discussion, intellectuals of today's Global North commonly lack the capacity to entertain such a belief. Neurosurgeon Eben Alexander III reports that before his own direct experience of God (when a catastrophic illness shut down his brain for a week), patients who spoke of transcendent experiences elicited from him merely "wan, distracted" attention (2012, p. 139).

Alexander "knew" that the human mind was anchored in terrestrial, biological reality. He was impatient with any claims of experiencing heaven, unless he was "good-naturedly comforting someone" (2012, p. 140). Now he proffers that the normal human brain, as part of earthbound, biological existence, "blocks out, or veils, [the] larger cosmic background, just as the sun's light blocks the stars.... We can only see what our brain's filter allows through" (2012, p. 72). According to 2 Kings 6:8–23, Elisha's attendant at Dothan learns the selfsame truth. Up against a great Syrian army surrounding the city and needing reassurance, he evokes the empathy of Elisha, who prays for his eyes to open. Thereupon, "the LORD opened

the eyes of the servant, and he saw; the mountain was full of horses and chariots of fire all around Elisha" (2 Kgs 6:17).

The prospect that a revelation akin to that in 2 Kings 6:17 might actually occur raises suspicions about any thoroughgoing cultural relativist approach to interpreting prophecy. A veritable revelation is not reducible to a purely anthropological phenomenon. But even granting the possibility of contact with transcendence, a prophecy's intelligibility necessitates that it fit the cultural forms and historical setting of a human audience. A community is unlikely to preserve abstruse, irrelevant prophecy. It is no accident that Elisha's attendant reports seeing chariots; a report about modern helicopter gunships is unthinkable. Elisha himself envisioned his master Elijah as "the chariots of Israel and its horsemen" (2 Kgs 2:12).

Any valid hermeneutics must recognize (1) that Israelite prophecy is given in the cultural forms of an ancient people and (2) that prophecy's later interpreters are similarly ensconced in specific cultures. For example, translators drawn from the ranks of the exploited in South America might offer a substantially different rendering of Micah 2:8 from what we find in the New Revised Standard Version. They might well perceive the activism of the text, translating Micah's announcement at face value, "Recently my people have taken up arms against an enemy" (see Williams, *Syntax*, sec. 271b).

Actual contact with transcendent reality may feel overpowering and trouncing. Alexander, in deep coma, his brain out of the way, experienced divine communication as "an explosion…that blew through [him]." He writes, "These thoughts were solid and immediate—hotter than fire and wetter than water" (2012, p. 46). They were "wave-walls rolling through me, rocking everything around me" (2012, p. 160). Jeremiah experienced God's messages similarly, as an uncontainable burning in his very bones (Jer 20:9). Again, such prophetic experiences challenge any radical relativism that denies people can validly report on things outside their own restricted historical or cultural context. Those espousing a cultural relativist approach will emphasize Israelite prophecy's fit within its ancient milieu, rather than its reports of supracultural, collective relevance.

An approach oriented on historicism might propose that Israel's prophets were practiced "diviners," akin to the many ancient professionals within their milieu tasked with this art. An argument can be made, however, that the "Writing Prophets" were not primarily professionals cultivating an art (see Amos 7:14 NET, NLT). Prophecy, at least for a figure such as Jeremiah, was neither an art nor a science but what Abraham Heschel (1962, p. 26) describes as the "overwhelming impact of the divine pathos upon...mind and heart...and the unrelieved distress that sprang from [an] intimate involvement." The Jeremiahs of scripture had a "sense of being ravished or carried away by violence, of yielding to overpowering force against one's will" (Heschel, 1962, p. 114).

The God-messages of prophecy are often fraught with meaning. Alexander speaks of receiving a "seed" of "trans-earthly knowledge" that will take years "to come to fruition," "years to understand" (2012, p. 82). This seed-like quality of prophecy does not prevent prophets from applying their message in their immediate milieu, but it does mean that any one application of a revelation will not necessarily exhaust its meaning. The revelations have an expansive quality, which allows for a "fuller sense" (*sensus plenior*) and creates the prospect of multiple valid fulfillments. One small example is the shout of joy in Isaiah 54:1, which at first signifies the joy of Zion in the restoration era but later encompasses the joy of Israel's dead at their awakening (Isa 26:19, echoing Isa 54:1).

Prophetic oracles typically display concentrated poetic art, impressing readers with their three-dimensional character jammed with beauty, mystery, and multivalence. Princeton psychologist Julian Jaynes interpreted the alterity of archaic poetry as the voice of the gods, pushing inspired artistry to the lips (1976, p. 73). According to Jaynes, prophecy and poetry share a neurobiological commonality. Both connect to the selfsame area of the brain's right cerebral hemisphere, "Wernicke's area."

The phenomenon of prophecy does not stop with the prophetic perception of having experienced God's presence and power. Unlike the stereotypical mystic,

the prophets strongly invest in communication. With time, prophetic communication in Israel developed standardized oral forms, resulting in the various genres of prophecy that form criticism (*Formgeschichte*) identifies. The many forms of Israelite prophetic speech, to name just a few *Gattungen*, include two-part judgment oracles, trial speech, woe oracles, admonitions, dirges, and exhortations to conversion. Nonverbal communication is another means of prophetic intermediation. Isaiah famously goes barefoot and naked to convince King Hezekiah not to join a revolt against Assyria (Isa 20:2–4). Later, Jeremiah wears the yoke of a beast of burden to symbolize Judah's submission to Babylon (Jer 27).

Prophets, as noted, are messengers, who typically declare oracles prefaced with "Thus says the LORD" (Amos 1:3 and almost 300 other times in scripture). Physical tokens sometimes accompany a prophetic message to authenticate it or convey its potency. The queen of Mari sent the king some prophetic words of Shelibum accompanied by a lock of his hair and a piece of the hem from his tunic (Matthews and Benjamin, 2006, p. 344). Upon ascending alive to heaven, Elijah dropped his mantle to his successor, Elisha, who received his prophetic power (2 Kgs 2:13–14). Elisha sent his personal staff with his servant as an implement for raising a dead child to life (2 Kgs 4:29–31).

Prophetic communications are part of a larger pattern of social interaction. Effective prophetic channeling results in a chain of communication leading from the realm of the transcendent to the prophet, from the prophet to an audience, and then from the audience back to the prophet as feedback. The prophet may convey the feedback to God, and another cycle of revelation may commence. The chain of revelation, proclamation, and feedback generally does not continue indefinitely. It eventually ends either in supernatural confirmation of the prophetic word or in that word's disconfirmation.

The social interactions involved in prophecy may be complex. Some communications at Mari attest to the ongoing intermediation of prophets, who remain active delivering new revelations to address a changing situation. An official stationed at Kallassu writes to Zimri-Lim, Mari's king, "There is no reason for me not to continue to send my lord…the words of the *apilu* prophets" (Matthews and Benjamin, 2006, p. 342).

Sometimes a prophet's ostensive addressee is not the actual recipient of the message. In one Mari letter, for example, an official sends Mari's king a prophecy overtly directed against Babylon: "Babylon, what do you think you're doing? I [the god Dagon] will bring you down like a bird with a net" (Matthews and Benjamin, 2006, p. 344). Despite the named addressee, the letter went to King Zimri-Lim alone. The numerous biblical oracles against the nations, *Völkersprüche*, are comparable. Ezekiel's oracles against Tyre and Sidon (Ezek 28:11–19, 20–26), for example, appear tailored for a Phoenician audience. The magnificent royal cherub in Ezekiel 28:14 and 16 brilliantly mirrors Phoenician royalty's self-perception. These oracles aim primarily, however, to convey God's self-disclosure to Israel. Thus, Ezekiel 28:24–26 lets slip that with Phoenicia judged, God's covenant people "shall live in safety" and "know that I am the LORD their God."

Feedback from the prophet's audience may take multiple forms. The Mari letters show Zimri-Lim sometimes indifferent, or at least forgetful, in response to prophetic communications. One letter states, "Repeatedly I have written to the king about the gift of livestock which he promised to the sanctuary of Addu…Addu…is still waiting for this livestock" (Matthews and Benjamin, 2006, p. 342). In another letter, a prophet proclaims, "Dagan has sent me to…remind the king to offer a funeral sacrifice" (Matthews and Benjamin, 2006, p. 345). Biblical texts similarly portray audiences indifferent or hostile to prophets (Exod 4:1; 16:20; 2 Kgs 17:13; Jer 6:16–17; 11:7–8; Zech 1:4). Even supernatural confirmations of prophecies sometimes barely faze the people (1 Kgs 18:17; Amos 4:6–11; Jer 3:8).

David Petersen (1981) has persuasively argued that role theory better accounts for Israelite prophecy than other models, which may characterize prophecy as an office/institution, as a state of ecstasy/possession, as an ideal type (opposed to the priest), or as a charismatic style of leadership. Prophecy is a social function and behavior pattern, taken on by individ-

uals of varying social location, which entails channeling and intermediation. Contrary to much nineteenth-century criticism (e.g., Bernhard Duhm, *The Theology of the Prophets*, 1875), even priests may become prophets. Individuals may wear two hats: Samuel was a priest and a prophet, Ezekiel was a Zadokite priest of Jerusalem, Hosea was a peripheral Levite. Not all prophets were priests, of course: Deborah was a tribal authority figure; Micah was a village elder; Amos was a cattle broker (*nōqēd*, see 2 Kgs 3:4), perhaps a crown representative (Sweeney, 2000, p. 197).

Factors such as profession, age, and lineage have little bearing on eligibility for the prophetic office. Even gender is not a determining factor. Names of female prophets greatly outnumber male prophets in Neo-Assyrian texts, where female prophecy functions in much the same manner as male prophecy. In ancient Mari, however, prophetic circles with higher social status appear to have included proportionally fewer women. Significant female prophets in the Hebrew scriptures include Noadiah (Neh 6:14), Deborah, Huldah, Miriam, and "the prophetess" of Isaiah 8:3. The last appears to have been a significant public figure, not Isaiah's wife.

Varieties of Biblical Prophetic Theologies. A deep understanding of biblical prophecy requires grasping the diversity of prophetic theologies. The vassal covenant of Mount Sinai, a bilateral, suzerainty type of covenant, undergirds the theology of Deuteronomy and propels Jeremiah's prophetic vocation. On Mt. Sinai, the mount of the covenant ablaze with fire, Moses risked his life taking up the role of Deuteronomic prophet. He stood between Israel and the Lord, to declare to the people the words of the covenant (Deut 18:16–17; cf. 5:5, 22–31; 9:15; Exod 20:19). There, the divine presence passed before Moses and the divine name rang out in verbal revelation (Exod 33:19). Hence, Moses came to know the Lord by name, to latch on to God. In turn, God empowered him as a unique channel. Through Moses, God's voice, God's "irrepressible whisper" (1 Kgs 19:12), unleashed itself.

God's voice, God's verbal revelation, is central in the communion of God and Moses on Sinai. It is God's primary instrument of presence and relationship. Exodus 19:19 (a text in the "D" family) says that on

Sinai "Moses was speaking and God was answering him *with a voice*" (NET, emphasis added; cf. NIV). The divine voice is a mode of highly personal, yet fearsome, divine immanence. The voice of God utters the "sweet talk" of courtship (Hos 2:14), which occasions a barely fathomable intimacy between God and God's people.

Upon reflection, it is imminently reasonable to associate Moses and his role with prophecy. Prophets, after all, are essentially messengers or go-betweens, who channel God's words and will to Israel. This makes them ideal mediators of the covenant. Moses is the original, archetypal covenant mediator who gave his life to bring the covenant down from Sinai—he is the quintessential prophet. Deuteronomy 34:10 directly affirms the fact: "Never since has there arisen a prophet in Israel like Moses, whom the LORD knew face to face." Prophets such as Hosea naturally look back to Moses's prophetic example: "By a prophet the LORD brought Israel up from Egypt" (Hos 12:13).

What is most amazing about Moses is not the physical person (cf. Deut 1:9, 12) but the phenomenon of embodying God's irrepressible word. "Is not my word like fire, says the LORD, and like a hammer that breaks a rock in pieces?" (Jer 23:29). God's creative word must continue its work in the world, tearing down idolatry, renewing community, and ushering in God's reign. To ensure that this work continues, God promises to raise up repeatedly prophets in Moses's line to direct Israel's journey to its eschatological fulfillment.

Multiple scriptures bearing Sinai theology presuppose a line of "Mosaic" prophets: Exodus 19:9, 19; 20:18–21; 33:11; Numbers 12; Deuteronomy 5:5, 27; 18:15–22 (all E or D). Moses's role continues in figures such as Joshua (e.g., Josh 5:15), Samuel (e.g., 1 Sam 12:23), Elijah (e.g., 1 Kgs 19:8), Elisha (e.g., 2 Kgs 2:8, 14), and Huldah ("the [Mosaic] prophetess," 2 Kgs 22:14). Jeremiah, the greatest prophetic proponent of the Sinai covenant and Deuteronomy's theology, was perhaps the ultimate bearer of the Mosaic mantle. According to Jeremiah 1, the Lord stretched out the divine hand, touched Jeremiah's mouth, and inserted the divine word (v. 9). Mirroring Moses's precedent, Jeremiah directly receives God's revelation—hand-delivered

(see Deut 18:18). His book portrays him judging opposing prophets (who bear no such word) using criteria straight from Deuteronomy (Jer 28:9; Deut 18:22). As Kenton L. Sparks (1998, p. 274) summarizes, Jeremiah "granted the [Josianic] charter reform document, Deuteronomy, a central and authoritative role in his evaluation of Judean society."

Whereas God's voice and word are primary in Deuteronomy and Jeremiah, an alternative vassal covenant oriented on holiness undergirds the theology of the Holiness School (HS) and Ezekiel. In this covenant, God desires to be tangibly present to Israel and so attaches the divine self to the people's central shrine, calling it "my sanctuary" (Lev 19:30; 20:3; 26:2 all HS; Ezek 5:11; 8:6; 9:6; 23:39; 37:28). Sin and impurity remain a threat to God's presence, but God does definitively purpose to occupy the central Temple (Exod 25:8; 40:35 HS; Ezek 9:3; 10:4; 11:23).

The Lord resides in the Temple as the *kābôd*, that is, as a uniquely tangible presence (NRSV: "glory"), which is nothing less than God's embodied self (note the syntax of Exod 24:16 HS; Ezek 10:20). Unapologetically anthropomorphic, holiness texts describe God at the Temple smelling the smoking fat (Lev 17:6; 26:31 HS) and consuming sacrifices as food (Lev 21:6; Num 28:2 both HS; Ezek 44:7). God's bodily presence cannot help but powerfully impact the people. Notably, it exudes holiness, envisioned as a sort of communicable plasma (Lev 6:18 [MT v. 11] HS; Ezek 44:19; 46:20).

From the midst of Israel, God radiates the divine holiness out to the entire land and to every sector of society. At the same time, God's people should actively strive to emulate the holiness in their midst (see Lev 11:44; 20:7, 26 all HS; Ezek 37:27; 43:9). The operative focus is sanctification (for details, see the HS strand at Exod 31:13; Lev 21:23; Num 5:3; 35:34; cf. Ezek 37:28). The Lord's intent is to sanctify the entire community of faith as well as the land on which they live. Speaking of God's people, Ezekiel's God proclaims, "I, the LORD, sanctify them" (Ezek 20:12). Just so, in Leviticus 21:8 (HS), God exclaims, "I, who sanctify you, am holy."

The 48 chapters of Ezekiel's book trace an epic journey of the Lord's physical presence (*kābôd*). It abandons Judah, which is defiled by sin; travels to

Babylon, to be "a diminished sanctity" to the exiles (Ezek 11:1 NJPS); and finally, in a utopian vision, returns to indwell an ideal new Temple (Ezek 43:1–12). The movement of God relates directly to a divine requirement of ritual and ethical holiness. Idolatry is anathema to the *kābôd*, but defiling a neighbor's spouse is just as grievous (Ezek 18:6; cf. Lev 18:20 HS). One must worship God in truth but also refrain from oppression (Ezek 18:7; cf. Lev 25:17 HS), robbery (Ezek 18:7; cf. Lev. 19:13 HS), and loan-sharking (Ezek 18:8; cf. Lev. 25:36 HS). The courts must be just (Ezek 18:8; cf. Lev 19:15 HS).

Ezekiel insists that the exiles stop blaming their fate on the sins of their parents, take responsibility, and seize life. God's statement that "all lives are mine" (Ezek 18:4), that all individuals, as responsible agents, are God's to judge, strongly recalls Numbers 16:22 (HS). The latter text affirms that the Lord is the "God of the spirits of all flesh," that the Lord does not lump souls together for indiscriminate punishment. In Ezekiel 18, as in Numbers 16, those who separate themselves from all offenders against God's holiness will surely find salvation amid God's judgment (Num 16:24 HS).

The Priestly Torah (PT) and 2 Isaiah understand God's presence and covenant with Israel in an entirely different manner, presenting us with yet another biblical theology. For the Priestly Torah, the *kābôd* is neither terrestrial nor anthropomorphic but appears on earth only as a transient spectacle, in opaque clouds and smoke, pure light, and burning flames (e.g., Exod 24:15–18; Lev 9:23–24; 10:2; 16:2 all PT). Likewise 2 Isaiah insists that God has no form or body comparable to anything in earthbound experience (Isa 40:18, 25; 44:7–8; 45:18; 46:5; 66:1). The Holy One is so entirely other, in fact, that divinity, rising sheer above the self (e.g., Isa 40:22; 42:5; 44:24; 55:9), works to submerge the ego, and, ultimately, paves the way for human recognition of finitude and frailty (Isa 40:6–8; 41:14; 51:2, 12; 53:2; 57:15; 66:2).

Isaiah's numinous God is the selfsame aniconic deity framed by the wings of the Priestly Torah's cherubim. This is the Holy One, hidden behind a palpable emptiness, an emptiness directing the imagination toward the beyond (Isa 45:15; Exod 25:22 PT; Cook, 2008, p. 48). Israel Knohl (1995, pp. 146–47) is correct that

the Priestly Torah's vision of God is "impersonal" and "nonanthropomorphic," oriented on an encounter with "the holy and its awesomeness." So, too, Nahum M. Sarna (1986, p. 213) aptly captures the significance of the cherubim for the Priestly Torah, when he writes that they preserve God's "absolute incorporeality and the aniconic nature of the national religion." Israel's relationship with a numinous, hidden God fosters reverence among the people, a virtue that squelches pride and uplifts the humble and vulnerable (persistent values in texts such as Isa 42:3, 7; 50:4, 6; 53:12; 61:1–2).

Trusting in the transformative power of reverence, the Priestly Torah describes God giving Israel a testimony on Mt. Sinai (*'ēdût*; Exod 25:16, 21 NJB and NIV), not a "covenant." As Israel grows in virtue, the people will obey the God-given testimony with no thought of recompense, no thought of rewards and punishments. The idea of a bilateral, conditional covenant is similarly absent from 2 Isaiah. Neither the Sinai covenant nor Moses, the great prophetic covenantal mediator, figures overtly in chapters 40 to 66 of the Isaiah corpus.

Avoiding language of conditionality, contingency, and threat, both the Priestly Torah and 2 Isaiah stress instead the permanency of God's commitment to Israel. The only "covenantal" agreement of God with which they are familiar is the *bĕrît 'ôlām* ("everlasting covenant"; see Gen 9:16; 17:7, 13, 19; Isa 55:3; 61:8; cf. Isa 45:17; 51:7–8). Such a covenant is a unilateral grant, vouchsafing an enduring divine allegiance to Israel.

God's irrevocable agreement with Noah (Gen 9:8–17) is a fine example of the unconditional and eternal nature of covenants in the Priestly Torah. The unshakable quality of the Noah covenant made it the perfect model for the Isaiah group to illustrate the perpetuity of God's commitments. Referring directly to the Priestly Torah's text, Isaiah 54:9 reads, "Just as I swore that the waters of Noah would never again go over the earth, so I have sworn that I will not be angry with you and will not rebuke you."

Biblical Prophecy as Sacred Text, the Written Scripture of Synagogue and Church. Both synagogue and church, throughout their history, have encountered biblical prophecy most immediately as written scripture, not as pressing verbal announcement (prophecy's original form). Jews and Christians are "people of the book," communities formed around sacred texts. Judaism, from very early on, presupposed the nurturing role of the "Tanak"—the Torah, Prophets, and Writings. Christianity, for its part, cherished the selfsame writings and soon recognized a deep dependence on select additional ones, including epistles and gospels. Theological reflection on prophecy in both religions continues to revolve around studying archived sacred writings, which have been inherited as an abiding theological witness.

Prophecy's first, archaic context was the immediate historical experience of ancient Israelites. Today's theologians, however, may take into account a new context for prophecy within sacred canon, which shapes interpretation. Among many notable features, this new biblical context of prophecy includes appendices to prophetic oracles that widen their scope (e.g., Amos 9:11–15), powerful verbal echoes within prophetic collections that weave a widescreen drama (e.g., Isa 40:1 reverberates with Isa 12:1), and a literary setting within Israel's extended story that sparks readers' imaginations (e.g., Jonah's mention in 2 Kgs 14:25). Such features of prophecy's new biblical shape represent a valid interpretive context alternative to prophecy's original historical context.

Modern historical criticism as it has developed over recent centuries has often discounted prophecy's current setting within the rich intertextual web of Jewish and Christian scripture. Prophecy's first historical and social setting has often seemed more significant than its newer setting within scripture's internal system of cross-reference. Hermann Gunkel, a founder of modernist criticism, opined that "if contemporary readers wish to understand the prophets, they must entirely forget that the writings were collected in a sacred book centuries after the prophets' work.… [They] must *not* read their words as portions of the Bible but [rather]…in the context of the life of the people of Israel in which they were first spoken" (cited in Seitz, 2007, p. 221, emphasis added).

Gunkel's approach (form criticism) yields significant insights into prophetic literature, including helpful theological ones. It is reductionist to limit a biblical text to any one interpretive context, even if that context be the biblical canon. Isaiah 40:1–8, for example, is greatly illuminated through an application of Gunkel's tools. Through form criticism, the passage's confusing cacophony of anonymous voices becomes intelligible. The speaker is participating, through a visionary encounter, in dialog characteristic of a report of a prophetic commissioning (cf. 1 Kgs 22:19–23; Isa 6:1–13). We have here a prophetic figure receiving God's commission to preach comfort to the Babylonian exiles.

In a commissioning narrative, the supernatural beings of God's heavenly council typically speak with each other and with a human prophet. The metaphor in Isaiah 40:6 of God's people as "grass" comes into focus in such a generic context as the standard prophetic objection to a call (cf. Isa 6:5, 11). So, too, a historical context within the Babylonian Exile clarifies the text's grass metaphor as an expression of the Judean deportees' sense of great trauma and vulnerability (cf. Isa 40:27: 41:14; 49:4, 14; 51:2).

The grief of an exilic setting—the tragic sensibility that human life is as fragile as withering grass (Isa 40:6–7)—gives Isaiah 40 a "cutting edge." By fronting this context, interpreters realize that the prophecy represents challenge as well as comfort. Facing down exile, it calls God's people out from every culture that is alien and hostile to God. It commends God's people to embrace the frailty that their exile reveals to them. As Brueggemann (1988, p. 77) writes, 2 Isaiah "works to deabsolutize imperial modes of reality, so that fresh forms of communal possibility can be entertained."

For 2 Isaiah the virtue undergirding new communal possibility is reverence among the people, a squelching of pride, and an acceptance of vulnerability. To embrace vulnerability, the text proffers, is to open to that which transcends all imposed captivities, all imperialist claims to define reality. "The grass withers, the flower fades; but the word of our God will stand forever" (Isa 40:8). As reverence awakens through the power of Isaianic poetry, "One can hear the ecstatic sounds of Sarah now with child (54:1–3), and the flood waters of Noah subsiding (54:9–11)" (Brueggemann, 1988, p. 78).

A form-critical approach is helpful in highlighting a theological theme of homecoming out from culture hostile to God. It offers little, however, by way of a bridge to the distant, sweeping vista that Jews and Christians eventually perceived within Isaiah 40:1–8. In texts such as 1QS 8:13–14, Matthew 3:3, and Handel's *Messiah*, the prophecy of Isaiah 40 is no longer a mere text of homecoming from Babylonia but a vision of a far-flung future when God decisively redeems and comes to his people.

Contrary to an approach of historicism, which insists that Isaiah 40:1–8 is a "construct" of the Exile era, moored to a repatriation from Babylonia of Judean deportees, many later Jews and Christians have heard the text bearing witness to expansive wonder. In addition to 1QS 8 and Matthew 3, texts such as Sirach 48:24–25, *1 Enoch* 1:6, and Baruch 5:7 understand the text to prophesy the end of the age. Perhaps surprisingly, this theological reading is intelligible when Isaiah 40 is interpreted within its scriptural context, its context within the Isaianic scroll's web of intertextuality.

In its intertextual, scriptural context, Isaiah 40 represents a fulfillment of a passage from the start of Isaiah's book, Isaiah 12:1–6, which it directly cites. It understands the literary persona of the prophet Isaiah in chapter 12 to look out from the eighth century B.C.E. to envision God's towering sublimity (*gēʾût*) about to be made known globally (Isa 12:5). His vision of "comfort" from the Assyrian era (Isa 12:1) reveals an arcing divine plan extending out for centuries to Babylonian times (Isa 40:1) and beyond. Here, the life of faith is no mere ad hoc reaction to pressing concerns, such as the forced deportation imposed by Babylonia, but aligns with a long-range prophetic trajectory, aimed at God's global reign.

Just as Isaiah 40:1–8 echoes Isaiah 12:1–6, Isaiah 51:11 repeats the exact words of Isaiah 35:10. The vision of a joyous, eschatological homecoming of God's people is already announced in 1 Isaiah. This is prophecy understood as *foretelling*, not "forthtelling." God's trajectory of promise bursts beyond a mere political repatriation of exiles. Taking a widescreen view of history, Isaiah's literary persona announces his prophecy will push through the ages to a reign of "everlasting joy," when "sighing shall flee away" (Isa 35:10). Lest there be any confusion, this is not a historical claim about Isaiah 35's dating. Rather, I am describing a specific canonical shaping that beckons an expansive, theological reading of Isaiah's prophecy.

Other texts in Isaiah 40—66 expand on messianic visions within 1 Isaiah, such as the prophecy of Isaiah 11. Many modern scholars deny that the texts of 2 Isaiah know of any messiah, with the possible exception of King Cyrus, God's "anointed" (*māšîah*, Isa 45:1). J. J. M. Roberts (2002, p. 388), for example, insists that Isaiah 40—55 includes no oracles "expressing the hope for a new David." In fact, he writes, "Second Isaiah applied God's commitments to David to the nation as a whole (Isa 55:3), thereby implicitly renouncing the expectations for a new David." The canonical shape of Isaiah, however, resists this rather "flat," historicist reading. In the book's canonical form, Isaiah 49:22 directly cites and reaffirms the promise in Isaiah 11:10, 12 of God one day hoisting his messianic "signal." The "signal" is none other than the root of Jesse (Isa 11:10), the coming ideal David, scion of Jesse (Isa 11:1).

The first Servant Song in Isaiah 42:1–9 alludes to the messianic tradition of Isaiah 11 through half a dozen verbal and thematic correspondences. Isaiah 53:2 again echoes the passage in describing the Suffering Servant with a metaphor of new growth pushing up out of dead ground. Eventually the tradition of Isaiah 11 proved foundational in the vision of God's coming reign in Isaiah 65. After announcing God's imminent creation of new heavens and a new earth (v. 17), Isaiah 65 stipulates that God's reign will see the vision of Isaiah 11 fully and literally realized (v. 25). Isaiah 65:25 directly references and affirms Isaiah 11:6–9, summarizing the text in an alternative, postexilic Hebrew idiom.

The branch of Jesse in Isaiah 11 exhibits striking qualities of humility and reverence that reappear in the Servant Songs. This ruler is preoccupied not with pomp and glory but with absolute integrity. Revering the Lord (v. 2), he puts responsibility before privilege. In thoroughgoing other-centeredness, he stands up for the poor and afflicted, for those who have nothing to offer by way of buttressing his reign. This ruler will be a servant, understanding that true strength lies in acknowledging human frailty.

The examples of canonical shaping reviewed thus far have involved individual prophetic themes, specifically God's reign and messianism. Scripture's present shape, however, also addresses the larger question of the theological place of prophets and prophecy within the canon. The Hebrew Bible ends both the Pentateuch and the Prophets on very similar notes. Deuteronomy 34 and Malachi 4 each esteem both Moses, the founding patriarch of the covenant, and the prophets, the carriers of the covenant into the future. The effect is to pair Torah and prophecy as joint partners in scripture's theological revelation of God and God's ways.

Deuteronomy 34 speaks of Moses and prophets, figures inferior to Moses but prophets nonetheless. Likewise, Malachi 4 speaks of Moses, mediator of the Sinai experience, and of Elijah, the prophet of God's coming reign (see Mal 3:1; 4:5; cf. Mark 9:4, 11). Taken together, Deuteronomy 34 and Malachi 4 provide a double exhortation to the reader to hold the Torah and the Prophets in dialog. The two major bodies of scripture, Torah and Prophets, offer a twin witness to God's one covenantal purpose with Israel (see Chapman, 2000).

Posthistory, Reception, and Consequences of Biblical Prophecy. The rabbinic corpus reveals at several points a belief that, after Haggai, Zechariah, and Malachi, Israel entered an era when God stopped sending prophets to his people (especially relevant rabbinic texts expressing some such conviction include t. Soṭah 13.3; y. Soṭah 9.13, 24b; b. Sanh. 11a; Cant. Rab. 8:9 #3; S. ʿOlam Rab. 30). Until recently, a scholarly consensus accepted that Judaism from Second Temple times permanently shut down prophecy. For good reasons, the consensus is now questioned.

First, the influential view of F. M. Cross that Israelite prophecy and monarchy rose and fell together cannot sustain itself. The Hebrew prophets did place checks on Israelite kingship, but this sort of specialized function should not define what counts as prophecy. The monarchic era simply harbored the necessary social conditions for the role of prophecy, but starting after the Babylonian Exile many came to believe that

prophecy would flourish again only as the final countdown to God's reign began. They understood the community's present task as gathering up the prophets' instructions, teaching new generations the prophetic hope, and awaiting its fulfillment in God's reign.

The New Testament attests that the early Jewish followers of Jesus claimed that prophecy was flourishing once again in precisely such end-time circumstances. New Testament texts celebrating an outpouring of the spirit of prophecy in John the Baptizer, Jesus, and the apostles include Matthew 11:9–14; 14:5; 16:13–14; 21:11, 26, 46; John 1:19–26; 4:19; 6:14; 7:40–52; Acts 11:27–28; 13:1; 1 Corinthians 12–14; Ephesians 4:11; and Revelation 1:3; 18:20.

Second, equally problematic is the view that prophecy ceased in Second Temple times as a result of the ascendancy of the Torah. Scholars increasingly recognize the Torah's own lively, prophetic character, which allows it to stand as a canonical partner with prophecy. What is more, a supposed Torah–prophecy dichotomy fits too neatly with the dualistic opposition of priestly and prophetic ideal types (Idealtypus) developed by sociologist Max Weber (1864–1920). Scholars can no longer legitimately replay the Weberian typology, which reflected a contemporary bias in German historiography opposing priestly, institutional religion with a lively, vital impulse animating prophecy.

Even if many Jews of the Second Temple era believed that prophecy had now borne its full witness and must patiently await end-time fulfillment, the social "role" of prophecy did not fully cease with Zechariah, Malachi, and other Persian-era prophets. Evidence to the contrary includes texts such as Daniel 7–11, 1QpHab 7:4–5, references in Josephus, and the manner in which Philo likened his own inspiration to genuine prophecy. Individuals also appear in Second Temple times whom the Dead Sea Scrolls, Philo, and Josephus deem to be false prophets. One should distinguish between the closing of the prophetic canon of scripture and any supposed cessation of the social role of prophecy. Jews and Christians may readily affirm a closed canon while simultaneously allowing for modern-era prophets such as Abraham Heschel and Martin Luther King Jr.

As the preceding section on prophecy's "canonical context" made apparent, the history of the reception and impact of canonical prophecy begins already within the history of composition of the Bible itself. Isaiah 11 proved foundational in the Exile era's vision of the Lord's servant as a light to the nations in Isaiah 42:1–9. Still later, in the restoration era, the prophecy reappeared in the early apocalyptic oracle at the close of Isaiah 65. Isaiah 65:25 cross-references Isaiah 11:6–9 and summarizes its thrust using postexilic Hebrew.

As the scriptures, in their canonical form, spawned and nurtured early Judaism and its younger sibling, the newborn Christianity, biblical prophecy had a tremendous impact. The book of Isaiah, for example, elicited deep reflection from New Testament authors (more than 400 citations and allusions). Throughout Judaism's and Christianity's histories, Isaiah's book has commanded passionate attention from theological thinkers such as Irenaeus, Augustine, Aquinas, Nicholas of Lyra, Calvin, Luther, Gerhard von Rad, Martin Buber, Karl Barth, Abraham Heschel, Brevard Childs, and Benjamin Sommer.

One can scarcely overestimate the significance of the prophetic writings of scripture in the history of theology. Despite missteps such as supersessionism, the history of exegesis shows many profound instances of brilliance. John Chrysostom's Isaiah commentary, for example, renders the prophetic text faithfully and with inspired imagination. It takes seriously the human elements of Isaiah and the book's divine grace. God's self-revelation in Isaiah 6 is understood as an act of "condescension" (*sunkatastasis*), allowing the finite human mind to glimpse divine reality. Isaiah's prophecies are treasured as multilayered and multivalent, bearing a discrete immediate meaning as well as a fuller sense congruent with fulfillments at the coming of Jesus (Childs, 2004, p. 107). The relationship of prophecy to fulfillment is far from mechanical or mathematical, as the historically subsequent Enlightenment critique of Christianity will casually assume.

The Hebrew prophetic texts have made their theological impact felt far beyond the pens of scholarly interpreters. Christian iconography of the Middle Ages and the Renaissance, for example, displays sophisticated theological readings of the prophets, detailing how Jesus fulfills messianic prophecy. Powerful illuminations of Isaiah 11:1–5 depict a tree of Jesse forming a ladder for Jesus to descend to earth as God's divine messiah. Stained glass versions at Chartres and other Gothic cathedrals contain doves around Jesse's tree, illustrating the Lord's spirit empowering the Messiah (Isa 11:2). Mary appears in some versions of the tree, fulfilling the vision in Isaiah 7:14 of the maiden who is "with child." The Spirit sometimes descends on her as well as on Christ.

Present-day biblical theologians must not simply turn back the clock, of course, naively reviving these sorts of premodern religious traditions. The current challenge is to strike a balance between prophecy as anticipation (rich with profound revelations of God's coming reign, of the Messiah) and prophecy as self-standing (intrinsically revelatory of Yahweh, true God). Reducing the Hebrew prophets to mere exemplars of Israelite religion, or even to "forthtellers" rather than "foretellers," appears theologically tone-deaf. At the same time, it is supersessionism or worse to downplay prophecy's first historical Israelite contexts and its witness to God actively at work within those contexts.

Rationalist scholars disparage prophecy if they take it as having exhausted all authentic and inherent meanings in its first historical contexts. Christologically oriented scholars equally disparage prophecy if they reduce it primarily to mere inklings of what only Jesus and the New Testament reveal fully. Chrysostom had it right. Biblical prophecy is irreducibly vital, multilayered, and polyvalent. It remains both a source for encountering the prophets of history and a theological witness to divine thoughts and ways as high above human consciousness as the heavens are higher than the earth (Isa 55:9).

[*See also* Book of the Twelve (Minor Prophets); Covenant; Deuteronomy; Ezekiel; Isaiah; Jeremiah; Moses; *and* Preaching and Prophecy.]

BIBLIOGRAPHY

Ahn, John, and Stephen L. Cook, eds. *Thus Says the Lord: Essays on the Former and Latter Prophets in Honor of Robert R. Wilson*. Library of Hebrew Bible/Old Testament Studies 502. New York: T&T Clark, 2009.

Alexander, Eben. *Proof of Heaven: A Neurosurgeon's Journey into the Afterlife.* New York: Simon & Schuster, 2012.

Blenkinsopp, Joseph. *Opening the Sealed Book: Interpretations of the Book of Isaiah in Late Antiquity.* Grand Rapids, Mich.: Eerdmans, 2006.

Brueggemann, Walter. "Second Isaiah: An Evangelical Rereading of Communal Experience." In *Reading and Preaching the Book of Isaiah,* edited by Christopher R. Seitz, pp. 71–90. Philadelphia: Fortress, 1988.

Buber, Martin. *The Prophetic Faith.* Translated by Carlyle Witton-Davies. Harper Torchbooks 73. New York: Harper and Row, 1960.

Chapman, Stephen B. *The Law and the Prophets: A Study in Old Testament Canon Formation.* Forschungen zum Alten Testament 27. Tübingen, Germany: Mohr Siebeck, 2000.

Childs, Brevard S. *The Struggle to Understand Isaiah as Christian Scripture.* Grand Rapids, Mich.: Eerdmans, 2004.

Cook, Stephen L. *The Social Roots of Biblical Yahwism.* Society of Biblical Literature Studies in Biblical Literature 8. Leiden, The Netherlands: Brill, 2004.

Cook, Stephen L. *Conversations with Scripture: 2 Isaiah.* Anglican Association of Biblical Scholars Study Series. Harrisburg, Penn.: Morehouse, 2008.

Davis, Ellen F. *Swallowing the Scroll: Textuality and the Dynamics of Discourse in Ezekiel's Prophecy.* Sheffield, U.K.: Almond, 1989.

Day, John, ed. *Prophecy and Prophets in Ancient Israel: Proceedings of the Oxford Old Testament Seminar.* Library of Hebrew Bible/Old Testament Studies 531. New York: T&T Clark, 2010.

Gignilliat, Mark S. *Karl Barth and the Fifth Gospel: Barth's Theological Exegesis of Isaiah.* Farnham, U.K.: Ashgate, 2009.

Hayes, John H. "Prophecy and Prophets, Hebrew Bible." In *Dictionary of Biblical Interpretation,* edited by John H. Hayes, Vol. 2, pp. 310–317. Nashville, Tenn.: Abingdon, 1999.

Heschel, Abraham Joshua. *The Prophets.* New York: Harper & Row, 1962.

Hibbard, James Todd. *Intertextuality in Isaiah 24–27: The Reuse and Evocation of Earlier Texts and Traditions.* Tübingen, Germany: Mohr Siebeck, 2006.

Jaynes, Julian. *The Origin of Consciousness in the Breakdown of the Bicameral Mind.* Boston: Houghton Mifflin, 1976.

Knohl, Israel. *The Sanctuary of Silence: The Priestly Torah and the Holiness School.* Minneapolis: Fortress, 1995.

Matthews, Victor H., and Don C. Benjamin. *Old Testament Parallels: Laws and Stories from the Ancient Near East.* 3rd ed. New York: Paulist Press, 2006.

Nissinen, Martti, and Peter Machinist. *Prophets and Prophecy in the Ancient Near East.* Writings from the Ancient World 12. Leiden, The Netherlands: Brill, 2003.

Overholt, Thomas W. *Channels of Prophecy: The Social Dynamics of Prophetic Activity.* Minneapolis: Fortress, 1989.

Petersen, David L. *The Roles of Israel's Prophets.* Sheffield, U.K.: JSOT Press, 1981.

Rad, Gerhard von. *The Message of the Prophets.* Translated by D. M. G. Stalker. New York: Harper and Row, 1965.

Rendtorff, Rolf. "The Place of Prophecy in a Theology of the Old Testament." In *Canon and Theology: Overtures to Old Testament Theology,* translated and edited by M. Kohl, pp. 57–65. Minneapolis: Fortress, 1993.

Roberts, J. J. M. *The Bible and the Ancient Near East: Collected Essays.* Winona Lake, Ind.: Eisenbrauns, 2002.

Sarna, Nahum M. *Exploring Exodus: The Heritage of Biblical Israel.* New York: Schocken, 1986.

Seitz, Christopher R. *Prophecy and Hermeneutics: Toward a New Introduction to the Prophets.* Grand Rapids, Mich.: Baker Academic, 2007.

Sommer, Benjamin D. *A Prophet Reads Scripture: Allusion in Isaiah 40–66.* Stanford, Calif.: Stanford University Press, 1998.

Sparks, Kenton L. *Ethnicity and Identity in Ancient Israel: Prolegomena to the Study of Ethnic Sentiments and Their Expression in the Hebrew Bible.* Winona Lake, Ind.: Eisenbrauns, 1998.

Steck, Odil Hannes. *The Prophetic Books and Their Theological Witness.* Translated by James D. Nogalski. Saint Louis, Mo.: Chalice, 2000.

Sweeney, Marvin A. *The Twelve Prophets.* Vol. 1: *Berit Olam.* Edited by David W. Cotter. Collegeville, Minn.: Liturgical Press, 2000.

Sweeney, Marvin A. *Form and Intertextuality in Prophetic and Apocalyptic Literature.* Forschungen zum Alten Testament 45. Tübingen, Germany: Mohr Siebeck, 2005.

Williams, Ronald J., and John C. Beckman. *Williams' Hebrew Syntax.* Toronto: University of Toronto Press, 2007.

Wilson, Robert R. *Prophecy and Society in Ancient Israel.* Philadelphia: Fortress, 1980.

Stephen L. Cook

PROVERBS

See Wisdom Literature.

PSALMS

The remarkable complexity of the Psalter's theology results from three primary factors: the size of the corpus, its numerous literary genres, and the wide temporal range over which the Psalms were written and redacted. The Psalter contains a number of distinct poetic forms and, arguably, some of the earliest and latest literature within the Hebrew Bible. The Psalter also shows marks of significant editorial activity at several periods prior to its stabilization. While tradition has attributed the Psalter to David, the collection is more accurately understood as the product of Yahweh's faithful community across centuries of composition and redaction. Thus, the five books of the Psalter (Pss 1–41; 42–72; 73–89; 90–106; 107–150) constitute a repository of theology in song.

David and the Psalter. David features prominently in the Psalter, in part because of his reputation as a musician and singer of psalms attested elsewhere in the Hebrew Bible (e.g., 1 Sam 16:23; 18:10; 19:9; 2 Sam 1:17–27; 22:1–51; Amos 6:5). Notably, in the chronicler's reworking of the history of the monarchy, David appears as the figure who single-handedly instituted the music and worship of Yahweh in the Jerusalem cult (1 Chr 6:31–53; 15:16; 16:4–43; 25:1–31; cf. Ezra 3:10; Neh 12:24, 45–46). Within the Psalter itself, 73 discrete psalms contain the Hebrew superscription *lĕdāwīd*, a phrase that can be translated variously: "[written] by David," "to/for/of David," and "pertaining to David." Several psalms expand on this simple phrase by situating the psalm within a particular episode of David's life (Pss 3; 7; 18; 34; 51; 52; 54; 56; 57; 59; 60; 63; 142). Further evidence of David's connection to the Psalter comes at the end of the second book: "The prayers of David son of Jesse are ended" (Ps 72:20). While most of the psalms associated with David do indeed appear in books 1 and 2, there are nevertheless 16 other psalms with the superscription *lĕdāwīd* in books 3–5 (Pss 101; 103; 108; 109; 110; 122; 124; 131; 138–145).

Most scholars agree that the opening superscriptions, Davidic or otherwise, postdate the composition of their respective psalms. Indeed, there is scant evidence within the "Davidic" psalms to suggest that he wrote more than a handful of them (among the best candidates are Pss 2 and 18). While *lĕdāwīd* permits several translations, the association of these psalms with David reflects a growing tendency in the postexilic period and beyond to establish a single person as an author of a wide range of biblical literature (cf. Moses's association with the Pentateuch and Solomon's connection to the wisdom literature). The Septuagint bears witness to this process as it contains even more Davidic superscriptions, 87 in all, and well as Psalm 151, an additional psalm attributed to David that describes his life. Accordingly, the New Testament often describes David as the author of the Psalms (e.g., Matt 22:41–46; Acts 1:16–20; 2:25–29; Heb 4:7; cf. Sir 47:8–10).

When one considers the Psalter as preserved in the Masoretic Text, the association with David carries unique theological force. The superscriptions occur primarily (but not exclusively) in the first two books of the Psalter, a portion of the Psalter in which lament predominates. In these Davidic psalms, one often finds claims that God is absent (e.g., Ps 22:1), hidden (e.g., Ps 13:1), and even an oppressive force (e.g., Ps 39:9–13). Sentiments like these essentially call into question God's faithfulness. As such, they are deeply troubling for a community grounded in worship to Yahweh as the one true God. However, by attributing Davidic authorship to these psalms, the community boldly authorizes painful but deeply honest statements to and about God that emerge in the context of prayer. As the founder of Israel's golden age and God's anointed king, David is a singular individual. Yet he functions at the same time as a representative for the entire community, one whose voice could speak for all of those who struggled to live faithfully in relationship with Yahweh. As the tradition of Davidic authorship gradually encompassed the entire Psalter by the first century C.E., an even fuller vocabulary of prayer—from dire lament and exuberant praise—found its authorization in this uniquely representative figure.

Theology through Different Forms. To digest the theology of the entire Psalter, one must first analyze the main theological themes of various psalmic genres or forms—how, for example, the theology of lament psalms compares to the theology of wisdom psalms. Only after examining the particular theological themes of various genres can one discern how the final form of the Psalter prioritizes or shapes these themes. To be sure, establishing the theology of the psalms requires an analysis of the direct statements that the psalmists make about God. Yet it also requires an exploration of the different ways that the psalmists address God. Put differently, the theology of the psalms emerges as much from *what* the psalmists say about God as *how* the psalmists speak to and about God in the context of prayer. The following discussion surveys the theological themes of some of the most important psalmic genres (lament, praise, royal, and wisdom psalms) and then explores how the final editors of the Psalter shaped its theological witness.

Psalms of lament. Lament psalms comprise the most common genre within the Psalter. As such, they hold special importance for determining the overall theology of the psalms. At a fundamental level, the lament psalms—both communal and individual laments—express a "crisis theology," born in the midst of pain, isolation, shame, fear, and the experience of powerlessness. The powerlessness of the psalmist typically stands in sharp contrast to the power of the psalmist's enemies. In a paradigmatic fashion, Psalm 22 presents the asymmetric power dynamic of lament psalms with the help of vivid, imagistic language. The psalmist is a worm (v. 6); his body breaks down and ceases to function properly (vv. 14–17). Meanwhile, the psalmist's enemies are powerful and terrifying. They surround him like threatening beasts (oxen, lions, dogs) ready to rip the psalmist apart (vv. 12–13, 16, 20–21).

The power of the enemy and powerlessness of the psalmist could lead the psalmist to several theological conclusions. First, God is powerless to act on his behalf. Second, God is somehow not aware of his suffering. Third, God has knowingly abandoned him. Throughout the lament psalms, the psalmists make the second and third conclusions, but not the first.

Indeed, the structure and formal elements of a lament psalm contradict the notion that God is powerless. With Psalm 22 again providing an example, one can see how a psalm's invocation (vv. 1–2), complaint (vv. 1–2, 6–8, 12–18), and petition (vv. 11, 19–21) all confirm God's power implicitly. The very act of crying out to God presumes that God indeed exists in a relationship with the psalmist, that God can hear,

and that God is powerful enough to act in response. The other elements of the lament psalm affirm God's power explicitly. The confession of trust (vv. 3, 9–10) typically describes God's reputation for powerful action on behalf of the psalmist and throughout the history of community. Likewise the vow of praise (v. 22) presumes that God's transforming action is on the horizon. The psalmist exhibits such confidence in God's power that often this vow of praise morphs into outright praise (vv. 23–31). Thus, the entire lament psalm, in both implicit and explicit ways, affirms God's power to intervene in the life of the psalmist.

While the lament psalms continually assert the ultimate power of God (divine omnipotence), these texts do not speak with one voice about whether God is always aware of the psalmist's suffering and weakness vis-à-vis the enemies (divine omniscience and omnipresence). Many lament psalms ask God to look at the psalmist and listen to his plea, as if God simply does not know the extent of his suffering. The psalmist reasons that if God knew, then surely God would act. Thus, the rhetorical force of these lament psalms is aimed at provoking a divine response. The psalmist tries to capture God's attention, often by repeating verbs of hearing (e.g., Ps 5:1–2) and seeing (e.g., Ps 13:3; 25:18) in the imperative mood. According to the logic of the lament psalms, for God to see and hear, God must be present. So the psalmist portrays his or her suffering fundamentally as a problem of proximity. Since God is far off, trouble is near (see, e.g., Pss 10:1; 22:1, 11). If God were to come near, then the psalmist would certainly experience God's salvation.

Yet some lament psalms characterize divine proximity differently. God's presence may also be a source of suffering if the psalmist has transgressed God's law. In these cases, the psalmist pleads that God would "turn [God's] gaze away from me" (Ps 39:13) and "hide [God's] face from my sins" (Ps 51:9). Such texts clearly suggest that God is the agent of suffering, meting out painful judgment against the psalmist.

More often, however, the lament psalms picture a righteous speaker whose sufferings are largely unjustified (see, e.g., Pss 4:1, 3; 7:3–5; 17:1–6, 15). The psalmist characterizes this experience of suffering as godforsakenness. God has chosen to afflict the psalmist for no clear reason (e.g., Ps 88) or has intentionally left the psalmist alone with no protection or comfort (e.g., Pss 22:1; 71:9–11, 18). Remarkably, the psalmist continually cries out to an absent God and/or a God who has rejected him. Thus, the lament psalms, as a whole, witness a powerful example of human faithfulness to God in the midst of desperate suffering. The psalmists defiantly cling to God, struggling to understand God's actions even as they maintain that God's character is marked by steadfast love (ḥesed, e.g., Ps 6:4).

Psalms of praise. While the lament psalms often witness God's power implicitly (by calling out to an apparently absent God), the psalmists describe God's power explicitly through praise. In a variety of literary genres (e.g., hymns, historical psalms, psalms of thanksgiving, songs of Zion) the psalmists detail the character and acts of the Deity and call others to do likewise. As such, the psalms of praise rely on a distinctive mode of interpreting the world and recalling history. The world is fundamentally God's creation, and relatedly, history is a rehearsal of God's actions. Thus, the entire cosmos stages the ever-unfolding drama of God's activity.

The psalms of praise, in line with other ancient Near Eastern religious systems, picture God's creative work as establishing the ordered, inhabitable world amid the waters of chaos (e.g., Pss 24:1–2; 65:7; 89:8–11). This foundational act reveals the essential elements of the divine persona. From the very start, God has been bringing order out of chaos, exercising control over terrifying forces, setting things aright, and sustaining the world so that life can thrive.

God's creative actions happened at the dawn of history but are by no means limited to the past. Indeed, God's work extends into the present and the future since the forces of chaos that God ordered at creation still actively threaten the psalmist and the community. The psalmists picture these threats in myriad ways but especially through natural elements such as the waters (Ps 46:2–3) and the wilderness (Ps 107:35). Likewise, numerous human foes threaten God's order, on both the national (Pss 46:6; 124:2–3) and the individual (Ps 68:1–3, 21) levels. Despite these manifold threats, the psalms of praise recount God's inevitable power over all rival claims of authority.

A well-established pattern emerges in many of the psalms of praise whereby the psalmists conflate God's creative acts with God's activities on behalf of the community that has been called together through covenant. Psalm 136 provides a particularly clear example. God's ordering of the world at creation (vv. 1–9) reflects his conquest over the power of Egypt, the Sea of Reeds (or Red Sea), and the rulers of Canaan (vv. 10–23). These mighty acts highlight God's character—God's ever-enduring love (ḥesed) for the community.

Because God has acted so powerfully on the cosmic and geopolitical stage, the community can take courage, knowing that he gives protection when the forces of chaos threaten (see, e.g., Ps 46). Thus, in the liturgical act of glorifying God, the community actually exhorts itself. Yet, even as the community encourages itself through remembering God's actions, praise also reminds God of God's actions. Praise encourages God to continue to overcome chaos and (re)establish order.

Royal psalms. In both lament and praise, the psalmists portray God as heavenly king, the one who establishes and maintains dominion over the entire world. Several psalms presume that the dominion of Yahweh can be realized on earth through a royal representative, a Davidic king. These royal psalms are prayers for, by, and about the king, the anointed one (Heb. māšîaḥ, e.g., Pss 2:2; 45:7) who is designated as Yahweh's son (Ps 2:7).

Divine sonship comes with unrivaled authority and the responsibility of promoting God's ordering work in the world. This work consists primarily of winning military contests by means of God's empowerment (Pss 18:28–50; 72:8–11; 118:10–16). Of course, the king's victory translates into victory for the people as well, for the king serves as the "shield" of his people (Ps 84:9). Through the person of the king, God keeps the enemies at bay—enemies who are, in fact, the personification of the forces of chaos. So in battling these foes, the king plays an active role in maintaining the order that God established at the creation of the world and at the creation of the covenant community.

The king also functions as the guarantor of justice within the land. Psalm 101, for example, recounts the king's pledge to rule with integrity, to maintain his own righteousness, and to administer his government in ways that foster righteousness throughout the land (vv. 1–8). In essence, just administration means caring for the poor and rooting out systems of oppression (Ps 72:12–14). Indeed, the king stands in the highest office as an advocate for the lowest segment in the community, especially when the wealthy and powerful would seek to take advantage of them. In short, the king's activities on behalf of the poor and weak mirror God's own actions (cf. Ps 146:5–10), which are seen so clearly in the lament psalms as God protects the powerless psalmist from the powerful enemies.

The royal psalms suggest that the righteousness of the king will yield prosperity for the entire community—a fruitful land and a thriving economy. Yet, in fact, across the scope of biblical history, there were relatively few times, if any, when there was a king in Jerusalem who effectively represented the righteousness of God according to the standards of the royal psalms. After the Exile, the very office of king became obsolete. In this period and beyond, Yahweh's kingship became more important than that of an earthly king. Thus, Psalm 72, a royal psalm abounding with blessings on the king in verses 1–17, concludes by reframing the ideology of kingship with a claim that Yahweh "alone does wondrous things" (v. 18). Successive generations of readers subsequently read the psalms as expressing the characteristics of a future anointed leader (*māšîaḥ*, "messiah") who would one day serve as God's agent of justice in the world, the personification of divine order. This messianic reading may have contributed to the fact that many nonroyal psalms were secondarily associated with King David through the addition of superscriptions (among many examples, see Pss 4–6).

Wisdom psalms. The wisdom psalms bear close affinities to Old Testament wisdom literature (Proverbs, Job, Ecclesiastes) in that they suggest that the divine order manifests itself through human experience, by reflecting on the patterns of cause and effect that govern all life. Just as streams of water cause a nearby tree to thrive (Ps 1:3) and wind causes chaff to be driven off (Ps 1:4), the consequences of all human actions will manifest themselves over the course of time. Inevitably, God's justice endures.

These meditations on ultimate outcomes seem to emerge from a unique setting. Wisdom psalms—again, like the rest of the wisdom literature—do not necessarily presume a liturgical context, as do royal psalms and psalms of praise. Nor do these psalms derive from the crucible of suffering. Rather, the wisdom psalms offer observations about the world that come with the benefit of perspective and reflection (see, e.g., Ps 37:25). They reflect not a "crisis theology" but instead a "contemplative theology" nurtured through experience across time.

While these psalms have a unique social context, they share the Psalter's common theme of the polarity of the righteous and the wicked, the difference between those who respect and preserve God's order and those who sow chaos, violence, and lies. In the wisdom psalms, wicked behavior leads inexorably to calamity while righteousness leads to divine favor and prosperity (e.g., Pss 1:3–4; 32:10; 34:16–18, 21–22). Although these psalms trade in sharp contrasts between the righteous and wicked, the poets are not naive about the complexities of human experience. The psalmists acknowledge and affirm that the wicked do indeed prosper (Ps 73:4–12) and that the righteous suffer (e.g., Pss 34:17–19; 73:13–14). These psalms therefore validate the experience of suffering and disorder in the world, even as they proclaim confidently that the wicked ultimately fall by their own devices, or as Psalm 37:15 puts it, "their sword shall enter their own heart." When one pays careful attention to the patterns of cause and effect, one realizes the profoundly negative consequences of sin.

This observation confirms the veracity of the Law of God, the *tôrâ*, which provides the primary theme of three wisdom psalms, Psalms 1, 19, and 119. The structure of Psalm 19 celebrates God's order as revealed through the natural world (vv. 1–6, general revelation) and the Torah (vv. 7–14, special revelation). As such, the psalmist integrates different ways of observing God's order into one unified poetic form. Psalm 119 also embodies the divine order through its poetic structure. With 176 verses, this colossal alphabetic acrostic psalm mirrors the perfection of

God's Law, each eight-verse stanza beginning with a successive letter of the Hebrew alphabet. The complex structure of this wisdom psalm presents an orderly presentation of order itself—God's Law, God's very word to the community.

The Shape of the Psalter's Theology. The Psalter hinges on the central theme of God's power to create order in the world, although the various psalmic genres articulate this theme differently. In lament, the psalmists petition God to (re)introduce order in the midst of a desperately chaotic situation. The psalms of praise celebrate God's order as the psalmists recall history and observe nature. The royal psalms understand God's order to be realized in the office of the king. The wisdom psalms contemplate the order of God through reflection on the patterns of cause and effect and by meditating on the Torah.

Scholars have identified many other genres on the basis of literary structure, content, and, in some cases, putative ritual context. In each of these genres, the theme of God's ordering power takes a unique shape. Entrance liturgies (Pss 15; 24), for example, affirm the protecting presence of God in the sanctuary and establish the conditions under which worshippers may approach the majesty of God, "the king of glory" (Ps 24:7–10). Enthronement psalms (Pss 47; 93; 95–99) extol the dominion of God through the central phrase *yhwh mālak*: "Yahweh is king" or "Yahweh has become king." These psalms celebrate both the establishment of God's reign and its continuance year after year. Songs of trust (Pss 11; 16; 23; 62–63; 91; 121; 125; 131) highlight God's faithfulness and power in the midst of grave threats. Imprecatory psalms (Pss 12; 58; 69; 83; 94; 109; 129; 137), an important subgroup of lament psalms, employ powerful rhetoric to motivate God to act on the behalf of the righteous against individual and communal foes.

Taken together, the various psalmic genres serve a diverse community of faith. It includes within its ranks the powerful and the powerless, those who have sinned and those who have not, those who are suffering greatly and those who observe the suffering of others and can recall their own. This mixed chorus sings together across the five books of the psalms—more often in counterpoint than in steady, predictable monotone.

Moreover, this choir of psalmists sings across hundreds of years, with a sung theology that changes and develops over time. New and radically different songs arise as the result of changing historical contexts. Psalm 137, for example, confirms that new contexts (both temporal and geographical) require different songs from those sung in the past. After all, one cannot sing the songs of Zion by the rivers of Babylon (Ps 137:1, 3–4). In other instances, the psalmists sing old songs in new ways. While Psalm 51:1–17 presents the prayer of a penitent individual who is guilty of a host of sins, the later addition of the final two verses (vv. 18–19) completely reorients the psalm. The individual's prayer becomes the prayer of the entire community seeking restoration in the wake of corporate sin.

Thus, the Psalter's final form has indelibly shaped its theological witness. Readers must take into account the structure that the book of Psalms has assumed over time, particularly the way the Psalter begins and ends. The addition of Psalm 1 as an introduction to the entire Psalter casts the whole work as an expression on God's order in song. The five "Hallelujah psalms" (Pss 146–150) make praise the psalmists' ultimate statement. All human speech to and about God leads inexorably to doxology.

Yet these framing psalms do not mute the complexity of the Psalter. Nor do the psalms proceed in a uniform, homophonic expression of God's power. The oppressive darkness of Psalm 88:18 stands right next to the exuberant praise of Psalm 89:1. In a similar juxtaposition, Psalm 39:14 describes God's presence as an oppressive force. Yet God's presence is a source of salvation in the immediately following verses, Psalm 40:1–2. And for its part, Psalm 40 soon swings back to lament, with its final verses pleading for the saving presence of God while the psalmist endures desperate suffering (vv. 11–17). In short, the Psalter witnesses a thorough integration of lament and praise, such that neither lament nor praise exists on its own. Together they constitute the rhythm of the faithful life. The Psalter pulses with this rhythm as it works its way to the final tonic chord of praise.

This rhythm is intrinsic to life lived in covenant relationship with Yahweh. Historical and social situations change—the fall of the monarchy, the Exile, the destruction and rebuilding of the Temple, social disarray. Yet the community continues to resonate with the old songs. Indeed, these songs proved to be so significant for the community that some have been updated with additional verses to reflect the particularities of their current contexts (e.g., Pss 51:18–19; 89:38–52; cf. Ps 72:18–20).

Reshaping the Psalter's Theology. A survey of the early reception of the Psalter reveals how strongly its forms of prayer guided the piety and practice of ancient faithful communities. The importance of the psalms for Hellenistic Jews is reflected by the fact that there are more extant manuscripts of the psalms in Greek than any other Old Testament book. Likewise, the writers of the New Testament quote and allude to the book of Psalms more than any other text. That Jesus's words from the cross draw from Psalm 22:1 provides a compelling example of this practice (Matt 27:46; Mark 15:34). Similarly, at Qumran it seems that there was no more important biblical collection, with the Psalter appearing in some 39 manuscripts.

The discoveries at Qumran attest both the importance of psalms and the fact that the Psalter existed in different editions as late as the second century C.E. Moreover, at Qumran one can find numerous examples of hymns, songs, and liturgies that do not appear in the Psalter of the Masoretic Text but nevertheless rely on the tradition of the Hebrew psalmody (e.g., the thanksgiving psalms [*Hodayot*], the Songs of the Sabbath Sacrifice, and other prayers, incantations, and liturgies). These texts rehearse well-established psalmic themes, even as they modify and develop literary forms in a different historical and cultic environment.

To be sure, the Psalter's influence did not cease with ancient communities. For many worshipers today, the psalms play a central liturgical role, through either responsive reading or singing. In traditions where Christian hymns have largely replaced corporate singing of psalms, one can nevertheless discern numerous allusions and quotations of psalms. In other contexts as well, from concert halls to jazz clubs to prayer groups, these ancient songs are rehearsed and reshaped into new forms.

There are at least three reasons for the long and rich reception history of the Psalter. First, the Psalter's figurative language creates a sense of immediacy that draws its audience into a vivid world of images. Second, the musicality of the psalms endows them with a powerful mnemonic effect. Even in translation, the psalms encourage memorization and thus have a particular power to preserve and express the theology of the community. Third, the voice of the psalmist is often expressed in the first person. These pronouns (I/me/my, we/us/our) invite readers to be a part of the psalm, to give new voice to someone else's prayer to God. The psalms invite all who encounter them to take up the "I" as one's very own voice.

Indeed, this openness of the Psalter presses a final critical point. The Psalter uniquely translates the experience of a relationship with God from one context to the next, from an ancient faithful community to a contemporary one. Through both its form and content, the Psalter continues to summon its readers to express their relationship with God through the prayers and praises of generations past. In doing so, the Psalter orients us not only to the community of the past but also to the faithful community of the present, to all who cling, even tenuously, to the notion that God has the power to bring about order in the world.

[*See also* Cult and Worship; David; Eschatology; Exile and Dislocation; Expiation; Faith; Festivals and Holy Days; God and Gods; Jerusalem (Zion); Kings and Kingship; Sacrifice and Offerings; *and* Tabernacles, Temples, and Synagogues.]

BIBLIOGRAPHY
Brown, William P. *Seeing the Psalms: A Theology of Metaphor.* Louisville, Ky.: Westminster John Knox, 2002.
Brown, William P., ed. *Oxford Handbook of the Psalms.* Oxford: Oxford University Press, 2014.
Brueggemann, Walter. *The Psalms and the Life of Faith.* Edited by Patrick D. Miller. Minneapolis: Fortress, 1995.
Flint, Peter W., and Patrick D. Miller Jr., eds. *The Book of Psalms: Composition and Reception.* With the assistance of Aaron Brunell and Ryan Roberts. Vetus Testamentum Supplements 99. Leiden, The Netherlands: Brill, 2005.
Gillingham, Susan E. *Psalms Through the Centuries.* Oxford: Blackwell, 2008.
Jacobson, Rolf A., ed. *Soundings in the Theology of Psalms: Perspectives and Methods in Contemporary Scholarship.* Minneapolis: Fortress, 2010.

Janowski, Bernd. *Arguing with God: A Theological Anthropology of the Psalms*. Translated by Armin Seidlecki. Louisville, Ky.: Westminster John Knox, 2013.

Keel, Othmar. *Symbolism and the Biblical World: Ancient Near Eastern Iconography and the Book of Psalms*. Translated by Timothy J. Hallett. Winona Lake, Ind.: Eisenbrauns, 1997.

Kraus, Hans-Joachim. *Theology of the Psalms*. Translated by Keith R. Crim. Continental Commentary. Minneapolis: Augsburg, 1986.

McCann, J. Clinton. *A Theological Introduction to the Book of Psalms: The Psalms as Torah*. Nashville, Tenn.: Abingdon, 1993.

Miller, Patrick D. *They Cried to the Lord: The Form and Theology of Biblical Prayer*. Minneapolis: Fortress, 1994.

Westermann, Claus. *Praise and Lament in the Psalms*. Translated by Keith R. Crim and Richard N. Soulen. Atlanta: John Knox, 1981.

Joel Marcus LeMon

R

RECONCILIATION

Paul interprets God's saving work in Christ's death in terms of God's "reconciliation" of sinners to himself. He designates the apostolic ministry as "the ministry of reconciliation" and the gospel as "the word of reconciliation," and he teaches that by accepting it, sinners become reconciled to God and saved from divine wrath. Some biblical scholars have seen reconciliation as the central theme of Pauline soteriology or even all of biblical theology, and some theologians appreciate its particular usefulness for gospel preaching in the twenty-first century.

The Terminology. The Greek words *katallassein* ("to reconcile") and *diallassein* ("to reconcile," and their cognates and synonyms) have the fundamental meaning of "exchange" and were used for a change from a relationship of conflict and enmity to one of peace and friendship. Their use in Greco-Roman diplomatic contexts can be seen as the background of Paul's use of the *katallassein/katallagē* (to reconcile/reconciliation) terminology, but those words were only rarely attested in the Hellenistic diplomatic records. "Reconciliation" words are rarely used for divine–human relationship in the Hellenistic literature, but they are more commonly attested in Hellenistic Jewish literature in the form "God is reconciled" to Israel or to individuals at their repentance, prayer, or vicarious suffering (e.g., 2 Macc 1:5; 5:20; 7:32–38;

8:29; Philo, *Mos.* 2.166; *Praem.* 166; Josephus, *B.J.* 5.415, *Ant.* 6.143; 7.153; *Jos. Asen.* 11:18).

In the New Testament, Jesus exhorts reconciliation (*diallassein*) between neighbors (Matt 5:24; cf. Luke 12:58), and Paul promotes reconciliation (*katallassein*) between estranged couples (1 Cor 7:11; cf. Acts 7:26). Only in the Pauline corpus is the *katallagē* ("reconciliation") language used for the God–human relationship (Rom 5:1–11; 11:15; 2 Cor 5:11–21; cf. *apokatallassein* ["to reconcile"] in Eph 2:11–18 and Col 1:19–23). Paul always uses it in the forms that make it clear that God (the offended) is the subject of reconciliation and human beings (the offenders) the object: "God reconciled the world to himself" or "we were reconciled to God"—forms that are attested nowhere else. Since very few interpreters identify 2 Corinthians 5:18–21 or part of it (v. 19ab) as a pre-Pauline tradition, we may conclude that the *katallagē* and its cognates are uniquely Pauline in the New Testament.

Atonement and Reconciliation. In view of Paul's connection of God's reconciliation with Christ's vicarious death in 2 Corinthians 5:11–21 and Romans 5:6–11 (cf. Col 1:20–22; Eph 2:13–18), Paul has usually been understood to be relating God's work of reconciliation with Christ's atoning sacrifice. However, it has been suggested that Paul bases his reconciliation doctrine on a Hellenistic understanding of Christ's vicarious death as well as on noncultic interpretations of Isaiah 53 and the Last Supper. But there is no Hellenistic evidence for reconciliation wrought through someone's vicarious death, and the reference to the servant's death as 'ašam in Isaiah 53:10 is a metaphorical use of the atonement language for noncultic acts or events in the Old Testament (cf. also Isa 43:3–4, koper), such use being frequent in Judaism (e.g., 1QS 3:4–12; 8:3–4). It appears also in interpreting the meaning of the martyrs' deaths in 4 Maccabees 6:29 and 17:22 (cf. 2 Macc 7:32–38). Given this Old Testament–Jewish tradition, it is not unusual that in the New Testament Christ's death is interpreted in terms of an atoning sacrifice, sometimes with the explicit cultic terminology (hilasmos/hilaskesthai, "expiation/to expiate") applied to it (Heb 2:17; 1 John 2:2; 4:10).

Paul regularly uses cultic language metaphorically for Christ (1 Cor 5:7–8), the church (1 Cor 3:16), and Christian life and ministry (e.g., Rom 12:1; 15:16; 1 Cor 6:19; Phil 2:17). That Paul does the same for Christ's death is confirmed by his reference to it as "hilastērion ['expiation' or 'propitiation'] in his blood" in Romans 3:24–25 (cf. Lev 17:11). He clearly has that phrase in mind when he speaks of the "blood" of Christ as the means of God's "reconciliation" in Romans 5:6–10 (cf. Col 1:20–22; Eph 2:13–18). This connection of katallagē ("reconciliation") language with hilaskesthai ("to expiate") language clearly shows that he sees Christ's death as an atoning sacrifice. Thus, Paul develops his doctrine of reconciliation by representing Christ's death with the Greek concept of reconciliation that has been interpreted in terms of the Old Testament–Jewish tradition of atonement.

There is an essential continuity between Paul's doctrine of atonement/reconciliation and the atonement in the Old Testament Temple cult. First, one may observe God's gracious provision of the institution of atonement (Lev 10:17; 17:11). Then, the sacrificial animal stands as an inclusive substitute for the one offering the sacrifice, a substitute that includes the offerer. The inclusion takes place when the offerer identifies himself with the victim by laying his hands upon it. So the offerer dies the death of judgment for his sins in and through his inclusive substitute. Therefore Hofius (1989b) explains that "atonement is as such reconciliation…reconciliation with God of the sinner who has fallen to death" (p. 43).

A close correspondence has been drawn between this Old Testament atoning sacrifice and Paul's doctrine of the atonement in Christ in 2 Corinthians 5:11–21, by pointing to Paul's stress on Christ's atoning death as an inclusive substitute: God did not count humanity's trespasses against them (5:19b) but made Christ "sin" for them (5:21a). Thus, Christ "died for all; therefore all have died" (5:14). By dying in and with Christ, the inclusive substitute, the death of judgment as old sinful Adamic human beings, and rising to the new being in and through him (cf. Rom 6:3–11; Gal 2:19–20), believers become "new creation" (5:17). Paul expresses this outcome of Christ's atoning death in terms of believers becoming "God's righteousness" (5:21b), that is, their justification or restoration to the right relationship with God wherein they now live for him (or his Son Jesus Christ, 5:15). Paul refers to this whole event of the atonement as God's "reconciliation" of the world in and through Christ (5:18–19).

Paul's stress on God's provision of the atonement/reconciliation in Christ is in contrast to Hellenistic Jewish writers who thought of human beings reconciling God to themselves through repentance, prayer, or, in the case of 4 Maccabees 6:28–29 and 17:21–22 (cf. 2 Macc 7:32–38), even the martyrs' vicarious death. How did Paul uniquely come to interpret the saving event in Christ in terms of "reconciliation" and formulate his reconciliation doctrine in such contrast to his Hellenistic Jewish milieu?

The Origin of Paul's Reconciliation Doctrine. Some scholars take their clue in the Jesus tradition (his welcoming and forgiving sinners on God's behalf), particularly the early Christian confession of Jesus's death as vicarious atonement and Isaiah 40–66. Others point to the Damascus Christophany as its foundation, looking especially to 2 Corinthians 5:11–21, which is part of Paul's apostolic apologia (2 Cor 2:14—7:4). If 2 Corinthians 5:16–17 alludes to his Damascus experience, it is natural to see the subsequent three aorist participle phrases in 5:18–19 (katallaxantos [reconciled], dontos [gave], and themenos [gave/entrusted]) as referring to what happened to Paul at the Damascus event: God "reconciled [Paul] to himself," "gave [him] the ministry of reconciliation," and "set in [him] the word of reconciliation."

While Paul was literally acting as an "enemy" of God (Rom 5:10) in his persecution of God's church (cf. Gal 1:13; 1 Cor 15:8; Phil 3:6), God granted him forgiveness and appointed him an apostle. Thus, Paul found it most appropriate to express that divine salvation in terms of the Greek concept of "reconciliation." This experience led him then to interpret God's offering of Christ in terms of that concept (5:19ab), as well as to designate the gospel and apostleship likewise. Paul then found both Jesus tradition and scripture (esp. Isa 40–55) to confirm what he experienced at the Damascus revelation. So was born Paul's unique soteriological category "reconciliation" with his unique formula "God reconciled sinners to himself."

Reconciliation and Justification. In 2 Corinthians 5:11–21, Paul closely relates "reconciliation" and "justification" (note his elaboration of vv. 18–19a with v. 21) just as he relates it with "new creation" (vv. 17–18). The parallel statements in Romans 5:8–9 and 5:10 make the close relationship between "justification" and "reconciliation" even clearer.

Some scholars who are focused on the forensic meaning of "justification" (acquittal and granting of righteous status) regard reconciliation as a consequence of justification. Romans 5:1 is cited to support this view: "Therefore, since we are justified by faith, we have peace with God through our Lord Jesus Christ." However, this view ignores the fact that in a sense reconciliation is prior to justification. While Paul speaks of God reconciling the world to himself through Christ's atoning death (2 Cor 5:19ab), he does not speak of God justifying the world through it. Thus, while he equates Christ's atonement with God's work of reconciliation (cf. Rom 5:10), he does not do the same with justification (cf. Rom 5:8, 9a). Therefore, insofar as justification is based on Christ's atoning death (e.g., Rom 3:24–26; 4:25; 8:3–4; 2 Cor 5:21), God's historic work of atonement/reconciliation in Christ is prior to justification. So while "reconciliation" is used to refer to God's historic work of atonement in Christ itself (as well as to its actualized state with the believers), "justification" is used to refer only to a fruit of it.

Furthermore, if justification is understood as including the relational meaning of restoring sinners to the right relationship with God, reconciliation and justification may be said to refer to the same reality, the restored relationship between God and humans. In this view they may be regarded as two different metaphors distinguished only by their different nuances: "justification" conveying the nuance of the restored relationship being a "right" (just) relationship and "reconciliation," an amicable relationship.

Preaching "the Word of Reconciliation" as Part of God's Saving Work. God's historic work of reconciliation in Christ (2 Cor 5:19ab; Rom 5:10) is effected and sinners actually become reconciled to God only as they avail themselves of Christ's work by accepting "the word of reconciliation," the gospel that announces that historic work of God's reconciliation in Christ (2 Cor 5:18c, 19c, 20). Therefore, the atonement in Christ, "the ministry of reconciliation," and "the word of reconciliation" proclaimed in the apostolic church make up God's total work of reconciliation (cf. Rom 10:9–10, 14–15).

In Colossians, those who used to be "estranged" from and "hostile" to God, "doing evil deeds," have now been "reconciled" to him by accepting his universal "reconciliation" through Christ's atoning sacrifice. Since the purpose of reconciliation was for them to lead a holy and righteous life, they must remain in that life dedicated to God (Col 1:20–23). The Corinthian Christians also accepted "the word of reconciliation," but in view of their serious evil deeds, Paul urges them to actualize in their ongoing life what happened when they first converted; they must live in a way that consolidates peace with God rather than provoking God's wrath (2 Cor 5:20; 6:1).

Horizontal and Cosmic Reconciliation. Through the missionary preaching of the gospel, the Gentile Christians have become reconciled to God along with the remnant of Israel who have accepted the gospel by faith (see Rom 11:5). Thus, the believing Gentiles and the believing Jews have become united in the body of Christ and have been made citizens in God's kingdom or members of his household together. Ephesians 2:11–18 celebrates this outcome of the gospel as an actualization of God's work of reconciliation in Christ. Here, Christ's death is interpreted as having wrought reconciliation by abolishing the law that was functioning as "the dividing wall of hostility" between

Jews and Gentiles. So it has reconciled not only Jews and Gentiles (i.e., all humans) to God but also those two groups to each other and has brought "peace" both to the "vertical" God–human relationship and the "horizontal" Jew–Gentile relationship.

While Ephesians expounds the meaning of Christ's work of reconciliation for the "horizontal" relationship, Colossians does so by affirming its cosmic scope: God "reconcile[d] to himself all things, whether on earth or in heaven, by making peace by the blood of his cross" (1:20). This universalistic statement reaches well beyond the reference to "the world" in the sense of all humanity in 2 Corinthians 5:19. However, this reference to cosmic reconciliation envisions not a universal salvation ("all will be saved") but a restoration of universal peace in God's kingdom with all the powers in the cosmos brought to the proper relationship with (i.e., submission to) God their creator by the Lord Jesus, God's Son—a process that includes "destruction" of some "enemies" (1 Cor 15:23–28; cf. Rev 19:11—21:1).

Conclusion. On the Damascus road, Paul experienced God's saving grace in the form of reconciliation. This revelatory experience led him to interpret God's saving work in Christ in terms of the Greek concept "reconciliation." So was born Paul's unique doctrine of reconciliation. In the New Testament, the term "reconciliation" appears in only a few places in Paul's epistles, and it never appears in the Old Testament. However, because Paul uses reconciliation to interpret the meaning of the Old Testament institution of atonement and the early Christian confession of Christ's death as the eschatological atonement, reconciliation can be taken as an all-integrating category of his soteriology. This view is further supported by the following: (1) reconciliation refers to Christ's atonement itself as well as to its effect on humans and the world; (2) it not only is closely related to justification and new creation but can incorporate as well the other categories that also convey the sense of restoration to the proper relationship with God or making them God's people or children (sanctification and adoption); (3) it covers the horizontal relationships between social groups; and (4) it incorporates the cosmic dimension. So, along with "redemption,"

"reconciliation" can be seen as one of the most comprehensive categories of all biblical soteriology.

[*See also* Ecclesiology; Forgiveness; Justice, Justification, and Righteousness; Peace; Redemption; *and* Soteriology.]

BIBLIOGRAPHY

Bash, Anthony. *Ambassadors for Christ*. Tübingen, Germany: Mohr Siebeck, 1997.

Breytenbach, Cilliers, "Salvation of the Reconciled." In *Grace, Reconciliation, Concord: The Death of Christ in Graeco-Roman Metaphors*, pp. 171–186. Supplements to Novum Testamentum 135. Leiden, The Netherlands: Brill, 2010a.

Breytenbach, Cilliers. "Versöhnung, Stellvertretung und 'Sühne'." In *Grace, Reconciliation, Concord: The Death of Christ in Graeco-Roman Metaphors*, pp. 11–33. Supplements to Novum Testamentum 135. Leiden, The Netherlands: Brill, 2010b.

Constantineanu, Corneliu. *The Social Significance of Reconciliation in Paul's Theology: Narrative Readings in Romans*. London: T&T Clark, 2010.

Gunton, Colin E., ed. *The Theology of Reconciliation*. London: T&T Clark, 2003.

Hofius, Otfried. "Erwägungen zu Gestalt und Herkunft des paulinischen Versöhnungsgedankens." In *Paulusstudien*, pp. 1–14. Tübingen, Germany: Mohr Siebeck, 1989a.

Hofius, Otfried. "Sühne und Versöhnung." In *Paulusstudien*, pp. 33–49. Tübingen, Germany: Mohr Siebeck, 1989b.

Kim, Seyoon. "2 Cor. 5:11–21 and the Origin of Paul's Concept of 'Reconciliation.'" *Novum Testamentum* 39 (1997): 360–384.

Porter, Stanley E. "Paul's Concept of Reconciliation, Twice More." In *Paul and His Theology*, edited by Stanley E. Porter, pp. 131–152. Pauline Studies 3. Leiden, The Netherlands: Brill, 2006.

Seyoon Kim

REDEMPTION

"If the Church is right about him…the man we hanged was God Almighty. So that is the outline of the official story…this terrifying drama of which God is the victim and hero" (Sayers, 1993, p. 116). The drama of redemption is the lead story of the Bible.

Any account must do justice not only to the narrower meaning of the Hebrew (*pādâ, gāʾal, kāpar*) and Greek ([*ex*]*agorazein, hilas-komai/-tērion,* [*apo*]*lytrōsis, paradidōmi*) terms translated as "buy [back]/redeem," "atone/purify/place of atonement," "redemption/ransom," "deliver over to death" but also to the central, integrating significance of redemption for the whole of scripture. One must grasp the polyvalent images of God's efforts at "at-one-ment" with his alienated, hostile, degenerating world of "creation." But arguably more than any other metaphor—whether "salvation," "reconciliation," "Christus Victor," or "justification"—"redemption" divulges the necessity for God to be both "victim" and "hero," to create new life precisely through God's own death. "Redemption" most poignantly reveals the rationale for God's self-sacrifice and the character of God's unprecedented love for his creation. As both "axis" and "linchpin" for the larger biblical narrative, "redemption" coordinates the variety of ways the Bible speaks of God's restoring of the estranged, dysfunctional cosmos.

The Bible as the Story of Redemption. When the Christian Old Testament and New Testament were commingling in their earliest forms, Irenaeus (ca. 130–ca. 202 C.E.) was one of the first to articulate this overarching plot: "Because of [God's] measureless love, [God] became what we are in order to enable us to become what he is" (*Haer.* 5. Pref.). An inescapable truth of redemption is the requirement that God somehow start over, re-create the human being, restock the experiments of human societies from *within* the very "being" of the human creature. Only by accomplishing in advance what human beings themselves could not perform does God's "redemption" reset the "default position" for a fallen, hapless humanity.

If classic descriptions of "God" are allowed—that than which nothing greater can be conceived, a Creator all-powerful, knowing, just, loving—how could such a deity "pay" or suffer loss when such a God is under obligation to nothing or no one outside of God's own being? I will sketch three overlapping attempts to explain God's "fix" for the botched human experiment through God's entering creation more

immanently than before. Such explanations illuminate the inescapable conditions of the human predicament as well as the raison d'être of God's costly suffering to reclaim what God had intended for creation.

Redemption through re-creation. Although God fashioned human beings to embody his own image and likeness by his own word (Gen 1:26–27), they deliberately disobeyed God's intention for their life. Lost in ignorance, they began to return to the nonbeing from which God had created them. Like Irenaeus but with greater nuance, Athanasius (ca. 293–373 C.E.) weaves a meta-narrative of how God himself had to become intimately united with his own creation by being born of a human mother in such a way that God might re-create the human person from within. The God–human "takes back" the human creature by destroying human corruptibility and its consequences by the death of death, effected through Christ's own death and rising up through the power of the Spirit in accord with the will of the one Father (*Inc.* 29). Thus, a trinitarian formulation of God incarnate becomes necessary in order to conceptualize God's reconstitutive, life-giving Spirit in the "life-soul" of the redeemed human being.

Redemption through satisfaction of God's honor. In *Cur Deus Homo?* Anselm of Canterbury (1033–1109) argues that God had to become a human being to reclaim an objective honor disgraced by humanity's shameful violation of God's infinite majesty. No finite human could approximate returning that honor to an infinite God. Jesus had to encompass humanity, full and perfected, without guilt or guile, as well as the full stature of God. Only then could the innocent, totally undeserved death offered freely by such a human–God pay the immeasurable penalty and "redeem" the satisfaction of God's infinite honor on behalf of all sinful humankind. God "takes back" God's honor through infinite cost.

Redemption through the justice of God's reign. Instead of emphasizing a change of God's status (Anselm) or indwelling re-creation (Athanasius), twentieth-century theologies of liberation stress the realization of God's justice among a people who fulfill God's creation in human history. Similar to Abelard's (1079–1142) moral appeal from the powerful examples of God's love in the prophets and the Christ who provoke humans to live justly with God and neighbor, Jesus's solidarity with sinners and outcasts, culminating in crucifixion and resurrection, motivates others to follow the same path of suffering and vindication. Whether it is the obedience of God's people to serve the poor, the ethnically oppressed, or women and other disenfranchised groups, the death and resurrection of Jesus is less the redemptive event than an expression of Jesus's full obedience to God's justice, which unleashes a powerful "taking back" of an unjust world.

Redemption as New Life through Suffering and Death. The New Testament's earliest formulations of redemption claim bluntly that Christ or the Son of God died or "was delivered over" or "gave himself up" or "suffered" for the sins of humankind "according to the scriptures" (1 Cor 15:3; Rom 8:32, echoing Gen 22:16; 1 Pet 2:21, citing Isa 53:9; cf. Rom 4:25; 5:6, 8, 10; 14:9; 1 Cor 8:11; 2 Cor 5:14, 15; Gal 2:20; Eph 5:2, 25; 1 Thess 4:14; 5:10). These declarations make sense only within the larger biblical semantic field of "redemption."

Terms of redemption in the Hebrew Bible and Septuagint (OT). The Hebrew verb *pādâ*, which occurs in the Torah's legal stipulations, denotes "ransom by the payment of a price," similar to a commercial transaction, and refers to release from human obligation or restitution of forfeited animals. In principle, anyone can "buy back" what has been forfeited. (The Code of Hammurabi indicates such practice beyond Israel.) Objects of redemption are as diverse as humans from slavery (Exod 21:8), firstborn sons (13:13b, 15) or animals (13:13a), and those under the penalty of death (e.g., 21:29–30). When God is the subject, the shift from literal payment to figurative cost becomes evident through God's special covenantal commitment (Ps 111:9) or gratuitous rescue of the oppressed (Isa 29:22; Ps 25:22). God's gracious release of Israel from Egyptian slavery should motivate obedience to the justice of this God who, without obligation, "takes Israel back." Thus, the Hebrew Bible speaks of the release of Israel's slaves (Deut 15:15), atonement for murder (21:1–9), rectification of injustices against neighbor and resident aliens (24:10–22; cf. 2 Sam 7:23), and calls for servant Israel's repentance (Ps 78:42; Mic 6:4). God's unfettered choice to redeem in the past forms the template for deliverance in the future: from the Exile (Neh 1:4–10; Ps 107:2; Jer 31:11; Zech 10:8), from Assyria and its own idolatry (Hos 7:13; 13:14), and from violation of righteousness (Isa 1:27; 50:2; 51:11).

The Hebrew verb *gāʾal* is distinguished by its nearly exclusive application to family law: enacted through a member of the clan, normally the oldest male relative is the *gōʾēl*. Many of the circumstances of "taking back through financial sacrifice" (Heb. *pādâ*) apply to the *gōʾēl*: the redemption of a family member from slavery (Lev 25:47–49); property lost through poverty or extortion (25:25); a widow, without male heir, through levirate marriage (Gen 38; Deut 25:5–10; Ruth 3:9–4:6); family honor violated from outside the family (thus, the *gōʾēl haddām* who avenges family blood by slaying the murderer: Num 35:16–28; Judg 8:18–21; 2 Sam 14:10–11). Similarly, God "takes back" stolen land from orphans (Prov 23:10–11). As Israel's *gōʾēl* from Egyptian slavery (Ps 78:35; cf. Deut 24:18 [*pādâ*]), God champions the cause of the oppressed and poor, even the resident alien, by extending redemption of the "covenant family" beyond Israel (Deut 24:14–18; Ps 72:12–14).

Especially in Isaiah 40–66 "God" or "the LORD" is Israel's *gōʾēl* or "kinsman." The remarkable concentration on this redemptive functionary (13 occurrences) in such a short section of the Bible is telling. By electing this people and forming them into a covenant family, God is under special obligation to "redeem" them as "my own" (Isa 43:1; 44:24). God is Israel's father and mother (43:1; 44:24; 63:9, 16) and must discipline them as a parent (48:17), handing them over for punishment for their sin. Yet God is also Israel's "husband," who must "take her back" from the shame of widowhood so that the whole earth might honor the name of Israel's God (49:26; 54:4–5). For Israel there is no God comparable, who out of sheer love and joy "redeems" and "lifts up" the nation from its wretchedness, even as "rebellious children" (41:14; 44:6; 48:20; 52:3, 9; 54:7–8; 63:8–9). Like the *gōʾēl*'s decisive liberating from Egypt, God will again be their "redeemer" through a "new exodus," restoring Israel to its familial inheritance as a "new creation"(43:14; 44:22–24; 51:10; 60:16; 62:12). Through all these redemptive initiatives, God as *gōʾēl* engages Israel as witness both to itself and to the nations, particularly through a mysterious, anointed "servant": a figure that encompasses the whole nation, a smaller group within, and an individual whose rejection apparently is tied to the means of the redeeming *gōʾēl* (42:1–4; 44:24–26; 49:7). The result will be a powerful victory for justice with "the LORD" reclaiming God's honor when the whole world acclaims the "Redeemer of Israel" as Lord (*kyrios*) of all (45:20–26; 47:4; 59:20–21; 63:4).

The Hebrew noun *kōper* refers to a "sum of money" or "substitute" to ransom a forfeited life, whether human or animal. A *kōper* can serve as a substitute for punishment (Exod 30:12), loss of life (Job 33:24), or exile at the expense of Israel's enemies (Isa 43:3–4). Some offenses—willful murder (Num 35:31), adultery (Prov 6:35)—brook no such substitute. The Day of Atonement features a "place of atonement" (*kāppōret* = *hilastērion* [LXX]), sprinkled with the blood of a calf (for the priests) and from one of two goats (for the people of Israel and "the holy place") in order to "purify" or "atone for" (*kipper* = *exilaskomai* [LXX]) sin as expiation/propitiation for an entire year (Lev 16:1–34). The high priest then lays both hands upon the head of the other goat, places all of Israel's sins upon it, and sends it out into the wilderness as a "scapegoat" (Heb. *azazel*, 16:8). In the Roman period this scapegoat was slain, apparently by being pushed over a cliff (*1 En.* 10:4–5; Philo, *Plant.* 61; *m. Yoma* 6.6).

Terms of redemption in the New Testament. Adopting Old Testament and later Jewish metaphorical use of "purchase" (*agorazein*), Paul elevates God's redemption to unparalleled significance. He transforms the ordinary term for "buying" in the marketplace into God's "buying" Israel and the nations "back" through the Son of God's own death (Rom 7:14; 1 Cor 6:20; 7:23).

Humanity's intransigence to God's will (Rom 1–3) has led to their being "sold into slavery under sin" (7:14; cf. 1:24, 26, 28) out of which Christ's lifeblood and resurrected life has procured their release: "you were bought with a price" (1 Cor 6:20; 7:23a). Now, however, this freedom from slavery is God's taking back of humanity for a new bondage as God's own servants. This "purchased" deliverance places even a human "slave" into a higher, paradoxically freer status. A slave in this life need not despair since, together with free persons, such a one has been transferred to a new household to become a "slave of Christ" (7:21–24). Although there are faint echoes of sacral manumission in Greek papyri from Delphi and elsewhere, for Paul, God—not the owner of the slave—initiates the sale (cf. the *gōʾēl*). God is the buyer, not the seller; the Lord Jesus is the new "owner," not the patron deity who "sponsors" the transaction. Most notably, unlike Greek practice, there is no period of half-freedom (*paramonē*) in which the previous owner retains certain controlling rights: "Do not continue to be slaves of human masters!" (7:23b).

In Galatians 3:13 "Christ has redeemed us [*exagorazein*] from the curse of the law by becoming a curse for us [*hyper hymōn*]." By "hanging on the tree," Israel's anointed absorbs God's curse of those who do not obey the law (cf. Deut 21:23c). This substitutionary "for us" is thus a "buyout" or "ransom price" for the removal of the curse of death in exchange for "the blessing to Abraham" and "the promise of the Spirit" (Gal 3:14). That Paul has the ransom and scapegoat of the Day of Atonement in mind becomes more evident in Galatians 4:4–7, where he twice uses the form *ex-apostellō* (Greek "send out"), found only here instead of the verb *apostellō* ("send") or *pempō* ("send" or "appoint"), which he normally uses. These exceptional occurrences can be explained by the same formulation of the "sending out of something" that results in another's redemption (cf. the sin-laden scapegoat of Lev 16, "sent out" [*ex-apostellō*] into the wilderness to redeem Israel). By "sending out" his son, God "buys out" (*exagorazein*) those captive under the law to grant them a new family status (cf. Exod 15:16 [LXX]). This new inheritance is the "adoption" (*huiothesia*) by which God again "sends" his Son through his Spirit, who utters the new family cry of freedom, "Abba" ("Beloved Father"). The *gōʾēl*'s rescue of Israel as covenant family through an anointed servant (Isa 42; 44; 49) is now consummated in the cry of adoption with Christ, the "elder brother," whose death and resurrection re-create a new solidarity among all the families of the earth (Rom 8:17, 29b; Gal 3:28–29; Eph 1:5–7; 3:15; cf. the anticipatory Jewish adoption of a slave: "He will become my son" [Elephantine, Brooklyn-Papyrus No. 8]).

Paul combines two rather rare Greek words, *hilastērion* and *apolytrōsis* (Rom 3:24–26; 8:23), which are developed further in Hebrews (9:5, 15; cf. 1 Cor 1:30; Eph 1:7, 14; 4:30; Col 1:14; Heb 9:11–14; 11:35). Since all humanity must "shut their mouths" (Rom 3:19) before God's "justice" or "rightness," God intervenes by "putting forward" Christ Jesus as a place of atonement (*hilastērion* = Heb. *kāppōret*) "through his blood as a demonstration of God's righteousness" in order to show that God is himself right and makes right those who have "faith in Jesus" (3:25–26; cf. Isa 52:3). God is both victim and victor (cf. Rom 1:1–4: "the gospel of God…concerning his Son"). The relation between the servant of Isaiah 53:11cd, "the right one [who] carries sins," and God who declares him "to be right" by his self-sacrifice as a scapegoat is undoubtedly mirrored here (cf. 2 Cor 5:21). The result is the redemption (*apolytrōsis*) for all by the "sacrifice of atonement by his blood" (Rom 3:24; cf. Ps 48 [LXX 49]:8–9). The Day of Atonement is realized eschatologically and universally. Paul depicts "those living by [this] faithfulness," alongside the whole creation, as "groaning…toward adoption [*huiothesia*], the [completed] redemption [*apolytrōsis*] of our bodies" (Rom 8:23).

Hebrews extends the metaphors of "ransom price" and "propitiatory/expiatory sacrifice," with Jesus, both high priest and victim, entering the "heavenly Holy of Holies" (9:3–5: *hilastērion*): "He entered once for all…not with the blood of goats and calves, but with his own blood, thus obtaining eternal redemption [*lytrōsis*].…For this reason he is the mediator of a new covenant…because a death has occurred that redeems [*apolytrōsis*] them from the transgressions under the first covenant" (9:11–15). Already in 4 Maccabees 17:21–22 (first century B.C.E.) the blood of the Maccabean martyrs had been deemed "ransom" (*antipsychon*) and "propitiatory atonement" (*hilastērion*), saving Israel from their enemies (cf. 1 John 2:2; 4:10 [*hilasmos*]; Heb 2:17 [*hilaskomai*]).

In Romans 8:32 Paul's seemingly gratuitous reference to God "not sparing" [*pheidomai*] "his own Son but gave him up for all of us" undoubtedly invokes God's "sparing" [*pheidomai*] of Isaac (Gen 22:16, LXX) while specifying Christ Jesus as the greater "sin offering for all." God's "giving up" or "handing over" (*paradidōmi*) Christ (Rom 8:32) likely refers to the "servant" of Isaiah 53:6 (cf. 52:13, "my son" [*pais*, LXX])

whose "sin offering for the many" shows God to be "right" (*dikaios*) in Romans 8:33 (cf. Isa 53:10–11b). Contrary to Torah's prohibition of the sacrifice of the firstborn (Lev 18:21), the death of God's "own" effects redemption, with his Son thereby becoming the "firstborn among many brothers and sisters" (Rom 8:23, 29b–32; cf. Isa 53:12). The reason for God's doing this is based squarely upon "the love of God" (Rom 8:35, 39). Paul's radical notion of God's life as "forfeit" for "the many" may have influenced both Petrine and Johannine tradition (1 Pet 2:21, 24; 3:18; 2 Pet 2:1; Rev 5:9).

All four Gospels portray Jesus as a slave or servant voluntarily giving his life to be "delivered over" (*paradidotai*) to death (Mark 10:33//Matt 20:18//Luke 18:32; John 18:30; cf. Isa 53:12). For Mark (10:45) and Matthew (20:8) Jesus is a "ransom" (*lytron*) "for the many." Luke presents Jesus in the temple as God's firstborn Son, redeemed in accordance with the firstborn spared at Passover (2:7, 22–24; cf. Exod 13:15), and, later in that Gospel, on an "exodus" journey of redemption (*lytrōsis/lytroomai*), to be enthroned upon the cross for the forgiveness or release of Israel and the nations (23:42–45; 1:68; 2:38; 9:31, 51; 24:21; cf. Acts 7:35; 20:28). In the Fourth Gospel the Baptist introduces Jesus as the "lamb [*amnos*] of God who carries away [*airō*] the sin of the world" (John 1:29; cf. Isa 53:7); Jesus declares his mission to be "finished" as "blood and water" flow from his side, apparently just when the Passover lambs are being slaughtered (John 19:30–34).

A Credo of Redemption. In one of his final communications Paul renders a "hymn of Christ" (Phil 2:6–11) to a status-saturated, Roman-dominated church at Philippi. While explicit terms of "purchase" are missing, Paul recites his Gospel's upside-down story of redemption, which this status-inverted ode epitomizes: the "form of God," revealed as Christ Jesus, "deprives" God (*heauton ekenōsen*, v. 7a) of any recognition of his status as God. Here alone in scripture is God so utterly degraded. In the divine form "perceived to be as a human being" (v. 7d), God submits to the lowest conceivable status: the slave's death of crucifixion (v. 8). God humiliates himself to the most disgraceful status imaginable and is actually shamed to death. But as a logical and ontological consequence of God's self-sacrifice, God exalts the hanging Christ Jesus to the highest honor of all, crowned with the name that only God can claim, Lord (*kyrios*) of all (vv. 9–11). Now the lowest form of subhuman life has disclosed the most sublime power of the character of God. In this terrifying drama the God who graces creation with his self-giving death as victim—empowering humankind to be "reformed" from "the body of humiliation" to the "honor-shaped body of Christ" (3:10–11, 21)—is indeed God the hero.

[*See also* Atonement; Christology; Creation; Cult and Worship; Eschatology; Exile and Dislocation; Expiation; Festivals and Holy Days; Freedom and Slavery; Honor and Shame; Inheritance (Heir); Isaiah; Justice, Justification, and Righteousness; Lamb of God; Lord; Pauline Letters; Priests and Priesthood; Reconciliation; Sacrifice and Offerings; Servant of God; *and* Sin.]

BIBLIOGRAPHY

Boff, Leonardo. *Jesus Christ Liberator: A Critical Christology for Our Time.* Maryknoll, N.Y.: Orbis, 1978.

Collitz, Hermann, Friedrich Bechtel, and Johannes Fürchtegott Baunack. *Sammlung der griechischen Dialekt-Inschriften.* Göttingen, Germany: Vandenhoeck & Ruprecht, 1905.

Cone, James H. *Black Theology and Black Power.* Maryknoll, N.Y.: Orbis, 1969.

Falk, Daniel K. "Festivals and Holy Days." In *The Eerdmans Dictionary of Early Judaism*, edited by John J. Collins and Daniel C. Harlow, pp. 636–645. Grand Rapids, Mich.: Eerdmans, 2010.

Kraeling, E. G. H. *The Brooklyn Museum Aramaic Papyri: New Documents of the Fifth Century B.C. from the Jewish Colony at Elephantine.* New Haven, Conn.: Yale University Press, 1953.

Moessner, David P. "Turning Status 'Upside Down' in Philippi: Christ Jesus' 'Emptying Himself' as Forfeiting Any Acknowledgment of His 'Equality with God' (Phil. 2:6–11)." *Horizons in Biblical Theology* 31 (2009): 123–143.

Pax, P. E. "Der Loskauf: Zur Geschichte eines neutestamentlichen Begriffes." *Antonianum* 37 (1962): 239–278.

Sayers, Dorothy. "The Greatest Drama Ever Staged." In *Spiritual Writings*, selected and introduced by Ann Loades, pp. 115–118. Cambridge, Mass.: Cowley, 1993.

Schüssler-Fiorenza, Elisabeth. *In Memory of Her: A Feminist Theological Reconstruction of Christian Origins.* New York: Crossroad, 1983.

Tolmie, D. François. "Salvation as Redemption: The Use of 'Redemption' Metaphors in Pauline Literature." In *Salvation in the New Testament: Perspectives on Soteriology*, edited by Jan van der Watt, pp. 247–269. Supplements to Novum Testamentum 121. Leiden, The Netherlands: Brill, 2005.

Yamayoshi, Tomohisa. *Von der Auslösung zur Erlösung: Studien zur Wurzel PDY im Alten Orient und im Alten Testament.* Wissenschaftliche Monographien zum Alten und Neuen Testament 134. Neukirchen-Vluyn, Germany: Neukirchener, 2013.

Young, Frances. "Redemption—The Starting-point of Christian Theology, I." *Expository Times* 88 (1976–1977): 360–364.

David P. Moessner

REMNANT

A recurring theme in the Old Testament concerns a small group of people, a remnant (Heb. *šĕʾêrît, šĕʾār, pĕlêṭâ*), who survive God's angry response to exterminate an entire population. According to some Old Testament traditions, the level of human corruption, referring to a particular nation or all of humankind, grows to such enormous proportion that eradication appears to be God's only choice. The remnant, the righteous few, is understood as the "seed" for re-creating the former community. This annihilation is reported as something that happened in the past, is imminent in the present, or will take place in the future. The massacre can affect the world at large or the nations surrounding Israel. Most frequently, however, God's anger is unleashed against his own people so that only a remnant will escape the devastating consequences. God's judgment reducing the people of Israel to a remnant can be read against the background of the covenant (treaty) he made with them at the time of Moses (Exod 6:2–13). Obedience to the stipulations of the covenant ensures blessings and prosperity; disobedience leads to a shattering outcome (Deut 28:1–45). The theme of the remnant is most prevalent in the Latter Prophets, particularly Isaiah. The remnant community represents the flipside of God's intention to tear down and destroy. God's mercy is directed to a few survivors, whom he will use to reconstitute the community, linking it to the past. The motif of remnant also occurs in later Jewish literature. However, in the New Testament remnant (Gk *leimma*) occurs only twice. For some contemporary Christian groups, such as the Seventh-day Adventist Church, identification with the remnant has been central to their own religious self-understanding.

Genesis. God's twofold action of near total annihilation and preservation of a remnant occurs for the first time after the creation of the earth and its inhabitants. God despairs of humankind because of its wickedness on the earth (Gen 6:5) but recognizes that "Noah was a righteous man, blameless in his generation" (Gen 6:9). Therefore, "He blotted out every living thing that was on the face of the ground, human beings and animals and creeping things and birds of the air.... Only Noah was left, and those that were with him in the ark" (Gen 7:23; see Sir 44:17). This remnant that survives in the ark receives God's blessing, and God commands Noah and those with him to be "fruitful and multiply" and to "fill the earth" (Gen 9:1).

The theme of the remnant also occurs in the Genesis story of the creation of Israel. Near the end of Genesis a famine in the land threatens the family of Jacob/Israel, who travel to Egypt for food. They meet Joseph, whom his brothers had sold into slavery and who has risen to be lord of Pharaoh's house. Joseph then explains that all this had happened at God's direction: "God sent me before you to preserve for you a remnant on earth, and to keep alive for you many survivors" (Gen 45:7; see Amos 5:15 and Sir 47:22).

Isaiah. Annihilation and survival are expressed in a variety of ways. The name of Isaiah's son, Shear-Yashub ("a remnant will return"), who accompanies Isaiah in his meeting with King Ahaz (Isa 7:3), encapsulates the disconcerting double meaning of remnant as the extermination of the many and the survival of the few. The book describes the way Yahweh will use Assyria, the rod of his anger (Isa 10:5), to devastate Judah (Isa 7:18–25). Although the people of Israel "were like the sand of the sea, only a remnant... will return" (Isa 10:22). Yahweh will provide a highway from Assyria and the surrounding nations "to recover the remnant that is left of his people" (Isa 11:11). This remnant of survivors will be different from those who were destroyed. They will rely on "the Holy One of Israel" (Isa 10:20) and return to "the mighty God" (Isa 10:21). When King Hezekiah beseeches Isaiah to offer a "prayer for the remnant that is left" (Isa 37:4; see 2 Kgs 19:4), Yahweh's response is that "the surviving remnant of the house of Judah shall again take root downward, and bear fruit upward for from Jerusalem a remnant shall go out, and from Mount Zion a band of survivors" (Isa 37:31–32; see 2 Kgs 19:30–31).

While the first part of Isaiah concerns the remnant surviving Assyrian invasion, the second part of the book focuses on "the remnant of the house of Israel," who are now in Babylonian exile. Yahweh addresses them in the second person as those "who have been borne by me from your birth, carried from the womb; even to your old age I am he, even when you turn gray I will carry you. I have made, and I will bear; I will carry and will save" (Isa 46:3–4). These verses echo God's earlier promise to the survivors in Egypt (Gen 45:7) to preserve Jacob/Israel as a remnant on earth.

Micah and Zephaniah. The remnant motif in Micah and Zephaniah emphasizes the weak, the lowly, and the humble. The remnant will gain strength and be purged of the transgressions of those who originally turned Yahweh's anger against them. In Micah the remnant is depicted as those who are lame and cast off (4:7) but will become strong like the lion in the forest (5:5–8). The restored remnant is described as an ideal community that will do no wrong and utter no lies (Zeph 3:13).

Jeremiah. In some passages Jeremiah speaks positively about the remnant that will return to the homeland and be fruitful and multiply (23:3; 31:7). However, his angry words are frequently directed to the present community to which Jeremiah himself belongs, the remnant in Jerusalem who survived Babylonian invasion. Yahweh will direct Babylon to cut down the existing remnant in Judah, as the grape-gatherer prunes the branches (6:9). "Death shall be preferred to life by all the remnant that remains" (8:3). Those who remain in Jerusalem are like bad figs that cannot be eaten (24:8). After Gedaliah is installed as governor by the Babylonians, Jeremiah's message changes. The remnant that now attempts to save itself by fleeing to Egypt (42:15, 17) will perish by famine and sword (44:7, 12) "so that none of the remnant of Judah who have come to settle in the land of Egypt shall escape or survive or return to the land of Judah" (44:14).

Haggai, Zechariah, and Ezra. Both Haggai and Zechariah are concerned with rebuilding the Temple at the time of restoration after the Babylonian Exile. Haggai exhorts Zerubbabel, the governor of Judah; the high priest Joshua; and the remnant of the people to begin work on building the house of Yahweh (Hag 1:12, 14; 2:2). This remnant has returned at the beginning of the rebuilding of the past community. Zechariah picks up Haggai's proclamation that the remnant will be blessed with prosperity and peace. According to Zechariah, Yahweh will now deal with the remnant as he dealt with his people in the former days (Zech 8:6, 11). By that he means, "there shall be a sowing of peace; the vine shall yield its fruit, the ground shall give its produce, and the skies shall give their dew; and I will cause the remnant of this people to possess all these things" (8:12). In a less optimistic fashion, Ezra speaks of the respite that God has given to the returned remnant in Jerusalem.

This survey of remnant in the Old Testament is based on the appearance of the word "remnant" in the texts. In these texts "remnant" refers to a specific group of survivors in an identifiable period of time. God's twofold actions of judgment and mercy are understood on a historical level.

Remnant in the Pseudepigrapha, the Qumran Literature, and the New Testament. The remnant motif is also found in later Jewish literature and the New Testament. A new dimension emerged in scholarship when scholars identified in this literature what is often referred to as "remnant theology." In their assessment of the literature, remnant has taken on an eschatological dimension; the remnant is the righteous community whom God will restore at the end of time. In addition, scholars argue that each of the different Jewish groups (Essenes, Pharisees, and emergent Christianity) understood themselves as the righteous remnant, the restored Israel.

Some scholars have argued that this remnant theology was central to the thought of Jesus and the New Testament writers (for an overview see Watts, 1988). Interpreting the church as remnant served the pur-pose of demonstrating how early Christianity came to understand itself as a continuation of ancient Israel and its traditions. However, the notion of a prevailing remnant in early sectarian Judaism as a key for understanding New Testament theology has been seriously challenged. Scholars have shown that the Pseudepigrapha and Qumran literature evince no notion that a Jewish sectarian group understood itself as the "eschatological remnant," the "true Israel." Others have argued that the same is true for the Rabbinic literature. If early Christianity saw itself as the eschatological remnant, this would have been unique among the sectarian groups of that time.

Furthermore, the language associated with remnant is lacking in the New Testament. Remnant occurs only two times in the New Testament (Rom 9:11; 11:5) in a section of Paul's letter to the Romans concerning the status of Jews in the present community. He quotes a passage from Isaiah saying that, although the people of Israel were like the sand of the sea, a remnant will return (Rom 9:11; Isa 10:22), and he argues that God's mercy has always preserved a remnant of his people. Similarly, in the present situation God's mercy has preserved a righteous remnant of Israelites like Paul himself (Rom 11:5).

The Remnant and Theology. In modern theology, the concept of remnant has played only a peripheral role. When it appears, it tends to be loosely associated with the biblical texts surveyed above. The remnant is central, however, to Seventh-day Adventism. The crucial verse is Revelation 12:17, which in the King James Bible reads, "And the dragon was wroth with the woman, and went to make war with the remnant of her seed [NRSV "rest of her children"], which keep the commandments of God, and have the testimony of Jesus Christ." The Adventists see themselves as this remnant that has been called in the last days to keep the commandments of God and the faith of Jesus. While this text appears to have little or no affiliation with the remnant motif in the Old Testament, Adventist scholars such as Gerhard Hasel (1972) have written definitive studies on remnant in the Old Testament.

Karl Rahner, a Roman Catholic theologian, appealed to the Old Testament notion of remnant as the basis for his argument that the universal church could be present in the local parish. The Anglican practical theologian Martin Thornton appealed to the notion of remnant in Isaiah and the other prophets to bolster his notion that in present-day parishes the remnant is that small group of parishioners who are supremely devoted and play a significant role with their intense spirituality for the church as a whole. While both theologians base their ideas on the Old Testament texts, neither of these views of the remnant fits the view of Old Testament remnant outlined above, particularly the notion that the remnant is what remains after God's near extermination of a community.

Assessment. To trace a motif such as remnant from the Old Testament through to Jewish thought at the time of emergent Christianity is fraught with difficulties, particularly when the motif is constructed by scholars where the language for remnant is not used. Tracing a continuous line of development can unwittingly become the construction of thought that serves the purpose of the interpreter.

The idea of the "remnant" and the concomitant destruction raises serious issues. Often, the grace afforded the remnant is emphasized and the annihilation of men, women, children, babies, and even flocks in the field is glossed over. The morality of our own times normally requires that brutality, even toward "enemies," be condemned. Some have seen the ruthlessness of such monstrous acts of destruction by God as reflecting the ancient world of warfare when such brutality was "the way the game was played" in the ancient Near East. Building kingdoms meant wiping out entire populations. That very explanation ought to be, one would think, the reason for denouncing such annihilation, regardless of the survival of a "remnant." There are those even in contemporary times, however, who celebrate this kind of violence and revel in it. The Left Behind novels of Tim LaHaye and Jerry Jenkins, which have sold millions of copies, celebrate the violence leading up to the restoration of the remnant of the Jews to the Promised Land with the associated desolation associated with the horrific wiping out of everyone who is not part of the remnant.

[*See also* Apocalypticism; Book of the Twelve (Minor Prophets); Isaiah; Judaism; Paul; *and* Tradition.]

BIBLIOGRAPHY

Clements, Ronald E. "'A Remnant Chosen by Grace' (Romans 11:5): The Old Testament Origin of the Remnant Concept." In *Pauline Studies: Essays Presented to Professor F. F. Bruce on His 70th Birthday*, edited by Donald A. Hagner and Murray J. Harris, pp. 106–121. Grand Rapids, Mich.: Eerdmans, 1980.

Hasel, Gerhard Franz. *The Remnant: The History and Theology of the Remnant Idea from Genesis to Isaiah*. Berrien Springs, Mich.: Andrews University Press, 1972.

Huebsch, Robert William. "The Understanding and Significance of the 'Remnant' in Qumran Literature: Including a Discussion of the Use of this Concept in the Hebrew Bible, the Apocrypha and the Pseudepigrapha." Ph.D. diss., McMaster University, 1981.

Meyer, Ben F. "Jesus and the Remnant of Israel." *Journal of Biblical Literature* 84 (1965): 123–130.

Watts, James W. "The Remnant Theme: A Survey of New Testament Research, 1921–1987." *Perspectives in Religious Studies* 15 (1988): 109–129.

Edgar W. Conrad

REPENTANCE

Repentance in the Bible and in Jewish and Christian theological traditions refers to the determination to change the direction of one's life by turning away from spiritual rebellion or moral wrongdoing and turning toward God in renewed obedience and deeper devotion. It has an internal or subjective dimension (regret for past wrongs and a commitment to future change) and an external or behavioral dimension (a new pattern of conduct befitting the restored relationship with God). A demand for repentance may be addressed to individuals or to the faith community as a whole, and a positive response to it is often marked by ritual or symbolic practices of various kinds. Theologically, repentance is equally grounded in the justice of God, which holds wrongdoers accountable for their choices, and the grace of God, which delights to show mercy and restore the penitent to right standing (Exod 34:5–7; Rom 2:2–5).

There is a rich vocabulary in the Bible for repentance and its components, and the concept of repentance may be present in texts even when the terminology is not used. Two key terms for repentance in the Old Testament are *nāḥam*, "to be sorry for something" or "relent from something," which accents the affective dimension of regret, sorrow, or pity (e.g., Gen 6:6; Exod 32:14; Jer 8:6; Job 42:6), and *šûb*, "to turn" or "return," which captures the effective dimension of a redirected life (e.g., 1 Kgs 8:33, 35; Ezek 3:19; Hos 6:1). In the Septuagint, *nāḥam* was almost exclusively translated by the Greek verb *metanoeō*, "change one's mind," while *šûb* was almost invariably translated with *epistrephō* or *apostrephō*, to "turn, turn back." By the beginning of the Christian era, *metanoeō* ("repent") and *metanoia* ("repentance") had come to denote a fundamental change of mindset leading to a corresponding change of lifestyle. The metaphorical use of *epistrephō* had much the same force (cf. Acts 3:19; 28:27).

Repentance in the Old Testament. As a covenantal concept, repentance in the Bible is a thoroughly relational category. Through the Sinai covenant, God has taken Israel as his treasured possession (Exod 19:5), setting his heart on her in unmerited love (Deut 7:7; 10:15) and demanding her wholehearted love in reply (Deut 10:12). When the covenant people transgressed the terms of the covenant specified in the law, they broke faith with God and stood in need of reconciliation and restoration to righteous standing. Repentance was the means of achieving this relational repair (Jer 3:22; Hos 14:4).

Repentance played an important role in the regular rhythms of cultic worship (Lev 5:5; Num 5:7; 15:27), especially on the Day of Atonement (Lev 16:21). True repentance required inward contrition of heart and outward confession of wrongdoing and was often accompanied by tangible expressions of regret, such as the bringing of gifts and offerings, times of fasting, weeping and mourning, the tearing of garments, and the wearing of sackcloth and ashes (e.g., Hos 14:2; Joel 2:12–13). Where the wrongdoing had caused injury to others in the community, repentance required restitution to the victim as well as sacrificial atonement (Num 5:6–7; Lev 6:1–7; cf. Matt 5:23–24). The Prophets were insistent that all cultic expressions of repentance and atonement were ineffectual without such corresponding deeds of justice and righteous-

ness, which alone were proof of inward change (Mic 6:6–8; Hos 6:6; Jer 6:20; 7:21–26; 14:12; Isa 1:1–17; Pss 40:6; 50:1; 51:16–18). The so-called *Miserere* of Psalm 51 has long been seen as the classic expression of the penitent heart ("miserere" is the initial word of Vulgate translation, *Miserere mei Deus*, "Have mercy on me O God").

For the nation as a whole, repentance is predominantly pictured as a "turning away" from idolatry and wickedness and "turning back" to God in renewed loyalty and obedience (e.g., Josh 22:16; 23:12; 1 Kgs 9:6–7; Jer 3:7; 15:7; Hos 6:1; 7:10; Amos 4:6). Failure to repent brings divine judgment, including exile from the land (e.g., Deut 28:1—30:5), but there is no strict theory of retribution at work. While repentance may sometimes avert or postpone divine punishment (2 Sam 12:13; 1 Kgs 21:28–29; Joel 2:13), at other times it does not. So virulent is the nature of sin and so deep-seated is Israel's corporate solidarity in its grip that even repentance may not be enough to staunch sin's destructive aftereffects, which ripple out through the social fabric of the community and down through the generations (Exod 34:7; Lev 26:39–40; Num 14:18; Jer 11:14).

For this reason, Israel's ultimate hope for salvation rests not on her capacity for repentance, as much as it was required, but on the promises and character of God who, despite all, remains steadfastly faithful to the covenant relationship and has a predilection for mercy (Deut 4:31; Isa 43:25; cf. Rom 3:1–8). Since the need for repentance exists only because of the stubbornness and hardness of the human heart (Hos 10:2; 13:6; Jer 5:23; 17:9; 49:16; Obad 1:3), the remedy must ultimately lie in God's gift of a new heart and a new spirit, within the context of a new or renewed covenant relationship (Deut 30:6; Ps 51:10; Ezek 11:19–20; 36:24–28; 37:14; Jer 31:31–34).

Repentance in the New Testament. The predominant meaning of repentance (*teshuvah*) in early Judaism was one of turning from sin and returning to God, manifest chiefly in renewed obedience to the law. Though it is a human action, ultimately it is God who gives repentance (Wis 12:19; *Sib. Or.* 4:168; *b. Sanh.* 107b) or at least the opportunity to repent (Wis 11:23; 12:10;

Sir 48:14–15; *Let. Arist.* 188), just as it is God who grants forgiveness and salvation to those who are repentant.

The demand for repentance was a dominant theme in the preaching of John the Baptist (Mark 1:4–9; Matt 3:7–12; Luke 3:1–11); over half of the references to repentance in the Gospels are associated with John's ministry. Believing eschatological judgment to be imminent, John summoned his hearers to a decisive act of repentance, accompanied by verbal confession of sins and baptism in water, leading to the forgiveness of sins. Crucially for John, repentance had to manifest itself ethically in bearing "fruit worthy of repentance," that is, in righteous behavior with respect to one's relationship to others (Matt 3:7–8; Luke 3:7–14). John's demand for repentance was universal in scope. It applied equally to blatant sinners, to the crowds, and to the religious elites. To resist the call was to invite divine reprisal (Matt 3:7, 10–12; Luke 3:7, 9, 16–17).

According to the Gospels, Jesus accepted the heavenly origins of John's baptism (Mark 11:29–32) and, apparently much to John's own surprise (Matt 3:14), submitted himself to baptism in preparation for his own public proclamation of repentance and faith (Mark 1:9). Like John, Jesus directed his call to the whole nation and understood repentance to entail both a decisive commitment to God's eschatological purposes and a new pattern of righteous living befitting God's rule.

But Jesus's call was distinctive in that it was predicated not on the impending wrath of God but on the already present reality of God's saving power. "The time is fulfilled; the Kingdom of God has drawn near. Repent and believe in the good news" (Mark 1:15 NRSV). The primary motivation for repentance was not fear of future judgment, even if disaster would ensue for those who refused to listen (Matt 11:20–24; 12:39–42; Luke 13:1–5). Rather, it was the good news that a new phase in salvation history had arrived, requiring a positive decision to embrace the reign of God and its revolutionary implications. The enactment of this repentance was through "following" Jesus and "believing" in him as the one who mediates participation in God's Kingdom and its blessings and who defines its moral and social requirements.

Several of Jesus's parables portray the dynamics of individual repentance. The parable of the two sons (Matt 21:28–32) illustrates the change of mind required. The parable of the tax collector and the Pharisee (Luke 18:9–14) dramatizes the humility and truthfulness involved. But it is the parable of the prodigal son (Luke 15:11–32) that most profoundly illuminates what is entailed. In his derelict state, the sinful boy finally chooses to return to the one he has injured—"I will get up and go to my father" (v. 18)—a response that underscores the relational as well as the volitional character of repentance. The boy's penitence is expressed in a verbal confession of wrongdoing: "Father I have sinned against heaven and before you; I am no longer worthy to be called your son; treat me like one of your hired hands" (vv. 18–19, 21). This confession captures three crucial elements of repentance—an acceptance of moral guilt, the recognition that others have been injured by the misconduct, and an acknowledgment that foundational relationships have been damaged and need to be repaired. The prodigal's proposal that he should henceforth serve as a hired worker further implies a commitment to an ongoing correction of life and possibly to restitution to his victim.

For Jesus, then, the call to repentance was occasioned by the in-breaking of God's eschatological Kingdom in his own person and mission. For the early church, the call to repentance was grounded in God's saving initiative in the life, death, and resurrection of Christ, which required a response of repentance from Israel (Acts 5:31; 13:24) and from "all people everywhere" (Acts 17:30; cf. 11:18; 26:20; 1 Thess 1:9–10). The language of repentance peppers the book of Acts, the Epistles, and the Apocalypse. It is used in two main connections. The first is for an initial, positive response to the gospel, entailing confession of sins, baptism in water, and commitment to the community of faith. Initial repentance could be termed "conversion" because it involved a fundamental reorientation of the person's entire existence in response to God's patience and kindness (Acts 17:30; Rom 2:4–5; 2 Pet 3:9). The second use of the terminology is for subsequent desistance from sin and recommitment to the community's norms of holiness (2 Cor 7:9–10; 12:21; Gal 6:1–2; 1 John 1:8–9; cf. Luke 17:3–4), which may be called "penitence."

Conversion and penitence have similar features, but the early church apparently saw something qualitatively distinctive about initial repentance. This is evident, for example, in the ambivalence in the New Testament over the standing of believers who had renounced their initial conversion, then subsequently relented and sought readmission to the community. Some in the church thought a second repentance, like a second virginity, was impossible in principle (Heb 6:1–6; cf. 3:12), even if the defector was penitent (Heb 12:17), whereas others considered a return to the fold to be feasible (Jas 5:19–20), even if difficult and unlikely (2 Pet 2:20–22).

Repentance in the Later Church. This same ambivalence is apparent in the postapostolic church as well, where several trajectories of understanding about repentance and penitence emerged. It was generally accepted that the initial commitment of baptism was an unrepeatable, irreversible act involving dedication to a blameless way of life. Some, like the later Tertullian, considered serious sins like apostasy, murder, and fornication to be irremediable (*Pud.* 9.20); others, like the Shepherd of Hermas, allowed for a "second repentance" for even serious sins but not for a third or fourth repentance (*Herm. Mand.* 4.3.3–6).

At the same time, it was obvious that baptismal purification did not confer instant perfection; and gradually, in both the East and the West, specific rituals of penance began to emerge. Penitential theology in the West was shaped by the teachings of Tertullian, Cyprian, Ambrose, and Augustine, which drew heavily on legal metaphors and categories. Penance was predominantly perceived as a way of appeasing the divine judge whose justice requires that all transgressions be punished (e.g., Tertullian, *Paen.* 6.4; 9.5). Penitential practices served as a form of, or substitute for, deserved punishment.

In the East, penance was also understood in more therapeutic terms, as a kind of medicine for the soul prescribed by the divine physician (e.g., Clement, *Strom* 2.27.1; 4.143.1; *Paed.* 1.64.4). Thus, they saw it as a life-

long process of healing and purification. Penitential thinking was most radically embraced by early Christian ascetics such as the desert fathers, who practiced extreme self-renunciation or "mortification" in the quest of *apatheia*, that simplicity of life in which love of God and neighbor are perfectly joined and untrammeled by physical needs and pleasures.

Initially in the ancient church penance was predominantly a public and communal affair, but from the seventh century onward the practice of private confession became more frequent. In 1215, the Fourth Lateran Council decreed that all Christians had to confess their sins to a priest at least once a year and perform the penance imposed on them. They also had to receive the Eucharist at least annually, leading to the widespread practice of the laity attending confession and doing penance during the season of Lent. The council did not prescribe any definitive theology of sacramental penance, but its practice came to include four distinct components: contrition, confession, satisfaction (or acts of penance), and absolution. Behind the sacrament lay an emphasis on God's retributive justice that requires punishment for sins, in this life and the next, and on God's gracious mercy that permits and empowers the penitent to avoid or reduce temporal punishment for postbaptismal sins through penitential works of satisfaction.

The Protestant Reformers objected strongly to this notion of cooperative grace and roundly rejected the sacrament of penance, not least for the abuses that surrounded the accompanying practice of purchasing indulgences. However, they continued to see value in the personal confession of sin to pastors or elders and in ritual or liturgical affirmations of penitence and forgiveness. Such penitence was not to be seen as a way of satisfying God's punitive justice but as a means of living out in daily life the sanctifying grace of God encountered in baptism (e.g., Luther, *Larger Catechism* 4:75; Calvin, *Institutes* 3.3).

All theological traditions have wrestled in different ways with the Bible's paradoxical affirmation that repentance is both a demand and a gift. It is a demand in that it is a free human response, obligated by the tension that exists between God's justice and holiness, on the one hand, and human perversity and pride, on the other. "You shall be holy for I am holy" (1 Pet 1:15). It is a gift in that it is evoked and enabled by God's prior grace. "The Kingdom of God has drawn near, repent and believe in the good news" (Mark 1:15). From the human side, repentance begins with a decisive act of turning away from sin and turning toward God and is followed by an obedient lifestyle in which the restored relationship to God is reaffirmed in acts of justice and goodness toward others. Both initial and ongoing expressions of repentance may be accompanied by tangible symbolic or ritual actions that manifest the volitional commitment involved and that declare the truth of human sinfulness and the merciful character of God's restorative justice.

[*See also* Apostasy; Atonement; Baptism; Discipleship; Ethics, Biblical; Forgiveness; Guilt and Innocence; *and* Soteriology.]

BIBLIOGRAPHY

Behm, J., and E. Wurthwein. "*metanoeō, metanoia.*" In *Theological Dictionary of the New Testament*, edited by Gerhard Kittel and Gerhard Friedrich, Vol. 4, pp. 975–1008. Grand Rapids, Mich.: Eerdmans, 1967.

Boda, Mark J., and Gordon T. Smith, eds. *Repentance in Christian Theology*. Collegeville, Minn.: Liturgical Press, 2006.

deSilva, D. A. "Repentance, Second Repentance." In *Dictionary of the Later New Testament and Its Developments*, edited by Ralph Martin and Peter H. Davids, pp. 1011–1015. Downers Grove, Ill.: InterVarsity, 1997.

Etzioni, Amaitai, and David E. Carney, eds. *Repentance: A Comparative Perspective*. Lanham, Md.: Rowman and Littlefield, 1997.

Lunde, J. "Repentance." In *Dictionary of Jesus and the Gospels*, edited by Joel B. Green and Scot McKnight, pp. 669–673. Downers Grove, Ill.: InterVarsity, 1992.

Marshall, Christopher D. *Faith as a Theme in Mark's Narrative*. Cambridge, U.K.: Cambridge University Press, 1989.

Marshall, Christopher D. *Compassionate Justice: An Interdisciplinary Dialogue with Two Gospel Parables on Law, Crime and Restorative Justice*. Eugene, Ore.: Cascade, 2012.

Merklein, H. "*Metanoia.*" In *Exegetical Dictionary of the New Testament*, edited by Horst Balz and Gerhard Schneider, Vol. 2, pp. 415–419. Grand Rapids, Mich.: Eerdmans, 1991.

Newman, Louis E. *Repentance: The Meaning and Practice of Teshuvah*. Woodstock, Vt.: Jewish Lights, 2010.

Sanders, E. P. *Jesus and Judaism*. London: SCM, 1985.

Christopher D. Marshall

RESURRECTION

A statement that death can be or has been overcome entails claims about not only the nature of death but also the nature of human life and existence and, ultimately, the nature of God's power. Given the character of those claims, anyone who reports an incidence of resurrection or interprets the belief must resort to metaphorical, symbolic, and analogical language because the phenomenon is beyond usual human experience. Further, the metaphysical nature of the claim and its analogical language inspire multiple, often conflicting interpretations, even among biblical authors. In effect, exposition of the belief belies exhaustion by any set of propositions.

Resurrection can be grouped with conceptions of postmortem existence, including immortality of the soul or spirit, reanimation of the body, transformation of the "self" into another form of existence, and some forms of reincarnation. However, in the contexts of ancient Judaism and early Christianity, resurrection refers more specifically to the particular belief that God can, has, and will raise human beings from the dead, transforming them into another form of existence. This belief, accordingly, affirms that God is creative, powerful, and trustworthy, a being justly committed to the ongoing relationship between itself and its creation. Simultaneously it is an expression of the goodness of that creation and a belief that no power, however inimical, can prevent its ultimate redemption and consummation.

In the Hebrew Bible these resurrection conceptions affirm God's covenant faithfulness and promises of Israel's restoration as a nation and people. In the New Testament these beliefs in God's covenant fidelity are extended to include all peoples. At the same time they are narrowed to a focus on God's resurrection of Jesus of Nazareth, which is understood as securing the covenant with Israel but also as the inauguration of a "new age" that will culminate in the general resurrection of the dead.

One characteristic feature of resurrection belief stands out in the New Testament materials: its disruptive force in human thought and history. Belief that Jesus was raised from the dead, never to die again, recalibrated every aspect of religious conviction and conception of social life, including understandings of God's actions in human history. Simultaneously holding that Jesus was crucified and raised from the dead required a reimaging of God's interactions with humanity, God's covenant with Israel, and the relationship of Israel to non-Jews. The particularity of Jesus as crucified and raised by God recast Israel's eschatological hopes and initiated a reorientation of its identity and social boundaries. In this regard, resurrection belief generated multiple and often competing understandings of its implications for the ethics of the resultant faith communities.

Resurrection in the Hebrew Bible. Israel's understandings of death and postmortem existence were variegated, ranging from viewing death as a natural termination of human physical existence to euphemistic ideas of "sleeping with one's ancestors," to a form of postmortem nether existence often referred to spatially as Sheol (Segal, 2004; Levenson, 1993). Moreover, the boundaries between life and death were not drawn with contemporary juridical or medical precision but by observing the waning of one's vitality. Thus, someone suffering from a severe malady was "in Sheol" (Ps 88:3–4, 6), that is, at "death's door." Those who had died perdured in Sheol, dwelling in a shadowy existence. While they were identifiable as individuals, they were neither fully alive nor in relationship with those who were.

Israel considered death a natural part of human existence and the fate of all human beings. Exceptions to this rule are Enoch and Elisha, who were translated from earthly to heavenly existence, thus bypassing death, and the resuscitations of a widow by Elijah (1 Kgs 17:17–24) and the Shunamite woman's son by Elisha (2 Kgs 4:18–37). However, these rare reports depict either a transportation to heaven prior to death or a temporary reanimation, rather than a permanent overcoming of physical death. In other words, death was a final reality, and postmortem imagery is usually metaphorical rather than literal.

Typically, then, "resurrection" belief was conceived less in terms of any particular individual and more in relationship to the restoration of Israel as a whole. It voiced a hope for a future when suffering, including that at the hands of Israel's national enemies, and death will be defeated (e.g., Isa 25:8–9) and Yahweh will reside peacefully with the covenant people.

Ezekiel 37:1–14. Ezekiel 37 depicts the prophet's vision of a valley full of dry bones. The eight references to the "bones" serve as a key to interpreting the passage. Ezekiel sees a mass of skeletal remains, not corpses. The bones are recombined into skeletal entities, and these are in turn enfleshed and inspirited. The entire group of reconstituted bodies is "the house of Israel" that God will restore. The image of resurrection (vv. 12–14) is clearly a metaphor for the reconstitution of Israel as a nation in right covenant relationship with God.

The imagery of the passage (especially v. 6: "breath in you") echoes Genesis 2:7, connecting the idea of "resurrection" with the creating power of God. In essence, the claim is a theological one. The God who can create the human being can also restore the nation of Israel through the same creative power.

The verses that follow identify the restoration as Israel's return from exile and its inhabitation of the Promised Land (vv. 12–14). Thus, resurrection is used metaphorically to reflect the conviction that God is steadfast in maintaining a relationship with Israel, regardless of the forces aligned against it.

Isaiah 26. The same image of corpses rising from the dust appears in Isaiah 26. The "Isaiah apocalypse" is part of a series of visions collected in chapters 24–27 and includes an apocalyptic psalm (26:4–19). These verses contrast the ways of the righteous and the conduct of the wicked (vv. 10–11). Following an acclamation of God's justice (vv. 12–15, 16–19), the contrast is extended by the examples of the dead who will not live (v. 14) and the nation that God has increased (v. 15). Verse 19 expands this image of restoration with the explicit language of resurrection, "Your dead shall live, their corpses shall rise…the earth will give birth to those long dead." Verses 20 and 21 then articulate the central point: Israel's period of distress is not its permanent condition; God will relieve Israel and eventually punish those who are now oppressing the nation.

The context suggests a metaphorical interpretation like that of Ezekiel, but unlike Ezekiel, here there is no explicit connection to the corporate entity as a whole. The vagueness of the reference to "the dead" (v. 19) does allow for a specific instance of resurrection, and scholars differ over whether Isaiah intended actual resurrection of dead people (Levenson, 1993, p. 198) or the restoration of Israel (Collins, 1993, pp. 394-395; Segal, 2004, pp. 259–261). The language in verse 19—"Your dead shall live, their corpses shall rise. O dwellers in the dust, awake and sing for joy! For your dew is a radiant dew, and the earth will give birth to those long dead"—recalls the imagery of Ezekiel 37. Still, the overall context, especially 26:21—27:13, suggests this reference is also better understood in a metaphorical manner.

Daniel 12:1–3. If Ezekiel 37 and Isaiah 26 use "resurrection" language symbolically to express belief in God's future deliverance of the Israelite nation, in Daniel 12:1–3 the belief in future restoration is made particular and for the first time in the Hebrew Bible a clear and explicit articulation of the resurrection of specific individuals occurs. While Daniel 12 is the most explicit expression of resurrection of the dead, it is best to consider it as the author's appropriation of already present beliefs to address the difficulties of his readers' situation, rather than a radical innovation. Still, it displays some significant innovations in the resurrection beliefs in Hebrew religious thought. First, while the redemption of the nation is not abandoned, resurrection is now focused on specific individuals. Second, the time frame is shifted from an unspecified future event to a time in the not distant future, thus moving eschatological redemption into human history. Third, resurrection is simultaneously a moment of redemption and judgment. God will raise both the righteous, thereby vindicating their lives and actions, and those who opposed these righteous ones (*maskîlîm*) so that they will

receive their just punishment. Resurrection still serves the notion of God's fidelity to covenant and justice, but it is now applied to individual actions rather than only to the corporate behavior of an entire people.

It is important to note what Daniel 12 does not say. Resurrection is limited to those who served God and those who acted against them. The verses were prompted by experiences of oppression, specifically those of Antiochus IV (r. 175–164 B.C.E.). As a result, Daniel 12 refers to a particular instance of redemption. It does not speak of a general resurrection of Israel as a whole or of a universal resurrection. Daniel is silent about the fate of the dead, except for the specific individuals he has in mind. The resurrection narration refers to judgment but is not made universal.

Daniel also leaves ambiguous the form of those who will be resurrected; they will be "like the stars," that is, in a glorified state. How this embodiment will be carried out, what it will entail, and what forms it will take are left unstated. Daniel also attaches no interpretation to this experience for anyone other than those who would be raised. While its vindication of martyrs signals a closure to a period of injustice and oppression, it makes no claims that it inaugurates a new age or the culmination of human history. Rather, the sole focus is on those who have suffered unjustly. The resurrection redresses injustice but is not a harbinger of the future. Such elaborations will come later in the Second Temple period, as seen in *1 Enoch* 22–27 and 102–104 and 2 Maccabees 7.

Resurrection in the New Testament. Texts such as Daniel 12, 2 Maccabees, and *1 Enoch* indicate that at least one segment of Second Temple Judaism believed in the individual bodily resurrection of the dead. However, this apocalyptic stream of thought and reflection was not the majority position. Indeed, while some Jews held to a possible form of immortality (e.g., Wisdom of Solomon 1–6), many Jews did not (e.g., the Sadducees; cf. Matt 22:23), and the bodily resurrection of the dead would have appeared as nonsensical to them as to most of the Greek religious and philosophical world.

Nevertheless, this strand of Judaism is the nexus in which Christian belief in resurrection arose and by which early Christians understood and expressed their belief in the resurrection of Jesus and the general resurrection from the dead (see Nickelsburg, 1992; 2006). To be sure, the catalyst for the New Testament resurrection beliefs was the experience of the resurrected Christ, but the religious thought of the Second Temple period provided the context for them to arise.

Every New Testament document refers to the raising of Jesus from the dead, at least implicitly; and the belief is considered foundational. However, the apologetic and catechetical purposes of the New Testament documents preclude a fully consistent presentation of a "doctrine of resurrection." Put succinctly, the extraordinary event of a person raised from the dead defies explication and description by ordinary language, but ordinary language is all that is available to those trying to construe the event and its meanings. Thus, the writers used figurative language and prevailing mythic imagery to express their primal belief that God raised Jesus from the dead. The writers diverged in their attempts at description and explanation, but they agreed that the "ordinary" must be understood in light of the extraordinary. Each writer refers to and depends on different aspects of the resurrection belief to address the needs of his or her audience. That is, the resurrection of Jesus becomes the defining matrix for lived reality. The documents reflect the plurality of ideas about and implications of this belief that early Christians all espoused. The most extensive treatments of the belief are found in the letters of Paul and the four Gospels, and this essay treats these materials as reflections of the varied resurrection beliefs that occur in the New Testament writings.

While Judaism used resurrection language to express its profound trust in God's fidelity, in the New Testament the resurrection of Jesus is the ultimate expression of that fidelity and the fundamental basis for that trust. Further, the hope of Israel's national restoration is now focused on the "already" event of Jesus's resurrection. The resurrection of Jesus is the dawn of a new eschatological age, in which the presence of God is immediately experienced and at the end of which all things will be united. This inaugural event is determinative for all history and all understandings of the human being before God. The internal and external

relationships of the early Christian communities were based on this originating belief.

New Testament authors' interpretations of the resurrection can be grouped under four headings: (1) a vindication of the life and death of Jesus, (2) the exaltation of Jesus as God's Christ or the cosmic Lord (*kyrios*), (3) the inaugural event of a general resurrection (usually those "in Christ" but occasionally in reference to a universal resurrection of all peoples), and (4) an eschatological event initiating a change in the course of human existence and the destiny of the cosmos. The ideas and interpretations of resurrection vary in detail of description and in development of the theological, social, and political implications. Indeed, the variations are themselves a form of interpretation. Still, there are important commonalities among these interpretations. First, the raising of Jesus is understood as the ultimate and unique revelatory event of God. As the key to understanding human history, it is not demonstrable by the tenets of human history. Second, while the event is acclaimed as having occurred within human history, it transcends that history. For the New Testament writers it is clear that Jesus alone has been raised from the dead and that this is the work of Israel's God. Third, the raising is not resuscitation but a full restoration of life that is not liable to death in the future. The empirical person has been transformed by God's act of resurrection.

Resurrection in Paul. The most extensive and varied set of theological reflections on the resurrection appears in Paul's undisputed letters. The death/resurrection/ascension complex is foundational to Pauline belief and thought. According to Paul, the resurrection of Jesus (never to die again, Rom 6:9) establishes that (1) Jesus's death is salutary and revelatory of the nature of God's actions toward and purpose for the creation and (2) Jesus is the Christ, God's designated agent now ascended and established as advocate and lord of the universe (Phil 2:10–11; see also Heb 5:7–9). These two tenets about Christ's resurrection are the touchstones for his teaching on righteousness, the mercy of God, the gift of the Spirit, communal ethics, and the future of human existence.

As extensive as his remarks are, the letters provide glimpses of Paul's notions of resurrection, not its fullest or systematized form. Paul wrote to address and correct the needs and beliefs of his congregations, and this affects his theological constructions, including those about resurrection. Thus, one cannot presume that what we find in his letters was all Paul thought about or might have emphasized about resurrection under different circumstances.

Given this caveat, one can extrapolate certain characteristic features of his statements on resurrection. Paul's reflections on resurrection are a combination of his understanding of Jesus as God's Christ, the experience of the Spirit now given to God's people, and his conceptions of the future existence of believers with God. These are part of a matrix of belief, but for clarification one can separate the strands he intertwined.

First, the resurrection of Jesus took place within human history. It was for Paul an objective event (1 Cor 15:3–7) that happened to a real person (Rom 1:3–4), albeit with cosmic consequences. The one descended from the flesh as "son of David" is declared [by God] through the power of the Spirit as the "Son of God" (Rom 1:3–4). Thus, objective experience of the raised Jesus was insufficient for one to comprehend the meaning of the resurrection. This fuller understanding came through revelatory experience of the Spirit (1 Cor 2:6–13; Gal 1:10). Second, the resurrection of Jesus inaugurates a new age of existence, which will soon be revealed fully at the Parousia of Christ (1 Thess 1:10; Phil 3:20–21). At present the new age is experienced in and through the Spirit of God (Rom 8:4–6, 9–11, 23). Christians thus participate in resurrection life through their incorporation into the raised Christ (Rom 6:1–14). Third, the new age reaches its cosmic culmination in a general resurrection of the dead, the first fruit of which is the raised Christ (1 Cor 15:20–23, 24–28).

Paul's teaching on the death and resurrection of Jesus incorporates early creeds and catechetical materials that preceded his letters (e.g., Rom 1:3–4; Phil 2:6–11; 1 Thess 4:14; 1 Cor 15:3–4). Basic to these materials is that the resurrection reverses the presumed verdict drawn from Jesus's death (1 Cor 1:18–30). Through the resurrection, God vindicates Jesus's righteous suffering and establishes his death by crucifixion as the criterion by which all human judgments are judged (2 Cor 5:14–21; Phil 3:7–11). The death of Jesus is not eradicated by the resurrection but reinterpreted as God's expression of the means and form of redemption.

This pattern is evident in Philippians 2:6–11, which exemplifies the humiliation, obedience, and exaltation of Jesus as cosmic lord. The hymn pivots around Christ's death by crucifixion (v. 8) and immediately announces God's response, "Therefore, God also highly exalted him and gave him the name that is above every name, so that at the name of Jesus every knee should bend, in heaven and on earth and under the earth, and every tongue should confess that Jesus Christ is Lord, to the glory of God the Father" (vv. 9–11). Here the resurrection is understood as cosmic exaltation (as is also the case in Rom 1:3–4).

The resurrection of Jesus is also the means to "obedience of faith" not only for Jews but also among the Gentiles "for the sake of his name" (Rom 1:5); that is, the power for redemption demonstrated in the resurrection of Jesus extends to all humanity. Moreover, in Romans 4:23–24 Paul draws on the words of Genesis 15:6 to argue that God's raising of Jesus establishes the death of Jesus as the means by which God liberates human beings from the bondage of trespass and establishes them as justly related to God. It is for this reason that Paul insists that the resurrection of Jesus is a reality in human history (cf. Rom 5:12–20), for, as he states to the Corinthian church, "If Christ has not been raised, your faith is futile and you are still in your sins. Then those who have died in Christ have perished. If for this life only we have hoped in Christ, we are of all people most to be pitied" (1 Cor 15:17–19).

In addition to understanding the resurrection as essential to human redemption, Paul connects it to the claim that physical death, while inevitable, is not the final state of human existence and to the expectation of the full disclosure of the reign of God at the Parousia, which will include the general resurrection. These beliefs are tied to the sense that the resurrection of Jesus expresses the fidelity of God to redeem the creation (Rom 8:18–25) and to maintain full intimate relationship with all God's people, renewing their mortal bodies with and through the Spirit (Rom 8:11).

The resurrection of Jesus thus simultaneously signifies the creative power of God to overcome death with life (Rom 4:16–25; 8:9–11) and the willingness of God to overcome the chasm of death to establish and maintain relationship with God's people, as Romans 8:31–39 so dramatically shows. Connected to the risen Christ through the ritual act of baptism, which unites the death of the individual with the death of Jesus, the believer is assured of participation in the glorified state of resurrection in the future (cf. Rom 6:1–14; Phil 3:20–21). At present, believers receive a down payment of that existence, the Holy Spirit (Rom 8:9; 2 Cor 5:5), which empowers them to live in right relationship with God (Rom 8:10–11, 12–17; Gal 5:1–26) and which eventually will result in their transformation (Rom 8:17; 2 Cor 4:16—5:5).

Paul speaks most distinctly about this transformation in 1 Corinthians 15, although even there his thoughts remain inchoate. He insists that a general resurrection is not only a possibility but also a future certainty because Jesus has been raised from the dead, demonstrating God's design for human existence beyond death (1 Cor 15:12, 20, 22). Relying on received tradition, Paul also insists that the resurrection of Jesus is an objective reality, verified through the testimony of eyewitnesses (vv. 3–7). He adds his own experience of the risen Christ, even though it was private, nonempirical, and individual, insisting that it be understood as part of the testimonial witness (vv. 8–11). This suggests that while the resurrection had coordinates within human temporal history, it was also something that transcended human history. As an eschatological event (i.e., beyond the nexus of historical events) it is more than an event that occurred in history: it is *the* event by which all history is interpreted and evaluated (2 Cor 5:16–21).

Finally, in this chapter Paul also insists that the future resurrected state of human beings is an embodied one (1 Cor 15:35–41). The resurrected body is not formed from flesh and blood as is the current empirical body; rather, it is composed of spiritual entities (vv. 42–46). Paul is thus arguing for a continuity of the empirical and the transformed self while also arguing for a discontinuity between the embodied forms of that self. That is, the one who dies is indeed the same one who will be raised, but the corruptible body of that self is replaced by an incorruptible, spiritual body

(vv. 53–54), one which is not vulnerable to death and is therefore suited to eternal existence with God (1 Cor 15:27; 2 Cor 5:4–8; Phil 3:21; 1 Thess 4:17). Unfortunately, the metaphorical nature of this passage and the ones to which it is compared makes a clear and concise summation of Paul's understandings of the future resurrected state exceedingly complicated.

These excerpts of Paul's letters demonstrate that the resurrection of Jesus is one of his fundamental interpretive lenses. Through it he understands the death of Christ; he evaluates the values of present physical existence; he develops an ethic of spiritual existence, both individual and communal; and he envisions future existence as an embodied ongoing relationship with God that cannot be severed, even by the powers inimical to that existence.

Resurrection in the Gospels. The Gospel tradition contains materials that reflect the matrix of Second Temple Jewish beliefs about resurrection set against the backdrop of the raising of Jesus. For example, Mark 5:21–43 relates the raising of Jairus's daughter with clear echoes of the resuscitations performed by Elijah and Elisha (1 Kgs 17:17–24; 2 Kgs 4:18–37). There are also predictions of a future redemption that mirror the martyrdom motifs in 2 Maccabees (e.g., Mark 8:34–35). While these underscore that Second Temple Jewish beliefs formed the context for New Testament reflections on resurrection, of interest are the reflections that pertain specifically to Jesus. Yet, the Gospels contain very few statements by Jesus about resurrection. Those that are present are connected to the vindication of Jesus following his death, prophetic materials referring to the future Kingdom of God, and controversies about the viability of belief in resurrection (e.g., Matt 22:23–33).

When the Gospels do focus on resurrection, it is in the context of Jesus's death, the empty tomb, and appearances by Jesus after his death. All the Gospels presume and mention the resurrection of Jesus, but each highlights different aspects of the event. For example, the best textual reconstructions of Mark's Gospel contain no post resurrection appearances, but these are emphasized in the other three Gospel accounts. Matthew uses them for apologetic purposes, while Luke differentiates the facets of resurrection, bodily redemption, and ascension/exaltation to demonstrate the coherency of God's actions in Christ.

Further, while all the Gospels contain an "empty tomb" narrative, their details differ markedly, even to the point of contradiction. This raises questions about their value for historical reconstructions, but the ubiquity of the reports points to an early belief that Jesus was buried and that his grave was discovered empty shortly afterward. (For a discussion of the issues pertaining to historicity see Bockmuehl, 2001.) In any case, it is clear that early Christians believed in the resurrection of Jesus, even if their means of expressing this belief differed in terms of both language and interpretation.

The Gospel accounts of postresurrection appearances amplify the mystery of resurrection. On the one hand, the raised Jesus is identifiable as the person the disciples knew and followed. On the other, the being before them is strikingly different in appearance and ability. It has been transformed by the power of God and displays superhuman capabilities.

The writers point to the continuity of the resurrected one with the one who died, while simultaneously noting that a transformation has occurred through their depictions of the postresurrection appearances. In every instance the resurrected body is markedly different from the entombed body. On the one hand, the person encountered is the Jesus his disciples knew, raised from the dead, and, on the other, the resurrected Jesus is unlike the body of any other human being. The resurrected being is neither an apparition nor a ghost but an embodied human being. The raised Jesus eats, drinks, speaks, and listens. At the same time his body is able to appear and disappear (Luke 24:13–15, 31), even pass through locked doors (John 20:19). He is a human being whose body has been transformed into a glorified state, the appearance of which instills fear in its viewers. This is clear from John's depictions of the raised Jesus's encounters with his disciples and Mary (cf. John 20:11–18, 19–23, 24–28; 21:1–14) as well as the appearance stories in Matthew (28:1–10, 16–20) and Luke (24:13–35, 36–49, 50–53). This typical response of fear and awe suggests that the disciples who experience the risen Jesus are experiencing the full expression of God's power to give life.

Thus, as one would expect, the theophany provokes awe, admiration, and fear.

The forms of these narratives suggest two additional points. First, the raised Jesus, by virtue of his enhanced existence, displays evidence of divine presence, and this implies that God has vindicated Jesus by overturning his execution by religious and political authorities. This is particularly evident in Jesus's predictions of his death (Mark 8:34—9:1; 9:30–32; 10:32–34 and parallels) and the claims made in the Acts speech by Peter at Pentecost (Acts 2:22–36). This follows the tradition of the redemption of the righteous sufferer and qualifies Jesus as God's anointed (see the allegorical references to Ps 118:22 in Mark 12:10//Matt 21:42//Luke 20:17 but particularly Acts 4:11 and 1 Pet 2:6, where this is made explicit). Second, the raised Jesus appears only to his followers, suggesting that comprehending resurrection requires more than seeing the empirical. To experience it one must have a context of faith in Jesus as God's Christ, and even then the resurrection experience transgresses the boundaries of human understanding (e.g., Luke 24:36–49; John 20:24–28; Acts 2:29–36).

The Gospels' presentation of the resurrection of Jesus also connects it to the in-breaking of the Kingdom of God and its consummation at the Parousia. Matthew makes this connection by his apocalyptic depiction of the dead rising after the resurrection of Jesus (Matt 27:52–53) as well as the final words of Jesus, who, as the resurrected one, now has *all* authority and who will be with the disciples to "the end of the age" (Matt 28:20). At that time the raised Lord will appear as the Son of Man in glory to judge all peoples (Matt 24:30–31; 25:31–46).

Finally, the Gospels' presentations of Jesus's empty tomb and post resurrection appearances serve apologetic purposes. The writers are aware of the incredulity of their claim and that other explanations for the empty tomb are more plausible (Matt 27:62–66; 28:11–15; John 20:1–2, 11–18). However, they reject explanations that involve human activity and attribute it to the exercise of divine power. This is symbolized by the presence of angelic figures at the tomb (Mark 16:5–8; Matt 28:2–8; Luke 24:4–11). Similarly, the movement of the stone sealing the tomb implies that this was not done by a human being but by divine power.

This exercise of power and sanction of Jesus as the Messiah is emphasized by Luke, especially in Acts 2:27, 31; 13:34–35, where the author appropriates Psalm 16:11 and emphasizes that God will not let the Holy One experience corruption. Acts 2:32–36 states the implications of this divine act. Raised from the dead by God (i.e., not experiencing corruption of the flesh), he is now "exalted at the right hand of God," made both "Lord and Messiah."

In Matthew and Luke, this empowerment is present during the life of Jesus but limited in scope until after his resurrection. In John, however, this is not the case. There from the beginning Jesus is the one raised from the dead but also the resurrection itself. That is, in him resides the full power for life, and it is already displayed during his life, as the raising of Lazarus makes clear. Mary awaits the day of resurrection, but Jesus corrects this anticipation and declares, "I am the resurrection and the life" (John 11:25). With this the Fourth Gospel interprets the raising of Jesus not as an exceptional instance of God's power but as the definitive example of a power that is always present in Jesus, the power of life. Thus, one experiences this reality now according to the Fourth Gospel (John 5:24; 11:26). Jesus, as the incarnate glory of God, possesses, while on earth, the capacity and authority over life and death (John 10:18). Here the full force of Israel's eschatological hope has been placed directly in the course of human history.

The preponderance of resurrection expressions in the Gospels focus on the aspects of God's sanction of Jesus as Messiah and on attributing this extraordinary display of power to God alone. Moreover, they place resurrection hope in the middle of human experience, and it becomes the key element for interpreting all that Jesus had taught or done prior to his death. That is, the raising of Jesus signals that God's authority is behind Jesus's ministry and death and, therefore, what Jesus has said is definitive. The authority is not found in the content of the teachings or in the display of miraculous behaviors but instead in the final sanction of power displayed by the resurrection.

Theological Reflections on Resurrection Beliefs. Resurrection belief in both testaments acclaims that God, as creator and sustainer of the universe, is and will remain true to the relationships God establishes with God's people and all creation. Thus, despite the course of human history, nothing, not even death, can sever that relationship. Resurrection belief is therefore a complex expression of a multitude of other beliefs including the sovereignty of God over creation and history, the trustworthiness of God to maintain and sustain covenant relationships, the power of God to create life, and the purposefulness that God ensures for individual lives and the universe. Resurrection belief therefore implies claims about the meaningfulness of existence, the triumph of justice, the goodness of creation, and the character of God as relational.

Belief in a resurrection streams from Second Temple Judaism and early Christianity. Still, in their particular expressions, the forms of this belief differ significantly. Within Judaism, resurrection was understood as a future possible reality, connected to the individual but more centrally to corporate judgment, resulting in either vindication or condemnation. Early Christianity shared this perspective but insisted that in the resurrection of Jesus this hope had been transferred into the present, located in one specific individual. The resurrection of Jesus established him as the designated agent of God and, thus, as advocate, judge, and means by which relationship with God would be secured.

Both Judaism and early Christianity understood resurrection as an overcoming of physical suffering and death, continuing in some form of beatific existence. Early Christianity understood this as somatic, while Jewish thought allowed both somatic and nonsomatic forms of postdeath existence. Finally, while early Christians understood resurrection belief as a fundamental tenet, Second Temple Judaism did not. In fact, it appears that only a minority of Jews held such a position.

In another distinction from its Jewish roots, early Christianity understood resurrection in relationship to the crucifixion of Jesus. That is, within Christianity it is best to consider the death/resurrection complex rather than to focus on either element in isolation. The interpretations of Jesus's death necessarily entail interpretations of his resurrection and vice versa. Consequently, expressions of belief in the resurrection are

Christological and theological claims. The resurrection of Jesus was interpreted as a vindication of Jesus and a guarantee of God's redemption of human beings through the death of Jesus. It was a sign of the defeat of all forces aligned against God, including death, and an acclamation of Jesus as God's cosmic lord.

These are metaphysical claims, entailing a worldview. As such they are claims about human history and God's control of it and destiny for it. As a result, while historical inquiry can provide evidence of this belief and suggest a catalyst for it, such inquiry cannot prove the claim or exhaust its existential meanings. The biblical materials make this clear. The biblical materials proclaim the truth of God's resurrection power; they do not seek to establish it by quantifiable and empirical arguments at the bar of human reason. This reminds us that the biblical materials are themselves interpretations of a presumed truth, albeit one held as fundamental. The interpretations, while theological, are neither systematic nor comprehensive. They are attempts to articulate deeply held convictions and to make sense out of profound experiences of something that transcends the empirically provable. They reflect the convictions of communities thrashed out in the midst of particular social and historical circumstances as a response to those conditions. In this sense, the resurrection is treated not as a doctrine in the biblical materials but as a lens to view the world in which these communities existed.

The biblical writers emphasize different aspects of this belief in order to ground, and sometimes correct, the convictions of their community members. As a result the authors reflect different, as well as differing, interpretations. The emphases focus on different aspects of resurrection, but they all entail implications for human existence, including respect for life, the enmeshment of human existence with the fate of the rest of creation, the relationship of the self to the body, the relationship of justice to human constructions of legal systems, and the ultimate value of the human in relationship to others.

[See also Anthropology; Apocalypticism; Body; Death and Dying; Eschatology; and Underworld and Hell.]

BIBLIOGRAPHY

Allison, Dale C. The End of the Ages Has Come: An Early Interpretation of the Passion and Resurrection of Jesus. Philadelphia: Fortress, 1985.

Allison, Dale C. Resurrecting Jesus: The Earliest Christian Tradition and Its Interpreters. New York: T&T Clark, 2005.

Alston, William P. "Biblical Criticism and the Resurrection." In The Resurrection: An Interdisciplinary Symposium on the Resurrection of Jesus, edited by Stephen T. Davis, Daniel Kendall, and Gerald O'Collins, pp. 148–143. New York: Oxford University Press, 1997.

Bieringer, R., V. Koperski, and B. Lataire, eds. Resurrection in the New Testament: Festschrift J. Lambrecht. Bibliotheca Ephemeridum Theologicarum Lovaniensium 65. Leuven, Belgium: Peeters, 2002.

Bockmuehl, Markus. "Resurrection." In The Cambridge Companion to Jesus, edited by Markus Bockmuehl, pp. 102–118. New York: Cambridge University Press, 2001.

Bryan, Christopher. The Resurrection of the Messiah. New York: Oxford University Press, 2011.

Catchpole, David. Resurrection People: Studies in the Resurrection Narratives of the Gospels. London: Darton, Longman & Todd, 2000.

Collins, John J. "The Root of Immortality: Death in the Context of Jewish Wisdom." Harvard Theological Review 71 (1978): 177–192.

Collins, John J. Daniel: A Commentary on the Book of Daniel. Minneapolis: Fortress, 1993.

Crossan, John Dominic. Jesus: A Revolutionary Biography. San Francisco: HarperSanFrancisco, 1994.

Davis, Stephen T., Daniel Kendall, and Gerald O'Collins, eds. The Resurrection: An Interdisciplinary Symposium on the Resurrection of Jesus. New York: Oxford University Press, 1997.

Johnston, Phillip S. Shades of Sheol: Death and Afterlife in the Old Testament. Downers Grove, Ill.: InterVarsity, 2002.

Levenson, Jon D. The Death and Resurrection of the Beloved Son: The Transformation of Child Sacrifice in Judaism and Christianity. New Haven, Conn.: Yale University Press, 1993.

Lichtenberger, Hermann, and Friedrich Avemarie, eds. Auferstehung-Resurrection. Tübingen, Germany: Mohr Siebeck, 2001.

Longenecker, Richard N., ed. Life in the Face of Death. Grand Rapids, Mich.: Eerdmans, 1998.

Lüdemann, Gerd. The Resurrection of Jesus: History, Experience, Theology. Translated by J. Bowden. Minneapolis: Fortress, 1994.

Lüdemann, Gerd. What Really Happened to Jesus: A Historical Approach to the Resurrection. Translated by

J. Bowden. Louisville, Ky.: Westminster John Knox, 1995.

Madigan, Kevin, and Jon D. Levenson. *Resurrection: The Power of God for Christians and Jews.* New Haven, Conn.: Yale University Press, 2008.

Martin-Achard, Robert. *From Death to Life: A Study of the Development of the Doctrine of the Resurrection in the Old Testament.* Translated by John Penney Smith. London: Oliver and Boyd, 1960.

Nickelsburg, George W. E. "Resurrection: Early Judaism and Christianity." In *Anchor Bible Dictionary*, edited by David Noel Freeman, Vol. 5, pp. 684–691. Nashville, Tenn.: Abingdon, 1992.

Nickelsburg, George W. E. *Resurrection, Immortality, and Eternal Life in Intertestamental Judaism and Early Christianity.* Cambridge, Mass.: Harvard University Press, 2006.

O'Collins, Gerald. *Interpreting the Resurrection: Examining the Major Problems in the Stories of Jesus' Resurrection.* New York: Paulist Press, 1988.

Perkins, Pheme. *Resurrection: New Testament Witness and Contemporary Reflection.* New York: Doubleday, 1984.

Segal, Alan. *Life after Death: A History of the Afterlife in the Religions of the West.* New York: Doubleday, 2004.

Vermes, Geza. *The Resurrection.* New York: Doubleday, 2008.

Wedderburn, A. J. M. *Beyond Resurrection.* London: SCM, 1999.

Wright, N. T. *The Resurrection of the Son of God.* Minneapolis: Fortress, 2003.

Steven J. Kraftchick

RETRIBUTION

See Reward and Retribution.

REVELATION

Revelation describes God's communication with humanity; it focuses on the unveiling of truths that otherwise would remain hidden. The presupposition of revelation is that God desires to be known by humans and that humans are able to comprehend something of God. Revelation is not an action in itself; God does not just "reveal." Revelation occurs through other actions: God is revealed in word, in deed, in Israel, and in Jesus Christ. Any discussion of revelation must account for the myriad ways in which God engages in revelation.

By the nature of the subject, revelation must be described through analogies. Analogies drawn from interpersonal communication seem most appropriate; nevertheless, analogies are always incomplete. Claiming that God speaks does not illuminate the means by which God speaks to Israel, a prophet, or a disciple. Instead, the claim is that God's revelation seems most like speech to the community or the one who receives it. Beyond analogies of communication, the analogy of sacrament is helpful for understanding God's revelation. God uses ordinary things to reveal gifts of grace.

Categories. Although revelation can be classified by either its content or the means through which humans experience it, the latter provides a more helpful focus here. Scholars have often split God's revelation into different categories based on God's action (i.e., word or deed). Alternatively, descriptions of God's revelation have been based on who understands it or how it is appropriated in human lives (e.g., general or specific revelation). Throughout scripture, however, God's revelation seeks the same salvific and redemptive ends regardless of appropriation. The categorization here reflects this cohesive purpose.

Essentially, the Bible attests to God's revelatory action in two primary ways: within communal instruments, such as worship, law, or tradition, and within an individual's personal experience. The first category involves revelation through Torah and cultus; the second category includes different aspects of personal experience in Israel and the church, whether connected to creation and wisdom, visions and dreams, or apocalyptic unveilings of heavenly secrets. The Old and New Testaments contain examples demonstrating the overlap between these two categories. In the prophetic tradition Torah and personal experience intersect. From a Christian perspective, these two categories are further united in the revelation of Christ, God's revealer (John 1:18), who encompasses all facets of God's revelation to humanity.

Biblical Contexts. As Genesis 1 demonstrates, God creates humanity as "very good" in a "good" creation (Gen 1:1—2:4a). A liturgical, poetic form of this creation account, reflected in some psalms, depicts creation as a means of revelation (Pss 8:3–4, 29, 104). Revelation is supposed to result in obeying and worshipping God (Gen 1:28—2:3; Exod 20:8–11; Pss 8:9; 29:1–2; 104:31–35). Here, creation points humanity to its Creator, who should be worshipped, and inspires joy in the recipients. While God's revelation in creation is oblique, it is fundamental for how Israel and the church (John 1:3; Rom 1:18–20; Heb 11:3) shape their view of the world. Yet, because this revelation is indirect, the appropriate response to this revelation is worship in community, which aids individuals in interpreting what they have experienced.

Worship is a key place of revelation in both the Old and New Testaments. The sacrificial system associated with tabernacle and temple is a fundamental means by which God is revealed to Israel (Exod 25:8; 29:42–46; 1 Kgs 8:10–13; Ps 68). Worship itself is grounded in Torah, which is the central revelation of God in the Old Testament. Torah demonstrates that God is active in history (e.g., Exod 20:1). Torah and God are nearly synonymous in Deuteronomy's description of what sets Israel apart from other nations: Israel's uniqueness is grounded in God's care, which in turn is revealed in Israel's God-given law (Deut 7:7–11).

Obedience to Torah is intended to produce the kind of nation that is holy—set apart for God's purposes—thus revealing God's character to the world (Isa 42:6–7). On the whole, however, the Old Testament tends to emphasize Israel's failure at this calling and God's faithfulness. Prophetic texts demonstrate God's revelation to individuals, sometimes within political or cultic structures (Isaiah [Isa 6–11], Ezekiel [Ezek 1:1–3]) and sometimes outside of them (Elijah [1 Kgs 17:1–7], Amos [Amos 7:14–15]). Furthermore, the prophetic form of God's revelation is primarily described in terms of truth-telling and exhortations of repentance. By their interpretation of signs, words, and actions, the prophets are an excellent reminder that God's revelation always requires interpretation (e.g., Isa 5:1–24; Jer 13:1–11; 18:1—19:15). They also remind Israel that sometimes the biggest challenge is not the interpretation of God's revelation but rather the obedience that it requires (Jer 7:5–15).

The Old Testament attests to more personal encounters of God's revelation as well. The theophanies to Moses (Exod 33:12—34:28) and Elijah (1 Kgs 19:9–18) demonstrate that God's revelation occurs but remains mysterious. Furthermore, these theophanies demonstrate that God's appearances are surprising and beyond human control. Though he makes the request to see God, Moses cannot see God's face (Exod 33:20–22); Elijah hears Yahweh in the sound of silence (1 Kgs 19:11–12; see also Job 38–41). Such experiences outside of human control sometimes occur as dreams—thus, Jacob (Gen 28:10–22) and Joseph (Gen 37:5–11; 40:1—41:36; cf. Matt 1:18–23).

The consummate interpreter of dreams is Daniel (Dan 2:1–45; 4:1–37; cf. 5:13–30), who also is portrayed as scripture's first apocalyptic visionary (Daniel 7–12). Apocalyptic literature, by its nature, is concerned with unveiling heavenly realities to help make sense of earthly experience. Texts from Qumran and 1 Enoch perpetuate the Old Testament's claims that God's revelation can occur either inside or outside typical community structures.

Some apocalyptic documents preserved by the Qumran community concentrate the interpretation of God's revelation as the responsibility of one person, the "teacher of righteousness" (1QpHab 6:12—7:5). Apart from this teacher, God's revelation is also manifested in the community's life in worship and Torah obedience, as well as the "mystery" that has been granted to the community. The content of this mystery is not disclosed, though it seems to be connected with God's activity in creating the world (4Q417.6, 11–13, 18).

In 1 Enoch, God's revelation produces primarily visionary experiences for a seer (especially 1 En. 1–36, 83–90), who discloses or keeps hidden God's revelation, based on God's command (1 En. 104:9–13; 4 Ezra 14:37–48; Rev 22:10). Sometimes these revelations seem related to historical events (e.g., Dan 11:2–39; 1 En. 89–90); at other times the seer is granted mystical revelations, like the secrets of the winds (e.g., 1 En. 41:3–4). The book 1 Enoch attests to a God who takes the seer up to heaven (e.g., 1 En. 39:3; cf. 2 Cor 12:1–10; Rev 4:1–2), revealing cosmic mysteries and God's activity on the other side of the veil.

In the New Testament, Paul uses the term *apocalypsis* to express God's action in revelation, declaring that the Gospel reveals both God's righteousness and wrath (Rom 1:17–18). The Gospel itself functions as God's revelation to the world. In general, the focal claim of New Testament texts is that the clearest revelation of God is found in Jesus, who unifies both God's word and deeds as the Word made flesh (John 1:14). Jesus is portrayed as a new giver and interpreter of Torah (Matt 5–7), a prophet like Elijah (Luke 7:11–17), and one who embodies God's love in washing disciples' feet and by dying, forsaken, on a cross (John 13:1–20; Matt 27:27–56). In the Fourth Gospel John the Baptist has come so that Jesus might be "revealed to Israel" (John 1:31). Jesus serves as the revealer of God, by interpreting God to those who believe in him (John 1:18) in created human form. Essentially, Jesus embodies all of the means of revelation represented in scripture.

Even though Jesus is central to the New Testament's conception of revelation, the Gospels are not cavalier about its comprehensibility. Jesus may reveal a mystery (cf. Mark 4:11; Eph 3:7–10), but it remains paradoxically mysterious nonetheless. Jesus's resurrection and the presence of the Spirit clear up confusion (e.g., Mark 13:9–12), but such clarification is neither automatic nor complete (1 Cor 13:12). In fact, all of the resurrection accounts describe much the same surprise and awe—and lack of comprehension—that we see in Old Testament accounts of theophany. In Luke 24, for example, Jesus explains "Moses and all the prophets" to two of his followers, but something kept "their eyes…from recognizing him" (24:27, 16). Later, their eyes are opened at the breaking of bread (24:31). The revelation of the resurrected Jesus's identity comes not in traveling on the road or even by Jesus's revealing of himself in scripture. Instead, it is through a meal, a sacrament-like feast, that Jesus reveals himself to these followers. Seeing Jesus again was a God-given revelation.

This Lukan narrative indicates how the same categories of revelation operative in the Old Testament are also present in the New Testament. While Jesus embodies both a personal revelation of God and Torah itself, Luke shows how Jesus's followers apprehended this revelation; often, the early church best understood Jesus in worship. This worship could be sacramental in character, as the overtones in Luke 24 imply, or it could be primarily oriented around words, as in Peter's sermon in Acts 2. Furthermore, as Acts 2 demonstrates, the availability of the Spirit to "all flesh" (Acts 2:17) highlights one of the engaging but perilous

aspects of revelation in both the Old and New Testaments: the prophetic edge of revelation often transcends the boundaries of traditional religious expectation. How much weight one gives to, or how one judges, the Spirit's revelation was as challenging in Israel and in the church as it is in the twenty-first century (cf. 1 John 4:7–21). However, it is important to note that prophetic revelation has always found a place in the tradition, despite that tradition's discomfort with it. Personal experience of God's revelation does not trump revelation found in the community's life of worship and obedience; indeed, they are found together. Luke, in particular, highlights the role of the Spirit in visions and in scriptural interpretation in community; the church needs both forms of revelation, each confirming the other (Acts 10–11; 15).

Lastly, it is important to consider the centrality of Jesus in the Christian understanding of revelation. The church claims that Jesus is the climactic revelation of God because he controls the interpretation of all other means of revelation: revelation takes place through Christ, whether that revelation occurs in worship, in reading scripture, or by experiencing the Spirit (2 Cor 3:14). Furthermore, Christ is also the one who reveals God's purposes for the present and future Kingdom of God (Matt 4:12–17; 24:1–51; Rev 1–5).

Postbiblical Contexts. The church retains a consistent tension between revelation via personal experiences of the Spirit and the more institutional aspects of revelation in word and sacrament. Particular aspects of revelation have been debated. Christian theologians, notably Karl Barth and his followers, have found it helpful to contrast the general revelation of God (i.e., in creation) with the specific revelation of God (i.e., in Jesus Christ), heavily privileging the latter. While this distinction can be advantageous in certain contexts, it is essential to note that, in the New Testament, God's revelation in creation points toward the redemption of the cosmos in Christ, while Christ points back to God's creating and sustaining action (Rom 8:18–39; Col 1:15–20).

A foundational idea of Christian theology is that God is willing to reveal his divine nature and attributes in a manner that is at least partially comprehensible by humans. The challenge is to make a place for different modes of revelation (creation, worship, Torah, prophecy, and apocalypse, all encompassed in Christ) and to realize that God's self-revelation occurs through the most ordinary of things: scriptural texts, words, bread and wine, humans, and all of creation. Recognizing God's extraordinary gifts of revelation in the ordinary leads to a sacramental understanding of revelation: perceiving God's revelation in these ordinary things is a gift of invisible grace in visible things, awaiting the time when all that has been made secret will be disclosed (Mark 4:22).

[*See also* Apocalypticism; Covenant; Cult and Worship; Decalogue; Epiphany; Eschatology; Glory; Grace; Knowledge; Lord's Supper; Mystery and Mystery Religions; *and* Scripture.]

BIBLIOGRAPHY

Abraham, William J. *Divine Revelation and the Limits of Historical Criticism.* Oxford: Oxford University Press, 1982.

Avis, Paul, ed. *Divine Revelation.* Grand Rapids, Mich.: Eerdmans, 1997.

Baillie, John. *The Idea of Revelation in Recent Thought.* London: Oxford University Press, 1956.

Barth, Karl. *Church Dogmatics* Vol. 1. Translated by Geoffrey W. Bromiley and T. F. Torrance. Edinburgh: T&T Clark, 1956.

Fackre, Gabriel. *The Doctrine of Revelation: A Narrative Interpretation.* Grand Rapids, Mich.: Eerdmans, 1997.

Gunton, C. A. *A Brief Theology of Revelation.* London: T&T Clark, 1995.

Pannenburg, Wolfhart, Rolf Rendtorff, Trutz Rendtorff, et al. *Revelation as History.* Edited by Wolfhart Pannenburg. New York: Macmillan, 1969.

Swinburne, Richard. *Revelation: From Metaphor to Analogy.* 2d ed. Oxford: Oxford University Press, 2007.

Laura C. Sweat

REVELATION, BOOK OF

See Apocalypticism.

REWARD AND RETRIBUTION

Pairing reward and retribution suggests an antithesis between salvation and judgment, but the Hebrew words translated "reward" can mean both payment for proper performance and requital for improper. The root *gml*, for example, is used in both ways when Saul admits that he has wronged David while David has shown him mercy (1 Sam 24:17–20). David himself claims the Lord has rewarded his righteousness (2 Sam 22:21 = Ps 18:20). The same root is used in Psalm 103:10 for God's requiting for sin.

The noun *pĕûllâ* can mean "wages," but a few times it means the good God has saved up for his people (Isa 40:10; cp. 62:11). It can also be used of judgment (e.g., Isa 65:7).

The primary meaning of *skr* (both noun and verb) is "hire" and, hence, payment for work. It shades over into "reward" in statements like Genesis 15:1, in which the Lord tells Abram that his faith will "pay off." Proverbs 11:18 assures the righteous of a sure compensation.

The Piel of *šlm* is used for a range of situations where (re)payment is involved. It means "produce what one promised" (Jonah 2:10; Eccl 5:4–5) or "pay off a debt" (2 Kgs 4:7; Jer 16:18; 32:18). It can be used in blessings calling down a divine reward for a good deed (Ruth 2:12; 1 Sam 24:19) but more often for the recompense of evil (Deut 32:14; 2 Sam 3:29).

The Hiphil of *šub* is often used for the "return" of evil deeds to haunt the doer. The idea of requital or recompense is that a person's untoward deeds will rebound on him or her (e.g., Judg 9:56; 1 Sam 25:39). Hosea uses it twice for Israel (4:9; 12:3).

The root *pqd* is used both for beneficial and retributive acts of God. God pays attention to a person or community (e.g., Gen 21:1; 50:24–25; in prophecy: Jer 29:10; Zech 10:3b), but much more often God's scrutinizes and judges (e.g., Exod 32:34; Isa 26:14; Job 7:18).

Translators have seldom used the word "retribution" for any of our words (Isa 66:6; Jer 5:9 in NRSV). Either "requite/requital" or "avenge/vengeance" have been preferred. The root *nqm* is normally translated "avenge/vengeance." The word can be used with a human subject (Judg 15:7; 16:28), but Yahweh is the subject far more often (e.g., Num 31:2; Judg 11:36; 2 Sam 4:8). Yahweh brings vengeance on his people for disobedience and betrayal (Lev 26:25; Isa 1:24; Jer 5:9; Ezek 24:8). Yahweh also avenges himself on foreign nations (e.g., Num 31:3; Deut 32:35), and judgment of the whole earth is a day of vengeance (Isa 34:8; Jer 46:10).

Old Testament Passages. The Israelites, as portrayed in the Old Testament, expected to reap a good, long, comfortable life for clinging to the Lord and abiding by his commandments. "And if you obey my commandments…[he] will give you rain in your land" (Deut 11:13). This "reward" was, of course, based upon God's generous gift of the land, of the law, and of election; God's grace precedes any action on Israel's part, but Israel must conform to God's will to continue to enjoy it.

The crisis came when God's protection and sustenance ceased, though the people insisted they had lived up to what was expected of them. This is the subject of Psalm 44: once God had shown Israel favor, but now he had cast them off (v. 9). The people insist they had been faithful to God and his covenant (vv. 17–19). They even swear an oath of clearance (vv. 20–22). All they could do was call upon the Lord to "wake up" (v. 23).

Individuals also expected rewards for living righteous and holy lives and were dumbfounded by serious reversals, for example, "I said in my prosperity, 'I shall never be moved.' By your favor, O LORD, you established me as a strong mountain; you hid your face, I was dismayed" (Ps 30:6–7). Job had a similar experience. Job recounts how well God had treated him and how he had lived an exemplary life and expected life to continue in the same vein until he died (29:18–20). But now he is even scorned by the wretched and persecuted by God (13:22–27); it took a divine revelation to resolve their conflict.

God also spoke to the people through the prophets. Amos, Hosea, Isaiah, Micah, Jeremiah, Ezekiel, and Zechariah all announced divine judgment before the calamity of defeat, death, and exile which befell Israel at the hands of Assyria and Judah at the hands of Babylon. Thus, despite protests like Psalm 44, the people know—or could know—why they suffered retribution rather than continuing in peace and prosperity. The words discussed here are clustered in these books. The only hope for the people of God was to endure the fires of judgment in order to be purified.

A few psalms absorbed the teaching of the prophets and the experience of exile. One can call their spirituality "penitential piety." The people pray in the spirit of repentance in Psalm 106 (also Isa 63:7—64:12; Neh 9:6–37), while individuals exemplify the penitential spirit in Psalms 51 and 130. Instead of protesting innocence and God's unreliability, these psalms acknowledge the sin of the speakers and seek healing and restoration. The Psalmist in Psalm 130:7–8 pleads with Israel to "hope in the LORD…he will redeem Israel from all his iniquities."

What kind of God rewards humans for faithfulness and obedience and requites them for evil deeds and indifference? In Exodus 34:6–7, the Lord himself describes the divine nature: "Yahweh, Yahweh, a God merciful and gracious, slow to anger, and abounding in steadfast love and faithfulness, keeping steadfast love for thousands, forgiving iniquity and transgression and sin, but who will by no means clear the guilty, visiting the iniquity of the fathers on the children and the children's children, to the third and fourth generation." The reward humans hope for is grounded in God's graciousness and love. He is even willing to forgive penitent sinners. Yet the Lord cannot indulge sin. Sin has consequences. Often the punishment of an oppressor is grace to the oppressed. And God himself has rights. Perhaps punishment is multigenerational because sin often is.

Postexilic Judaism. The exile of Judah had deep consequences for the subject of reward and retribution. Exile brought the monarchy to an end and with it various territorial and sociological features of Israelite identity. The Jewish population was scattered around the ancient world and forced to worship without a temple. When the Temple was rebuilt, it was a distant pilgrimage site for a majority of Jews. Divine law became the focus of loyalty and its practice the source for a distinctive identity. The Exile, because it was God's judgment, instilled a deep sense of guilt and prompted a passion to fulfill the commandments of God.

Reward and retribution gravitated more than before to divine law or Torah. The Pentateuch was set apart as written divine revelation and interpreted for its teaching of God's requirements of his people. E. P. Sanders (1977) names the religion of first-century Palestinian Judaism "covenantal nomism." God has chosen Israel as his witness in the world; this was a gracious gift, but it entailed commandments, which Israelites had to perform to remain in God's good graces. If an Israelite sinned, there were means of atonement, repentance, and forgiveness.

Promises of reward and warnings of retribution were essential to preaching the covenant. Within this life, individual Israelites could expect rewards for loyalty to God and obedience to his commandments, a privilege no non-Israelite enjoyed because non-Israelites were not under the law. On the other hand, an Israelite who broke faith or disobeyed faced retribution if he or she did not repent and wait upon God's forgiveness.

Although promise of rewards and warning of punishment might suggest Jews were given to self-righteousness, their prayers exhibited heartfelt humility and compunction. Before God, the worshipper knew that his or her righteousness was filthy rags. Salvation depended upon the mercy of God.

By the first century B.C.E., most Jews had accepted a doctrine of a future kingdom, in which the dead too would participate. Thus, the Tannaim frequently spoke of reward and retribution in the world to come. All Jews would be accepted into this kingdom if they had remained loyal and obedient and had sought divine forgiveness when they had sinned. Thus, Israelites would be saved by "grace," by participating in the grace shown Israel.

Opposite the Kingdom of God is Gehenna, a place of divine retribution. Threats of Gehenna are not systematic; definitely, wicked Gentile rulers belong there, as well as apostate Jews. The image of fire stands out.

There is really no place for most Gentiles in this scheme. Some teachers taught that no one who lacked the Torah would be saved. Others held out the prospect of salvation for "righteous Gentiles," though there is no measure for this righteousness.

Greek Vocabulary and New Testament Passages. The Greek word translated "reward" is *misthos*. In the Gospels it appears mostly in the Sermon on the Mount (Matt 5–7) and the Sermon on the Plain (Luke 6:17–38), paradigmatically in Matthew 5:12 and Luke 6:23, which promise reward in heaven.

The passages using "reward" show how the Jesus of the Gospels overturns normal expectations of rewards. Fulfilling normal social obligations is not enough;

radical obedience is necessary. A conclusion correlates appropriate behavior with the character of God (Matt 5:48; Luke 6:36). Similarly, only religious acts done solely for their devotion to God deserve reward.

As for Torah, Jesus says he does not intend to abolish the law but to fulfill it (Matt 5:17); anyone who relaxes the divine commandments is in trouble (Matt 5:19). However, elsewhere Jesus "relaxes" sabbath practices (Matt 12:1–8, 9–14; Mark 2:23–28; 3:1–6; Luke 6:1–5) and seems to dispense with etiquette and dietary laws altogether (Matt 15:1–20; Mark 7:1–23; Luke 11:38–39). Thus, what Jesus said seems to be compatible with the Gentile mission.

Paul did not abandon moral law (e.g., "what is good and acceptable and perfect," Rom 12:2), and his opposition to circumcision and dietary restrictions was based on his belief that Gentiles had access to God's saving grace without bearing the burden of Torah. Paul explicitly challenges the need for "works of Torah" for "justification" (*dikiosyné*) (Gal 2:15–16). Neither Gentiles nor Jews earn God's saving grace by compliance with the Law of Moses. Jewish Christians may continue to adhere to Torah; Paul himself was observant among fellow Jews, though not among Gentiles (1 Cor 9:19–23).

Paul puts "faith in Christ" in place of "works of Torah." He defines faith precisely in Romans 10:9: "if you confess with your lips that Jesus is Lord and believe in your heart that God raised him from the dead." Why is faith, rather than works of Torah, rewarded with salvation? First, it is available to all humans, not only the Jewish people. Second, neither Gentiles nor Jews have proven acceptable to God; if there is to be salvation, it must be God's unmerited gift. Faith is the acceptance of that gift.

Now I come to the other key word, *retribution*. The Greek noun *antapodoma* and the corresponding verb can be so translated; its general meaning is "repay/repayment." In the New Testament, the verb is found in quotes of Deuteronomy 32:35 (Rom 12:19; Heb 10:20). Romans 11:9 (citing Ps 69:22–23) uses the noun to mean retribution. A more common family of words is *ekdikéo/ekdikësis/ekdikos*. In the theological sense, Romans 12:19 is a key passage: "Beloved, never avenge yourselves, but leave it to the wrath of God; for it is written, 'Vengeance is mine, I will repay, says the Lord.'" In Revelation 6:10 martyrs cry for God's speedy intervention to avenge their blood (cf. Luke 18:7–8).

Jesus is famous for rejecting the poetic formula for retributive justice, "an eye for an eye and a tooth for a tooth" (Matt 5:38) in favor of returning good for evil (5:39–42, also vv. 43–48). Paul says the same in Romans 12:19, but he assures his audience that one does not thereby abandon the demand for justice; God will take care of it. Jesus too must have assumed divine retribution.

While Jesus does not seem to subscribe to any doctrine of rewards and punishments in history, he does identify with the apocalyptic scenario of a last judgment. Being closely allied with John the Baptist, whose primary message was that the present generation was in the midst of the final judgment of God, Jesus warned occasionally of a time of reckoning (e.g., Mark 8:38; Matt 12:41–42/Luke 11:31–32), though he emphasized the great boon of the coming of the Kingdom (e.g., Mark 1:15; Matt 13:44–46). One of the most poignant pronouncements of coming judgment is Jesus's lament over Jerusalem (Matt 23:37–39/Luke 13:34–35), which speaks of the city and the Jewish people in prophetic terms (cf. Jer 15:5–9). Though later interpreted as referring to an event of historical judgment, the saying was understood by the first generation of Christians as eschatological (cf. Mark 13:14–23).

Paul states his belief in a final judgment, "on that day when…God judges the secrets of [humans] by Christ Jesus" (Rom 2:16), substituting a "law written on the heart" as a measure of Gentile righteousness for the revealed law by which Jews live (see Rom 2:12–16). He concludes that no one could stand at the last judgment (Rom 3:20). Fortunately for humankind, God has provided an alternative, namely, justification and salvation by faith.

Paul's soteriology can be interpreted narrowly to mean that only those who have Jesus Christ as their patron will be saved (Rom 10:14–17). Yet, Paul now and then speaks of the salvation of all humans (e.g., Rom 5:18–21; 11:30–36). While these might be harmonized, it is probably better theologically to leave the ambiguity. If 1 Thessalonians 5, 2 Thessalonians, and 1 Corinthians 15 are considered, it seems likely that each

new theological or ecclesiastical issue called forth another scenario of how final judgment brings resolution to the tensions and conflicts of time.

The book of Revelation has numerous scenes of judgment, most often to shatter the power of collective evil. Faithful Christians are protected, though some may die in persecutions. At the very end, there are a series of judgments and probably non-Christians as well as Christians are accepted into the heavenly city. Personal salvation depends upon being among resisters of the demonic rulers of collective history.

Summation. The New Testament shares with the Old, and with Judaism, that those who do evil are to suffer consequences equal to the evil done and those who please the Lord will be rewarded. Judaism highlighted the role of Mosaic Torah in measuring human deeds. Jesus and the Christian authors of the New Testament still think of retribution but separate salvation from obedience to Torah. In its place is a law written on the heart. Paul asserts that no one can please God by righteous deeds; all must rely for salvation on God's gracious gift.

[*See also* Blessings and Curses; Decalogue; Election; Ethics, Biblical; Expiation; Good and Evil; Grace; Justice, Justification, and Righteousness; Redemption; Repentance; Salvation History; *and* Soteriology.]

BIBLIOGRAPHY

Arndt, William F., and F. Wilbur Gingrich. *A Greek–English Lexicon of the New Testament and Other Early Christian Literature.* Chicago: University of Chicago Press, 1957.

Carson, D. A., Peter T. O'Brien, and Mark A. Seifrid, eds. *Justification and Variegated Nomism.* Vol. 1: *The Complexities of Second Temple Judaism.* Grand Rapids, Mich.: Baker Academic, 2001.

Crenshaw, James. *Defending God: Biblical Responses to the Problem of Evil.* Oxford: Oxford University Press, 2005.

Jenni, Ernst, and Claus Westermann. *Theological Lexicon of the Old Testament.* 3 vols. Translated by Mark Biddle. Peabody, Mass.: Hendrickson, 1997.

Miller, Patrick D., Jr. *Sin and Judgment in the Prophets: A Stylistic and Theological Analysis.* Society of Biblical Literature Monograph Series 27. Atlanta: Scholars Press, 1982.

Patrick, Dale. *Redeeming Judgment.* Eugene, Ore.: Pick-wick, 2012.

Penchansky, David. *What Rough Beast? Images of God in the Hebrew Bible.* Louisville, Ky.: Westminster John Knox, 1999.

Sanders, E. P. *Paul and Palestinian Judaism: A Comparison of Patterns of Religion.* Philadelphia: Fortress, 1977.

Travis, Stephen. *Christ and the Judgment of God: The Limits of Divine Retribution in the New Testament.* Carlisle, U.K.: Paternoster; Peabody, Mass.: Hendrickson, 2009.

Yinger, Kent F. *Paul, Judaism, and Judgment According to Deeds.* Society of New Testament Monograph Series 105. Cambridge, U.K.: Cambridge University Press, 1999.

Dale Patrick

RIGHTEOUSNESS

See Justice, Justification, and Righteousness.

ROMANS

See Pauline Letters.

RUTH

See Megillot.

S

SABBATH

See Festivals and Holy Days.

SACRIFICE AND OFFERINGS

Even a cursory reading of both the Hebrew Bible and the New Testament underlines the importance of sacrifices and offerings in the biblical world. However, historically, exegetes and theologians have often struggled to understand the underlying rationale of ritual activities and prescriptions related to sacrifices and offerings because of two competing approaches: either scholars focused exclusively on the origins and *Sitz im Leben* ("life setting") of sacrifices and their "textuality" or, highly influenced by social studies and anthropology, they succumbed to the temptation to search for the grand rationale of sacrificial activity in religion per se, not paying sufficient attention to the details and nuances of biblical sacrifices and offerings. In order to avoid the pitfalls of the two extremes, this entry first situates sacrifices and offerings within the larger context of the religious worldview (or universe) of biblical religious activity, followed by a brief introduction to individual sacrificial types and their significance and meaning within the temple economy. Following this, the important innerbiblical prophetic critique of sacrifices and offerings will be revisited

as well as the New Testament's transformation of this highly significant ritual activity. The next section focuses upon the later extrabiblical reception within Judaism (e.g., at Qumran), early Christianity, as well as subsequent historical periods. Finally, the significance of sacrifices and offerings for a biblical theology is highlighted and their relevance for contemporary theology and culture discussed.

Sacrifices/Offerings, Ritual, and Biblical Theology. Sacrifices and offerings lie at the very heart of ritual activity, yet ritual is not limited to only these activities. The late twentieth and early twenty-first centuries have witnessed significant cross-fertilization between social science research and biblical studies. Ritual theory has informed numerous studies dealing with biblical ritual. Insights from these "exchanges" have influenced the thinking about sacrifices and offerings in the Bible, including the importance of carefully considering key elements of ritual (such as space, time, action, participants, objects, sequence, language, and sound) without overlooking the larger issue of ritual meanings or dimensions that undergird every ritual activity. Unfortunately, scholars influenced by Wellhausen (in the field of biblical studies) or Robertson Smith (in the area of religious studies) have often considered sacrifice an early and primitive stage in the evolution of religious thought and activity. In addition to overly evolutionist perspectives, reductionism focusing upon one model or theory represents another problematic aspect discussed in current scholarship. Interestingly, Girard's extremely influential model relied heavily on evolutionist underpinnings. Girard's focus on primal violence led him to interpret sacrifice as the transformation of the instinct of violence; this transformation then is a community's way of deflecting its own violent instincts on someone (mostly an animal) who becomes the scapegoat. Other scholars (e.g., Burkert, 1983) have suggested other anthropological models for the study of biblical sacrifice in order to discover the interpretational key that would unlock this ritual practice as noted in the texts of both the Hebrew Bible and the New Testament, yet none of these models has proven the one-for-all key to unlock the significance and meaning of sacrifice and offerings.

Dimensions such as gift giving, feeding of the gods, substitution, expiation, restoration of community or fellowship following the break in a relationship, restoring the right order of the world, or a symbolic system of imitating God along the lines of rules that are similar to biblical purity concerns and involving the divine presence are some of the suggested rationales of sacrifices and offerings. However, considering the wide range of linguistic expressions (i.e., terminology), vastly differing literary and historical contexts, an increasing appreciation of the complexity of ritual and its communicative functions, and the conscious decision to avoid reductionism, it seems more appropriate to describe a plethora of key elements of biblical sacrifice and offerings instead of searching for *the* overarching model or theory. Before attempting this descriptive task, however, it is important to consider the complex relationship between ritual and biblical theology, especially in view of the "textuality" of the biblical data. Anthropologists would affirm a close link between ritual activity and the worldview and thinking about the divine of a particular people. Utilizing the mainstay of fieldwork (including observation, interviews, and possibly even participation), they would argue for a likely link between practice and theology/ideology. Regrettably, in the past, biblical theologians have often ignored biblical ritual (including often biblical law) as a valid source of information regarding Israel's theology.

The often complex literary history—supposed and real—of a particular corpus and the repetitive nature of ritual texts have been major reasons for this neglect. Yet, what is done in worship and cult events (including sacrifices and offerings) is often more important than what is said. Action speaks louder than words; careful attention to the details of biblical ritual will significantly benefit the task of writing a comprehensive biblical theology.

Sacrifices and offerings were a common staple of religious expression in all ancient cultures inhabiting the Levant (including Egypt, Palestine, Syria, Anatolia, and Mesopotamia). Their existence is reflected in the pictorial and—not always as clear but definitely present—in the archaeological record (Porter and Schwartz, 2013). Offerings sought to establish or maintain communication with the deity and were often linked to specific times in the calendar (such as the Day of Atonement ritual in Leviticus 16 or the Akītu festival in Babylon) or were part of the strategy to respond to a specific crisis. They could occur in both a public and a private setting, as illustrated by the existence of incense altars, libation vessels, or libation pits in private homes in the material culture of the Levant. Good illustrations of this family religion activity are the abbreviated altar construction notices in Genesis 12:7, 8; 13:18; 22:9–10; 26:25, pointing to a more complex and elaborate sacrificial ritual involving purposeful communication with the covenant deity in the context of a clan or family. This description of patriarchal family religion in Genesis clearly illustrates family-centered sacrificial activities and introduces the reader to the wide spectrum of Hebrew sacrificial activity and terminology.

Sacrificial/Offering Types and Functions in the Hebrew Bible. A significant number of different terms are used in Hebrew and Greek to mark a sacrifice or offering. Some of the terms (e.g., *nesek*, "libation," and *minḥâ*, "grain offering") point to nonbloody offerings involving animals, vegetables, or fluids. In the following, the terms marking sacrifice or offering will be briefly introduced. The first term, linked to an offering, to appear in Genesis is *minḥâ*, "grain offering" or "offering per se." In Genesis 4:4–5 *minḥâ* is used to describe both an animal offering as well as the offering of produce. Leviticus 2:13 and 23:13, 18 describe a grain offering, which appears to be a more generic term for an offering (cf. Ezek 45:17; Isa 57:6; but 1 Sam 2:17 referring to an animal offering). The term *zebaḥ*, "sacrifice," appears repeatedly in the patriarchal narratives (Gen 31:54; 46:1). The verbal form is used constantly in the plague narrative (Exod 3—10) in the dialogue between Moses and Pharaoh that provided the rationale for Israel's release: the people had to go into the desert to "sacrifice" to Yahweh (e.g., Exod 5:3). The Passover sacrifice is called a *zebaḥ pesaḥ* (Exod 12:27), even though it appears as if *pesaḥ* represents the larger expression in most instances (Exod 12:21).

Another term, *šělāmîm*, "peace offering" or "fellowship offering," can occur with or without the generic *zebaḥ* (Exod 29:28; Lev 3:1). *Šělāmîm* appears also with *ʿōlâ*, often in public contexts involving the larger community (e.g., Exod 20:24; 24:5; 32:6; Josh 8:31; Judg 20:26). Exodus 24:5–8 describes how Moses sprinkled half of the blood of a combined *šělāmîm* and *ʿōlâ* offering upon the people—most likely to bind the people to the altar (where the other half of the collected blood had been sprinkled) and to the deity associated with the altar.

The *ʿōlâ*, "burnt offering," was completely burnt on the altar (Lev 7:8) and appears in public contexts involving a national crisis (1 Sam 7:9; 1 Kgs 18:38) or celebration (1 Kgs 9:25). The levitical legislation of the *ʿōlâ* (Lev 1:1–17; 6:8–13) indicates the animal type (male small herd animal or bird, without blemish) and highlights the purpose of the offering, namely, *lĕkappēr ʿālāyw*, "to make atonement for him" (Lev 1:4). The laying on of hands pointed to the substitutionary nature of the sacrifice. The blood manipulation subrite involved sprinkling the blood of the slaughtered animal around the altar base. The *ʿōlâ* was the most frequent sacrifice in the list of Israelite festivals (Num 28–29), involving also the daily *tamîd* (Num 28:1–8; cf. 2 Kgs 16:15).

The *ḥaṭṭāʾt* (Lev 4–5) represents another key sacrifice of the Hebrew Bible. Translation of the technical term has varied from "sin offering" to "purification offering." Milgrom's argument for the rendering "purification offering" has resonated with many scholars and is based on the fact that the *ḥaṭṭāʾt* was required in cases of material impurities (e.g., sacrifice for women after childbirth [Lev 12:6], people who had recovered from a skin disease [Lev 14:19] or from bodily discharges [Lev 15:15], people who had come into contact with a corpse [Num 19:14–17]) or in rituals that marked a changed status (e.g., ordination [Lev 8:14–15], the completion of a Nazirite vow [Num 6:11]). However, the specific association with the verb *ḥāṭāʾ*, "to sin," in Leviticus 4:2, 3, 23, 28 clearly describes a dimension beyond purity concerns. Kiuchi (2003) has suggested a different translation of the verb and the noun as "hiding oneself [before God]," which has, however, not garnered many supporters. In view of the diverse contexts of the *ḥaṭṭāʾt*, the best strategy may be to recognize the multivalency of the term and let the specific context determine the exact significance.

The use of the *ḥaṭṭāʾt* during the important Day of Atonement ritual (Lev 16:11–19) specifically indicates removal (or purification) of the sins of Israel, accumulated during the entire year, from the sanctuary. However, throughout the year, the *ḥaṭṭāʾt* removes evil and uncleanness from the offerer (Lev 12:7; 14:20). Finally, the *ḥaṭṭāʾt* marks diverse social strata as the animal that needed to be offered was distinct for different groups (i.e., an anointed priest [Lev 4:3–12], the congregation [Lev 4:13–21], a prince or tribal leader [Lev 4:22–26], and a common Israelite [Lev 4:27–35]). As was the case with the *ʿōlâ*, the *ḥaṭṭāʾt* often appears in conjunction with other offerings.

The *ʾāšām*, "reparation offering" or "guilt offering," involved not only a sacrifice but also the payment of a 20 percent penalty (Lev 5:16). The *ʾāšām* was only effective for unintentional sins (Lev 5:15), an important element that characterizes the entire Israelite sacrificial system: only unintentional sin could be atoned for by a sacrifice (Num 15:15–29, but note v. 30). The horizontal dimension of the sin or trespass, as well as the economic penalty included in addition to the cost of the sacrificial animal, underline the close integration of the sacrificial system into the ethos and larger tapestry of Israelite society.

The *nesek*, "libation offering," appears in patriarchal narratives and was not restricted to the sanctuary/temple (Gen 35:14, yet note that the narrative describing a similar activity in 28:18 utilizes a different term). The *nesek* appears repeatedly in offering lists (Lev 23; Num 28–29) for specific Israelite festivals. Interestingly, Israel's prophets include repeated references to libations in their critique of idolatrous cult practices (Jer 7:18; 19:13; 32:29; Ezek 20:28). Liquids played an important role in the ritual and cult of the Hebrew Bible. They were used to wash, bathe, purify, rinse, clean, swab, dip, soak, scrub, scour, anoint, smear, rub, or daub ritual participants, objects, or locations—typically in public settings. The pouring or smearing of a costly liquid (such as scented oil) before a deity often leveled the playing field (e.g., Lev 8:6–8 describes how both the altar and the priestly family are anointed using the same oil mixture) and indicated commitment and surrender, marked by deliberate wastefulness. Others have suggested that the libation (which often preceded other sacrifices) functioned as an "entrance fee" into the presence of the deity. The significant number of libation vessels or other utensils used in libation offerings in the material culture of Palestine during the Late Bronze and Iron Ages provides a helpful backdrop for the biblical data.

The final term that will be briefly discussed here does not describe a particular sacrificial type but rather focuses upon the modus operandi. The *qĕṭôrâ*, "incense," emphasized both the content and the manner of presenting it (Deut 33:10; 1 Sam 2:28). The verbal form often marks the burning (or "going up in smoke") of some parts of the sacrificial animal (e.g., Exod 28:13; Lev 1:9, 13, 15, 17). However, the *qĕṭôrâ* as an offering type was specifically connected to the altar of incense offering (Exod 30:1–10), providing a strong smell in the holy place of the sanctuary. It required the exclusive use of a special mixture of ingredients (Exod 30:34–38), making it "Yahweh's smell." The successful "turning into smoke" of sacrificial offerings was often described with the formulaic expression *lĕrêaḥ nîḥōaḥ*, "for a pleasing smell" or a "soothing aroma." The completion phrase is found in connection with the *ʿōlâ* (Exod 29:18, 41; Lev 1:9), *qorbān* (or "grain offering"; Lev 2:2, 9, 12; 6:8), *šĕlāmîm* (Lev 3:5, 16; 17:6), *nesek* (Num 15:7, 10, 13, 14; 28:24), and once with *ḥaṭṭāʾt* (Lev 4:31). The anthropomorphic metaphor suggests the notion of establishing a relation with the deity and always appears to mark the successful completion of the ritual—as commanded by Yahweh (see esp. Lev 8:21, where the completion formula is explicitly linked to the *lĕrêaḥ nîḥōaḥ* formula). Obedience to divine prescription results in divine recognition and acceptance of the offering. Notably, only male sacrificial animals were considered appropriate (Lev 1:3, 10; 4:23) for the *ʿōlâ* and the *ḥaṭṭāʾt*, while the *šĕlāmîm* could include either a male or a female animal (Lev 3:6). Gender relations are reflected in sacrificial requirements, even though most scholars would affirm that women could also participate in sacrificial rites.

Later Reception. The following section will highlight the prophetic critique of sacrifices and offerings within the Hebrew Bible, its interpretation in intertestamental Judaism, as well as the New Testament appropriation and adaptation of sacrificial practice and imagery.

Prophetic critique of sacrifice/offerings. Israel's prophets, at times, interacted critically with sacrificial rituals, suggesting (at minimum) the common practice of these rituals or their popular recognition. Some of these critiques decried the incongruence of ritual and ethics, juxtapositioning offerings and sacrifices with obedience (1 Sam 15:22). Samuel, representing both prophetic and priestly functions (e.g., 1 Sam 7:17; 9:12–13; 16:1–5), accuses King Saul of putting ritual performance over obedience to explicit divine commands. Samuel's critique is not directed against ritual per se but rather against Saul's stepping outside the agreed upon covenant relation. Interestingly, Samuel's symbolic act of tearing the hem off his robe when Saul clings to it (1 Sam 15:27–29) is immediately integrated into the divine message. Tearing rites were well known in Israel and the cultures surrounding Israel.

Hosea's iconic message to northern Israel in the eighth century B.C.E. employs a marriage metaphor for describing Yahweh's relation with his covenant people. The relationship between cult and ethics is highlighted by the use of *ḥesed*, "lovingkindness," and *daʿat*, "knowledge," set in opposition to *zebaḥ* and *ʿōlâ* in Hosea 6:6. The prophetic critique does not primarily contradict prior cultic legislation; rather, it appears to reiterate the basic principles laid down in the Pentateuchal laws and emphasizes discrepancies between the divine ideal and Israel's reality. Amos's dark critique of Israel's cult (Amos 5:21–27) continues the conversation between covenant partners. "*I* hate, *I* despise *your* festivals; and *I* take no delight in *your* solemn assemblies" (Amos 5:21; italics added; cf. Isa 1:15–18) highlights the difference between "yours" and "mine." Amos 5:24 provides the rationale of the divine disgust. The terms *mišpāṭ*, "justice," and *ṣĕdāqâ*, "righteousness," are not evidenced in the horizontal relations of the covenant people.

A distinct element of the prophetic critique can be found in Jeremiah 7:1–7, 21–28 and focuses not only on the well-known indictment of sacrificial practices without ethical repercussions but also on the Jerusalem Temple, or sacred space per se (cf. Jer 7:1–7, 21–28). Jeremiah's message highlights the fact that the right space, even one involving covenant promises (cf. Ps 132:13–14; 2 Sam 7:12–13), will not guarantee safety and salvation. Lifestyle change is required (Jer 7:3). Israel's prophets argued against the sacramental understanding of ritual and sacrificial offerings, disconnected from lifestyle and ethos.

Offerings and sacrifices in intertestamental Judaism. The breadth and width of intertestamental Judaism has been the subject of many volumes. Suffice to say that, instead of suggesting some type of normative Judaism, it would be more accurate to speak of a multiplicity of religious perspectives within Judaism. The discovery of the "sectarian" (in itself a problematic concept since it presupposes a clearly defined mainstream) Dead Sea Scrolls from Khirbet Qumran highlights some of the diversity. Elsewhere, Philo, a prominent member of the thriving Jewish community in Alexandria, Egypt, is well known for his allegorical interpretation of biblical texts and ritual. His hermeneutics suggested that many laws, rituals, and narratives of the Hebrew Bible had a deeper (or second) level of meaning beyond the literal. Apparently, Philo himself went to Jerusalem to "offer up prayers and sacrifices" (*Prov.* 2.64), yet it seems that he spiritualizes the sacrificial temple ritual, arguing that prayer is a superior sacrifice.

The religious community at Khirbet Qumran represents another important strand in the continuum of Jewish traditions in the intertestamental period. Based on analysis of the writings of the community, scholars have noted the "hegemony of ritual" at Qumran (Kugler, 2002). Khirbet Qumran's inhabitants focused particularly upon purity concerns, food preparation and ingestion, and the critical (or even hostile) relationship to the sacrificial ritual of the Jerusalem Temple (1QS IX 3–4; CD VI 11–15). They apparently expected the continued use of burnt and sin offerings in their eschatological perspective (1QM II 5) yet, similar to Philo, seemed to redefine sacrificial practices in terms of worship, prayer, and an ethical lifestyle following (most likely) the laws of the community (1QS IX 4–6). Their strict nonpriestly purity concepts clashed with other Jewish interpretations of the Law that were influenced by Hellenistic philosophy. Ultimately, it was a way of maintaining a particular religious identity in an ever-changing world that challenged basic Jewish concepts. The Qumran texts not only highlight the immense ritual density of life in the community but went, in many areas, beyond the legislation found in the Hebrew Bible. As noted by Bell (1997) and others, ritual intensification can function as a defense mechanism against secularization. Interestingly, a similar tendency can be found in Rabbinic literature which, following the destruction of the Temple in Jerusalem, dedicated an entire order of the Mishnah (i.e., *Qodašim*) to rulings governing sacrifices that could not be offered (because of the lack of temple and altar). Similar to earlier attempts, the sacrificial offering theology of the Hebrew Bible was reinterpreted to include prayer, fasting, good works, and Torah study.

New Testament transformation of sacrifice/offerings. Following the death of Christ, early Christians of (mostly) Jewish origin sought to adapt the basic concepts of Hebrew Bible sacrificial ritual to their changed perspective regarding the Messiah and his sacrifice. Christology and soteriology clearly top the list of inner-Christian conversations during that period, evidenced by the New Testament texts. The birth, ministry, and death of Jesus Christ are framed by the New Testament authors as fulfillment of prophetic texts of the Hebrew Bible. Fulfillment formulas mentioning specific prophets (e.g., Matt 4:14; 8:17; 12:17) or more general intertextual links (e.g., Matt 1:22; 2:15; Luke 18:31; John 13:18) focus particularly upon two important events: the Messiah's birth and death. Jesus is described as the "Lamb of God" in John 1:29, 36; Revelation 5:6; 7:14; 19:19; 22:1, 3, utilizing metaphorical language that clearly points to the sacrificial practice of the Hebrew Bible. The most obvious adaptation of Hebrew Bible sacrificial ritual to the substitutionary death of Jesus (echoing perhaps Isa 53:12) is represented in the Lord's supper texts (Mark 14:22–24; 1 Cor 11:23–25). Its clear link to the Passover celebration highlights the power of ritual innovation, where a known ritual is adapted to a new historical or theological reality. Later discussion in Christianity revolved around the issue of whether the Eucharist was a mere metaphor, a sacrament of sacrifice or a surrogate.

Key terms for sacrifice in New Testament Greek include *thysia* and *prosphora*. Paul beseeches his readers to present their bodies as a *thysian zōsan*, "a living sacrifice" (Rom 12:1), and tells his audience that he himself was being poured out as a drink offering (Phil 2:17). Ephesians 5:2 suggests that Christ's death was an offering and sacrifice (utilizing both key terms) to God for a sweet-smelling aroma, the Greek equivalent of the Hebrew *lĕrêaḥ nîḥōaḥ*, pointing to the successful completion of Jesus's sacrificial mission. By far the largest number of references to sacrifice and offerings can be found in the Epistle to the Hebrews, which focuses upon the high priestly function of Jesus (Heb 7) who is the "guarantee of a better covenant" (Heb 7:22). As a perfect high priest and sacrifice, Jesus does not need sacrifices covering his sins (Heb 7:28). Jesus's high priestly ministry is linked to the heavenly sanctuary that is connected to the divine presence (Heb 8:1–5). The author of Hebrews clearly navigates the Israelite sanctuary with its associated sacrifices and festivals with ease yet emphasizes the "better" (or "more excellent") nature of Jesus's ministry (Heb 8:6). Echoing the important function of blood in the sacrificial cult of the Hebrew Bible (Lev 17:11), Hebrews underlines the cleansing function of blood in the ministry of Jesus, whose

death is a one-time event, capable of accomplishing atonement (Heb 9:22–28). In fact, Hebrews 10:4 goes so far as to state that the blood of sacrificial animals in the Israelite cult could not really remove sin, a feat that could only be accomplished by the atoning death of Jesus (Heb 10:10).

Paul's reference to *hilastērion*, "propitiation," emphasizes the substitutionary element that is also present in the sacrificial cult of the Hebrew Bible (Rom 3:25–26). Interestingly, the close link to God's righteousness in Romans 3:25 connects to the important theodicy motif in the Day of Atonement ritual noted by Gane (2005). Substitution and expiation are also expressed by *hilasmos* (1 John 2:2; 4:10; cf. 2 Cor 5:21) and are associated with blood imagery (1 John 1:7).

In summary, the New Testament authors were not only familiar with the sacrificial/offering practices of the Hebrew Bible cult; they, in line with other Jewish groups during the intertestamental period, reinterpreted them. They clearly understood them as pointing to Jesus, the suffering Messiah, whose death, resurrection, and heavenly high priestly functions are described using language that is deeply rooted in the language and conceptual world of the Hebrew Bible. The close link to familiar ritual terminology and concepts suggests a proximity to the larger world of first-century B.C.E. Judaism. While the early Christian church recognized the completeness of Christ's substitutionary death in terms of the typological relationship between Hebrew Bible sacrificial systems (including altar, sanctuary, cult personnel, and cultic times/festivals), they remained rooted in the language and text of the Hebrew Bible and considered Christ's sacrifice the fulfillment of Messianic references found in the Hebrew Bible (Isa 53).

Postbiblical Reception. Sacrifice and offerings continued to be important topics in postbiblical periods because of their marked presence in the biblical text. The division adopted in this entry is primarily for the purpose of organization and does not suggest importance or relevance.

Patristic Christianity. Early Christianity often found itself in a tight spot between two worlds. A disdain for Judaism, as well as its problematic standing within the Roman Empire (esp. following the Jewish revolt in 73 C.E.), caused some church fathers to adopt an "anti-Jewish" stance, often leading to marked criticism of the Jewish temple economy (including sacrifices). Their metaphorical use of sacrificial terminology undermined any literal significance but marked an important theological process of reinterpretation, already present in early New Testament writings. Instead of literal sacrifices, offered in a specific geographical location, offering language is adopted to prayer, giving alms, fasting, financial support of the poor, or even martyrdom. At the same time, Greek philosophers begin to engage Christian leaders, leading to an even greater emphasis upon spiritualized "offerings"—"liberating" the Christian God from the notion of having to rely on gifts. Origen's allegorical method provided a way of transforming Hebrew Bible ritual or sacrificial texts directly to his immediate context and time (e.g., *Hom. Exod.* and *Hom. Lev.*). His hermeneutics does not aim at discovering the literal meaning of a specific text from the Hebrew Bible (which he read in the Greek of the Septuagint) but rather at edifying his Christian readers and jumping effortlessly from keywords to contemporary theological issues.

Medieval Christianity. By the seventh or eighth century C.E. Christianity had become the dominant religion in what used to be the Roman Empire. Monasticism was on the rise and scholars in these monasteries produced important texts that help us understand their hermeneutical and theological methods. One of the more important authors was the Venerable Bede from Northumbria, England. Utilizing the typical monastic *lectio divina* ("divine reading"), Bede spends significant space on explaining the function and meaning of the altar of burnt offerings and its vessels (*On the Tabernacle* 2.11). Every element of the ritual is applied to the individual Christian (e.g., the altar designates the "heart of the elect"). Medieval hermeneutics tended to atomize and randomly apply biblical text, without providing appropriate exegetical clues. For another important representative of medieval Christianity Anselm of Canterbury sacrifice (or Latin *sacrificium*) was a clear cipher for the Eucharist and for the offering of prayer and a contrite heart (*Epistles* 10, 65). The celebration

of the mass thus became the focal point of Christian worship and theology.

Protestantism. The Reformation was not only an important theological or social movement; it meant, above all, a hermeneutical sea change that challenged the importance of tradition over against *sola scriptura*. The translation of the biblical text in the vernacular in Germany, France, and England served as impetus and invitation to return to the Word. "Righteousness by faith" and the "priesthood of all believers" were rallying cries of the Protestant Reformation. In consequence, ritual (as the sacramental understanding of the Eucharist and the doctrine of transubstantiation) was considered unsympathetically, based in a deep-seated suspicion that wondered about righteousness by works in biblical texts emphasizing biblical law. This critical attitude toward all things ritual is still reflected in later Protestant scholarship, as well as in contemporary evangelical traditions (Klingbeil, 2007).

Critical scholarship. As already noted, Wellhausen's influential work grew out of a desire to describe the theological and historical development of Israel's religion. His emphasis on distinct sources and his decisions regarding the dating of biblical texts led him to characterize the Jewish religion as a decline from spontaneous and free worship in an early age to a highly regulated expression of religion (including sacrifice) that smothered true spirituality. Wellhausen's Protestant heritage may have led him to entertain such a negative notion of ritual per se, and this evolutionist paradigm has continued to inform Pentateuchal scholarship, even though it should be noted that current academic interest in ritual has opened the door for fruitful dialogue with anthropology and sociology, highlighting the complexity of ritual and its power to unite groups of people and give them an identity.

Sacrifice in Biblical Theology and Contemporary Culture. Both biblical theology and contemporary culture have at times struggled with sacrificial biblical ritual, for different reasons. Moderns and postmoderns relate differently to ritual as a whole and, more specifically, sacrifice. Some consider the sacrificial practices of the Hebrew Bible barbaric, bloody, boring, too complex, or simply irrelevant. Others wonder about the very essence of addressing through a physical ritual activity a divine being whose existence modern science cannot verify. Yet, further reflection reminds us of our own public rituals (just consider the Super Bowl in American football) and the need to decipher ritual and sacrificial activity appropriately (Bergen, 2005).

As already noted, most biblical theologians have long been focusing upon prophetic or wisdom literature instead of law or ritual and have highlighted the difference between the history of Israelite religion and biblical theology. While attempts at writing a more comprehensive biblical theology that pays attention to all types of genres and texts are encouraging, the "omnipresence" of sacrificial language and metaphors in both the Hebrew Bible and the New Testament clues the careful reader of the canonical text of the Bible to its conceptual importance. Sacrifice and offering represented a prime means of the human desire to "communicate" with the divine. At times, a sacrifice was meant to represent a gift; in other contexts the clear substitutionary notion involved in atonement reminds us of its role in taking care of the sin problem separating erring humans from a holy God. Sacrifice and offerings not only leveled the playing field in the Hebrew Bible (everybody had to offer a sacrifice when he or she sinned; the Day of Atonement affected the entire community) but also represented an important element of theodicy—God's vindication as the forgiver within the larger cosmos of his law. The transferral of the guilt and "stain" of Israel's sins upon the Azazel goat (Lev 16:20–22), representing the originator of sin, during the key Day of Atonement ritual was a yearly reminder to Israelites that the sin problem required more than the shedding of blood—it needed an ultimate purification and outside resolution.

Sacrificial activity, however, not only involved specific ritual action pointing to important theological concepts; the complex and prolific prescription of sacrificial law represented also an important rhetorical tool used to communicate divinely authorized texts (Watts, 2007). Thus, ritual and rhetoric went hand in hand in a process whose results we now recognize as canon.

Ultimately, sacrifice and offerings speak of the human need to reach out to the divine. The clear identification of Jesus as the "Lamb of God, taking away the sin of the world" (John 1:29) changes the equation dramatically. The New Testament's reuse of familiar sacrificial terminology and concepts inverts the familiar direction of humans seeking to connect to heaven (or the divine). Rather, New Testament authors highlight the complete opposite. It was really the Son of God who ultimately carried the sins of the world, denoting divine salvation and restoration of a broken relationship. This radical recycling of a well-known biblical concept continues to challenge readers and scholars engaging with the biblical text.

[*See also* Forgiveness; Guilt and Innocence; Leviticus and Numbers; Prayer; Priests and Priesthood; *and* Tabernacles, Temples, and Synagogues.]

BIBLIOGRAPHY

Anderson, Gary A. *Sacrifices and Offerings in Ancient Israel: Studies in Their Social and Political Importance.* Harvard Semitic Museum 41. Atlanta: Scholars Press, 1987.

Beckwith, Roger T., and Martin J. Selman, eds. *Sacrifice in the Bible.* Grand Rapids, Mich.: Baker Book House, 1995.

Bell, Catherine. *Ritual: Perspectives and Dimensions.* Oxford: Oxford University Press, 1997.

Bergen, Wesley J. *Reading Ritual: Leviticus in Postmodern Culture.* Journal for the Study of the Old Testament, Supplement Series 417. London: T&T Clark, 2005.

Burkert, Walter. *Homo necans: The Anthropology of Ancient Greek Sacrificial Ritual and Myth.* Translated by Peter Bing. Berkeley: University of California Press, 1983.

Douglas, Mary. *Leviticus as Literature.* Oxford: Oxford University Press, 1999.

Eberhart, Christian A., ed. *Ritual and Metaphor: Sacrifice in the Bible.* Society of Biblical Literature Resources for Biblical Studies 68. Atlanta: Society of Biblical Literature, 2011.

Gane, Roy E. *Cult and Character: Purification Offerings, Day of Atonement, and Theodicy.* Winona Lake, Ind.: Eisenbrauns, 2005.

Gilders, William K. *Blood Ritual in the Hebrew Bible: Meaning and Power.* Baltimore: Johns Hopkins University Press, 2004.

Girard, René. *Violence and the Sacred.* Baltimore: Johns Hopkins University Press, 1977.

Kiuchi, Nobuyoshi. *A Study of Ḥāṭāʾ and Ḥaṭṭāʾt in Leviticus 4–5.* Forschungen zum Alten Testament 2.2. Tübingen, Germany: Mohr Siebeck, 2003.

Klawans, Jonathan. *Purity, Sacrifice, and the Temple: Symbolism and Supersessionism in the Study of Ancient Judaism.* Oxford: Oxford University Press, 2006.

Klingbeil, Gerald A. *Bridging the Gap: Ritual and Ritual Texts in the Bible.* Bulletin for Biblical Research Supplements 1. Winona Lake, Ind.: Eisenbrauns, 2007.

Kügler, Joachim, ed. *Die Macht der Nase: Zur religiösen Bedeutung des Duftes.* Stuttgarter Bibelstudien 187. Stuttgart: Verlag Katholisches Bibelwerk, 2000.

Kugler, Robert A. "Making All Experience Religious: The Hegemony of Ritual at Qumran." *Journal for the Study of Judaism* 33 (2002): 131–152.

Milgrom, Jacob. *Leviticus 1–16.* Anchor Bible 3. New York: Doubleday, 1991.

Petropoulou, Maria-Zoe. *Animal Sacrifice in Ancient Greek Religion, Judaism, and Christianity, 100 BC to AD 200.* Oxford Classical Monographs. Oxford: Oxford University Press, 2008.

Porter, Anne, and Glenn M. Schwartz, eds. *Sacred Killing: The Archaeology of Sacrifice in the Ancient Near East.* Winona Lake, Ind.: Eisenbrauns, 2013.

Rodríguez, Ángel Manuel. *Substitution in the Hebrew Cultus and in Cultic-Related Texts.* Andrews University Seminary Doctoral Dissertation Series 3. Berrien Springs, Mich.: Andrews University Press, 1979.

Watts, James W. *Ritual and Rhetoric in Leviticus: From Sacrifice to Scripture.* Cambridge, U.K.: Cambridge University Press, 2007.

Wright Knust, Jennifer, and Zsuzsanna Várhelyi, eds. *Ancient Mediterranean Sacrifice.* Oxford: Oxford University Press, 2011.

Gerald A. Klingbeil

SALVATION HISTORY

The term "salvation history" (Ger *Heilsgeschichte*)—alternatively translated as "revelation history" or "revelation in history"—refers to an approach to biblical theology that focuses on particular "saving acts" or "revelatory acts" in the history of Israel or the early Christian community. Central to this view is a series of connected, intentional actions by which God reveals his nature and covenantal relationship to humanity. In the Old Testament these acts include Israel's election, the Exodus, covenant, exile, and restoration. In the New Testament the critical events are Jesus Christ's life and ministry, his death and resurrection, the church's formation, and the expansion of Christian faith to all peoples. In both testaments large narratives or narrative units carry the most weight. The main proponents of this view were G. Ernest Wright, Gerhard von Rad, and Oscar Cullmann.

Salvation History and the Biblical Theology Movement. Salvation history is best understood as part of the biblical theology movement of the mid-twentieth century, which itself was in part a reaction against earlier liberal theologies and the narrowly descriptive task of historical criticism. The biblical theology movement arose alongside a renewed interest in theology occasioned by the various impulses of neo-orthodoxy. Salvation history identified God's *activity* in critical events of faith communities as the "kernel" of theological reflection and interpretation.

G. Ernest Wright. Wright (1952) took issue with those who saw the focus of biblical theology on God's words. Instead, he understood God's self-revelation in Israel's history as central to Old Testament theology. He pointed to three key elements: (1) "The Old Testament betrays a peculiar attention to history and to historical traditions as the primary sphere in which God reveals himself" (p. 55); (2) God chose a people, first through Abraham and subsequently through Moses, by whom to accomplish God's purposes; and (3) that election was clarified by means of a covenant ceremony at Sinai, which presented legal expectations of Israel. Wright regarded Jesus's ministry and death as the central element of the New Testament, connected to the Old Testament by means of a carefully controlled typology.

Gerhard von Rad. In what many consider the pre-eminent Old Testament theology for the latter half of the twentieth century, von Rad (1962) developed a "consistently *heilsgeschichtlich* approach" (Barr, 1999, p. 32). Rejecting a systematic description of Israel's faith, von Rad focused instead on the formative influence of certain events on Israel's reflection on its relationship with God. While focusing on the narrative of God's "saving events," von Rad critically viewed the ways in which traditions about these events developed over time. For him, Israel developed its unique self-consciousness, especially in opposition to Canaanite religions, through normative confessions ("credos") closely linked to covenantal or liturgical acts. This focus on the interpretation of the events in successive confessional situations allowed for an emphasis on both God's activity and the growth in traditions over time. Based on the historical–critical methods of scholarship, von Rad's interest lay in the dynamic ways by which Israel reused traditional materials to assert a coherent theological self-definition.

Oscar Cullmann. For Cullmann (1951–1967), a key feature of the Bible's presentation of God's intervention in human activity is a series of events, organized in a linear progression across time. He argued that this linear concept of redemptive time stood in sharp contrast to a Hellenistic view of time that is circular or repetitive. For Cullmann, the Christ-event—Jesus's life, death, and resurrection—constitutes the central historical fact that forces a new conceptualization of how God acts with humanity. All biblical history is redemptive history because it both moves toward, and lays a foundation for, the Christ-event; from that event salvation history then flows out, influencing subsequent actions within the church.

This progressive movement in history is similar to the Jewish concept of history, but Cullmann asserts that the Christ-event transforms a purely future orientation to one in which history has reached its culmination. Christ has become the critical point—the midpoint—of all time: all subsequent events are reinterpreted in terms of that singular event. As a result, the New Testament regards all time as having reached its culmination in Christ. Future expectation is not thereby ended but transformed: Christians live now in an intermediate period. Opposing a purely existential view of the Christ-event or a purely eschatological view, Cullmann argued that "eternity" is not something outside of time but is, rather, the full comprehension of that historical time in which God works redemptively.

While each of these examples of a salvation-history approach to biblical theology has unique features, some common elements bind them together.

1. All share a perception that God interacts with humans primarily through events or actions. Usually these are summarized in a short list of key turning points in Israel's history or in the history of Jesus and the church.

2. All recognize a strong unity across the entire Bible based on God's activity. While the main arguments for salvation history have been made from the perspective of either the Old Testament or the New Testament, Wright, von Rad, and Cullmann agree that the concept of salvation binds the testaments together. All are committed to a larger project of biblical theology.

3. Against many systematic approaches, these scholars share the belief that such theology cannot simply describe elements of Israel or Christianity's faith. Salvation history seeks to understand God's unfolding engagement with the world.

Critiques of Salvation History. There have been numerous critiques of salvation history. Here are some of the most important.

1. The linear recital of "saving events," even if dynamically conceived (von Rad), seems to point to a progression of God's revelation in a series of positive events. But the Bible's historical narrative may also be seen as a story of problems in the elect communities' understanding of God: as much *unheilsgeschichte* as *heilsgeschichte*. This critique raises questions about how useful the concept of salvation history is for a unified theology of the Bible. In particular, Ulrich Luz (1968) argues that Paul's view of history is primarily one of faithlessness, containing only occasional indications of positive revelation in history. Luz's view, however, primarily adopts the perspective of human action and reception, not of God's activity.

2. Perhaps the most serious questions about salvation history concern the precise role that historicity and historical reconstruction should play in theology. It has been suggested that Wright, and perhaps Cullmann, operated with a naive or innocent view of the relationship between the biblical narrative and history. For both scholars, the problem of

historical reconstruction was not seriously engaged. This is not surprising, given the relationship of salvation history to the biblical theology movement and the latter's origination as a reaction against the excesses of the historical–critical method. Von Rad's approach to the biblical text is better nuanced, acknowledging the ongoing process of traditioning: Israel's core confessions were reworked in subsequent historical situations.

But how secure is our understanding of what actually happened? Since the core events contained in both Wright's and von Rad's "recitals" of tradition come from early in Israel's history, any reconstruction of what happened during Israel's formative period is less than secure. The critical period of the Exodus and conquest, usually considered central in salvation history, is contested by historians. What happens to "salvation in history" if historical confirmation remains uncertain or if there is evidence that undermines one or another event? In the New Testament "the acts of God" are sketched in a minimal way. Historical Jesus research offers support for the main outlines of the Christ-event. But how dependent is the theological enterprise on the teaching of Jesus or the historicity of Acts? At issue is whether a theology based on history is dependent on factual reconstruction.

3. Gilkey (1961) challenged the use of texts in constructing salvation history, arguing that biblical theologians were not consistent in how they used evidence of "revelation by the special activity of God." How do proponents of salvation history imagine that God speaks or acts: audibly and physically, or metaphorically? Rather than offering examples of God's self-revelation by direct actions, salvation historians have often drawn on naturalistic explanations for "what God actually does": acts subsequently understood to be mighty acts. Gilkey argues that this proposal becomes circular or ontologically confused: Does revelation come through the events themselves, or does it rest only on the events' faithful interpretation, without which God's activity could not be so recognized? If events can be interpreted only through the prism of a prior understanding of God's nature, then such acts are not revelatory but in fact subjective.

4. Equally perplexing is the nature of history as a literary activity. Even if various biblical documents are intended to be "historical," what is "history" and how is it constructed? Postmodern historians have emphasized that authorial subjectivity and subjective interpretation of events are essential aspects of historiography. Historical writing, like all discourse, is linguistic and inherently relativized. Anticipating postmodern objections to a foundationalist approach to biblical history, Barr argued that the "long narrative corpus of the Old Testament seems…to merit the title of story rather than history" (1976b, p. 1). To use Frei's term, biblical narrative is not historical but "history-like" (1974).

5. Cullmann's emphasis on linear time, especially as reflective of a uniquely "Hebraic" perspective, has suffered extensive criticism. Barr (1961, pp. 11–20) raised serious questions about this entire characterization of time and history, with respect to both Hebrew and Greek thought. Barr argued that such proposals, based on an inadequate understanding of how languages work, were focused too narrowly on individual words rather than larger semantic units. Barr's semantic argument undermined the distinguishing feature of biblical history asserted by Cullmann.

6. A fundamental challenge for any biblical theology is the ability of its organizing principle to explain the coherence among the Bible's disparate documents and genres. Many have questioned the degree to which salvation history meets this challenge. For example, the emphasis on a basic narrative of God's actions on behalf of Israel tends to minimize some important Old Testament material: it is difficult to fit wisdom literature into a salvation-history framework. Although Sirach (ca. 200 B.C.E.) offers historical examples of wise people, wisdom in general emphasizes nonhistorical explanations of humanity's relationship with God. Likewise, creation and law are largely left out of a salvation-history approach to theology.

Similar concerns may be raised of salvation history's scope in the New Testament. Because this approach focuses primarily on narrated events, priority is given to the Gospels and Acts. Does salvation history do justice to the concerns expressed in the Pauline and Catholic Epistles? While they certainly reflect on Jesus and the kerygma about his ministry, death, and resurrection, the epistles develop interests and themes quite distinct from the Gospels' core narrative. How well does salvation history address Paul's concern for inclusion of Gentiles, questions about the law's value, or ecclesiological concerns such as the nature of the church and its unity? Luke–Acts has strongly influenced constructions of salvation history in the New Testament; yet many contend that precisely this construction, along with that in the Pastoral letters, represents a later, "early catholic" approach that is in fundamental tension with Paul and an earlier Gospel like Mark.

7. Does the salvation-historical approach sufficiently address the hermeneutical need of biblical theology to bridge the gap, distinguished by Stendahl (1962, pp. 421–422), from descriptive explanation of the text to making normative sense of it for modern readers? Stendahl critiqued many such approaches for not treating seriously the descriptive task but granted that Cullman's biblical theology well described how the categories of time and history are central to the world in which the New Testament arose. Stendahl, nevertheless, believed that Cullmann and the salvation-historical approach in general tended to remain locked within the descriptive task, without serious reflection on what their descriptive observations might mean for a normative understanding of God's activity in the Bible.

A Possible Future for Salvation History. Because of many of the preceding critiques, the concept of salvation history has fallen from favor in current biblical theology. But perhaps there is room to consider some renewed role for this concept in the Bible's own project of describing God's relationship with humanity.

It can certainly be asserted that, taken as a whole, the Old Testament does construct a "history-like" narrative that traces God's involvement with humanity: beginning with creation, God is shown as interacting first with the patriarchs, then with Israel in the Exodus and conquest, and later with its development as a nation-state. This narrative continues to the Exile, followed by the nation's restoration. Thus, there is a narrative arc that encompasses the various materials of the Torah, the Deuteronomistic history, the Chronicler, and Ezra–Nehemiah. The Old Testament offers a story of God's election of a specific people, with covenantal initiatives that progressively impose responsibilities on God's chosen people. By engaging the failures of covenantal obedience and speaking to renewed covenantal relationships, the prophets also participate in this grand narrative arc.

The "actions" of election, making covenant, judgment, and covenant renewal are the core elements in the story of God's engagement with Israel. Features of this narrative arc can be seen in repeated confessions (von Rad's "credos"), including a late instance in Nehemiah 9 that reaches back to creation and extends the recital of Israel's vicissitudes through exile and return. Various prophetic critiques and interpretations of events during their lifetimes adopt this "history-like" perspective on God's reaction to Israel's observance of covenantal requirements.

In a similar way, the New Testament's fourfold gospel—despite differences in details, timelines, and theological emphases—testifies to the centrality of the narrative of Jesus's life, death, and resurrection. The centrality of this narrative arc is emphasized in Acts, which claims a direct "continuation" of that narrative (Acts 1:1–4), and can also be found in Paul's letters and the Catholic Epistles, which demonstrate that believing communities continued to reflect on the core events of the Christ-event.

A crucial element in both history and narrative is temporal progression. Events are given importance within a temporal framework, sequences of events suggest patterns and trajectories, and characters develop across time. We make sense of events and characters within "history-like," narrative contexts. This temporal progression in the Bible points to a future hope but also engages the past through interpretation and comparison as a means of creating meaning. Old Testament narratives often reflect on God's involvement in past events as a way of understanding current events; they also anticipate God's continued future involvement. Similarly, the New Testament links itself extensively back to the Old Testament, tracing temporal patterns and events that interpret Jesus; the New Testament looks forward as well so that a "historical" or "narrative" pattern is built into its expectation of continued activity. This temporal progression is central to a theology of the Bible.

Is this progression "history," strictly speaking? The most substantive critiques of salvation history have focused on the difficulty of linking the theology of God's activity with what "actually happened," judged in accordance with modern historiography. Certainly, there are problems here; the use of the term "history" may itself be problematic. Nevertheless, central to the biblical "story" are the acts of God on behalf of his people. As Hengel (2003) notes, God's actions in history are not obvious at the time: God is a *deus absconditus*. These "mighty acts" are not of the sort that can be historically objectified; rather, they are recognized as God's doing, viewed through the eyes of faith. But they are central to the Bible's theology.

In some ways a salvation-history model may still inform biblical theology. First, recognition of the Bible's essentially narrative nature points to the importance of narrative approaches to theology. Continued work on how narratives construct meaning, by means of plot or character development, may enhance this perspective. Focusing on a "history-like" narrative instead of on "history" might also address Gilkey's critique.

Second, postmodern approaches to history, which focus on the essentially subjective construction of narrative histories, serve as a critique of foundationalist approaches to history. On the other hand, many critiques of salvation history (e.g., that it is not truly "historical") have themselves presupposed a foundationalist approach to history. Postmodern critiques may modify the tendency to place too much emphasis, positively or negatively, on historical data, highlighting instead the meaning that historians construct.

Third, the understanding of biblical narratives as "history-like" might be enhanced by attention to the role of "witness" or "testimony" (thus, Schuele's [2008] review of von Rad's theology). The concept of testimony links historical experience and tradition in a way that is not simply descriptive but focuses on the presence or reality of God in the narrative pattern.

Any biblical theology seeks to capture the essence of the Bible's theological core. The diverse nature of the Bible makes that difficult. Salvation history found a means to explore helpfully much of the Bible's central thrust. Perhaps there is a place for continued exploration from this perspective.

[*See also* Allegory and Typology; Apocalypticism; Catholic Epistles; Covenant; Creation; Deuteronomy; Election; Exile and Dislocation; Exodus; Ezra, Nehemiah, and 1 and 2 Chronicles; Genesis; Hermeneutics, Biblical; Luke–Acts; Pauline Letters; Prophets and Prophecy; Redemption; Revelation; Soteriology; Story and Memory; *and* Witness.]

BIBLIOGRAPHY

Barr, James. *The Semantics of Biblical Language*. Oxford: Oxford University Press, 1961.

Barr, James. "Revelation in History." In *The Interpreter's Dictionary of the Bible*, suppl. vol., edited by Keith Crim, pp. 746–749. Nashville, Tenn.: Abingdon, 1976a.

Barr, James. "Story and History in Biblical Theology." *Journal of Religion* 56 (1976b): 1–17.

Barr, James. *The Concept of Biblical Theology: An Old Testament Perspective*. Minneapolis: Fortress, 1999.

Brueggemann, Walter. *Theology of the Old Testament*. Minneapolis: Fortress, 1997.

Bultmann, Rudolf. *Theology of the New Testament*. 2 vols. Translated by K. Grobel. New York: Charles Scribner's Sons, 1951–1955.

Carson, D. A. "Biblical Theology." In *Dictionary of Biblical Criticism and Interpretation*, edited by Stanley E. Porter, pp. 35–41. London: Routledge, 2007.

Childs, Brevard. *Biblical Theology in Crisis*. Philadelphia: Westminster, 1970.

Conzelmann, Hans. *The Theology of St. Luke*. London: Faber and Faber, 1960.

Cullmann, Oscar. *Christ in Time*. London: SCM, 1951.

Cullmann, Oscar. *Salvation in History*. London: SCM, 1967.

Dever, William G. "Biblical Theology and Biblical Archaeology: An Appreciation of G. Ernest Wright." *Harvard Theological Review* 73 (1980): 1–15.

Dunn, James D. G. *Unity and Diversity in the New Testament: An Inquiry into the Character of Earliest Christianity*. Philadelphia: Westminster, 1977.

Dunn, James D. G. *New Testament Theology: An Introduction*. Nashville, Tenn.: Abingdon, 2009.

Frei, Hans. *The Eclipse of Biblical Narrative: A Study in Eighteenth and Nineteenth Century Hermeneutics*. New Haven, Conn.: Yale University Press, 1974.

Gilkey, Langdon. "Cosmology, Ontology and the Travail of Biblical Language." *Journal of Religion* 41 (1961): 194–204.

Hasel, Gerhard F. "The Relationship between Biblical Theology and Systematic Theology." *Trinity Journal* 5 (1984): 113–127.

Hengel, Martin. "'Salvation History': The Truth of Scripture and Modern Theology." In *Reading Texts, Seeking Wisdom*, edited by David F. Ford and Graham Stanton, pp. 229–244. Grand Rapids, Mich.: Eerdmans, 2003.

Hinze, Bradford E. "The End of Salvation History." *Horizons* 18, no. 2 (1991): 227–245.

Kraftchick, Steven J. "Facing Janus: Reviewing the Biblical Theology Movement." In *Biblical Theology: Problems and Perspectives*, edited by Steven J. Kraftchick, Charles D. Myers Jr., and Ben C. Ollenburger. Nashville, Tenn.: Abingdon, 1995.

Luz, Ulrich. *Das Geschichtsverständniss des Paulus*. Munich: Christian Kaiser, 1968.

Mead, James K. *Biblical Theology: Issues, Methods, and Themes*. Louisville, Ky.: Westminster John Knox, 2007.

Miller, Ed L. "Salvation-History: Pannenberg's Critique of Cullmann." *Iliff Review* 37, no. 1 (1980): 21–25.

Morgan, Robert. "Theology (NT)." In *Anchor Bible Dictionary*, edited by David Noel Freedman, Vol. 6, pp. 473–483. New York: Doubleday, 1992.

Perdue, Leo G. *The Collapse of History: Reconstructing Old Testament Theology*. Minneapolis: Augsburg Fortress, 1994.

Rad, Gerhard von. *Old Testament Theology*. 2 vols. Translated by D. M. G. Stalker. New York: Harper & Row, 1962.

Reventlow, H. G. "Theology (Biblical), History of." In *Anchor Bible Dictionary*, edited by David Noel Freedman, Vol. 6, pp. 483–505. New York: Doubleday, 1992.

Schuele, Andreas. "Theology as Witness: Gerhard von Rad's Contribution to the Study of Old Testament Theology." *Interpretation* 62 (2008): 256–267.

Stendahl, Krister. "Biblical Theology, Contemporary." In *Interpreter's Dictionary of the Bible*, edited by G. A. Buttrick, Vol. 1, pp. 418–432. Nashville, Tenn.: Abingdon, 1962.

White, Hayden. *Figural Realism: Studies in the Mimesis Effect*. Baltimore: Johns Hopkins University Press, 1999.

Wright, G. Ernest. *God Who Acts: Biblical Theology as Recital*. London: SCM, 1952.

Wright, N. T. *The New Testament and the People of God*. Minneapolis: Fortress, 1992.

Mark A. Matson

1 AND 2 SAMUEL

See Historical Narratives (Joshua—2 Kings).

SATAN

The name "Satan" derives from the Hebrew noun *śāṭān*, meaning "adversary" or "accuser." In the Hebrew Bible, this term is applied to both human (1 Sam 29:4; 2 Sam 19:23 [EV 22]; 1 Kgs 5:18 [EV 5:4]; 11:14, 23, 25; Ps 109:6) and celestial figures. The term is generally translated *diabolos* (which can also mean "slanderer") in the Septuagint, where unlike the Hebrew, it is often used as a proper noun. In the New Testament, *Diabolos* and the Greek transliteration *Satanas* are used interchangeably of the same celestial figure (see Rev 12:9).

Ancient Near Eastern Background. Two ancient Near Eastern concepts contribute significantly to the developing understanding of Satan. First, the widespread ancient Near Eastern concept of the divine council (e.g., the "sons of El" in the *Ba'al Cycle*; cf. Ps 82) introduces the role of celestial figures in the legal maintenance of earthly justice. Second, with greater influence on pseudepigraphal and New Testament texts, is the combat myth, in which a heroic, often divine, figure defeats a powerful adversary, such as Marduk's slaying of Tiamat in *Enuma Elish* or Ba'al's similar conquest of Yam in the *Ba'al Cycle* (see Forsyth, 1987). For biblical references to this myth, though without an explicit connection between the opponent and Satan, see Psalms 74:13–15 and Isaiah 27:1 and 51:9.

Hebrew Bible. The four passages that use the term *satan* to refer to a celestial figure all understand him primarily in terms of that first legal motif above, though they do not all necessarily refer to the same figure. In fact, with the exception of 1 Chronicles 21:1, the definite article accompanying the term likely indicates it was not considered a proper noun. In the earliest reference, the angel of the Lord "took a stand in the way as his adversary [śāṭān]" (Num 22:22; cf. v. 32) to block Balaam and his donkey on their journey so that he may remind him to speak only Yahweh's words. In Zechariah 3:1–7, the celestial satan figure now opposes the angel of the Lord in a dispute apparently over whether Joshua is worthy to serve as high priest. Yahweh decides in Joshua's favor and rebukes the satan (v. 2).

The third and most famous reference to the satan in the Hebrew Bible appears in Job 1–2. Here, a more developed satan character plays a similar accusatory role in the divine council. The satan appears among the "sons of God" as they present themselves before Yahweh and takes up his prosecutorial role by responding to Yahweh's praise of his servant Job with the suggestion that Job's fear of God is motivated only by his divinely bestowed material blessings. He proposes that Job's piety be tested by removing them, and Yahweh agrees on the condition that the satan not afflict Job's person. After a persistently pious Job passes this first test (1:21), the satan continues to question Job's devotion, so God allows him to afflict Job's body but not take his life. Job again responds submissively (2:10), and the satan is not mentioned again in the book. Here, the satan's activity is subjected to divine control and Job's pious responses to his affliction attribute the cause of his suffering to Yahweh alone, a view endorsed by the biblical narrator (2:10).

The final mention of a celestial satan occurs in 1 Chronicles 21:1. Though the parallel account in 2 Samuel 24:1 attributes David's desire to take the illicit census that leads to the death of 70,000 Israelites to Yahweh's provocation, the Chronicler blames "Satan" (the lack of the article here is generally seen to indicate a proper name, though Day [1988, pp. 127–145] disagrees). Though a desire to distance Yahweh from evil may have motivated this change, the Chronicler maintains Yahweh's role in other morally trou-

bling episodes (e.g., 2 Chr 18:22; cf. 1 Kgs 22:23). Instead, a desire to present David's relationship with Yahweh more favorably may better represent a consistent motivation throughout his work.

Second Temple Judaism. First Chronicles 21:1 may suggest the beginnings of Satan's convergence with the devil, the apotheosis of evil and supreme supernatural opponent of God, which is continued in the texts from later Second Temple Judaism (Sacchi, 1990, p. 223). The foisting of Yahweh's more questionable activities on a demonic figure is more explicit in the book *Jubilees* (second century B.C.E), where a figure named Mastema (as a noun, the word means "hatred"; cf. Hos 9:7) is given responsibility for ordering Abraham to sacrifice Isaac (*Jub.* 17:16; cf. Gen 22:1) and attacking Moses on his way to Egypt (*Jub.* 4:2; cf. Exod 4:24), among other things. Mastema is one of a host of demonic figures that infest texts from this period. These include Satan, now definitely as a personal name and connected explicitly with evil (*Jub.* 10:11; 23:29; cf. *As. Mos.* 10:1); Shemihaza or Asael, who leads the rebellious watcher angels in the book of *Enoch* (third century B.C.E); and Belial/Beliar ("the Worthless One") in the Qumran literature (e.g., 4QFlor 1:7–13, 1QS 2:19; cf. 2 Cor 6:15), who developed from an abstract concept into the personification of evil identified with the Angel of Darkness, who opposes the Prince of Light (1 QS 3:20–21). The growing interest in demonic opposition to God during this period may result from the influence of Persian Zoroastrian dualism.

The watcher myth, which appears with variations in *1 Enoch* (6–16) and *Jubilees*, offers an elaborate version of the myth of fallen angels, in which a group of angels lusts after human women and descends to have intercourse with them. The entry of evil into the world and divine judgment for the angels both result. Some version of the watcher myth is evident in Genesis 6:1–4, where "the sons of God" are said to bear children by "the daughters of man." For allusions to this myth in the New Testament, see Jude 6, 2 Peter 2:4, and Revelation 12:4.

The metaphysical dualism of apocalyptic literature raised the question of whether history was within the scope of human responsibility or merely a battleground for supernatural powers (Forsyth, 1987, p. 148). Sirach (ca. 180 B.C.E) testifies to an opposing trend, an internal ethical dualism, in which Satan is treated as a metaphor for impious instincts. Thus, Sirach 21:27 declares, "When an ungodly person curses an adversary [or "Satan," *ho satanas*], he curses himself." This tendency is taken up in Rabbinic Judaism, in which Satan receives little emphasis as a personified opponent to God, instead generally replaced by an internal conflict between the inclination to good (*yēṣer hāṭob*) and the inclination to evil (*yēṣer hāraʿ*).

New Testament. The tension between metaphysical and ethical dualism is reflected in the New Testament. Satan rules over a kingdom opposed to God. He is identified with Beelzebul, "the ruler of the demons" (Luke 11:15–19; Matt 12:24–27; Mark 3:22–26), and is called the "ruler of this world" (John 12:31; 14:30; 16:11; cf. 1 John 5:19), "the god of this world" (2 Cor 4:4), and "the prince of the power of the air" (Eph 2:2). The implicit hostility between God and the satan in Zechariah 3 and Job 1–2 is explicit in the New Testament. Satan is called an enemy (Matt 13:39), the evil one (Matt 13:38), an adversary (1 Pet 5:8), a murderer, and the father of lies (John 8:44) and is associated with heresy (Rev 2:24). He and his demons have the power to "enter" people, as Satan does with Judas (Luke 22:3; John 13:27; cf. Mark 5:12–13; Luke 8:30–32), and drive them to evil and destructive behavior. Satan even appears to have rights that limit the power of God, such as an obligated release from his chains to stage a final rebellion (Rev 20:3).

However, when Paul emphasizes Adam's sin (Rom 5:18; cf. 1 Cor. 15:21–22) and not the fall of the angels, as in *Enoch* and *Jubilees*, as the cause of human suffering, he shifts responsibility for evil on to humanity (Forsyth, 1987, p. 278). Believers, therefore, are obliged to resist Satan (Eph 4:27; 6:11–13; Jas 4:7; 1 Pet 5:8–9) and given a message that has the authority to rescue people from Satan's power (Acts 26:18). That power is limited. Several texts present Satan as subject to God's will. God uses him for discipline (1 Cor 5:5; 1 Tim 1:20), and though Satan asks to "sift" Peter, Jesus's intercession is able to deliver him (Luke 22:32). Satan has been judged (John 16:11), and he will even-

tually be defeated. Mixing much of the earlier imagery used for Satan together, including both the celestial accuser and primeval combatant from the ancient Near East, Revelation 12 depicts a battle between the archangel Michael and a great dragon: "The great dragon was thrown down, that ancient serpent, who is called the Devil and Satan, the deceiver of the whole world—he was thrown down to the earth, and his angels were thrown down with him…the accuser of our comrades has been thrown down" (vv. 9–10; cf. Rev 20:2, 10; Matt 25:41).

Patristic Literature. This assimilation of various traditions into the depiction of a single powerful opponent of God continued in the early church. However, the church fathers faced a theological challenge: give Satan too much power and risk setting up an independent rival evil force in the cosmos (the Gnostic heresy) as well as removing ethical responsibility from humanity, but give Satan insufficient power and risk making people responsible for their own salvation (the Pelagian heresy) and God liable for evil. These early interpreters developed a narrative solution to this dilemma by gradually developing a full "biography of Satan" (Kelly, 2006; cf. Forsyth, 1987, p. 403) through pulling together the various biblical references to Satan and filling in the gaps with further biblical passages and vestiges of extrabiblical traditions.

First, Satan was associated with the serpent that tempted Adam and Eve in Genesis 3 and was thereby involved in their sin. This link, though suggested by recurring imagery in several passages (e.g., Rom 16:20; Rev 12:9) and Satan's reputation for temptation (e.g., Matt 4:1–11), is nowhere explicitly made in the Bible. Justin Martyr and Tertullian initially claimed that Satan's involvement in the first couple's fall caused his own. Later, however, Cyprian and Irenaeus claimed Satan's initial transgression was an earlier jealousy of Adam (cf. Wis 2:24), a view developed in *The Life of Adam and Eve* (ca. fourth century C.E.) and the Qurʾan. By associating Satan with the "Lucifer" (lit. "Day Star") of Isaiah 14:4–20, however, Origen suggested Satan's original sin was pride. Though this text originally referred to the king of Babylon (v. 4), the mythological description of a figure who had "fallen from heaven"

(v. 12) made it easily transferrable to Satan. Ezekiel 28:11–19, originally addressed to the prince of Tyre (v. 2), was similarly considered a description of Satan's pride. Interpreted this way, it also placed Satan in the garden of Eden (v. 13) and affirmed that he was initially created good (v. 15). This double fall, first of Satan and his angels and then of humanity through Satan's deception, enabled God to be the creator of both all things and only good things since Satan fell of his own volition, as did Adam and Eve, though influenced by Satan's temptation. Thus, Augustine writes, "Who made the devil? He himself, for the devil was made not by his nature but by sin" (*Gen. Man.* 2.28). However, lest this emphasis on choice lead to a Pelagian optimism in human nature, Augustine also affirmed that after Adam's fall, all humans were infected with sin and thus under the power of Satan, only to be delivered through the ransom paid by Christ's death.

Later Interpretation. Though the traditions associated with Satan continued to accumulate in the centuries that followed, including the addition of Satan's role as punisher of the dead in hell (Kelly, 2006, pp. 229–241), his basic biography was generally consistent in the church until the Enlightenment, when belief in Satan began to decline, gradually replaced with biological, sociological, and psychological causes of evil (Russell, 1977, pp. 26–31). The horrors of the twentieth century appear, however, to have created a new openness to the existence of transcendent evil (Russell, 1977, p. 32), as demonstrated by several recent polls indicating that over 70 percent of Americans believe in the existence of Satan (De La Torre and Hernández, 2011, p. 3).

In recent research, several scholars in a "quest for the historical Satan" (De La Torre and Hernández, 2011) have attempted to untangle the various aspects of the Satan figure that were intertwined in his development. A range of "Satans" have resulted, which include Satan as the shadow of God (Russell, 1977), the opponent in the combat myth (Forsyth, 1987), the "demonization" of internal opponents (Pagels, 1996), the prodigal son of God (Nielsen, 1998), the accuser (Kelly, 2006), and the trickster (De La Torre and Hernández, 2011). This variety points to the complex mix of diverse traditions, biblical and otherwise, that contributes to the theological conception of Satan, who "collects in himself very reasonable demands of human thought confronted with the problem of evil" (Sacchi, 1990, p. 231).

[*See also* Devils and Demons; God and Gods; Good and Evil; *and* Underworld and Hell.]

BIBLIOGRAPHY

Day, Peggy Lynne. *An Adversary in Heaven: Śāṭān in the Hebrew Bible.* Harvard Semitic Monographs 43. Atlanta: Scholars Press, 1988.

De La Torre, Miguel A., and Albert Hernández. *The Quest for the Historical Satan.* Minneapolis: Fortress, 2011.

Forsyth, Neil. *The Old Enemy: Satan and the Combat Myth.* Princeton, N.J.: Princeton University Press, 1987.

Kelly, Henry Ansgar. *Satan: A Biography.* Cambridge, U.K.: Cambridge University Press, 2006.

Nielsen, Kirsten. *Satan—The Prodigal Son? A Family Problem in the Bible.* Biblical Seminar 50. Sheffield, U.K.: Sheffield Academic Press, 1998.

Pagels, Elaine H. *The Origin of Satan.* London: Allen Lane, Penguin, 1996.

Russell, Jeffrey Burton. *The Devil: Perceptions of Evil from Antiquity to Primitive Christianity.* Ithaca, N.Y.: Cornell University Press, 1977.

Sacchi, Paolo. "The Devil in Jewish Traditions of the Second Temple Period (c. 500 BCE–100 CE)." In *Jewish Apocalyptic and Its History*, translated by William J. Short, pp. 211–232. Journal for the Study of the Pseudepigrapha, Supplement Series 20. Sheffield, U.K.: Sheffield Academic Press, 1990.

Will Kynes

SCRIPTURE

In the Bible itself, the word "scripture" in the singular usually refers to a particular passage from the Old Testament (e.g., Mark 12:10; 15:28), but the church came to use the word to refer to the Old and New Testaments as a whole. The New Testament uses the plural "scriptures" to refer to Judaism's sacred writings (e.g., Mark 12:24; 14:49), which correspond approximately to what Christians call the Old Testament (I include the word "approximately" because it is not known whether the extent of these writings in New

Testament times exactly corresponded to the bounds of the Torah, the Prophets, and the Writings as these are accepted in Judaism and are the collection termed in Christian parlance "the Old Testament").

Memory, History, Witness, Tradition. Theology has traditionally used categories such as "authority," "inspiration," and "revelation" in order to understand the theological status of the scriptures; but these need to be supplemented with other categories in order to do justice to the scriptures' own nature. In particular, these categories do not satisfactorily illumine the narrative works that occupy the first half of each testament.

Memory. Those narrative works embody the memory of Israel and of the early Christian church concerning key events of their story as the community corporately wished it to be remembered. The works suggest that Jewish and Christian faith focuses on certain sequences of past events that the narratives relate. The faith emerging from them does not center on timeless statements about God or on obeying certain behavioral imperatives. It involves seeing particular events and interactions between God and people as foundationally important guides for living.

The Old Testament narratives comprise two multipart works, the books from Genesis to Kings and the books of Chronicles, Ezra, and Nehemiah. Both begin from creation but focus on the story of Israel down to the time of the author and readers. The first highlights the time of Abraham and Jacob, Moses, Joshua, and David; the second highlights the time of David, Ezra, and Nehemiah. Both works attach importance to the events that are remembered and to the significance of their memory for succeeding centuries, in particular for the time of author and readers. Both also reflect the interaction between the events and the community's life over the intervening centuries. Scholarly study has attempted to trace that interaction by dating the sources that lie behind the works, but changing views on the nature of that process suggest that we are not in a position to uncover this history; the only certainty is the narrative we have.

The two works assert the importance of the fact that God made a commitment to Israel's ancestors in order to pursue a purpose for the whole world that he had created, then delivered Israel's ancestors from serfdom, instructed them about their community life, settled them in their own land, set up a stable government, instructed them about building a sanctuary, let their life unravel so that they lost their land, then partially reestablished them. Such a summary combines the stories told by the two works. The first story extends from creation to the fall of Jerusalem in 586 B.C.E. and thus tells of the failure of God's plan to fulfill his purpose for the world (Rudolf Bultmann spoke of the Old Testament story as a whole as the failure of God's plan, but the description applies strictly more to the first of these two great narrative works). It is a formulation of the way the narrative's authors in the Exile wished the story to be understood by their generation, who needed to own their responsibility for its shape, to reaffirm their trust in the divine promises it nevertheless incorporates, and to make a new commitment to God. The second of the two works focuses on the period from David onward and takes the story beyond the fall of Jerusalem into the time when the community has been restored in order to suggest a different way of remembering the story for a generation that needed both encouragement and direction.

The earliest known designation for the first of these narratives treats it as a two-part work, "The Torah" (Genesis to Deuteronomy) and "The Former Prophets" (Joshua, Judges, Samuel, Kings). The Hebrew word *torah* was rendered into Greek and other languages by words meaning "law," which give a false impression of its nature. As a title for Genesis—Deuteronomy as a whole, Torah suggests "teaching" that puts a framework of narrative around large tracts of instruction regarding the life of the community and of individuals. As a title for Joshua—Kings, "Former Prophets" perhaps suggests a prophetic perspective on Israel's story. Chronicles–Ezra–Nehemiah is then part of "the Writings," the miscellany of scrolls that closes the Torah, the Prophets, and the Writings.

History, witness, tradition. In the context of modern study these two works came to be viewed as "histories," a term that recognizes one aspect of their significance but obscures another aspect. Seeing them as history recognized the importance of historical events to Israel's faith and to the story these scriptures tell. Timeless theological statements and behavioral expectations such as "Yahweh our God Yahweh one" (Deut 6:4; all translations are the author's), "You shall love Yahweh your God" (Deut 6:5), and "Love your neighbor as someone like yourself" (Lev 19:18) are given their content and grounds by means of historical statements about the way Yahweh acted in creating the world and taking Israel out of serfdom. The archetypal illustration is the declaration that opens the Decalogue, "I am Yahweh your God who brought you out of the country of Egypt" (Exod 20:2), which is the basis for the expectations that follow.

The description of the narratives as "witness" links with that significance of them. There are several senses in which theology can speak of the witness of the scriptures or the witness of a particular book. The word can imply that the scriptures are only a witness, not the reality; it can also imply that a particular book gives one partial witness, while another gives a different partial witness. When the scriptures themselves use the term "witness," they do so in another connection. The Israelites are Yahweh's witnesses to the fact that Yahweh has spoken and then delivered (e.g., Isa 43:10–12); the Twelve are witnesses to Jesus's resurrection (e.g., Acts 1:8, 22; 2:32). They are able to give testimony to things they have seen. In life in general, the testimony of other people is indispensable to most of our knowledge of events in the world. The scriptures' witness to Yahweh's acts in Israel and in the New Testament events is one key instance of the indispensable nature of witness.

It is the task of witnesses to "pass on" what they have seen; witness becomes tradition. Most Israelites did not experience the Exodus; the people who did experience it passed on an account to their children, and they to their children, and so on. Most believers in Jesus did not meet him; the people who did meet him passed on an account to others, and they passed it on to yet other people, and so on. In each case they did so in a way that suggested the significance of the

events to the ongoing needs of the community. In due course the testimony came to be written down, possibly in part to ensure that the tradition did not get lost in a time of crisis and in part to ensure that the process of updating did not fatally compromise the tradition's reliability as testimony.

While there is thus a close relationship between scripture and tradition, the scriptures also use the term "tradition" in a negative way. The New Testament warns readers about Jewish and Christian traditions that are alien to the scriptures. In the history of theology, tradition has also been distinguished from scripture as a supplementary source of truth—for instance, in its affirming that the primacy of the pope and the bodily assumption of Mary are traditions that can and must be accepted or are interpretations of the scriptures that are hallowed by tradition.

There is yet another sense in which "tradition," like "witness," is a term that can be used to avoid giving the scriptures too absolute a position. There are various traditions of faith in the world, such as Buddhist traditions and Native American traditions. The biblical tradition is one of these faith traditions alongside others. This way of using the idea of tradition contrasts with the use of the idea to safeguard the scriptures' authenticity. It presupposes that many or all traditions have some value and that no single one should be absolutized.

The history in the scriptures and our history. We cannot verify most of the testimony that has been passed on in the biblical tradition. Indeed, the scholarly community regards much of it as falsified, while many ordinary readers instinctively doubt elements in the narrative such as the account of God creating the world over a six-day period a few thousand years ago. In light of such scholarly work and such human instincts, one might see the narratives as more like movies that are "based on fact" than documentaries. In such works the basic historical reference of the story is vital, but so is the way the story has been retold so as to have an impact on the audience. Even the account of creation expresses facts, such as the fact that God created the world, acted in a purposeful way, brought into being something that was "good," made men and women in the image of God, and so on. With regard to subsequent parts of the narrative that are nearer to being historical in a modern sense, their being "based on fact" without being thoroughly factual does not compromise the indispensability of the witness or the memory that they pass down. It is important that it does not do so because of that characteristic of Christian faith that we have noted, that Christian faith is centrally a gospel, the report of a piece of news, of things that happened.

In his book *The Eclipse of Biblical Narrative*, Hans Frei identified a fundamental change that came about in Christian thinking about scriptural narrative in the eighteenth century. Until that time, Christian belief took for granted that the narrative corresponded to what actually happened and that our story needs to be seen in the context of that story. In the eighteenth century both unities came apart.

Henceforth scholarship distinguished between the story and the history that lay somewhere behind it and had to decide which mattered more. The importance of history to modern thinking made it inevitable that scholarship focused on discovering the actual history rather than the not wholly historical story. We have noted that two centuries of intensive study have unfortunately proved only that the attempt to trace the actual history of Israel or the actual history of Jesus cannot reach definitive results. There has been no progress in the investigation, and we have no basis for thinking that there will ever be progress. The material frustrates the quest. It was in part for this reason that the late twentieth century saw a turn back to an interest in the narrative that tells the story rather than the events that might lie behind the narrative. The disillusion also coheres with the quest's not yielding results that made it possible to use the scriptures in theology, spiritual formation, or preaching.

This fact in turn links with the other unity that came apart. From the eighteenth century onward, Christian instinct was to interpret the scriptural story in light of our story rather than the other way around. In other words, we assume that our understanding of our story is true and we evaluate the truth of the scriptural story in light of that understanding. This

takes us into a consideration of traditional ways of thinking about the status of the scriptures.

Authority. In recent centuries in Christian thinking the notion of authority has been of paramount importance in connection with the scriptures. The idea of authority suggests that the scriptures have the right to determine what people believe and what they do. How is it possible to tell people what they must believe? Perhaps only God might be able to do so, and belief in the scriptures' authority implies that it is God's authority that they mediate. On what basis can one say that God's authority lies behind the scriptures?

Authority to shape belief. The scriptures themselves are familiar enough with the notion of authority (e.g., Matt 8:9; 21:23), and it is therefore striking that they do not speak of their authority—for instance, when the New Testament refers to the Torah, the Prophets, and the Writings. On the other hand, the New Testament does use the expression "it is written" in referring to them (e.g., Matt 4:1–11), which conveys the implication, "so that settles it." Elsewhere the phrase "it is written" occurs in connection with declarations about the future; events take place "as it is written" (Luke 18:31). Sometimes it does refer to theological statements (e.g., Rom 1:17).

One can say, then, that Jesus and the New Testament writers do assume that the Torah, the Prophets, and the Writings have the authority to determine what people should believe and do. It is logically impossible for there to be an equivalent statement within the scriptures about the New Testament having this authority. It is the post–New Testament church that attributes such authority to the writings that make up the New Testament. Does authority therefore lie in the church that attributes the authority? The church has usually taken the view that the authority lies inherent in the scriptures themselves; the church is simply rubber-stamping it.

That understanding points to an alternative way of construing the notion of authority. When people describe Jesus as speaking with authority (Matt 7:29), they do not mean he is an accredited expert like a scribe. They yield to his teaching because it has a compelling profundity and wisdom. Many or most or all of the biblical documents seem likely to have gained their authority among Israelites by a parallel dynamic. At some points an official body, such as the Persian authorities, may have decreed that the Torah had authority in Jerusalem; likewise the churches eventually became involved in discussing whether different Christian writings should have an official position in their scriptures. The process whereby scriptures became authoritative thus involved two stages. Individual writings found informal appreciation; later, a collection received formal recognition. Reference to the canon of scripture implies this second stage. Possibly the Jewish community went through a similar two-stage process, but we do not have records of discussions parallel to the ones that happened in the churches.

Theologically, there is a further basis for applying the notion of authority to the scriptures. Their status in Christian faith and theology issues from the nature of Christian faith as a gospel, a message that hinges and focuses on things that happened in a particular past. The writings of other religious groups can be true and edifying, but they cannot tell us this gospel. James Barr has further commented that what counts as Christian faith is not whatever the church now may think but what the first Christians articulated in light of their proximity to Jesus's own time and to his acts and their involvement in the beginnings of the church. Christian faith is a historical faith in the sense that it focuses on who Jesus was, what he said, what happened to him, what he achieved, and how his significance was articulated in the context of these events. The authority of the scriptures lies in their being able to tell us what the first generations of Christians articulated, as writings from 1,000 or 2,000 years later cannot. It is not an argument for the authority of the particular writings in the New Testament (e.g., as opposed to other gospels) but an argument for the authority of a collection of documents of this kind as opposed to later Christian writings or non-Christian writings.

This principle does not imply the scriptures must be the writings that come from those closest to the

events. It can take time for the significance of events to emerge. The authority of the Torah, the Prophets, and the Writings lies in their significance for an understanding of Yahweh's dealing with Israel through its history from its beginnings to the Greek period, even though the books themselves mostly come from long after many of the events to which they refer. The authority of the New Testament lies in their capacity to testify to Christian beginnings.

Authority to shape behavior. Jewish thinking in terms of the authority of the Torah moves in a different direction. The first occurrences of the phrase "it is written" in the New Testament draw our attention to the fact that in everyday speech "authority" connotes the right to tell people what they should do. While the Torah does have the framework of a narrative, it is dominated by vast tracts of instruction material. And while "law" is a misleading umbrella term for the Torah, even for its instruction material with its exhortations and rules for life, it is not unreasonable to characterize the Torah as designed to give direction for the life of the people of God. The scriptures lay down the stances people should take to God and to one another.

Sometimes they do so without giving reasons. The Torah three times tells Israelites not to cook a baby goat in its mother's milk, without saying why (Exod 23:19; 34:26; Deut 14:21). Paul says that women should remain silent in the churches (1 Cor 14:34). In both cases, we can only guess at the reasons for the commands. The Torah says that people should love their neighbors, and the New Testament agrees but again does not give reasons (Lev 19:18; Mark 12:31). Both the Torah and the New Testament assume that this expectation about loving one's neighbor is self-evident and needs no explaining. Perhaps they make the same assumption about those other commands whose rationale is not obvious to readers in an urbanized Western context.

Sometimes the scriptures do give reasons when they lay down the law. It is because the Israelites were serfs in Egypt and their God got them out of that serfdom that they should care for their own bondservants and for other needy people; it is because Jesus loved the disciples that they should love one another. The scriptures likely take these commands also to be obvious expectations of humanity. They are not distinctive of the scriptures. What the scriptures do is provide extra arguments for fulfilling such expectations.

There are scriptural commands or beliefs that readers may find uncongenial, which leads into consideration of the relationship between scriptural authority and other authorities. The question of authority came into prominence in theology in the West at the time of the Protestant Reformation, which raised questions concerning the authority of the scriptures and the authority of the church or of the pope or of church tradition. As the Enlightenment developed, Richard Hooker expressed the question in terms of the relationship of scripture, tradition, and reason. The Wesleyan Quadrilateral speaks in terms of the relationships between scripture, tradition, reason, and experience.

These two or three or four loci of authority are not simply alternatives. Christian thinking and behavior are properly subject to all these influences; the practice of the scriptures themselves justifies that fact. One way to think of their interrelationship is to ask about the dynamic balance between them. Which source has decisive influence on thinking and behavior at crucial points? Another way is suggested by the word "canon." In origin it is the Greek word for a ruler. To describe scripture as "canon" is to give it a decisive role in another sense: where there is a clash between scripture, tradition, reason, and experience, scripture has the last word.

In the twenty-first century in the West, it is clearer that the formulations of tradition, reason, and experience are all shaped by the culture in which people live, like the scriptures themselves, so that the question might be put more simply in terms of the relationship of the scriptures in their culture and us in our culture. At one level, this relationship then compares with the relationship between the scriptures and movements such as feminism and postcolonialism. At another level, it concerns the relationship between the scriptures and Western assumptions such as the importance of the individual, of human

choice, of the possibility of progress toward peace and justice, and of the rejection of violence. There are overlaps between the scriptures and these movements and assumptions, but there are also ways in which the scriptures imply a need to qualify their assertions or in which the movements imply a need to qualify the scriptures' authority. Modern theology thus has to decide between giving final authority to ways of thinking that emerge from our culture or to ways of thinking that emerge from the scriptures. More realistically, it lives in an ongoing dialogue over such questions.

Yet another related insight that emerges from twenty-first-century Western awareness is that authority is not a very useful category for thinking about theology. The idea that something or someone can tell us what to think now seems odd and is hardly required by the scriptures themselves.

Inspiration. The explicit scriptural background to the idea of the inspiration of the scriptures comes in the description of every (Old Testament) scripture as *theopneustos*, in 2 Timothy 3:16, the first known occurrence of this word. It is usually taken to mean "God-breathed"; but 2 Peter 1:21 speaks of the scriptural prophets being "moved by the Holy Spirit" (the verb in this passage might be more forcibly translated "carried"), and *theopneustos* may similarly suggest "blown over by God." This understanding would fit references in the Prophets themselves. In the more usual understanding, the idea is that the words in the scriptures were breathed out by God.

How inspiration may work. The prophets have at least three ways of describing the origin of their words. First, sometimes they say "Yahweh has said this," speaking like a king's messenger. Now a king need not dictate the words of his message but rather provide the gist of it; the messenger formulates the words. That fact does not compromise the message's authenticity; the messenger's words count as the king's words and have the force of the king's words. Second, sometimes the scriptures refer to God speaking "by means of" a prophet, more literally, "by the hand of" the prophet (e.g., Hag 1:1) or "by the mouth of" someone (e.g., Acts 1:16). Here God is using the person as an instrument, like a ventriloquist. The prophet does not formulate the words but simply opens the mouth and out the words come. Third, sometimes prophets speak words that they themselves simply devise. Whereas in other contexts they speak of what Yahweh is saying, here they speak as their own "I." The book of Jeremiah provides examples as it records the prayers and reflections of Jeremiah. When the idea of inspiration is extended to other forms of writing that appear in the scriptures such as narratives, acts of praise, and letters, this last form of inspiration is the one that applies. The speaker or writer takes the initiative, but God works through the person.

Following on the development of biblical criticism in the nineteenth century, some theologians inferred from "God-breathed" that the scriptures must be infallible (the word "inerrant" subsequently comes into usage in this connection). This inference seems unjustified. On the one hand, the scriptures speak of Yahweh arousing Sennacherib to do his work and see Nebuchadnezzar as Yahweh's servant, without implying a validation of all that these conquerors do or of the way they do it. Indeed, the prophets critique the acts in question. The scriptures could be God-breathed yet compromised by the fact that they more literally emerge from human mouths. It need not be so; perhaps the words are exactly what God wants said and the narratives are infallible or inerrant. But describing them as "inspired" does not in itself carry this implication.

Powerful words. The context of 2 Timothy 3:16 suggests that the point about declaring scriptures to be *theopneustos* lies elsewhere. The scriptures' inspiration explains the counterintuitive claim that these "sacred writings" are able to convey a wisdom that leads to salvation "in Christ Jesus"—who was not born when they were written—and it undergirds the subsequent declaration that they are therefore "useful for teaching, rebuking, correcting, and training in right living" for believers in Jesus. The involvement of God's Spirit accounts for these scriptures' capacity to be significant far beyond their original context and audience. The point is made elsewhere by speaking more directly of the involvement of God's Spirit in the generating of the scriptures. It was "by the Holy Spirit"

that God spoke in Psalm 2, which explains the extraordinary fact that it describes the activity of people persecuting believers in Jesus (Acts 4:25–26; cf. 28:25; Mark 12:36; Heb 3:7; 9:8).

Something that "Yahweh has said" can naturally be described as "Yahweh's word" (e.g., 1 Kgs 18:1; Isa 1:10) or occasionally "God's word" (e.g., 1 Sam 9:27; 1 Kgs 12:22). In the New Testament "God's word" can refer to a particular scripture (Mark 7:13; John 10:35), but it more characteristically denotes the message about Jesus (e.g., Acts 4:31; 6:2). The convention of describing the scriptures as a whole as "God's word" does not correspond to the scriptures' own usage, although the description of them as "God's words" would be an unexceptionable extension of the scriptural usage.

What is the point about referring to a message as "the word of God" or "the word of Yahweh"? One answer is that a message from God characteristically declares or implies a divine intention—either a promise or a warning. Its being God's message draws the listeners' attention to the fact that the word will find fulfillment because God does as he says. The other answer is that listeners are therefore advised to take the message seriously and give it the appropriate response of trust and expectation or of repentance and turning to the right way.

Revelation. As is the case with authority and inspiration, the idea of revelation does appear within the scriptures but in more concrete and narrower connections than the one that has classically obtained in discussion of the scriptures' theological nature. In the Christian thinking of the medieval period, revelation was commonly set alongside reason; these were two complementary sources of truth. Modernity was more inclined to set revelation and reason over against one another; the relationship became more fraught.

The scriptures sometimes speak of God revealing himself in the sense of personally appearing to a person (e.g., Gen 35:7), but they more often speak of God revealing something in words spoken into someone's ear (e.g., 1 Sam 9:15). Twentieth-century theology further debated the question whether revelation lay in God's words as preserved in the scriptures or in

God's acts as reported in them. Within the scriptures themselves, both are involved and each is dependent on the other. When God reveals something, the revelation commonly concerns something God intends to do (e.g., Isa 22:14). The event then provides evidence that the revelation was real. Conversely, when God acts, this act is characteristically preceded by a revelation concerning the event and commonly followed by a comment on the event's significance. This sequence reflects the fact that the event would not in itself reveal anything unless it was accompanied by some words. There is thus a close relationship between talk in terms of revelation and the Prophets' more characteristic talk in terms of "Yahweh's word."

The noun "revelation" is used in a similar way to refer to coming events in the introduction to the book known as Revelation, "the revelation of Jesus Christ which God gave him to show his servants what must soon take place" (Rev 1:1). But the book also "reveals" much more than events to come in the future. In Rabbinic thinking, "revelation" applied to "things above and below, things in front and behind"—that is, both heaven and hell and both the past (especially creation) and the future (especially the end times). In other words, it covers anything that human beings could not know by using their human insight.

Once more, then, the use of the term "revelation" to refer to the scriptures as a whole does not link very well with their own use of the word, partly because the word's use in theology reflects issues in later contexts. But the idea of revelation is useful for conveying the sense that one discovers from the scriptures things that one would not have guessed or worked out.

Theological study has commonly made a distinction between general revelation and special revelation. Although the scriptures do not use the words in this way, the categorization fits some assumptions that appear there. A prophet such as Amos and a writer such as Paul assume that the world in general is aware of the basic truths about God and about human obligation. People do not need a special revelation in order to know that God is real and is powerful, moral, and compassionate or to know

that adultery, false witness, and torture are wrong, though such awarenesses can be surrendered and lost. These truths are aspects of human awareness like the awareness that we exist. One can think of them as the general revelation available to all humanity through being made in God's image. Further, the scriptures assume that there are truths about life and the world that human beings discover by looking at the world itself and by reflecting on human experience. It is the truths that cannot be discovered in this way (the "things above and below, things in front and behind") that are the subjects of special revelation.

Praise and Protest. A surprising feature of the collection of writings called "holy scriptures" is the presence among them of substantial material that addresses God, as opposed to narrating the story of God's involvement with people or laying down God's expectations of people or conveying messages God has given. The Psalms are the main such repository, but Lamentations takes the same form; Job and Ecclesiastes also largely comprise protest.

While the New Testament quotes the Psalms in the conviction that they have a similar nature to prophecy as God's words (e.g., Acts 1:20; 2:25–31), the form of the Psalms suggests that most of them began life as prayers and praises addressed to God. Apparently, the Israelite community believed them to be prayers and praises that were acceptable to God and could model proper prayer and praise. The form of the Psalter as a whole reflects this conviction. It comprises five books of praise and prayer, with "Amen" codas after Psalms 41, 72, 89, and 106 to mark this structure (the headings "Book One" and so on that appear in English translations make the point explicit, but the "Amen" codas themselves are part of the Hebrew text). The five books of praise and protest thus correspond to the five books of the Torah. They offer instruction on praise and prayer in the form of 150 examples of praise and protest that the community has recognized as acceptable to God and in keeping with the Torah and the Prophets.

The fact that they address God in confrontational ways and ask God for things that seem scandalous to modern readers has raised the question whether they are present in the Psalter as examples of prayers that people prayed rather than of prayers whose content God approves. But there is only a quantitative difference between the protests in the Psalms and ones that appear elsewhere, including the New Testament (Rev 6:9–11), so this "solution" to that modern problem seems implausible. There is a link with the fact that the Psalms comprise the densest collection of theological affirmations in the scriptures. It would be ironic if they are present in the scriptures only as examples of the way people prayed, not as embodying what may properly be said of God. The Psalms have been thought to provide evidence for some theological ideas such as divine omniscience that have been favored by theologians and ordinary people but are hard to find in the scriptures, but ironically, the chief proof text for this idea (Ps 139:1) works in the opposite direction in that it describes God as getting to know about the psalmist and, thus, as not knowing about the psalmist through an inherent omniscience. The Psalms make other scandalous statements about matters such as God's abandonment or sleepiness (which Christian thinking commonly reformulates as apparent abandonment or sleepiness).

The Scriptures and Theology. This article has been considering ways in which one might look at the scriptures theologically. The converse question is, How do we look at theology scripturally? What is the relationship between scripture and theology?

Biblical theology and systematic theology. Theology in the West developed through an interaction between a Middle Eastern way of thinking and a European way of thinking. The creeds and the doctrines they presuppose, such as the Trinity, reflect the process whereby the thinking embodied in the scriptures came to be formulated in conceptual categories that were recognizable to Christian leaders familiar with Greek thinking, hence the use of terms such as "hypostasis" and "persona." It was a necessary aspect of the contextualization of the gospel in their context.

One difficulty with this particular form of contextualization was that these European categories obscured the vivid and dynamic content of what the scriptures communicate. Theology had to focus on problems such as the sense in which Jesus could be both divine and human or the sense in which God can be both one and three, which easily distract from conveying a sense of the vigorous presentation of God and of Jesus in the scriptures. Images and metaphors become analytic concepts. Doctrines of the atonement find it difficult to convey the lively nature of Paul's account of the significance of Jesus's execution.

It was also hard for these European categories to preserve the centrally narrative character of the scriptural message. The creeds illustrate the difficulty. While they do justice to the narrative character of Jesus's own life, they do not set it in the context of the story that runs through the scriptures as a whole. There are no narrative statements about God, only about Jesus.

Making a distinction between systematic theology and biblical theology might be expected to help with this difficulty. Systematic theology is a discipline that seeks to express the nature of Christian faith as a coherent whole in light of the categories of analytical Western thinking and concepts. Biblical theology might then be seen as a discipline that seeks to express the nature of Christian faith as a whole in the terms of the scriptures themselves. In practice, however, attempts at biblical theology also reflect the categories and concepts of Western thinking. Partly out of an awareness of this difficulty, ventures into biblical theology are inclined to stop short of outlining one biblical theology and more often seek to describe a set of biblical theologies (plural): the theologies of Genesis and Jeremiah, of Paul and John, of Old Testament and New Testament.

We have noted that one theological significance of the prominence of narrative in the scriptures is the fact that theological statements need to do justice to the fact that Jewish and Christian faith centrally involves committing oneself to the vital importance of something that happened in the past. Another theological significance of the prominence of narrative is that narrative makes it possible to discuss theological questions in a way that does justice to their depth and complexity. The narrative account of Moses's interaction with Pharaoh in Exodus, for instance, constitutes a nuanced discussion of the interrelationship between divine sovereignty and human responsibility; but it is hard to preserve the subtlety of this presentation when one abandons narrative form. The same applies to the Sinai narrative in Exodus with its discussions of the idea of God's presence and of the various possible responses God can make to the rebellion of his people. It applies to the discussion in Job of the meaning of human suffering and of its implications for an understanding of God's relationship with us, which is presented as a kind of debate in which all the participants make significant contributions even if some are more relevant than others to Job himself. It applies to the juxtaposition of Jesus's ministry of power and then his submission to martyrdom in the two halves of Mark's Gospel.

Unity and diversity. The common Christian designation of the scriptures (plural) as "scripture" (singular) implies a unity about the collection of works as a whole. But one characteristic that imperils the idea of their having authority or being inspired or constituting a divine revelation is the diversity and inconsistency they manifest. Thus, some parts of the Old Testament emphasize the importance of offerings in the Temple, while other parts declare that these do not matter. In the New Testament, Paul declares that people are put right with God through faith alone and not by doing the right thing and adds that people need only to consider the story of Abraham to see that it is so. James declares that people are put right with God by doing the right thing and not by faith alone and adds that people need only to consider the story of Abraham to see that it is so. In response to an awareness of such diversity, one might choose between different texts, see them as witnessing to different aspects of what is truthful and right, or see them as reflecting different contexts. One problem that then emerges is that readers are likely to focus on the affirmations they appreciate and already affirm and to discount the ones for which they care less, instead of focusing on the ones they are inclined to discount.

Yahweh's discourse to Job points to a further insight and a further question. As a human being, Yahweh points out, Job has only a very small place in the world and only a very partial understanding of God and his ways in the world. In a postmodern context, the partial nature of what we perceive has become central to our awareness. This awareness heightens the importance of that scriptural way of doing theology that recognizes complexity and seeks to analyze it, rather than thinking it can be resolved. This awareness also links with the classic postmodern suspicion of meta-narratives, if by a "meta-narrative" one means a total system or theory or explanation of reality.

In connection with the scriptures, it is appropriate also to use the term "meta-narrative" in the narrower sense of an overarching story and then to note that suspicion of meta-narratives encourages a questioning of the kind of meta-narrative that has emerged from theology and has aimed to encapsulate the scriptural message (e.g., creation, fall, redemption, second coming). It provides another stimulus to the recognition that this summary of the implicit meta-narrative of the scriptures is oversimplified. The scriptures themselves incorporate a series of "local narratives" and do not construct a grand narrative out of them. We might, indeed, more tentatively infer from the scriptures a meta-narrative (in the more literal sense) that does more justice to the scriptures' many local narratives—a narrative about creation; human rebellion; God's promises to Israel's ancestors; God's involvement with Israel itself; Israel's exile and restoration; Jesus's coming, ministry, martyrdom, and resurrection; the outpouring of God's spirit and the spreading of the Jesus story; and the prospect of his final appearing and our resurrection. Christian faith does affirm such a narrative insofar as this is a proper summary of the narrative that we might infer from the scriptures. It is a grand narrative within which Christians live.

The Scriptures of the Old Covenant and of the New. The diversity and inconsistency within the scriptures emerge particularly clearly in differences between the two testaments. Corresponding to the nature of the scriptures themselves are several ways of seeing the relationship between the testaments.

Continuity and difference. Between them they give a prominent place to the story of Israel, of Jesus, and of the early church; and the New Testament sees its story as the continuation of the story in the Torah, the Prophets, and the Writings. John Bright thus sees the scriptures as a drama in which the Old Testament is act one and the New Testament act two. While the Old Testament story hardly requires continuation in a story such as that in the New Testament, it is possible to argue that the Old Testament story does not reach closure and needs some form of continuation. Genesis—Kings ends with exile and a coda telling only of the release of the Davidic king. Chronicles–Ezra–Nehemiah relate the restoration of Judah but close with Judah still chafing under Persian authority and needing the further action of reformers such as Nehemiah. It is then possible to see the story of Jesus and the early church as bringing the restoration of Judah. Yet the New Testament's story also does not reach closure. Judah is not free of the Roman yoke and does not recognize its Messiah; the church does not look like a community in which the new covenant has become a reality. The New Testament does make clear that one cannot understand its story except as the continuation of the Old Testament story. It is the narrative link between the two testaments' stories that requires Christian faith to give a status to Israel's scriptures that it does not give to the religious traditions of other nations.

Another New Testament way of making a link with the Old Testament is to note that promises expressed in the Old Testament are fulfilled within the New. Thus, Mark begins with a reference to God's promise to send a messenger who would herald the Lord's own coming and sees John the baptizer as fulfilling this role. Similarly, in the Gospel of Luke, when John is born, his father sees his birth as an indication that God has acted "as he said through his holy prophets" (Luke 1:70). In parallel with the way the story in the New Testament links with that in the Old, it is not simply the case that Old Testament promises are fulfilled in the New. Fulfillment is a motif within the Old Testament itself, and living in hope in light of God's promise is a feature of New Testament faith.

Christians often think in terms of the Old Testament God being wrathful and the New Testament God being loving, but such distinctions hardly survive a reading of the scriptures themselves. Jewish readers are not inclined to see the God of the Torah, the Prophets, and the Writings as wrathful. Neither does the New Testament itself make this contrast. Whereas God spoke piecemeal through the Prophets and has now spoken through a Son (Heb 1:1), the content of the speaking is the same. Further, wrath is a prominent theme in the New Testament. It is Jesus who introduces into the scripture the idea that God sends people to hell. This particular fact does link with the one major theological difference between the testaments, which is that the Torah, the Prophets, and the Writings assume that when people die they simply go to Sheol or Hades, whereas the New Testament is able to declare a new piece of news, that God has "given us a new birth into a lively hope through the resurrection of Jesus Christ from the dead" (1 Pet 1:3). It is this fact to which Hebrews testifies, in declaring that the new covenant is better than the old. The two testaments thus complement each other: Dietrich Bonhoeffer noted that it was only when God had driven home in the Old Testament the importance of this life that he could risk entrusting people with the news about resurrection life.

Vision and accommodation. In laying out God's expectations, Jesus declares, "You have heard it said, but I say" (see Matt 5:21–48) and at first sight may seem to be introducing a higher standard than the Old Testament. But it is hard to locate any point at which his expectations are not already expressed in the Old Testament. For instance, it has already urged that people forswear anger and lust, that their word should be trustworthy, that they should be forgiving rather than seek redress, and that they should love their enemies. There are other points at which the Old Testament approves of redress and of attacks on enemies; but then, there are also points at which the New Testament indicates an acceptance of slavery and of the submission of wives to husbands in a way that implies a lower standard than the Old Testament. Both Old and New have mixed standards.

One clue that Jesus offers to the inconsistency in the instructions in the Torah comes in connection with divorce (e.g., Mark 10). Some Pharisees note that Deuteronomy 24 permits divorce; Jesus notes that Genesis 1–2 implicitly rules it out. Jesus's comment is that Genesis indicates what God intended from the beginning, while Deuteronomy makes allowance for the human stubbornness that causes divorce. On another occasion he identifies the command to love God and to love one's neighbor as the commands in the Torah on which the rest of the Torah and the Prophets depend, and one could infer that Deuteronomy's regulation about a divorce certificate is an expression of love in the way it provides some evidence of status to a woman who has been divorced. Thus, aspects of the Torah are expressed in a way that reflects God's intent for creation, while other aspects make allowance for human sinfulness. The same is true about the New Testament. The vocation of interpretation involves perceiving how expectations in both Testaments relate to the creation ideal and how they make that allowance.

If there is a difference between the testaments concerning God's expectations, it lies not in their levels but in their foci. The Old Testament speaks both to the obligations of the individual and to those of the nation. It is the duty of the individual to be forgiving (as Joseph is in relation to his brothers); it is the duty of the nation or the local community to see that justice is done in a way that honors "an eye for an eye." The New Testament does not speak to the government of life in the city or the village or to the administration of justice as, for example, it does not offer any regulations to control slavery.

A related difference is the two testaments' approach to worship and purity. In both areas the early church reverts to something like the pattern of the time of Abraham, though it also takes for granted participation in the ongoing worship in the Temple. After the destruction of Jerusalem the post–New Testament church in due course follows the line taken by the Old Testament: building churches, appointing priests, and developing set forms of worship. The purity rules are even more unequivocally annulled in the New Testament. These rules were designed as an adjunct to God's missional purpose, which involved keeping Israel distinct from the nations in order to attract the nations. In Acts God inverts his strategy; the purity rules are annulled in order to serve that same missional purpose.

As the account of God's activity in effecting his purpose for the world and as his commentary on that purpose and its implications for his people, the scriptures tell the story in whose context the church is invited and challenged to live if it wants to be Christian.

[*See also* Authority and Order; Canon; Hermeneutics, Biblical; Story and Memory; Torah; *and* Witness.]

BIBLIOGRAPHY

Abraham, William J. *Canon and Criterion in Christian Theology.* Oxford and New York: Oxford University Press, 1998.

Barr, James. *The Bible in the Modern World.* London: SCM; New York: Harper, 1973.

Barr, James. *The Scope and Authority of the Bible.* Philadelphia: Westminster, 1980. Also published as *Explorations in Theology* 7. London: SCM, 1980.

Barr, James. *Holy Scripture: Canon, Authority, Criticism.* Philadelphia: Westminster; Oxford: Oxford University Press, 1983.

Bartlett, David. L. *The Shape of Scriptural Authority.* Philadelphia: Fortress, 1983.

Bauckham, Richard, and Benjamin Drewery, eds. *Scripture, Tradition and Reason A Study in the Criteria of Christian Doctrine.* Edinburgh: T&T Clark, 1988.

Berkouwer, G. C. *Holy Scripture.* Grand Rapids, Mich.: Eerdmans, 1975.

Bonhoeffer, Dietrich. *Letters and Papers from Prison.* London: Collins, 1962.

Brenneman, J. M. *Canons in Conflict.* Oxford and New York: Oxford University Press, 1997.

Bright, John. *The Authority of the Old Testament.* Nashville, Tenn.: Abingdon; London: SCM, 1967.

Brown, William P., ed. *Engaging Biblical Authority.* Louisville, Ky., and London: Westminster John Knox, 2007.

Brueggemann, Walter. *The Book that Breathes New Life.* Minneapolis: Fortress, 2005.

Bultmann, R. "Prophecy and Fulfillment." In *Essays on Old Testament Interpretation.* Edited by C. Westermann.

London: SCM, 1963. Also published in *Essays on Old Testament Hermeneutics* (Richmond, Va.: Westminster John Knox, 1963), pp. 50–75.

Frei, Hans. *The Eclipse of Biblical Narrative.* New Haven, Conn., and London: Yale University Press, 1974.

Fretheim, Terence E., and Karlfried Froehlich, eds. *The Bible as Word of God in a Postmodern Age.* Minneapolis: Fortress, 1998. Reprint, Eugene, Ore.: Wipf and Stock, 2002.

Goldingay, John. *Theological Diversity and the Authority of the Old Testament.* Grand Rapids, Mich.: Eerdmans; Carlisle, U.K.: Paternoster, 1986.

Goldingay, John. *Models for Scripture.* Grand Rapids, Mich.: Eerdmans; Carlisle, U.K.: Paternoster, 1994.

Green, Joel B., and Max Turner, eds. *Between Two Horizons.* Grand Rapids, Mich.: Eerdmans, 1999.

Jodock, Darrell. *The Church's Bible.* Minneapolis: Fortress, 1989.

Martin, Lee M., and James A. Sanders, eds. *The Canon Debate.* Peabody, Mass.: Hendrickson, 2002.

Packer, J. I. *"Fundamentalism" and the Word of God.* London: IVF; Grand Rapids, Mich.: Eerdmans, 1958.

Pannenberg, Wolfgang, ed. *Revelation as History.* New York and London: Macmillan, 1968.

Reventlow, H. Graf. *The Authority of the Bible and the Rise of the Modern World.* London: SCM, 1984; Philadelphia: Fortress, 1985.

Robinson, H. W. *Inspiration and Revelation in the Old Testament.* Oxford and New York: Oxford University Press, 1946.

Schneiders, Sandra M. *The Revelatory Text.* 2d ed. Collegeville, Minn.: Liturgical Press, 1999.

Warfield, Benjamin B. *The Inspiration and Authority of the Bible.* Philadelphia: Presbyterian and Reformed, 1948; London: Marshall, 1951.

Wright, N. T. *Last Word.* San Francisco: Harper, 2005.

John Goldingay

SERVANT OF GOD

The Old Testament names various persons "servant of the Lord." But the history of interpretation has assigned a special importance to the figure in Isaiah 40–55 who is given this title. Ancient readers generated this history, readers who lived in a God-ordered world spoken of in sacred texts. Thus, for the heirs of this tradition, the topic has a theological significance inseparable from the history of interpretation, a history fundamentally shaped by the book of Isaiah itself.

The Servant of the Lord in 2 Isaiah. In contrast to most premodern readers, many scholars now interpret the servant passages of Isaiah 40–55 in the light of the formation of the book of Isaiah. Isaiah is widely regarded as a composite work. Chapters 1–39 (1 Isaiah) preserve the original sayings of the eighth-century prophet Isaiah alongside later additions; chapters 40–55 (2 Isaiah) derive from a prophet active at the end of the Babylonian Exile and include later material as well; chapters 56–66 (3 Isaiah) stem from some time in the postexilic period or later.

As scholarly views regarding the relationship of these three parts of the book have changed, so too have interpretations of the servant. Bernhard Duhm's commentary helped transform the interpretive context of the servant passages in two respects. First, Duhm assured the separation of chapters 1–39 from 40–66 by upholding the view that both halves of the book developed independently from each other, being joined secondarily only at a late date. Second, Duhm judged several of these servant passages to be later additions, which he called the "servant of Yahweh songs" (42:1–4; 49:1–6; 50:4–9; 52:13—53:12). Hence, Duhm's highly influential compositional model effectively cut these texts off from both 1 and 2 Isaiah. Both became largely irrelevant as literary contexts for understanding these "Servant Songs," whose true home (according to Duhm) had been lost to history.

Duhm's model remains influential, though not for the most part in its original form. Many in the twenty-first century think chapters 40–66 were composed in the light of material in 1 Isaiah. And those who have not outright rejected Duhm's theory of separate "songs" now usually see these passages as having been integrated into their present context by editorial reinterpretation. For instance, many regard Isaiah 42:5–9, 49:7–13, and 50:10–11 as secondary elaborations of 42:1–4, 49:1–6, and 50:4–9. Other texts seem to presuppose these "songs" (e.g., 42:3//51:4b; 42:4//51:5b; 50:8a//51:5a; 50:9b//51:6b, 8a) so that either these "songs" were never independent of 2 Isaiah or these passages were written after the "songs" were inserted (cf. 51:16a//49:2a; 59:21).

Accordingly, scholars now read the servant passages in the light of their broader context in the book. For instance, whereas Duhm did not identify the servant of 42:1–4 as Israel, many later scholars did, finding support in the context of 2 Isaiah. Just as Isaiah 42:1 speaks of "my servant" and "my chosen one," so Isaiah 41:8 refers to Israel as "my servant," whom "I have chosen" (author's translation). In both, God will "uphold" (*tāmak*) the servant (41:10; 42:1), a verb used only one other time in the book and therein a different connection (33:15). All of this suggests that the servant of 42:1–4 has been identified as Israel. Whether this identification was the original intention of the passage or the product of secondary editorial interpretation is difficult to know. In short, the literary context of the book is now being given its due weight in the interpretation of 2 Isaiah's servant passages.

Causes of interpretive disagreement. The servant passages of 2 Isaiah have produced a host of differing interpretations. Is the servant all Israel, part of Israel, the prophets, the priests, a Judean king, the Persian king Cyrus, the Messiah, a prophet, the prophet who wrote 2 Isaiah, a disciple, or someone else? No small share of the responsibility for this profusion of conflicting interpretations must be assigned to Duhm's theory, which left these texts without context and thus open to an almost endless number of competing understandings. At the same time, however, the texts themselves present serious difficulties for the reader. While some passages clearly identify Israel as the servant, others leave the referent unspecified and seem to speak of an individual, despite the fact that all of the passages share a similar literary profile. Moreover, in some instances, scholars detect multiple roles combined in a single passage, which may have been original or the result of editing. The editing of 2 Isaiah raises the possibility that the identity of the servant shifted in the process of composition, leaving us with composite portraits. The interpretive disagreement surrounding these passages also derives from the much older debate between Jews and Christians over the identity of the servant.

Key interpretive issues. Interpretations of 2 Isaiah's servant typically handle at least three analytically distinct but related exegetical issues. Does the referent of the word "servant" in 2 Isaiah remain the same or change? How are role and identity related in 2 Isaiah's "servant" texts? Does the "servant" refer to a group or an individual?

Constant or changing referent. Does every occurrence of the word "servant" have the same referent throughout 2 Isaiah, or does the referent change? A high level of continuity between the relevant passages is clear. God will "show his glory" through his servant (44:23; 49:3), "helping" and "upholding" him for success (41:9–10; 42:1–6; 44:2; 49:5, 8; 50:7–9; 52:13; 53:10). Opponents of God's servant will not succeed but rather perish (41:11–13; 50:8–11; cf. 51:7–8). By means of God's servant, divine "instruction" and "justice" will go forth, providing a "light" to the nations (42:1–4, 6; 49:6, 8; 51:4–5). The servant is "despised" and "kings" will "see" (49:7//52:15; 53:3). He does not raise his voice when faced with adversity (42:2–4//53:7). For many scholars, however, such continuity has not translated into a continuity of identity, some discerning more than one figure behind 2 Isaiah's servant passages. Much of the continuity in these texts deals with the divine purpose, rather than necessarily the identity of the servant. Indeed, without mentioning any such agent, Isaiah 51:4–5 states that God himself will carry out the task initially assigned to servant Israel, a point made through deliberate allusion to Isaiah 42:1–4.

Role and identity. What is the relationship between role and identity in the servant passages? The complex nature of this relationship is illustrated well by Isaiah 42:1–4(9). Here, the portrait of the servant draws on the description of the Davidic king in Isaiah 11:1–10. In both texts, the "spirit" of God is placed "upon" the figure, in 11:1–10, so that he can "judge" (*yišpôṭ*) and, in 42:1–4, so that he can bring forth "justice" (*mišpāṭ*). The allusion suggests the servant receives the role initially given to the king, a point strengthened if 42:5–9 alludes to 9:1–2. In support of this, many note that the multiple features ascribed to the servant here can only be applicable all at once to a royal figure: in the Old Testament, some kings have a similar presentation (e.g., 1 Sam 9:17), are endowed with the "spirit" (e.g., 1 Sam 16:16), and are titled "my servant" and "my chosen one" (e.g., Ps 89:3, the only other biblical example outside 2 Isaiah where these phrases stand in parallel in the singular). Thus, Isaiah 42 probably offers a royal portrait of the servant. However, according to many scholars, it would be wrong to infer from this royal portrait that the passage now has in mind an individual king since the context indicates that the servant here is Israel (e.g., 41:8–10). This may be related to Isaiah 55:3–5, where the "sure mercies of David" are promised to the people if they obey, which could indicate that the people themselves will inherit the role once enjoyed by King David.

While role and identity, therefore, ought to be recognized as distinct categories, they are nevertheless closely related, as in Isaiah 49:1–6 and 50:4–9, where the servant reflects on his prophetic ministry in the first person—a fact suggesting to many scholars that this is the prophet responsible for 2 Isaiah. Thus, his commission to "return" (lĕšôbēb) Jacob to God (49:5) corresponds exactly with the divine word uttered by the prophet, "return [šûbâ] to me, for I have redeemed you" (44:22). And his equipping with a "learned tongue" to help the "weary" (yāʿēp) with a word (50:4) coincides precisely with the prophet's assurance that God "gives strength to the weary [yāʿēp]" (40:29), an adjective only occurring these two times in the book. For many, once this identification has been made, the identity of the suffering servant of 52:13—53:12 comes into sharper focus. The prophet who reflects on the futility of his ministry in 49:4 and his sufferings in 50:6 is now remembered in 52:13—53:12 for his sufferings and death on behalf of others, in which capacity his life is remarkably called an ʾāšām (53:10), a word variously rendered as "guilt offering" or "restitution." Reinforcing the prophet's relationship to the suffering servant are the parallels each share with Jeremiah (Isa 49:1//Jer 1:5; Isa 53:7–8//Jer 11:19).

Individual or group. Does "servant" in 2 Isaiah refer to an individual or a group? In many instances, 2 Isaiah explicitly identifies God's "servant" as Israel (41:8–9; 42:18–25; 43:10 [cf. v. 1]; 44:1–2, 21; 45:4; 48:20; 49:3). However, all of these identifications (except 49:3) occur in chapters 40–48, which leaves 50:4–11 and 52:13—53:12. In these passages, if the "you" is Israel,

then his/my "servant" must be somebody else (50:10; 52:13–15). (Emending "you" to "him" in 52:14 finds very little support in the manuscript evidence.) Isaiah 52:13—53:12 also distinguishes the servant from the speakers: "surely he bore our sicknesses" (53:4). Accordingly, only Isaiah 49:1–6 calls the servant "Israel" (v. 3) within Isaiah 49–55. Yet, even here a straightforward identification with the nation is complicated by verse 5, "and now, says the LORD who formed me in the womb to be his servant in order to bring Jacob back to himself." According to this verse (on the syntax, see Hermisson, 2003, pp. 359–360), the servant has a mission to the people of Israel, which forces a distinction between the two. For these reasons, many reasonably identify the servant as the nation Israel in 40–48 but as somebody else in 49–55, be it an individual or a subgroup within Israel.

The servant in 2 Isaiah's strategy. Is there a strategy behind 2 Isaiah's use of the term "servant"? Several scholars understand the servant passages in the light of the widely acknowledged division within 2 Isaiah between chapters 40–48 and 49–55. Thus, Peter Wilcox and David Paton-Williams (1988) argue that the servant is Israel in 40–48 but the prophet in 49–55. In their view, chapters 40–48 identify Israel as the servant with a mission to the nations, a mission that, because of the people's failure, is then transferred to the prophet in 49–55. Hence, Isaiah 40–48 concludes by accusing the people of disobedience in chapter 48, and Isaiah 49–55 begins with a redefinition of the prophet's mission to include the Gentiles in 49:5–6. This, they argue, explains the odd statement in 49:3–5 where the servant is Israel but also has a mission to Israel. This contradiction—supported by nearly all manuscript evidence—is only apparent, they argue, because verse 3 gives the title "Israel" to the prophet, rather than to the nation. "By the redefinition of his mission to include the nations, and by his designation as 'servant of the Lord,' the prophet has become [the true] Israel" (Wilcox and Paton-Williams, 1988, p. 92). For this reason, one ought to read the word "Israel" in verse 3 not as a vocative ("You are my servant, [O] Israel") but as "a predicate, parallel to 'servant' ('You are my servant, [you are] Israel')" (p. 93). This is why chapters 40–48 explicitly identify the servant as Israel, whereas 49–55 never do this, except in 49:3 where, by all accounts, a transformation of the ministry of the speaker takes place: the speaker now has, alongside a ministry to Israel, a mission to the Gentiles, which he formerly did not have (v. 6), a task earlier assigned to Israel (42:1–4, 6).

The History of Interpretation. The earliest interpreters of 2 Isaiah's servant could have been the editors responsible for 2 Isaiah's present shape. Whether as a result of editing or simply as the original intention, the portrait of the servant served as a paradigm for those in the broader community already in 2 Isaiah itself, a move perhaps invited by the dual application of "servant" to the nation and an individual. In Isaiah 50:4–11, the prophet, God's "servant," states, "Behold, the LORD God will help me.... Behold, all of them [his opponents] will wear out like a garment; a moth will eat them" (v. 9). His confidence expressed here becomes a lesson for the community addressed immediately following this in 51:1–8. Clearly alluding back to the words of the servant, this passage instructs those "who pursue righteousness" and "seek the LORD" (vv. 1, 7) not to fear "the reproach of man" nor "their reviling" because "the moth will eat them like a garment; and like wool a moth will eat them," and unlike the earth, which "will wear out like a garment," God's "salvation will be forever" (vv. 6–8). Here, the portrait of the servant becomes a paradigm for the community, precisely the relationship that also seems to have been set up between the suffering servant and those addressed by the divine introduction to 52:13—53:12: "Just as many [*rabbîm*] were appalled at you, so his appearance was marred unlike that of a man ... so he shall sprinkle/startle many [*rabbîm*] nations" (52:14–15). This comparison comes immediately after an announcement of the servant's future exaltation in 52:13, suggesting the comparison aims to encourage those addressed. This paradigmatic feature of the servant's portrait in 2 Isaiah seems to have become a basic assumption for much subsequent interpretation as various communities sought to understand themselves and their circumstances in the light of these texts.

Third Isaiah. Being written later, 3 Isaiah interprets 2 Isaiah's servant, apparently according to the paradigmatic presentation of the servant in chapters 40–55. In Isaiah 61, a figure describes his ministry in language borrowed almost entirely from 2 Isaiah, especially the servant passages. Hence, "the spirit of the LORD God is on me" (61:1) echoes "I have put my spirit on him" (42:1). Accordingly, many of the tasks assigned to the servant in 2 Isaiah are taken up by this figure: ministry to the "faint" (42:3//61:3), proclaiming release to the "prisoners" (49:9//61:2), rebuilding in the time of "favor" (Isa 49:8//61:2, 4). The preaching ministry of the servant in 49 and 50 is also taken up by the figure of 61, who, like the prophet behind chapters 40–55, has been called "to proclaim" (40:2–6//61:1–2), "to preach good news" (40:9; 41:27; 52:7//61:1), and "to comfort" (40:2; 48:13; 51:3, 12, 19; 52:9; 54:11//61:2) those who "mourn."

Like the voice behind Isaiah 61, these mourners are to emulate 2 Isaiah's servant: they will be a "planting" to "glorify" God (44:23; 49:3//60:21; 61:3) and a "light" to the "nations" (42:6; 49:6//60:1–3). Because they emulate God's servant, they will inherit the promises made to that figure. It is fitting, then, that those "who mourn over Zion" in 61:2–3 are identified as the "servant of the LORD" in 3 Isaiah (66:10–14), a righteous remnant called "a seed from Jacob" (65:9). Unlike their opponents, these servants obeyed the message of the prophet (55:8–9//65:1–2, 10–15), and so, some have argued, are his "seed," that is, disciples, thus fulfilling what was promised of the suffering servant in 53:10, "he shall see seed" (see also 42:1; 51:16a [cf. 49:2]//59:20–21). However, there is more at work in the reception here than mere emulation. When 3 Isaiah speaks of "the servants of the LORD," it limits what was promised to the whole nation (the servant) in 2 Isaiah to a righteous remnant (the servants) from that group. Thus, in 2 Isaiah God promises to save the whole nation, "Jacob/Israel," whom alone he calls "my servant" and "my chosen one" (42:1; 43:20; 45:4); but in Isaiah 65:9–10 God promises to spare a righteous "seed" from Jacob, a "seed" God calls "my servants" and "my chosen ones" (cf. 56:1–8; 59:20–21; 65–66). They, and not the wicked among the people, shall inherit the land.

Daniel. After the book of Isaiah was finished, the reception of 2 Isaiah's servant continued. It continued, however, under pressure from the new literary shape and interpretation given the servant by 3 Isaiah, where in order to receive the promise of old that servant had to be emulated. A striking example of this can be found in the final vision accounts of the book of Daniel, which are thought to stem from the Hellenistic period (ca. 167 B.C.E.) and borrow heavily from the book of Isaiah.

An especially dense cluster of such borrowings comes in Daniel 12:1–3, which patterns the fate of the righteous on that of the suffering servant in Isaiah 52:13—53:12, a move invited by the Isaianic passage itself (on 52:13–15 in this respect, see above). Just as "the righteous one, my servant, will make the many righteous [*yaṣdîq...lārabbîm*]" (Isa 53:11), so those resurrecting to eternal life "make the many righteous [*maṣdîqê hārabbîm*]" (Dan 12:2–3). They are "the insightful ones" (*hammaśkīlîm*), a title from Isaiah 52:13: "my servant will prosper [*yaśkîl*] and be high and lifted up." The Daniel author probably understood the verb in Isaiah 52:13, "be high" (*yārûm*), as a reference to the resurrection of the suffering servant ("he will rise") and this on the basis of Isaiah 26:19, which the Daniel author cites: those who abide in the "dust" will "awake" (Isa 26:19//Dan 12:2). Moreover, "the insightful ones" of Daniel, who are to resurrect to eternal life, take their name from precisely that verse promising the exaltation of the servant (52:13). Such an exegetical deduction will have arisen in response to the tension inherent in the Isaiah passage itself: if the servant died, what did it mean that he would "be high/rise" (52:13; 53:8–9, 10–12)? This tension remains an interpretive problem, some favoring resurrection and others regarding the language about death as merely metaphorical.

Daniel takes the servant of Isaiah 52:13—53:12 as a model for the righteous, being influenced by 3 Isaiah, which regards 2 Isaiah's "servant of the LORD" as a model for the righteous "servants of the LORD." Hence, just as 3 Isaiah contrasts the wicked with God's "servants" who "do" and "hold firm" God's "covenant" (Isa 56:2, 4, 6; cf. 65:8–16; 66:1–15, 22–24), so Daniel contrasts "those who act wickedly toward the covenant" with "the people who know their God" who "hold firm and do," a group including "the insightful ones [*maśkîlê*]

of the people who instruct the many [*lārabbîm*]," an identity echoing the suffering servant (Dan 11:32–33). Just as the opponents of God's servants will become an eschatological "abomination" (Isa 66:24), so the adversaries of "the insightful ones" will resurrect to everlasting "abomination" (Dan 12:2), a word occurring only these two times in the Old Testament. And just as the "servant" and (after him) the "servants" would "shine" in Isaiah (42:6; 49:6; 60:1–3), so too would "the insightful ones" in Daniel 12:3. Thus, when the author of Daniel patterned the righteous after 2 Isaiah's servant, he was influenced by the same move made in 3 Isaiah.

Other Second Temple interpreters. Embedded in both 3 Isaiah and Daniel, then, is a reading pattern grounded in emulating 2 Isaiah's servant. Likely under the influence of one or both of these texts, subsequent interpretation continued to portray various figures and groups after the pattern of the Isaianic servant. In this respect, they understood themselves and their world to be a function of what was (as they saw it) recounted in scripture.

Such an interpretation appears in several Second Temple texts (ca. 515 B.C.E.–70 C.E.), some being written very close in time to the book of Daniel, a few perhaps even before it. Thus, *1 Enoch* 37–71 arguably alludes to 2 Isaiah's servant in portraying the "son of man," a figure clearly related to the "son of man" in Daniel 7 (e.g., "a light to the nations" [*1 En.* 48:4//Isa 42:6; 49:6]). (Later, in the New Testament, Isaiah's servant and Daniel's "son of man" are combined in the person of Jesus.) The Wisdom of Solomon was influenced by 3 Isaiah's "servants" theme (Isa 56:4–5// Wis 3:14). It encourages the righteous suffering community (Wis 3:1–9) with a portrait of the exemplary righteous "servant" patterned after the suffering servant in Isaiah 52:13–53:12 (Wis 1–6). The Jewish community who lived near the Dead Sea also derived their identity from this stream of interpretive tradition: the *Rule of the Community* (1QS) names the master "the instructor" (*maśkîl*) and the sect "the many" (*hārabbîm*), echoing precisely those texts in Isaiah 52:13—53:12 that are taken up by Daniel 11–12. Arguably, other texts preserved by this community also testify to something similar.

Clearly, then, 2 Isaiah's servant functioned as a pattern after which subsequent interpreters understood the identity of various individuals and groups; why they did so is not always transparent. Was the servant (perhaps taken as a figure of the past) seen as worthy of emulation? Or, alternatively, were these early readers interested in disclosing the identity of this mysterious figure? For instance, when Sirach, a Second Temple writing, combines allusions to Elijah's eschatological advent in Malachi 4 with the mission of the servant in Isaiah 49:6 "to restore the tribes of Jacob" (Sir 48:10), does it mean to say that 2 Isaiah's servant is Elijah or that Elijah only emulates this servant? Perhaps the allusion to Isaiah here is too subtle for a certain answer (cf. Mark 1:2–3).

The New Testament. The servant in 2 Isaiah enjoyed a long history of interpretation in subsequent Judaism, being identified variously as Israel, the Messiah, or other figures. In antiquity, however, the interpretation of the servant was perhaps most productive among early Christians (some being Jewish), who understood Jesus and themselves in the light of these Isaianic texts, a move that would shape subsequent Christian theology ever after. New Testament authors appeal to 2 Isaiah's servant to explain Jesus's healing ministry (Matt 12:18–21//Isa 42:1–4), the divine presentation of Jesus after his baptism (Mark 1:1//Isa 42:1), and the ministry of the apostle Paul (2 Cor 6:2//Isa 49:8). Especially important was the portrait of the suffering servant (Isa 52:13—53:12), which they allude to or cite in order to illuminate Jesus's healing of the sick (Matt 8:17), his being arrested (Luke 22:37), the unbelieving response to his miracles (John 13:38), the giving of his life as "a ransom for many" (Mark 10:45), the negative reception of the gospel (Rom 10:16), Paul's mission to the Gentiles (Rom 15:21), and the righteousness to be gained by faith in Christ (Rom 3:21–26).

In many instances, the New Testament seems to follow the argument structure of Isaiah 40–66, where 2 Isaiah's "servant" is to be emulated by 3 Isaiah's "servants." Thus, Luke–Acts regards both Jesus and those he commissions, the apostles, as a light to the Gentiles (Luke 2:29–32; Acts 13:47; 26:17–23//Isa 42:6; 49:6). In 1 Peter 2:21–25 the righteous sufferings of

Christ are described, with Isaiah 53:5–12 as an "example" to be followed by believers who suffer unjustly. Philippians 2:5–11 also exhorts believers to follow the example of Christ, who left his exalted status, humbling himself by taking on the form of a "slave/servant," submitting himself to death, but then being exalted above all with a name above every name, at which "every knee should bend" and "every tongue confess that Jesus Christ is Lord" (Isa 45:23; 52:13—53:12). The name above every name may reflect an inner-Isaianic development of Isaiah 6:1 where God is "high and lifted up," language borrowed by the exaltation of the servant in 52:13 and transformed into a divine name in 57:15. Acts 8:27–39 may also testify to 3 Isaiah's influence on the reception history of 2 Isaiah's servant. Just as Isaiah 56:1–8 offers "foreigners" and "eunuchs" the opportunity to become "servants" of the Lord, so Acts 8:27–39 tells how an Ethiopian eunuch read a passage about the suffering servant (Isa 53:7–8), inquired as to the identity of this figure, and, upon being told the good news about Jesus from this passage, was baptized by Philip (cf. Luke 4:21// Isa 61:1–2).

The writers of the New Testament relied on these Isaianic texts to explain Jesus, themselves, and the early church. Whether or not Jesus understood his own life in the light of these texts has long been a matter of debate, though a positive answer is favored by the long history of just such a reading of 2 Isaiah's servant in the pre-Christian period.

[*See also* Exile and Dislocation *and* Isaiah.]

BIBLIOGRAPHY

Beuken, Willem A. M. "Servant and Herald of Good Tidings: Isaiah 61 as an Interpretation of Isaiah 40–55." In *The Book of Isaiah*, edited by J. Vermeylen, pp. 411–440. Leuven, Belgium: Leuven University Press, 1989.

Blenkinsopp, Joseph. *Opening the Sealed Book: Interpretations of the Book of Isaiah in Late Antiquity.* Grand Rapids, Mich.: Eerdmans, 2006.

Dell, Katharine J. "The Suffering Servant of Deutero-Isaiah: Jeremiah Revisited." In *Genesis, Isaiah and Psalms: A Festschrift to Honour Professor John Emerton for His Eightieth Birthday*, edited by Katharine J. Dell, Graham Davies, and Yee Von Koh, pp. 119–134. Leiden, The Netherlands: Brill, 2010.

Driver, Samuel R., and A. Neubauer. *The Fifty-Third Chapter of Isaiah According to the Jewish Interpreters.* Vol. 2: *Translations.* Oxford and London: James Parker, 1877.

Duhm, Bernhard. *Das Buch Jesaja übersetzt und erklärt.* 4th ed. Göttingen, Germany: Vandenhoeck & Ruprecht, 1922.

Haag, Herbert. *Der Gottesknecht bei Deuterojesaja.* Erträge der Forschung 233. Darmstadt, Germany: Wissenschaftliche Buchgesellschaft, 1985.

Hermisson, Hans-Jürgen. *Deuterojesaja.* Vol. 2: *Jesaja 45, 8–49,13.* Biblischer Kommentar Altes Testament 11. Neukirchen-Vluyn, Germany: Neukirchner Verlag, 2003.

Mettinger, Tryggve N. D. *A Farewell to the Servant Songs: A Critical Examination of an Exegetical Axiom.* Lund, Sweden: CWK Gleerup, 1983.

Nickelsburg, George W. E. *Resurrection, Immortality, and Eternal Life in Intertestamental Judaism and Early Christianity.* Expanded ed. Cambridge, Mass.: Harvard University Press, 2006.

Sommer, Benjamin D. *A Prophet Reads Scripture: Allusion in Isaiah 40–66.* Stanford, Calif.: Stanford University Press, 1998.

Steck, Odil Hannes. *Gottesknecht und Zion: Gesammelte Aufsätze zu Deuterojesaja.* Tübingen, Germany: Mohr Siebeck, 1992.

Stromberg, Jacob. *An Introduction to the Study of Isaiah.* London: T&T Clark, 2011a.

Stromberg, Jacob. *Isaiah after Exile: The Author of Third Isaiah as Reader and Redactor of the Book.* Oxford: Oxford University Press, 2011b.

Stuhlmacher, Peter, and Bernd Janowski, eds. *The Suffering Servant: Isaiah 53 in Jewish and Christian Sources.* Grand Rapids, Mich.: Eerdmans, 2004.

Teeter, Andrew. "Isaiah and the King of As/syria in Daniel's Final Vision: On the Rhetoric of Inner-Scriptural Allusion and the Hermeneutics of 'Mantological Exegesis.'" In *A Teacher for All Generations: Essays in Honor of James C. VanderKam*, edited by Eric F. Mason and Samuel I. Thomas, pp. 169–199. Leiden, The Netherlands: Brill, 2012.

Wilcox, Peter, and David Paton-Williams. "The Servant Songs in Deutero-Isaiah." *Journal for the Study of the Old Testament* 42 (1988): 79–102.

Williamson, Hugh G. M. *The Book Called Isaiah: Deutero-Isaiah's Role in Composition and Redaction.* Oxford: Clarendon, 1994.

Williamson, Hugh G. M. *Variations on a Theme: King, Messiah and Servant in the Book of Isaiah.* Carlisle, U.K.: Paternoster, 1998.

Jacob Stromberg

SEXUALITY

Because the Bible is a collection of books containing multiple voices collected over centuries, it contains different and even opposing viewpoints on many topics, including this one. God declares all creation good (Gen 1:31), and part of fruitful creation is to multiply. The perspective is male, and biblical laws sought to maintain the binary distinction between male and female present in creation and to channel male sexual energy into marriage, family, reproduction, and child rearing. But Genesis describes male dominance as a result of the fall. Sexual mutuality is regained in the Song of Songs, which affirms mutual sexual desire. In other works, sexual potency indicates power: Solomon's 700 wives and 300 concubines, for example, symbolize the power of his rule. In the New Testament, purity concerns prevail. Jesus affirms marriage and sexual continence for followers while condemning divorce, adultery, and desire for another man's wife. But in the resurrection there will be no marriage, he tells followers. Assuming the transience of the present age, Paul promotes sometimes marriage and sometimes abstention.

Language. To understand the distance that separates the Bible from our world, consider the language different biblical books use to speak about marriage and family. The Hebrew language has no verb "to marry" and no nouns "marriage" or "family," nor does it have a specific word for wife or husband. Instead, we find a type of sentence, "X takes Y as his woman" (e.g., Gen 28:2; Matt 1:20), in which a man is the subject and a woman, the object. The sentence infers ownership (of a woman by a man) in a context of marriage. This is language of social exchange, not individual affections. If the man has more than one wife, then he possesses more than one woman. The sentence also implies patrilocality: the bride moves to the house of the groom, where the new unit creates what we might call an extended family. In the household of this extended family are also slaves who relate socially and sexually to the man.

Both in Hebrew (the language of the Hebrew Bible or Old Testament) and in Greek (the language of the Second or New Testament), the word for man (Heb.

'iš; Gk *anēr*) is translated "husband" when translators deem it appropriate. Similarly, words for woman (Heb. *'išâ*; Gk *gunē* like the Latin word *mulier* used in the Vulgate) indicate both "woman" and "wife." Hebrew and Greek societies probably assume that all men and women are married. There is no word in Greek or Hebrew that exactly corresponds to the modern word "family"; the closest Greek word, *oikia*, or *oikos*, means variously household or house, like *bet* in Hebrew, which similarly means house and can be used for household in the sense of family lineage. "Marriage" is a contemporary word implying a unit that does not convey the notion of possession found in biblical texts. Even if the woman is taken by a man from close kinship groups, other women in the household (slaves and dependents) relate to the man as inferior and subordinate. This implies sexual availability: Abraham, for example, has sex with Hagar, an Egyptian slave in his household (Gen 16); Jacob has sex with Bilhah and Zilpah, two female slaves (Gen 30). Biblical texts do not describe or reflect on being single. Women are not autonomous beings in that world. Biblical laws stipulate female virginity (Deut 22:13–22) and therefore control of women's bodies.

Adultery. Adultery, the sexual congress of a male with a married or betrothed woman, is severely punished (Exod 20:14; Lev 20:10) as a crime of property, not sexual, offense. The property in question is the woman's sexuality, which her husband, not she herself, owns. Hence, adultery occurs when a man has sexual relations with a woman married (or "owned") by another man (Deut 22:22–24). If the woman is a slave, widow, or prostitute, then no crime has taken place. If the woman is under the authority of her father, then the man must pay the woman's father a bride-price and take her into his household as his woman or wife unless the father refuses (Exod 22:16–17; Deut 22:28–29). But laws against adultery, Jesus says, are not the point. Sexually desiring another man's wife contravenes God's law (Matt 5:27). Control and regulation of male sexual intent is the issue.

Regulation of male sexual desire includes all forms of child sexual abuse, probably including pederasty (Mark 9:42–48 identifies one who puts a "stumbling block" before "little ones"). Further, John the Baptist

(and presumably Jesus) condemns Herod Antipas for marrying his brother's wife (Mark 6:17–18) on grounds of incest (Lev 18:16). We know Jesus opposes divorce.

Marriage and Polygyny. Genesis identifies human physicality in two creation stories. The second creation account of Genesis 2 shows a concern for relationship, "it is not good that the man should be alone" (Gen 2:18). So God created woman to be a suitable companion to man. Taking a rib out of his side, God fashions a woman. Their sexual connection is explained positively: "therefore a man leaves his father and his mother and clings to his wife and they become one flesh" (Gen 2:24). The man and the woman are thus "bone of my bones, and flesh of my flesh." Some may see this as "hetero-normative marriage," but the text does not speak of marriage. Even if we infer marriage from statements about the man and the woman (2:25, "the man and his wife were both naked, and were not ashamed"), what is normative about a rib-less male who "clings to his wife" as a means to wholeness? Genesis 3 describes patriarchy and hierarchical sexual relations as a result of human disobedience, not sexual relations. Descriptions of barren women in subsequent narratives (Sarah, Rebecca, Rachel, Leah, Hannah, and Elizabeth) indicate that reproduction is not a male accomplishment but a blessing from God.

A positive view of sexual relations continues in the Song of Songs read descriptively not allegorically. In it, a woman pursues a man for sexual relations. The text speaks of the erotic yearning of the man and the woman rather than sexuality per se. Nothing in the text speaks of marriage or procreation. By speaking positively about longing, the text provides the only biblical metaphysics of sex: "Love is strong as death, passion fierce as the grave....Many waters cannot quench love, neither can floods drown it" (Song 8:6–7).

Reflecting ancient Hebrew and later Greek and Roman cultures, the Bible considers marriage as a social and legal agreement to secure alliances, to engender children and through them future generations, to care for the elderly, and to make provision for the inheritance of property. It cements political alliances and connects clans. To the marriage a bridegroom brings a betrothal gift or "bride-price" that compensates for the loss of a daughter to her family of origin. Examples include Jacob, who gives 14 years of labor to Laban in exchange for Leah and Rachel in Genesis 29; Deuteronomy 22:29, which stipulates 50 shekels as the proper "bride-price"; and David, who gives Saul 100 Philistine foreskins for his daughter Michal. The bride brings to the marriage a dowry (property, clothing, jewelry, household goods) as security in case of widowhood or divorce.

Marital delight is clear. Sarah remembers sexual pleasure with Abraham (Gen 18:12). New bridegrooms are exempt from military campaigns for a year in order to cause their wives to rejoice (Deut 20:7; 24:5). Intact families demand sexual fidelity, and the best way to ensure this is for the man to find sexual satisfaction in marriage (Prov 5:18–19). Women's sexuality is guarded. A woman's virginity before marriage ensured identification of the paternity of her first child. Biblical laws discourage (but do not prohibit) adultery of married men (Deut 22:28). The commandment "You shall not covet your neighbor's wife" (Exod 20:17) is directed at husbands, not wives. While polygyny (one man possessing sexual rights over many women) exists in the case of Israelite kings (David and Solomon) and patriarchs (Abraham), it may depend on the man's wealth, the need for alliances (in the case of rulers), and women's shorter life spans. Marriage of one man and one woman is assumed in Genesis 2:24 and the Song of Songs.

It seems that both men and women could divorce. Deuteronomy 24:1–4, often cited as a divorce text, actually describes the case of a man seeking to remarry the same woman. The Elephantine papyri (sixth century B.C.E.) from a Judean settlement in Egypt contain documents in which a woman divorces her husband. Given the importance the Hebrew Bible accords to marriage, it is no surprise that the Bible commends having children, particularly sons (Gen 1:28; Ps 127:3–5). It is never too late: Sarah conceives at the age of 90 with God's help (Gen 17), thus fulfilling God's promise to Abraham that his descendants would be as numerous as the stars of heaven (Gen 17; 22). At the same time, biblical texts describe the dangers of childbirth and high child mortality in a society with a life expectancy of 30 years for

women and 40 for men. To order sexuality, laws forbade sexual contact with women during menstruation (Lev 18:19), that is, at times less likely to result in conception. This also helps explain the prohibition of same-sex relations (Lev 18:22–23). Nevertheless, in a culture that values sons, Ruth 1:16–17 describes the loyal refusal of Ruth to leave her mother-in-law Naomi in language that is often read aloud in Christian weddings. Naomi's neighbors describe Ruth as worth more than seven sons to her mother-in-law (Ruth 4:15). In fact, by describing strong bonds of affection between Ruth and Naomi and between David and Jonathan (2 Sam 1:25–26), it may be that behind the texts some same-sex friendships express more companionship than does marriage.

In the New Testament, Jesus values marriage (John 2:1–12) and is described as a bridegroom in the Gospels (John 3:29; Mark 2:20). The Gospels preserve Jesus's citation of Genesis 1:27 and 2:24 describing marriage as an indissoluble bond sanctioned by God. We know Jesus opposes divorce (Mark 10:1–9). As we noted, John the Baptist (and presumably Jesus) condemns Herod Antipas's marriage of his brother's wife on grounds of incest (Lev 18:16; Mark 6:17–18). In the resurrection Jesus says that there will be no marriage (Mark 12:25; Matt 22:30).

Rape. Several narratives describe attempted or real rape of men and women by predatory males. In Genesis 19, inhabitants of the cities of Sodom attempt to rape divine beings under the protection of Lot. Although the divine beings manage to escape, such evil inhospitality secures the city's destruction. Judges 19 describes the gang rape and murder of the Levite's concubine in Gibeah. The depravity of the attack indicates a premonarchic state of tribal warfare as in the following narrative the tribe of Benjamin is almost eradicated. After Amnon rapes his halfsister Tamar (2 Sam 13), the narrative describes his change from lust to loathing.

God. From a theological perspective, the Bible understands God to be alone. But the monotheism of postexilic prophetic literature in 2 Isaiah is challenged by other passages: Ezekiel 1:27, for example, describes the divine loins; Yahweh is metaphorically husband and father to Israel in, for example, Hosea, while in the New Testament Jesus is God's Son. Historically, the God of the Hebrew Bible exists with a consort: at Kuntillet 'Ajrud, for example, archaeologists have found an eighth-century B.C.E. depiction of two figures with the inscription "Yahweh and his Asherah." But the Bible itself contains other, more female images of a God of mercy (*rahamim*) connected to the Hebrew word for "womb," *rehem*. An older description has God in labor pains while giving birth to Israel (Deut 32:18, NJPS). Male and/or female, the Bible goes to great lengths not to describe God as sexually active, although occasional statements indicate that biblical writers experimented: "I have produced a man with the help of the LORD," Eve exclaims in Genesis 4:1.

Paul, Deutero-Paul, and the Pastoral Epistles. Paul shares a Jewish belief in the goodness of God's creation, of which marriage—and sexual relations within marriage—is a part. In Paul's letters, women and men experience sexual desire or "burning." But because marriage and sexual relations are part of the present transitory age, Paul deems marriage inferior to singleness. Sexual intercourse outside marriage with any woman is immorality (*porneia*), and Paul cites Genesis 2:24 to argue that sex with an immoral woman creates a bond that undoes the bond of that man with Christ (1 Cor 6:16–17).

Paul sees same-sex intercourse in Romans 1 as a confusion reflecting disorder that ensues when people exchange worshipping God for idols. His assessment is that such relations transgress Leviticus 18:22 and 20:13, pervert God's intention, and thus bring shame on all parties. Like contemporary Stoic philosophers, Paul advocates self-control of passions and avoidance of excess. Marriage is a remedy for those unable to practice restraint. First Corinthians 7:1–5 indicates that his response to a Corinthian statement, "It is good not to touch a woman," includes admonitions to mutual care, respect, and agreement in contexts of marriage and pleasing the Lord. Perhaps because of the shortness of time, Paul does not discuss procreation as reason for marriage (cf. Jer 16:1–2).

Behind and in the New Testament, we see married, widowed, and single women in leadership positions: Prisca and her husband, Aquila, were associated with house churches in Ephesus and Rome (1 Cor 16:19; Rom 16:3–5); Nympha hosts an assembly in her house (Col 4:15); Lydia, a household owner whose household probably included slaves, deals in purple cloth in Thyatira (Acts 16:11–15, 40); and Junia was an apostle before Paul with her husband, Andronicus (Rom 16:7). We can see the contours of households and family life in the world of the New Testament when we read household codes prescribing household relations by including slaves, former slaves, clients, and dependent workers in a household. If they were read aloud in assemblies, the household codes directly addressed wives, children, fathers, and slaves as well as husbands as heads of households. How would Nympha react when she heard in Colossians 3:18, "Wives, be subject to your husbands, as is fitting in the Lord!" Did it have an effect on her life, or was it simply repeated traditional teaching?

First Peter 3:1–2 and 1 Timothy 6:1–2 reveal that wives have joined different assemblies (churches) without their husbands, indicating that some women made independent choices to join groups. We may compare Luke 8:1–3, where Joanna, wife of Herod's steward Chuza, is one of the followers of a peripatetic Jesus. If Joanna follows the mission as a woman who has separated from her husband, then perhaps Luke is emphasizing the magnitude of personal sacrifice that disciples are willing to make; but then, where is Joanna getting the resources she is using to support the mission? Independently wealthy women did exist in Jesus's world, but one of the socioeconomic reasons for opposition to divorce was the destitution it often imposed on a divorced woman. Another possibility is that Joanna has not, in fact, separated from her husband but has gone on a mission with Chuza's permission or perhaps even under his direction. Luke may be implying that Chuza approves of the mission sufficiently to be willing to second his wife to it and undergo the consequent deprivation. However things stand with Chuza, Joanna, unlike other disciples, is not described as having left anything; she remains "the wife of Chuza," and she witnesses the empty tomb in Luke 24:10.

The letter to the Ephesians contains a "household code" in which duties for household members are described, particularly the married couple, whose relationship is compared to Christ and the church. Here, the metaphor of Israel as God's wife, familiar in Hosea, is recast not in terms of faithfulness or unfaithfulness but in language of hierarchy, respect, and love. In fact, although there is language of mutual submission in reverence of Christ for husband and wife (Eph 5:21), and although there is no verb in the Greek text of Ephesians 5:22 (a fact ignored by most modern translations), wives are still enjoined to be inferior in their subjection to husbands in everything as the church is to Christ (5:24). Husbands are to love their wives and make them holy as Christ purifies the church, his body (5:25–27). For the author of Ephesians, a patriarchal household reflects the relationship of Christ to the church. To what extent this reinterprets Paul is a matter of debate.

The author of the Pastoral Epistles (1, 2 Timothy and Titus) commends self-control (*sophrosunē*) as a key virtue, particularly in relation to sexuality (2 Tim 1:7; Titus 1:8; 2:2; 12). The self-control of older men (Titus 2:2) is not that of younger women. Their self-control is being chaste in relation to their husbands and in managing the household (Titus 2:4–5).

Eunuchs. Jesus commends voluntary eunuchs to the disciples in Matthew 19:12. This leads us to conjecture that disciples as eunuchs exist in the Matthean community. They have voluntarily given up all honor deriving from family, possessions, and wealth and are exclusively loyal to the kingdom. Honor and status (central values in the world of the New Testament) derive from the heavenly Father. Status acquired through proximity and service to the heavenly Father cannot be passed to one's heirs. To Peter's poignant question posed after Jesus's teaching about eunuchs, "Look, we have left everything and followed you. What then will we have?" Jesus offers status and power, not in this world but in the next. Jesus promises Peter that when the Son of Man is seated on the throne of his glory, those followers will also sit on 12 thrones, "judging the 12 tribes of Israel. And every one who has left houses or brothers or sisters or father or mother or children or lands, for my name's sake, will receive a

hundredfold, and will inherit eternal life" (19:27–29). If some of Matthew's disciples are taking Jesus's injunctions seriously enough to make themselves the equivalent of children or slaves, they have no heirs or possessions in this life.

In Matthew 19:12, Jesus is not talking about single people, be they unmarried or widowed, or people with celibate vocations. There are many other ways to commend sexual continence; for example, Paul boasts of his unmarried state and praises the single person and the widowed without ever mentioning eunuchs. We must survey roles and functions of eunuchs in Israelite, Persian, Hellenistic Greek, Nubian, Byzantine, and Chinese history.

If eunuchs are full members of the Matthean community, then we see roles and titles in the whole Gospel differently. Matthew's community is neither ascetic nor celibate: the passage includes children in the community, and mothers are an important part of the whole Gospel. The injunction of Matthew 23:9, to call no man father on earth, "for you have one Father—the one, in heaven," is often understood to describe Matthew's community as one of equals under one heavenly Father. Those who obey the command to "call no one your father" must also surrender their own right to be called father with all attendant privileges. They must surrender also their claim on their offspring, who become children of the one Father in heaven. A begetter's responsibility for care and nurturing of the children remains part of his responsibility toward the whole community, but he has become, effectively, Isaiah's "dry tree," a eunuch. Here is another way that some "make themselves eunuchs" for the sake of the kingdom. In a community where some cannot beget, one way to ensure equality may be to require that all surrender the privilege of fatherhood.

Jesus's commendation of those who become eunuchs specifically undermines male heterosexual privilege. At the heart of Jesus's message commending certain social behaviors for men and women lies a refusal to claim the privilege and power of the father, which belong only to God. In contemporary discussions of sexual identity, Matthew 19 reminds us that Jesus commends to some of his disciples the absolute severing of family ties and complete subordination for the sake of the kingdom.

Importance of the Topic. Despite all attempts to make it say more, the Bible really has very little interest in sexuality. Exhortations to practice acts of charity are far more prevalent in the Bible than injunctions to be fruitful and multiply.

In her 1992 book *In the Wake of the Goddesses: Women, Culture and the Biblical Transformation of Pagan Myth*, Tikvah Frymer-Kensky argues that because Israel's God incorporated all the character and functions of the female goddesses, gender disappears from biblical monotheism. Consequently, in the recitation of the Genesis creation narrative, for example, humans need not be concerned about creation or continuity of fertility in the earth. Epitomized in the creative word, God has power over fertility, creation, and reproduction. Israel's heroes Isaac, Jacob, Joseph, Samson, and Samuel are all born after divine action opens wombs that were closed. Stories of their birth convey the message that God alone can cause conception. As for gender, she argues that the Bible does not see men and women as being different in essence. They are socially unequal, and women are subordinate; but they are not inferior in any intellectual or spiritual way. She sees the Bible's positive evaluation of women as one of the beneficial effects of biblical monotheism, but she also notes negative effects of the Bible's removal of gender from the divine, particularly the fact that the Bible, and Judaism and Christianity in general, have so little to say about such important things as human sexuality and reproduction. "The Bible never really incorporates sexuality into its vision of humanity or its relationship with the divine," she writes (p. 187).

Similarly, the New Testament says little about human sexuality. A Christian doctrine of marriage developed well after the time of the New Testament, namely, in the patristic and early medieval periods. Attempts to ground Christian definitions of the sacrament of marriage in Paul's counsel that marriage was safer than unconsidered celibacy (in 1 Cor 7), in the metaphor of the marriage of Christ and the Church in Ephesians 5, and in Jesus's prohibition of divorce (Mark 10:2–9; Matt 19:3–9 [cf. 5:31–32]; Luke 16:18) were made well after the time of the New Testament. These texts do not together or separately comprise a coherent statement on marriage, nor were they intended to. Attempts to use, for example, Jesus's statements to uphold the sanctity of heterosexual marriage must heed one thing: Jesus's statements link marriage and divorce. Jesus never considers marriage apart from divorce. Even if Jesus's prohibition of divorce views it as a concession to human failure to live out marriage, divorce/marriage is a given in all three Gospels.

If we recognized that sexuality is marginal in biblical tradition, that the Bible has no vision to help integrate human sexuality, and that a Christian theology of the sacrament of marriage is patristic and medieval, what might be the consequences for our contemporary debates about sexuality in the church and elsewhere? One is that because sexuality seems to be of no great concern to either God or Jesus according to the biblical record, we need to recognize this gap before we rush to fill it. Minding this gap helps us understand that while the Bible recognizes the power of the erotic (think of the biblical laws regulating sexual behavior and the statement in the Song of Songs, "for love is stronger than death"), it is in fact the ideations, imaginations, and fantasies of scholars and religious people that have created modern discourses about sexuality in ancient Israel or in the New Testament. Rather than promoting discourses that regulate and restrict human sexual behavior, we could affirm that a gap is a space into which we must put different discourses, so we can be intentional about what we are doing. Minding the gap helps us understand that, except for pederasty and adultery, we have no biblical mandate to argue on the basis of sexual practice for the exclusion of anyone from Christian communities or for the exclusion of ourselves from community with others. Precisely because of this gap we can afford inclusion to differently constituted families and households.

[*See also* Anthropology; Ethics, Biblical; Family; Honor and Shame; Image of God; *and* Marriage.]

BIBLIOGRAPHY

Brown, Peter. *The Body and Society: Men, Women, and Sexual Renunciation in Early Christianity*. New York: Columbia University Press, 1988.

Coogan, Michael. *God and Sex: What the Bible Really Says*. New York: Twelve, 2010.

Frymer-Kensky, Tikvah. *In the Wake of the Goddesses: Women, Culture, and the Biblical Transformation of Pagan Myth*. New York: Free Press, 1992.

Loader, William. *Sexuality and the Jesus Tradition*. Grand Rapids, Mich.: Eerdmans, 2005.

Loader, William. *Sexuality in the New Testament: Understanding the Key Texts*. Louisville, Ky.: Westminster John Knox, 2010.

Loader, William. *The New Testament on Sexuality*. Grand Rapids, Mich.: Eerdmans, 2012.

Menn, Esther. "Sexuality in the Old Testament: Strong as Death, Unquenchable as Fire." *Currents in Theology and Mission* 30, no. 1 (February 2003): 37–45.

Osiek, Carolyn, and David L. Balch. *Families in the New Testament World: Households and House Churches*. Louisville, Ky.: Westminster John Knox, 1997.

Rogers, Jack. *Jesus, the Bible, and Homosexuality: Explode the Myths, Heal the Church*. Louisville, Ky.: Westminster John Knox, 2009.

Trible, Phyllis. *God and Rhetoric of Sexuality: Overtures to Biblical Theology*. Philadelphia: Fortress, 1985.

Deirdre Good

SHAME

See Honor and Shame.

SICKNESS, DISEASE, AND HEALING

From what we know of their neighboring cultures, people represented in the Bible held less complex views of sickness and healing. Convinced of the goodness and power of God, biblical writers saw illness primarily as evil, an aberration or the consequence of sin, but also as a means of grace. Healing was an expectation of God, if not in the present then a hope for the future. Because of the sheer number of healing stories associated with him, Jesus dominates the biblical motif of healing.

Understanding the portrayal of disease and healing in the Bible requires considering not only other ancient views but also the cultural, linguistic, and geographical distances of the current reader from the text. For example, translating *selēniazomai* ("moonstruck," only at Matt 4:24; 17:15) as "epileptic" does not take into account the ancient understanding of the impact of the stars and planets on human health (cf. Plutarch, *Mor.* 3.10.658 E–F).

Hebrew Bible. A number of medical papyri reflect a culture probably familiar to the Hebrews in Egypt. For example, an unfinished reference book, the sixteenth-century B.C.E. hieratic Edwin Smith Papyrus, systematically lists 48 injuries, perhaps resulting from battle, including fractures, dislocations, open wounds, and abscesses. Then, from the Nineveh palace library of Ashurbanipal (r. 668–627 B.C.E.), with whom the Hebrews likely had contact (2 Chr 33:10–13), cuneiform tablets list in detail diseases of the head, including headache and hair loss; of the eyes, including dryness, inflammation, and secretion; and of the ears, throat, neck, stomach, bowels, feet, and legs.

In Hebrew, however, medical descriptions are generally confined to broad terms, for example, "weak" (or "ill," *ḥālāh*, Gen 48:1) and "injure" (*nāgap*, Exod 21:22; or "strike," 1 Sam 25:38). Although common ailments such as colds or headaches go unmentioned, particular sicknesses or conditions are recognizable in the text: for example, sciatica (Gen 32:25–32), a plague or epidemic (2 Sam 24:15; 1 Kgs 8:37), possibly a subarachnoid hemorrhage (2 Kgs 4:17–37), dysentery and prolapse of the rectum or large intestine (2 Chr 21:15, 18–19), perhaps a stroke (1 Sam 25:37–38), being deaf (*ḥērēš*, Exod 4:11; Lev 19:14), and mental impairment (*šiggāʾôn*, Deut 28:28). It is generally agreed that leprosy (Hanson disease) was not known before the sixth century C.E. Biblical "leprosy" (*ṣāraʿat*, Lev 13–14; *lepra*, Matt 8:3) was probably an imprecise term covering color changes in clothing (Lev 13:47–49), walls of houses (Lev 14:34–57), and human skin, where the condition could be a boil (Lev 13:18; Job 2:7), a burn (Lev 13:24), ringworm or sycosis (Lev 13:29), or dermatitis (Lev 13:36).

Much of the illness depicted in the Hebrew Bible is caused by humans: war (Josh 6:21; 1 Sam 11:2), massacres (2 Kgs 8:12; 25:7), military sieges (2 Kgs 6:24–32), slavery (Jer 48:7; Joel 3:6; Amos 1:6), and cruel kings (Jer 22; Ezek 34). Accidents also brought wounds (Exod 21:22, 28). However, so-called natural causes are not invoked. Nevertheless, poor hygiene and diet would have contributed to epidemics, and flies infecting eyelids and corneas would have brought blindness. If not congenitally blind, old age (1 Sam 4:15; 1 Kgs 14:4) or perhaps cataracts (Tobit 2:10) robbed others of their sight.

Even if disease is attributed to a supernatural being, God is still taken as responsible for the agent and the sickness (Deut 28:28; 1 Sam 16:14–23; 2 Kgs 6:18; Job 2:6–7; Joel 3:5–6; Amos 1:6; cf. Gen 16:2). Concomitantly, sickness can be explained as the result of rebellion (Exod 8:2; 15:26) or sin against God (Deut 28:15, 22; 1 Kgs 8:33–47; 14:1–14; 2 Chr 21:11–15). However, though from early (Exod 15:26) to later (Sir 38:9–10) times a connection was made between sin and sickness, uncertainty about the relationship is an important theme in Job (22:5–11; 34:5–9). In any case, Hebrew Bible regulations require care of the sick and diseased (Lev 19:14; Deut 27:18; Job 29:15).

Healing. The breadth of the notion of healing as restoration in the Old Testament is expressed in the frequently occurring term *rāpā'*. The term could be used of, for example, recovery from injury (Exod 21:19), the healing of a boil (Lev 13:18) or skin condition (Num 12:13), repairing an altar (1 Kgs 18:30), making water drinkable (2 Kgs 2:21), land restored after drought (2 Chr 7:14), and repairing pottery (Jer 19:11).

Treatments prescribed by ancient Egyptian physicians, who were highly regarded, include the earliest known references to sutures, splints and braces, and cauterization. In one case, along with an anointment and poultice, an incantation is recommended (Edwin Smith Papyrus, case 9). The prescriptions in Assyrian cuneiform tablets typically involved anointment of a preparation combined with the recitation of a brief charm. Though the Hebrews did not appear to sanction charms, they also sought healing from readily available substances, such as mandrake (Gen 30:14–16) and balm or mastic (Jer 46:11). They also used bandages (Ezek 30:21). Also, the hygienic implications of laws (Lev 12:1–5, 13–15; 19:1–22; Num 5:1–5) can reasonably be seen as contributing to better health.

As would be expected of a major ancient deity, Yahweh is widely portrayed as the one who heals. Therefore, the sick prayed to God (Isa 38:1–5, 16–17/2 Kgs 20:1–6). However, the sick sought healing from other individuals, who were sometimes viewed positively (Jer 8:22; Ezek 30:21) and sometimes not (2 Chr 16:12; Job 13:4). Among those consulted for healing were prophets (2 Kgs 4:32–34; 5:1–27).

However, unlike Egyptians, whose medical personnel involved physicians, priests, and magicians (Ebers Papyrus 99; cf. Edwin Smith Papyrus 1, gloss A), and Cyrus II (Persian king from ca. 558 to 529 B.C.E.), who was apparently accompanied by physicians (Xenophon, *Cyr.* 1.6.15), the Hebrews did not have professional healers. Their priests functioned more as observers (Lev 13–14). Later, under Greek influence the Hebrews applauded the physicians who were chiefly pharmacists (Sir 38:8) with skills dependent on God (38:1).

Consistent with both early Mesopotamian and later Greek cultures, in early Hebrew Bible traditions those seeking healing, including for infertility (1 Sam 1), probably attended the temples. Before the sweeping reforms of Hezekiah (king of Judah, ca. 715–ca. 686 B.C.E.), the Jerusalem Temple contained a bronze serpent once used for healing (Num 21:9) and to which offerings were more recently made, perhaps still for healing (2 Kgs 18:4). Hezekiah's cleansing of the Jerusalem Temple, however, probably signaled a change in the central Temple's function. For not only is healing sought apart from the Temple (1 Kgs 8:37–39), but the sick are likely excluded from it (Lev 14:46; 15:31; Num 5:2; 2 Chr 26:16–21; 2 Sam 5:8).

Future hopes. In the face of disappointment and difficult times, including sickness and disease, biblical writers anticipated a better future. Isaiah anticipated blind eyes seeing, the ears of the deaf hearing, the lame leaping as a hart, and the tongue of the stammerer speaking plainly (Isa 35:5–6; cf. 30:26; 42:18; 58:8; Jer 30:17; 33:6). Healing was also expected in *Jubilees* (23.26, 29; cf. *4 Ezra* 7.21; 8.53). For those responsible for the Qumran texts, sight for the blind, straightening for the twisted (4Q521 2.2.8), and healing (CD 8.4), including for the badly wounded (2.2.12), is anticipated. In one text, healing is the principal characteristic of the eschaton (1QS 4.6). Some references to healing were probably initially only metaphors for the future; others would be rendered hollow if not taken literally (e.g., 1QS 4.6; Philo, *Praem.* 15.85–90). Moreover, early Christians interpreted the future hope of healing as at least partly fulfilled in the miracles said to be conducted by Jesus and his followers (e.g., Matt 11:5/Luke 7:22; Justin, *1 Apol.* 22, 48.2, 54.10; *Dial.* 69.3–3; Tertullian, *Adv. Jud.* 9; *Apol.* 21.14–17; *Marc.* 4.24.12, 4.26; *Res.* 20.6).

New Testament. The motif of sickness and healing is related primarily to the pre-Easter ministry of Jesus. Healing was a tangible expression of the Kingdom of God he and his immediate followers announced and was part of Paul's Gospel.

Jesus. Beyond assuming that some sickness involved unclean spirits (Matt 12:22/Luke 11:14) or lack of a sense of forgiveness (Mark 2:1–12), Jesus is said to resist theorizing about the cause of sickness, refusing to link sin and sickness (Luke 13:4; John 9:1–3). It is generally, though not unanimously, agreed that Jesus was well known as a healer.

Though we know of no healer of the period with a reputation equal to that of Jesus, his methods were the stock-in-trade of healers: touching and laying on of hands (1QapGen 20.28–29; Mark 1:31, 41), applying spittle (Tacitus, *Hist.* 4.81; Dio Cassius, *Roman History*, 66.8; Mark 7:33; 8:23), and words of command, especially in exorcisms (Mark 1:25; 5:8, 9; 9:25). A number of sayings likely originating from Jesus show that he took the healings (Matt 11:2–6/Luke 7:18–23), particularly the exorcisms, as the present realization of God's eschatological reign (Matt 12:28/Luke 11:20).

As some sicknesses isolated sufferers from the community and cult (Lev 13:3; 21:17–24; 1QSa 2.3–11; Luke 17:12), healing constituted religious and relational restoration (Mark 1:31). In contrast to the apparent high cost of medicine, healing by Jesus and his followers was notable for depending on faith (Mark 5:25–34) not fees, which continued to be abhorred (Acts 8:14–24; *Did.* 11.6). In view of what Jesus said (Mark 6:6b–13) and from the expectation that in the eschaton sickness would be eliminated, it is not surprising that the New Testament portrays early Christians involved in healing (see Acts).

Paul. The earliest known Christian writer, Paul, considered sickness part of the fallen order (2 Cor 4:16–17) and at least sometimes caused by sin (Rom 1:18–23; 1 Cor 10:1–14; 11:27–32). Nowhere does Paul suggest that demons cause sickness, though he indirectly attributes his thorn in the flesh (probably a physical illness) to "a messenger of Satan."

Physical sickness had a considerable impact on Paul's life. First, sickness humbled him and caused him to see himself as weak (2 Cor 12:1–10). Second, Paul's illness was not healed (12:9). However, third, through his illness he was able to boast in the ongoing experience of God's grace, or the power of Christ, apparent in his weakness (12:8–10). Fourth, for Paul sickness could be an opportunity to proclaim the Gospel (Gal 4:13). Fifth, his illness caused him to fear rejection (Gal 4:13–14). Sixth, Paul mentions God's mercy causing Epaphroditus, his coworker, to recover from near death, relieving Paul of sorrow (Phil 2:27).

Paul's only direct mention of healing is as one of the "charismata," or gifts of the Spirit (1 Cor 12:9, 28, 30). However, over against his competitors ("superapostles," *huperlian apostoloi*), who probably claimed to perform healings (2 Cor 11:5; 12:11), Paul never made such a claim. When he mentions powers or signs and wonders, which might reasonably be thought to include healing, he says God supplied them (Gal 3:5). Alternatively, Paul uses the passive, "were performed" (*kateirgasthē*, 2 Cor 12:12), implying that it was God, not him, who was responsible for healing. In a letter written by one of Paul's followers, wine is prescribed for frequent sickness (1 Tim 5:23).

Mark. The earliest Gospel writer, Mark, saw sickness as caused by sin (2:1–11) and bringing uncleanliness (1:23, 40–45; 5:1–3). He depicts Jesus as a powerful healer, but the healings are ambiguous in that they provide a great variety of responses, including conflict with authorities (3:6, 22). Apart from exorcisms, all healings involve some expression of trust in Jesus. Faith appears essential not only to gain Jesus's willingness (9:14–29) but also his ability to heal (6:6) so that the healings are both a summons and a demand for faith and repentance. Forgiveness can be equivalent to healing (2:1–11), which, in turn, brings cleanliness (1:44). In particular, the healing involved in exorcism was, as for Matthew and Luke, the eschatological destruction of Satan (3:23–27; Matt 12:28//Luke 11:20). Also as for Matthew (Matt 10:1–42) and Luke (Luke 9:1–6, 10–11; 10:1–12, 17–20), Mark considers that in Jesus the followers of Jesus have a mandate and model to heal the sick (Mark 3:14–15; 6:7–13).

Matthew. The portrait of Jesus by Matthew does not give healing a high profile. Yet, as a healer Jesus acts mightily not only as Messiah (9:27; 12:23; 15:22; 20:30–31) but as God himself among his people because of who he is, evident in that faith is not needed for him to heal (8:14–15).

Luke. The author of Luke blurs the distinction between kinds of sicknesses so that exorcisms become healings (9:42; 13:10–17) and healings become exorcisms (4:39; 6:17–19). Though not all diseases are given a demonic dimension (5:12–16; 17:11–19), Luke more clearly than the other Gospel writers portrays sickness as part of the spiritual oppression God's people suffer (4:18). The healings, which bring salvation (sometimes termed "mercy," 17:13; 18:38–39), show Jesus to be the compassionate Messiah and identify him as God at work. As in Matthew, healings do not illustrate or demonstrate, but are themselves, the good news (Matt 12:28//Luke 11:20). In turn, healing both prepares for and produces faith. In Acts, the healings remain part of Luke's "show-and-tell" view of the Gospel; they are part of the "signs and wonders" that authenticate the messengers and the divine origin of the Gospel (Exod 4:1–17). In turn, the healings cause amazement and create faith (Acts 3:8; 9:35, 42; 19:17).

The Fourth Gospel. Along with the other miracles of Jesus, the Fourth Gospel takes the healings as part of the message of Jesus that requires explanation. As signs, the healings point not only to the presence of God (John 4:23; 5:25; 12:30–31) but also to the identity or glory (John 2:11) of Jesus and his filial relationship, even identity, with the Father. Healing, as in the Septuagint (Hab 1:15), is the salvific work of God (John 9:4). The healings reach a crescendo in the raising of Lazarus (John 11:1–57), which becomes the prism through which to understand both the preceding healings and the Parousia (John 13—14) as centered in the person and work of Jesus. Given the magnitude of the healings in this Gospel (John 4:46–54; 5:5;

9:32; 11:17), it is not surprising the Fourth Gospel includes no exorcisms.

James. In directing the "weak" (*astheneō*, Jas 5:14) to call the elders and saying the "ill" or "discouraged" (*kamnō*) will be "saved" or "healed" (*sōzō*, Jas 5:15), James probably has in mind the sick who are prayed over in faith or trust (5:15; cf. 1:6). They are to be anointed with oil either as an active agent in healing (Isa 1:6; *b. Šabb.* 53b; *PGM* IV.3007–3020) or as a symbol of God's presence (Exod 30:29). The resulting healing, as necessary, includes forgiveness (Jas 5:15), appearing to connect sin and sickness (cf. Mark 2:5; John 5:14; 9:2–3; 1 Cor 11:30).

First Peter. This letter has the phrase "by his wound [*mōlōps*, singular] you were healed" (1 Pet 2:24; cf. Isa 53:5, *Barn.* 7.2). Whatever kind of healing is in mind, it is closely related to freedom from sin, the immediate and dominant concern of the writer (1 Pet 2:22–25).

Revelation. The book of Revelation uses the phrase "smear your eyes with salve in order to see" (Rev 3:18) as a metaphor for curing the spiritual blindness of readers in Laodicea, where perhaps eye ointments were readily available to the readers from a nearby medical school (Strabo, *Geogr.* 12.8.20). Later, in another metaphor portraying wholeness and the absence of all need in the heavenly city, the writer says the leaves of the tree of life are healing to the nations (Rev 22:2; cf. Ezek 47:12).

Late Antiquity. With the fall of Jerusalem (70 C.E.) and the decline of the centralized priesthood, Jews increasingly sought charismatics for personal help, including healing (e.g., *m. Ber.* 5.5). Jews are depicted as using artifacts and incantations (Josephus, *Ant.* 8.46–49) and Christians as practicing "magic" (*periergos*, Acts 19:19) for healing. Writing between the end of the first and the end of the second centuries, the Christian Apostolic Fathers express remarkably little interest in sickness and healing. Though there is no mention of his miracles, Jesus is seen as the only physician (Ign. *Eph.* 7.2) or healer (*Diogn.* 9.6), and God is asked to heal the sick (*1 Clem.* 59.4). *Barnabas* (14.7–9) refers to sickness and healing but only as a metaphor for being ransomed from the darkness. Polycarp (*Phil.* 6.1) directs the presbyters in Philippi to visit the sick as part of being compassionate and honorable.

For the Shepherd, sins (Herm. *Vis.* 1.9), afflictions (Herm. *Mand.* 49.2; *Sim.* 66.4), evil (Herm. *Vis.* 3.1), and ignorance (Herm. *Sim.* 60.3–4) are healed by God. The Shepherd also says that encouraging the weak or sick (*kamnō*) is part of living for God (Herm. *Mand.* 38.10).

In the second and early third centuries the Christian Apologists sought to make a reasoned defense of Christianity to outsiders. For Quadratus, the truth of the work of "our Savior" is linked to his healings of individuals, some of whom were still alive at the time of his writing (Eusebius, *Hist. Eccl.* 4.3.2). Justin Martyr (2 *Apol.* 6) placed great weight on Jesus's healings, including exorcisms, to support the claim that Jesus is the Son of God, Savior, and God's anointed. Similarly, a little later Origen (ca. 185–ca. 254 C.E.) used the healings to substantiate the Holy Spirit appearing to Jesus and took the healings by Jesus's followers, including in Origen's own time, as explaining the spread of Christianity (*Cels.* 1.46, 67). In this period baptism became linked with healing (Hippolytus, *Trad. ap.* 20).

Though challenged by their traditions (cf. Job), Jews could see illness as the result of sin (*b. Šabb.* 55a). Nevertheless, it was widely held that bile, contaminated food, and bodily discharges (*b. Ber.* 25a, *Šabb.* 109b, *'Abod. Zar.* 30a), for example, and the blood in particular, were natural causes of sickness, leading to frequent bloodletting (*b. Šabb.* 129b). Though suffering was valued (*b. Sanh.* 101b), restoring a person's body was an obligation (*b. B. Qam.* 85a; cf. Deut 22:2), even to the non-Jew (*'Abod. Zar.* 26a; cf. Lev 25:35), and great attention was given to medication (*b. Giṭ.* 70a, *'Abod. Zar.* 30a). Also, the physician was highly regarded (*b. Sanh.* 17b), and mental well-being was as important as well as bodily health (*b. Sanh.* 100b).

Medieval Period. Augustine of Hippo (354–430 C.E.), whose thinking permeated the period, supposed that sickness was caused by the ignorance and sin characteristic of the fallen human condition (*Civ.* 22.22). Cures came about "through the name of Christ, sometimes through his sacraments and sometimes through the intercession of the relics of his saints," and through prayer (*Civ.* 22.8). Like earlier followers of Jesus, individuals such as the hermit Hospicius (d. ca. 580 C.E.) healed "In the name of my lord Jesus Christ" (Gregory

of Tours, *History of the Franks*, 6.6). Perhaps because of the breakdown in confidence in the hierarchy of the imperial church, these revered individuals were increasingly relied upon for healing. Their ability to heal through touch or the sign of the cross, for example, came to be seen to result from humility and identifying with the suffering (Bonaventure, *Life of St. Francis*, 2.6–7, 12.9–10). Materials associated with these people—including water, spittle, tears, food, clothes, and their tombs—were also thought to have healing properties. Gregory of Tours found relief from dysentery and high fever in a drink including dust from the tomb of Martin (*De Virtutibus S. Martini*, 2.1). Though iconoclasts saw them as idols (Gregory I, *Epistles* 9.105, 11.13), healing was also sought through icons. A 12-year-old with bubonic plague, set before an icon of Christ from which fell drops of dew, was immediately healed (*Life of St. Theodore of Sykeon*, 8).

From the time of Paul, the Eucharist had been associated with health and sickness (1 Cor 11:30); by the end of the period the bread was taken to have healing properties so powerful that, as in a story told by Caesarius of Heisterbach (ca. 1180–1240), a woman was said to be cured by an abbot who had contact with the host the previous day (*Libri VIII miraculorum*, 1.9). Some maintained that illness had a pedagogical function (Barsanuphius, d. 540, *Letters* Epp. 189, 613; Isaac of Nineveh, d. ca. 700, *Ascetic Homilies* 5.68–70; cf. Job, 2 Cor 12:9). Moses Maimonides (Moses ben Maimon, 1135–1204), a rabbi and a physician, took sickness to result from natural causes and injury but primarily from sin. Health to serve God came not through miracles but through regulating life according to the laws of hygiene.

Thomas Aquinas (ca. 1225–1274) was the first to theorize about miracles since Augustine and depended on him for the view that illness was the result of the Fall (*Summa Theologiae* 2.1.82.1). He explained healings as confirming the preachers' words so faith could be confirmed (*Summa Contra Gentes* 154.8). However, due to is dependence on the closed naturalistic system of Aristotle, Aquinas never mentions healing as part of the Christian life after the time of the apostles. At the end of the period, as part of his primitivism or call to return to the church in the book of Acts,

Erasmus of Rotterdam (ca. 1466–1536) attacked seeking healing through external forms as misplaced faith and magic. He also encouraged self-care and valued the medical profession.

Early Modern Period. Martin Luther (1483–1546) said the devil "beats our bodies with various plagues" (*Tischreden* 4.3945). Though he considered a good diet the best medicine (3.3801), he valued doctors, but not their high fees and failure to take into account Satan's involvement in sickness, which required the higher remedy of faith and prayer (4.4784). Still, Luther also saw sickness as educational and almost indispensable in knowing God (3.543, 21.299–300). Joseph Caro (1488–1575) noted that, for Jews, care of the sick was to take precedence over even the needs of the synagogue. John Calvin (1509–1564) acknowledged that sickness, frequently the result of sin, afflicts even the regenerate (*Institutes of the Christian Religion*, 3.3.10). He considered the healings related to relics to be utterly false because they led people away from the worship of God. Like the rest of the miracles, Calvin supposed that, since the time of the apostles, the gift of healing had vanished (4.19.18). Catholicism countered what it saw as a weakness in Protestantism not only by promoting the miraculous, including healing, as a tool of evangelism but also by answering Luther's attacks on the cult of saints by deploring the fabrication of miracles among Catholic priests.

Enlightenment. Coexistent with a skeptical intellectual climate, British and American revivalism (e.g., Jonathan Edwards, 1703–1758, and John Wesley, 1703–1791) reported miraculous healings. Wesley considered sin and sickness, as well as salvation and healing, to be of a piece so that sin was a wound or disease as much as a cause of guilt (Outler, 1984, 1.586). Salvation was not merely future deliverance from hell but included the present "restoration of the soul to its primitive health" (11.106) by the Great Physician (19.99). Taking the early church as a model for his time, it is not surprising that his journal contains stories of healings (19.32, 191, 194; 21.345–46). He also set up clinics for the poor (9.275) and, along with promoting holistic medical care as part of his ministry, advised what would now be seen as superstitious cures. For example, anointing with wine and the boiled juice of ground ivy was expected to cure melancholy (*Primitive Physick*).

Contemporary and Global Perspectives. Karl Barth (1886–1968) understood sickness and healing in the light of Jesus Christ and scriptures. Sickness, a "sign of the power of chaos and nothingness" (*Church Dogmatics*, 3.4, 368), a forerunner of death, is a sign of God's righteous wrath and judgment. However, even the seriously ill are not rendered inhuman (366–367), and all learn that neither this life nor our lives are in our hands (374). In scriptures Barth saw a place for both medicine and hygiene (360–361) and the call to be healthy through binding the forces of sickness in Jesus Christ and his sacrifice (367–368).

In contrast to Barth, Karl Rahner (1904–1984) wrote that sickness does not necessarily arise out of a person's guilt and is not always an expression of psychic conflicts. But sickness always exposes the person of faith to ultimate dependence on God and to a readiness for death and eternal life. Faith, in its calming effect, may bring healing in a psychological manner or as a miracle. He identified the saving force of faith as the greatest healing miracle.

A small but increasing number of theologians and interpreters of the Bible can be classified as "renewalist," belonging to Pentecostal denominations, or "charismatics" from traditional churches. In the face of Western skepticism, they generally share the view that the reported supranatural experiences of the followers of Jesus in the New Testament, including healings, remain viable models. Representative of Pentecostals, John Christopher Thomas (b. 1955) takes sickness to originate in sin, divine chastisement, or the demonic. Thomas concludes that healing may come through prayer, confession, or, in a minority of cases, exorcism. Some renewalists take healing (along with forgiveness) to be granted, while others see that it is merely possible, through the atoning death of Jesus; a minority see no place for modern medicine.

Compassion and practical care have remained consistent responses to sickness and disease by interpreters of the Bible. However, while those in the developing world more nearly mirror biblical views, particularly since the Enlightenment, Western thinkers have generally had an uneasy relationship with miraculous healing.

[*See also* Blessings and Curses; Death and Dying; Honor and Shame; Reward and Retribution; *and* Sin.]

BIBLIOGRAPHY

Avalos, Hector. *Illness and Health Care in the Ancient Near East: The Role of the Temple in Greece, Mesopotamia, and Israel.* Harvard Semitic Museum Monograph 54. Atlanta, Ga.: Scholars Press, 1995.

Brown, Michael L. *Israel's Divine Healer.* Grand Rapids, Mich.: Zondervan, 1995.

Dorff, Elliot N. "The Jewish Traditions." In *Caring and Curing: Health and Medicine in the Western Religious Traditions*, edited by Ronald L. Numbers and Darrel W. Amundsen, pp. 5–39. Baltimore: Johns Hopkins University Press, 1986.

Föller, Oskar. "Martin Luther on Miracles, Healing, Prophecy and Tongues." *Studia Historiae Ecclesiasticae* 31 (2005): 333–351.

Hejzlar, Pavel. "John Calvin and the Cessation of Miraculous Healing." *Communio Viatorum* 49 (2007): 31–77.

Kelsey, Morton T. *Healing and Christianity: In Ancient Thought and Modern Times.* New York: Harper & Row, 1973.

Maddox, Randy L. "John Wesley on Holistic Health and Healing." *Methodist History* 46 (2007): 4–33.

Messer, Neil G. "Toward a Theological Understanding of Health and Disease." *Journal of the Society of Christian Ethics* 31 (2011): 161–178.

North, Robert. "Medicine and Healing in the Old Testament Background." In *Medicine in the Biblical Background*, pp. 9–68. Analecta Biblica 142. Rome: Biblical Institute, 2000.

Outler, Albert, et al., eds. *The Works of John Wesley.* Nashville, Tenn.: Abingdon, 1984–.

Pilch, John J. *Healing in the New Testament: Insights from Medical and Mediterranean Anthropology.* Minneapolis: Fortress, 2000.

Porterfield, Amanda. *Healing in the History of Christianity.* Oxford: Oxford University Press, 2005.

Rahner, Karl. "The Saving Force and Healing Power of Faith." In *Theological Investigations*, Vol. 5, pp. 460–467. London: DLT; New York: Seabury, 1966.

Sigerist, Henry E. *A History of Medicine.* 2 vols. New York: Oxford University Press, 1951–1961.

Thomas, John Christopher. *The Devil, Disease and Deliverance: Origins of Illness in New Testament Thought.* Journal of Pentecostal Theology Supplement 13. Sheffield, U.K.: Sheffield Academic Press, 1998.

Twelftree, Graham H. *In the Name of Jesus: Exorcism among Early Christians.* Grand Rapids, Mich.: Baker Academic, 2007.

Walsham, Alexandra. "Miracles and the Counter-Reformation Mission to England." *Historical Journal* 46 (2003): 779–815.

Ward, Benedicta. *Miracles and the Medieval Mind.* Philadelphia: University of Pennsylvania Press, 1987.

Wilkinson, John. *The Bible and Healing: A Medical and Theological Commentary.* Grand Rapids, Mich.: Eerdmans, 1998.

Graham H. Twelftree

SIN

This article provides an overview of the Bible's teaching on sin by taking a canonical-thematic approach, that is, a focus on the theme of sin as it occurs in the different canonical sections of the Bible in its final form. As an overview, it concentrates on major themes and refers to the secondary literature for more detailed discussion.

The Story of Sin: A Biblical Overview. "Sin 'offends God not only because it bereaves or assaults God directly, as in impiety or blasphemy, but also because it bereaves and assaults what God has made'" (Plantinga, 1995, p. 16). This well captures the biblical understanding of what sin is: anything contrary to God and his purpose for this world. And since that purpose is for humanity to reflect his character and enjoy perfect harmony with God, other people, and creation, sin is consistently described as ruining and destroying these very things: people become a broken and marred image of their Creator, break fellowship with God and rebel against him, commit great treachery and harm against one another, and rule over the creation as a despot instead of as a benevolent king. Sin defaces the sinner and acts as a relational poison with fatal consequences.

This becomes clear when sin is set in the context of the entire Bible. The bookends of the Bible describe a world without sin. In Genesis 1–2, God creates a world of perfect order that he deems "very good" (1:31). It includes man and woman, whom he makes in his image to reflect his good and benevolent rule over all he has made (1:26–27). His posture toward them is one of blessing, providing them with rich companionship in each other (2:18–25), placing them in the luxuriant garden of Eden (2:4–17), promising them fruitfulness of womb and a special role in the creation (1:28–30), and walking with them as their God

(3:8; cf. Lev 26:12). The picture is one in which humanity enjoys perfect harmony with God, one another, and the creation.

The Bible's last two chapters paint the same picture for those who follow Jesus (Rev 21–22). As in Eden, the new heavens and earth have a river and tree of life (Rev 22:1–2; cf. Gen 2:9, 10) and humanity once again walks in perfect fellowship with God (Rev 21:3, 7; 22:3–4), serves him faithfully and extends the rule of God and of the Lamb over all of creation (Rev 22:3–5; cf. 20:4), and experiences a world in which death, mourning, crying, and pain are no more (21:4; cf. 22:3). It is a restoration to Eden where humanity once more enjoys perfect harmony with God, one another, and the creation.

What happens in between these bookends is the story of humanity's sin and God's response to it. Sin enters the story at Genesis 3 and casts a shadow of darkness and death over the entire story until Revelation 21. God's response is immediate. As soon as humanity rebels (Gen 3:6–7), God brings his justice to bear against sin (3:14–19) but also shows mercy to the sinful (3:21), makes clear he will one day defeat sin fully and finally through humanity's seed (3:15), and reissues his original creational commands to a succeeding generation (9:1–3; cf. 2:28–30).

God follows this pattern consistently. In the Old Testament, he not only brings his justice to bear against sin but also extends mercy and forgiveness to the penitent (Exod 34:6–7; Ps 32:2–5). What is more, he repeatedly calls a person, or group of people, to establish his Kingdom in the world, a kingdom in which sin is banished and the seeds of righteousness are sown, watered, and cultivated in order that humanity can again feast on Eden's fruit (Gen 17:1–8; Exod 19:4–6; Lev 26:3–13; 2 Sam 7:8–29).

In the New Testament, Jesus becomes God's ultimate answer to humanity's sin. By sending Jesus to be a sacrifice for sin, God demonstrates his love for sinful humanity and his desire for them to be reconciled to him (Rom 5:8). By sending Jesus to be king of his Kingdom (Luke 1:32–33), he gives him the authority to remove and banish sin (Matt 9:2–8) and to establish a community that puts God's good and just Kingdom on full display (Matt 5:16; Eph 5:8–10; Titus

2:14; 1 Pet 2:9–12) and that seeks to repatriate the rest of humanity to it (Matt 28:18–20). It is this king who will come again to banish sin and all its effects and return his servants to an Eden in which sin will never be named again (Rev 21–22).

With this overview in place, we may now turn to see how individual sections of the Bible contribute to it.

Sin in the Old Testament. We begin with a general consideration of the Old Testament's vocabulary and metaphors for sin and then consider how different sections of the Old Testament speak about it.

Vocabulary and metaphors. The Old Testament has at least 10 different terms for sin (see Luc, 1997, pp. 87–89). If phrases are also included, the list climbs to more than 50 (Swanson, 1997, §§88.289–88.318, cited in Boda, 2009, p. 6n16). This rich vocabulary indicates not only that sin is "a central theme of [Old Testament] theology" (Cover, 1992, p. 31) but also that it is a complex reality that manifests itself in a myriad of ways.

The most commonly occurring terms are words built on the Hebrew roots *ḥṭʾ* ("to miss [a mark]"), *ʿwh* ("to bend, twist, turn aside"), and *pšʿ* ("to break with, rebel"), though more important than their root is the way these words were used in specific contexts (for which, see Knierim, 1997a–c). Most broadly speaking, however, these terms refer to some sort of offense or wrong, and over the course of the Bible, they are used to refer to wrongs committed solely against God (*ḥṭʾ*: 1 Kgs 16:13; *ʿwh*: Jer 11:10; *pšʿ*: Ezek 2:3) as well as to wrongs against other humans (*ḥṭʾ*: Num 12:11; *ʿwh*: Isa 59:3; *pšʿ*: 1 Sam 25:28). Significantly, they occur together in some contexts to describe sin in its totality, as happens most famously when the Lord declares that he "forgives iniquity [root *ʿwh*], transgression [root *pšʿ*] and sin [root *ḥṭʾ*]" (Exod 34:7, NASV; Knierim, 1997b, p. 410). God's forgiveness to those who repent is as multifaceted as the sins they commit (Pss 32:5; 103:3; 130:4; cf. 1 John 1:9).

Alongside of specific terms, the Old Testament frequently uses metaphors to describe sin. Certain metaphors focus on the ways in which sin is against God: it is to rebel against him (Ezek 2:3), to forsake and despise him (Isa 1:4), and to break covenant faith with him (Deut 31:16). Idolatry in particular is described as forsaking the Lord (Judg 10:10) and as an act of spiritual prostitution and adultery (Lev 17:7; Hos 4:11–12;

Ezek 16:15–22). Sin is not first and foremost the breaking of a rule but the breaking of a relationship, an act of treachery against one's king and Creator.

Other metaphors focus on what sin does to those who commit it: it defiles both them (Ps 51.2; Ezek 14:11; 37:23) and the land on which they commit it (Lev 18:24–27; Isa 24:5), ensnares and rules over them (Ps 119:133; Prov 5:22), causes them to stumble (Ezek 7:19), makes a separation between them and God (Isa 59:2), and causes them to rot (Ezek 24:23). Sin is utterly self-destructive.

The Old Testament also uses a large number of metaphors to describe the ways in which God rescues the penitent from their sin: he cleanses it (Ps 51:2; Isa 4:4), removes it from them as far as the east is from the west (Ps 103:12), blots it out (Isa 44:22), treads it under foot and casts it into the heart of the sea (Mic 7:19), covers it (Ps 32:1), and remembers it no more (Jer 31:34). Ultimately, God himself must rescue humanity from sin's penalty and power.

Torah (Genesis—Deuteronomy). Sin is a major theme in the Bible's opening books. They first introduce us to sin (Genesis) and then devote a great deal of time to its description and how it should be addressed (esp. Leviticus and Numbers).

Genesis. Sin slithers its way into the biblical story in Genesis 3. It is characterized by disobedience to God's commands (3:11) and results in horrific consequences for humanity, including punishment from God (3:16–19) and a threefold alienation: from God (3:8–10), from one another (3:7, 12, 16), and from the creation (3:17–18; cf. Cover, 1992, p. 36). It is a complete reversal of God's intention for humanity as set out in Genesis 1–2, a point underscored by other tragic reversals in the opening chapters.

Genesis 1–2	Genesis 3
Living in a fruitful garden (2:15)	Cast out of the garden (3:23–24)
Naked and no shame (2:25)	Naked and ashamed (3:7)
Multiplying (1:28)	Pain in childbirth (3:16)
Keeping a fruitful garden (2:15)	Working the thorn-infested ground (3:17–19)
Taken out of the ground and given life (2:7)	Dying and returning to the ground (3:19)

Genesis 3 also tells us that en evil personality is at work in the world that is opposed to God (3:4–5) and seeks to ruin humanity and creation by means of sin (cf. 3:1–5 with 3:6–19; see Collins, 2006, pp. 170–172). Many of the New Testament authors will return to this theme (as will Job in a unique way; Job 1–2). But Genesis 3 makes equally that clear God will one day vanquish this evil one through the seed of the woman (3:15) and will in the meantime continue to care for sinful humanity (3:21; cf. Palmer, 2000, p. 416). God's response of mercy in the face of humanity's sin will be an ongoing theme in the rest of the biblical story.

Once sin enters the world, it spreads like a lethal virus to succeeding generations: Cain murders his brother (4:7), Lamech's vengeance knows no bounds in its violence (4:23), and humanity as a whole has an inclination of the heart that leans to evil all the time (6:5) and pollutes the earth so badly that God must wash it in a cosmic act of judgment (7:6–24). As Clines aptly notes, "The flood is only the final stage in a process of cosmic disintegration that began in Eden" (1978, p. 75).

But once more, sin will not have the last word. The Lord reissues the creation mandate to Noah (9:1–3) and affirms that humanity is still in God's image (9:6). And even when humanity plunges again headlong into sin (11:1–9), the Lord's response is not only to judge (11:8–9) but also to raise up a faithful line (11:20–32), through whom "the seed" of the woman can bring about blessing to the earth (12:3). No matter how sinful humanity becomes, God's ultimate plan for humanity in Eden is not thwarted because God responds in grace to humanity's sin (see further Clines, 1978, pp. 76–79).

Exodus to Numbers. These books discuss sin much more specifically for three reasons: (1) the tabernacle (the Israelites' worship center) is now up and running and with it a place to make sacrifice for sin; (2) the Lord now dwells in their midst (Exod 40), and this underscores the necessity of dealing properly with sin; and (3) the Israelites sin greatly during this time.

Broadly speaking, these books identify three categories of sin and how to deal properly with them (Sklar, 2012). For each category, repentance and atonement are necessary. "Repentance is the means by which sinners turn from their rebellion and realign themselves with the mission the Lord has given them, and atonement is the means by which sin and impurity are removed, so that fellowship with the Lord can continue and his people can engage fully in his purposes for them" (Sklar, 2014, p. 55).

Category of sin	Example	How to atone
Unintentional sin (Lev 4:2, 13; 5:14; Num 15:22; etc.)	Perhaps not realizing you were ritually impure and failing to deal with it properly	Repentance, confession, sacrifice (Lev 5:5, 10; Num 15:25)
Intentional but not (necessarily) apostate sin (Lev 5:1; 6:1–7)	Failing to testify about a crime (Lev 5:1)	Repentance, confession, sacrifice (Lev 5:5–6; 6:6–7)
Apostate sin (Num 15:30)	Refusing to enter the Promised Land (Num 14:1–35)	Sacrificial atonement not possible (cf. Num 15:22–28 with 15:30–31), but a mediator could intercede on the repentant sinner's behalf (Num 14:13–20)

These books also note that sin can defile the sinner (Lev 16:30) as well as the land (Lev 18:25–29; Num 35:33; cf. Ezek 36:17–18). As in Genesis 3, humanity's sin causes the world itself to suffer.

Two specific sins are especially significant in these books: (1) the Israelites' idolatry with the golden calf (Exod 32), by which they forsook the Lord (32:7–10) and broke their covenant with him (cf. 32:19b), and (2) their refusal to obey the Lord's command to enter the Promised Land (Num 14:1–4), by which they rejected his covenant promises and thus the Lord himself (14:8–12). Sin often manifests itself as a betrayal of covenant faithfulness and, when done against the Lord, as treason against the covenant king.

Deuteronomy. As the Pentateuch draws to a close, the covenant people are again confronted with the choice of Eden: "See, I set before you today life and prosperity, death and destruction" (Deut 30:15). Sadly, the Lord himself states, they will soon choose the latter (31:14–22); and the prophetical books will bear this out. But he is equally clear this is not the choice they have to make (30:11, 14). Those who are in covenant relationship with God can choose to follow him and not be devoured by the sin that crouches at their door (cf. Gen 4:7).

Former Prophets (Joshua—Kings). These books tell the Israelites' story from their entry into the Promised Land (Josh 3) to their exile from it as a result of their sin (2 Kgs 17; 25). Sin is a major theme: "From the beginning Israel forgets, rebels, hustles, craves, tests, envies, forsakes, despises, disbelieves, grumbles, disobeys, abandons, angers, provokes, compromises, nauseates (Ps 106)" (Goldingay, 2006, p. 254).

By far the most common sin mentioned is idolatry. It is the very last thing Joshua warns them about (Josh 24:14–27) and yet the very thing they rush into just two chapters later (Judg 2:11–13). It recedes into the background during David's reign (1 Sam 16—2 Sam 24) but surges forth again under his son, Solomon (1 Kgs 11:1–8, 31–33). And despite brief periods where some kings encourage the Israelites to faithfulness (2 Kgs 18:1–6; 23:1–25), their idolatrous tendencies are encouraged by most kings, especially Jeroboam (1 Kgs 12:25–33) and Manasseh (2 Kgs 21:1–9). Significantly, idolatry is given as the prime reason the Israelites were exiled (2 Kgs 17:7–18; 21:10–15; 23:26–27), and the cycle of Eden continues: rebels are again banished from the Promised Land.

These books also explain that the Lord responds to the Israelites' idolatry, and to sin in general, in various ways (see Boda, 2009, pp. 186–188). These include providing faithful leadership (Josh 24:14–28; Judg 2:11–19; 1 Sam 7:1–4), providing Israel his Word (Josh 1:7–9; 2 Kgs 17:13; 22:1–23:25), and bringing judgment and discipline to bear (Judg 2:11–15; 1 Sam 3:11–14; 15:24–29; 2 Kgs 17:7–18). In each case, the Israelites are to respond with repentance, and this underscores a key biblical theme: the Lord constantly calls his sinful people to return to him; even with judgment, his ultimate goal is not destruction but restoration (Boda, 2009, p. 189; see Judg 10:10–16; 1 Sam 7:2–17; 12:8–11; 1 Kgs 8:33–36, 46–53).

Latter Prophets (Isaiah—Ezekiel, the 12 Minor Prophets). While these prophets also focus on idolatry, in which the sinner deals faithlessly with God (Isa 2:8; Ezek 5:11; Mic 1:7; Hos 8:4), they also list dozens of other sins, in many of which the sinner deals faithlessly with people. A majority of these sins fall into one of three general categories: violence, sexual immorality, and oppressing others (for a representative sample, see Ezek 18:10–13; 22:1–12). Within this third category, it is significant to note how often the prophets rebuke those who sin against others for the sake of financial gain, especially those weaker than themselves (Isa 3:14–15; Amos 5:11–12; 8:4–6; Mic 7:3; cf. 1 Tim 6:10). The gross injustice that results from human greed is not simply a modern phenomenon.

The prophets' solution is not sacrifice. The people's sins had reached a level of rank apostasy, for which there was no sacrifice (see "Exodus to Numbers"), and their religious rites were offensive because they were not accompanied by covenant faithfulness (Isa 1:11–15; 58:1–5; Jer 7:4–11). Instead, the Israelites were to repent by turning from evil and practicing good (Isa 55:7; Amos 5:14–15; Mal 3:6–12) and to put their hope in the Lord's compassion and love (Jer 31:3, 20; Hos 11:1–11; Mic 7:18–20). The Lord would bring calamity to bear against them to punish their sin (Isa 10:1–3; Jer 5:9–11) but also to discipline, correct, refine, and restore them (Hos 3:3–5; Jer 5:3; Mal 3:2–4; Hos 6:1–3; Goldingay, 2006, pp. 335–342). He also promises to give them a new heart so they could walk faithfully with him (Isa 44:1–5; Jer 24:1–7; 31:33–34; Ezek 36:26–28) and speaks of a coming servant who would bear on himself the people's sin so that they might be healed (Isa 53:4–5, 8; cf. Lev 16:21–22). These last observations in particular emphasize another biblical theme: while sinners must repent of their sin, the Lord himself must ultimately deal with their sin and enable them to live righteously.

Writings. This section may be divided between those books that are highly poetic in nature (Psalms, Proverbs, Job) and those which are related to Israel's later history (Lamentations, Daniel, Ezra, Nehemiah, Chronicles).

Psalms, Proverbs, Job. These books often contrast the "wicked" (or "sinner") and the "righteous." The wicked are those who are characterized by committing great evil, not only against God but especially against others (Pss 10:3–11; 14:1–7; Prov 20:19; 21:10; see also Cover, 1992, p. 37). By way of contrast, the righteous are characterized by repenting of their sin (Ps 32:3–6), walking in the Lord's ways (1:1–6), and thus acting justly toward others (37:21; Job 29:11–17; Prov 29:7).

Generally speaking, the wicked will face God's judgment in this life and the righteous will experience his blessing (Pss 1; 11:4–7; 34:15–22; 37; 64; 92:5–15). Theologians call this the "retributive principle"; it emphasizes, among other things, that wickedness is to be avoided at all costs and righteousness pursued with all one's strength.

Proverbs usually speaks from the perspective of this principle. It frequently speaks of wisdom and righteousness (1:3, 7; 2:1–20) as well as folly and wickedness (4:14; 19:3; 28:26). The former lead to life; the latter, to death (3:33; 10:16, 27) (though Proverbs is aware of exceptions; 20:22; 21:6 [cf. Boda, 2009, p. 374]).

Many of the psalms also speak from the perspective of this principle, for example, the frequent calls for the Lord to judge the wicked and to vindicate the righteous (10:1–18; 17:1–15; 22:1–21; 74:1–23). But these very calls make clear that the righteous often suffer and the wicked often prosper, meaning that the retributive principle is just that: a principle, not a law.

The book of Job emphasizes this. His friends conclude his suffering is due to his sin (11:13–20; 22:4–11), but the opening chapters make clear that Job is upright (1:1, 5, 8; 2:3) and that his suffering is due to other factors (Job 1–2). His friends were right to think that suffering can be connected to sin but wrong to think the connection is automatic (see Kidner, 1985, p. 61). Those who suffer are sometimes the most upright, a fact meant to encourage the righteous sufferer and to warn others against easy and automatic judgments that link a person's suffering to his or her sin.

Books relating to Israel's later history (Lamentations, Daniel, Ezra, Nehemiah, Chronicles). While suffering is not an automatic sign of sin, it certainly can be, and many of the remaining books in the writings—which come after the apostate Israelites have been exiled from their land—explain how sinners are to respond to the Lord's judgment. Lamentations emphasizes not only that Jerusalem's destruction is the Lord's judgment for the Israelites' sin (1:5, 8–9, 12–15, 17–18; 2:1–10, 17–22) but also that the proper response is to accept it as the Lord's discipline (3:25–30, 39), repent of wickedness (3:40), and look to the Lord with hope for deliverance (3:20–24, 31–36).

Many of these themes are found in the lengthy penitential prayers recorded in Daniel, Ezra, and Nehemiah. While these prayers have distinct emphases (see Boda, 2009, pp. 465–468, 475–480, 483–488), they also overlap significantly.

Physical posture in prayer: fasting, sackcloth, ashes, physical disfiguration (all signs of mourning)	Ezra 9:3; 10:6; Neh 1:4; 9:1; Dan 9:3
Confession: past and present generations have not followed the Lord's commands given through Moses and the prophets	Ezra 9:6–7a, 10–11a; Neh 1:6b–7; 9:16–17a, 26, 28a, 29b, 30b, 33–35; Dan 9:5–6, 7b–8, 9b–11a
Acknowledgment of the Lord's righteousness and that Israel's suffering is just	Ezra 9:7b, 13; Neh 1:8b; 9:27a, 28a, 30b, 33; Dan 9:7a, 11b–13a, 14, 16
Acknowledgment of the Lord's mercy and covenant faithfulness to Israel (at times even in the midst of their sin)	Ezra 9:8–9; Neh 1:5; 9:32; Dan 9:4, 15a

Chronicles underscores these themes and emphasizes not only that repentance involves humbling oneself before the Lord but also that he is quick to respond with forgiveness and grace (2 Chr 12:1–7; 33:10–13; 34:23–28). Once more, the Lord's ultimate goal in judgment is restorative: he desires not to crush his sinful people but to call them back to life-giving fellowship with him.

Sin in Intertestamental Literature. It is appropriate to say a brief word on the topic of sin as found in Jewish literature coming after the time of the Hebrew Bible and before—or in some cases during or just after—the writing of the New Testament.

Apocrypha and Pseudepigrapha. This literature dates roughly from 300 B.C.E. to 200 C.E. In it, "the [Old Testament] Law continued to be the measuring rod of good and evil (Sir 35:1; 41:8; *Pss. Sol.* 14:2)," though it is also true that "a tendency emerges to describe sin more abstractly, as a force or realm that is antagonistic to both God and humanity" (Harrington, 2010, p. 1230; cf. *T. Jud.* 20:1).

There is also much more discussion, especially in the Pseudepigrapha, on why sin and evil are so common in the world. Charlesworth (1983) identifies at least four explanations: because of Eve's sin (*LAE* 18:1; cf. Sir 25:24), because of Adam's sin (*4 Ezra* 3:20–22; cf. 7:118–119), because individuals choose to sin (*2 Bar.* 54:15, 19; cf. *1 En.* 98:4–5), and (based on a certain understanding of Gen 6:1–7) because of the involvement of evil angels with humanity (*1 En.* 54:6; 64:1–2; cf. 6:1—16:4). Common to all of these is the view that God is not the source of human sin or evil, an idea in keeping with the Old Testament and perhaps especially relevant to Jews who lived during a time when God's people were experiencing much suffering (cf. Charlesworth, 1983).

Dead Sea Scrolls. In the Dead Sea Scrolls (ca. third century B.C.E. up to 70 B.C.E.), human sin is described sometimes as stemming from larger spiritual forces battling one another (cf. 1QS 3:20–24 with 1QM 17:6–7) and at other times "as an inherent human condition in which each person must struggle from birth (1QH^a 12:29–30)" (Harrington, 2010, p. 1230). Sin results in various forms of divine judgment (1QH^a 7:29; 12:35; CD 1:3–4; 1QS 2:8) or in being ostracized from the community (1QS 5:13–14), and the proper response to it is to confess, "plead for mercy, swear never to sin again, and pray for divine aid in the future (1QH^a 4:18–24; 6:17; 14:6; cf. CD 15:3)" (Harrington, 2010, p. 1231; she notes that sacrificial atonement was not an option because this community was opposed to the Jerusalem priesthood).

Uniquely, some of the documents from Qumran expanded the relationship between moral wrongdoing and ritual impurity: "in the Hebrew Bible, moral impurity and ritual impurity remained distinct: Sin did not produce ritual impurity, sinners were not ritually defiling, and sinners did not need to be purified. At Qumran, sin was considered to be ritually defiling, and sinners had to purify themselves" (Klawans, 2000, p. 90). In this community, sin thus expands in scope and the means of dealing with it must expand as well (repentance and ritual cleansing).

Sin in the New Testament. As we did with the Old Testament, we begin with a general consideration of the New Testament's vocabulary and metaphors for sin and then consider how different sections of the New Testament speak about it.

Vocabulary and metaphors. Like the Old Testament, the New Testament also has a rich vocabulary for sin: Louw-Nida lists 30 individual terms in its general entry on "sin, wrongdoing, guilt" (1989, §88.289–88.318) and scores of other terms to describe more specific sins (§88.105–88.288; for a discussion of the most commonly occurring terms, see Günther, 1986, and Bauder, 1986). This shows again how central sin is to the New Testament story and how many different forms it takes. "Humans have discovered an astonishing number of ways to manifest their estrangement from their creator" (Moo, 2013, p. 111).

The most commonly occurring terms for sin in the New Testament are found in the word groups related to the nouns *hamartia* ("sin, sinfulness"), *adikia* ("wrongdoing, unrighteousness, injustice"), *parabasis* ("transgression"), and *paraptōma* ("offense, wrongdoing, sin"). Taken together, these terms refer to a large range of offenses against God and against people (see entries in BDAG and again Günther, 1986; Bauder, 1986).

The real damage caused by sin becomes especially clear when the New Testament's metaphors for it are also considered, many of which overlap with those of the Old Testament. Significantly, just as God is the positive answer to sin in the Old Testament metaphors, the positive answer to sin in the New Testament metaphors is Jesus.

As the context of these verses demonstrates, all these metaphors are held together by Jesus's sacrificial death and resurrection from the dead, by which he fully atoned for sin and demonstrated his power over it (see Peterson, 2012, pp. 273–549). Believing in

If sin...	Jesus...
brings death,	gives life (Rom 6:23; Eph 2:5; Col 2:13)
is disease,	is cure (1 Pet 2:24)
defiles,	cleanses (1 Cor 6:11; Heb 10:22; 1 John 1:9)
is darkness,	is light (John 3:19; 8:12; 12:46)
is a condemning burden,	bears it (Heb 9:28; 1 Pet 2:24)
is our hostility to God, making us his enemies,	reconciles us to God and makes peace (Rom 5:1–11; 2 Cor 5:16–21)
is slavery,	redeems, frees, and claims sinners as his own (Mark 10:45; John 8:34–36; Acts 20:28; Titus 2:13–14; Rev 1:5–6; Peterson, 2012, p. 274)
calls for penalty,	pays it (Rom 3:25–26; Gal 3:13; 1 Pet 2:24; 3:18)
is oppression by evil forces,	defeats them (Eph 2:1–5; Rev 12:9–11)

Jesus thus becomes humanity's hope for forgiveness from sin and for victory over it. As the following overview shows, this is emphasized in every section of the New Testament.

Synoptic Gospels and Acts. If the Lord's purpose in creation was for humanity to reflect his character so that the world was filled with his kingdom of love, mercy, goodness, justice, and peace (see above, "The Story of Sin: A Biblical Overview"), the Gospels emphasize that the Lord has sent Jesus as the long-awaited king of that Kingdom and to inaugurate it in a way the world has never seen (Matt 1:16–17, 21; Mark 1:1–15; Luke 1:32–33; note that the Hebrew word "Messiah" and the Greek word "Christ" are ways of referring to this long-awaited king). This means that sin must be banished and righteousness flourish, and Jesus accomplishes this in various ways.

As king, Jesus has authority to forgive the Kingdom's subjects (Matt 9:2–8). Indeed, his very name means "the Lord saves" (1:21). Unexpectedly, he does not do this simply by divine decree but by sacrificing himself for sinners so they may be forgiven (26:28; Mark 10:45). This is seen as an expression of God's love and mercy for sinful humanity (Luke 1:77–79). God is both righteous judge and merciful savior, the latter of which the religious leaders often failed to understand (Matt 9:11–13; Luke 7:36–50; 15:1–32).

But Jesus also brings justice to bear against sin (Matt 3:11–12; 24:36–51; Luke 13:1–9). To avoid it, sinners must repent of sin and follow him, the one who can save them from sin and lead them in righteousness (Matt 4:17; Mark 2:15–17; Luke 9:23–26; 24:47). This explains why one of the most frequently mentioned sins in the Gospels is to reject Jesus (Matt 9:1–8; 21:28–46; Mark 3:1–6; Luke 4:14–30). To reject the Lord's king is to reject the Lord himself (Luke 10:13–16).

Jesus also emphasized that repenting from sin includes both heart and life. To a religious culture focused on ritual purity of the body, Jesus underscored that sin is a moral impurity that begins in the heart (Matt 12:34–35; Mark 7:14–23). Repentance thus involves an internal reorientation of the heart to God's ways (Matt 5:21–22, 27–28; Mark 7:6b–7). And because righteousness is demonstrated by action, repentance also involves turning away from sinful acts toward just acts (Luke 3:3–14; 19:8–10). Luke's Gospel especially emphasizes that this will involve repenting of the love of money by caring for the less fortunate (12:33; 14:12–14; 16:14–15, 19–31). Those who understand God's mercy and love toward them in Jesus cannot help but show this same mercy and love to others.

In Acts, Jesus is again presented as the one who can save from sin's penalty. People must therefore repent and put their faith in Jesus, the long-awaited king who can forgive their sins (5:31; 10:43; 16:31; 17:30–31). As in the Gospels, a primary sin is refusal to repent and believe the good news about Jesus (3:1–4:22; 17:18–32; 19:23–41). Those who do repent and believe began to live uprightly (19:17–20), shown again especially in caring for the poor (2:45; 4:32–37; 20:35). Jesus therefore inaugurates God's Kingdom in that his followers have their sins forgiven through him (the banishment of sin) and follow him in demonstrating God's character of justice, mercy, and love to the world (the manifestation of righteousness).

Johannine literature. We may divide this literature into the Gospel of John, the letters of John (1–3 John), and the book of Revelation.

Gospel of John. John's Gospel repeats many of the above themes: Jesus is the king who has authority to forgive sins (1:49; 5:21; 6:40; 18:36), he makes this forgiveness possible by presenting himself as a sacrificial lamb to take away sin (1:29), and God's provision of Jesus to do this is a sign of God's love for sinners (1:29; 3:14–16). In addition, John has an especially strong focus on sin as darkness and Jesus as the light that delivers people from its darkness (1:5; 3:19–20; 8:12; 12:46) and on Jesus as the Son of God who perfectly represents the Father and who is sent by the Father to rescue people from sin (3:16–18; 5:19–24; 6:35–40; 8:36; 20:31). In keeping with this, the most frequently occurring sin in this Gospel is disbelieving Jesus and his teaching (6:66; 7:2–5, 32; etc.). It is also the most severe because it is to reject God himself and God's own plan of salvation from sin, leaving the sinner under God's judgment (3:31–36; 8:24; 12:44–50), the very thing from which Jesus came to deliver people (3:17; 12:47). Repentance thus involves changing one's mind about Jesus, believing in him as God's provision of forgiveness for sin, and following him (3:15–18; 8:12; 10:27–30; 12:26; 20:31).

First to Third John. The letters of 1–3 John also make clear that forgiveness for sin happens by believing in Jesus, who is both the advocate for sinners and the sacrifice for their sins (1 John 2:1–2; 4:10) and thus serves as both prophetic and priestly intercessor (cf. Exod 32:11–14; Num 16:46–47) and as atoning sacrifice (cf. Lev 17:11). These letters also emphasize that those who follow Jesus no longer "walk in the darkness" (i.e., have lives characterized by sin) but "walk in the light" (i.e., have lives characterized by righteousness) (1 John 1:5–7; 2:6, 29; 3:6–10; 3 John 1:11). Repenting from sin involves not only rooting out evil but also producing a harvest of good.

Revelation. Revelation emphasizes that Jesus, by his sacrificial death, frees his followers from sin's domain (death) and transfers them to the Lord's domain (life) (5:9–10; 7:14–17). Jesus's followers thus turn away from practicing sins, which are listed in several places and include idolatry, demon worship, magic, sexual immorality, murder, and lying (9:20–21; 21:8; 22:15). Those who reject Jesus and practice such things can expect to face God's judgment, which is seen as an expression of his justice (16:7; 18:5, 20; 19:2) and will come at levels both local (2:16, 22–23) and worldwide

(9:1–11; 14:9–11). God will bring his justice to bear against sin in a full and final way.

Revelation also returns to a theme found in Genesis: there is an evil one who leads people into sin (12:9; 20:2–3; cf. Gen 3:1–7) but who will be defeated by the seed of the woman (cf. Gen 3:15). This seed is Jesus (Rev 12:4–5), who both vanquishes the evil one (12:9–10) and leads his followers to do the same (12:10–11; cf. Beale, 2011, p. 220). To follow the evil one in sinful ways is thus a losing battle, with great suffering to come, while following Jesus leads to the blessing for which humanity was created: a life free from the curses of sin and pain and death and full of the blessings of peace and joy and perfect fellowship with God and the Lamb (7:15–17; 21:1–5; 22:1–5).

Paul and later Pauline letters (Romans—Philemon). Like the rest of the New Testament, the 13 letters traditionally attributed to Paul emphasize that sin is humanity's fundamental problem and that Jesus is the only solution. With reference to God, sin is a failure to reflect his glorious character into the world (Rom 3:23; Moo, 2013, p. 115), a denial of who he is (1:18–23), and a choice to indulge in evil rather than obey his commands (1:28–32; Eph 2:3). With reference to others, sin consists in various activities that bring harm to others (Rom 3:13–17; Gal 5:19–21; 2 Tim 3:1–5), in contrast to showing them God's love and care (cf. Eph 4:32—5:2 with 4:28–31). While all of these things call forth God's righteous judgment (Rom 1:18; 2:2; 6:23a), he also demonstrates his love to sinful humanity by providing Jesus as an atoning sacrifice (5:8). Jesus takes the punishment due for sin (5:6–9; 1 Thess 5:9–10) and makes a way for his followers to be considered righteous (Rom 4:5–8; 2 Cor 5:18–21) and to be adopted as God's children (Rom 8:14–17; Gal 4:1–7; Eph 1:5). Those who do follow him are not characterized by wickedness but by following Jesus in reflecting God's own character into the world (Gal 5:16–24; Eph 4:20—5:2; Col 3:10–17; Titus 2:14), in this way returning to God's purpose in creation (cf. Col 3:10 with Gen 1:26). Repentance is thus turning from sin, believing in Jesus as the savior from sin, and following him in righteous living.

These letters also describe sin from other angles. Sometimes they speak of sin with regard to Old Testament law. The law defines what sin is and makes clear that all are sinners because all have broken the law (Rom 3:20, 23; 7:7; Gal 3:22). And because law-breaking leads to curse (Gal 3:10; cf. Deut 27:26), it is impossible to be saved by it. Salvation comes only by faith in Jesus who took the law's curse on himself in his sacrificial death (Gal 3:13; Titus 2:14).

Sin is also spoken of by making a contrast between two men: Adam and Christ (Rom 5:12–21). Adam first sinned and by this means introduced death into the world, "and so death spread to all people because all sinned" (5:12 lit.). Conversely, Christ came as the sinless second Adam, making a way for sin to be forgiven by the sacrifice of himself. Those who remain "in Adam" remain in the realm of death; those who are "in Christ" by faith are now considered righteous and enter the realm of life (5:15–19; cf. 3:23–26; 5:6–9; 1 Cor 15:22).

In addition to Jesus's sacrificial death, these letters speak of his resurrection as central to dealing with sin. This is because death results from sin (Rom 5:12; 1 Cor 15:56; cf. Gen 2:17; 3:19). If you cannot defeat death, you have not defeated sin. By his resurrection from the dead, Jesus shows he has defeated sin; he shares this victory with those who follow him and will thus be raised from the dead at the last day (1 Cor 15:20–23, 53–57).

In terms of what leads to sin, these letters identify internal and external factors. Internally, people are led into sin by the desires of "the flesh" (Rom 8:5–8; 1 Cor 3:3; Gal 5:17, 19–21), that is, the "natural human condition…[that is] determined by the perspective of this world, in contrast to the world to come" (Moo, 2013, p. 120). Jesus addresses this by granting his followers the Spirit, who enables them to put to death the deeds of the flesh and walk in God's righteous path (Rom 8:1–11; Gal 5:16, 22–25). This in turn means "[sin's] presence and action in the Christian are only the death throes of a mortally wounded foe" (Bromiley, 1988, p. 525).

Externally, these letters speak of an evil one who tempts people to commit sin (2 Cor 2:11; 1 Thess 3:5; 2 Tim 2:26) and, more generally, of evil spiritual forces and powers that the believer battles against (Eph 6:12; see Moo, 2013, pp. 126–127). God has defeated all of these evil forces in Jesus, meaning Jesus's followers are delivered from their tyranny and declared to be forgiven citizens of Jesus's Kingdom: "He has rescued us from the power of darkness and transferred us into the kingdom of his beloved Son, in whom we have redemption, the forgiveness of sins" (Col 1:13–14; cf. Gal 1:4; Eph 2:1–7; Col 2:15).

General letters and Hebrews (James—2 Peter, Jude). As with the other biblical books, each of these letters has unique emphases when discussing sin. James emphasizes that sins are the fruit of the heart's evil desires (1:13–15, 21; 3:14–16; 4:1–2) and that sinners must repent by rooting them out of their lives as they humble themselves before the Lord and his word, knowing that the Lord himself will draw near to help in the battle against sin (1:21; 4:6–10). James also warns strongly against sins directed at others (1:26; 2:1–13; 3:1–12; 4:11; 5:1–6), making clear that those who practice such things do not truly follow God because they deny the "royal law found in scripture, 'Love your neighbor as yourself'" (2:8; cf. 1:26–27; 2:14–26). For James, faith in God and righteous action toward others go hand in hand, while sinful action toward others is a clear sign of a lack of true faith in God.

Both 1 and 2 Peter emphasize that Jesus is the one who saves from sin (1 Pet 2:24; 3:18; 2 Pet 1:1) and sets his followers apart to live righteous lives (1 Pet 1:13–17; 2:11–12; 3:8–9; 2 Pet 1:5–9). God's salvation from sin is always tied to his mission of establishing his righteous Kingdom in this world through his people. Also, 2 Peter warns that false prophets and false teachers will lead people into all sorts of sins (2:1–22) and that they and those who follow them will face judgment (2:9b–13a). Holding firm to the apostles' teaching is thus central to avoiding sin.

Jude emphasizes the same, warning of false believers who are characterized by immorality and false teaching, especially a denial of Jesus Christ as Lord (1:4, 8, 10–13, 16). Jude is clear that these things lead to God's judgment (1:5–7, 13–15) and exhorts believers to avoid such sin by abstaining from any type of immorality (1:23) and by remaining faithful to the apostles' teaching (1:3, 17–20). His letter ends with strong encouragement that the Lord himself helps his people to avoid sin and to be faithful (1:24).

Like much of the New Testament, Hebrews is clear that Jesus's followers must turn from sin (12:16; 13:4) and practice love and good deeds (10:24). But it especially emphasizes their need to remain faithful to Jesus (2:1–4; 3:6—4:14; 10:19–39; 12:1–29), supporting this with two complementary points. First, in contrast to the Old Testament sacrificial system, which has sinful priests (who must sacrifice for their own sins) and sacrifices that result only in external ritual cleansing (not internal conscience cleansing), Jesus is a sinless priest who gave his own life as the perfect sacrifice for sin that can fully cleanse a sinner's conscience (4:15; 7:26–27; 9:7–14, 25–28; 10:1–14). Belief in Jesus is now the God-appointed way of dealing with sin, which leads to the second point: to turn away from Jesus is to turn away from the only means of forgiveness for sins available and thus to experience God's judgment for sin (2:1–3a; 3:1—4:13; 10:26–31). Once again, only Jesus can solve humanity's problem with sin.

Sin Today. I have noted that the Bible presents sin as self-destructive to the sinner and as ruining and destroying the sinner's relationship to God, to others, and to the creation. Since the Bible's completion, the discussion of sin has had a long and complex history in the biblical faiths (for an overview of the discussion in Judaism, see Jacobs, 2007, pp. 624–625; Wigoder, 2002, p. 723; in Christianity, see Connolly, 2005, pp. 1116–1120). The challenge these faiths have faced throughout the centuries has been to maintain all of the above aspects of the biblical teaching.

In the past two centuries especially, it seems that conservative expressions of biblical faith have tended to place strong emphasis on sin as personal rebellion against God and on the corresponding destructive judgment sinners will experience. At the same time, liberal expressions have tended to place strong emphasis on sin being embodied in social and environmental injustice and on the corresponding existential destruction of the self that sinners experience for living inauthentic lives. But the biblical witness is that all of these emphases are true. Accordingly, God calls people, on the one hand, to acknowledge and turn from their sinful rebellion against him, in all its myriad and dark manifestations, and to look to him as the only one who can fix their sin problem and deliver them from its power. On the other hand, God also calls them to walk with him, to transcribe his character into the world not only at the personal level but also at the social level, so that the blessing of Eden might flow as far as the curse is found. God's call is always salvific and missional, a call out of sin and toward his original purpose in creation: for humanity to reflect his character into the world so that it might be filled with his goodness, justice, love, and mercy—all this for God's glory and humanity's blessing (Williams, 2005, pp. 59–62, 137–139).

To be authentically human is to participate fully in this mission. "Real freedom is the right to be properly related to God, to other human beings, and to the world about" (Williams, 2005, p. 153). It is this type of freedom that Jesus speaks of when he says, "Come to me, all you that are weary and are carrying heavy burdens, and I will give you rest. Take my yoke upon you, and learn from me; for I am gentle and humble in heart, and you will find rest for your souls. For my yoke is easy, and my burden is light" (Matt 11:28–30). It is an invitation to be delivered from sin's burden and to follow Jesus as he teaches his followers how to fulfill their mission of relating properly to God, to others, and to the world. It is for this, not for sin, that humanity has been created.

[*See also* Adam (Primeval History); Atonement; Blessings and Curses; Cult and Worship; Devils and Demons; Ethics, Biblical; Expiation; Forgiveness; Good and Evil; Guilt and Innocence; Idols and Idolatry; Redemption; Sacrifice and Offerings; Satan; *and* Sickness, Disease, and Healing.]

BIBLIOGRAPHY

Bauder, W. "παράπτωμα." In *The New International Dictionary of New Testament Theology*, edited by Colin Brown, Vol. 3, pp. 585–587. Grand Rapids, Mich.: Zondervan, 1986.

Beale, G. K. *A New Testament Biblical Theology: The Unfolding of the Old Testament in the New*. Grand Rapids, Mich.: Baker Academic, 2011.

Boda, Mark J. *A Severe Mercy: Sin and Its Remedy in the Old Testament*. Winona Lake, Ind.: Eisenbrauns, 2009.

Bromiley, G. W. "Sin." In *The International Standard Bible Encyclopedia*, edited by G. W. Bromiley, Vol. 4, pp. 518–525. Grand Rapids, Mich.: Eerdmans, 1988.

Charlesworth, James H., ed. *The Old Testament Pseudepigrapha*. Vol. 1: *Apocalyptic Literature and Testaments*. New York: Doubleday, 1983.

Clines, David J. A. *The Theme of the Pentateuch*. Journal for the Study of the Old Testament, Supplement Series 10. Sheffield, U.K.: Sheffield Academic Press, 1978.

Collins, C. John. *Genesis 1–4: A Linguistic, Literary, and Theological Commentary*. Phillipsburg, N.J.: P&R, 2006.

Connolly, Hugh. "Sin." In *Encyclopedia of Christianity*, edited by John Bowden, pp. 1114–1120. Oxford: Oxford University Press, 2005.

Cover, Robin C. "Sin, Sinners (OT)." In *The Anchor Bible Dictionary*, edited by David Noel Freedman, Vol. 6, pp. 31–40. New York: Doubleday, 1992.

Goldingay, John. *Old Testament Theology*. Vol. 2: *Israel's Faith*. Downers Grove, Ill.: InterVarsity, 2006.

Günther, W. "ἀδικία." In *The New International Dictionary of New Testament Theology*, edited by Colin Brown, Vol. 3, pp. 573–576. Grand Rapids, Mich.: Zondervan, 1986.

Günther, W. "ἁμαρτία." In *The New International Dictionary of New Testament Theology*, edited by Colin Brown, Vol. 3, pp. 577–583. Grand Rapids, Mich.: Zondervan, 1986.

Günther, W. "παράβασις." In *The New International Dictionary of New Testament Theology*, edited by Colin Brown, Vol. 3, pp. 583–585. Grand Rapids, Mich.: Zondervan, 1986.

Harrington, Hannah. "Sin." In *The Eerdmans Dictionary of Early Judaism*, edited by John J. Collins and Daniel C. Harlow, pp. 1230–1231. Grand Rapids, Mich.: Eerdmans, 2010.

Jacobs, Louis. "Sin: Rabbinic Views." In *Encyclopaedia Judaica*, 2d ed., edited by Fred Skolnik, Vol. 18, pp. 624–625. Detroit: Macmillan Reference USA, Thomson Gale; Jerusalem: Keter, 2007.

Kidner, Derek. *The Wisdom of Proverbs, Job and Ecclesiastes*. Downers Grove, Ill.: InterVarsity, 1985.

Klawans, Jonathan. *Impurity and Sin in Ancient Judaism*. New York: Oxford University Press, 2000.

Knierim, Rolf. "עָוֹן ʿāwōn perversity." In *Theological Lexicon of the Old Testament*, edited by Ernst Jenni and Claus Westermann, translated by Mark E. Biddle, Vol. 2, pp. 862–866. Peabody, Mass.: Hendrickson, 1997a.

Knierim, Rolf. "חטא ḥṭʾ to miss." In *Theological Lexicon of the Old Testament*, edited by Ernst Jenni and Claus Westermann, translated by Mark E. Biddle, Vol. 1, pp. 406–411. Peabody, Mass.: Hendrickson, 1997b.

Knierim, Rolf. "פֶּשַׁע pešaʿ crime." In *Theological Lexicon of the Old Testament*, edited by Ernst Jenni and Claus Westermann, translated by Mark E. Biddle, Vol. 2, pp. 1033–1037. Peabody, Mass.: Hendrickson, 1997c.

Louw, Johannes P., and Eugene A. Nida, eds. *Greek–English Lexicon of the New Testament: Based on Semantic Domains.* 2d ed. New York: United Bible Societies, 1989.

Luc, Alex. "חָטָא *ḥāṭāʾ*." In *New International Dictionary of Old Testament Theology & Exegesis*, edited by Willem A. VanGemeren, Vol. 2, pp. 87–93. Grand Rapids, Mich.: Zondervan, 1997.

Moo, Douglas J. "Sin in Paul." In *Fallen: A Theology of Sin*, edited by Christopher W. Morgan and Robert A. Peterson, pp. 107–130. Wheaton, Ill.: Crossway, 2013.

Palmer, C. E. "Clothes." In *New Dictionary of Biblical Theology*, edited by T. Desmond Alexander and Brian S. Rosner, pp. 416–418. Downers Grove, Ill.: InterVarsity, 2000.

Peterson, Robert. *Salvation Accomplished by the Son: The Work of Christ.* Wheaton, Ill.: Crossway, 2012.

Plantinga, Cornelius, Jr. *Not the Way It's Supposed to Be: A Breviary of Sin.* Grand Rapids, Mich.: Eerdmans, 1995.

Sklar, Jay. "Sin and Atonement: Lessons from the Pentateuch." *Bulletin for Biblical Research* 22, no. 4 (2012): 467–491.

Sklar, Jay. *Leviticus: An Introduction and Commentary.* Downers Grove, Ill.: InterVarsity, 2014.

Swanson, James. *Dictionary of Biblical Languages with Semantic Domains: Hebrew (Old Testament).* Electronic ed. Oak Harbor, Wash.: Logos Research Systems, 1997.

Wigoder, Geoffrey, ed. "Sin." In *The New Encyclopedia of Judaism*, pp. 722–723. New York: New York University Press, 2002.

Williams, Michael D. *Far as the Curse Is Found: The Covenant Story of Redemption.* Phillipsburg, N.J.: P&R, 2005.

Jay Sklar

SLAVERY

See Freedom and Slavery.

SON OF GOD

The New Testament's presentation of Jesus as Son of God reflects a mosaic of perspectives forged from the Hebrew Bible and Septuagint. That portrait focuses on key historical moments (resurrection, crucifixion, baptism, conception) in which Jesus was "made" Son of God as well as formulates proto-orthodox beliefs in Jesus's eternally "begotten" divine nature. These Christological developments emerged from a diverse milieu of Jewish, Greek, and Roman concepts of filial relations in heavenly and earthly realms. Boundaries between divine and human spheres were more porous in antiquity than moderns typically allow; familial associations of exceptional human beings with deities had as much to do with positions of worldly power as with speculations about metaphysical essence.

Jewish Contexts. The Hebrew Bible occasionally portrays a divine council of heavenly beings surrounding, yet subordinate to, the supreme Creator God as "sons of God" (*ʾĕlōhîm*) or "sons of the Most High" (*ʾelĕyôn*; Gen 6:2, 4; Job 1:6; 2:1; 38:7; Pss 29:1; 82:1, 6; 89:6–7). While these figures usually function as God's faithful, worshipful servants, in two cases they precipitously fall from favor: either as sexual predators upon human daughters, resulting in titanic offspring (*nĕpilîm*, "fallen ones" [Gen 6:4]), or as unjust national gods partial to the wicked and sentenced to die "like mortals, and fall like any prince" (Ps 82:2, 6–7).

The Creator God enters into a covenantal bond with the people of Israel as his collective "firstborn son" (*bēn bĕkôr*). The pivotal adoptive moment occurs when God rescues his kidnapped "son" from Egyptian slavery (Exod 4:22; Hos 11:1), thereby granting Israel a peculiar privileged, responsible status in God's household. Unfortunately, Israel does not always prove to be a faithful "son," prompting disciplinary and restorative action from the ever loyal and loving Father (Jer 3:19; 31:9, 20; Hos 11:1–9).

During Israel's monarchical period the people's role as God's "son" begins to crystallize in the person of the king. The prophet Nathan brokers a new covenant between God and David's royal house, promising an unending succession of David's biological and God's adoptive heirs: "I [the Lord God] will establish the throne of his kingdom forever. I will be a father to him, and he shall be a son to me" (2 Sam 7:13–14). This covenant comes to be celebrated in coronation ceremonies that reinforce adoptive relations with anointing rituals: "The kings of the earth set themselves…against the LORD and his anointed [*māšîaḥ*]…. 'I have set my king on Zion, my holy hill.'

I will tell of the decree of the LORD: He said to me, 'You are my son [*běnî*]; today I have begotten you'" (Ps 2:2, 6–7). Thus, the roles of "Messiah" ("anointed one") and "son of God" converge, though not necessarily with eschatological overtones: the focus falls on "today," not the future. Likewise, "today" precludes pushing "begotten" backward to some preternatural birth or primordial divinization. In Psalm 2 "begotten" is functionally equivalent to "adopted."

Other psalms, however, intensify the filial metaphor. Addressing the God-blessed monarch, Psalm 45 suddenly declares, "Your throne, O God, endures forever and ever" (45:6). This statement accords the king God's full authority, if not identity with God. Immediately the Psalmist qualifies the divine–human royal relationship: "Therefore God, your God, has anointed [*māšîaḥ*] you" (45:7). In any case, God and Israel's king enjoy a special, intimate bond. Reflecting exilic struggles over the demise of Davidic rule and apparent abrogation of God's covenant with his "firstborn [*běkôr*], the highest of the kings of the earth," Psalm 89 lodges a poignant lament against God for rejecting "his anointed" and pleads for God to remember his covenant, rescue his people, and restore the Davidic kingdom (89:26–27, 38–52). Hope begins to sprout for an eschatological redeemer, a new Messiah-Son from the line of David (cf. Pss 132:10–18; 144:9–10; Ezek 37:24–28; Amos 9:11–15).

The Septuagint (LXX), Dead Sea Scrolls, and other early Jewish writings more boldly hint of an ontological union between God and his anointed Davidic "son." The Septuagint maintains the identity of the Davidic regent as God's "begotten" (*gegennēka*) son, "God" (*theos*), and God's "firstborn" (*prototokos*) in Psalms 2:7, 45:6, and 89:27, respectively, without demurral (LXX Pss 2:7; 44:7; 88:28). The Septuagint clarifies the obscure Hebrew of Psalms 110:3 concerning the origins of the eternal royal priest and conqueror of enemy kings: "From the womb, before Morning-star, I [the Lord] brought you forth [*exegennēsa*]" (LXX Ps 109:3). In Isaiah 9:6, which originally envisioned a historical, human son of David (probably Hezekiah), crowned with the honorifics of "Wonderful Counselor, Mighty God, Everlasting Father, Prince of Peace," the Septuagint, composed long after the Davidic–Judahite

kingdom's fall, reads, "He is named Messenger/Angel [*angelos*] of the Great Counsel" (9:5)—perhaps suggesting a heavenly, angelic agent of God's peaceful reign.

Scriptural interpretation in the Dead Sea Scrolls further promotes an eschatological son of God. The *Florilegium* (4Q174) identifies God's Davidic son (2 Sam 7) and the God-anointed king (Ps 2) as the Messiah-Savior of Israel "at the end of time." However, this royal figure, the "branch of David," will work in tandem with a priestly "interpreter of the Law." The *Aramaic Apocalypse* (4Q246) provides the most direct, titular use of "the Son of God." Also called "the Son of the Most High," this warrior-ruler will determine the fate of the nations. But it is not certain to whom the "Son of God" refers in this fragmentary text. Alluding to Daniel 7 and the Maccabean crisis, this so-called Son of God may refer to Antiochus IV, the Hellenist tyrant and divine claimant who sought to "trample" the Jews. More likely, this "Son of God" is aligned with the celestial "one like a son of human being" appointed by God to establish an "eternal kingdom" for God's beleaguered people (Dan 7:13–27). Ultimate victory, however, results from the mighty intervention of the "Great God" (4Q246 col. II; cf. Dan 2:45).

Other Jewish apocalypses challenged oppressive Roman rule. *Psalms of Solomon* envisions a messianic, Davidic son appointed by God "to rule over your servant Israel…to destroy the unrighteous rulers, to purge Jerusalem from Gentiles" (17:21–22). While alluding to God's covenant with David (2 Sam 7) and the anointed king's "iron rod" conquest (Ps 2), the *Psalms* do not explicitly designate the Messiah as "son of God" (17:4, 24). Divine filial language is reserved for Israel "as a beloved son" (13:9), "a firstborn son, an only child" (*huion prototokon monogenē*, 18:4). Fourth *Ezra* first anticipates God's revelation of "my son the Messiah," who will restore and rule over Israel for 400 years. Although an extraordinary figure, perhaps with a pre-existent heavenly pedigree, this messianic son remains mortal, destined to die at the end of his long reign (7:28–29). But in the seer's penultimate vision, "something like the figure of a man" comes in "the clouds of heaven," mirroring Daniel's son of Man (13:3; cf. Dan 7:13). Also identified as "my Son" ("my" = that of "the Most High"), this figure will judge the ungodly nations, redeem God's people, and establish God's peaceable "creation" (13:25–26, 32, 37, 52). In the meantime, this Son of the Most High lives in heaven with the faithful (14:9). There is no further hint of the Son's mortality.

The wisdom traditions generally take a broader cosmological and less eschatological view. Wisdom is personified as the Lord's first-begotten child and creative partner "before the beginning of the earth," albeit as a feminine figure (Heb. *ḥokmāh*; Gk *sophia*), not as son of God (Prov 8:22–31; cf. Sir 24:1–9; Wis 7:21–27). Sirach extols Moses as a "God-beloved" hero "brought forth" (*exagō*) by the Lord and "made...equal in glory to the holy ones" or angels (Sir 45:1–2). The Wisdom of Solomon presents yet another divine filial figure: the anonymous "righteous man" (*dikaios*), a "servant" or "child [*pais*] of the LORD" who is vindicated as a "son of God" (*huios theou*). This figure functions as a "gentle" prophet, calling people back to God's just way. In turn, however, his hearers "make trial of his forbearance" and "condemn him to a shameful death." His hope rests in the ultimate deliverance of his Father God (Wis 2:12–20; cf. Isa 52:13—53:12).

Greek and Roman Contexts. Zeus, son of Cronus and Rhea, emerged as the supreme head of the Greek pantheon on Mount Olympus and became a prolific father of divine and mortal offspring, male and female. On the mortal side, myths abounded affiliating Zeus with various Hellenist rulers. Arrian recounts Alexander the Great's trek to an oracle in Libya, where he confirmed his true father to be Ammon-Re, the Egyptian deity equivalent to Zeus; Alexander also ratified his ancestral line to Perseus and Herakles, other sons of Zeus known for their military prowess (*Anab.* 3.3–4). Plutarch reports the legend tracing Alexander's origin to Zeus's impregnating the mortal Olympias via a thunderbolt or a serpent before her marriage to Philip of Macedon (*Alex.* 3–6). Alexander's Ptolemaic successors in Egypt also claimed the titles "son of Re" and "son of Zeus." Seleucid rulers in Syria-Palestine took a similar line, though not with explicit filial language. Antiochus IV promoted himself as "Epiphanes" or "God Manifest," esteeming himself "greater than any god" (Dan 11:36), though not directly as "son of Zeus." He did, however, rechristen the Jerusalem sanctuary as "the temple of Olympian Zeus" and coerced Jews to celebrate the festival of Dionysus there (2 Macc 6:1–11).

Certain teachers and healers accrued a measure of divine status by their beneficent wisdom and power. The philosopher and physician Empedocles (ca. 490–430 B.C.E.), renowned for his good deeds and healing oracles, claimed to be widely venerated as "an immortal god, mortal no more" ("Purifications," frag. 112). Diogenes Laertius relates an Athenian myth, via Speucippus, suggesting that Plato (ca. 427–ca. 348 B.C.E.) was conceived in his mother Perictione's womb by the god Apollo instead of by his putative human father Ariston (*Lives and Opinions of Eminent Philosophers*, 3.2). The popular medical cult hero Asclepius, to whom healing shrines were dedicated throughout the Hellenistic world, was thought to be the son of Apollo and the mortal Arsinoe (alternatively, Chronis); eventually he was elevated by Zeus to the Greek pantheon because of his therapeutic powers (Hesiod, *Catalogue of Women*, frag. 63; scholiast on Pindar, *Pyth.* 3.14).

Appropriating Greek mythology, the Romans advanced the divine ruler cult with unprecedented zeal. Although some regimes pressed emperor worship more vigorously than others, propaganda of the emperor's august status and supreme power permeated the state-controlled public media displayed on coins, inscriptions, statues, monuments, temples, and other shrines and in theatrical productions and political speeches.

Tracing his ancestry through Aeneas and Venus and garnering the title of *Pontifex Maximus*, Julius Caesar was officially declared *divus Iulius* by the Roman senate after his assassination (44 B.C.E.). His successor, Octavian, staked his claim as Caesar Augustus to equal divine status, buttressed by his filial bond to Julius and Apollo, his military conquests, and his numerous public works and civic benefactions. The common coin (*denarius*) of the day presented his laurel-crowned head on one side and the inscription "Son of God, Father of the Fatherland" (*Divi Filius*, *Pater Patriae*) on the other. Notably, Octavian's divine sonship was legally certified through adoption. Though having a biological son (Caesarion), Julius adopted his great-nephew Octavian on the basis of merit to inherit his supreme authority. Likewise, Octavian bequeathed the empire to his adopted son Tiberius. In Roman society adoption did not imply weak, second-class status but rather the legitimate prerogative of the patriarchal family head (*paterfamilias*) to designate his primary heir (see Peppard, 2011b).

The New Testament. Paul ascribes to Jesus the title "Son of God" infrequently by comparison to "Lord" and "Christ" (2 Cor 1:19); sometimes Paul conjoins all three titles (Rom 1:3–4). In his earliest New Testament writing (ca 50 C.E.), addressed to the Thessalonian church "in God the Father and the Lord Jesus Christ," Paul commends the believers' repudiation of false gods "to serve a living and true God, and to wait for his Son from heaven, whom he raised from the dead—Jesus" (1 Thess 1:1, 9–10). This text establishes the primary eschatological context of Paul's understanding of God's Son, grounded in Jesus's resurrection from the dead, exaltation to heaven, and expected glorious return to earth (cf. 2:19; 3:13; 4:15–17; 5:23). In 1 Corinthians Paul envisions this reappearance as a climactic world-changing event, when God's Son "hands over the kingdom to God the Father, after he has destroyed every ruler and every authority and power," and then resubmits himself to his Father's rule "so that God may be all in all" (15:24–28). However, Paul also believed that the "end" had already commenced with Christ's resurrection, when God's "Son…descended from David according to the flesh…was declared [designated] to be Son of God with power" (Rom 1:3–4).

For Paul, therefore, the resurrection marks the pivotal, adoptive Son-of-God moment for Jesus. While affirming Jesus's royal Davidic lineage and that "God sent his Son, born of a woman" (Gal 4:4), Paul shows comparatively little interest in Jesus's filial origins. The action of God's "sending" his Son need not imply dispatching Jesus from heaven to earth; most likely, it simply conveys Jesus's commission to advance God's rule. On the rare occasions when Paul hints at Jesus's heavenly preexistence, he does not use sonship language (1 Cor 8:5–6; 2 Cor 4:4; Phil 2:6–11). A possible exception arises in Colossians 1:15–20. Of disputed provenance (possibly post-Paul), this poetic text extols God's regnant "beloved Son" (1:13) as the "image of the invisible God, the firstborn [*prototokos*] of all creation" through whom "all things have been created" (1:15–16). While this statement suggests God's primordial "begetting" of Jesus after the fashion of Wisdom, a few lines later the Pauline author returns to more familiar resurrection moorings, identifying Jesus as "firstborn [*prototokos*] from the dead" (1:18). In turn, this "firstborn" image shifts the focus forward to the resurrection of other sons and daughters in God's "large family" (Rom 8:29) of redeemed, "adopted" children, entitled to joint inheritance with Jesus of the bountiful kingdom of "Abba, Father" (Rom 8:12–17, 28–32; Gal 4:4–7).

Mark. Like Paul, Mark has no interest in Jesus's birth but does backshift the dynamic, formative "Son-of-God" moment to Jesus's baptism. As Jesus emerges from the water, the Holy Spirit descends upon him and the heavenly voice announces, "You are my Son, my Beloved; with you I am well pleased [or am pleased to choose (*eudokeō*)]" (Mark 1:10–11). God thus adopts and certifies Jesus as the chosen heir of God's realm in continuity with royal Davidic sons (Ps 2:7). The baptismal voice echoes another scriptural strain of leadership, represented by God's Spirit-anointed servant-son (*pais*) as "chosen" to rule justly through humble and peaceful, not iron-fisted, means (LXX Isa 42:1–4; cf. 52:13—53:12; Wis 2:12–20).

While Mark offers further supernatural confirmation of Jesus's filial inheritance of God's mighty power (5:7; 9:7), he places greater emphasis on Jesus's suffering and rejection as God's Messiah and "beloved Son" by Israel's religious leaders (12:6–8; cf. 8:31; 9:31; 10:33–34). The conflict comes to a head at Jesus's trial before the Jewish Council with the high priest's interrogation, "Are you the Messiah, the Son of the Blessed One?" Jesus's straightforward response, "I am"—his only "I"-declaration of Sonship in Mark's narrative—provokes charges of blasphemy and cries for capital punishment (14:61–65). At the climax of his crucifixion, however, as Jesus is mocked as the failed "Messiah" and "King of the Jews" and wracked by his own doubts of God's support (15:25–34), the attending Roman centurion, of all people, is moved to confess, "Truly this man was God's Son!" (15:39). While this comment might be taken as ironic insult, the final indignity of a defeated king, the motivating factor of the way Jesus "breathed his last"—precipitating a top-to-bottom rip of the Temple curtain—suggests the officer's overwhelming conviction of Jesus's divine filial power manifested through death.

Like Paul, Mark believes in Jesus's vindication through resurrection and anticipated return to consummate God's reign on earth. But Mark prefers to cast the future eschatological figure as "Son of Man" rather than "Son of God." Mark's only use of "the Son" *simpliciter* pairs him with the angels who do not know the Father's appointed time for the Son of Man's return (13:32; omitted by Luke and in some mss of Matthew).

Common material in Matthew and Luke. Two passages in Q confirm Jesus's vocation as Son of God on ethical and epistemological grounds, demonstrating his faithful doing and knowing of God's will. First, Satan tests Jesus's mettle as "the Son of God" (Matt 4:3, 5/Luke 4:3, 9) by tempting him to use his power for self-serving ends and to obtain authority over all earthly kingdoms by worshiping the devil. But at every turn Jesus eschews self-advancement, proving to be God's obedient Son in the wilderness, as firstborn Israel often failed to be, and a loyal son of God in the Davidic covenantal line, exclusively devoted to God, Israel's true king (Matt 4:1–11/Luke 4:1–13).

Second, in another rare self-disclosure of divine Sonship in the Synoptics, Jesus claims intimate knowledge of the heavenly Father's will and the exclusive right to reveal this wisdom "to whom the Son chooses" (Matt 11:25–27/Luke 10:21–22). As in the temptation scene, the present reality, not the preternatural origin, of Jesus's role as God's son is emphasized. Also in view is the implicit solidarity of the Son with those who do the Father's will, as disclosed and embodied by Jesus. Faithful followers of Jesus also become "sons [*huoi*] of the Father/Most High" (Matt 5:45/Luke 6:35; cf. the gender-inclusive formulation in Matt 12:48–50/Luke 8:20–21).

Matthew. In reporting Jesus's baptism, Matthew shifts the Father's personal statement in Mark ("You are my Son") to a more public announcement ("This is my Son") and stresses the Son's obedience to the Father's will (a baptism "to fulfill all righteousness"), reinforced in the ensuing temptation incident (Matt 3:13–17). But Matthew's story of Jesus's divine Sonship goes back further, to his conception by God's Spirit in the virgin Mary's womb, apart from normal marital relations (1:20–25). Jesus is thus directly "begotten" by God and a mortal female, recalling myths of Greek and Roman heroes. But Matthew grounds this miraculous nativity in scriptural prophecy: "Look, the virgin shall conceive and bear a son, and they shall name him Emmanuel" (Matt 1:23; cf. Isa 7:14). Yet Matthew raises this oracle to a higher key with the note of divine paternal conception (Matt 1:20). Isaiah simply envisioned a "young woman" (Heb. *'almāh*) or "virgin" (Gk *parthenos*) conceiving a son by normal means, whose name would provide an assuring sign of God's presence (Emmanuel = "God with us"), not of God's paternity. On the human side, Matthew tracks Jesus's Messianic-Davidic lineage through Mary's husband Joseph, not through Mary herself (1:1–17, 20). Thus, Joseph effectively assumes the legal role of *paterfamilias*. In Matthew, therefore, metaphors of conception and adoption merge. Jesus is "begotten" by the Spirit as God's Son and "made" David's son by Joseph.

Matthew depicts the salutary, powerful dimensions of Jesus's divine Sonship in two episodes featuring Peter and in the events surrounding Jesus's death. Peter makes a stumbling attempt to join Jesus in his supernatural walk on the stormy sea, prompting Jesus's rescue and consequent worship by all the disciples, who confess, "Truly you are the Son of God" (14:22–33). Jesus the Son thus demonstrates his authority over primordial chaotic forces, commonly imagined as turbulent, monster-infested waters, and stakes his counterclaim to Caesar as rightful ruler over the seas and everything in them. Soon thereafter, in the region of Caesarea Philippi, where Herodian rulers had built temples devoted to worshipping Caesar Augustus on sites formerly dedicated to the Greek god Pan, Peter boldly asserts to Jesus, "You are the Messiah, the Son of the living God." Jesus acknowledges this Messiah–Son identification as a revelation from "my Father in Heaven" and as the foundation of the church and "Kingdom of Heaven" that will prevail against all diabolical powers (16:13–20).

In this authoritative mode, however, Jesus immediately turns to predict his looming suffering and violent death. Although he also forecasts his resurrection, Peter rebukes him for his defeatist attitude (16:21–23). Jesus's self-prophecy crystallizes at his trial as the high priest eggs him on to certify "if you are the Messiah, the Son of God" (26:63, echoing the devil's taunt in 4:3, 5) and at his crucifixion as bystanders and two bandits dying with him join the religious hierarchs in ridiculing his claim to be God's Son (27:38–44). But as in Mark, the centurion has the final word—"Truly this man was God's Son" (27:54, echoing 14:33)—this time catalyzed by seismic natural and supernatural effects as Jesus expired, including the resurrection of "saints" from the dead (27:51–54).

Luke and Acts. Like Matthew, Luke begins the story of Jesus with his Spirit-conception in Mary's virginal womb, though he describes the Spirit's activity more dramatically as one that will "come upon" and "overshadow" Mary (Luke 1:35). Through the angelic herald Gabriel, Luke also identifies Jesus from birth as "Son of the Most High" and "Son of God" (1:32, 35), precisely matching the messianic titles in 4Q246. Luke also stresses Jesus's Davidic lineage and rightful inheritance of his throne forever (1:32). Like Matthew, Luke tracks Jesus's Davidic ancestry through Joseph; but Luke differs in plotting a reverse trajectory from the legal paternity of Joseph (3:23; cf. 4:22) all the way back to "son of Adam, son of God" (3:38). Here "son of God" reflects Jesus's solidarity with all humanity created, like Adam, in God's image. Luke thus affirms Jesus's full divine and human identity through a conceptual mix of natural and supernatural, adoptive-genealogical, and Spirit-generative models.

Elsewhere Luke generally parallels the synoptic affirmations of Jesus as God's Son in his baptism (3:22), exorcisms (4:41; 8:28), transfiguration (9:35), and trial (22:70). For Luke, as for Paul, the titles "Lord" and "Christ" overshadow "Son of God," although this does not diminish the functional importance of Jesus's intimate relationship with the Father. At the

crucifixion Luke replaces Jesus's piercing lament of God-forsakenness (Mark 15:34/Matt 27:46) with two direct appeals to the Father, the last a deep expression of trust: "Father, into your hands I commend my spirit" (23:46). In response, the centurion praises God and announces, "Certainly this man was innocent [*dikaios*]," not that he was "Son of God." Luke cares less about ascribing the title "Son of God" to Jesus than describing his exemplary character after the fashion of the suffering righteous (*dikaios*) servant-son of God in Isaiah 53 and Wisdom 2.

This emphasis on Jesus's role as "Righteous One" resurfaces in the preaching of the early church in Luke's second volume (Acts 3:14; 7:52; 22:14). The focus on Jesus as "Son of God" remains comparatively muted, appearing only twice as part of Paul's message. In his first sermon in a Damascus synagogue, Paul flatly says about Jesus, "He is the Son of God" (Acts 9:20). He elaborates this theme in Pisidian Antioch (Acts 13:33–35), declaring Jesus's resurrection as the decisive moment of his installment as God's "begotten" royal son, in fulfillment of Psalm 2:7 (together with LXX Isa 55:3 and Ps 16:10) and parallel to Romans 1:3–4 (Acts 13:33–35).

Johannine literature. The Johannine prologue extols the eternal unity of Father and Son "in the beginning," their partnership in creating "all life," and the Son's incarnation in Jesus Christ, who thereby "has made [the Father] known" to humanity (John 1:1–18). While the Fourth Gospel repeatedly reinforces the Son's oneness and equality with the Father (5:18; 10:30, 33–38; 14:10; 17:20–24) and the first Johannine letter concludes with a clear confession that the "Son Jesus Christ…is the true [*alēthinos*] God and eternal life" (1 John 5:20), John never speculates on the "natures" of the Father and Son. Their divine bond is more functional than metaphysical, a oneness of purpose and action. Jesus is vindicated as God's Son because he speaks the words of God and shows "many good works from the Father" (John 10:30–38; cf. 14:10–12). Moreover, in this dynamic union Jesus the Son still assumes a submissive, obedient place before the Father, "doing nothing on his own, but only what he sees the Father doing" (5:19) and seeking to honor the Father rather than to advance his own glory (8:28–29,

49–54). In turn, the heavenly patron-Father "loves the Son and has placed all things in his hands" (3:35) and will glorify the Son (5:22–23; 17:1–5).

Beyond affirming the Son's coexistence with the Father from "the beginning" (1:1; cf. 8:56–58), John has nothing more to say about the Son's origins. He accepts Jesus's full humanity as "the [divine] Word [*logos*] became flesh" (1:14 KJV) but has no interest in the mechanics of Jesus's human birth. In the lone reference to Jesus's birth, the focus falls on Jesus's royal purpose in being "sent" into the world, rather than on his conception. Responding to Pilate, Jesus says, "You say that I am a king. For this I was born, and for this I came into the world" (18:37). John does identify Jesus as the *monogenēs*, Son of God (1:14, 18; 3:16, 18), by which early Christian tradition closely linked Jesus's relationship with God as eternally "begotten [*gennēthenta*] not made" ("only begotten" in KJV). Strictly speaking, however, *monogenēs* in biblical Greek simply means "only" or "unique," without any "genetic" specification. When John uses "begotten" (*gennaō*) language, he applies it not primarily to Jesus but to all "born of God": believers in Jesus's name (1:12–13; 3:3–8; 1 John 2:29; 3:9; 4:7; 5:1, 4, 18).

Jesus the Son plays the major role in "begetting" other divine children, not by virtue of his own "begottenness" but through his action as savior and mediator of eternal life, preparing the way for others to "come to the Father" (14:6) and become one in God's family, as the Son and Father are one (17:22–23; cf. 1 John 4:7–15). This inheritance of divine or eternal life by faith in God's Son has a strong eschatological thrust that breaks into the present (John 3:36; 5:24; 6:47) and is consummated in the future "when the dead will hear the voice of the Son of God and … live" (5:25; cf. 6:40).

Hebrews. Rivaling John's prologue in poetic grandeur and Christological transcendence, the opening of Hebrews exalts Jesus the Son as "the reflection of God's glory and the exact imprint of God's very being [*hypostasis*]" throughout eternity (Heb 1:3): from the beginning, as the one through whom God "created the worlds," to "these last days," as the one by whom God has ultimately spoken to the world and who was exalted to God's right hand after atoning for humanity's

sin (1:1–4). This eternal Son who came to earth and returned to heaven thus commands the worship of all beings, including angels, Moses, Abraham, and Levi. Citing Deuteronomy 32:43 and identifying its "him" with God's Son, the writer of Hebrews exhorts, "Let all God's angels [*angeloi*; "sons of God" (*huioi theoi*) in LXX] worship him" (Heb 1:6). Whereas Moses was a model "faithful … servant [*therapōn*]" in God's family, Jesus outranks him as a faithful son [*huios*] "over God's house as a son" (3:5–6 NIV). Whereas Abraham and, by lineal extension, the priestly patriarch Levi paid homage to the mysterious king-priest Melchizedek (Gen 14:18–20), Jesus proves to be the highest "priest forever, according to the order of Melchizedek" (Heb 7:1–17; Ps 110:4). The family "resemblance" (7:3, 15) of Jesus the Son of God and Melchizedek the "priest of the Most High God" (7:1) extends to Melchizedek's eternal nature: "without father, without mother, without genealogy, having neither beginning of days nor end of life" (7:3).

Complementing this mythic Christology is a deep grounding of Jesus the incarnate Son in the thick soil of human nature and need. Balancing his seeming lack of origins as the eternal Son, Jesus also appears in Hebrews as God's "firstborn [*prototokos*] into the world" (1:6), who was "appointed heir of all things" and "inherited" his superior identity, not least that of the promised Davidic Messiah "anointed" and "begotten" by God according to 2 Samuel 7:14 and Psalms 2:7 and 45:5–7 (all cited in Heb 1:2–9). As in the Old Testament, divine "begetting" of David's son denotes "adoption" as a full heir, not generation in any biological sense. Though the exalted Son-Messiah, Jesus did not lord his position over his subjects but, rather, became like God's flesh-and-blood "children" (*paidia*) "in every respect" save personal sinfulness, even unto death, in order that he might eradicate their "fear of death" (2:11–18). And as the "great high priest who has passed through the heavens, Jesus the Son of God" does not forget his "weak" earthly brothers and sisters but sympathetically intercedes for them (4:14–18). Such concern is neither contrived nor condescending but springs from learned experience of the human condition: "although he was a Son, he learned obedience through what he suffered" (5:8).

From the New Testament to the Nicaean Creed. In the roughly two centuries spanning the period from the completed New Testament to the establishment of Nicaean orthodoxy, doctrines about Jesus the Son of God were solidified in debate over Christ's "essential" relationship to God ("begotten" or "adopted/made," consubstantial or subordinate) and to the created, material world (Jewish or gnostic, holistic or dualistic). Overall the proto-orthodox early church fathers affirmed the New Testament's composite portrait of Jesus: preexistent with the Creator God of the Hebrew Bible, involved in creating and sustaining the material world, conceived by the Spirit and born of the virgin Mary, royal son of David by divine (Ps 2:7) and human adoption (Joseph's line), fully divine and fully incarnate (not just "seeming" so, as Docetists claimed), Son of God and Son of Man, firstborn of a great family of human sons (and daughters) sharing the inheritance of God's Kingdom. Like the New Testament authors, patristic writers ranged across the metaphorical and conceptual spectrum to grasp Jesus's filial relationship to God, with no qualms that adoptive Sonship and collective brotherhood diminished Christ's supreme glory.

Patristic Christianity held in tension Jesus's intimate, "begotten" union with the Father alongside his submissive, secondary position before the singular Most High God. Thus, Justin Martyr proclaims Jesus worthy of worship as "the Son of the true God himself" and "a crucified man [occupying] a place second to the unchangeable and eternal God, the Creator of all" (*1 Apol.* 13). Tertullian identifies Christ the Son with the "substance of the Word" with qualification: "while I recognize the Son, I assert his distinction as second to the Father" (*Prax.* 7.9). Origen contends that, while the Father and Son enjoy a oneness of thought and will, "the Son is not mightier than the Father, but inferior [or subordinate] to him [citing John 14:28]....None of us is so insane as to affirm that the Son of Man is Lord over God" (*Cels.* 8.12, 15).

Such nuanced reflections about Jesus's subordinate relationship to the Father, which became most associated with the Alexandrian presbyter Arius in the early fourth century, proved too messy for the more philosophically purist clerics who dominated the church council at Nicaea (325 B.C.E.). The resulting creed, which has carried the day in orthodox Christian thought to the present, confesses the "one Lord, Jesus Christ, the only-begotten [*monogenē*; Lat *unigenitum*] Son of God, begotten [*gennēthen*] of the Father before all worlds, God of God, Light of Light, very [*alēthinon*] God from very God, begotten [*gennēthenta*] not made, being of one substance [*homoousion*; Lat *consubstantialem*] with the Father." The New Testament connotation of *monogenēs* as "only, unique" carries in the creed the heavier metaphysical freight of "only-begotten" within the one true divine "substance" (*homoousion*, a term the New Testament never uses). Nicaean orthodoxy precludes anything that might cast the slightest shadow over Jesus's utter uniqueness as God's eternally begotten, uncreated Son. As Alexander, bishop of Alexandria, wrote in response to Arius, "[The] Sonship [of our Savior], naturally partaking in paternal divinity, is unspeakably different from the sonship of those who, by his appointment, have been adopted as sons. He is by nature immutable, perfect, and all-sufficient, whereas men are liable to change, and need his help" ("Letter of Alexander," cited in Theodoret, *Hist. eccl.* 1.4). Jesus the Son's solidarity with humanity as "firstborn" among many sons and daughters is thus suppressed to protect Jesus's incomparable divine essence.

[*See also* David, Son of; Kings and Kingship; Lord; *and* Son of Man.]

BIBLIOGRAPHY

Angel, Andrew R. "*Crucifixus Vincens*: The 'Son of God' as Divine Warrior in Matthew." *Catholic Biblical Quarterly* 73 (2011): 299–317.

Brown, Raymond E. *The Birth of the Messiah: A Commentary on the Infancy Narratives in the Gospels of Matthew and Luke.* 2d ed. New York: Doubleday, 1993.

Brown, Raymond E. *An Introduction to New Testament Christology.* New York: Paulist Press, 1994.

Collins, Adela Yarbro. "Mark and His Readers: The Son of God among Jews." *Harvard Theological Review* 92 (1999): 393–408.

Collins, Adela Yarbro. "Mark and His Readers: The Son of God among Greeks and Romans." *Harvard Theological Review* 93 (2000): 85–100.

Collins, Adela Yarbro, and John J. Collins. *King and Messiah as Son of God: Divine, Human, and Angelic Messianic Figures in Biblical and Related Literature*. Grand Rapids, Mich.: Eerdmans, 2008.

Collins, John J. *The Scepter and the Star: Messianism in Light of the Dead Sea Scrolls*. 2d ed. Grand Rapids, Mich.: Eerdmans, 2010.

Dunn, James D. G. *Christology in the Making: A New Testament Inquiry into the Origins of the Doctrine of the Incarnation*. 2d ed. Grand Rapids, Mich.: Eerdmans, 1996.

Fockner, Sven. "Reopening the Discussion: Another Conceptual Look at the Sons of God." *Journal for the Study of the Old Testament* 32 (2008): 435–456.

Hengel, Martin. *The Son of God: The Origin of Christology and the History of Jewish Hellenistic Religion*. Translated by John Bowden. Eugene, Ore.: Wipf & Stock, 1976. English translation of *Der Sohn Gottes. Die Enstehung der Christologie und die jüdische-hellenistische Religiongeschichte*, first published 1975.

Kuhn, Karl A. "The 'One Like a Son of Man' Becomes the 'Son of God.'" *Catholic Biblical Quarterly* 69 (2007): 22–42.

Levin, Yigal. "Jesus, 'Son of God' and 'Son of David': The 'Adoption' of Jesus into the Davidic Line." *Journal for the Study of the New Testament* 28 (2006): 415–442.

Matera, Frank J. *New Testament Christology*. Louisville, Ky.: Westminster John Knox, 1999.

Peppard, Michael. "Adopted and Begotten Sons of God: Paul and John on Divine Sonship." *Catholic Biblical Quarterly* 73 (2011a): 92–110.

Peppard, Michael. *The Son of God in the Roman World: Divine Sonship in Its Social and Political Context*. Oxford: Oxford University Press, 2011b.

Pietersma, Albert, and Benjamin G. Wright, eds. *A New English Translation of the Septuagint*. Oxford: Oxford University Press, 2007.

Vermes, Geza. *The Complete Dead Sea Scrolls in English*. Rev. ed. London: Penguin, 2011.

Vermes, Geza. *Christian Beginnings: From Nazareth to Nicaea*. London: Penguin, 2012.

F. Scott Spencer

SON OF MAN

"Son of Man" (*ben adam, bar enash, ho huious tou anthopou*) is a Semitic idiom that normally refers to a human being or to someone's humanity. "Sons of men" is the plural form. "Human" and "humans" or other gender-inclusive translations are also appropriate English renderings so that "son of a human" is a reasonable and legitimate translation, even as "son of man" remains the traditional rendering. The central debate among scholars surrounds whether or not Jesus's use of the expression builds upon messianic expectations in the Hebrew Bible.

Key Passages. In the book of Ezekiel, God addresses the prophet as "son of man" 93 times. The expression connotes the prophet's limited humanity. One finds a parallel in Daniel 8:17: "Understand, son of man, that the vision is for the end-time" (unless otherwise noted, translations of biblical texts are the author's literal translations). In neither does the phrase have messianic implications. Several passages in the Hebrew Bible, the New Testament, and Second Temple Judaism use "son of man/sons of men" in the same way to refer to human beings or to one's humanity. A few examples will suffice. Numbers 23:19 contrasts God with human beings with two parallel phrases: "human" and "son of man." Isaiah 51:12, 52:14, and 56:2 all make the same parallel. Psalm 8:4 provides the perfect example: "What is a human that you are mindful of him or a son of man that you care for him?" Here "human" and "son of man" clearly define one another. Other passages include Jeremiah 49:18; 50:40; 51:43; Psalms 146:3; Job 16:21; 25:6; Daniel 2:38; Wisdom of Solomon 9:6; Mark 3:28; Ephesians 3:5; 1QS 11; *1 Enoch* 39:1, 5; 42:2; 64:2 (twice); 69:6, 8, 12, 14; *Apocalypse of Peter* 5; *Apocalypse of Paul* 7; and *Testament of Abraham* 2:6 (Turner translation in *AOT*).

However, much debate has surrounded the interpretation of Daniel 7:13: "As I looked in the night visions, I saw one like a son of man coming on the clouds of heaven." Christian tradition asserts that Daniel 7:13 is a messianic prediction of the coming of Jesus, that is, Jesus is the Danielic Messiah, the Son of Man. Scholars have offered several different interpretations. Some thought "son of man" was a messianic title with its roots in ancient Near Eastern cosmic speculation, while others argued for a Canaanite background, still others argued for a more general ancient Near Eastern royal man myth. Finally, some argued for a heavenly divine agent such as the archangel Michael, the heavenly patron of Israel (see Dan 10:13; 10:21; 12:1; 1QM 17.5–8; 11QMelch; *T. Mos.* 10:2; *T. Ab.* 1:6; 2:1–3).

A New Assessment. A key problem is that too few exegetes recognize the difference between generic phrases (son of man/sons of men), on the one hand, and comparisons (e.g., "one like a son of man [Dan 7:13]" or "one having the appearance of a man" [Dan 8:15 RSV]), on the other, and the fact that several Jewish and Christian writings dated between 200 B.C.E. and 200 C.E. recognized and consistently maintained this distinction. Several writers from this period used various types of comparisons to describe heavenly beings in human likeness. Probably following Ezekiel (1:26), Daniel employs comparisons to denote angels in human likeness ("one like a human being in 7:13, "Then someone appeared standing before me, having the appearance of a man" in 8:15, "Then one in human form touched my lips" in 10:16, "Then one in human form touched me and strengthened me" in 10:18). Both *1 Enoch* 46 and *4 Ezra* 13 reinterpret Daniel 7:13, and both use comparisons in the process: "whose face had the appearance of a man" (*1 En.* 46:1 [Knibb translation in *AOT*]) and "something like the figure of a man" (*4 Ezra* 13:3). In like manner, the *Apocalypse of Abraham* 10:4 reads, "The angel he sent to me in the *likeness of a man* came, and he took me by my right hand and stood me on my feet" (*OTP*, italics added).

Three additional Jewish writings from this period further substantiate this argument. Philo of Alexandria employs a comparison while discussing the three angels who visited Abraham in Genesis 18: "(T)hough incorporeal, they assumed human form" (*Abr.* 118, LCL). The *Testament of Abraham* 2:3 describes the archangel Michael "like a handsome soldier" (*AOT*). Finally, the *Martyrdom and Ascension of Isaiah* 4:2 describes Beliar (Satan) thusly: "He will descend from his firmament in the *form of a man*" (*OTP*, italics added). Some Second Temple Jewish traditions held that Satan resided in heaven and Satan's fall from heaven would be a sign of the end times (e.g., Luke 10:18; Rev 12:7–10).

Philippians, Revelation, and Acts used comparisons in the same manner. Paul, using an early Christian hymn, incorporated at least two comparisons in Philippians 2:7–8. First, Paul affirms that Jesus relinquished his equality with God and was "born in human likeness. And being found in human form." Revelation 1:13 and 14:14 also echo Daniel 7:13 when they use the expression "like a son of man." While Revelation 1:13 is clearly messianic, there is some debate whether Revelation 14:14 depicts Christ or an angel. However, all agree that Revelation 1:13 and 14:14 refer to heavenly beings in human form. Without any messianic connotations whatever, Acts 14:11 shows that comparisons were intelligible in the broader society. After Barnabas and Paul heal someone, the crowd proclaims, "The gods, being in human-likeness, have come down to us."

In sum, writings from various perspectives, social locations, and different genres (including apocalypses, letters, testaments, histories, and religiophilosophical apologies) employed comparisons to denote heavenly beings in human likeness. While *1 Enoch*, *4 Ezra*, Revelation, and perhaps the *Apocalypse of Abraham* have been influenced by Daniel 7:13, Paul, Acts, Philo, the *Testament of Abraham*, and the *Martyrdom and Ascension of Isaiah* do not display any influence of Daniel 7:13. Rather, they reflect a more general perception that heavenly beings take human form when descending into human society. To say heavenly beings take human form in first-century Roman society was not a reference to some sort of hypostasis, nor was it an early form of Docetism. For these writers, it merely conveyed that humans perceived heavenly beings as other, real human beings. It did not connote a lower status or that they were not real but that their appearance had changed in order to interact with humans.

More importantly, several of these works employ both the generic meaning of being human and comparisons ("one like a son of man" or a similar phrase) without confusing their roles and functions: Daniel 2:38 and 8:17 have the generic meaning, while 7:13, 8:15, 10:16, and 10:18 are comparisons; *1 Enoch* 39:1, 5; 42:2; and 64:2 are generic references and 46:1, a comparison; *Testament of Abraham* 2:6 is a generic reference, while 2:3 presents the archangel Michael in human form (cf. 10:15). We can also add Mark 3:28 to this list. Mark employs the generic meaning in 3:28, which is not to be confused with Jesus, "*the* Son of Man," in passages such as Mark 10:33–34. *Testament of Abraham* 2:6 is most interesting in that in one passage we find an archangel in human form and the generic reference "sons of men" to denote human beings: "Abraham said to the Prince [i.e., Michael], 'Greetings, most honourable soldier, [whose face] shines like the sun and [whose form is] more handsome than any of the sons of men: you are welcome indeed'" (*AOT*). These examples demonstrate that ancient writers consciously and consistently used the two types of expressions differently. However, those works specifically interpreting Daniel 7:13 share common exegetical features which relate directly to the Synoptic Son of Man tradition.

Interpreters of Daniel 7:13. The *Similitudes of Enoch*, *4 Ezra*, and Revelation share several exegetical features. First and foremost, each interprets the "one like a son of man" as the messiah (*1 En.* 52–53; *4 Ezra* 12–13; Rev 1:13). Second, each uses a comparison ("one like a son of man") to do so (*1 En.* 46:1; *4 Ezra* 13:3; Rev 1:13). Third, the messiah is an eschatological judge (*1 En.* 45:3; 46:2–6; 62:3–16; 69:27–29; *4 Ezra* 13:37–38; cf. 12:32–33; Rev 1:16). Fourth, the messiah gathers together an elect community (*1 En.* 48:4; 62:12–13; *4 Ezra* 13:12–13; Rev 1:13, 20; 14:14–16). Fifth, the messiah makes war against the enemies of righteousness (*1 En.* 48:9; *4 Ezra* 13:8–11, 34–38; Rev 1:7, 16; 14:19–20). Additionally, *1 Enoch* equates the chosen/elect/righteous one with its messianic Son of Man (e.g., chs. 51–52) who sits on a throne (e.g., 45:3; 55:4; 61:8; 69:27–29), rules the universe (e.g., 46:3; 62:6–7), is a revealer (e.g., 46:3), and is preexistent (e.g., 48:2–6). Revelation shares two of these additional features with *1 Enoch*: the messiah is a revealer (*1 En.* 46:3; Rev 1:19) and rules the universe (*1 En.* 46:3; Rev 1:13–20). Revelation 1:7 and 14:14 also share with *4 Ezra* 13:3 the belief that the messiah in human likeness traveled via clouds. These commonalities point to a common exegetical tradition about the meaning of Daniel 7:13 within first-century C.E. Judaism and Christianity. This tradition also shared messianic expectations with other traditions at the time.

These writers were not systematic theologians employing technical terms for a closed community of specialists. Rather, they were religious thinkers who sought to influence a more general audience and employed materials and traditions in various ways to convey their respective messages. That is why they used different comparisons to convey similar concepts and ideas.

The Synoptic Son of Man. Consensus scholarly opinion holds that there are three types of Son of Man sayings in the Synoptic Gospels: (1) present sayings, those which speak of the Son of Man being present at the moment; (2) future/eschatological sayings that refer to a future, coming heavenly redeemer; and (3) suffering sayings that connote the coming passion of the Son of Man. According to Christian tradition the synoptic Son of Man sayings fulfilled the prophecy of Daniel 7:13, and "Son of Man" was a pre-Christian messianic title. Some scholars have totally affirmed the tradition, while others have doubted the authenticity of all the Son of Man sayings. Still others have argued that some from one or more of these types of sayings go back to Jesus and not early Christian tradition. Often the positions say more about the exegete than Jesus.

The Johannine Son of Man. In the Gospel of John, "Son of Man" is clearly a messianic title, a more developed concept of Christ than one finds in the Synoptic Gospels. However, the Johannine tradition is not totally separate from what preceded it.

A. Y. Collins (2009) argues that the Johannine Son of Man has three roles and that two of them clearly reflect contact with the exegetical tradition surrounding Daniel 7:13. First, she states that the Johannine Son of Man functions as an eschatological judge. Collins argues further that John 5:27 is an allusion to Daniel 7:13–14 because *huios anthropou* ("son of man") does not have a definite article (that is, has "*a* son of man" rather than "*the* son of man") and thus follows the examples of the Old Greek and the Greek translation attributed to Theodotion, which also read *huios anthropou*. She persuasively argues that the Father giving authority to the Son of Man is akin to the Ancient of Days giving authority to the "one like a son of man." All these features are reminiscent of Daniel 7:13–14.

John's Gospel, again theologically more advanced than the Synoptics, provides an exception. John 5:27 reads, "And he [God] has given him authority to execute judgment, for he is [the] Son of Man [*huios anthropou*]." Here, as in John 9:5 (*phos eimi tou kosmou* ["I am the light of the world"]), there is no definite article; however, within the context of John's Gospel to leave out the definite article when translating the Greek into English would not do justice to the Christological meaning of these passages (see also John 10:36).

Additionally, Collins argues that the Son of Man is exalted in John 3:14–15, 8:28, and 12:34 (cf. 12:32). "Lifting up" carried the double meaning of physical lifting and exaltation. She argues correctly that the Gospel of John perceives the crucifixion as ultimately leading to the exaltation of Jesus and that these sayings are equivalent to the Synoptic passion predictions. Another form of exaltation is Jesus's glorification (12:23; 13:31) where the death of Jesus leads to his ultimate glorification.

Finally, the Johannine Son of Man was preexistent (3:13; 6:61–62). Commenting upon John 3:13, Collins writes that if John held "the view that the 'one like a son of man' in Dan 7:13 was preexistent" as in *1 Enoch* 37–71 and *4 Ezra*, "the descent of that heavenly being may have been identified with the incarnation of the Logos" (Collins, 2009, p. 347). Moreover, the ascent in John 6:61 might also reflect the influence of Daniel 7:13. Similarly, the messianic son of man in *1 Enoch*, again interpreting Daniel 7:13, is also presented as preexistent (e.g., *1 En.* 48:2–6).

An Assessment. The synoptic tradition is more complex than earlier interpreters recognized. There are actually two types of present sayings and five types of eschatological sayings. The first type of present saying is unembellished: "Foxes have holes, and birds of the air have nests; but the Son of Man has nowhere to lay his head" (Luke 9:58); "The Son of Man came eating and drinking, and they say, 'Look, a glutton and a drunk, a friend of tax collectors and sinners!'" (Matt 11:19). The second type of present saying has the Son of Man possessing authority. Matthew 9:6 states, "But so that you may know that the Son of Man has authority on earth to forgive sins." Similarly, Mark 2:28 reads, "so the Son of Man is lord even of the sabbath."

The five types of eschatological Son of Man sayings all understand Jesus to be the messiah. (1) The Son of Man is an eschatological judge (e.g., "Be alert at all times, praying that you may have the strength to escape all these things that will take place, and to stand before the Son of Man" [Luke 21:36]). (2) The Son of Man is enthroned (e.g., "Jesus said, 'I am; and you will see the Son of Man seated at the right hand of the Power and coming with the clouds of heaven'" [Mark

14:62]). (3) The Son of Man travels via clouds (see Mark 14:62 above and 13:24–27; Matt 24:30). (4) The Son of Man gathers an elect community as in Matthew 24:31 ("and he [the Son of Man] shall send out his angels with a loud trumpet call and they will gather his elect from the four winds, from one end of heaven to another"). (5) Finally, the Son of Man shall come with glory ("Those who are ashamed of me…, the Son of Man will be ashamed of them when he comes in his glory and the glory of the Father and the holy angels" [Luke 9:26]).

In addition to the present and eschatological saying types, the suffering Son of Man sayings constitute a third type of synoptic Son of Man saying generally recognized by the scholarly community. These are actually prophecies (e.g., Matt 17:12; 26:2; Mark 10:33–34; Luke 9:22; 18:31–34). While no parallels exist in the tradition as with the generic use of "son of man" and the comparisons ("one like"), it must be said that the tradition has an abundance of prophecies.

The present son of man sayings (those that acknowledge that Jesus is the Son of Man) reflect the generic use of "son of man" in Judaism and early Christianity. They connote Jesus as a member of the human community. However, Jesus has made them forms of self-reference. This probably was inspired by "son of man" as a form of direct address to the prophets Ezekiel and Daniel. Jesus presents himself as the new prophet of spiritual renewal and restoration.

The eschatological synoptic son of man sayings belong to the comparisons tradition, especially those works interpreting Daniel 7:13. Jesus (1) is the messiah (e.g., Luke 22:67–69), (2) travels via clouds (e.g., Mark 14:62), (3) is an eschatological judge (e.g., Matt 16:25–28), (4) gathers an elect community (e.g., Matt 13:37–39), (5) is an enthroned king (e.g., Matt 19:28), and (6) comes in glory (e.g., Luke 9:26). Five of these six features (all except coming in glory), as noted earlier, appear in the interpretation of Daniel 7:13 in the *Similitudes of Enoch*, *4 Ezra*, and Revelation.

Daniel 7:13, when viewed in context, probably refers not to the messiah but to an archangel, probably Michael, as in Daniel 10:13. The other comparisons in this section of Daniel (8:15; 10:16, 18) all refer to angels. Second Temple Jewish writers, living under the rule of Gentile foreigners, interpreted the passage messianically (the *Similitudes of Enoch*, *4 Ezra*, and Revelation). Some Jews applied it to Enoch (*1 En.* 71), while Christians, including Jewish followers of Jesus, applied this messianic interpretation to Jesus of Nazareth (Rev 1).

In the Synoptic Gospels, "son of man" probably has its genesis as a self-reference by Jesus. It denoted Jesus's self-awareness as a restoration figure and simultaneously set him apart from other "sons of men" as a special emissary from God. The present sayings and the eschatological sayings were probably blended in the process of transmitting oral Aramaic sayings into written Hellenistic Greek gospels. The unembellished present sayings have the highest probability of authenticity. They do not display much, if any, influence of early Christian traditions. The present sayings that add that Jesus has authority reflect the early Christian kerygma. They have a higher probability of authenticity if Jesus possessed a high degree of messianic consciousness.

The five types of eschatological sayings derive from the same exegetical tradition of Daniel 7:13 identified earlier in *1 Enoch*, *4 Ezra*, and Revelation. While the synoptic eschatological sayings do not employ comparisons, the functions of the messiah are strikingly similar to those identified earlier. The synoptic Son of Man is an eschatological judge (e.g., *1 En.* 45:3; *4 Ezra* 13:37–38; Rev 1:16; Matt 16:27–28), is enthroned (e.g., *1 En.* 45:3; 55:4; 61:8; Mark 14:62), travels via clouds (e.g., *4 Ezra* 13:3; Rev 1:7; 14:14; Matt 24:30), gathers an elect community (e.g., *1 En.* 48:4; *4 Ezra* 13:12–13; Rev 1:13; Matt 24:31), and will come in glory (e.g., Luke 9:26). The Synoptics share four of the five functions, and traveling with clouds points toward a Danielic origin for this exegetical tradition. Some have argued that Jesus was referring to someone else in these sayings because all are in the third person. While at first this seems plausible, it is not as helpful as it might seem since all the son of man sayings in the Gospels are in the third person. Jesus could just as well have been referring to himself in the third person. On the other hand, he could have been referring to a heavenly redeemer other than himself and the early church applied these sayings to Jesus. It is difficult to decide because it is difficult to find an interpretation that does not conform to the theological perspective of the interpreter.

No suffering son of man sayings exist outside the Gospels. Coupled with the fact that these sayings re-

flect the early Christian proclamation about Jesus, they have a low probability of authenticity. If that be the case, they are examples of *ex eventu* prophecies (prophecies after the fact), a prominent feature of many apocalypses. However, they are prophecies, and prophets did not always foresee a comfortable future for themselves (e.g., Isa 6:9–13; cf. Rev 10:8–10). If these sayings are generally authentic, Jesus consciously understood himself to be the messiah, the Son of Man of the later Danielic tradition in *1 Enoch* 37–71, *4 Ezra*, and Revelation. Thus, he foresaw an inglorious end for himself. If these sayings are inauthentic, they reflect the early church's understanding of the meaning and significance of Jesus of Nazareth for humanity.

The Johannine son of man sayings also reflect the messianic interpretation of Daniel 7:13 in Second Temple Judaism. The Son of Man as eschatological judge has been identified in *1 Enoch* 37–71, *4 Ezra*, Revelation, and the Synoptics; it goes back to the comparisons tradition. The exaltation of Jesus the Son of Man in John is comparable to the Son of Man coming in glory in the Synoptics (e.g., Luke 9:26). Both speak of the reexaltation of the Son of Man to divine status. Finally, preexistence is a feature of John and *1 Enoch* 48:2–6, further supporting the argument that the Johannine son of man tradition has its roots in the interpretation of Daniel 7:13 in the first Christian century.

[*See also* Angels; Christology; David, Son of; Ezekiel; Servant of God; *and* Son of God.]

BIBLIOGRAPHY

Borsch, Frederick Houk. *The Son of Man in Myth and History*. Philadelphia: Westminster John Knox, 1967.

Bultmann, Rudolf. *Theology of the New Testament.* 2 vols. New York: Scribner, 1951–1955.

Burkett, Delbert. *The Son of Man Debate*. Cambridge, U.K.: Cambridge University Press, 1999.

Caragounis, Chrys C. *The Son of Man*. Wissenschaftliche Untersuchungen zum Neuen Testament 38. Tübingen, Germany: Mohr Siebeck, 1986.

Casey, Maurice. *The Solution to the Son of Man Problem*. New York: T&T Clark, 2007.

Charlesworth, James H., ed. *The Old Testament Pseudepigrapha*. 2 vols. Garden City, N.Y.: Doubleday, 1983–1985.

Collins, Adela Yarbro "Son of Man." In *New Interpreters' Dictionary of the Bible*, edited by Katherine Doob Sakenfeld, Vol. 5, pp. 341–348. Nashville, Tenn.: Abingdon, 2009.

Collins, John J. "The Son of Man in First Century Judaism." *New Testament Studies* 38 (1992): 448–466.

Collins, John, J. *Daniel.* Hermeneia. Minneapolis: Fortress, 1993.

Colpe, C. "*Ho huios tou anthropou.*" In *Theological Dictionary of the New Testament,* edited by Gerhard Kittel and Gerhard Friedrich, Vol. 8, pp. 406–430. Grand Rapids, Mich., Eerdmans, 1972.

Hare, Douglas R. A. *The Son of Man Tradition.* Minneapolis: Fortress, 1990.

Higgins, A. J. B. *The Son of Man in the Teaching of Jesus.* Cambridge, U.K.: Cambridge University Press, 1980.

Hooker, Morna D. *The Son of Man in Mark: A Study of the Background of the Term "Son of Man" and Its Use in St. Mark's Gospel.* Montreal: McGill University Press, 1967.

Käsemann, Ernst. "Problem of The Historical Jesus." In *Essays on New Testament Themes,* pp. 15–47. London: SCM, 1964.

Kearns, Rollin. *Die Entchristologisierung des Menschensohnes.* Tübingen, Germany: Mohr Siebeck, 1988.

Lindars, B. "Re-enter the Apocalyptic Son of Man." *New Testament Studies* 22 (1975): 52–72.

Mowinckel, S. *He That Cometh.* New York: Abingdon, 1954.

Schmidt, Nathaniel. "Was *bar nash* a Messianic Title?" *Journal of Biblical Literature* 15 (1896): 36–53.

Schmidt, Nathaniel. "The 'Son of Man' in the Book of Daniel." *Journal of Biblical Literature* 19 (1900): 22–28.

Schnackenburg, R. "The 'Son of Man' in the Fourth Gospel." In *The Gospel According to St. John,* Vol. 1, pp. 5529–5543. New York: Herder & Herder, 1968.

Slater, Thomas. "One Like a Son of Man in First Century CE Judaism." *New Testament Studies* 41 (1995): 183–198.

Slater, Thomas. "Comparisons and the Son of Man." *Bible Bhashyam* 24 (1998): 67–78.

Slater, Thomas. *Christ and Community: A Socio-historical Study of the Christology of Revelation.* London: T&T Clark, 1999.

Sparks, H. F. D., ed. *The Apocryphal Old Testament.* Oxford: Clarendon, 1984.

Vermes, G. "The Use of *bar nas/bar nasa* in Jewish Aramaic." In *An Aramaic Approach to the Gospels and Acts,* 3d ed., edited by Matthew Black, pp. 310–320. Oxford: Clarendon, 1967.

Walker, William O., Jr. "The Son of Man: Some Recent Developments." *Catholic Biblical Quarterly* 45 (1983): 584–560.

Thomas Slater

SONG OF SONGS

See Megillot.

SOTERIOLOGY

Dealing with soteriology of the New Testament provides numerous challenges. A first challenge lies with the diversity in definition. The concept of soteriology (*sōtēr* + *logos*) in the New Testament may focus on different aspects related to salvation. This might range from the focus falling on the moment of change to the total process of being changed, living as a saved person up to the final eschatological outcome. Both positive spiritual and physical change might be included. In this article emphasis will fall on the event or moment of salvation, although watertight differentiation is not always possible. The "moment of salvation" is seen as that point in a person's life where radical change takes place that moves one away from something very negative and distressful to a positive position.

A second challenge is the diversity in and of the documents of the New Testament. The complex soteriological landscape does not lend itself to précis form. The multifaceted levels of diversity, theological and linguistic alike, cannot simply be "synchronized." Neither are the documents of the New Testament (abstract) theological treatises. They should rather be seen as reflecting the integration of the message into the particular situations of the people involved in the original communication process. Thus, a truly diverse soteriological landscape is birthed as individual situations play a decisive role in how the message of the Christ-event is expressed. The documents address different issues, employing different linguistic styles, thereby creating different foci—although they are part of the canon, they were not written as a unity or as a planned, coherent body of thought. Changing circumstances influenced the character of linguistic or conceptual expressions. When circumstances changed, concepts and language also changed.

The commonality of the canonical documents lies in the shared tradition, which was interpreted and applied according to the needs of specific situations. This makes the use of generic statements problematic since the finer nuances of the different writings stand in danger of being compromised, especially in a short theological overview article like this one. While a degree of careful synthesis will be attempted, diversity will be acknowledged by constantly referring to the different books when presenting similarities. The focus will not fall on detailed nuances or differences between the different documents (which is more an exegetical than a specifically theological procedure). Since the focus in this article is more theological than exegetical (although the former is based on the latter), tendencies within the New Testament will be described that arise from a fairly broad level of abstraction.

The Soteriology of the Synoptic Gospels. Each of the Synoptic Gospels has a distinct approach to salvation but certain theological aspects can be identified as common to them all in different degrees. The Gospels are biographical narratives (*bioi*) in which the soteriological dynamics are developed in the actions, relations, and words of the characters. This implies that Jesus healing a person, the change of social affiliation by a person, or simply deciding to follow Jesus might all be ways to express salvation within the narrative. In other cases, Jesus as a character in the narrative might explain salvation through his sermons or invitations by, for instance, saying that whoever believes will receive eternal life or inviting someone to follow him. Some of the commonalities among the Synoptic Gospels will now receive attention.

Jewish scriptures fulfilled—salvation dawned. An overlap on the conceptual level among all the Gospels is that God's salvation has dawned, as was promised by the Jewish scriptures. This forms an important framework within which the salvific work of Jesus is presented and serves as proof of the continuity of God's plan in the midst of the Christ-event.

Both Mark and Matthew emphasize the significance of the Old Testament prophecies and locate the salvific actions of Jesus solidly within the promise that Yahweh will return to Zion to save his people and establish his Kingdom (Mark 1:15; Matt 1:22–23; 2:19–23). Likewise, Luke emphasizes the long history of God with his people. His narration of the Christ-event, like that of Mark, shows a special focus on the fulfillment of the prophecies of hope for salvation (Luke 1:13–17, 68–75; 2:9–14; 24:44). God stands central in this process as the absolute source of salvation.

Ultimately salvation goes back to him, although Jesus is the agent in and through whom salvation is realized.

Christological centrality: Israel's narrative expressed and redefined in Christ. Situating the salvific events against the backdrop of Old Testament prophecies highlights the eschatological nature of the presence of Christ. As promised, God is indeed triumphantly returning to his people as an act of divine power in and through the deeds and words of Jesus.

As Mark and Matthew aptly describe, salvation means the coming of God's Kingdom, his eschatological reign (Mark 1:14–15; 9:47; 10:24–25). God's reign includes Israel's return from exile, with evil defeated and God returning to his people. This will be consummated with the return of the Son of Man (Mark 8:38–9:1; 13:24–27), which marks the point of final judgment of the enemies of God (Mark 13:24–27). John the Baptist already pronounced the eschatological judgment of Jesus (Matt 3:11–12; Luke 3:16–17). It is Jesus's ability to forgive sin that saves believers from judgment and allows them to participate in the community of Jesus (Mark 2:10; 8:35–37; 9:43, 45; 10:17). Matthew's approach is a bit different. He retells the history of Joshua being sent by God as Moses's successor to save Israel. The healing of Israel now takes place through Jesus (Matt 1:22–23). He brings the good news of the Kingdom, bringing the "little ones" into the household of God, the king.

Luke's story of salvation shares the concerns of Mark and Matthew but has a broader focus. He describes God's restoration through Jesus (Luke 2:30; 3:6) as part of God's salvific history with Israel (Luke 1:69–79) that reaches all levels of society, not only the spiritual but also the physical. Above all, their position before God is restored through Jesus, who has the power to forgive sins. For Luke it remains important that it is God who saves (Luke 1:47, 68–79).

Faith in Jesus is required. Salvation deals with becoming part of the new people of God. This presupposes a decisive turn toward God and away from one's previous existence, with all the implications associated with such a change. Different concepts are used in the Gospels to describe this decisive change. "Faith" is the most common term used to mark the turning point, while terms like "conversion" and "following Jesus" are also used. These terms focus on the acceptance of and association with Jesus.

For Mark, salvation flows from a reaction of faith in Jesus as the Son of Man. It implies unconditional acceptance of God's power as is seen and expressed in Jesus as the bearer of the Spirit (Mark 2:1–5; 5:21–24; 5:25–34; 11:23–25; 10:27). God himself stands behind salvation, while Jesus, as God's eschatological messenger, acts as mediator of God's favor. As Savior he provides salvation in the narrower sense of healing as well as in the broader sense of salvation from sin. This creates new existential opportunities for believers. Conversion is not simply turning away from personal sin but also communal: Israel is challenged radically to surrender its way of being Israel and to trust Jesus for his way. The idea of following Jesus (Mark 8:34; 10:21–24, 28–31) therefore functions as an alternative description of salvation, implying readiness to die for Jesus (Mark 8:34–35) and sharing communal life with him (Mark 1:16–19; 2:14–15; 10:28–29; 15:41).

Matthew largely follows Mark with choice also being important—people must choose between the old and new Moses, with all the implications associated with such a choice. To accept Jesus as the Davidic Messiah—the one whom God has commissioned to save Israel from their sin—leads to salvation, a life in the presence of the God-with-us. The call to follow Jesus with total dedication up to the point of death (including carrying one's cross), expresses the nature of choosing for Jesus (Matt 8:19–22; 16:24–25; cf. 19:27–30). Luke likewise emphasizes the importance of faith in Jesus, starting with responding to the message of Jesus (Luke 24:45–47). Through this trust in him people can consistently rely on his ability to help (Luke 18:1–8).

People who decide to follow Jesus should follow him unconditionally. Nevertheless, God's role in this process of choice, conversion, or faith is not excluded; on the contrary, God remains the savior-king.

The presence of evil. The presence of Satan and evil forms the backdrop of salvation in the Gospels and is the contrast to the presence of God in Christ. The soteriological narrative unfolds in the context of conflict with and eventual victory over evil.

In Mark the focus on Satan's role is toned down after Jesus's victory in the wilderness (Mark 1:12–13). Although Satan does not disappear from the narrative, Mark is more concerned about Jesus's redemptive actions than about Satan's cosmic defeat. The need for salvation stays bound to the presence of Satan, even though Mark does not see Satan as the sole source of evil. Evil also originates in the human heart and so not only with Satan. Nevertheless, through Jesus evil is overpowered and salvation becomes possible. Mark's perspective of history, where the present is typified by the absence of the risen Jesus who will return in the future, leads him to see the present time as one of imminent danger of the loss of salvation (Mark 4:16–19; 10:30; 13:6–13, 19–20; 14:27). Believers must remain faithful (Mark 13:5, 9, 23, 34, 37) and proclaim the gospel (8:34, 38). Nevertheless, Mark looks forward to Satan's final defeat in the end time. Matthew follows Mark, with the exception that the salvific Christ remains with his people even in the time after the resurrection (Matt 28:20). In Luke Satan remains in active conflict with Jesus up to the final stages of that Gospel, although the victory of Jesus and his disciples is already pronounced in Luke 10:17–18, where Jesus watched the devil falling from heaven like a flash of lightning.

Salvation through Jesus. In all the Gospels Jesus is the purveyor of salvation—the presence of the good news is Christologically defined. Faith in Jesus, accepting his message and following him, forms the basis of salvation in the Gospels. Although there is consensus about the centrality of Jesus, views on his role, position, and work are developed and expressed in different ways in the respective Gospels.

In Mark the presence of Jesus is beneficial (is salvific) and is described in terms of his role as wonder worker, savior, and proclaimer. Through Jesus's presence the Kingdom of God is mediated proleptically (Mark 1:13; 6:30–44; 8:1–9; 14:25); his healings and exorcisms anticipate the final eschatological salvation (Mark 7:31–37). By giving his life as ransom for many he saves his people from the power of the devil (10:45), and his disciples partake in this salvific presence (Mark 4:35–41; 6:7–13, 45–51). The verb *sōzein* in Mark refers to "saving life" from, for instance, physical hazards (Mark 3:1–6; 5:21–24, 35–43; 5:25–34; 6:53–56; 10:46–52) or from God's final judgment (cf. Mark 8:35, 38; 10:26; 13:13, 20).

Matthew to a large extent follows Mark but has his own emphasis in presenting the material, as is also the case with Luke. In the Matthian birth narrative the baby is named Jesus (which means "God is savior," Matt 1:18–24) who will save his people from their sins, implying that God will eschatologically save his people through Jesus as his salvific instrument. God similarly turns toward the nations (Matt 21:41–45; 22:7–10; 28:19), establishing the universality of salvation.

The deeds of Jesus. The deeds of Jesus have salvific significance, especially the miracles and signs that illustrate the presence and salvific power of God in him. In Mark a distinction could be made between "provisional" and "definitive" salvific works. "Provisional" salvation refers to healing people, bringing people back to life and restoring their wholeness, although they will eventually die again. The ongoing destructive process in this world is temporarily neutralized. As part of the gift of the Messianic age, these healing actions of Jesus are directly related to the forgiveness of sin. "Definitive" salvation is eternal salvation. It is the protection of life from the threat of death. Within this framework, Jesus's power to forgive sin should be understood (Mark 2:10; Matt 1:21; 26:27–28).

According to Luke, Jesus brings liberation to his people through his deeds and especially his ability to forgive sin and give life. As the Gospel for the underdogs, Luke describes salvation along two lines, physical and spiritual; not only physical and mental restoration takes place (Luke 6:9; 8:36; 8:48, 50) but also spiritual restoration, which means forgiveness of sin (Luke 7:50), atonement, and eternal life—hence a total restoration on all levels of society and life.

The cross and salvation. The cross events play varying roles in the narratives of all the Gospels, although there are notable differences regarding the presentation and interpretation of the cross. Mark focuses on the suffering and servitude for others (Mark 10:45; see the only other reference to the meaning of Jesus's death in Mark 14:25, where Jesus refers to his drinking of the cup). Jesus is able to save others because he died. He is king not in spite of but because he gives up his life for others. Authority is expressed in service. In Matthew salvation is expressed in the "forsaken" Jesus on the cross, signaling God's paradoxical saving presence (Matt 27:45–50). He does not focus further on the cross except in linking it to the destruction of the Temple (27:51) and, thus, to the conflict between the followers of the "new Moses" and their opponents.

No significant emphasis is found in Luke on the salvific function of the cross, at least not to the extent of Mark or Matthew. Some scholars (building on this view in Conzelmann, 1960) claim that Luke does not focus on the atonement power of the cross of Christ at all. No direct soteriological significance is drawn from Jesus's suffering or death, except that it might be exemplary. Others argue that Luke had a redemptive understanding of Jesus's death (with supporting evidence from Acts), although the disciples did not understand the necessity of Jesus's suffering.

The different Gospels, then, clearly present their material on this central issue in different ways and allot different emphases to the reality of the cross within the process of salvation. Nevertheless, they share the conviction that the cross events are central in the Jesus narrative.

Resocialization as an essential part of salvation. In the context of God returning to his people, it is not surprising that salvation is described in terms of belonging to a new group, often expressed in well-known Jewish concepts (such as the shepherd and his sheep and eating together), but consistently associated with Jesus as God's Son and Messiah. Jesus inaugurates God's salvation in Israel and the world by means of establishing new relations. Boundaries are transcended and new relations between God and humans, as well as among humans themselves, are established, even outside existing familial and national boundaries. These relationships introduce demands of new loyalties, new responsibilities, new ethics, and new behavior.

In Mark this radical change is described as receiving life and status, which means a change in one's state of being. In this new state of being the disciples constitute a new community, which is understood by

Mark as an eschatological family (Mark 10:30). Matthew's story follows the same lines but also confronts people with the quest for membership in the true Israel. Choosing Jesus, as the "new Moses," results in being a disciple of the Kingdom of heaven (for discussion of Jesus as the new Moses in Matthew).

Like the other Synoptic Gospels, Luke describes salvation as taking place through the presence of Jesus; his presence introduces the Kingdom of God on several levels. After accepting the message of Jesus in faith, baptism and the bestowal of the Spirit follow and believers are incorporated into the Christian communities, inter alia expressed through their participation in communal meals. Believers become members of this new Kingdom that constitutes their newfound social and religious reality. Although the consummation still lies in the future, changing the present reality is emphasized. This is not only a spiritual change but also a physical one in diverse ways, that is, economically, socially, politically.

Soteriology in Pauline Literature. Discussions on Pauline soteriology are usually influenced by the complex nature of the terminology, development of ideas, and structure of thought inherent to the Pauline materials, as well as the relationship between the so-called Pauline and Deutero-Pauline letters. For the sake of this theological presentation, the Pauline and Deutero-Pauline letters will be treated together as part of a related theological developmental process.

In spite of their variety, virtually all the letters share certain common theological features on a higher level of abstraction. The intention here is not to focus on small exegetical detail or the finer developments in soteriological thought but rather to consider possible similarities, while not denying the differences. The soteriological emphasis often shifts within a letter or between letters, which focuses on a specific aspect of Pauline soteriology, for instance, the formation of a new relationship, purification from sin, or deliverance from evil. These and similar aspects must be noted but not isolated from the soteriological dynamics as a whole. Paul offers an integrated and complex picture of the soteriological dynamics that emphasizes not only the complex process of deliverance but also the consequences of this deliverance.

Paul's soteriology is characterized by the number of images that express the dynamics of the soteriological process (e.g., justification, reconciliation, slavery, filial expressions). This lends power and richness to his soteriological descriptions. These metaphors or images sometimes overlap semantically—they address the same issue in different ways—for instance, the images of moving from slave to child or enemy to friend in essence express the same idea, namely, restoration (or establishment) of a relationship. The added power of the imagery nevertheless lies in the finer nuances of the imagery: changing from a slave to a child carries a different sociocultural nuance from the change from an enemy to a friend. Although these nuances cannot be worked out here, they should receive due attention in closer exegetical analyses.

A common line that runs through Pauline soteriological thought (although with varying intensity) is a negative assessment of the human condition, which is remedied by a graceful God through Jesus with the result that the saved people enjoy a new status and consequently positive (eschatological) relationships with God and one another. This is a broad outline, but it is time and again developed in different ways by means of different images.

A negative assessment of the human condition. Salvation has to do with a negative spiritual assessment of the human condition that includes behaviors from which people are to be saved. They are viewed as ungodly and weak sinners who live in hostility toward God (Rom 1:18–32; 8:1–8; Gal 1:4). Paul regards humans as accountable to God, and their sin constitutes guilt before (Rom 3:9–20), alienation from, and enmity between humans and God (Rom 1:18—3:20). This condition has a corporate as well as an individual aspect—humanity is indeed in trouble—"all have sinned" (Rom 3:23). Humans need to be freed from their condition of slavery (Gal 3:21—5:1), their own sinfulness and sinful nature (Rom 8:3, 7), their own lack of knowledge (Titus 2:11–14), and, indeed, their enmity and alienation from God. Inherently part of this negative situation is humanity's bondage to cosmic powers (Gal 4:3, 8; Col 2:8, 20; 1 Cor 15:24). Paul is therefore acutely aware of the active presence of negative influences and powers within humans from which they need to be saved. Not the least of these powers is personified in the law and expressed in the flesh from which people need to be freed (Rom 8:1–8; Gal 3:12–13).

Benefaction as gracious act. Because of the negative anthropological frame of Pauline soteriology, gracious action from God is needed (Rom 5:15–21; Eph 2:8). Exactly because of the negative condition of humans, divine grace is the basis for salvation for all—humans cannot be saved by their own effort (Eph 2:8; 1 Tim 2:4; Titus 3:5). Without God people have no hope (Eph 2:12) and remain in darkness (Col 1:13). Only a gracious God can change people and secure a future for them. While the initiative lies with God, it leads to a process in which Jesus, the Spirit, and humans are all involved (Rom 5:8–11; 2 Thess 2:13). Within the framework of ancient gracious benefactorism, Paul develops the idea of the gracious God who benefits people who do not deserve it (Rom 11:33–37). In the face of consistent ingratitude God freely bestows favor to everybody through Christ. This runs contrary to expectations within ancient Mediterranean societies. There is now equal access for all to God's favor, irrespective of the status or behavior of the beneficiaries. No restrictions are set on the availability of grace; God wants everybody to be saved (1 Tim 2:3–4; 4:16; Titus 2:11). This does not imply, however, that all will be saved because this grace calls for fitting responses. Believers are put in a new sphere of *gratia continua* in which corresponding human reaction is required. Paul's attitude toward the Jewish Law, especially in the light of the grace of God, cannot be discussed in any detail here but should be mentioned as a central soteriological theme in Paul (Rom 3:19–31; Gal 2:16—5:1).

Christ as savior. Paul reserves the word "savior" (*sōtēr*) for God (e.g., 1 Tim 1:1; 2:3–4; Titus 1:3; 2:10; 3:4) and Jesus (e.g., Phil 3:20; 2 Tim 1:10; Titus 1:4; 2:13; 3:6), which is notable because it was a term used widely for gods and some heroes in ancient times. The pivotal point of Pauline soteriology is that God's salvation is mediated or made possible through Christ

(Rom 3:21–25; 8:1–4; 1 Cor 1:30–31; 2 Cor 5:19; Gal 4:4–5; Col 1:13–14; 1 Tim 1:15; 2:5–6). Salvation is offered "in Christ" (Col 2:5–15; 2 Tim 2:10; 3:15). The old existence (through a prolepsis of the eschatological judgment) is terminated, which makes possible a newly created humanity in Christ (2 Cor 5:17–19).

Salvation through Christ is consistently linked to faith in Jesus and what he did (Rom 1:16–17; 3:26; 5:1; 10:9; 1 Cor 15:1–2; Gal 2:16; Eph 2:8). For Paul, the cross and resurrection of Jesus are central (1 Cor 2:1–4; 15:1–34; 2 Cor 4:10; Gal 6:14; Phil 3:10). Faith results from the proclamation of the message of and about Jesus Christ (Rom 10:14–17; 1 Cor 1:21; 15:1–2; Col 1:5–8; 2 Tim 1:8–9). In this way Paul's soteriology also relates to practical aspects like preaching the gospel.

Paul makes extensive use of forensic imagery in his treatment of soteriology. It could even be regarded as a central aspect of Pauline soteriology, especially in Romans. God, the Creator, is judge of all humanity. Humanity is guilty of sin and therefore accountable to God for its sins. Although God as judge shows no favoritism, the norms he uses are colored by grace and he consciously places himself on the side of the accused who are in Christ. In spite of this gracious process, the integrity of the juridical process is not compromised since redemption and atonement come through Christ. That is why justification must be appropriated by faith. The believer receives a new identity and status with God and lives in a restored relationship with God, which will be confirmed at the final judgment.

A second aspect of salvation is Paul's concept of reconciliation. The image of reconciliation expresses the transition from enmity to friendship (Rom 5:8–11; 2 Cor 5:18–20). Within the ancient sociocultural framework, the process of reconciliation described the restoration of relations between humans who were in conflict. Paul applies this sociocultural phenomenon to the movement from enmity to peace and friendship between God and humans. God is the agent of this reconciliation, acting through the death of Christ (Rom 3:24–26) to bring restoration for humanity (with eschatological effects).

A third perspective on this change of position from negative to positive, implying a radical reversal of status, is expressed by means of socioeconomic imagery. The picture of humanity in a hopeless situation of slavery forms the framework of the imagery of paying a price. Christ intercedes with the required payment and transforms the status of believers from slavery to being free people in the presence of God (1 Cor 6:19–20; 7:20–24). This is not unrestricted freedom but rather a life lived under new obligations to God (Rom 6:16–23).

Another set of images expressing the change that takes place through salvation by Christ is linked to filial language. In 1 Thessalonians, salvation is expressed in terms of a new family, which emphasizes the new relationship between God and believers. Because believers are drawn into a group that resembles an ancient family, their behavior should also be positive toward one another, reflecting the behavioral expectations within an ideal family. The image of adoption expresses this social change (Gal 4:4–7; Eph 1:13–14). The resulting intimate relationship also implies that children of God share the fate of Jesus, including his death and resurrection. Resurrection will consummate the salvation they have appropriated (1 Thess 4:18). In this way the dynamics of salvation are expressed in terms of the most basic social order in Paul's world. Although coming from a different semantic field (i.e., creation), the image of becoming a new creation expresses the radical break with the past and the dynamics of a new beginning with God (2 Cor 5:17; see also Eph 2:10, 14–15). Within the context of 2 Corinthians 5, this opens up a new reality of relationships with God.

Salvation also comes through victory over the powers of this world. Colossians describes humans as being in a cosmic "prison" superintended by hostile spiritual presences and evil powers. They are oppressed by the rule of these powers. Salvation from God comes through the power of Christ, who as the image of God is far superior to all these powers. Through Christ those who were alienated from God have now been reconciled (Col 2:9–15) and those who were separated from God or who were foreigners to his covenant have been brought near (Col 1:12–14, 21–23). Believers now live in the presence of the Son of God (Col 2:20—3:4). Even though their "lives"

are with God in the present, the fullness of this presence will be revealed in the eschatological future.

Pauline literature employs a number of other metaphors to describe salvation. Colossians describes salvation as new life in Christ, emphasizing the salvific and victorious role of the cross and resurrection of Jesus (Col 1:18–23; 2:11–15). As Jesus died and was raised, believers died and were raised to the new reality in Christ (Col 2:11–15; 3:1–4) with their sins forgiven. The resurrection of Jesus forms a crucial point in Pauline thought, theologically explaining the origin and effects of salvation (see also Rom 8:11; 1 Cor 15; Eph 2:5–6). Linked to the cross, the reference to the expiation of human sin through the blood of Jesus also forms a significant element in the soteriological dynamics of Paul (Rom 3:25; 5:9). By the blood of Jesus believers are redeemed, forgiven, and justified; and by his death former sinners are reconciled to God (Rom 5:8–10; Eph 1:7; Col 1:21–22). Through the blood of Jesus the new covenantal community is established. It is within this community that believers experience the eschatological presence of the risen Jesus (1 Cor 11:25; 2 Cor 5:18). Colossians 1:20 suggests an even wider, cosmic reconciliation through Jesus's death and the blood of his cross.

In all these images the position and actions of Jesus are constitutive. This leads to a new way of existence in which believers find themselves resocialized within the divine reality.

New people in Christ and in relation to God—a matter of resocialization. A basic concept in the soteriology of Paul is the status change that salvation brings about because of the establishment of a completely new relationship between the believer and God through Christ or, in other words, resocialization. This new status is instituted unreservedly, whether it is the result of payment, forensic activities, reconciliation, or becoming part of God's family. All these images point to restored relationships between God and humanity, as well as among believers themselves, based on the changed status and identity of believers. Social and ethical responsibilities are correspondingly adjusted.

Characteristic of this change is the so-called already-not-yet situation, namely, that definitive change has occurred in the present, but full consummation still awaits. Salvation is indeed visible in the present already (Rom 10:10), but it is not yet the full picture. The moment of salvific change introduces a process that is drawn toward and is fulfilled with the final return of Jesus (Rom 8:18–39; 1 Cor 15:22–28).

Although the moment of change from a negative to a positive position is an important focus in Paul's soteriological thought, it should not be seen in isolation. It is, rather, part of a continuing process that involves the whole life of the saved people (Phil 2:12). It forms a coherent process, starting with the change. Malherbe (2005) illustrates how the process of learning is intrinsic to the eternal plan of God (2 Tim 3:14–15). The gracious God appears in history with the consequence that conditions of knowledge change. Knowledge of truth becomes possible, with baptism and the Spirit standing central to this process. The initiative starts with God, and through Jesus the Spirit is given in baptism. Through the learning process people are guided in the art of living. In many cases the ontological status of a believer (being saved and having life already—Rom 6:4; Col 2:12–15) should be seen in light of his or her ethical status as the believer continues to experience the challenges of living in an imperfect world inhabited by powers and spirits (Rom 6:4–6; 7:6; 8:1–16; Phil 2:12–13; Col 2:2—3:4; Titus 4:18). This dynamic soteriological process finds its consummation in the return of Christ and the final judgment (Rom 5:9; 13:11–14; 14:10–12; 1 Cor 1:7–8; 5:5; 15:12–58; 2 Cor 5:10; Phil 3:10–11, 20–21; 1 Thess 1:10; 4:13—5:11; 2 Thess 2:1–12).

Although Paul does not use a single or even a coherent set of images to express his soteriological thought, there is a discernible unity amid the diversity, even if it is on a certain level of abstraction. The theological unity can broadly be described in this way: the dire position of humans is changed by the gracious salvific actions of God, which restore relationships and change enmity into peace and friendship. The believers' newly acquired position obligates them to act according to their status. Within this narratological framework, the finer detail of Paul's soteriology is presented. Different aspects of this process are presented through different images, each with a focus of its own.

The Johannine Literature (Gospel, Letters, and Revelation). A negative anthropology also underlies the soteriological thinking of John. This is expressed in different ways, for instance, that people are spiritually in darkness, are blind, or are dead (John 3:17–21; 5:25; 9:1–41; 12:49–50; 14:9–11). A loving God solves this dire situation by sending his Son to this world to make God, the Father, known and thus convey salvation in the form of eternal life (John 1:1, 18; 3:16; 14:6–14). Soteriology is thus Christologically determined with Jesus as the center of God's salvific presence in this world. Jesus is the savior (*sōtēr*) of the world (John 4:22), who comes to reveal the God of Israel, Abraham (John 8:33, 39–40, 51–56), and Moses (John 1:17; 5:45–47). Where God and Jesus are, there salvation is. This is possible since the presence of the Father and Son is experienced through the presence of divine qualities like life, light, and truth (John 8:12; 14:6). Where the light shines through darkness or the truth is accepted, life results since Jesus as the way, the truth, and the life (14:6) gives life to those who believe (John 3:16, 35–36; 5:26; 6:57).

Jesus is the giver of salvation since, as the unique Son of God who was in the bosom of the Father (John 1:18), he is the Word (John 1:1), life (John 14:6), light (John 8:12), and the one sent by the Father (John 3:16). He not only received life from the Father (John 5:25; 6:57) but also received the power over life and death (John 5:21; 10:17–18). As the resurrection and the life, he gives life (John 12:25–26). Within this constellation, Jesus does not need to "earn" salvation through his death or by atonement but has the power of God to convey eternal life (salvation) to those who believe even before his death on the cross. The soteriological function of the cross in John is therefore disputed. Some argue that there are undertones of atonement in the gospel and clear indications thereof in the letters (1 John 2:2; 4:10). Since the cross is the place where Jesus's identity will be revealed (John 8:28), it has a definite revelatory function; it is the "sign" that shows people the true identity and divine origin of Jesus, which should result in believing in him (John 7:39; 8:54; 11:4; 12:16, 23; 13:31, 32; 17:1, 5) and thus receiving life (John 20:30–31).

John expresses the moment of change, when people move from death to life (John 5:24), by combining two concepts, namely, *faith* and spiritual *birth* from above. Thus, he focuses on the human and divine aspects of salvation (John 1:12–13). By having faith in Jesus, a person is spiritually born from above and receives eternal life (John 20:31; 3:35–36; see also 5:24). Birth as the point of existential change leads to eternal life, which forms part of the larger filial imagery John uses to express the process of salvation. The metaphorical nature of terminology like "birth of God," "eternal life," "children of God," and "God becoming our Father" is directly related to familial imagery. Receiving eternal life means becoming a child of God within the family of God, including everything such a new relationship offers. The believer lives within this new existential reality of the family of God, and his or her life is determined by it.

In this way John metaphorically activates a basic ancient social institution, the family, to express the nature of the salvific process. Believers are now able to partake in the reality of God, being born of God and thus being resocialized in terms of that spiritual family toward which they now orient their lives. This analogy functions in multiple ways: the familial obedience expected from a child to his or her father is now expected from the believer to God, the Father; as a father protects his children, the Father will protect the believers, and so on. Believers must now love their brothers and sisters since the Father and the Son love them. This mutual love constitutes the essence of the ethical expectations within the family of God (John 13:34–35).

The Apocalypse of John describes the Christian community as experiencing both internal and external crises. Through salvation and their consequent relation to God and Christ, the church's identity as the people of God is established and serves as a point of orientation, encouragement, and support within their conflicts. Salvation comes from God (Rev 7:10; 19:1) and is constituted through the blood of the Lamb that was slain but lives in order to ransom people for God from every tribe, tongue, and nation (Rev 5:8–13; see also 1:5), those people whose names are written in the book of life (Rev 3:5; 20:12). Within the apocalyptic framework, the message of salvation links the role of the Lamb to the eschatological unfolding of God's plan leading to the final judgment (Rev 19–20) and

consummation in the new Jerusalem (Rev 21:1—22:5). This should motivate believers to persevere amid harsh and hostile conditions in this world (Rev 21:7) that could encourage apostasy (see the content of the letters to the seven churches, e.g., 2:11). Revelation is rich in images that express soteriological perspectives, such as marriage (Rev 19:5–10), administrative recording of names (Rev 20:12), building structures (Rev 3:12; 21), freedom from slavery (Rev 1:6; 5:9), imperial actions (Rev 3:21), numbers (Rev 7:4, 9; 14:1), and clothing (Rev 2:10; 3:4; 19:8).

Because of the crisis situation within which believers find themselves, Revelation emphasizes the perseverance that will lead believers to ultimate eschatological victory (Rev 2:26–27). Believers should remain in the love they had at first (Rev 2:4) or else the lamp stand (= congregation) will be removed from its place (Rev 2:5).

Further Mosaic: Hebrews, Other General Epistles. Hebrews expands and enriches the New Testament's soteriological mosaic. Again, it is a matter of unity amid diversity. Differences in genre, situations addressed, as well as chosen language contribute toward a diversity that colors the soteriology.

Hebrews expresses salvation in language and imagery that is linked to the story of Israel's journey through the dessert. Thus, it employs, for example, the language of sacrifice, covenant, tabernacle, offerings, high priest (Heb 8:1—10:22). The principal source for this imagery is the story of Israel's liberation from bondage in Egypt. Believers are encouraged to persevere in faith on their own journey to rest and glory. On this journey they experience certain challenges but also are offered explicit hope and an eschatological future.

Sin and death, which are associated with unbelief and faithlessness, are barriers to overcome in this life since they lead to wrongful actions and are sources of impurity and defilement. The program of salvation in Hebrews has its origins in God but is realized through Christ (Heb 5:7–9; 9:28). The faithful God delivers sinners from the oppression of evil powers through Christ, who, as the pioneer (Heb 2:10) in the battle against Satan, overcame the power and bondage of Satan through his incarnation, suffering, death, resurrection, and mediation as high priest (Heb 2:14–18). The image of Jesus as the once-for-all single sacrifice for sins explains his salvific activity within the framework of priestly language (Heb 10:11–12). He appears in the presence of God, both as high priest and as sacrifice (9:12–14, 23–28; cf. Lev 16). Covenantal language is also employed with Jesus as the mediator of the new covenant (8:8–13; cf. Jer 31:31–34). Believers will receive the eternal inheritance through his death (Heb 9:15–16; 12:24). As the resurrected Christ, he sits at the right hand of God until the final victory, when his enemies will be made a stool for his feet (Heb 10:12–13). Believers can be assured that there in the heavenly sanctuary Jesus appears in the presence of God on their behalf on the basis of his own sacrifice (Heb 9:24–28).

Faith, as the assurance of things hoped for (Heb 11:1–2, 7; 4:2–3; 10:19–20), forms the basis of the obedience and perseverance of believers (see the examples in Heb 11) in the current world but also creates expectations for the future. With this faith relationship between believers and God, believers are delivered from judgment and encouraged to persevere in the hope of what is to come. Their hope is that they will share in the heavenly glory in the everlasting presence of God. Although the destruction of the evil powers is not yet complete, it is nonetheless foreshadowed by the power of deliverance. Final fulfillment awaits believers as they embark as the new Israel on a journey through this world to a glorious city to come (Heb 13:14). The break with their former Jewish heritage, represented by the Jerusalem Temple, is most probably illustrated by Jesus who suffered outside the camp where they will also be (Heb 13:12–14). Believers can face the ongoing threat of sin by persevering faithfully in anticipation of the final fulfillment of God's promises. Although they already experience liberation, they experience difficulties because they are still on their way to their glorious destiny (Heb 13:13–16).

According to James, believers receive a new identity as the first fruits of a new Israel (Jas 1:18). New social borders are created that are defined according to the wisdom of God (Jas 4:13–18). People are saved from evil and the devil though faith in Jesus (Jas 2:23), and the authenticity of faith is measured according to works (Jas 2:14–26). This letter stands in the Jewish wisdom tradition, which means that perfection, wholeness, and completeness are important (Jas 1:21, 26; 4:7–8, 10). Absolute loyalty, which is publicly and corporately displayed, is therefore required (Jas 1:12, 27). Thus, the community's existence, as well as ultimate salvation, is ensured (Jas 5:7–8).

The image of the family of God also dominates in 1 Peter. People who are dead in sin, also called slaves to sin, are born into the family of God (1 Pet 1:3, 23; 2:2) through faith in Jesus (1 Pet 1:9) who died for their sins once for all (1 Pet 3:18). This possibility of spiritual birth is directly related to the resurrection of Jesus from the dead (1 Pet 1:30; 3:21–22). Expressed differently, through his blood believers are ransomed from their previous futile ways (1 Pet 1:18–19), being dead to sin so they can live to righteousness (1 Pet 2:24). This new reality of being in the family of God and experiencing the privileges linked to this reality forms the core of how salvation is expressed. Further, 1 Peter pictures God as the *patria potestas* who redeems believers (former slaves) into his household through the blood of Jesus, with clear covenantal undertones (1 Pet 2:9–10; cf. Exod 19:6). The Father-king graciously transforms the saved into his nation (1 Pet 2:9–10). The salvific events of bringing people to God and making them alive in the spirit are graphically presented in a comparison between Noah and what happens at baptism (1 Pet 3:18–22; cf. Gen 6–8). There are also smaller images that are used, like sheep that are returned to the shepherd (1 Pet 5:1–5) or people who are healed through the wounds of Christ (1 Pet 2:24). Full salvific consummation will take place in the last time (1 Pet 1:5) with the eschatological coming of the Lord and consequent judgment (1 Pet 4:5; 2 Pet 3:13–18). Second Peter 1:4 describes believers as "participants of the divine nature."

In spite of the diversity in these different documents, they all emphasize the problem of sin that needs to be overcome through faith in Jesus. On this basis God will restore the relationship between him and these believers. He gives them a new identity, resulting in a redefinition of their social status. In the letters of John and Peter this resocialization is formulated in terms of the family of God, while Hebrews uses the image of the eschatological people of God.

Some Concluding Remarks. With the necessary acknowledgment of the different approaches to and expressions of salvation in the New Testament, a basic "master narrative" can be identified, although on a higher level of abstraction. Diversity is either explicitly or implicitly framed within this broader "master narrative."

The negative anthropological perspective of a stressed or even nonexistent relationship between humans and God presupposes and invites soteriological activity. This alienation or stressed relation with God becomes evident in the behavior of people. Salvation is aimed at restoring (or creating) this relationship, which will become evident in the lives of the people on both the spiritual and the physical levels. People are not able to restore this relationship on their own but need a gracious God to initiate the process of salvation. Motivated by love and grace, God does initiate this process. His plan is put into action through Jesus, who mediates God's salvation through his message and deeds. Through Jesus the relationship between believers and God is (re)established with eschatological and eternal results—believers will be with God forever. For the relationship to endure, certain ethical conditions must be met. Final consummation is still awaited, but believers are already experiencing the presence of this new era and should accordingly live in loyalty and obedience within this glorious salvific reality.

Key moments in this "master narrative" can be expressed in many different ways; for instance, the negative situation of people may be expressed in images of being dead, in darkness, in slavery, in the flesh or sin or of being judicially guilty, depending on the semantic domains a particular author uses to express his ideas. The same is the case with other key moments in the "master narrative," for instance, in describing how salvation was accomplished: a ransom price was paid, a person was born again, a person was reconciled or justified, sin was washed away.

There is merit, nonetheless, in taking seriously the conceptual reality that particular images introduce. The means of expressing an idea (the literary image itself) should be distinguished from the content of the expression (message). Obviously, images are not comprehensive but have a limited scope of expression and should not be overinterpreted. Each image contributes in its own way to the full soteriological landscape. The resulting soteriological mosaic should be carefully constructed because different authors describe the same landscape with different imagery and conceptual expressions.

[*See also* Anthropology; Atonement; Baptism; Christology; Conversion; Discipleship; Ecclesiology; Election; Eschatology; Expiation; Forgiveness; Freedom and Slavery; Gospel; Grace; Guilt and Innocence; Holy Spirit; Hope; Inheritance (Heir); Justice, Justification, and Righteousness; Reconciliation; Redemption; Repentance; *and* Sin.]

BIBLIOGRAPHY

Best, Ernest. *The Temptation and the Passion: The Markan Soteriology.* Society for New Testament Studies Monograph Series 2. Cambridge, U.K.: Cambridge University Press, 1965.

Breytenbach, J. Celliers. "Salvation of the Reconciled." In *Salvation in the New Testament: Perspectives on Soteriology*, edited by Jan G. van der Watt, pp. 271–286. Supplements to Novum Testamentum. Leiden, The Netherlands: Brill, 2005.

Burnett, Gary W. *Paul and the Salvation of the Individual.* Biblical Interpretation Series 57. Leiden, The Netherlands: Brill, 2011.

Conzelmann, Hans. *The Theology of St. Luke.* New York: Harper & Row, 1960.

de Villiers, Pieter G. R. "Safe in the Family of God: Soteriological Perspectives in 1 Thessalonians." In *Salvation in the New Testament: Perspectives on Soteriology*, edited by Jan G. van der Watt, pp. 305–330. Supplements to Novum Testamentum. Leiden, The Netherlands: Brill, 2005.

Doble, Peter. *The Paradox of Salvation: Luke's Theology of the Cross.* Society for New Testament Studies Monograph Series 87. Cambridge, U.K.: Cambridge University Press, 1996.

du Toit, Andrie B. "Forensic Metaphors in Romans and Their Soteriological Significance." In *Salvation in the New Testament: Perspectives on Soteriology*, edited by Jan G. van der Watt, pp. 213–246. Supplements to Novum Testamentum. Leiden, The Netherlands: Brill, 2005.

du Toit, David S. *Der abwesende Herr: Strategien im Markusevangelium zur Bewältigung der Abwesenheit des Auferstandenen.* Neukirchen, Germany: Neukirchener Verlag, 1996.

Fritzen, Wolfgang. *Von Gott verlassen? Das Markusevangelium als Kommunikationsangebot für bedrängte Christen.* Stuttgart: Kohlhammer, 2008.

Green, Joel B. *The Theology of the Gospel of Luke.* New Testament Theology. Cambridge, U.K.: Cambridge University Press, 1995.

Joubert, Stephan J. "*Charis* in Paul." In *Salvation in the New Testament: Perspectives on Soteriology*, edited by Jan G. van der Watt, pp. 187–211. Supplements to Novum Testamentum. Leiden, The Netherlands: Brill, 2005.

Köstenberger, Andreas J. *The Missions of Jesus and the Disciples According to the Fourth Gospel.* Grand Rapids, Mich.: Eerdmans, 1998.

Malherbe, Abraham J. "'Christ Jesus Came into the World to Save Sinners': Soteriology in the Pastoral Epistles." In *Salvation in the New Testament: Perspectives on Soteriology*, edited by Jan G. van der Watt, pp. 331–358. Supplements to Novum Testamentum. Leiden, The Netherlands: Brill, 2005.

Sellner, Hans Jörg. *Das Heil Gottes: Studien zur Soteriologie des lukanischen Doppelwerks.* Beihefte zur Zeitschrift für die neutestamentliche Wissenschaft und die Kunde der älteren Kirche 152. Berlin: De Gruyter, 2007.

Tolmie, D. François. "Salvation as Redemption: The Use of 'Redemption' Metaphors in Pauline Literature." In *Salvation in the New Testament: Perspectives on Soteriology*, edited by Jan G. van der Watt, pp. 247–269. Supplements to Novum Testamentum. Leiden, The Netherlands: Brill, 2005.

van Aarde, Andries G. "*Ihsous*, The Davidic Messiah, as Political Saviour in Matthew's History." In *Salvation in the New Testament: Perspectives on Soteriology*, edited by Jan G. van der Watt, pp. 7–31. Supplements to Novum Testamentum. Leiden, The Netherlands: Brill, 2005.

van der Watt, Jan G. *Family of the King: Dynamics of Metaphor in the Gospel According to John.* Leiden, The Netherlands: Brill, 2000.

van der Watt, Jan G., ed. *Salvation in the New Testament: Perspectives on Soteriology.* Supplements to Novum Testamentum. Leiden, The Netherlands: Brill, 2005.

van Zyl, Hermie C. "The Soteriology of Acts: Restoration to Life." In *Salvation in the New Testament: Perspectives on Soteriology*, edited by Jan G. van der Watt, pp. 133–160. Supplements to Novum Testamentum. Leiden, The Netherlands: Brill, 2005.

Waetjen, Herman C. *The Letter to the Romans: Salvation as Justice and the Deconstruction of Law.* New Testament Monographs. Sheffield, U.K.: Sheffield Phoenix, 2011.

Williams, Martin. *The Doctrine of Salvation in the First Letter of Peter.* Society for New Testament Studies Monograph Series 149. Cambridge, U.K.: Cambridge University Press, 2011.

Wolter, Michael. *Paulus: Ein Grundriss seiner Theologie.* Neukirchen, Germany: Neukirchener Verlag, 2011.

Jan G. Van der Watt

STORY AND MEMORY

This entry contains two subentries: Old Testament *and* New Testament.

Old Testament

In biblical studies, story or narrative is typically regarded as fiction (Byrskog, 2000), which complicates its relationship to history (Baer, 2000; Barstad, 2008, 2012), cultural memory (Davies, 2008), and cultural trauma (Alexander, 2004). In other circles, however, story or narrative goes beyond the fictional category. Elements of narrative theology take precedence, with faith and (grammatical-historical) scholarship navigating the message or lesson to be learned for current and future generations. Scholarship that fully accepts the category of story or narrative without questioning the status quo of fiction requires critical redress since some elements of fiction are based on real persons, events, or scenarios. In fact, in recent scholarship, fiction is said to be twice as true as fact, generating powerful cognitive and emotional simulation (Oatley, 1999). Ethnographic fiction (based on real people), for example, has been shown to heighten authorial presence, thus providing greater analytic possibilities (Gray, 2004). Conversely, scholarship that completely rejects the category of story or narrative as fiction requires close scrutiny of its scope and purpose. The best way of describing and understanding story or narrative in the Old Testament is through the context of scripture, that is, its ancient Near Eastern and Mediterranean environments or, more broadly, anthropology and sociology of religion.

The stories in the Old Testament are about a social group of people, ancient Israel/Judah, and their experiences in various cultural settings and historical periods. Those stories and narratives were preserved through oral tradition, eventually written down, forming a text, which in turn was redacted and further expanded to be culturally relevant and religiously inspirational for current and future generations. Those stories, read with a canonical consciousness, became authoritative and binding, scripture for the Jewish and Christian communities. Although critical scholars may see stories in the Old Testament as fiction, many in faith communities would say otherwise. This fundamental canonical precept should be remembered when referencing these ethnographic cultural stories with rich layers of rituals, myths, and symbols.

The definition of "culture" is complex. Using a social scientific perspective, which focuses on historical shifts that directly influence intellectual, spiritual, and aesthetic developments, Williams (1976) has noted that "culture" is one of the two or three most complicated words to define in the English language. Geertz's construction of culture as a system or a web of influence that is spun to express views on life has been an important cornerstone (Geertz, 1973). The German concept of *Kultur* adds value and moral progress to the definition. French scholars Maurice Halbwachs (1992) and Pierre Nora have placed memory and the location of memory on the intellectual map. Karl Mannheim, a Hungarian scholar who chose exile in Germany over converting to communism and later studied with Alfred Weber, the brother of Max Weber, has provided one of the most original constructs, "generation unit."

Although Connerton (1989) describes three types of individual memory (personal, cognitive, habit), Halbwachs demonstrated that memory stems from social belonging. Collective memory is framed through family, royal, and nonroyal settings (Smith, 2002) and passed down by community, by space, or from (a distant) land. Assmann's (1998) concept of mnemohistory has provided new insights on remembering significant past events that are formative for shaping cultural and social relevancy in the present. Mnemohistory carefully studies memory through the traditional storyline, cultural web of influence, intertex-

tuality, and diachronic and synchronic readings. With emphasis placed on the importance of the present's reception of the past, historical reconstruction is not dismissed. As part of cultural memory, mnemohistory has a formative and prominent presence in the social sciences, history, political science, philosophy, theology, and biblical studies. In this piece, ancient Israel/Judah's mnemohistory is presented through cultural memory and cultural trauma.

In literary circles, cultural memory focuses on cognitive framing and language or communicative action. Memory is not necessarily located in the mind of a literary character or actor but in the *discourse* (in the text or in the present) about the past. The overarching cultural memory of the southern kingdom of Judah is the discourse on the loss of the nation and monarchy (597 B.C.E.), the Temple and its religious institutions (586 B.C.E.), and especially its people, including the poor—the people of the land (597, 587, and 582 B.C.E.). The language of exile or forced migration is the dominant subject matter of cultural memory and source of trauma for ancient Israel/Judah. With the loss of people, especially children (Ps 137:8–9), an entire generation—dashed or smashed against the walls of Jerusalem—unresolved cultural trauma echoes across time. It is not so much traumatic effects but traumatic affects notes Sztompka (in Alexander et al., 2004). With significant segments of ancient Israel/Judah's cultural memory representing these losses and this pathos, the scribes who controlled the narrative selected additional social memories to build around this national story.

According to Alexander, drawing on the catastrophic 9/11 event as the backdrop to the theory on cultural trauma, there is a genuine struggle for collective meaning and understanding. Identifying the nature of the pain, the nature of the victim, and the responsibility that comes with the knowledge of collective disruption and social crisis is what he calls the "trauma process." Central to this process are the "carrier groups" who articulate the claim and speak out on behalf of the affected to a wider audience or public (Alexander et al., 2004). In the context of ancient Israel/Judah, the nature of the pain was physically caused by the Babylonians. But internally, community leaders and scribes placed the blame on the previous generations' iniquities. Both victim and the source of the pain, the carrier groups as the canonical authors or editors present their cultural memory as a record and guide for future generations. Should a similar traumatic event occur, turning to the scrolls for comfort and how to respond collectively is the first step in a genuine struggle to understand.

Cultural Memory. Cultural memory is an amalgamation of truth and fiction, historical details, and folklore motifs, all framed in authentic propaganda or ethnic nationalism (Hendel, 2001). Quoting the social construction of reality theorist Thomas Luckmann, Assmann notes that "Memory is the faculty that enables us to form an awareness of selfhood (identity), both on the personal and collective level" (Assmann, 2008, p. 109). Assmann adds that identity is established by "time." Time is measured in a triad of inner subjectivity time, social time, and historical/mythical-tradition/cultural time. These three sets are further equated with individual memory, communicative memory, and cultural memory. Identity formation is thus inner self, social self, and cultural identity. In sum, cultural memory begins with history, myth-tradition, and cultural time, which then leads to the epicenter, cultural memory, thus forging cultural identity. Cultural memory serves consciousness on both the social and communicative levels as a bridge to time and identity. On the social side, social time produces a social self, a person as a carrier of social roles, producing communicative memory (like the collective memory of the Exile, what I call "exilic" or "Diaspora generational consciousness").

Assmann (2008) and others credit the art historian Aby Warburg (Gombrich, 1986) with coining the term "social memory." For Warburg, images or, more technically, "iconic memory" and the study of the "afterlife" were cultural objectives, carriers of memory. This was "*mnemosyne*," the Greek term for memory, but also the mother of the nine Muses. However, the term "cultural memory" was never used by Warburg. Only in the last 20 years, in conjunction with "time, identity, and memory" and "personal, social, and cultural" has "cultural memory" been in circulation. Assmann (2011) focuses on the power of remembering and

forgetting that establishes structural amnesia. He undertakes a case study of four cultures: Greek, Israelite, Egyptian, and Hittite. Two cultures (Greek and Israelite) survive, and two are almost completely forgotten. Greece and Israel are remembered because of their respective canons. The telling and retelling of stories as memory figures, real or inventive, has the power to sustain a culture.

Jan Vansina (1985), a cultural anthropologist, has traced cultural memory through the medium of the oral traditions of an African society. His findings are not surprising. In the presentation of the past, which is framed in communicative action, the past recedes deeper and deeper into the background, becoming more vague and less lucid the farther back in time one goes. According to Vansina, this social construction of reality through oral tradition is limited to three generations. This is telling. Biblical scholars will recall the phrase down to "the third or fourth generation" (e.g., Gen 15:16; Exod 20:5; 34:7; Num 14:18; Deut 5:9). It is not arbitrary that the patriarchal narrative is framed in three generations: the God of Abraham, Isaac, and Jacob; even some of the letters in the New Testament (e.g., Ephesians) are dated to the third or fourth Christian generation. We often say and even hear the phrase "the God of Abraham, Isaac, and Jacob," but rarely is Joseph, progenitor of the fourth generation, added to this formulaic expression. Perhaps this is the difference between a truly oral society and a society that is in transition to the written text.

In *Exile as Forced Migrations* (Ahn, 2011), I concluded my study on the exilic period with the third-generation Judeo-Babylonians. The methodology reflects contemporary migration and generational studies that conclude with the third generation and internal biblical witnesses that suggest the exilic experience lasted three generations. By the time of the fourth generation, there is usually full upward socioeconomic and political ascension, as in the story of Joseph. The addition of the fourth generation Joseph novella (Gen 37–50) to the third generation's Jacob cycle (Gen 25–36) suggests that the fourth generation clearly wanted also to be remembered. In short, the biblical construct of the three or four generations may be read literally as three or four generations that produced the text or more precisely as three and a half generations—that is, with 20 years marking each generation and the "1.5" generation 10 years, the first, 1.5, second, and third generations constitute "70 years" (Jer 25:11–12; 29:10), a holistic generational marker indicating that there were in fact three and a half generations in Babylon before a group was motivated to return home. Of the three or four generations, it is the third generation that permanently defines where home is for the collective community—either in that habitual place of residence or somewhere else. For example, "Jacob" returns home (Gen 49:29–33), whereas Joseph marries Asnath, the daughter of an Egyptian priest (Gen 41:45), for upward social and political mobility and becomes a citizen of Egypt (Gen 50:22–26).

A salient feature of exilic or Diaspora generational consciousness—the complex and significant relationship of dislocation and identity—is preserving and passing down the unapologetic individual and collective human experiences of forced migrations for future generations. Like the remains of any material culture or layering a text, a previous generation's disposition or experience is always honored, even if there are variances. Diaspora study is truly global in nature, bridging scores of major and minor issues, which are often hidden or veiled in communities. Geopolitics, hybridity, nomadism, creolization, and symbols—including the interpreting of sacred texts—are all involved. There is much complexity since phenomenology is involved. From searching for a home in a state of homelessness to seeking out welcome and acceptance in new places of residence, the chief questions are, Will "we" be fully accepted? And one day, can "we" also become hosts?

Exilic or Diaspora generational consciousness is a product of cultural anthropology and cultural memory. This memory dominates the Old Testament, beginning in Genesis. Acknowledging and going beyond ancient Near Eastern parallel accounts, Genesis 1 and 2 may be reread as the creation account of one nation separated by space and time: the Judeo-Babylonians in Babylon (Gen 1) and the Judeans in the land (Gen 2).

In the poetic narrative that begins in Babylon after the three displacements in 597, 587, and 582 B.C.E., the upper and skilled classes of Judeans experienced derivative forced migrations, a static migration resulting from a cartographical redrawing of borders (after a war) in 597 B.C.E. when Jehoiachin relinquished his throne to save his people and nation (2 Kgs 24:12). The type of displacement that the first wave of forced migrants (the king, his royal family, the scribes, priests, prophets, skilled classes, and military personnel) experienced is best classified as development-induced displacement, which results in development-induced displaced persons. For the socioeconomic development of Babylon, the first wave of Judeans was displaced and resettled as human capital to rehabilitate war-torn cities from a previous generation of conflict between the Babylonians and Assyrians.

At the center of the Babylonian economy was the maintenance of its extensive primary, secondary, and tertiary irrigation canals along with infrastructure and building projects surrounding Nippur, Chebar Canal/River (Al Yahudu texts; Ezek 1:1; 3:15; 10:15, 20, 22; 4:3), and other areas. The groups of people that arrived 10 and 15 years later or possibly other waves of migrants not recorded in the Old Testament experienced purposive forced migration (587/582) as punishment for rebellion, revenge, political gain, or control (Zedekiah's rebellion and Gedaliah's murder; 2 Kgs 24:20; 25:25; Jer 41:2). The people of 587 and 582 are best described as internally displaced persons. Often identified as the underclass or out-group, powerless victims, internally displaced persons technically do not cross an international border, although they collectively relocate. In our case, from the periphery of the empire to the center, the 587 and 582 groups that resettled in Babylon are to be distinguished from the 582 group of Judeans led by Johanan, including Jeremiah, who voluntarily fled to Tahpanhes, Egypt (Jer 43). In response to forces of political or natural oppressions of tyranny, warfare, domestically or climate-related change, people who migrate voluntarily encounter responsive forced migration. It should be noted that responsive forced migration is a voluntary migration, in contrast to derivative forced migration and purposive forced migration, which are involuntary. This last group is best described as refugees since they crossed an international border and found refuge in Egypt.

	597 B.C.E.	*587 B.C.E.*	*582 B.C.E.*
Judeo-Babylonians	DFM	PFM	PFM
	DIDPs	IDPs	IDPs
Judeo-Egyptians (or			RFM
those who fled to			Refugees
the coastlands)			
Judeans (in the land)	DFM	DFM	DFM

DFM, derivative forced migration; PFM, purposive forced migration; DIDP, development-induced displaced person; IDP, internally displaced person; RFM, responsive forced migration.

The Babylonians used forced migration for political and economic control. From a Judeo-Babylonian perspective, however, forced migrations saved lives. In due course, the children and grandchildren of the 597 group would learn and master the languages, culture, customs, and traditions of their host country. They integrated fully into Babylonian life but maintained their own Judean culture, language, as well as a higher version of a transcendent, all-powerful God. But they never forgot the experience of their parents' "formlessness and void" (Gen 1:2), symbolic mythopoetic chaos and evil. The community transcended this initial experience, seeing the good with each succeeding generation as they indeed became fruitful and multiplied.

The *Sitz im Leben* ("setting in life") of Genesis 2 may be the Judeans who survived and remained in the land after the multiple displacements. They too experienced derivative forced migrations upon reallocation of borders or more simply an exile-less exile. In the land, in the aftermath of the destructions of 586 and 582, there would have been considerably fewer opportunities for upward socioeconomic advancement in comparison to the Judeo-Babylonians or even Judeo-Egyptians. It is difficult to assess fully if life was better, comparable, or worse than it was for the underclasses of 587 and 582 displaced to Babylon. With the conflagration of the king's house and all houses in Jerusalem, including the dismantling of the

walls of Jerusalem (Jer 39:8), resulting in the collapse of the economy (housing market), and even with a modicum of hope in Mizpah as a new center for economic activity, the situation in Judah could not have continued without any disruption, as depicted by Barstad (2012). With the majority of the upper and skilled classes removed from the land (597), what sociologists call a "brain [and skill] drain," and the removal of any genuine hope for a prosperous future by displacing intelligent youths and teens to Babylon (e.g., Daniel), there would have been considerable discontinuity in Judah (Ahn, 2012). Jeremiah 39:10 notes that the poor were given vineyards and fields to survive. In the social construction of reality for the poor Judeans in the land, if there was any true continuity, that continuity is preserved in the language of victimization, "punishment down to the third or fourth generation."

The social contexts of these two communities may be the settings of Genesis 1 and 2. Genesis 2's anthropomorphic projection of the LORD God may be drawn from the simple image of a poor farmer working the soil in the context of the sixth century B.C.E. Conversely, Genesis 1 has parallels with not only the Babylonian creation epic, which the scribes likely knew from their time in Babylon, but also, in due course, subsequent generations of upper-class and skilled Judeo-Babylonians who experienced a very good life in a new land with a new understanding, purpose, and even rest. Genesis 1 captures this social (re)construction of a rich, complex, ordered, and highly evolved social world. The two separated communities in Babylon and Judah were nevertheless united under transnationalism that extends beyond borders. Cultural memory of the Exile is additionally referenced in Genesis 3 and 4, the stories of Adam and Eve and of Cain and Abel—the first two generations.

In short, Adam and Eve are individually punished for their sins. Then, collectively, they are forced to migrate from the Garden of Eden (Gen 3:24). This can be read as the community being forced to leave the land of Judah, collectively as the first generation. In the next episode of the generational story, after killing his brother, Cain too is displaced and forced to leave the presence of an established community. He resettles in the east (Gen 4:16) and starts life anew, a possible mnemohistory of how a second-generation exilic community arrived in the east. There are two central messages in these two stories. First, infraction against the law (Gen 3) and humanity (Gen 4) leads to expulsion from one's habitual place of residence, resulting in exile or forced migration. The second message, which is more controversial, may be phrased as a question: Are a previous generation's sin and the current generation's sin inherited and literally passed down from the parents to children, extending from generation to generation, even to Noah and his children? The answer comes only later, from second- or third-generation exilic authors who reject the notion that sin can be passed down intergenerationally (Ezek 18:2; Jer 31:29–30). Perhaps this explains the genealogical or generational lists (Gen 4:17–26; 5:1–32; 10:1–32; 11:10–32) that demonstrate that even if there is wrongdoing in one generation, there is still an opportunity for blessing and progeny in the next.

The predominant cultural memory in Genesis 1–11 is exile or forced migration where sin is passed down generationally. From a Judean point of view, the sin and exile of previous generations should not be projected onto their community. Those exiled to Babylon or elsewhere deserved such retribution. As Judeans who were not exiled but instead remained in the land, they were different. However, the Judeo-Babylonian point of view is precisely the opposite. Because there is nothing left in the land and because the king and the majority of the elites were all now in Babylon, exile is more an opportunity for new life than a punishment for past sins. Interestingly, the first generation of Judeo-Babylonians appears to concur and even endorse this precept (Ps 137). Then, with the transitional generation, the view gradually changes: "For surely I know the plans I have for you, says the LORD, plans for your welfare and not for harm, to give you a future with hope" (Jer 29:11).

During the time of the second generation, a radical new position develops: forced migrations happened because they, the second (and subsequent)-generation Judeo-Babylonians, are precious and

loved by God (Isa 43). Children born in Babylon in the sixth century B.C.E., or in any contemporary immigrant context to first-generation parents for that matter, collectively have the same dream of succeeding and going beyond the starting point of their parents. The desire to succeed is driven in part by witnessing the struggles and sacrifices of the parents' generation. As a bridge to the third generation, the dual consciousness to take care of one's parents when they are old and to support the future generation fosters a unique drive in all second generations across cultures and time. Empirical research shows that second generations outperform all other generations (Ahn, 2011). Yet, in order to move forward, the central ideology that needs to be emended or rejected is the notion that they must bear their parents' sin. Such a view would directly impinge on their future. Fueled by positivism and hope, it would be this particular generation in Babylon that would truly understand and reform the authority of the king to the authority of scripture (597), transform religiosity from outward sacrifice to inward prayer (587), and form a new collective consciousness (Ahn, 2013).

The story of Noah's flood (Gen 6–10) may be reread as a narrative of the complete destruction of the southern kingdom of Judah. Engulfed and forced to migrate across the waters, Noah's family may symbolically represent the last legitimate Davidic dynasty, Jehoiachin and his family. However, even after land is reached, problems emerge. Reframed as a return migration narrative, upon return to Yehud, indeed, unresolved past and new problems reemerge. The primeval history concludes where it began, in Babel (Babylon) (Gen 11).

Genesis 11 is a carefully woven story about language and building in Shinar, a code word for Babylon. It draws the reader's attention to the vocabularies, syntax, and semantics of both Genesis 1 and 2, while centrally preserving a Judeo-Babylonian cultural memory of language confusion and physically rebuilding or reconstructing cities near Nippur (Pearce, 2006).

A new cultural memory of Diaspora generational consciousness begins in Genesis 12 with the stories of Abraham and Sarah; Isaac and Rebecca; Jacob, Leah (Zilpah), and Rachel (Bilhah); and Joseph (Aseneth) (Gen 12–50). From a cultural memory point of view, the entire book of Genesis is about exile—forced migrations (Gen 1–11) and return migrations (Gen 12–50) framed in generation units. Each generation responds to its own set of circumstances and experiences in various cultural settings, with encounters often repeating in current and ensuing generations (e.g., in sister wife stories; see Gen 12:10–20; 20:1–18; 26:1–13).

Exodus marks yet another new story, with a new leader, Moses, whose Sargon-like birth narrative makes him a greater-than-life figure. Redeemed from the "waters," he too would experience forced migration, until he is called to return to Egypt to deliver his people from slavery. His leadership is passed down to Joshua, a transitional figure who represents what anthropologists and sociologists call the forgotten 1.5 generation. Joshua is neither first nor second generation. Then, the second-generation leaders, the elders who are born in the wilderness, transition to the third generation, the judges, the generation that was ultimately replaced by the monarchy. Finally, the fourth generation, the kings, have their own generational history, which concludes with the Exile or forced migrations in 597, 587, and 582 B.C.E. (2 Kgs 24–25) completing the full cycle of exilic or Diaspora generational consciousness.

In the wilderness (Numbers), the first-generation Israelites wander and complain. The wilderness wandering tradition is remembered as a period of punishment, though not without hope. The same potential of not being able to enter the Promised Land rests on the second-generation Israelites. A key episode is sparked by the second-generation Gadites and Reubenites, who request land and permanent residence in the Transjordan. Moses interprets their request as a threat to the promise and rejects their initial proposal. With tension and conflict rising, the second-generation Gadites and Reubenites make a counterproposal: they will help all Israel claim land in the Cisjordan, and when each tribe has settled down, they will return home, to the other side of the Jordan, to their wives, children, cattle, and goods. Moses

agrees and blesses them (Num 32). This is one of the most important yet least understood chapters in the entire book of Numbers. This narrative is likely a retrospection, cultural memory from the period of the third- or fourth-generation Judeo-Babylonians in Babylon, questioning and rejecting the collective call to return to the land of Yehud (Isa 40–55). A compromise was reached, a provisional turn to Yehud so that they could in fact return home.

Cultural memory of exilic generational consciousness is particularly evident in the prophets (Isaiah, Ezekiel, Jeremiah). The sour grapes metaphor—"The parents have eaten sour grapes, and the children's teeth are set on edge" (Jer 31:29; Ezek 18:2)—stipulates that each generation is now responsible for its own action, thereby rejecting the first-generation notion that sin is passed down to the second generation, then the third, and so on. By analogy, as referenced above, the very notion of exile as forced migrations changed from sin and punishment to a purpose for good (Jer 29).

The ensuing generations in Babylon build on the 1.5 generation's diligent work ethos and prayer life. This 1.5 generation kept the separated communities together by preserving exchanges of letters and a key historical moment, including an unsuccessful bid to return after only a few years in Babylon (Ahn, 2011). The second generation would eventually see their lives as a new creation (Isa 43)—the best and worst of both Judean and Babylonian life. Born in Babylon to privileged parents of 597, this particular in-group would be the recipients of the stipulations and codes. They would be the ones who eventually crystallized monotheism. At some point, there was no longer any need to keep up with news taking place in Judah. The third generation will be reviewed more thoroughly below, but in passing we may note that even Ezekiel's spiritual temple is a reminder that Judeo-Babylonians/Persians need not return to Jerusalem to rebuild a physical temple. God's spiritual temple is found where the community resides with memory.

The wisdom tradition also echoes the memory of the Exile. The book of Job is read through the experience of Judah's forced migration. Job says he did not sin, which equates him to a second- or third-generation

Judeo-Babylonian perspective on their struggle to understand the calamity and existing hardship. God eventually sides with Job. Qoheleth, which at times is archaic and at times reads like a translated Aramaic text or, in certain chapters, like modern Hebrew, casts a long shadow from Solomon to the Persian or Hellenistic era. "*Habel*" (e.g., 1:2: "all is vanity [*habel*]") and "chasing after the wind" have socioeconomic ramifications and convey cultural memory of a failed and corrupt monarchy (Barber, 2008), the reason and cause for the displacement of the nation. Diaspora themes also occur in Tobit, 1 Esdras, Prayer of Azariah, Bel and the Dragon, Song of the Three Children, Susanna, Judith, and the *Letter of Aristeas*. They all pertain to the reality of everyday life, coping with hardships, challenges of society, and figuring out how to be live as minorities wanting to become a significant in-group in a changing world.

The Damascus Document (CD) opens with a reference to 390 years since Nebuchadnezzar, which is immediately followed by a marker of generational consciousness, "20 years" (cf. Num 1:20; 14:29; CD 1.5–6). The context behind this community's document may be voluntary displacement and resettlement to the coastland or Damascus (CD 8.6–10) as an alternative option to Egypt. If one group did in fact escape to the coastlands or Damascus, they may be a precursor to the Essenes; and this document may be an earlier form of the *Rule of the Community* (1QS). The Qumranites also voluntarily fled and lived in exile, in forced migration, as an ethnic enclave generating economic output, rituals, and copying and writing scripture and other texts. Lastly, in 1 and 2 Peter, the sojourners or foreigners are seen as a second- or third-generation or third- or fourth-generation community of believers. They too experience marginalization. The community is encouraged to live in the hope of their priesthood, waiting until the Lord's "return." Indeed, the dominant cultural memory in scripture is exile and return (exilic or Diaspora generational consciousness).

Marcus Hansen's law of third generation (more commonly known as what the son or daughter wishes to forget the grandson or granddaughter reclaims) coupled with Mary Douglas's definition of "home"

finds application in the third- and subsequent-generation Judeo-Babylonians (Ahn, 2011, pp. 223–255). Babylon or Persia became home. As Vansina pointed out, by the time of the third generation memory fades and the notion of homeland recedes until it is no longer pertinent in the present. The habitual place of residence had become home. But to justify home on the other side of the Jordan (Persia), like the Gadites and Reubenites (Num 32), the upper class (descendants of 597) agrees *to turn* to Yehud only provisionally, to fulfill the words of Isaiah. This was a "temporary return" over against the more "permanent return" migration for those who never made it in Babylon. The suffering community, the descendants of 587/582 labeled as "Jacob" in Isaiah 40–55 would finally experience "comfort" like their elite counterpart, "Israel."

Consistently in Isaiah, where both Jacob and Israel appear together, there are subtle but noticeable differences. For example, "Fear not, you *worm* Jacob, you *men* of Israel" (41:14, italics added); "he who *created* you, O Jacob, he who *formed* you, O Israel" (43:1); "*did not call* upon me, O Jacob; but you *have been weary* of me, O Israel" (43:22); "Therefore I profaned the princes of the sanctuary, and have given Jacob *to the curse* and Israel *to reproaches*" (43:28); "But hear, O Jacob *my servant*, Israel *my chosen!*" (44:1); "the Lord has *redeemed* Jacob and will be *glorified in* Israel" (44:23); "Jacob *my servant*, Israel *my chosen*" (45:4); "O house of Jacob, who are *called by the name of Israel*, and who came from the loins of Judah" (48:1); "And now the Lord says, who formed me from the womb to be his servant, *to bring Jacob back to him*, and that Israel *might be gathered to him*" (49:5); and "*raise up the tribes* of Jacob and to *restore the preserved* of Israel" (49:6).

In the book of Isaiah, all verbs attributed to Jacob are slightly inferior or subservient to those that predicate Israel. Jacob needs to be brought back to God; he is part of Israel, but Israel is never a part of Jacob. Jacob needs to be redeemed and transformed, whereas Israel is consistently the chosen. Jacob will then be glorified in Israel, and it is exclusively and only Jacob who will in essence leave Babylon with shouts of joy: "Go out from Babylon, flee from

Chaldea, declare this with a shout of joy, proclaim it, send it forth to the end of the earth; say, "The LORD has redeemed his servant Jacob!'" (Isa 48:20). The suffering underclass, the third- and fourth-generation descendants of 587 and 582, would finally have the opportunity for economic and social restoration.

Convincing the upper class "Israel" to finance the expensive return migration to the fringes of the Persian Empire involved much risk, with the possibility of little or no return on their involvement and investment. Fulfilling Isaiah's utopian vision of a new creation through a gradual return migration by imitating the system of forced migration for socioeconomic gain after several generations may have been the template behind the gradual return migrations. His vision would have been a new model to unite all the scattered communities in Babylon, Egypt, and the coastlands or Damascus with those in Yehud. However, the story of the return migrations is one of mismanagement and leadership failure. It would take decades, until the time of Ezra and Nehemiah when economic recovery would arrive through religious-class-ethnic segregation.

According to Vansina (1985), all such known forms of traditions and the past are rendered, actualized, or performed within a community through storytelling, songs, dances, rituals, and masks and by narrators, bards, mask carvers, and scribes. Such events produce cultural memory. According to Nora, most *lieux de mémoire* ("locations of memory") function to invent and serve nation-states. In 1984, Nora was particularly concerned with the rapid disappearance of French national memory in the face of European integration. His concern was perhaps similar to that of the Judeo-Babylonians or Judeo-Egyptians integrating into the larger Babylonian/Persian or Egyptian cultural setting. He writes, "[It] seemed to me to call for an inventory of the sites where it [the national memory] was selectively incarnated. Through human willpower and the work of centuries, these sites have become striking symbols: celebrations, emblems, monuments, and commemorations, but also speeches, archives, dictionaries, and museums" (cited in den Boer, 2008, p. 21). His observations may extend to the most terrible *lieux de mémoire* in the twentieth century (Verdun and

Auschwitz). Whether in an individual state or a collective European *loci memoriae*, the next generation needs teachers to help retrieve its cultural memory. The question is not only "why" did this horrific event in the past happen but also "how" do we construct life in the aftermath of its ruins. Somehow victims discover the courage to live, even though living is harder than dying; and by choosing to live and move forward, they become in turn a carrier group. Nevertheless, although the admonition lesson may be to "forget the former things and behold the new" (Isa 43:18–19), the memory of trauma says otherwise.

Cultural Trauma. According to Wulf Kansteiner and Harald Weilnbock (2008, p. 229), the humanities and the social sciences have failed to develop an interdisciplinary concept of trauma primarily because they have leaned too heavily on Hollywood's glamorized portrayal of traumatic events. Popularization of postmodern trauma discourse in the humanities is marred by a lack of critical self-reflection. The new meta-narrative is now cultural trauma. Instead of liberating literature and exposing ideological biases and blind spots, cultural trauma functions as a point of reentry, reestablishing a traditional textual exegesis built on philology. This is not bad for traditionalists or exegetes. But for theorists, theory should never regress. Attempting to be significant without forward progress is really no progress at all.

For Caruth (1996), traumatic experiences comprise two components, the mental and physical, which can never be fully reconciled. A terrible mental or physical ailment can successfully be overcome, but somehow and somewhere a new set of symptoms will arise tangentially to the original injury. Echoing Paul de Man, Caruth says that a failure to reconcile that terrible ailment is a rare opportunity, "a valuable moment of authenticity," because only at such moments of humanity's truest collapse, under the total weight of our cultural system, can scholarship truly grasp this system disintegration. The only time one can truly witness cultural trauma is when it is never resolved. Such an opportunity to witness and record is invaluable. Any viable solution to verbalize or resolve or integrate the traumatic experience will potentially destroy the value of trauma. Trauma is "revelation that teaches us about limits and possibilities of human culture" (1996, p. 238). Caruth adds, it is rather apocalyptic "grasped only in the very inaccessibility of its occurrence" (1996, p. 18).

The primary critique focuses on Caruth's deconstruction of benefiting from unresolved emotional, mental, and physical collapse. The moral conundrum is that there is neither acknowledgment of the pain nor resolution for the individual or community experiencing the trauma. From the perspective of victims, the exploitation of their trauma for purely scientific or intellectual reasons shows little or no sympathy or empathy for the deeper truths of their experiences (Kansteiner and Weilnbock, 2008). Think of exploiting the traumatic experience of Holocaust survivors in order to construct a grand theory on cultural trauma. To do so would be "sacrilegious" (Baer, 2000, p. 27). The sharp criticism and the dangers of the use of cultural trauma are warranted and noted. Weinberg (1999), a literary anthropologist, suggests that trauma is an indispensable conceptual tool and "subscribes to the construct of a poststructuralist code of ethics by promising to do anything he can to prove trauma's incurability." The takeaway from Weinberg is that the "contradictory logic of trauma, philosophy and history tries to make us forget about the traumatic flipside of all memory whereas in literature, there is a most honest and productive home for exploring trauma and memory" (Caruth, 2013). These are some of the sharp edges of this antianalytical and antiempirical philosophical background in cultural trauma studies. The advocates of the concept of cultural trauma acknowledge that it is extremely difficult to access and understand trauma but also that it must remain inaccessible to memory and cultural representation (Weinberg, 1999, p. 204). These advocates, agreeing with psychologists and therapists, note that traumatic experiences are captured and represented in "everyday narrative language."

A noticeable feature in the wilderness wandering tradition is the presentation of the experience of not having water and food and threats of safety through everyday language of complaint or murmur. For many in developed nations, not having access to water, food, or safety is difficult to understand fully. For a Third World nation or especially an ancient community physically on the move from Jerusalem to Babylon, the serious threat of not having access to water, food, and safety invites a lasting traumatic experience. The repeated psychological trauma that the community experienced daily, in search of water and food to sustain themselves on the long arduous journey to begin life as corvée, is disquieting.

Leading up to the story of Marah, a short interpolation sets the narrative in context: "They walked three days in the wilderness and found no water" (Exod 15:22c). A careful reading will reveal that the aforementioned generic wilderness is distinctive to verse 22b, where the wilderness of Shur is referenced. Introducing the story of Marah (Exod 15:22–26), the original core of the text begins, "When they came to Marah [*mārātâ*; with the directive *hā*; cf. Jer 4:17 and Hos 14:1], they could not drink its water because it was bitter [*mārâ*, or "rebellious"]. That is why it was called Marah," a cultural memory story that tells the experience of collective or cultural trauma, going three days into the wilderness and not finding water. Marah may be a direct reference to the Akkadian *Marrâtim* (Babylon), the land by the *nar Marrâtu*, "the bitter river" (near or actually the Persian Gulf—southern Babylon [BDB 601]). This geographical language of exilic generational consciousness is very much like the opening words in Psalm 137, "By the irrigation canals of Babylon, 'there' we wept and also lived when we remembered Zion" (author's translation). In Psalm 137 there is lament, but in the Marah story the people collectively "complain." Then, Moses cries out to God, and God intercedes and tells Moses to cast a tree or wood into the bitter or hard water to make it soft or potable. Understandably, the Israelites repeatedly complain, literally on every other page throughout the wilderness journey to and from Sinai or possibly from Jerusalem to Babylon or from Babylon to Jerusalem.

The language of murmur or complaint (*lwn*) unifies the wilderness narratives. In the pre-Sinai collection or exilic layer each complaint story has an identical form: (1) a genuine human need or threat, (2) collective complaint by the people to the leader, (3) Moses turns to God to echo the complaint, (4) God provides a solution to Moses, (5) Moses performs an act, and (6) the threat is resolved. In post-Sinai or possibly postexilic, early return migration stories, punishment is added to the narratives (e.g., fiery serpents, death for Korah's rebellion or cultural revolution). Many Exodus and Numbers commentators note how ungracious the Israelites are. They lack faith and trust in God even after immediately witnessing an act of salvation history (Exod 15:1–21). The Israelites are portrayed as complaining or nagging teenagers, an ungrateful community. This is precisely the point that Martin Noth made when he noted that the wilderness stories are late, a secondary insertion that has little or nothing to do with the Exodus event. What is central is the traumatic experience of not having water, and when they did find water, that water was either highly acidic or salt-ridden.

I have suggested that a segment of the community worked and lived by the irrigation canals of Babylon (Jacob) for several generations. Imagine a father, son, and grandson, all collectively working side by side on the irrigation canals—not just one or two families but an entire underclass of Judeo-Babylonians. The cultural trauma of looking for water has turned to a cultural trauma of having discovered bitter water. The powerful story of Marah and other wilderness wandering stories each have a social construction of reality. Sadly, Exodus and Numbers commentators have sided with God and not with the physical and psychological needs of the people. And because God intervened to address the problem of water, food, or threat, commentators have noted that the trauma was in fact healed. But the language of complaint suggests otherwise; it prevents the cultural trauma from being quickly discarded or even alleviated.

Conclusion. The story of the Old Testament is about exile and return (forced and return migrations), a human phenomenon that is still witnessed and discussed today. Cultural memory stories have the ability to tell and retell cultural trauma, subtly and overtly. In the collective memory of the community in Babylon, for the third- or fourth-generation Judeo–Babylonians/Persians, their very first concern upon hearing the words to return to Yehud is the traumatic experience of the previous generation's experience in the wilderness. The cultural trauma of

looking for water during the wilderness wandering period was not erased from memory. Isaiah, for example, exhorts those exiled in Babylon to prepare a direct way or highway in the wilderness. The wilderness will become a pool of water. The prophet promises (Isa 40:3; 41:18–19; 43:19–20) the wilderness (land of Judah) will become like Eden (Isa 51:3). These words address a past generation's trauma, a trauma that reverberated in the memory of the third and fourth generations.

Broadly speaking, the Old Testament may be viewed as an anthropological and sociological response to the sixth-century experience of exile or forced migrations. As a biblical anthropology, this cultural memory, as Assmann has noted, is instrumental in shaping not only Israel's cultural identity but also eventually its institutionalized rituals, myths, and writings and symbols.

[*See also* Exile and Dislocation; Exodus; Identity; Land; *and* Tradition.]

BIBLIOGRAPHY

Ahn, John. *Exile as Forced Migrations: A Sociological, Literary, and Theological Approach on the Displacement and Resettlement of the Southern Kingdom of Judah.* Beihefte zur Zeitschrift für die Alttestamentliche Wissenschaft 417. Berlin: De Gruyter, 2011.

Ahn, John. "Exile." In *Dictionary of the Old Testament: Prophets*, edited by Mark Boda and J. McConville, pp. 196–204. Downers Grove, Ill.: InterVarsity, 2012.

Ahn, John. "Diaspora." In *The Oxford Encyclopedia of Biblical Interpretation*, edited by Steve McKenzie. New York: Oxford University Press, 2013.

Ahn, John. "Ezekiel 15." In *The Prophets Speak on Forced Migrations*, edited by Mark Boda, Frank Ames, John Ahn, et al. Atlanta: Society of Biblical Literature, forthcoming.

Alexander, Jeffrey C., Ron Eyerman, Bernhard Giesen, et al. *Cultural Trauma and Collective Identity.* Oakland: University of California Press, 2004.

Assmann, Jan. *Moses the Egyptian: The Memory of Egypt in Western Monotheism.* Cambridge, Mass.: Harvard University Press, 1998.

Assmann, Jan. "Communicative and Cultural Memory." In *Cultural Memory Studies: An International and Interdisciplinary Handbook*, edited by Astrid Eril and Ansgar Nünning, pp. 109–118. Berlin: De Gruyter, 2008.

Assmann, Jan. *Cultural Memory and Early Civilization: Writing, Remembrance, and Political Imagination.* Cambridge, U.K.: Cambridge University Press, 2011.

Baer, Ulrich. *"Niemand zeugt für den Zeugen": Erinnerungskultur und historische Varantwortung nach de Shoah.* Frankfurt: Suhrkamp, 2000.

Barstad, H. *History and the Hebrew Bible: Studies in Ancient Israelite and Ancient Near Eastern Historiography.* Forschungen zum Alten Testament 61. Tübingen, Germany: Mohr Siebeck, 2008.

Barstad, H. "The City State of Jerusalem in the Neo-Babylonian Empire: Evidence from the Surrounding States." In *By the Irrigation Canals of Babylon: Approaches to the Study of the Exile*, edited by John Ahn and Jill Middlemas, pp. 34–48. Library of Hebrew Bible/Old Testament Studies 526. New York: T&T Clark, 2012.

Byrskog, Samuel. *Story as History—History as Story: The Gospel Tradition in the Context of Ancient Oral History.* Wissenschaftliche Untersuchungen zum Neuen Testament 123. Tübingen, Germany: Mohr Siebeck, 2000.

Caruth, Cathy. *Unclaimed Experience: Trauma, Narrative, and History.* Baltimore: Johns Hopkins University Press, 1996.

Caruth, Cathy. *Literature in the Ashes of History.* Baltimore: Johns Hopkins University Press, 2013.

Connerton, Paul. *How Societies Remember.* New York: Cambridge University Press, 1989.

Davies, Philip. *Memories of Ancient Israel: An Introduction to Biblical History—Ancient and Modern.* Louisville, Ky.: Westminster John Knox, 2008.

den Boer, Pim. "Loci memoriae—Lieux de mémoire." In *Cultural Memory Studies: An International and Interdisciplinary Handbook*, edited by Astrid Eril and Ansgar Nünning, pp. 19–25. Berlin: De Gruyter, 2008.

Geertz, Clifford. *The Interpretation of Culture.* New York: Basic Books, 1973.

Gombrich, Ernest H. *Aby Warburg: An Intellectual Biography.* Chicago: University of Chicago Press, 1986.

Gray, Ross. "No Longer a Man: Using Ethnographic Fiction to Represent Life History Research." *Auto/Biography* 12 (2004): 44–61.

Halbwachs, Maurice. *On Collective Memory.* Edited and translated by Lewis A. Coser. Chicago: University of Chicago Press, 1992.

Hendel, Ronald. "The Exodus in Biblical Memory." *Journal of Biblical Literature* 120 (2001): 601–622.

Kansteiner, Wulf, and Harald Weilnböck. "Against the Concept of Cultural Trauma." In *Cultural Memory Studies: An International and Interdisciplinary Handbook*, edited by Astrid Eril and Ansgar Nünning, pp. 229–241. Berlin: De Gruyter, 2008.

Oatley, K. "Why Fiction May Be Twice as True as Fact: Fiction as Cognitive and Emotional Simulation." *Review of General Psychology* 3, no. 2 (1999): 101–117.

Pearce, Laurie. "New Evidence for Judeans in Babylonia." In *Judah and the Judeans in the Persian Period*, edited by Oded Lipschits and Manfred Oeming, pp. 399–411. Winona Lake, Ind.: Eisenbrauns, 2006.

Smith, Mark. "Remembering God: Collective Memory." *Catholic Biblical Quarterly* 64 (2002): 631–651.

Vansina, Jan. *Oral Tradition as History.* Madison: University of Wisconsin Press, 1985.

Weinberg, Manfred. "Trauma—Geschichte, Gespenst, Literatur—und Gedächtnis." In *Trauma: Zwischen Psychoanalyse und kulturellem Deutungsmuster*, edited by Elizabeth Bronfen, Brigit Erdle, and Sigrid Weigel, pp. 173–206. Cologne: Böhlau, 1999.

Williams, Raymond. *Keywords: A Vocabulary of Culture and Society.* New York: Oxford University Press, 1976.

John Ahn

New Testament

A story or a narrative is always fictional, even one portraying historical events in the Bible or elsewhere (Backhaus and Häfner, 2009). As fiction, story refers to reality in different ways. Some stories are pure fantasy, employing figurative language and images that have no connection to everyday experience. Such stories are often labeled "fiction." Other stories seek to report faithfully what happened, reflecting memories of eyewitnesses, literary documents, and oral tradition that have been used as sources in redactional processes and literary composition. To some extent these compositions create their own narrative fiction by redacting and composing the material in a certain order. In addition, some stories imitate reality with more or less rhetorical finesse and, while not necessarily presenting what really happened in the past, appear quite realistic (Auerbach, 1946; Frei, 1974; Ricoeur, 1983–1985).

The Referentiality of Story and Memory. Certain stories reflect the memory of individuals and groups, creatively negotiating with contemporary experiences and values. They exhibit a "mnemo-historical" narrative consisting of a symbiosis of the past as it really happened and of the past as a social construction in the present (Kelber, 2005). Past and present realities interact, creating a complex web of historical reminiscences. The ensuing story depends on the referentiality of memory for its own potential of communicating what really happened. This mnemonic referentiality is of greatest significance for understanding the New Testament's four Gospels and their relationship to the reality they claim to depict and for conceptualizing the historical dimension of large narrative sections of the Hebrew Bible.

Mnemonic referentiality is thus closely linked to various kinds of story making. Scholars of memory note that memory tends to arrange the past in series of small or large episodes taking place at a certain time and place. To the extent that memory is autobiographical, enabling the individual to travel backward in time, episodic memory may be distinguished from a broader, wide-ranging notion of semantic memory (Tulving, 1972; Rubin, 1986). People link their personal experiences to historical events and regard past episodes of their lives as belonging to significant times and places. They tend to think of themselves as temporal beings; their unceasing creation of stories of the past in which they were involved plays an important part in how they build and maintain a personal sense of belonging (Hinchman and Hinchman, 1997).

To a significant degree autobiographical memory and episodic memory are social constructions. Halbwachs (1950, pp. 35–40; 1952) distinguished between autobiographical memory, historical memory (the past to which we have no "organic" relation), and collective memory (the past forming our realities); he pointed out that individuals remember as members of groups. Autobiographical memory is social: the mental act of remembering includes social aspects; the memory of individuals in social contexts is larger than the individual yet related to her or him.

As a social construct, memory is also narrative in character. Not only do individuals' contemporary circumstances play a significant part in mnemonic negotiations with the past; others' experiences and interpretation of the past also interact in the creation of new stories. Memory entails interpreted ex-

periences not made by the remembering self and includes so-called observe memories, which are channeled through cognitive processes and direct telling or streams of oral tradition. Thus, memory seeks plotted patterns into which each element of the past can be meaningfully integrated, becoming itself a narrative entity that creates and negotiates collective senses of identity. This broader category of narrative memory may be distinguished from episodic memory, which focuses on autobiographical recollections. Narrative memory manifests itself unevenly, based on how strongly people relate themselves to their own past and to others' experiences of things that happened. However, the literary composition and oral performance of a mnemo-historical story like a Hebrew Bible narrative or a New Testament Gospel are manifestations of how different mnemonic versions of the past, embodied in tradition, interacted with the memory of the author and the performer of the story, stimulating the creation of new narrative configurations. The referentiality of story and memory is, therefore, a complex web of social and narrative constructions that refer to past reality indirectly, through representation and interpretation.

The Narrativity of Recall. Modern theories of episodic and narrative memory emphasize the social forces that bear on the formation of memory and tend toward narrativization. Since memory nourishes and is nourished by story making, narrativity is a constitutive element of the ability to recall items of the past.

Accurate memory was considered a matter of honor in ancient Greece and Rome; it also carried a significant religious value in ancient Israel and in rabbinic circles. The ability to remember was often commented upon and was related to various narrative strategies. We find a subtle awareness of the way memory navigates narratively between past and present in the earliest systematic reflection on memory and recollection in ancient Greece. While neglected at first, Aristotle's (ca. 384–322 B.C.E.) treatise *de Memoria et Reminiscentia* came to strongly influence philosophical thinking on memory (Bloch, 2007; King, 2009). Reacting against Plato's idea (*Theatetus,*

Philebus) that memory applies equally to sensations of the past, the present, and the future, Aristotle differentiates memory (*mnēmē*), memory of the past, from recall (*anámnēsis*), the recollective process through which one find one's way by means of association and order among the contents of memory.

The notion of time is crucial in Aristotle's reflection on how the past interacts with the present. Time not only helps to distinguish memory and perceptions about the present from expectations for the future; it also defines the process of recollection itself. The first step in this process is to find a starting point. This can be done either by means of logical association—e.g., from milk to white, from white to mist, thence to moist, from which one remembers autumn (the "season of mists")—or by establishing a point in the middle of the events from which one can reach in any direction (Sorabji, 2004, pp. 31–34). Aristotle stresses that it is necessary to have a sense of time (*Mem. rem.* 452b.7). The recollective process thus arranges the past in accordance with implicit narrative structures between the images themselves, with a sense of temporal distance between past and present. Recollection occurs when the movement between images of the past corresponds with the cognition of time. It was this idea that Augustine (354–430 C.E.) developed in books 10 and 11 of his *Confessions*: especially in book 11 he insisted that time is an entity in memory because through memory a person is able to sense the duration of an event or the interval of time, then arrange the past according to sequential structures between perceptions of past events, based on a sense of temporal distance and interaction between the past and the present.

Aristotle was aware of the technique of mnemonic loci: a widespread method for accurate recall that illustrates the tendency in antiquity to remember the past according to narrative plots. Cicero said that Simonides of Ceos (ca. 556–468 B.C.E.) was able to identify Scopas and other people on whom the roof of a banqueting hall collapsed because he remembered the places where they had been sitting (*De or.* 2.86.352–353). According to one mnemonic technique, the speaker was encouraged to imagine mental places with sufficient concreteness and detail to visu-

ally associate the things or words to be recalled at a certain moment. The most common mnemonic locus was a house with several rooms and paintings, which evoke memory and trigger recollection. Based on the insight that memory tends to create mental sites with episodic features, this technique reflects an awareness that memory seeks to organize the past according to narrative patterns.

The example of mnemonic loci indicates how closely narrative memory is related to visual memory: the use of mental images resembling real objects in mnemonic negotiations. People in antiquity knew that narrative memory functions recollectively through visualization. A good illustration is Lucian's *Wisdom of Nigrinus* (second century C.E.), wherein Lucian recounts a visit he paid to the Platonic philosopher Nigrinus in Rome and the effect his discourse had upon him. Lucian describes how he calls to mind Nigrinus's words, daily repeating them two or three times. Lucian keeps the philosopher in view like a beacon's fire; he imagines Nigrinus seated beside himself in whatever he is doing (*Nigr.* 6–7). Nigrinus's oral delivery had affected him so deeply that even in times of pressure he remembered the philosopher's face and the sound of his voice. Lucian's attempt to remember the words of Nigrinus was part of a mnemonic process of visualizing the past event of having seen and heard him.

In Christian literature we find a similar visual process in Eusebius's quotation of how Irenaeus (ca. 130–202 C.E.), in a letter to Florinus, relates that he carries in his memory Jesus tradition from Polycarp. As a young boy Irenaeus learned this tradition by meticulously observing Polycarp: the place where he taught, how he came in and out, his way of life, what he looked like, and so forth. In this way Irenaeus made notes in his heart (upomnematizomenos…en tē eme kardia) of the things he heard (*Hist. eccl.* 5.20.5–7). He remembered them by mentally visualizing the performer in certain situational settings.

Mnemonic Negotiation and Story Making in the Jesus Tradition. Research suggests that the Hebrew Bible was formed not only through copying of texts but also, even primarily, through repeated use of information transmitted by memory (Carr, 2005, 2011).

Tradition and text passed from one generation to the next by performance and memory; scribal revisions visible in the texts of the Hebrew Bible are traces of memory variants occurring in the course of mnemonic transmission. According to this view, the Hebrew Bible came down to us through the sorts of transmission processes characteristic of oral–written literature of long duration. Just as the prophetic writings testify to prophetic followers adapting the remembered tradition from the prophetic master to various situations (e.g., Isa 8:16) and integrating it into what came to constitute short biographical narratives, elsewhere tradition is also a manifestation of mnemonic negotiation adaptable to various circumstances and forms of narrativity. Both modern theories of memory and ancient descriptions of memory and recall point to the social and narrative character of many tradition-based constructions of the past.

These insights open up the study of mnemonic negotiations embodied in the Jesus tradition (Kirk, 2009), but we must beware of one-sided emphases. Oral tradition is essentially a mnemonic entity; work on the Jesus tradition pays attention to the social and collective memory of the early Christ-believers and to the strong influence of their present conceptions upon their constructions of the past (Kirk and Thatcher, 2010). Building on Halbwachs's presentist approach to memory, many scholars argue that the social environment of memory censored the vision of the past embodied in the oral Jesus tradition in a way that made it conform entirely to the values and narrative plot structures of the remembering individual and group. While acknowledging an important aspect in the mnemonic power of the social environment, this idea is at odds with the historiographical criterion, established in a long line of historical Jesus research, which suggests that tradition-based information about Jesus has a claim to authenticity if it is dissimilar from and embarrassing to early Christian tendencies. A more balanced perspective is required, one that carefully looks at the early Christian discipline of creating a narrative symbiosis from both the available mnemonic tradition and particular social forces, each simultaneously interacting with the other.

Rather than assuming that memory fostered only fluctuating occurrences of mnemonic negotiations and story making among the early Christ-believers, there is reason to believe that initial impressions of the words and deeds of Jesus were gradually formed according to available narrative patterns that were familiar to people with elementary education, then elaborated and narratively expanded into more extensive gospel stories (Byrskog, 2010). To be sure, comparison with illiterate singers and Homeric poets suggests that random performances based on brief, memorized formulae, fitted into new narrative figurations, could take place when early Christ-believers gathered to recall and celebrate the memories of Jesus (Lord, 1960; Foley, 1985). But performances could also be more systemized, relying on the skilled use of manuscripts or oral tradition by trained lectors.

The *Progymnasmata*, rhetorical exercises in the elementary education of the Greek schools, mentions two narrative categories requiring some deliberate structuring: *chreia* and *diēgēma*. Both of these forms are narrative in character. Theon of Alexandria (first century C.E.) defined the *chreia* as "a concise statement or action which is well-aimed, attributed to a specified character or something analogous to a character" (Spengel, 1854, p. 96, lines 19–21). The attribution is what differentiates the *chreia* from the maxim and provides it with a small narrative core. Even in a short *chreia* there was often a participial clause that accompanied the attribution and described the author. An exercise requiring students to expand the *chreia* for the sake of producing a persuasive argument—an elaboration (*ergasia* thus, Hermogenes of Tarsus, second century C.E.)—added descriptive details about the author's credentials and circumstances or enlarged the dialogue into a little story with dramatic traits of its own. Alternatively, a longer story could be abbreviated into a pointed *chreia*. Through its attribution to a specific character, the *chreia* had an implicit narrativity that could be developed and again condensed in various rhetorical contexts.

People in late Greek and Roman antiquity distinguished the *chreia* from the *diēgēma*, which Theon defines as "an explanatory account of matters which have occurred or as if they occurred" (Spengel, 1854, p. 78, lines 16–17). The *diēgēma* explained something by reference to a more extended narrative presentation consisting of six elements: the person(s), the action, the place, the time, the manner, and the cause of the things narrated. A narrative lacking any of these was considered deficient. To each of these elements were added a number of properties. Thus, the narrative must also be clear, credible, and, if possible, concise.

Of these two narrative categories, the *chreia* is most pertinent to the New Testament. While the *diēgēma* is not to be confused with literary narratives such as the Gospels but seen in relation to the *narratio* of rhetorical speeches, the *chreia* was a smaller unit, suited as a building block in various compositions and performances. The two categories had no immediate generic relationship, and the *diēgēma* falls into the background as a formal category for conceptualizing the Gospels' formation as historicized *bioi* (Byrskog, 2006).

The closest literary relative of the *chreia* was the *apomnēmoneuma,* a broad literary genre applied to a number of writings. There was a general awareness that the *apomnēmoneuma* was different from, yet similar to, the *chreia.* Like the *chreia*, it is an action or saying that is useful for living; however, according to Theon, it is also distinguished from the *chreia* by being "sometimes expanded" and "remembered by itself" (Spengel, 1854, p. 97, lines 3–7). The second point probably indicates that, unlike the *chreia*, the *apomnēmoneuma* was complete with the identity of the character to which it is attributed. The difference was mostly a matter of length. *Chreiai* that were expanded into longer stories were thought to be memorable and therefore sometimes labeled *apomnēmoneumata.*

In addition to their narrative form, a shared feature of the *chreia* and the *apomnēmoneuma* was that both had to do with memory: they provided formal links between mnemonic negotiation and story making. The term *apomnēmoneuma* communicated the idea that the writing in question rested or sought to rest on personal reminiscence of the things themselves or on the oral tradition about them. The *chreia* could be seen as an *apomnēmoneuma*

precisely because it was easy to remember. The third-century C.E. fragment Oxyrhynchus Papyrus 85 articulates this idea when it responds to the question why the *chreia* is an *apomnēmoneuma* by stating that "it is kept in mind" (*apomnēmoneutai*).

In his introduction to the *Progymnasmata*, Theon placed the *chreia* among the first of his exercises because it was easy to remember and therefore suitable to provide the essential skills for the other exercises. The mnemonic character of the *chreia* comes to the surface especially in the exercise requiring students to recite it from memory. For Theon this is the first of eight gradually more difficult exercises with the *chreia*. Recitation is obvious, he says, "because we try to the best of our ability to report clearly the assigned *chreia* in the same words or in others as well" (Spengel, 1854, p. 101, lines 7–9). Recitation of the *chreia* in the classroom probably adhered closely to the words of the teacher who provided it, but recitation with other words was also permissible. The emphasis fell on clarity.

The *chreia* thus links memory and story making. It constitutes a form that could be used to gradually shape the remembered impact of Jesus and the ensuing mnemonic negotiation among his followers into smaller or larger narrative units. Papias (early second century C.E.) was convinced that the Gospel of Mark consisted of *chreiai* from Peter that the author wrote down from memory (Eusebius, *Hist. eccl.* 3.39.15). Justin Martyr (ca. 100–165 C.E.) called the Gospels *apomnēmoneumata*, believing that the Gospel of Mark comprised the reminiscences of Peter (*Dial.* 106.3). Research has shown that the earliest Gospel in fact contains stylized *chreiai* and therefore betrays traces of the way the Jesus tradition was shaped and transmitted. What Mark remembered and tried to write down, according to Papias, were well-aimed sayings or actions attributed to a specific character. Considering the rhetorical quality and elaborative potential of the *chreia*, it was natural to expand the collection of such memorable anecdotes into stories of a more literary and hermeneutically profound kind.

Memory as Part of the Story. The Gospel of Mark testifies to how memory and story were linked in the forms used in tradition and composition. Adopting a technique as old as Deuteronomy (e.g., 5:15; 8:12; 15:15), Luke–Acts and the Johannine literature indicate this linkage by giving prominence to memory in the stories themselves. The prologue of Luke–Acts, with its emphasis on what had been transmitted from eyewitnesses and ministers of the word (Luke 1:2), accords with the peculiar accent on memory and witnessing in the ensuing narrative. The liturgical and Christological dimension of memory indicated in the command to celebrate the Lord's supper in memory of Jesus (Luke 22:19; cf. 1 Cor 11:24–25) is related to the remembrance of Jesus's words elsewhere in Luke–Acts. At a climactic point in Luke (24:6–8), the women are to remember, and do remember, that Jesus, while still in Galilee, said that the Son of Man must be handed over to the sinners, crucified, and on the third day rise again. Later, Peter tells how he remembered the word of the Lord (Acts 11:16). Likewise, in his speech to the Ephesian elders, Paul urges remembrance of the words of the Lord Jesus (Acts 20:35).

The motif of witnessing broadens the mnemonic focus to include more than the Lord's sayings. The apostles are witnesses of the resurrection, but this event is not seen in isolation from Jesus's entire ministry. The decisive criterion for electing a new apostle is that this person must have accompanied the disciples during all the time that Jesus went in and out among them, beginning from the baptism to the day of his ascension (Acts 1:21–22). Accordingly, when Peter testifies about Jesus, he rehearses Jesus's entire ministry and summarizes the apostolic testimony in broad terms: "We are witnesses to all that he did both in Judea and in Jerusalem" (10:39). The words that are to be remembered and the resurrection to which they should bear testimony are integral to the total impact of Jesus's appearance in word and deed. Memory manifests itself as a witness to Jesus's earthly ministry from the beginning. It does not merely quote his sayings and report about his deeds; memory reconfigures his life.

We find a similar mnemonic trajectory in John. Early in that Gospel the author adds a reference to what the disciples remembered after Jesus was raised from the dead (2:22). This seemingly unnecessary excursion into the extradiegetic future points to the mnemonic link between history and faith. A

similar thing appears later in the story, when the author tells the audience that after Jesus was glorified the disciples remembered (12:16). Memory is used as a means of retrospectively realizing what had essentially happened.

The Fourth Evangelist validates this epistemologically mnemonic activity in two ways. First, he has Jesus point out that he says things in order that the disciples shall remember that he told them so when the hour comes (16:4a; cf. 15:20). Just as he says things to the disciples to prevent their stumbling (16:1), so he also says things to them in order that they should remember them. Intersected with this mnemonic feature is, second, the reminding and didactic function of the Paraclete. Jesus forecasts that the Holy Spirit will teach the disciples everything and that this teaching, in effect, means that the Spirit will remind them of everything that he had said to them (14:26). The disciples' future mnemonic activity is a spiritual activity stimulated by the Paraclete's teaching. Such memory carries a strong theological nuance, anchoring what Jesus says in a divinely, spiritually sanctioned process of traditioning and reconfiguration.

This "mnemonic theology" concerns more than Jesus's sayings. As shown by the intricate relationship between remembering and testifying, it includes Jesus's activity from the beginning. The Spirit reminds the disciples of what Jesus had said (14:26); it also testifies on Jesus's behalf so that the disciples, too, will testify (15:26–27) because they have been with Jesus from the beginning.

This interplay between memory and testimony among the disciples corroborates John's understanding of the gospel. Not only do characters within the story give testimony; the author or someone close to him regards the story as continuous with these testimonies. Jesus tells Peter that the beloved disciple will remain until he comes (21:20–24); this disciple is the one who is testifying to "these things" and has written them. The beloved disciple had been with Jesus during all the decisive events so that the things to which he testifies and the things he has written become one and the same. The author and others ("we," 21:24) regarded the finished story as a reflection of the disciples' inspired reminiscences and testimonies. They shaped the story to convey the idea that memory provided the spiritual path from the Jesus of history to the finished gospel about his life, death, and glorification. This memory was textualized and momentarily frozen when the gospel was finally redacted, not as a nonnegotiable and unchangeable written record but as an infusion of the mnemonic history into the written story itself.

The authors of Luke–Acts and the Fourth Gospel thus relate mnemonic activity to the witnessing about Jesus's earthly ministry from its beginning to its end, including central parts of his *bios* into this witnessing activity. Memory has become a theological and hermeneutical category, forming a "mnemonic trajectory" that unites the early Christians' sense of history with their present time in narrativizing processes of interpretation and reconfiguring of the life, death, and resurrection of Jesus (Byrskog, 2012).

Story as Memory—Memory as Story. Biblical scholars have often looked at memory in terms of memorization of isolated items, especially of Jesus sayings, producing a strange dichotomy between sayings material and narrative material. But, as we have seen, memory functions in processes of negotiation between the past and the present, where the narrative representation of the past plays a crucial role. This "narratization" of memory tells both a story about the past and a story about the past's relation to the present. Whether one speaks of ancient Israel or the early church, memory is constitutive of the construction of narrative identity.

It comes as no surprise, therefore, that narrative entities, which normally relate events to one another according to a sense of time and causality, are part of the mnemonic trajectory of the early Christians. The appreciation of memory—seen in Papias's view of the Markan story, Justin's labeling of the Gospels as memoirs, and the mnemonic signals encoded in the narratives of Luke–Acts and John—indicates a sensitivity to the remembering process as a narrative form of mnemonic negotiation. The production of briefer or longer narratives in ancient Israel and among early Christ-believers was not seen as an activity separated from memory; rather, those narratives were considered a dynamic result of recurrent processes of mnemonic activity.

Finally, several short narratives in the Hebrew Bible and, in particular, the gospels' stories betray the same kind of referentiality as does memory. Just as memory refers to the past through mental representation and narrative interpretation, so also the Gospels tell about Jesus by employing images and narrative fiction as means to communicate in the present what happened in the past. Modern stories about the past are further removed from the currencies of memory and tradition than their ancient counterparts, betraying the effect of a Western print mentality that culminated before the occurrence of computer-based forms of communication. Yet there is enough similarity between ancient and modern correlations of memory and story to indicate that the creation of the Gospels' narratives did not constitute a break with the mnemonic hermeneutics of pregospel tradition. The Gospels' literary character flowed out of earlier forms of individual and collective mnemonic negotiations, manifested in tradition and reflecting an ongoing search for Christian identity. Since these negotiations—and to some extent the brief biographical sections in the prophetic literature—reconfigured the sayings and events of a person who was deeply venerated, whose life and death were of crucial significance to the traditionists, memory interacted with story from the moment that eyewitnesses and others framed history into oral anecdotes and narratives of what Jesus said and did and of what happened to him (Byrskog, 2000).

[*See also* Deuteronomy; John and the Johannine Epistles; Judaism; Luke–Acts; Mark; Prophets and Prophecy; *and* Tradition.]

BIBLIOGRAPHY

Auerbach, Erich. *Mimesis: Dargestellte Wirklichkeit in der abendländischen Literatur.* Bern, Switzerland: A. Francke Verlag, 1946.

Backhaus, Knut, and Gerd Häfner, eds. *Historiographie und fiktionales Erzählen: Zur Konstruktivität in Geschichtstheorie und Exegese.* 2d ed. Biblisch-Theologische Studien 86. Göttingen, Germany: Vandenhoeck & Ruprecht, 2009.

Bloch, David. *Aristotle on Memory and Recollection: Text, Translation, Interpretation, and Reception in Western Scholasticism.* Philosophia antiqua 110. Leiden, The Netherlands: Brill, 2007.

Byrskog, Samuel. *Story as History—History as Story: The Gospel Tradition in the Context of Ancient Oral History.* Wissenschaftliche Untersuchungen zum Neuen Testament 123. Tübingen, Germany: Mohr Siebeck, 2000.

Byrskog, Samuel. "Performing the Past: Gospel Genre and Identity Formation in the Context of Ancient History Writing." In *History and Exegesis: New Testament Essays in Honor of Dr. E. Earle Ellis for His Eightieth Birthday,* edited by Sang-Won Son, pp. 28–44. New York: T&T Clark, 2006.

Byrskog, Samuel. "The Transmission of the Jesus Tradition: Old and New Insights." *Early Christianity* 3 (2010): 1–28.

Byrskog, Samuel. "From Memory to Memoirs: Tracing the Background of a Literary Genre." In *The Making of New Testament Christianity: Conflicts, Contacts, and Constructions. Essays in Honor of Bengt Holmberg,* edited by Magnus Zetterholm and Samuel Byrskog, pp. 1–21. Coniectanea biblica New Testament Series 47. Winona Lake, Ind.: Eisenbrauns, 2012.

Carr, David M. *Writing on the Tablet of the Heart: Origins of Scripture and Literature.* Oxford: Oxford University Press, 2005.

Carr, David M. *The Formation of the Hebrew Bible: A New Reconstruction.* Oxford: Oxford University Press, 2011.

Foley, John Miles. *Oral-Formulaic Theory and Research: An Introduction and Annotated Bibliography.* Garland Folklore Bibliographies 6. New York: Garland, 1985.

Frei, Hans W. *The Eclipse of Biblical Narrative: A Study in Eighteenth and Nineteenth Century Hermeneutics.* New Haven, Conn.: Yale University Press, 1974.

Halbwachs, Maurice. *La mémoire collective.* Paris: Presses Universitaires de France, 1950. Published posthumously by Jeanne Alexandre (born Halbwachs).

Halbwachs, Maurice. *Les cadres sociaux de la mémoire.* Paris: Presses Universitaires de France, 1952. First published 1925.

Hinchman, Lewis P., and Sandra K. Hinchman, eds. *Memory, Identity, Community: The Idea of Narrative in the Human Sciences.* Albany: State University of New York Press, 1997.

Kelber, Werner H. "The Works of Memory: Christian Origins and MnemoHistory—A Response." In *Memory, Tradition, and Text: Uses of the Past in Early Christianity,* edited by Alan Kirk and Tom Thatcher, pp. 221–248. Society of Biblical Literature Semeia Studies 52. Atlanta: Society of Biblical Literature, 2005.

King, R. A. H. *Aristotle and Plotinus on Memory.* Quellen und Studien zur Philosophie 94. Berlin: De Gruyter, 2009.

Kirk, Alan. "Memory." In *Jesus in Memory: Traditions in Oral and Scribal Perspectives,* edited by Werner H. Kelber and Samuel Byrskog, pp. 155–172. Waco, Tex.: Baylor University Press, 2009.

Kirk, Alan, and Tom Thatcher. "Jesus Tradition as Social Memory." In *Memory, Tradition, and Text: Uses of the Past in Early Christianity,* edited by Alan Kirk and Tom Thatcher, pp. 25–42. Society of Biblical Literature Semeia Studies 52. Atlanta: Society of Biblical Literature, 2010.

Lord, Albert B. *The Singer of Tales.* Cambridge, Mass.: Harvard University Press, 1960.

Rubin, David C., ed. *Autobiographical Memory.* Cambridge, U.K.: Cambridge University Press, 1986.

Sorabji, Richard. *Aristotle on Memory.* 2d ed. London: Duckworth, 2004.

Spengel, L. *Rhetores Graeci.* Vol. 2. Leipzig: Teubner, 1854.

Tulving, E. "Episodic and Semantic Memory." In *Organization of Memory,* edited by Endel Tulving and Wayne Donaldson, pp. 381–403. New York: Academic Press, 1972.

Samuel Byrskog

Tabernacles, Temples, and Synagogues

In the worldview of ancient Near Eastern cultures, the temple, whether fixed or moveable, served as the earthly residence of the divinity or divinities worshipped by the attendant community. It functioned for the community as an *axis mundi*, a place of intersection and interaction between heaven and earth. For this reason, temples were often built on mountaintops, where earth and sky met, though they could be constructed at any location where a human–divine encounter was believed to have occurred.

Although built by human hands, temples were considered the property of the resident divinity and assigned a higher status than estates that remained in human possession. Movement from the profane realm of common humanity to the sacred domain of the divine often required purity rituals and sacrificial offerings. Human conduct within the temple precincts was highly regulated, to prevent offending the deity. Special castes of human attendants enforced temple laws, overseeing prescribed rituals; violators typically faced severe punishment.

The benefits emanating from these sacred structures were perceived as paramount. Within the temple precincts, all persons, items, and lawful proceedings were considered protected by the deity. This belief promoted a sense of stability and security within the community. In turn, the temple precincts became a venue where official deliberations took place, public and private monies were secured, and community records were kept. The temple often functioned as a place of refuge for those fleeing creditors or other litigants and even as a center of commerce, especially for sacrificial goods associated with the temple.

Though important, such public benefits were ancillary to the temple's principal function: to serve as a place where both the individual worshipper and the reverent community could receive the deity's blessings. In this human–divine interaction, the community or its individual members offered worship through a combination of prayers and sacrificial rituals in the hopes of receiving divine favor, particularly in the granting of various petitions for protection from enemies, prayers for a bountiful harvest, and entreaties for forgiveness of sins. At the temple, heavenly powers were invoked to effect changes within the earthly realm that were deemed beyond human ability to enact.

In addition to a principal temple, deities of the ancient Near East were commonly worshipped in secondary estates, either along the periphery of the immediate community or near the center of distant colonies. These shrines functioned similarly to the central sanctuary, though usually on a smaller, more limited scale. They provided more immediate access to the deity for those not dwelling near the main temple. In addition, they expanded spatially the deity's power. The main sanctuary thus served as the central pillar supporting the sacred canopy over the community; distant shrines extended that canopy outward.

While the foregoing traits were common to all temples of the ancient Near East, those of the Israelites were distinguished by adherence to monotheism and prohibition against idolatry. Most ancient Near Eastern cultures erected temples to individual gods from a larger pantheon, each shrine replete with graven images of the resident deity. Israelite sanctuaries, by contrast, were dedicated to the one God of Jewish monotheism, who was never directly depicted. Over time, and not without controversy, Jewish monotheism became equated with worship of the one God at a single, central temple located in Jerusalem. By the Greco-Roman period, most Jews believed that only there could sacrificial rituals be lawfully conducted.

Proto-Temples in the Patriarchal Narratives. In the Old Testament's narrative world, temples initially play a minor role because of the nomadic origins of the patriarchs and their clans. The Genesis accounts refer mostly to temporary altars (*mizbēaḥ*) or pillars (*maṣṣēbāh*) such as those constructed by Noah (Gen 8:20), Abram/Abraham (12:7–8; 13:4, 18; 22:9), Isaac (26:25), and Jacob (28:18–22; 31:45–51; 33:20; 35:1–20). These structures were built upon places where the patriarchs had experienced an encounter with God and had rendered sacrifices as an act of worship.

Despite their infrequent appearance in the early biblical narrative, these ad hoc altars or pillars embodied one of the defining elements of a temple: they formed a nexus connecting the earthly and heavenly realms, as illustrated in Jacob's dream of a ladder between heaven and earth upon which the angels of God ascended and descended (Gen 28:12). Because of their association with patriarchal encounters of the divine, several of these sites—including those at Jerusalem (equated with Mt. Moriah, Gen 22:2, 9; 2 Chr 3:1; cf. Josephus, *Ant.* 1.226) and Bethel (Gen 28:19; Judg 20:26; 1 Kgs 12:29—13:5)—would later become major cultic centers.

Exodus and the Appearance of the Tabernacle. While altars and pillars play a limited but important role in the patriarchal accounts, the notion of a more permanent sacred sanctuary makes a sudden and prominent appearance in the Exodus narratives. When first appearing to Moses at the base of Mt. Horeb (Sinai), God orders him to lead the Israelites out of bondage in Egypt to that same mountain to worship him (Exod 3:1–12). After this has been accomplished, God again appears to Moses on Mt. Sinai, commanding him to construct a sanctuary so that God might dwell among the people after their departure from the holy mountain (25:8). Specifically, Moses is instructed to build an ark to contain the covenant tablets received on the mountain (25:10–22), as well as a golden incense altar and table for bread offerings (25:23–30; 30:1–6) and a lampstand containing seven lamps (25:31–37). These are to be placed inside a tabernacle (*miškān*)—also known as a "tent of meeting" (*'ōhel mô'ēd*, e.g., 227:21)—fashioned from various fabrics and animal skins, then draped upon detachable frames (chs. 26–27). Subsequently, the Israelites constructed these items from their donations (chs. 35–36). The tabernacle and its furnishings were erected and consecrated at a ceremony featuring burnt offerings on an altar in front of the shrine's entrance, all enclosed by a surrounding screen (40:1–33). During this consecration, God's glory (*kābôd*) settled upon the tabernacle in the form of a cloud (40:34). Henceforth, the tabernacle would serve as a portable temple, essentially allowing the Israelites to extend the human–divine interaction beyond the initial covenant encounter at Mt. Sinai.

Following the departure from Horeb, the tabernacle served as the place where God and Moses would thereafter communicate (Exod 33:8–11; Lev 1:1). Yet it was Moses's brother Aaron and his sons who were consecrated as priests of the tabernacle (Exod 28:41; 40:13). Assisting them were fellow clansmen from the tribe of Levi, who were also consecrated for more restrictive service in the tabernacle (Num 8:5–26). Together, these appointed castes and their male descendents were charged with overseeing and enacting all sacrifices. Leviticus and Numbers enumerate ritual specifics, detailing daily (Num 28:1–8), weekly (Lev 23:3; Num 28:9–10), monthly (Num 28:11–15), and annual (Lev 23:4–44; Num 28:16—29:40) sacrifices, as well as special-purpose offerings (Lev 1–7, 12–15, 21). The latter, including sin and guilt offerings, were mostly associated with purity strictures, some of which were required only of tabernacle functionaries (Lev 21) but others for all Israelites (Lev 4–7, 11–15). Some purity regulations, such as the kosher laws (Lev 11), were mandated for all times and places; others were prescribed only for lawful entry into the tabernacle (thus, the requirement to bathe beforehand: Exod 30:18–21; Num 19:13).

The Tabernacle in the Promised Land. At the end of Deuteronomy, just prior to his death, Moses takes Joshua inside the tabernacle to commission him as his successor (31:14). Following the Israelites' initial conquests in Canaan, Joshua built an altar on Mt. Ebal and held a covenant renewal ceremony there and on nearby Mt. Gerizim (Deut 11:29; Josh 8:30–35; cf. Josh 24). Although these sites would eventually become a unified cultic center for the Samaritans (2 Macc 6:2; Josephus, *Ant.* 11.310, 12.257–261), in the conquest narratives the tabernacle is finally placed at Shiloh (Josh 18:1; 19:51), which is proclaimed as the only legitimate place for sacrificial worship (Josh 22:19, 29). Nevertheless, during the period of the judges and early monarchy, several other sacrificial sites (Judg 6:24; 13:20; 21:2–4; 1 Sam 7:17; 14:35) are approvingly mentioned as functioning alongside the main cultic center at Shiloh (1 Sam 1–4).

Following his capture of Jerusalem, David moved the ark to the conquered city, placing it in a new tent (2 Sam 6:17–19; 1 Chr 16:1–6). During his reign sacrifice was offered separately before the ark in Jerusalem and at the tabernacle in Gibeah (1 Chr 16:39–40). Under Solomon, the two sacred artifacts were briefly reunited at the dedication of Solomon's Temple (1 Kgs 8:4; 2 Chr 5:5). The ark was placed in the new inner sanctuary; presumably, the tabernacle was broken down and stored inside the sacred structure that superseded it.

Solomon's Temple. Solomon constructed his Temple (*hêkāl*), "the house of Yahweh" (*bêt Yahweh*), on the hill overlooking Jerusalem. Soon known as "Mount Zion," the site recalled the original meeting between God and Israel at Mt. Sinai (cf. Ps 48:1–2; Isa 4:5). The construction of this grand edifice was said to have taken seven years (1 Kgs 6:37–38). To judge from detailed descriptions, the Temple preserved the tabernacle's general contours, with an inner "holy of holies"

for the ark; an outer sanctuary for the incense altar, shewbread table, and menorahs; and an outside porch overlooking the main altar (1 Kgs 6; 7:15–51; 2 Chr 3–4).

Despite these similarities to its moveable predecessor, Solomon's Temple was more extravagantly embellished with gold and contained several new, distinctive features. Within the Temple itself, a pair of towering golden cherubim flanked the ark in the holy of holies (1 Kgs 6:23–28); walls and doors were carved with images of "cherubim, palm trees, and open flowers" (1 Kgs 6:29; cf. 6:32); 10 menorahs illuminated the whole (2 Chr 4:7). Outside, two huge bronze pillars (cryptically named "Jachin" and "Boaz"), detailed with pomegranates, supported the porch's canopy (1 Kgs 7:15–22; 2 Chr 3:15–17). These overlooked the large main altar, made of bronze (2 Chr 4:1), as well as an enormous bronze "sea" (water reservoir) supported by a dozen oxen figurines (1 Kgs 7:23–26; 2 Chr 4:2–5). The artistic motifs of palm trees, cherubim, and other flora recall the Garden of Eden, the place where God first communed with Adam and Eve (Gen 2) and where sacrifice had first been offered because of sin (Gen 3:21). Solomon's desire to portray the Temple as a "portal to Eden" (cf. Isa 51:3; Lam 2:6), overcame the biblical prohibition against graven images a breach that would not be reopened in future iterations of the Temple.

At its completion, Solomon assembled all the people for the structure's dedication. After overseeing extensive animal sacrifices, the king offered a lengthy prayer, inviting the Almighty to be present from heaven in his newly constructed house (1 Kgs 8:22–29). Solomon prayed that the Temple would become a meeting place between God and his people; that God would thereafter accept the worship and sacrifices offered in its precincts; and that the Almighty would always consider favorably petitioners' pleas for such things as the forgiveness of sins, protection from enemies, and relief from pestilence and plague (8:30–40). Solomon also asked that these blessings be extended to reverent foreigners (8:41–43) and to distant worshippers who prayed in the direction of the new Temple (8:44–53; cf. Dan 6:10), thus extending outward the Temple's power and sanctity.

The people reportedly left this ceremony with hearts filled with joy over the Almighty's presence in the new Temple (1 Kgs 8:66). Such delight is conveyed in many of the psalms, some of which may have originated during this period, later to be sung regularly in the Temple courts by the Levitical choir (Josephus, *Ant.* 11.80). Some psalms reveal that petitioners drew comfort and strength from communing with the Almighty in the Temple: "How lovely is your dwelling place, O LORD of hosts! My soul longs, indeed it faints for the courts of the LORD" (Ps 84:1–2a; cf. 18:6; 42:1–4). Still other psalms portray supplicants as offering gratitude to God in the Temple for his granting of their requests (e.g., 66:13–16; 116:1, 18–19). Elsewhere the Psalmist "bow[s] down toward your holy temple in awe of you" (5:7), asking only "to live in the house of the LORD all the days of my life, to behold the beauty of the LORD, and to inquire in his temple" (27:4; cf. 26:8; 42:4; 122:1). These poetic utterances reveal how the Temple served as a place where worshippers encountered God in a deeply personal and spiritual manner.

Despite the esteem with which Solomon's Temple was held, with the division of the monarchy, rival cultic sites in the northern kingdom emerged at Bethel and Dan (1 Kgs 12:29–33). During this period, "high places" (*bāmâ*) also proliferated in both the northern and southern kingdoms. While these local centers of sacrifice had existed prior to the construction of the Jerusalem Temple (1 Kgs 3:2), they appear to have increased in number with the growth of the population. After the Temple's establishment, however, they are no longer regarded as benign entities in the biblical narrative. Deemed as idolatrous, these sites become targets for the Deuteronomist, who assesses each monarch by his success or failure in destroying them (e.g., 1 Kgs 15:14; 22:43). Their presence, as well as general idolatry and apostasy, were later cited as reasons for the First Temple's demise (Ezek 6) at the hands of Nebuchadnezzar in 587 B.C.E.

Temples and Synagogues in the Postexilic Period. With the return of the exiles under Cyrus, Zerubbabel led the drive to rebuild Solomon's Temple between 520 and 516 B.C.E. (Ezra 3–6; cf. Hag 1–2; Zech 4). The Samaritans offered to help in the effort but were rebuffed. This led to their opposition to the enterprise: evidently, they saw a reconstructed Jerusalem Temple as a rival to their own cultic site on Mt. Gerizim (Ezra 4). During the fourth century B.C.E. the Samaritans built their own temple on that mountain (cf. Josh 8:30–35) under the leadership of Manasses, a former high priest of the Jerusalem Temple (Josephus, *Ant.* 11.310). The Jewish high priest John Hyrcanus destroyed the Samaritan temple in 128 B.C.E., resulting in intensified enmity between the two groups (Josephus, *Ant.* 13:254–256).

In the early second century B.C.E., another former high priest, Onias IV, constructed a rival temple in the Egyptian region of Leontopolis (Josephus, *Ant.* 13:65–71, *B.J.* 7.423). This temple existed until 74 C.E., when the Romans demolished it. Even earlier, in the fifth century B.C.E., a Jewish colony erected a sacrificial temple to "Yaho" farther south in Elephantine. After an Egyptian force destroyed the complex in 410 B.C.E. (*ANET*, 491–492), it was never rebuilt.

Despite the existence of these rival temples, during the postexilic period a majority of Jews increasingly viewed sacrificial worship outside the Jerusalem Temple as unlawful: overwhelmingly, they participated in the regular Temple festivals at Jerusalem (Sir 50:14–21, Philo, *Spec.* 1.70) and fought boldly against Antiochus IV (r. ca. 175–164 B.C.E.) when he outlawed Jewish worship and desecrated the Temple. Subsequently, it was cleansed, and the sacrifices were reinstituted (1 Macc 1:10—4:61).

During this same period an acceptable ancillary emerged: assemblies of sabbath worshippers, gathered at peripheral locations, whose members did not offer sacrifice, aside from a figurative "sacrifice of the lips" (Philo, *Spec.* 1.272). The model for such assemblies was likely Ezra and Nehemiah's rededication of the Jerusalem Temple, where the reading and explication of the Torah took place, not on the Temple Mount but in the square before the distant Water Gate (Neh 8:1–8; cf. 1 Esd 9:38; Josephus, *Ant.* 11.154–158). In subsequent years, similar assemblies proliferated among the public squares in other locales (Philo, *Legat.* 315; Josephus, *Ant.* 16.167–168, 172–173). Many of these eventually moved into purpose-built structures that became known as "prayer halls" (*proseuchē*), "synagogues" (*synagōgē*), and even "temples" (*heiron*), all of which are attested in literary and epigraphic evidence as early as the third century B.C.E. While there is ample evidence that these structures were classified as sacred (i.e., in divine possession) and that religious rituals took place inside of them, the exercise of actual sacrificial worship appears to have been excluded from them—even those of the separatist Essenes, who built their own synagogues (Philo, *Prob.* 80–83; Josephus, *B.J.* 2.128–132). By the first century C.E., scores of synagogues were scattered throughout the Jewish homeland and Diaspora (Philo, *Mos.* 2.216; *Legat.* 311–313; Acts 15:21), with all but the sectarian branches coexisting harmoniously with the Jerusalem Temple and its priestly hierarchy (Philo, *Legat.* 191).

The Temple of Herod. When Zerubbabel first rebuilt the Temple, some of those present for the laying of the foundations, remembering the grandeur of Solomon's Temple, wept in sorrow over the meager appearance of the new structure (Ezra 3:12–13). Five centuries later, Herod the Great (r. 37–4 B.C.E.) may have felt likewise, for he embarked on an ambitious project to totally reconstruct the Temple shrine and its surrounding courts (Josephus, *Ant.* 15.380–425). Beginning in 20 B.C.E. 1,000 priests labored to rebuild the central shrine, a task that was completed within 18 months. Out of respect for tradition, the new shrine retained its predecessor's modest size; nevertheless, it was constructed with even larger quantities of gold than in Solomon's Temple. Unlike Solomon's version, the holy of holies was kept empty: neither the lost ark nor the pair of cherubim was replicated. Moreover, only one menorah—not Solomon's 10—lit the holy place containing the incense altar and shewbread table. In strict conformity to the second commandment (Exod 20:4; Deut 5:8), absent also were the bronze pillars and oxen figurines.

In contrast to the relatively conservative design of the central shrine, the surrounding courts were dramatically expanded to encompass a massive 35 acres—a size unparalleled among temple precincts in the Greco-Roman world. These courts were arranged according to gradations of purity: only priests were allowed in the area closest to the altar and shrine, male Israelites in the first portico, all Israelites in the second, and persons of any nation in the enormous outer courts, which were ringed by towering colonnades.

Their construction continued well past Herod's lifetime; final features were not completed until just prior to the outbreak of the Jewish Revolt in 66 C.E. (Josephus, *Ant.* 20.219).

As during the earlier Greco-Roman period, all sacrificial ritual for the nation took place within the Temple precincts. In time, however, many other public functions took place in the Second Temple. Some were more overtly religious in nature, such as the reading and explication of scripture (Josephus, *Ant.* 4.209–210) and the offering of prayers (Luke 18:10; Acts 3:1). Others were what might anachronistically be labeled as "secular," such as the Temple's function as a public archive and treasury (1 Macc 14:27–45; Josephus, *C. Ap.* 1.30–36; *B.J.* 6.282), the central council hall (Josephus, *B.J.* 5.144, 6.354), and supreme judicial court (Josephus, *B.J.* 4.336; Acts 6:14–16). With the exception of sacrificial ritual, all these functions are attested for the coexisting synagogues (e.g., Josephus, *Ant.* 14.260, 16.43–44, 16.164, *Vita* 276–303; Philo, *Legat.* 133). Thus, when Titus demolished the Jerusalem Temple in 70 C.E., much of Jewish religious and public life was able to continue within these ancillary sacred structures. Even sacrifice could be figuratively enacted within the synagogues, through the offering of prayers and the scholarly study of Temple ritual. The latter eventually resulted in the production of the Mishnah, the Tosefta, and the Talmuds.

Christian Relations with the Temple and the Synagogues. Within the New Testament, the Temple is sometimes portrayed in a positive light. In Luke's infancy narrative (1:5–23), the angel Gabriel appears to Zechariah inside the Temple's holy place as the priest offered incense and the people worshiped outside. Joseph and Mary render the customary purification sacrifices inside the Temple, where Simeon and Anna greet them kindly (2:22–38). The young Jesus carries on lengthy religious discussion inside the Temple, which he calls his "father's house" (2:42–50).

Although the adult Jesus continued to worship and teach in the Temple and in synagogues (e.g., Matt 21:23; Luke 4:16; John 7:37), his relationship with the leaders of these institutions seems to have become largely oppositional (e.g., Matt 21:12–13; Luke 13:14–16). A similar observation could be made vis-à-vis the earliest Christians (e.g., Acts 3:1—4:21; 13:43–45; Rev 2:9; 3:9). When early attempts at persuading the religious hierarchy of Jesus's messianic identity failed and as the new faith attracted Gentile converts, Christians broke their ties with Jewish institutions and began to meet exclusively in their own religious assemblies or "churches" (*ekklēsia*; e.g., Gal 1:2; 1 Cor 1:2; Acts 8:1; 18:4–7; cf. Prov 5:14, LXX).

While moving away from the Temple and its cult, Christians increasingly understood the purpose of these institutions as fulfilled in the death and resurrection of Jesus Christ. Some Christian writers regarded Titus's destruction of the Jerusalem Temple as vindicating this view: the future Roman emperor had been an instrument of God's judgment upon the Temple (cf. Matt 24; Mark 13; Luke 21), from whose inner sanctuary the Almighty had already departed (Mark 15:38; cf. Josephus, *B.J.* 6.299). Despite this negative assessment, many New Testament authors did not abandon the language or imagery of the Temple and its cult; instead, they reinterpreted them, with Christ absorbing the role of the Temple (John 1:15; 2:21), the high priesthood (Heb 5:5–6), the feasts (John 7:37–38; 1 Cor 5:7–8), and the sacrificial offerings (Rom 3:24–25; Rev 13:8). Although the earthly Temple had been destroyed, the true Temple of Ezekiel's vision (Ezek 40–48; cf. Philo, *Spec.* 1.66–68) remained in the heavenly dwellings, where Christ reigned victoriously (Rev 7:15–17; cf. Heb 8:5; 9:24).

During the period when Christ's second coming was believed imminent (1 Thess 4:14–17), Christian assemblies met in domestic residences (Rom 16:5; 1 Cor 16:19; Col 4:15; Phlm 1:2). The construction of standing worship centers may have been regarded as counter to Jesus's great commission to preach the gospel to the ends of the earth (Matt 28:16–20; Acts 1:8), especially if the present earth and heaven were soon passing away (Rev 21:1). In addition, there emerged a utopian understanding of God's presence as not confined to a particular place but present within the bodies of individual believers (themselves viewed as temples: 1 Cor 3:16–17; 6:19; 1 Pet 2:4–5) and especially within the community of believers, wherever they gathered (Rom 12:5; 1 Cor 12:12–27).

This utopian view was predominant for the first three centuries C.E. (*Barn.* 16.1–10; Origen, *Cels.* 8.19).

The imperial patronage of monumental church construction under Constantine (r. 306–337) recalled the return of the Jewish exiles under Cyrus and marked, for Christians, the reassertion of a locative understanding of divine presence. Thus, at the dedication of a church at Tyre, Eusebius of Caesarea likened the endeavor to Zerubbabel's reconstruction of the Jerusalem Temple (*Hist. eccl.* 10.4.2–6, 69–72). Henceforth, the architects and builders of the Constantinian period drew inspiration from the Old Testament accounts of the tabernacle and Temple, constructing within their churches new altars, not for the sacrifice of animals but for the celebration of the Eucharist, the holy rite recalling Christ's sacrifice and victory over death (1 Cor 11:23–26). With the construction of these sacred buildings, the *axis mundi* had returned, providing worshippers once more with a fixed passageway between heaven and earth.

Contemporary Relevance. Within both Judaism and Christianity, there remains a tension between a locative and a utopian understanding of divine presence. Although both traditions discern God's presence within the gathering of its worshippers in any location, certain buildings or monuments retain a heightened sense of sacredness. For Jews, the Western Wall of the destroyed Jerusalem Temple remains the most sacred spot for worship. Likewise, many Christians consider the Church of the Holy Sepulcher, built over the rock of Calvary and the empty tomb, to be the holiest place in all of Christendom. To a lesser degree, synagogues and churches associated with other sacred events and holy persons are viewed similarly, as are any structures built to serve as a "temple" or "house of God." These contrasting viewpoints, holding in tension human perceptions of God's immanence and transcendence, continue to influence contemporary theology.

[*See also* Cult and Worship; Deuteronomy; Ecclesiology; Expiation; Ezra, Nehemiah, and 1 and 2 Chronicles; Festivals and Holy Days; Forgiveness; Glory; Guilt and Innocence; Heaven and Earth; Holiness; Idols and Idolatry; Jerusalem (Zion); Judaism; Leviticus and Numbers; Lord's Supper; Prayer; Priests and Priesthood; Psalms; Sacrifice and Offerings; Sin; *and* Theophany.]

BIBLIOGRAPHY

Ben-Dov, Meir. *In the Shadow of the Temple: The Discovery of Ancient Jerusalem.* 1st U.S. ed. New York: Harper & Row, 1985.

Binder, Donald D. *Into the Temple Courts: The Place of the Synagogues in the Second Temple Period.* Dissertation Series 169. Atlanta: Society of Biblical Literature, 1999.

Biran, Avraham, Inna Pommerantz, and Hannah Katzenstein, eds. *Temples and High Places in Biblical Times: Proceedings of the Colloquium in Honor of the Centennial of Hebrew Union College-Jewish Institute of Religion, Jerusalem, 14–16 March 1977.* Jerusalem: Nelson Glueck School of Biblical Archaeology of Hebrew Union College–Jewish Institute of Religion, 1981.

Day, John, ed. *Temple and Worship in Biblical Israel.* Library of Hebrew Bible/Old Testament Studies 422. London and New York: T&T Clark, 2005.

Eliade, Mircea. *The Sacred and the Profane: The Nature of Religion.* New York: Harcourt, Brace & World, 1959.

Eliade, Mircea. "Sacred Architecture and Symbolism." In *Symbolism, the Sacred, and the Arts,* edited by Mircea Eliade and Diane Apostolos-Cappadona, pp. 105–129. New York: Crossroad, 1985.

Fine, Steven, ed. *The Temple of Jerusalem: From Moses to the Messiah: In Honor of Professor Louis H. Feldman.* Brill Reference Library of Judaism 29. Leiden, The Netherlands, and Boston: Brill, 2011.

Klawans, Jonathan. *Purity, Sacrifice, and the Temple: Symbolism and Supersessionism in the Study of Ancient Judaism.* Oxford and New York: Oxford University Press, 2006.

Levine, Lee I. *The Ancient Synagogue: The First Thousand Years.* 2d ed. New Haven, Conn.: Yale University Press, 2005.

McReady, Wayne O., and Adele Reinhartz, eds. *Common Judaism: Explorations in Second-Temple Judaism.* Minneapolis: Fortress, 2008.

Neusner, Jacob. *Method and Meaning in Ancient Judaism.* Brown Judaic Studies 10. Missoula, Mont.: Scholars Press, 1979.

Runesson, Anders. *The Origins of the Synagogue: A Socio-historical Study.* Coniectanea Biblica 37. Stockholm: Almqvist & Wiksell, 2001.

Runesson, Anders, Donald D. Binder, and Birger Olsson. *The Ancient Synagogue from Its Origins to 200 C.E.: A Source Book.* Ancient Judaism and Early Christianity 72. Leiden, The Netherlands, and Boston: Brill, 2008.

Sanders, E. P. *Judaism: Practice and Belief, 63 BCE–66 CE.* London: SCM; Philadelphia: Trinity Press International, 1992.

Schwartz, Daniel R., and Zeev Weiss, eds. *Was 70 CE a Watershed in Jewish History? On Jews and Judaism before and after the Destruction of the Second Temple.* Ancient Judaism and Early Christianity 78. Leiden, The Netherlands, and Boston: Brill, 2012.

Stambaugh, John E. "The Functions of Roman Temples." In *Aufstieg und Niedergang der romischen Welt: Geschichte und Kultur Roms im Spiegel der neueren Forschung, Teil II, Bd. 16, Religion: Heidentum,* edited by Hildegard Temporini and Wolfgang Haase, pp. 554–608. Berlin: Walter de Gruyter, 1978.

Wardle, Timothy. *The Jerusalem Temple and Early Christian Identity.* Wissenschaftliche Untersuchungen zum Neuen Testament 2, Reihe 291. Tübingen, Germany: Mohr Siebeck, 2010.

Donald D. Binder

TEMPLE

See Tabernacles, Temples, and Synagogues.

THEODICY

See Good and Evil *and* Justice, Justification, and Righteousness.

THEOLOGY, BIBLICAL

This entry contains two subentries: Old Testament *and* New Testament.

Old Testament

"Biblical theology" refers to the systematic theological exposition of the Bible. The Bible appears in a variety of forms in Judaism and the various streams of Christianity. Consequently, the scope and concerns of biblical theology must be defined in relation to each tradition. Biblical theology in Judaism encompasses the theological exposition of the Tanak, the Jewish version of the Bible that comprises the 24 books of the Masoretic Text of the Bible in Hebrew and Aramaic. Biblical theology in Christianity encompasses the theological exposition of the books of both the Old Testament and the New Testament. In the Protestant traditions, biblical theology takes up the 39 books of the Old Testament and the 27 books of the New Testament. The quasi-canonical status of the Apocrypha in

Protestant Bibles entails that its treatment is optional in Protestant biblical theology. Because the Roman Catholic Church considers the Apocryphal books to be fully canonical, their treatment is essential in a Roman Catholic biblical theology. Christian biblical theology ideally treats the books of the Bible in relation to the principal versions and languages in which they are written and read, e.g., the Hebrew and Aramaic Masoretic Text, the various versions of the Greek Septuagint, the Syriac Peshitta, the Latin Vulgate, the Ethiopic Bible.

The Origins of Biblical Theology in the Sixteenth to Eighteenth Centuries. Christian Old Testament theology originated during the mid-sixteenth through the eighteenth centuries as a part of the larger field of Christian biblical theology. Christian biblical theology per se has its roots in the early Protestant Reformation, which was concerned with challenging the dominance of dogmatic theology in the Roman Catholic Church by establishing sacred scripture as the basis for Christian theology, faith, and practice. Martin Luther's principle of *sola scriptura*, "scripture alone," constituted one of the ideals of the early Protestant Reformation; but subsequent Protestant orthodoxy followed Philipp Melanchthon's attempts to systematize Luther's understanding of the Bible by developing its own dogmatic theology in which selected biblical passages would be employed as "proof texts" to justify the dogmatic principle or doctrine in question. Such use of *dicta probantia* was derived from earlier medieval practice, and it presupposed that the Bible in its entirety—and every individual statement therein—constituted the universally true, sacred, infallible, and authoritative word of God. As a result, early Protestant orthodoxy saw no need to treat individual passages from the Bible in relation to the historical, cultural, literary, or theological contexts and concerns in which they were written and to which they were addressed. Every statement from scripture must be considered in relation to the whole as a true witness to God's relationship with humanity through Christ. Therefore, the Old Testament was effectively subsumed into the concerns of the New Testament and ultimately to the dogmatic theological concerns of Protestant orthodoxy through the seventeenth century.

Greater attention to the reading and study of scripture within Protestant Christianity prompted greater awareness of the historical dimensions of the writings of the Bible. Baruch Spinoza (1632–1677), a Dutch Jew whose works were widely read by Christians, was a key figure in the discussion who called for a reading of the Bible based on reason that would separate the universal truths of the Bible from the particular teachings of its historical context. Protestant thinkers increasingly came to realize that the Bible was not written as a book of systematic theological doctrine but instead presented an account of God's relationship with humanity through the course of history from creation through the revelation of Christ. Johannes Cocceius (originally Koch, 1603–1669) recognized the importance of the relationship between God and humanity defined as *foedus*, "league," "federation," or "covenant," throughout the Bible, and therefore proposed that "covenant" become the fundamental concept upon which the teachings of the Bible must be understood. Cocceius distinguished two basic covenants in the relationship between God and humankind. The first was the covenant of works (*foedus operum*) or the covenant of nature (*foedus naturae*), which was in force from creation to the fall of Adam. The second was the covenant of grace (*foedus gratiae*), which began with Adam's fall, included the revelation of the Law of Moses, and reached its fullest expression in Christ's self-sacrifice to expiate the sins of humanity. Cocceius set the fundamental patterns for the development of modern Old Testament theology by emphasizing both covenant and the salvation history or *Heilsgeschichte* of the relationship between God and humankind.

The Development of Old Testament Theology in the Eighteenth through the Early Twentieth Centuries. Many contemporary theologians identify Johann P. Gabler (1753–1826) as the founder of the field of biblical theology, but his work clearly presupposes earlier currents of thought. Gabler was influenced by Kant's understanding of empirical reason and ethical idealism. He therefore did not set out to define biblical theology as a field in its own right; rather, he was concerned with defining a secure basis for formulating dogmatic theology by first establishing its foundations in the Bible. His 1787 inaugural lecture at the

University of Altdorf, "An Oration on the Proper Distinction Between Biblical and Dogmatic Theology and the Specific Objectives of Each," argues for a distinction between biblical and dogmatic theology based upon the distinction between the human or historical concerns and the core divine or universal concerns expressed within the Bible (Sandys-Wunsch and Eldredge, 1980). Gabler challenged Luther's principle of *sola scriptura* by emphasizing the interrelationship between the historical concerns of biblical exegesis that identified what the biblical authors thought about matters of theology and the didactic concerns of dogmatic theology that would employ the universal truths of the Bible to address the needs of the contemporary world.

Increasing concern with the rationalist and historical dimensions of philosophy and theology appeared throughout the nineteenth century. Friedrich Schleiermacher's (1768–1834) work was particularly influential at this time. His interest in constructing a true Christianity based on the experience of absolute dependence on God prompted him to reject the teachings of the Old Testament as primitive fetishism that provided the basis for the development of true Christianity. The work of Georg Wilhelm Friedrich Hegel (1770–1831), which emphasized the role of the absolute spirit (of God) in the unfolding historical progress of humankind, was also influential. Hegel argued that the Germanic nations of Protestant northern Europe were the heirs of the Greeks and Romans who embodied the spirit of developing human intellectual freedom. The Old Testament was a product of Oriental fetishism, but it nevertheless provided a historical foundation for the unfolding of the absolute spirit in German Protestantism.

The predominance of historical work in Old Testament studies in general, buttressed by the increasing knowledge of the history and literature of the ancient Near Eastern and Greco-Roman worlds, prompted an eclipse in the field of Old Testament theology in the late nineteenth century as scholars increasingly turned their attention to the historical development of the Old Testament from its earliest stages through the beginning of the Christian era. In the view of many theologians at this time, the Old Testament was a relic of the primitive past that was increasingly irrelevant at the dawn of the newly emerging modern world.

Old Testament Theology in the Twentieth Century. World Wars I and II, the Shoah (Holocaust), the potential for nuclear destruction, and other factors played important roles in prompting theologians to recognize the fundamental problems with models of human progress in the late nineteenth and early twentieth centuries. The result was a return to questions of theology as a basis for engaging religious traditions to interpret both the past and the modern world. Consequently, the twentieth century saw a reinvigoration of the fields of biblical theology in general and Old Testament theology as theologians debated the question of the interrelationship between historical knowledge of religion and theological understandings of revelation in relation to biblical interpretation.

As a consequence of this discussion and the perceived need to address questions of biblical theology in the aftermath of World War I, Eichrodt produced his still influential Old Testament theology in 1933–1939. He attempted to provide a methodological synthesis in Old Testament theology that would combine engagement with history of religions research with concern for the revelatory character of the New Testament. Eichrodt continued to express the prevailing anti-Semitism of his day by not taking up the relationship between the Hebrew Bible and postbiblical Judaism, which he characterized as having a "torso-like appearance…in separation from Christianity."

Eichrodt focused on "covenant" as the basic concept for his systematic exposition of the Old Testament. He argued that a "cross-cut" method would demonstrate the unity of a fundamental concept throughout the various writings of the Old Testament and would best facilitate the exposition of the constancy and basic character of the Old Testament as a self-contained entity despite the ever-changing historical conditions that led to its production. Eichrodt considered the Hebrew term *běrît*, "covenant," as the best expression of the living process of the relationship between God and the human world that manifests itself throughout the Old Testament. He therefore organized his theology around three fundamental themes: (1) God and the people, expressed as the people of Israel or the national concept of Israel; (2) God and the world, expressed in terms of God's relationship with all of humanity and the cosmos; and (3) God and human beings, expressed in terms of the relationship between God and the individual human being. This organization of his work reflected Eichrodt's concern with one of the fundamental theological problems of Christianity, viz., the interrelationship between the "particularism" of the nation Israel and the "universalism" of all humankind as collective and as individual. Such a concern likewise reflected the question of Germany's unification in central Europe during the late nineteenth and early twentieth centuries and its growing hostility to recognizing the legitimacy of Jews as a distinct people and to integrating them into the German nation. Eichrodt was severely criticized for imposing a concept that did not account adequately for the entire Old Testament. Nevertheless, his theology constitutes a highly systematized account of the means by which the holy, all-powerful, sovereign, and infinite author of creation relates to the vulnerable, educable, and finite Israel and humanity in the world.

The widespread silence of the Christian churches during the Nazi period prompted some pointed rethinking of systematic theology as Christian and Jewish theologians explored new means to articulate a theological worldview as a consequence of Germany's actions during World War II. Karl Barth (1932–1970) highlighted the importance of the proclamation of the word of the transcendent and holy God as the central task of Christian theology and preaching. Dietrich Bonhoeffer's (1972) writings and his execution by the Nazis stimulated considerable reflection on theological questions of social justice and the need to assert divine presence in the world. Wolfhart Pannenberg's (1975) reflections on God's role in history expressed the theological return to history in the face of an increasingly secular and technological world. Abraham Joshua Heschel's (1962) focus on divine pathos in the face of evil and the efforts of the divine to enter into relationship with humans prompted both Jews and Christians to posit a far more intimate relationship between God and human beings. Richard

L. Rubenstein (1966) pointed to divine absence in the world in the aftermath of the Shoah and its implications for constructing Jewish identity and Judaism's relationship with Christianity.

The World Council of Churches played an important role in stimulating thought on the relevance of the Bible to the modern world. Such reflection stimulated the so-called biblical theology movement during the 1950s and 1960s as interpreters turned to the Bible as a basis for discerning divine purpose for the world. Theodorus Christian Vriezen (1949; 1970) emphasized the Christian character of Old Testament theology and the concept of the communion between God and human beings as the fundamental kerygmatic proclamation of the relationship between God and humankind. George Ernest Wright (1952) argued that the Bible is not the word of God. Instead, it constitutes a confessional record of the acts of God as they actually happened and were portrayed in the Old Testament. His 1969 study emphasized three basic concepts of God in the Old Testament: God the Creator, who sets the structure of the universe to which humans must conform; God the Lord or divine monarch, who establishes a covenant relationship with humanity; and God the warrior, who combats human sin in an effort to redeem the world. Edmond Jacob (1955) drew heavily on ancient Near Eastern mythology to focus on God's freedom and sovereignty in the Old Testament in which God sets the parameters of the relationship to which human beings respond. Following Vatican II, John L. McKenzie (1955; 1974) was the first Roman Catholic biblical theologian to move beyond dogmatic categories in his attempts to focus on the experience by Israel of the Deity in the Old Testament with particular emphasis on cultic matters, law, and holiness.

Gerhard von Rad (1957–1960; 1972) was the most influential Old Testament theologian of the twentieth century. His *Heilsgeschichtlicher* or salvation-historical approach embraced the dichotomy between the picture of ancient Israelite history and religion developed by modern historical scholarship and the kerygmatic understanding of the Deity in history as proclaimed in the Old Testament. His early form- and tradition-critical work on the Hexateuch pointed to the confessional role of the statement in Deuteronomy 26:5–9 concerning the Deity's acts on Israel's behalf during the ancestral, Exodus, and wilderness periods until the entry into the Promised Land as the basis for Israel's understanding of the Deity. The biblical writings displayed tremendous diversity in theological outlook because of their long tradition-historical development in a variety of historical and institutional settings. Therefore, there was no center to the Old Testament. The historical dimensions of the Old Testament nevertheless point to a theological view grounded in history from the time of creation, through Israel's historical experience, and beyond. Von Rad was heavily criticized for marginalizing concepts that demonstrated stability rather than change in the relationship between the Deity and Israel or the world, creation, and the wisdom literature in particular. He therefore subsequently produced a third volume devoted to the wisdom literature but nevertheless characterized wisdom as Israel's response to the Deity's acts in history. Von Rad's *Heilsgeschichtlicher* model nevertheless provided the primary counterpoint to Eichrodt's covenant model throughout the twentieth century.

Other theologies written during the late twentieth century followed upon the work of von Rad. Walther Zimmerli (1972) highlighted the central concern of what the Old Testament says about God by emphasizing classical Reformed theological themes in an attempt to counter von Rad. Zimmerli's work focused instead on the absolute free sovereignty and grace of God, the revelation of the divine name to Israel, Israel's ungrateful response leading to divine judgment, and the salvation offered to the entire world. Georg Fohrer (1972) attempted to identify two centers to the Old Testament in "the rule of God" and "communion with God," which emphasized prophecy as the reappearance of Mosaic religion in a purified form that would counter the nationalist-religious ideology of state. Claus Westermann (1978) attempted to combine systematic and diachronic approaches in an effort to present God's saving action in history; God's blessing in creation; God's judgment and compassion; the human response to God in words, action, and reflection; and the relationship between the Old Testament and Jesus Christ. Hartmut Gese (1977) focused on the tradition-historical stream of development from the Old Testament to the New. Horst Dietrich Preuss (1991–1992) emphasized Israel's election in the Old Testament as a basis to trace the election of humanity in the New Testament. Erhard Gerstenberger (2001) abandoned any attempt to define a center to the Old Testament and instead examined the theologies represented throughout the social history of ancient Israel.

Developments in the Late Twentieth and Early Twenty-First Centuries. The dominance of historical models for Old Testament theology came under challenge in the late twentieth century as theologians sought to address their shortcomings. Newer canonical, cosmological, and dialogical models (including feminist, Jewish, African American, Asian, and postcolonial models) emerged during the late twentieth and early twenty-first centuries (Perdue, 1994; 2005).

Brevard Childs (1970; 1985; 1993) called for a focus on the Christian canon as the central concern of biblical theology in an attempt to recover the Christian character of Old Testament theology. In his view, the canonical text of the Bible—and not the reconstructed history of Israel or the purportedly original texts that had informed the work of the biblical theology movement—stood as the product of Christian faith throughout history. Childs understood biblical theology to include both the Old and the New Testaments. He nevertheless sought to provide a basis for interpretation of the Old Testament in its own right as Christian scripture in conversation with the New Testament and the *Wirkungsgeschichte* or later actualization of scripture in the Christian community. Childs's work has been sharply criticized as an attempt to abandon the historical character of scripture, although his inclusion of historical issues in his treatment of texts indicates that this is not his agenda. Most importantly, his emphasis on the *substantia*, which he understands as the divine reality to be found in the Bible, has left him open to charges of subjectivity (Barr, 1999). Nevertheless, Childs's canonical model provides a means to overcome the selective systematic and historical foci of earlier theologies.

It also recognizes the interpretative afterlife of the Bible in the communities for which it serves as sacred scripture.

Childs's work has been followed by that of other scholars who have also focused on canonical issues. James A. Sanders (1972; 1984) did not produce a full theology, but he moved beyond Childs's monolithic focus on the Western Protestant canon to stress the importance of the various textual and canonical forms of the Bible and their impact on Christian and Jewish believing communities. Rolf Rendtorff's (2001) concentration on the Masoretic form of the Bible as a canonical model for Old Testament theology provided the opportunity for Judaism and Christianity to engage in a common reading of their shared sacred scripture. Marvin A. Sweeney (2012) took the canonical structure of the Tanak and the intertextual dialog among its books as the bases for a distinctively Jewish biblical theology. He proposes that a similar model might be employed to construct Christian biblical theologies.

One of the major problems to emerge in biblical theology in general and Old Testament theology in particular during the course of the twentieth century is the recognition that the ideal patterns of God's relationship with humanity and creation have largely failed to be realized. Past models have generally been content to characterize the question of theodicy as one of human sin, but the moral questions raised about divine absence in relation to the Shoah have prompted reconsideration of divine power and righteousness in the Bible. Scholars are increasingly interested in investigating the theological significance of the wisdom and creation texts and the issues that they raise as an essential element of biblical theology. Rolf P. Knierim (1995) moved beyond the historical work of von Rad to point to the cosmological foundation of the Deity's world order in justice and righteousness as a means to define human responsibility in the world of creation. Jon D. Levenson (1985; 1988) pointed to the role of the Jerusalem Temple as the sacred center of creation as well as of the nation Israel and to the importance of the Deity's daily struggle against evil to maintain creation's holy and moral integrity. Bernhard W. Anderson (1999) focused on the different understandings of covenant in the Old Testament as a means to define the relationship between the Deity and Israel and the crisis provoked by the manifestation of evil in the world of creation. James Crenshaw (2005) highlighted the importance of the question of theodicy in the Old Testament, which asserts divine righteousness as a means of defending God. Marvin A. Sweeney (2008) emphasized the role that human beings must play to ensure the well-being of the world when God fails to act in the face of evil.

Finally, the inclusion of previously marginalized groups, including women, Jews, African Americans, and theologians from cultures outside of Europe and North America, points to dialogical models for Old Testament theology that bring the unique perspectives of each group into the discussion. Feminist theological scholarship has emerged as an especially powerful voice, prompting theologians to rethink basic understandings of God and the web of relationships between and among God and human beings. Phyllis Trible (1978; 1984) pointed out that texts must be read from multiple perspectives depending on the context of the reader and that the feminine characters of God and key figures in the Bible as well as the interrelationships between God, humans, and texts are frequently overlooked because of the limits of our gendered hermeneutical perspectives. Jewish biblical theology appears in the works of Heschel, Levenson, and Sweeney as well as in the work of Michael Fishbane (2003), who emphasized the interrelationships between biblical and rabbinic literature. Randall C. Bailey's (2000) approach to African American biblical interpretation of the Bible exposes white supremacist presuppositions in current biblical scholarship and pointed to the role of African American ideological criticism in the reading of biblical texts. Fernando Segovia (2000) pointed to Third World perspectives in the theological reading of biblical literature. The volume of essays edited by Mary F. Foskett and Jeffrey Kuan (2006) explored the possibilities for Asian forms of biblical theology. Finally, Walter Brueggemann (1997) took up the differing perspectives in the reading of the Bible that underlie each of the preceding approaches to biblical theology. Brueggemann emphasized that the discipline of theology is fundamentally discourse concerning God, which prompts him to examine the communicative functions of various writings of the Hebrew Bible. His purpose is to bring their differing perspectives together in theological dialog or testimony concerning God and God's relationship to the world.

Although the theological study of the Hebrew Bible has prompted a very intense and variegated discussion over the past centuries, continuing work at the outset of the twenty-first century promises continuing engagement in the field.

[*See also* Adam (Primeval History); Canon; Covenant; Creation; Ethics, Biblical, *subentry* Old Testament; Judaism; Salvation History; *and* Wisdom Literature.]

BIBLIOGRAPHY

Surveys of Research

Barr, James. *The Concept of Biblical Theology: An Old Testament Perspective.* Minneapolis: Fortress, 1999.

Graf Reventlow, Henning. *Problems of Old Testament Theology in the Twentieth Century.* Philadelphia: Fortress, 1985. English translation of *Hauptprobleme der alttestamentliche Theologie im 20. Jahrhundert*, first published in 1983.

Hasel, Gerhard. *Old Testament Theology: Basic Issues in the Current Debate.* 4th ed. Grand Rapids, Mich.: Eerdmans, 1991.

Perdue, Leo G. *The Collapse of History: Reconstructing Old Testament Theology.* Minneapolis: Fortress, 1994.

Perdue, Leo G. *Reconstructing Old Testament Theology: After the Collapse of History.* Minneapolis: Fortress, 2005.

Studies

Anderson, Bernhard W. *Contours of Old Testament Theology.* Minneapolis: Augsburg Fortress, 1999.

Bailey, R. C. "Academic Biblical Interpretation among African Americans in the United States." In *African Americans and the Bible: Sacred Texts and Sacred Textures*, edited by Vincent L. Wimbush, pp. 696–711. New York: Continuum, 2000.

Barth, Karl. *Church Dogmatics.* 5 vols. Edinburgh: T&T Clark, 1936–1977. English translation of *Kirchliche Dogmatik*, first published in 1932–1970.

Bonhoeffer, Dietrich. *Letters and Papers from Prison.* Edited by Eberhard Bethge. New York: Macmillan, 1972.

Brueggemann, Walter. *Theology of the Old Testament: Testimony, Dispute, Advocacy.* Minneapolis: Fortress, 1997.

Childs, Brevard S. *Biblical Theology in Crisis.* Philadelphia: Westminster, 1970.

Childs, Brevard S. *Old Testament Theology in a Canonical Context.* Philadelphia: Fortress, 1985.

Childs, Brevard S. *Biblical Theology of the Old and New Testaments: Theological Reflection on the Christian Bible.* Minneapolis: Fortress, 1993.

Crenshaw, James L. *Defending God: Biblical Responses to the Problem of Evil.* New York: Oxford University Press, 2005.

Eichrodt, Walther. *Theology of the Old Testament.* 2 vols. Translated by J. A. Baker. Philadelphia: Westminster, 1961–1967. English translation of *Theologie des Alten Testaments*, first published in 1933–1939.

Fishbane, Michael. *Biblical Myth and Rabbinic Mythmaking.* Oxford and New York: Oxford University Press, 2003.

Fohrer, Georg. *Theologische Grundstrukturen des Alten Testaments.* Berlin: De Gruyter, 1972.

Foskett, Mary K., and Jeffrey Kah-Jin Kuan, eds. *Ways of Being, Ways of Reading: Asian American Biblical Interpretation.* Saint Louis, Mo.: Chalice, 2006.

Gerstenberger, Erhard S. *Theologies in the Old Testament.* Translated by John Bowden. Minneapolis: Augsburg Fortress, 2002. English translation of *Theologies im AT: Pluralität und Synkretismus alttestamentlichen Gottesglaubens*, first published in 2001.

Gese, Hartmut. *Essays on Biblical Theology.* Minneapolis: Augsburg Fortress, 1981. English translation of *Zur biblische Theologie: Alttestamentliche Vorträge*, first published in 1977.

Heschel, Abraham J. *The Prophets.* New York: Harper & Row, 1962.

Jacob, Edmund. *Theology of the Old Testament.* Translated by Arthur W. Heathcote and Philip A. Allcock. London: Hodder & Stoughton, 1958. English translation of *Théologie de l'ancien Testament*, first published in 1955.

Knierim, Rolf P. *The Task of Old Testament Theology: Method and Cases.* Grand Rapids, Mich., and Cambridge, U.K.: Eerdmans, 1995.

Köhler, Ludwig. *Old Testament Theology.* Translated by A. S. Todd. Philadelphia: Westminster, 1957. English translation of *Theologie des Alten Testament*, first published in 1936.

Levenson, Jon D. *Sinai and Zion: An Entry into the Jewish Bible.* Minneapolis: Winston, 1985.

Levenson, Jon D. *Creation and the Persistence of Evil: The Jewish Drama of Divine Omnipotence.* New York: Harper & Row, 1988.

McKenzie, John L. *The Two-Edged Sword: An Interpretation of the Old Testament.* Milwaukee, Wis.: Bruce, 1955.

McKenzie, John L. *A Theology of the Old Testament.* Garden City, N.Y.: Doubleday, 1974.

Pannenberg, Wolfhart. *Faith and Reality*. Philadelphia: Westminster John Knox, 1977. English translation of *Glaube und Wirklichkeit*, first published in 1975.

Preuss, Horst Dietrich. *Old Testament Theology*. 2 vols. Louisville, Ky.: Westminster John Knox, 1995–1996. English translation of *Theologie des Alten Testaments*, first published in 1991–1992.

Rad, Gerhard von. *Old Testament Theology*. 2 vols. Translated by D. M. G. Stalker. New York: Harper & Row, 1962–1965. English translation of *Theologie des Alten Testaments*, first published in 1957–1960.

Rad, Gerhard von. *Wisdom in Israel*. Philadelphia: Abingdon, 1972. English translation of *Weisheit in Israel*, first published in 1970.

Rendtorff, Rolf. *The Canonical Hebrew Bible: A Theology of the Old Testament*. 2 vols. Translated by David E. Orton. Leiden, The Netherlands: Deo, 2005. English translation of *Theologie des Alten Testaments: Ein kanonischer Entwurf*, first published in 2001.

Rubenstein, Richard L. *After Auschwitz*. Indianapolis, Ind.: Bobbs-Merrill, 1966.

Sanders, James A. *Torah and Canon*. Philadelphia: Fortress, 1972.

Sanders, James A. *Canon and Community: A Guide to Canonical Criticism*. Philadelphia: Fortress, 1984.

Sandys-Wunsch, John, and Laurence Eldredge. "J. P. Gabler and the Distinction Between Biblical and Dogmatic Theology: Translation, Commentary, and Discussion of His Originality." *Scottish Journal of Theology* 33 (1980): 133–144.

Segovia, Fernando F. *Decolonizing Biblical Studies: A View from the Margins*. Maryknoll, N.Y.: Orbis, 2000.

Sweeney, Marvin A. *Reading the Hebrew Bible after the Shoah: Engaging Holocaust Theology*. Minneapolis: Fortress, 2008.

Sweeney, Marvin A. *Tanak: A Theological and Critical Introduction to the Jewish Bible*. Minneapolis: Fortress, 2012.

Trible, Phyllis. *God and the Rhetoric of Sexuality*. Philadelphia: Fortress, 1978.

Trible, Phyllis. *Texts of Terror: Literary-Feminist Readings of Biblical Narratives*. Philadelphia: Fortress, 1984.

Vriezen, T. C. *An Outline of Old Testament Theology*. 2d ed. Newton, Mass.: Branford, 1970. English translation of *Hoodlijnen der theologie van het Oude Testament*, first published in 1949.

Westermann, Claus. *Elements of Old Testament Theology*. Translated by Douglas W. Stott. Atlanta: John Knox, 1982. English translation of *Theologie des Alten Testament im Grundzügen*, first published in 1978.

Wright, George Ernest. *God Who Acts: Biblical Theology as Recital*. London: SCM, 1952.

Wright, G. Ernest. *The Old Testament and Theology*. New York: Harper & Row, 1969.

Zimmerli, Walther. *Old Testament Theology in Outline*. Translated by David E. Green. Atlanta: John Knox, 1978. English translation of *Grundriss der alttestamentlichen Theologie*, first published in 1972.

Marvin A. Sweeney

New Testament

Biblical theology seeks the Word of God in the written words of human beings collected in the Old and New Testaments. It looks for the unity of the Bible in the plurality of biblical books and the two testaments. In doing so, biblical theology is engaged to orientate Christian living and teaching in the testimonies of faith which are collected in the holy scripture.

The Challenges. The Bible itself asserts that the Word of God is present in every time and place; it is "living and active, sharper than any two-edged sword" (Heb 4:12). A theological concept of canon, truth, and inspiration depends on this biblical theology of the Word of God.

The Word of God. In the New Testament, the Word of God is seen in the face of Jesus Christ, God's icon (2 Cor 4:4; Col 1:15; cf. John 12:45; 14:9). Because of Jesus's incarnation, proclamation, service, death, and resurrection, the Word of God sounds in the proclamation of the gospel, which is, in Paul's words, "the power of God for salvation to everyone who has faith" (Rom 1:16). The Word of God needs witness by human beings for human beings. This human mediation is not a problem to be solved but the very truth of God's revelation because the human Jesus himself spoke God's Word (cf. Matt 5:1–2) and sent his disciples to proclaim the gospel to all Israel (Matt 10:5–15//Luke 10:4–12; cf. Mark 6:6b–13//Luke 9:2–5) and, after Easter, to all nations (Matt 28:16–20; Luke 24:46–47; Acts 1:8). Their preaching and teaching, starting with the vivid remembrance of Jesus's mission, is the object and medium of the New Testament writings. Every book of the New Testament is totally human, conditioned by the culture of its genesis. The Word of God is not only a part of that human witness but also the source and the horizon of the New Testament. As St.

Augustine commented, "God speaks through a human being in human fashion; and speaking thus he seeks us" (Civ. 17.6.2: CSEL 40.2.228).

The canon. According to the biblical writings themselves, the Word of God is found not exclusively in the holy scriptures but also in the creation (cf. John 1:1–5; Rom 1:20), in the consciousness of human beings (Rom 2:14ff.), and in human cultures (Acts 14:15–17; 17:26–28). For the community of believers, however, the Holy Bible is a special repository of God's Word; it is the "canon," i.e., the guideline of all ecclesial teaching, the touchstone of all Christian life, and the signpost of every conversion and reform in the church. Through critical study, biblical theology helps the community orient its faith. It also has to inform the society about the mission and ethos of the church in relation to scripture, the first authority of her teaching.

The process of assembling the canon was lengthy. In earliest Christianity the "scripture(s)" was the Bible of Israel, later called the "Old Testament." This is the case despite the facts (1) that the list of books in the Hebrew Bible was somewhat fluid both in early Judaism and in early Christianity, especially in the Wisdom writings, and (2) that the New Testament quotations of the Old Testament were in Greek, more or less in the tradition of the Septuagint. Marcion rejected the authority of the Old Testament; but the vast majority of the church recognized the Bible of Israel as testimony of the one God, the Creator and Lord of the world.

In the New Testament books, "scripture" appears as a pluriform unity that testifies to the truth of God. These books contain no critique of or reaction against any "Old Testament" book or teaching. The emergence of the New Testament was a process of reception in the Christian communities; it began with the writing of the books and came to a preliminary end in the fourth century (Athanasius). The collection has three centers: the four Gospels, the "Catholicon" with Acts and the Catholic Letters, and the Corpus Paulinum. Ancient canon lists and manuscripts show that there was a general acceptation of most of the New Testament writings with the exceptions of Hebrews (and some of the shorter Catholic Epistles) and Revelation. Some lists and manuscripts include some "apocryphal" texts (such as the *Shep-*

herd of Hermas or the *Letter of Barnabas*), which were not finally accepted as canonical. In addition, some more or less gnostic groups made it necessary to discuss "apocryphal" gospels, letters, and acts.

Truth. The Word of God, heard with the ears of biblical authors and readers, is true in itself. Therefore, the Bible, understood theologically, testifies to the truth revealed by God. Biblical theology, listening to the Word of God in scripture, searches for the truth of the Bible. The biblical theologian must resist the temptation of a fundamentalism that tries to monopolize the biblical message by severing the threads of conversation with other religions, philosophies, and worldviews. To overcome this temptation, theologians employ the methods of critical reading and maintain interdisciplinary dialogue, which is the job of exegesis in biblical theology. The problem of understanding the very "truth" of the Bible arises because there are some clear mistakes in the Bible, for instance, the name of the priest in Mark 2:26 was not "Abiathar" but Ahimelech (1 Sam 21:2). In modern times such mistakes seem to destroy the credibility of scripture. Biblical theology has struggled to distinguish between "correctness" in historical, biological, geographical, and similar matters, on the one side, and "truth" in a theological sense, on the other side, without introducing a dualistic separation between faith and history. Modern theology recognizes that the "truth" of the Bible is "salvation truth," which God reveals in scriptures (for Catholic theology see Vat. II, *Dei verbum* 12). Therefore, the challenge of biblical theology can be seen as identifying and interpreting the biblical text in relation to the truth that frees (John 8:32).

Inspiration. Biblical theology needs a concept of inspiration that is rooted in the witness of the biblical writings. Key texts such as 2 Timothy 3:16–17 and 2 Peter 1:20–21 promote a personal and ecclesial understanding of inspiration: God enables human beings to say his Word in their words in order to build up the faith of recipients. This concept is in tension with an understanding of inspiration that sees it as a direct deposit of knowledge about God, like that of Philo (*Moses* 2.188ff.; *Decalogue* 18) or of 2 Esdras 14:38–44. Instead, it is closer to the idea of Josephus in which the prophets both receive a word from God and relate their own observations (*Ag. Ap.* 1.37–41). A biblical theology that is true to the biblical text must criticize theories that neglect the human factor and construct a theory that articulates the capacity of some persons to speak and write in a way that hearers and readers are able to recognize the Word of God in what they have spoken or written.

The Special Question. From a New Testament point of view, the special issue is the relationship between the witness about Jesus Christ in the New Testament and the Old Testament witness about the history of Israel with God. Biblical theology must address the question of how to read the Old Testament as the first part of holy scripture, written "before Christ," and how to read the New Testament as the second part of the same holy scripture, written "in Christ."

Old and new. The theological relationship between the "Old" Testament and the "New" Testament is complicated because Jesus claims for his ministry the "new" of God's eschatological action (Mark 2:22) and proclaims the gospel as the dynamic realization of God's promise; he has not come "to abolish the law or the prophets…but to fulfill" (Matt 5:17–20). The newness of the gospel reflects the eschatological event of Jesus's mission; at the same time it is an eschatological affirmation of the "scripture" because it reveals the righteousness of God, who is true.

Because of this theological structure, the relationship between the two testaments in the one Bible is both problematic and unbalanced. It is problematic because in the first century the terms "Old Testament" and "New Testament" are not used as labels for the two collections of books. Hebrews, however, compares the former covenant, which was weak because it was unable to forgive sins in an eschatological way, with the Christ covenant, which is strong because it overcomes sin and brings life to its best end, the presence of God (Heb 9:1—10:18). The relationship between the Old Testament and New Testament is unbalanced because, in the view of the early Christian writings, there is a (more or less open) unity of "the Torah of Moses, the prophets, and the psalms" (Luke 24:44), while the New Testament is *in statu nascendi.*

Nevertheless, it is possible to discuss the relation between the two because the "scriptures" are a refer-ence point sui generis for the New Testament writings. Furthermore, early Christian literature (whose most important products are later collected as the New Testament) built a network of references to the Old Testament.

Theological significance. Three things make discussion of the relationship between the two testaments in the one holy scripture theologically significant. First, for Jesus, Paul, and the other apostles, as well as for the Evangelists, a constructive relationship with the Bible of Israel is essential for their own message and theology. Examples of this relationship include the present form of the New Testament starting with a genealogy of Jesus from Abraham (Matt 1:1–17), which is a short summary of the history of Israel; Jesus's double commandment, which is a combination of Deuteronomy 6:4–5 and Leviticus 19:18 (//Mark 12:28–34); the New Testament justification theology, which is grounded in an exegesis of Genesis 15:6 (Rom 4:3; 9:22; Gal 3:6; cf. Jas 2:23); and the final vision of Revelation, which recalls Isaiah's heaven and new earth (Rev 21:1–8; Isa 65:17; 66:2).

Second, the relationship between the Old and New Testaments is the core of the relationship between Jews and Christians. The Old Testament is the full Bible for Jews who have their own traditions of interpretation. Jesus and the early church establish a new hermeneutic that included an eschatological reading of the Jewish Bible, which was familiar in some tendencies of Second Temple Judaism, and a Christological reading, which was prepared by Jesus and elaborated by the first Christian theologians. To describe the hermeneutical relationship of the two testaments in the perspectives of both, Jewish and Christian exegesis is a cornerstone of an interreligious dialogue between Jews and Christians.

Third, reflection on the relationship between the two testaments in one and the same Christian Bible is an essential aspect of a theological understanding of the Bible as holy scripture. The dimensions of time and space are essential in the Christian Bible: the Christ-event marks a cut and a bridge in time between "before" and "after" as well as between heaven and earth. From a New Testament perspective, Jesus Christ is the perfect reader of scripture and the central key for understanding its truth of salvation. On the other side, the so-called Old Testament provides the special key to understanding the gospel through the traces of God's righteousness present there and through interpreting the mission to all nations as fulfillment of God's promise.

Traditional Answers. In the traditional hermeneutic, understanding begins with the New Testament and goes back to the Old Testament. Following the New Testament, this method portrays Jesus Christ as the true reader and exegete of the Jewish Bible. The leading idea was that scripture had two meanings, the literal sense and the spiritual sense (Origen, *Princ.*). In Platonic theory the truth is present but hidden in the letter and opened in the Spirit. In this way the Torah, especially with its commandments about pureness and holiness, sacrifice and priesthood, violence and punishment, was interpreted as symbolic of a truth that was perfectly revealed by Jesus Christ: the truth of faith, love, and hope. In ancient times this hermeneutic of the twofold sense of the scripture realized the possibility of a coherent interpretation of the Bible as a whole—in the way of the *interpretatio Christiana*. The dogmatic, ethical, and eschatological content of the Bible could be identified in the interpretations of the ecclesial tradition.

The anchor of this interpretation is the New Testament itself. Paul argues sometimes from the literal sense (Gal 3:16) and sometimes with the spiritual meaning, especially with a typological (1 Cor 10:1–13) or allegorical (Gal 4:21–31) interpretation. These methods were not unusual in the Judaism of his time, especially among Pharisees and the Qumran community. The distinctive element of the New Testament is its Christological reference.

In the twenty-first century, the problems inherent in this model of interpretation are clear. (1) Because scripture is read with the eyes of the present ecclesial faith, it is difficult to distinguish between scripture and tradition; this differentiation is necessary in critical theology, although the richness and critical function of the "canon" need explication and communication. (2) While the special link between the literal and the spiritual sense is unclear, a methodical reading needs transparency and clarity.

(3) It is problematic to emphasize a Christological understanding, even though the gospels portray Jesus himself engaged in dialogue with scripture and contemporaneous Jewish interpretation.

The traditional answer is of historic importance, and it remains relevant insofar as it asks in which ways other hermeneutical models can ascertain the actual meaning of scripture. Interpreters need new approaches that integrate the historical dimension of biblical theology and the dialogue between the two testaments, including the dialogue between Jewish and Christian theology about hermeneutical methods.

Historical–Critical Models. Humanism inspired Western theology to study anew the original languages of scripture. For the New Testament two scholars were of most importance: Francisco Jiménez (Ximenes) de Cisneros in Spain, who in 1514 finished the New Testament of the later published Complutensian Polyglot Bible, and Erasmus from Rotterdam, who in 1516 published the critical Greek New Testament (*Novum Testamentum omne*) that became the basis of Luther's translation into German. The Enlightenment critiqued the ideas of revelation and (verbal) inspiration. The critique of David Hume and others was directed against the miracles of Jesus, the resurrection and empty tomb, the virginity of Mary, and other accounts of the miraculous. The breakthrough of historical thinking (Johann Gustav Droysen, Wilhelm Dilthey, and Paul Yorck von Wartenburg), however, contributed the possibility of a historical reading of the Bible that also has a theological impact.

The concept of historical–critical exegesis arose in this context. Its relation to biblical theology created great tensions and great opportunities. On the one side, the historical approach seemed to neglect theological exegesis and the orientation of the canon as a whole. In the nineteenth century William Wrede (1897) claimed a pure *Religionsgeschichte* as the consequence of an objective science that must be independent from church authority. In the twentieth century Räisänen (1990) pled for exegesis beyond theology in favor of hermeneutical fairness and a sense of interreligious rapprochement. On the other side, traditional Catholic exegesis tried to avoid historical–critical exegesis in order to maintain the theological substance of the

Bible; this was the policy of the Pontifical Biblical Commission, from their foundation in 1902 until the mid-twentieth century. Both extremes are problematic because they assume an understanding of truth, inspiration, authority, and theology that is nonhistorical, while in the biblical teaching the relationship to historicity is essential.

Between these extremes a wide and seminal field of interaction between historical–critical exegesis and biblical theology was cultivated in modern Protestant theology. The doctrine of *sola scriptura* seems to require the search for the dogmatic substance of Christian faith in the Bible, especially in the New Testament. A paradigm was the idea of Heinrich Julius Holtzmann (1911). He sought to identify the *Lehrbegriffe* ("religious teachings") which should fit together as parts of a coherent system of original theology. The problem with this concept is twofold: (1) it is self-contradictory for these concepts to be the result of historical and philological research and then to stand as eternal pillars of theological truth, and (2) the resultant theology should genuinely reflect the meaning of the text but is in reality a mirroring of Protestant grace theology seen with the eyes of a nineteenth-century German academic. Weinel (1928) tried to integrate the Old Testament programmatically into Christian biblical theology, but he did so at the cost of reducing it to some ethical principles influenced by Kant. Thus, biblical theology lost the elements of redemption theology and Christology. Adolf Schlatter (1909) tried to integrate a historical reconstruction of the teaching of Jesus and the teaching of the apostles with a theological interpretation of the revelation event. This attempt is significant in principle but problematic insofar as it gives little place to the Old Testament and fails to include a dialogue with tradition, especially its ecumenical aspects. Nineteenth-century research did more to demonstrate the problems of a hermeneutical integration of biblical theology and New Testament exegesis than it did to contributing ideas for fruitful dialogue.

Theological Models. The problems of a theologically oriented exegesis were carefully analyzed by Rudolf Bultmann (1984). His hermeneutical decision was significant in itself. He argued that the theology of the New Testament must be independent of the results of research regarding historical events and tradition-historical relations; it must interpret only the kerygma, and it has to do it through an existentialist interpretation (*existentiale interpretation*) so that modern-day people can hear the gospel. The consequences are threefold: (1) Bultmann underestimated the New Testament's relationship to the Old Testament because the Old Testament seems to be only a presupposition, not a vital element of New Testament theology; (2) Bultmann depended on a philosophical anthropology without criticizing it from the perspective of biblical theology; and (3) Bultmann pleaded for modernity but did not reflect on how hearing the Word of God in the present needs historical thinking.

Bultmann's concept was nevertheless very influential. German "New Testament theology" is particularly inclined to highlight the "newness" of the gospel to such an extent that it concentrates only on the New Testament. Georg Strecker (1996) stresses the critique of law by Jesus and Paul as a reason for this emphasis. Ferdinand Hahn (2011a; 2011b) argues for this "newness" from the eschatological character of Jesus's mission, death, and resurrection. Udo Schnelle (2007) underlines the influence of Hellenistic traditions in the formation of the New Testament as evidence of this "newness." The problem of these sharp differentiations between the two testaments is that they presuppose an understanding of "unity" that is too static. What these views see correctly, however, is (1) that the New Testament insists that "everything has become new" (2 Cor 5:17) and (2) that the Bible is not a closed shop of tradition building but a communication platform of interchange and identity building.

In a critique of Bultmann's "sublime Docetism" (Ernst Käsemann), other scholars place New Testament theology within a horizon of biblical theology. The concepts, however, are different. Hans Hübner (1990–1995), influenced by Hans Georg Gadamer's hermeneutic of *Wirkungsgeschichte* ("reception history"), distinguishes between the *Vetus Testamentum in se* ("Old Testament in itself"), which would be of only historical interest, and the *Vetus Testamentum in Novo receptum* ("Old Testament as received in the New"), which would belong to the center of New Testament theology. This distinction is important for identifying the way the New Testament authors understood and used the Old Testament; but the sharp distinction between *in se* and "reception" does not fit the New Testament itself, which sees the Old Testament as unity. Influenced by Pietism, Peter Stuhlmacher (1991–1995) follows the signs of the New Testament writings when he programmatically interprets essential New Testament texts and motives in the light of the Old Testament, identifying the confession of the One God as the core of the New Testament. Influenced by Wolfhart Pannenberg, who transformed Hegel's philosophy of history into history as revelation, Ulrich Wilckens (2001–2009) built his *Theology of the New Testament* on a historical approach that finds theology in the process of the communication of revelation. He traces a process that starts with Jesus as he is seen in the gospels, moves to his death and resurrection as they are interpreted in the New Testament, and then moves through the ongoing tradition that results in the formation of the canon. In this tracing of early theology, he integrates the Old Testament as theological testimony that essentially belongs to the New Testament. Stuhlmacher and Wilckens manage to integrate historical research and theological orientation, but their hermeneutics minimizes the differences between the two testaments and lacks a dialogue with the Jewish exegesis of the "Old Testament."

Wilhelm Thüsing (1981–1999), in dialogue with Karl Rahner, focused on Jesus himself as the theocentric nerve of biblical theology. The theological dimension of the historical context is essential for Jesus.

Canonical Approaches. Two Old Testament scholars, Brevard S. Childs (1992) and James A. Sanders (1987), have made proposals of biblical theology that are important for New Testament theology. Childs favors a hermeneutic of complementarity between Old Testament and New Testament theologies. This concept is interesting insofar as it maintains the dogmatic status of the Old Testament for Christian faith and doctrine, but it is problematic insofar as it reduces theology to the teaching portions of the text without integrating the narrative and historical elements of the biblical books into its theological system. Sanders rejects a purely textual orientation,

arguing that the people of God are the primary readers addressed by the Bible, and they are called to construct its theological meaning. This view has the advantage of integrating the text into a context whose primary task is the construction of meaning. But this approach does not take sufficient account of the need to develop a Christian theology of Israel in order to avoid a substitution hermeneutic. In addition, it needs criteria for differentiating between scripture and tradition.

Canonical approaches may offer new insights if both testaments are reconstructed as reception of the gospel and if the biblical theology of the Word of God is methodically integrated into a biblical theology of the New Testament. Then it would be possible to combine historical positions and interactions with the theological perspectives and positions of the New Testament writings in their own relation to the gospel. In this way a network of different theologies in the time of Jesus and the apostles and their first successors can be recognized that needs the Old Testament, in both its Jewish and Christian interpretations, as its counterpart and communication partner. In this way biblical theology is not the last norm but the essential orientation of theological thinking and Christian life.

[*See also* Canon; Christ; Christology; Covenant; Eschatology; Gospel; Hermeneutics, Biblical; *and* Scripture.]

BIBLIOGRAPHY

History of Research

Kümmel, Werner Georg. *Das Neue Testament: Geschichte der Erforschung seiner Probleme.* Orbis Academicus. Freiburg, Germany: Verlag Karl Alber, 1970. First published 1958.

Merk, Otto. *Biblische Theologie des Neuen Testaments in ihrer Anfangszeit: Ihre methodischen Probleme bei Johann Philipp Gabler und Georg Lorenz und deren Nachwirkungen.* Marburger Theologische Studien 9. Marburg, Germany: Elwert, 1972.

Reventlow, Henning Graf. *Epochen der Bibelauslegung.* Vol. 1: *Vom Alten Testament bis Origenes*; Vol. 2: *Von der Spätantike bis zum ausgehenden Mittelalter*; Vol. 3: *Renaissance, Reformation, Humanismus*; Vol. 4: *Von der Aufklärung bis zum 20.* Munich: Beck, 1990–2001.

Strecker, Georg, ed. *Das Problem der Theologie des Neuen Testaments*. Wege der Forschung 367. Darmstadt, Germany: Wissenschaftliche Buchgesellschaft, 1975.

New Testament and Biblical Theology

Auwers, J.-M., and H. J. de Jonge, eds. *The Biblical Canons*. Bibliotheca ephemeridium theologicarum Lovaniensum 163. Leuven, Belgium: Peeters, 2003.

Berger, Klaus. *Theologiegeschichte des Urchristentums: Theologie des Neuen Testaments*. Tübingen, Germany: Francke Verlag, 1996.

Bultmann, Rudolf. *Theologie des Neuen Testaments (1948–1953)*. Edited by Otto Merk. Tübingen, Germany: J. C. B. Mohr, 1984.

Caird, G. B. *New Testament Theology*. Edited by L. D. Hurst. Oxford: Clarendon, 1994.

Childs, Brevard S. *Biblical Theology of the Old and New Testaments: Theological Reflection on the Christian Bible*. London: SCM, 1992.

Dormeyer, Detlev. *Einführung in die Theologie des Neuen Testaments*. Darmstadt, Germany: Wissenschaftliche Buchgesellschaft, 2010.

Gnilka, Joachim. *Theologie des Neuen Testaments*. Herders Theologisher Kommentar zum Alten Testament Supplementband 5. Freiburg, Germany: Herder, 1994.

Goppelt, Leonhard. *Theologie des Neuen Testaments*. Edited by Jürgen Roloff. Uni-Taschenbücher 850. Göttingen, Germany: Vandenhoeck & Ruprecht, 1978.

Hahn, Ferdinand. *Theologie des Neuen Testaments*. Vol. 1: *Die Vielfalt des Neuen Testaments*. Tübingen, Germany: Mohr, 2011a. First published 2002.

Hahn, Ferdinand. *Theologie des Neuen Testaments*. Vol. 2: *Die Einheit des Neuen Testaments*. Tübingen, Germany: Mohr, 2011b. First published 2002.

Holtzmann, Heinrich Julius. *Lehrbuch der neutestamentlichen Theologie*. 2 vols. Edited by Adolf Jülicher and Walter Bauer. Tübingen, Germany: Mohr (Siebeck), 1911.

Hübner, Hans. *Biblische Theologie des Neuen Testaments*. Vol. 1: *Prolegomena*; Vol. 2: *Die Theologie des Paulus und ihre neutestamentliche Wirkungsgeschichte*; Vol. 3: *Hebräerbrief, Evangelien und Offenbarung, Epilegomena*. Göttingen, Germany: Vandenhoeck & Ruprecht, 1990–1995.

Ladd, George Eldon. *A Theology of the New Testament*. Grand Rapids, Mich.: Eerdmans, 1974.

Marshall, I. Howard. *New Testament Theology: Many Witnesses, One Gospel*. Downers Grove, Ill.: InterVarsity, 2004.

Pontifical Biblical Commission. *The Interpretation of the Bible in the Church*. Boston: Pauline Books & Media, 1993.

Pontifical Bible Commission. *The Jewish People and Their Sacred Scriptures in the Christian Bible*. Boston: Pauline Books & Media, 2001.

Räisänen, Heikki. *Beyond New Testament Theology*. London: SCM, 1990.

Sanders, James A. *From Sacred Story to Sacred Text*. Philadelphia: Fortress, 1987.

Schlatter, D. A. *Die Theologie des Neuen Testaments und die Dogmatik*. 2 vols. Gütersloh, Germany: Bertelsmann, 1909.

Schnelle, Udo. *Theologie des Neuen Testaments*. Göttingen, Germany: Vandenhoeck & Ruprecht, 2007.

Segalla, Giuseppe. *Teologia Biblica del Nuovo Testamento*. Turin, Italy: Elledici, 2006.

Söding, Thomas. *Einheit der Heiligen Schrift? Zur Theologie des biblischen Kanons*. Quaestiones Disputatae 211. Freiburg, Germany: Herder, 2005.

Strecker, Georg. *Neutestamentliche Theologie*. Edited by Friedrich Wilhelm Horn. Berlin: De Gruyter, 1996.

Stuhlmacher, Peter. *Biblische Theologie des Neuen Testaments*. Vol. 1: *Grundlegung: Von Jesus zu Paulus*; Vol. 2: *Von der Paulusschule zur Johannesoffenbarung*. Göttingen, Germany: Vandenhoeck & Ruprecht, 1991–1995.

Thüsing, Wilhelm. *Die neutestamentlichen Theologien und Jesus Christus: Grundlegung einer Theologie des Neuen Testaments*. Vol. 1: *Kriterien aufgrund der Rückfrage nach Jesus und des Glaubens an seine Auferweckung*; Vol. 2: *Programm einer Theologie des Neuen Testaments mit Perspektiven für eine Biblische Theologie*; Vol. 3: *Einzigkeit Gottes und Jesus-Christus-Ereignis*. Münster, Germany: Aschendorff, 1981–1999.

Weinel, H. *Biblische Theologie des Neuen Testaments: Die Religion Jesu und die Urchristentums*. Tübingen, Germany: Mohr (Siebeck), 1928.

Wilckens, Urich. *Theologie des Neuen Testaments*. 2 vols. Neukirchen-Vluyn, Germany: Neukirchener, 2002–2009.

Wrede, William. *Über Aufgabe und Methode der sogenannten Neutestamentlichen Theologie*. Göttingen, Germany: Vandenhoeck & Ruprecht, 1897.

Thomas Söding

THEOPHANY

The word is derived from the Greek *theos* ("god") and *phainein* ("to appear"). It appropriately denotes those passages in scripture that describe some visible evidence of God's presence on earth, although it is often used more freely, with reference to divine speech, without anything being said of sight. In spite of such explicit statements as "no one shall see me and live" (Exod 33:20b) and "No one has ever seen God" (John 1:18), scripture records various visible manifestations that are identified with the real presence of God. The authors ordinarily do so very carefully, lest they write anything that might support idolatry. Yahweh could not be represented by anything in creation (Deut 4:15–19), but they seem to have found it necessary to record accounts of the personal appearance of God within the created world. No author reveals a sense of uneasiness about reporting divine speech. At Sinai, all the people heard God speak (Deut 4:12; 5:24). God spoke when there were as yet no ears to hear (Gen 1:3–19), and he is fully known through his Word (John 1:1, 14, 18). Auditions are often reported in a remarkably matter-of-fact way, but when something is visible, that is another matter. They were events that evidently had to be reported, sometimes with remarkable boldness but usually very cautiously, for they ran the risk of making Yahweh seem to be like the gods of the nations who took on human or even animal forms.

"Theophany" is not a form-critical term, for it is applied to a variety of literary types that speak of God's appearance on earth. This article will use the question of visibility as a way to organize various forms of divine self-manifestation, following the literal meaning of "theophany"—appearance of God—and of the introductions to several Old Testament texts: "and Yahweh/God appeared" (rā'â, nip'al; lit. "was seen"). This will emphasize the issue for the writers, whether there is anything about God himself that can be seen.

Sound without Sight. There are narratives set in daily life, called "theophanies" by some scholars, in which God is said to have appeared to an individual; but nothing is said about what that person may have seen (Gen 12:7; 17:1; 26:2, 24; 35:9; 48:3). Other texts do not even introduce the divine message with "appear." For example, God was present with Adam and Eve in the garden, so some identify this as a theophany; but we are told that they heard God, not that they saw anything (Gen 3:8, 10). The Lord came and stood by Samuel's bed in the night (1 Sam 3:10), suggesting that God may have assumed a human form; but the author of the passage will say only that the Lord revealed himself to Samuel by "the word" (1 Sam 3:21). In spite of the verb "appear" that is sometimes used, these texts speak only of a God who is known by his word.

The Divine Messenger. A similar genre, also set in daily life, involves the appearance of an angel (mal'āk, lit. "messenger"), who speaks the word of God. As human messengers spoke the words of the ones who sent them, so angels spoke God's own word, in the first person; but they were intermediaries, not to be identified with God (note the words of the angel in Judg 6:11–23). Hagar described her experience in the wilderness as a theophany: "Have I really seen God and remained alive after seeing him?" But the author wrote that she saw an angel (Gen 16:7–13). Manoah said, "We shall surely die, for we have seen God," even though the author of the story says repeatedly that he and his wife saw an angel, who is also simply called a man (Judg 13:3–22). The angel who confronted Balaam is said to have carried a sword, so presumably this was a human-like figure (Num 22:22, 31–35). Joshua also encountered a man carrying a sword who identified himself as "commander of the army of the LORD" (Josh 5:13–15), and whenever anything is said in the Old Testament about what an angel looks like, he is called a man (Dan 8:15; 9:21; 10:16, 18; Zech 1:8; cf. Mark 16:5; Luke 24:4).

We do not know what the angel who appeared to Abraham from heaven (Gen 22:11–12) or the one who spoke to Joseph in a dream (Gen 31:11–13) looked like. In Exodus 3:2–4, an angel of the Lord appeared to Moses "in a flame of fire out of a bush," so Moses saw a figure of some sort; then God called to him out of the bush. The passage thus begins with a suggestion that God addressed Moses via an angel, but what follows is all introduced as the direct speech of the Lord. The use of "angel" in verse 2 thus seems to be an example of biblical authors' tendencies to avoid suggesting that God is visible in any way.

Two possible exceptions to the above statement appear in Genesis. When "the LORD appeared to Abraham" in Genesis 18:1–2, he saw three men, to whom he offered the appropriate hospitality. In a tantalizing way, the author seems to identify one of the three men as Yahweh himself (vv. 13, 17, 20, 22–33). If the two angels of Genesis 19:1 are supposed to be identified with the other two men of chapter 18, then the author has quite boldly claimed that Yahweh might appear on earth in the form of a man who would even eat and drink as Abraham's guest (18:8). This is so unusual that many interpreters prefer to speak of all three of the men as angels.

Even less clear is the narrative in Genesis 32:24–30 since it all took place in the dark. Without any reason provided, an unidentified man wrestled with Jacob until daybreak. He refused to give Jacob his name but did bless him, leading Jacob to believe he had been in the presence of God: "I have seen the God face to face, and yet my life is preserved." Jacob's affirmation includes three important issues in the study of theophany. (1) To see God is potentially life-threatening, as Hagar and Manoah had said (but no one is ever said to die that way). (2) "Seeing" need not mean actual physical sight since Jacob's experience happened in the dark. Other texts will provide abundant support for the use of "see" to mean experience or understand. (3) "Face to face" also need not involve sight but is an idiom for close personal communication (see Exod 33:11). Note that Hosea either knew a variant form of the story or refused to take Jacob's statement literally, for his recounting of the patriarch's career states, "He strove with the angel and prevailed" (Hos 12:4). The stories about angels are thus not full theophanies, but they need to be included in the study since they are one way that the writers of scripture could insist that God does draw close to people, sometimes using a human form to do so, while mostly succeeding quite well in protecting his otherness.

The Disruption of Nature. A very different genre depicts the coming of the Lord, to save or to judge, in powerful poetry that describes the uproar in nature—storm and earthquake—caused by his coming. God is given a personality that is not emphasized (or usually even mentioned) in the other texts that concern us. He is angry (Ps 18:7; Isa 13:9, 13; 30:27; 59:17; Jer 10:10; 23:19–20//30:23–24; Ezek 38:19; Nah 1:2, 6; Hab 3:8, 12) and has come, is coming, or will come to annihilate his enemies (Isa 13:11; Jer 51:29; Ezek 38:22; Nah 1:2–3, 8) and/or to save those who call upon him (Ps 18:16–19; Nah 1:7; Hab 3:13). A few passages explicitly describe God as a warrior with some visible human qualities (Ps 18:14; Isa 59:15b–20; 63:1–6; Hab 3:8–15).

In one sense, these texts fit the definition of theophany. They are descriptions of the appearance of God on earth. They do not contribute much, however, to the question this article is tracing: does scripture ever really claim that God has been visible to anyone and, if so, in what form was he seen? The authors need not have witnessed in full the scenes described in these poems. They use in creative ways the terrifying natural phenomena that everyone in the Middle East had experienced, combining them occasionally with the divine warrior theme that was a well-known part of the cultural environment, in order to glorify the God whom psalmists and prophets believed was truly the master of the entire cosmos and the upholder of justice.

A few of the poets claim to have experienced the theophany. The longest and most impressive passages, Psalm 18:7–16 and Habakkuk 3:3–15, do make that claim; but the psalmist's description of his distress and his salvation (18:4–5, 16) strongly suggests that although he had intense feelings of God's presence, all the language in verses 4–16 is purely figurative. Habakkuk seems to be describing a vision of the coming of the mighty divine warrior, and its effects on him are remarkable (3:16–19); but he introduces his reaction to it all with "I hear" (3:16). He does not say what he has heard.

With one exception these poems do not introduce a message from God, as the types discussed earlier have done. The exception is Psalm 50:1–3, which although just a fragment, does introduce a divine word by speaking of God coming (from Zion) and shining forth with a devouring fire and a mighty tempest.

Texts such as Psalms 18, 29, 50, and 77; Habakkuk 3; and the fragmentary theophanies elsewhere in the Psalter (Pss 68:7–8; 97:2–5; 114:3–8; 144:5–7; cf. Deut 33:2; Judg 5:4–5) strongly suggest that they are poems produced by visionaries for use in worship. They described the overwhelming power of God so effectively that prophets also used elements of the same language when they announced the imminent coming of Yahweh to judge his people (Amos 1:2; Mic 1:2–4) or the nations (Isa 13:9–13; 30:27–33; 50:2–3; 59:15b–20; 63:1–6; Jer 23:19–20//30:23–24; Ezek 38:19–23; Joel 3:16; Nah 1:3–8; Zech 9:14).

At Mt. Sinai. Most of the natural phenomena that are described in the poems also were present when God appeared at Mt. Sinai. Yahweh manifested himself by coming down (*yārad*) to the top of the mountain "in the sight of all" (Exod 19:11, 20), and his presence was made known by a trumpet blast (*yōbēl* in 19:13b; *šōpār* in 19:16, 19; 20:18), probably a warning signal here, blown on a ram's horn by someone, not some natural phenomenon. "In the sight of all" were thunder, lightning, cloud (19:16; 20:18; 24:15, 18), smoke, fire (19:18; 20:18; 24:17), and earthquake (19:18), daunting indications that Yahweh was present; but he was hidden in thick darkness (20:21). When God spoke with Moses on the mountain it was in the midst of a cloud (19:9; 24:15–18) or thick darkness, so at this point in Exodus there is no suggestion that Moses saw God. That will come in Exodus 33.

This is a major, audible self-revelation of God, for all the people are said to have heard his voice, speaking the Ten Commandments (Exod 20:1). Deuteronomy emphasizes that it was a personal experience of God but only through a voice, with nothing of God himself visible. "You heard the sound of words but saw no form; there was only a voice" (Deut 4:12; cf. 4:15–19, 33, 36; 5:22). The natural phenomena of the poetic theophanies and the Sinai event reveal the matchless power of Yahweh, but they also hide him. The Sinai event becomes revelation (unlike the poems, except for Ps 50) because God speaks.

Exodus 24:9–11. The structure of Exodus 19–34 has frustrated every scholar who has tried to explain it. It appears that here and there the final author has included fragments of very old traditions, thinking it was necessary to preserve them even though they did not fit very well. Once such text is Exodus 24:9–11. It does not fit the context at all. Seventy-four men go up the mountain and apparently have a vision of heaven there, for nothing is said of cloud or fire or deep darkness. The author dares to write that they saw God and even that God had feet, but beyond that he will describe only "something like a pavement of sapphire stone." This put the men in great danger, but "God did not lay his hands" on them; and they participated in some sort of meal in God's very presence: "also they beheld God, and they ate and drank." This

amazing experience is left without any explanation or consequence. Since the mention of shining pavement suggests they saw a vision of heaven, this passage would not fit the definition of theophany as an appearance of God on earth; but like the other visions to be discussed, it is important for its suggestion that God might be seen in something like a human form.

Exodus 33. The golden calf incident (Exod 32) led to a long discussion between God and Moses (Exod 32:7–14; chs. 33–34) over the question of whether there could be any future relationship between God and these people. Divine presence became the subject of a difficult conversation between Moses and God, now located in the tent of meeting, which stood outside the camp. This can be called another theophany. It has a unique form, and it includes many of the terms associated with theophany elsewhere: *pānîm* (face, presence; Exod 33:11, 14, 15, 20, 23), glory (33:16, 22), pass before (*'ābar*; 33:19, 22; 34:6), and see God (33:20, 23; 33:18). The conversation is full of non sequiturs, very likely because the author has taken on the very risky task of claiming to record a closer personal encounter between a human being and God than we can find anywhere else. Once God had assured Moses that he would continue to go with the people (33:12–17), Moses responded, "Show me your glory, I pray" (33:18). God's glory then passed by (*'ābar*) Moses in a completely mysterious way. Since "no one shall see me and live" (33:20), Moses could be permitted to see God's back but not God's face. We are not told whether that actually happened (33:21–23 and see the continuation in 34:1, 5, 8–9).

Glory, fire, cloud. Interpreters have always taken this to be a request for a personal, mystical experience of God, even surpassing his "face-to-face" conversations (Exod 33:11). Moses and all the people had already seen God's glory, however (16:7, 10; 24:16–17) and would see it again (29:43; 40:34–35). The glory in the cloud had accompanied them through the wilderness this far, and Moses's request ought to be understood simply as an appeal for the journey to recommence under God's guidance; and it does (34:9). Glory and fire, often associated with a cloud (Exod 16:10; 24:15–18; 40:34–38; Num 16:42; Deut 5:4), were evidence for the presence of the Lord but hid him from sight. In Exodus

24:17 and 29:3; Deuteronomy 5:24; and Ezekiel 1:27–28, 10:4, and 43:2 glory is a blinding light, associated with the supernatural fire that appears elsewhere in theophanies. That glory is always visible (Lev 9:6, 23–24; Num 14:10, 22; 16:19, 42; 20:6; Deut 5:24; 1 Kgs 8:11; cf. Luke 2:9), so these passages are typical of most theophanies: God appears but is hidden.

Fire represented the presence of the Lord in the unique covenant-making ceremony recorded in Genesis 15. Abraham saw in a vision "a smoking fire pot and a flaming torch" (15:17), surely not to be taken as the form of God in any sense but as a sign of his presence.

Face, presence. The word *pānîm* ("face") in Exodus 33 deserves attention for the ways it is used with reference to the presence of God, for other authors will speak of seeing God's face. The word is used idiomatically many times, to mean "presence," not one's literal face. As a synecdoche, *pānîm* refers to the whole person, so "face to face" means in close personal contact, not always involving sight (e.g., Gen 32:30; Num 14:14; Deut 5:4; Ezek 20:35). It is *pānîm* that is translated "presence" in Exodus 33:14, 15, but something more physical seems to be meant by "you cannot see my face" and "my face shall not be seen" (33:20, 25). The use of "back" as the counterpart of "face" may just tell us that there is no vocabulary available to provide an actual description of Moses's unique relationship with God.

Elijah at Horeb/Sinai. The contrast between sight and sound reappears in another theophany at what is presumably the same mountain (1 Kgs 19:1–18). When Queen Jezebel threatened Elijah's life after his victory in the contest with the prophets of Baʿal on Mt. Carmel, he fled to Horeb, the mountain of God, "and behold, the LORD passed by" (19:11; lit.). Then there was wind, earthquake, and fire; but the Lord was not in them. Translating the Hebrew very literally, what followed was "a sound of thin silence" (19:12). Into that numinous silence came the voice of the Lord. All the uproar may perhaps just identify that mountain as the mountain of Moses, for the Lord is known only through his word.

Dreams and Visions. Dreams and visions do not fit some definitions of theophany since everything is in the mind, not a physical appearance on earth. But they need to be compared with the other texts because of the many parallels between them and because they contribute something to the question of whether and how God may actually make himself known to humans.

Dreams. Sometimes God spoke in a dream, and nothing is said about sight (Gen 20:3; 1 Kgs 3:5; cf. Num 12:6; Job 33:15–17; Joel 2:28). Jacob, however, saw in his dream a ladder connecting earth with heaven, and we are told that the Lord stood (*niṣṣāb*) beside or above him (the preposition *ʿal* can be translated either way) and spoke with him (Gen 28:10–22). Presumably he saw a figure of some sort, but nothing is described. In the book of Job, Eliphaz claimed to have experienced a vision of the night in which a mysterious form appeared and spoke to him (Job 4:12–21). He left unsaid whether he thought that form represented God's own presence.

Visions. Others speak of visions in which they did see God, in human form. Micaiah, son of Imlah, boldly claimed, "I saw the LORD sitting on his throne" (1 Kgs 22:19–23). He added nothing more of what he saw; the rest of his vision was entirely speech. Isaiah's similar vision ("I saw the LORD sitting on a throne") includes one not particularly helpful detail: "the hem of his robe filled the temple" (Isa 6:1). Amos introduced a word from God in the briefest way: "I saw the LORD standing beside the altar" (Amos 9:1).

Ezekiel's vision contained a great deal more detail, although he carefully qualified everything he said. Although he claimed to have seen "something that seemed like a human form" seated above the likeness of a throne, his summary of the vision provided a triple qualification of everything: "This was the appearance of the likeness of the glory of the LORD" (Ezek 1:28).

Daniel would not say outright that he saw God in his vision, and in fact everything in Daniel 7 is symbolic. The beasts in Daniel 7:3–8 represent the four world empires, the "one like a human being" (lit. "son of man," 7:13) represents the people of the holy ones of the Most High (7:27); so the ancient one is not God but represents God, and his white clothing and hair are to be interpreted symbolically, not taken as descriptive (7:9). No symbol but a human being could be taken to represent God however.

Seeing God. Some of the psalms speak of Israelite worshippers seeing God in the Temple, and those remarkable statements have sometimes been explained as the effects of a theophany of some sort that occurred during worship. One of them is a direct statement of something that has happened: "So I have looked upon you in the sanctuary, beholding your power and glory" (Ps 63:2). Another affirms the possibility: "For the LORD is righteous; he loves righteous deeds; the upright shall behold his face" (Ps 11:7). Others speak of it as a hope (Pss 17:15; 27:4, 13; 42:2). The proposal that they speak of life after death has little to support it. The language of each text suggests that the psalmists refer to an experience in worship (esp. Pss 27:4 and 63:2), but they do not contain any of the terms associated with theophanies elsewhere. Since the verbs for seeing do not always refer to something visible but can refer to something understood (Gen 2:19; Hab 2:1; like the English "I see") or experienced (Ps 89:48, "see death"; Jer 5:12), it seems most likely that the psalmists used the words only to speak of a close personal experience of God's presence. If so, they contribute to the study of theophany evidence that "see God" could be used rather freely and not literally.

The author of the book of Job wrote of seeing and hearing God in a way that deserves a brief comment. Scholars sometimes refer to God's response to Job as a theophany since it begins, "Then the LORD answered Job out of the whirlwind" (Job 38:1). What follows is a long speech that calls upon Job to hear and answer, not to see anything; but Job 38 makes a new use of the language describing God's mastery of the natural world, so it seems likely that the author did intend to remind readers of theophanies—times when God came to save—even though here he mostly challenges Job. If theophany does lie in the background, it helps to account for Job's reaction: "I had heard of you by the hearing of the ear, but now my eye sees you" (42:5).

We have seen that God's essential manifestation of himself is by word, not by sight; and God has spoken at length here. Job seems to reverse that, making sight superior to sound, but this is not a puzzle if seeing is used as it is in the Psalms, to refer to an intensely powerful experience of the presence of God.

The reminder of theophanies in Job 38 would thus lead readers to understand Job's "seeing" as comparable to the life-changing, numinous experiences recorded in Psalm 18:49, Isaiah 6:5 and 8, Ezekiel 2:1, and Habakkuk 3:16–19.

The New Testament. Theophanies as they are described in the Old Testament do not occur in the New Testament, but reflections of them appear here and there. God addressed people via angels, not in person (Matt 1:20; 2:13; 28:2; Luke 1:11, 26; 2:9; a young man, Mark 16:5; men, Luke 24:4). The Transfiguration took place on a mountaintop, Jesus's clothing became dazzling white, a cloud overshadowed them, and a voice came from heaven (Mark 9:2–8 and pars.). Predictions of the coming of the Son of Man contain parallels to Old Testament accounts of the coming of God: "Then they will see the Son of Man coming in clouds with great power and glory" (Mark 13:26; cf. Matt 16:27; 25:31; Mark 8:38; 14:62; Luke 9:26; 21:27).

The author of Revelation reported a vision similar to those of the prophets and Daniel. He saw in heaven someone seated on a throne (4:2), surrounded by lightning and thunder (4:5), who is addressed by the elders in heaven as "our Lord and our God" (4:11; cf. 11:16). He looks like jasper and carnelian, another way of introducing brilliance of some sort into any effort to speak of a God who is in some way visible (4:3).

The delicate subject of seeing God does reappear. When Jesus said, "Blessed are the pure in heart, for they will see God" (Matt 5:8), this was certainly an eschatological promise. But in the Gospel according to John, Jesus said, "Whoever has seen me has seen the Father" (John 14:9; cf. 12:45; 14:11), so some scholars speak of Jesus himself as a theophany. What John understood by that quotation is explained, to a considerable extent, in the prologue to his gospel (1:1–18). He claims that the classic (though partial) theophany, God's manifestation of himself to Moses at Sinai, has now been made perfect with the coming of Jesus. The key words of Exodus 33–34 reappear in John 1:14, 16–18:

- "Glory": John 1:14; Exodus 33:18, 22
- "Grace": John 1:16; Exodus 33:19
- "Grace and truth": John 1:14, 17; Exodus 34:6 ("Faithfulness" is derived from a root that also means "truth")

- "See God": John 1:18; Exodus 33:20
- "Know God": John 1:18; Exodus 33:13

The insistence of the Old Testament that God can be known by humans through his Word was taken as John's starting point (1:1–5). He alluded to the theophanies that spoke of divine self-manifestation on earth, claiming something related to them but very new. When the Word became flesh, God became visible in a way that could not have been imagined earlier.

Theophany, Epiphany, and *Shekinah* in Postbiblical Literature. The term "theophany" occurs in the liturgy of the Eastern Orthodox Church, essentially meaning "revelation," for it is the name of the feast celebrated on January 6 in commemoration of the baptism of Jesus. The gospel texts describing his baptism are understood to be the record of the first revelation of God as Trinity: God the Son present on earth in the man Jesus, God the Father speaking from heaven, and God the Holy Spirit manifested visibly as a dove.

On the same date, other churches celebrate the Feast of Epiphany, a term related in meaning to theophany. The word "theophany" does not occur in the New Testament, but "epiphany" does appear in the Pastoral Epistles, denoting Christ's appearance on earth. Forms of the word *epiphaino* were widely used in Hellenistic Greek to denote helpful appearances on earth of various deities, and perhaps its association with other gods accounts for its limited use in the New Testament. It is used of the advent of Christ in 2 Timothy 1:10 and of his eventual return, in the last days, in 1 Timothy 6:14, 2 Timothy 4:1 and 8, and Titus 2:13. But the church has made a special use of the term, for the Feast of Epiphany is so called because it celebrates the appearance on earth of God to the Gentiles, viz., the visit of the Magi to the child Jesus in Bethlehem (Matt 2:1–12). The reports of Jesus's birth and baptism that have led to the use of these two terms in the liturgy do not reflect the language of the theophanies of the Old Testament in any significant way.

If the accounts of the appearances of the risen Christ in the gospels (and Acts 1) were intended to be understood as Thomas did, encounters with "my Lord and my God" (John 20:28), then the Old Testament theme of seeing God has reappeared. The way

these accounts are told bears scarcely any relationship to Old Testament theophanies however. For example, although there are hints of it in the empty tomb stories (the earthquake in Matt 28:2), when Jesus appears there is no cosmic upheaval and no sense of danger at being in the presence of God. The account of Christ's Ascension into heaven (Acts 1:9–11; Luke 24:21) was presumably intended to instruct the church that Christ would not appear on earth again until the eschaton. In spite of that, many reports of Christ's bodily appearance (distinct from visions) have been offered, from early times to the present. The question of their authenticity need not concern us here. They deserve a brief reference because they represent claims to have seen God, that is, the Son of God, Jesus, here on earth and because they differ significantly from Old Testament theophanies.

Bright light is the most consistent element of continuity. There are various other unexplainable features, but the figure the reporters usually see is a man with long hair, a beard and mustache, wearing a white robe and sandals—remarkably ordinary. References to fear and the sense of danger at being in the presence of God are not prominent, although the figure sometimes is judgmental. Usually he is a loving person who has come to help. That much is parallel to many theophanies, in which God comes to save; but the experience is expressed in very different language. Claims to have seen Jesus are controversial; but a more extreme one, a claim to have seen God in his fullness, is likely to be completely rejected by most Christians, so the cautions expressed in the theophanic language of the Old Testament still prevail.

The rabbis were concerned that passages in the Hebrew Bible that spoke of God appearing to humans might lead to idolatry, so they were careful to protect God's transcendence while at the same time finding it necessary to affirm his presence with his people. When "seeing God" appeared in the Hebrew text, the Aramaic translations (Targums) supplied "seeing the glory of God"; and when God was said to come to, dwell in, or leave a place, the word *shekinah* was substituted for "God" or the Tetragrammaton. The word, which means "presence," does not occur in the Hebrew Bible but was widely used in Judaism. God's *shekinah* was present everywhere but appeared with special intensity in the tabernacle and the Temple (e.g., *Num Rab.* 13.6). It would leave Israel as a result of injustice (*Sipra* 88d fin; *Deut Rab.* vi.14) but even accompanied Israel into exile in spite of their sins because of God's love (*Sipre Num* 161, f.62b–63a). It was present in the synagogue and with any individual seriously at prayer. "If two sit together and words of the Law [are spoken] between them, the Divine Presence rests between them" (*m. ʾAbot* 3.2). It was perceived by faith, not by sight, so the rabbis offered a quite negative answer to the question about seeing God.

[*See also* Angels; Apocalypticism; Exodus; Ezekiel; God and Gods; Heaven and Earth; Revelation; *and* Wisdom Literature.]

BIBLIOGRAPHY

Barr, James. "Theophany and Anthropomorphism in the Old Testament." *Vetus Testamentum Supplements* 7 (1960): 31–38.

Cherbonnier, Edward Lass. "The Logic of Biblical Anthropomorphism." *Harvard Theological Review* 55 (1962): 187–206.

Eaton, J. H. "The Origin and Meaning of Habakkuk iii." *Zeitschrift für die alttestamentliche Wissenschaft* 76 (1964): 144–171.

Eidevall, Gören. "Horeb Revisited: Reflections on the Theophany in 1 Kings 19." In *Enigmas and Images: Studies in Honor of Tryggve N. D. Mettinger*, edited by Göran Eidevall and Blazenka Scheuer, pp. 92–111. Winona Lake, Ind.: Eisenbrauns, 2011.

Hamori, Esther. *"When Gods Were Men": The Embodied God in Biblical and Near Eastern Literature.* Beihefte zur Zeitschrift für die alttestamentliche Wissenschaft 384. Berlin: De Gruyter, 2008.

Jeremias, Jorg. *Theophanie: Die Geschichte einer alttestamentliche Gattung.* Wissenschaftliche Monographien zum alten und neuen Testament 10. Neukirchen-Vluyn, Germany: Neukirchener Verlag, 1965.

Johnson, Aubrey R. "Aspects of the Use of the Term PNYM in the Old Testament." In *Festschrift Otto Eissfelt*, edited by Johann Fück, pp. 155–159. Halle, Germany: Max Niemyer, 1947.

Polak, Frank. "Theophany and Mediator: The Unfolding of a Theme in the Book of Exodus." In *Studies in the Book of Exodus: Redaction—Reception—Interpretation*, edited by Marc Vervenne, pp. 113–147. Bibliotheca Ephemeridum Theologicarum Lovaniensium 126. Leuven, Belgium: Leuven University Press, 1996.

Savran, George W. *Encountering the Divine: Theophany in Biblical Narrative.* London: T&T Clark, 2005.

Schmid, H. "Gottesbild, Gottesschau und Theophanie." *Judaica* 23 (1967): 241–254.

Smith, M. S. "'Seeing God' in the Psalms: The Background to the Beatific Vision in the Bible." *Catholic Biblical Quarterly* 50 (1988): 171–183.

Wiebe, Phillip H. *Visions of Jesus: Direct Encounters from the New Testament to Today.* New York and Oxford: Oxford University Press, 1997.

Donald E. Gowan

1 THESSALONIANS

See Pauline Letters.

2 THESSALONIANS

See Deutero-Pauline Letters.

1 AND 2 TIMOTHY

See Deutero-Pauline Letters.

TITUS

See Deutero-Pauline Letters.

TORAH

The term "Torah," primarily used in Jewish rather than Christian settings, has at least four connotations. First, it refers to the "written Torah" (Heb. *tôrâ šěbiktav*), the first section of the Jewish Bible: *Bereshit* (Genesis), *Shemot* (Exodus), *Vayikra* (Leviticus), *Bemidbar* (Numbers), and *Devarim* (Deuteronomy). The Hebrew titles derive from the first major word in each book. In reference to this entire collection, "Torah" appears not in these volumes themselves but in later Hebrew (biblical) literature such as Isaiah 5:24 and 30:9, Malachi 3:22 (Christian Bibles 4:4), Psalms 19:8 (19:7), Ezra 7:6, Nehemiah 8:1, and elsewhere, where it is frequently glossed with phrases such as "of Moses" or "of Yahweh." Traditional Judaism regards the Torah as the preeminent revelation of the divine to Moses and, therefore, as more important than the other parts of the Jewish Bible, or Tanak (an acronym for Torah, Nevi'im [Prophets], and Ketuvim [Writings]).

For Judaism Torah connotes, second, this material's interpretation: the "oral Torah" (Heb. *tôrâ šĕbi ʿal peh*; sometimes called, under Christian influence, "oral law"). According to the Mishnaic tractate *Pirqe Avot* (1.1), "Moses received the Torah from Sinai and transmitted it to Joshua; Joshua to the elders; the elders to the prophets; and the prophets handed it down to the men of the Great Assembly," in a chain of tradition that culminates with Rabbinic Judaism and its heirs. Discussion of two Torahs, one "written" and one "oral," appears classically in *b. Šabbat* 31a. Thus, Jewish references to "Torah" may refer not just to the first five books but also to the entire compendium of Jewish teaching, from *Bereshit* through rabbinic commentaries and even more broadly to teachings that continue to this day.

The oral Torah provides instruction on how to understand the written. For example, Exodus 20:10 forbids "work" on the sabbath; the Mishnah (*m. Šabb.* 7.2–4) defines what constitutes work. Exodus 21:24, Leviticus 24:20, and Deuteronomy 19:21 mandate in certain cases of physical injury a penalty of "eye for eye, tooth for tooth"; the Mishnah (*m. B. Qam.* 8.1) insists that these injunctions signal legal principle, not physical mutilation: "He who injures his fellow is liable to [compensate] him on five counts: injury, pain, medical costs, loss of time [i.e., income], and indignity." The "tradition of the elders" mentioned in the gospels (Mark 7:3, 5; cf. Matt 15:2) suggests a similar, postbiblical interpretive collection.

A third connotation of Torah is the scroll upon which these first five books are inscribed and from which certain verses, standardized across Jewish communities, are chanted in Hebrew on Mondays, Thursdays, and more extensively on the sabbath (Saturday). Using quills, specially trained scribes inscribe the Hebrew letters onto a scroll of sewn-together sheets of parchment made from the skin of a kosher animal (e.g., sheep, cattle).

The term "Torah" itself derives from a Hebrew root meaning "to shoot" (as with an arrow) or "to throw" (as in casting lots in seeking divine instruction). From this idea of "hitting the mark" or, colloquially, "straight shooting," a fourth meaning of Torah is "teaching," "guide," or "instruction": those teachings that, to continue the metaphor, keep one on target in relation to correct living. The term is used in this sense in Isaiah 51:4 (general instructions for a global audience), Hosea 4:6 (sacerdotal instruction) and 8:1 (covenantal terms), Amos 2:6–12 (moral injunctions), Habakkuk 1:4 (ethics), and Proverbs 1:8 (parental advice): "Hear [*šĕmaʿ*], my child, your father's instruction (Heb. *mûsar*), and do not reject your mother's teaching [*tôrâ*]."

When the written Torah was translated into Greek, likely beginning in the third century B.C.E., Jewish translators rendered the word "Torah" not as "instruction" or "teaching" but as "law" (Gk *nomos*). At that time *nomos* connoted philosophical and theological as well as legislative elements, not "law" in the strict sense of a list of rules. However, for parts of the postbiblical Christian tradition, Torah—understood as law—came to be associated with legalism and negatively juxtaposed to grace, despite the fact that "grace" (Heb. *ḥēn*, typically translated in the LXX as *charis*) is a component of written Torah (see Gen 6:8; Exod 33:17). There are numerous positive references to the "law" (i.e., Torah) in the New Testament (e.g., Matt 5:17–18; Rom 7:12). Torah grounds the ethical exhortation in the Epistle of James:

> You do well if you really fulfill the royal law according to the scripture, "You shall love your neighbor as yourself" [Lev 19:18]. But if you show partiality, you commit sin and are convicted by the law as transgressors. For whoever keeps the whole law but fails in one point has become accountable for all of it. For the one who said, "You shall not commit adultery" [Exod 20:14; Deut 15:18], also said, "You shall not murder" [Exod 20:13; Deut 5:17]. Now if you do not commit adultery but if you murder, you have become a transgressor of the law. (Jas 2:8–11)

However, other New Testament verses (e.g., John 1:17; Rom 8:2; 10:4; Eph 2:15), taken out of context, have led to unfortunate stereotyping.

At least by the time of the Tertullian (ca. 160–ca. 225), Christians referred to the written Torah not only as the "Law" but also as the "Pentateuch," from the Greek terms for "five" (*penta*) and "scroll," "jar," or "vessel (*teuchos*). Other designations for the written Torah, found in the New Testament, include "the book of Moses" (Mark 12:26) and just the eponymous "Moses" (Acts 15:21; 2 Cor 3:15).

Consistent with distinctions in terminology, Judaism and Christianity traditionally display different understandings of Torah's import. Rabbinic tradition insists that the Torah is one of the three pillars, along with Temple service and deeds of loving kindness, by which the world is sustained (*Pirqe Avot* 1.2). Although Jesus's followers eventually rejected Marcion's dismissal of Israel's scriptures, they nevertheless relegated Torah to a secondary (compared to the NT) or tertiary (compared to the NT, the Prophets, and Psalms) place. These followers, especially those from Gentile origins, ignored much of the Torah's legal material because they did not regard its practices (e.g., circumcision, dietary regulations, ritual purity), designed to keep Israel distinct among the nations, as applicable to them. Whereas, against Marcion, most early Christians insisted on the Torah as sacred, they rejected Jewish readings that disagreed with their own messianic presuppositions. For example, according to Paul (2 Cor 3:15–16), when (nonmessianic) Jews read "Moses" (i.e., Torah), "a veil lies over their minds; but when one turns to the Lord, the veil is removed."

Historical Development. Although the written Torah itself does not claim Mosaic authorship, the tradition developed that Moses received the text, in toto, on Sinai. Well-known passages such as Exodus 20:2–17, the Decalogue or "Ten Commandments," are introduced with the affirmation, "Then God spoke all these words" (Exod 20:1). Moses's mediation is suggested by passages such as Exodus 24:4 ("Moses wrote down all the words of the LORD"), Joshua 8:31 (the "book of the Torah of Moses") (lit. trans.), and Ezra 6:18, which refers to the "Book of Moses" (lit. trans.). Mosaic authorship is also suggested in Mark 12:26 and Acts 15:21, as well as by Josephus (*Ant.* 4) and Philo (*Moses*).

Parts of rabbinic tradition teach that the Torah both existed prior to its revelation to Moses and was the blueprint by which God created the world (*Lev. Rab.* 19.1; cf. *Pirqe Avot* 3.14). This attribution of preexistence may have developed under the influence of Proverbs 8:22, a hymn to Wisdom: "Yahweh created me at the beginning of his work, the first of his acts of long ago." Torah became, and in Jewish circles remains, connected to the concept of Wisdom. Similarly, parts of early Christian tradition taught that Jesus, who functions as Wisdom incarnate or the divine Word, was an agent of creation (John 1:1; cf. Phil 2:6). *Pirqe Rabbi Eliezer* 11 proposes that when God stated, "Let us make humankind" (Gen 1:26), he was in dialogue with the Torah.

The Septuagint (Deut 33:2 [at Sinai, "the angels were with God"]) and following it the New Testament (Acts 7:53; Gal 3:19; Heb 2:2) likely gave rise to the idea that Moses received the Torah via an angelic intermediary. Josephus (*Ant.* 15.136) quotes Herod the Great as affirming, "We have learned from God the most excellent of our doctrines [Gk *dogmaton*], and the most holy part of our law, by angels from God."

Today, outside of most representatives of Orthodox Judaism and very conservative Christian circles, the written Torah is recognized not as a singular work divinely dictated to Moses but rather as a compendium of sources from different periods. This recognition is not only a product of the Enlightenment: *Fourth Ezra* (= 2 *Esdras*), a late first-century C.E. text, posits that the original Torah was destroyed when the Babylonians sacked Jerusalem (586 B.C.E.) and that Ezra the scribe rewrote the text upon the return of the exiled community to Jerusalem. The church father Clement of Alexandria (ca. 150–ca. 215) claimed that Moses would not have written Genesis 9, for surely the claim that Noah had become drunk was a lie that Moses never would have perpetrated.

Anachronisms also produced early doubts about Mosaic authorship. Genesis 12:6 states that the Canaanites were "then"—that is, not at the time of the author—in the land, and several premodern rabbis (e.g., Ibn Ezra [1089–1164]) recognized that the verse must postdate Moses. Nor did they find it likely that Moses wrote of his own death and burial (Deut 34:5–8), although one tradition suggests that he wrote these divinely dictated lines with tears in his eyes; another, more practically, suggests Joshua penned the last few verses (*b. Menaḥ.* 30a).

More secularly oriented scholarship argues that the Torah was written over several centuries. Scholars have long noticed varying names for the Deity (e.g., Yahweh, Elohim, El Shaddai), accompanied by variations in theology, repetitions (Isaac's receipt of his name in Gen 17, 18, 21; the Decalogue's reappearance in Exod 20:2–17 and Deut 5:6–21 [cf. Exod 34:14–26]), inconsistencies (whether the animals were created before [Gen 1] or after [Gen 2] humanity; Moses's encounter with the Deity on Mt. Sinai [Exod 19] or Mt. Horeb [Deut 1]), additional anachronisms (domesticated camels in texts set in the Late Bronze Age; references to the Philistines, who arrived long after the putative time of Moses), and connections between material in the Torah and in later biblical books. It was also considered unlikely that Moses, had he authored the written Torah, would have referred to himself in the third person.

In 1651 Thomas Hobbes (1588–1679) claimed much of the Pentateuch was post-Mosaic; shortly thereafter, likely independently, Baruch Spinoza (1632–1677) reached the same conclusion. Nineteenth-century source critics posited multiple sources extending from Genesis into the Deuteronomistic History (Joshua, Judges, 1–2 Samuel, 1–2 Kings). In 1878 Julius Wellhausen (1844–1918), following a number of other source critics, posited what has come to be called the "documentary hypothesis," which argues that at least four sources comprise the Torah.

The first source, labeled "J" or the "Jahwist" for its use of Yahweh (*Jahveh* in German) as the Deity's name in Genesis 2 and elsewhere, is typically dated to the early monarchy (ca. 850 B.C.E.) and located within Judean court circles; its probable basis in the land of Judah serves as an additional mnemonic for J. The E source, named for its use of Elohim (God) for the Deity in Genesis 1 and elsewhere until Exodus 3 (the theophany at the burning bush), is usually understood as being derived from the northern kingdom of Israel, also known as Ephraim (another mnemonic), with a date in the early eighth century. Wellhausen hypothesized that, when Israel fell to Assyria in 722,

northern refugees brought E to Judah, where J and E were combined.

The Deuteronomist, or D source, represents the bulk of the book of Deuteronomy and is connected to the Deuteronomic History. The notice in 2 Kings 22:8–13 that Hilkiah, a priest during the reign of Josiah (r. ca. 632–609 B.C.E.), found "the book of the Torah" (Heb. *sēfer hatôrâ*) while engaged in Temple restoration suggests a possible origin at least for Deuteronomy.

Finally, the P or Priestly source, which focuses on teachings in Leviticus and portions of Numbers concerning holiness, sacrifice, purity, and the priesthood, is dated to the Babylonian Exile (587–538 B.C.E.) or the early Second Temple period. A compilation of J, E, D, and P—that is, a rudimentary version of what we call the written Torah—may underlie the comment in Nehemiah 8:1–3 that Ezra assembled the people in Jerusalem and read to them "the book of the Torah of Moses."

Today, scholars proffer numerous modifications to the documentary hypothesis: some posit a source underlying both J and E, others doubt the existence of E, others divide the sources differently across chapters, and still others date J to the sixth century rather than the tenth. Those wishing to retain Mosaic authorship speak of Moses's own use of sources or take a literary approach and suggest that changes in style, repetition, and rephrasings are all part of Moses's literary style.

Biblical Content. The Torah begins with the creation of the world and details elements of the primeval history (e.g., the garden of Eden, the Flood, the Tower of Babel; a mix of J and P). For each major encounter between God and humanity, relationships are strained but never fully broken. Adam and Eve disobey the commandment concerning the forbidden fruit; they are expelled from Eden, but God goes with them (Gen 2–3). Cain kills his brother Abel, but he receives a mark of protection from God (Gen 4). The generation of Noah proves so wicked that God undoes creation by flooding the earth with the waters of chaos initially separated on the first day of creation (Gen 1:6–7), but Noah and his family remain safe on the ark. Upon their disembarkation, God makes a covenant with

Noah—and hence with all humanity—never again to destroy the earth by flood (Gen 6–9). At this time as well, God curses Canaan, Noah's grandson (Gen 9:20–27): an etiology for the Israelites' settlement in the land once called Canaan. Following the incident of the Tower of Babel (Gen 11:1–9), an anticipation of the abuses of the Babylonian Empire and its eventual destruction, Genesis (12–50) focuses on the family of Abraham, his son Isaac, his grandson Jacob, and Jacob's sons and grandsons, who become the eponymous ancestors of the 12 tribes of Israel.

In Genesis (15:1–21; 17:1–27) God establishes with Abraham and his progeny an irrevocable covenant that guarantees descendants and land as well as proclaims that Abraham and his children are to be a blessing to other nations. The events in the lives of Abraham, his wife Sarah, his cowife (and Sarah's slave) Hagar, and their children find recapitulations in the later sections of Torah as well as in the Deuteronomistic History; thus, the Torah presents itself as having both internal consistency and connections with the later parts of the Bible. For example, Sarah abuses her Egyptian slave Hagar (Gen 16), just as the Egyptians, in Exodus (1:13–14; 2:23–25), will abuse Sarah's descendants. Abraham and Sarah expel Hagar and her son Ishmael from their camp (21:8–14); in a few generations the Ishmaelites will sell Joseph, Abraham and Sarah's great-grandson, into slavery in Egypt (37:25–28).

Genesis also anticipates much later material. The binding of Isaac (Gen 22) prefigures the actual sacrifice of Jephthah's daughter (Judg 11). The rape (or seduction) of Dinah, in which Jacob, her father, refuses to take action and Dinah's brothers slaughter Shechem and all the men of his city (Gen 34), prefigures the rape of David's daughter, Tamar, by her half-brother, the crown prince Amnon; David's refusal to intervene; Amnon's murder; and the ensuing civil war started by Tamar's brother, Absalom (2 Sam 13–18). Genesis ends with the descent of Abraham's grandson Jacob and his extended family to Egypt to escape famine in Canaan and their settlement in the land of Goshen by Joseph, Jacob's son, who had risen to second-in-command of Egypt.

Exodus 1–2 recounts how, generations later, a new pharaoh enslaved the Israelite population, then ordered that all their male children be killed. Saved by the collaborative effort of his mother, his sister, and Pharaoh's daughter, Moses is raised in the royal household. After killing a slave master he found abusing an Israelite slave, then fleeing to Midian to avoid punishment, Moses experiences a theophany on Mt. Horeb (i.e., Sinai): from a burning bush, Yahweh commissions him to liberate the Israelite slaves (Exod 3). A battle of wills ensues between Pharaoh, whom the Egyptians regarded as divine, and the God of Israel. Israel's God strikes the Egyptians with nine plagues; warned of the tenth plague, the slaughter of the firstborn of Egypt (an echo of the murder of the Israelite infants), Moses instructs his fellow Israelites to slaughter a lamb and place its blood on their doors so that the angel of death will pass over their homes. The Israelites flee to the Red Sea; pursued by Pharaoh's chariots, they experience a miracle when God parts its waters. Israel escapes Egypt under the leadership of Moses, his brother Aaron, and his sister Miriam (Exod 5–15).

In the wilderness between Egypt and the Promised Land, Moses ascends Sinai/Horeb to receive another covenant, this one between God and the people of Israel (Exod 19–20). The bulk of the content from the middle of Exodus through the end of Deuteronomy consists of legal and sacerdotal material. Among the central laws are the Decalogue (Exod 20:1–17; Deut 5:6–21), the commands to love both one's neighbor and the stranger (Heb. *gēr*) in the community "because you were strangers in the land of Egypt" (Lev 19:33–34), civil laws (Exod 21–23), instructions on the construction of the wilderness sanctuary that houses the copies of these laws (ch. 25), and detailed discussions of the holy, the priesthood, and the sacrificial system (chs. 26–40). Exodus promises a good life in the land for those who follow its instructions but expulsion if the people transgress. While the covenant of the land is permanent, residential rights can be suspended.

The word *Deuteronomy* derives from a Greek term meaning "second law." To some extent this book is a recapitulation of earlier narrative and legal material, here presented as Moses's farewell speech. The reference to "Torah" in Deuteronomy 4:44 ("This is the Torah that Moses set before the Israelites") has initially this narrow sense of Deuteronomy alone, not the full written Torah.

Much of the material in the Torah has counterparts in other ancient Near Eastern literature. Genesis 1 holds similarities to Babylonian cosmogony in the *Enuma Elish*; Noah (Gen 6–9) resembles other flood survivors such as the Sumerian Ziusudra, the Akkadian Utnapishtim in the *Epic of Gilgamesh*, and the Old Babylonian and Neo-Assyrian Atrahasis. The third-century B.C.E. Babylonian historian Berossus records a flood story, as do many cultures throughout the world.

Legal collections were a standard part of ancient Near Eastern literature, ranging from Sumerian texts as early as ca. 2100 B.C.E. (Ur-Namma) to the famous Babylonian Code of Hammurabi (ca. 1750 B.C.E.) to later materials from neo-Assyrian and neo-Babylonian courts to the Persian period. The Code of Hammurabi, engraved on an eight-foot stele, depicts the enthroned sun god Shamash, before whom stands Hammurabi; drawing a connection with the giving of the Torah to Moses would not be inappropriate. The Demotic Chronicle (ca. 519 B.C.E.) records a directive from Darius I of Persia to his colonial governor in Egypt that "the former laws of Egypt until the 44th year [526 B.C.E.] of Pharaoh Amasis" be compiled. Such instruction may have been a partial impetus for the redaction of the various laws now present in Torah. According to the Talmud (*Mak.* 23b), God gave Moses 613 commandments (Heb. *miṣvōt*, sing. *miṣvâ*), which can be divided into 248 positive commandments (e.g., "Honor your father and your mother") and 365 negative ones (e.g., "You shall not steal"). The number 248 is said to correspond to the number of bones in the human body; 365, to the days in a solar year.

The Torah ends with Moses in Moab, on Mt. Nebo, overlooking "the whole land: Gilead as far as Dan" (Deut 34:1). Yahweh reiterates the promise of the land to the patriarchs and their descendants, telling Moses, "I have let you see it with your eyes, but you shall not cross over there" (v. 4). Moses dies and is buried in an unknown place. This ending, with Moses overlooking the land, is recapitulated by the ending of the Tanak. Although medieval manuscripts vary in the order of the books of the Ketuvim, eventually Jewish communities settled the ending in 2 Chronicles 36:23: the edict of Cyrus of Persia that the Jews exiled to Babylon return to their homeland. "Whoever is among you of all his people, may Yahweh his God be with him. Let him go up [to Jerusalem]." The Christian Old Testament, ending with Malachi (cf. 4:5/Matt 3:1–5) rather than 2 Chronicles, loses this echo of the Torah as well as the Torah's emphasis on the homeland.

Also signaling the Torah's central place in the Jewish canon is the opening of the other two sections of the Tanak. Nevi'im (Prophets) commences with the book of Joshua, which begins by encouraging behavior "in accordance with all the Torah [NRSV: "law"] that my servant Moses commanded you," for "this book of Torah [NRSV: "book of the law"] shall not depart out of your mouth; you shall meditate on it day and night, so that you may be careful to act in accordance with all that is written in it" (1:7a–8a). Ketuvim begins with Psalms; Psalm 1:2 reads, "For in the Torah of Yahweh is his delight and on his Torah he meditates day and night."

Postbiblical Context. From the time of Ezra (ca. fifth century B.C.E.), Jews have proclaimed Torah in communal settings. Specially trained readers learn correct pronunciation as well as the cantillation (which varies among the Jewish communities, such as the Sephardic and the Ashkenazic) with which the text is chanted in the synagogue.

The Mishnah does not detail how the readings were to be divided for liturgical proclamation. Postbiblical Jewish sources suggest two cycles: a triennial cycle, used in the land of Israel, with the Torah readings divided into 154 sections, and an annual cycle, used in Babylon, in which the readings were divided into 54 portions to be read each consecutive sabbath (a double portion being read in some weeks). Possibly Acts 15:21 reflects some such liturgical system. The Babylonian divisions eventually became standardized across the Jewish world.

In Orthodox congregations the entire Torah is read on a yearly cycle; Conservative and Reform congregations use a triennial cycle (comparable to years A, B, and C in Christian churches' common lectionary) so that one-third of the designated section is read each sabbath. There are also special readings for holidays; on Saturday afternoons as well as Monday and Thursday mornings in Orthodox and most Conservative synagogues, the first section from the next sabbath is read. Each Torah portion for the sabbath or a holiday has an accompanying *haftarah* ("ending," "finish"), a reading from the Prophets (Nevi'im), much as Christian lectionaries pair readings from across the Christian canon. The annual cycle is completed on Simchat Torah ("rejoicing of the Torah"), 23 days after Rosh Hashanah, the new year. Following the reading of the last verses of Deuteronomy, the opening verses of Genesis are read.

In synagogues the Torah scroll is adorned with a special cover, sash, and ornaments. It is housed in an ark (*aron ha-kodesh*); when it is time during the service for it to be read, it is removed from the ark. When the scroll is lifted up, the congregation stands (see Neh 8:5). Thus, the Torah reading becomes the focal point of the service, just as the Eucharist is in Catholic settings and the sermon is among Protestants. In each case, the divine word is made present to the congregation.

The Torah retains permanent value in both Jewish and most Christian traditions. Isaiah 2:3 (cf. Mic 4:2) insists that, in the eschatological age, God will teach Torah to the Gentile nations. While the New Revised Standard Version renders the last section of this verse as "For out of Zion shall go forth instruction," the Hebrew literally states, "For out of Zion shall go forth Torah." (This line is recited in synagogue worship when the scroll is removed from the ark.) According to Jeremiah 31:33, Torah remains constant but will be inscribed on the heart, not inculcated by teaching. The New Revised Standard Version reads, "I will put my law within them, and I will write it on their hearts"; the Hebrew reads, "I will put my Torah within them." In the Sermon on the Mount (Matt 5:17–18), Jesus insists, "Do not think that I have come to abolish the law or the prophets; I have come not to abolish but to fulfill. For truly I tell you, until heaven and earth pass away, not one letter, not one stroke of a letter, will

pass from the law until all is accomplished." "Law" and "prophets" can refer to the first two sections of the Tanak (Torah and Nevi'im), but at the time of Matthew's composition, it may have referred to all the books, including those now found in the third division (the Ketuvim), regarded as sacred (cf. Luke 24:44).

[*See also* Covenant; Decalogue; Deuteronomy; Education; Ethics, Biblical; Ezra, Nehemiah, and 1 and 2 Chronicles; Festivals and Holy Days; Genesis; God and Gods; Grace; Hermeneutics, Biblical; Historical Narratives (Joshua—2 Kings); Israel and Israelites; Jeremiah; Jerusalem (Zion); Judaism; Land; Leviticus and Numbers; Matthew; Moses; Priests and Priesthood; Sacrifice and Offerings; Scripture; Story and Memory; Tabernacles, Temples, and Synagogues; *and* Wisdom Literature.]

BIBLIOGRAPHY

Alter, Robert. *The Five Books of Moses: A Translation with Commentary*. New York: Norton, 2004.

Baden, Joel S. *The Composition of the Pentateuch: Renewing the Documentary Hypothesis*. Anchor Yale Bible Reference Library. New Haven, Conn.: Yale University Press, 2012.

Berlin, Adele, Marc Zvi Brettler, and Michael Fishbane, eds. *The Jewish Study Bible*. Oxford: Oxford University Press, 2004.

Dozeman, Thomas B., Konrad Schmid, and Baruch J. Schwartz, eds. *The Pentateuch: International Perspectives on Current Research*. Tübingen, Germany: Mohr Siebeck, 2011.

Edelman, Diana V., Philip R. Davies, Christophe Nihan, et al. *Opening the Books of Moses*. Sheffield, U.K.: Equinox, 2012.

Eskenazi, Tamara Cohn, and Andrea L. Weiss, eds. *The Torah: A Women's Commentary*. New York: Women of Reform Judaism, 2008.

Fox, Everett. *The Five Books of Moses: Genesis, Exodus, Leviticus, Numbers, Deuteronomy*. New York: Schocken, 2000.

Friedman, Richard Elliott. *Commentary on the Torah with a New English Translation*. New York: HarperCollins, 2003.

Goldstein, Elyse M., ed. *The Women's Torah Commentary: New Insights from Women Rabbis on the 54 Weekly Torah Portions*. Woodstock, Vt.: Jewish Lights, 2000.

Heschel, Abraham Joshua. *Heavenly Torah: As Refracted Through the Generations.* Edited and translated from the Hebrew, with commentary, by Gordon Tucker with Leonard Levin. New York and London: Continuum, 2006.

Knoppers, Gary, and Bernard M. Levinson, eds. *The Pentateuch as Torah: New Models for Understanding Its Promulgation and Acceptance.* Winona Lake, Ind.: Eisenbrauns, 2007.

Lim, Timothy. *The Formation of the Jewish Canon.* Anchor Yale Bible Reference Library. New Haven, Conn.: Yale University Press, 2013.

McEntire, Mark H. *Struggling with God: An Introduction to the Pentateuch.* Macon, Ga.: Mercer University Press, 2008.

Ska, Jean Louis. *The Exegesis of the Pentateuch: Exegetical Studies and Basic Questions.* Tübingen, Germany: Mohr Siebeck, 2009.

Van Wijk-Bos, Johanna W. H. *Making Wise the Simple: The Torah in Christian Faith and Practice.* Grand Rapids, Mich.: Eerdmans, 2005.

Zucker, David J. *The Torah: An Introduction for Christians and Jews.* New York: Paulist Press, 2005.

Amy-Jill Levine

TRADITION

In connection with the Bible, the term "tradition" can mean at least two different things. "Tradition" can refer to the oral and written discourse that existed before the library of biblical books was collected into a single volume; such prebiblical traditions were passed around among religious communities, and some of these traditions were incorporated into the emerging biblical canon. There is thus tradition in the sense of something that existed prior to the Bible and that helped to shape it. Especially in later theological reflection, "tradition" can also mean the totality of Christianity except the Bible: the accumulated record of rites, reflection, and history, but not the text that is, in many ways, their source. This raises the question of how the Bible and tradition relate to each other. Various answers have been given to this question in the history of Christian thought, and the major Christian churches have taken specific stances on this issue.

Tradition before and within the Bible. Traditional material fed into the Hebrew Bible. For instance, various literary strata are visible within the Old Testament's first books. Based on their distinctive theological perspectives and specific names for God, J. Wellhausen (1844–1918) identified four literary sources for the Pentateuch: J (Yahwist), E (Elohist), D (Deuteronomist), and P (Priestly). While subsequent scholarship has debated the details of Wellhausen's documentary hypothesis, its basic point—that the Old Testament is the product of primitive source material—is widely acknowledged outside of fundamentalist circles.

At the same time, the Old Testament itself adopts an attitude toward tradition, often addressing the topic explicitly. This is so because the Jewish people are constituted by virtue of their collective memory of events that founded their community. Israel remembers its deliverance from Egypt by observing the Passover. In addition, the people's life after the Exodus was governed by a legal code that members of the community needed to learn and to pass on to subsequent generations. Because of these circumstances, the Old Testament itself emphasizes tradition as the transmission of a particular narrative and a set of practices (Deut 11:18–21). This tradition stresses the uniqueness of Jewish practices and prohibits Israel's assimilation to other forms of life (thus, Deut 12:30).

The New Testament attests to traditional elements, teachings circulated within the early Christian communities, which chronologically precede the now canonical text. The opening verses of Luke's Gospel claim that integrated summaries of the deeds and teachings of Jesus were already in circulation, even before the composition of his Gospel, having been assembled by the earliest followers of Jesus and "handed on" to later ones (1:2). Likewise, the Fourth Gospel announces its own limitations of coverage and admits that those who encountered Jesus while he was alive saw him do many things that did not enter into the Gospel narrative (John 20:30; 21:25). Twenty-first-century biblical scholarship aims to reconstruct the history of the oral forms and written sources that surrounded and fed into the formation of the biblical text in its present shape.

While the Bible sometimes acknowledges its character as a produced text, the New Testament preserves divergent strands of thought about tradition. Some seem positive; others, negative. Jesus's explicit comments about tradition express disapprobation for the specific traditional practices in question. In Mark 7:6–8 he takes the Pharisees to task for following what he calls "human tradition" while neglecting genuinely divine commands that remain binding. The target of Jesus's criticism is the Pharisees' custom of excusing children from the obligation to care for their parents in cases where the children have dedicated themselves to religious service. It would be too much, however, to see in Jesus's words, here or elsewhere, a simple conflation of all tradition with practices that were merely human rather than divinely sanctioned. To construe Jesus's attitude toward tradition as a blanket rejection is to underestimate his own embeddedness in Jewish tradition. His ministry was an effort to realign an existing form of life and thought around himself or God's kingdom, not an attempt to abolish any systematic approach to interpreting and applying the Law. Still, in a much later context, Protestants picked up on Jesus's anti-tradition rhetoric and brought it to bear against their Roman Catholic opponents.

In Pauline texts the author more typically depicts tradition as a normative standard. Tradition takes three different forms. First, *kerygmatic* tradition consists of compressed summaries of the basic Christian message, with a special focus on the death and resurrection of Jesus Christ (1 Cor 15:3–8). This form of tradition may be articulated in a variety of ways, but it is, in one shape or another, foundational for the other modes of tradition. Second, *ecclesial* tradition refers to practices that followers of Jesus would perform and reflect upon in an attempt to remember him. The observance of the Lord's Supper, discussed in 1 Corinthians 11:23–26, is an example of such a church tradition. Third, *ethical* tradition means individual or corporate behavior that endeavors to be faithful to the model that Jesus himself set and that Paul sought to transmit to others so that they might ultimately imitate Jesus by following his apostle (1 Cor 4:16; Eph 4:20–21; Phil 2:5). The language of tradition generally has a positive valence in Pauline texts, notwithstanding Paul's portrayal of his own conversion experience as one that did not depend upon human agency, and in spite of his frequent stress on the freedom that life in the Spirit brings to the Christian life. For the apostle, "where the Spirit of the Lord is, there is freedom" (2 Cor 3:17); yet it is also true that the Spirit's work does not ultimately overthrow the authority of the church's various forms of tradition but rather works through them.

Tradition after the Bible and in Relation to It. Thus, on the one hand, the Bible preserves traditions that existed prior to its formation and in a sense is constituted by them, at least in part. Christian theology, however, eventually developed a distinction between the biblical canon and the sum total of all theological thought and religious practice apart from it. Viewed from this vantage point, the Bible serves as a generative, founding text for the Christian tradition, and it becomes possible to inquire into the relationship between the Bible itself and the post-biblical tradition. There have been four historically influential ways of construing the relationship between the Bible and tradition, when tradition stands for the entirety of Christianity apart from its sacred text. Those four views, in roughly chronological order of development, are as follows.

Coincidence. This view, developed in the patristic period, sees the genuine apostolic tradition as coinciding with the Bible in its substantive content. The basic claim is that the Bible is materially sufficient (its contents requiring no supplementation from additional sources) but also formally insufficient, for it requires an authorized interpretation. The hermeneutical function of tradition in relation to the Bible is to offer a construal of the overall message of scripture. In this way, tradition does not dictate the interpretation of each individual detail of the biblical text, but instead preserves the essential pattern that emerges when the text's various parts are interrelated to one another. Irenaeus illustrates this by comparing his overall schematization of scripture to a key for assembling a mosaic (*Haer.* 1.9.4). Those who possess the key will not try to piece together the colored tiles of the mosaic into the picture of a fox when the finished product should represent a king's face instead.

Constructing the proper picture out of the pieces supplied may still require some ingenuity, though the work of assembling the pieces proceeds on the basis of a rough, prior knowledge of the resulting picture.

The coincidence view emerged especially from Irenaeus's polemical engagement with the Valentinian Gnostics. What legitimates apostolic tradition, for Irenaeus, is that in its oral form it matches up with the teaching of scripture. It is the bishops, above all, whose teaching is inherited from the apostles and, thus, coincides with it in content. The rule of faith is a summary of their teaching that serves as the key to assembling the mosaic of scripture. Irenaeus saw the gnostic view of tradition as adding something new to the Bible—indeed, something that conflicts with elements of the text, especially its portrayal of a single God across the two testaments. The coincidence view was the dominant position, at least among the orthodox, during the patristic period.

Supplementary. In this view, also known as the "two-source" view of revelation, tradition supplies further content that supplements the biblical canon materially. Accordingly, the Bible is insufficient both materially and formally. This view became popular in the medieval period and had as its purpose vindicating the teaching office of the church. Such vindication was important for those who saw the official teaching of the church as going beyond what the text of scripture could justify. A supplementary role for tradition served to fill the gap between the biblical text and the teaching of the contemporary church. The supplementary view of tradition rose to ascendancy after the Council of Trent (1545–1563), though Tridentine decrees themselves admit of more than one possible reading on this subject. Following Trent, Catholic theologians almost always read the council's canons as teaching the supplementary position, which provided a strong counter to the Reformation. But because the results of the council could also be understood to propound the coincidence view, it was possible for Roman Catholic theology to swing back to that position, which it ultimately did.

Basil of Caesarea's treatise *On the Holy Spirit* (375) is often claimed as patristic precedent for the supplementary view because he advocates that theological teaching about the Spirit can find its "source" either in the written text of the Bible or in the liturgical practices of the church. Read in this way, Basil goes beyond the Bible to find a basis for approving worship of the Holy Spirit. Yet this is a misrepresentation of the Cappadocian's teaching: when he refers to "sources," he means sources of actual verbal formulae. So, for Basil, the presence in the liturgy of certain locutions provides warrant for their being valid theological forms; however, they only entered into the liturgy because they have a basis in biblical teaching, which propounds similar ideas using different verbal forms.

Ancillary. The ancillary view is operative when tradition, as represented by the teaching of the church fathers or the decisions of ecclesial councils, is viewed as an eminently helpful guide but not an absolutely binding criterion for the Bible's interpretation. This is essentially the position of the magisterial Reformers, such as Luther and Calvin. The radical Reformers tried to reduce the role of tradition further, seeing the magisterial Reformers as maintaining a problematic proximity to their Catholic opponents. For Luther and Calvin, scripture is both formally and materially sufficient, needing interpretation but not interpretation by any ecclesial authority. Scripture alone serves as the finally authoritative source of and norm for Christian doctrine, though tradition may serve in a subsidiary role. The main line of the Protestant tradition had a complaint, not against tradition per se, but against many of the teachings of contemporary Roman Catholicism. The reformers wanted to turn the church away from what they regarded as late medieval innovations, which they understood as undermining the gospel, and to return to the Bible and the church fathers, the latter being good (if not perfect) guides to the former. Thus, the Protestants viewed history in such a way as to see it—or at least compelling segments of it, such as the early church—as being on their side.

Neither Luther nor Calvin was a conciliarist, for they did not believe that a duly assembled and constituted council of the church would necessarily reach a correct decision. Councils are constituted by human beings and subject to making mistakes. Their decisions are binding only insofar as they concur with the teachings of the Bible, which the Reformers take to be perspicuous, providing guidance that is sufficiently clear that conscientious and holy readers can find the answers that they need to questions pertaining to the Christian life. While the ancillary position is close to the coincidence view, it diverges insofar as it does not presume the theological rectitude of the contemporary church.

Developmental, or unfolding. The thrust of this view is that doctrine develops over the course of time as implications of assertions and practices are teased out and brought to bear in new circumstances. This fourth view is not so much a whole new option, standing as a possibly independent way to relate the Bible and the postbiblical tradition. It usually serves to enrich the coincidence view with the insights of modern historical consciousness. It was propounded first by John Henry Newman (1801–1890) and remains an important view, especially among Roman Catholics. Newman developed categories for thinking about legitimate developments because modern research made it difficult to conceive of the early church as theologically uniform—was tradition really what has been believed "everywhere, always, and by all" (Vincent of Lérins, d. ca. 445)— and as a framework that could provide a set of norms for a church almost two millennia removed from its founding events and texts. Unlike any of the preceding views, the developmental view conceded that tradition is not static in the sense of preserving teaching without in any way modifying it. Legitimate changes were possible: they include any alterations that unpack the original teaching and apply them in new contexts. Other changes count as corruptions.

Further Developments and a Question about Future Research. The twentieth century saw a convergence between Protestant and Roman Catholic thinking on tradition that resulted in part from ecumenical dialogue between the two churches. The documents of Vatican II minimize the distinction between the Bible and tradition, and Roman Catholic theology generally has moved away from the supplementary view. For their part, Protestants have moved away from the antitradition polemics of the Reformation, seeing tradition as a way that apostolic teaching has de facto been legitimately transmitted to the present. The rise of hermeneutics has contributed to Protestants' (and Catholics') willingness to see tradition in a positive light, as it is now common for readers of the Bible to acknowledge that their preunderstanding of scripture has been formed by the history of its interpretation. Differences nevertheless remain. While Vatican II underscores the magisterium's position as the final court of appeals in adjudicating the meaning of Christian teaching, for Protestants scripture alone functions in this way. An important question at present is how future debates about tradition will be shaped now that the momentum behind the ecumenical movement has waned.

[*See also* Authority and Order; Canon; Covenant; Ecclesiology; Ethics, Biblical; Gospel; Hermeneutics, Biblical; Identity; Israel and Israelites; Judaism; Lord's Supper; Story and Memory; *and* Torah.]

BIBLIOGRAPHY
Bauckham, Richard. "Tradition in Relation to Scripture and Reason." In *Scripture, Tradition and Reason*, edited by Benjamin Drewery and Richard Bauckham, pp. 117–145. Edinburgh: T&T Clark, 1988.
Calvin, Jean, and Jacopo Sadoleto. *A Reformation Debate: Sadoleto's Letter to the Genevans and Calvin's Reply.* Edited by John C. Olin. New York: Fordham University Press, 2000.
Congar, Yves. *Tradition and Traditions: An Historical and a Theological Essay.* London: Burns & Oats, 1966.
Florovsky, Georges. *Bible, Church, Tradition: An Eastern Orthodox View.* Collected Works of Georges Florovsky 1. Belmont, Mass.: Nordland, 1972.
Hanson, R. P. C. *Tradition in the Early Church.* London: SCM, 1962.
Lane, A. N. S. "Scripture, Tradition and Church: An Historical Survey." *Vox Evangelica* 9 (1975): 37–55.
Newman, John Henry. *An Essay on the Development of Christian Doctrine.* 6th ed. Notre Dame, Ind.: University of Notre Dame Press, 1989.
Williams, Daniel H. *Retrieving the Tradition and Renewing Evangelicalism: A Primer for Suspicious Protestants.* Grand Rapids, Mich.: Eerdmans, 1999.

Darren Sarisky

TRINITY

The Trinity refers to the "one God, the Father" (1 Cor 8:6), the "one LORD, Jesus Christ" (1 Cor 8:6), and the "one Spirit" (Eph 4:4) of Christian worship and confession. A doctrine of the Trinity is an effort to think through the mutual relatedness of these three, for the purpose of showing that the church's worship of Jesus Christ and the Holy Spirit accords with the Father's one, eternal deity (cf. Deut 6:4; Mark 12:29). The doctrine of the Trinity, in the singular, refers to the set of (partly disputed) affirmations that have the highest degree of ecumenical authority: in briefest compass, that the Trinity exists eternally as three persons in one substance. Christians have not generally supposed that any doctrine of the Trinity, even the most authoritative, can exhaustively describe the Trinity itself. Rather, the doctrine's role is more modest. It permits Christians to profess faith in the Father, the Son, and the Holy Spirit without obscuring the mystery of their common life by neglecting either the diversity of persons, on the one side (the error of modalism), or the unity of divine essence and deity, on the other (the error of subordinationism).

The Unity of the Old and New Testaments and the Multidimensionality of Salvation. The Christian confession of the Trinity rests on the combined testimony of the Old Testament and the New Testament. In the Old Testament the central story of salvation is the Exodus. God lays claim to being uniquely God and makes good on that claim by delivering Israel from bondage and leading it to a land of life and blessing. Thereafter, the Old Testament reverberates with the memory and hope of a God who saves in just this way: "in every place where I cause my name to be remembered, I will come to you and bless you" (Exod 20:24). Salvation becomes a three-dimensional affair, as it were, encompassing the knowledge of God's uniqueness, the experience of God's presence, and participation in God's blessings.

Turning to the New Testament, one readily recognizes the three basic dimensions of biblical salvation. Like the Exodus, the gospel of Jesus Christ is about how the "one God and Father of all" (Eph 4:6) makes himself known by a dramatic act of deliverance (the

cross and resurrection) and an extravagant gift of blessing and life (the outpouring of the Spirit). But the Testaments differ quite remarkably as well. In the Old Testament salvation in all its dimensions is routinely predicated of a single divine "I" who speaks with a single voice: "*I* cause my name to be remembered," "*I* come," "*I* bless." In the New Testament one continues to hear this same voice: for example, it speaks from above in response to Jesus's prayer outside the Temple in Jerusalem (John 12:28). Moreover, the voice from above says much what it said before when inaugurating the day of salvation: "I have glorified [my name], and I will glorify it!" But the New Testament differs markedly from the Old Testament with respect to the other two dimensions of salvation. Even as "God Most High" (Mark 5:7) remains the active source of his saving presence and blessing, these latter dimensions of salvation become rigorously aligned with figures who act in their own right and speak in their own voices. God's saving presence coincides with his sending of Jesus of Nazareth and God's blessing, with the outpouring of the Holy Spirit (Gal 4:4–6).

In sum, the New Testament portrays not only salvation as three-dimensional but also, in some remarkable way, the agent of salvation. God, Jesus Christ, and the Holy Spirit are one in accomplishing salvation; together they receive creation's worship and praise. Yet each is distinct, playing a different role in salvation and receiving worship and praise in different ways. This rich, multidimensional apprehension of the God who saves by Christ and the Spirit gives rise to the doctrine of the Trinity. At heart, that doctrine is an effort to think through the implications of this distinctively Christian apprehension of God's being and activity.

In what follows, we explore three different ways in which the writers of the New Testament portray the mutual relatedness of God, Christ, and the Spirit. Each begins with an Old Testament antecedent, even as it transforms that antecedent in the light of God's sending of Christ and the Spirit.

The Tetragrammaton and Salvation as the Manifestation of God's Uniqueness. One particularly important strand of New Testament testimony begins with God's personal proper name, YHWH, henceforth indicated by the traditional surrogate LORD. Although we have referred to the divine agent in the Old Testament merely as "God," the Old Testament itself repeatedly emphasizes the fact that the LORD, and no other, is God. The LORD is differentiated from other gods by the fact that he alone bears this name. The name thus becomes the linguistic token par excellence of God's oneness and uniqueness. A prime testimony is the Shema, Israel's primordial confession of faith: "Hear O Israel, the LORD is our God, the LORD alone" (Deut 6:4). Over the long course of Israel's history, the name also became the token par excellence of God's salvation. If the LORD is one and unique, the way he demonstrates this is precisely by bringing glory to this name. The later prophets anticipate a day when the LORD will so manifest his uniqueness, enact his presence, and bestow his blessing that the whole earth will be filled with the knowledge of the LORD (e.g., Isa 40–55; Hab 2:14).

Jews of the Second Temple period typically showed reverence for God by avoiding direct use of the name "YHWH." Instead, they employed some other contextually appropriate surrogate in its place, such as "Lord" when reading scripture (Luke 4:8, 12, 18, 19) or "the Blessed One" or "the Power" in free discourse (Mark 14:61–62). Far from indicating a lack of interest in the divine name, this practice signaled a heightened concern for its holiness and sanctity. Significantly, the practice also afforded Jews, including the writers of the New Testament, a powerful mode of theological expression.

Consider, for example, the extraordinary role many New Testament writers assign to the surrogate term "Lord," especially when quoting Old Testament verses that contain the name. In some instances New Testament writers cites Hebrew scripture to refer to "God on high": that is, the God whom Jesus himself worships and serves. This is the case when Jesus admonishes the devil in the wilderness: "As it is written, 'Worship the Lord your God, and serve only him'" (Matt 4:10; cf. Deut 6:13). In other cases "Lord" serves to disambiguate the identity of God's Spirit from other spirits: thus, Jesus reads from the scroll of Isaiah in the synagogue in Nazareth, "The Spirit of the Lord is upon me, because he has anointed me to bring good news to the poor" (Luke 4:18; cf. Isa 61:11). In still

other cases, something more remarkable happens: New Testament writers cite scripture in such a way that the periphrastic "Lord" demands to be understood as Jesus himself, as though he were himself the bearer of the divine name "YHWH." Paul employs the usage frequently, glossing the confession "Jesus is Lord" by citing Joel 2:32, "Whoever calls on the name of the Lord shall be saved" (Rom 10:13). But Matthew, Mark, and Luke do much the same thing by putting the words "Prepare the way of the Lord" (Matt 3:3 parr.) near the outset of their gospels. For the Synoptic Evangelists, the one sent to prepare the Lord's way is John the baptizer, not Jesus. Jesus, in some extraordinary sense, is the saving advent of the Lord himself.

But how can this be? How can Jesus be sent by the Lord, be anointed by the Spirit of the Lord, and yet himself *be* the Lord of Old Testament attestation? Most New Testament passages make little apparent effort to answer this question; they merely affirm that it is so. Prominent among these is Paul's creed-like reformulation of the Shema: "For us there is one God…and one Lord, Jesus Christ" (1 Cor 8:6). This confession, among the oldest in the New Testament, simply places Jesus inside Israel's ancient confession of faith alongside the one God.

Other passages, however, do shed light on how both Jesus and the God to whom he prays can bear the same divine name. Key to these passages is the idea that God has given his own personal name to Jesus, with the result that God's saving self-manifestation to creation transpires in and through its recognition that Jesus is Lord. We encounter this astonishing idea in Philippians 2:5–11 and again in John 17, among the earliest and latest New Testament writings. According to Paul, God gave Jesus "the name above every name" (i.e., YHWH) after his exaltation from death so that all creation might confess him to be "Lord" to the "glory of God the Father" (Phil 2:11). We find a similar idea in John, where Jesus speaks of "your name that you have given me," in consequence of which he and the Father are "one" (17:11, 12). Unlike Philippians, the Fourth Gospel suggests that Jesus received the divine name prior to the commencement of his earthly ministry—indeed, even before the world began: "Before Abraham was, I am" (John 8:58, "I am" being yet another contextually appropriate surrogate for the divine name, based on allusion to Exod 3:14–15).

In such texts we see New Testament writers using the motif of God's name to reflect on the mutual relationship of God and Jesus in a highly sophisticated way. What God and Jesus have in common that makes them worthy of worship is the one divine name, "the name above every name," the Tetragrammaton. What makes them distinct is how they relate to the one name: one gives it, and the other receives it. Substitute "essence" (*ousia, substantia*) for "name," and one has something very much like the idea of essential communication (*communicatio essentiae*), which becomes a central pillar of the church's established doctrine of the Trinity. This idea traces the life of the Trinity back to an act of primordial generosity, whereby the one unoriginate God eternally shares or communicates the essence of his deity (his "name") with the Son and the Spirit, thereby multiplying the number of those who bear the divine essence without dividing the essence itself, which remains perfectly "one" (cf. John 17:11).

Kinship Terminology and Salvation as the Enactment of Divine Presence. Important as it was, the motif of the divine name could not say everything. In particular, it did not lend itself to expressing how God, Christ, and the Spirit could be sufficiently different from one another to play distinct roles in the work of salvation, to speak with different voices, and, above all, to have mutual dealings with one another. To illuminate this dimension of the gospel, centered in salvation as fellowship with God, New Testament writers drew upon another ancient strand of Old Testament theology: its language of divine kinship.

In the Old Testament kinship primarily concerns how human beings relate to one another, not how God relates to human beings. God creates Adam and Eve; he does not beget them—it is the lot of human creatures, not God, to experience the vicissitudes of parental love, sibling jealousy, fratricide, reconciliation, and so on. Nevertheless, if natural kinship is foreign to God in the Old Testament, a kind of adoptive kinship is not. By dint of love and good pleasure, God may supervene upon natural family ties and make himself the divine father of an otherwise ordinary human being, making that creature his earthly child.

This is precisely what God does in relation to the people Israel (Exod 4:22), then again to the Davidic king (2 Sam 7:14). In this way, the vagaries of kinship come to characterize the already messy relations between God and humankind. God, for his part, fulfills the role of a loving and protective divine father, liberating Israel from bondage in Egypt and showering his chosen children with his best gifts, including (according to some texts) God's own Spirit (Isa 11:1–2). But nation and king, for their part, often prove less than ideal sons, repeatedly failing to demonstrate the loyalty, love, and obedience they should.

In the New Testament the language of divine kinship vividly differentiates actors. As Father and Son, God and Jesus play distinct yet mutually interactive roles in the gospel's drama of life and death, estrangement and reconciliation. At the same time God and Jesus enact kinship in ways different from their Old Testament antecedents. For one thing, both Father and Son abundantly fulfill their obligations to each other, thanks (according to several New Testament traditions) to the Father's gift of the Spirit to Jesus (Mark 1:10; Matt 4:1; Luke 4:1, 14, 18). For another, the humiliation that Jesus suffers as the Son of God arises not from his own estrangement from the Father but from his overcoming the estrangement of others. Most extraordinarily, Christ is not first a son of Adam who becomes a Son of God, thanks to God's adoptive love for him. Rather, he is first God's Son who becomes a son of Adam, thanks to God's adoptive love for the world (cf. John 3:16; Luke 1:26–56; 2:1–38; 3:23–38; John 3:16; Gal 4:4).

Matthew and Luke signal the priority of Christ's divine Sonship by means of the nativity stories (Matt 1:18—2:23: Luke 1–2); other texts speak more radically of Christ preexisting as the Son of God even before the creation of the world (John 1:14, 18; Heb 1:2). In both cases a key point for later Trinitarian theology is this: the loving communion of Father, Son, and Holy Spirit is the starting point of the story of salvation, not its outcome. The distinctions that mark their life together belong to the God who saves, not to the world that is saved. This insight is what Christian theologians later sought to express by affirming that the God who saves by sending his Son and Spirit into the world lives eternally as three persons (*tres personae, tria hypostases*): Father, Son, and Holy Spirit.

Wisdom Language and Salvation as the Gift of Life. The writers of the New Testament drew upon yet a third strand of Old Testament testimony that would prove important for the development of the doctrine of the Trinity: the motif of divine wisdom, which undergirds the cosmic order and directs it toward life. Wisdom tradition helped mediate the unity and diversity emphasized in the motifs already examined. At the same time wisdom tradition harbored a crucial ambiguity that would bedevil later Christian theologians: What exactly was the relation between God and the wisdom by which he created the world? Was wisdom inherent in God's very identity as God? Was it the first and greatest of all creatures other than God? Or was it, perhaps, something else in between?

The Old Testament does not offer clear answers to these questions. On the one hand, the God of the Old Testament is inherently wise, as he is inherently good, mighty, and just (Job 12:13). God no more needs to create his own wisdom than he needs to create his own word or spirit. In this sense the Old Testament wisdom traditions tend by their very nature to presuppose and emphasize the unity of God much more strongly than does its language of God's fatherhood, which inevitably entails a contrast with some all-too-human child.

On the other hand, the unity of God and wisdom is not absolute. This is especially true in a set of remarkable texts that portray divine Wisdom as a kind of heavenly offspring, or creation, who exists alongside God before the world's creation (Job 28; Prov 1, 8, 9; Bar 3:9—4:4; Sir 24; Wis 7:7—9:18). The precise nature of wisdom's origin from God is mysterious and obscure. It is described as a creating, setting up, coming forth, and so on—all in a single text (Prov 8:22–31 LXX). Adding to Wisdom's mystery is her quicksilver persona. Although always concerned with the things that lead to life, she is sometimes concretely personal and other times immaterial and conceptual. Lady Wisdom speaks out in the public streets like an Old Testament prophet: first threatening and cajoling, then comforting with food and wine (Prov 1–9). In a more "demythologized" vein she is described as "a breath

of the power of God," "a pure emanation of the glory of the Almighty," "a reflection of eternal light," and "an image of his goodness" (Wis 7:22, 25–26) who confers "immortality," "joy," and "gladness" (Wis 8:16–17).

Turning to the New Testament, I have already noted that the preexistent Christ is sometimes described in terms of divine Sonship, indicating that Christ was the Son of God before he was a son of Adam (Heb 1:5; 1 John 4:9). Nevertheless, it is an interesting fact that New Testament writers commonly eschew the language of divine kinship when describing the preexistent Christ and instead employ the vocabulary of the Old Testament wisdom tradition. They do this, however, in a highly selective way. Gone is any suggestion of the preexistent Christ as a heavenly consort, offspring, or companion of God, whether male or female, who speaks and acts in his own right. What remains is the more rarified vocabulary of wisdom speculation in its "demythologized" form. The preexistent Christ is said to be "the image of the invisible God" (Col 1:15), "the reflection of God's glory" (Heb 1:3), "the exact imprint of God's very being" (Heb 1:3), "in the form of God" (Phil 2:6), and, of course, "the Word" (John 1:1, 14) "who sustains all things" (Heb 1:3) and brings "peace" (Col 1:20), "life," and "light" (John 1:4).

The selective use of wisdom tradition by New Testament writers had at least two important consequences. First, it permitted, even if it did not strictly require, an affirmation of Christ's full and equal dignity in relation to God. Second, it provided a way of thinking about God and Christ—and, by implication, the Spirit—that tempered and combined the emphases of unity and distinction that I have already noted. If the motif of the divine name anticipates what later Christian tradition would call the one essence of God and if the motif of divine kinship anticipates what it would call the three persons or hypostases, the motif of divine wisdom suggests a kind of mediating path between these two insights. God, Christ, and the Spirit simply are the one divine essence, each in a distinct mode of being (*tropos hyparcheos*) that is determined by their mutual relationships to one another.

From the Scriptures to the Nicaean–Constantinopolitan Creed (381). A very great distance between what the New Testament affirms about God, Christ, and the

Spirit and the later doctrine of the Trinity is sometimes supposed. In reality, that doctrine represents a fairly straightforward effort to work out the implications of the biblical testimony just reviewed. God is one, not many. Yet salvation in all its dimensions is the joint work of God, Christ, and the Spirit, whom together the church worships and adores. How can this be?

The doctrine of the Trinity answers this question by staking out what is, in effect, a mediating position between two exegetical extremes. One extreme emphasizes the unity of Father, Son, and Spirit but so forcefully that it denies any ultimate differences between them. The other extreme acknowledges ultimate differences between Father, Son, and Spirit but so forcefully that it denies that any but the Father is truly and fully divine. These two positions have come to be known, respectively, as *modalism* and *subordinationism*. The orthodox doctrine of the Trinity identifies both alternatives as heretical misreadings of the biblical evidence and aims to steer a middle course between them.

Of the two extremes, modalism (or Sabellianism, as it was known before the modern era) was the first to provoke opposition and proved on the whole easier to deal with. Arguably, modalism's great strength was (and is) its conceptual simplicity. For modalists such as Sabellius (fl. ca. 215), the one God of the Bible may appear now as "Father," now as "Son," now as "Spirit," according to the needs of humankind; but the different names do not pick out anything ultimately real in God, for God in himself is simply and perfectly one. However, this conceptual clarity comes at a high and fairly obvious price.

All the strands of New Testament evidence I have reviewed distinguish how God, Christ, and the Spirit relate to one another, not just to the world. This is clearest in the case of the kinship language of Father and Son, but it is also true of the other idioms (e.g., God as giver of the divine name, Christ as its receiver; God as source of wisdom, Christ as wisdom itself). If Father, Son, and Spirit refer indistinguishably to the same reality, then their mutual dealings with one another are really only a kind of make-believe and it is the Father and Spirit who died on the cross as much as the Son. Such a reading of the Bible undercuts the dramatic distinctions that make the gospel of Jesus Christ a narratable story of salvation in the first place. The North African theologian Tertullian (ca. 160–225 C.E.) devised a terminology to make these points against modalism. He used the Latin term "person" (*persona*) to identify Father, Son, and Spirit in their irreducible distinctiveness and the term "substance" (*substantia*) to express what they are or had in common that made them one and worthy of worship. Tertullian's language endured in the Latin West, while Christians in the East eventually arrived at comparable terms (*hypostasis, ousia*). The language supplied a form of discourse that lent itself to further development and eventual encapsulation in a simple formula: the Trinity (another word introduced by Tertullian) is "one substance in three persons."

Still, the rejection of modalism did not settle everything. There remained another way of making sense of basic Christian convictions that eventually provoked even fiercer debate. Like Tertullian and the antimodalists, subordinationism affirms real distinctions between God, Christ, and the Spirit; but it carries this insight to the point of asserting that God is more truly divine than Christ and the Spirit. God is not only the source of Christ and the Spirit, as the biblical evidence clearly suggests (sons come from fathers, words from speakers, and so forth), but also, by virtue of being their source, their superior in deity.

Like modalism, subordinationism is not without its attractions. The assumption that divinity is an elastic category admitting of degrees was widespread in the ancient world; it provided many Christians with a natural, seemingly unproblematic way of understanding the one God's relation to his own (slightly inferior) Word and Spirit. Furthermore, as we have seen, scripture itself seems at times to suggest such a view, especially in passages informed by wisdom tradition (cf. Prov 8:22; Col 1:15).

Still, subordinationism conceals a lurking problem. Recall that, in the Bible, salvation encompasses three interrelated dimensions: knowledge of God's uniqueness, experience of God's presence, and participation in God's life-giving blessings. The *novum* of the New Testament is that God accomplishes all this by sending his own Word and Spirit into the world. But if the

Word and the Spirit are truly inferior to God, as subordinationism maintains, then the salvation they bring must also be less than fully divine. Christ and the Spirit can enact an attenuated version of divine presence and blessing, perhaps; but the fullness of God's presence and blessing remains remote and unavailable, even after the incarnation and the outpouring of the Spirit at Pentecost. In short, subordinationism is a problem for soteriological reasons. It endangers the unity, reality, and fullness of salvation as fellowship with God.

Nevertheless, the weaknesses of this position remained largely unexplored until Arius (ca. 250–336 C.E.) forced Christians to think through the issue without recourse to the idea of a sliding scale of deity. Arius, a proponent of subordinationism, held that the proper context for thinking about God's relation to Christ and the Spirit was not the dubious idea of degrees of uncreated deity but rather the Bible's basic distinction between creator and created. On this point, Arius's intervention was decisive, and subsequent theologians largely followed his lead. But having thus successfully reframed the issue, Arius failed to persuade the church to adopt the subordinationist viewpoint itself. Faced with the stark choice of declaring Christ to be either a creature of God or a cocreator with him, the bishops assembled at the Council of Nicaea in 325 chose the latter view; and they did so, at least in part, for the sort of soteriological reasons previously noted.

The Nicaean Creed makes the case against Arius's view of Christ by drawing on all three strands of biblical testimony identified in this article. In the process, it effectively makes the case against modalism, too. In 381 the Nicaean Creed was revised at the Council of Constantinople for the purpose of defending the status of the Holy Spirit, who was then subject to subordinationist interpretation as well. The expanded creed, most correctly called the Nicaean–Constantinopolitan Creed, soon became the preeminent standard of Trinitarian orthodoxy and remains so.

The literary backbone of the Nicaean–Constantinopolitan Creed ("We believe in one God...and one Lord Jesus Christ") is an almost verbatim citation of 1 Corinthians 8:6, which in turn is Paul's Christologically enhanced paraphrase of Israel's Shema, "Hear O Israel: The LORD is our God, the LORD alone" (Deut 6:4). The words include Christ in the confession of the one God, accord him the dignity of the divine name (indicated by the surrogate "Lord"), and thereby imply his inclusion in God's deity, if any words can. In 381 the Nicaean Creed's original, lapidary confession, "We believe in the Holy Spirit," was augmented to include the confession that the Holy Spirit is "the Lord," thereby according it, too, a dignity equal to that of God and Christ.

The creed also gives prominent place to the kinship language of "Father" and "Son." The composers of the creed home in on the term "beget" to make the anti-Arian case. The Son is "begotten, not made": this distinguishes the Father's relationship to the Son from that of every created thing and places both Father and Son on the creator side of the creator/creature distinction. Moreover, the Son is "eternally begotten" of the Father, excluding the idea of the Son's origin in time and implying that the Father has always been Father and the Son always Son. In 381 the creed was augmented to affirm that the Holy Spirit "proceeds from the Father, and with the Father and Son is worshipped and glorified," again according the Spirit a dignity equal to that of God and Christ, this time with reference to practices of worship. Christians in the West eventually began to confess that the Holy Spirit proceeds "from the Father and from the Son [filioque]," an addition that contributed substantially to the Great Schism of 1054 between Eastern and Western portions of the church.

Finally, the creed evokes the imagery and rhetoric of Old Testament wisdom in its declaration that Christ is "God of God, Light of Light, Very God of Very God" and that the Holy Spirit is the "Giver of Life." Here, Christ is named three times, each time in a way that entails a corresponding naming of God. The "anti-Arian" point is made by employing the same divine names for both God and Christ, while the work of differentiating them is performed by grammatical case, or, in English translation, by the preposition "of."

Alongside its rich use of biblical language, the creed uses one nonbiblical term to make the case against subordinationism. The word appears at the end of a long string of Christological affirmations, where at last it is said that the Son of God is "of one essence" (*homoousion*) with the Father. This affirmation has sometimes been thought to demonstrate the great intellectual gulf that separates the creed from the Bible; actually, it is best understood as a fairly modest elucidating comment. If Christ is "Light of Light" and bearer of the divine name "Lord" and eternally begotten of the Father, then this is as much as to say that he shares in the Father's one eternal deity: he is "of one essence" with the Father.

In its basic rudiments, then, the doctrine of the Trinity is neither especially complicated nor far distant from the plain sense and implication of scripture as a tiding of salvation. On the one hand, it affirms, against a modalist reading of the Bible, that the Father, the Son, and the Holy Spirit are genuinely distinct: otherwise, how could the Father really send the Son and Spirit into the world? On the other hand, against a subordinationist reading of the Bible, it affirms that the Son and Holy Spirit share fully in the Father's one eternal deity: otherwise, how could their sending be good news?

[*See also* Christology; Creation; Deuteronomy; Deutero-Pauline Letters; God and Gods; Gospel; Hermeneutics, Biblical; Holy Spirit; John and the Johannine Epistles; Lord; Luke–Acts; Mark; Matthew; Pauline Letters; Redemption; Salvation History; Son of God; Soteriology; Theology, Biblical; Wisdom; Wisdom Literature; *and* Word (Logos).]

BIBLIOGRAPHY

Anatolios, Khaled. *Retrieving Nicaea: The Development and Meaning of Trinitarian Doctrine.* Grand Rapids, Mich.: Baker Academic, 2011.

Bauckham, Richard. *Jesus and the God of Israel.* Grand Rapids, Mich.: Eerdmans, 2008.

Beeley, Christopher, *Gregory of Nazianzus on the Trinity and the Knowledge of God: In Your Light We Shall See Light.* Oxford: Oxford University Press, 2008.

Gieschen, Charles A. "The Divine Name in Ante-Nicene Christology." *Vigiliae Christianae* 57 (2003): 115–158.

Hurtado, Larry. *Lord Jesus Christ: Devotion to Jesus in Earliest Christianity.* Grand Rapids, Mich.: Eerdmans, 2003.

Pelikan, Jaroslav. *The Christian Tradition: A History of the Development of Doctrine.* Vol. 1: *The Emergence of the Catholic Tradition (100–600).* Chicago: University of Chicago Press, 1975.

Soulen, R. Kendall. *The Divine Name(s) and the Holy Trinity.* Vol. 1: *Distinguishing the Voices.* Louisville, Ky.: Westminster John Knox, 2011.

Studer, Basil. *Trinity and Incarnation: The Faith of the Early Church.* London: T&T Clark, 1994.

Widdicombe, Peter. *The Fatherhood of God from Origen to Athanasius.* Oxford: Oxford University Press, 2000.

Yeago, David S. "The New Testament and the Nicene Dogma: A Contribution to the Recovery of Theological Exegesis." In *The Theological Interpretation of Scripture: Classic and Contemporary Readings*, edited by Stephen E. Fowl, pp. 87–100. Cambridge, U.K.: Blackwell, 1997.

R. Kendall Soulen

TRUTH

The two biblical words rendered in English as "truth" are ʾemet (Hebrew) and *alêtheia* (Greek); ʾemet and the closely related term ʾemunâ are cognates of the verb ʾaman, "to be steady or firm." In its most basic sense ʾemet refers to firmness, trustworthiness, or faithfulness. The Greek term *alêtheia* is a compound noun consisting of the alpha-privative ("not") and the root *lêth-*, "to obscure, to hide, or to forget." Thus, *alêtheia* refers to something that is neither obscure nor hidden. That which is true is plain and clear; *alêtheia* is usually translated as either "truth" or "reality."

Truth in Classical and Hellenistic Contexts. In the earliest Greek literature the notion of truth is very simply the opposite of a lie, as in Homer's phrase "to speak the truth" (*alêtheiên katalexai*; e.g., *Il.* 24.407). Very soon, however, the term acquires technical meanings in Greek philosophy. A particular concern for philosophers is the relationship between truth and knowledge. The cosmological poem of Parmenides, transmitted under the false title "On Nature," shows the basic contours of the problem. The goddess Justice warns the poem's reader of a difference between *alêtheiê* and human opinions, in which there is nothing *alêthês*. Both the senses and human convention deviate from *alêtheiê*, "reality." Our habits and perceptions lead us into a false world, away from what is real.

Plato (ca. 427–ca. 348 B.C.E.) develops a similar line of thought. For him, the term *alêtheia* can be translated to mean either "truth" or "reality," and his understanding of *alêtheia* depends on his distinction between "being" and "becoming." The world available to the senses is a world in flux, merely "becoming." Trees, mountains, the bodies of animals—all such things are impermanent. They "become" for a while, and then they are gone. In contrast to this world of impermanent "becoming," Plato posits a world of permanence and perfection unavailable to the senses, the realm of true "being." Because our senses can mislead us and can perceive only the impermanent realm of change, the senses lead only to opinions (*doxai*) about things that are relatively good or relatively beautiful. But if the human eye leads only to opinions, the eye of the soul is different. The soul's eye perceives a realm lying beyond human experience. This is the realm of the objective, perfect good and the objective, perfectly beautiful: what Plato sometimes calls "the Good itself" (*auto to kalon*). Perception of this realm leads not to subjective opinion (*doxa*) but to objective knowledge (*epistêmê*): the realm of what is "true" or "real." In an important comment in *The Republic* (508D–509A), Plato says that knowledge (*epistêmê*) and truth (*alêtheia*) are related to the Good in the same way that light and vision are related to the sun. In general, for Plato, *alêtheia* is either knowledge of what is real/true or reality/truth itself.

Thinkers contemporary with the New Testament follow Plato, especially Philo of Alexandria (ca. 13 B.C.E.–ca. 50 C.E.), who also closely associates what is accessible to the senses (*orata*) with mere opinion (*doxa* or *dokêsis*), while what is accessible to the mind (*noêta*) is associated with *epistêmê* and *alêtheia* (*Det.* 162, *Praem.* 28). A different approach to the same problem occupies other thinkers around the time of the New Testament, especially the Epicureans, Stoics, and Skeptics. These schools are preoccupied with the delineation of a "criterion of truth." Epicurus is the innovator in this pursuit. For him, the key term in epistemology is *kanôn*. A *kanôn* was a tool for making a straight line or for measuring, much like our modern ruler. Its close synonym in Epicurus's thought is "criterion": a final arbiter in determining truth, something a priori requiring neither defense nor support, which could uphold what is true or convict what is false (see Lucretius, *De rerum natura* 4.469–521).

These criteria of truth are themselves not open to debate but are considered self-evident. The three criteria posited by Epicurus are sensations (*aisthêseis*), preconception (*prolêpsis*), and feelings (*pathos*). If our sensations lead us to an improper judgment, then the fault lies not with the sensations, which are accurate, but with the judgment founded upon them.

The Stoics develop this program in a slightly different direction. While believing that there are criteria of truth that help us to judge what is true from what is false, they differ from Epicurus in claiming that sense impressions themselves can be either true or false; thus, Stoics identify the criterion among cognitive impressions. The Skeptics, by contrast, chose instead to suspend all judgment (Plutarch, *Adv. Col.*, 1122A–F); their purpose was to destroy any foundation that other philosophers established in order to force their opponents into an ever-expanding, infinite regression of argument. The pursuit of a final criterion of truth would occupy early Christian theologians in the second century C.E. and beyond.

Truth in the Old Testament. In the Septuagint *alêtheia* generally translates *ʾemet*, though sometimes other cognates are used (especially *alêthinos*, *alêthôs*, or *alêtheuein*). The noun *ʾemet* occurs in the Old Testament more than 100 times. It refers to something solid, valid, or binding—hence, "true." It is especially important as a legal term—thus, Deuteronomy 22:20, where a matter is said to rest on whether a "charge is true" as opposed to false. Similarly, Deuteronomy 13:14 and 17:4 refer to a matter confirmed by inquiry, thereby made trustworthy. A witness to the facts of a case is called "a truthful witness" (Prov 14:25). From this basic sense derive others. When a prophet speaks, as ratified by the mother of the child saved by Elijah (1 Kgs 17:24), "the word of the LORD" is called *ʾemet*: that word is truly present in the mouth of the prophet.

Related to this legal sense is the term's religious connotation. Because God is true (Isa 65:16), anyone who follows God is also required to be true and to seek God's truth (Pss 25:5; 51:6; 86:11). The one who speaks truth (*ʾemet*) in his or her heart is ritually permitted to dwell on the holy hill (Ps 15:2). In Hosea 4:1 this religious notion of truth is also linked to knowledge of God: because there is no *ʾemet* in the land, there is no knowledge of God. The religious nuance of *ʾemet* is further extended to include all of Israelite religion, as in Daniel 8:12: the truth is "cast to the ground," where *ʾemet* seems to refer to the entire complex of Israelite religious life.

Truth in the New Testament. In the New Testament the term *alêtheia* occurs 109 times. The vast majority of its occurrences appear in the Johannine and Pauline corpora. The term occurs 47 times in letters attributed to Paul and 44 times in the Gospel and Letters of John. Of the remaining 18 uses, only 7 occur in the Synoptic Gospels.

In Romans 1:18–19 Paul refers to those "who by their wickedness suppress the truth. For what can be known about God is plain to them." Here, truth is linked to knowledge of God, as it is in both Old Testament and Greek thought. Similarly, Paul distinguishes false belief or misunderstanding from what he calls "the truth of the Gospel" (Gal 2:5, 14). Hebrews 10:26 refers to "receiving the knowledge of the truth" in a context that relies on baptismal imagery, which suggests that the phrase refers to conversion. The very similar phrase "come to the knowledge of the truth" seems to function in the same way in the Pastoral Epistles (1 Tim 2:4; see also 1 Tim 4:3; 2 Tim 2:25; 3:7).

The idea that one might possess knowledge of the truth or might know the truth is also common in the Johannine writings (John 8:32; 17:3; 1 John 2:21; 2 John 1). The Gospel and Letters of John rely on a relatively small storehouse of vocabulary that is used repeatedly, and *alêtheia* is one of these key Johannine terms. Jesus is called "the truth" (14:6), the "true bread" (6:32), and the "true vine" (15:1), where the understanding seems to be that he is the "real" manna, and so forth. The Paraclete is also called the "Spirit of truth" (14:17; 16:13). Some key phrases of Johannine terminology depend on Semitic usage. In the Gospel's prologue, for instance, the phrase "grace and truth" (1:14, 17) seems dependent on the combination of the Hebrew terms *ḥesed* and *ʾemet* (Exod 34:6). Both the Fourth Gospel and 1 John refer to doing the truth (John 3:21; 1 John 1:6), another Semitic idiom (2 Chr 31:20; Neh 9:33) common in later Jewish writings (Tob 4:6; 1QS 1.5, 5.3, 8.2).

A broad range of significance attaches to Pilate's famous question "What is truth?" (John 18:38). When Pilate asks Jesus that question, he is assigning himself to a particular group in the Fourth Gospel. Jesus testifies to what he has seen, yet not everyone receives his testimony. Those who do receive it recognize that God is true (*alêthês*); those who do not receive it fall under the wrath of God (3:31–36) and are condemned in judgment. Testimony, judgment, and truth cohere even more closely in John 8:14, "Even if I testify on my own behalf, my testimony is valid [*alêthês*]," and in 8:16, "Yet even if I do judge, my judgment is valid [*alêthinê*]". When Pilate asks "What is truth?" he falls under judgment.

Truth in Postbiblical Thought. In second-century debates between orthodoxy and heresy, the concern among Hellenistic philosophers for finding a "criterion of truth" becomes central among early Christian theologians. Irenaeus argues that the Gnostics would develop a new line of argument in every debate (*Haer.* 1.18.1, 1.21.5), leading to the same infinite regress that the Skeptics developed in their debates with Stoics and Epicureans. In response, Irenaeus and others establish as the "criterion of truth" the "rule of faith." Irenaeus writes in regard to gnostic readings of scripture, "Anyone who keeps unswervingly in himself the canon of truth [*kanona tês alêtheias*]…will restore each of the passages [of scripture] to its proper order and, having fit it into the body of truth" (*Haer.* 1.9.4).

Finally, it should be emphasized that the Christian pursuit of truth is not merely an intellectual enterprise, focused on theology and biblical hermeneutics. The criterion of truth also applies to the Christian life. Reflecting on the work of St. Silouan (1866–1938) of Mt. Athos, the ascetical writer Archimandite Zacharias writes, "With apostolic conviction, St. Silouan…says somewhere that the criterion for the presence of the Holy Spirit, the criterion of the truth, is the love for one's enemies" (2006, p. 4).

[*See also* Faith; John and the Johannine Epistles; Justice, Justification, and Righteousness; Knowledge; Pauline Letters; *and* Witness.]

BIBLIOGRAPHY

Behr, John. *The Way to Nicaea.* Crestwood, N.Y.: St. Vladimir's Seminary Press, 2001.

Brown, Raymond E. *The Gospel According to John.* Anchor Bible 29 and 29A. New York: Doubleday, 1970.

Dodd, C. H. *The Interpretation of the Fourth Gospel.* Cambridge, U.K.: Cambridge University Press, 1953.

Lincoln, Andrew T. *Truth on Trial: The Lawsuit Motif in the Fourth Gospel.* Grand Rapids, Mich.: Baker Academic, 2000.

Long, A. A., and D. N. Sedley, trans. and eds. *Translations of the Principal Sources with Philosophical Commentary.* The Hellenistic Philosophers 1. Cambridge, U.K.: Cambridge University Press, 1987.

Osborn, Eric F. "Reason and the Rule of Faith in the Second Century AD." In *The Making of Orthodoxy: Essays in Honor of Henry Chadwick,* edited by Rowan Williams, pp. 40–61. Cambridge, U.K.: Cambridge University Press, 1989.

Quell, G., G. Kittel, and R. Bultmann. "*alêtheia.*" In *Theological Dictionary of the New Testament,* edited by Gerhard Kittel and Gerhard Friedrich, Vol. 1, pp. 232–247. Grand Rapids, Mich., Eerdmans, 1964.

Zacharias, Archimandrite. *The Enlargement of the Heart.* South Canaan, Pa.: Mount Thabor Pub., 2006.

George L. Parsenios

TWELVE, BOOK OF THE

See Book of the Twelve (Minor Prophets).

U

UNDERWORLD AND HELL

Notions of the underworld and hell developed considerably over time. A shadowy underworld as a destiny for all in ancient Israel developed to the separate fates for the righteous and the wicked of Second Temple Judaism and early Christianity then to the classical doctrines of heaven, and hell and on to diverse modern perspectives.

Hebrew Bible. The Hebrew Bible generally reflects the majority ancient Near Eastern view that death led to a gloomy underworld, termed *sheol*. However, in contrast to the extant literature of surrounding cultures, the Hebrew texts show little interest in the underworld itself. *Sheol* and its synonyms (mainly *šaḥat* and *bôr*) only occur about 120 times, often in parallel, a paltry total given the pervasiveness of death as both event and theme. Also, there is scant description of the underworld itself and only in two prophetic texts. In one, the weak, somnolent "shades" (Heb. *rĕpāʾîm*) are roused to greet a newcomer and then only to tell the Babylonian king that he has become as weak as them (Isa 14:9–10). In the other, dead warriors by national group lie motionless in a vast cavern (Ezek 32:17–32). While *sheol* is occasionally presented as eager to swallow its victims (Hab 2:5), it is never portrayed as a place of punishment. Instead, the dominant emphasis is that death is the end of all meaningful existence (e.g., Pss 39:13; 88:18), since the underworld and its denizens are cut off from Yahweh with no possibility of further praise or prayer (e.g., Ps 6:5; Isa 38:18).

Sheol is the only fate envisaged in most of the Hebrew Bible, but somewhat surprisingly it is not viewed neutrally; rather, those consigned there are predominantly the ungodly, while psalmists repeatedly plead for deliverance from it. These pleas may simply be for temporal respite, nevertheless the pattern remains striking. Only four apparently righteous people explicitly envisage descent there: Jacob, Hezekiah, Job, and a despairing psalmist (Gen 37:35; Isa 38:10; Job 14:13; Ps 88:4), all arguably assuming themselves under divine judgment. This interpretation is supported by the various different phrases used later for Jacob's demise as his life ends happily (Gen 46–49). The same element of judgment may also explain an early exilic psalmist's consignment of all humanity to *sheol* (Ps 89:48–49). Only the sceptical Qoheleth gives an unqualified universal perspective (Eccl 9:10), though interestingly the book of Ecclesiastes alone also suggests postmortem judgment (Eccl 3:17; 12:14).

There are occasional hints of an alternative fate. Enoch and Elijah apparently survived death (Gen 5:24; 2 Kgs 2:11), but they remained unexplained exceptions and never became paradigmatic for other faithful Israelites. A few psalmists may have envisaged some continuation of communion with Yahweh (Pss

16:10; 49:13–15, the latter in explicit contrast to the "foolhardy"). Undeveloped comments on divine power over death (Deut 32:39; 1 Sam 2:6; also Isa 25:8) plus the portrayal of postexilic national restoration as resurrection (Ezek 37:12) may well have fostered the apocalyptic notion of individual resurrection, first of the faithful only (Isa 26:19; cf. v.14) and then of a multitude, some to "everlasting life" and others to "everlasting contempt" (Dan 12:2).

Many scholars attribute the Hebrew Bible's relative disinterest in the underworld to the Deuteronomists' reforming zeal, and argue for a much greater interest in death activities in preexilic Israel (ancestor cults, food for the dead, necromancy, etc.), as elsewhere in the ancient Near East (e.g., Stavrakopoulou, 2010). This plurality of belief and practice was inimical to the Deuteronomists and therefore written out of their record. Alternatively, others defend the texts' own perspective of a genuinely ancient disinterest (Johnston, 2002).

Emerging Judaism. The traditional Israelite view is maintained in the early second century B.C.E. by Jesus ben Sira: "From the dead, as from one who does not exist, thanksgiving has ceased" (Sir 17:28). While this approach is rare in the contemporary and later literature, it persisted as one perspective within Judaism and was held by the later Sadducees, whose rationale was both explicitly theological (absence of resurrection in the Torah) and implicitly political (belief in resurrection facilitates insurrection).

By contrast, Second Temple texts reveal an increasing fascination with the afterlife, as portrayed in visions of the future conveyed by various ancient and supernatural figures (see Nickelsburg, 2007; Bauckham, 1998). These contain two significant developments concerning the underworld: its compartmentalization and the emergence of punishment for the wicked. This is well illustrated in the composite *1 Enoch*, which notes several compartments in Hades (*1 En.* 22; the text mentions both "three" and "four" places) and an abyss of fire (*1 En.* 21, 90). Other texts mention wrath (1QH 3:25–36), fire (4Q184 1:7), worms and pain (Jdt 16:17; cf. Isa 66:24), beating and torment (*Apoc. Zeph.* Sahidic B:2, Akhmimic 11:2). There are also various references to resurrection, both for

the righteous only (2 Macc 7:9, 14) and for all (*T. Benj.* 10:7–8, *Sib. Or.* 4:182). Somewhat differently, the more Hellenistic Wisdom of Solomon (3:1–5) speaks of the immortality of souls of the righteous, although with the specific Jewish perspective that "in the time of their visitation…they will govern nations" (3:7–8).

Scholars attribute the development of the concept of separate fates for the righteous and the wicked, however these groups are delineated, to three main influences. Firstly, and most widely, there is the influence of other religions and worldviews, notably Persian Zoroastrianism and Greek immortality, possibly also Canaanite dying-and-rising deities (as Ugaritic Ba'al) and Egyptian afterlife belief. Secondly, there is the effect of the severe Antiochene persecution, reflected initially in the books of Daniel and Maccabees with their Israelite responses to unjust foreign rulers and persecution. And thirdly, there is the development from hints in the Hebrew Bible, as already noted. Most scholars combine these influences with various weighting, but Levenson (2006) argues strongly for a distinctly inner-Israelite theological development.

New Testament and Early Christian Texts. The New Testament builds on the perspectives of early Judaism, although it introduces a new theology and uses distinctive vocabulary. In the gospels Jesus speaks repeatedly of separate fates for the godly and for sinners, the distinction being implicit in context and/or linked to their responsiveness to God. The apostles, particularly Paul, expound the distinction more in terms of faith in Jesus Christ and his salvific death. Those who believe will go to heaven when they die, to be with God eternally. Those who do not will go to what is usually described as Gehenna, Hades, a place of torment and agony, or more simply everlasting destruction.

The Greek term *géenna* clearly derives from the Hebrew *gê hinnōm* ("valley of Hinnom"). This was situated to the immediate southwest of Jerusalem, was reputedly a site of child sacrifice and the Molech cult (e.g., Jer 7:31–32; 32:35), and was possibly the locale envisaged in Isaiah's portrayal of the undying worm and unquenchable fire (Isa 66:24). It is often suggested that the Hinnom valley became Jerusalem's garbage dump, which constantly smoldered,

UNDERWORLD AND HELL 401

and that this contributed to the Greek term's meaning. This is certainly feasible, although it lacks early attestation and to our knowledge was first proposed by Kimhi (ca. 1200 C.E.). In any case, the prophetic eschatology cited above sufficiently explains the meaning of *géenna*. The Greek term was first used in the New Testament, while its Latin derivative appears in the later Christian apocalypse of 2 Esdras (7:36). Gehenna occurs 12 times in the New Testament, mostly in four dominical pericopae, and clearly indicates a place for the reprobate (e.g., Mark 9:43–48, citing Isa 66:24). The only other reference is James 3:6, where it sets the tongue on fire.

The Greek term *hades* occurs 11 times, in three synoptic and three other contexts. Two of the former clearly imply a place of punishment since unbelieving citizens of Chorazin, Bethsaida, and Capernaum will fare far worse in their consignment to Hades than those of ancient wicked cities, and the rich man who ignored Lazarus in life suffers torment there (Luke 10:13–15; 16:23). The other contexts seem to envisage Hades more like the Hebrew *sheol* (Matt 16:18; Acts 2 and 1 Cor 15, quoting Ps 16 and Hos 13, respectively; and four times in Rev, always coupled with death). Some scholars therefore perceive a clear New Testament distinction between Hades as a provisional disembodied state and Gehenna as eternal destruction of body and soul. However, most argue instead for a substantial overlap of the terms, especially given the Lucan texts.

The Synoptic Gospels contain several vivid descriptions of the fate of the ungodly, involving variously eternal punishment, unquenchable fire, the undying worm, outer darkness, weeping, and gnashing of teeth (e.g., Matt 3:12; 8:12; 13:42; 18:8; 22:13). This terminology is echoed occasionally in Hebrews (10:27) and the Catholic Epistles (Jude 7) and repeatedly in Revelation (e.g., 14:10). A few texts envisage the dead awaiting judgment (e.g., 1 Pet 2:4–5), while one notes that after death Jesus preached to the imprisoned pre-Noahite spirits (1 Pet 3:19)—although whether to offer salvation or proclaim judgment is a well-known *crux interpretum*.

Elsewhere in the New Testament, however, significantly different language occurs. The Johannine literature eschews mention of Gehenna, Hades, torment, fire, etc. and instead portrays unbelief as death, judgment, and perishing (conversely, belief as salvation and life). Acts also avoids all reference to hell: the apostolic preaching focused on resurrection and salvation, with scant, undeveloped references to divine judgment. The Pauline corpus mentions fire once, in reference to testing the work of believers (1 Cor 3:13), and envisages "anguish and distress for everyone who does evil" in the paradigmatic Romans 2:9. However, and surprisingly so in light of common modern perceptions, it never speaks of hell per se. It frequently mentions the wrath of God, judgment, condemnation, death, perishing, and everlasting destruction but seldom that which follows judgment.

Christian Theology. Early postapostolic Christian literature affirms the New Testament portrayal of distinct afterlife fates, with eternal death and punishment for the wicked. Most early Christian texts portray this, for example, *Epistle of Barnabas*, *1* and *2 Clement*, the Ignatian letters, *Martyrdom of Polycarp*, *Shepherd of Hermas*, and notably the writings of Justin Martyr and Tertullian. (The *Didache* is exceptional in mentioning only the resurrection of the righteous.) In an era of frequent suffering and intermittent persecution, faith was bolstered by the prospect of blissful heaven for the faithful and fearful hell for the impenitent.

The classical doctrine of hell as eternal conscious punishment was further developed by Augustine within a systematic theological framework. Original sin and human depravity mean that all people deserved hell, while substitutionary atonement and divine predestination mean that some are gifted heaven. Augustine argued extensively and vehemently against the theology of Pelagius, that one could be virtuous and hence avoid hell by human willpower. While Augustine's view largely prevailed in later theology, the debate reemerged at various times, for example, in the early sixteenth century between the humanist Erasmus and the reformers Luther and Calvin, in the late seventeenth between Jesuits and Jansenists, and generally from the Enlightenment on between conservative and liberal Christians.

Meanwhile there gradually developed in Christian tradition the concept of purgatory: an intermediate state after death, in which souls are purged of sin and prepared for heaven. Its roots and rationale can be traced back to foundational texts and early traditions, but the doctrine emerged in mature form only in the twelfth century. An emphasis on the torments experienced in the purgatorial process, described like hell itself in ever more lurid detail, led to its common bracketing with hell. However, Griffiths (2008) demonstrates that it should instead be bracketed with heaven for which it is the antechamber, as well understood by the visionary poet Dante.

Over the twentieth century, Christian views changed significantly. While creeds and doctrinal statements generally maintain classical positions on hell, the majority of practising Christians in Western traditions have serious misgivings. Many then adopt alternatives, even if these are seldom developed theologically. Of these, three views are common: (1) universalism, that is, all go to heaven, immediately or eventually; (2) near-universalism, that is, all but the most evil go to heaven; and (3) annihilationism, that is, those who do not go to heaven are annihilated, either immediately on death or after final judgment. This third view has gained ground in conservative Protestant circles, although it has also met strong opposition. From the later twentieth century onwards there has also been a new wave of scholarly study examining hell theologically and philosophically (e.g., Kvanvig, 1993). The Hebrew concept of a shadowy underworld has long been superseded. The Christian concept of hell remains a matter of contention.

[*See also* Death and Dying; Devils and Demons; Heaven and Earth; *and* Monsters.]

BIBLIOGRAPHY

Bauckham, Richard. *The Fate of the Dead: Studies on the Jewish and Christian Apocalypses.* Leiden, The Netherlands: Brill, 1998.

Bernstein, Alan E. *The Formation of Hell: Death and Retribution in the Ancient and Early Christian Worlds.* Ithaca, N.Y.: Cornell University Press, 1993.

Casey, John. *Afterlives: A Guide to Heaven, Hell, and Purgatory.* Oxford: Oxford University Press, 2009.

Griffiths, Paul J. "Purgatory." In *The Oxford Handbook of Eschatology*, edited by Jerry L. Walls, pp. 427–445. Oxford: Oxford University Press, 2008.

Johnston, Philip S. *Shades of Sheol: Death and Afterlife in the Old Testament.* Leicester, U.K.: Apollos, 2002.

Kvanvig, Jonathan L. *The Problem of Hell.* New York: Oxford University Press, 1993.

Levenson, Jon D. *Resurrection and the Restoration of Israel: The Ultimate Victory of the God of Life.* New Haven, Conn.: Yale University Press, 2006.

Nickelsburg, George W. E. *Resurrection, Immortality, and Eternal Life in Intertestamental Judaism and Early Christianity.* 2d ed. Cambridge, Mass.: Harvard University Press, 2007.

Segal, Alan F. *Life After Death: A History of the Afterlife in Western Religion.* New York: Doubleday, 2004.

Stavrakopoulou, Francesca. "'Popular' Religion and 'Official' Religion: Practice, Perception, Portrayal." In *Religious Diversity in Ancient Israel and Judah*, edited by Francesca Stavrakopoulou and John Barton, pp. 37–58. London and New York: T&T Clark, 2010.

Philip S. Johnston

VIOLENCE

Violence is ubiquitous in the biblical record. We may distinguish between paradigmatic, quasi-historical stories of violence and eschatological violence attributed to God or divine agents.

Human Violence. The first eruption of violence in the biblical narrative is the murder of Abel by his brother Cain. Remarkably, in this case, the murderer is protected by divine decree: "Whoever kills Cain will suffer a sevenfold vengeance" (Gen 4:15). A few chapters later, in the covenant with Noah after the flood, we meet the more typical biblical norm: "Whoever sheds the blood of a human, by a human shall that person's blood be shed" (Gen 9:6). Pentateuchal laws specify the death penalty for a wide range of offences, social, sexual, and religious (Exod 21:12–32; 31:14–15; Lev 20:2, 10–16, 22; 24:16; Num 1:51; 3:10, 38; 18:7; Deut 21:18–21; 22:22, 25). In this light it is clear that Exodus 20:13 (Deut 5:17), usually translated "Thou shalt not kill," is not an absolute prohibition against taking human life; it should instead be translated "Thou shalt not murder," as in the NRSV. By ancient standards, biblical law is not exceptionally harsh. In fact, the law of *talion*, specifying "eye for eye and tooth for tooth" (Exod 21:23–24), is meant to moderate retribution; and the Bible never prescribes the death penalty for property crimes. Nonetheless, the Bible does not affirm a right to life: Exodus 22:29–30 demands the sacrifice of firstborn sons as well as the firstborn of animals, a law later revoked (Exod 34:20, "the firstborn of your sons you shall redeem"). The issue of human sacrifice is dramatized most famously in the story of Abraham and Isaac (Gen 22:1–14). Abraham is not ultimately required to sacrifice Isaac, but he is praised for his willingness to do so, an ambivalence to human sacrifice that troubles the modern reader.

Even more distressing for the modern reader is the biblical account of the conquest of Canaan. According to Deuteronomy, the pre-Israelite inhabitants were to be put to the ban: "when the LORD your God gives them over to you and you defeat them, then you must utterly destroy them. Make no covenant with them and show them no mercy" (Deut 7:2–6). The ban (*herem*), the practice whereby the defeated enemy was dedicated for destruction, is also attested in a Moabite inscription from the ninth century B.C.E.: King Mesha boasts that, when he took Nebo from Israel, he killed all the men, boys, women, girls, and maidservants, for he had devoted them to destruction to his god Chemosh. Thus, the destruction had a sacrificial character: sometimes demanded by the deity (as with Amalek in 1 Sam 15:3), sometimes proposed as a human offering to win the deity's support ("If you will indeed give this people into our hands, then we will utterly destroy their towns," Num 21:1). The ban presupposes "a God who appreciates human sacrifice" (Niditch, 1993, p. 50). Deuteronomy rationalizes the practice to some degree. In Canaan, "you must not let anything that breathes remain alive . . . so that they may not teach you to do all the abhorrent things that they do for their gods" (Deut 20:16–18). Ethnic cleansing is the way to ensure cultic purity. In some cases the destruction is justified as punishment for lack of hospitality or as a preemptive measure to avoid trouble in the future (Num 33:55).

According to the book of Joshua, Joshua implemented these commandments by a sweeping, violent conquest of Canaan, "not leav[ing] any who breathed" (Josh 11:14). It now appears, however, that this is not a reliable historical account but, rather, an ideological fiction from a much later time. The archeological evidence does not support the account of a sweeping, violent conquest of Canaan. There is much to be said for the view that neither Deuteronomy nor Joshua was intended to incite actual violence against other peoples; rather, they were written to intimidate those who might resist the Deuteronomic view of cultic orthopraxy: "For you are a people holy to the LORD your God (Deut 7:6). But as Barr points out, "The problem is not whether the narratives are fact or fiction, the problem is that, whether fact or fiction, the ritual destruction is commended" (1993, p. 209). The idea that violent conquest can be justified by divine command or divine providence is rightly seen as morally problematic by modern readers because the divine mandate dovetails too neatly with the interests of those who report it.

The story of the conquest of Canaan has often been taken as paradigmatic. Mattathias, father of the Maccabees, emulated the zeal of Phinehas, who punished sexual impropriety by running through an Israelite man and a Midianite woman with his spear (Num 25:6–8; cf. 1 Macc 2:26). Likewise, the revolutionaries of the Roman period were known as Zealots. Much later, the conquest of Canaan provided a paradigm for Puritan conquests in America and Ireland, for the Boers in South Africa, and for Israeli settlers in contemporary Palestine.

A Violent God. As evidenced in the Song of Moses, the God of Israel was conceived as a warrior from the earliest times (Exod 15:3). A god who was worthy of worship had to be able to take care of his people by defeating their enemies. Many of the great myths of the ancient Near East described primeval combat between divine beings—Marduk and Tiamat in Babylonia, Baal and Yamm in Canaan—in which the "good" god obtained universal kingship by killing or subduing his rivals. Similar stories were told about Yahweh in ancient Israel, although we know them only through allusions in poetic books: "Was it not you who cut Rahab in pieces, who pierced the dragon?" (Isa 51:9). A prophetic poem from the postexilic period compares the divine warrior to a person treading the wine press: "Why are your robes red, and your garments like theirs who tread the wine press? . . . I trod them in my anger and trampled them in my wrath; their juice spattered on my garments and stained all my robes" (Isa 63:2–3). If God was a model for human behavior, it was a violent model.

Fantasized Violence. For most of the biblical period, however, the people of Israel and Judah were the victims of violence rather than its perpetrators. The violence encountered in the prophetic and apocalyptic writings is primarily fantasized violence, to be executed by God in the future. When the Assyrians and Babylonians brought Israel and Judah to the brink of extinction, the power of their God was brought into question. Consequently, the prophetic and apocalyptic texts of the Second Temple period are replete with gory fantasies of divine vengeance. In Ezekiel 38–39 the quintessential Gentile ruler Gog is left with his troops on the mountains of Israel for the birds of prey and wild animals to devour. In Joel 3 the Lord will gather all the nations for judgment in the valley of Jehoshaphat. In Zechariah 12 a plague will strike all the nations that make war against Jerusalem: their flesh shall rot while they are still on their feet, their eyes shall rot in their sockets, and their tongues shall rot in their mouths. This tradition of violent fantasy reaches a climax in the book of Revelation, which fantasizes the destruction of the Whore of Babylon (Rome) and pictures Christ as a warrior who comes from heaven on a white horse, with a sword coming out of his mouth for striking down the nations (Rev 17:1–18; 19:11–21).

Fantasized violence does not necessarily lead to violent action. In many cases apocalyptic literature recommends quietism in the present, in anticipation of divine vengeance to come. This is true of Revelation, which holds up the crucified Messiah, the Lamb that was slain, as the model to be emulated. "Vengeance is mine," says the Lord in Deuteronomy 32:35, where he also promises to avenge the blood of his children (32:43). This literature exhibits an intrinsic connection between present forbearance and eschatological vengeance. As Stendahl observes (1962, pp. 344–345), "With the Day of Vengeance at hand, the proper and reasonable attitude is to forego one's own vengeance and to leave vengeance to God. Why walk around with a little shotgun if the atomic blast is imminent?"

The teaching of Jesus, as portrayed in the Gospels, is decidedly nonviolent: "Do not resist an evildoer. If anyone strikes you on the right cheek, turn the other also" (Matt 5:39). When a follower draws his sword in the garden to resist those who have come to arrest him, Jesus says, "Put your sword back into its place; for all who take the sword will perish by the sword" (Matt 26:52). The Evangelists clearly distinguish Jesus from Jewish revolutionaries who engaged in armed rebellion against Rome. (Compare also the pointed contrast with Barabbas, whom the populace chooses over Jesus in Matt 27:15–23.) One enigmatic saying of Jesus might suggest that he endorsed violent resistance to Rome: "Do not think I have come to bring peace on earth. I have not come to bring peace but the sword" (Matt 10:34). But this aphorism is hard to reconcile with the dominant portrayal of Jesus in the Gospels.

The followers of Jesus, however, could not entirely dispense with violence. Paul endorsed the teaching of Jesus that one should not repay anyone for evil, but he supplied a new rationale: "Leave room for the wrath of God . . . for by doing this you will heap burning coals on their heads" (Rom 12:19–20; cf. Prov 25:21–22). This reflects the typical apocalyptic mentality in which violence is deferred to the final judgment but not rejected. The book of Revelation may be exceptional in its violent imagery but not in its desire for violent punishment of the wicked.

Opinions differ sharply as to the ethics of fantasized violence. Some argue that it is therapeutic for the oppressed and provides a necessary outlet in the absence of violent action. Nonetheless, indulgence in fantasized violence is surely conducive to hatred, and that can erupt into violence when circumstances allow. It encourages the demonization of the other that is at the heart of religious violence, even if it only rarely spills over into violent action.

Violence and Hermeneutics. Theologians deal with scriptural portrayals of violence in various ways. Some argue for a link between monotheism and violence; however, ancient polytheistic societies, such as Assyria, were often even more violent than the monotheistic religions. Intolerant monotheism can give rise to violence, but so can any other intolerant ideology. Some are content to denounce "the dark side of the Bible" (Lüdemann, 1997). Others point out, quite correctly, the diverse attitudes to violence in scripture and in Jewish and Christian traditions of its interpretation. The command to annihilate the Canaanites relates to a specific situation in the past and cannot be applied automatically to modern Israeli/Palestinian conflict. For Christians, Jesus's teaching on love of enemies and turning the other cheek (Matt 5:39, 44) takes priority over the Old Testament's violent commandments. As Williams argues, "the biblical witness to the innocent victim and the God of victims demystifies and demythologizes the sacred social order" in which violence is grounded (1991, p. 243, building on the work of René Girard). Yet, the Christian Bible concludes with the judgment scene in Revelation, in which the Lamb that was slain returns as the heavenly warrior with a sword for striking down the nations. Violence is not the only model of behavior on offer in the Bible, but it is by no means marginal or negligible; and it can be applied in ways that are destructive as well as salutary.

[*See also* Apocalypticism; Comfort and Mourning; Peace; Persecution; Politics and Systems of Governance; *and* War (Holy War).]

BIBLIOGRAPHY

Amanat, Abbas, and John J. Collins, eds. *Apocalypse and Violence*. New Haven, Conn.: Yale Center for International and Area Studies and the Council on Middle East Studies, 2002.

Assmann, Jan. *Moses the Egyptian: The Legacy of Egypt in Western Monotheism.* Cambridge, Mass.: Harvard, 1997.

Barr, James. *Biblical Faith and Natural Theology.* Oxford: Clarendon, 1993.

Boustan, Raʿanan S., Alex Jassen, and Calvin J. Roetzel, eds. *Violence, Scripture, and Textual Practices in Early Judaism and Christianity.* Leiden, The Netherlands: Brill, 2010.

Collins, John J. *Does the Bible Justify Violence?* Minneapolis: Fortress, 2004.

Greenberg, Moshe. "On the Political Use of the Bible in Modern Israel: An Engaged Critique." In *Pomegranates and Golden Bells: Studies in Biblical, Jewish, and Near Eastern Ritual, Law, and Literature in Honor of Jacob Milgrom,* edited by David P. Wright, David Noel Freedman, and Avi Hurvitz, pp. 466–469. Winona Lake, Ind.: Eisenbrauns, 1995.

Lüdemann, Gerd. *The Unholy in Holy Scriptures: The Dark Side of the Bible.* Louisville, Ky.: Westminster John Knox, 1997.

Matthews, Shelly, and E. Leigh Gibson, eds. *Violence in the New Testament.* London: T&T Clark, 2005.

Niditch, Susan. *War in the Hebrew Bible: A Study in the Ethics of Violence.* New York: Oxford University Press, 1993.

Schwartz, Regina. *The Curse of Cain. The Violent Legacy of Monotheism.* Chicago: University of Chicago Press, 1997.

Seibert, Eric A. *Disturbing Divine Behavior: Troubling Old Testament Images of God.* Minneapolis: Fortress, 2009.

Stendahl, Krister. "Hate, Non-retaliation, and Love: 1QS X, 17–20 and Rom 12:19–21." *Harvard Theological Review* 55 (1962): 343–355.

Williams, James G. *The Bible, Violence, and the Sacred: Liberation from the Myth of Sanctified Violence.* San Francisco: HarperSanFrancisco, 1991.

John J. Collins

Vows

See Oaths and Vows.

WAR (HOLY WAR)

The Hebrew word for war (*milḥamâ*) appears more than 300 times in the Old Testament. The parallel Greek term (*polemos*) occurs only 16 times in the New Testament, but it is a crucial part of the Gospels, Epistles, and Revelation. Thus, war is a major subject throughout the Bible. It is at the center of many of the narratives in the Old Testament, and it occupies much attention in both testaments as a concern in regard to human political conflict and as a figurative expression of the spiritual struggle against forces of evil. One of the great challenges in interpreting the Bible, however, is to determine when accounts of war should be read as literal presentations of martial conflict between two human parties and when the description of war is intended as an emblem of the struggle for spiritual and religious purity. The problem is complicated by the apparent approval of war in some cases as divinely sanctioned action that was intricately connected to the spiritual lives of those who carried it out (Deut 7:1–11).

War may be defined narrowly as "the attempt by one nation to impose its will on another by force" (Yadin, 1963, p. 1). The Bible contains many examples of this state-versus-state conflict (2 Kgs 3:4–27; 17:5–23; 18:13—19:37; cf. Isa 36–37), but it also is replete with accounts of coercive action by smaller parties that would nonetheless be counted as war: Israel's patri-archs against other groups in Canaan (Gen 14), warlords fighting in mercenary roles (Judg 11:1–33; 1 Sam 27), Israel in intertribal conflict (Judg 21:8–12), and Israel as a confederation of tribes defending themselves in the wilderness (Exod 17:8–16) or capturing the city states of Canaan (Josh 6). Thus, warfare in the societies that produced the Bible is perhaps best plotted on a scale with state-sponsored war led by career military figures to accomplish political goals on one end of the spectrum and war waged by smaller groups to settle feuds, seek revenge, or capture resources on the other (Niditch, 1993, pp. 16–17).

Nature of Warfare in the Biblical World. Wars in the Bible included battles in the open field and assaults on fortified cities. Both types of conflict were important, but the latter are most closely associated with state-sponsored warfare.

Weapons and soldiers. The Bible as well as sources outside the Bible give evidence of implements soldiers used in warfare. There are also ample data for understanding how soldiers protected themselves in battle.

Protection and weapons in hand-to-hand combat. Soldiers preparing for battle in the closest contexts wore armor and helmets (1 Sam 17:5–6, 38; cf. Eph 6:11–17). Armor consisted of a solid breastplate and scales to cover other areas (1 Sam 22:34) or a coat of mail (1 Sam 17:5, 38; Yadin, 1963, Vol. 1, p. 15). A shield might be used in place of armor to reduce the weight on the body (see Yadin, 1963, Vol. 2, p. 293). The most common weapons in such settings were the axe, mace, sword, and spear (1 Sam 17:7, 39).

Longer-range weapons. The use of weapons that could reach the enemy from longer range was important for both open-field conflict and attacks on and defense of cities. The bow was perhaps the most important weapon in this regard since some bows had an effective range of 300 meters or more (Yadin, 1963, Vol. 1, p. 7). The sling also could fire missiles at great distances. Slings were simple to construct, and ammunition could be simply collected, not produced. Finally, the javelin (as opposed to the spear) could be launched into an enemy line or into a fortification much like an arrow, although with less distance.

Mobility. The quick movement of forces in battle was facilitated by two primary tools: the chariot and the horse. Chariots provided both speed to move and a platform from which to fire on an enemy. They required a driver, who controlled the vehicle, and a soldier (usually a bowman), who fired; but they offered great accuracy with quick movement. The horse allowed a soldier to operate alone, but the dual role of using the weapon and controlling the animal reduced effectiveness.

Siege warfare. Attacks on fortified cities required a distinct set of strategies and actions. When a city was shut up, the assaulting army might attack directly and immediately. With artillery fire as cover (from bowmen, slingers, and javelin throwers), soldiers tried to approach and breach the city wall by scaling it, undermining it, or creating an opening in it. A primary weapon in this effort was the battering ram. A simple version was simply a fortified shelter for soldiers who hit and chipped away at the wall with a pole from inside. More complex battering rams were machines on wheels the army hoisted up a ramp constructed for the purpose. Soldiers inside the machine would then hammer the wall with a large ram that moved as a swing. This technique was commonly used by the Assyrians and Babylonians, as their artwork illustrates (see Yadin, 1963, Vol. 2, pp. 314–315). Perhaps the most famous use of siege ramp and battering ram was in the Roman capture of Masada ca. 73 C.E.

Defensive structures. Residents of cities typically constructed fortifications to prevent an enemy from breaching the city walls and thus entering and capturing the settlement. Walls were built of stone, but they could also be covered with metal to enhance their strength. Thus, when God promises Jeremiah he will be a "wall of bronze," the reference is to his ability to withstand attack from hostile opponents (Jer 15:20). In some cities a second wall was constructed parallel to the first, and the space between the two was portioned for storage or living quarters. This so-called casemate structure is represented in the description of Rahab's house in Joshua 2:15: "her house was on the outer side of the city wall and she resided within the wall itself." Another strategy for enhancing the defenses of city walls was to partition the city with a set of inner walls so that invaders who breached the outer wall encountered yet another wall in the inner fortress.

The most vulnerable part of a city's defensive system was the city gates. Invaders could breach the wall most easily where there was already an opening, so the gate was fortified in ways the rest of the wall was not. Remains at Gezer, Hazor, and Megiddo reveal gates with three chambers through which invaders had to pass in order to enter the city (see Yadin, 1963, Vol. 2, pp. 370–379).

In addition to enhancing the strength of walls, efforts were made to prevent invaders from approaching the wall in the first place. Cities were built on hills or elevated areas, which made approach more difficult. In addition to this natural defensive feature, it was common to alter hillsides beneath portions of city walls that might be targets of attack. The hill was made steep, covered with clay, and then packed so that the approach to the wall was slick and footing was difficult. The history of warfare in the biblical world is characterized by such efforts to improve fortifications, matched by the development of war techniques and implements.

The Ethics of War. Numerous Old Testament passages speak either directly or indirectly about standards of conduct in war. An example of indirect discussion of this issue is the series of oracles in Amos 1:3—2:6. Amos's larger purpose is to indict Israel for its economic injustice, but he does so by drawing a parallel between Israel's mistreatment of the poor and Israel's neighbors' atrocities in battle. The collection of oracles seems to assume internationally recognized standards by which nations could be judged in their conduct of war (Barton, 2003, pp. 77–129). The breaches of standards Amos highlights include breaking treaties (Amos 1:11), taking whole populations into exile (Amos 1:6, 9; exile typically included only the most powerful and influential citizens), mistreating the bodies of dead enemies (Amos 2:1), and abusing vulnerable members of conquered peoples (i.e., "ripped open pregnant women in Gilead"; Amos 1:13).

Deuteronomy 20 and 21 discuss directly certain practices of war, presumably to guide the Israelites as they engaged their enemies in battle. For example, the Israelites are ordered to offer terms of peace to any town they approach. They could attack the town only if the residents refused the terms of peace (Deut 20:10). When the Israelites besieged a city, they were not allowed to cut down fruit trees as part of the siege. They were only to fell non-fruit-bearing trees to use them for siege works (Deut 20:13–14). These chapters also regulate how the Israelites were to treat women captured in battle: if an Israelite man found desirable a woman from a conquered people, he could take her as his wife only after allowing her a period of mourning for her dead family members (21:12–13; cf. Judg 5:30). But under no circumstances was the man to treat her as a slave. If he was displeased with her as a wife, he was required to set her free (21:14).

It is impossible to know how such laws were applied or even to what extent they were real laws. It is generally acknowledged that Deuteronomy is unique in literature of this period and in the region of western Asia in its inclusion of written regulations for war. In the case of the regulation against destruction of fruit trees, however, the law seems to stand against the command of Elisha in 2 Kings 3 to destroy fruit trees as part of a battle strategy and thus may represent an internal debate about proper behavior in war. What is certain is that the Deuteronomic law speaks against the Assyrian practice of ecocide in conducting wars (Wright, 2008, p. 456). As Jacob Wright argues, this seems to reflect the unique concern of Deuteronomy's authors both to restrain the violence of war and to codify that restraint (2008, p. 458).

Holy War and the Ban. War in the Bible is sometimes associated directly with the actions of God, and God officially sponsors warfare by his people. This type of conflict is sometimes called "holy war."

The concept of holy war. The expression "holy war" refers to the practice of war for God's purposes or with God's help, and it carries the assumption that God is unambiguously on the side of one party in the conflict. Some scholars have argued that holy war was a central feature of Israel's earliest religious experience (see von Rad, 1991, pp. 41–51). Reference to "the Book of the Wars of the LORD" may give evidence that this was so (Num 21:14). According to this understanding of Israel's history, the Israelites (primarily in the time depicted in Judges) were united by a loose confederation in a tribal league. They came together under leaders like Othniel (Judg 3:7–11), Deborah (Judg 4—5), and Gideon (Judg 6:11—8:35) to fend off enemies, with God fighting for them (see the summary of this reconstruction in Bright, 1981, pp. 162–173). Scholars now generally question this view of Israel's formative period and the place of holy war in it (see the incomplete list of tribes in Judg 5:15–18 and the charge that some tribes did not participate).

What is clear, however, is that such divinely sponsored war is presented in numerous passages that depict the early period of Israel's history. Perhaps the key feature of such warfare is expressed in Moses's words to the Israelites in Exodus 14:14: "The LORD will fight for you, and you have only to keep still." In the so-called holy war God went before the army and did the fighting. The main role of humans was to trust in God and to be faithful to divine instruction (Josh 1:1–9). Soldiers purified themselves as if to perform the duties of a priest (Josh 3:5). After the account of the Exodus and wilderness period, God's presence in such conflicts was symbolized by the Ark of the Covenant that went before the army (Josh 6:6; 1 Sam 4:1b–11). The clearest example of an extended conflict that follows this pattern is the story of Israel's conquest of Canaan (Josh 1—12; Judg 1:1—3:6). Although the narrative describes the Israelites as part of the fight, God fights and defeats the enemy. So at Jericho, without any human effort to breach the walls of the city, "the wall fell down flat" (Josh 6:20). In a subsequent battle the Lord threw hailstones upon the enemy so that "there were more who died because of the hailstones than the Israelites killed with the sword" (Josh 10:11).

The ban. A particularly disturbing feature of Israelite war practice is the ban, which entailed the ritual annihilation of the enemy as a way of giving thanks to God for victory in battle. The Hebrew verb *ḥāram* means "to devote to destruction," and the noun that derives from it (*ḥerem*) is used to denote persons or objects as "devoted things" (that is, set apart for destruction). The practice is known outside the Bible on a victory stela erected by King Mesha of Moab. Mesha declared that his god Chemosh gave him victory, and he devoted his enemy to destruction in return. Numbers 21:1–3 says the Israelites enacted the ban in the same way in their battle with the king of Arad.

The greatest ethical challenge of the ban is due to the fact that the ban appears as a requirement for the Israelites during the conquest of Canaan. Whereas Numbers 21:1–3 presents the Israelites initiating the practice of the ban, as part of a vow to receive God's help, Moses orders the practice of the ban at all times in the conquest. In Deuteronomy 7:2 Moses gives the Israelites strict instructions about how to treat the people in the land of Canaan: "when the LORD your God gives them over to you and you defeat them, then you must utterly destroy them. Make no covenant with them and show them no mercy." There are questions, however, as to the historical reality behind this command and whether or not it was actually implemented in Israel's occupation of Canaan.

War as Allegory of Spiritual Life. Many early Jewish and Christian interpreters argued that Moses's order to kill the Canaanites is not to be read literally. Perhaps most famously, Origen asserted that the entire account of Israel's conquest of Canaan was a figurative account of the battle with temptations, part of the Christian's effort not to be "conformed to this world" (Rom 12:2; Origen, *Hom. Josh.* 26–33). For Origen the order to put the residents of the land under the ban was a figurative way of saying that the Christian must purge the self of all that would hinder pure devotion to God. Thus Origen said, "within us are the Canaanites; within us are the Perizzites; here (within) are the Jebusites" (Origen, *Hom. Josh.* 34; see also Hoffman, 1999, p. 197).

Although many modern scholars reject Origen's interpretation as an attempt to countermand the clear message of the text, there is good reason to affirm his interpretation, at least in the case of Deuteronomy 7:1–11. Immediately following Moses's command to put the residents of the land under the ban, Deuteronomy 7:3–5 explains what *ḥerem* means in two stipulations, neither of which involves taking life. The first stipulation is a statement against intermarriage (vv. 3–4). Marrying those living in the land would lead to religious unfaithfulness. The second stipulation is to destroy the sacred objects of the residents of Canaan: "break down their altars, smash their pillars, hew down their sacred poles, and burn their idols with fire" (v. 5). Thus, the only things "devoted to destruction" are the religious objects associated with the worship of foreign deities.

Adding to the notion that the ban is figurative, many scholars conclude that Deuteronomy and the conquest account in Joshua were composed largely during the reign of Josiah in the late seventh century B.C.E. The main feature of Josiah's reign was a set of religious reforms meant to purify and standardize Judah's religious practices (2 Kgs 23). His orders centered precisely on the destruction of sacred objects and sanctuaries associated with heterodox religious practices.

Josiah was dealing not with Canaanites in the land but with his own people who often practiced the worship of their God with elements of the worship of Baʿal and other deities. Hence, Origen's allegory really does capture the meaning of the text, a meaning that points away from violence and bloodshed.

God's Relationship with War. In addition to God's sponsorship of war, God is sometimes depicted acting directly as a warrior. This type of portrait of God is typical of ancient Near Eastern religions. Most significant, however, are the ways the biblical God appears differently in relation to war compared to other deities.

Creation by word instead of combat. The Bible's picture of God in relation to war is complex. The Bible opens with a remarkable picture of God *not* engaging in conflict. Genesis 1:1—2:4a shows God ordering the disordered elements not only with words but also with invitations: "Let the earth put forth vegetation" (1:11) and "let the waters bring forth swarms of living creatures" (1:20; see also 1:9, 14, 24). This portrait of God creating stands in sharp contrast to the account in the Babylonian creation epic in which Marduk, the chief Babylonian deity, created by doing battle with the chaos monster Tiamat. Since Genesis 1:1—2:4a and the Babylonian account present a near identical order of events and since the biblical author was likely an exile in Babylon, it seems likely that the first creation story was intended as a reaction to the story of Marduk's creation by combat.

God as warrior. But many passages describe and depict God as a warrior. The first occurrence of the idea is in the so-called Song of the Sea in Exodus 15:1–18 (v. 3). The warrior label is communicated in three words woodenly translated, "the LORD is a man of war" (author's translation). The warring activity of God appears in this song as it does typically in other texts as well. God makes war in two ways. First, God expressed power directly in action against Pharaoh and his forces. For instance, verse 1b declares "I will sing to the LORD, for he has triumphed gloriously; horse and rider he has thrown into the sea". Again in verse 4a the passage declares, "Pharaoh's chariots and his army he cast into the sea". Second, the song shows God using the nonhuman world as an instrument in divine warfare. Statements to this effect punctuate the poem: "The floods covered them" (v. 5a); "At the blast of your nostrils the waters piled up, the floods stood in a heap; the deeps congealed in the heart of the sea" (v. 8); "You blew with your wind, the sea covered them" (v. 10a); "You stretched out your right hand, the earth swallowed them" (v. 12).

After the end of the poem, a summary statement reiterates the point: "When the horses of Pharaoh with his chariots and his chariot drivers went into the sea, the LORD brought back the waters of the sea upon them; but the Israelites walked through the sea on dry ground" (v. 19). Thus, in this concluding account of God's defeat of Pharaoh, Pharaoh's immediate foe

is the nonhuman world itself. The power of God is displayed mainly in his ability to direct the elements against the Egyptian king. For other examples of God acting similarly to a warrior, see Psalms 29 and 68.

God's reign and the end of warfare. Despite the prominence of God acting as a warrior in the Old Testament, there are also many passages that present God's ultimate goal as to end war and conflict. Images of the peaceable kingdom in Isaiah 11:1–9 provide one example. The final stanza of Psalm 46 speaks about how God intends to end human violence (vv. 8–11). This section seems to address the nations directly with a series of imperatives: "Come, behold the works of the LORD; see what desolations he has brought on the earth" (v. 8). The "desolations" mentioned here may at first seem to point to God's destructive actions as the divine warrior. A close reading of the verses that follow, however, seems to say just the opposite. Reference to the desolations of God leads directly to statements about God bringing peace to the world. Hence, the word "desolations" (*šammôt*) was perhaps intended to be sarcastic. It is the nations who bring desolation through their wars, and God brings all of that to naught. In other words, the reference to desolation is, in essence, an indictment of the nations' attempts to control each other by violent means. This becomes clear in verses 9 and 10. Verse 9 declares, "He makes wars cease to the end of the earth; he breaks the bow, and shatters the spear; he burns the shields with fire." This verse draws on the image of the ruler in the ancient Near East for whom warfare is crucial for protecting the people and for securing the land; God's works entail bringing war to an end. Unlike the picture such kings painted of themselves, however, God does not just bring peace for his own people by defeating other people. Rather, God establishes peace as the norm in all the earth.

Verse 10 continues and clarifies this message with an order to the nations to cease fighting. Traditionally rendered "be still," the first expression in the verse is better translated "stop" or "let it go" (*harpû*). The word literally means "let drop." In some passages the word refers to the hands that hold weapons of war (2 Sam 24:16 = 1 Chr 21:15). In the context of Psalm 46 this imperative seems to order the nations to cease their dependence on warfare and destruction. James L. Mays sums up the message of this verse: "Cease your warring! Stop your attacks! Leave off your vain attempts to subject history to your power. There is but one power exalted over the earth and nations. Only one is God—the one whose work is the destruction of weapons and whose help is the refuge of those who recognize that he is God" (1994, p. 184).

Spiritual Warfare and the Battle with Evil. In the New Testament the battle with evil is sometimes depicted as a war between God's forces and the forces of evil. This is presented most dramatically in the apocalyptic material in which warfare occurs in the heavens between divine and demonic forces. Revelation 12:7 contains perhaps the most direct statement: "And war broke out in heaven; Michael and his angels fought against the dragon." When the dragon was thrown to earth, Revelation 12:17 says, "Then the dragon was angry with the woman, and went off to make war on the rest of her children, those who keep the commandments of God and hold the testimony of Jesus" (cf. Rev 13:7). In this case war is not human activity but something reserved for God in God's efforts to secure the world under divine rule. Ephesians 6:10–20 does say humans have a role in such warfare but are simply to abide in God's protection, that is, to "put on the whole armor of God" (v. 11). Although this passage uses the language of battle ("our struggle [*palē*, lit. "wrestling" or "battle"] is not with flesh and blood"), the Christian is to "be strong in the Lord" (v. 10). Furthermore, the elements of armor to be put on are characterized as "whatever will make you ready to proclaim the gospel of peace" (v. 15). Hence, the human is called simply to trust God and wait for God's acts of salvation. The command cannot be construed as a call to fight against earthly expressions of evil. To the contrary, the battle is purely spiritual and is waged by God alone.

[*See also* Apocalypticism; Exile and Dislocation; Foreigner; Historical Narratives (Joshua—2 Kings); Israel and Israelites; Persecution; *and* Salvation History.]

BIBLIOGRAPHY

Barton, John. *Understanding Old Testament Ethics: Approaches and Explorations.* Louisville, Ky.: Westminster John Knox, 2003.

Bright, John. *A History of Israel.* 3d ed. Philadelphia: Westminster, 1981.

Craigie, Peter C. *The Problem of War in the Old Testament.* Grand Rapids, Mich.: Eerdmans, 1978.

Creach, Jerome F. D. *Joshua.* Interpretation: A Bible Commentary for Teaching and Preaching. Louisville, Ky.: Westminster John Knox, 2003.

Creach, Jerome F. D. *Violence in Scripture.* Interpretation: Resources for the Use of Scripture in the Church. Louisville, Ky.: Westminster John Knox, 2013.

Hoffman, Yair. "Deuteronomistic Conception of the Herem." *Zeitschrift fur die Alttestamentliche Wissenschaft* 111 (1999): 196–210.

Lind, Millard C. *Yahweh Is a Warrior: The Theology of Warfare in Ancient Israel.* Scottsdale, Penn.: Herald, 1980.

Lohfink, Norbert. "חָרַם ḥāram." In *Theological Dictionary of the Old Testament*, edited by G. Johannes Botterweck and Helmer Ringgren, translated by David E. Green, Vol. 5, pp. 180–199. Grand Rapids, Mich.: Eerdmans, 1986.

Mays, James Luther. *Psalms.* Interpretation: A Bible Commentary for Teaching and Preaching. Louisville, Ky.: Westminster John Knox, 1994.

Miller, Patrick D. *The Divine Warrior in Early Israel.* Cambridge, Mass.: Harvard University Press, 1973.

Niditch, Susan. *War in the Hebrew Bible: A Study in the Ethics of Violence.* New York: Oxford University Press, 1993.

Rad, Gerhard von. *Holy War in Ancient Israel.* Translated and edited by Marva J. Dawn. Grand Rapids, Mich.: Eerdmans, 1991.

Stern, Philip D. *The Biblical Ḥerem: A Window on Israel's Religious Experience.* Brown Judaica Series 211. Atlanta: Scholars Press, 1991.

Walzer, Michael. *In God's Shadow: Politics in the Hebrew Bible.* New Haven, Conn.: Yale University Press, 2012.

Wright, Jacob L. "Warfare and Wanton Destruction: A Reexamination of Deuteronomy 20:19–20 in Relation to Ancient Siegecraft." *Journal of Biblical Literature* 127, no. 3 (2008): 423–458.

Yadin, Yigael. *Warfare in Ancient Israel in the Light of Archaeological Study.* 2 vols. Translated by M. Pearlman. New York: McGraw-Hill, 1963.

Jerome F. D. Creach

WEALTH AND POVERTY

The distribution of resources in a society is always a complex matter, and the biblical world was no exception. The economy of ancient Israel and then in Judah during the Second Temple period (when Jesus lived) revolved around the agricultural cycle, animal husbandry, and harsh conditions for all but a small minority of the populace. The challenging terrain for farming and the incursion of foreign powers made it difficult for households to avoid poverty. Stratification played a divisive role in the society, leading to hardship for many, especially when those with means oppressed or cheated vulnerable persons. In both testaments, one finds regular acknowledgment of these realities and in many cases a depiction of stark inequality.

When considering wealth and poverty in the Bible, four recurrent themes are worth noting from the outset: (1) a "justice" (Heb. *mišpāṭ*) principle that advocates a fair and equitable distribution of resources, such that no one hoards too much and persons can avoid destitution; (2) God taking the side of those who suffer from poverty, even becoming their legal advocate; (3) wariness about the corrupting nature of money and how it can distract someone from faithful living; (4) an emergent belief in certain Jewish and Christian texts that immortality provides eternal consolation, especially for those righteous persons who have suffered the devastating effects of poverty. The first three themes appear in the legal collections, prophetic texts, and wisdom literature of the Hebrew Bible as well as in the New Testament (especially the Gospels) and the postbiblical literature of the Second Temple period. The fourth theme appears only in texts beyond the Hebrew Bible, with the exception of the book of Daniel.

Hebrew Bible. A variety of terms in biblical Hebrew describe these economic polarities. With regard to wealth, some designations refer to actual material holdings, including *ḥayil* ("strength" or "wealth"), *ʿōšer* ("riches"), *kābōd* ("glory" or "wealth"), *kōaḥ* ("strength" or "wealth"), *hôn* ("riches"), and the noun *kesep*, which can mean either "silver" or "money." The range of some of these terms indicates semantic overlap between physical strength and material holdings. In other words, some of the vocabulary related to power has both a physical and a material connotation. In addition, certain roots have adjectival forms that denote a wealthy individual, such as *ʿāšîr* ("rich person").

With regard to poverty, key terms include *dal/dallâ* ("poor," "poor one"), *rāš/rîš* ("poor one," "poverty"), *ʿānî* ("poor" or "afflicted"), and *ʾebyôn* ("needy"). Certain phrases are quite descriptive of what it means to be poor, such as *ḥăsar leḥem*, which literally means "one who lacks bread."

Along with these key Hebrew words for wealth and poverty, related terms include *nešek* ("interest"), *śākār* ("wages"), and the verb *ʿārab* ("to stand surety"). Moreover, the biblical texts indicate that some categories of people are more susceptible to poverty, such as slaves, "resident aliens" (*gērîm*), widows, and orphans. On the other side, kings, noble persons, large landowners, and in certain instances priests have greater resources.

Biblical law. All three sections of the Hebrew Bible (Torah, Prophets, Writings) deal with wealth and poverty issues, including candid acknowledgments of social realities and prescriptive solutions for a fairer society. With regard to the biblical laws on wealth and poverty, there is special concern for the plight of the poor. In the Covenant Code from Exodus (20:19–23:33), the earliest collection of laws in the Bible, one finds specific commands on this topic: "You shall not wrong or oppress a resident alien, for you were aliens in the land of Egypt. You shall not abuse any widow or orphan" (22:21–22 [Heb. vv. 20–21]). The society of ancient Israel was built around a "house of the father" (Heb. *bêt ʾāb*) structure, which consisted of household units with kinship ties and usually a patriarch at the head of a hierarchical grouping. This system was patrilocal, such that women who married became members of their new husband's household, and patrilineal because family identity and any inheritance generally passed from the father to his son(s). Consequently, those who did not enjoy a connection to a functioning "house of the father" faced precarious circumstances. This is a primary reason that the laws of the Pentateuch single out widows, orphans, and resident aliens as needing special protection because these persons were most susceptible to isolation and destitution. They lacked the security of a functioning household.

Other laws in the Covenant Code are equally cognizant of the vulnerability of poor persons: "If you lend money to my people, to the poor among you, you shall not deal with them as a creditor; you shall not exact interest from them" (Exod 22:25). The Hebrew word for interest (*nešek*) can also describe the bite of a serpent, thereby offering an incisive commentary on the behavior of certain lenders.

Such laws pertaining to wealth and poverty have "justice" as a baseline goal. "Justice" in the Hebrew Bible can mean more than the act of deciding a case; it frequently indicates "fairness," with special attention to those on the margins. The stipulations of Deuteronomy are pertinent here as these build on the Covenant Code and single out those most likely to be poor: "You shall not deprive a resident alien or an orphan of justice; you shall not take a widow's garment in pledge" (Deut 24:17). Because God's defining characteristics are "justice and righteousness" (e.g., Ps 99:4: "Mighty king, lover of justice, you have established equity; you have executed justice and righteousness in Jacob"), because God acted within history to redeem a chosen people from Egypt, those who are part of the covenant community of Israelites have to follow their Creator's lead in seeking to ameliorate the effects of poverty. One biblical scholar (Pleins, 2001) calls this a "theology of obligation," such that humanity must limit the frequent inclination to take advantage of vulnerable persons for financial gain.

Another famous example of this emphasis on justice and advocacy for the poor is the Jubilee year legislation from the Holiness Code in Leviticus (25:1–26:2). The lengthy description in this chapter requires forgiveness of all loans, including interest, and restoration of all lands every 50 years. Such a bold requirement recognizes the tendency in many agrarian economies for land and resources to become concentrated in the hands of the few, especially when interest charges and debt slavery widen the gap between rich and poor. Since there are no extracanonical references to the Jubilee year as actual practice, many biblical scholars doubt that such a bold remission actually occurred; but it does reflect the goals of debt forgiveness and minimizing poverty.

A related practice is the sabbatical year, a law of forgiving debts every seven years and letting farmlands lie fallow (Exod 23:10–11; Deut 15:1–6; Lev 25:1–7, 20–22). This law of "release" (*šĕmiṭâ*) appears in later texts (1 Macc 6:49; Josephus, *Ant.* 11.342–343; 12.378; 14.202–203), suggesting that such requirements resonated with later interpreters, even if the widespread adoption of the sabbatical year is uncertain.

With regard to the charitable responsibilities of wealthier persons, the biblical laws require contributions to priests, Levites, widows, and others who do not own property. According to Deuteronomy 14:22, persons have to donate one-tenth (i.e., tithe) of their annual produce for Jerusalem during the year. In a similar statement, a law in Leviticus requires that one-tenth of produce, "whether seed from the ground or the fruit from the tree, are the LORD's" (Lev 27:30). This statement implies a regular priestly claim to such proceeds. These and similar passages affirm the significance of owning land in the ancient Near East and the need to support those who do not since they are the most susceptible to poverty.

In assessing these various passages, the goal of an egalitarian society is persistent, as many of the regulations acknowledge stratification and enmity between rich and poor. The laws depict oppression of the poor and failure to help the most vulnerable members of the society as an abrogation of responsibility to the God of "justice and righteousness." Yet this material in the Pentateuch does not necessarily categorize financial holdings as inherently evil. In fact, many of the biblical narratives include material favors from God as part of the covenant blessing (e.g., God's treatment of Abraham in Gen 12:1–4).

Prophetic books. Nowhere in the Bible are economic inequality and treatment of the poor more passionate topics than among the prophets of ancient Israel. The most vocal commentary comes from such figures of the eighth century B.C.E. as Amos, Hosea, Micah, and Isaiah. These prophetic figures had their careers during a time of economic polarization. Various kings and wealthy citizens of Israel and Judah centralized power and expanded the role of the elite and mercantile classes. During this period, the prophet Samuel's earlier warnings about the king taking vital goods from the populace (e.g., 1 Sam 8:17) were verified. Such figures as Jeroboam II of Israel

(r. ca. 786–746 B.C.E.) and Uzziah of Judah (r. ca. 783–743 B.C.E.), along with their associates, established fortresses throughout the region, usurped land belonging to small farmers through a variety of tactics, and built opulent houses for themselves. Wine production increased during the eighth century, as well as the making of olive oil. I am not talking about the same level of conspicuous consumption that often takes place in our modern context, but the eighth century marks a period of wealth disparity and redistribution in both Israel and Judah. There is a key term for this development: "latifundialization." This refers to a process in which the plight of the lower classes, especially subsistence farmers, worsens as they lose access to arable land, often through deceptive tactics. In most premodern societies, including ancient Israel and Judah, agrarian households required at least a small plot of land in order to maintain their viability and "house of the father" structure. During the period of these prophets, the concentration of land and resources into the hands of a few threatened their very survival.

Such developments incensed prophets like Amos, who provides perhaps the most colorful commentary on wealth, poverty, and the process of latifundialization. Despite coming from Judah, Amos had his career in the northern kingdom of Israel; and he leveled specific indictments against the wealthy:

> because they sell the righteous for silver,
>   and the needy for a pair of sandals—
> they who trample the head of the poor into
>   the dust of the earth,
>   and push the afflicted out of the way;
> father and son go in to the same girl,
>   so that my holy name is profaned;
> they lay themselves down beside every altar
>   on garments taken in pledge;
> and in the house of their God they drink
>   wine bought with fines they imposed.
>   (Amos 2:6–8)

Amos takes aim here at bribery, corruption, sexual assault against the vulnerable, conspicuous consumption—all issues that frequently characterize an era of marked stratification. Moreover, those wealthy persons oppressing the poor should not believe that showy displays of piety can atone for their ruthless behavior: "I hate, I despise your festivals, and I take no delight in your solemn assemblies" (5:21). According to Amos, God longs for a day in which "justice roll down like waters, and righteousness like an everflowing stream" (Amos 5:24). This means something quite specific for the prophet. Amos seeks *mišpāṭ*, fairness in society, so that all voices are heard and institutional corruption and mistreatment of the poor will cease.

The prophets Micah and Isaiah bring a similar message. In the late eighth century, Micah sees many of the same injustices in Judah that Amos had witnessed a few decades earlier. This prophet is a vocal defender of the rights of small farmers and their households, who had been working the same plot of land for centuries according to the "house of the father" structure. Micah promises that God will punish any rapacious individuals who bilk land from those who depend on it (Mic 2:1–5). The famous declaration that the Lord only requires that a person commit "to do justice, and to love kindness, and to walk humbly with your God" (6:8) often yields a sentimental interpretation in contemporary circles. Yet the prophet's articulation of this requirement is anything but syrupy: in a specific indictment of the people in Micah 6, God seeks a society where human beings live into long-standing covenant stipulations, including care for the poor. The passion of these prophets on wealth and poverty issues inspired future believers, including Jesus and the New Testament authors.

Wisdom literature. The sapiential works of the Hebrew Bible, most notably the book of Proverbs, contain a more ambiguous presentation on wealth and poverty. Because this is a collection of sayings, edited by scribes over many centuries, the reader should not expect uniformity across the text. Yet the contradictory sayings on wealth and poverty are striking. In certain maxims, wealth functions as a blessing for virtuous behavior and awe before God (i.e., "fear of the Lord"). For example, "The reward for humility and fear of the LORD is riches and honor and life" (Prov 22:4). Along the same lines, those who adopt corrupt behavioral patterns will not enjoy the benefits of wealth (e.g., Prov 1:10–19, and the young man who falls in with the wrong crowd). Yet other sayings highlight the superiority of wisdom over wealth: "How much better to get wisdom than gold! To get understanding is to be chosen rather than silver" (16:16). Such statements appear to contradict the maxims about wealth as a reward for wisdom.

Still another set of sayings presents a more realistic description of wealth and poverty: "The field of the poor may yield much food, but it is swept away through injustice" (13:23). Here, and in similar maxims, one finds an honest assessment of wealth and poverty in relation to human behavior. Moreover, as with the Torah and many of the prophets, the sages responsible for Proverbs cite the Deity as siding with the poor. God becomes the advocate who "pleads their cause" (Prov 23:11).

Other sayings address the reasons a person becomes rich or poor. One frequent trope is that industrious behavior leads to material gain and laziness results in penury. The person whose work ethic resembles that of an ant will prosper (Prov 6:6–9), while those with questionable habits, especially when alcohol is involved, will never become wealthy (e.g., Prov 21:17; cf. 23:20–21).

In assessing all of these sayings, it becomes clear that the book of Proverbs affirms contradictory beliefs: a casual connection between virtuous behavior and wealth as well as an acknowledgment that the poor often suffer grievous harm, even when they have not sinned. This tension does not indicate an obtuse perspective in Proverbs but rather a goal to instill honest behavioral patterns, guarantee some sort of connection between a person's character and his or her earthly rewards, and affirm divine fairness. These are often contradictory goals. The presentation in Proverbs demonstrates the difficulty of formulating a social ethics when so much wealth is attained through illicit means.

The book of Ecclesiastes, written by a sage after the Babylonian Exile, is even more candid about the dangers of wealth and poverty in a society. The author of this text assumes that the wealthy will not always play fairly (Eccl 5:8; 9:13–16) and that the wisdom of the poor individual will not resonate with the public (Eccl 9:15). Since death strikes everyone in equal measure and even the wealthy have to leave

their possessions behind, the best option for all persons is to take delight in family, friendships, and whatever their resources allow them to do, "for there is no work or thought or knowledge or wisdom in Sheol, to which you are going" (9:10).

Other Second Temple Texts. The Jewish sage Ben Sira (second century B.C.E.) comments on wealth and poverty issues in the spirit of Proverbs and Ecclesiastes. Unlike these earlier books, his discourse explicitly utilizes the Torah in formulating a belief that almsgiving and generosity are paramount. Ben Sira does not view accumulation as evil: "Riches are good if they are free from sin" (Sir 13:24). Yet this sapiential author does not view this as a likely possibility: "As a stake is driven firmly into a fissure between stones, so sin is wedged in between selling and buying" (Sir 27:2).

An even more revolutionary development occurred during the third and second centuries B.C.E. Because of the emergence of apocalyptic ideas within the traditions of early Judaism, certain authors began to promise eschatological reward for the righteous elect. The corpus of Enochic works includes some passages in this regard, most notably from the Epistle of Enoch. In this text, a series of woe oracles in the tradition of earlier prophets depicts a stark contrast between the wealthy and the poor. The wealthy may have enjoyed lucrative earthly success, but this apocalyptic text offers a reversal at the end of days: "from your riches you will depart, because you have not remembered the Most High in the day of your riches" (1 En. 94:8). Casting the poor as the elect class, this text offers eternal recompense for those righteous who have suffered during their lifetime: "you will shine like the luminaries of heaven; you will shine and appear, and the portals of heaven will be opened for you" (1 En. 104:2). Such statements provide an eschatological horizon for the poor to receive blessings. Similar pronouncements occur in the corpus of the Dead Sea Scrolls, especially in the sapiential text 4QInstruction.

New Testament. The New Testament writers and Jesus himself drew upon this eschatological framework to discuss wealth and poverty, especially in the Gospels. In the famous passage addressing judgment and the separation of the sheep and the goats, the litmus test for salvation is not knowledge or creedal statements but care for the poor: "just as you did it to one of the least of these who are members of my family, you did it to me" (Matt 25:40). The ones who deny such aid receive terrible punishment in an "eternal fire" (v. 41).

The most sustained engagement with wealth and poverty in the New Testament occurs in the Gospel of Luke. Like the Epistle of Enoch, the Sermon on the Plain contrasts the fate of the wealthy and the poor in eschatological terms: "Blessed are you who are poor [ptōchos], for yours is the kingdom of God" (Luke 6:20). In contrast, "But woe to you who are rich [plousios], for you have received your consolation" (6:24). These woe oracles regarding the wealthy are in the same tradition as the Epistle of Enoch.

The parable of the rich man and Lazarus (Luke 16:19–31) offers the clearest and perhaps the most famous example in the New Testament of this eschatological framework. The wealthy man clothed "in purple and fine linen" (v. 19) does not live into the justice requirements from the Torah, as evidenced by his callous neglect of the poor fellow (Lazarus) who suffers at the gate outside of his house (v. 20). When death occurs for these individuals, the rich man faces the same fate as the wicked in Matthew 25, eternal "agony" in the fiery flames of hell/Hades (Luke 16:24–25), while Lazarus "was carried away by the angels to be with Abraham" (v. 22). The emphasis on the "theology of obligation" in the Torah and the Prophets is apparent in this passage. Jesus cites the rich man's brothers as fully culpable for their actions because of the clear template in Jewish tradition: "They have Moses and the prophets; they should listen to them" (v. 29). These earlier voices in the Hebrew Bible had called such behavior into question; the fundamental difference in Luke is that there are now eternal repercussions related to wealth and poverty.

The book of Acts continues the Lukan tradition of paying attention to these concerns. In the midst of all the signs and wonders, an important observation appears in 4:32: "Now the whole group of those who believed were of one heart and soul, and no one claimed private ownership of any possessions, but everything they owned was held in common [koina]." This last word, koina, is from the same Greek root as koinonia.

Koinonia can mean "association" or "fellowship" and is often used to refer to the solidarity that the first believers had with one another. In this early portion of Acts, we hear of the followers of Jesus that "They devoted themselves to the apostles' teaching and fellowship [koinonia], to the breaking of bread and the prayers" (2:42). This was communal living at its most basic, with no great disparities in wealth and a clear sense that the resurrection miracle demanded solidarity. Such language is in the spirit of Jesus's more radical commandments earlier in Luke: "Sell your possessions, and give alms" (12:33).

The apostle Paul also speaks of wealth and poverty, again with an emphasis on not hoarding more than one requires in order to live. His clearest articulation of this belief is in 2 Corinthians: "I do not mean that there should be relief for others and pressure on you, but it is a question of a fair balance between your present abundance and their need, so that their abundance may be for your need, in order that there may be a fair balance" (8:13–14).

Engaging the Biblical Witness on Wealth and Poverty. The relevance of this material from scripture continues to be a divisive issue. Some modern-day prophets, such as Martin Luther King Jr., sought to live into the mandate of the prophets and New Testament through direct action and a focus on civil and economic rights. His "Letter from Birmingham City Jail," for example, highlights the pursuit of justice in prophets like Amos. The efforts of Clarence Jordan to enact communal living on Koinonia farms in Americus, Georgia, are another example of direct imitation in this regard. Jordan attempted to model this community after the first disciples.

Even with these examples, the disconnect between our global economy and an agrarian, small-village society that relied on household stability and bartering is striking. With worldwide communication and transportation operating at such an advanced level, some have argued that these laws and principles in the Bible are anachronistic, having no relevance in our more sophisticated context. The ability to conduct financial transactions with the click of a button and the intricate network of international commerce differ sharply from the regional economy of the biblical world. In the debate about the fairness and efficacy of various types of economic structures, the content of these ancient laws and oracles is rarely invoked as a guidepost beyond religious circles. Even among those who take the Bible seriously as scripture, the notion of using it as a blueprint for addressing the complexities of modern stratification seems far-fetched to many.

Yet there are still many similarities between the biblical world and ours when it comes to wealth and poverty, primarily as the result of stark inequality and the timelessness of human behavior. The daily challenges for many persons, especially in the Third World, resemble quite closely the situation of poverty for many of the characters in the Bible. Moreover, the charging of exorbitant interest rates on loans to the poor by ruthless creditors is a clear example of continuity. Witness the frequency of "payday lending" to low-income borrowers in the United States. Many who study this material are coming to believe that these ancient voices can indeed provide a template, with a relentless focus on love of God and neighbor and an obligation to seek fairness in every society.

[*See also* Eschatology; Ethics, Biblical; Freedom and Slavery; Justice, Justification, and Righteousness; Labor; *and* Mercy and Compassion.]

BIBLIOGRAPHY

Baker, David L. *Tight Fists or Open Hands? Wealth and Poverty in Old Testament Law*. Grand Rapids, Mich.: Eerdmans, 2009.

Fox, Michael V. *Proverbs*. 2 vols. Anchor Yale Bible 18A, 18B. New Haven, Conn.: Yale University Press, 2000–2009.

Goff, Matthew J. *The Worldly and Heavenly Wisdom of 4Q Instruction*. Studies on the Texts of the Desert of Judah 50. Leiden, The Netherlands: Brill, 2003.

Lehtipuu, Outi. *The Afterlife Imagery in Luke's Story of the Rich Man and Lazarus*. Supplements to Novum Testamentum 123. Leiden, The Netherlands: Brill, 2005.

Nickelsburg, George W. E. "Revisiting the Rich and the Poor in 1 Enoch 92–105 and the Gospel According to Luke." *Society of Biblical Literature Seminar Papers* 37 (1998): 2:579–605. First published in *New Testament Studies* 25 (1978–1979): 324–344.

Nickelsburg, George W. E., and James C. VanderKam. *1 Enoch: A New Translation*. Minneapolis: Fortress, 2004.

Pleins, J. David. *The Social Visions of the Hebrew Bible*. Louisville, Ky.: Westminster John Knox, 2001.

Premnath, D. N. *Eighth Century Prophets: A Social Analysis*. Saint Louis, Mo.: Chalice, 2003.

Sandoval, Timothy J. *The Discourse of Wealth and Poverty in the Book of Proverbs*. Biblical Interpretation Series 77. Leiden, The Netherlands: Brill, 2006.

Weinfeld, Moshe. *Social Justice in Ancient Israel and the Ancient Near East*. Minneapolis: Fortress, 1995.

Samuel L. Adams

WISDOM

The words for wisdom in Hebrew, *ḥokmâ*, and in Greek, *sophia*, have a long and complex pedigree within the Jewish and Christian scriptures. The Hebrew word and its cognates (*daʿat*, translated "knowledge"; *bînâ*, "understanding"; *musar*, "discipline"; *ʿăṣâ*, "advice, counsel") represent more than their corresponding English words. They stand for the ideology and worldview of a distinct group within Israel, a group with its own language and its own concerns. Nevertheless, the Israelite sages worshipped Yahweh as their national God and identified themselves as Israelites. The sages assumed God's existence, even as they grieved over God's betrayal or as they protested God's absence.

Biblical wisdom enables the most mundane tasks such as weaving a tapestry or fitting a wooden joint. In Exodus God describes the chief builder of the Tabernacle as wise:

> The LORD spoke to Moses: See, I have called by name Bezalel…and I have filled him with divine spirit, with ability [*ḥokmâ*], intelligence [*bînâ*], and knowledge [*daʿat*] in every kind of craft, to devise artistic designs, to work in gold, silver, and bronze, in cutting stones for setting, and in carving wood, in every kind of craft. (Exod 31:1–5)

The wisdom of Bezalel enables his skill with materials. The New Revised Standard Version here translates *ḥokmâ* as "ability."

Wisdom also asks the big questions. It addresses all of life, although with two stipulations: first, that the information is to be used and, second, that divine guidance originates from observation of God's creation, reading the book of nature.

In addition to this wide-ranging definition, there is a wisdom worldview. This worldview, although distinctly Israelite and Yahwist, differed at key points with others. The most powerful Israelite institutions, such as the prophetic guild and the priesthood, saw the world differently. Wisdom distinguished itself from prophecy in that it was received through no special divine messenger. Rather, God embedded knowledge in the structure of things. The wise person observes discerned patterns, which he or she extrapolates into principles. The wise ones live according to these principles. Hebrew wisdom ignores the cult, scarcely mentioning temples or sacrifice. This differentiates the sage from the priest.

This article examines wisdom as it pertains to the Bible. It divides into three parts: (1) the wisdom people—Which Israelites saw themselves as repositories of cultural learning? Who wrote the wisdom books?—(2) the wisdom books—the wise produced five books, which are the best sources for Israelite wisdom and represent Israelite wisdom: Job, Proverbs, Ecclesiastes, Sirach (Ben Sira, also named Ecclesiasticus, the Wisdom of Jesus Ben Sira, or Sirach), and the Wisdom of Solomon (other books in the Bible give evidence of wisdom influence as well)—and (3) the wisdom ideas—a survey of a few key issues about which the sages debated.

The Wisdom People. In the biblical stories of the kings (1, 2 Sam; 1, 2 Kgs), people known as counselors (Heb. *yaʿaṣ*) serve the king. Narrators described these counselors using wisdom words. For example, King David's general hired the wise woman (Heb. *ʾiššâ ḥokmâ*) of Tekoa to use her linguistic and psychological skills to persuade the king to allow his exiled son Absalom to return to Jerusalem (2 Sam 14:1–20). In another narrative, King David pits one counselor against another. By this strategy, he defeats his son in a civil war: "Now in those days the counsel that Ahithophel gave was as if one consulted the oracle of God; so all the counsel of Ahithophel was esteemed, both by David and by Absalom" (2 Sam 16:23). Ahithophel had joined Absalom's rebellion against the king. David sent another sage, Hushai, instructing him to persuade Absalom to ignore his lead counsel,

Ahithophel. Because Absalom listened to Hushai and not Ahithophel, Ahithophel committed suicide (2 Sam 17:1–23). In another example, the young prince Amnon needed advice as to how to seduce his half-sister, Tamar. He came to his friend Jonadab, "a very crafty man" (*ʾyš ḥakam*; 2 Sam 13:3), for advice. It is highly plausible to identify the counselors in 1 and 2 Kings and 1 and 2 Samuel as some of those responsible for writing the Hebrew wisdom books. These counselors made up part of an identifiable and distinct group or movement within Israel. The English "the wise, sages" translates the Hebrew *ḥăkamîym*.

The tradition of Israelite wisdom goes back to Solomon. Both Jewish and Christian traditions trace three of the wisdom books to him. Proverbs has collections that claim to trace back to the king. Ecclesiastes begins with narration from a king of Israel, son of David, wealthy and bored. Wisdom has the name in the title. The wisdom books of Proverbs, Ecclesiastes, and Wisdom thereby claim implicitly that Solomon wrote them. However, Solomon's time predates most of the wisdom writing by centuries.

First Kings depicts Solomon as a wise king:

> God gave Solomon very great wisdom, discernment, and breadth of understanding as vast as the sand on the seashore, so that Solomon's wisdom surpassed the wisdom of all the people of the east, and all the wisdom of Egypt. (1 Kgs 4:29–31)

He asked God for wisdom and received it (1 Kgs 3:5–15). He made wise judicial decisions (1 Kgs 3:16–28). When the queen of Sheba visited him, she marveled at his wisdom: "your wisdom and prosperity far surpass the report that I had heard" (1 Kgs 10:7). These stories portray Solomon as the patron saint of biblical wisdom.

The claim of Solomonic authorship for any of these wisdom texts therefore enabled the sages to connect with the earlier wisdom tradition and give the weight of authority to their writing. The real authors of wisdom books were Israelites from the tenth century B.C.E. (a few proverbs) until the second or first century B.C.E. (Wisdom). Two different kinds of people wrote most of the wisdom texts: first, village elders whose poetic couplets connect to rhythms of agricultural life and village economics and, second, members of the royal court. There later emerged a third source, professional scribes who ran schools and regarded themselves as the intellectual class.

The village elder wielded authority not only because of advanced age but also because of recognized abilities. These elders became the repository of the community's ethos and a source of counsel as to its application to daily life decisions. With the rise in Israel of monarchy and the spread of cities, there arose need for an educated managerial class and for teachers. They called the ones who filled that need ḥăkamîym ("sages"). These individuals also served as diplomats and royal counselors. They became the first Israelite scientists, observing, cataloguing, and recording what they saw.

It is difficult to discern at what point Israelite education became formalized. Some form of schools emerged perhaps by the time of Ecclesiastes or earlier, in connection with the training of bureaucrats and children in the royal court. One of the early editors of Ecclesiastes implies that he ran a school: "Besides being wise, the Teacher also taught the people knowledge, weighing and studying and arranging many proverbs. The Teacher sought to find pleasing words, and he wrote words of truth plainly" (Eccl 12:9–10). Some years later, Ben Sira advertised his school's benefits for potential students: "Draw near to me, you who are uneducated, and lodge in the house of instruction [a phrase meaning "school"]....Hear but a little of my instruction, and through me you will acquire silver and gold" (Sir 51:23, 28).

Some deny the existence of this wisdom class. Norman Whybray (1974) makes the strongest case for this alternate way of seeing the authorship of the wisdom books. He maintains that there was no specific wisdom class distinguished from other theological groupings in Israel. Rather, the literate elite wrote the books. The key obstacle to Whybray's thesis is the exclusion of covenant references in Hebrew wisdom. This might suggest that the writers did not share common traditions with the writers of the king stories, the ancestral stories, or the Moses stories, or the prophets. He explains this odd omission as a result of the requirements of the wisdom genre: the type of lit-

erature they were writing precluded their mentioning covenant stories. Writers of wisdom knew the stories, and they believed them. However, they deliberately excluded such stories in their wisdom writing. In a similar way, a lover would not include stock quotes in a letter to his or her beloved. In Greek wisdom, the sages no longer observed this presumed generic prohibition. Whybray's position portrays Israel as a less diverse and more coherent place. Others see Israel as a place where wisdom struggled against others over how best to define and understand Yahweh. A distinct wisdom class remains the likeliest explanation for the existence of the wisdom books. However, given the paucity of information regarding the activities of a sage class, any description must have a speculative element.

Sages embrace and learn from other cultures. As evidence of this, note that Job and Agur (the declared author of Prov 30) are both non-Israelites. Egyptian writing influenced biblical wisdom, which suggests that the sages had deep roots and long-standing connections to the Egyptian wisdom tradition. For example, sages copied verses from the Egyptian *Instructions of Amenemopet* nearly verbatim in Proverbs (22:17–23:11). The Deuteronomist compared Solomon's wisdom to Egyptian wisdom (1 Kgs 4:29–31).

Two prophets mentioned sages in their writings. Neither prophet liked or approved of the wise. Isaiah, writing in the eighth century B.C.E., said, "The wisdom of their wise shall perish, and the discernment of the discerning shall be hidden" (Isa 29:14). Over two centuries later, in the sixth century B.C.E., Jeremiah writes this antiwisdom screed:

The wise shall be put to shame, they shall be dismayed and taken; since they have rejected the word of the LORD, what wisdom is in them? (Jer 8:9)

Thus says the LORD: Do not let the wise boast in their wisdom, do not let the mighty boast in their might, do not let the wealthy boast in their wealth. (Jer 9:23)

Concerning Edom, thus says the LORD of hosts: Is there no longer wisdom in Teman? Has counsel perished from the prudent? Has their wisdom vanished? (Jer 49:7)

These prophetic diatribes give evidence that the wise existed as a definable group. They borrowed from Egyptian culture and favored an Egyptian military alliance. The prophets who mention the wise (Isaiah and Jeremiah) show contempt for their ideas. They charged that the sages set their wisdom against God. They accused the sages of claiming to be wiser than God.

The sages had a unique position in Israel, open to the wider international community. They existed as part of Israelite society and yet different. The sages maintained a tradition parallel to old stories of ancestors, prophets, and kings. The wisdom creation narrative (Prov 8; Job 38–41) differs from Genesis 1 (the seven-day creation story) and Genesis 2 (the garden of Eden narrative). The sages regarded with some disdain or indifference mystical or intuitive sources of religious information (such as the prophets claimed). The Hebrew wisdom books question the very foundations of Israelite belief. The later, more pious scribes, who edited these texts, preserved this seditious material in their canon because they regarded such opinions as legitimate expressions of the wisdom tradition.

The sages are anthropocentric. They looked to human subjective experience as their primary measuring rod to determine wisdom. They elevated human experience so that it determined their theology. For instance, Job insists that his friends must take into account his suffering in their description of how God governs. Is God good by definition, or does one evaluate God by a standard of goodness external to God? Job accuses God of misbehavior, which means that he had a human standard external to God as a measure of how God should behave. On the other hand, Job's friends claimed that God's actions, by definition, must be meretricious.

The Wisdom Books—Differences between Hebrew and Greek Wisdom. In many ways, the first three books chronologically, Job, Proverbs, and Ecclesiastes, differ considerably from the last two, Sirach and Wisdom. They differ in language. The first three are written in Hebrew. Although Sirach began as a Hebrew original, his grandson translated the book into Greek, and the Greek version took precedence. These two books, Sirach and Wisdom, henceforth called "Greek wisdom," differed from Hebrew wisdom in the way they addressed the old questions. They reflected the dramatically different cultural environment in which they lived, dominated by the expanding Greek empire. To distinguish these two expressions of biblical wisdom, I call the earlier three books, Job, Proverbs, and Ecclesiastes, "Hebrew wisdom."

Both Greek wisdom books build upon Greek philosophical concepts. Sirach introduces the notion of personal authorship. Wisdom refers to an afterlife. These are new ideas that, subsequent to the writing and wide circulation of Hebrew wisdom, came to wisdom following Alexander's conquest of Palestine in 333 B.C.E.

The Greek wisdom books give evidence that a sea change took place in the wisdom community because of Greece's cultural domination of Palestine. Unlike the Hebrew wisdom books, these later books identify wisdom with Torah and embrace the distinctions of Israelite/Jewish theology. This imposed Greek (Hellenistic) culture significantly shaped the writings of Israelite sages.

The primary source for wisdom in Israel is the wisdom books themselves. They use wisdom words, such as "wisdom," "understanding," "knowledge," and "counsel"; and they concern themselves with issues traditionally associated with wisdom, such as how to achieve the good life, the problem of evil, and, related to that, the doctrine of retribution. In these five wisdom books, the sages debated the merits of various wisdom propositions.

Here follows a brief introduction to wisdom issues traced through each of the books. This does not serve as an introduction to scholarship regarding the books themselves but only in their relationship to the sages' unique contribution to wisdom in Israel.

Proverbs. Proverbs consists of five unequal collections, most of them with distinct introductions and conclusions. For instance, one collection begins, "These are other proverbs of Solomon that the officials of King Hezekiah of Judah copied" (Prov 25:1). These collections come from different periods in Israel's history. Scholars dispute their exact dating, but most would regard chapters 10–21 as the earliest written, many originating in a village setting. However,

Proverbs also contains courtly advice and theological speculation that comes from an urban culture. Proverbs divides humanity into two groups; depending upon behavior, one shows oneself as either wise or foolish. The wise follow the right path, learning from their elders and carefully observing life and learning from it. The foolish go on the path to destruction.

Countering one another in Proverbs are two mythic women, Lady Wisdom (ḥokmâ) and "the strange woman" (ʾšâ zarâ). Lady Wisdom invites young men to her feast, promising them riches and success if they respond to her invitation. The strange woman invites hapless youth into her parlor for a night of unrestrained sex.

> Come, let us take our fill of love until morning; let us delight ourselves with love.... With much seductive speech she persuades him.... Right away he follows her, and... bounds like a stag toward the trap until an arrow pierces its entrails... for many are those she has laid low, and numerous are her victims. Her house is the way to Sheol, going down to the chambers of death. (Prov 7:18–27)

On one level, these two represent the goddesses of wisdom and folly. On another, they personify human impulses that draw one to constructive or destructive ends. (Lady Wisdom appears elsewhere in wisdom literature, discussed under "The Wisdom Ideas.")

Job. The book depicts Job as a righteous man, blessed by God, who for no apparent reason is struck with tragedy and terrible illness. Many such stories in the ancient Near East depict an innocent sufferer who complains to the gods. Then they restore the sufferer to a previous position of wealth and comfort. The book of Job exposes the central tension within the wisdom tradition between the insights passed on as traditional knowledge and those from personal subjective experience. Admonitions in Proverbs reflect such traditional knowledge: "Trust in the LORD with all your heart, and do not rely on your own insight. In all your ways acknowledge him, and he will make straight your paths. Do not be wise in your own eyes; fear the LORD, and turn away from evil" (Prov 3:5–7). Job's friends defend the principle that the elders passed down—that only the sinner suffers. Job and

Job's friends represent competing sides in the debate (Job 3–37). Traditional wisdom affirms a balance in the universe. God directs existence so that results follow reliably from their antecedent actions. In other words, people get what they deserve. Sages base this wisdom principle on generations of observation. Therefore, one might infer regarding a suffering individual that he or she in some manner caused his or her own suffering. The friends argue this—that Job must have done something wrong to merit his suffering. The structure of reality, as understood by the sages, demands that kind of balance. The Hebrew sages did not have the option to say that God would balance things after death. The sages relied on only what they could observe. Wisdom, written in the second or first century B.C.E., introduced the concept of a reward and punishment in the hereafter.

Job agreed that the universe should work like that, a place where everybody gets what they deserve. However, his personal experience contradicted the cumulative insights of his wisdom community. Job's friends had no right to try and explain Job's experience, his suffering. Rather, Job's suffering must instruct them. Human experience provides a source of divine wisdom, according to the sages. Job wants to learn the meaning of his suffering. He turns first to his friends. Failing that, he addresses God. The friends give him only platitudes that fix the blame upon him. However, when God finally appears, he bullies Job and answers none of his questions. Does one force the evidence to fit the overall principles (the friends), or does one adjust the principles to account for human subjectivity/experience (Job)? Job and his friends debate this.

The resolution to the debate remains ambiguous. The framing narrative of Job declares Job's innocence, and that his suffering does not result from any bad behavior: "The LORD said to Satan, 'Have you considered my servant Job? There is no one like him on the earth, a blameless and upright man who fears God and turns away from evil'" (Job 1:8). The friends provide no adequate explanation for Job's suffering. God does not answer Job's questions. There are two traditional interpretations of God's speeches (Job 38–41). Some say that the fact that God appeared to Job provides him with an adequate answer. Alternatively, the content of God's speeches puts Job in his place. God is busy governing the universe. Job is only a very small part of it. Job responds to God's speech: "I had heard of you by the hearing of the ear, but now my eye sees you; therefore I despise myself, and repent in dust and ashes" (Job 42:5–6). Some see this as capitulation and confession of sin. However, God speaks to the friends in the next line: "you have not spoken of me what is right, as my servant Job has" (Job 42:7). The wisdom of the book of Job puts forward a negative theology, which deconstructs and refutes the prevailing wisdom principle that evil/foolish people suffer while good/wise people are rewarded.

Ecclesiastes. In traditional wisdom, things happen for a reason. The book of Job questioned the rosy picture offered by the earlier sages. Ecclesiastes goes much further. It calls into question the entire wisdom enterprise. The author, called Qoheleth, "the Teacher," offers little solace. He leaves readers without certainty. He first appears in the guise of the great and wealthy King Solomon but a Solomon who had become jaded and cynical. He could fulfill his every desire. "All is vanity [*hăbel*]," he says, and this becomes a repeating chorus throughout the book. "Vanity of vanities…all is vanity" (Eccl 1:2; 12:8).

The king tries out all the things that might lead to human happiness and fulfillment—wealth, fame, pleasure, companionship, children—but finds them all wanting, "chasing after wind" (Eccl 1:14). This is wisdom at its most skeptical. Qoheleth concludes that the reality of death renders all meaning pointless. Once dead, it no longer matters whether one acted in a manner good or bad, wise or foolish. It does not even matter whether one had been an animal or a human.

> For the fate of humans and the fate of animals is the same; as one dies, so dies the other. They all have the same breath, and humans have no advantage over the animals; for all is vanity. All go to one place; all are from the dust, and all turn to dust again. Who knows whether the human spirit goes upward and the spirit of animals goes downward to the earth? (Eccl 3:19–21)

Qoheleth questions whether meaning or honest happiness is possible. He shares his observations with ruthless honesty.

The ending of the book enjoins piety and preaches divine retribution:

> The end of the matter; all has been heard. Fear God, and keep his commandments; for that is the whole duty of everyone. For God will bring every deed into judgment, including every secret thing, whether good or evil. (Eccl 12:13–14)

In this, a final editor (ch. 12 refers to Qoheleth in the third person) continues the debate and tries to pull the book back into some semblance of traditional orthodoxy.

Ben Sira. Sirach occupies a transitional position between Hebrew and Greek wisdom. The Greek version of the book (the only one extant until the late nineteenth century) translates a Hebrew original: "You are invited therefore to read it with good will and attention, and to be indulgent in cases where, despite our diligent labor in translating, we may seem to have rendered some phrases imperfectly" (Prologue). The original Hebrew version was discovered in a Cairo synagogue. Sirach equates wisdom (*sophia*) with Torah. He tells a story of a time when Lady Wisdom looked for a home. Yahweh told her to locate her home in Jerusalem: "Then the Creator of all things gave me a command, and my Creator chose the place for my tent. He said, 'Make your dwelling in Jacob, and in Israel receive your inheritance'" (Sir 24:8). Sirach concludes, "All this [his previous discussion of Lady Wisdom] is the book of the covenant of the Most High God, the law that Moses commanded us as an inheritance for the congregations of Jacob" (Sir 24:23). Previous to this, wisdom held a strict division between itself and Torah. Now, that division has sundered.

Wisdom of Solomon. Written in the Greek language, Wisdom (second or first century B.C.E.) makes a final effort to solve the perennial wisdom conundrum known as the problem of evil. Do God and the universe reward good and punish evil? Why do the innocent suffer? The author of Wisdom introduces the idea of punishment and reward in an afterlife. The innocent might suffer now, and the evil remain unpunished. However, after they die, in some reckoning, everyone will get what he or she deserves.

Previously, sages based their findings on observation. However, one cannot observe the afterlife.

Therefore, by introducing this idea, the author of Wisdom shifted the conceptual framework of wisdom. The author argues this point by telling the story of a righteous person and his disreputable friends. They found his presence disturbing, so they decided to test his claim of divine protection: "he calls the last end of the righteous happy, and boasts that God is his father. Let us see if his words are true, and let us test what will happen at the end of his life" (Wis 2:16–17). They captured him, tortured and killed him, and believed they had proven their point, that no reward came to the wise or righteous. A few chapters later though, these same individuals have some sort of vision and see their righteous friend now enjoying eternal life with the angels.

> Then the righteous will stand with great confidence in the presence of those who have oppressed them and those who make light of their labors. When the unrighteous see them, they will be shaken with dreadful fear, and they will be amazed at the unexpected salvation of the righteous. (Wis 5:1, 2)

They see their own prospects as grim, but they cannot change their fate: "But the righteous live forever, and their reward is with the LORD; the Most High takes care of them" (Wis 5:15).

Wisdom outside the wisdom corpus. Many have found wisdom influence in other parts of the Bible. However, most of these similarities are not significant but rather result from all Israelites sharing a common culture and vocabulary. Nonetheless, some texts specifically address wisdom issues.

Psalm 73. This psalm confronts the same issues as the authors of Job and Ecclesiastes. The psalmist struggles with the success of wicked people, while he tries to remain pious in the midst of suffering.

> But as for me, my feet had almost stumbled;
>   my steps had nearly slipped.
> For I was envious of the arrogant;
>   I saw the prosperity of the wicked.
>   (Ps 73:2–3)

Whereas the sages scarcely mentioned the Temple, the psalmist finds solace there. Under its influence, he sees the wicked from a divine perspective.

> …until I went into the sanctuary of God;
>   then I perceived their end.
> Truly you set them in slippery places;
>   you make them fall to ruin.
>   (Ps 73:17–18)

He takes comfort that God will enforce a balanced and fair result. Other wisdom psalms might include Psalms 37 and 49, and indeed, this is an ill-defined and much-debated category.

Joseph (Gen 37–50) and Daniel (Dan 1–6). Some suggest that the narrative stories about Joseph and Daniel provide examples to instruct potential scribes/sages. Both of them in foreign courts show great skill in navigating palace politics, thus providing an example for potential court bureaucrats. However, these stories differ from wisdom texts. Each court narrative places its protagonist in opposition to the wise men and magicians of Egypt (in the case of Joseph) or Babylon (in the case of Daniel). These young Israelites continually bested the wise ones in the royal courts. Their information came from God by means of revelation, not observation or mastery of a skill: "And Joseph said to them, 'Do not interpretations belong to God?'" (Gen 40:8). Although these stories have wisdom as a subject, they do not share wisdom sensibilities.

The garden of Eden narrative (Gen 2–3). One of the main characters, the serpent, is a symbol for wisdom in the ancient Near East. In Genesis, the serpent offers to the first humans the knowledge of good and evil. "Knowledge of good and evil" means wisdom. The serpent demonstrates its own wisdom by its insight into Yahweh's ways. However, the humans, by following the serpent's advice, lose paradise. In the garden of Eden, the narrator describes the serpent as "crafty" (Heb. *ārum*; 3:1), another synonym for wise. The word might suggest dishonesty, but it need not. The serpent as a potent but destructive force suggests the author viewed the wisdom tradition with suspicion.

The Wisdom Ideas. Sages believed that God built the knowledge of how to live into the fabric of existence and that careful observation would uncover that knowledge, yielding right understanding. They did not resort to supernatural revelation. In contrast to the prophets, their knowledge came from two sources:

first, the results of careful observation for the purpose of discerning patterns of cause and effect and, second, the body of accumulated knowledge and experience built upon the tradition of sages who came before. No new generation had to discover afresh principles such as "work diligently and as a result prosper." The wisdom community expected the young sage to submit to the wisdom of elders who had mastered the wisdom tradition before them. However, because of their commitment to honest observation and ruthless questioning, the sages often challenged the prevailing wisdom tradition of their elders based on their subjective experience. Observation leads the sages to raise the question, Why are things the way they are instead of how they should be?

Wisdom questions. In Hebrew wisdom, the sages raise certain questions. What behaviors lead to success and prosperity? And, underlying that, does the universe make sense? Is it fair? Is there justice? Are the ways of God and of the universe knowable, discoverable? Are God's ways predictable? Are they reliable? Is the wisdom enterprise a valid way to yield useful knowledge? What, if anything, gives meaning to life? By contrast, the Hebrew sages did not ask other questions: What is the relationship of one's personal story to the stories of the ancestors? In what way does Torah give structure and meaning to life? What rituals and Temple behavior does God require? How might participation in ritual make one whole?

Accessibility of wisdom. Sages argued repeatedly whether God treats human beings fairly. If the answer was yes, that God governs rationally, then is it possible for humans to apprehend that rationality? The debate occurred between those who believed that God's ways were hidden and completely unavailable and those who argued that diligent seeking would bring results. Those for hidden wisdom said, "The human mind plans the way, but the LORD directs the steps" (Prov 16:9) and "All our steps are ordered by the LORD; how then can we understand our own ways?" (Prov 20:24). Those who felt the task was possible said, "The beginning of wisdom is this: Get wisdom, and whatever else you get, get insight" (Prov 4:7). One of Job's friends enters the argument on the side of wisdom's possibilities: "You shall come to your grave in ripe old age, as a

shock of grain comes up to the threshing floor in its season. See, we have searched this out; it is true. Hear, and know it for yourself" (Job 5:26–27). Yet, Job 28 argues the opposite: "Where then does wisdom come from? And where is the place of understanding? It is hidden from the eyes of all living, and concealed from the birds of the air" (Job 28:20–21).

Problem of evil—doctrine of retribution. In Job, the friends believed that suffering came because of human misbehavior. Job faced his own irrational suffering, and he concluded that the world was a dangerous and unpredictable place. Ecclesiastes went further, claiming that humans gain nothing by becoming wise or good. Qoheleth saw no lasting benefits to being born a human and not an animal. For Qoheleth, all life rings hollow when faced with the inevitability of death: "For who knows what is good for mortals while they live the few days of their vain life, which they pass like a shadow? For who can tell them what will be after them under the sun?" (Eccl 6:12). Ecclesiastes rejects wisdom's relative optimism. Most of Proverbs portrays God as governing with wisdom, although some argued that God's wisdom remained obscure. However, Job wonders why the older affirmations do not seem to apply in his case. Qoheleth rejects altogether the affirmation that God rules reliably and fairly. Sirach and Wisdom, both pious, pull the tradition back toward confidence in God's governance, away from doubt.

Ḥokmâ. Notable in wisdom literature is the figure of Ḥokmâ, woman wisdom. She appears as a young child in a creation account (Prov 8:29–30) and again in later wisdom books (Sir and Wis) as the personification of wisdom, an aspect of God. The language used elevates her to the highest level in the divine hierarchy:

when he marked out the foundations of the earth, then I was beside him, like a master worker; and I was daily his delight, rejoicing before him always. (Prov 8:29–30)

I came forth from the mouth of the Most High, and covered the earth like a mist. I dwelt in the highest heavens, and my throne was in a pillar of cloud. Alone I compassed the vault of heaven and traversed the depths of the abyss. (Sir 24:3–5)

For she is a breath of the power of God, and a pure emanation of the glory of the Almighty; therefore nothing defiled gains entrance into her. For she is a reflection of eternal light, a spotless mirror of the working of God, and an image of his goodness. (Wis 7:25–26)

The Christian community took these phrases and constructed a language to describe Jesus of Nazareth.

He is the image of the invisible God, the firstborn of all creation; for in him all things in heaven and on earth were created…all things have been created through him and for him. He himself is before all things, and in him all things hold together. (Col 1:15–17)

The creation account at the beginning of the Gospel of John owes more to wisdom creation than anything in Genesis. The "word," in Greek *logos*, has a meaning similar to *ḥokmâ* in Hebrew. However, unlike *ḥokmâ* or *sophia* (the Greek word for wisdom), *logos* is masculine. Like *ḥokmâ*, Lady Wisdom, in Proverbs 8, the *logos* too is present at creation. As *sophia* in the Wisdom becomes God's instrument of creation, so too does the *logos*: "In the beginning was the Word [*logos*]….He was in the beginning with God. All things came into being through him, and without him not one thing came into being" (John 1:1–3). Also like *ḥokmâ* in Proverbs 8, the *logos* is the link between God and humanity: "And the Word became flesh and lived among us, and we have seen his glory" (John 1:14).

Legacy. Although not all sages rebelled, the very structure of wisdom leads inevitably to a rejection of some of Israel's foundational theological principles. Reality becomes a problem when one uses reified standards to determine how the world works. It is tempting to modify one's perception of reality to conform to ideology. Wisdom, by its methodology (reading from the book of nature), works against such dishonesty. Even Greek wisdom books showed themselves supple in the face of an overwhelming culture.

Wisdom asked the hard questions, and the keepers of the wisdom tradition had the intellectual courage and integrity to keep a record of the previous debates, however unorthodox, in their literature. They recognized that many dissonant voices coexist simultaneously side by side. No one answer may continue long unchallenged. Wisdom, in contrast to piety or submission, looks outside its own community and tries out multiple answers to the ancient questions.

The sages engaged in a ruthless, painful examination of uncomfortable truths. They thereby functioned as a reality check to protect against excessive dogmatism or rigid fundamentalism. That is wisdom.

[*See also* Anthropology; Creation; Education; Family; Friendship; Knowledge; Reward and Retribution; Theology, Biblical; Theophany; Wisdom Literature; *and* Word (Logos).]

BIBLIOGRAPHY

Collins, John. *Jewish Wisdom in the Hellenistic Age.* Louisville, Ky.: Westminster John Knox, 1997.

Crenshaw, James L. *Studies in Ancient Israelite Wisdom.* Library of Biblical Studies. New York: Ktav, 1976.

Crenshaw, James L. *Old Testament Wisdom: An Introduction.* 3d ed. Louisville, Ky.: Westminster John Knox, 1981.

Crenshaw, James L. "Wisdom in the Old Testament" and "Wisdom Literature." In *Mercer Dictionary of the Bible*, edited by Watson Mills, pp. 961–965. Macon, Ga.: Mercer University Press, 1990.

Dell, Katharine J. *Get Wisdom, Get Insight: An Introduction to Israel's Wisdom Literature.* London: Darton, Longman and Todd, 2000.

Di Lella, Alexander A. "Conservative and Progressive Theology: Sirach and Wisdom." *Catholic Biblical Quarterly* 28, no. 2 (April 1966): 139–154.

Fox, Marvin V. *A Time to Tear Down and a Time to Build Up: A Rereading of Ecclesiastes.* Grand Rapids, Mich.: Eerdmans, 1999.

Good, Edwin M. *In Turns of Tempest: A Reading of Job.* Stanford, Calif.: Stanford University Press, 1990.

Gordis, Robert. *Koheleth—The Man and His World: A Study of Ecclesiastes.* 3d ed. New York: Schocken, 1968.

Koch, Klaus. "Is There a Doctrine of Retribution in the Old Testament?" In *Theodicy in the Old Testament*, edited by James Crenshaw, translated by Thomas A. Trapp, pp. 57–87. Philadelphia: Fortress, 1983.

Lang, B. *Wisdom and the Book of Proverbs: An Israelite Goddess Redefined.* New York: Pilgrim, 1986.

Murphy, Roland E. "Introduction to Wisdom Literature." In *The New Jerome Biblical Commentary*, edited by Raymond Brown, pp. 447–452. Englewood Cliffs, N.J.: Prentice Hall, 1990.

Murphy, Roland E. *The Tree of Life: An Exploration of Biblical Wisdom Literature*. Anchor Bible Reference Library. New York: Doubleday, 1990.

Penchansky, David. *Betrayal of God: Ideological Conflict in Job*. Louisville, Ky.: Westminster John Knox, 1990.

Penchansky, David. *Introduction to Hebrew Wisdom: Conflict and Dissonance in the Hebrew Text*. Grand Rapids, Mich.: Eerdmans, 2012.

Rad, Gerhard von. *Israelite Wisdom*. Nashville, Tenn.: Abingdon, 1992.

Skehan, Patrick W., and Alexander A. DiLella. *The Wisdom of Ben Sira*. Anchor Bible. New York: Doubleday, 1987.

Tsevat, Matitiahu. "The Meaning of the Book of Job." *Hebrew Union College Annual* 37, no. 1 (1966): 73–106.

Whybray, R. H. *The Intellectual Tradition in Israel*. Berlin and New York: De Gruyter, 1974.

Winston, David. *The Wisdom of Solomon*. Anchor Bible. New York: Doubleday, 1979.

David Penchansky

WISDOM LITERATURE

Wisdom theology springs from a particular worldview associated with the biblical and extracanonical wisdom literature. I take this to be primarily Proverbs, Job, Ecclesiastes, Ben Sira, and the Wisdom of Solomon, although there is some debate as to which texts should be included, largely because of a lack of agreement as to what precisely makes up the "wisdom literature" and its parameters. There is also a remarkable lack of consensus among scholars about the precise nature of wisdom theology, given the slippery definition of the wisdom category. Various definitions for "wisdom" have been suggested, such as "nonrevelatory speech" (Crenshaw, 2010), "a practical knowledge of the laws of life and of the world based on experience" (von Rad, 1972), or "a style of intellectual and spiritual quest" (Whybray, 1994); but each definition suffers from being too broad. There is debate too as to whether the wisdom worldview belongs to a specific context of sages or scribes and how far it is distinct from other biblical worldviews and syntheses of material.

The wisdom category was originally posited on the grounds of difference from other material. In the early nineteenth century these were often designated "poetical books" and included Psalms and Song of Songs. Another categorization used was "didactical," and this ultimately evolved into the "wisdom" category that we use today. It seems to spring from the mid-nineteenth century in an attempt to categorize biblical material from a universal, humanistic, and philosophical standpoint. Delitzsch (1874) claimed that Bruch (1851) "was the first to call special attention to the Chokma or humanism as a peculiar intellectual tendency in Israel" (p. 14; see discussion in Kynes, 2015), but interestingly Delitzsch included the Song of Songs, which is usually ranked outside the corpus. Of course, the earliest grouping of the material was in reference to the ostensible "author," Solomon, who supposedly penned Proverbs, Ecclesiastes, the Song of Songs, and the Wisdom of Solomon. This would bring the Song of Songs into the definition as Delitzsch suggested. There may be some merit in returning to this, but then identifying the "theology" of a category solely based on authorial attribution would be a somewhat forced undertaking.

The wisdom material is characterized by a notorious lack of historical reference to Israel and its kings/leaders, cult, and institutions, although that sweeping statement has been challenged in certain quarters (e.g., Perdue, 1977, in reference to the cult). Wisdom theology has often been downgraded as "second class" as opposed to the mainstream of Old Testament theology and, with its close links to Egypt and Mesopotamia, regarded as that part of the Old Testament to be branded "international" in a derogatory way, with little thought that actually much of the Old Testament has ancient Near Eastern roots and connections.

It is helpful to look at how scholarship has evolved with its definition of wisdom theology since the rise of biblical scholarship in the late nineteenth century. There is a certain subjectivity in the characterization depending on the time and context of the interpreter, as I shall attempt to show; but at the same time I believe that there is some objectivity to be had. Key theological connections have traditionally been made of wisdom theology with creation and with the concept of order in the world.

In the late nineteenth century (up to the 1930s) it was almost universally thought that the wisdom literature was a late development, the successor to the law and the prophets (e.g., Cheyne, 1887). The sages were seen as the spiritual heirs of the prophets but with an interest in law, especially Deuteronomic law, as indicated by references in both Proverbs (especially 1–9) and Job. The key difference with this literature was the individual slant given on issues pursued in a more communal context by their predecessors, perceived as a development in a utilitarian direction. The happiness of the self was of prime concern, and this was to be gained by following the path of wisdom on a strict scheme of retribution.

The good were rewarded by God, the wicked punished—and even when that scheme seemed to be in question, as in the book of Job, the happy ending to that book confirmed its reliability. Although the doctrine of retribution went through a bout of questioning in Job and Ecclesiastes, it was pulled back into line by Ben Sira and the Wisdom of Solomon. Job was popular as the challenge to the retributive principle, but it was that principle that held the field among scholars seeking to characterize the material (e.g., Bauer, 1838). The relationship of the wisdom books, notably Proverbs, to philosophy was of interest (hence the origin of the wisdom term) in a post-Enlightenment age when rationality was high on the agenda. Despite this emphasis, the divine origin of the wisdom literature as "revelation" was stressed, in just the same way that prophecies and legal material were "revealed."

It was perceived by early scholars that God appeared in these wisdom books as the creator and that this was a factor that made them different. However, the salvation history element of the later wisdom books and the alignment with the Torah in Ben Sira were also seen as part of the picture. This creation emphasis fitted in with an interest in the universal flavor of the material, which bolstered the alignment with philosophy. Indeed, the perception that these books were universal and more philosophical than historical led in turn to a late dating and a recognition that much of the Old Testament was influenced by the sages. Meinhold (1908) argued, for example, that there was a wisdom layer in most of the Old Testament, while Bauer (1838) saw Proverbs as at the

apex of the development toward universalism, with Job as an even more masterful achievement in relation to questions raised by suffering individuals. Wisdom material was often downgraded as too pragmatic and utilitarian, lacking the theological sophistication of prophecy. A late dating also tended to align it with the kind of legalism criticized by Jesus in his encounters with the Pharisees and Sadducees—not that this material was particularly legalistic, but it was a rigid system of reward and punishment nonetheless.

A sea change in the evaluation of wisdom theology came in the 1960s with the work of Gerhard von Rad and Hans H. Schmid. These scholars evaluated wisdom's theology very differently and in many ways set up the tensions that are still noticeable in the discussion today. Von Rad (1972) stressed the theology of creation in wisdom as contrasted with salvation history or *Heilsgeschichte*. He saw creation as a relatively late concern in Israel, predominant from the time of the Exile as the starting point of the *Heilsgeschichte*, but found in the latest part of Proverbs, chapters 1–9. Schmid (1966) opposed von Rad's assessment of creation theology in wisdom literature as essentially late arguing, on the basis of ancient Near Eastern parallels, largely with Egyptian literature, that creation was a foundational and early idea for wisdom, found in the oldest sayings in Proverbs. However, he used the terminology of "world order" rather than creation, again harking back to Egyptian ideas. He introduced the idea that order was as essential a part of the definition of wisdom as "creation."

Also at this time the impact of the discovery of the *Instruction of Amenemope* in 1923 (Erman, 1924) was being felt, and there was a move toward assessing wisdom theology in the light of that work. Proverbs 22:17—23:22 was considered by many to be dependent on Amenemope and to shed light therefore on teaching methods and the transmission of material by sages in Proverbs. This is what led to the idea that wisdom literature had more in common with "foreign" material than other parts of the Old Testament, until, that is, the integration with Israelite thought in Ben Sira and the Wisdom of Solomon. Anderson (1967) tried to find a middle path between the views of von

Rad and Schmid by asserting that early nature of ideas of creation as primitive order in the wisdom literature was a separate and parallel strand of thought alongside the *Heilsgeschichte*.

The scope of the definition of wisdom theology continued to be an issue. How wide should the net be cast? Should wisdom psalms, wisdom narratives (e.g., the succession narrative of 2 Sam 7–20 and 1 Kgs 1–2), and wisdom influences in the eighth-century prophets all be included? Crenshaw (2010) has long maintained that a narrow definition of wisdom literature and, hence, of wisdom theology is needed. His primary focus is the question of the God–human relationship, notably in terms of theodicy, as raised in the book of Job. Other scholars (e.g., Morgan, 1981) have cast the net much more widely, and there has been a fresh emphasis on the nineteenth-century interest in relationships with law, psalmody, and prophecy, using the modern terminology of intertextuality (Dell and Kynes, 2012). Opinions on dating have swung to and fro, with some seeing wisdom as essentially a redaction of other texts and others seeing it as a formative influence on other texts.

Von Rad's emphasis on creation theology as a late-comer to *Heilsgeschichte* and the resulting divide in thought between creation and history became a commonplace of the debate in the twentieth century. Brueggemann (1997) used these two categories as trajectories for his Old Testament theology. Gemser (1938) and Westermann (1982) used the language of *Heilsgeschichte* as a horizontal line cut by the vertical line of the ahistorical at significant points. It is interesting that it is in the later wisdom literature itself that the two are brought together, a fact often overlooked by scholars who overcharacterize the ideological divide in the material. Murphy (1994) has consistently maintained the unity of the two concepts of creation and history in the Old Testament, refusing to see wisdom literature as outside the historical process. The uniting theme of covenant has been used by some (e.g., Murray, 1992) as a way to link creation with history, but this concept appears to be lacking in the wisdom literature.

Another issue in regard to the wisdom material is how anthropocentric it is—an aspect that Zimmerli

(1978) has consistently maintained. He famously wrote, "Wisdom thinks resolutely within the framework of a theology of creation" (p. 146). The word "secular" has even been used. Others have pointed out the centrality of God in the wisdom material even if God is, at times, behind the scenes. God is certainly not behind the scenes in Job, which contains the only example of a lengthy theophany with God speaking in the Old Testament. Zimmerli had an opponent in the 1960s in Gese (1958), who stressed world order springing from the divine as a key theme of the wisdom worldview. He drew, like Schmid (1966), on Egyptian ideas, this time on the concept of *Ma'at*, a principle of order that later became a goddess in Egyptian thought. To this he likened Woman Wisdom in Proverbs 1, 3, and 8. This led to Koch's (1983) characterization of wisdom theology as having at its heart the "act–consequence" relationship whereby all actions have consequences that can be known. This is overturned in Job, but it is still, Koch argued, the presupposition of the material. The idea of essentially secular roots for wisdom fitted into this scheme, taken up by others as a possible first stage of wisdom that was later "theologized" by literary stages and redaction (Whybray, 1994; McKane, 1965, in reference to Proverbs in particular). Perdue (1977) tried to hold anthropology and theodicy in tension in his evaluation of wisdom theology. Schwab (2013) prefers to speak of relational eudemonism—a concern for relationship with the divine that is essentially self-interested, although this assessment is mainly based on the theology of Proverbs.

The idea of wisdom representing some kind of natural law, rather than revealed law, has also emerged in modern times (e.g., Crenshaw, 1976), notably in relation to the book of Job. God's relationship to the world is, in this scheme, seen as a more "scientific," creational one than as a revealed process over time. The concept of a known order given to the world once for all by God both in the creation and in society tends to dominate a more inductive, revelatory model. There has been a challenge to both aspects of this. First, a questioning of the centrality of the creation/order motif has come notably from Weeks (2010), who does not believe that wisdom contains a creation theology. He returns to the older idea that creation is used as a frequent metaphor or illustration and does not provide an overarching theme. Second, Fox (1995) has challenged the ideas of act–consequence and world order, arguing that the Egyptian parallels themselves were overplayed and misinterpreted. In this view the wisdom quest is seen as a more piecemeal and inductive one. While these approaches are helpful correctives to an oversystematization of wisdom's theology, I argue that they are not successful in challenging the primacy of creation and order as the two keynotes of wisdom theology, themes found throughout the wisdom corpus.

There has been interest in the way that wisdom forms character, stressing afresh its ethical aspect (Brown, 1996). This interest puts the emphasis back on the human quest for wisdom and the process of shaping and reshaping character in relation to the perceived world. The intersection between the individual and the community is key, as is the emphasis on the moral traits that ethical character shaping engenders. Indeed, the nature of wisdom as moral guidance is another overarching concern in the literature. Characters are in transition, shaped by moral guidance and by interaction with people and events. There is then a key "social" aspect in that wisdom is about living in harmony with others and about relationships, human and nonhuman. Imagery from the natural world and of animals is a regular theme, often used to illustrate human character traits.

One problem with the characterization of a "wisdom theology" is that the wisdom books are all very different. The evaluation of wisdom tends to use the book of Proverbs as a starting point with the assumption that the other books follow this same path of thought. Arguably, however, this is not the case, except in a very broad definition of wisdom theology (e.g., the God–human relationship). Proverbs is itself made up of a number of very different sections. The more theological part in Proverbs 1–9 has often been the place to look for wisdom theology, with the figure of Wisdom, the mediator between God and humanity, being a central motif. However, there are long sections of maxims that appear relatively unrelated one to another on a range of practical topics, and then

there are separate sections attributed to Agur, king of Massa, and to another king, Lemuel, which may suggest some royal context.

The book of Job does not have the practical, ethical stance of Proverbs; rather, it is a story with an extended dialogue. To be sure, the question of retribution is raised in a major way, but so too are questions about disinterested righteousness ("Does Job fear God for nothing?" Job 1:9), divine and human interaction, and God's justice. Job has a strong relationship with both Deuteronomy and the Psalms, which extends beyond a narrow set of wisdom genres (Dell, 1991), although there is a "hymn to wisdom" in chapter 28.

Ecclesiastes cites the occasional proverb, but much of the book criticizes what might be regarded as traditional wisdom theology. The Creator God is largely behind the scenes in this book. The human condition is at the forefront, with issues of the meaning of life, the place of enjoyment, the vanity of life, the inevitability of death, and the value of work on the agenda. While there is an interest in the doctrine of retribution, it is not center stage as it is in Proverbs.

Ben Sira or Ecclesiasticus in the Apocrypha returns to the kind of proverbial wisdom found in Proverbs and yet takes the new step of equating wisdom with the Torah. In this masterstroke it connects the saving history and the characters of that history with wisdom and the keeping of the Torah. This, according to Ben Sira, is the path to wisdom. With this connection, however, wisdom loses its universal character.

The Wisdom of Solomon turns the figure of Wisdom into an attribute of God and, thus, emphasizes the divine aspect of wisdom theology. In the connection of prayers and the cult, a strong link is forged with Israelite tradition. Wisdom theology, then, is not a monochrome concept; instead, it is one that changed and developed over time, criticizing and reinventing itself. This is what makes it so hard to define as an overall concept—any characterization does not adequately represent every sum of every part.

Important questions continue to be debated. Who generated this wisdom material? What kind of worldview did the sages have? Indeed, who were these sages? Did they emerge at the time of Solomon as an educated group around the king and court that had the responsibility of gathering traditional proverbial material together? Was wisdom theology then the province of the elite and of the literate? While the written material might suggest this, the nature of proverbs as oral and disseminated in families and possibly schools mitigates against this conclusion. Wisdom theology appears to have been an alternative worldview that had a practical, ethical aspect in everyday life. It would have been far from the mind of those putting proverbs into practice to reflect on an overall theology of this material, even though their worldview consistently promoted behavior of a moral nature that led to the good and ultimately to "life." Wisdom seems to have had a particular context in the training of the young on the "path to life," a training in making good choices and being aware of inappropriate temptations (such as Wisdom's opposite number, Woman Folly). Education therefore seems a real possibility as to context, whether that be at the grass-roots level or in royal schools.

In sum, "order" and "creation" are useful terms when seeking to characterize wisdom theology and a notion of a dialectic between God and humanity, between the theocentric and the anthropocentric. Wisdom is certainly about relationship—with others, with oneself, with the divine—but it is also essentially practical, about real human life and making choices for good or ill.

[*See also* Education; Ethics, Biblical, *subentry* Old Testament; Good and Evil; Theology, Biblical, *subentry* Old Testament; *and* Tradition.]

BIBLIOGRAPHY

Anderson, Bernhard W. *Creation versus Chaos: The Reinterpretation of Mythical Symbolism in the Bible.* New York: Association Press, 1967.

Bauer, G. L. *Theology of the Old Testament.* London: Charles Fox, 1838.

Brown, William. *Character in Crisis: A Fresh Approach to the Wisdom Literature of the Old Testament.* Grand Rapids, Mich.: Eerdmans, 1996.

Bruch, J. F. *Weisheits-Lehre der Hebräer, ein Beitrag zur Geschichte der Philosophie.* Strassburg, Austria: Treutel & Würtz, 1851.

Brueggemann, Walter. *Theology of the Old Testament.* Minneapolis: Fortress, 1997.

Cheyne, T. K. *Job and Solomon.* London: Kegan Paul, Trench, 1887.

Crenshaw, James L. "Popular Questioning of the Justice of God in Ancient Israel." In *Studies in Ancient Israelite Wisdom*, edited by James L. Crenshaw, pp. 289–304. New York: KTAV, 1976.

Crenshaw, James L. *Old Testament Wisdom.* 3d ed. Louisville, Ky.: Westminster John Knox, 2010.

Delitzsch, Franz. *Biblical Commentary on the Proverbs of Solomon.* 2 vols. Clark's Foreign Theology Library 43, 47. Edinburgh: T&T Clark, 1874.

Dell, Katharine. J. *The Book of Job as Sceptical Literature.* Beihefte zur Zeitschrift für die Alttestamentliche Wissenschaft 197. Berlin: De Gruyter, 1991.

Dell, Katharine, and Will Kynes. *Reading Job Intertextually.* Library of Hebrew Bible/Old Testament Studies 574. London: Bloomsbury, 2012.

Erman, Adolf. "Eine ägyptische Quelle der 'Spruche Salomos.'" *Sitzungsberichte der preussischen Akademie der Wissenschaften, Philosophisch-historischen Klasse* 15 (1924): 86–93.

Fox, Michael "World Order and *Ma'at*: A Crooked Parallel." *Journal of the Ancient Near Eastern Society* 23 (1995): 31–48.

Gemser, Bruce. *Sprüche Salomos.* Handbuch zum Alten Testament 16. Tübingen, Germany: Mohr Siebeck, 1938.

Gese, Hartmut. *Lehre und Wirklichkeit in der alten Weisheit.* Tübingen, Germany: Mohr, 1958.

Koch, Klaus. "Is There a Doctrine of Retribution in the Old Testament?" In *Theodicy in the Old Testament*, edited by J. L. Crenshaw, pp. 57–87. London, SPCK, 1983. First published in German in 1955.

Kynes, Will. "The Nineteenth-Century Beginnings of 'Wisdom Literature' and Its Twenty-First-Century End?" In *Angles on Israelite Wisdom: Proceedings of the Oxford Old Testament Seminar*, edited by John Jarick. London: Bloomsbury, forthcoming.

McKane, William. *Prophets and Wise Men.* Studies in Biblical Theology 44. London: SCM, 1965.

Meinhold, H. *Die Weisheit Israels.* Leipzig, Germany: Quelle & Meier, 1908.

Morgan, Donn F. *Wisdom in the Old Testament Traditions.* Atlanta: John Knox, 1981.

Murray, Robert. *The Cosmic Covenant.* Heythrop Monographs 7. London: Sheed and Ward, 1992.

Murphy, Roland E. "Wisdom Literature and Biblical Theology." *Biblical Theology Bulletin* 24 (1994): 4–7.

Perdue, Leo G. *Wisdom and Cult.* Society of Biblical Literature Dissertation Series 30. Missoula, Mont.: Scholars Press, 1977.

Rad, Gerhard von. *Wisdom in Israel.* Translated by J. D. Martin. Harrisburg, Pa.: Trinity Press International, 1972. First published in German in 1970.

Schmid, Hans H. *Wesen und Geschichte der Weisheit.* Beihefte zur Zeitschrift für die Alttestamentliche Wissenschaft 101. Berlin: Alfred Töpelmann, 1966.

Schwab, Zoltan. *Towards an Interpretation of the Book of Proverbs: Selfishness and Secularity Reconsidered.* Winona Lake, Ind.: Eisenbrauns, 2013.

Weeks, Stuart. *An Introduction to the Study of Wisdom Literature.* London: T&T Clark, 2010.

Westermann, Claus. *Elements of Old Testament Theology.* Atlanta: John Knox, 1982.

Whybray, R. Norman. *The Composition of the Book of Proverbs.* Journal for the Study of the Old Testament, Supplement Series 168. Sheffield, U.K.: Sheffield Academic Press, 1994.

Zimmerli, Walter. *Old Testament Theology in Outline.* Translated by David E. Green. Edinburgh: T&T Clark; Atlanta: John Knox, 1978. First published in German in 1972.

Katharine J. Dell

WITNESS

In the ancient legal sphere, witnessing (Heb. *ʿēd*; Gk, *martys*) involved personal testimony from eyewitness knowledge of a fact or an event. At trial, the prosecution was required to produce firsthand corroborating evidence—contradictory testimony was inadmissible—from at least two witnesses to establish the guilt of a person accused of a crime (Deut 19:15; Prov 19:28; Matt 18:16; 26:65; Mark 14:63; Acts 6:11–14; 2 Cor 13:1; 1 Tim 5:19), especially a capital offense (Num 35:30; Deut 17:6; Matt 26:59–66; Mark 14:53–64; Heb 10:28). Witnesses could also be called by the defense (Prov 14:25). Evidence, therefore, consisted of affirmation by individuals of a fact's veracity, which was subject to examination. If confirmed by another, a reasonable judge could rely upon the witnesses' testimony. No witness was required against a woman charged with adultery (Num 5:11–31). In capital crimes the witnesses also initiated execution of the party found guilty (Deut 17:7; John 8:7; Acts 7:58). Only free men of integrity were qualified as witnesses (Josephus, *Ant.* 4.8.15). As in Mesopotamian law, there were no explicit rules of evidence in Israel. Witnesses were not put under oath, but false testimony was proscribed (Exod 20:16; 23:1–3; Deut 5:20; Prov 6:16, 19;

12:17; 14:25; 19:5, 9; 21:28; 25:18; Sus 28—62), as was the withholding of evidence (Lev 5:1; Prov 29:24). Conviction of false witness carried with it a penalty identical to that faced by the accused (Deut 19:16–21; Sus 60–62). Frequent references to false testimony suggest that it was not uncommon or, at least, that witnessing was in many instances viewed skeptically (1 Kgs 21:8–14; Pss 27:12; 35:11–12; Prov 6:19; 12:17, 19; 14:25; 19:5, 9; 21:28; Matt 26:59–60; Mark 14:55–59; Acts 6:12–14).

Legal agreements like business contracts utilized witnesses to provide evidence of the transaction. Qualified men witnessed the consent of the parties, although the number of witnesses was not stipulated and, therefore, could be more or fewer than two (Gen 23:10–20; Ruth 4:7–12; Isa 8:1–2). Witnesses drew up, signed, or sealed contracts, deeds, and letters of divorce (Deut 24:1–3; Jer 32:9–12). Sometimes the physical witness or memorial of a transaction consisted of an animal sacrifice (Gen 21:30) or an inanimate object, such as a sandal, pillar, altar, or pile of rocks (Gen 31:44–52; Deut 25:7–10; Josh 22:26–34; Ruth 4:9; Isa 19:19–20). The tablets of the Decalogue were called the "tables of testimony/witness" (Exod 32:15), and the Ark of the Covenant was referred to as the "tabernacle of testimony/witness" (Exod 25:16, 21; Num 17:19, 22, 23 [MT; 17:4, 7, 8 LXX]). Witnessing, whether testimony or object, served as proof of an accusation or transaction (Gen 31:44; Deut 31:24–29; Josh 24:26–27; Mark 6:11).

Religious Connotations. Gods in the ancient world were frequently called upon to act as witnesses to treaties, solemn declarations or understandings, and oaths. False oaths or breaches of agreement were believed to bring divine punishment upon the offender. Likewise Israel's God was asked to act as a witness to such events (Judg 11:10; 1 Sam 12:5–6). Similar to the juridical sense, God was adjured to be a witness, often for the prosecution, to confirm proper or improper conduct or the truth of what was said (Gen 31:50; 1 Sam 12:5; 20:23, 42; Jer 29:22–23; 42:5; Mic 1:2; Mal 2:13–16; Rom 1:9; 2 Cor 1:23). For example, God was called as a witness against Israel's misconduct (Jer 29:23; Mic 3:8; Mal 3:5). Indeed, God's law itself served as a witness against Israel's past and future rebelliousness (Deut 31:25–29). Also, Job called God as witness to his innocence (Job 16:19). Classical and Hellenistic philosophers were often witnesses to beliefs held rather than to events. They expressed commitment to these views by conduct faithful to their convictions, whatever their personal circumstances. For instance, Stoics—regardless of what fate befell them—were called to testify to divine control of the cosmos against those who would dispute it. Similarly, for Israel's prophets God's sovereignty was not an observable fact but a statement of faith based on their experience of the world and God's self-revelation. In this way Israel was considered a witness to God as the Lord of history and Israel's deliverer, savior, and redeemer (Isa 43:9–13; 44:7–11).

New Testament Meanings. In the New Testament witness retains its juridical sense of those who testify, especially at a trial, to what they have seen or heard (Matt 18:16; 26:65; Mark 14:53–64; Luke 11:48; Acts 6:11–14; 7:58; 2 Cor 11:1; 1 Thess 2:10; 1 Tim 5:19; 6:12; 2 Tim 2:2; Heb 10:28). God is called as witness to conduct or truth (John 5:31–47; 8:18; 15:26 [the Spirit]; Acts 13:22; 15:8–9; Rom 1:9; 2 Cor 1:23; Phil 1:8; 1 Thess 2:5, 10; Heb 11:4–5, 39); others bear witness to truths about God (John 3:11; Rev 11:3). Two or three witnesses should be consulted in settling disputes between community members (Matt 18:16). By contrast, the high priest judges that Jesus's personal testimony precludes the need of witnesses at his trial (Matt 26:65; Mark 14:63). In a twist, the tombs honoring prophets serve as witness to their murder by their Jewish ancestors (Matt 23:31; Luke 11:48).

Witness takes on several distinctive meanings in the New Testament. Jesus himself is witness to the truth and to the Father (John 3:11, 31–34; 5:36; 8:12–19; 10:25; 18:37; Rev 1:5; 3:14). The apostles are chosen by God to be witnesses to Jesus (Acts 5:32; 10:41). In the juridical sense they are witnesses in defense of Jesus (Acts 3:14–15; 5:30–32). Moreover, they are eyewitnesses to the historical events of his life, including his ministry, arrest and trial, crucifixion, resurrection, and ascension (Luke 24:48; John 15:27; 19:31–37; 21:24; Acts 1:8, 21–22; 2:32; 4:33; 5:31; 10:39–42; 13:27–31; 1 Pet 5:1; 1 John 1:1–3; 4:14). As believers—together with all believers—they are also witnesses in faith to the significance of Jesus (John 1:6–9, 15–28, 32–34; 3:26–30;

5:33; 1 John 1:2; 4:14; 5:10–12). The apostles are empowered to witness by the Spirit (Acts 1:8; 2:14–21), who inspires them (Matt 10:16–20; Luke 12:11–12; Acts 6:10), gives them courage (Acts 4:13–33), and bears witness with them (John 15:26; Acts 5:32). The Spirit, together with water (baptism) and blood (Eucharist), witnesses to the power of Christ's saving death (1 John 5:7–8). Paul, too, is considered a witness in Acts (14:4, 14; 22:15; 26:16), although he never refers to himself as such in his letters. He does, however, claim apostleship in the same sense as that attributed to him and the 12 apostles in Acts—namely, he saw the risen Lord and was called directly and equally by God for God's work (1 Cor 9:1–2; Acts 9:5–6, 15–16; 13:2–3; 22:10–15; 26:16–18; Rom 1:1–6; Gal 1:1, 12, 15–19; 1 Cor 15:3–11). Nevertheless, unlike the other apostles, Paul is a historical witness only with respect to his experience of Christ on the road to Damascus (Acts 9:3–7); otherwise, his witnessing concerns faith in the crucified and risen Christ (Acts 22:15).

A Martyrological Sense. The development of a martyrological sense of witness in the postbiblical period is anticipated in the New Testament. The writer of 1 Peter refers to himself as "a witness of the suffering of Christ" (1 Pet 5:1), which suggests that he is more than an eyewitness: as a proclaimer of the gospel he participates in Christ's suffering. The idea of sharing in Christ's suffering appears elsewhere in the New Testament, even though it is not explicitly connected to witnessing (2 Cor 1:5; Col 1:24; 1 Pet 2:21). Acts 22:20 calls Stephen a witness to Christ, that is, someone who dies for proclaiming Christ (Acts 7:2–60). This sense occurs as well in Revelation: John is instructed to write to the Christ-believing community at Pergamum of the witness Antipas, who was killed (Rev 2:13). Jesus himself is the "faithful witness" (Rev 1:5; 3:14), the one whose witness unto death serves as the model for Christ-believers to follow (Rev 6:9; 12:11, 17). Later, John mentions Christ's two witnesses who will prophesy during the end time and be slain by the beast (Rev 11:3–7), as well as the woman (Rome) "drunk with the blood of the saints and the blood of Jesus' witnesses" (Rev 17:6). Such references, in combination with increasing persecution of the Christian community, led to the development of the meaning of witness as "martyr" by the middle of the second century C.E. (*Mart. Pol.* 19:1).

[*See also* Apostasy; Apostleship; Baptism; Blessings and Curses; Christology; Decalogue; God and Gods; Guilt and Innocence; Holy Spirit; John and the Johannine the Epistles; Lord's Supper; Luke–Acts; Matthew; Oaths and Vows; Pauline Letters; Persecution; Prophets and Prophecy; *and* Wisdom.]

BIBLIOGRAPHY

Brown, Raymond E. *The Epistles of John.* Anchor Bible 30. Garden City, N.Y.: Doubleday, 1982.

Edwards, Douglas R. "Witness." In *Harper's Bible Dictionary*, edited by Paul J. Achtemeier, p. 1138. San Francisco: Harper & Row, 1985.

Greenberg, Moshe. "Witness." In *The Interpreter's Dictionary of the Bible*, edited by George Arthur Buttrick, Vol. 4, p. 864. Nashville, Tenn.: Abingdon, 1962.

Johnson, Luke Timothy. *The Gospel of Luke.* Sacra Pagina 3. Collegeville, Minn.: Liturgical Press, 1991.

McKenzie, John L. "Witness." In *Dictionary of the Bible*, pp. 933–935. Milwaukee, Wisc.: Bruce, 1965.

Strathmann, Hermann. "μάρτυς, μαρτυρέω, μαρτυρία, μαρτύριον." In *Theological Dictionary of the New Testament*, edited by Gerhard Kittel and Gerhard Friedrich, Vol. 4, pp. 474–508. Grand Rapids, Mich.: Eerdmans, 1967.

Trites, Allison A. "Witness." In *New Interpreter's Dictionary of the Bible*, edited by Katharine Doob Sakenfeld, Vol. 5, pp. 875–876. Nashville, Tenn.: Abingdon, 2009.

Verheul, A. "Witness." In *Encyclopedic Dictionary of the Bible*, edited by Louis F. Hartman. Translated by Eamonn O'Doherty, cols. 2591–2593. New York: McGraw-Hill, 1963.

William Sanger Campbell

WORD (LOGOS)

The importance of Logos, or "Word," for theology arises from its use in the prologue of the Gospel according to John (1:1): "In the beginning was the Word, and the Word was with God and the Word was God." This verse encapsulates the Gospel's Christology, which claims that Jesus, the Son of God, not only was sent by the Father but is in some significant sense one with him. This bold claim and the language used to express it, rooted in the theology of Hellenistic Judaism, fueled Christian theological debates through the end of antiquity and remains a fertile source of contemporary theological reflection.

Background. The pre-Socratic philosopher Heraclitus, whose work survives in fragments, held that behind the constantly changing phenomenal world resides a unifying force, which he labeled the "Logos" (Diogenes Laertius, *Lives and Opinions of Eminent Philosophers*, 9.1.1). This term, which ordinarily referred to speech or its content, suggested that the unifying force manifested a rational order. Heraclitus's lapidary sayings were later used in the more systematic doctrine of the Stoics, who held that whatever exists is material, although some matter is inert and some active, a distinction roughly analogous to modern conceptions of mass and energy. The Stoics gave many labels to the energy that pervades, unites, and shapes all things. In a demythologizing mood they called it "Zeus," the king of the gods (Cleanthes, "Hymn to Zeus," from Stobaeus, *Ecl.* 1.1.12; "Zeno," in Diogenes Laertius, *Lives and Opinions of Eminent Philosophers*, 7.1.88). In more naturalist terms they labeled it *pneuma*, or "spirit." *Pneuma*, which was not immaterial but rather something like a fine gas or electrical charge, worked in an orderly way. It could be described as the *logos spermatikos*, "seminal principle," dictating from within the comprehensible patterns in nature (Diogenes Laertius, *Lives and Opinions of Eminent Philosophers*, 7.135–136). Those principles functioned as what moderns call "laws of nature" as well as ethical norms, endowing the world with rational order.

Stoic teaching about the immanent *pneuma* attracted Jews of the Hellenistic period, who used it to explain aspects of their native tradition in its new environment. The Wisdom of Solomon (late first century B.C.E. or early first century C.E.) wrestled with questions of theodicy, offering an apology for Jewish history as a process guided by divine wisdom (Gk, *sophia*). In doing so its author adapted an ancient hymn to divine wisdom, inspired by Proverbs 8, and presented Sophia not as a quality of God's existence but as something much like the Stoic notion of a pervasive force. In her was a "spirit [*pneuma*] intelligent, holy, unique" (Wis 7:22), which "pervades and penetrates all things" (7:24). She is "a breath of the power of God, and a pure emanation of the glory of the Almighty" (7:25), and "a reflection of eternal light…an image of his goodness" (7:26). Although this language, echoed in the New Testament in Hebrews 1:3, does not identify Wisdom as the Logos, it is clearly inspired by Stoic ideas.

Philo of Alexandria (ca. 13 B.C.E.–ca. 50 C.E.) followed the path opened by the Wisdom of Solomon. His philosophical framework, known as Middle Platonism, sought to harmonize Plato's teachings with Stoicism and other Hellenistic philosophies. Plato's *Timaeus* recounted a story of creation potentially compatible with Genesis but problematic for monotheists. Plato's creator, the Demiurge or Craftsman, does not make the world ex nihilo but contemplates and then replicates transcendent principles, the Forms or Ideas, in preexisting, unruly matter (*hyle*). Thus, the Demiurge is hardly the absolute sovereign of the universe. Following other Middle Platonists, Philo solved the problem by holding that the Forms were not eternal, independent entities but actually Ideas in the Creator's mind. Philo called that realm of Ideas "Wisdom" (*Creation*, 148) but also, and more commonly, the Logos: "Word" or "Reason" (*Creation*, 24–25, 36).

Once Platonic forms were construed as divine thoughts, other resources of Stoicism became useful to Philo. Building on the etymology of Logos, the Stoics explained the intimate relationship between thought and speech: thought was "embedded speech" (*logos endiathetos*); speech was "expressed thought" (*logos prophorikos*; Philo, *Migration*, 71–73). This distinction, later useful for Christian theologians striving to explain Christ's divinity, provided Philo a way of describing the divine presence in creation and in Torah while preserving God's transcendence. What bridged the gap was the Logos, which mediated the Platonic world of ideas, the word in God's mind, and Stoic *pneuma*, the "reason" breathed into creation as "seminal principles" (Philo, *Creation*, 43) and expressed

in Torah. Philo personifies and celebrates the Logos as "archangel," a mediator neither "uncreated as God nor created" (*Heir*, 205–206), the soul's "bride" (*Posterity*, 78), or "High Priest" (*Flight*, 108–112). He even calls the Logos God's "firstborn son" (*Confusion*, 146–147; *Agriculture*, 51) and a "second God" (*QG*, 2.62).

The Johannine Appropriation. The Logos of John's prologue alludes to Genesis 1:3, 6, 9, where God's speech brings creatures into being. Yet the Logos is not simply an abstraction for the divine voice. It is modeled on celebrations of Divine Wisdom in the Jewish tradition, particularly for her role as an instrument of creation. The affirmation of John 1:3–4, "all things were made through him, and without him not a single thing came to be," echoes the description of Wisdom's role in Proverbs 8:22–31. Other Christians made similar claims without referring to the Logos (1 Cor 8:6; Heb 1:2–3). John was probably influenced by a form of wisdom speculation not unlike Philo's, whose philosophical formulation of the sapiential tradition provides analogies with the Johannine prologue as well as resources for its interpretation by early Christians.

The prologue's most dramatic affirmation about the Logos, that it has become incarnate, echoes two earlier wisdom hymns. The verb for "dwelt among us" in John 1:14, *eskênosen* ("pitched a tent"), corresponds to the action described in Sirach 24:8–12, where Divine Wisdom "pitches her tent" in Israel as Torah. John's formulation suggests that Jesus now functions as Torah, a claim reinforced by the contrast between Jesus and Moses in John 1:17. The contention that Jesus stands in place of Torah is part of the Gospel's overall strategy to invest Jesus with the significance of central elements in Israel's sacred tradition. A second element of the prologue echoes Wisdom of Solomon 7:27, which celebrates Sophia who "in every generation…enters into the souls of faithful men and makes them friends of God and prophets." The Logos does something similar in John but in a more radical fashion—entering into Jesus's flesh (*sarx*, John 1:14). That incarnation makes possible something of universal import, analogous to the empowerment of Wisdom's prophets. What the Gospel promises as a result of the incarnation of the Logos is the ability of human beings to become "children of God" (John 1:12). That promise, repeated in the dialogue between Jesus and Nicodemus about birth from "water and Spirit" (3:5), is made possible by the effusion of the spirit that comes from Jesus crucified (19:30) and resurrected (20:22). The "holy spirit" poured forth through Christ, effecting forgiveness of sins (John 20:23), constitutes the final form of John's version of Wisdom and Logos. His use of such traditions transforms them by linking them to Christ's death and resurrection.

Attributes of the Logos, "light" and "life" (John 1:4), appear later in the Gospel to define the significance of Jesus. These elements resemble Philo's Logos and its evocation of Platonic Ideas or Forms. Although the Logos is not explicitly present in the rest of John, the claims made about it—that it was "with God" (1:1), that it resides in the "bosom of the Father" (1:18), that it "was God" (1:1)—are echoed in the Gospel's affirmations that Jesus and the Father "are one" (John 10:30) and in Jesus's use of the name by which God revealed himself, "I am" (John 8:58; cf. Exod 3:14). Particularly in his treatment of the love command and the relationship between Father and Son, John's interpretation of the Logos becomes clear. The relationship of Jesus to God is best understood not in terms of a metaphysical scheme but rather as a personal relationship. The love that Father and Son shared before the world's foundation (17:24) is what Jesus, by his command (13:34) and example (15:12–13), invites the disciples to embrace. That abiding love is the true character of the Spirit poured forth at Easter, the true content of the divine Word.

John's articulation of a "high" Christology stimulated subsequent debates. What kind of relationship is implied by being "with" or "toward" God (1:3)? What is the sense of "God" when predicated of the Logos (1:3)? Does it mean "fully divine" or simply "godlike"? Such questions would trouble later theologians.

The Logos in the Second Century. As a designation of Jesus's divine dimension with many Hellenistic resonances, Logos proved useful to second-century Christian apologists. Attempting to show that acceptance of Christianity was a reasonable decision,

they claimed that Christ's person and teaching gave focused expression to the divine will supporting all creation and accessible to any rational soul. This stance, echoing Stoic notions, made Christianity comprehensible but risked sacrificing Christ's uniqueness. The tension faced by the apologists surfaces in some modern forms of theology and contemporary efforts at interreligious dialogue, in which the claims of Christianity are reduced to truths generally accessible to reason.

Other implications of Logos language proved helpful to patristic theologians. To explain how Christ's divinity was compatible with monotheistic belief, they used images of continuity and discontinuity. The relationship between God and God's Word, the offspring of the Father, resembles that of the sun to its rays (Athenagoras, *Leg.*, 10.1) or a fire and a kindled flame (Justin Martyr, *Dial.*, 61.2; Tatian, *Oration*, 5.1). Similarly, the Logos *endiathetos*, within the mind of God and therefore part of God from all eternity, is one with the Logos *prophorikos*, or Word incarnate (Theophilus, *Autol.*, 22).

Not all theologians who used Logos language stood in the tradition that came to define Christian thought. The second century saw various speculative systems flourish, among them the school of Valentinus, an Alexandrian teacher active in Rome. The doctrines his disciples developed, built on the mythology of earlier "Gnostics," were deemed heretical by such theologians as Irenaeus, Clement of Alexandria, Tertullian, and Origen. At the heart of this controversy were claims about the relationship of God to creation. The Valentinians explained the human condition as the result of devolution from a transcendent first principle. The process started with a flaw in the divine realm caused by an entity known as Sophia (Wisdom). Creation involved the imprisonment of spiritual substance in matter by the machinations of an inferior deity: a Demiurge, identified with the God of the Old Testament and inimical to the true, spiritual God. Criticism by heresiologists led the anonymous third-century author of the *Tripartite Tractate* from Nag Hammadi (NHC I,5) to recast Valentinian theology in terms of the Logos as an element of the Godhead who supervised not a hostile devolution but a process overseen by beneficent divine providence.

The Logos in Trinitarian and Christological Controversies. The situation of Christian theologians changed in the early fourth century when the emperor Constantine first tolerated (r. 306–337 C.E.), then increasingly supported, the church. Having gained control over the whole empire in 324 C.E., he summoned Christian bishops to a council at Nicaea in 325, in part to deal with a theological controversy troubling Alexandria. The dispute focused on the teachings of a charismatic presbyter, Arius, who denied the full divinity of the Son. Nicaea affirmed the Son's divine status, though it would take more than another half-century for the Christian doctrine of God to be fully defined.

The controversy rested in part on implications of Logos terminology widely used in the previous two centuries. Stoic doctrines about thought and speech offered a model of continuity helpful for describing the relationship between divine and human in the person of Jesus; when applied to the relationship between Father and Son in the Godhead, however, the model created difficulties. The unity of thought and speech combines elements that are temporally distinct; thought usually exists before speech. This relationship suggests that the Logos had a moment of becoming. If so, "there was," as Arius said, "when the Son was not" (Socrates Scholasticus, *Ecclesiastical History*, 1.5). If so, the Son is not coeternal with the Father and, therefore, not in the full sense "divine." The same problem affected other terms used to describe the relationship between Father and Son, particularly Nicaea's affirmation that the Son was "begotten." Many theologians may have thought of the Logos that became incarnate in Christ as in some sense a lesser deity than the Father, like Philo's "second god." For that position they could find Johannine support in Jesus's statement that "the Father is greater than I" (John 14:28). Defenders of the Nicaean position explained that verse as a reference to Christ's human nature. The resolution of the debate finally affirmed that the relationship of Father to Son is an eternal one, not something subject to temporal change.

Following the Council of Constantinople (381 C.E.), theological debate turned to the relationship between divinity and humanity in Christ. This dispute may be partially understood as an attempt to explain John's affirmation, "the Word became flesh" (1:14). Did the Logos assume human flesh, effectively displacing a human soul and creating a divinized entity (a notion that influenced Alexandrian Christology)? Or does "flesh" mean something more like "human nature" generally, including a human will or soul (the position favored at Antioch)? Such debates were largely resolved at the Council of Chalcedon (451 C.E.), which affirmed that in the one person of Christ were united both fully divine and fully human natures. That position thereafter defined Christology in the Latin and Greek orthodox churches, though it was rejected by eastern Monophysite churches.

The history of Logos terminology used in the early Church, based on John 1:1–18, highlights the significance of claims made about Jesus in that passage and the difficulties of working out those claims' implications. The issues involved, concerning the relationship of Jesus to God and the very character of God, remain central to theology.

[*See also* Christology; Creation; Flesh; Holy Spirit; John and the Johannine Epistles; *and* Knowledge.]

BIBLIOGRAPHY

Anatolios, Khaled. *Retrieving Nicaea: The Development and Meaning of Trinitarian Doctrine*. Grand Rapids, Mich.: Baker, 2011.

Attridge, Harold W. "Philo and John: Two Riffs on One Logos." *Studia Philonica Annual* 17 (2005): 103–117.

Borgen, Peder. *Logos Was the True Light and Other Essays on the Gospel of John*. Trondheim, Norway: Tapir, 1983.

Engberg-Pedersen, Troels. "*Logos* and *Pneuma* in the Fourth Gospel." In *Greco-Roman Culture and the New Testament: Studies Commemorating the Centennial of the Pontifical Biblical Institute*, edited by David Edward Aune and Frederick E. Brenk, pp. 27–48. Supplements to Novum Testamentum 143. Leiden, The Netherlands, and Boston: Brill, 2012.

Koester, Craig. *The Word of Life: A Theology of John's Gospel*. Grand Rapids, Mich.: Eerdmans, 2008.

Reinhartz, Adele. *The Word in the World: The Cosmological Tale in the Fourth Gospel*. Society of Biblical Literature Monograph Series 45. Atlanta: Scholars Press, 1992.

Rusch, William G. *The Trinitarian Controversy*. Philadelphia: Fortress, 1980.

Winston, David. *Logos and Mystical Theology in Philo of Alexandria*. Cincinnati, Ohio: Hebrew Union College Press, 1985.

Young, Frances M. *From Nicaea to Chalcedon: A Guide to the Literature and Its Background*. Philadelphia: Fortress, 1983.

Harold W. Attridge

WORSHIP

See Cult and Worship.

Topical Outline of Contents

This outline provides a general overview of the conceptual scheme of *The Oxford Encyclopedia of the Bible and Theology*, listing the title of each entry and sub-entry. The topical categories are not mutually exclusive, and some entries are listed in more than one section. Entries in the encyclopedia are organized alphabetically. Entries in this outline are arranged under the following headings:

Biblical Figures
Biblical Places
Biblical Sources
Biblical Themes
Cult and Worship
Deities and Demons
Economic, Juridical, Political, and Social Issues

BIBLICAL FIGURES

Abraham
Adam, Last
Adam (Primeval History)
Angels
Christ
David
David, Son of
God and Gods
Holy Spirit
John the Baptist
Lamb of God

Lord
Mary
Moses
Paul
Peter
Satan
Servant of God
Son of God
Son of Man
Trinity

BIBLICAL PLACES

Canaan and Canaanites
Eden
Heaven and Earth

Israel and Israelites
Jerusalem (Zion)
Underworld and Hell

BIBLICAL SOURCES

Book of the Twelve (Minor Prophets)
Catholic Epistles

Deuteronomy
Deutero-Pauline Letters

BIBLICAL THEMES

Adoption
Allegory and Typology
Anger
Anthropology
Apocalypticism
Apostasy
Apostleship
Asceticism
Authority and Order
Baptism
Blessings and Curses
Body
Call
Canon
Christology
Comfort and Mourning
Conversion
Covenant
Creation
Cult and Worship
Day of the LORD
Death and Dying
Discipleship
Ecclesiology
Education
Election
Epiphany
Eschatology
Ethics, Biblical
    Old Testament
    New Testament
Exile and Dislocation
Faith
Family
Fear
Flesh
Forgiveness
Friendship
Genealogy
Gentiles

Glory
Good and Evil
Gospel
Grace
Heaven and Earth
Hermeneutics, Biblical
Holiness
Holy Spirit
Honor and Shame
Hope
Hospitality
Identity
Idols and Idolatry
Image of God
Inheritance (Heir)
Joy
Judaism
Knowledge
Labor
Land
Life and Life Force
Light and Darkness
Love
Marriage
Mercy and Compassion
Miracles
Monsters
Mystery and Mystery Religions
Parable
Prophets and Prophecy
Reconciliation
Redemption
Remnant
Repentance
Resurrection
Revelation
Reward and Retribution
Salvation History
Scripture
Sexuality

CULT AND WORSHIP

DEITIES AND DEMONS

ECONOMIC, JURIDICAL, POLITICAL, AND SOCIAL ISSUES

DIRECTORY OF CONTRIBUTORS

Samuel L. Adams
Union Presbyterian Seminary
Fools and Foolishness; Wealth and Poverty

John Ahn
Austin Presbyterian Theological Seminary
Story and Memory: Old Testament

O. Wesley Allen Jr.
Department of Homiletics and Worship, Lexington Theological Seminary
Preaching and Prophecy

Peter Altmann
Department of Theology, University of Zurich
Nature and Natural Resources

Harold W. Attridge
Yale Divinity School, Yale University
Word (Logos)

John M. G. Barclay
Department of Theology and Religion, Durham University
Grace

David L. Bartlett
Columbia Theological Seminary, Emeritus
Minister and Ministry

Stephen C. Barton
Department of Theology and Religion, Durham University
Authority and Order

Timothy Beal
Case Western Reserve University
Monsters

Mary Ann Beavis
Department of Religion and Culture, St. Thomas More College
Freedom and Slavery

John Bergsma
Department of Theology, Franciscan University of Steubenville
Covenant

Donald D. Binder
Historic Pohick Church, Virginia
Tabernacles, Temples, and Synagogues

C. Clifton Black
Department of Biblical Studies, Princeton Theological Seminary
Mark

Ryan P. Bonfiglio
Columbia Theological Seminary
God and Gods; Idols and Idolatry

Sarah Jane Boss
Department of Humanities, University of Roehampton
Mary

Linda McKinnish Bridges
Wake Forest University School of Divinity
Comfort and Mourning

Brendan Byrne

Jesuit Theological College

Gospel

Samuel Byrskog

Centre for Theology and Religious Studies, University of Lund

Story and Memory: New Testament

Douglas A. Campbell

Duke University Divinity School

Faith

William S. Campbell

University of Wales Trinity Saint David

Identity

William Sanger Campbell

Department of Theology & Religious Studies, The College of St. Scholastica

Witness

David B. Capes

Department of Theology, Houston Baptist University

Lord

Greg Carey

Lancaster Theological Seminary

Anger

John T. Carroll

Bible Department, Union Presbyterian Seminary

Luke–Acts

Warren Carter

Brite Divinity School, Texas Christian University

Politics and Systems of Governance

Ellen T. Charry

Princeton Theological Seminary

Hermeneutics, Biblical

Stephen J. Chester

North Park Theological Seminary

Conversion

Bruce Chilton

Department of Theology, Bard College

Abraham

Andrew D. Clarke

Department of Divinity and Religious Studies, University of Aberdeen

Apostleship

Ron Clements

King's College, Emeritus

Decalogue

Richard J. Clifford

School of Theology and Ministry, Boston College

Genesis

John J. Collins

Yale Divinity School

Violence

Raymond F. Collins

Department of Religious Studies, Brown University (Visiting Scholar)

Catholic Epistles

Edgar W. Conrad

School of History, Philosophy, Religion & Classics, University of Queensland

Remnant

Stephen L. Cook

Virginia Theological Seminary

Prophets and Prophecy

Robert B. Coote

San Francisco Theological Seminary

Land

Charles H. Cosgrove

Garrett-Evangelical Theological Seminary

Ethics, Biblical: New Testament

L. William Countryman

Church Divinity School of the Pacific; Graduate Theological Union, Emeritus

Marriage

Jerome F. D. Creach

Pittsburgh Theological Seminary

Oaths and Vows; War (Holy War)

Gregory W. Dawes

Department of Philosophy, University of Otago

Body

Martinus C. de Boer

Vrije Universiteit Amsterdam

Christology

Katharine J. Dell

Faculty of Divinity, University of Cambridge

Wisdom Literature

Walter Dietrich

Institut für Bibelwissenschaft, Universität Bern

Justice, Justification, and Righteousness:
Old Testament

Daniel R. Driver

Tyndale University College & Seminary

Forgiveness

James D. G. Dunn

Durham University, Emeritus

Adam, Last

Susan Eastman

Duke University Divinity School

Mercy and Compassion

Mark W. Elliott

School of Divinity, University of St. Andrews

Atonement

C. A. Evans

Acadia Divinity College, Acadia University

Kingdom of God (Heaven)

Everett Ferguson

Abilene Christian University, Emeritus

Mystery and Mystery Religions

Karin Finsterbusch

Institut für Evangelische Theologie, Universität Koblenz-Landau

Deuteronomy

Paula Fredriksen

Department of Comparative Religion, The Hebrew University, Jerusalem

Christ

Erhard S. Gerstenberger

Philipps-Universität Marburg

Cult and Worship

Robert Karl Gnuse

Department of Religious Studies, Loyola University, New Orleans

Kings and Kingship

John Goldingay

School of Theology, Fuller Theological Seminary

Scripture

Deirdre Good

General Theological Seminary

Sexuality

Donald E. Gowan

Pittsburgh Theological Seminary, Emeritus

Theophany

Klaus B. Haacker

Kirchliche Hochschule Wuppertal/Bethel

Justice, Justification, and Righteousness: New Testament

Anselm C. Hagedorn

Humboldt-Universität zu Berlin

Foreigner

Scott Hahn

University of St. Mary of the Lake, Mundelein Seminary; Franciscan University of Steubenville

Covenant

Martien A. Halvorson-Taylor

Department of Religious Studies, University of Virginia

Exile and Dislocation

James E. Harding

Department of Theology and Religion, University of Otago

Body

Daniel J. Harrington

School of Theology and Ministry, Boston College

Lamb of God

Camilla von Heijne

Department of Diaconal Studies, Church Music, and Theology, Ersta Skondal University

Angels

Suzanne Watts Henderson

Department of Philosophy and Religion, Queens University of Charlotte

Discipleship

J. Todd Hibbard

Department of Religious Studies, University of Detroit Mercy

Apocalypticism

Thomas Hieke

Johannes Gutenberg-Universität Mainz

Genealogy

Morna D. Hooker

Robinson College, University of Cambridge

Paul

Denise Dombkowski Hopkins

Wesley Theological Seminary

Blessings and Curses

Arland J. Hultgren

Luther Seminary

Parable

Michael B. Hundley

Georgetown University

Heaven and Earth

Susan E. Hylen

Candler School of Theology, Emory University

Glory

Bernd Janowski

Evangelisch-Theologische Fakultät, Eberhard Karls Universität Tübingen

Anthropology

David Janzen

Department of Philosophy and Religious Studies, North Central College

Festivals and Holy Days

Luke Timothy Johnson

Candler School of Theology, Emory University

Ecclesiology

J. J. Johnston

Acadia University

Kingdom of God (Heaven)

Philip S. Johnston

Department of Divinity, University of Cambridge

Underworld and Hell

Joel Kaminsky

Department of Religion, Smith College

Election

Craig S. Keener

Asbury Theological Seminary

Miracles

Micah D. Kiel

Department of Theology, St. Ambrost University

Devils and Demons

Seyoon Kim

Fuller Theological Seminary

Reconciliation

Gerald A. Klingbeil

Andrews University

Sacrifice and Offerings

Marjo C. A. Korpel

Protestantse Theologische Universiteit

Light and Darkness

Steven J. Kraftchick

Candler School of Theology, Emory University

Resurrection

Will Kynes

Whitworth University

Satan

André LaCocque

Chicago Theological Seminary, Emeritus

Eden; Guilt and Innocence

Peter Lampe

University of Heidelberg; University of the Free State

Peter

Phillip Michael Lasater

Theologische Fakultät, Universität Zürich

Fear

Anthony Le Donne

University of the Pacific

David, Son of

Joel Marcus LeMon

Candler School of Theology, Emory University; University of Stellenbosch

Psalms

Mark Leuchter

Department of Religion, Temple University

David

Martin Leuenberger

Eberhard Karls Universität Tübingen

Day of the LORD

Amy-Jill Levine

Divinity School, Vanderbilt University

Torah

John R. Levison

School of Theology, Seattle Pacific University

Holy Spirit

Oded Lipschits

Institute of Archaeology, Tel Aviv University

Israel and Israelites

Maggie Low

Trinity Theological College, Singapore

Barrenness

Jack R. Lundbom

University of Cambridge; Garrett-Evangelical Theological Seminary

Jeremiah

Ulrich Luz

University of Bern

Matthew

Christopher D. Marshall

Victoria University of Wellington

Repentance

Mark A. Matson

Milligan College

Salvation History

S. Dean McBride Jr.

Union Presbyterian Seminary, Emeritus

Exodus

Mark McEntire

College of Theology and Christian Ministry, Belmont University

Ezra, Nehemiah, and 1 and 2 Chronicles

J. Richard Middleton

Northeastern Seminary at Roberts Wesleyan College

Image of God

Mitzi L. Minor

Memphis Theology Seminary

Lord's Prayer

David P. Moessner

Texas Christian University

Redemption

Francis J. Moloney
Australian Catholic University, Emeritus
Love

Kenneth Ngwa
Drew Theological School
Knowledge

B. J. Oropeza
Department of Biblical Studies, Azusa Pacific University
Apostasy

Carolyn Osiek
Brite Divinity School, Texas Christian University, Emerita
Family

George L. Parsenios
Princeton Theological Seminary
Truth

Dale Patrick
Department of Philosophy and Religion, Drake University, Emeritus
Reward and Retribution

David Penchansky
Theology Department, University of St. Thomas
Good and Evil; Wisdom

Pheme Perkins
Department of Theology, Boston College
Baptism; Lord's Supper

John J. Pilch
Odyssey Program, Johns Hopkins University
Hospitality; Labor

Sandra Hack Polaski
Southeastern Commission for the Study of Religion
Call

Emerson B. Powery
Department of Biblical and Religious Studies, Messiah College
Persecution

Mitchell G. Reddish
Department of Religious Studies, Stetson University
Hope

Paul L. Redditt
Georgetown College; Baptist Seminary of Kentucky
Book of the Twelve (Minor Prophets)

Calvin J. Roetzel
Department of Classical and Near Eastern Studies, University of Minnesota, Emeritus
Eschatology; Gentiles

Thomas Römer
Collège de France; Faculty of Theology and Religious Sciences, University of Lausanne
Historical Narratives (Joshua—2 Kings); Leviticus and Numbers

Deborah W. Rooke
Regent's Park College, University of Oxford
Priests and Priesthood

Clare K. Rothschild
Department of Theology, Lewis University
John the Baptist

Darren Sarisky
Faculty of Divinity, University of Cambridge
Tradition

Annette Schellenberg
San Francisco Thological Seminary
Adam (Primeval History); Megillot

Matthew Richard Schlimm
University of Dubuque Theological Seminary
Ethics, Biblical: Old Testament

Konrad Schmid
University of Zurich
Creation

Andreas Schuele
University of Leipzig; University of Stellenbosch
Isaiah; Life and Life Force

Robert Paul Seesengood

Department of Religious Studies, Albright College

Friendship

Jeffrey S. Siker

Department of Theological Studies, Loyola Marymount University

Judaism

Judy Yates Siker

San Francisco Theological Seminary

Holiness

Matthew L. Skinner

Luther Seminary

Death and Dying

Jay Sklar

Covenant Theological Seminary

Sin

Thomas Slater

McAfee School of Theology, Mercer University

Son of Man

D. Moody Smith

Duke University Divinity School, Emeritus

John and the Johannine Epistles

Thomas Söding

Ruhr-Universität Bochum

Theology, Biblical: New Testament

R. Kendall Soulen

Wesley Theological Seminary

Trinity

F. Scott Spencer

Baptist Theological Seminary at Richmond

Son of God

Gregory E. Sterling

Yale Divinity School, Yale University

Allegory and Typology

Todd D. Still

George W. Truett Theological Seminary, Baylor University

Epiphany

Brent A. Strawn

Candler School of Theology, Emory University

Canaan and Canaanites

Gail P. Streete

Department of Religious Studies, Rhodes College, Emerita

Asceticism; Deutero-Pauline Letters

C. A. Strine

University of Sheffield

Ezekiel

Jacob Stromberg

Duke University

Servant of God

Jerry L. Sumney

Lexington Theological Seminary

Adoption; Inheritance (Heir); Pauline Letters

Willard M. Swartley

Department of the Bible, Anabaptist Mennonite Biblical Seminary, Emeritus

Peace

Laura C. Sweat

School of Theology, Seattle Pacific University

Revelation

Marvin A. Sweeney

Claremont School of Theology

Moses; Theology, Biblical: Old Testament

James W. Thompson

Graduate School of Theology, Abilene Christian University

Expiation

Graham H. Twelftree

School of Divinity, Regent University

Sickness, Disease, and Healing

Jan G. Van der Watt

Radboud University Nijmegen

Soteriology

Jacques Vermeylen

Brussels

Jerusalem (Zion)

Robert Wall

Seattle Pacific University

Canon

David F. Watson

United Theological Seminary

Honor and Shame

Rodney A. Werline

Barton College

Prayer

Robert Williamson Jr.

Department of Religious Studies, Hendrix College

Education

Carla Swafford Works

Wesley Theological Seminary

Joy

Richard A. Wright

Oklahoma Christian University

Flesh

INDEX

Page numbers in boldface refer to the main entry on the subject. Page numbers in italics refer to illustrations and tables.

infant and childhood deaths, **1**:14
  Roman emperors, **1**:15
  Hebrew Bible, **1**:14
    Israel as God's son, **1**:14
    king as God's son, **1**:14
    lack of examples, **1**:14
  huiothesia (to take a son), **1**:14; **2**:225, 226
  metaphorical usage, by Paul, **1**:15–16
    believers as heirs of God, **1**:16
    Israel as God's son, **1**:15–16
    Spirit and eschatological salvation, **1**:16
  ontological nature of Christ, debates, **1**:16
  Pauline letters, **1**:15–16
adrogatio, **1**:14
adultery
  Bathsheba affair, **1**:193–95, 197, 577; **2**:11, 135
  Decalogue, **1**:214
  idol worship, **1**:509, 512
  Jeremiah, **1**:544
  marriage after divorce, **1**:285
  Old Testament ethics, **1**:274
  prostitution and, **2**:56
  sexuality, **2**:286
  slavery and, **1**:380
  witness and, **2**:432
adversary (*śāṭān*), **1**:23, 229, 320; **2**:265
Aeneid (Virgil), **1**:44, 71
aeshma daēva (demon of wrath), **1**:230
agalliasis/agalliaō (joy), **1**:558
Agamben, Giorgio, **1**:411
Agnus Dei, **2**:27
Ahasuerus, **1**:26, 294, 405–6; **2**:81, 93
Ahimelech, **2**:174, 365
Ahn, John, **2**:334–35, 342
Ahura Mazda (Lord of Wisdom), **1**:185; **2**:46
Akhenaten, **2**:124
Akkadians
  biblical creation and flood narratives,
    1:166–67
  creation topic in theology, **1**:166–67
  cults, **1**:179
  language
    clay tablets, **1**:537
    education, Old Babylonian period, **1**:249–50, 251
    palāḫu (fear), **1**:344, 345, 346

prophecies
  Dynastic Prophecy, **1**:43
  Uruk Prophecy, **1**:43
  Sargon of Akkad, **2**:10, 12, 112
akolouthein (to follow), **1**:232, 234–35. *See also*
    discipleship
ʾālâ, **1**:84, 152; **2**:131. *See also* oaths and vows
alêtheia (truth), **2**:394–95, 396
Alexander III, Eben, **2**:202, 203
Alexander the Great, **1**:547, 565; **2**:176, 310
allegory and typology, **1**:17–20
  adoption, usage by Paul
    believers as heirs of God, **1**:16
    Israel as God's son, **1**:15–16
    Spirit and eschatological salvation, **1**:16
  allegoresis, **1**:17–20
  Aristobulus, **1**:18
  "diaretic" allegory, **1**:17
  early Christianity, allegoresis, **1**:19–20
  Greco-Roman world, allegoresis, **1**:17–18
  Hellenistic Judaism, allegoresis, **1**:18–19
  Heraclitus, **1**:17, 18, 20
  Homeric epics, **1**:17, 18
  metaphors
    church as body of Christ, **1**:90–91
    Eden as metaphor for the good, **1**:248
    exile as, **1**:292–93
    slave metaphors, **1**:381
  metaphors for God (Hebrew Bible), **1**:414–16
    gardener, shepherd, parent (sustenance
        metaphors), **1**:415–16
    king, judge, warrior (governance metaphors),
        1:415
  Neoplatonists, **1**:18
  Origen, **1**:19
    allegory examples, **1**:458
    Israel's conquest of Canaan, **2**:410
    sacrifice and offerings, **2**:257
    Song of Songs, bodily language of, **1**:88
  parables, **1**:19
  Philo of Alexandria, **1**:18–19
  Plato, **1**:17
  Pseudo-Aristeas, **1**:18
  Song of Songs, **1**:459
  Stoics, **1**:17–18

cultic-priestly motif, **1:**520–21. *See also* image of God (*imago Dei*)

cultural memory. *See* story and memory: Old Testament

cultural trauma, **2:**340–42

cultural universals, **1:**498

curses. *See* blessing and curse

Cushites, **1:**369

Cybele (goddess), **2:**120

Cynics, **2:**61

Cyprian, **1:**49, 500; **2:**54, 171, 233, 266

Cyril of Alexandria, **1:**3; **2:**81

D

Dagon (god), **1:**414; **2:**204

daimōn, **1:**229, 230, 330. *See also* devils and demons

Daniel. *See also* apocalypticism; prophetic literature

    angels, **1:**21, 22, 23, 24

    apocalypticism, **1:**43, 45–46, 263–64

    Diaspora narrative, **1:**293

    Kingdom of God concept, **2:**5

    Kingdom of God language, **2:**3

    resurrection in, **2:**236

    sin in, **2:**301–2

    Son of Man (Daniel 7:13), **2:**318

    wisdom (Daniel 1–6), **2:**424

Dante's *Divine Comedy*, **1:**231

darkness. *See* light and darkness

David, **1:189–97**. *See also* David, Son of; Solomon

    Absalom

        beauty of, **1:**88

        caught in oak tree, **1:**452

        hair of, **1:**55, 88

        rebellion, against David, **1:**193–94; **2:**11, 381, 419

    adultery, **1:**194

    "apology of David," **1:**189

    Bathsheba affair, **1:**193–95, 197, 577; **2:**11, 135

    battle against Amalekites, **1:**190, 306; **2:**94, 174

    in Chronicles, **1:**195–96

    as controversial figure, **1:**197

    Davidic covenant, **1:**158, 189, 197, 564–66

    early career, **1:**190–91

    God as king, **2:**2

    Goliath and, **1:**79, 88, 190–91, 192

    Hebrew Bible, **1:**189

"house of David," victory stele at Tell Dan (1963), **1:**546

Jesse (David's father)

    branch of, **2:**208–9

    prominent villager, **1:**189

    root of, **1:**128; **2:**208

    stump of, **1:**127, 577

    tree of, illuminations of, **2:**210

Jesus's connection, **1:**196

just king, **1:**576–77

Kings, book of, **1:**195

māšîaḥ (anointed), **1:**126–27, 134, 198

as messiah, **1:**126–27, 134, 195, 198

Michal and, **1:**80, 88, 191; **2:**287

Nabal and, **1:**191, 367, 428

New Testament, **1:**196

old man, **1:**195

outlaw years, **1:**191–92

Philistines

    David's service, **1:**191–92

    foreskins, as bride-price for Michal, **1:**88; **2:**287

in Psalms, **1:**195–96; **2:**212

in rabbinic literature, **1:**196–97

in Samuel, **1:**189–95

Saul

    Amalekites battle, **1:**190, 306; **2:**94, 174

    David's place in Saul's court, **1:**190–91

    Michal (daughter), **1:**80, 88, 191; **2:**287

    persecution of David, **1:**191–92

    Saul's family tree, **1:**394

Succession Narrative, **1:**190, 193–95; **2:**429

as symbol of national existence, **1:**195

Tamar's rape, by Amnon, **1:**79, 194; **2:**287, 381, 419

United Monarchy, **1:**189, 192–93, 534, 535, 538; **2:**163

Uriah the Hittite, **1:**194–95, 257, 446, 577; **2:**11, 135, 156

David, Son of, **1:197–200**

    introduction, **1:**197

    Jesus as, **1:**199–200

    as political and/or messianic type, **1:**197–98

    as sapiential and/or exorcist type, **1:**198–99

day/night rhythm, **1:**32

Day of Atonement. *See* Yom Kippur

day of Enlil, **1:**201

day of Ištar, **1:**201

Ruth
   described, **2**:90–91
   friendship and, **1**:385
   genealogies, **1**:393–94
   religious constructions of status, mocking
     of, **1**:402
   scholarship, **2**:94
  Song of Songs (Canticles, Song of Solomon)
   allegory, **1**:459
   anthropological statements and perspectives
     in, **1**:38
   body as object of erotic gaze, **1**:88
   canonization, **2**:90
   described, **2**:91–92
   dove in, **1**:490
   Eden, **1**:246
   "enclosed garden," **2**:82
   eroticism in, **1**:88, 160, 459; **2**:91, 286, 290
   fidelity within marriage, **1**:160
   friendship metaphor, **1**:385
   honor and shame, **1**:493
   image of God, **1**:38
   Immaculate Conception, **2**:84
   Lady Wisdom as ideal spouse, **1**:160
   liturgical use, **2**:90
   marriage, **1**:160; **2**:59, 78
   Passover, **2**:90
   scholarship, **2**:94
   "sealed fountain," **2**:82
   sexuality, **2**:285, 286, 287, 290
   sexual love, **2**:59, 78
   social equality and, **1**:341
   unusualness of, **2**:91
   as wisdom literature, **2**:427
Meister Eckhart, **1**:388
Melanchthon, Philipp, **2**:358
Melchizedek
  as chief of heavenly armies, **1**:22
  Jesus compared to, **2**:314
  in paradise of Eden, **1**:247
  Shem, **1**:2
Melito of Sardis, **1**:354, 570
mĕl'ākîm (angels), **1**:23
memory. *See* scripture; story and memory
men, angels as, **1**:21

Menzies, Robert P., **1**:482
mercy and compassion, **2**:95–98
  classical and Hellenistic contexts, **2**:95
  divine mercy: Hebrew Bible, **2**:95–96
  divine mercy: New Testament, **2**:96–97
   Pauline letters, **2**:96–97
  God's character: merciful and gracious, **1**:417
  human mercy/compassion, **2**:97–98
mercy seat, **1**:62, 308, 312, 313; **2**:144
merism
  good and evil, **1**:428, 431; **2**:44
  light and darkness, **2**:43, 44
mĕšārîm, **1**:574, 578. *See also* justice, justification, and
   righteousness: Old Testament
Mesopotamia. *See also* ancient Near East
  Adam/Primeval Human in, **1**:4–5
  Adapa myth, **1**:247
  anthropology, Old Testament, **1**:31
  apocalypticism, **1**:43
  Atrahasis epic
   Adam/Primeval Human, **1**:5
   creation-flood story, **1**:396–97
   death and life span, **1**:397
   fertility and barrenness, gods' responsibility,
     1:79
   humans, as slaves to gods, **1**:396
   learning, Mesopotamian education, **1**:249
  creation topic in theology, **1**:166
  education in, **1**:249–50
  Enlil (god), **1**:181, 201, 263, 397, 451, 452
  Enmeduranki, **1**:43
  Enūma Eliš
   Adam/Primeval Man, **1**:5
   creation account, **1**:167, 170–71
   Exodus compared to, **1**:298–99
   temple construction for gods, **1**:315
  fear, **1**:345–46
  Genesis revision of Mesopotamian theology,
    1:396–98
  Gilgamesh Epic
   Adam/Primeval Human, **1**:4
   continuous scribal authorship, **1**:298
   creation-flood story, **1**:396
   "Eden" and, **1**:246
   Enkidu and Gilgamesh, **1**:4, 384, 385